D0950012

Cinema Sequels and Remakes, 1903–1987

Cinema Sequels and Remakes, 1903–1987

by
Robert A. Nowlan
and
Gwendolyn Wright Nowlan

McFarland & Company, Inc., Publishers
Jefferson, North Carolina, and London

British Library Cataloguing-in-Publication data available

Library of Congress Cataloguing-in-Publication Data

Nowlan, Robert A.
Cinema sequels and remakes, 1903–1987.

Includes index.
1. Motion picture sequels.
2. Motion picture remakes.
I. Nowlan, Gwendolyn Wright, 1945–
II. Title.
PN1995.9.S29N69 1989 791.43'75 88-42640

ISBN 0-89950-314-4 (lib. bdg.; 50# acid-free natural paper) 

Printed in the United States of America.

McFarland & Company, Inc., Publishers
Box 611, Jefferson, North Carolina 28640

In
memory of our mothers

Marian Juanita Shields Nowlan
and
Gertrude Margaret Evans Lawson

Acknowledgments

We appreciate the kindness of Morris Everett of Cleveland, Ohio, who has generously allowed us to use his splendid motion picture stills. Our research efforts have been enhanced by the assistance of Fred Leskowitz, Thomas Clarie, and particularly Claire Bennett, the quality of whose assistance has only been matched by her encouragement.

Contents

Introduction

The motion picture industry has wholeheartedly endorsed the adage "Imitation is the sincerest form of flattery" by returning again and again to stories which had already been filmed—sometimes successfully, sometimes not. The new productions have not always been faithful re-creations as in the case of 1952's *The Prisoner of Zenda* which was a scene-for-scene remake of the 1937 classic. Just as often, the setting has been completely changed as is the case with the caper classic *The Asphalt Jungle* (1950) which in 1958 showed up as the western *The Badlanders.*

Other examples of remaking movies include the production of a musical version of a previously filmed story as with 1948's *Summer Holiday,* a tuneful retelling of Eugene O'Neill's *Ah, Wilderness!* which was filmed in 1935. Then there are movies which are not so much remakes as the telling of the same basic story from a different point of view. For instance, *My Darling Clementine* and *Gunfight at the OK Corral,* both westerns, deal with the showdown between Wyatt Earp and Doc Holliday, and the Clanton gang.

In terms of sequels, a popular device has been to revisit a story by introducing a son or daughter faced with similar problems as were their parents in earlier movies. Examples include *Son of Monte Cristo* and *Dracula's Daughter.* Sequels also are designed to follow the further adventures of a character as in the case of *The Bell's of St. Mary's,* which allowed audiences to further enjoy Bing Crosby's performance as the charming Catholic priest introduced in *Going My Way.* If this device is used more than once or twice, what we have is a series. The basic difference between a sequel and one film in a series is that in the former, the story of a previous movie is continued in some way, whereas in the case of the latter, there is no real connection between the films, save some central characters who reappear. In the James Bond movies, for instance, 007, Miss Moneypenny, M and Q have for the most part been constants.

While sources exist which list remakes and sequels of certain movies, the sheer number of such entries seemingly has forced the authors of these materials to merely give the most basic information about the movies, the source of their story, their year of release and production company or country of origin. This book will include such information, but in addition will provide a description of the story of the movies and their remakes or sequels, a comparison of the productions, and for each movie featured, its director, screenwriter, main characters and the leading performers in the films.

To produce a source with so much information makes it necessary to limit the number of primary films in one volume, leaving other pictures and their remakes and sequels for a second or even third volume to be produced at a later time. Having made this decision, we adopted the following guiding definition of which movies will be included in this first volume. All films, silent or sound, from the genres of drama, action-adventure, romance, comedy or thriller, which have at least one English-speaking sound remake or sequel, will be treated as primary films, and together with their remakes and sequels will be featured. The entries in the book will be an alphabetical listing of the movies, with listings of remakes and sequels giving a reference to the primary film where they are discussed.

Although many genres for primary films have been excluded for this volume, the book does include certain musicals, westerns, horror and science fiction films when these are remakes or sequels to some given primary film. Every effort has been made to include every primary film and remake or sequel which satisfies our criteria, but we are certain that some of our readers will feel that we have omitted a movie which meets our definition. If so, the omission is merely an oversight and we would be happy to learn of such instances. On occasion, we found claims of remakes or sequels of movies mentioned in one or another of our sources which was never corroborated by any other authority. Rather than to repeat what may be a fiction, we have chosen not to honor any claim of remakes or sequels unless it is made in more than one reliable source.

Readers will note that the extent of the commentary for the various entries varies greatly. This is deliberate, with greater discussion being given to movies which have had the greatest impact on the motion picture industry. This doesn't mean that they are the authors' personal selection for the best movies—only that we feel there is more that can and should be said about the particular movies.

The Films

A

Abbott and Costello Meet Dr. Jekyll and Mr. Hyde *see* **Dr. Jekyll and Mr. Hyde**

1 Abie's Irish Rose

Based on Anne Nichols' play. Story: Abie falls in love with and marries Rosemary despite the strongly bigoted objections of their respective fathers, Solomon Levy and Patrick Murphy. Insults fly faster than the humor and it's more than a little embarrassing to endure the admittedly funny slurs flung against Jews and Catholics by these two early-day Archie Bunkers. The example of the youngsters finally wins over the older generation to a certain grudging acceptance of the marriage and mutual respect.

Paramount, 1928 (original). Silent. Director: Victor Fleming; screenwriter: Anne Nichols. Cast: Jean Hersholt (Solomon Levy), Charles Rogers (Abie Levy), Nancy Carroll (Rosemary Murphy), J. Farrell MacDonald (Patrick Murphy), Bernard Gorcey (Issac Cohen), Ida Kramer (Mrs. Issac Cohen).

• ***Abie's Irish Rose*** (remake). United Artists, 1946. Director: A. Edward Sutherland; screenwriter: Anne Nichols. Cast: Joanne Dru (Rosemary), Richard Norris (Abie), Michael Chekhov (Solomon Levy), J.M. Kerrigan (Patrick Murphy), George E. Stone (Issac Cohen), Vera Gordon (Mrs. Cohen).

Anne Nichols' stage play was extremely successful, but the work did not transfer well to the screen. In the silent version, audiences had to read the title gags written by Julian Johnson and Herman Mankiewicz, which didn't have the same force as the spoken word on stage. Nevertheless the performances of Jean Hersholt and Bernard Gorcey were outstanding. Nancy Carroll and Charles Rogers made a pleasant young couple and MacDonald was amusing if predictable as the comic Irishman. The film lacked much of a climax, resolving itself when the two bigoted fathers demanded to see their grandchild, fighting over the sex of the infant. All was forgiven when the young couple produced twins, a boy and a girl.

The later version was no improvement on the silent. The exaggerated comedy was still filled with racial and religious prejudice but the producers insisted on pushing a message of brotherhood. Among other things they made certain the youngsters were nondiscriminatingly married, having them undergo ceremonies by a minister, a rabbi and a Catholic priest.

About Face *see* **Brother Rat**

2 The Absent-Minded Professor

Based on a story by Samuel W. Taylor. Story: A slightly addled professor at a small college invents a substance, "flubber," with some remarkable qualities. When applied to the soles of shoes it allows the wearer to soar high in the air and also allows the prof's ancient Model-T Ford to fly. You see, flubber means flying rubber. This discovery saves the institution of higher learning from embarrassing itself on athletic fields and allows it to prosper financially, even if the use of flubber does seem to be inconsistent with NCAA rules.

Walt Disney, 1961 (original). Director: Robert Stevenson; screenwriter: Bill Walsh. Cast: Fred MacMurray (Prof. Ned Brainard), Nancy Olson (Betsy Carlisle), Keenan Wynn (Alonzo Hawk), Tommy Kirk (Biff Hawk), Leon Ames, Elliot Reid, Edward Andrews, Wally Brown, Ed Wynn.

• ***The Son of Flubber*** (sequel). Walt Disney, 1963. Director: Robert Stevenson; screenwriter: Bill Walsh. Cast: Fred MacMurray (Prof. Ned Brainard), Nancy Olson (Betsy Brainard), Keenan Wynn (Alonzo Hawk), Tommy Kirk (Biff Hawk), Leon Ames, Joanna Moore, William Demarest, Paul Lynde, Ed Wynn.

In this squeaky-clean screwball comedy, MacMurray proves his ability to play comedy even if it is of a low variety. His stereotyped absent-minded professor even forgets to show up for his wedding to Nancy Olson. His "flubber" allows Metcalf College's undersized basketball players to soar over their giant opponents to victory. Keenan Wynn plays an exasperated heavy with Tommy Kirk as his good "Joe College" son.

In the sequel, the gags and the participants are much the same. Only now Olson has changed from MacMurray's patient fiancée to his impatient wife and flubber saves the day on the football field when a new variety, which can also make rain, inflates the team's fullback who truly flies over the heads of opposing linemen. Both films are wholesomely filled with sight-gag slapstick.

3 The Abysmal Brute

Based on a story by Jack London. Story: At a time when boxing was basically brute strength against brute strength, Pat Glendon was successful in preventing his opponents from marring his handsome features until he falls for a girl from a family which considers him something of a brute and low-class creature because of his profession. While not an ignorant, pain-absorbing animal like Rocky Balboa, his attention to the young beauty puts him down for the count of nine before he rises from the canvas and pulverizes his adversary.

Universal, 1923 (original). Silent. Director: Hobart Henley; adapted by A.P. Younger. Cast: Reginald Denny (Pat Glendon, Jr.), Julienne Scott (Marion Sangster), Buddy Messenger (Buddy Sangster), David Torrence, Charles French, Crauford Kent.

• ***Conflict*** (remake). Universal, 1937. Director: David Howard; screenwriters: Charles Logue and Walter Weems. Cast: John Wayne (Pat Glendon), Jean Rogers (Maude), Tommy Bupp (Tommy), Ward Bond (Carrigan), Eddie Borden, Frank Sheridan.

In the silent version, Denny is the James J. Corbett–like pugilist who on the night of a fight attends dinner at the home of Julienne Scott and her prominent family. Not suitably attired and refusing wine and eating lightly because of the up-coming boxing match, he suffers the verbal abuse of the spoiled brother, Buddy, and the dinner discussion about a brute who is fighting that evening, the family being unaware that he is the brute they are so uncharitably describing. When his identity is discovered, the girl is at first appalled but later agrees to attend the match. While the fight is in progress, he pays too much attention to her and is almost knocked out. Remembering himself, he comes off the canvas to destroy his opponent. The girl is impressed.

In *Conflict,* also based on London's story, Wayne is a stooge for a traveling boxer, Bond. The Duke shows up in a town or logging camp and impresses one and all with his strength and fighting ability and when Bond shows up offering a prize to anyone who can beat him, his new friends push forward Wayne, placing bets with the boxer's manager that John will win. Then Wayne goes into the tank, throws the fight and the conspirators move on to a new location to find new suckers. Jean Rogers plays a reporter for a San Francisco newspaper who intends to unmask the racket. In a logging camp that Wayne has infiltrated, she and young Tommy Bupp change Wayne; when Bond arrives, John double-crosses him, winning the match and the girl.

4 Accent on Youth

Based on the play by Samson Raphelson. Story: The secretary to a middle-aged playwright falls in love with him, thus paralleling his new play about an older married man who deserts his wife for a young girl. The playwright loves her but believing he is too old for her, encourages her to marry a young, wealthy actor. She does, but a few months later she divorces her husband and returns to the playwright.

Paramount, 1935 (original). Director: Wesley Ruggles; screenwriters: Herbert Fields and Claude Binyon. Cast: Sylvia Sidney (Linda Brown), Herbert Marshall (Steven Gaye), Phillip Reed (Dickie Reynolds), Astrid Allwyn (Genevieve Gaye), Holmes Herbert, Catherine Doucet, Ernest Cossart, Donald Meek.

• ***Mr. Music*** (remake). Paramount, 1950. Director: Richard Haydn; screenwriter: Arthur Sheekman. Cast: Bing Crosby (Paul Merrick), Nancy Olson (Katherine Holbrook), Charles Coburn (Alex Conway), Ruth Hussey (Lorna Marvis), Robert Stack (Jefferson Blake), Tom Ewell, Ida Moore, Charles Kemper.

• ***But Not for Me*** (remake). Paramount, 1959. Director: Walter Lang; screenwriter: John Michael Hayes. Cast: Clark Gable (Russel Ward), Carroll Baker (Eleanor Brown), Lilli Palmer (Kathryn Ward), Lee J. Cobb, Barry Coe, Thomas Gomez.

Although the synopsis of the story doesn't reveal it, this is a lightweight comedy. On the stage, the lead roles of the secretary and the playwright were at various times played by Constance Cummings and Nicholas Hannen, Greer Garson and Nicholas Hannen, and Grace Kelly and Jerome Cowan. In the 1935 film version Sylvia Sidney and Herbert Marshall were featured in the roles and gave bright, witty performances.

The play was reworked in 1950 as a musical starring Bing Crosby as a middle-aged songwriter who needed Nancy Olson's prodding to complete his songs. The musical pieces, which were no great shakes, included "Accidents Will Happen," "Wouldn't It Be Funny" and the title song. Guests in the pleasant but somewhat bland production included Groucho Marx, Dorothy Kirsten, Peggy Lee, and Marge and Gower Champion.

In 1959, Clark Gable portrayed a washed-up Broadway producer who is loved and abetted by young drama student and secretary, Carroll Baker. It lacked both the wit and gaiety of the original story.

Aces High *see* **Journey's End**

Achsuuse Unterm Gulgen *see* **Kidnapped**

Acht Maedles im Boot *see* **Eight Girls in a Boat**

Across to Singapore *see* **All the Brothers Were Valiant**

5 The Admirable Crichton

Based on the play by Sir James M. Barrie. Story: Crichton is the butler in the home of the Earl of Loam, and does not share his employer's democratic notions that all men are to be treated equal. He and the cockney maid, Tweeney, who loves him, join the Earl and his three daughters on a world cruise. They are shipwrecked on an uninhabited island, where efficient and competent Crichton is quickly established as the natural leader of the stranded band. One of the daughters, Lady Mary, is greatly impressed by his commanding ways and intends to marry him when they are rescued. However when a rescue ship appears, Crichton reverts to his very proper butler-position and marries the maid when, after reaching London, everyone resumes their usual social status.

• ***The Admirable Crichton*** (remake). Jury Pictures, 1918. Silent. Director: G.B. Samuelson; screenwriter: Kenelm Foss. Cast: Basil Gill (Crichton), Mary Dibley (Lady Mary), Lennox Pawle (Lord Loam), Lilian Hall-Davis, James Lindsay.

• ***Male and Female*** (remake). Paramount, 1919. Silent. Director: Cecil B. DeMille; screenwriter: Jeanie Macpherson. Cast: Thomas Meighan (Crichton), Gloria Swanson (Lady Mary), Lila Lee (Tweeny), Theodore Roberts (Earl of Loam), Raymond Hatton, Mayme Kelso, Robert Cain, Bebe Daniels.

• ***We're Not Dressing*** (remake). Paramount, 1934. Director: Norman Taurog; screenwriters: Benjamin Glazer, Horace Jackson, Francis Martin and George Marion, Jr. Cast: Bing Crosby (Stephen Jones), Carole Lombard (Doris Worthington), George Burns (George), Gracie Allen (Gracie), Ethel Merman (Edith), Leon Errol, Jay Henry, Raymond Milland.

• ***Our Girl Friday (The Adventures of Sadie—USA)*** (remake). Renown Pictures, 1953. Director and screenwriter: Noel Langley. Cast: Joan Collins (Sadie Patch), George Cole (Jimmy Carroll), Kenneth More (Pat Plunkett),

Robertson Hare, Hermione Gingold, Walter Fitzgerald, Hattie Jacques, Felix Felton.

• ***The Admirable Crichton*** (remake). Columbia, 1957. Director: Lewis Gilbert; screenwriter: Vernon Harris. Cast: Kenneth More (Crichton), Cecil Parker (Lord Loam), Diane Cilento (Tweeney), Martita Hunt (Lady Brocklehurst), Sally Ann Howes (Lady Mary), Jack Watling, Gerald Harper, Mercy Haystead, Miranda Connell, Peter Graves, Miles Malleson.

The 1918 release was a faithful reproduction of the play, which followed shorter film productions entitled *Back to Nature* (1912), *Shipwrecked* (1913), *A Man of Her Choice* (1914), and *Master and Man* (1915).

In DeMille's 1919 version, the Barrie story was interspersed with imaginative flashbacks to Babylonian biblical days and became one of the biggest box-office hits of the silent era.

In the Crosby version of 1934, greater emphasis was placed on the comedy aspects of the fantasy, supplied by Burns and Allen. Songs by Harry Revel and Mack Gordon included "Love Thy Neighbor," "She Reminds Me of You," "Once in a Blue Moon," and "Good Night, Lovely Little Lady."

The 1953 film was a coy sexual farce about four shipwrecked survivors washed up on a deserted island, starring Joan Collins before she turned deliciously bitchy.

In 1957, Kenneth More took over the part of the talented manservant and seemed very much at home as the boss of the shipwrecked aristocrats, but when the rescue ship is spotted, he appears in the best finery that he can salvage and with a towel over his arm serves what passes for cocktails to his employers.

Adult Version of Dr. Jekyll and Mr. Hyde *see* **Dr. Jekyll and Mr. Hyde**

Adventure in Iraq *see* **The Green Goddess**

Adventure in Manhattan *see* **Three Hours**

Adventure Island *see* **Ebb Tide**

6 Adventures of a Rookie

Based on a story by William Bowers and M. Coates Webster. Story: Brown, Carney and Martin appear as a trio of recruits who have a series of misadventures at an induction center and training camp, usually caused by the antics of Brown and Carney with Martin a somewhat innocent bystander along for the ride. They resolve their various jams and board a transport for overseas duty. It's a standard army comedy with the expected military gags and only a few pleasant surprises.

RKO, 1943 (original). Director: Leslie Goodwins; screenwriter: Edward James. Cast: Wally Brown (Jerry Miles), Alan Carney (Mike Sturgeon), Richard Martin (Bob Prescot), Erford Gage (Sgt. Burke), Margaret Landry (Peggy

Linden), Patti Brill (Patsy), Rita Coprday (Ruth), Robert Anderson, John Hamilton, Ruth Lee, Lorraine Krueger.

• ***Rookies in Burma*** (sequel). RKO, 1943. Director: Leslie Goodwins; screenwriter: Edward James. Cast: Wally Brown (Jerry), Alan Carney (Mike), Erford Gage (Sgt. Burke), Claire Carleton (Janie), Joan Barclay (Connie), Ted Hecht (Capt. Termura).

The material is aged and the direction by Goodwins doesn't help. It's a corny story lacking the yuks found in other films that presented similar situations. In the sequel, Brown and Carney are captured in Burma by the Japanese along with Sgt. Gage, but manage to escape and pick up two stranded showgirls as they are chased by their former captors. Ah, war is hell.

The Adventures of Arsene Lupin *see* Arsene Lupin

Adventures of Don Juan *see* Don Juan

The Adventures of Ichabod and Mr. Toad *see* The Headless Horseman

The Adventures of Mr. Pickwick *see* The Pickwick Papers

Adventures of Prince Ahmed *see* Aladdin and His Magic Lamp

The Adventures of Robin Hood *see* Robin Hood

The Adventures of Sherlock Holmes *see* Sherlock Holmes

The Adventures of Tom Sawyer *see* Tom Sawyer

7 The Adventures of the Wilderness Family

Based on an original story by Stewart Raffil. Story: A modern couple with two children are sick of the smog, hassle and crime of Los Angeles. Since their daughter has a serious respiratory problem and needs fresh, clean air if she is to be cured, they sell everything and move to a log cabin in the Rocky Mountain region. Here they must deal with cultural shock and the dangers of an existence in the wild.

Pacific International, 1975 (original). Director and screenwriter: Stewart Raffil. Cast: Robert Logan, Susan Damante Shaw, Holleye Holmes, Ham Larsen, Buck Flower, William Cornford, Heather Rattray.

• ***Further Adventures of the Wilderness Family*** (sequel). Pacific International. Director and screenwriter: Frank Zungia. Cast: Robert Logan, Susan D. Shaw, Heather Rattray, Ham Larsen, Buck Flower, Brian Cutler.

• ***Mountain Family Robinson*** (sequel). Pacific International. Director and screenwriter: John Cotter. Cast: Robert Logan, Susan D. Shaw, William Bryant, Heather Rattray, Ham Larsen, Buck Flower.

These are three beautifully photographed, naive family stories with the two sequels being clones of the first. The pretty scenery and the animals compensate for the fact that there is little in any of the three movies of dramatic significance. One film would have probably sufficed, but it's difficult to argue with the success of these Swiss Family Robinson–like productions.

An Affair to Remember *see* **Love Affair**

8 The Affairs of Annabel

Based on the story and characters created by Charles Hoffman. Story: Frantic press agent Lanny Morgan attempts to gain front page coverage for his client, film star Annabel, by plopping her into real situations which will attract attention. One of his schemes is to have her serve a short term in a reformatory but her suffering is for naught when the film project for which she is preparing is shelved. Next, Morgan arranges for her to become a maid in a household which is soon terrorized by two fugitive kidnappers who browbeat Annabel into becoming an unwilling accessory. Her frantic pleas for help from Morgan go unheeded as he misunderstands her plight. There is considerable excitement, humor and gunplay before the gangsters are captured.

RKO, 1938 (original). Director: Ben Stoloff; screenwriters: Bert Granet and Paul Yawitz. Cast: Jack Oakie (Lanny Morgan), Lucille Ball (Annabel), Ruth Donnelly (Josephine), Bradley Page (Webb), Fritz Feld (Vladimir), Thurston Hall (Major), Elizabeth Risdon, Granville Bates, James Burke.

• ***Annabel Takes a Tour*** (sequel). RKO, 1938. Director: Lew Landers; screenwriters: Bert Granet and Olive Cooper from a story by Joe Bigelow. Cast: Jack Oakie (Morgan), Lucille Ball (Annabel), Ruth Donnelly (Josephine), Bradley Page (Webb), Ralph Forbes (Viscount), Frances Mercer, Donald McBride, Alice White, Pepito.

The Affairs of Annabel is a fast-paced, breezy farce with good performances from Ball as the scatterbrained film star, Oakie as the Svengali-like press agent, Donnelly as a wise-cracking secretary, and Page, Feld and Hall as various Hollywood caricatures. It affectionately poked fun at the movie business and was planned as the first of a "B" comedy series.

All ideas of this faded with the arrival a few months later of the sequel, entitled *Annabel Takes a Tour.* This production has press agent Morgan continuing his zany plots to keep his client's name on page one. While on a personal appearance tour, Morgan sets up a phony romance between Annabel and a viscount who writes steamy love novels. Everything goes well with the romance until Annabel takes it seriously and announces she wishes to give up her career and marry him. Her dreams are shattered when the viscount's wife and children arrive along with process servers. Annabel makes a hasty retreat to Hollywood. The sequel lacked the nonstop wackiness of the original and was the only film to lose money for RKO in 1938.

After the Thin Man *see* **The Thin Man**

9 Against All Flags

Based on the novel by Aeneas MacKenzie. Story: Naval officer Hawke allows himself to be thrown out of the service in disgrace so he may infiltrate a pirate stronghold which plans to sabotage their fortifications. One of the pirate leaders, Brasiliano, suspects he is a spy, but he is saved from death by the beautiful female buccaneer, Spitfire Stevens, whom he romances as he carries on his undercover work. The pirates capture the ship of the Mogul of India carrying the latter's daughter and a dozen harem girls. The princess fits in with the others and Hawke attempts to prevent the pirates from learning her true identity. This is misinterpreted by Spitfire and her jealousy almost blows his cover before he can spike the pirates' guns. Eventually a British warship arrives and defeats the pirates. As his award for his performance, Hawke is given custody of Spitfire, ensuring a happy ending.

Universal Pictures, 1953 (original). Director: George Sherman; screenwriters: Aeneas MacKenzie and Joseph Hoffman. Cast: Errol Flynn (Brian Hawke), Maureen O'Hara (Spitfire Stevens), Anthony Quinn (Roc Brasiliano), Mildred Natwick (Molvina MacGregor), Alice Kelley (Princess Patma), Robert Warwick (Captain Kidd), Harry Cording, John Anderson, Phil Tully, Lester Matthews.

• ***The King's Pirate*** (remake). Universal Pictures, 1967. Director: Don Weiss; screenwriter: Paul Wayne. Cast: Doug McClure (Lt. Brian Fleming), Jill St. John (Jessica Stephens), Guy Stockwell (John Avery), Kurt Kasznar (Zucco), Mary Ann Mobley (Princess Patma), Richard Deacon, Torin Thatcher, Diana Chesney, Ivor Barry, Sean McClory.

Flynn was a bit past his prime for playing a swashbuckler but his performance held up rather well. Maureen O'Hara looked as fiery as her name and Alice Kelley made a yummy Princess Patma. The story is old hat but did provide a pleasant Saturday afternoon diversion for those who couldn't get enough of romantic adventure. In the remake there was little excitement, with McClure, St. John and Stockwell seemingly miscast. As for Mary Ann Mobley, her appearance in harem pants might have won her the evening gown competition but her acting wouldn't have been well-received in the talent competition of the Miss America pageant.

10 The Age of Innocence

Based on a novel by Edith Wharton and a play by Margaret Ayer Barnes. Story: Socially prominent Newland Archer, although engaged to May Mingott, falls in love with charming Countess Ellen Olenska who has left her brutish Polish husband. His efforts to escape his engagement are frustrated by his family and circumstances and he marries May hoping to forget Ellen. But in a subsequent meeting they decide to go away together. Visiting Ellen, May informs her that she is expecting a baby. Ellen decides to give up Archer and return to her husband. Newland repents and vows to be worthy of his wife.

Warner Bros., 1924 (original). Silent. Director: Wesley Ruggles; screenwriter: Olga Printzlau. Cast: Elliott Dexter (Newland Archer), Beverly Bayne (Countess Ellen Olenska), Edith Roberts (May Mingott), Willard Louis, Fred Huntley, Gertrude Norman, Sigrid Holmquist, Stuart Holmes.

• ***The Age of Innocence*** (remake). RKO, 1934. Director: Philip Moeller; screenwriters: Sarah Y. Mason and Victor Heerman. Cast: Irene Dunne (Ellen),

John Boles (Newland Archer), Julie Haydon (May Welland), Lionell Atwill, Laura Hope Crews, Helen Westley.

The 1924 psychological melodrama of Bohemian living sacrificed plot for character development but was sufficiently shocking for the times to maintain audiences' interest. The remake teamed the stars of another weeper, *Back Street*, but Irene Dunne and John Boles couldn't make the new vehicle rival that success. The film is ponderous and, unfortunately, devoid of any real emotion. The predictable female-oriented drama did not require the number of handerkerchiefs that the producers expected. It is told in flashback with Boles as an elderly Archer, relating the story to a grandchild, already familiar with the situation, who has run across gramp's long-lost love.

11 Ah, Wilderness!

Based on the play by Eugene O'Neill. Story: Eugene O'Neill's most uncharacteristic play, a comedy, is the story of adolescent Richard Miller whose attempts to share his poetry and modest radical nature with the girl of his dreams, Muriel McComber, is frustrated by her father who does not approve of the boy's ideas. Crushed, he gets drunk and takes up with Belle, a down-on-the-heels scarlet woman. Richard is fortunate to have a loving and understanding family, each of whom in their own way prove their concern is more for the boy's well-being than his encounter with sin. Of particular help to the hung-over lad is his tippling uncle Sid Davis who has been there before on many occasions.

MGM, 1935 (original). Director: Clarence Brown; screenwriters: Albert Hackett & Frances Goodrich. Cast: Wallace Beery (Sid Davis), Lionel Barrymore (Nat Miller), Eric Linden (Richard Miller), Aline MacMahon (Lily Davis), Cecilia Parker (Muriel), Spring Byington, Mickey Rooney, Helen Flint, Charles Grapewin, Bonita Granville.

• ***Summer Holiday*** (remake). MGM, 1948. Director: Rouben Mamoulian; screenwriters: Albert Hackett, Frances Goodrich & Ralph Blane. Cast: Frank Morgan (Sid Davis), Walter Huston (Nat Miller), Mickey Rooney (Richard Miller), Agnes Moorehead (Lily Davis), Gloria De Haven (Muriel), Selena Royle, Butch Jenkins, Marilyn Maxwell, John Alexander, Shirley Johns.

Although Wallace Beery was the nominal star of the 1935 film and its story consisted of more than just Richard's fall into a mild degradation, this episode best illustrates the charm and poignancy of a turn-of-the-century life in the small Connecticut town. It may or may not be an accurate depiction of American values and rituals in a simpler time, but should have been.

The 1948 musical remake is basically a star vehicle for the then very popular Mickey Rooney who played the bratty younger brother in the earlier version. The songs are nothing special, although Marilyn Maxwell as the tart, Belle, does a nice job with "I Think You're the Sweetest Kid I've Ever Known" as she puts the make on the young innocent. Rooney enthusiastically sings "You Mustn't Be Afraid to Fall in Love" to Gloria De Haven as Muriel, as they dance happily across a field. At the Fourth of July picnic, the male members of the cast give a rousing rendition of "This Independence Day" and in a clear take-off of Judy

Wallace Beery as Uncle Sid (middle) shows a little tenderness to Aline MacMahon as Cousin Lily, while Spring Byington, Lionel Barrymore and Bonita Granville look on in Ah, Wilderness! *(MGM, 1935).*

Garland's "The Trolley Song" from *Meet Me in St. Louis,* Rooney treats the audience to "Stanley Steamer."

The casting in the two films was far from perfect and both versions look at life through rose-colored glasses, making audiences nostalgic for experiences they may never have known but which seem most appealing and typically American. Worse frauds have been filmed than making things seem better than they really were.

Ain't Misbehavin *see* **Pygmalion**

12 Airplane

Based on an original screenplay by Jim Abrahams, David Zucker and Jerry Zucker. Story: The plot of this film is definitely secondary to bits of business meant to satirize and parody just about every film ever made. Ted Striker arrives at an airport to find his girl Elaine has left him because she can no longer stand living with a coward. Seems that during the war, a command decision made by flyer Striker resulted in the death of several of his men. Ever since, he has been afraid to fly. Nevertheless, he boards the plane and when the pilot, co-pilot, navigator and many passengers become seriously ill because of food

Butch Jenkins (center) uses a program as a spy glass to get a better look at his brother (Mickey Rooney) on the occasion of the latter's high school graduation. Other members of the proud family are, from left to right, Shirley Johns, Selena Royle, Jenkins, Agnes Moorehead, Michael Kirby and Anne Francis. Behind Jenkins is John Alexander.

poisoning, he's called on to save everyone by landing the plane. He is assisted in this by a zany ground crew and an arrogant pilot on the ground, whom he despises, who must talk him down.

Paramount, 1980 (original). Director and screenwriters: Jim Abrahams, David Zucker and Jerry Zucker. Cast: Robert Hays (Ted Striker), Julie Hagerty (Elaine), Lloyd Bridges (McCroskey), Peter Graves (Captain Oveur), Kareem Abdul Jabbar (Murdock), Leslie Nielsen (Dr. Rumack), Robert Stack, Lorina Paterson, Ethel Merman, Steven Strucker.

• ***Airplane II: The Sequel*** (sequel). Paramount, 1982. Director and screenwriter: Ken Finkleman. Cast: Robert Hays (Ted Striker), Julie Hagerty (Elaine), Lloyd Bridges (McCroskey), Peter Graves (Captain Oveur), William Shatner, Steven Strucker, Sonny Bono, Raymond Burr, Chuck Connors, Rip Torn, John Dehner, Kent McCord, John Vernon, Chad Everett.

Beginning as a parody of the *Airport* films, this production of sophomoric skits was so far out it was in. For some the fun was to identify the particular film that was being satirized at a given moment. What made it work was that everyone acted as if the zany behavior was quite normal. Some of the funny scenes involved the crew of the cockpit and a small boy who was visiting them.

Then too the automatic pilot who had a mind of his own and a yen for Julie Hagerty was also quite amusing. The flashback scene where Striker and Elaine first meet in a Casablanca-like bar, turning into a take-off of *Saturday Night Fever*, complete with Striker dancing like John Travolta to the strains of the Bee Gees' "Staying Alive," is a scream. By the time the producers tried to repeat their success with *Airplane II: The Sequel*, the satire was getting a bit weak and audiences knew what to expect as the routines became more predictable and many of the gags from the first film were repeated.

Airplane II: The Sequel *see* **Airplane**

13 Airport

Based on the novel by Arthur Hailey. Story: In this "Grand Hotel on an airport concourse," despondent D.O. Guerrero has taken out a large insurance policy on himself, and has boarded a plane carrying a bomb. The drama deals with those on the ground who know what he's up to and those in the air who must try to stop him. The bomb goes off, he's blown away, the plane is severely damaged and now the problem is how to bring it down during a bad storm.

Universal Pictures, 1970 (original). Directors: George Seaton and Henry Hathaway; screenwriter: George Seaton. Cast: Burt Lancaster (Mel Bakersfield), Dean Martin (Vernon Demerest), Jean Seberg (Tanya Livingston), Jacqueline Bisset (Gwen Meighan), George Kennedy (Patroni), Helen Hayes (Ada Quonsett), Van Heflin (D.O. Guerrero), Maureen Stapleton (Inez Guerrero), Barry Nelson, Dana Wynter, Lloyd Nolan, Barbara Hale, Gary Collins.

• ***Airport 1975*** (sequel). Universal Pictures, 1974. Director: Jack Smight; screenwriter: Don Ingalls. Cast: Charlton Heston (Murdock), Karen Black (Nancy), George Kennedy (Patroni), Efrem Zimbalist, Jr. (Stacy), Gloria Swanson (Herself), Susan Clark (Mrs. Patroni), Helen Reddy (Sister Ruth), Linda Blair (Janice), Dana Andrews (Scott Freeman), Roy Thinnes, Sid Caesar, Myrna Loy, Ed Nelson, Nancy Olsen, Larry Storch, Martha Scott.

• ***Airport '77*** (sequel). Universal Pictures, 1977. Director: Jerry Jameson; screenwriters: Michael Scheff and David Spector. Cast: Jack Lemmon (Don Gallagher), Lee Grant (Karen Wallace), Brenda Vaccaro (Eve Clayton), Joseph Cotton (Nichilas St. Downs, III), Olivia de Havilland (Emily Livingston), Darren McGavin (Stan Buchek), Christopher Lee (Martin Wallace), Robert Foxworth, Robert Hooks, Monte Markham, Kathleen Quinlan, Gil Gerard, James Stewart.

• ***The Concorde-Airport '79*** (sequel). Universal Pictures, 1979. Director: David Lowell Rich; screenwriter: Eric Roth. Cast: Alain Delon (Metrand), Susan Blakely (Maggie), Robert Wagner (Kevin), Sylvia Kristel (Isabelle), George Kennedy (Patroni), Eddie Albert (Eli), Bibi Andersson (Francine), Charo, John Davidson, Andrea Marcovicci, Martha Raye, Cicely Tyson, Jimmie Walker, David Warner, Mercedes McCambridge, Avery Schreiber.

In the first picture, Helen Hayes won an Academy Award for Best Supporting Actress and Maureen Stapleton, also nominated, gave her competition for the award. In the second of these airborne melodramatic disaster films, a private plane collides with a commercial jet, killing the cockpit crew, leaving it up to stewardess Karen Black to fly the plane. The third film has a private airliner loaded with guests and art treasures hitting an oil rig and settling underwater on a sandbank. Finally, if the Concorde had as many problems in flying from Washington to Paris as it does in the movie, it would be permanently grounded. These all-star pictures are not good, but they are entertaining. In 1980 and 1982, Paramount brought out the parodies, *Airplane* and *Airplane II: The Sequel,* although the originals were often unintentionally funny themselves.

Airport 1975 ***see*** **Airport**

Airport '77 ***see*** **Airport**

Aladdin ***see*** **Aladdin and His Wonderful Lamp**

14 Aladdin and His Wonderful Lamp

Based on the *Tales of the Arabian Nights.* Story: Aladdin, the son of a Baghdadian tailor, falls in love with a princess and although she is smitten as well, her father, the Sultan, will not sanction the match. The princess' throne is threatened by an usurper but Aladdin puts everything right and wins the princess with the assistance of a genie confined in a magic lamp found by our hero.

• ***Aladdin and His Wonderful Lamp*** (remake). Fox Pictures, 1917. Silent. Directors: C.M. and S.A. Franklin. Cast: Francis Carpenter (Aladdin), Fred Turner (Mustapha, the tailor), Virginia Corbin (Princess Badr al-Budur), Alfred Paget (The Sultan), Elmo Lincoln (The Genie), Violet Radcliffe, Buddy Messinger, Lewis Sargent.

• ***1001 Nights*** (remake). Columbia Pictures, 1945. Director: Alfred Green; screenwriters: Wilfred Pettitt, Richard English and Jack Henley. Cast: Cornel Wilde (Aladdin), Evelyn Keyes (The Genie), Phil Silvers (Abdulah), Adele Jergens (Princess Armina), Dennis Hoey (The Sultan/Prince Hadji), Dusty Anderson, Phillip Van Zandt, Rex Ingram, Gus Schilling, Nestor Paiva.

• ***Aladdin and His Wonderful Lamp*** (remake). Monogram Pictures, 1952. Director: Lew Landers; screenwriters: Howard Dimsdale and Millard Kaufman. Cast: Patricia Medina (Jasmine), John Sands (Aladdin), Richard Erdman (Mirza), John Dehner (Bokra), Charles Horvath (The Genie), Billy House, Ned Young, Noreen Nash.

• ***Wonders of Aladdin*** (remake). Lux Films/Embassy/MGM, Italy. Director: Henry Levin; screenwriter: Luther Davis. Cast: Donald O'Connor (Aladdin), Noelle Adam (The Princess), Vittorio de Sica, Aldo Fabrizi, Michele Mercier.

Other filmings of the Aladdin story were made in England in 1898, 1923 (entitled *One Arabian Night*) and once again in 1952 simply as *Aladdin.* An independent American production was made in 1923. India made versions of the story in 1926, 1930, 1933, 1935, 1939, 1951, 1955, 1957, 1963 and 1965. Germany's two versions, both called *Adventures of Prince Ahmed,* were made in 1926 and 1942. The former, by Lotte Reiniger, was the only feature-length silhouette film ever made. In addition, versions of the legend were made in Holland in 1936, in the Philippines in 1947, in Hungary in 1955, a

French-Italian version in 1961, a French production in 1969, and a Russian version in 1967.

The 1917 filming of *Aladdin and His Wonderful Lamp* was a Fox Kiddies Feature with the main parts played by children who did so with much enthusiasm but not much acting ability. The sets were impressive and the production ran nearly two hours.

Columbia's 1945 version took a great many liberties with the story including having the genie played by curvaceous red-head Evelyn Keyes who did her best to thwart Aladdin's wedding plans with Princess Armina. Another feature was when she turned Aladdin into a Baghdadian crooner, much to the delight of screaming harem cuties. Phil Silvers made no attempt to alter his act to fit the period but his bits were considered hilarious at the time.

In 1952, the interest centered more on the Princess, portrayed by the beautiful Patricia Medina, than Aladdin, only adequately played by the soon-to-be-forgotten John Sands. This time Aladdin is a pick-pocket who falls for the daughter of the Caliph. John Dehner, a suitor of the princess, more interested in her throne, is a properly dastardly villain. *Wonders of Aladdin,* despite Donald O'Connor's good intentions and hectic action, is a flat, charmless piece which only appealed to the most undemanding kiddies.

Alaska Seas *see* **Spawn of the North**

The Alf Garnet Saga *see* **Till Death Do Us Part**

15 Alfie

Based on the play by Bill Naughton. Story: Where glib, cynical, cockney Alfie is concerned, women are just "birds" to be enjoyed and discarded. His involvement with quiet Gilda results in her pregnancy. Although Alfie does not desert her and instead helps her through the pregnancy and deeply cares for their child, he cannot make a permanent or exclusive commitment to her. He seduces rather plain, married Lily and when she becomes pregnant, arranges for an abortion. At other times he becomes involved with women who are as casual about love and sex as is he. In one case he serves as a gigolo for a rich American widow, Ruby, who dumps him when her interest lags. Through all of this the audience is subtly brought to the realization of the emptiness of Alfie's life, something he suspects but is helpless to change.

Paramount/Sheldrake, 1966 (original). Director: Lewis Gilbert; screenwriter: Bill Naughton. Cast: Michael Caine (Alfie), Vivien Merchant (Lily), Shirley Ann Field (Carla), Millicent Martin (Siddie), Jane Asher (Annie), Julie Foster (Gilda), Shelley Winters (Ruby), Eleanor Bron, Denholm Elliott.

• ***Alfie Darling*** (remake). EMI/Signal, 1975. Director and screenwriter: Ken Hughes. Cast: Alan Price (Alfie), Jill Townsend (Abby), Paul Copley (Bakey), Joan Collins (Fay), Shelia White (Norma), Annie Ross (Claire), Hannah Gordon, Rula Lenska.

Alfie was a rather startling and somewhat upsetting work when released in 1966. Here is a person of obvious charm incapable of any real feelings for a woman. His casual movement from one affair to another was due to amorality, not immorality. The picture gave an affirmative answer to the question posed in the words of the extremely popular title song, "What's it all about Alfie? Is it just for the moment we live?" The subject of the film wasn't casual sex and the breakdown of moral standards but rather the emptiness of spirit of life when there is no involvement. We know that Alfie has some understanding of this because much as the chorus in a Shakespearean play he occasionally discusses his feelings in an aside to the camera and audience.

The remake is a crude and vulgar rip-off with no subtlety and no point. Here Alfie is a teamster who drives a huge trailer truck between London and various other cities. He has a female sleeping companion at every stop but no interest in any of them. Ultimately he finds a girl, Abby, who at least initially resists his charms but as so many before succumbs to his persistence. They plan to marry but she dies in a plane crash. If there's a message here, it must be that it's better not to get involved, because then there can be no loss.

Alfie Darling *see* **Alfie**

16 Alf's Button

Based on a serial written by W.A. Darlington. Story: Private Alf Higgins, serving in France during World War I, discovers a button on his uniform which when rubbed conjures up a genie. This helpful fellow from Aladdin Lamp days propels Alf and his buddy Bill into a series of fantastic and supposedly hilarious adventures.

• ***Alf's Button*** (remake). Gaumont, Great Britain, 1930. Director: W.P. Kellino; screenwriter: L'Estrange Fawcett. Cast: Tubby Eldin (Pvt. Alf Higgins), Alf Goddard (Bill Grant), Nora Swinburne (Lady Isobel), Polly Ward (Liz), Humberson Wright (Eustace), Jimmy Nervo, Teddy Knox, Cyril McLaglen, Gypsy Rhouma, Peter Hadden, Annie Esmond, Merle Oberon.

• ***Alf's Button Afloat*** (remake). Gainsborough, 1938. Director: Marcel Varnel; screenwriters: Marriott Edgar, Val Guest and Ralph Smart. Cast: Bud Flanagan, Chesney Allen, Jimmy Nervo, Teddy Knox, Charles Naughton and Jimmy Gold (The Crazy Gang), Alastair Sim (The Genie), Wally Patch, Peter Gawthorne.

Darlington's fantastic adventure farce was first filmed as a silent in 1921 at Hepworth Films with Leslie Henson as Alf. It earned a great deal of money for its producers at its release and many subsequent re-issues. The 1930 talkie, while not quite as successful, did have its funny moments with this updated Aladdin's lamp story. In 1938, musical hall headliners, The Crazy Gang, appear as six itinerant brothers who join the Marines by mistake and find a brass button that once was part of Aladdin's magic lamp. When it is rubbed, a genie appears who develops a taste for Hollywood gangster films and because he usually misunderstands commands, his granting of the brothers' wishes brings them embarrassment along with riches. It's a lot of laughs for those who like low-brow British humor.

Algiers *see* **Pepe-Le-Moko**

Ali Baba and the Forty Thieves *see* **Chu Chin Chow**

Alias French Gertie *see* **Smooth As Satin**

17 Alias Jimmy Valentine

Based on the play by Paul Armstrong and a story by O. Henry. Story: While planning a bank job with his cronies, master safecracker Jimmy Valentine falls in love with Rose Lane and decides to put his criminal days behind him and marry the girl. He secures a position as an assistant cashier in the bank of a small town and reverts to his real name, Lee Randall. Police detective Doyle, suspicious of the "retirement" of the famous criminal, tracks him down. Somehow Randall is able to convince Doyle that his suspicions that he is the infamous Jimmy Valentine are false but then Randall risks exposure by breaking into the vault of his employer to rescue a little girl who had been accidently imprisoned within. Convinced by this act of heroism that Randall is sincere about his retirement, Doyle leaves the ex-safecracker to his future with Rose.

• ***Alias Jimmy Valentine*** (remake). MGM, 1920. Silent. Director: Edmund Mortimer; screenwriter: Finis Fox. Cast: Bert Lytell (Lee Randall, alias Jimmy Valentine), Vola Vale (Rose Lane), Wilton Taylor (Inspector Doyle), Eugene Pallette (Red Jocelyn), Marc Robbins (Bill Avery), Robert Dunbar, Winter Hall, James Farley.

• ***Alias Jimmy Valentine*** (remake). MGM, 1929. Director: Jack Conway; screenwriters: Sarah Y. Mason and A.P. Younger. Cast: William Haines (Randall—Jimmy Valentine), Lelia Hyams (Rose), Lionel Barrymore (Doyle), Karl Dane (Swede), Tully Marshall (Avery), Howard Hickman, Billy Butts, Evelyn Mills.

• ***The Return of Jimmy Valentine*** (sequel). Republic Pictures, 1936. Director: Lewis D. Collins; screenwriters: Jack Natteford and Olive Cooper. Cast: Roger Pryor (Gary Howard), Charlotte Henry (Midge Davis), Robert Warwick (Jimmy Davis), James Burtis (Mac), Edgar Kennedy (Callahan), J. Carroll Naish (Tony Scrapelli), Lois Wilson, Wade Boteler.

Alias Jimmy Valentine was first filmed in 1915 by World Pictures with Robert Warwick as the "cracksman." Warwick reclaimed the role in the 1936 production of *The Return of Jimmy Valentine.* In that story, a newspaper, having difficulty competing with radio for advertisers, offers a large reward to anyone who can locate the long-absent safecracker Jimmy Valentine. It turns out that it is the paper's own star reporter who, after a relentless search, locates Jimmy Davis (played by Robert Warwick) and is certain he is Valentine. Naturally, Davis, totally reformed, doesn't want to be re-discovered and is content in retirement. He has a lovely daughter, Midge, played by Charlotte Henry of *Alice in Wonderland* fame, for whose love the reporter allows the aging ex-criminal his peace and amonymity.

The 1920 and 1929 films were very faithful to Paul Armstrong's play, both with capable casts, even though the characters seem basically stereotypes, particularly the role of the detective Doyle who is sort of a flat-footed Inspector Javert. The 1929 version was the first sound film produced by MGM and it's clear that the studio had a great deal to learn about the new technique.

Alias Nick Beal *see* **Faust**

18 Alias the Deacon

Based on the play by John B. Hymer and Leroy Clemens. Story: The Deacon, a professional cardsharp and gambler, meets John Adams, a young hobo, and Nancy, a girl disguised as a boy, when he rescues her from tramps who have discovered her sex. The Deacon recognizes the girl as his daughter whom he hasn't seen since she was a child; he stays at the hotel where she has taken a job as a clerk in order to protect her. Meanwhile, John Adams, who loves Nancy, has taken a job working in a garage. In an effort to get money to make a home for himself and Nancy, he suffers a terrible beating in a prize fight. The fight promoter, Cunningham, refuses to pay up and arranges to have John arrested on some trumped-up charges. The Deacon gets Cunningham into a poker game, wins all of the promoter's money and gets him to confess that he framed John. The Deacon turns Cunningham in to the authorities and, content that his daughter will be taken care of well by John, skips town to avoid the police who by now are onto his profession.

Universal, 1927 (original). Silent. Director: Edward Sloman; screenwriter: Charles Kenyon. Cast: Jean Hersholt (The Deacon), June Marlowe (Nancy), Ralph Graves (John Adams), Myrtle Stedman (Mrs. Clark), Lincoln Plummer (Cunningham), Ned Sparks, Tom Kennedy, Maurice Murphy, George West.

• ***Half a Sinner*** (remake). Universal, 1934. Director: Kurt Neumann; screenwriters: Earle Snell and Clarence Marks. Cast: Berton Churchill (The Deacon), Joel McCrea (John Adams), Sally Blane (Phyllis), Spencer Charters (Jim Cunningham), Mickey Rooney (Willie), Alexandra Carlisle (Mrs. Clark), Gay Seabrook, Russell Hopton, Guinn Williams, Bert Roach, Walter Brennan.

• ***Alias the Deacon*** (remake). Universal, 1940. Director: Christy Cabanne; screenwriter: Nat Perrin. Cast: Bob Burns (Deke Caswell), Mischa Auer (Andre), Peggy Moran (Phyllis), Dennis O'Keefe (Johnny Sloan), Virginia Brissac (Elsie Clark), Bennie Bartlett, Spencer Charters, Thurston Hall, Guinn Williams, Ed Brophy.

The 1927 filming of this comedy-melodrama has Jean Hersholt as something of a sanctimonious flim-flam man. By 1934, Berton Churchill, re-creating his 1925 stage role, poses as a hillbilly deacon, rather loveable as he only trims those who deserve it. In 1940, Bob Burns put a great deal of his radio-comedy persona into the role, passing off humorous comments which at the time were considered topical. In every production, the role of the Deacon dominates proceedings, almost as if the screenwriters had wearied after they perfected this part and had little energy left to bring much life to the other main characters. The flaws in the three filmings lay with the romantic scenes and characters, where in the sound versions the dialog isn't too convincing. Some of the character roles are well handled; in particular Myrtle Stedman as the hotel owner in the silent production, Guinn Williams as the boxer in both talkies and Mischa Auer as a slapstick local barber in the 1940 picture.

L'Alibi *see* **Alibi**

19 Alibi

Based on the story by Marcel Achard. Story: Professor Winkler, a sinister mind-reader, commits a murder to cover up an earlier slaying. He provides himself with an alibi by paying Parisian night-club hostess Helene a large sum of money to say he spent the night of the killing with her. It's Inspector Calas' responsibility with the help of his assistant Laurent to learn the facts of the case and bring the villain to justice.

• ***L'Alibi*** (original). B-N Films, France, 1938. Director: Pierre Chenal; screenwriters: J. Companeez and R. Juttke. Cast: Erich von Stroheim (Professor Winkler), Louis Jouvet (Inspector Calas), Jany Holt (Helene), Albert Prejean (Laurent), Phillippe Richard, Margo Lico, Florence Marly.

• ***Alibi*** (remake). Republis/Corona, Great Britain, 1943. Director: Brian Desmond Hurst; screenwriters: R. Carter and J. Companeez. Cast: Margaret Lockwood (Helene), Hugh Sinclair (Inspector Calas), Raymond Lovell (Professor Winkler), James Mason (Laurent), Enid Stamp-Taylor, Hartley Power, Jane Carr, Rodney Ackland, Edana Rommey.

The 1938 French film was released in the U.S. with subtitles which weren't always the most grammatical or the best translations. Von Stroheim was convincingly menacing as the mystic and Jany Holt was plausible as the hostess who wasn't too particular how she earned her keep. The dialogue, while rather risque for the time, was essential to the plot. The photography and lighting left a great deal to be desired, especially in close-ups. This complaint carried over to the 1943 remake which also seemed to suffer from poor judgement in the cutting room. While the performances of Lockwood, Sinclair and Lovell were strong, director Hurst did not provide the tenseness in the unravelling of the story that was called for.

20 Alice Adams

Based on the novel by Booth Tarkington. Story: Frustrated by her cloddish family's modest means and constantly embarrassed by her vulgar brother, Alice Adams builds romantic dreams and attempts to give the impression that her family is both socially and economically more prominent than they are. She particularly wishes to impress Arthur Russell, the man she has her heart set on winning as a husband. At a dinner party, Russell discovers the truth about Alice and is disgusted by the behavior of her family. Russell abandons Alice, who finally realizes that she has only been fooling herself, and accepts her fate to be doomed to a dull unprosperous life in a hick town.

Associated Exhibitors, 1923 (original). Silent. Director and screenwriter: Rowland V. Lee. Cast: Florence Vidor (Alice Adams), Vernon Steele (Arthur Russell), Claude Gillingham (Virgil Adams), Harold Goodwin (Walter Adams), Margaret McWade (Mrs. Adams), Thomas Ricketts, Margaret Landis, Gertrude Astor.

• ***Alice Adams*** (remake). RKO, 1935. Director: George Stevens; screenwriters: Dorothy Yost, Mortimer Offver and Jane Murfin. Cast: Katharine Hepburn (Alice Adams), Fred MacMurray (Arthur Russell), Fred Stone (Mr. Adams), Frank Albertson (Walter Adams), Anne Shoemaker (Mrs. Adams), Evelyn Venable, Carles Grapewin, Grady Sutton.

Booth Tarkington produced a sociological study of life in a small town and the silent film was true to his realistic approach with impressive performances given by Florence Vidor as the girl who chooses to live in a dream world and Harold Goodwin as the brother who is a boorish, constant reminder of the truth about her family and herself that she wishes not to believe. By 1935, the producers wished to emphasize the romantic aspects of the story for their young star, Katharine Hepburn, and so changed the ending. Although it didn't seem plausible or a promising match, what with the naive escapism of Alice and her family's unappealing nature, the picture ends with a final fade-out clinch and Russell whispering, "I love you, Alice." Hepburn was nominated for an Academy Award for this picture, and although her performance was a bit more appealing than that in *Morning Glory*, for which she won an Oscar, she did not take home another one this time. MacMurray, on loan from Paramount, was so impressive that his standing with his home studio was greatly enhanced. The picture remains a fine exhibition of the talent and beauty of the great actress when she was young.

Alice's Adventures in Wonderland *see* Alice in Wonderland

21 Alice in Wonderland

Based on the books of Lewis Carroll. Story: Alice follows a white rabbit down a hole into a world where she has several strange and wonderful encounters with the likes of Humpty Dumpty, the Mock Turtle, the Mad Hatter, the March Hare, Tweedledum and Tweedledee, the Queen of Hearts, and other curious creatures.

Hepworth, Great Britain, 1903 (original). Silent. Directors: Cecil Hepworth and Percy Stow; screenwriter: Cecil Hepworth. Cast: May Clark (Alice), Cecil Hepworth (Frog), Mrs. Hepworth (White Rabbit/Queen), Norman Whitten (Fish/Mad Hatter), Stanley Faithfull, Geoffrey Faithful.

• ***Alice in Wonderland*** (remake). Paramount Pictures, 1933. Director: Norman Z. McLeod; screenwriters: Joseph L. Mankiewicz and William Cameron Menzies. Cast: Charlotte Henry (Alice), W.C. Fields (Humpty Dumpty), Cary Grant (Mock Turtle), Gary Cooper (White Knight), Edward Everett Horton (Mad Hatter), Edna May Oliver (Red Queen), Jack Oakie (Tweedledum), Leon Errol (Uncle), Charles Ruggles (March Hare), May Robson (Queen of Hearts), Louise Fazenda (White Queen), Ned Sparks (Caterpillar), Alison Skipworth (Duchess), Richard Arlen, Roscoe Ates, William Austin, Billy Barty, Billy Bevan, Colin Campbell, Harvey Clark, Jack Duffy, Alec B. Francis, Skeets Gallagher, Raymond Hatton, Charles Butterfield, Lucien Littlefield, Mae Marsh, Polly Moran, Jackie Searl, Ford Sterling.

• ***Alice in Wonderland*** (remake). Walt Disney/RKO, 1951. Directors: Clyde

Geronomi, Hamilton Luske and Wilfred Jackson; screenwriter: uncredited. Cast: Voices of: Kathryn Beaumont (Alice), Ed Wynn (Mad Hatter), Richard Haydn (Caterpillar), Sterling Holloway (Cheshire Cat), Jerry Colonna (March Hare), Verna Felton (Queen of Hearts), Pat O'Malley (Walrus, Carpenter, Tweedleedum and Tweedleedee), Bill Thompson (White Rabbit/Dodo), Heather Angel (Alice's sister), Joseph Kearsn, Larry Grey, Queenie Leonard, Dink Trout, Doris Lloyd, James Macdonald, Pinto Colvig.

• ***Alice's Adventures in Wonderland*** (remake). Shaftel/Twentieth Century–Fox, Great Britain, 1972. Director and screenwriter: William Sterling. Cast: Fiona Fullerton (Alice), Hywell Bennett (Duckworth), Michael Crawford (White Rabbit), Robert Helpmann (Mad Hatter), Michael Horden (Mock Turtle), Lewis Carroll (Michael Jayston), Davy Kaye (Mouse), Dudley Moore (Dormouse), Spike Milligan (Gryphon), Dennis Price (King of Hearts), Ralph Richardson (Caterpillar), Flora Robson (Queen of Hearts), Peter Sellers (March Hare), Rodney Bewes, Ray Brooks, Peter Bull, Julian Chagrin, Freddie Earle, Roy Kinnear, Patsy Rowlands, Dennis Waterman, Frank and Freddie Cox.

This children's classic and equally fanciful companion piece *Alice Through the Looking Glass* has also been brought to the screen with varying degrees of success in 1909, 1910, 1915, 1927, 1928, 1948, 1951, 1966, 1972, 1976 and 1978. Today anyone who would say, "I love all children—except boys!" as did the Reverend Dodgson (Lewis Carroll) would likely find himself with quite a bit of explaining to do—for instance, whether he had a "Lolita" complex. But churchman and mathematician Dodgson apparently was not really a dirty old man. His inspiration for his masterpiece was Alice Liddell, daughter of the dean of Christ Church, and in particular by a trip upriver from Oxford to Godstow he took with her and her sisters on July 4, 1862. These masterful children's classics, among the most frequently translated books of all time, are at the same time tomes of modern logic, with every syllogism used by the author perfectly correct—even if nonsense.

Usually the 1933 Paramount production receives the most critical attention, but the Disney piece has plenty of supporters. Of help to this production was the excellent animation, the fine voices of a strong cast of character performers and the music of Bob Hilliard and Sammy Fain, including "I'm Late," "In a World of My Own" and "The Walrus and the Carpenter"; Don Raye and Gene De Paul's "Twas Brillig"; and "The Unbirthday Song" by Mack David, Al Hoffman and Jerry Livingston. The 1972 British version starts out brightly enough, but quickly settles down into just a parade of characters and performers trying very hard to be noticed in their cameo-like roles.

Alice Through the Looking Glass *see* **Alice in Wonderland**

All Night Long *see* **Othello**

All That Money Can Buy *see* **Faust**

22 All Quiet on the Western Front

Based on the novel by Erich Maria Remarque. Story: As World War I begins, a German high school teacher whips his male students into a frenzy of patriotism and en masse they join the army. They soon discover the reality of war, its brutality and meaninglessness, as one by one they are picked off and die in the trenches. Only one of the boys, Paul Baumer, makes it back home alive and that is only on a brief furlough from the madness. His disillusionment with war is only made greater when he discovers those on the home-front still see it as a glorious and glamorous struggle. His former teacher is now in the process of haranguing more young scholars, now no more than sixteen years old, to take up arms for the Kaiser and country. Baumer speaks the truth about the absurdity and horror of battle, only to be accused of being a coward. Wearily, he makes his way back to the front, where he is killed by a French bullet just as he is about to feed a little bird on the trunk of a tree. And so ends this classic antiwar piece, with kindness and death.

Universal Pictures, 1930 (original). Director: Lewis Milestone; screenwriters: George Abbott, Maxwell Anderson and Dell Andrews. Cast: Lew Ayres (Paul Baumer), Louis Wolheim (Katczinsky), John Wray (Himmelstross), Slim Summerville (Tjaden), Arnold Lucy (Kantorek), Russell Gleason (Muller), Raymond Griffith (Gerard Duval), Ben Alexander (Kemmerick), Owen Davis, Jr., Beryl Mercer, William Bakewell, Joan Marsh, Scott Kulk, Yola D'Avril, Walter Browne Rogers.

• ***The Road Back*** (sequel). Universal, 1937. Director: James Whale; screenwriters: R.C. Sherriff and Charles Kenyon. Cast: John King (Ernst), Richard Cromwell (Ludwig), Slim Summerville (Tjaden), Andy Devine (Willy), Barbara Read (Lucy), Louise Fazenda (Angelina), Noah Beery, Jr. (Wessling), Maurice Murphy (Albert), John Emery (Capt. Von Hagen), Etienne Girodot, Lionel Atwill, Henry Hunter, Spring Byington, Frank Reicher.

Little can be added to the millions of words that have been written describing the impact of the most influential antiwar film ever made. It was with some bravery that the producers decided to film this story at all, and even more so in not pulling any punches as to how gruesome and repulsive war is, and that the laying down of the lives of young boys is despicable, no matter how much one loves his country or how horrible the enemy. The fact that its message has not been heeded and many more young boys have had to sacrifice their lives and ambitions since its filming in no way diminishes the power of the movie. If it cannot influence those in power who decide to pursue a warlike posture, at least it should be seen by all young boys, so they will not be misled into believing that going into battle is glorious and high-minded.

In 1937, Universal filmed the sequel, *The Road Back*, based on a follow-up novel by Erich Maria Remarque dealing with the question: What happens to men when they return from war? By this time, it wasn't as popular to be antiwar, what with the conflicts already enjoined throughout the war and the very real likelihood that another world war would have to be fought.

In making political compromises, the producers weakened the story of German boys returning home after having survived four years in the trenches.

Despite some outstanding sequences, such as the one when Captain Van Hagen dismisses the 30-odd men left in his battalion and the ghosts of hundreds, dimly outlined, also line up, the film does not develop a strong, compelling story and hardly builds to any point, finishing with a weak and disappointing ending. Hollywood would have to wait another nine years before the readjustment of war veterans would be handled with care and sensitivity in *The Best Years of Our Lives.*

Rather than inadequately describe the emotions that *All Quiet on the Western Front* draws from its audiences and come up far short, we offer the following quotes, spoken by Lew Ayres as Paul Baumer, to sum up the picture. In speaking to the students in his old school while on furlough, Baumer deglamorizes war by advising them, "When it comes to dying for your country, it's better not to die at all." And speaking of how it is at the front, "We live in the trenches out there. We fight—we try not to be killed, but sometimes we are—that's all." Especially moving is Baumer's pleading with the dead French soldier (played superbly by Raymond Griffith) he has killed:

> When you jumped in here, you were my enemy—and I was afraid of you. But you're just a man like me and I killed you. Forgive me, comrade. Say that for me. Say you forgive me! Oh, no, you're dead! You're better off than I am—you're through—they can't do any more to you now. Oh, God! Why did they do this to us? We only wanted to live, you and I. Why should they send us out to fight each other? If we threw away these rifles and these uniforms, you could be my brother, just like Kate and Albert. You'll have to forgive me comrade.

23 All the Brothers Were Valiant

Based on a story by Ben Ames Williams. Story: Joel Shore is appointed captain of a whaling schooner once commanded by his elder brother who has been lost at sea. With his wife, Priscilla, he sets sail, seeking whales. Priscilla believes that Joel is somewhat cowardly and when the ship picks up brother Mark, she is drawn to his manliness. Mark incites the crew to a mutiny when Joel refuses to alter course to search for a cache of pearls that Mark describes. During the mutiny, Mark redeems himself by coming to the aid of his brother but falls overboard and Joel is unsuccessful in his attempts to rescue the lost man. Priscilla finally realizes that her husband is brave and they sail off towards a happy future.

Metro Pictures, 1923 (original). Silent. Director: Irvin V. Willat; screenwriter: Julien Josephson. Cast: Malcolm McGregor (Joel Shore), Billie Dove (Priscilla), Lon Chaney (Mark Shore), William H. Orlamond (Aaron Burnham), Robert McKim (Finch), Robert Kortman, Otto Brower, Curt Renfeld.

• ***Across to Singapore*** (remake). MGM, 1928. Silent. Director: William Nigh; screenwriter: Ted Shane. Cast: Ramon Novarro (Joel Shore), Joan Crawford (Priscilla), Ernest Torrence (Mark Shore), Frank Currier (Jeremiah Shore), Dan Wolheim (Noah Shore), Duke Martin (Matthew Shore), Edward Connelly, James Mason.

• ***All the Brothers Were Valiant*** (remake). MGM, 1953. Director: Richard Thorpe; screenwriter: Harry Brown. Cast: Robert Taylor (Joel Shore), Stewart

Granger (Mark Shore), Ann Blyth (Priscilla), Betta St. John (Native Girl), James Whitmore (Fletcher), Kurt Kasznar (Quint), Lewis Stone (Capt. Holt), Robert Burton, Peter Whitney, John Lupton, James Bell.

Each of the three film versions of this whaling adventure story pleased audiences looking for exciting escapism. Each successive version was played for more hokum but it didn't detract from the enjoyment of the story. In the 1928 version, Joel and Priscilla weren't married. In fact she was unwillingly engaged to Mark, who had been abandoned in Singapore by his crew. Joe sails with Priscilla to find his brother and when the reunion is accomplished, Mark sees how things are and steps aside so that Joel and Priscilla can be together.

In the 1953 Technicolor picture, much is made of the differences in personalities of the two brothers, with Mark being the more interesting, particularly to Priscilla, the young bride of the steady but unexciting Joel. In the end she decides that dullness isn't all that bad and that her husband is actually a brave and valiant man. Part of the film deals with Mark's adventures while stranded and how he discovers the fortune in pearls which he wishes to use his brother's ship to reclaim. While lost he dallied with a beautiful native girl, played with great sexy innocence by Betta St. John. The special effects, the excitement of the danger of the whaling game and the climactic mutiny are as exciting sequences as could be hoped for by any audience.

None of the performers can be accused of giving stellar acting performances, although in such a story little emoting is expected. Still, the three pairs of brothers and their conflicts were well-handled by McGregor and Chaney, Novarro and Torrence, and Taylor and Granger respectively. As for the females, little was demanded of them, other than to look attractive and be confused in their feelings for the pairs of brothers. In this respect, Dove, Crawford and Blyth were more than adequate.

24 Almost a Honeymoon

Based on a play by Walter Ellis. Story: A young British man-about-town has let his flat to an engaged couple. The girl decides to spend the eve before her wedding at the flat. The young man, having forgotten that he has let his flat because he had been drinking rather more than usual, decides to go home and sleep it off. Such trifling circumstances are the basis for the somewhat expected hilarity when the man and girl discover they are sharing the same bedroom.

Wardon Films, England, 1930 (original). Director and screenwriter: Monty Banks. Cast: Clifford Mollison, Dod Watts, Donald Calthrop, Lamont Dickson, Pamela Carme, C.M. Hallard, Winifred Hall, Edward Thane.

• ***Almost a Honeymoon*** (remake). Pathe, England, 1938. Director: Norman Lee; screenwriters: Kenneth Horne and Ralph Neale. Cast: Tommy Trinder, Linden Travers, Edmond Breon, Frederick Burtwell, Vivienne Bennett, Arthur Hambling, Betty Jardine, Ian Fleming.

It's a frisky farce with slick and daring dialog for the times, with all the stops pulled out to titillate audiences with bedroom humor, clever lines and too much slapstick. The same ground has been covered on so many occasions since, making these movies terribly dated. Gags tend to repeat as if the directors were afraid that the pace of the pieces was such that the audiences may have missed them the first time through. Both versions seem too long with plenty of examples of remarkably bad timing.

25 Almost Human

Based on the story "The Bar Sinister" by Richard Harding Davis. Story: A real bitch, Maggie, lures champion Regent Royal from his luxurious home to the old barn where she resides. After having his way with her, Regent Royal finds his way home. The result of the affair is a pup, named Pal, who is soon abandoned by his mother. In a park, Pal takes up with Mary Kelly, a homeless orphan, who is rescued by John Livingston, the master of Royal Regent, when she almost drowns trying to save a child. John takes Mary home, where she is not welcomed by John's mother. Nevertheless they fall in love and, disinherited when they marry, accept employment as a chauffeur and maid in an aristocrat's home. At a party, Mary misinterprets John's attention to a former sweetheart and leaves him to work for a doctor in whose home she has their baby. Pal is eventually able to get the young couple back together and Mrs. Livingston relents and blesses the marriage.

Pathe, 1927 (original). Silent. Director: Frank Urson; screenwriter: Clara Beranger. Cast: Vera Reynolds (Mary Kelly), Kenneth Thomson (John Livingston), Claire McDowell (Mrs. Livingston), Majel Coleman (Cecile Adams), Hank (Pal, a dog), Paul (Regent Royal, a dog), Trixie (Maggie, a dog).

• ***It's a Dog's Life*** (remake). MGM, 1955. Director: Herman Hoffman; screenwriter: John Michael Hayes. Cast: Jarma Lewis, Jeff Richards, Edmund Gwenn, Dean Jagger, Richard Anderson, Sally Frazer, J.M. Kerrigan.

It stretches credibility that anyone would film such a story once, let alone twice. Neither version will become a cult film nor will their canine heroes and heroines rival Rin-Tin-Tin or Lassie. The 1955 film was meant for the second-line theaters content to run "B" pictures. Jarma Lewis, a fetching brunette who never got any better roles, was stuck with dull Jeff Richards who had somewhat better luck because of his muscular build. The only other thing that can be said of the movie is that the terrier had all the best lines and expressed the greatest range of emotions.

Aloha *see* **Aloha Oe**

26 Aloha Oe

Based on an original story by J.G. Hawks and Thomas H. Ince. Story: A successful lawyer, dependent on strong liquor and drugs, takes a sea voyage to a remote South Seas island where he becomes a beachcomber, falls for the daughter of the native chief and is proclaimed the Sun God's son. Homesick, he goes back home to face a welcome that soon has him scurrying back to his happy island and native bride.

England, 1915 (original). Silent. Director: Thomas H. Ince; screenwriters: J.G. Hawks and Thomas H. Ince. Cast: Willard Mack (the attorney), Enid Markey (his native wife).

• ***Aloha*** (remake). Tiffany Films, 1931. Director: Al Rogell; screenwriters: Leslie Mason and W. Totman. Cast: Ben Lyon, Raquel Torres, Robert Edeson, Alan Hale, Thelma Todd, Marion Douglas, Dickie Moore.

The sound feature, a knockdown of more successful films such as *White Cargo,* borrows from the Ince piece, but prefers an unhappy ending, forcing the native girl, played by Torres, to pay for the affair and child she has with married man Lyon. She hurls herself into a volcano before her suddenly conscious-stricken lover can arrive to save her. Critics were unanimous in the belief that even the most nondiscriminating viewers would walk out in disgust from this poorly made film. Apparently, not many ever paid the price of admission in the first place.

27 Aloma of the South Seas

Based on the play by John B. Hymer and Leroy Clemens. Story: Aloma, a beautiful dancer on Paradise Island, jealously guarded by her native lover, Nuitane, is defended from the unwanted advances of Red Malloy, a dishonest trader, by Bob Holden, an American seeking to forget an unhappy love affair. When his former love, Sylvia, and her husband Van Templeton show up, Aloma, who by now has fallen in love with Bob, is tricked into a brief affair with Van. Bob, who realizes that he still loves Sylvia, is lost at sea with Van when their canoe capsizes. Aloma and Sylvia are drawn together in a common bond of grief. But when Bob reappears, he goes off with Sylvia and Aloma returns to Nuitane.

Paramount, 1926 (original). Silent. Director: Maurice Tourneur; screenwriter: James Ashmore Creelman. Cast: Gilda Gray (Aloma), Warner Baxter (Nuitane), William Powell (Van Templeton), Percy Marmont (Bob Holden), Julienne Johnston (Sylvia), Harry Morey (Red Malloy), Joseph Smiley, Frank Montgomery, Madame Burani, Ernestine Gaines.

• ***Aloma of the South Seas*** (remake). Paramount, 1941. Director: Alfred Santell; screenwriters: Frank Butler, Seena Owen and Lillian Hayward. Cast: Dorothy Lamour (Aloma), Jon Hall (Tanoa), Lynne Overman (Corky), Phillip Reed (Reno), Katherine de Mille (Kari), Fritz Leiber (High Priest), Dona Drake, Esther Dale, Pedro de Cordova.

In the remake, Dorothy Lamour, the queen of the sarong, is the bride chosen at childhood for the son of the chief of a South Seas island. Tanoa, as he is called, has been away for 15 years in the United States getting an education and has no intention of marrying someone whom he has never met. Naturally, he meets Aloma, without knowing she's his intended, and falls in love with her. His slippery cousin, Reno, tries to break up the affair, and is banned from the island. This villain returns to disrupt the wedding and makes the gods angry, setting off an eruption from the local volcano. Somehow the marriage party survives but not before many others meet a fiery fate.

Both versions of the story offer colorful sets and pretty people who have their simple lives thrown into turmoil by disasters.

Always a Bride *see* **Brides Are Like That**

Always Goodbye *see* **Gallant Lady**

Always in My Heart *see* **Daughters Courageous**

Les Amants Terribles *see* **Private Lives**

28 Amateur Gentleman

Based on the book by Jeffrey Farnoul. Story: Barnabas Barty, son of an innkeeper and former bare-knuckles boxer, inherits a fortune and moves to London to learn to become a gentleman. He meets Lady Cleone Meredith with whom he falls deeply in love and Viscount Devenham from whom he purchases a high-spirited horse, which he enters in a steeplechase. His rival for both Lady Cleone and the steeplechase is Sir Mortimer Carnaby, a vicious enemy. Trying to be helpful, Barnabas offers to repay the debts of Lady Cleone's brother Ronald but because of the influence of Mortimer, Ronald refuses the kind gesture. Barnabas' horse wins the steeplechase and Lady Cleone. Infuriated, Mortimer buys up Ronald's notes and has the creditor threaten Ronald with imprisonment. Desperate, Ronald kills the creditor, then follows Barnabas to Mortimer's country house where Ronald and Mortimer kill each other. Disillusioned by London society, Barnabas returns to his village, followed closely by Lady Cleone who only wants to be with him.

• ***Amateur Gentleman*** (remake). First National Pictures, 1926. Silent. Director: Sidney Olcott; screenwriter: Lillie Hayward. Cast: Richard Barthelmess (Barnabas Barty), Dorothy Dunbar (Lady Cleone Meredith), John Miljan (Viscount Devenham), Gardner James (Ronald), Nigel Barrie (Mortimer Carnaby), Brandon Hurst, Billie Bennett, Herbert Grimwood, Gino Corrado, Sidney De Gray, John Peters.

• ***Amateur Gentleman*** (remake). Criterion Film Productions/United Artists, 1936. Director: Thornton Freeland; screenwriters: Clemence Dane and Sergei Nolbandon. Cast: Douglas Fairbanks, Jr. (Barnabas Barty), Elissa Landi (Lady Cleone), Hugh Williams (Ronald), Natty Bell (Gordon Hawkes), Frank Pettingell (John Barty), Basil Sydney (Chichester), Athole Stewart, Coral Brown, Irene Brown, Margaret Lockwood, Esme Percy.

A brief silent production of *Amateur Gentleman* was released in England in 1920.

Barthelmess, a dependable but not very exciting actor, played the role of Barnabas with great seriousness, whereas Fairbanks possessed a lightness of touch that allowed a little humor into the proceedings. In the remake, Barnabas is required to rescue his father from hanging on a false charge and unmask the real culprit. Both versions dealt intelligently with severely dated material and the directors deserve praise for keeping the plot from too badly showing its age.

29 The Amazing Quest of Mr. Ernest Bliss

Based on the novel by E. Phillips Oppenheim. Story: Bored millionaire Ernest Bliss bets that he can live on his own earnings for a year. He takes numerous different jobs, but loses the bet when he feels he must give money to his girlfriend, Frances, for an operation for her invalid sister.

Hepworth/Imperial, Great Britain, 1920 (original). Silent. Director: Henry Edwards; screenwriter: E. Phillips Oppenheim. Cast: Henry Edwards (Ernest Bliss), Chrissie White (Frances Clayton), Gerald Ames (Dorrington), Mary Dibley (Kate Brent), Reginald Bach (Jack Brent), Henry Vibart, Douglas Munro, Mary Brough, Stanley Turnbull, Gerald Hillier.

• ***The Amazing Quest of Mr. Ernest Bliss*** (remake). Garrett-Klement Pictures, Great Britain, 1936. Director: Alfred Zeisler; screenwriter: John L. Balderston. Cast: Cary Grant (Ernest Bliss), Mary Brian (Frances), Henry Kendal (Lord Honiton), Leon M. Lion (Donnington), Garry Marsh, John Turnbull, Iris Ashley, Arthur Hardy, Frank Stanmore.

The silent production was released both as a five-reel feature and a serial. The amount of the bet made by Ernest Bliss was £25,000. Cary Grant's portrayal in the remake didn't seem to justify the trouble of bringing him home to England to make a movie. He didn't do much for the picture and it didn't do much for him.

30 American Graffiti

Based on an original screenplay by George Lucas. Story: On the eve of their departure for college, three boys try to crowd into one night all of the memories they can of their home area and the girls they have known and wished to know. One, Curt, spends the evening chasing a blonde in a big car who has given him the come-on, but he never catches up with her. Another, Steve, is spending the evening with his steady, Laurie, and all does not go well when he suggests that while he is away, they date others. The third, Terry the Toad, hooks up with brassy and none-too-bright Debbie who is, nevertheless, too smart for him and his amorous plans. There is a fourth boy, John, who has graduated some years earlier and is the owner of the fastest car on the strip, making him the number one "cool" character around. He gets stuck with the underaged and wise-mouthed Carol as he cruises around awaiting a challenge from an out-of-town dude with a souped up car dying for a race with the number one man. Throughout the often hilarious action, a steady stream of rock and roll music is heard coming from a station with Wolfman Jack as the disc jockey. In the end, reluctant Curt flies off to college with Steve deciding to go to school near home so he can be with Laurie.

Universal/Lucasfilm/Coppola Co., 1973 (original). Director and screenwriter: George Lucas. Cast: Richard Dreyfuss (Curt Henderson), Ronny Howard (Steve Bolander), Paul Le Mat (John Milner), Charles Martin Smith (Terry the Toad Fields), Cindy Williams (Laurie Henderson), Candy Clark (Debbie), Mackenzie Phillips (Carol Morrison), Bo Hopkins (Joe), Harrison Ford, Wolfman Jack.

• ***More American Graffiti*** (sequel). Universal/Lucasfilm, 1979. Director and screenwriter: B.W.L. Norton. Cast: Ron Howard (Steve Bolander), Paul Le Mat (John Milner), Candy Clark (Debbie), Mackenzie Phillips (Carol Morrison), Bo Hopkins (Joe), Charles Martin Smith (Terry Fields), Cindy Williams (Laurie Bolander).

American Graffiti was a mammoth success with Academy Award nomina-

Pregnant Sylvia Sidney appears to have a premonition that lover Phillips Holmes will cause her death so he can be with Frances Dee in An American Tragedy *(Paramount, 1931).*

tions for Best Picture, Screenplay and Directing as well as for Candy Clark as Supporting Actress. None won but that takes nothing away from this marvelous slice of nostalgia for the early sixties. None of the kids were really bad and adults could laugh at their mischieviousness along with the newer generations who liked the music and the fact that all the leading performers were young like them. The sequel was a mistake, being a series of vignettes about what happened to the likeable characters a few years later. They had grown dull, that's what happened to them. Forgeting this pointless sequel, one can still take pleasure in the original and the advertising cry, "Where were you in '62?"

31 An American Tragedy

Based on the novel by Theodore Dreiser. Story: Clyde Griffiths, reared in the moralistic teachings of his evangelistic parents in a small town, finds a job in a factory where he meets Roberta Alden. Professing his love, he seduces her

Don't let those smiles fool you in A Place in the Sun *(Paramount, 1951). Montgomery Clift will wish he had never hooked up with his pregnant girlfriend (Shelley Winters) once he meets society girl Elizabeth Taylor.*

but becomes disenchanted with the relationship when he meets society beauty Sondra Finchley. When Roberta discovers she is pregnant and insists that Clyde marry her, he takes her out on a lake and when the boat capsizes, he allows her to drown. Although he denies murdering the poor girl, he is convicted of the crime and executed in the electric chair.

Paramount, 1931 (original). Director: Josef von Sternberg; screenwriters: Samuel Hoffenstein and Josef von Sternberg. Cast: Phillips Holmes (Clyde Griffiths), Sylvia Sidney (Roberta Alden), Frances Dee (Sondra Finchley), Irving Pichel, Claire McDowell, Wallace Middleton, Frederick Burton, Vivian Winsten.

• ***A Place in the Sun*** (remake). Paramount, 1951. Director: George Stevens; screenwriters: Michael Wilson and Harry Brown. Cast: Montgomery Clift (George Eastman), Elizabeth Taylor (Angela Vickers), Shelley Winters (Alice Tripp), Anne Revere, Raymond Burr, Herbert Heyes, Keith Brasselle, Lois Chartrand, Sheppard Strudwick, Frieda Inescourt.

Theodore Dreiser unsuccessfully attempted to prevent the release of the 1931 film on the grounds that his story had been distorted to depict Griffiths as a mean and despicable individual rather than indict American society as was the author's intention. Although the film was critically acclaimed, audiences of the time did not like unhappy endings and it was a box-office failure.

In the 1951 remake, the three leading actors—Clift as the victim of his own ambition, Taylor as the stunningly beautiful socialite and Winters as the unfortunate, abandoned, pregnant girlfriend—each gave first rate performances. Clift and Winters were nominated for Academy Awards but both lost. Clift's performance was one of quiet desperation, finally accepting his punishment even though he had not actually performed the crime, but willed it. Winters, who previous to this role had played several blonde sexpots, gave ample evidence of her acting ability. Taylor never looked more lovely, making many males in the audiences anxious to help hold poor Shelley under the water.

Amorous Adventures of Don Quixote and Sancho Panza *see* **Don Quixote**

32 And Then There Were None

Based on the book and play *Ten Little Indians* by Agatha Christie. Story: Ten assorted characters have been invited to spend the weekend on a lonely island off the English coast. None know the identity of their host, but they soon learn by listening to a phonograph record that he knows them well, including their most guilty secrets. He announces that they have been sentenced to death. Marooned on the island from which there is no escape, one by one they are murdered in accord to the lines of the nursery rhyme "Ten Little Indians." After a few deaths, and unable to find anyone else on the small island, the survivors become convinced that their mysterious host is one of them, so they not only have to fear the unknown but each other. The resolution of the mystery and whodunnit is revealed in a surprise ending.

Twentieth Century–Fox, 1945 (original). Director: Rene Clair; screenwriter: Dudley Nichols. Cast: Barry Fitzgerald (Judge Quineannon), Walter Huston (Dr. Armstrong), Louis Hayward (Philip Lombard), Roland Young (Blore), June Duprez (Vera Claythorne), C. Aubrey Smith (General Mandrake), Judith Anderson (Emily Brent), Mischua Auer (Prince Starloff), Richard Haydn (Rogers), Queenie Leonard (Mrs. Rogers).

• ***Ten Little Indians*** (remake). Tenlit Productions, 1966. Director: George Pollock; screenwriters: Peter Yeldham and Harry Alan Towers. Cast: Wilfrid Hyde-White, Dennis Price, Stanley Holloway, Leo Genn, Shirley Eaton, Hugh O'Brian, Daliah Lavi, Fabian, Mario Adorf, Marianne Hoppe.

• ***Ten Little Indians (And Then There Were None)*** (remake). Avco/Embassy, 1975. Director: Peter Collinson; screenwriter: Peter Welbeck (Harry Alan Towers). Cast: Oliver Reed, Richard Attenborough, Elke Sommer, Herbert Lom, Gert Frobe, Stephane Audran, Charles Aznavour, Adolfo Celi, Alberto de Mendoza, Maria Rohm.

Although critics were not enthusiastic at the time of its release, and some were even so dastardly as to name the mysterious murderer in their reviews, this Rene Clair–directed piece has become a classic of the whodunnit school and is, without a doubt, the best filming of an Agatha Christie story. The cast works together beautifully. Each character comes to life and while audiences have no particular sympathy for any of them and their predicament, there is considerable rooting interest in the discovery of the killer before the last little

Indian is disposed of. The characters are all quite interesting, although some don't last long. Self-preservation, not the protection of the other victims, motivates the majority of these doomed people. When the butler Rogers is killed, Judith Anderson's complaint is, "What can they do now that the last servant is gone?"

The remakes were both disappointing, particularly the 1975 version. The only screams heard when this was playing were in disgust from audiences who noticed that this otherwise fine cast appeared little interested in the proceedings. The 1965 screening was somewhat better but could not touch the original for quality or suspense. In it the ten found themselves trapped together in a remote and inaccessible house in the Austrian Alps, while in the last remake, it was an isolated Persian hotel that acted as the setting for the killings.

Andy Hardy Comes Home *see* **A Family Affair**

Andy Hardy Gets Spring Fever *see* **A Family Affair**

Andy Hardy's Blonde Trouble *see* **A Family Affair**

Andy Hardy's Private Secretary *see* **A Family Affair**

33 Angel

Based on an original story by Robert Vincent O'Neill. Story: Angel is a high school honor student by day and a miniskirted hooker on Hollywood Boulevard at night. She has chosen her profession to pay for her expenses at a fancy private school she was attending when her parents deserted her. Her companions on the strip are a weird assortment of oddballs, all of whom appear to have hearts of gold. They include a transvestite, her butch and gruff landlady, and an aging ex-stuntman who believes that he is legendary gunman Kit Carson. A police detective is anxious to get Angel off the street, particularly so because a madman is killing hookers. Eventually Angel and her friends corral the culprit with Angel in high heels and tight skirt, a large six-gun in her grasp, chasing the murderer dressed in Hare Krishna garb down a crowded street.

New World/Adam's Apple Productions, 1983 (original). Director and screenwriter: Robert Vincent O'Neill. Cast: Donna Wilkes (Angel-Molly), Cliff Gorman (Lt. Andrews), Dick Shawn (The Transvestite, Mae), Rory Calhoun (The Quick-Draw Expert, Kit), Susan Tyrrell, John Diehl.

• ***Avenging Angel*** (sequel). New World/Adam's Apple Productions, 1985. Director and screenwriter: Robert Vincent O'Neill. Cast: Betsy Russell (Angel-Molly), Rory Calhoun (Kit Carson), John Diehl (Billy Boy), Susan Tyrrell (Solly), Ossie Davis, Barry Pearl, Steven Porter, Tim Rossovitch, Ross Hagen.

This kiddie porn flick delivered a lot less than its advertisements promised in the way of shocking material. Wilkes is rather sexy in a cute Lolita-way and not really bad despite her way of making a living. She and her cronies on the strip, although not in the mainstream of American morality, have their own very special code of behavior and a loyalty that's actually laudable. It's an exploitation film and that is sure, but it's not truly offensive. In the sequel, Angel, now played by the more sultry and sexy Betsy Russell, goes back on the street to avenge the death of the police detective who had helped her in the original. She succeeds in bringing the murderer to justice with the help of her unusual set of friends, in particular Rory Calhoun as the aging gunfighter, who is a very appealing character.

Angel and Sinner *see* **The Woman Disputed**

An Angel from Texas *see* **The Butter and Egg Man**

Angel on My Shoulder *see* **Here Comes Mr. Jordan**

Angel Street *see* **Gaslight**

Angels Wash Their Faces *see* **Angels with Dirty Faces**

34 Angels with Dirty Faces

Based on an original story by Rowland Brown. As boys, Rocky Sullivan and Jerry Connelly were close friends and tough kids. One day they were chased after a theft with Rocky caught while Jerry escaped. In the ensuing years Rocky goes through a series of reform schools and prisons while Jerry, answering his vocation, becomes a priest. The story picks up when Rocky is released from prison, having taken the fall for the gang headed by Mac Keefer and crooked lawyer James Frazier. Expecting to get his share of the gang's take for the years he kept his mouth shut in prison, Rocky moves back into his old neighborhood to wait to be paid off. He immediately becomes a hero to a bunch of larcenous punks that Father Connelly is trying to save from ending up like Rocky. When Frazier and Rocky's other ex-friends decide to bump Rocky off rather than cut him into their profits, Rocky coldbloodedly goes on a murdering rampage. He is caught and sentenced to the chair. Father Connelly pleads with his old friend to do the decent thing and act the coward as he goes to his death so as to destroy the hero-worship of the boys in the neighborhood. Rocky refuses and with his usual jaunty step and don't-give-a-damn attitude begins his walk down the last mile. Suddenly Rocky screams that he doesn't want to die and has to be pulled into the execution room and placed in the chair, bawling his eyes out. When the boys read that Rocky died a coward, it looks as if Father Connelly has won this round in their moral redemption.

Warner Bros., 1938 (original). Director: Michael Curtiz; screenwriters: John Wexley and Warren Duff. Cast: James Cagney (Rocky Sullivan), Pat O'Brien (Father Jerry Connelly), Humphrey Bogart (James Frazier), Ann Sheridan (Laurie Ferguson), George Bancroft (Mac Keefer), Billy Halop (Soapy), Bobby Jordan (Swing), Leo Gorcey (Bim), Gabriel Dell (Pasty), Huntz Hall (Crab), Bernard Punsley (Hunky).

• ***Angels Wash Their Faces*** (sequel). Warner Bros., 1939. Director: Ray Enright; screenwriters: Michael Fessier, Niven Busch and Robert Buckner from an idea by H. Jonathan Finn. Cast: Ann Sheridan (Joy Ryan), Billy Halop (Billy Shafter), Bernard Punsley (Sleepy Arkelian), Leo Gorcey (Leo Finnegan), Huntz Hall (Huntz), Gabriel Dell (Luigi), Bobby Jordan (Bernie), Ronald Reagan (Pat Remson), Bonita Granville (Peggy Finnegan), Eduardo Ciannelli (Martino), Frankie Thomas (Gabe Ryan).

James Cagney was masterful in his role as the tough mobster and killer from New York's Tenderloin whose pet greeting "Whaddaya hear? Whaddaya say?" summed up his breezy attitude towards his work and people in general. Before he is to face death in the electric chair, he tells boyhood friend Jerry Connelly, "You know Jerry, I think, in order to be afraid, you got to have a heart. I don't think I got one. I had that cut out of me a long time ago." This comment gives conflicting signals as to whether he went to the chair as a coward because he really was one or because at the last moment he decided to honor Jerry's request to act in such a way as to kill the hero-worship of the boys in the neighborhood. Cagney was the good-bad man while Bogart portrayed the bad-bad man whose death almost seemed justified, at least by the limited code of behavior existing between gangsters. Pat O'Brien, who was always at home with his collar turned, gave a strong performance as the priest. The Dead End Kids' act as young street-smart punks had not yet begun to wear thin or turn into a comedy routine as it shortly would in a series of second-run features.

Angels Wash Their Faces isn't a sequel in the usual sense as none of the characters from *Angels with Dirty Faces* repeated their part. However, the featuring of Ann Sheridan and the Dead End Kids in roles very similar to those they had played in the first film, makes it plain that the producers were attempting to capitalize on the success of the Cagney picture. Audiences weren't fooled and the absence of star names such as Cagney, O'Brien and Bogart limited its success. In this film, the boys are on the side of the law, although their means to their end of thwarting crooked politicians are somewhat questionable. In neither film did Sheridan do anything to enhance the image of "The Oomph Girl" which would be established for her during World War II, but she did demonstrate some acting ability. Ronald Reagan, included to provide some love interest for Sheridan, had little to do.

35 The Animal Kingdom

Based on the play by Philip Barry. Story: In this smart comedy, intellectual publisher Tom Collier marries Cecelia Henry when his mistress, Daisy Sage, goes to Europe to study art. His demanding wife acts more like a mistress than Daisy who always seemed to demonstrate the virtues of a good wife. After having all he can take of the wily Cecelia, he leaves a check on the mantel for her for services rendered and goes back to "his wife," Daisy.

RKO, 1932 (original). Director: Edward H. Griffith; screenwriter: Horace Jackson. Cast: Leslie Howard (Tom Collier), Ann Harding (Daisy Sage), Myrna Loy (Cecelia Henry), William Gargan, Neil Hamilton, Henry Stephenson, Ilka Chase.

Irene Dunne insists that Rex Harrison honor his pledge to provide her with a house outside of the palace in Anna and the King of Siam *(20th Century–Fox, 1946).*

• ***One More Tomorrow*** (remake). Warner Bros., 1946. Director: Peter Godfrey; screenwriters: Charles Hoffman & Catherine Turney. Cast: Dennis Morgan (Tom Collier), Ann Sheridan (Christie Sage), Alexis Smith (Cecelia Henry), Jack Carson, John Loder, Thurston Hall, Jane Wyman, Reginald Gardiner.

Leslie Howard repeated his stage role in the 1932 film version and critics and fans alike felt his casting and that of Ann Harding were perfect. Myrna Loy, who up to this time had been stuck in various exotic roles as orientals, was properly seductive in one of her first important Caucasian roles. The dialogue was smart and the film was greatly helped by the fine supporting work of William Gargan and Ilka Chase who reprised the roles they had played on Broadway.

The 1946 remake was a bowdlerized version and as such rather lost the point of the relationship between Collier and his two women. Dennis Morgan appears as a wealthy playboy who marries a left-wing photographer and buys up her magazine. Neither Sheridan nor Smith were allowed to seem too much like a mistress, nor ever much of a wife.

36 Anna and the King of Siam

Based on Margaret Landon's book. Story: In 1862, British widow Anna Leonowens accepts a position as teacher of the 67 children of the King of Siam. She and her son Louis find Siam to be a backward country ruled by a near-

Deborah Kerr seems shocked by the attitude of Yul Brynner in the musical The King and I *(20th Century–Fox, 1956), as a number of his many wives, dressed in Western finery, mingle in the background.*

barbaric monarch who treats his wives, concubines and all others as his virtual slaves. She is particularly appalled at his treatment of his wife Tuptim when he discovers she loves another, younger man. Anna's initial revulsion for the King changes slowly to respect as she discovers his thirst for knowledge and desire to bring his country into the nineteenth century. The two become friends, with Anna offering the King sound advice on the adoption of Western ways. When the King dies, Anna, who has lost her son, stays on to help the young Prince who has assumed the royal duties.

Twentieth Century–Fox 1946 (original). Director: John Cromwell; screenwriters: Sally Benson and Talbot Jennings. Cast: Irene Dunne (Anna Owens), Rex Harrison (King Mongkut), Linda Darnel (Tuptim), Gale Sondergaard (Lady Thiang), Lee J. Cobb (The Kralahome), Mikhail Rasmumny (Phra Alack), Richard Lyon (Louis), Tito Renaldo, Addison Richards, William Edmunds, Leonard Strong.

• ***The King and I*** (remake). Twentieth Century–Fox, 1956. Director: Walter Lang; screenwriter: Ernest Lehman, De Luxe Color. Cast: Deborah Kerr (Anna Leonowens), Yul Brynner (The King), Rita Moreno (Tuptim), Terry Saunders (Lady Thiang), Martin Benson (Kralahome), Carlos Rivas (Lun Tha), Rex Thompson (Louis), Patrick Adiarte (Prince Chulalongkorn), Geoffrey Toone, Alan Mowbray.

Anna and the King of Siam was based on Margaret Landon's best-selling 1944 biography, which in turns was based on Anna Leonowen's original book, *The English Governess at the Siamese Court.* The 1946 movie was a lavish production with bravura performances by Irene Dunne and Rex Harrison in the leading roles and excellent support from the likes of Linda Darnell and Lee J. Cobb. This film proved the inspiration for the Broadway musical *The King and I* when Gertrude Lawrence, who had obtained the stage rights for the work, persuaded Richard Rodgers and Oscar Hammerstein to develop a musical from the book. The production was to be Miss Lawrence's last, as she died during the run of the show. Yul Brynner exploded onto the scene as the King, with his bald head and oriental looks making his performances most credible. The musical remained on Broadway for 1,246 performances.

Brynner was signed to repeat the role of the King in the movie version of the smash hit, with Deborah Kerr cast as Anna. The latter's singing voice was dubbed by Marni Nixon, who had done similar chores for any number of non-singing actresses in musicals. The film was a delight if a trifle long. The Rodgers and Hammerstein numbers, including "Hello, Young Lovers," "Something Wonderful," "Getting to Know You," "Shall We Dance," "A Puzzlement," "The March of the Siamese Children," and "The Small House of Uncle Thomas," were lavishly staged. Yul Brynner won an Academy Award for his performance, as did Alfred Newman and Ken Darby for musical direction. Deborah Kerr was nominated for a Best Actress Oscar, Leon Shamroy for his photography and the film itself for Best Picture.

37 Anna Christie

Based on the play by Eugene O'Neill. Story: Abandoned as a child by her sea-faring father, Anna Christie was raised by cruel and harsh poverty-stricken relatives from whom she escapes to become a prostitute. She finds her father, Chris, who now abandons his boozing mistress, Marthy Owen, when Anna agrees to go to sea with him. Anna meets and falls in love with rugged Irish sailor Mat Burke. The two men fight over possession of Anna, who rebels against her father's past neglect and Mat's possessiveness. Leaving her father, she and Mat plan to make a new life together.

First National Pictures, 1923 (original). Silent. Director: John Griffith; screenwriter: Bradley King. Cast: Blanche Sweet (Anna Christie), George F. Marion (Chris Christopherson), William Russell (Mat Burke), Eugenie Besserer (Marthy Owen), Chester Conklin, George Seigmann, Ralph Yearsley.

• ***Anna Christie*** (remake). MGM, 1930. Director: Clarence Brown; screenwriter: Frances Marion. Cast: Greta Garbo (Anna Christie), George F. Marion (Chris Christopherson), Charles Bickford (Mat Burke), Marie Dressler (Marthy Owen), James T. Mack, Lee Phelps.

Blanche Sweet was well-received as Anna, described by one critic as "glowing with the idea of her love" for William Russell as Burke. George Marion, re-creating his stage role, was described as the perfect picture of a seafaring man who blames the sea for everything that happens. He is impressive when he explains to his daughter, with his limited vocabulary, the pleasure of a trip on a coal barge. Eugenie Besserer is admirable as the slovenly drinking companion to Chris. Russell is convincing playing Mat as a tower of strength.

Audiences had anxiously awaited Garbo's first talking role and were not disappointed when in a low, almost masculine voice she demands of a bartender: "Give me a whiskey, and don't be stingy." Garbo suited her actions to her words and her performance was well received and still impresses today. Marion, a little older, is still wonderful as the seaman who believes his Anna is the personification of purity, even though out of his sight she tells his mistress, Marthy (played brilliantly by Marie Dressler), "You're me, forty years from now." Bickford is splendid as the powerful physical specimen Mat.

A German-language version of this film was released in 1930, starring Garbo as Anna, Hans Junkermann as Mat, Salka Viertel as Marthy and Theo Shall as Chris. A Japanese version called *Fog in the Harbor* was released in 1923.

38 Anna Karenina

Based on the novel by Leo Tolstoy. Story: Anna Karenina, wife of Russian government official Alexei Karenin, deserts her loveless marriage to an older man to have an affair with dashing Count Alexey Vronsky, by whom she has a daughter. Her husband refuses to allow her to see their son Seryozha. Living in Moscow in virtual social isolation with Vronsky, Anna becomes despondent when she believes that her lover is growing tired of the affair and throws herself under the wheels of a passing train.

• ***Anna Karenina*** (remake). Russia, 1914. Silent: Director: Vladimir Gardin. Cast: Maria Germanova (Anna Karenina), Vladimir Shaternikov (Count Vronsky), M. Tarnarov (Karenin).

• ***Anna Karenina*** (remake). Fox Films, 1915. Silent. Director: J. Gordon Edwards. Cast: Betty Nansen (Anna Karenina), Richard Thornton (Count Vronsky), Edward Jose (Karenin).

• ***Love*** (remake). MGM, 1927. Silent. Director: Edmund Goulding; screenwriter: Francis Marion. Cast: Greta Garbo (Anna Karenina), John Gilbert (Count Vronsky), George Fawcett (Grand Duke), Emily Fitzroy (Princess Betsy), Brandon Hurst (Karenin), Phillipe de Lacy (Serezha).

• ***Anna Karenina*** (remake). MGM, 1935. Director: Clarence Brown; screenwriters: Clemence Dane, Salka Viertel and S.N. Behrman. Cast: Greta Garbo (Anna Karenina), Fredric March (Count Vronsky), Basil Rathbone (Karenin), Freddie Bartholomew (Sergei), Maureen O'Sullivan (Kitty), May Robson, Reginald Owen, Reginald Denny.

• ***Anna Karenina*** (remake). London Films, 1948. Director: Julien Duvivier; screenwriters: Jean Anouilh, Guy Morgan and Julien Duvivier. Cast: Vivien Leigh (Anna Karenina), Kieron Moore (Count Vronsky), Ralph Richardson (Karenin), Sally Ann Howes (Kitty), Niall MacGinnis, Martita Hunt, Marie Lohr, Michael Gough.

Besides those mentioned above, *Anna Karenina* was filmed in 1910 in both Russia and Germany, in 1911 in France, in 1917 in Italy, in 1919 in Germany, in 1920 in Hungary, in 1934 in France, in 1936 in Austria under the name *Manja*

Walewska, in 1952 in India, in 1953 in U.S.S.R., in 1956 in Argentina, in 1961 in the United Arab Republic and in 1967, 1971 and 1975 in U.S.S.R.

In 1915, Betty Nansen's performance as Anna was described as one which could not be improved upon. The 1927 filming, which was entitled *Love,* paired the famous screen lovers Garbo and Gilbert, but it was not favorably reviewed, with most critics agreeing that Gilbert overplayed the role of Vronsky. In 1935, Garbo was presented with the New York Film Critics Circle's first annual award as best actress for her subtle and restrained performance as Anna in MGM's 1935 remake. March was far superior to Gilbert in the role of Vronsky and Rathbone was a more than adequate Karenin. The 1948 British version starring Vivien Leigh was generally panned, with the complaint that both Leigh and Kieron Moore were not up to the roles and compared rather badly to the commanding performance of Ralph Richardson as Karenin.

Annabel Takes a Tour *see* **The Affairs of Annabel**

39 Anne of Green Gables

Based on books by L.M. Montgomery. Story: Little orphan girl Anne arrives in a New England town to stay with a brother and sister. The child gradually wins over the rather stiff couple with her affectionate and demonstrative habits. Anne grows into a beautiful girl, very popular with the boys. Shortly after graduation from high school, her foster parents lose all their money and the brother dies of a heart attack. Anne is forced to take a position as a teacher to support herself and her "aunt." She is forced to give a whipping to the son of a family that never liked her. The boy breaks away, hops a hay wagon, falls off, breaking his arm and blames everything on Anne. The boy's father and a crowd of angry citizens converge on Anne's house where the aunt is recuperating from an operation and requiring quiet. Anne meets the noisy crowd with a shotgun but agrees to go off with them for her aunt's sake. A preacher who had seen the accident clears up the matter to everyone's satisfaction.

Realart Pictures, 1919 (original). Silent. Director: William Desmond Taylor; screenwriter: Frances Marion. Cast: Mary Miles Minter (Anne Shirley), George Stewart (Gilbert Blythe), Marcia Harris (Marilla Cuthbert), Frederick Burton (Matthew Cuthbert), F.T. Chailee, Lelia Romer, Lincoln Stedman.

• ***Anne of the Green Gables*** (remake). RKO, 1934. Director: George Nichols, Jr.; screenwriter: Sam Mintz. Cast: Anne Shirley (Anne Shirley), Tom Brown (Gilbert Blythe), O.P. Heggie (Matthew Cuthbert), Helen Westley (Marilla Cuthbert), Sara Haden, Murray Kinnell, Gertrude Messinger, June Preston, Charley Grapewin.

• ***Anne of Windy Poplars*** (sequel). RKO, 1940. Director: Jack Hively; screenwriters: Michael Kanin and Jerry Cody. Cast: Anne Shirley (Anne Shirley), James Ellison (Tony Pringle), Henry Travers (Matey), Patric Knowles (Gilbert Blythe), Slim Summerville (Jabez Monkman), Elisabeth Patterson, Louise Campbell, Joan Carroll, Katherine Alexander.

The murder of the director of the silent picture, William Desmond Taylor, was one of the great mysteries and scandals of the 1920s, involving the star of this picture, Mary Miles Minter, in a role not as sweet as she appeared in the film. Minter was meant to be a Mary Pickford clone but even if the still-unsolved murder hadn't occurred she would never had been much competition for "America's Sweetheart."

Anne Shirley, born Dawn Paris, assumed the name of her character in the remake and its sequel. Critics described the first film as "wholesome, sympathetic and heart-tugging." They also noted that the picture, now transferred to Prince Edward Island, Canada, wasn't really a drama, rather more a sentimental biography, which made its successful transfer to the screen even more impressive.

By 1940, critics found the sequel to be "dull and uninteresting, belonging to the pre-gaslight era in which the story is laid." Other words used to describe the film included, "tepid," "rambling" and "pointless." In this film, Anne has taken the position of vice-principal in a rural town and becomes caught in the middle of a local feud involving the ruling family of the community. As is her nature, she maintains her "Pollyanna" attitudes and unbelievably wins over all with her sweetness and good nature.

Anne of the Thousand Days ***see*** **The Private Life of Henry VIII**

Anne of Windy Poplars ***see*** **Anne of the Green Gables**

Annie ***see*** **Little Orphan Annie**

Another Part of the Forest ***see*** **The Little Foxes**

Another Thin Man ***see*** **The Thin Man**

Any Man's Wife ***see*** **Michael O'Halloran**

Any Which Way but Loose ***see*** **Every Which Way but Loose**

Any Which Way You Can ***see*** **Every Which Way but Loose**

40 The Apple Dumpling Gang

Based on the novel by Jack M. Bickham. Story: Gambler Russel Donovan inherits the responsibility of three orphaned youngsters who co-own a gold mine. It's a predictable western comedy with plenty of comical antics by two bumbling crooks, Theodore and Amos, played respectively by Don Knotts and Tim Conway. It's strictly a no-harm, no-foul film which amused youngsters and TV situation comedy–addicted adults.

Buena Vista/Walt Disney, 1975. Director: Norman Tokar; screenwriter: Don Tait. Cast: Bill Bixby (Russel Donovan), Susan Clark (Magnolia), Don Knotts (Theodore), Tim Conway (Amos), David Wayne (Colonel T.T. Clydesdale), Slim Pickens, Harry Morgan, John McGiver, Marie Windsor, Iris Adrian.

• ***The Apple Dumpling Gang Rides Again*** (sequel). Buena Vista/Walt

Disney, 1979. Director: Vincent McEveety; screenwriter: Don Tait. Cast: Tim Conway (Amos), Don Knotts (Theodore), Tim Matheson (Private Jeff Reid), Kenneth Mars (Marshall), Elyssa Davalos, Jack Elam, Robert Prine, Harry Morgan, Ruth Buzzi.

In the sequel, the two incompetent western crooks, Theodore and Amos, land in more trouble trying to go straight. Neither film is really a western, just television comedies on the big screen with Knotts and Conway acting their familiar characters polished on *The Andy Griffith Show* and *The Carol Burnett Show*, respectively. They're good clean fun, pointless and silly.

The Apple Dumpling Gang Rides Again *see* **The Apple Dumpling Gang**

41 The Arab

Based on a play by Edgar Selwyn. Story: To punish his son Jamil for robbing a desert caravan, Bedouin chief Sheik of El Khyrssa gives the young man's favorite horse to the robbery victim who in turn sells it to a Turkish general, who makes it a present to Christian missionary teacher Mary Hilbert. When Jamil finds that Mary has his horse, he takes it from her and forces her to walk home through the desert. This little tiff out of the way, he falls in love with her and saves her life and that of her father by calling on his Bedouin tribesmen when the Turkish Governor leads a massacre against the Christians. The old sheik dies and Jamil bids Mary farewell, off to assume his heritage as the new ruler.

Paramount/Lasky, 1915 (original). Silent. Director: Cecil B. DeMille; screenwriters: Edgar Selwyn and Cecil B. DeMille. Cast: Edward Selwyn (Jamil), Horace B. Carpenter (Sheik of El Khyrssa), Gertrude Robinson (Mary Hilbert), Theodore Roberts (Turkish Govenor), Milton Brown, Billy Elmer, Sydney Deane.

• ***The Arab*** (remake). MGM, 1924. Silent. Director and screenwriter: Rex Ingram. Cast: Ramon Novarro (Jamil), Alice Terry (Mary Hilbert), Maxudian (The Govenor), Jean De Limur (Hossein), Paul Vermayal, Adelgui Millar, Gerald Robertson, Paul Francesci, Justa Uribe.

• ***The Barbarian*** (remake). MGM, 1933. Director: Sam Wood; screenwriters: Anita Loos and Elmer Harris. Cast: Ramon Novarro (Jamil), Myrna Loy (Diana), Reginald Denny (Gerald), Louise Closser Hale (Powers), C. Aubrey Smith, Edward Arnold, Blanche Frederici.

DeMille's and Selwyn's 1915 silent production was a great success with audiences fascinated by the mores and what was presented as the more open sexual attitudes of the Arab world, where lust without sweet love was accepted.

In the first remake Jamil is played by Ramon Novarro (brought to films as competition for Rudolph Valentino), and he demonstrates that he can flare his nostrils as well as Rudy when he observes the delicious-looking Alice Terry. In the next version, the desert lord is reduced to being a guide in an Egyptian city by behavior considered unseemingly by his father, and falls for a half-caste girl with a European fiancé. The film has a great number of beatings, draggings and kidnappings before things are resolved. Myrna Loy, who played many mixed-blood girls, pleased male members of the audiences at least in a provocative if somewhat discreet nude scene when she took a bath in an ornate sunken pool with only blossoms on the surface of the water for modesty's sake.

42 Arabian Nights

Based on the legends. Story: Two brothers, Haroun-Al-Raschid and Kamar, both aspire to the caliphate. When Haroun is supposedly killed by Kamar, the former is rescued by a band of entertainers and is nursed back to health by lovely Scheherazade, who hopes to make a high-placed marriage. She falls in love and Ali Ben Ali becomes Haroun's close friend. From here on out it's a series of fast-paced intrigues, chases, battles and the final reinstatement of Haroun to his position of Caliph.

• ***Arabian Nights*** (remake). Universal Pictures, 1942. Director: John Rawlins; screenwriter: Michael Hogan. Cast: Jon Hall (Haroun-Al-Raschid), Maria Montez (Scheherazade), Sabu (Ali Ben Ali), Leif Erickson (Kamar), Billy Gilbert (Ahmad), Edgar Barrier (Nadan), Richard Lane, Turhan Bey, John Qualen, Shemp Howard, Thomas Gomez.

• ***A Thousand and One Nights*** (remake). Columbia Pictures, 1945. Director: Alfred E. Green; screenwriter: Wilfrid H. Pettitt. Cast: Cornel Wilde (Aladdin), Evelyn Keyes (the Genie), Phil Silvers (Abdullah), Adele Jergens (Princess Armina), Dusty Anderson, Dennis Hoey, Phillip Van Zandt, Gus Schilling, Nestor Paiva, Rex Ingram, Richard Hale, John Abbott, Shelley Winters.

• ***The Desert Hawk*** (remake). Universal Pictures, 1950. Director: Frederick de Cordova; screenwriters: Aubrey Weisberg, Jack Pollexfen and Gerald Drayson Adams. Cast: Yvonne De Carlo (Princess Scheherazade), Richard Greene (Omar), Jackie Gleason (Aladdin), George Macready (Prince Murad), Rock Hudson (Captain Ras), Carl Esmond, Joe Besser, Ann Pearce, Marc Lawrence, Lois Andrews, Frank Puglia.

• ***The Golden Blade*** (remake). Universal Pictures, 1953. Director: Nathan Juran; screenwriter: John Rich. Cast: Rock Hudson (Haroun), Piper Laurie (Princess Khairuzan), Gene Evans (Hadi), Kathleen Hughes (Bakhamra), George Macready (Jafar), Steven Geray, Alice Kelley, Lori Nelson, Anita Ekberg, Erika Norden, Valerie Jackson, Vic Romito.

The previously named films are just a few among the numerous movies loosely based on this or that tale from the Arabian Nights. Others include films by that name in 1920, 1924, 1926, 1972 and 1980. In 1926, there was a production entitled *Tales of 1001 Arabian Nights;* in 1935, *The Black Rose;* and in 1960, *Sabu and the Magic Ring.* Other movies dealing with Aladdin, Scheherazade or Ali Baba have their own entries in this book.

Are These Our Parents? ***see*** **Where Are Your Children?**

Arenes Sanglantes ***see*** **Blood and Sand**

Aren't We All ***see*** **A Kiss in the Dark**

43 Arsene Lupin

Based on the play by Maurice LeBlanc and Francis de Croisset. Story: Arsene Lupin is the named signed by a gentleman thief, the Duke of Charmerace, to notes he leaves behind when he robs the rich. His exploits become so daring and outrageous that he is pursued by the leading French detective, Guerchard. He is almost caught stealing the Mona Lisa.

• ***Arsene Lupin*** (remake). MGM, 1932. Director: Jack Conway; screenwriters: Carey Wilson, Lenore Coffee and Bayard Veiller. Cast: John Barrymore (Duke of Charmerace/Arsene Lupin), Lionel Barrymore (Detective Guerchard), Karen Morley (Sonia), John Miljan, Tully Marshall, Henry Armetta, George Davis, John Davidson, James Mack.

• ***Arsene Lupin Returns*** (sequel). MGM, 1937. Director: George Fitzmaurice; screenwriters: James K. McGuinness, Howard Emmett Rogers and George Harmon Coxe. Cast: Melvyn Douglas (Arsene Lupin), Warren William (American detective), Virginia Bruce, John Halliday, Nat Pendleton, Monty Woolley, George Zucco.

• ***Enter Arsene Lupin*** (sequel). Universal Pictures, 1944. Director: Ford Beebe; screenwriter: Bertram Millhauser. Cast: Charles Korvin (Arsene Lupin), Ella Raines (Stacie), G. Carroll Naish (Ganimard), George Dolenz, Gale Sondergaard, Miles Mander, Leland Hodgson, Tom Pilkington, Lillian Bronson, Holmes Herbert.

The French Jewel thief was portrayed in silents in 1917 by Earle Williams, in *The Teeth of the Tiger* in 1919 by David Powell, and by Wedgewood Newell in 1920. Other sound versions had Robert Lamoureux in the title role in *The Adventures of Arsene Lupin* in 1957 and Jean-Claude Brialy in *Arsene Lupin Contre Arsene Lupin* in 1962.

The best of the lot was the feature starring the Barrymore brothers. It was their first picture together and they played off each other very well, resulting in the movie being a big hit. The Melvyn Douglas sequel was meant to be the start of a series but the poor script about the reformed jewel thief who helps an American detective track down a French criminal was a disappointment. Even worse was Universal's entry which has virtually unknown actor Charles Korvin as the renowned jewel thief who steals, then returns, a woman's emerald when he discovers that she is about to inherit a fortune and other relatives are planning her death. He prevents her demise.

Arsene Lupin Contre Arsene Lupin *see* **Arsene Lupin**

Arsene Lupin Returns *see* **Arsene Lupin**

As You Desire Me *see* **This Love of Ours**

44 As You Like It

Based on the play by William Shakespeare. Story: Rosalind, the niece of a wicked duke, is banished to the Forest of Arden by her uncle. Disguised as a man for her own protection, she meets the man of her dreams, Orlando, also hiding in the forest. Orlando loves Rosalind, but does not recognize her in her disguise. Together the "men" discuss Orlando's love—which Rosalind is secretly testing.

• ***Love in a Wood*** (remake). London/Diploma, Great Britain, 1915. Silent. Director: Maurice Elvey; screenwriter: Kennelm Foss. Cast: Elisabeth Risdon (Rosalind), Gerald Ames (Orlando), Vera Cunningham (Celia), Frank Stanmore (Touchstone), Kenelm Foss (Oliver), Cyril Percival, Dolly Tree.

• ***As You Like It*** (remake). Inter Allied/20th Century–Fox, 1936. Director: Paul Czinner; screenwriters: Carl Mayer and R.J. Cullen. Cast: Elizabeth Bergner (Rosalind), Laurence Olivier (Orlando), Henry Ainley (Banished Duke), Sophie Stewart (Celia), Mackenzie Ward (Touchstone), Leon Quartermaine (Jacques), Richard Ainley, Felix Aylmer, Aubrey Mather, Fisher White, George Moore Marriott, John Laurie, Lionel Braham.

Shakespeare's play was also filmed in 1908, 1912 and 1913. The 1916 version was a modern dress production. In the 1936 film, Elizabeth Bergner looked quite fetching in men's clothes, but audiences may find Olivier's acting too frenzied. The film received mixed reviews, but more agreed that the photography, production design and music were particularly good.

Asi Es la Vida ***see*** **What a Man**

45 The Asphalt Jungle

Based on a book by W.R. Burnett. Story: Aging criminal mastermind Doc Riedenschneider, just out of prison, has a plan for one last big heist before he retires. He is backed in this venture by an influential lawyer, Alonzo D. Emmerich, who agrees to fence the jewelry that is to be stolen. Emmerich is actually flat-broke and sees this as a way to recoup his previous financial standing. It's in the back of his mind to doublecross the thieves. Riedenschneider puts together a gang of losers including a "hooligan" named Dix Handley. They pull off the heist but from that point everything starts to unravel. The cops aren't as dumb as the crooks believe and one by one the members of the gang are picked up or picked off. Emmerich, disgraced, commits suicide; Dix, fatally wounded, tries to escape with the help of the girl who loves him, Doll Conovan, and takes a long time to die. Doc almost gets away but is thwarted by staying too long in a roadside dive watching a pretty young thing dance.

MGM, 1950 (original). Director: John Huston; screenwriters: Ben Maddow and John Huston. Cast: Sterling Hayden (Dix Handley), Louis Calhern (Alonzo D. Emmerich), Jean Hagen (Doll Conovan), Sam Jaffe (Doc Erwin Riedenschneider), James Whitmore (Gus Minissi), John McIntire (Police Commissioner Hardy), Marc Lawrence (Cobby), Barry Kelly (Lt. Dietrich), Anthony Caruso (Louis Ciavelli), Marilyn Monroe (Angela Phinlay).

• ***The Badlanders*** (remake). MGM, 1958. Director: Delmer Daves; screenwriter: Richard Collins. Cast: Alan Ladd (Peter Van Hock), Ernest Borgnine (John McBain), Katy Jurado (Anita), Claire Kelly (Ada Winton), Kent Smith (Cyril Lounsberry), Nehemiah Persoff (Vincente), Robert Emhardt (Sample), Anthony Caruso (Commanche), Adam Williams (Leslie).

• ***Cairo*** (remake). MGM, 1963. Director: Wolfe Rilla; screenwriter: Joanne

Court. Cast: George Sanders, Richard Johnson, Faten Hamama, John Meillon, Eric Pohlman, Walter Rilla.

• ***Cool Breeze*** (remake). MGM, 1972. Director and screenwriter: Barry Pollack. Cast: Thalmus Rasubla, Judy Pace, Jim Watkins, Lincoln Kilpatrick, Sam Laws, Margaret Avery, Wally Taylor, Raymond St. Jacques.

Most film buffs know that *The Asphalt Jungle* is supposedly the first film to show the development and performance of a criminal caper from the point of view of the criminals. It's also common knowledge that in this film, Marilyn Monroe used her small part as Louis Calhern's mistress to great advantage, opening the door to her ultimate super-star status. Less written about are the performances-of-their-lives by actors like Marc Lawrence and Anthony Caruso, who before and after this movie were stuck with roles of little importance and not the type with which to demonstrate one's acting abilities. In fact, all the performers seemed to be at the top of their game and for this, one must credit the superb directing talents of John Huston.

The western remake *The Badlanders* is the story of Alan Ladd and Ernest Borgnine, two ex-cons released from a Nevada prison with dreams of revenge and larceny on their minds. They plan to rob a gold mine by blasting a hole in the side of a mountain adjacent to a shaft filled with workmen and cart away a ton of ore, making their escape with the help of a Mexican carnival. The film has a nice blend of humor, poignancy and action without resorting to a bunch of western clichés.

The movie *Cairo* transports the story to the Egyptian city where crooks plan to steal Tutankhamen's jewels from a museum. It was well-produced and had its moments but by now the story is much too familiar and almost done to death. In 1972, *Cool Breeze,* an almost all-black version of *The Asphalt Jungle,* was produced, being fairly faithful to the original, although the crooks were supplied with a sort of altruistic motive. They wanted the profits of their heist to pay to establish a black people's bank. The film had a great deal of brutal sex and allowed the underworld mastermind to get away with the jewels and continue his preoccupation with juicy young girls.

The Astonished Heart *see* **Tonight at 8:30**

46 At the Villa Rose

Based on the novel by A.E.W. Mason. Story: When a rich widow is murdered, her companion Celia Harland, a fraudulent medium, is suspected of the crime. Celia has disappeared along with the victim's jewels, but she has been kidnapped by the real murderer because it is believed she has the lady's gems. Inspector Hanaud rescues Celia, reconstructs the seance at which the widow died and tricks the killer into betraying himself.

Stoll, Great Britain, 1920 (original). Silent. Director: Maurice Elvey; screenwriter: Sinclair Hill. Cast: Manora Thew (Celia Harland), Langhorne Burton (Harry Weathermill), Teddy Arundell (Inspector Hanaud), Norman Page (Julius Ricardo), Joan Beverley, Eva Westlake, Kate Gurney, J.L. Boston.

• ***At the Villa Rose*** (remake). Twickenham/Warner Bros., Great Britain,

1930. Director: Leslie Hiscott; screenwriter: Cyril Twyford. Cast: Norah Baring (Celia Harland), Austin Trevor (Insp. Hanaud), Richard Cooper (Ricardo), Barbara Gott (Mme d'Avray), Francis Lister, Amy Brandon Thomas, Violet Farebrother.

• ***At the Villa Rose*** (remake). Associated British Productions, Great Britain, 1939. Director: Walter Summers; screenwriter: Doreen Montgomery. Cast: Kenneth Kent (Insp. Harland), Judy Kelly (Celia Harland), Walter Rilla (Ricardo), Peter Murray Hill (Harry Wethermill), Antoinette Cellier (Adele Rossignol), Clifford Evans, Martita Hunt, Ruth Maitland, Ronald Adam.

This well-liked thriller about jewel thieves who frame a fake medium for the murder of a widow was set in France. It's one of the drawing-room murder mysteries where the clever detective rounds up the suspects and tricks the guilty party in giving herself or herself away.

Atom Man vs. Superman ***see*** **Superman**

47 Auntie Mame

Based on the book by Patrick Dennis and the play by Jerome Laurence and Robert E. Lee. Story: Young Patrick Dennis is sent to live with his bohemian Auntie Mame, when his parents are killed in an accident. She has no use for conventions and is particularly aggravating to the boy's financial guardian, a bank official named Babcock. Patrick is an observer to her many strange parties and her outrageous guests, including always tipsy actress Vera Charles. When the Great Depression hits, Mame's money is wiped out and she must find a job, something for which she is totally unfit. Fortunately, she meets Beauregard Burnside, a Southerner, whose fortune was not wiped out in the stock market crash. He takes her home to meet his family and she successfully bluffs her way through a fox hunt, even ending up with the fox. Mame and Beauregard are married and travel throughout the world while Patrick is away at school growing up. On one of these trips, Beauregard is killed, but Mame need never again worry about money. Instead, she becomes concerned with the now grown-up Patrick who has become engaged to a bigoted and ignorant girl from a bigoted and ignorant rich family. With a little help from Mame and her still-zany cast of hangers-on, Patrick matures and finds a girl much more suitable.

Warner Bros., 1958 (original). Director: Morton Da Costa; screenwriters: Betty Comdon and Adolph Green. Cast: Rosalind Russell (Mame Dennis), Forrest Tucker (Beauregard Burnside), Coral Browne (Vera Charles), Fred Clark (Mr. Babcock), Roger Smith (Patrick Dennis as an adult), Patric Knowles (Lindsay Woolsey), Peggy Cass (Agnes Gooch), Jan Handzlik (young Patrick), Joanna Barnes (Gloria Upsen).

• ***Mame*** (remake). Warner Bros., 1974. Director: Gene Saks; screenwriter: Paul Zindel. Cast: Lucille Ball (Mame Dennis), Beatrice Arthur (Vera Charles), Robert Preston (Beauregard), Jane Connell (Agnes Gooch), Bruce Davison, Kirby Furlong, Doria Cook, John McGiver, Joyce Van Patten.

Rosalind Russell was a delight as the very zany free-spirit who possesses a good heart and a sincere love for her nephew rivaling her zest for life. Mame

Two unidentified performers take bows with Rosalind Russell (second from right) and Coral Browne in Auntie Mame *(Warner Bros., 1958).*

seems a wonderful person to visit but not someone you'd want to live with. The remainder of the cast was quite good, with Coral Browne as the ever-drunken actress, Peggy Cass as the plain girl who "lived" and wanted to know what she should do after that, and Joanna Barnes as the very nasal and obnoxious fiancée of grown-up Patrick. Weakest in their roles were the two actors who portrayed Patrick. They seemed the kind of youngsters who would bore a wonderful dame like Mame.

In the musical remake, Lucille Ball was much too old for the part and would have looked it as well, had not specially gauzed lenses been used to hide her aged features. She apparently saw no reason to play Mame any differently than the characters she had been impersonating since the success of her first television hit, *I Love Lucy*. Beatrice Arthur as Vera Charles and Jane Connell as Agnes Gooch, who had played the roles on Broadway, gave the most enjoyable performances although Robert Preston, ever dependable, did a nice job as Beauregard. The songs by Jerry Herman included the title number and the quite popular "If He Walked Into My Life."

Avenging Angel *see* **Angel**

Lucille Ball gets hot at a party, singing "It's Today" in her appearance as the title character in Mame *(Warner Bros., 1974).*

48 The Aviator

Based on the play by James Montgomery. Story: Wishing to assure the sale of a book on the wartime experiences of an anonymous aviator, the publishers convince successful writer Robert Street to be credited with its authorship. Street knows nothing about aviation, but the book becomes an overnight success. He consents to pose for some publicity pictures sitting in the cockpit of a plane. He accidently starts the plane, creating an incredible demonstration, landing in a haystack. A race is arranged pitting Street against a French flyer and after a series of hair-raising and hilarious complications, Street abandons his pose.

Warner Bros., 1929 (original). Director: Roy Del Ruth; screenwriters: Robert Lord and Arthur Caesar. Cast: Edward Everett Horton (Robert Street), Patsy

Ruth Miller (Grace Douglas), Johnny Arthur (Hobart), Lee Moran (Brown), Edward Martindel, Armand Kaliz, Kewpie Morgan, Phillips Smalley.

• ***Going Wild*** (remake). Warner Bros., 1930. Director: William A. Seiter; screenwriter: Humphrey Pearson. Cast: Joe E. Brown (Rollo Smith), Laura Lee (Peggy), Walter Pidgeon (Ace Benton), Frank McHugh (Ricky Freeman), Arthur Hoyt (Robert Story), Lawrence Gray, Ona Munson, Mary Boley, Johnny Arthur.

Edward Everett Horton was an enjoyable and unique comedian who always made his presence known in his many supporting roles. He also had a career as the leading performer in several amusing little comedies such as *The Aviator.* He inevitably pleased audiences with his portrayals of fussy men, thrust into trying situations which they somehow managed to survive.

In the remake, Joe E. Brown is mistaken for a famous aviator. Pleased with the admiration coming his way, he accepts the situation and finds himself involved in an air race and a $25,000 wager with Walter Pidgeon. His girl, Laura Lee, substitutes herself for his mechanic who was trying to teach Brown how to fly, and between them they drive Pidgeon out of the air with their wild gyrations. Unable to land, she accidently pulls the parachute ring and they safely float to the ground as Brown proposes marriage and Lee accepts. There was a French version of this film released in 1931.

Le Avventure e gli Amori de Miguel Cervantes *see* **Don Quixote**

49 The Awful Truth

Based on the play by Arthur Richman. Story: In this screwball comedy of marital errors, Norman and Lucy Slatterly file for divorce when the former becomes irrationally jealous because of the latter's innocent flirtation with Rufus Kempster. During the year they must wait for the interlocutory decree to be finalized, Lucy, annoyed with her husband's attentions to femme fatale Josephine Trent, decides to win him back by fanning his jealousy once again by accepting a marriage proposal from dull Daniel Leeson. Unhappy with their new romantic interests, Norman and Lucy realize that they are still in love and reconcile, now aware that love comes with mutual trust, the awful truth they must accept.

Producers Distributing Company, 1925 (original). Silent. Director: Paul Powell; screenwriter: Elmer Harris. Cast: Warner Baxter (Norman Slatterly), Agnes Ayres (Lucy Slatterly), Philips Smalley (Rufus Kempster), Raymond Lowney (Daniel Leeson), Winifred Bryson (Josephnie Trent), Carrie Clark Ward.

• ***The Awful Truth*** (remake). Pathe, 1929. Director: Marshall Neilan; screenwriters: Arthur Richman and Horace Jackson. Cast: Henry Daniell (Norman Warriner), Ina Claire (Lucy Warriner), Paul Harvey (Dan Leeson), Judith Vosselli (Josephine Trent), John Roche (Jimmy Kempster), Theodore von Eltz, Blanche Frederici.

• ***The Awful Truth*** (remake). Columbia, 1937. Director: Leo McCarey; screenwriter: Vina Delmar. Cast: Cary Grant (Jerry Warriner), Irene Dunne

(Lucy Warriner), Ralph Bellamy (Daniel Leeson), Molly Lamont (Barbara Vance), Joyce Compton (Dixie Belle Lee), Alexander D'Arcy, Cecil Cunningham, Esther Dale.

• ***Let's Do It Again*** (remake). Columbia, 1953. Director: Alexander Hall; screenwriters: Mary Loos and Richard Sale. Cast: Jane Wyman (Constance Stuart), Ray Milland (Gary Stuart), Aldo Ray (Frank McGraw), Leon Ames (Chet Stuart), Valerie Bettis (Lilly Adair), Tom Helmore (Courtney Craig), Karin Booth, Mary Treen, Richard Wessel.

The 1925 movie was considered consistently amusing if of small moment, with Warner Baxter playing the role of a man who deserved to lose his wife because of his lack of trust in her. Agnes Ayres played a wife worth keeping and audiences were delighted as she taught her jealous husband a much-needed lesson.

Ina Claire re-created her stage role in Pathe's 1929 talkie and her performance was generally praised although the quality of the sound was not consistent and demonstrated that the motion picture industry had much to learn about the new phenomenon.

The 1937 version is considered to be one of the best examples of the crazy comedies produced in the era. Grant and Dunne were experts at the genre and played together beautifully. Bellamy, as the stooge used to make Grant jealous, was comfortable in one of his most consistent roles, the other man who wouldn't get the girl because of his innate dullness.

By 1953, the age of the screwball comedy had past and adding a few inferior songs such as "I'm Taking a Slow Burn" and "Zamesi Puberty Ritual" didn't help the production. It was pleasant enough but lacked the bite of the earlier attempts.

B

50 Babbitt

Based on the novel by Sinclair Lewis. Story: George F. Babbitt is a respected and prosperous middle-aged real-estate man in the city of Zenith. He's a rather boring and narrow-minded man who, growing tired of the routine of family life, feels that he has missed something important. He takes the usual avenue, beginning an affair with vampish Tanis Judique, with whom he plans to run away and discover his lost youth. However, responding to the pleas of his son, he returns to his ill and ever-faithful wife, confesses that he has acted foolishly and once again settles in to the comforts of family life.

Warner Bros., 1924 (original). Silent. Director: Harry Beaumont; screenwriter: Dorothy Farnum. Cast: Willard Louis (George F. Babbitt), Mary Alden (Mrs. Myra Babbitt), Carmel Myers (Tanis Judique), Raymond McKee (Theodore Roosevelt Babbitt), Maxine Elliott Hicks, Virginia Loomis, Robert Randall, Cissy Fitzgerald, Gertrude Olmstead, Lucien Littlefield.

• ***Babbitt*** (remake). Warner Bros./First National, 1934. Director: William Keighley; screenwriters: Mary McCall, Jr., Tom Reed and Niven Busch. Cast:

Guy Kibbee (George F. Babbitt), Aline MacMahon (Myra Babbitt), Claire Dodd (Tanis Judique), Glen Boles (Ted Babbitt), Maxine Doyle, Minna Gombell, Alan Hale, Berton Churchill, Russell Hicks, Nan Grey.

Neither Willard Louis nor Guy Kibbee were very successful in breathing life into their character, although both looked the part. Both versions are a bit tedious and slow-paced and seem to lack the irony and cynicism of the novel. The ladies, first Mary Alden and Carmel Myers, followed by Aline MacMahon and Claire Dodd, were more satisfactory in their roles than the nominal stars. George F. Babbitt made an additional film appearance in the 1960 production of Sinclair Lewis' *Elmer Gantry* with Edward Andrews doing a first rate impersonation of the pompous businessman.

Baby, Take a Bow *see* **Square Crooks**

51 Bachelor Mother

Based on an original story by Felix Jackson. Story: When shopgirl Polly Parrish finds a baby on her doorstep and takes it in, she is thought to be the mother. The department-store owner's son, David Merlin, takes an interest in her predicament and offers his help, resulting in him being believed to be the child's father. The two fall in love and marry, giving the baby parents.

RKO Pictures, 1939 (original). Director: Garson Kanin; screenwriter: Norman Krasna. Cast: Ginger Rogers (Polly Parrish), David Niven (David Merlin), Charles Coburn (J.B. Merlin), Frank Albertson, E.E. Clive, Edward Coplan, Jr.

• ***Bundle of Joy*** (remake). RKO Pictures, 1956. Director: Norman Taurog; screenwriters: Norman Krasna, Robert Carson and Arthur Sheekman. Cast: Eddie Fisher (Dan Merlin), Debbie Reynolds (Polly Parrish), Adolphe Menjou (J.B. Merlin), Tommy Noonan, Nita Talbot, Una Merkel, Melville Cooper.

Bachelor Mother was filled with rather spicy dialogue and double entendres but these were broad enough not to offend the family trade. It's a fine comedy and still enjoyable to watch. Rogers, Niven and Coburn give appealing and extravagant performances. The remake teamed America's perfect young couple, peppy and cute Debbie Reynolds and her singing-star husband, Eddie Fisher. Although tame in comparison to the original farce, it still pleased most audiences. The musical numbers, however, were only so-so.

Bachelor's Folly *see* **The Calendar**

Back at the Front *see* **Up Front**

Back from Eternity *see* **Five Came Back**

52 Back Street

Based on the novel by Fannie Hurst. Story: Ray Schmidt meets businessman Walter Saxel in 1900. They begin an affair which will last for the better part of twenty-five years. Saxel is a selfish man who, despite what appears to be a genuine love for Ray, marries another woman because the move will further his career ambitions. While Saxel prospers and achieves his life's goals, Ray gives up her opportunities with other suitors to stay in the "back streets" of her lover's life. They discuss his getting a divorce but as she sees he really doesn't have the heart for it, she does not push the matter. She acquiesces to all of his wishes. As his children grow to adulthood, they become aware of this shadow in their father's life and attempt to persuade her to give him up. Saxel learns of this and tries to explain his needs for Ray. When he is stricken by a fatal stroke, he convinces his son to phone Ray so he can hear the voice of the woman he loves once more. She hears him breathe his last on the phone.

Universal Pictures, 1932 (original). Director: John M. Stahl; screenwriter: Gladys Lehman. Cast: Irene Dunne (Ray Schmidt), John Boles (Walter Saxel), June Clyde (Freda Schmidt), George Meeker (Kurt Schendler), Zasu Pitts (Mrs. Dole), Shirley Grey (Francine), Doris Lloyd (Mrs. Saxel), William Bakewell, Arletta Duncan, Walter Catlett.

• ***Back Street*** (remake). Universal Pictures, 1941. Director: Robert Stevenson; screenwriters: Bruce Manning and Felix Jackson. Cast: Charles Boyer (Walter Saxel), Margaret Sullavan (Ray Smith), Richard Carlson (Curt Stanton), Frank McHugh (Ed Porter), Frank Jenks, Tim Holt, Peggy Smith, Esther Dale, Nell O'Day.

• ***Back Street*** (remake). Universal Pictures, 1961. Director: David Miller; screenwriters: Eleanore Griffin and William Ludwig. Cast: Susan Hayward (Rae Smith), John Gavin (Paul Saxon), Vera Miles (Liz Saxon), Charles Drake (Curt Stanton), Virginia Grey (Janie), Reginald Gardiner, Robert Eyer, Natalie Schafer.

This winning tearjerker's three film productions were all interesting but the best was the 1941 version starring Margaret Sullavan and Charles Boyer. This pair was best at making audiences believe that a woman would sacrifice so much for so little for the man she loved. Boyer's selfishness was tempered with a genuine and lasting love of the woman he kept in the back streets. Boseley Crowther described the film as "the quintessence of what is known as the 'woman's picture'." This is arguably the best film of Sullavan's career of being one of the screen's great tragediennes.

Irene Dunne's performance in the 1932 original was commendable but John Boles didn't seem the kind that could sustain such a woman's interest for a long period of time. Some critics objected that in the 1961 film, Susan Hayward didn't suffer very much and in fact, considering her clothes and living arrangements, had fallen into the lap of luxury rather than a back street. While this criticism is justified, a greater problem with the '61 piece was that audiences couldn't see Hayward as the kind of woman who would put aside her own ambitions to be at the beck and call of a selfish man, and particularly one as uninteresting as John Gavin.

Back to Bataan *see* **Bataan**

53 Bad Day at Black Rock

Based on the story "Bad Time at Hondo" by Howard Breslin. Story: One hot

As Charles Boyer and family (son Tim Holt and wife Nella Walker to his left; daughter Nell O'Day to his right) are debarking, his long-time mistress, Margaret Sullavan, is nowhere to be seen. Smart money has it that she's not too far away, however, in Universal's 1941 production of Back Street.

summer day, one-armed war veteran John J. Macreedy steps off the train at the tiny California town of Black Rock. He is there to present a medal, won by a dead Japanese-American in his command, to the boy's parents. His arrival is met with great suspicion and hostility by the local residents. When no one will give him any answers to his questions about the Japanese couple and he is taunted by a couple of the local bullies, he shows what a one-armed man trained in the martial arts can do. He finally succeeds in getting to the couple's farm only to find that it had burnt to the ground, years before. He discovers that a gang of the local residents had killed the Japanese couple and burnt their home in a rage after Pearl Harbor. To protect their guilty secret, the leader, Reno Smith, decrees that Macreedy must be killed. He is almost successful, but John J. turns the tables on him.

MGM, 1954 (original). Director: John Sturges; screenwriter: Millard Kaufman. Cast: Spencer Tracy (John J. Macreedy), Robert Ryan (Reno Smith), Anne Francis (Liz Wirth), Dean Jagger (Tim Horn), Walter Brennan (Doc Velie), John Ericson (Pete Wirth), Ernest Borgnine (Coley Trimble), Lee Marvin (Hector David), Russell Collins, Walter Sande.

• ***Platinum High School*** (remake). MGM, 1961. Director: Charles Haas;

John Gavin is embarrassed when his long-time mistress, Susan Hayward, sees his wife (Vera Miles) intoxicated in the 1961 Universal production of Back Street.

screenwriter: Robert Smith. Cast: Mickey Rooney (Steven Conway), Terry Moore (Jennifer Evans), Dan Duryea (Major Redfern Kelly), Conway Twitty (Billy Jack Barnes), Warren Berlinger (Chip Hastings), Yvette Mimieux (Lorinda Nibley), Jimmy Boyd, Richard Jaeckel, Chris Dark, Elisha Cook, Jr.

Bad Day at Black Rock is one of the most suspenseful films ever made. Every performance in this gripping, tight-paced movie is top notch with Tracy's and Ryan's being superb. The photography is outstanding and the expectancy that builds is as grueling as the desert heat depicted. In the disguised remake, Mickey Rooney visits an island off the California coast, the site of an expensive military school, where the son he has never known died. During his stay, he realizes that his son's death was not the accident described but a murder, the result of hazing. Both the students and the officials of the school had conspired to keep their involvement and guilt a secret. This version of the story didn't generate much audience interest and garnered even less critical praise.

54 Bad Girl

Based on a book by Vina Delmar and the play by Vina Delmar and Brian Marlow. Story: A pair of uneducated youngsters meet on a Coney Island boat, spend the night together and hastily marry. Their adjustment to marriage is difficult, particularly when it's discovered that a baby is on the way. Through a misunderstanding, neither feels the other wants the baby. But once it arrives they settle down to domestic life with all of its daily problems.

Fox Pictures, 1931 (original). Director: Frank Borzage; screenwriter: Edwin Burke. Cast: Sally Eilers (Dorothy Haley), James Dunn (Eddie Collins), Minna Gombell, William Pawley, Frank Darien.

• ***Manhattan Heartbeat*** (remake). Twentieth Century–Fox, 1940. Director: David Burton; screenwriters: Harold Buchman, Clark Andrews, Jack Jungmeyer, Jr., and Edith Skouras. Cast: Robert Sterling (Johnnie), Virginia Gilmore (Dottie), Joan Davis (Edna), Edmund MacDonald, Don Beddoe, Paul Harvey, Irving Bacon.

There was a Spanish version, *Marida y Mujer,* of the film released in 1932. There really isn't much to the story and filming it didn't make it any better. Of the two versions, the first is preferable, showing a bit more sparkle in the almost verbatim transcription of the play's dialog. James Dunn (in his first movie) and Sally Eilers provided some modest comedy as the two ungrammatical and almost inarticulate young kids, bewildered by marriage and its responsibilities. In the remake, the couple wasn't presented as quite as untutored and the film had to depend on Joan Davis to provide what humor it contained.

55 The Bad News Bears

Based on an original screenplay by Bill Lancaster. Story: Morris Buttermaker, former minor league baseball player now down on his luck, is hired to coach the worst Little League team. These are no Disney kids, but rather real youngsters. That means they bitch and moan, cheat, roughhouse, use four-letter words and at the right time play some winning baseball.

Paramount Pictures, 1976 (original). Director: Michael Ritchie; screenwriter: Bill Lancaster. Cast: Walter Matthau (Morris Buttermaker), Tatum O'Neal (Manda Whurlitzer), Vic Morrow (Roy Turner), Joyce Van Patten (Cleveland), Ben Piazza (Councilman Whitehead), Jackie Earle Haley (Kelly Leak), Alfred Lutter, Brandon Cruz, Chris Barnes, Erin Blunt, Gary Lee Cavagnaro, Quinn Smith, Scott Firestone, David Pollock.

• ***The Bad News Bears in Breaking Training*** (sequel). Paramount Pictures, 1977. Director: Michael Pressman; screenwriter: Paul Brinkman. Cast: William Devane (Mike Leak), Clifton James (Sy Orlansky), Jackie Earle Haley (Kelly Leak), Jimmy Baio (Carmen Ronzonni), Chris Barnes (Tannar Boyle), Erin Blunt, Jamie Escobedo, George Gonzales, Alfred Lutter, Brett Marx, David Pollock, Quinn Smith.

• ***The Bad News Bears Go to Japan*** (sequel). Paramount Pictures, 1978. Director: John Berry; screenwriter: Bill Lancaster. Cast: Tony Curtis (Marvin Lazar), Jackie Earle Haley (Kelly Leak), Tomisaburo Wayakam (Coach Shimrau), George Wyner, Lonny Chapman, Matthew Douglas Anton, Erin Bluntl.

The first film was a rough-and-tough star comedy with Matthau and O'Neal fighting each other as much as they did opposing teams. The two sequels were certainly unnecessary, being far-fetched stories of this once-worst team, now becoming one of the best. In the second, the Bears are invited to play in the Houston Astrodome, but they need a coach. William Devane, looking as he did in his Jack Kennedy role, obliges. In the final (we hope!), the team is invited to a Little League World Series in Japan; winning more through luck than skill.

The Bad News Bears in Breaking Training *see* **The Bad News Bears**

The Bad News Bears Go to Japan *see* **The Bad News Bears**

Bad Sister *see* **The Flirt**

56 Badger's Green

Based on the play by R.C. Sherriff. Story: Developers wish to take over the village green where the cricket-loving inhabitants of Badger's Green hold their matches. In a Romeo and Juliet–like bit, the protest leader's son falls in love with the daughter of the developer. Everything is resolved to the villager's satisfaction when they are victorious in a crucial cricket match against a strong opponent.

British and Dominions/Paramount British, 1934 (original). Director: Adrian Brunel; screenwriters: R.F. Davis and Violet Powell. Cast: Valerie Hobson, Bruce Lister, Frank Moore, David Horne, Sebastian Smith, John Turnbull, Wally Patch.

• ***Badger's Green*** (remake). General Film Distributors, 1948. Director: John Irwin; screenwriter: William Fairchild. Cast: Barbara Murray, Brian Nissen, Garry Marsh, Kynaston Reeves, Laurence Naismith, Mary Merrall, Jack McNaughton.

Both versions of the story are barely feature length, running just a little over an hour. They are pleasant little rural comedy-dramas not meant to be taken too seriously. It is amusing to see how even long-standing feuds are forgiven to present a united front by the villagers against the developers who would ruin their cricket field.

The Badlanders *see* **The Asphalt Jungle**

Badshah Dampati *see* **The Hunchback of Notre Dame**

57 Ball of Fire

Based on the original story "From A to Z" by Billy Wilder and Thomas Monroe. Story: Professor Bertram Potts and seven colleagues are compiling a book of slang, when they discover that locking themselves up for years to prepare their work has resulted in their being unaware of the new lingo of the day. Potts' venture into the world for research results in meeting Sugarpuss O'Shea, a burlesque stripper involved with gangsters, who nevertheless is "hep" to what's the latest jive. She moves in with Potts and his seven colleagues to hide out from the authorities who wish to question her about the illegal activities of her mobster fiancé, Joe Lilac. Lilac, figuring that a wife can't testify against her husband, decides it's time to tie the knot. In the meantime, however, Sugarpuss has fallen for the innate goodness of Potts, who is called on to outsmart Lilac and his hoods.

RKO, 1941 (original). Director: Howard Hawks; screenwriters: Charles Brackett and Billy Wilder. Cast: Gary Cooper (Professor Bertram Potts),

Barbara Stanwyck (Sugarpuss O'Shea), Dana Andrews (Joe Lilac), Oscar Homolka (Prof. Gurkakoff), Henry Travers (Prof. Jerome), S.J. Sakall (Prof. Magenbruch), Tully Marshall (Prof. Robinson), Leonid Kinsky (Prof. Quintano), Richard Haydn (Prof. Oddly), Aubrey Mather (Prof. Pengram), Allen Jenkins, Dan Duryea, Kathleen Howard, Mary Field.

• ***A Song Is Born*** (remake). RKO, 1948. Director: Howard Hawks; screenwriter: Harry Tugend. Cast: Danny Kaye (Professor Hobart Frisbee), Virginia Mayo (Honey Swanson), Steven Cochran (Tony Crow), Benny Goodman (Prof. Magenbruch), Hugh Herbert (Prof. Twingle), J. Edward Bromberg (Dr. Elfini), Felix Bressart (Prof. Gurkakoff), Ludwig Stossel (Prof. Traumer), O.Z. Whitehead (Prof. Oddly), Esther Dale, Tommy Dorsey, Louie Armstrong, Lionel Hampton, Charley Barnett, Mel Powell, Buck & Bubbles.

Both screenings took a simple gag and played it for all it was worth, perhaps more than it was worth. The Cooper-Stanwyck version was the last of the successful and fondly recalled screwball comedies, so popular in the thirties. The odd assortment of timid and not-of-this-world professors being charmed by the brassy and street-smart stripper had many fine moments.

In the remake, the academic types are now busily compiling a history of music, but are made aware by a pair of with-it window washers, that they have completely missed "swing" and the other hot music of the period. Kaye in his role as the youngest of the researchers sets out to see what they have been missing, and besides the music he finds the delectable Virginia Mayo, a nightclub singer. Like Stanwyck before her, she needs a safe hideout because her gangster lover, Steve Cochran, has committed a murder which the D.A. wants to question her about.

As did Stanwyck before her, Mayo falls for the professor and he and his colleagues thwart the gangster. The remake abounded with talented musicians who put on a jam session that sealed the crooks' fate. The new songs written for the film weren't anything special; it's a shame that the "cats" weren't given the opportunity to play some of their own hits.

Although these two films were based on an original story by Wilder and Monroe, both owed a lot to *Grimm's Fairy Tales* and Walt Disney's animation masterpiece *Snow White and the Seven Dwarfs.* You could almost pick out Doc, Grumpy, Dopey, Sleepy, Happy, Sneezy and Bashful from among the two sets of professors, although neither Sugarpuss nor Honey had the innocence and sweetness of Snow White.

58 The Ballet Girl

Based on the novel by Sir Compton MacKenzie. Story: Set in London in 1900 when no good girl would enter certain music halls, Jennie, despite her mother's dire warnings of the danger of the life, joins the *corps de ballet* of the Orient Theater under the name of La Syrena. She meets a sculptor, Robert Frazer, becomes his model, falls in love with him, but won't move in with him. He abandons her. Disillusioned and burdened with caring for a crippled sister, Jennie marries a dour Cornish farmer, Zachary Trewhello, whom she does not love. She gives up her life on the stage to live with the bigoted man, but refuses to truly be his wife. The sculptor shows up, the romance warms up again, and when the jealous husband sees the two talking together on the seashore, he kills her.

World Films, 1916 (original). Silent. Director and screenwriter: William A. Brady. Cast: Alice Brady (La Syrena–Jennie), Holbrook Blinn (Zachary Trewhello), Fred Pearl (Robert Frazer), Julia Stuart (Mrs. Raeburn), Harry Dawes, Laura McClure, Jessie Lewis, Alec B. Francis.

• ***Dance Pretty Lady*** (remake). Great Britain, 1932. Director and screenwriter: Anthony Asquith. Cast: Ann Casson (Jennie), Carl Harbord (Maurice), Michael Hogan (Trewhello), Moore Marriott, Flora Robson, Sunday Wilshin, Rene Ray, Leonard Brett.

• ***Carnival*** (remake). Two Cities Films, Great Britain, 1946. Director: Stanley Haynes; screenwriter: Eric Maschwitz. Cast: Sally Gray (Jenny), Michael Wilding (Maurice Avery), Stanley Holloway (Charlie Raeburn), Bernard Miles (Trewhello), Jean Kent, Catherine Lacey, Nancy Price, Hazel Court.

These melodramas are no great shakes and the performances, especially in the 1946 film, strangely inappropriate for the intended seriousness of the piece. Don't wait up late to catch them on TV.

The Band Wagon *see* **Dancing in the Dark**

The Bandits of Sherwood Forest *see* **Robin Hood**

The Bandits of Corsica *see* **Robin Hood**

The Barbarian *see* **The Arab**

59 Barefoot Boy

Based on a poem by John Greenleaf Whittier. Story: Twelve-year-old Dick Alden, mistreated by his stepfather and falsely accused by the townspeople of setting fire to the schoolhouse, runs away from home, vowing revenge. Years later he returns, planning to shut down the mill he has inherited which supplies employment for those who had humiliated him earlier. However, his love for his childhood sweetheart causes him to change his mind and he resolves to no longer live in the past.

Columbia, 1924 (original). Silent. Director: David Kirkland; screenwriter: Wallace Clifton. Cast: John Bowers (Dick Alden), Marjorie Daw (Mary Truesdale), Sylvia Breamer (Milicent Carter), George McDaniel (Rodman Grant), Raymond Hatton, Tully Marshall, George Periolat, Virginia True Boardman.

• ***Barefoot Boy*** (remake). Monogram, 1938. Director: Karl Brown; screenwriter: John T. Nevine. Cast: Jackie Moran (Billy Whittaker), Marcia Mae Jones (Pige Blaine), Claire Windsor (Valerie Hale), Ralph Morgan (John Hale), Bradley Metcalf (Kenneth Hale), Charles D. Brown, Helen Mackellar, Frank Puglia, Matty Fain.

The original production is a homey piece in which love triumphs over hatred but it stretches the point more than a little bit. In the remake, the boy doesn't grow up but has plenty of adventures, including invading a haunted house and clearing a wrongly imprisoned man convicted of stealing some bonds. Jackie Moran is wholesome and lively but that's not enough to make the remake a very interesting picture.

60 The Barker

Based on the play by Kenyon Nicholson. Story: Nifty Miller, self-proclaimed world's greatest carnival barker, ends his longtime affair with hula dancer Carrie when his son Chris arrives at the carnival to spend his summer vacation from law school. To punish her ex-lover, Carrie pays the show's beautiful snake charmer, Lou, to captivate the son. After awhile, to her amazement, Lou realizes that she has fallen in love with Chris. They leave the carnival, marry, and she supports him in law school by performing her act in a nightclub. Nifty, in a drunken rage, quits as the barker but when he hears how inferior his replacement is, returns to this craft of ballyhoo.

First National Pictures, 1928 (original). Director: George Fitzmaurice; screenwriter: Benjamin Glazer. Cast: Milton Sills (Nifty Miller), Dorothy Mackaill (Lou), Douglas Fairbanks, Jr. (Chris), Betty Compson (Carrie), S.S. Simon, George Cooper, John Irwin, Sylvia Ashton, Tom Dugan.

• ***Hoopla*** (remake). Fox Pictures, 1933. Director: Frank Lloyd; screenwriter: Bradley King. Cast: Preston Foster (Nifty Miller), Clara Bow (Lou), Richard Cromwell (Chris), Minna Gombell (Carrie), Roger Imhof, Herbert Mundin, James Gleason, Florence Roberts.

• ***Billy Rose's Diamond Horseshoe*** (remake). Twentieth Century–Fox, 1945. Director and screenwriter: George Seaton. Cast: Betty Grable (Bonnie Collins), Dick Haymes (Joe Davis, Jr.), Phil Silvers (Blinky Walker), William Gaxton (Joe Davis, Sr.), Beatrice Kay (Claire Williams), Carmen Cavallaro, Hal K. Dawson, Margaret Dumont, Roy Benson.

Critics were pleased with the original version of this story of life within a traveling tent show, praising the work of Milton Sills, Dorothy Mackaill and Douglas Fairbanks, Jr. However, they did note that the sound quality was such as to have them prefer that the movie had been made as a silent feature as originally planned.

In her last film, Clara Bow strained to give a decent performance as the hard-boiled carnival dancer paid to seduce the barker's son and it showed. The other leading performers also seemed lost in this out-dated melodrama.

In the 1945 Technicolor musical remake, Betty Grable portrays a nightclub singer who gives up her career for medical student Dick Haymes. In this version, the leads were much more genteel than in the previous filmings. Lavish musical numbers by Mack Gordon and Harry Gordon included "I Wish I Knew," "The More I See You," "Play Me an Old Fashioned Melody" and "Welcome to the Diamond Horseshoe."

61 The Barretts of Wimpole Street

Based on the play by Rudolf Besier. Story: Puritanical Edward Moulton-

Barrett is a tyrant in his Victorian Wimpole Street home, inflicting harsh and unreasonable demands on his children with the exception of the eldest, invalid Elizabeth, whom he dearly and perhaps unnaturally loves. His preference for the frail Elizabeth is deeply resented by the other children. Elizabeth shares her poetry in a correspondence with fellow poet Robert Browning, who falls in love with her when he comes to visit. Mr. Barrett in a jealous rage rails against their romance, but Browning pleads with Elizabeth to escape from her prison and marry him. She agrees when she realizes that her father's great affection and concern for her is incestuously motivated.

MGM, 1934 (original). Director: Sidney Franklin; screenwriters: Donald Ogden Stewart, Ernst Vajda and Claudine West. Cast: Norma Shearer (Elizabeth Moulton-Barrett), Fredric March (Robert Browning), Charles Laughton (Edward Moulton-Barrett), Maureen O'Sullivan, Katherine Alexander, Ralph Forbes, Una O'Connor, Marion Clayton, Ian Wolfe.

• ***The Barretts of Wimpole Street*** (remake). MGM, 1957. Director: Sidney Franklin; screenwriter: John Dighton. Cast: Jennifer Jones (Elizabeth Moulton-Barrett), Bill Travers (Robert Browning), John Gielgud (Edward Moulton-Barrett), Virginia McKenna, Maxine Audley, Michael Brill, Kenneth Fortescue.

The Moulton-Barrett family was none too pleased with the treatment of their grandfather in the play, and in the original stage production and subsequent film productions some references to his behavior were toned down. But as Charles Laughton observed, even if the dialogue was softened, they couldn't keep the glint from his eyes when looking at Norma Shearer as his daughter. Critics felt Laughton was masterful in the role of a man who was not allowed any sympathetic characteristics. Shearer was compared unfavorably with Katherine Cornell who had made the role of Elizabeth her own on the stage, although it was admitted that Shearer's performance was quite touching. March's reviews were more mixed. Some critics found him a virile and interesting Browning, while others felt he was merely reading his lines without giving them meaningful expression.

Sidney Franklin, the director of the 1934 film, was also responsible for the remake, but the addition of Cinemascope and Metrocolor did not overcome the obvious miscasting of the leading performers and the too-Freudian emphasis on the father-daughter relationship. It was judged a boring film made in an era that had no use for Victorian melodrama.

Barricade ***see*** **The Sea Wolf**

62 The Barrier

Based on a novel by Rex Beach. Story: During a storm off the coast of Alaska, cruel sea captain Dan Bennett forces his wife to work along with his seamen and she is fatally hurt in an accident. Seaman John Gaylord, who has loved the woman, agrees to take her child away from its father. Years later, the child Necia has grown into a beautiful young woman, believing that Gaylord is her father. She is loved by half-breed Poleon Doret, but she's interested in a young Virginia aristocrat stationed in Alaska, Lt. Meade Burrell. Predictably, her real

Charles Laughton as Edward Moulton-Barrett, center, shows his disapproval of Fredric March (as Robert Browning), who insists on courting Norma Shearer (as Elizabeth Barrett) in The Barretts of Wimpole Street *(MGM, 1934).*

father shows up and spills the beans that Necia's mother was an Indian. Burrell is stunned by the news. Thinking he no longer loves her, Necia leaves with her brutish father. When Captain Bennett's ship gets caught in an ice jam, his crew deserts, but Burrell arrives to rescue Necia. Bennett dies and the lovers are happy together once again.

Rex Beach Production, 1917 (original). Silent. Director: Edgar Lewis; screenwriter: A. Gil-Speer. Cast: Mabel Julienne Scott (Meridy/Necia), Russell Simpson (John Gaylord/John Gale), Howard Hall (Dan Bennett/Ben Stark), Victor Sutherland (Lt. Meade Burrell), Mitchell Lewis (Poleon Doret).

• ***The Barrier*** (remake). MGM, 1926. Silent. Director: George Hill; screenwriter: Harvey Gates. Cast: Norman Kerry (Meade Burrell), Harry B. Walthall (Gale Gaylord), Lionel Barrymore (Stark Bennett), Marceline Day (Necia), Mario Carillo (Poleon), Bert Woodruff, Princess Neola.

• ***The Barrier*** (remake). Paramount, 1937. Director: Leslie Selander; screenwriters: Bernard Schubart, Harrison Jacobs and Mordaunt Shairp. Cast: Leo Carillo (Poleon Doret), Jean Parker (Necia), James Ellison (Lt. Burrell), Robert Barrat (John Gale), Otto Kruger (Stark), Andy Clyde, Addison Richards, Sara Haden.

All three films presented an exciting story with plenty of action and actors

Jennifer Jones as Elizabeth Barrett smiles up at her unhappy-looking father, John Gielgud, who intends his piercing stare to put the fear of God into the hearts of his other children and Jones' suitor, Bill Travers (as Robert Browning), directly across the room from him in The Barretts of Wimpole Street *(MGM, 1957).*

competent for their parts. It seems unlikely, however, that the story will ever be filmed again, as the problems of a half-caste have been presented on too many occasions, usually poorly. The 1937 version was shot in Mt. Baker National Park, Washington, and has some beautiful photography.

63 The Barton Mystery

Based on the play by Walter Hackett. Story: A man is wrongly accused of a murder committed by a girl who finally admits her guilt, but a fake medium's inspiration helps her prove that the victim was a blackmailer whom she killed in self-defense.

Stoll, Great Britain, 1920 (original). Silent. Director: Harry Roberts; screenwriter: R. Bryon-Webber. Cast: Lyn Harding (Beverley), Hilda Bayley (Ethel Standish), Vernon Jones (Phyllis Grey), Maud Cressall (Mrs. Barton), Edward O'Neill (Richard Standish), Arthur Pusey (Harry Maitland), Ernest A. Cox, Eva Westlake, Austen Camp.

• ***The Barton Mystery*** (remake). British & Dominion/Paramount, Great Britain, 1932. Director: Henry Edwards; screenwriter: uncredited. Cast: Ursula Jeans (Ethel Standish), Ellis Jeffreys (Lady Marshall), Lyn Harding (Beverley),

Ion Swinley (Richard Standish), Wendy Barrie (Phyllis Grey), Joyce Bland (Helen Barton), Tom Helmore, O.B. Clarence, Franklyn Bellamy, Wilfred Noy.

These are pretty tame mystery stories with nothing very remarkable about either version. The performances are adequate to the material and conversely, but it doesn't seem that it will ever prove necessary to bring the Hackett play to the screen again.

64 The Bat

Based on the play by Mary Roberts Rinehart and Avery Hopwood and the novel *The Circular Staircase* by Mary Roberts Rinehart. Story: It's the yarn about a mysterious and energetic thief who disguises himself as a giant bat. Wealthy spinster Cornelia Van Gorder hires Detective Anderson to guard her rented summer home from mysterious nightly intruders searching for a large amount of money stolen from the local bank. During a violent summer storm, Cornelia and her terrified maid Lizzie decide that someone is in the house, which they search and find a secret room and the missing money. They maintain a vigil in the secret room and "The Bat" is finally captured.

(Aka: ***The Circular Staircase***). Selig Pictures, 1915 (original). Silent. Director: Edward Le Saint. Cast: Eugenie Besserer (Aunt Ray), Stella Razetto (Gertrude Innes), Guy Oliver (Halsey Innes), Edith Johnson (Louise Armstrong), William Howard, George Hernandez, Bertram Grassby.

• ***The Bat*** (remake). United Artists, 1926. Silent. Director: Roland West; screenwriter: Julien Josephson. Cast: Louise Fazenda (Lizzie Allen), Emily Fitzroy (Cornelia Van Gorder), Jack Pickford (Brooks), Eddie Gribbon (Detective Anderson), Kamiyama Sojiin, Jewel Carmen, Robert McKim.

• ***The Bat Whispers*** (remake). United Artists, 1930. Director and screenwriter: Roland West. Cast: Chester Morris (Detective Anderson/The Bat), Una Merkel (Dale Van Gorder), Maude Eburne (Lizzie Allen), Grayce Hampton (Cornelia Van Gorder), William Bakewell (Brooks), Hugh Huntley, Gustave von Seyffertitz, Richard Tucker.

• ***The Bat*** (remake). Allied Artists, 1959. Director and screenwriter: Crane Wilbur. Cast: Vincent Price (Dr. Malcolm Wells), Agnes Moorehead (Cornelia Van Gorder), Gavin Gordon (Lt. Anderson), John Sutton (Warner), Lenita Lane (Lizzie Allen), Elaine Edwards, Darla Hood, John Bryant, Harvey Stephens.

The first film version, made in 1915, took the title of Mary Roberts Rinehart's 1908 novel which she and Avery Hopwood adapted in 1920 for a three-act play called *The Bat.*

The 1926 presentation of the mystery kept audiences guessing as to the identity of "The Bat," laying a few false clues that made even Miss Van Gorder seem a suspect. The film was described as spine-tingling and the performances of Emily Fitzroy and Jack Pickford were singled out for special praise.

By 1931, audiences found the new wide-screen presentation, now called *The Bat Whispers,* causing more giggles than shivers. It was judged as working too hard to be frightening, instead becoming hectic nonsense which even the suspense of uncovering the identity of the mysterious Bat could not salvage, although the camera work and sets were considered excellent.

In the 1959 remake, Agnes Moorehead is a lady mystery writer who rents a spooky old house and finds herself and her guests at the mercy of a maniac frantically searching the house for stolen money. It's a typical Vincent Price thriller of the era.

The Bat Whispers *see* **The Bat**

65 Bataan

Based on a screenplay by Robert D. Andrews. Story: Thirteen soldiers representing various ethnic, religious and racial origins hold a bridge on Bataan against the advancing Japanese and are killed, one by one. During the lulls in the fighting, the survivors get very philosophical, and wave the flag in a clear effort to strengthen the resolve of members of the audience to win the war.

MGM, 1943. Director: Tay Garnett; screenwriter: Robert D. Andrews. Cast: Robert Taylor, George Murphy, Thomas Mitchell, Lloyd Nolan, Lee Bowman, Robert Walker, Desi Arnaz, Barry Nelson, Philip Terry.

• ***Back to Bataan*** (sequel). RKO, 1945. Director: Edward Dmytryk; screenwriters: Ben Barzman and Richard Landau. Cast: John Wayne, Anthony Quinn, Beulah Bondi, Fely Franquelli, Leonard Strong, Richard Loo, Philip Ahn, Lawrence Tierney, Paul Fix.

The first film seems to be an uncredited remake of *The Lost Patrol.* Of the genre of films about doomed Americans holding out as long as possible against superior odds, it is the most intelligent and interesting. The second film, not actually a sequel to the first, has John Wayne and a small force of Filipino guerillas harrassing the Japanese on Bataan during the war. The Japanese are portrayed as unbelievably cruel barbarians, and the picture's mission to intensify the hatred of them is successfully achieved.

66 Battle Circus

Based on a story by Allen Rivkin and Laura Kerr. Story: Major Jed Webbe is a tough Army surgeon assigned to a Mobile Army Surgical Corps in Korea. Simultaneous with the arrival of helicopters filled with wounded soldiers from the front is the appearance of a group of relief nurses including Lt. Ruth McCara who is thrilled with the prospect of service to humanity. Webbe takes an immediate interest in the young nurse, particularly because of the unnecessary risks she takes. He starts a succession of passes at the girl to relieve the monotony of his duties. Initially she resists his advances but as the war progresses, so does their romance.

MGM, 1952 (original). Director and screenwriter: Richard Brooks. Cast: Humphrey Bogart (Major Jed Webbe), June Allyson (Lt. Ruth McCara), Keenan Wynn (Sgt. Orville Statt), Robert Keith (Lt. Col. Hillary Whalters), William Campbell, Perry Sheehan, Patricia Tiernan, Adele Longmire, Ann Morrison.

• ***M*A*S*H*** (remake). Twentieth Century–Fox, 1970. Director: Robert Altman; screenwriter: Ring Lardner, Jr. Based on a novel by Richard Hooker. Cast: Donald Sutherland (Hawkeye Pierce), Elliott Gould (Trapper John), Tom

Perry Sheehan and June Allyson listen attentively as Humphrey Bogart discusses his toast in Battle Circus *(MGM, 1952).*

Skerritt (Duke), Sally Kellerman (Major Hot Lips Houlihan), Robert Duvall (Major Frank Burns), Jo Ann Pflug (Lt. Dish), Rene Auberjonois (Dago Red), John Schuck (Painless Pole), Gary Burghoff (Radar O'Reilly).

While *M*A*S*H* is not really a remake of *Battle Circus* and is based on a different source, there is enough to connect the two movies. Both deal with the monotony, boredom, frustration and horror of war. Both view love as a "for-the-time-being" kind of thing. Both deal with trying to patch-up young men who are dying without knowing what it is for and why it is happening to them. Both show the great tension and exhaustion that goes with the assignment.

The Bogart vehicle is the more dramatic of the two and is presented in a more serious vein. *M*A*S*H* is a black comedy with an existentialist message. It has no real plot and in fact no beginning or end. The war and the dying soldiers are there when Hawkeye Pierce arrives and they are there when he departs. In between, he and the other doctors, nurses and military personnel cope as best they can with an impossible situation. There is no dignity in being a physician in a medical madhouse and civilized behavior would seem out of place. The humor is cruel and cynical, as when Radar arranges to broadcast Margaret Houlihan and Frank Burns' love-making to the entire camp or when it is arranged to have Hot Lips give an unexpected nude show as she is taking her shower. The football game in the second half of the picture is the weakest point

*Some of the leading performers of M*A*S*H (20th Century–Fox, 1970), strike a pose not seen in the movie. From left to right, Fred Williamson, Sally Kellerman, Elliot Gould, Donald Sutherland, Jo Ann Pflug and Tom Skerritt.*

of the picture. It reduces the film from a serious statement about war to just another of the many zany college football game sequences seen in many movies of the 30s.

The Battling Bellhop *see* **Kid Galahad**

The Bawdy Adventures of Tom Jones *see* **Tom Jones**

67 The Beachcomber

Based on the book *Vessel of Wrath* by W. Somerset Maugham. Story: Ginger Ted is a drunken beachcomber on a tiny Dutch island in the Pacific with an eye for the local cuties. His behavior is the despair of the only other white inhabitants on the island, a dour, bigoted Welsh minister, Dr. Jones, and his militant spinster sister, Martha. They wish him deported for corrupting the natives. The new government official of the area arrests Ted when he wrecks the grog shop. However, an epidemic sobers him, and he ends up marrying the spinster and returning to England to run a pub.

• ***The Beachcomber (Vessel of Wrath)*** (original). Mayflower Company, 1938. Director: Erich Pommer; screenwriter: Bartlett Cormack. Cast: Charles

The Geste brothers, in their English home before setting out for adventure with the French Foreign Legion, are from left to right, Digby, played by Neil Hamilton, Michael "Beau," played by Ronald Colman and John, played by Ralph Forbes. Beau Geste, *Paramount, 1926.*

Laughton (Ginger Ted), Elsa Lanchester (Martha Jones), Tyrone Guthrie (Dr. Jones), Robert Newton (Controleur), Dolly Mollinger (Lia), Rosita Garcia (Kati), J. Solomon, Fred Groves, Eliot Makeham, Mah Foo, Ley Oh.

• ***The Beachcomber*** (remake). United Artists, 1955. Director: Muriel Box; screenwriter: Sydney Box. Cast: Robert Newton (Ted), Glynis Johns (Martha), Donald Sinden (Edward Gray), Paul Rogers (Owen), Donald Pleasence (Tromp), Walter Crisham, Michael Hordern, Auric Lorand, Tony Quinn, Ah Chong Choy.

Laughton gives a first-rate salty and comical performance as the disreputable wastrel. Elsa Lanchester is the fiercely virtuous spinster who comes to love the scruffy beachcomber. The film has many of the aspects of the 1951 smash *The African Queen.* In the 1955 programmer, Robert Newton moves up in the cast from his 1938 appearance as the government official to the rascally Ted and is quite good at it, demonstrating his usual flamboyant style, no doubt playing the drunken scenes from personal memory.

68 Beau Geste

Based on the novels of Sir Percival Christopher Wren. Story: A relief

The Geste brothers, Digby (Robert Preston), Beau (Gary Cooper) and John (Ray Milland) are reunited in a French Foreign Legion barracks in Beau Geste, *Paramount, 1939.*

detachment of the French Foreign Legion under the command of Major de Beaujoulis arrives at remote Fort Zinderneuf to find each embrasure of the fort manned by a dead soldier. The buglar is sent to investigate, but when he does not return, the major scales the wall and finds the fort's commander, Sgt. Lejaune, dead, killed by a French bayonet. Near his body is that of another dead Legionnaire. While the major is opening the gate, both bodies disappear. Later, when the detachment is again in the desert, the fort catches fire and is destroyed.

The story flashbacks to England some 15 years earlier, where the three Geste brothers are being raised by their aunt, Lady Brandon, who also cares for her ward, Isobel. Beau and Digby have a pact that the first to die is to be given a Viking's funeral consisting of a dog being placed at the foot of the deceased and both bodies burned on a pyre. Beau accidently learns that his aunt has sold the family's priceless sapphire, the "Blue Water," and has substituted a worthless imitation in its place. Years later when the boys are grown to young men, John and Isobel plan to marry. A message arrives that long-absent Lord Brandon is coming for the sapphire which he plans to sell. Beau takes the imitation but denies having done so. During the night each of the boys leaves a note claiming that he alone had taken the stone and is off to join the Foreign Legion.

The Geste's are under the command of "the cruelest beast and the bravest soldier," Lejaune. When Arabs attack the fort, he places dead men at each embrasure to make the enemy feel the fort is still fully manned. When Beau is fatally wounded, Lejaune searchs his body for the jewel he believes the dead man possesses. John kills the desecrator and flees into the desert. The buglar with the relief attachment is none other than Digby, who, seeing his dead brother, remembers his promise; using the sergeant as the cur, he gives Beau a Viking's funeral and then joins John in the desert, although only the latter makes it back to England and his beloved Isobel.

Famous Players–Lasky/Paramount, 1926 (original). Silent. Director: Herbert Brenon; screenwriter: Paul Schofield. Cast: Ronald Colman (Michael "Beau" Geste), Neil Hamilton (Digby Geste), Ralph Forbes (John Geste), Noah Beery (Sgt. Lejaune), Alice Joyce (Lady Brandon), Mary Brian (Isobel), Norman Trevor (Major de Beaujoulis).

• ***Beau Sabreur*** (sequel). Paramount, 1928. Silent. Director: John Waters; screenwriter: Tom Geraghty. Cast: Gary Cooper, Evelyn Brent, Noah Beery, William Powell, Roscoe Karns.

• ***Beau Ideal*** (sequel). RKO, 1931. Director: Herbert Brenon; screenwriter: Paul Schofield. Cast: Lester Vail, Ralph Forbes, Don Alvarado, Loretta Young, Irene Rich.

• ***Beau Geste*** (remake). Paramount Pictures, 1939. Director: William A. Wellman; screenwriter: Robert Carson. Cast: Gary Cooper (Beau Geste), Robert Preston (Digby), Ray Milland (John), Brian Donlevy (Sgt. Markoff), Heather Thatcher (Lady Brandon), Susan Hayward (Isobel), James Stephenson (Major de Beaujoulis).

• ***Beau Geste*** (remake). Universal Pictures, 1966. Director and screenwriter: Douglas Heyes. Cast: Telly Savalas, Guy Stockwell, Doug McClure, Leslie Nielsen, Leon Gordon, Michael Constantine.

• ***Last Remake of Beau Geste*** (remake). Universal Pictures, 1977. Director: Marty Feldman; screenwriters: Marty Feldman and Chris J. Allen. Cast: Marty Feldman, Michael York, Ann-Margret, Peter Ustinov, Trevor Howard, James Earl Jones.

The 1939 version is a faithful remake of the silent classic. It's ironic that Colman with his cultured British-speaking voice was not heard and Cooper with his Western accent tried to speak like a well–brought up Englishman. Both Colman and Cooper were spectacular as the valiant Beau. As their brothers, Hamilton and Forbes, and Preston and Milland respectively, were more than adequate. Deserving particular praise are Beery and Donlevy as the cruel, brilliant military villains.

In *Beau Sabreur,* Cooper takes on the role of Major de Beaujoulis who is sent to the Sudan to negotiate a treaty with a powerful and treacherous sheik, played nastily by Beery. *Beau Ideal* dealt with the further adventures of the surviving Geste brother, John (once again played by Ralph Forbes), and his efforts to get back to his beloved Isobel, now portrayed by lovely Loretta Young. In 1966, a low-budget remake was made by Universal featuring Telly Savalas as the cruel sergeant who appeared more mad than evil. The story reduced the number of

Geste brothers to two, no doubt in an economy move, played by Stockwell and McClure. The 1977 spoof-parody, exhibiting the multi-dimensional talents of crazy Marty Feldman as writer, director and star, had an impressive cast, each seemingly caught at a low point in their career.

Beau Ideal *see* **Beau Geste**

Beau Sabreur *see* **Beau Geste**

La Beaute Du Diable *see* **Faust**

69 Beauty and the Boss

Based on the play *Church Mouse* by Ladislaus Fodor and Paul Frank. Story: Viennese bank president Baron von Ullrich finds the various beautiful girls that he has employed to be his secretary to be so distracting that when plain-looking Susie Sachs applies for the job he hires her on the spot. But Susie blossoms into the prettiest girl in the office. In her transformation, she is assisted by Polly, the baron's current mistress who used to be his secretary. She is so successful in describing how to become attractive and snare a man, that Susie takes the Baron away from her and the two are married.

Warner Bros., 1932 (original). Director: Roy Del Ruth; screenwriter: Joseph Jackson. Cast: Marian Marsh (Susie Sachs), Warren William (Baron Von Ullrich), Mary Doran (Polly), Charles Butterworth, Frederick Kerr, Lillian Bond, Polly Walters, Robert Grieg, Yola D'Avril, Barbara Leonard.

• ***The Church Mouse*** (remake). Warner Bros./First National, 1934. Director: Monty Banks; screenwriter: W. Scott Darling. Cast: Laura la Plante, Ian Hunter, Jane Carter, Edward Chapman, Clifford Heatherley, John Batten, Gibb McLaughlin, Monty Banks, Florence Wood.

The theme of this "Cinderella" story is about 180 degrees from *Nine to Five*. Here, every young stenographer wants only to please the boss, hoping he will notice her and propose marriage. Warren William proposed many things to the girls in his office, but until Marian Marsh comes along, marriage is not among them. The lines in this formula comedy were considered rather saucy for the times, particularly Mary Doran's description of her love techniques. In the amusing remake, Laura la Plante plays the dowdy secretary who through instructions on beauty and catching a man by Jane Carter, blossoms into an irresistible beauty and lands the banker, played by Ian Hunter.

70 Becket

Based on Jean Anouith's *Becket, ou L'Honneur de Dieu*. Story: In twelfth-century England, Norman King Henry II is at odds with the church because he spends most of his time in frivolous activities with his Saxon friend Thomas Becket, who also advises him on matters of state. Angered when the church refuses to allocate funds for Henry's battle with France, the king appoints Thomas Chancellor of England, in which post Becket fights the church on Henry's behalf. When the Archbishop of Canterbury dies, Henry appoints

Becket to the post, hoping to control the church. Becket, protesting that he cannot serve both God and the King, resigns as Chancellor and henceforth opposes Henry's attempts to tax the church and punish its priests. Frustrated, Henry impulsively calls for the elimination of this meddlesome priest and four of his barons oblige, killing Becket before the altar in Canterbury Cathedral. Stricken by the loss of his friend, Henry submits to flogging by Saxon monks and then proclaims Becket a saint.

Paramount Pictures, U.S./Great Britain, 1964 (original). Director: Peter Glenville; screenwriter: Edward Anhalt. Cast: Richard Burton (Thomas Becket), Peter O'Toole (King Henry II), John Gielgud (King Louis VII of France), Donald Wolfit (Gilbert Folliot, Bishop of London), Martita Hunt (Queen Matilda), Pamela Brown (Queen Eleanor), Paola Stoppa (Pope Alexander III), Gino Cervi, David Weston, Felix Aylmer, Percy Herbert, Niall MacGinnis, Christopher Rhodes, Peter Jeffrey, Michael Miller, Peter Prowse, Sian Phillips.

• ***The Lion in Winter*** (remake). Haworth/Avco Embassy, Great Britain, 1968. Director: Anthony Harvey; screenwriter: James Goldman, based on his play of the same name. Cast: Peter O'Toole (King Henry II), Katharine Hepburn (Queen Eleanor of Aquitaine), Jane Merrow (Princess Alais), John Castle (Prince Geoffrey), Timothy Dalton (King Philip of France), Anthony Hopkins (Prince Richard the Lion-Hearted), Nigel Stock (William Marshall), Nigel Terry (Prince John), Kenneth Griffith, O.Z. Whitehead, Kenneth Ives.

Academy Award nominations for *Becket* were for Best Picture, Best Direction (Glenville), Best Photography (Geoffrey Unsworth), Best Musical Score (Laurence Rosenthal), Best Screenplay (Edward Anhalt), Best Actor (Burton and O'Toole) and Best Supporting Actor (Gielgud). Only Anhalt won.

Katharine Hepburn won an Oscar, as did screenwriter Goldman and John Barry for the musical score for *The Lion in Winter*. It was nominated for Best Picture, Best Direction (Harvey) and Best Acting (O'Toole). It is the story of a Christmas court at Chinon Castle to which Henry II calls his wife, Eleanor of Aquitaine, whom he has held imprisoned for 10 years for her part in civil wars and plots against him. The purpose of the court is to decide which of Henry's remaining three sons will be named his heir to the throne. He holds all three sons in low esteem. The protagonists plot to attain their own selfish ends, using the sons as pawns in their game of intrigue.

Becky Sharp *see* **Vanity Fair**

Bedazzled *see* **Faust**

71 Bedtime for Bonzo

Based on a story by Raphael David Blau and Ted Berkman. Story: Psychology professor Peter Boyd uses a chimp named Bonzo to prove that environment, not heredity, determines a child's future. The only housekeeper he can employ to nursemaid the chimp is pretty ex-farm girl Jane. The presence of both Bonzo and Jane in the professor's house breaks up his engagement to Valerie

Tillinghast, but as would be expected Jane gets the professor and they go on a honeymoon with Bonzo.

Universal Pictures, 1951 (original). Director: Frederick de Cordova; screenwriter: Val Burton. Cast: Ronald Reagan (Professor Peter Boyd), Diana Lynn (Jane), Walter Slezak (Prof. Hans Neumann), Lucille Barkley (Valerie Tillinghast), Bonzo, Jesse White, Herbert Heyes, Herbert Vigram, Harry Tyler.

• ***Bonzo Goes to College*** (sequel). Universal Pictures, 1952. Director: Frederick de Cordova; screenwriters: Leo Lieberman and Jack Henley. Cast: Maureen O'Sullivan (Marion Drew), Charles Drake (Malcolm Drew), Edmund Gwenn (Pop Drew), Gigi Perreau (Betsy Drew), Gene Lockhart, Irene Ryan, John Miljan, Bonzo, Jerry Paris, Guy Williams.

It's beguiling nonsense and not exactly the sort of thing for which the president of the United States wishes to be remembered. But then it is a family story, and what a family! In the sequel of sorts, Bonzo escapes from a sideshow where his mental prowess is questioned by a pair of sharpies and takes up residence with the granddaughter of a college's football coach. Bonzo easily passes the college's entrance exams and becomes the team's star quarterback. Ah, yes, suspicions confirmed. Does the NCAA know about this?

Behind the High Wall *see* **The Big Guy**

Behind the Iron Mask *see* **The Iron Mask**

72 Behold My Wife

Based on the book *The Translation of a Savage* by Sir Gilbert Parker. Story: Frank Armour, the son of an English family, migrates to Northwest Canada. During his absence his fiancée breaks their engagement to marry another with the concurrence of his own family. Outraged, Frank marries a half-breed, Lali, and sends her back to live with his family. Frank's brother Richard takes responsibility for the girl and instructs her in civilized ways and in no time she becomes quite acceptable in polite society. Meanwhile, Frank lives a self-destructive existence until reformed by an English surveyor who cuffs Frank severely every time he attempts to take a drink. They return to England where Frank discovers that Lali has borne him a son. They settle down as man and wife for real this time.

Paramount, 1920 (original). Silent. Director and screenwriter: George Medford. Cast: Mabel Julienne Scott (Lali), Milton Sills (Frank Armour), Winter Hall (General Armour), Elliot Dexter (Richard Armour), Helen Dunbar (Mrs. Armour), Ann Forrest (Marian Armour), Maud Wayne (Julia Haldwell).

• ***Behold My Wife*** (remake). Paramount, 1934. Director: Mitchell Leisen; screenwriters: Grover Jones and Vincent Lawrence. Cast: Sylvia Sidney (Tonita Stormcloud), Gene Raymond (Michael Carter), Juliette Compton (Diana Carter-Curson), Laura Hope Crews (Mrs. Carter), H.B. Warner (Mr. Carter), Monroe Owsley (Bob Prentice), Kenneth Thomson, Ann Sheridan, Dean Jagger, Eric Blore.

The story has the sentimental quality of *The Squaw Man* but with a happy ending. In the remake, Michael Carter wishes to marry a pretty stenographer but his wealthy American family won't hear of it. He marries an Indian girl, Tonita, to embarrass his family even though he doesn't love her. While living with his family, Tonita gets drawn into a murder case. It seems her married sister-in-law has shot and killed her lover. Tonita, trying to prove her value to the family, tells the police that she did the shooting. Learning of this, Michael goes to the police station and confesses he's the gunman. The wise police leave the couple alone with a hidden microphone and in a short time have the whole story and the young couple find they are really in love. The story is not to be taken too seriously but each version was satisfactory entertainment for the times in which they were released.

73 Bella Donna

Based on the novel by Robert S. Hichens and the play by James Bernard Fagan. Story: Bella Donna's first husband is convicted of throwing one of her admirers into a Venetian canal. The adventuress then marries engineer Nigel Armine and sails with him to Egypt, where she becomes infatuated with Mahmoud Baroudi. The latter convinces Bella Donna to poison her already ill husband, but he is saved when a friend correctly diagnoses his problem. Bella Donna flees to Baroudi's tent but finds him in the arms of another woman and not interested in any further involvement with her because of her failure to shed her husband. She turns and wanders off into the desert alone.

• ***Bella Donna*** (remake). Famous Players/Paramount Pictures, 1923. Silent. Director: George Fitzmaurice; screenwriter: Ouida Bergere. Cast: Pola Negri (Bella Donna), Conway Tearle (Mahmoud Baroudi), Conrad Nagel (Nigel Armine), Adolphe Menjou (Mr. Chepstow), Claude King (Dr. Meyer Isaacson), Lois Wilson, Macey Harlam, Robert Schable.

• ***Bella Donna*** (remake). Gaumont-British, 1934. Director: Robert Milton; screenwriter: H. Fowler Mear. Cast: Mary Ellis (Mona Chepstow), Conrad Veidt (Mahmoud Baroudi), Cedric Hardwicke (Dr. Isaacson), John Stuart (Nigel Armine), Rodney Millington, Michael Shepley, Jeanne Stuart.

• ***Temptation*** (remake). Universal Pictures, 1946. Director: Irving Pichel; screenwriter: Robert Thoren. Cast: Merle Oberon (Ruby), George Brent (Nigel), Charles Korvin (Baroudi), Paul Lukas (Isaacson), Leonore Ulric, Arnold Moss, Ludwig Stossel, Gavin Muir, Ilka Gruning, Robert Capa.

Bella Donna was also filmed in 1915 and 1918. The story of infidelity, wifely treachery and rejection was a popular vehicle for Pola Negri. The critics were divided in their opinion of the 1934 British remake. It had a fine cast but the story no longer held much interest. *Temptation* wasn't tempting. By 1946, the story seemed completely ridiculous, not even good soap opera material. Merle Oberon was, as usual, quite lovely to look at.

La Belle Lola ***see*** **Camille**

74 Belles of St. Trinian's

Based on a screenplay by Frank Launder, Sidney Gilliat and Val Valentine, inspired by the cartoons of Ronald Searle. Story: The little horrors of St. Trinian's, a British school for girls, foil the plot to steal the favorite horse in a big race. There is a battle royal between the girls of the fourth form and the girls of the sixth form. The prime mover in the dastardly horse stealing plot is the headmistress' bookmaker brother.

British Lion/London Films, 1954 (original). Director: Frank Launder; screenwriters: Frank Launder, Sidney Gilliat and Val Valentine. Cast: Alastair Sim (Miss Fritton/Clarence Fritton), Joyce Grenfell (Sergeant Ruby Gates), George Cole (Flash Harry), Hermione Baddeley (Miss Browder), Betty Ann Davies (Miss Waters), Renee Houston (Miss Brimmer), Beryl Reid (Miss Wilson), Irene Handl (Miss Gale), Mary Merrall (Miss Buckland), Joan Sims (Miss Dawn), Balbina, Jane Henderson, Diana Day, Jill Braidwood, Annabelle Covey, Jauline Drewett, Jean Langston, Lloyd Lamble, Richard Wattis, Guy Middleton, Eric Pohlmann.

• ***Blue Murder at St. Trinian's*** (sequel). British Lion, 1958. Director: Frank Launder; screenwriters: Launder, Val Valentine and Sidney Gilliat. Cast: Terry-Thomas (Rommey), George Cole (Flash Harry), Joyce Grenfell (Sgt. Gates), Alastair Sim (Miss Fritton), Sabrina (Virginia), Lionel Jeffries (Joe Mangan), Ferdy Mayne, Lloyd Lamble, Thorley Walters, Cyril Chamberlain, Judith Furse, Richard Wattis, Guido Lorraine, Lisa Gastoni, Jose Read, Dillya Laye.

These first two St. Trinian films were followed up in 1961 with *Pure Hell at St. Trinian's* and in 1966, *The Great St. Trinian's Train Robbery.* But by the time of these two, the gag and novelty of bringing the Ron Searle cartoon schoolgirls to life on the screen had worn quite thin. In the sequel, the little fiends find their school in a state of siege. Their headmistress, Miss Fritton, amusingly played by Alastair Sim, is in jail and pending the arrival of a new headmistress the police and the army have been called out to keep order at the school. The girls have arranged to win a contest whose first prize is a trip to Rome. One of the fathers who has pulled off a jewel heist signs on as chaperone. It has some good lines, amusing situations and some of the students, unlike in the Searle cartoons, are quite easy on the eye.

Belles on Their Toes ***see*** **Cheaper by the Dozen**

The Bells of St. Mary's ***see*** **Going My Way**

The Beloved Rogue ***see*** **If I Were King**

75 Beloved Vagabond

Based on the novel by William J. Locke. Story: Gaston de Nerac is jilted by his sweetheart, Joanna, who marries a count to save her father from financial ruin. Gaston takes to the road, teaming up with Blanquette, an orphan whose grandfather had founded an orchestra that our gentleman tramp takes over. Later his old love, now a widow, returns to the scene but he realizes that he loves Blanquette.

Astra-National, Great Britain, 1923 (original). Silent. Director: Fred Leroy

Ramon Novarro as Ben Hur and May McAvoy as Esther embrace in Ben Hur *(MGM, 1926).*

Granville; screenwriter: Frank Miller. Cast: Carlyle Blackwell (Gaston de Nerac), Madge Stuart (Blanquette), Phyllis Titmuss (Joanna Rushworth), Sydney Fairbrother (Mrs. Smith), Albert Chase (Asticot), Owen Roughwood, Hubert Carter, Cameron Carr, Irene Tripod.

• ***Beloved Vagabond*** (remake). Toeplitz, Great Britain, 1936. Director: Kurt Bernhardt; screenwriters: Wells Root, Arthur Wimperis, Hugh Mills and Walter Creighton. Cast: Maurice Chevalier (Gaston de Nerac), Betty Stockfeld (Joanna Rushworth), Margaret Lockwood (Blanquette), Desmond Tester (Asticot), Austin Trevor (Count Verneuil), Peter Haddon, Charles Carson, Cathleen Nesbitt.

For the remake, the critics couldn't agree. Some felt it was the best work that Chevalier had done to date, while others found his performance and the film "trite and tedious." The truth depends upon how one feels about Chevalier. If you like him, you'll like the film. If not, well, it is a bit trite and tedious.

Ben *see* **Willard**

76 Ben-Hur

Based on the novel by General Lew Wallace. Story: In Jerusalem, Ben-Hur, of the Jewish house of Hur, develops a friendship with a Roman centurion,

Charlton Heston as Ben Hur and Haya Harareet as Esther share meaningful looks as they realize for the first time that they are in love, in Ben Hur *(MGM, 1959).*

Messala. When a loose tile from the Hur home is accidently knocked free and falls on and kills a Roman officer, Messala has the entire Hur family arrested. Ben-Hur is sentenced to the galleys but on the way is given a drink and comfort by Jesus Christ, refreshing his spirits. When Ben-Hur saves the life of the galley ship's commander, Arrius, the latter adopts Ben-Hur as his son and takes him to Rome, where the young man becomes wealthy and popular as a charioteer. Ben-Hur takes revenge on his old enemy by defeating Messala in a spectacular chariot race. Back in Jerusalem, Ben-Hur is recognized by his mother and sisters who have become lepers. They are taken to be cured by a follower of Christ, Esther, and the family returns to the palace of Hur.

• ***Ben-Hur*** (remake). MGM, 1926. Silent. Director: Fred Niblo; screenwriters: Bess Meredith and Carey Wilson. Cast: Ramon Novarro (Ben-Hur), Francis X.

Bushman (Messala), May McAvoy (Esther), Betty Bronson (Mary), Claire McDowell (Princess of Hur), Kathleen Key (Tirzah), Carmel Myers (Iras), Mitchel Lewis (Sheik Ilderim), Frank Currier (Arrius), Nigel De Brulier (Simonides), Leo White, Charles Belcher, Dale Fuller, Winter Hall.

• ***Ben-Hur*** (remake). MGM, 1959. Director: William Wyler; screenwriter: Karl Turberg. Cast: Charlton Heston (Judah Ben-Hur), Jack Hawkins (Quintas Arrius), Stephen Boyd (Messala), Haya Harareet (Esther), Hugh Griffith (Sheik Ilderim), Martha Scott (Miriam), Sam Jaffe (Simonides), Cathy O'Donnell (Tirzah), Finlay Currie (Balthasar), Frank Thring, Terence Longden, Andree Morell, Marina Berti.

The Wallace story was first filmed by Kalem Pictures in 1907. The 1926 version was the silent screen's biggest spectacular, running 170 minutes, with magnificent sets and even a color sequence. The sea battle and the chariot race are the most memorable images of the epic. The remake was just as spectacular, running 217 minutes, winning the best picture Academy Award as well as oscars for director Wyler, photographer Robert Surtees, composer Miklos Rosza, and for acting, Charlton Heston and Hugh Griffith. It is reported that before settling on Heston, the producers had sought Rock Hudson, Marlon Brando and Burt Lancaster for the lead. It is an exciting film, but not a great one. It lumbers on and every now and then throws in some much-needed action. Griffith acted, Heston reacted, but one shouldn't really expect great histrionics in an epic.

Bengal Tiger *see* **Tiger Shark**

77 Benji

Based on a screenplay by Joe Camp. Story: It's a simple tale (sorry about that) of a mongrel dog who saves two children from kidnappers and as a reward is adopted by the children's family. Not much happens, the camera just follows the dog, who is a surprisingly good actor.

Mulberry Square, 1974 (original). Director and screenwriter: Joe Camp. Cast: Higgins (Benji), Patsy Garrett (Mary), Allen Fiuzat (Paul), Cynthia Smith (Cindy), Peter Breck (Dr. Chapman), Frances Bavier, Terry Carter, Edgar Buchanan, Tom Lester, Christopher Connelly, Deborah Walley.

• ***For the Love of Benji*** (sequel). Mulberry Square, 1977. Director and screenwriter: Joe Camp. Cast: Higgins (Benji), Patsy Garrett (Mary), Cynthia Smith (Cindy), Allen Fiuzat (Paul), Ed Nelson (Chandler), Art Vasil, Peter Bowles, Bridget Armstrong, Mihalis Lambrinos.

In the sequel, Benji gets lost in the Greek Islands and tangles with international criminals. If you like cute little dogs, these films will be pleasant—otherwise you may become sick to your stomach. Keep alert, the little fellow was back on the screen in 1987. Isn't that a rather long life span for the breed?

78 Berkeley Square

Based on the play by John L. Balderston, adapted from Henry James' *The*

Sense of the Past. Story: When American Peter Standish, fascinated by the eighteenth century, inherits his British ancestral home in Berkeley Square, he enters his own past and falls in love with Helen Pettigrew, a girl of two hundred years ago. When Helen dies, Peter reverts to his twentieth-century self and rejects marriage to his fiancée, Marjorie Frant, in order to spend his life with the memory of his long-gone true love.

Fox, 1933 (original). Director: Frank Lloyd; screenwriters: Sonya Levien and John L. Balderston. Cast: Leslie Howard (Peter Standish), Heather Angel (Helen Pettigrew), Valerie Taylor (Kate Pettigrew), Irene Browne (Lady Anne Pettigrew), Betty Lawford (Marjorie Frant), Colin Keith-Johnston, Ferdinand Gottschalk, Beryl Mercer, Samuel S. Hinds, Alan Mowbray.

• ***I'll Never Forget You (The House in the Square)*** (remake). Twentieth Century–Fox, 1951. Director: Roy Baker; screenwriter: Ranald MacDougall. Cast: Tyrone Power (Peter Standish), Ann Blyth (Helen Pettigrew/Martha Forsyth), Michael Rennie (Roger Forsyth), Beatrice Campbell (Kate Pettigrew), Irene Browne (Lady Anne Pettigrew), Dennis Price, Raymond Huntley, Kathleen Bryon.

Leslie Howard, who had played the role of Peter Standish both in London and New York, gave a magnificent and believable performance as the time traveler who could never forget the girl he met when he had taken the place of his ancestor. The *New York Times* chose *Berkeley Square* as one of the ten best pictures of 1933, praising its "poetic charm, gentle humor and appealing pathos."

The remake with Tyrone Power suffered almost completely negative reviews with the handsome leading man's performance described as "monotonous." Critics were also not happy with the decision to film the eighteenth-century sequences in Technicolor and the modern ones in black and white.

In 1980, Christopher Reeve appeared as a playwright who finds a way to go back in time to find the girl, played by Jane Seymour, whom he loved in a previous incarnation. Entitled *Somewhere in Time,* the film was based on Richard Matheson's novel *Bid Time Return,* which was clearly a variation on *Berkeley Square.*

79 The Best People

Based on a play by David Grey and Avery Hopwood. Story: In this romantic comedy, wealthy Mrs. Lenox plans for her children to marry within their class, but daughter Marion is in love with the chauffeur, Henry Morgan, while son Bertie has this thing for show girl Alice O'Neil. Marion's sometime fiancé, Arthur Rockmere, arranges for Marion's father and her puritanical uncle Throckmorton to meet with Alice and her show-girl friend Millie in a hope of buying off Alice. Bertie gets wind of this and arrives at the meeting where things get out of hand and all land up in jail. Finally the father realizes that his children need the common sense of those they have fallen in love with and so Bertie is allowed to marry Alice and Marion to marry Henry. Throckmorton, not to be outdone, marries Millie.

Paramount/Famous Players-Lasky, 1925 (original). Silent. Director: Sidney

Olcott; screenwriter: Bernard McConville. Cast: Warner Baxter (Henry Morgan), Esther Ralston (Alice O'Neil), Kathlyn Lenox (Mrs. Lenox), Edward Davis (Bronson Lenox), Margaret Morris (Marion Lenox), Joseph Striker (Bertie Lenox), Larry Steers (Uncle Throckmorton), William Austin (Arthur Rockmere), Margaret Livingston (Millie Montgomery).

• ***Fast and Loose*** (remake). Paramount, 1930. Director: Fred Newymeyer; screenwriters: Doris Anderson and Preston Sturges. Cast: Miriam Hopkins (Marion Lenox), Carole Lombard (Alice O'Neil), Frank Morgan (Bronson Lenox), Charles Starrett (Henry Morgan), Henry Wadsworth (Bertie Lenox), Winifred Harris (Carrie Lenox), Herbert Yost (George Grafton), David Hutcheson (Lord Rockingham), Ilka Chase (Millie Montgomery).

The films are pleasant, light entertainment of how unruly children of wealth may still have better sense in choosing their life partners than their parents. In the remake, Miriam Hopkins was making her screen debut and critics withheld judgement, believing they would have to see her in additional films before they could tell if she would be a successful screen personality. Carole Lombard was appreciated for her performance as the show girl as was Frank Morgan as the father and Ilka Chase as Alice's friend, Millie.

Between Two Worlds ***see*** **Outward Bound**

80 Beverly Hills Cop

Based on a screenplay by Daniel Petrie, Jr. Story: Axel Foley is a street-wise black Detroit police detective, specializing in entrapment and tactics of questionable legality, who takes a leave of absence to track down those responsible for the death of a close friend. His quest takes him to the plush and unfamiliar territory of Beverly Hills, California, and a cocaine smuggling caper.

Paramount Pictures, 1984 (original). Director: Martin Brest; screenwriter: Daniel Petrie, Jr. Cast: Eddie Murphy (Axel Foley), Judge Reinhold (Det. Billy Rosewood), John Ashton (Sgt. Taggart), Lisa Eilbacher, Ronny Cox, Steven Berkoff, James Russo.

• ***Beverly Hills Cop II*** (sequel). Paramount Pictures, 1987. Director: Tom Scott; screenwriters: Eddie Murphy and Robert D. Works. Cast: Eddie Murphy (Axel Foley), Judge Reinhold (Billy Rosewood), Jurgen Prochnow (Maxwell Dent), John Ashton (Taggart), Ronny Cox, Allen Garfield, Brigitte Nielsen, Dean Stockwell.

Eddie Murphy demonstrated his unique comical style and fine sense of timing in *48 Hours* and *Trading Places*, but despite the fabulous box-office success of his 1984 picture, which was repeated with the sequel, Murphy in these pictures is just as much a stereotype as Stepin Fetchit ever was. The latter was a frightened, slow, dumb and shiftless "nigger." In *Beverly Hills Cop* I and II, Murphy is just a foul-mouthed, sexist con man whose sense of what is right or wrong depends on whether you're his friend or his enemy. Audiences laugh hysterically at Murphy's genitalia and scatological humor much as they must have when they were adolescents, the proper age group to appreciate his unoriginal material. It's a shame, because he has given promise of being a great comical find. It appears success too soon has made him satisfied with getting the cheap laughs at the expense of others in his movies, all of whom are merely pawns for him to use.

In the sequel, Murphy's friend Ronny Cox is shot by beautiful, tall blonde Brigitte Nielsen as part of something called the alphabet crimes. Murphy comes running back to Beverly Hills as fast as he can con his chief, takes possession of a mansion in which to live, and picks up his Abbott and Costello sidekicks (Judge Reinhold and John Ashton) to bask in his sunlight as he shows how clever he is by outsmarting all of the dumb honkies. He has a lot of fun commenting on Sylvester Stallone's ex-wife Brigitte Nielsen, a six-foot beauty who kills on the command of master criminal Jurgen Prochnow, and serves as a target for Murphy's sexual barbs. Both films feature modern Keystone Kops set loose to destroy the city with cement trucks and blow away the baddies with an arsenal which would please the Contras. Murphy is Dirty Harry with a dirty mouth—and he's becoming something of a bore as he goes through the same routine in each of his movies.

Beverly Hills Cop II *see* **Beverly Hills Cop**

Beyond the Poseidon Adventure *see* **The Poseidon Adventure**

81 Big Brother

Based on a book by Rex Beach. Story: Gangster Jimmy Donovan is made guardian of Midge, the-seven-year-old-brother of Jimmy's friend Big Ben Murray. Jimmy decides to go straight so he can give the child a decent life but the authorities have other ideas. It isn't until Donovan proves his sincerity by recovering a payroll stolen by some of his former cronies that he is allowed to keep the boy and win his girl, Kitty.

Paramount/Famous Players-Lasky, 1923 (original). Silent. Director: Allan Swan; screenwriter: Paul Sloane. Cast: Tom Moore (Jimmy Donovan), Edith Roberts (Kitty Costello), Raymond Hatton (Cokey Joe Miller), Joe King (Big Ben Murray), Mickey Bennett (Midge Murray), Charles Henderson, Paul Panzer, Neill Kelley.

• ***Young Donovan's Kid*** (remake). RKO, 1931. Director: Fred Niblo; screenwriter: J. Walter Ruben. Cast: Richard Dix (Jim Donovan), Jackie Cooper (Midge Murray), Marion Shelling (Kitty Costello), Frank Sheridan (Father Dan), Boris Karloff (Cokey Joe), Dick Rush, Fred Kelsey, Wilfred Lucas.

The original production was a sweet, sentimental film with enjoyable performances from all concerned. But in the remake, it was all Jackie Cooper's picture. Cooper is so winning in his performance that everyone in the audience wants to protect this ragged, dirty and crisp-tongued youngster. Richard Dix even goes so far as getting shot so he can keep the kid.

82 The Big Guy

Based on the story "No Power on Earth" by Wallace Sullivan and Richard K.

Polimer. Story: Prison captain Bill Whitlock is taken hostage during a breakout. He steals $250,000 of the escaped prisoner's loot. Young con Jimmy Hutchins, who had innocently become enmeshed in the break and a subsequent murder, is convicted as an accomplice, and sentenced to die. Whitlock is made warden of the prison and must struggle with his conscience as his knowledge of the affair could save the boy's life. He finally makes a confession—but at the hour the youth and a trusty make a break for freedom. The warden dies in a pitched battle with the crazed trusty and the boy's life is saved.

Univeral Pictures, 1939 (original). Director: Arthur Lubin; screenwriter: Lester Cole. Cast: Victor McLaglen (Warden Bill Whitlock), Jackie Cooper (Jimmy Hutchins), Ona Munson (Mary Whitlock), Peggy Moran (Joan Lawson), Edward Brophy (Dippy), Jonathan Hale, Russell Hicks, Wallis Clark, Alan Davis.

• ***Behind the High Wall*** (remake). Universal Pictures, 1956. Director: Abner Biberman; screenwriter: Harold Jack Bloom. Cast: Tom Tully (Wardern Frank Carmichael), Sylvia Sidney (Anne McGregor), John Gavin (Johnny Hutchins), John Larch (William Kiley), Barney Phillips, Ed Kemmer, Don Beddoe.

McLaglen gives a vigorous performance as the man who is forced to choose between keeping stolen loot which will take care of him and his sick wife for the rest of their days or save an innocent man's life. Cooper is no longer the appealing kid but his performance has the same earnest quality that so endeared him to audiences when he was younger. The remake of the glum melodrama is a cheaply made but capably presented "B" picture meant to be a second feature.

83 Big Hearted Herbert

Based on a story by Sophie Kerr and the play by Sophie Kerr and Ann Richardson. Story: One-time plumber Herbert Kainess has seen his business grow until he is the prosperous owner of a bathroom facilities factory. Rather than being thankful for his good fortune and eager to shower his family with the luxuries his money can buy, he has become miserly and of ill disposition whenever money must be spent. When his daughter gives a party to announce her engagement, his grumbling about expenses, crude manners and domineering attitude ruin the affair. That's the last straw and his family plot to teach him a lesson. A few days later he brings home to dinner his best out-of-town customer and the man's wife. The family dresses poorly and serves the simplest fare, with the family's servants pulled-up to the table. They explain they are just simple folk, not wanting much and not into spending money for unnecessary things. When the man and his wife leave, Herbert is furious, but before he can blow his top, his family explains some important facts of life to him and he vows to completely reform.

Warner Bros., 1934 (original). Director: William Keighley; screenwriters: Lillie Harward and Ben Mackson. Cast: Aline MacMahon (Elizabeth Kainess), Guy Kibbee (Herbert Kainess), Patricia Ellis (Alice Kainess), Helen Lowell (Martha), Phillip Reed (Andrew Goodrich), Robert Barrat, Henry O'Neill.

• ***Father Is a Prince*** (remake). Warner Bros./First National, 1940. Director: Noel Smith; screenwriter: Robert E. Kenit. Cast: Grant Mitchell, Nana Bryant, John Litel, George Reeves, Jan Clayton, Lee Patrick, Billy Dawson.

Some of Kibbee's blustering is funny and Aline MacMahon is her usual loyal and wise self, but the film's comedy is not sustained and there are large gaps where it seems everyone, including the performers, is waiting for something to happen. The remake isn't any better, although Mitchell and Bryant struggle valiantly with weak comedy material. In this case the father's selfishness almost results in his wife's breakdown and death, which are not exactly yuk-producing topics. Of course all ends well in this simple story.

84 The Big Sleep

Based on a book by Raymond Chandler. Story: Tough private-eye Philip Marlowe is hired by wealthy General Sternwood to deal with a blackmailer who has compromising pictures of the General's youngest daughter, Carmen. He soon discovers that her older sister, Vivien, is also somehow at risk. The blackmailer, one Geiger, is murdered and Marlowe finds Carmen in the dead man's house, completely smashed. He takes her home and engages Vivien in a conversation which raises more questions than answers. She appears anxious to have him off the case. Ignoring her suggestion, Marlowe finds that a second man has made blackmail threats against Carmen. This leads Marlowe, Vivien and a drunken Carmen to a confrontation with a couple of Geiger's employees, Joe Brady and Agnes, who are now in possession of the blackmailer's files. Marlow threatens Brady with implication in the murder of Geiger if he doesn't talk but before he can tell what he knows, he's also killed. Next stop is a gambling casino run by Eddie Mars, where Vivien is losing heavily without any apparent concern. Marlowe eventually gets a confession from Mars about his involvement in the various plots and pushes him out the door where he is gunned down by his own men; Marlowe and Vivien, meanwhile, wait patiently for the police to arrive.

Warner Bros., 1946 (original). Director: Howard Hawks; screenwriters: William Faulkner, Leigh Brackett and Jules Furthman. Cast: Humphrey Bogart (Philip Marlowe), Lauren Bacall (Vivien Sternwood), John Ridgeley (Eddie Mars), Martha Vickers (Carmen Sternwood), Dorothy Malone (bookstore proprietress), Patricia Clarke (Mona Mars), Regis Toomey (Bernie Ohls), Charles Waldron (General Sternwood), Charles D. Brown, Louis Jean Heydt, Elisha Cook, Jr.

• ***The Big Sleep*** (remake). United Artists, 1978. Director and screenwriter: Michael Winner. Cast: Robert Mitchum (Philip Marlowe), James Stewart (General Sternwood), Sarah Miles (Vivien), Candy Clark (Carmen), Oliver Reed (Eddie Mars), Diana Queek (Mona Mars), Richard Boone, John Mills, Richard Todd, Edward Fox, John Justin, Harry Andrews.

The plot of the 1946 film was so convoluted that mystery writer Raymond Chandler, on seeing it, confessed he couldn't figure out who the murderer was in the film based on his book. This defect, which might have proven fatal for any other film, hardly mattered in this case. The appeal of the complex mystery

Humphrey Bogart gives Lauren Bacall a light in The Big Sleep *(Warner Bros., 1946).*

wasn't whodunnit but the incredibly entertaining and sharp dialogue, particularly that given to Bogart as Marlowe. Interchanges and characterizations rather than events were stressed and if all the questions weren't answered by the end, few in the audience or among the critics seemed to mind. One of the most enjoyable sequences is when Marlowe, on stake-out, finds he has time for a bit of dalliance with the attractive bookstore proprieteress, played perfectly by Dorothy Malone. It's a classic in the *film noir* genre and is still very popular today, a major piece in the cult fabric which has been woven around Bogart since his death.

In the remake, the action is moved from 1940 California to 1977 London with basically the same story. This production isn't strong enough to withstand the intrinsic weaknesses of the story and the performers, although an impressive cast, don't seem to understand what is expected of them and apparently director Winner was unsuccessful in instructing them. Robert Mitchum, who had scored big in an earlier remake of a classic Marlowe film *(Farewell My Lovely)*, seems to be merely going through the motions this time. Sarah Miles and Candy Clark as the spoiled daughters are unappealing and Jimmy Stewart's role isn't big enough to have much impact on the production. The first version was a flukey hit, the remake, mostly, hit and miss.

Charlotte Sternwood (Sarah Miles) listens apprehensively as Philip Marlowe (Robert Mitchum) relates the history of the gun she holds in The Big Sleep *(United Artists, 1978).*

85 A Bill of Divorcement

Based on a play by Clemence Dane. Story: Hillary Fairfield returns to his home after having spent many years in a mental institution to discover his wife has divorced him and is planning to remarry. He meets for the first time his grown-up, strong-willed daughter who is also engaged to be married. When the daughter, Sydney, discovers that her father's illness is due to heredity and not shell-shock as she had been led to believe, she calmly and frankly explains to her fiancé that she cannot marry him and risk bringing children into the world, with the possibility that they and their mother might develop mental disorders. She instead plans to stay with her father and take care of him.

• ***A Bill of Divorcement*** (remake). RKO, 1932. Director: George Cukor; screenwriters: Howard Estabrook and Harry Wagstaff Gribble. Cast: John Barrymore (Hillary Fairfield), Billie Burke (Margaret Fairfield), Katharine Hepburn (Sydney Fairfield), David Manners (Kit Humphrey), Henry Stephenson (Dr. Alliot), Paul Cavanaugh, Elizabeth Patterson, Gayle Evers, Julie Haydon.

• ***A Bill of Divorcement*** (remake). RKO, 1940. Director: John Farrow; screenwriter: Dalton Trumbo. Cast: Maureen O'Hara (Sydney Fairfield), Adolphe Menjou (Hillary Fairfield), Fay Bainter (Margaret Fairfield), Herbert Marshall (Gray Meredith), Dame May Whitty, Patric Knowles, C. Aubrey Smith, Ernest Cossart.

There was a silent production of the Clemence Dane play in 1922 with

Constance Binney as Sydney, Malcolm Keel as Hillary and Fay Compton as Margaret Fairfield. The 1932 feature was the movie debut for Katharine Hepburn and Billie Burke's first sound film. It was immediately apparent that Miss Hepburn was something special. She had an angular beauty and obvious intelligence. Her New England accent was distinctive, although found to be harsh and grating by some critics. It didn't matter if critics and audiences approved or disapproved of her and her mannerisms, she was all they could talk about and the picture was clearly hers. Barrymore, here cast in a role that was more of the type his brother, Lionel, might play, was more reserved than in his usual flamboyant performances. It is among his finest screen characterizations. Billie Burke made her character flighty and distracted, a device which would prove familiar to audiences throughout her career. A Czech version of this film was released in 1933.

The 1940 remake was predicted to do for Maureen O'Hara, in her first major starring role, what the earlier version had done for Hepburn. Not quite, as it turned out, although O'Hara's performance was quite good as were those of Adolphe Menjou and Fay Bainter in the roles of the sacrificing girl's parents. O'Hara took full advantage of her meaty role to demonstrate that she was more than just a spectacular beauty as seen as the poor dancing girl, Esmerelda, in *The Hunchback of Notre Dame.*

Billion Dollar Brain *see* **The Ipcress File**

86 Billy Jack

Based on an original screenplay by T.C. Frank (Tom Laughlin) and Teresa Christina (Delores Taylor). Story: Billy Jack is a half-breed Vietnam veteran who roams the Arizona desert protecting the "freedom school" run by his erstwhile girl friend Jean Roberts, and populated by runaway youths whose liberal views apply only to what they believe in. They and Billy Jack have no tolerance for dissenting views, and anyone who thinks otherwise better run when he kicks off his footwear and gives a demonstration of his Bruce Lee imitation. On the other hand the local townspeople are as bigoted, racist and reactionary as could ever be created as "strawmen" with whom Billy Jack must deal.

Warner Bros., 1971 (original). Director: T.C. Frank (Tom Laughlin); screenwriters: Frank and Teresa Christina. Cast: Tom Laughlin (Billy Jack), Delores Taylor (Jean Roberts), Clark Howat (Sheriff Cole), Bert Freed (Stuart Posner), Julie Webb, Ken Tobey, Victor Izay, Debbie Schrock, Stan Rice, Teresa Kelly.

• ***The Trial of Billy Jack*** (sequel). Taylor/Laughlin, 1974. Director: Tom Laughlin; screenwriters: Laughlin and Delores Taylor. Cast: Tom Laughlin (Billy Jack), Delores Taylor (Jean Roberts), Victor Izay (Doc), Teresa Laughlin (Carol), Russell Lane (Russell), Michelle Wilson (Michelle), William Wellman, Jr., Geo Anne Sosa, Lynn Baker, Riley Hill.

As bad as the first mish-mash was, it far surpasses the sequel, in which Laughlin continues playing the half-breed as a latter-day Christ short on tolerance, understanding and forgiveness, brought to trial on trumped-up charges. He also endures the trials of his ancient ancestors with their unusual rituals of pain. Laughlin got one last chance to play the role in *Billy Jack Goes to Washington,* a very poor knockdown of Frank Capra's *Mr. Smith Goes to Washington.*

Billy Jack Goes to Washington *see* **Mr. Smith Goes to Washington**

87 Bird of Paradise

Based on a play by Richard Walton Tully. Story: Johnny Baker is the skipper of a yacht carrying a group of American passengers that sails into port at a South Seas atoll. Here he meets Luana and immediately falls in love with her. The customs of the natives and the Americans are in sharp contrast, particularly in terms of romance and courtship. The tribal dance of wild abandonment followed by wholesale love-making would affect any red-blooded man. Johnny and Luana enter into a sort of premarital trial relationship to determine if they are suited for each other and are blissfully happy until the island's volcano becomes active. Luana, believed by the natives to be the bride of the volcano, must sacrifice herself by jumping into its mouth to appease its deity. She performs her duty to save her people.

RKO, 1932 (original). Director: King Vidor; screenwriters: Wells Root, Leonard Praskins and Wanda Tuchok. Cast: Dolores Del Rio (Luana), Joel McCrea (Johnny Baker), John Halliday (Mac), Richard "Skeets" Gallagher (Chester), Lon Chaney, Jr. (Thornton), Bert Roach, Napoleon Pukui, Sofia Ortega.

• ***Bird of Paradise*** (remake). Twentieth Century–Fox, 1951. Director and screenwriter: Delmer Daves. Cast: Louis Jourdan (Andre Laurence), Debra Paget (Kalua), Jeff Chandler (Tenga), Everett Sloane (The Beachcomber), Maurice Schwartz (The Kahuna), Jack Elam, Prince Lei Lani, Otto Waldis, Mary Ann Ventura.

Dolores Del Rio was not a particularly good actress and she had a difficult accent, but she was a spectacular exotic beauty who looked very much at home in this romantic piece where she had little to say, at least with her voice. She is a delightful eyeful in the sequence in which she and McCrea make love underwater. McCrea's trim figure was certainly enough to please the ladies of the audiences. Among film firsts, this picture had the first comprehensive start-to-finish musical sound score.

In the remake, a new character, Tenga (played exceptionally well by Jeff Chandler), was introduced. He, of the royal family of the isle, returns home after an attempt at stateside living with his friend Andre, whom he introduces to his lovely sister Kalua, and nature does the rest. The young lovers' romance is marred by the dislike of the local medicine man and Kalua's inability to have a child. She solves this problem by bringing a number-two wife home for Andre. When her sacrifice to the volcano is called for, she calmly says goodbye to her lover and goes bravely to her death. Debra Paget as Kalua looks very good in her form-fitting garb and Louis Jourdan makes a handsome foreigner left behind to be consoled by a wise and patient Jeff Chandler.

The Birds and the Bees *see* **The Lady Eve**

88 The Biscuit Eater

Based on a story by James Street. Story: Two boys, one white, one black, devote themselves to training an unwanted pup to become a champion bird dog. Interesting sequences in the picture include the dog's rescue from a weird swamp hermit and its competition in show-dog field trials. She dies, but leaves a litter of pups to soften the sadness.

• ***The Biscuit Eater (God Gave Him a Dog)*** (original). Paramount, 1940. Director: Stuart Heisler; screenwriters: Lillie Hayward and Stuart Anthony. Cast: Billy Lee, Snowflake, Cordell Hickman, Helene Millard, Lester Matthews, Richard Lane, William Russell, Earl Johnson.

• ***The Biscuit Eater*** (remake). Disney Studios, 1972. Director: Vincent McEverty; screenwriter: Lawrence Edward Watkin. Cast: Johnny Whittaker, Earl Holliman, Lew Ayres, Godfrey Cambridge, Patricia Crowley, Beah Richards.

The 1940 feature was a surprising hit, due mainly to the natural performance of Billy Lee and the picturesque setting in rural sections of Georgia. The Disney remake didn't seem to move anyone despite a very decent cast, each of whom tried very hard. Whittaker seemed to be trying too hard but all audiences saw was acting, not feeling.

89 Black Beauty

Based on a book by Anna Sewell. Story: The story of Black Beauty traces his life from a colt to a thoroughbred and deals with the various people, kind and cruel, who have owned him, including an aristocrat, a London cabby and a kid farmer.

• ***Black Beauty*** (remake). Vitagraph, 1921. Silent. Director: David Smith; screenwriter: William B. Courtney. Cast: Jean Paige (Jesse Gordon), James Morrison (Harry Blomefield), George Webb (Jack Beckett), Bobby Mack (Derby Ghost), John Steppley (Squire Gordon), Colin Kenny, Leslie T. Peacock, Adele Farrington.

• ***Black Beauty*** (remake). Monogram, 1933. Director: Phil Rosen; screenwriter: Charles Logue. Cast: Esther Ralston (Leila Lambert), Alexander Kirkland (Henry Cameron), Hale Hamilton (Bledoe), Gavin Gordon (Captain Jordan), Don Alvarado, George Walsh.

• ***Black Beauty*** (remake). Twentieth Century–Fox, 1946. Director: Max Nossek; screenwriters: Lillie Howard and Agnes Christine Johnston. Cast: Mona Freeman (Anne Wendon), Richard Denning (Bill Dixon), Evelyn Ankers (Evelyn Carrington), Charles Evans (Squire Wendon), J.M. Kerrigan, Moyna Macgill, Terry Kilburn.

• ***Black Beauty*** (remake). Twentieth Century–Fox, 1957. Director: Harold Schuster; screenwriter: Steve Fisher. Cast: Johnny Crawford, Mimi Gibson, John Bryant, Diane Brewster, J. Pat O'Malley, Russell Johnson, Ziva Rudann.

• ***Black Beauty*** (remake). Paramount, 1971. Director: James Hill; screenwriter: Wolf Mankowitz. Cast: Mark Lester (Joe Evans), Walter Slezak

(Hackenschmidt), Peter Lee Lawrence (Gervaise), Ursula Glas (Marie), Patrick Mower, John Netleton.

The sentimental story of the trials and tribulations of the beautiful horse has also been filmed in Britain in 1906 and 1910 and in the United States as *Your Obedient Servant* by Edison Studios in 1917. In the 1921 silent, Beauty's winning of the big race results in the solution of a robbery and a happy ending for the young couple that own the animal. In the 1933 version, Beauty is badly treated by a series of cruel owners and is rescued just in time for a happy ending as he is being shipped to work in a bullring. In the 1946 production, Mona Freeman is forced to save the horse from a spectacular stable fire. In the 1957 feature, it's Black Beauty that brings together a bitter boy and his widowed father. In the 1971 movie, Beauty is forced to kill an evil young squire who hates horses. All in all, through this series of films, Black Beauty has had a full life.

The Black Bird *see* **The Maltese Falcon**

90 Black Caesar

Based on an original screenplay by Larry Cohen. Story: Like Edward G. Robinson in *Little Caesar,* black gangster Tommy claws his way to the top of the rackets in New York's Harlem. Unlike Robinson he doesn't get his just deserts at the end of the picture.

American International, 1973 (original). Director and screenwriter: Larry Cohen. Cast: Fred Williamson (Tommy), D'Urville Martin (Rev. Rufus), Julius Harris (Gibbs), Don Pedro Colley (Crawdaddy), Gloria Hendry (Helen), Art Lund (McKinney), Val Avery, Minnie Gentry, Philip Roye, William Wellman, Jr.

• ***Hell Up in Harlem*** (sequel). American International, 1973. Director and screenwriter: Larry Cohen. Cast: Fred Williamson (Tommy), Julius W. Harris (Papa Gibbs), Gloria Hendry (Helen), Margaret Avery (Sister Jennifer), D'Urville Martin (Rev. Rufus), Tony King, Gerald Gordon.

Unfortunately, this film and its sequel, in which Williamson is now trying to clean up Harlem by killing anyone who gets in his way, is fairly typical of the black exploitation films of the time. The men were ruthless mobsters and the women often as not merely whores. Fred Williamson, in playing the lead, showed all the finesse that he had developed when hammering opposing running backs while playing professional football.

91 The Black Pirate

Based on a story by Elton Thomas. Story: The only survivors of a Spanish vessel captured on the high seas are Michel and his father. These two are marooned on an island. When the father dies, Michel swears vengeance. He joins a pirate band and proves his worth by single-handedly capturing a merchant ship. Henceforth, he is called the Black Pirate. Michel falls in love with a girl on the captured ship (the Princess). He is captured by the same crew of bloody-thirsty pirates that he and his father had encountered and is forced to

Is it the beauty of the lost colt in the 1946 20th Century–Fox production of Black Beauty *which causes the looks of astonishment on the faces of Richard Denning and Mona Freeman?*

walk the plank. He swims to shore, gathers some men and leads them swimming underwater back to the ship, winning the day and rescuing his love. At this point he reveals to the girl that he is a Spanish duke, proposes marriage and she accepts.

United Artists, 1926 (original). Silent. Director: Albert Parker; screenwriters: Lotta Woods, Jack Cunningham and Elton Thomas. Cast: Douglas Fairbanks (The Black Pirate/Michel), Billie Dove (The Princess), Anders Raudoff (Pirate Leader), Donald Crisp (McTavish), Tempe Pigott, Sam De Grasse, Charly Stevens, Charles Belcher, Fred Becker.

• ***The Crimson Pirate*** (remake). Warner Bros., 1952. Director: Robert Siodmak; screenwriter: Roland Kibbee. Cast: Burt Lancaster (Vallo), Nick Cravat (Ojo), Eva Bartok (Consuelo), Torin Thatcher (Humble Bellows), James Hayter, Leslie Bradley, Margot Grahame, Noel Purcell, Frederick Leister.

Fairbanks père was at his swashbuckling best in this exciting pirate movie. His infectious grin and steely determination marked him as the heroic person he impersonated. The battle scenes were stunning and their techniques borrowed by many other producers of action-adventure films. The remake was an out-and-out comedy spoof of the genre, with Lancaster so informing the audiences of the intentions during the opening credits. Burt is Vallo, an

Walter Slezak and Ursula Glas as his daughter admire the luckless horse Black Beauty in the 1971 Tigon British/Chilton production of the film of that name.

acrobatic fellow, known as the Crimson Pirate, who at least initially hopes to play both sides against the middle in a profitable way in the struggle of island rebels and the navy of the King of Spain. Finally deciding to assist the underdog in the dispute, Vallo and his men fight the Spaniards with primitive machine guns, tanks, submarines, high explosives and a balloon. It's all good fun with Lancaster and his friend from his circus days, Nick Cravat, tumbling and flying through the air with great good humor.

The Black Rose *see* **Arabian Nights**

92 The Black Stallion

Based on an original screenplay by Melissa Mathison, Jeanne Rosenberg and

William D. Wittliff. Story: Some 40 years ago, a boy and his father are traveling aboard a ship in the Mediterranean whose other passengers drink, gamble and speak in tongues foreign and frightening to a young boy. Their prize possession is a magnificent black stallion. After a ferocious storm, the ship catches fire and sinks. The stallion saves the boy, pulling him to a deserted island. Here a great friendship develops. When they are rescued, the boy is reunited with his mother and meets an old horse trainer who believes he can make the stallion a champion racer. Reminiscent of *National Velvet,* the horse wins a big race with the boy as the jockey.

United Artists/Orion Zoetrope, 1979 (original). Director: Carroll Ballard; screenwriters: Melissa Mathison, Jeanne Rosenberg and William D. Wittliff. Cast: Kelly Reno (Alec Ramsey), Mickey Rooney (Henry Dailey), Teri Garr (Alec's mother), Clarence Muse (Snoe), Hoyt Axton (Alec's father), Michael Higgins (Neville), Cass-ole (the Black Stallion).

• ***The Black Stallion Returns*** (sequel). Coppola/Zoetrope/MGM-UA, 1983. Director: Robert Dalva; screenwriters: Richard Kletter and Jerome Kass. Cast: Kelly Reno, Allen Goorwitz, Ferdy Mayne, Woody Strode, Vincent Spano.

Seeing the *Black Stallion* is like seeing two pictures. The first half is a breathtakingly beautiful gem, described as a joy to behold. Once the horse and boy are rescued it becomes the familiar story of the trials and tribulations of getting a horse ready to win an important race. Nevertheless, it's special, something many people probably overlooked, believing it would be just another hokey, boy meets horse, boy loses horse, boy gets horse feature. That description better fits the sequel in which Alec Ramsey, once again played by Kelly Reno, is now a teenager who loses the black stallion in Morocco and has a heck of a time getting him back. Where the original is a delight, the sequel is disappointingly predictable.

The Black Stallion Returns *see* **The Black Stallion**

93 Black Tulip

Based on the novel by Alexandre Dumas. Story: In Holland in 1672, a Royalist and a tulip merchant unsuccessfully attempt to discover the secret of black tulips by jailing a young tulip cultivator.

Granger-Binger, Great Britain, 1921 (original). Silent. Director: Frankland A. Richardson; screenwriter: Marjorie Bowen. Cast: Zoe Palmer (Rosa), Gerald McCarthy (Cornelius van Baerle), Frank Dane (Prince William), Harry Walter (Issac Boxtel), Edward Verkade (Cornelius de Witt), Dio Huysmans (John de Witt), Coen Hissink (Gryphus).

• ***Black Tulip*** (remake). Fox British, Great Britain, 1937. Director: Alex Bryce; screenwriter: uncredited. Cast: Patrick Waddington (Cornelius), Ann Soreen (Rosa), Campbell Gullan (Boxtel), Jay Laurier (Gryphus), Wilson Coleman (Cornelius de Witt), Bernard Lee (William of Orange), Florence Hunt (Julia Boxtel), Ronald Shiner, Aubrey Mallalieu.

The films didn't really have much to do with the Dumas novel, nor were they of much excitement or interest. While the authors of this book greatly admire the tulips that grace their yard each spring, trying to imagine intrigue over their secret, even the rare black tulip, is difficult.

94 The Black Watch

Based on a story by Talbot Mundy. Story: Captain King of the Black Watch Regiment of the British Army is given a secret assignment in India just as his company is called to fight in France at the outbreak of war. As a result he is considered a coward by his fellow officers, particularly when he becomes involved in a drunken brawl in which he apparently kills another officer. All of this is to throw suspicion off of him as he contrives to avert a rebellion. He enlists the aid of Yasmani, who has a yen for the Captain. She is believed by her tribesmen to be a goddess who will lead them in victory against the English. When, with her assistance, King is able to put down the revolt, her followers kill her.

Fox Pictures, 1929 (original). Director: John Ford; screenwriter: John Stone. Cast: Victor McLaglen (Captain Donald Gordon King), Myrna Loy (Yasmani), Dave Rollins (Lt. Malcolm King), Roy D'Arcy (Rewa Chunga), Mitchell Lewis (Mohammed Khan), Cyril Chadwick, Claude King, Francis Ford, Walter Long, David Torrence.

• ***King of the Khyber Rifles*** (remake). Twentieth Century–Fox, 1953. Director: Henry King; screenwriters: Ivan Goff and Ben Roberts. Cast: Tyrone Power (Captain King), Terry Moore (Susan), Michael Rennie (Brigadier General Maitland), John Justin (Lt. Heath), Guy Rofle (Kurram Khan), Richard Stapley, Murray Matheson, Frank de Kova, Argentina Brunetti.

The Ford film is a good adventure yarn but not among his best works. McLaglen, who is not usually thought of as a leading man by audiences more familiar with his many fine supporting roles, was properly courageous and Myrna Loy, in another of her exotic roles, was quite lovely. In the remake, Captain King is a half-caste assigned to a native regiment, the Khyber Rifles. The English general's daughter becomes interested in King, although falling in love with a native, "just isn't done." King must rescue her from the clutches of his foster-brother, Kurram Khan, and lead his troops into battle against this tribal leader with only knives as weapons. His native troops refuse to use their new rifles because they believe the shell casements have been treated with the grease of the forbidden pig fat. Guess who wins?

95 Blind Alley

Based on the play by James Warwick. Story: Escaped killer Hal Wilson, his girl friend, Mary, and members of his gang take refuge in the secluded Long Island home of psychiatrist Dr. Anthony Shelby. The gangsters plan to use the home as a hide-out until a boat can come, on which they plan to escape from the police. During their two-day wait, Dr. Shelby discovers that Wilson suffers from recurring nightmares. The psychiatrist explores the killer's subconscious and reveals the man's jealousy of his tramp of a mother and his hatred of his cruel father. In a rage and unable to cope with his feelings, he kills Mary and then, totally confused, turns the gun on himself and commits suicide.

Columbia, 1939 (original). Director: Charles Vidor; screenwriters: Philip MacDonald, Michael Blankfort and Albert Duffy. Cast: Chester Morris (Hal Wilson), Ralph Bellamy (Dr. Anthony Shelby), Ann Dvorak (Mary), Joan Perry (Linda Curtis), Melville Cooper, Rose Stradner, John Eldridge, Ann Doran, Marc Lawrence, Stanley Brown, Scotty Beckett, Milburn Stone.

• ***The Dark Past*** (remake). Columbia, 1948. Director: Rudolph Mate; screenwriters: Philip MacDonald, Michael Blankfort and Albert Duffy. Cast: William Holden (Al Walker), Nina Foch (Betty), Lee J. Cobb (Dr. Andrew Collins), Adele Jergens (Laura Stevens), Stephen Dunne, Lois Maxwell, Barry Kroeger, Steven Geray, Wilton Graff.

The play on which the films were based was one of the first to use psychoanalysis as a weapon against crime. The 1939 version was given faint praise by most critics with Chester Morris being accused of over-acting. The 1948 remake fared somewhat better, being called tense and gripping. The performances of Lee J. Cobb as the psychiatrist and William Holden as the killer were considered excellent. The film took a fresh look at a familiar situation, which was also explored in *The Small Voice* the same year, in *The Desperate Hours* in 1955, and several other films.

Blonde Trouble *see* **June Moon**

96 Blood and Sand

Based on the novel *Sangre y Arena* by Vincente Blasco Ibanez. Story: Young matador Juan Gallardo marries his childhood sweetheart, Carmen, just as his fame in the bull ring is reaching its peak. He is happy and successful and adored by the fans, but succumbs to the charms of the passionate vamp Dona Sol. His wife leaves him but comes back to nurse him when he is gored by a bull. She pleads with him to retire and incidentally give up Dona Sol, but he refuses. His affair affects his artistry and his popularity declines. One day in the ring, he is distracted by the sight of Dona Sol in the stands with a handsome young stranger. Dona Sol's attention span for men is just not very long. He does not see the charge of the bull and is mortally wounded. He dies in the arms of his wife, but not before telling her she has been his only true love, and hearing the cheers of the throngs for a new favorite.

• ***Blood and Sand*** (remake). Paramount/Famous Players–Lasky, 1922. Silent. Director: Fred Niblo; screenwriter: June Mathis. Cast: Rudolph Valentino (Juan Gallardo), Lila Lee (Carmen), Nita Naldi (Dona Sol), George Field (El Nacional), Rosa Rosanona (Señora Augustias), Walter Long, Leo White, Charles Belcher, Jack Winn.

• ***Blood and Sand*** (remake). Twentieth Century–Fox, 1941. Director: Rouben Mamoulian; screenwriter: Jo Swerling. Cast: Tyrone Power (Juan), Linda Darnell (Carmen), Rita Hayworth (Dona Sol), Nazimova (Señora Augustias), Anthony Quinn (Manola de Palma), John Carradine (El Nacional), Lynn Bari, Laird Cregar, J. Carroll Naish.

A silent version of the work was made in Spain in 1912 under the title *Arenes Sanglantes*. In the 1922 work, Valentino superbly demonstrates his star quality even if by today's standards his performance would be seen as a bit on the hammy side. Lila Lee is effective as the sweet and patient wife and Nita Naldi is a hot and sexy piece of baggage. Screenwriter Mathis' ending was with the death of Juan, but director Niblo opted for a happy fade-out in which Juan recovers, retires and settles down happily with his wife. The public seemed pleased with the decision.

In the elaborate 1941 production, almost 30 minutes were consumed with a sort of prologue dealing with Juan and Carmen's childhood. Juan, son of a bullfighter killed in the ring, is poor and illiterate, but he seems to have inherited some special skills and Spanish charisma. He's out of his league with sophisticated Dona Sol who enjoys playing with and discarding handsome men who fall in love with her and her obvious sexual charms. Carmen's quiet loyalty and devotion to her husband can hardly be expected to compete with the excitement of Dona Sol. The three main performers are each in their own way quite good, but the acting laurels go to Nazimova, John Carradine, Laird Cregar and J. Carroll Naish, who give their relatively small roles some real life.

97 The Blue Angel

Based on the book *Professor Unrath* by Heinrich Mann. Story: Professor Immanuel Rath falls hopelessly for the tawdry charms of cabaret singer Lola, whom his students have been nightly sneaking away to see. This causes him to lose his teaching position. He and Lola are married and he is reduced to selling postcards of his wife from table to table in the various seedy clubs where she appears. The manager decides to put Rath in the show, making him a clown, whose specialty is mimicking a rooster. When the troupe is again to appear in the professor's home town, his role is given prominent billing in the hope of attracting his former students. This degradation and the fact that his cheap wife is now having an affair with another performer completely unhinges the pedagogue, who runs from the stage to strangle Lola when he sees her in an embrace with her latest lover. Rath is taken away in a straightjacket but later released. He makes his way back to his former classroom and dies at his desk.

• ***The Blue Angel*** (remake). Paramount, 1930. Director: Josef von Sternberg; screenwriter: Robert Liebmann. Cast: Emil Jannings (Prof. Immanuel Rath), Marlene Dietrich (Lola Froblich), Kurt Gerron (Kiepert), Rosa Valetti, Hans Albers.

• ***The Blue Angel*** (remake). Twentieth Century–Fox, 1959. Director: Edward Dmytryk; screenwriter: Nigel Balchan. Cast: Curt Jurgens (Professor), May Britt (Lola), Theodore Bikel (The Manager), John Banner, Fabrizzio Minoni, Ludwig Stossel.

The 1930 production was actually a remake of the UFA German film, starring Jannings and Dietrich. The difference was in emphasis. In Germany, the film was to spotlight Jannings, making his first talkie movie. In Hollywood, von Sternberg, recognizing the potential international star he had under contract, and shifted the story to make Dietrich the more important player. He even put her on a diet, reasoning that Americans wouldn't care for the rather plump girl who appeared in the German version. It is said that Jannings never forgave von

Sternberg for this. There is little doubt that von Sternberg knew what he was doing. Dietrich became the personification of sensuality as the coarse, disdainful temptress, strutting the stage and seductively saddling a chair while singing "Falling in Love Again" and "Beware of Blonde Women."

The remake was an ill-advised venture, attempting to present the story in a "realistic" style, updating the story, and even giving it a happy ending of sorts when the professor's former colleagues rescue him from his unfaithful bride and restore him to his teaching position. While Curt Jurgens was credible in his performance, May Britt's sensuality seemed like a baby-doll's in contrast to that of the incomparable Dietrich.

98 The Blue Bird

Based on a play by Maurice Materlinck. Story: Two ill-behaved children have a dream in which they seek the Blue Bird of Happiness. They travel to many magic places in their search, including the home of Mr. and Mrs. Luxury, the Palace of Joys and Delights, the World of the Dead, of Night, the Forest, the Future and the Land of Un-Born Children before discovering that if they don't find the Blue Bird of Happiness at home, they will never find it.

• ***The Blue Bird*** (remake). Paramount/Artcraft, 1918. Silent. Director and screenwriter: Maurice Tourneur. Cast: Robin MacDougall (Tyltyl), Tula Belle (Mytyl), Edwin E. Reed (Daddy Tyl), Emma Lowry (Mummy Tyl), William J. Gross, Florence Anderson, Edward Elkas, Katherine Bianchi, Lillian Cook, Gertrude McCoy.

• ***The Blue Bird*** (remake). Twentieth Century–Fox, 1940. Director: Walter Lang; screenwriter: Ernest Pascal. Cast: Shirley Temple (Mytyl), Johnny Russell (Tyltyl), Spring Byington (Mummy Tyl), Gale Sondergaard (Tylette), Eddie Collins (Tylo), Nigel Bruce, Sybil Jason, Jesse Ralph, Helen Ericson, Laura Hope Crews.

• ***The Blue Bird*** (remake). Twentieth Century–Fox/U.S.S.R., 1976. Director: George Cukor; screenwriters: Hugh Whitmore and Alfred Hayes. Cast: Elizabeth Taylor (Queen of Light/Mother/Maternal Love/Witch), Jane Fonda (Night), Todd Lookinland (Tyltyl), Patsy Kenset (Mytyl), Ava Gardner, Cicely Tyson, Robert Morley, Harry Andrews, Will Geer.

The play *The Blue Bird* has never successfully been brought to the screen and it's unlikely that it ever will. This whimsical story and morality lesson's theme was better handled in *The Wizard of Oz*. Besides the productions mentioned above, the story was brought to the screen in 1910 in Great Britain and in 1911 in Russia. The film was the first box-office flop of Shirley Temple's career, in part because of the story and in part because the curly-haired one was growing up and wasn't quite as cute. In fact she was out-cuted by her co-star, Johnny Russell. The film had imaginative sets and was visually beautiful but not enough

Opposite, top: *Wicked Lola, played by Marlene Dietrich, vamps her professor and every other male in the vicinity in the 1930 German* UFA *production* The Blue Angel. Bottom: *May Britt unsuccessfully attempts to recapture the seductiveness of wicked Marlene Dietrich as Lola in the 1959 20th Century–Fox remake of* The Blue Angel.

people seemed to care. Even having Gale Sondergaard and Eddie Collins accompany the two children on their dream adventure as the family's cat and dog didn't help. The joint U.S.–U.S.S.R. venture in 1976 was a costly flop that didn't even improve East–West relations. Both the story and the production were seen as trite and unappealing to the small number of people who actually paid to see it.

99 The Blue Lagoon

Based on the novel by H. DeVere Stacpoole. Story: Two children, Emmeline Foster and Michael Reynolds, are among the passengers on a ship sailing in the Pacific, when the ship catches fire and is lost. The children are rescued by an old sailor, Paddy Button. After drifting for days, they sight land, an uninhabited island. Confident that they will be rescued, the trio go about exploring the island, but as the days and months go by, they resign themselves to a marooned life on the island. The sailor dies and the children are left to fend for themselves. Years go by and the youngsters are now adolescents, beginning to notice each other sexually. They have a baby and attempt to escape their long-time home in a hand-made boat. They are picked-up and returned to a civilization from which they had been absent for many years. The story of their adjustment is not told, although it might have made an interesting epilogue.

• ***The Blue Lagoon*** (remake). G.F.D./J. Arthur Rank, Great Britain, 1949. Directors: Frank Launder and Sidney Gilliat; screenwriters: Frank Launder, John Baines and Michael Hogan. Cast: Jean Simmons (Emmeline Foster), Donald Houston (Michael Reynolds), Susan Stranks (Emmeline as a child), Peter Jones (Michael as a child), Noel Purcell (Paddy Button), James Hayter, Cyril Cusack, Nora Nicholson, Maurice Denham.

• ***The Blue Lagoon*** (remake). Columbia Pictures, 1980. Director: Randal Kleiser; screenwriter: Douglas Day Stewart. Cast: Brooke Shields (Emmeline), Christopher Atkins (Richard), Leo McKern (Paddy), William Daniels (Arthur), Elva Josephson (young Emmeline), Glenn Kohan (young Richard).

Stacpoole's romantic tale of the blossoming of unsupervised young love was first filmed as a silent in England in 1923. The 1949 version was a rather chaste edition of the story, suggesting more than is shown. Jean Simmons' growing allure in a tight-fitting sarong did not go unnoticed by Donald Houston, but their lovemaking was more spiritually depicted than graphic. Such was not the case of the 1980 remake, where nudity and passion were frankly displayed by Brooke Shields (or at least her double) and Christopher Atkins. Some critics objected to this, but it probably was more realistic to expect adolescents without parental interference or anyone to teach them sexual etiquette to behave naturally rather than with some learned modesty. The remake can be faulted on other grounds, however. Neither Shields nor Atkins were very skilled performers and other than watch two rather well-developed youngsters and the beautiful scenery, there's not much happening in the film.

Blue Murder at St. Trinian's *see* Belles of St. Trinian's

100 Blue Skies

Based on the story "The Matron's Report" by Frederick Hazlitt Brennan. Story: It's the tale of children in an orphanage and their antics to outsmart the matron and get themselves adopted. When a rich daddy shows up, the boy exchanges his foundling outfit with the girl's and she's adopted instead of him.

Fox Pictures, 1929 (original). Silent. Director: Alfred L. Werker; screenwriter: John Stone. Cast: Carmencita Johnson (Dorothy May), Freddie Frederick (Richard), Ethel Wales (Matron), Helen Twelvetrees (Dorothy May), Frank Albertson (Richard Lewis), Rosa Gore, William Orlamond, Evelyn Hall, Claude King.

• ***Little Miss Nobody*** (remake). Twentieth Century–Fox, 1936. Director: John Blystone; screenwriters: Lou Breslow, Paul Burger and Edward Eliscu. Cast: Jane Withers (Judy Devlin), Jane Darwell (Martha Bradley), Ralph Morgan (Gerald Dexter), Sara Haden (Teresa Lewis), Harry Carey (John Russell), Betty Jean Hainey, Thomas Jackson, Jackie Morrow, Jed Prouty.

Blue Skies takes the unusual approach of having a first sequence showing the children and their antics with the matron and a second in which Helen Twelvetrees and Frank Albertson assume the roles of the two main children while the other kids remain as they are. It's a novel idea but it didn't make for good cinema. In the remake, Hollywood's number-two child star, Jane Withers, portrays a spirited young girl whose misconduct only occurs for a good reason, such as helping someone else or bedeviling a baddie. She escapes from the orphanage and when found is put on trial, only to discover the prosecuting attorney is her real father. Jane tries hard and gives her usual good performance but it doesn't make for a picture of lasting impression.

101 Bluebeard's Eighth Wife

Based on a book by Alfred Savoir. Story: Mona de Briac, daughter of an impoverished French nobleman, is induced to marry millionaire American John Brandon. She discovers that he has been married and divorced seven times before, choosing and paying for wives as he would a new car. She is so outraged that she tries to force him to give her a divorce but he really loves her and refuses. From then on, it's only a story of how they will finally reconcile and settle down to wedded bliss.

Paramount/Famous Players–Lasky, 1923 (original). Silent. Director: Sam Wood; screenwriter: Sada Cowan. Cast: Gloria Swanson (Mona de Briac), Huntley Gordon (John Brandon), Charles Green (Robert), Lianne Salvor (Lucienne), Paul Wegel, Frank Butler, Irene Dalton.

• ***Bluebeard's Eighth Wife*** (remake). Paramount, 1938. Director: Ernst Lubitsch; screenwriters: Charles Brackett and Billy Wilder. Cast: Claudette Colbert (Nicole de Loiselle), Gary Cooper (Michael Brandon), Edward Everett Horton (De Loiselle), David Niven (Albert De Regnier), Elizabeth Patterson, Herman Bing, Warren Hymer.

It's a light and sometimes entertaining comedy but basically a one-idea film with the outcome pretty obvious once the initial gag is revealed. Even with the sure touch of Lubitsch and the talents of Charles Brackett and Billy Wilder, the remake is merely a slightly amusing picture. As for the original, Gloria Swanson had better material to work with and in this one she had to struggle to bring forth the few laughs it produced.

102 Body and Soul

Based on an original story by Abraham Polansky. Story: Young boxer Charlie Davis emerges from the amateur ranks and after a series of knockouts is ready to take on the middleweight champion. But to get his chance at the crown, he is forced to sell a 50 percent interest in himself to a gambler named Roberts who makes it a habit of owning fighters and deciding when they will win and when they will lose. Davis becomes the champ because the gambler has the fix in with the incumbent who expects to be carried by Davis and lose the fight without getting hurt. Instead he is given a brutal beating by Davis and dies of a head injury. When the gambler decides it's Davis' turn to vacate his title, Charlie agrees to the arrangement, with the understanding that a big bet will be placed for him to lose. However, when Davis discovers that the gamblers have double-crossed him, he kayoes the contender.

United Artists, 1947 (original). Director: Robert Rosen; screenwriter: Abraham Polansky. Cast: John Garfield (Charlie Davis), Lilli Palmer (Peg Born), Hazel Brooks (Alice), Anne Revere (Anna Davis), William Conrad (Quinn), Lloyd Goff (Roberts), Joseph Pevney, Canada Lee, Art Smith, James Burke.

• ***Body and Soul*** (remake). Cannon/Golan/Globus, 1981. Director: George Bowers; screenwriters: Leon Isaac Kennedy and Abraham Polansky. Cast: Jayne Kennedy, Muhammed Ali, Michael Gazzo, Perry Lang, Kim Hamilton, Peter Lawford, Danny Wells, Johnny Brown.

Garfield is convincing in this typical yarn about what a dirty and crooked racket is professional boxing. Many such films were made but the Robert Rosen picture is just about the best of the sub-genre. Beside Garfield, others in the cast who give good accounts of themselves include Canada Lee as the doomed middleweight champion whom Garfield killed, William Conrad as Garfield's manager, Anne Revere as his mother and Lloyd Goff as the gambler. Lilli Palmer seemed miscast but made an attractive appearance. Despite giving credit to screenwriter Polansky, the remake is qualitatively inferior to the original. It is the story of an amateur boxer who turns pro to earn money for an operation needed by his kid sister. To give you an idea of the level of this sentimental piece, Muhammad Ali, playing himself, distinguishes himself as the best actor in the piece.

103 Bonne Chance

Based on an original story by Sacha Guitry. Story: Claude is a Parisian artist who shares a lottery ticket with a girl he has befriended. The ticket wins and the two are a million francs richer. They decide to spend all the money in a quick vacation before she marries her fiancé. They travel as brother and sister but after a point they drop the sibling routine.

Guitry Production, 1935 (original). Director and screenwriter: Sacha Guitry.

Cast: Sacha Guitry (Claude), Jacqueline Delubac (Marie), Numes, Jr. (Prosper), Robert Darthez, Pauline Carton, Antoine.

• ***Lucky Partners*** (remake). RKO, 1940. Director: Lewis Milestone; screenwriters: Allan Scott and John van Druten. Cast: Ronald Colman (David), Ginger Rogers (Jean), Jack Carson (Freddie), Spring Byington, Cecilia Loftas, Harry Davenport.

Using the Sacha Guitry film as a foundation, the 1940 movie has Colman as a Greenwich Village painter who shares a sweepstakes ticket with Rogers, whom he has just met. They jest that if they win, they will go away together on a marvelous vacation. They win and then have to convince Rogers' none-too-bright fiancé, Carson, that it will be just an innocent jaunt. Their trip together sinks Carson as they end up in a fade-out clinch. The French version was considered a bit too racy for American audiences, as there was no mistaking that the couple did more than hold hands. In the American remake, decorum was maintained but not without many near misses.

Bonnie and Clyde *see* **The Bonnie Parker Story**

104 The Bonnie Parker Story

Based on the screenplay by Stan Shpetner. Story: Waitress Bonnie Parker is led into a life of violent crime when society sends her husband, Duke Jefferson, up the river for 175 years. She quickly becomes hardened, smokes big black cigars and handles a tommy gun expertly. Her savagery puts her on a one way trip to oblivion.

Allied Artists, 1958 (original). Director: William Witney; screenwriter: Stan Shpetner. Cast: Dorothy Provine (Bonnie Parker), Jack Hogan (Guy Darrow), Richard Bakalyan (Duke Jefferson), Joseph Turkel (Chuck Darrow), William Stevens, Ken Lynch, Douglas Kennedy, Patt Huston, Joel Colin, Jeff Morris, Jim Beck.

• ***Bonnie and Clyde*** (remake). Warner Bros.–7 Arts, 1967. Director: Arthur Penn; screenwriters: David Newman and Robert Benton. Cast: Warren Beatty (Clyde Barrow), Faye Dunaway (Bonnie Parker), Michael J. Pollard (C.W. Moss), Gene Hackman (Buck Barrow), Estelle Parsons (Blanche), Denver Pyle (Frank Hamer), Dub Taylor (Ivan Moss), Evans Evans, Gene Wilder, James Stiver.

Both films are fictional accounts of the exploits of Bonnie Parker, but the earlier version chose to give her a husband and change her companion in crime's surname to Darrow. Dorothy Provine made a sultry Bonnie, but nothing to compare to the job done by Faye Dunaway with the same part. The Warren Beatty production won Academy awards for Burnett Guffey for Best Photography and for Estelle Parsons for Best Supporting Actress. The nominations for Oscars went to the writers, director, Beatty, Dunaway, Pollard, Hackman and the picture. The exceptional film is technically brilliant, and totally new in concept and execution. The characters are fully developed. There is time for humor and tenderness as well as the shocking violence that begins when Beatty blows a man away who is on the getaway car's running board and ends when Beatty and Dunaway are riddled to pieces in a ballet of bullets and death at the end of the film. The chase scenes accompanied by Lester Flatt and Earl Scruggs' "Foggy Mountain Breakdown" work to perfection. The atmosphere of the midwest and southwest countryside and small-town life of the 30s is beautifully presented. It is simply one of the best movies made in the crime genre.

Bonzo Goes to College *see* **Bedtime for Bonzo**

Born for Trouble *see* **Jailbreak**

105 The Bosun's Mate

Based on a story by W.W. Jacobs. Story: A retired bosun, George Benn, hires ex-soldier Ned Travers to burgle widow Mrs. Walters' inn, so the former can impress the lady when he routs the invader. Things get a bit muddled in the execution.

London Films, Great Britain, 1914 (original). Silent. Director: Harold Shaw; screenwriter: W.W. Jacobs. Cast: W.H. Berry (George Benn), Mary Brough (Mrs. Walters), Wyndham Guise (Ned Travers), Charles Rock, George Bellamy, Judd Green, John East, Brian Daly.

• ***The Bosun's Mate*** (remake). Anvil/GFD, Great Britain, 1953. Director and screenwriter: Richard Warren. Cast: Cameron Hall (George Benn), Barbara Mullen (Mrs. Walters), Edwin Richfield (Ned Travers), George Woodridge.

The long time between filmings did not improve the story. It's just a simple comedy with not many big laughs, whether with titles or sound.

The Bounty *see* **Mutiny on the Bounty**

106 Boy's Town

Based on a story by Dore Schary and Eleanore Griffin. Story: While comforting a man who is about to be executed in the electric chair, Father Flanagan is haunted by the man's bitterness about his boyhood which he believes to be the reason he has ended up the way he has. From then on and against great odds and opposition, Flanagan works to establish a community where troubled boys can live and grow into decent adults. When his community is established, his conviction that "there's no such thing as a bad boy" is severely tested by the arrival of Whitey Marsh, kid brother of an imprisoned gangster who wants nothing more than to grow up to be just like his brother. Through Flanagan's patience and guidance and Whitey's run-in with some of his brother's former associates, Whitey's reformation is accomplished.

MGM, 1938 (original). Director: Norman Taurog; screenwriters: John Meehan and Dore Schary. Cast: Spencer Tracy (Father Flanagan), Mickey Rooney (Whitey Marsh), Henry Hull (Dave Morris), Leslie Fenton (Dan Farrow), Bobs Watson (Pee Wee), Gene Reynolds, Edward Norris, Adison Richards, Jonathan Hale.

• ***Men of Boy's Town*** (sequel). MGM, 1941. Director: Norman Taurog;

screenwriter: James Kevin McGuinness. Cast: Spencer Tracy (Father Flanagan), Mickey Rooney (Whitey Marsh), Bobs Watson (Pee Wee), Larry Nunn (Ted Martley), Darryl Hickman (Flip), Henry O'Neill, Mary Nash, Lee J. Cobb.

Although there was a Father Flanagan and there is a Boy's Town, this picture is not a biography in the usual sense. The tear-jerking melodrama instead concentrates on the work of Father Flanagan, using a fictitious Whitey Marsh to make the point. The film was so successful that a sequel was almost demanded. Spencer Tracy as Father Flanagan had played a priest before and seemed quite comfortable in the role of the no-nonsense but sensitive and caring cleric. Mickey Rooney, at the peak of his popularity, scored once again as the bad boy who was redeemed. In the sequel, the now completely reformed Whitey Marsh leaves Boy's Town briefly to practice the precepts of its founder and help in fund-raising for the institution. Arriving at the school is a crippled lad (Larry Nunn), his injury sustained in a reform school beating, who is somewhat understandably bitter. Never fear, Flanagan, Marsh and the other boys eventually bring him around and he is rehabilitated both spiritually and physically.

The Brasher Doubloon *see* **Time to Kill**

107 The Brass Bottle

Based on a book by F. Anstey. Story: Some 6,423 years ago, Fakresh-el-Aumash was corked up in a brass bottle which was flung into deep waters. In present-day England, young architect Horace Myers comes into possession of the bottle and when he stumbles in his unpretentious abode, the bottle is smashed and the genie is released, offering to give the architect anything he wishes as a reward for setting him free. Besides customers, which Fakresh supplies, Horace wishes permission from Professor Hamilton to marry his daughter, Marjorie. Appearing before Professor Hamilton in modern dress, Fakresh asks for the maiden's hand for his young master. The professor refuses so Fakresh turns him into a jackass. He reverses the transformation when Horace and Marjorie discover the jackass in her father's study. Horace, trying to make a good impression, invites Professor Hamilton, his wife and daughter to take dinner with him at his apartment. He leaves the details to Fakresh who turns the apartment into an Arabian palace, complete with Nubian slaves and dancing girls. All of the silliness is eventually resolved with Horace getting Marjorie and Fakresh moving on to adjust to his new surroundings.

• ***The Brass Bottle*** (remake). First National, 1923. Silent. Director and screenwriter: Maurice Tourneur. Cast: Ernest Torrence (Fakresh-el-Aumash), Tully Marshall (Professor Hamilton), Harry Myers (Horace Ventimore), Barbara LaMarr (Marjorie Hamilton), Ford Sterling, Charlotte Merriam.

• ***The Brass Bottle*** (remake). Universal Pictures, 1964. Director: Harry Keller; screenwriter: Oscar Bradley. Cast: Tony Randall (Harold Ventimore), Burl Ives (Fakresh-el-Aumash), Barbara Eden (Sylvia Kenton), Kamala Devi (Tezra), Edward Andrews (Professor Anthony Kenton), Ann Doran, Richard Erdman, Kathie Browne.

There was a silent version of the film produced in 1914. The 1923 film is an entertaining piece with fine performances from Ernest Torrence as the genie and Tully Marshall as the professor. The young lovers, Harry Myers and Barbara La Marr, have little to do, save looking bewildered and startled, respectively. Except for moving the locale of the story to America, the remake was pretty much the same. In this version, Barbara Eden, who was soon to make her name as Jeannie in TV's "I Dream of Jeannie," left the wearing of harem pants to some other fetching beauties. Tony Randall re-created his usual role of a rather fussy but-not-quite-with-it young man. Burl Ives came across quite nicely as the genie and Edward Andrews was properly blustery as the put-on father who is turned into a jackass.

108 The Brat

Based on the play by Maude Fulton. Story: It's the "Cinderella" tale of a poor young girl, called the Brat, who gets in trouble over some unpaid bills, but is rescued by wealthy novelist MacMillan Forester, who falls in love with her.

• ***The Brat*** (remake). Fox Film Corporation, 1931. Director: John Ford; screenwriters: Sonya Levien and S.N. Behrman. Cast: Sally O'Neil (The Brat), Allan Dinehart (MacMillan Forester), Frank Albertson (Stephen Forester), Virginia Cherrill (Angela), June Collyer, J. Farrell MacDonald, Mary Forbes, Albert Gran.

• ***A Girl from Avenue A*** (remake). Twentieth Century–Fox, 1940. Director: Otto Brower; screenwriter: Frances Hyland. Cast: Jane Withers (Jane), Kent Taylor (MacMillan), Katharine Aldridge (Lucy), Elyse Knox (Angela), Laura Hope Crews, Jessie Ralph, Harry Shannon, Vaughn Glaser, Rand Brooks.

The Brat was first produced by MGM in 1919. The 1931 film was a light comedy drama that succeeded at the box office without much critical acclaim. The remake was an opportunity for Jane Withers to show her peculiar and delightful comedy talent. She appears as a street-wise urchin who is taken in by a wealthy but eccentric family in the hope that she could inspire a playwright son, Kent Taylor, by teaching him slang. She succeeds in this Pygmalion-like story.

The Breaking Point *see* **To Have and Have Not**

109 Brewster's Millions

Based on the novel by George Barr McCutcheon and the play by Winchell Smith. Story: Monte Brewster is informed that he must spend one million dollars left to him by his grandfather in one year in order to inherit seven million dollars from his uncle. The hitch is he must have nothing to show for it at the end of the year. It's to be gone and he is to own nothing that it bought. Initially, Monte's luck is all bad: Everything he does to unload the dough backfires and earns him more, which he then must also dispose of. He's almost done in by well-meaning friends to whom he is not allowed to explain why he is acting so bizarre. They try to secretly save and invest some of his fortune so he'll have something when he comes to his senses. He just makes it at the last moment—and comes into some real money.

• ***Brewster's Millions*** (remake). Paramount Pictures, 1921. Silent. Director: Joseph Henabery; screenwriter: Walter Woods. Cast: Roscoe "Fatty" Arbuckle (Monte Brewster), Betty Ross Clark (Peggy Gray), Fred Huntley (Mr. Brewster), Marian Skinner (Mrs. Brewster), James Corrigan (Mr. Ingraham), Jean Acker (Barbara Drew), Charles Ogle, Neely Edwards, William Boyd, L.J. McCarthy, Parker McConnell, John MacFarlane.

• ***Miss Brewster's Millions*** (remake). Paramount Pictures, 1926. Silent. Director: Clarence Badger; screenwriter: Lloyd Corrigan. Cast: Bebe Daniels (Polly Brewster), Warner Baxter (Thomas B. Hancock, Jr.), Ford Sterling (Ned Brewster), Andre de Beranger (Mr. Brent), Miss Beresford (landlady).

• ***Brewster's Millions*** (remake). British and Dominion, Great Britain, 1935. Director: Thorton Freeland; screenwriters: Clifford Grey and W. Wilhelm. Cast: Jack Buchanan (Jack Brewster), Lili Damita (Rosalie), Nancy O'Neil (Cynthia), Sydney Fairbrother (Miss Plimsole), Ian McLean (McLeod), Fred Emney (Freddy), Allan Aynesworth, Lawrence Hanray, Dennis Hoey, Henry Wenman.

• ***Brewster's Millions*** (remake). United Artists, 1945. Director: Allan Dwan; screenwriters: Sig Herzig and Charles Rogers. Cast: Dennis O'Keefe (Monty Brewster), Helen Walker (Peggy Gray), Eddie "Rochester" Anderson (Jackson), June Havoc (Trixie Summers), Gail Patrick (Barbara Drew), Mischa Auer (Michael Michaelovich), Joe Sawyer, Nana Bryant, John Litel, Herbert Rudley, Thurston Hall.

• ***Brewster's Millions*** (remake). Universal Pictures, 1985. Director: Walter Hill; screenwriters: Herschel Weingrod and Timothy Harris. Cast: Richard Pryor (Montgomery Brewster), John Candy (Spike Nolan), Lonette McKee (Angela Drake), Stephen Collins (Warren Cox), Pat Hingle (Edward Roundfield), Tovah Feldshuh (Marilyn), Hume Cronyn (Rupert Horn), Jerry Orbach (Charley Pegler), Joe Grifasi, Peter Jason, David White, Jerome Dempsey, David Wohl.

The story of a man ordered to spend a million to earn seven million was first screened in 1914. Over the years, the sex and color of Brewster has changed, as has the amount he or she must spend and the amount he or she will receive if successful. After the first picture, the time frame was reduced to thirty days and the various ways the money is spent becomes a function of the time frame in which the production is set. Brewster's ability to meet the provisions of the will are threatened both by friends and selfish outside agents, whom he (or she) almost accidently outwits. The 1935 British version with Jack Buchanan is a musical. In 1985, Richard Pryor is a minor league baseball pitcher who realizes his ambition to pitch against the Yankees (since he wears a Chicago Cubs' uniform top most of the time, he may be trying to avenge the Cubs' 1932 World Series loss to the Yanks). He also is almost elected mayor of New York, but convinces people to vote for "None of the above." Arguably the best of the various versions is the 1945 feature with the delightful actor Dennis O'Keefe. It hasn't the production values of the 1985 piece, but it is fondly remembered as a scream.

Bride by Mistake *see* **The Richest Girl in the World**

Bride of the Regiment *see* **The Lady in Ermine**

110 Brides Are Like That

Based on the play *Applesauce* by Barry Connors. Story: Bill McAllister is a pleasant but shiftless young man who believes that he can get anything he wants through flattery. Among other things, he convinces his rival for the affection of Hazel Robinson that the man is too lofty an individual to be caught in the trap of marriage. He dishes out the "applesauce" and everyone laps it up.

Warner Bros., 1936 (original). Director: William McGann; screenwriter: Ben Markson. Cast: Ross Alexander (Bill McAllister), Anita Louise (Hazel Robinson), Joe Cawthorn (Fred Schultz), Gene Lockhart (John Robinson), Kathleen Lockhart (Mrs. Ella Robinson), Mary Lou Treen, Alma Lloyd, Craig Reynolds, Richard Purcell.

• ***Always a Bride*** (remake). Warner Bros., 1940. Director: Noel M. Smith; screenwriter: Robert E. Kent. Cast: Rosemary Lane (Alice Bond), George Reeves (Michael Stevens), John Eldridge (Marshall Winkler), Virginia Brissac (Lucy Bond), Francis Pierlot, Oscar O'Shea, Ferris Taylor, Joseph King.

The subject of the two films is flattery and the producers would have us believe that people would actually fall for such outrageous gee-gaw. It's an amicable story which grows tiresome long before the finish of either film. In the remake, George Reeves, who would later gain some fame for his portrayal of Superman, failed to impress in his first leading role. But he is able to flatter himself into becoming the mayor of his town—Isn't that the way with all politicians?

111 The Bridge of San Luis Rey

Based on the novel by Thornton Wilder. Story: The Bridge of San Luis Rey, built by the Incas and blessed by St. Louis, stands on the high road of Peru and to the villagers, represents their communication with God. On July 20, 1714, the bridge collapses, hurling five people to their death. Since the tragedy occurred on the feast day of St. Louis the villagers see the event as a forewarning of their imminent doom. They come to Father Juniper for spiritual guidance. The priest delves into the background of the five victims to learn what brought them to their fate with the bridge. His conclusion is that man can never fully understand God's ways or purposes. He tells the villagers that there is a land of the living and a land of the dead and the bridge between them is love.

MGM, 1929 (original). Part talkie. Director: Charles Brabin; screenwriter: Alice D.G. Miller. Cast: Lily Damita (Camila), Ernest Torrence (Uncle Pio), Raquel Torres (Pepita), Don Alvardo (Manuel), Duncan Renaldo (Esteben) Henry B. Walthall (Father Juniper), Michael Varitch (Viceroy), Emily Fitzroy (Marquess), Jane Winton (Dona Clara), Gordon Thorpe (Jamie), Mitchell Lewis (Captain Alvardo).

• ***The Bridge of San Luis Rey*** (remake). United Artists, 1944. Director: Rowland V. Lee; screenwriter: Howard Estabrook. Cast: Lynn Bari (Michaela), Akim Tamiroff (Uncle Pio), Francis Lederer (Manuel/Esteben), Nazimova (The Marquess), Blanche Yurka (The Abbess), Donald Woods (Brother

Juniper), Louis Calhern (The Viceroy), Emma Dunn, Barton Hepburn, Joan Lorring, Abner Biberman, Minerva Urecal.

Director Charles Brabin added a few minutes of talk after the film was completed. Neither version of the Pulitzer Prize–winning novel was very successful, either artistically or at the box office. Most critics agree that of the two, the silent version is the better, believing that Brabin is more successful in getting the performers to breathe life into their characters. It has long proven difficult to film allegorical, spiritual stories without looking too reverent or too superficial. Such is the case with these two pictures. There is a definite unevenness in both in telling the multi-plotted story. Among the performers who distinguished themselves with their efforts were Ernest Torrence and Henry B. Walthall in the original, and Akim Tamiroff and Donald Woods in the remake. But these performers had the most interesting roles, Uncle Pio and Father/Brother Juniper, respectively.

Brief Encounter *see* **Tonight at 8:30**

British Intelligence *see* **Three Faces East**

112 Broadway

Based on the play by Philip Dunning and George Abbott. Story: Billie Moore, a dancer in the Paradise nightclub, witnesses the murder of gangster "Scar" Edwards by bootlegger Steve Crandall. However, it is her dancing partner, Roy Lane, who is arrested for the murder by detective Dan McCorn. When Crandall confesses he killed her lover, dancer Pearl shoots and kills him but is released when McCorn, who has become infatuated with Pearl, calls Crandall's killing a suicide.

Universal, 1929 (original). Director: Paul Fejos; screenwriters: Edward T. Lowe and Charles Furthman. Cast: Glenn Tyron (Roy Lane), Evelyn Brent (Pearl), Merna Kennedy (Billie Moore), Thomas Jackson (Dan McCorn), Robert Ellis (Steve Crandall), Otis Harlan, Paul Porcasi, Marion Lord, Fritz Feld, Leslie Fenton.

• ***Broadway*** (remake). Universal, 1942. Director: William A. Seiter; screenwriters: Felix Jackson and John Bright. Cast: George Raft (George), Pat O'Brien (Dan McCorn), Janet Blair (Billie Moore), Broderick Crawford (Steve Crandall), Marjorie Rambeau (Lil), Anne Gwynne (Pearl), S.Z. Sakall, Edward S. Brophy, Marie Wilson.

The 1929 film was handsome entertainment and became one of the biggest box-office grossers of the year. The performance of Robert Ellis as the murdering bootlegger was extremely good. His show of nervousness as he is being tracked down by the avenging Pearl is done to great advantage. Evelyn Brent as Pearl is splendid as the determined dancer who tells Crandall to turn his face to her so he can see her shoot him.

The remake was revised to allow George Raft to recall his life as a dancer in New York at the time of prohibition, and in particular a murder involving gangsters and chorus girls. While effectively staged, the film did not generate much excitement and has generally been forgotten.

113 Broadway Bill

Based on a story by Mark Hellinger. Story: Dan Brooks, the troubled and broke owner of race horse, Broadway Bill, needs to scrounge up the entry fee for a big race. The horse is attached because Brooks hasn't paid the feed bill. Brooks is jailed for fighting with the sheriff but is released just in time. To add to his troubles, gamblers have got to the jockey to throw the race. Despite all the misfortunes and jams of Brooks, the horse wins the race but dies as a result of his victory. There is still a happy ending as Brooks gets the girl, Alice, who shares his love of horses.

Columbia, 1934 (original). Director: Frank Capra; screenwriter: Robert Riskin. Cast: Warner Baxter (Dan Brooks), Myrna Loy (Alice), Walter Connolly (J.L. Higgins), Helen Vinson (Margaret), Douglas Dumbrille (Eddie Morgan), Raymond Walburn, Lynne Overman, Clarence Muse, Margaret Hamilton.

• ***Riding High*** (remake). Paramount, 1950. Director: Frank Capra; screenwriter: Robert Riskin. Cast: Bing Crosby (Dan Brooks), Coleen Gray (Alice Higgins), Charles Bickford (J.L. Higgins), Frances Gifford, Raymond Walburn, William Demarest, Clarence Muse, Margaret Hamilton, Douglas Dumbrille.

Both of Capra's efforts to bring this horse-racing story to the screen were quite successful. He deserves most of the credit for producing such fast-paced entertainment. Audiences were able to enjoy humor, adventure, suspense and a good cry all for the price of one admission. In both cases, Dan Brooks is hooked up with a woman who doesn't understand and doesn't appreciate his racing interests, but in each case he ends up with a woman who shares his enthusiasm. In the remake, Crosby, as one would expect, is called upon to sing, the best effort being "Sunshine Cake" by Johnny Burke and Jimmy Van Heusen. Also, as might be expected, Crosby is more easygoing than the more intense Warner Baxter. In the remake there's a very funny scene between Crosby and Demarest and Walburn, with both sides trying to con money from the other.

Broadway Musketeers *see* **Three on a Match**

114 Broken Blossoms

Based on the book *The Chink and the Child* by Thomas Burke. Story: Set in foggy Limehouse, the film is the story of a Chinese boy who has a pure and almost holy love for a young girl. She lives with her father, a brutish boxer, who when learning that his daughter is the beloved of a "chink" beats her to death. The boy takes revenge by killing the father and then committing suicide.

Griffith/Artcraft/United Artists, 1919 (original). Silent. Director and screenwriter: D.W. Griffith. Cast: Lillian Gish (The Girl), Richard Barthelmess (The Chinaman), Donald Crisp ("Battling" Burrows), Arthur Howard, George Beranger, Norman "Kid McCoy" Selby.

• ***Broken Blossoms*** (remake). Twickenham Films, 1936. Director: Hans

Brahm; screenwriter: Emlyn Williams. Cast: Dolly Haas (Lucy), Emlyn Williams (Chen), C.V. France (High Priest), Basil Redford (Mr. Reed), Edith Sharpe (Mrs. Reed), Ernest Jay (Alf), Bertha Belmore, Gibb McLaughlin, Ernest Sefton, Donald Calthrop.

Griffith's sensitive direction resulted in a film which is considered a silent classic. In it he makes a plea for nonviolence and racial tolerance. Gish's performance is among her very best. Her fragile beauty and sad expression still melt the hearts of audiences. Griffith was supposed to direct the remake but quit the film after a dispute with Emlyn Williams, and Hans Brahm took over. It's a shame that audiences were denied the opportunity to see what the old master could do with this story using sound. Perhaps he wouldn't have succeeded any more than did Brahm, who did come up with a stylish film, because the story is really only a maudlin, old-fashioned piece for which no remake was necessary. Williams wasn't very convincing as a Chinese lad. While Barthelmess's impersonation was a stereotype, at least he appeared oriental. Williams' effeminate portrayal might have been of any nationality but some felt he sounded Welsh. As for Dolly Haas, her delivery of lines makes one yearn for the silents.

115 Broken Dishes

Based on the play by Martin Flavin. Story: Henpecked Cyrus Bumpstead is constantly nagged by his shrewish wife who tells her daughters that she should have married long-gone Chester Armstrong, whom she describes as both a genius and an Adonis. Of his daughters, only Elaine sympathizes with her father and one night during their nightly dishwashing she seeks her father's permission to marry Bill Clark, whom Mrs. Bumpstead despises. While the mother and the other two daughters are at the movies, Cyrus, who has just arrived home from a lodge meeting where he had met and drunkingly inbibed with the self-same Chester Armstrong, arranges for the preacher to perform a wedding ceremony for his daughter and her love. When Mrs. Bumpstead arrives home finding her daughter married and all the dishes broken by her clumsy husband and new son-in-law, she is furious. However, to her dismay, the worm turns and Cyrus asserts himself, whereas Chester Armstrong calls Mrs. Bumpstead an old crow and is discovered to be a swindler who has spent many a year in jails, to which the police intend to return him.

• ***Too Young to Marry*** Warner Bros., 1931 (original). Director: Mervyn LeRoy; screenwriter: Frances E. Faragoh. Cast: O.P. Heggie (Cyprus Bumpstead), Loretta Young (Elaine Bumpstead), Grant Withers (Bill Clark), Emma Dunn (Mrs. Bumpstead), Richard Tucker (Chester Armstrong), J. Farrell MacDonald, Lloyd Neal, Virginia Sale, Aileen Carlisle, Frank Darien.

• ***Love Begins at Twenty*** (remake). First National Pictures, 1936. Director: Frank MacDonald; screenwriters: Tom Reed and Dalton Trumbo. Cast: Hugh Herbert (Horatio Gillingwater), Warren Hull (Jerry Wayne), Patricia Ellis (Lois Gillingwater), Dorothy Vaughn (Evalina), Mary Treen, Hobart Cavanaugh, Clarence Wilson, Robert Gleckler.

In the *Too Young to Marry* version of the play *Broken Dishes*, O.P. Heggie can be faulted for overacting in this family farce with a plot which has too often been overdone in the ensuing years. It might have been a pilot for one of the many TV situation comedies of the 50s and 60s which depicted the father as a bumbling loser who had to be managed by his clever and overbearing wife and children. Nevertheless, lovely Loretta Young is always something to look at and Emma Dunn was quite efficient as the domineering wife.

The remake, *Love Begins at Twenty,* was meant to be a quickly made "B" picture and it looked it. Woo-wooing Hugh Herbert merely repeated his patented performance and the other members of the cast did nothing to distinguish themselves.

116 The Broken Melody

Based on the play by Herbert Keith and James Leader. Story: Exiled Prince Paul returns to his faithful shopkeeper wife, Bianca, after having written an opera for flirtatious singer Gloria.

Welsh-Pearson-Elder/Paramount Pictures, Great Britain, 1929 (original). Silent. Director: Fred Paul; screenwriters: Fred Paul and Thomas Coutts Elder. Cast: Georges Galli (Prince Paul), Audree Sayre (Bianca), Enid Stamp-Taylor (Gloria), Cecil Humphreys, Mary Brough, Albert Brouett.

• ***The Broken Melody*** (remake). Twickenham/AP&D, Great Britain, 1934. Director: Bernard Vorhaus; screenwriter: Vera Allinson, Michael Hankinson and H. Fowler Mear. Cast: John Garrick (Paul Verlaine), Margot Grahame (Simone St. Clair), Merle Oberon (Germaine), Austin Trevor (Pierre), Charles Carson, Harry Terry, Andrea Malandrinos, Tonie Edgar Bruce.

Although director Vorhaus is credited with the story for the second film, the themes of the two movies are similar enough to believe that he was inspired by the first. In his version a composer kills his wife's lover, is sent to Devil's Island, escapes, finds happiness with another woman, writes an opera, and is allowed to go free when the governor of Devil's Island recognizes him and chooses to say nothing. He must be a real music lover.

117 The Broken Wing

Based on a play by Paul Dickey and Charles Goddard. Story: When American airplane pilot Philip Marvin crashes his plane on a ranch near the Mexican border, Inez, the foster daughter of the owner of the ranch, nurses him back to health. Although revolutionary leader Captain Innocencio Dos Santos has made his romantic intentions clear to the girl, Inez has been hoping for someone better, and believes that Marvin is the answer to her prayer. Suffering from amnesia, Marvin is held for ransom by Dos Santos, but the caballero is outsmarted by American secret servicemen and Inez gets her man.

B.P. Schulberg Productions, 1923 (original). Silent. Director and screenwriter: Tom Forman. Cast: Kenneth Harlan (Philip Marvin), Miriam Cooper (Inez Villera), Walter Lang (Capt. Dos Santos), Richard Tucker, Edwin J. Brady, Ferdinand Munier, Evelyn Selbie.

• ***The Broken Wing*** (remake). Paramount, 1932. Director: Lloyd Corrigan; screenwriters: William Slavens McNutt and Grover Jones. Cast: Lupe Velez

(Lolita), Leo Carrillo (Capt. Innocencio Dos Santos), Melvyn Douglas (Phil Marvin), George Barbier, Willard Robertson, Arthur Stone, Soledad Jiminez, Claire Dodd, Pietro Sosso.

Both films feature stereotypes of Mexicans which were in vogue at the times of their release. In particular, in the remake, Leo Carrillo portrayed a Cisco Kid–like outlaw and Lupe Velez was her usual fiery self. Melvyn Douglas, as the aviator, looked like he wished he was in another picture. They don't make movies like these anymore—fortunately.

118 Brother Rat

Based on a play by John Monks, Jr. and Fred F. Finklehoff. Story: It's the tale of the high jinks of three cadets at Virginia Military Institute who have girl trouble, money trouble, class trouble, faculty trouble, sports trouble, etc. The star baseball player is secretly married, his wife is going to have a baby and he's in danger of flunking out. Everything is favorably resolved before the end of the film.

Warner Bros., 1938. Director: William Keighley; screenwriters: Richard Macaulay and Jerry Wald. Cast: Priscilla Lane (Joyce Winfree), Wayne Morris (Billy Randolph), Johnnie Davis (A. Furman Townsend, Jr.), Jane Bryan (Kate Rice), Eddie Albert (Bing Edwards), Ronald Reagan (Dan Crawford), Jane Wyman (Claire Adams), Henry O'Neill, Gordon Oliver, Larry Williams.

• ***Brother Rat and a Baby*** (sequel). Warner Bros., 1940. Director: Ray Enright; screenwriters: John Monks, Jr. and Fred F. Finklehoff. Cast: Priscilla Lane (Joyce Winfree), Wayne Morris (Billy Randolph), Eddie Albert (Bing Edwards), Jane Bryan (Kate Edwards), Jane Wyman (Claire Terry), Ronald Reagan (Dan Crawford), Peter B. Good, Arthur Treacher, Moroni Olsen, Jessie Busley.

• ***About Face*** (remake). Warner Bros., 1952. Director: Roy Del Ruth; screenwriter: Peter Milne. Cast: Gordon MacRae (Tony), Eddie Bracken (Biff), Dick Wesson (Dave), Virginia Gibson (Betty), Phyllis Kirk (Alice), Aileen Stanley, Jr. (Lorna), Joel Grey, Larry Keating.

Eddie Albert re-created his stage role as Bing Edwards and if anything was even funnier as the expectant father who must also deal with his lack of academic abilities and the big baseball game. Wayne Morris appears as the ringleader of the trio of cadets who is always getting them into trouble. Ronald Reagan, the easygoing member of the crew, is always ready to go along with the plans of the others. The females are all hugable but aren't required to do too much.

In the sequel, Albert, Morris and Reagan are out of school but act as if they were still in their dorm plotting how to outfox the faculty. In the real world, their antics are not so amusing, although Morris tries to maintain his juvenile antics abetted by Albert's baby, played winningly by Peter B. Good. All thoughts of a *Brother Rat* series were put to rest by this vehicle.

The Technicolor musical remake in 1952 just didn't work. With the exception of the ballad "If Someone Had Told Me," the songs were forgettable. Bracken, the expectant father, didn't possess Albert's charm, but the film was also hurt by the times. It was difficult several years after World War II to believe that anyone would be so whiney about his impending parenthood. In a small part as a put-upon underclassman, Joel Grey was excellent in this otherwise pretty but dull film.

Brother Rat and a Baby *see* **Brother Rat**

119 Brown on "Resolution"

Based on a novel by C.S. Forrester. Story: In 1893, the daughter of a London grocer meets a young naval lieutenant who takes her to dinner and spends the remaining days of his leave with her. At the end of this time he goes off to sea, never to see her again, and she delivers the seaman's son. Years later, the boy becomes a sailor and when war is declared he is the only survivor of his torpedoed ship, saved by the German ship that sunk her. The German cruiser puts into an isolated island, Resolution, to repair the damages suffered in battle. The boy escapes with a gun and one by one picks off the seamen working on the cruiser and the members of the search party sent to find him. His plan is to delay the German departure until a British ship can catch up with them. He succeeds in this but is killed. The captain of the British ship which blows the German cruiser out of the water gives full credit for the victory to the boy. When the captain discovers his own watch on the dead boy's body, he realizes that he is his son.

Gaumont-British Productions, 1935 (original). Director: Walter Forde; screenwriter: J.O.C. Orton. Cast: Betty Balfour (Elizabeth Brown), John Mills (Albert Brown), Barry MacKay (Lt. Somerville), Jimmy Hanley, H. Marion Crawford, H.G. Stoker, Percy Walsh, George Merritt, Cyril Smith.

• ***Sailor of the King*** (remake). Twentieth Century–Fox, 1953. Director: Ray Boulting; screenwriter: Valentine Davies. Cast: Jeffrey Hunter, Michael Rennie, Wendy Hiller, Bernard Lee, Peter van Eyck, John Horsley, Patrick Barr.

In this tribute to the valor of the English seaman, young John Mills gives a superb performance in a most engrossing film. The others in the cast are quite good and the movie is well worth seeing again. In the remake, Jeffrey Hunter is the young seaman, Wendy Hiller his mother, Michael Rennie the unaware father, and the conflict World War II. The story basically follows the same plot although in this version, the boy survives and at the end of the film, he stands in Buckingham Palace to receive a medal, next to Rennie, without either knowing of their relationship. Once again, the performances are excellent.

120 Brown Sugar

Based on the play by Lady Arthur Lever. Story: When Lord Sloane marries showgirl Stella Deering, his parents—The Earl and Countess of Knightsbridge—do not approve. But when the actress takes the blame for her husband's brother's gambling debts, her stern mother-in-law realizes she undervalued the girl and begs for forgiveness.

British Super/Jury, Great Britain, 1922 (original). Silent. Director: Fred Paul; screenwriter: Walter Summers. Cast: Owen Nares (Lord Sloane), Lilian

Hall-Davis (Stella Deering), Eric Lewis (Earl of Knightsbridge), Henrietta Watson (Countess of Knightsbridge), Margaret Halstan, Cyril Dane, Eric Leighton, Gladys Harvey, Louise Hampton.

• ***Brown Sugar*** (remake). Twickenham/Warner Bros., Great Britain, 1931. Director: Leslie Hiscott; screenwriter: Cyril Twyford. Cast: Constance Carpenter (Lady Stella Stone), Francis Lister (Lord Sloane), Allan Aynesworth (Lord Knightsbridge), Helen Haye (Lady Knightsbridge), Cecily Byrne, Eva Moore, Chili Bouchier, Gerald Rawlinson, Alfred Drayton, Wallace Geoffrey.

Neither version of this stale, drawing room romance will thrill audiences. The characters and their behavior are totally predictable and the only thing uncertain for the audience is, if they can sit through the entire movie.

121 The Buccaneer

Based on the screenplay by Jeanie Macpherson, Edwin Justus Mayer, Harold Lamb and C. Gardner Sullivan. Story: During the War of 1812, pirate Jean Lafite, whose headquarters are in the bayous near New Orleans, is approached by the British for aid. Instead, in part because of his love for the governor's daughter and partially because of his admiration for American democratic principles, he sides with Andrew Jackson in the defense of New Orleans, in a battle that took place after the war was officially over.

Paramount Pictures, 1938 (original). Director: Cecil B. De Mille; screenwriters: Jeanie Macpherson, Edwin Justus Mayer, Harold Lamb and C. Gardner Sullivan. Cast: Fredric March (Jean Lafite), Akim Tamiroff (General You), Walter Brennan (Andrew Jackson), Franciska Gaal, Margot Grahame, Ian Keith.

• ***The Buccaneer*** (remake). Paramount Pictures, 1958. Director: Anthony Quinn; screenwriters: Jesse L. Lasky, Jr. and Bernice Mosk, based on the earlier screenplay. Cast: Yul Brynner (Jean Lafite), Charles Boyer (General You), Charlton Heston (Andrew Jackson), Claire Bloom, Inger Stevens, Henry Hull, E.G. Marshall.

The remake demonstrated that Brynner looked better when bald. He was adequate in the part of the dashing pirate, as was Fredric March before him, but in both films it was General You, Lafite's second in command, who stole the show. In the first, Akim Tamiroff, a fine character actor, was convincing as the loyal former gunner for Napoleon Bonaparte. Charles Boyer, happy that he wasn't called on to appear as the great lover, was appealingly bombastic as Brynner's friend and comrade-in-arms. The action in both films is enjoyable and one can forgive the fact that both are clearly studio-bound.

122 Buck Privates

Based on an original screenplay by Arthur T. Horman. Story: Two dimwitted and crooked sidewalk tie-salesmen accidently join the army to escape the authorities. After going through the now-painfully familiar training camp hilarities they (by accident) become heroes. The love interest in the film is provided by a triangle consisting of a spoiled socialite, his ex-body guard and a girl singer. Plots in Abbott and Costello pictures were never very important or tight and this is true in this, their first starring movie.

Universal Pictures, 1941 (original). Director: Arthur Lubin; screenwriter: Arthur T. Horman. Cast: Bud Abbott (Slicker Smith), Lou Costello (Herbie Brown), Lee Bowman (Randolph Parker, III), Alan Curtis (Bob Martin), Jane Frazee (Judy Gray), The Andrews Sisters (themselves), Nat Pendleton, Samuel S. Hinds, Harry Strang, Nella Walker, Leonard Elliott.

• ***Buck Privates Come Home*** (sequel). Universal Pictures, 1947. Director: Charles T. Barton; screenwriters: John Grant, Frederic J. Rinaldo and Robert Lees from a story by Richard Macaulay and Bradford Ropes. Cast: Bud Abbott (Slicker Smith), Lou Costello (Herbie Brown), Tom Brown (Bill Gregory), Joan Fulton Shawlee (Sylvia Hunter), Nat Pendleton, Beverly Simmons, Don Beddoe, Don Porter, Donald MacBride.

Abbott and Costello had made their screen debut in 1939 in *One Night in the Tropics*, but it was with *Buck Privates* that movie audiences first were treated to some of the classic routines the boys had polished on the vaudeville circuit. The romantic angle included in this film was an obvious device by the producers to hedge their bet, not knowing if the antics of the boys could carry the picture. It turns out that they could and the love story was the least interesting part of the film. Far more enjoyable were the Andrews Sisters who gave out with "I'll Be with You in Apple Blossom Time" and "Boogie Woogie Bugle Boy of Company B." Jane Frazee chipped in with "I Wish You Were Here."

In the sequel the boys are discharged and team up with an army buddy to go into midget car racing. They have smuggled a French war orphan into the country and can use all the dough they can get their hands on to keep her. The feature has a good final chase as well as several flashbacks to *Buck Privates*. Not among their best features, the film did provide more of the entertainment a public had grown to enjoy, featuring Abbott as the not-quite-honest dude who was always taking advantage of the terribly dumb and immature Costello.

Buck Privates Come Home *see* **Buck Privates**

Bulldog at Bay *see* **Bulldog Drummond**

123 Bulldog Drummond

Based on the stories by "Sapper" (Herman Cyril McNeile). Story: Bored with civilian life after World War II, Bulldog Drummond, a young British Army officer, advertises for adventure. He is approached by an American girl, Phyllis Benton, whose uncle, Hiram J. Travers, is being held prisoner by Dr. Larkington, a sadistic physician, and his confederate, Peterson. These two plan to torture Travers until he gives up his fortune. After several thrilling adventures, debonair Drummond rescues Travers and takes a personal vengeance on the villains. He wins Phyllis' love and the eternal gratitude of Travers.

• ***Bulldog Drummond*** (remake). Goldwyn Productions/United Artists, 1929. Director: F. Richard Jones; screenwriters: Wallace Smith and Sidney Howard. Cast: Ronald Colman (Bulldog Drummond), Joan Bennett (Phyllis Benton),

Lilyan Tashman (Erma), Montagu Love (Peterson), Lawrence Grant (Dr. Larkington), Claude Allister (Algy), Charles Sellon (Travers), Wilson Benge, Adolph Milar, Tetsu Komai.

• ***Bulldog Drummond Strikes Back*** (sequel). Twentieth Century–Fox, 1934. Director: Roy Del Ruth; screenwriter: Nunnally Johnson. Cast: Ronald Colman (Hugh Drummond), Loretta Young (Lola Field), Warner Oland (Prince Achmed), Charles Butterworth (Algy), Una Merkel (Gwen), C. Aubrey Smith (Inspector Nielson), Kathleen Burke, Arthur Hohl, George Regas, Ethel Griffies, Mischa Auer.

• ***Bulldog Drummond Comes Back*** (sequel). Paramount Pictures, 1937. Director: Louis King; screenwriter: Eward T. Lowe. Cast: John Barrymore (Colonel Nielson), John Howard (Bulldog Drummond), Louise Campbell (Phyllis Clavering), Reginald Denny (Algy Longsworth), E.E. Clive (Tenny), J. Carroll Naish (Mikhail Valdin), Helen Freeman, Zeffie Tilbury, John Sutton, Rita Page, Iva Henderson, John Rogers.

The adventures of the fascist-like Bulldog Drummond have been brought to the screen many times. Among these are a 1922 silent with Carlyle Brackwell; 1925s *The Third Round* with Jack Buchanan; a lost Fox film; *Temple Tower* with Kenneth MacKenna in 1930; *Drummond* in 1934 with Ralph Richardson; the 1934 spoof *Bulldog Jack* starring comic Jack Hulbert; *Bulldog at Bay* in 1937 with John Lodge as the title character; another 1937 film with Ray Milland as Drummond *(Bulldog Drummond Escapes);* a cheap remake of the 1937 Lodge film in 1947 with Ron Randell; Tom Conway in the role of Drummond in 1948s *The Challenge;* Walter Pidgeon starring in 1951s *Calling Bulldog Drummond* and 1967s *Deadlier Than the Male* with Richard Johnson.

In the first of the two sequels featured in this entry, Drummond postpones his honeymoon to investigate a mysterious London house, kidnappings and disappearing bodies. Colman plays the role handsomely and even though it is gallant nonsense, the movie is enjoyable and has its share of comical moments. In the second sequel, John Howard as Drummond is victimized by two criminals who seek revenge for the gentleman adventurer having caused the hanging of a relative. The villains kidnap Louise Campbell, who plays Drummond's love, to provoke him and after leading him and Algy through a series of terroristic incidents, capture these two as well. All are rescued by Drummond's friend, Inspector Nielson, portrayed by John Barrymore, who looks like he enjoyed donning the various disguises that he wore in the movie.

Bulldog Drummond Comes Back *see* **Bulldog Drummond**

Bulldog Drummond Escapes *see* **Bulldog Drummond**

Bulldog Drummond Strikes Back *see* **Bulldog Drummond**

Bulldog Drummond's Secret Police *see* **Bulldog Drummond**

Bulldog Jack *see* **Bulldog Drummond**

Bullets for O'Hara *see* **Public Enemy's Wife**

Bundle of Joy *see* **Bachelor Mother**

Bunker Bean *see* **His Majesty, Bunker Bean**

124 Bureau of Missing Persons

Based on an original screenplay by Robert Presnell. Story: A woman seeks her husband, who is missing. Coincidentally, he's been murdered and she is wanted for murder herself. The Bureau of Missing Persons receives a ransom note, dictating that a certain amount of money is to be paid to kidnappers by attaching the bucks to a carrier pigeon. Unperturbed by this ridiculous demand, the Bureau chief charters a plane and follows the bird to the hideout of the crooks, thus solving the case.

Warner Bros./First National, 1933 (original). Director: Roy Del Ruth; screenwriter: Robert Presnell. Cast: Bette Davis, Pat O'Brien, Glenda Farrell, Lewis Stone, Alen Jenkins, Ruth Donnelly, Hugh Herbert, Alan Dinehart, Marjorie Gateson, Tod Alexander.

• ***Missing Witnesses*** (remake). Warner Bros./First National, 1937. Director: William Clemens; screenwriters: Kenneth Gamet and Don Ryan. Cast: John Litel, Jean Dale, Dick Purcell, Raymond Hatton, Shelia Bromley, William Haade, Harland Tucker, Ben Welden.

It's not clear if the producers of this quickie meant it to be comedy but the story was certainly laughable. Bette Davis, the nominal star, didn't show up until the film had used up a half-hour of celluloid and then had only a few scenes. Bette not only might like to forget this entry in her filmography but probably has. The remake, if one chooses to call it that, deals with the investigation of the protection rackets and the witnesses needed to close down operations. It's another quickie that had little to say.

125 Burlesque

Based on the play by George Manker Watters and Arthur Hopkins. Story: Bottle-scarred second-rate burlesque comedian Skid Johnson and his long-suffering wife, Bonny, play tank towns across the country until he is offered a feature role in a Broadway show. Surprisingly, he becomes a star and takes up with old flame Sylvia Marco. Bonny files for divorce and Skid's bouts with drinking abort his new career, reducing him once again to the burlesque circuit. Realizing that Skid can't cope on stage or in life without her, Bonny drops her divorce proceedings and planned marriage to a wealthy cattleman and takes him back.

• ***The Dance of Life*** (original). Paramount, 1929. Directors: John Cromwell and Edward Sutherland; screenwriter: Benjamin Glazer. Cast: Hal Skelly (Ralph "Skid" Johnson), Nancy Carroll (Bonny Lee King), Oscar Levant (Jerry Evans), Dorothy Revier (Sylvia Marco), James Quinn, Charles D. Brown, Ralph Theadore, Al St. John.

• ***Swing High, Swing Low*** (remake). Paramount, 1937. Director: Mitchell

Leisen; screenwriters: Virginia Van Upp and Oscar Hammerstein, II. Cast: Carole Lombard (Maggie King), Fred MacMurray (Skid Johnson), Charles Butterworth (Harry), Jean Dixon (Ella), Dorothy Lamour (Anita Alvarez), Cecil Cunningham, Harvey Stevens, Charles Arnt, Franklin Pangborn.

• ***When My Baby Smiles at Me*** (remake). Twentieth Century–Fox. Director: Walter Lang; screenwriter: Lamar Trotti. Cast: Betty Grable (Bonny), Dan Dailey (Skid Johnson), Jack Oakie (Bozo), June Havoc (Guzzie), James Gleason, Richard Arlen, Vanita Wade, Kenny Williams, Jean Wallace.

Hal Skelly repeated his stage role and Nancy Carroll stood in for Barbara Stanwyck in the first filmed version of *Burlesque,* which was called *The Dance of Life* so as not to offend potential customers who considered even the name burlesque somewhat risque. It's difficult to understand why such a lovely and sensitive girl as played by Carroll would stick with a lousy bum like Skelly's character, but then love is blind, at least in the movies. Oscar Levant made his debut film appearance and showed glimpses of the sarcastic and insecure character he would play so often. The film was given "A" production values by Producer David O. Selznick, even having a two-color Technicolor sequence for one of the musical numbers.

The 1937 production of the backstage drama, entitled *Swing High, Swing Low,* had Fred MacMurray and Carole Lombard as married entertainers stranded in Panama, who part when he is offered a trumpeting job on Broadway. She divorces him, he falls on bad times, recovers, and wins her back. This version of *Burlesque* was slanted more towards comedy than the previous filming. Musical numbers included the title song by Leo Robin and Ralph Rainger and "Spring Is in the Air" by Ralph Freed and Charles Kisco.

In *When My Baby Smiles At Me,* Betty Grable and Dan Dailey are a vaudeville couple who are happy together until he becomes successful in a Broadway show. He begins to drink and becomes an alcoholic. She divorces him and plans to marry a rancher but Dailey's friend Jack Oakie gets him back on stage. The attempt isn't successful until Betty comes back to him as his partner. Musical numbers include the title song by Harry Von Tilzer and Andrew B. Sterling, and "By the Way, What Did I Do?" by Mack Gordon and Joseph Myrow.

But Not for Me *see* **Accent on Youth**

126 But the Flesh Is Weak

Based on the play *Truth Game* by Ivor Novello. Story: This is the tale of a pair of father and son fortune hunters on the prowl in London society for some rich quarry. They have nothing to offer save their personalities, which prove to be quite enough as they each find a wife, the son's being for love, the father for the real thing, money.

MGM, 1932 (original). Director: Jack Conway; screenwriter: Ivor Novello. Cast: Robert Montgomery (Max), Nora Gregor (Rosine), Heather Thatcher (Lady Joan), Edward Everett Horton (Sir George), C. Aubrey Smith (Florian), Nils Asther (Prince Paul), Frederick Kerr, Eva Moore, Forrester Harvey.

• ***Free and Easy*** (remake). MGM, 1941. Director: George Sidney; screenwriter: Marvin Borowsky. Cast: Robert Cummings (Max Clemington), Ruth Hussey (Martha Gray), Judith Anderson (Lady Joan Culver), C. Aubrey Smith (the Duke), Nigel Bruce (Florian Clemington), Reginald Owen, Tom Conway, Forrester Harvey.

Both films are hurt by a weak story with little action and basically inept acting. Other than that there's little to complain about. In the original, Robert Montgomery is the charming young fortune hunter with designs on Heather Thatcher, but who ends up happily with Nora Gregor, who is also seeking a meal ticket. C. Aubrey Smith played dear old dad also looking for any convenient female with a bankroll. In the remake, the son is Robert Cummings, the target is Judith Anderson, the consolation prize Ruth Hussey, and poppa is played by Nigel Bruce.

127 The Butter and Egg Man

Based on the play by George S. Kaufman. Story: Small-town hotel clerk Peter Jones realizes his lifetime ambition to become a Broadway producer when Jack McLure sells him a play he's certain will fail. Peter falls in love with the show's leading lady, Mary Martin, and when it becomes a smash, he sells back his share to McLure for a large profit and heads back to Chillicothe, Ohio, with Mary as his bride.

First National Pictures, 1928 (original). Silent. Director: Richard Wallace; screenwriter: Adelaide Heilbron. Cast: Jack Mulhall (Peter Jones), Greta Nissen (Mary Martin), William Demarest (Jack McLure), Gertrude Astor.

• ***The Tenderfoot*** (remake). Warner Bros., 1932. Director: Ray Enright; screenwriters: Arthur Caesar, Monty Banks and Earl Baldwin. Cast: Joe E. Brown (Peter Jones), Ginger Rogers (Ruth), Lew Cody (Sam Lehman), Vivian Oakland (Miss Martin), Robert Grieg, Wilfred Lucas, Spencer Charters.

• ***Dance, Charlie, Dance*** (remake). Warner Bros., 1937. Director: Frank MacDonald; screenwriters: Crane Wilbur and William Jacobs. Cast: Stuart Erwin (Andy Tucker), Jean Muir (Mary Mathews), Glenda Farrell (Fanny Morgan), Allen Jenkins (Alf Morgan), Addison Richards, Charles Foy, Chester Clute.

• ***An Angel from Texas*** (remake). Warner Bros., 1940. Director: Ray Enright; screenwriters: Fred Niblo, Jr. and Bertram Millhauser. Cast: Eddie Albert (Colman), Rosemary Lane (Lydia), Wayne Morris (McClure), Jane Wyman (Marge), Ronald Reagan (Allen), Ruth Terry, John Litel, Hobart Cavanaugh.

• ***Three Sailors and a Girl*** (remake). Warner Bros., 1953. Director: Roy Del Ruth; screenwriters: Roland Kibbee and Devery Freeman. Cast: Jane Powell (Penny), Gordon MacRae (Jones), Gene Nelson (Twitch), Sam Levene (Joe Woods), Jack E. Leonard (Parky), George Givot, Veda Ann Borg, Archer MacDonald.

Warner Bros. got the most out of George S. Kaufman's simple comedy, filming it six times. The one not mentioned above was called *Hello Sweetheart*, filmed in 1936 for release in Great Britain, directed by Monty Banks and starring Claude Hulbert, Gregory Ratoff and Jane Carr. The Joe E. Brown version had Mr. Big Mouth as a stupid cowboy who finds himself involved with a group of gangsters when he backs a Broadway show featuring Ginger Rogers. The 1937 film lacked Kaufman's famous satirical wit, featuring instead Stu Erwin as an innocent and gullible "angel" conned into investing his money in a failing Broadway show.

In the 1940 movie, Eddie Albert is the yokel who arrives in New York with $20,000 to visit his stage-struck girl friend, Rosemary Lane, and to buy a hotel, but instead is talked into buying a piece of a show to star his gal by shoestring producers Wayne Morris and Ronald Reagan. Finally, in 1953, Gordon MacRae, Gene Nelson and fat comic Jack E. Leonard are the three sailors who put their savings into a musical being promoted by Sam Levine. It's a flop, but with the help of MacRae's girl, Jane Powell, the boys turn it into a hit. Songs by Sammy Cahn and Sammy Fain that helped include: "There Must Be a Reason," "Face to Face," "Home Is Where the Heart Is," "My Heart Sings" and "Show Me a Happy Woman and I'll Show You a Miserable Man."

By the Light of the Silvery Moon *see* **Penrod**

C

Cabaret *see* **I Am a Camera**

Caesar and Cleopatra *see* **Cleopatra**

Cafe Hostess *see* **Her Man**

128 Caged

Based on an original screenplay by Virginia Kellogg and Bernard C. Schoenfeld. Story: Marie Allen, innocently involved in a hold-up of a boy friend, is sent to a prison for women. She is placed in a cell block supervised by sadistic guard Evelyn Harper, who does favors for prisoners who have the means with which to bribe her. Terrified by what has happened to her, Marie attempts to stay out of trouble, but here that is impossible. Her only hope is to be paroled. When this is denied her, she discovers ways to survive in the hell-hole. Not a criminal when she entered, on her eventual release she has become a hardened woman who looks like a good bet of landing back in the joint before long.

Warner Bros., 1950 (original). Director: John Cromwell; screenwriters: Virginia Kellogg and Bernard V. Schoenfeld. Cast: Eleanor Parker (Marie Allen), Agnes Moorehead (Ruth Benton), Hope Emerson (Evelyn Harper), Jan Sterling (Smoochie), Ellen Corby (Emma), Lee Patrick (Elvira Powell), Betty Garde, Olive Deering, Jane Darwell, Gertrude Michael, Shelia Stevens.

• ***House of Women*** (remake). Warner Bros., 1962. Director: Walter Doniger; screenwriter: Crane Wilbur. Cast: Shirley Knight (Erica), Andrew Duggan (Warden Cole), Constance Ford (Sophie Brice), Barbara Nichols (Candy Kane), Margaret Hayes (Zoe Stoughton), Jeanne Cooper (Helen Jennings), Virginia Gregg, Patricia Huston, Jason Evers.

Although derived from different screenplays, these two women's prison stories are very similar, dealing with an innocent girl brutalized by the conditions and lack of hope that accompany being placed behind bars at the mercy of dangerous fellow inmates and cruel guards. In the second film, Shirley Knight as the pregnant girl unwittingly involved in a crime, for which she is imprisoned, attracts the attention of the warden, who falls for her and helps plead her case with the parole board. This version of the story doesn't have the chilling impact of *Caged.* In some ways the fact that the setting is a prison seems almost incidental. In the original, Eleanor Parker did a nice job, changing from the frightened, naive girl into a tough broad who could take care of herself. As the sadistic guard, Hope Emerson is mean enough to cause nightmares of being under her control.

Cain and Mabel *see* **The Great White Way**

Cairo *see* **The Asphalt Jungle**

129 The Calendar

Based on the play by Edgar Wallace. Story: In this racehorse melodrama, a girl trainer helps prove that a horse's owner did not deliberately hobble his horse so it would lose a race. The main part of the film is a moderately interesting trial by the Jockey Club.

Gainsborough-British Lion, 1931 (original). Director and screenwriter: T.H. Hunter. Cast: Herbert Marshall (Garry), Edna Best (Mollie), Anne Grey (Wenda), Gordon Harker, Nigel Bruce.

• ***The Calendar*** (remake). GFD/Rank-Gainsborough, Great Britain, 1948. Director: Arthur Crabtree; screenwriter: Geoffrey Kerr. Cast: Greta Gynt (Wenda), John McCallum (Garry), Raymond Lovell (Willie), Sonia Holm (Mollie), Leslie Dwyer, Charles Victor, Felix Aylmer, Sydney King.

The 1931 version, also known as *Bachelor's Folly,* is hardly memorable, although the performances by Herbert Marshall as the horse's owner and Gordon Harker as a burglar-butler are quite good. In the remake, gold digger Wenda jilts racehorse owner Garry when he loses most of his money. While drunk, Garry buys a suggestion by his valet to pull his horse entered for an important race to get a better price at its next outing. This gets him in a jam, which requires burglary, forgery and the help of female trainer Sonia Helm to bail Garry out. The comedy angles of both films could have used some work. These are just old-fashioned melodramas which have not stood the test of time.

130 The Call of the Wild

Based on a book by Jack London. Story: Buck, a young Saint Bernard, becomes the lead dog of prospector Jack Thornton's dogsled. Thornton and his friend Shorty set out to find gold, but first come across Claire, adrift in the woods after losing her husband, who turns out to be the man with a claim for the gold being sought. The three become partners but need money for equipment and supplies. This they get from an Englishman named Smith, whom

Buck once bit, for which he wishes to kill the dog. Smith bets Thornton $1000 against the dog that Buck can't pull a 1000-pound load over the course of 100 yards. Buck, seeming to sense the importance of the task both to him and Thornton, comes through with a mighty effort to win the bet. After an arduous trek, Thornton, Shorty and Claire arrive at the cabin that marks the site of the gold find. While Shorty returns to Dawson to file a claim, Thornton and Claire, who have been falling in love, madly and passionately make love. The husband, Blake, believed dead, arrives, followed shortly by Smith and his men intent on having the gold for themselves. They shoot Blake and holdup Thornton but get their comeuppance when they are drowned, pulled down by the weight of the gold dust they carry on their persons, when their canoe capsizes. Blake survives and Claire chooses to stay with her husband. Thornton must console himself with his dog and his considerable fortune.

Hal Roach Studios, 1923 (original). Silent. Director and screenwriter: Fred Jackman. Cast: Buck (himself), Jack Mulhall (John Thornton), Walter Lang (Hagin), Sidney D'Albrook (Charles), Laura Roessing (Mercedes), Frank Butler (Hal).

• ***The Call of the Wild*** (remake). Twentieth Century– Fox, 1935. Director: William Wellman; screenwriters: Gene Fowler and Leonard Praskins. Cast: Clark Gable (Jack Thornton), Loretta Young (Claire Blake), Jack Oakie (Shorty Hoolihan), Reginald Owen (Smith), Frank Conroy (John Blake), Katherine DeMille, Sidney Toler, James Burke, Charles Stevens, Lalos Encinas.

• ***The Call of the Wild*** (remake). Massfilms/CCC/Izaro/Oceania/UPF, 1971. Director: Ken Annakin; screenwriters: Harry Alan Towers, Wyn Wells and Peter Yeldman. Cast: Charlton Heston, Michelle Mercier, Raimund Harmstorf, George Eastman.

The description of the story given above is that of the best production of the Jack London work, namely the one starring Clark Gable and Loretta Young. Both the 1923 silent and the 1971 film are closer to the book than the Wellman-directed picture, but this is a case in which the screenwriters improved on the story by deviating from it to provide more adventure and romance. The dog still plays a prominent role and finds romance with a she-wolf but the picture clearly centers on the heroic Gable and the lovely Young. The silent was a satisfying dog picture while the joint British, German, Spanish, French and Italian venture with Charlton Heston was generally judged to be unsatisfactory, with neither the dog nor the humans of much interest.

131 Called Back

Based on the novel by Hugh Conway and the play by Comyns Carr. Story: While in a trance, a rich young Englishman, Gilbert Vaughan, recuperating after being blinded, "sees" the murder of his mad wife's brother by her evil uncle, Dr. Manuel Ceneri.

London Films, Great Britain, 1914 (original). Silent. Director: George L. Tucker; screenwriter: Comyns Carr. Cast: Henry Ainley (Gilbert Vaughan), June Gail (Pauline March), Charles Rock (Macari), George Bellamy (Dr. Manuel Ceneri), Vincent Clive (Anthony March), Ackerman May, Judd Green.

• ***Called Back*** (remake). Real Art/Radio, Great Britain, 1933. Directors: Reginald Denham and Jack Harris; screenwriter: Denham. Cast: Franklin Dyall (Dr. Jose Manuel), Lester Matthews (Gilbert Vaughan), Dorothy Boyd (Pauline March), Anthony Ireland (Anthony March), Francis L. Sullivan, Ian Fleming, Margaret Emden, Geoffrey Goodhart.

The remake is an attempt to modernize the rather far-fetched yarn (once a very popular novel), but the effort is not too successful. The setting is changed from Italy to Spain (now that's modernization), Gilbert is only temporarily blind, and the heroine isn't mad, just merely unhappy. The evil uncle kills his nephew, squanders his niece's money and puts Gilbert in danger, but pays for his crimes by being executed in Russia.

Calling Bulldog Drummond ***see*** **Bulldog Drummond**

Calling Philo Vance ***see*** **The Kennel Murder Case**

Camelot ***see*** **Knights of the Round Table**

132 Cameo Kirby

Based on the play by Booth Tarkington and Harry Leon Wilson. Story: Gambler Cameo Kirby, playing a card game with Colonel John Randall and crooked player Colonel Moreau, wins, but Randall loses his homestead to Moreau. Kirby, planning to return it to Randall, wins the deed to the property from Moreau, but Randall in desperation has committed suicide. Kirby kills Moreau in a duel and takes refuge in the Randall country home where Colonel Randall's heirs turn on him, believing that he had killed Moreau in cold blood. However, Kirby is able to justify himself and marries Adele, Randall's daughter.

Fox Film Corp., 1923 (original). Silent. Director: John Ford; screenwriter: Robert N. Lee. Cast: John Gilbert (Cameo Kirby), Gertrude Olmstead (Adele Randall), Alan Hale (Colonel Moreau), Eric Mayne (Colonel Randall), William E. Lawrence, Richard Tucker, Phillips Smalley, Jack McDonald, Jean Arthur.

• ***Cameo Kirby*** (remake). Fox Film Corp., 1930. Director: Irving Cummings; screenwriter: Marion Orth. Cast: Harold Murray (Cameo Kirby), Norma Terris (Adele Randall), Douglas Gilmore (Jack Moreau), Robert Edeson (Colonel Randall), Myrna Loy, Charles Morton, Stephin Fetchit, George MacFarlane, John Hyams.

Except for the addition of dialog and a few songs, the remake is much the same as the silent version of the story of an honest gambler who almost gets lynched for doing the honorable thing, and not only saves his life but wins the daughter of the man to whom he had hoped to return the deed to his cotton plantation, won from him by an unscrupulous gambler in a crooked game. The story was also filmed by Paramount in 1914.

133 The Cameraman

Based on a screenplay by Clyde Bruckman, Lew Lipton and Richard Schayer. Story: Luke Shannon is a tintype photographer who falls in love with

Sally, a secretary with Hearst Newsreel. He sells his camera so that he can buy an old movie camera, hoping to sell some of his footage to Hearst and afford to marry his girl. Sally gives Luke a tip that a tong war in Chinatown is about to break out. Luke risks his skin to cover all the dangers of this feud and then discovers that he has no film in his camera. The next day, while filming a regatta, Luke must rescue Sally, who has fallen overboard from the boat of a cowardly Hearst cameraman who deserts her to save himself. As a hero, Luke gets a job and his girl.

MGM, 1928 (original). Silent. Director: Howard Sedgwick; screenwriters: Clyde Bruckman, Lew Lipton and Richard Schayer. Cast: Buster Keaton (Luke Shannon), Marceline Day (Sally), Harold Goodwin (Stagg), Harry Gribbon (Cop), Sidney Bracy (Editor).

• ***Watch the Birdie*** (remake). MGM, 1950. Director: Jack Donohue; screenwriters: Ivan Tors, Devery Freeman and Harry Ruskin. Cast: Red Skelton (Rusty Cammeron/Pop Cammeron/Grandpop Cammeron), Arlene Dahl (Lucia Corlane), Ann Miller (Miss Lucky Vista), Leon Ames (Grantland D. Farns), Pam Britton (Mrs. Shanway), Richard Rober, Dick Wessel.

Keaton in his "Lonesome Luke" role still breaks audiences up with his deadpan expression and hilarious antics. He produced the film and so had control over its quality, which if not quite on a par with his *The General* is at least an excellent silent visual comedy. In the remake, Skelton is the operator of a photography store who comes to the assistance of Arlene Dahl, head of a home-building project, whose plans are being threatened by the shady dealings of crooked land speculators. The film has style and Skelton proves once again that he is a great clown. A standout in this cornball comedy is Ann Miller, always ready to show her beautiful gams in a cheesecake picture for any sponsor.

134 Camille

Based on the play by Alexandre Dumas, fils, adapted from his novel *La Dame aux Camelias.* Story: Beautiful Parisian courtesan Marguerite Gautier, known as La Dame aux Camelias or simply Camille because of her fondness for camelias, is supported by a series of lovers, including Baron de Varville. One day at the theater she meets dashing young Armand Duval and they both fall deeply in love. While spending time in the country with Armand, she is visited by his father, who tells her if Armand marries her his career and whole life will be ruined. She leaves him, lying by telling him she prefers the rich men of Paris. She contracts tuberculosis, is forced to sell her possessions and is left alone, forgotten by all the men who once showered attention on her. Dying, she cannot forget Armand, who, when he learns of her condition, comes to her and pledges his eternal love. She dies happily, knowing that Armand still loves her.

• ***La Dame aux Camelias*** (original). Denmark Films, 1907. Silent. Director: Viggo Larsen. Cast: Oda Alstrup (Marguerite Gautier), Lauritz Olsen (Armand Duval).

• ***La Dame aux Camelias*** (remake). Italy, 1909. Silent. Director: Ugo Falena. Cast: Vittoria Fepanto (Marguerite Gautier), Alberto Nipoti (Armand Duval).

• ***La Dame aux Camelias*** (remake). French-American Film Co., 1912. Silent. Directors: Andre Calmettes and Henri Pouctal. Cast: Sarah Bernhardt (Marguerite), Paul Capellani (Armand), Henri Desfontaines (Count de Varville), Henri Pouctal (M. Duval).

• ***Camille*** (remake). Champion Film Co., 1912. Silent. Director: Herbert Brendon; screenwriter: Lawrence McGill. Cast: Gertrude Shipman (Marguerite), Irving Cummings (Armand), Arthur Evers (Count de Varville), Susanne Willis (Madame Prudence), Evelyn Frances (Nichette), Lawrence McGill (M. Duval), John Genung, Charles Hopkins, Mary Hall.

• ***Camille*** (subtitle: ***A Modern Camille***) (remake). World Film Corporation, 1915. Silent. Director: Albert Capellani; screenwriter: Frances Marion. Cast: Clara Kimball Young (Marguerite), Paul Capellani (Armand), Robert Cummings (M. Duval), Frederick C. Truesdale (Count de Varville), Lillian Cook, Louise Ducey, William Jefferson, Stanhope Wheatcroft, Edward Kimball, Dan Baker, Beryle Morhage, Ruth Gordon.

• ***Camille*** (remake). Italy, 1915. Silent. Director: Baldassare Negroni. Cast: Helen Hesperia (Marguerite), Gustavo Serena (Armand).

• ***Camille*** (remake). Italy, 1915. Silent. Director: Gustavo Serena. Cast: Francesca Bertini (Marguerite), Gustavo Serena (Armand).

• ***Camille*** (remake). Fox Film Co., 1917. Silent. Director: J. Gordon Edwards; screenwriter: Adrian Johnson. Cast: Theda Bara (Marguerite), Albert Roscoe (Armand), Walter Law (de Varville), Alice Gale, Claire Whitney, Glenn White.

• ***Primavera, die Kameliendame*** (remake). Germany, 1917. Silent. Director: Paul Leni. Cast: Erna Morena (Marguerite), Harry Liedtke (Armand).

• ***Camille*** (remake). Metro Pictures, 1921. Silent. Director: Ray C. Smallwood; screenwriter: June Mathis. Cast: Alla Nazimova (Marguerite), Rudolph Valentino (Armand), Arthur Hoyt (de Varville), William Orlamond (M. Duval), Zeffie Tillbury (Madame Prudence), Rex Cherryman, Edward Connelly, Patsy Ruth Miller.

• ***The Lover of Camille*** (remake). Warner Bros., 1924. Silent. Director: Harry Beaumont; based on Sacha Guitry's play *Deburau*. Cast: Monte Blue (Jean Gaspard Deburau), Marie Prevost (Marie Duplessis), Williard Louis (Robillard).

• ***Camille*** (remake). Sweden, 1925. Silent. Director: Olof Molander. Cast: Tora Teje (Marguerite), Uno Henning (Armand), Ivan Hedqvist (M. Duval), Sven Bergvall (de Varville).

• ***Camille*** (remake). First National Pictures, 1927. Silent. Director: Fred Niblo; screenwriter: Fred De Gresac. Cast: Norma Talmadge (Marguerite), Gilbert Roland (Armand), Rose Dione (Prudence), Oscar Beregi (de Varville), Lilyan Tashman (Olympe), Maurice Costello (M. Duval), Harvey Clark, Helen Jerome Eddy, Alec B. Francis, Albert Conti.

• ***La Dame aux Camelias*** (remake). France, Films Fernand Rivers Productions. Director: Fernand Rivers; screenwriter: Albert Gance. Cast: Yvonne Printemps (Marguerite), Pierre Fresnay (Armand), Jane Marken (Prudence), Andre Dubosc (Le Duc), Irma Genin (Nichette), Andree Lafayette (Olympe),

Edy Debray (de Varville), Lugne-Poe (M. Duval), Roland Armontel, Armand Lurville, Pierre Morin.

• ***Camille*** (remake). MGM, 1936. Director: George Cukor; screenwriter: Zoe Akins. Cast: Greta Garbo (Marguerite), Robert Taylor (Armand), Lionel Barrymore (M. Duval), Laura Hope Crews (Prudence), Henry Daniell (de Varville), Elizabeth Allen (Nichette), Jessie Ralph, Rex O'Malley, Douglas Walton, E.E. Clive, Leonore Ulric, Russell Hardie, Martin Ballou, Joan Brodel, June Wilkins.

• ***The Lost One (La Traviata)*** (remake). Columbia Pictures, Italy, 1948. Director: Carmine Gallone; libretto: F.M. Piave; music: Giuseppe Verdi. Cast: Nelly Corradi (Violetta Valery), Gino Mattera (Alfredo Germont), Manfredi Polverosi (Georg Germont), Flora Marino (Flora Bervoix), Massimo Serato, Nerio Bernardi, Onelia Fineschi (singing voice of Violetta), Tio Gobbi (singing voice of Georg Germont).

• ***La Dame aux Camelias*** (remake). France, 1952. Director and screenwriter: Raymond Bernard. Cast: Micheline Presle (Marguerite), Roland Alexandre (Armand), Gino Cervi (M. Duval), Jean Paredes (de Varville).

• ***Camelia, Passion Sauvage*** (remake). Mexico, 1952. Director: Roberto Gavaldon. Cast: Maria Felia (Camelia), Jorge Mistral (Rafael).

• ***Fille d'Amour*** (remake). France-Italy, 1953. Director: Vittorio Cottafavi. Cast: Barbara Laage (Rita), Armando Francioli (Armand).

• ***La Belle Lola, une Dame aux Camelias*** (remake). Spain-Italy-France, 1962. Director: Alfonso Balcazar. Cast: Sarita Montiel (Lola-Marguerite), Antonio Cifariello (Armand).

• ***La Traviata*** (remake). B.L. Vision/I.C.I.T. Films, Italy, 1967. Director: Mario Lanfranchi; libretto: Mario Lanfranchi; music: Giuseppe Verdi. Cast: Anna Moffo (Violetta), Franco Bonisolli (Alfredo Germont), Gino Bechi (Georg Germont), Mafalda Micheluzzi (Flora Bervoix), Gianna Lollini, Afro Poli, Arturo La Porta, Glauco Scarlini.

Other screen versions of *Camille* were made in China in 1930 under the name *Wild Grass;* in Germany the same year as *The Red Peacock;* in Egypt in 1941 as *La Dame aux Camelias;* in Mexico in 1944 as *La Dame de las Camelias;* in Italy in 1953 as *La Traviata, la Signorasenza Comelie;* in Argentina in 1953 as *La Mujer de las Camelias;* in a French-Italian production in 1953 as *Fille d'Amour, Traviata '53;* an independent production called *Camille 2000* in 1969; and a Greek production in 1968 called *The Girl at Luna Park.*

Marguerite Gautier has been played with varying degrees of success by many of the finest stage and film dramatic actresses. Producers seem to believe that audiences will never tire of the tragic story of a kept woman who dies just when she has found real love. Of the productions, those most favorably reviewed include the productions starring Sarah Bernhardt (1912), Alla Nazimova (1921), and Greta Garbo (1936).

Nazimova's version modernized the story and her performance was described by *Variety* as "the finest acting with which the silver screen has been graced." Surprisingly, the film eliminated the famous scene of Camille dying in Armand's arms.

The 1924 Warner Bros. production was not based on Dumas' play but rather on *Deburau* by Sacha Guitry. However, it does have its Camille who has an affair with Deburau, a famous clown of the French stage; she takes him for everything, and years later dies in his arms.

The First National release of 1927, starring Norma Talmadge, was judged to be lacking in vitality and the punch to make it a first class piece of film. Miss Talmadge was described as never more beautiful and Gilbert Roland as quite handsome, but the famous death scene left critics unmoved. As the most famous of modern Camilles, Greta Garbo was nominated for an Academy Award for her performance but did not win. *New York Times* critic Frank S. Nugent described her performance as "eloquent, tragic, yet restrained." He adds that "she is as incomparable as legend tells us that Bernhardt was." Howard Barnes of the *New York Herald Tribune* said: "As the tragic Dumas heroine, she floods a romantic museum piece with glamor and artistry, making it a haunting and moving photoplay by the sheer magic of her acting."

135 The Cannonball Run

Based on an original screenplay by Brock Yates. Story: There really is no story to this noisy, light-hearted romp which in many ways resembles the star's *Smokey and the Bandit* films. However, this one appears to be made up as it goes along. Familiar celebrities, either as themselves or one of their recognizable characters, are entries in an illegal coast-to-coast race. Their adventures are pointless and the whole film rests on a series of visual gags, old at the time of the Keystone Kops.

Golden Harvest Productions, 1980 (original). Director: Hal Needham; screenwriter: Brock Yates. Cast: Burt Reynolds, Roger Moore, Farah Fawcett, Dom DeLuise, Dean Martin, Sammy Davis, Jr., Jack Elam, Adrienne Barbeau, Terry Bradshaw, Jackie Chan, Jamie Farr, Bert Convy, Peter Fonda, Molly Picon.

• ***The Cannonball Run II*** (sequel). Golden Harvest, 1983. Director: Hal Needham; screenwriters: Hal Needham, Albert S. Ruddy and Harvey Miller. Cast: Burt Reynolds, Dom DeLuise, Sammy Davis, Jr., Dean Martin, Jamie Farr, Telly Savalas, Shirley MacLaine, Frank Sinatra, Susan Anton, Catherine Bach, Richard Kiel, Tim Conway, Sid Caesar, Don Knotts, Ricardo Montalban, Jim Nabors.

In the remake, an Arab sheik (whose son Jamie Farr didn't win the first race) puts up a million-dollar prize for a Cannonball Run II to give the lad another chance. It's even more disjointed than the original, if that's possible. Both features consist of a series of nonperformances by groups of well-known movie and TV personalities who seemingly have gotten together to see just how gullible the public really is. Quite a bit, considering the success at the box office of these movies.

The Cannonball Run II *see* **The Cannonball Run**

Captain Applejack *see* **Strangers of the Night**

136 Captain Blood

Based on the book *Captain Blood, His Odyssey* by Rafael Sabatini. Story: Young Irish physician Peter Blood is exiled as a slave to Barbados for doctoring a wounded political enemy of the English king. He is bought by Colonel Bishop at the request of his niece Arabella, who finds him spirited and interesting. After suffering greatly in the service of the cruel Bishop, he leads a group of other slaves in an escape, captures a Spanish galleon and terrorizes Caribbean privateers. He is offered a commission in the English Navy, defeats the French at Port Royal, is rewarded by being named the governor of Jamaica and marries Arabella.

Vitagraph Co. of America, 1924 (original). Silent. Director: David Smith; screenwriter: Jay Pilcher. Cast: J. Warren Kerrigan (Captain Peter Blood), Jean Paige (Arabella Bishop), Charlotte Merriam (Mary Traill), James Morrison (Jeremy Pitt), Allan Forrest (Lord Julian Wade), Bertram Grassby (Don Diego), Wilfrid North (Colonel Bishop), Jack Curtis, Otto Matieson, Robert Bolder.

• ***Captain Blood*** (remake). Warner Bros., 1935. Director: Michael Curtiz; screenwriter: Casey Robinson. Cast: Errol Flynn (Peter Blood), Olivia de Havilland (Arabella Bishop), Basil Rathbone (Levasseur), Lionel Atwill (Colonel Bishop), Ross Alexander (Jeremy Pitt), Guy Kibbee (Hagthorpe), Henry Stephenson (Lord Willoughby), Robert Barrat, Hobart Cavanaugh, Donald Meek, J. Carroll Naish, Pedro de Cordova.

• ***Fortunes of Captain Blood*** (remake). Columbia Pictures, 1950. Director: Gordon Douglas; screenwriters: Michael Hogan, Robert Libott and Frank Burt. Cast: Louis Hayward (Captain Peter Blood), Patricia Medina (Isabelita Sotomayer), George Macready (Marquis de Riconete), Alfonso Bedoya, Dona Drake, Lowell Gilmore, Wilton Graff, Curt Bois, Lumsden Hare, William Bevan.

• ***Captain Pirate*** (remake). Columbia Pictures, 1952. Director: Ralph Murphy; screenwriters: Robert Libott, Frank Burt and Meredyth Lucas. Cast: Louis Hayward (Peter Blood), Patricia Medina (Dona Isabela), John Sutton (Hilary Evans), Charles Irwin, George Givot, Rex Evans, Ted de Corsia, Malu Gatica, Sven Hugo Borg.

In addition to the films mentioned above, Errol Flynn's son Sean appeared in *Son of Captain Blood* in 1962. While the lad had his father's good looks and smile, he did not have that special ingredient that made the elder Flynn such a winning performer. We suppose it's called "star quality." *Captain Blood* (1935) is the film that established Flynn as a star. He was so handsome and charming that both men and women were delighted with him. It is safe to say that he was an original and his unique talents thrilled audiences for years to come in many exciting adventure and action films.

The silent film starring Kerrigan as Peter Blood was also an exciting piece of film, with the leading performer in good form. Louis Hayward, a minor swashbuckler, appeared in the role twice. In the first he preys on Spanish ships rather than French, but other than that the story is much as before. In his second appearance, he comes out of retirement to hunt down a new pirate, played by John Sutton, who has been using Blood's name as he made brutal raids on

In one of her usual poses at this point in her career, Olivia de Havilland looks up admiringly at Errol Flynn, her hero in Captain Blood *(Warner Bros., 1935).*

a series of coastal towns. Can't have someone sullying one's bad name, can one?

Captain Clegg *see* **Dr. Syn**

137 Captain January

Based on a story by Laura E. Roberts. Story: Lighthouse keeper Jeremiah Judkins finds a little girl washed ashore, tied to a spar. He adopts the child, calls her Captain January, and she helps him run the lighthouse. One night he falls asleep and the light goes out, resulting in the beaching of a yacht. One of the passengers, Isabelle Morton, sees the child and identifies her as the daughter of her sister who was killed in a sea accident. The sister takes her niece with her, but the youngster is unhappy in her new home. At the first opportunity she makes her way back to the lighthouse keeper. Isabelle and her husband, seeing the close bond between the child and Judkins, make room for him in their home so they can be together.

Principal Pictures, 1924 (original). Silent. Director: Edward F. Cline; screenwriters: Eve Unsell and John Grey. Cast: Hobart Bosworth (Jeremiah Judkins), Baby Peggy (Captain January), Irene Rich (Isabelle Morton), Lincoln Stedman, Harry T. Morey, Barbara Tennant, John Merkyl, Emmett King.

Louis Hayward and Patricia Medina look deeply into each other's eyes in Fortunes of Captain Blood *(Columbia, 1950). Louis doesn't seem to be enjoying himself too much, however.*

• ***Captain January*** (remake). Twentieth Century–Fox, 1936. Director: David Butler; screenwriters: Sam Hellman, Gladys Lehman and Harry Tugend. Cast: Shirley Temple (Star), Guy Kibbee (Captain January), Slim Summerville (Captain Nazro), June Lang (Mary Marshall), Buddy Ebsen (Paul Roberts), Sara Haden, Jane Darwell, Jerry Tucker, Nelle Walker, George Irving.

The silent version is a sweet, sentimental story, guaranteed to pull a few tears from even the most hardened soul. In the remake, Kibbee, the Captain January of this piece, and Summerville are two crusty old seamen who share a deep love for the baby named Star, reared by Kibbee until a mean truant officer puts a scare into the proceedings. Buddy Ebsen and June Lang provide the little love angle in the story that's not directed towards the precocious child, played winningly by the little trooper Shirley Temple. Shirley dances a cute routine with Ebsen and she sings "Codfish Ball" and "The Right Somebody to Love."

Captain Pirate ***see*** **Captain Blood**

Captain Sinbad ***see*** **Sinbad the Sailor**

138 The Card

Based on the novel by Arnold Bennett. Story: Denny Machin, son of a washerwoman, progresses to the position of mayor by using his wits. He turns his back on a countess and a gold digger and marries the daughter of a man who once sacked him when he was his future father-in-law's clerk.

Ideal, Great Britain, 1922 (original). Silent. Director: A.V. Gamble; screenwriter: Eliot Stannard. Cast: Laddie Cliff (Denny Machin), Hilda Cowley (Ruth Earp), Joan Barry (Nellie Cotterill), Mary Dibley (Countess of Chell), Sydney Paxton (Councillor Cotterill), Dora Gregory, Norman Page, Arthur Cleave, Jack Denton, Frank Goddard.

• ***The Card*** (remake). British Film Makers, Great Britain, 1952. Director: Ronald Neame; screenwriter: Eric Ambler. Cast: Alec Guinness (Edward Henry Machin), Glynis Johns (Ruth Earp), Valerie Hobson (Countess of Chell), Petula Clark (Nellie Cotterill), Edward Chapman, Veronica Turleigh, George Devine, Joan Hickson, Frank Pettingell, Gibb McLaughlin, Michael Horden, Alison Leggatt, Wilfrid Hyde-White, Henry Edwards.

In the remake, Guinness' cheeky performance is most engaging and makes this basically a one-character farce. All other members of the cast are there so that Sir Alec can play off of them—and he does it admirably.

139 The Cardboard Lover

Based on the play *Dans sa candeur naive* by Jacques Deval. Story: Sally, an American making the grand tour of Europe, sets her cap for French tennis star Andre. Sally finds that Andre's sweetheart, Simone, is not true to him. Andre hires Sally to keep him away from Simone and the girl really takes her job seriously, dogging the couple no matter where they go. She even moves into Andre's house to convince Simone that he is through with her. Andre comes to love his eccentric employee and marries her.

Cosmopolitan/MGM, 1928 (original). Silent. Director: Robert Z. Leonard; screenwriter: F. Hugh Herbert. Cast: Marion Davies (Sally), Jetta Goudal (Simone), Nils Asther (Andre), Andres de Segurola, Tenen Holtz, Pepe Lederer.

• ***The Passionate Plumber*** (remake). MGM, 1932. Director: Edward Sedgwick; screenwriter: Laurence E. Johnson. Cast: Buster Keaton (Elmer), Jimmy Durante (McCracken), Irene Purcell (Patricia), Polly Moran (Albine), Gilbert Roland, Mona Maris, Maude Eburne.

• ***Her Cardboard Lover*** (remake). MGM, 1942. Director: George Cukor; screenwriters: Jacques Deval, John Collier, Anthony Veiller and William H. Wright. Cast: Norma Shearer (Consuelo Croyden), Robert Taylor (Terry Trindale), George Sanders (Tony Barling), Frank McHugh, Elizabeth Patterson, Chill Wills.

The story was also filmed in England in 1929 as *Her Cardboard Lover* and a French version, *Le Plombier Amoureux,* was made in 1932. One might believe that any story which was filmed this many times must have something going for it. One would be wrong. The comedy is paper-thin and even with the teaming of Buster Keaton and Jimmy Durante, the movie is left with a silly plot and few laughs. In his version, Keaton is led on by Irene Purcell to make her boyfriend, Gilbert Roland, jealous. Sadly, Norma Shearer chose the vehicle to be her last movie, retiring from films at the age of 42, still looking lovely. Her swan song was a box-office failure.

The Caribbean Mystery *see* **Murder in Trinidad**

140 Un Carnet du Bal

Based on an original screenplay by Julien Duvivier and others. Story: Having recently been widowed, Christine Sugere discovers an old dance program from her first ball of many years before. Her memories of the ball have been enhanced by the passage of time. Determined to seek out the six men who were on her card and recapture the romance of the well-remembered ball, she is disenchanted when she discovers her beaux leading mediocre and even questionable lives. Finally realizing the futility of living in an idealized past, she finds purpose in life in helping the son of her recently deceased husband whom she loved.

Production Sigma, France, 1937 (original). Director: Julien Duvivier; screenwriters: Jean Sarment, Pierre Wolff, Bernard Zimmer, Henri Jeanson and Julien Duvivier. Cast: Marie Bell (Christine Sugere), Francoise Rosay (Mme. Audie), Louis Jouvet (Jo-Pierre Verdier), Harry Baur (Fr. Alain Regnault), Pierre-Richard (Eric Irvin), Raimu (Patusset), Pierre Blanchar (Dr. Thierry), Fernandel (Fabien Coutissol), Robert Lynes, Roger Legris.

• ***Lydia*** (remake). United Artists, 1941. Director: Julien Duvivier; screenwriters: Ben Hecht and Sam Hoffenstein. Cast: Merle Oberon (Lydia MacMillan), Edna May Oliver (Granny), Alan Marshal (Richard), Joseph Cotten (Michael), Hans Yaray (Frank), George Reeves (Bob), John Halliday, Sara Allgood, Billy Ray, Frank Conlan.

Duvivier's French production consists of eight episodes, not all of equal quality. At the time of its release, the film was given high praise and many honors. Seen today, it doesn't hold up well, but it is a wonderful opportunity to see a distinguished cast of French stars in one film. The remake, *Lydia,* is quite good, with Merle Oberon aging from 20 to 60 in the story of a woman recalling the lovers in her life over that period, including Joseph Cotten as a young physician who falls in love with her first, followed by George Reeves as a Harvard athlete, and Hans Yaray as a blind musician, whom she inspires to write a concerto. But, the most memorable is Alan Marshal as a seafaring lover, who, when she brings together these men of her past, doesn't recall the romance. Oberon is excellent in this interesting character study.

Carnival *see* **The Ballet Girl**

Carousel *see* **Liliom**

141 The Carpetbaggers

Based on the novel by Harold Robbins. Story: In an obvious effort to fictionalize the life of Howard Hughes, this *film à clef* is the story of Jonas Cord, Jr., an unemotional man who inherits his father's fortune and runs it into some real money by shrewd business transactions and a complete lack of concern for whomever he hurts in the process. His treatment of women is about as insensitive as can be imagined. He enters the movie business and as with everything else he is successful, but compulsively so. By the end of the picture, he has lost every friend and loyal associate he has ever made, surrounded instead by mere retainers.

Paramount, 1964 (original). Director: Edward Dmytryk; screenwriter: John Michael Hayes. Cast: George Peppard (Jonas Cord, Jr.), Alan Ladd (Nevada Smith), Robert Cummings (Dan Pierce), Martha Hyer (Jennie Denton), Elizabeth Ashley (Monica Winthrop), Lew Ayres (McAllister), Martin Balsam (Bernard B. Norman), Carroll Baker (Rina Cord), Ralph Taeger, Archie Moore, Leif Erickson, Tom Tully.

• ***Nevada Smith*** (prequel). Paramount, 1966. Director: Henry Hathaway; screenwriter: John Michael Hayes. Cast: Steve McQueen (Nevada Smith/Max Sand), Karl Malden (Tom Fitch), Brian Keith (Jonas Cord), Arthur Kennedy (Bill Bowdre), Suzanne Pleshette (Pilar), Raf Vallone (Father Zaccardi), Janet Margolin, Pat Hingle, Howard Da Silva, Martin Landau, Paul Fix, Sam Sand.

Hollywood was able to get two pictures from Harold Robbins' seamy novel. The first tells the story of the rise and rise of Jonas Cord, an unfeeling and cruel man to whom money is just a way to keep score as he wheels and deals in a series of business ventures. Most of these are begun because of Cord's incredible curiosity and a compulsion to be all-knowledgeable about the project; he is free to do precisely what he wishes, until such time as he becomes bored with it. His reaction to women and friends is precisely the same. In the prequel, Steve McQueen is Max Sand, whose parents were slaughtered by a band of outlaws. As Nevada Smith he tracks each down and exacts his revenge. In the process he is befriended by Jonas Cord, Sr., who is met briefly in the Peppard movie as the vicious and hard-hearted daddy who marries Junior's love.

Peppard is perfectly cold and unemotional as the unfeeling tycoon. Alan Ladd, in his last movie, demonstrates he still possesses some star quality as the aging Nevada Smith who becomes a movie star, portraying his own Western character. In the prequel, Steve McQueen rivals Peppard for never putting on a happy face.

142 Carrefour

Based on a story by Hans Kafka. Story: A French manufacturer who suffered shell-shock during World War I suddenly finds himself the center of a blackmail plot. He is accused of having been a pre-war criminal whom the police still seek. The victim takes his accusers to court and he wins his defamation case when a stranger comes forth to testify that he was with the criminal when he died. The stranger, who turns out to be a more clever blackmailer than the first, then tells the manufacturer that indeed he is the sought criminal. The manufacturer is about to turn the stranger over to the police when the latter whistles a tune that brings back a memory of the former's pre-war activities. Resigned to the fact that before he had lost his memory, he was a criminal and fearing he will not be allowed to continue his rehabilitated life, the manufacturer makes a decision to turn himself in to the authorities. Before he is forced to act on this plan, he is reprieved when the manufacturer's former mistress, now the mistress of the stranger, shoots and kills the latter.

Eclair-Journal, France, 1932 (original). Director: Kurt Bernhardt; screenwriter: Hans Kafka. Cast: Charles Vanel, Jules Berry, Suzy Prim, Tania Fedor, Marcelle Geniat, Jean Caludio, J. Tissler, Argentin, Otto Walburg, Paul Amiot.

• ***Dead Man's Shoes*** (remake). Associated British Films, 1939. Director: Thomas Bentley; screenwriters: Hans Kafka and Nina Jarvis. Cast: Leslie Banks (Roger de Vetheuil), Joan Marion (Viola de Vetheuil), Geoffrey Atkins (Paul de Vetheuil), Wilfred Lawson (Lucien Sarrou), Judy Kelly (Michelle Allan), Nancy Price, Walter Hudd, Peter Bull, Henry Oscar, Ludwig Stossel.

• ***Crossroads*** (remake). MGM, 1942. Director: Jack Conway; screenwriter: Guy Trosper. Cast: William Powell (David Talbot), Hedy Lamarr (Lucienne Talbot), Claire Trevor (Michele Allaine), Basil Rathbone (Henri Sarrou), Margaret Wycherly (Mme. Pelletier), Felix Bressart, Sig Rumann, H.B. Warner, Phillip Merivale, Vladimir Sokoloff.

The French filming of Kafka's tale of a man with a double personality is intriguing melodrama, although the remakes are more pedestrian. In the roles of the manufacturer, strange witness and mistress, Charles Vanel, Jules Berry and Suzy Prim, respectively, give thoughtful performances. The British version is less impressive and the U.S. production with William Powell as a prominent French Foreign Office official having suffered amnesia in a train accident is only so-so, despite the surprise ending in which Powell vindicates himself of charges of having been a criminal before losing his memory.

143 Carry on Nurse

Based on an idea by Patrick Cargill and Jack Searle. Story: The film consists of a series of farcical, childish, and hilarious episodes which take place in a British men's hospital ward. It makes fun of all the shortcomings of socialized medicine, teaching hospitals, pompous doctors, authoritarian head nurses, sexy angels of mercy, operations, bedpans, pills, examinations, temperature takings, and weird patients. It runs the gamut from slapstick to burlesque-house humor. The bawdy, suggestive and naughty business is the kind of thing one expects from British TV comedian Benny Hill, but is done better here.

Anglo Amalgamated/Governor Films, 1960 (original). Director: Gerald Thomas; screenwriter: Norman Hudis. Cast: Shirley Eaton (Dorothy Denton), Kenneth Connor (Bernie Bishop), Hattie Jacques (Matron), Charles Hawtrey (Hinton), Terence Longdon (Ted York), Bill Owen (Percy Hickson), Leslie Phillips (Jack Bell), Joan Sims (Stella Dawson), Kenneth Williams (Oliver Reckitt), Wilfrid Hyde-White, Susan Stephen, Nichael Medwin, Susan Beaumont, Ann Firbank, Joan Hickson, Irene Handl, Cyril Chamberlain, Rosalind Knight.

• ***Twice Around the Daffodils*** (remake). Anglo Amalgamated, 1962. Director: Gerald Thomas; screenwriter: Norman Hudis. Cast: Juliet Mills (Catty), Donald Sinden (Ian Richards), Donald Houston (John Rhodes), Ronald Lewis

(Bob White), Kenneth Williams (Harry Halfpenny), Andrew Ray (Chris Walker), Lance Percival (George Logg), Joan Sims (Harriet), Jill Ireland (Janet), Nanette Newman, Amanda Reiss, Shelia Hancock, Renee Houston, Mary Powell.

Carry on Nurse is one of the most popular of the many *Carry On* films, proving a big box-office hit in the United States. To celebrate the use to which a daffodil is put to make fun of a patient with a private room in the film, employees of many theaters passed out daffodils to customers on leaving the auditorium. To enjoy this work, it's best to be in a silly, slightly raunchy mood. The second film, with the same director and screenwriter while not quite a remake or sequel, attempted to do for a TB sanatorium what the original did for a general hospital. It is based on the play *A Ring for Catty*, by Patrick Cargill and Jack Searle, who had the idea for *Carry on Nurse*. As a satirical piece using sight gags to make fun of most everything in British society, it was not as successful at the box office as the previous work.

Casbah *see* **Pepe-le-Moko**

The Case of the Black Parrot *see* **In the Next Room**

144 The Cat and the Canary

Based on the play by John Willard. Story: The family of Ambrose West gather at his Hudson River castle, Glencliff Manor, for a midnight reading of his will. Having feared hereditary insanity in his family, he has left everything to a distant relative, Annabelle West. Attempts are made to drive Annabelle mad when it is learned that a second will exists which decrees that she will be disinherited if she proves mentally unbalanced. She is terrorized, a cousin is attacked by a "monster," the lawyer disappears and murder is committed before one of the relatives is exposed as being behind the bizarre happenings.

Universal Pictures, 1927 (original). Silent. Director: Paul Leni; screenwriters: Robert F. Hill and Alfred A. Cohn. Cast: Laura La Plante (Annabelle West), Creighton Hale (Paul Jones), Martha Mattox ("Mammy" Pleasant), Tully Marshall (Roger Crosby), Arthur Edmund Carewe (Harry Blythe), Flora Finch (Susan Sillsby), Gertrude Astor, Forrest Stanley, George Seigmann, Lucien Littlefield.

• ***The Cat Creeps*** (remake). Universal, 1930. Director: Rupert Julien; screenwriters: Gladys Lehman and William Hurlibut. Cast: Helen Twelvetrees (Annabelle West), Raymond Hackett (Paul Jones), Blanche Frederici ("Mammy" Pleasant), Lawrence Grant (Roger Crosby), Theodore von Eltz (Harry Blythe), Elizabeth Peterson (Susan Sillsby), Lilyan Tashman, Neil Hamilton, Montague Love, Jean Hersholt.

• ***The Cat and the Canary*** (remake). Paramount, 1939. Director: Elliot Nugent; screenwriters: Walter De Leon and Lynn Starling. Cast: Paulette Goddard (Joyce Norman), Bob Hope (Wally Campbell), Gale Sondergaard (Miss Lu), John Beal (Fred Blythe), Douglass Montgomery (Charlie Wilder), Elizabeth Patterson (Aunt Susan), Nydia Westman, George Zucco, John Wray.

• *The Cat and the Canary* (remake). Gala/Grenadier Productions, Great Britain, 1979. Director and screenwriter: Radley Metzger. Cast: Honor Blackman, Michael Callan, Edward Fox, Wendy Hiller, Beatrix Lehmann, Olivia Hussey, Daniel Massey, Carol Lynley, Peter McEnery, Wilfrid Hyde-White.

Critics praised the filming of the mystery drama *The Cat and the Canary* in 1927, being particularly impressed with director Leni's clever shift of the character's moods so that by the end, everyone is properly suspected of being the villain.

The sound remake in 1930 is not in any way memorable, consisting of pedestrian performances and unimaginative directing. The best thing about actress Twelvetrees was always her name.

The 1939 version remains a classic, mostly due to the decision to play the story for laughs, supplied by the very talented Bob Hope. His one-liners such as "They tell me he was so crooked that when he died they had to screw him into the ground," and his comeback to the question if he believed that dead people came back ("You mean like Republicans") not only had audiences in stitches but eased the tension of a still very scary movie. Paulette Goddard's performance is much more than a foil to Old "ski-nose." She manages to look delectable even when on the verge of hysterics. Of the supporting performers, no one could ever approach Sondergaard for looking sinister.

The 1979 remake couldn't find the magic even though it had an impressive cast. Despite a spirited beginning, rather than add to the production values the performers get in the way of each other, resulting in a weary film.

The Cat Creeps *see* **The Cat and the Canary**

Catch My Soul *see* **Othello**

Caught in the Draft *see* **Fog Over Frisco**

145 Ceiling Zero

Based on a play by Frank Wead. Story: This salute to the pioneers in the early days of commercial airline flights zeros in on Dizzy Davis, a daring if not always rational pilot, a whiz with the ladies, and the man who is indirectly responsible for the death of a close friend. In the end, his heroic demise atones for his indiscretions, signaling the message that commercial flying is safe if the pilots are a part of a cooperative team.

Warner Bros., 1936. Director: Howard Hawks; screenwriter: Frank Wead. Cast: James Cagney (Dizzy Davis), Pat O'Brien (Jake Lee), June Travis (Tommy Thomas), Stuart Erwin (Texas Clarke), Barton MacLane (Al Stone), Henry Wadsworth, Martha Tibbet, Isabel Jewel, Craig Reynolds, Richard Purcell.

• ***International Squadron*** (remake). Warner Bros., 1941. Director: Lewis Seiler; screenwriters: Barry Trivers and Kenneth Gamet. Cast: Ronald Reagan (Jimmy Grant), Olympe Bradna (Jeanette), James Stephenson (Squadron Leader), William Lundigan (Lt. Rog Wilkins), Joan Parry (Connie), Reginald Denny (Wing Commander), Cliff Edwards, Julie Bishop, Michael Aines.

These are examples of formula pictures. The audience is tipped off early as to what to expect. With a name like Dizzy, one just knows that Cagney is into one of his cocky roles in which no one can tell him anything. It's a foregone conclusion that O'Brien will play a level-headed official who admires Cagney personally but doesn't care for his behavior. Stu Erwin acts and looks so innocent that one just knows he will prove expendable and serve as an object lesson to the irresponsible Cagney, who before the fade-out will redeem himself by paying with his life. The remake, while perhaps a little less obvious because the players are not as familiar, also has enough clues to make it better than an even bet. Shortly into the movie, Ronald Reagan, a brash pilot who has joined the International Squad of the RAF, will cause the death of some innocent because of his refusal to live by the rules and he in turn will suffer an end in the air trying to make amends for his blunders.

Cesar *see* **Fanny**

The Challenge *see* **Bulldog Drummond**

Challenge for Robin Hood *see* **Robin Hood**

146 Challenge to Lassie

Based on the book *Greyfriar's Bobby* by Eleanor Atkinson. Story: In Scotland of the 1800s, Jock Gray, a sheepherder, raises Lassie from a puppy and trains her to become a first-rate sheepdog. When Gray is killed after a beating by thugs, he is buried in the churchyard at Greyfriar. Lassie takes up a position as sentinel of his grave, sleeping near her master every night. John Traill, innkeeper and friend of Jock's, cares for the dog, but the animal runs afoul of local ordinances which make it illegal for dogs to run loose and especially to make the graveyard their home. An overzealous policeman, Sgt. Davie, takes Lassie into custody. At a hearing to decide what is to be done with the dog, the magistrate is impressed and touched when the children of the village come forth with their pennies to pay for a license to save Lassie. His ruling is that Lassie is to have the freedom of the city with a special collar proclaiming the right.

MGM, 1949 (original). Director: Richard Thorpe; screenwriter: William Ludwig. Cast: Edmund Gwenn (John Traill), Donald Crisp (Jock Gray), Geraldine Brooks (Susan Brown), Reginald Owen (Sgt. Davie), Alan Webb, Ross Ford, Henry Stephenson, Alan Napier, Sara Allgood.

• ***Greyfriar's Bobby*** (remake). Walt Disney/Buena Vista, 1961. Director: Don Chaffey; screenwriter: Robert Westerby. Cast: Donald Crisp (James Brown), Laurence Naismith (Mr. Traill), Alec MacKenzie (Old Jock), Duncan MacRae (Constable MacLean), Andrew Cruickshank, Gordon Jackson, Rosalie Crutchley, Freda Jackson.

Both versions of the story possess considerable charm and heart. The low-key approaches to this story (based on fact) allow for several talented character actors to develop wonderfully real identities. The performances of Gwenn, Crisp and Owen in the original are beautiful, while in the remake, where the dog is now a Skye terrier, Crisp and Naismith are impeccable as two high-principled and stubborn men who fight over the loyal dog.

147 The Champ

Based on an original story by Francis Marion. Story: Andy is a down-and-out boxer, raising his ten-year old son, Dink, who in turn takes care of his drunken, gambling father, affectionately called Champ by the lad. The love between the two is very special. When the boys want a horse, Champ wins one for him, which the boy names Little Champ. At a race in which the horse is entered, they run into Champ's ex-wife and her new husband. She wants her son back but he can't adjust to life away from his father. Dink returns in time to be with Champ, who collapses and dies after winning a brutal match. Dink then goes to live a less exciting but normal life with his mother and stepfather.

MGM, 1931 (original). Director: King Vidor; screenwriter: Leonard Praskins. Cast: Wallace Beery (Champ/Andy), Jackie Cooper (Dink), Irene Rich (Linda), Roscoe Ates (Sponge), Edward Brophy (Tim), Hale Hamilton (Tony).

• ***The Clown*** (remake). MGM, 1952. Director: Robert Z. Leonard; screenwriter: Martin Rackin. Cast: Red Skelton (Dodo Delwyn), Jane Greer (Paula Henderson), Tim Matheson (Dink Delwyn), Loring Smith (Goldie), Philip Ober (Ralph Henderson), Lou Lubin, Jonathan Cott, Don Beddoe, Steve Forest.

• ***The Champ*** (remake). United Artists, 1979. Director: Franco Zeffirelli; screenwriter: Walter Newman. Cast: Jon Voight (Billy), Faye Dunaway (Anne), Ricky Schroeder (T.J.), Jack Warden (Jackie), Arthur Hill (Mike), Strother Martin, Joan Blondell, Mary Jo Catlett, Elisha Cook.

Wallace Beery won an Academy Award for his performance as the irresponsible but lovable boxer. Jackie Cooper, one of the best cryers of child actors, caused many in the audience to reach for their hankies in this frightfully sentimental picture. In the remake, the role was given to Ricky Schroeder, who's usual expression is one of perplexity rather than sorrow. Jon Voight and Faye Dunaway should have fired their agents for getting them involved in this ancient story. Voight plays a Florida horse trainer who has a chance as a championship boxer and Dunaway is his disapproving ex-wife. In the disguised remake, Skelton portrays an alcoholic comedian, inspired by his son into making a comeback. It's pure bathos with Skelton on the downswing of his movie career.

148 The Charge of the Light Brigade

Based on the poem by Alfred, Lord Tennyson. Story: Major Geoffrey Vickers, who has witnessed the slaughter of men, women and children after they had surrendered their isolated garrison outpost to the evil Indian ruler Surat Khan, switches the orders of the British high command. As a result, a force of 600 cavalrymen ride into the "valley of death" at Balaclava during the Crimean War, to face cannon and a force five times their number. Vickers' reason for this is that his old enemy, Surat Khan, is with the Russian troops, and the major wishes his troops to have their revenge for the massacre of their friends and family

That great child weeper Jackie Cooper gently reaches out and touches his father, washed-up prizefighter Wallace Beery in The Champ *(MGM, 1939).*

members. Before going into battle, Vickers makes certain that he saves the life of his younger brother, Captain Perry Vickers, who shares the love of Elsa Campbell, to whom Geoffrey was engaged before she met his dashing brother.

• ***The Charge of the Light Brigade*** (remake). Warner Bros., 1936. Director: Michael Curtiz; screenwriters: Michel Jacoby and Rowland Leigh. Cast: Errol Flynn (Major Geoffrey Vickers), Olivia de Havilland (Elsa Campbell), Patric Knowles (Capt. Perry Vickers), Donald Crisp (Colonel Campbell), Henry Stephenson (Sir Charles Macefield), C. Henry Gordon (Surat Khan), Nigel Bruce, David Niven, Spring Byington, G.P. Huntley, Jr., E.E. Clive, Lumsden Hare.

• ***The Charge of the Light Brigade*** (remake). United Artists/Woodfall, Great Britain, 1968. Director: Tony Richardson; screenwriter: Charles Wood. Cast: Trevor Howard (Lord Cardigan), Vanessa Redgrave (Clarissa), John Gielgud

Ricky Shroeder and his father, boxer Jon Voight, are counting the house instead of listening to manager Jack Warden between rounds in The Champ, *(MGM, 1979).*

(Lord Raglan), Harry Andrews (Lord Lucian), Jill Bennett (Mrs. Duberly), David Hemmings (Captain Nolan), Peter Bowles, Mark Burns, Howard Marion Crawford, Mark Dignam.

Silent versions of the story of the famous Crimean charge at Balaclava were made in 1903, 1912, 1914, and 1928, the latter going by the name *Jaws of Hell.*

Whereas the 1936 film depicts the brave charge of the 600 (which inspired Tennyson's poem) to be the act of a single man intent on revenge for an earlier tragic defeat, the 1968 version lays the blame at the foot of the generals and colonial officials as well as those in charge back in England who didn't understand the situation. In either case, as is usually true in war, brave young men go to their certain death, unaware of why or what is hoped to be accomplished with their sacrifice.

The film ensured the incomparable Flynn's superstar status and one can't imagine any other performer who could pull off such an outrageous stunt and have audiences accepting it as not only plausible but heroic. Others in the cast whose performances deserve note include C. Henry Gordon as the wily native leader, a baddy if ever there was one, and Donald Crisp as the noble Colonel Campbell. He bravely consoles his men as they await their executions by the conquerors to whom they had surrendered with a false promise that they would be treated fairly as prisoners of war. In the several films that Olivia de Havilland made with Flynn, little was expected of her, except to be a staunch supporter and admirer of the great hero. This film was no exception and her performance gave only little hint of the tremendous acting ability she would display in years to come. Patric Knowles was as handsome as Flynn and almost as dashing, but there was only room for one such romantic hero in Hollywood.

The remake contained some splendid moments but on the whole was rather disappointing. No one in the cast, certainly not David Hemmings, had the charisma of Flynn. The whole thing seemed to lack direction as if the producers and director were trying to tell several stories, rather than one rousing adventure yarn.

149 Charley's Aunt

Based on the play by Brandon Thomas and the musical version by George Abbott. Story: Oxford University students Charley Wykeham and Jack Chesney have won the permission of Stephen Spettigue to have his niece, Amy, and his ward, Kitty, visit them at school, assured that Charley's wealthy widowed aunt, Donna Lucia d'Alvadorez, on her way from Brazil, will be serving as chaperone. When Donna Lucia's arrival is delayed, the boys convince classmate Lord Fancourt Babberley to impersonate her. Jack's financially strapped father, Sir Francis Chesney, visits him and vies with Spettigue for the affection and millions of Donna Lucia, who is Babberley in drag. When Donna Lucia arrives, she sizes up the situation and presents herself as Mrs. Beverly-Smythe. Jack's father falls in love with Mrs. Beverly-Smythe, whom he believes to be as impoverished as himself. Meanwhile, infatuated by the phony Donna Lucia, Spettigue agrees to the engagements of his niece to Charley and his ward to Jack. Donna Lucia reveals her true identity and accepts Sir Francis' marriage proposal. At last Lord Babberley is free of his disguise and is able to turn his attentions to his true love, Ela Delahay.

Christie Film Company, 1925 (original). Silent. Director: Scott Sidney; screenwriter: F. McGrew Willis. Cast: Sydney Chaplin (Lord Fancourt Babberley), Mary Akin (Amy Spettigue), Eulalie Jensen (Donna Lucia d'Alvadorez), Priscilla Bonner (Kitty Verdun), David James (Jack Chesney), Jimmy Harrison (Charley Wykeham), James E. Page (Stephen Spettigue), Phillips Smalley (Sir Francis Chesney), Ethel Shannon (Ela Delahay).

• ***Charley's Aunt*** (remake). Christie Film Company, 1930. Director: Al Christie; screenwriter; F. McGrew Willis. Cast: Charles Ruggles (Lord Fancourt Babberley), June Collyer (Amy Spettigue), Doris Lloyd (Donna Lucia), Flora Sheffield (Kitty Verdun), Rodney McLennon (Jack Chesney), Hugh Williams (Charley Wykeham), Halliwell Hobbes (Mr. Spettigue), Phillips Smalley (Sir Francis Chesney), Flora Le Breton (Ela Delahay).

• ***Charley's (Big Hearted) Aunt*** (remake). Gainsborough Films, 1940. Director: Walter Forde; screenwriters: Marriott Edgar and Val Guest. Cast: Arthur Askey (Arthur Linden-Jones), Phyllis Calvert (Betty Forsythe), Richard Murdoch (Stinker Burton), Moore Marriott (Jerry), Graham Moffatt (Albert Brown), Jeanne de Casalis (Aunt Lucy), J.H. Roberts, Felix Alymer, Wally Patch.

• ***Charley's Aunt*** (remake). Twentieth Century–Fox, 1941. Director: Archie

Mayo; screenwriter: George Seaton. Cast: Jack Benny (Fancourt "Babbs" Babberley), Anne Baxter (Amy Spettigue), Kay Francis (Donna Lucia), Arleen Whelan (Kitty Verdun), James Ellison (Jack Chesney), Richard Haydn (Charley Wykeham), Edmund Gwenn (Mr. Spettigue), Laird Cregar (Sir Francis Chesney), Ernest Cossart, Morton Lowry, Lionel Pape.

• ***Where's Charley?*** (remake). Warner Bros., 1952. Director: David Butler; screenwriter: John Monks, Jr.. Cast: Ray Bolger (Charley Wykeham), Allyn McLerie (Amy Spettigue), Margaretta Scott (Donna Lucia), Mary Germaine (Kitty Verdun), Robert Shackleton (Jack Chesney), Horace Cooper (Mr. Spettigue), Howard Marion Crawford (Sir Francis Chesney), Henry Hewitt, H.G. Stoker, Martin Miller.

• ***Charley's Tante*** (remake). Constantin Release, Germany, 1956. Director: Hans Qest; screenwriter: Gustav Kampendonk. Cast: Walter Giller (Charley Sallmann), Hertha Feiler (Charlotta Ramirez), Elisa Loti (Ulla), Henry Ruchmann (Dr. Dernberg), Ina Peters (Britto), Ruth Stephen (Mona), Hans Leibelt, Claus Biederstaedt.

• ***La Marraine de Charley*** (remake). Plazza-Fides Films, France, 1959. Director: Pierre Chevalier; screenwriters: Jean Girault and Pierre Chevalier. Cast: Fernand Raynaud (Charley), Anne Auberson (Rosie), Pierre Bertin (de St. Servan), Jean-Pierre Cassel (Claude), Sacha Briquet (Jacques), Claude Vega (Lue), Jean Juillard (Raymond), Renee Caron (Annick), Monique Vita (Minou), Albert Michel, Germaine Delbat, Lucien Barjon.

Other versions of *Charley's Aunt* were produced in Sweden in 1926; in Germany in 1934 as *Charley's Tante;* in France in 1935 as *La Marriane de Charley;* in Austria in 1963 as *Charley's Tante* and in Spain in 1967 as *Charley's Aunt in a Mini-Skirt.*

The first screen version of *Charley's Aunt* starred Charlie Chaplin's older brother Sydney as the gentleman in drag. The same production company remade a sound version in 1930 with Charles Ruggles swishing the famous skirts. Jack Benny donned curls and the ever-present costume in the 1941 version and was judged to be at his funniest. With Ray Bolger re-creating his Broadway success, the person of Lord Babberley had disappeared and Charley Wykeham moved center stage to impersonate his aunt. The Technicolor film was a delight, particularly when the Frank Loesser songs such as "Once in Love with Amy" were sung and danced by Bolger. The various foreign film versions made certain cultural adjustments in the play, but kept the basic plot, sharing the laughs of this preposterously simple and charming story with the whole world.

Charley's Aunt in a Mini-Skirt *see* **Charley's Aunt**

Charley's Big Hearted Aunt *see* **Charley's Aunt**

Charley's Tante *see* **Charley's Aunt**

150 Charlie Chan Carries On

Based on the novel by Earl Derr Biggers. Story: In what amounts to being the true start of a long series of movies featuring Charlie Chan, the Honolulu Oriental detective solves a murder mystery that baffles Scotland yard. A wealthy American is found dead in a London hotel and the corpse is the only one in the film that doesn't have at least one wisecrack in this flippant but entertaining mystery. The plots of Charlie Chan movies hardly matter. Of far more importance is what quaint aphorisms will the non–Oriental, who portrays Chan, utter as he resolutely moves towards the solution to the crime.

Fox Film Corp., 1931 (original). Director: Hamilton McFadden; screenwriters: Philip Klein and Barry Connors. Cast: Warner Oland (Charlie Chan), John Garrick (Mark Kenaway), Marguerite Churchill (Palema Potter), Warren Hymer (Max Minchin), Marjorie White (Sadie Minchin), C. Henry Gordon, William Holden, George Brent, Peter Gawthorne, John T. Murray.

• ***Charlie Chan's Murder Cruise*** (sequel). Twentieth Century–Fox, 1940. Director: Eugene Ford; screenwriters: Robertson White and Lester Ziffren. Cast: Sidney Toler (Charlie Chan), Marjorie Weaver (Paula Drake), Lionel Atwill (Dr. Suderman), Sen Yung (Jimmy Chan), Robert Lowery (Dick Kenyon), Don Beddoe, Leo G. Carroll, Cora Witherspoon, Kay Linaker.

In the second film, a Scotland Yard inspector is killed in Charlie's Honolulu office just as he is about to reveal his plan to trap a murderer on a world cruise party. When a member of the party is strangled in his hotel room, Charlie joins the cruise and by the time the ship ties up in San Francisco, he's ready for the denouement.

Charlie Chan's Courage *see* **The Chinese Parrot**

Charlie Chan's Murder Case *see* **Charlie Chan Carries On**

151 The Charm School

Based on a story by Alice Duer Miller. Story: Car salesman Austin Bevans inherits a girl's school and since he feels that acquiring grace is more important than acquiring knowledge for girls, he throws out the academic program and turns the institution into a charm school. He falls for one of the students, Elsie, whose grandfather gives Austin a job when a new will is discovered, dispossessing him of the school. Elsie is disappointed in this, because her grandfather had treated Austin as an inferior, but she comes around and they plan to marry.

Famous Players/Paramount Pictures, 1921 (original). Silent. Director and screenwriter: James Cruze. Cast: Wallace Reid (Austin Bevans), Lila Lee (Elsie), Adele Farrington (Mrs. Rolles), Beulah Bains, Edwin Stevens, Grace Morse, Patricia Magee.

• ***Someone to Love*** (remake). Famous Players/Paramount Pictures, 1928. Silent. Director: F. Richard Jones; screenwriters: Keene Thompson and Monte Brice. Cast: Charles "Buddy" Rogers (William Shelby), Mary Brian (Joan Kendricks), William Austin (Aubrey Weems), Jack Oakie (Michael Casey), James Kirkwood, Mary Alden.

• ***Sweetie*** (remake). Paramount Pictures, 1929. Director: Frank Tuttle; screenwriters: George Marion, Jr. and Lloyd Corrigan. Cast: Nancy Carroll

(Barbara Pell), Stanley Smith (Biff Bentley), Jack Oakie (Tap-Tap Thompson), Helen Kane (Helen Fry), Stuart Erwin, William Austin, Wallace MacDonald, Charles Sellon.

• ***Collegiate*** (remake). Paramount Pictures, 1936. Director: Ralph Murphy; screenwriters: Walter DeLeon and Francis Martin. Cast: Jack Oakie (Jerry Craig), Joe Penner (Joe), Ned Sparks ("Scoop" Oakland), Frances Langford (Miss Hay), Betty Grable (Dorothy), Lynne Overman, Betty Jean Cooper, Mack Gordon.

These inconsequential pieces of fluff are entertaining in a small way but do not leave a lasting impression. In the first remake, Rogers is a music store clerk who impresses Mary Brian's father by affirming that he won't ask for her hand until he has made a success of himself. Through a misunderstanding, Brian believes he's a fortune hunter and breaks off their relationship. He becomes the director of an exclusive girl's school and when Brian learns that she has misjudged Rogers they get her father's permission to marry. In the second remake, the sexes are changed to have perky Nancy Carroll as a chorus girl who inherits a college. The early talkie is filled with flappers and songs such as George Marion, Jr., and Richard Whiting's "My Sweeter Than Sweet" and Al Lewis, Abner Silver and Al Sherman's "He's So Unusual" boop-boop-a-booped by Helen Kane. In the third remake, finally making it to the leading role, Jack Oakie inherits a girl's school and converts it into a music and dancing school with himself as Dean. The two best Mack Gordon and Harry Revel songs were "You Hit the Spot" and "I Feel Like a Feather in the Breeze." Then of course there is the matter of the legs of a young Betty Grable.

The Chaser ***see*** **The Nuisance**

Chayka ***see*** **The Seagull**

The Cheap Detective ***see*** **The Maltese Falcon**

152 Cheaper by the Dozen

Based on the novel by Frank B. Gilbreth, Jr. and Ernestine Gilbreth Carey. Story: It's the nostalgic, romanticized reminiscences of Frank Jr. and Ernestine Gilbreth of their lives with their parents, Frank and Lillian Gilbreth, and their ten brothers and sisters. Their parents are efficiency experts who pioneered time motion studies. The film is full of amusing episodes involving the domestic adjustments needed to cope with such a large, loving family, ending on a sad note with the death of the father.

Twentieth Century–Fox, 1950 (original). Director: Walter Lang; screenwriter: Lamarr Trotti. Cast: Clifton Webb (Frank Bunker Gilbreth), Myrna Loy (Mrs. Lillian Gilbreth), Jeanne Crain (Ann Gilbreth), Betty Lynn (Libby Lancaster), Edgar Buchanan (Doctor Burton), Barbara Bates (Ernestine), Mildred Natwick, Sara Allgood, Anthony Sykes, Roddy McCaskill, Norman Ollestad.

• ***Belles on Their Toes*** (sequel). Twentieth Century–Fox, 1952. Director: Henry Levin; screenwriters: Phoebe and Henry Ephron. Cast: Jeanne Crain

(Ann Gilbreth), Myrna Loy (Lillian Gilbreth), Debra Paget (Martha), Jeffrey Hunter (Dr. Bob Grayson), Edward Arnold (Sam Harper), Hoagy Carmichael (Tom Bracken), Barbara Bates (Ernestine), Robert Arthur (Frank Gilbreth), Verna Felton, Roddy McCaskill, Tina Thompson, Teddy Driver, Tommy Ivo.

Neither film is really a biopic of the Gilbreth family, any more than TV's *The Waltons* is the true story of Earl Hamner, Jr.s', clan. Instead the two films are fictionalized features based on real people and events fondly remembered. In the sequel, the story of the Gilbreth family continues after the father's death, concentrating on the awakening of feelings of love by the eldest daughter, Ann, and the courtship of the still very attractive mother by businessman Sam Harper, played by Edward Arnold. Although fond of him, Lillian is much too busy raising her large brood of children, pursuing her career and lecturing on women's rights. These are sweet, old-fashioned stories of life in a small town with people surrounded by family and friends, which if not as it really was, is how many with romantic notions believe it should have been.

153 The Cheat

Based on the story by Hector Turnbull. Story: Wealthy South American beauty Carmelita De Cordoba is disinherited by her father when she elopes with New York broker Dudley Drake, rather than marry the elderly man to whom she is promised. In need of money, she falls into the clutches of Rao-Singh, a crook posing as an Indian prince. When she seeks to repay him with mere money, he refuses her check and cruelly brands her with the family crest as a cheat. Carmelita shoots and wounds the bogus prince, with Drake arriving in time to take the rap. He is acquitted at his trial when Carmelita shows the brand on her shoulder and her tormentor is attacked by an angry courtroom mob.

Famous Players–Lasky/Paramount Pictures, 1923 (original). Silent. Director: George Fitzmaurice; screenwriter: Ouida Bergere. Cast: Pola Negri (Carmelita De Cordoba), Jack Holt (Dudley Drake), Charles De Roche (Claude Mace/Prince Rao-Singh), Dorothy Cummings, Robert Schable, Charles Stevenson.

• ***The Cheat*** (remake). Paramount Pictures, 1931. Director: George Abbott; screenwriter: Harry Harvey. Cast: Tallulah Bankhead (Elsa Carlyle), Irving Pichel (Hardy Livingston), Harvey Stephens (Jeffrey Carlyle), Jay Fassett, Ann Andrews, Arthur Hohl, Willard Dashiell, Robert Strange.

The first to film the story of a woman suffering a branding at the hands of an oriental rather than sacrifice her virtue was Cecil B. De Mille in 1915, who always knew that a lot of good sex could be portrayed on screen as long as you made it clear you were against it. His stars were Fannie Ward and Hollywood's only Japanese star, Sessue Hayakawa. Prints of this film vividly show the power of the latter as an actor usually forced to portray villains with lustful designs on lily-white ladies. The story is implausible and particularly so with Tallulah Bankhead, as audiences found it hard to swallow that the latter would become virginal when she had a quick way to pay back the loan of funds to replace those she had stolen from a charity bazaar to pay off her gambling debts. Some felt that she had already compromised her morality just a bit.

154 Cheating Cheaters

Based on the play by Max Mancin. Story: A crooked lawyer gets a young woman, Ruth, acquitted of a shoplifting charge and places her with the Brocktons, a gang of crooks. They move into a seaside home, planning to steal the jewels of the Palmer family, who live next door. To help the plan along, Ruth flirts with Tom Palmer, who becomes infatuated with her and wants her to run away with him, but she refuses. Tom is caught red-handed in the Brockton mansion stealing their jewels at the very same time the Brocktons are robbing the Palmer home. Everyone is arrested and Ruth reveals that she is actually an undercover detective. She arranges for Tom to be paroled in her custody and they are off to be married.

Selig Productions, 1919 (original). Silent. Director: Allan Dwan; screenwriter: Kathryn Stuart. Cast: Clara Kimball Young (Ruth Brockton), Anna E. Nilsson (Grace Palmer), Jack Holt (Tom Palmer), Frederick Burton (George Brockton), Frank Campeau (Steve Wilson), Nicholas Dunaew, Mayme Kelso, Tully Marshall, Edwin Stevens, Jess Singleton.

• ***Cheating Cheaters*** (remake). Universal Pictures, 1927. Silent. Director: Edward Laemmle; screenwriter: James T. O'Donohue. Cast: Betty Compson (Nan Carey), Kenneth Harlan (Tom Palmer), Sylvia Ashton (Mrs. Brockton), Erwin Connelly (Mr. Brockton), Maude Turner Gordon (Mrs. Palmer), E.J. Ratcliff (Mr. Palmer), Lucien Littlefield, Eddie Gribbon, Cesare Gravine.

• ***Cheating Cheaters*** (remake). Universal Pictures, 1934. Director: Richard Thorpe; screenwriters: Gladys Unger and Allen Rivkin. Cast: Fay Wray (Nan Brockton), Cesar Romero (Tom Palmer), Hugh O'Connell (Steve Wilson), Henry Armetta (Tony Verdi), Francis L. Sullivan (Dr. Brockton), Wallis Clark, John T. Murray, George Barraud, Minna Gombell.

The idea of two gangs of jewel thieves plotting to rob each other with a mysterious female detective thrown in for good measure would seem to suggest that some decent comical situations might evolve. Perhaps they did at the time the story was filmed in 1919, but by the time of the sound version in 1934, the plot was rather creaky and even the surprises weren't surprising. Critics praised Clara Kimball Young for her performance in the original, appreciated Betty Compson in the first remake, and yawned in speaking of Fay Wray in the last version. It does seem that there might be a possibility here, if the girl was played by someone like Barbara Streisand's character in *What's Up Doc.*

155 Chicago

Based on the play by Maurice Watkins. Story: Amos Hart steals money from the safe of his lawyer, Flynn, an unscrupulous man who, for a large sum of money, promises to get Hart's wife, Roxie, acquitted of the murder of her lover, car salesman Casley. Roxie enjoys all the attention and publicity of the trial but despite all the evidence against her she is found not guilty. At home after the trial, two detectives arrive to accuse Amos of the theft of the lawyer's money but the maid, Katie, has removed it before they can begin a search. After they are gone, Amos announces he is through with Roxie, who is still basking in her notoriety, and will marry Katie.

Pathe/De Mille Pictures, 1927 (original). Silent. Director: Frank Urson; screenwriter: Lenore J. Coffee. Cast: Phyllis Haver (Roxie Hart), Victor Varconi (Amos Hart), Eugene Pallette (Casley), Robert Edeson (Flynn), Virginia Bradford (Katie), Clarence Burton, Warner Richmond, T. Roy Barnes, Sidney D'Albrook, Otto Lederer, May Robson.

• ***Roxie Hart*** (remake). Twentieth Century–Fox, 1942. Director: William A. Wellman; screenwriter: Nunnally Johnson. Cast: Ginger Rogers (Roxie Hart), Adolphe Menjou (Bill Flynn), George Montgomery (Homer Howard), Lynne Overmann (Jake Callahan), Nigel Bruce, Phil Silvers, Sarah Allgood, William Frawley, Spring Byington, Ted North, Helene Reynolds, George Chandler.

The original had its many good moments as a rather ridiculous satire of American jusisprudence, with fine performances from most of the cast. In the remake, the emphasis is placed on Roxie's trial, which she really enjoys. She's a dancer accused of a murder committed by her husband and she believes the publicity will be good for her career. She's more than willing to go along with any silly stunt suggested by cynical reporters as long as it lands her on the front page of their newspapers. In a courtroom travesty, Menjou, as her lawyer, has her use an unborn child gag to sway the jury's sympathy and she is acquitted. When the trial is over she dumps her husband in favor of cute reporter Montgomery, who has fallen in love with her. Wellman's direction keeps this farce moving at a frantic pace.

156 Chick

Based on the novel by Edgar Wallace. Story: College hall porter Chick Beane comes into a peerage and is exploited by a gang of financial sharks. He supports a child welfare bill, and marries Gwenda Maynard posing as a widow.

British Lion, Great Britain, 1928 (original). Silent. Director: A.V. Bramble; screenwriter: Eliot Stannard. Cast: Bramwell Fletcher (Chick Beane), Triliby Clark (Gwenda Maynard), Chili Bouchier (Minnie Jarvis), Rex Maurice (Marquis of Mansur), Edward O'Neill, John Cromer.

• ***Chick*** (remake). British and Dominions/United Artists, Great Britain, 1936. Director: Michael Hankinson; screenwriters: Irving Leroy, Daniel Wheddon, Gerard Fairlie, Cyril Gardner and D.B. Wyndham-Lewis. Cast: Sydney Howard (Chick Beane), Betty Ann Davies (Peggy), Fred Conyngham (Sir Anthony Monsard), Cecil Humphries (Sturgis), Mai Bacon, Wallace Geoffrey, Aubrey Mather.

The two versions of the Edgar Wallace novel attempt to demonstrate, but are not completely successful, that an average person with a bit of gumption can handle not only the pressures of a peerage but also see through the plot of some crooks who claim to have found oil on the lord's estate.

Chicken Wagon Family *see* **The Dixie Merchant**

A Child Is Born *see* **Life Begins**

Child of Divorce *see* **Wednesday's Child**

157 La Chienne

Based on the novel by Georges de la Fouchardiere. Story: Middle-aged bank clerk Legrand interrupts a pimp beating his prostitute, Lulu, and then falls for the wily girl. He is induced to embezzle money to buy her gifts. Her demands become more frequent and expensive and when Legrand discovers that she has not broken her relationship with her pimp, Dede, he stabs her to death. The police arrest Dede for the murder and when Legrand maintains his silence, the man is sent to the guillotine. Nagged with guilt and the shame his actions have brought him, Legrand becomes a derelict.

Braunberger-Richebe, 1931 (original). Director and screenwriter: Jean Renoir. Cast: Michel Simon (Legrand), Janie Mareze (Lulu), Georges Famount (Dede), Magadeleine Berubet, Jean Gehret.

• ***Scarlet Street*** (remake). Universal Pictures, 1945. Director: Fritz Lang; screenwriter: Dudley Nichols. Cast: Edward G. Robinson (Christopher Cross), Joan Bennett (Kitty March), Dan Duryea (Johnny Prince), Margaret Lindsay, Rosalind Ivan, Jess Barker, Arthur Loft, Samuel S. Hinds, Vladimir Sokoloff.

Not subject to the demands of the Hays Office, *La Chienne* was considered a bit too racy for American audiences, not only because of the presence of a pimp and a prostitute, but also because the guilty party was not punished in accordance with the Motion Picture Code of Decency. In the remake, Robinson, a married clerk, is dragged down to degradation by a scheming Bennett. He is a brilliant artist who allows her to sign his work as her own. When they begin to sell and Robinson discovers that Duryea is behind the scheme, he murders her and allows Duryea to be executed for the crime. He is tormented by the knowledge of what he has done and the fact that he can't sell his paintings, for fear the authorities will figure what really happened. The latter film, a fine example of *film noir,* was brilliantly directed by Lang and acted by Robinson, Bennett and Duryea. It's a gloomy piece but extremely entertaining.

158 The Children's Hour

Based on the play by Lillian Hellman. Story: In Hellman's play, the setting is a girl's school run by two young, unmarried women about whom a spiteful child spreads the rumor than they are involved in a lesbian relationship. The lie causes the closing of the school and the suicide of one of the teachers.

• ***These Three*** (original). United Artists, 1936. Director: William Wyler; screenwriter: Lillian Hellman. Cast: Miriam Hopkins (Martha Dobie), Merle Oberon (Karen Wright), Joel McCrea (Dr. Joseph Cardin), Catherine Doucet (Mrs. Lily Mortar), Alma Kruger (Mrs. Tilford), Bonita Granville (Mary Tilford), Marcia Mae Jones (Rosalie Wells), Carmencita Johnson, Mary Ann Durkin, Margaret Hamilton, Marie Louise Cooper.

• ***The Children's Hour*** (remake). United Artists, 1961. Director: William Wyler; screenwriters: Lillian Hellman and John Michael Hayes. Cast: Shirley MacLaine (Martha Dobie), Audrey Hepburn (Karen Wright), James Garner

(Dr. Joseph Cardin), Karen Balkin (Mary Tilford), Fay Bainter (Mrs. Tilford), Miriam Hopkins (Lily Mortar).

Hollywood believed that Samuel Goldwyn had gone mad when he bought the Hellman play with the stipulation, from the Hays Office, that any film produced from it could not use either the title or the lesbian angle. Goldwyn was wise enough to realize that the story was about the effect of a vicious lie, not the nature of the lie, and so he hired Hellman to write a screenplay in which the rumor of misconduct by the teachers was based on the more acceptable notions of heterosexual misbehavior. Fifteen years later, director Wyler was able to use the original title and original premise but it didn't make it a better drama than the bowdlerized version.

Although the performances of Miriam Hopkins and Merle Oberon as the accused teachers in the 1936 film were among their very best, as was that of Alma Kruger as the grandmother who believes her granddaughter's malicious lie, the most memorable performances for many were those of Bonita Granville as the sadistic child and Marcia Mae Jones as her disciple. Granville masterfully portrayed the truly malevolent youngster, establishing herself with this role as Hollywood's little female brat in many pictures to follow. Jones was superb as the fearful child, coerced due to her weakness to back up the lies of the dominant Miss Granville. In this film, the producer and director opted for what seems a cop-out "happy" ending, allowing Oberon and her fiancé to reunite, but despite this the movie is a powerful statement. For those who like to spot boo-boos in movies, catch Margaret Hamilton as the maid pulling on Bonita Granville to lock her in her room after her grandmother has, to her mortification, finally understood that the child is a pathological liar who, with the grandmother's help, has nearly ruined the lives of three innocent people. Rather than speak the girl's character name, Hamilton says, "Come here, Bonita."

In the remake, the reference to lesbianism was allowed and the one teacher, MacLaine as Martha Dobie, did commit suicide after deciding that at least on her part, there might have been some truth to the accusation of an "unnatural relationship," even though it had not been acted upon. The performances were generally credible, with Fay Bainter as the grandmother and Miriam Hopkins, here playing the silly aunt of one of the teachers, really quite excellent. Unfortunately, Karen Balkin, as the malicious child, did not produce a performance as memorable as had Bonita Granville.

159 The Chinese Bungalow

Based on the play by Marian Osmond and James Corbett. Story: When Englishwoman Charlotte comes to China to stay with her sister Sadie who has married a Chinese millionaire, Yuan Sing, she discovers that Sadie is having an affair with a neighboring planter, Harold Marquess. The mandarin, by now in love with his sister-in-law, poisons Harold. The planter's brother, Richard (also in love with Charlotte), and Sing drink to her from goblets, one of which they know contains poison, and Sing dies.

Stoll, Great Britain, 1926 (original). Silent. Director: Sinclair Hill; screenwriters: Marian Osmond and James Corbett. Cast: Matheson Lang (Yuan Sing),

Genevieve Townsend (Charlotte), Juliette Compton (Sadie), Shayle Gardner (Richard Marquess), George Thirlwell (Harold Marquess), Malcolm Tod, Clifford McLaglen.

• ***The Chinese Bungalow*** (remake). Neo-Art, Great Britain, 1930. Directors and screenwriters: J.B. Williams and Arthur W. Barnes. Cast: Matheson Lang (Yuan Sing), Jill Esmond (Jean), Anna Neagle (Charlotte), Ballard Berkeley (Richard Marquess), Derek Williams (Harold Marquess).

• ***The Chinese Bungalow*** (remake). Pennant/British Lion, Great Britain, 1940. Director: George King; screenwriters: A.R. Rawlinson and George Wellesley. Cast: Paul Lukas (Yuan Sing), Jane Baxter (Charlotte Merrivale), Robert Douglas (Richard Marquess), Kay Walsh (Sadie Merrivale), Wallace Douglas (Harold Marquess).

By the last production of this silent classic, the piece was definitely an antique and betrayed values and attitudes no longer current. The acting was fine, but it's not the kind of story or movie that wears well as the years pass.

160 The Chinese Parrot

Based on a book by Earl Derr Biggers. Story: Sally Randall, who 20 years earlier had married the man who was her father's choice rather than the man she loved (Philip Madden), is now a widow and financially strapped. She is forced to sell her priceless pearls. She is astonished to discover that her long-ago sweetheart, who has never forgiven her, is to be the buyer. The pearls have been entrusted to a Chinese detective, Charlie Chan, and the sale is contingent on Sally delivering the pearls to Madden's desert home. He is taken prisoner by some crooks, one of whom, Jerry Delaney, assumes his identity, and awaits the arrival of Sally and the pearls. The jewels are stolen by various parties before Chan can put everything right, aided by a Chinese parrot who witnessed the kidnapping and tells Chan about it.

Universal/Jewel, 1927 (original). Silent. Director: Paul Leni; screenwriter: J. Grubb Alexander. Cast: Marian Nixon (Sally Randall Phillimore), Florence Turner (Sally Phillimore, older), Hobart Bosworth (Philip Madden/Jerry Delaney), Kamiyama Sojiin (Charlie Chan), Edward Burns, Albert Conti, Fred Esmellon.

• ***Charlie Chan's Courage*** (remake). Twentieth Century–Fox, 1934. Director: George Hadden; screenwriter: Seton I. Miller. Cast: Warner Oland (Charlie Chan), Drue Leyton (Paula Graham), Donald Woods (Bob Crawford), Paul Harvey, Murray Kinnell, Harvey Clark.

• ***Castle in the Desert*** (remake). Twentieth Century–Fox, 1942. Director: Harry Lachman; screenwriter: John Larkin. Cast: Sidney Toler (Charlie Chan), Arleen Whelan (Brenda Hartford), Richard Deer (Carl Dethridge), Douglas Dumbrille (Manderley), Henry Daniell (Watson King), Sen Yung (Jimmy Chan), Edmund MacDonald, Lenita Lane, Ethel Griffies.

The oriental detective Charlie Chan, created by Earl Derr Biggers, made his first film appearance as a minor character played by George Kura in *House Without a Key.* His role in *The Chinese Parrot* was definitely supporting, but beginning in 1931, with *Charlie Chan Carries On* with Warner Oland in the title role, the detective was the leading figure. In his first of 16 appearances as Chan, Oland delivers the expensive jewelry to a prospective buyer and has to solve a murder. Sidney Toler took over as Chan in 1938, and the remake, *Castle in the Desert,* was about the best of the 21 he made for Twentieth Century–Fox and Monogram. In this version, murders take place in the remote castle of an eccentric millionaire. Chan and his son Jimmy discover that the homicide was caused by a poisoned wine potion.

161 The Chinese Puzzle

Based on the play by Leon M. Lion and Marion Bower. Story: Li Chung, a Chinese mandarin, is involved in negotiations with the British foreign office. He discovers that information about a treaty is being leaked to the press. He traces the source of the leak to the son of an old friend, and in return for past favors, takes the blame himself.

Ideal, Great Britain, 1919 (original). Silent. Director and screenwriter: Fred Goodwins. Cast: Leon M. Lion (Marquis Li Chung), Lilian Braithwaite (Lady de la Haye), Milton Rosner (Sir Roger de la Haye), Sybil Arundale (Naomi Melsham), Charles Rock, Dora de Winton, Reginald Bach, Sam Livesey, Alexander Sarner.

• ***The Chinese Puzzle*** (remake). Twickenham, Great Britain, 1932. Director: Guy Newall; screenwriter: H. Fowler Mear. Cast: Leon M. Lion (Marquis Li Chung), Lilian Braithwaite (Lady de la Haye), Elizabeth Allan (Naomi Melsham), Austin Trevor (Paul Markatel), James Raglan, Jane Welsh, C.M. Hallard, Mabel Sealby, Charles Carson, George Carr.

These are films of stereotypes and hold little interest for audiences of today. The story, the style, the acting is just too old fashioned even to be considered quaint.

The Chinese Ring *see* **Mr. Wong in Chinatown**

The Chocolate Soldier *see* **The Guardsman**

162 A Christmas Carol

Based on the novel by Charles Dickens. Story: Ebenezer Scrooge is a miserly, friendless man who grossly underpays and mistreats his clerk, Bob Crachit. Scrooge is particularly outraged by Christmas and all of its trappings, which he describes as "humbug." One Christmas Eve he is visited by the ghost of his deceased partner, Jacob Marley, who is doomed to an afterlife of restless wandering because of his miserable and grasping nature while alive. He warns Scrooge that such a fate awaits him unless he changes his life. Marley's ghost foretells the coming of three spirits who will further instruct Scrooge. The first, the Spirit of Christmas Past, shows Scrooge his past loveless and unloving life. The Spirit of Christmas Present shows Scrooge the happiness of Bob Crachit's poor family on the special day, even that of the youngest son, Tiny Tim, a cripple with little chance of surviving. The Spirit of Christmas Yet-to-Come reveals Tiny Tim's death and that of the unmourned Scrooge. Awakening, Scrooge resolves to change his ways and to be a friend to man and particularly to Bob Crachit and his family and as is noted, "he was as good as his word" and came to celebrate Christmas as well as did any man.

• ***Scrooge*** (remake). Zenith Films, 1913. Silent. Director: Leedham Bantock; screenwriter: Seymour Hicks. Cast: Seymour Hicks (Ebenezer Scrooge), William Lugg, J.C. Buckstone, Dorothy Buckstone, Leedham Bantock, Leonard Calvert, Osborne Adair, Adela Measer.

• ***A Christmas Carol*** (remake). Fenning London Films, 1914. Silent. Director and screenwriter: Harold Shaw. Cast: Charles Rock (Ebenezer Scrooge), George Bellamy (Bob Crachit), Mary Brough (Mrs. Crachit), Edna Flugarth (Belle), Franklyn Bellamy (Fred), Edward O'Neill (Jacob Marley), Arthur Cullin, Windham Guise, Acheton Tonge.

• ***The Right to Be Happy*** (remake). Universal Pictures, 1916. Silent. Director and screenwriter: Rupert Julian. Cast: Rupert Julian (Scrooge), John Cook (Bob Crachit), Claire McDowell (Mrs. Crachit), Frankie Lee (Tiny Tim), Harry Carter (Jacob Marley), Emory Johnson (Fred), Francillia Billington, Roberta Wilson.

• ***Scrooge*** (remake). Twickenham Pictures, England, 1935. Director: Henry Edwards; screenwriters Seymour Hicks and H. Fowler Mear. Cast: Seymour Hicks (Scrooge), Donald Calthrop (Bob Crachit), Barbara Everest (Mrs. Crachit), Philip Frost (Tiny Tim), Mary Glynne (Belle), Robert Cocharan (Fred), Marie Ney, Oscar Ashe, C.V. France, Garry Marsh, Eve Gray.

• ***A Christmas Carol*** (remake). MGM, 1938. Director: Edwin L. Marin; screenwriter: Hugo Butler. Cast: Reginald Owen (Scrooge), Gene Lockhart (Bob Crachit), Kathleen Lockhart (Mrs. Crachit), Terry Kilburn (Tiny Tim), Leo G. Carroll (Marley's Ghost), Barry Mackay (Fred), Lynne Carver, Ann Rutherford, Lionel Braham, D'Arcy Corrigan, Ronald Sinclair.

• ***A Christmas Carol*** (remake). United Artists–Hurst, England, 1951. Director: Brian Desmond Hurst; screenwriter: Noel Langley. Cast: Alastair Sim (Scrooge), Mevyn Johns (Bob Crachit), Hermione Badderley (Mrs. Crachit), Glyn Dearman (Tiny Tim), Kathleen Harrison (Mrs. Dibler), Jack Warner (Mr. Jorkins), Michael Horden (Jacob Marley), Clifford Mollison (Mr. Wilkins), George Cole (Young Scrooge), Rona Anderson (Alice), Brian Worth (Fred), Carol Marsh (Fan), Michael Dolan (Christmas Past), Francis De Wolff (Christmas Present), Roddy Hughes (Mr. Fezziwig), Miles Malleson (Old Joe), Ernest Thesiger (Undertaker).

• ***Scrooge*** (remake). Waterbury–Cinema Center Films, 20th Century–Fox, 1970. Director: Ronald Neame; screenwriter: Leslie Bricasse. Cast: Albert Finney (Scrooge), Alec Guinness (Marley's Ghost), David Collins (Bob Crachit), Frances Cuka (Mrs. Crachit), Edith Evans, Kenneth More, Paddy Stone, Michael Medwin, Laurence Naismith, Richard Beaumont, Aston Rodgers, Suzanne Neve.

Other film versions of *A Christmas Carol* were made in 1901 in England; in 1908 by Essanay Studios; in 1910 by Edison Studios; in 1910 in Italy as *Dream of Old Scrooge;* in 1912 in the United States; in 1923 in England as *Scrooge;* in 1947 in Spain; and in various television productions, perhaps the best of which was made in 1984, starring George C. Scott as Ebenezer Scrooge.

In one of the many versions of the Dickens classic, Reginald Owen as Scrooge and Terry Kilburn as Tiny Tim are at the center of a celebration of various Cratchits and Scrooge's nephew and his wife in A Christmas Carol *(MGM, 1938).*

The early silent filmings of *A Christmas Carol* were generally well-received but some critics complained that the 1916 effort, *A Right to Be Happy*, was produced in sunny California and the Christmas scenes didn't look quite right. Seymour Hicks produced and starred as Scrooge in a silent version of the story in 1913 and a talkie in 1935. Reginald Owen made an admirable Scrooge in the 1938 Hollywood screening, ably supported by a fine cast headed by Gene Lockhart as the hapless Bob Crachit. In many minds, the definitive screen Scrooge is Alastair Sim in the 1951 British film. Sim's nasty nature and his redemption were both completely believable and the other members of the cast, down to the smallest parts, seemed to ideally capture the mood of the Dickens masterpiece. For many families, Christmas wouldn't be Christmas unless this version is viewed at least once on television during the holiday season. Albert Finney's performance in the 1970 musical version cannot be faulted but the music is not memorable. Songs by Leslie Bricasse include "I Hate People," "I Like Life" and the best of the bunch, "Thank You Very Much."

163 Chu Chin Chow

Based on the play by Oscar Asche and Frederick Norton, and legends. Story: It's the tale of Ali Baba and a slave girl, Zahrat, who foils a robber, Abu

Hassan, posing as a mandarin he has killed. She discovers that he has hidden his 40 thieves in large oil jars. She arranges that they don't leave the jars alive.

• ***Chu Chin Chow*** (remake). Graham/Wilcox, Great Britain, 1923. Silent. Director and screenwriter: Herbert Wilcox. Cast: Betty Blythe (Zahrat), Herbert Langley (Abu Hassan), Randle Ayrton (Kasim Baba), Eva Moore (Alcolma), Judd Green (Ali Baba), Olaf Hytten (Mukbill), Jeff Barlow, Jameson Thomas, Dora Levis, Dacia.

• ***Chu Chin Chow*** (remake). Gainsborough, Great Britian, 1934. Director: Walter Forde; screenwriters: Edward Knoblock and L. DuGarde Peach. Cast: George Robey (Ali Baba), Fritz Kortner (Abu Hassan), Anna May Wong (Zahrat), John Garrick (Nur-al-din), Pearl Argyle (Marjanah), Malcolm MacEachern, Dennis Hoey, Francis L. Sullivan.

• ***Ali Baba and the Forty Thieves*** (remake). Universal Pictures, 1944. Director: Arthur Lubin; screenwriter: Edward L. Hartmann. Cast: Marie Montez (Amara), Jon Hall (Ali Baba), Turhan Bey (Jamiel), Andy Devine (Abdullah), Kurt Katch (Hulagu Khan), Frank Puglia (Cassim), Fortunio Bonanova (Baba), Moroni Olsen, Ramsey Ames, Chris-Pin Martin, Scotty Beckett.

• ***Son of Ali Baba*** (remake). Universal Pictures, 1952. Director: Kurt Neumann; screenwriter: Gerald Drayson Adams. Cast: Tony Curtis (Kashma Baba), Piper Laurie (Kiki), Susan Cabot (Tala), William Reynolds (Mustafa), Hugh O'Brien (Hussein), Victor Jory, Morris Ankrum, Philip Van Zandt, Leon Balasco.

• ***Thief of Damascus*** (remake). Columbia Pictures, 1952. Director: Will Jason; screenwriter: Robert E. Kent. Cast: Paul Henreid (Abu Andar), John Sutton (Khalid), Jeff Donnell (Scheherazade), Lon Chaney (Sinbad), Robert Clary (Aladdin), Philip Van Zandt (Ali Baba), Elena Verdugo, Helen Gilbert, Edward Colmans.

• ***The Sword of Ali Baba*** (remake). Universal Pictures, 1965. Director: Virgil Vogel; screenwriters: Edmund Hartmann and Oscar Brodney. Cast: Peter Mann (Ali Baba), Jocelyn Lane (Amara), Frank McGrath (Pindar), Gavin MacLeod (Hulagu Khan), Frank Puglia (Prince Cassim), Peter Whitney, Greg Morris, Frank De Kova.

The story of Ali Baba and the forty thieves has also been told in movies in 1902, 1907, 1911, 1918, 1926, 1934, 1937, 1939, 1941, 1954, 1963, 1967, and 1971. The 1934 British version of *Chu Chin Chow* was a musical comedy and while the 1944 film wasn't meant to be a comedy, audiences laughed anyway. In it the thieves are the protectors of Ali Baba, not his enemies. At least Marie Montez looked great, particularly in her bathing scenes. The remaining films twisted and turned the Ali Baba legends as if they were wet rags, trying to get the last drop of a storyline out of them. They served the purpose of being entertaining to children at Saturday afternoon matinees.

The Church Mouse *see* **Beauty and the Boss**

164 Cipher Bureau

Based on a story by Monroe Shaff. Story: Phillip Waring is the cipher bureau officer in charge of U.S. counterespionage. The film reveals how he frustrates the complicated and devious spies intent on discovering this country's secrets. A lot of time is spent explaining how codes are deciphered and how even broadcast music can serve as a medium for spies to transmit messages. Waring's brother, Paul, a naval lieutenant, is duped by a modern Mata Hari, but is saved from total disgrace by his brother.

Grand National Pictures, 1938 (original). Director: Charles Lamont; screenwriter: Arthur Hoerl. Cast: Leon Ames (Phillip Waring), Charlotte Wynters (Helen Lane), Joan Woodbury (Therese Brahm), Don Dillaway (Paul Waring), Tenen Holtz, Gustav von Seyffertitz, Walter Bohn, Si Wills, Peter Lynn.

• ***Panama Patrol*** (sequel). Grand National Pictures, 1939. Director: Charles Lamont; screenwriter: Arthur Hoerl. Cast: Leon Ames (Phillip Waring), Charlotte Wynters (Helen Lane), Weldon Heyburn (Lt. Murdock), Adrienne Ames (Lia Maring), Abner Biberman, Hugh McArthur, Donald Barry, Richard Loo.

The sequel is just more of the same, featuring Leon Ames as an army major in the intelligence agency and Charlotte Wynters as his aide; they must put off their wedding plans as they use their skills to foil a ring of Oriental spies and saboteurs intent on destroying the Panama Canal. The two films are fairly exciting, but the average viewer may conclude that he or she has learned more about deciphering codes than one ever wanted to know.

165 The Circle

Based on the play by W. Somerset Maugham. Story: At the end of the nineteenth century, Hugh Portenous, who was to be the best man at the wedding of Lady Catherine to Lord Cheney, convinces her that he is the best man and they run off to elope. Thirty years later, Elizabeth, the wife of the couple's son, Arnold, is thinking of following their lead and running out on her husband to be with Edward Lutton. She invites her in-laws for a visit to see how their marriage had survived the years. What she sees convinces her to go with Lutton, but her husband disguises himself as the chauffeur, drives the couple to a secluded spot and thrashes Lutton. He takes his wife home with him. Seeing him in a new light, she is content to resume their marriage.

MGM, 1925 (original). Silent. Director: Frank Borzage; screenwriter: Kenneth B. Clarke. Cast: Eleanor Boardman (Elizabeth), Malcolm McGregor (Edward Lutton), Eugenie Besserer (Lady Catherine), George Fawcett (Portenous), Creighton Hale (Arnold), Alec Frances, Otto Hoffman, Eulalie Jensen.

• ***Strictly Unconventional*** (remake). MGM, 1930. Director: David Burton; screenwriters: Sylvia Thalberg and Frank Butler. Cast: Catherine Dale Owen (Elizabeth), Paul Cavanaugh (Ted), Tyrell Davis (Arnold Champion-Cheney), Lewis Stone (Clive Champion-Cheney), Ernest Torrence, Alison Skipworth.

Neither version of the Maugham play worked well, both being too stagey for the screen. In the remake, ambitious Elizabeth makes good her escape from her boring, puritanical husband, despite the pleas of her in-laws and his belated attempts at heating up their sex life. Marriage never looked more boring.

The Circular Staircase *see* **The Bat**

166 Circus Days

Based on the book *Toby Tyler* by James Otis. Story: Toby Tyler runs away from an uncle who has mistreated him and joins a circus, selling lemonade. Eventually his talents are recognized and he becomes a star clown. Toby's adventures with the strange and wonderful people of the traveling circus is the only notable plot device.

First National, 1923 (original). Silent. Director: Edward F. Cline; screenwriters: Edward F. Cline and Harry Weil. Cast: Jackie Coogan (Toby Tyler), Barbara Tennant (Ann Tyler), Russell Simpson (Eben Holt), Claire McDowell (Martha Holt), Cesare Gravina, Peaches Jackson, Sam De Grasse, De Witt Jennings, Nellie Lane, William Barlow.

• ***Toby Tyler*** (remake). Walt Disney, 1959. Director: Charles Burton; screenwriters: Bill Walsh and Lillie Hayward. Cast: Kevin Corcoran (Toby Tyler), Henry Calvin (Ben Cotter), Gene Sheldon (Sam Treat), Bob Sweeney (Harry Tupper), Richard Eastham (Colonel Sam Castle), Barbara Baird (Mme. Jeanette), Dennis Joel (M. Ajax), James Drury, Edith Evanson, Tom Fadden.

For anyone old enough to remember how important it was to children of small towns when the circus came to town, these pictures will be viewed with nostalgia. Otherwise one might note that there's nothing much to them. Coogan with his pouty look was always worth watching. Kevin Corcoran is cute, if you like cute kids, but his co-star of sorts, a monkey named Mr. Stubbs, grows old very quickly. In the Disney version, Toby's aunt and uncle from whom he ran away really love the boy and want him back, but the owner of the circus has found Toby to be a big draw in a bareback riding act and doesn't want to let him go. The alternate title, *Ten Weeks with a Circus*, gives the clue as to what happens by the end of the picture.

167 The City of Beautiful Nonsense

Based on the novel by E. Temple Thurston. Story: Pledged to marry a rich man to save her father from ruin, Jill is nevertheless pursued from London to Venice by poor composer John Grey, who loves her. He ultimately wins her love in return.

Hepworth, Great Britain, 1919 (original). Silent. Director: Henry Edwards; screenwriter: E. Temple Thurston. Cast: Henry Edwards (John Grey), Chrissie White (Jill Dealtry), James Lindsay (Skipworth), Henry Vibart (Thomas Grey), Gwynne Herbert, Douglas Munro, Stephen Ewart, Teddy Taylor.

• ***The World of Wonderful Reality*** (remake). Hepworth, 1924. Silent. Director and screenwriter: Henry Edwards. Cast: Henry Edwards (John Grey), Chrissie White (Jill Dealtry), James Lindsay (Skipworth), Henry Vibart (Thomas Grey), Gwynne Herbert, Stephen Ewart, Violet Elliott.

• ***The City of Beautiful Nonsense*** (remake). Butcher's Film Service, 1935. Director: Adrian Brunel; screenwriter: Donovan Pedelty. Cast: Emlyn Williams (Jack Grey), Sophie Stewart (Jill Dealtry), Eve Lister (Amber), George

Carney (Chesterton), Marie Wright, Eric Maturin, J. Fisher White, Daisy Dormer, Hubert Harben, Margaret Damer, Derek Oldham.

John Grey finally convinces Jill to follow her heart, rather than her sense of obligation to marry a man she doesn't love to help her father, when she is moved by his father's dying words to the young couple who he believes are already married: "Build your life on love as I have built mine. Build your children on love, as I have built mine." The 1919 piece was for its time a flawless production and the succeeding remakes were fine for what they were, old fashioned love stories.

168 Clarence

Based on the play by Booth Tarkington. Story: Mr. Wheeler hires an ex-soldier, Clarence, as a handyman for his home. The latter falls in love with Violet Pinney, the governess, whom Mrs. Wheeler suspects of having designs on her husband. When Clarence and Violet prevent the Wheelers' daughter, Cora, from eloping with Mr. Wheeler's private secretary, Hubert Stem, Stem decides to check up on Clarence. He learns that the army is seeking a deserter, Charles Smith; Stem convinces Mr. Wheeler he is actually Clarence. But a letter arrives revealing Clarence to be a college professor about to regain his position. He asks Violet to marry him and she accepts the proposal.

Paramount/Famous Players, 1922 (original). Silent. Director: William De Mille; screenwriter: Clara Beranger. Cast: Wallace Reid (Clarence Smith), Agnes Ayres (Violet Pinney), May McAvoy (Cora Wheeler), Kathryn Williams (Mrs. Wheeler), Edward Martindel (Mr. Wheeler), Adolphe Menjou (Hubert Stem).

• ***Clarence*** (remake). Paramount, 1937. Director: George Archainbaud; screenwriters: Seena Owen and Grant Garrett. Cast: Roscoe Karns (Clarence Smith), Eleanore Whitney (Cora), Eugene Pallette (Mr. Wheeler), Johnny Downs (Bobbie), Inez Courtney (Della), Charlotte Wynters (Violet), Spring Byington (Mrs. Wheeler).

Clarence, also filmed by Paramount in 1931, is a comedy about a tempermental family, all of whom suspect each other of being unfaithful. Wallace Reid, a popular silent star, would be tragically dead of drug dependency within a year. In the remake, Roscoe Karns, not the leading man type, disappointed. But as the material available for this screwy comedy wasn't much, this may explain why he got the role.

Class of '44 *see* **Summer of '42**

169 Claudia

Based on the play by Rose Franken. Story: Charming but immature Claudia, married to architect David, still reacts childishly to life, which causes considerable concern to her husband and mother. Her emotional and spiritual maturing process is ultimately achieved with her discovery that she is pregnant, her mother is dying of cancer and she can't make her husband jealous by flirting with a British author. Although the story has many soap opera ingredients, it also has its light comical moments.

Twentieth Century–Fox, 1943 (original). Director: Edmund Goulding; screenwriter: Morrie Ryskind. Cast: Dorothy McGuire (Claudia Naughton), Robert Young (David Naughton), Ina Claire (Mrs. Brown), Frank Tweddell (Fritz), Olga Baclanova (Madame Daruschka), Reginald Gardiner, Jean Howard, Elsa Janssen.

• ***Claudia and David*** (sequel). Twentieth Century–Fox, 1946. Director: Walter Lang; screenwriters: Rose Franken and William B. Meloney. Cast: Dorothy McGuire (Claudia), Robert Young (David), Mary Astor (Elizabeth Van Doren), John Sutton (Phil Dexter), Gail Patrick, Florence Bates, Rose Hobart, Harry Davenport.

Dorothy McGuire repeated her Broadway role as the child-bride in both the 1943 filming and its 1946 sequel. Attempts were made to get Cary Grant to portray her husband, but when he wasn't available the choice fell to Robert Young, who brought an interestingly bemused and exasperated quality to the role. McGuire, in her film debut, was appealing and made the experience of the film acceptable to wartime audiences who enjoyed stories of families that successfully coped. The sequel continued the sugary story of the young wife and her patient husband. While it's unlikely that either film would much appeal to today's audiences, the story did possess a certain warmth and homeyness that might be appreciated by those seeking a clean love story.

Claudia and David *see* **Claudia**

170 Cleopatra

Based on legends and a screenplay by Waldemar Young and Vincent Lawrence. Story: In competition with her brother for the throne of Egypt, Cleopatra turns to Julius Caesar to make her sole ruler. She captures the heart of the Roman general who plans to marry her, but he is assassinated before he can follow through. Cleopatra then turns her attentions to Mark Antony, but this romance turns out badly as well and she is forced to commit suicide by allowing an asp to bite her bosom.

• ***Cleopatra*** (remake). Paramount Pictures, 1934. Director: Cecil B. De Mille; screenwriters: Waldemar Young and Vincent Lawrence. Cast: Claudette Colbert (Cleopatra), Henry Wilcoxon (Mark Antony), Warren William (Julius Caesar), Gertrude Michael, Joseph Schildkraut, Ian Keith, C. Aubrey Smith, Leonard Mudie, Irving Pichel, Arthur Hohl.

• ***Cleopatra*** (remake). Twentieth Century–Fox, 1963. Director: Joseph L. Mankiewicz; screenwriters: Mankiewicz, Randall MacDougall, Sidney Buchman and others. Cast: Elizabeth Taylor (Cleopatra), Richard Burton (Mark Antony), Rex Harrison (Julius Caesar), Pamela Brown, George Cole, Hume Cronyn, Cesare Danova, Kenneth Haigh, Andrew Keir, Martin Landau, Roddy McDowall, Robert Stephens, Francesca Annis, Martin Benson, Herbert Berghof.

Other actresses who have portrayed the sultry Egyptian queen include

Helen Gardner in 1911; Theda Bara in 1917; Vivien Leigh in *Caesar and Cleopatra* in 1945; Rhonda Fleming in *Serpent of the Nile* in 1953; Hedy Lamarr in *The Story of Mankind* in 1957 and Amanda Barris in the 1963 spoof *Carry on Cleo.* Cecil B. De Mille's 1934 production demonstrates all of the excesses of the famous director but few of his achievements. While Colbert as Cleopatra was okay and Warren William was a passable Caesar, Henry Wilcoxon acted like what he was, a relative of the director. De Mille's epic was exceeded in vulgarity and poor acting by the 1963 film, notable only for the off-screen shenanigans of Burton and Taylor. It is a non-spectacular spectacle of over four boring hours, with the Todd-AO making Taylor's more than ample bosom and Burton's knobby knees dominate the screen.

171 Cleopatra Jones

Based on a story by Max Julien. Story: It's a comic-strip black exploitation story about a black female CIA agent, Cleopatra Jones, who battles drug dealers led by a villain called Mommy.

Warner Bros., 1973. Director: Jack Starrett; screenwriter: Max Julien. Cast: Tamara Dobson (Cleopatra Jones), Bernie Casey (Reuben), Shelley Winters (Mommy), Brenda Sykes (Tiffany), Antonio Fargas (Doodlebug), Bill McKinney, Dan Fraser, Stafford Morgan, Mike Warren, Albert Popwell.

• ***Cleopatra Jones and the Casino of Gold*** (sequel). Warner Bros., 1975. Director: Chuck Bail; screenwriter: William Tennant. Cast: Tamara Dobson (Cleopatra Jones), Stella Stevens (Dragon Lady), Tanny (Mi Ling), Norman Fell (Stanley), Albert Popwell, Caro Kenyatta, Chan Sen, Christopher Hunt, Lin Chen Chi, Liu Loke Hua.

Tamara Dobson, an Amazon beauty, deserved something better than this trashy nonsense. The films also showed how far the careers of Shelley Winters and Stella Stevens had fallen. In the sequel, the latter gets hers from the sexy and deadly Miss Dobson. About the only thing positive to say about the dim-witted second feature is it offered work to actors of two minority groups.

Cleopatra Jones and the Casino of Gold *see* **Cleopatra Jones**

The Clown *see* **The Champ**

172 The Clue of the New Pin

Based on the novel by Edgar Wallace. Story: The body of a wealthy eccentric is found by his nephew in a locked vault, with the key to the room on a table next to the deceased. A will is found leaving everything to the man's ward, Ursula Ardfern, which makes her the number one suspect, but the murderer turns out to be the nephew.

British Lion, Great Britain, 1929 (original). Director: Arthur Maude; screenwriter: Kathleen Hayden. Cast: Benita Hume (Ursula Ardfern), Kim Peacock (Tab Holland), Donald Calthrop (Yeh Ling), John Gielgud (Rex Trasmere), H. Saxon-Snell, Johnny Butt, Colin Kenney.

• ***The Clue of the New Pin*** (remake). Merton Park, Great Britain, 1961.

Director: Allan Davis; screenwriter: Philip Mackie. Cast: Paul Daneman (Rex Lander), Bernard Archard (Supt. Carver), James Villiers (Tab Holland), Catherine Woodville (Jane Ardfern), Clive Morton, Wolfe Morris, Leslie Sands, Ruth Kettlewell.

In the first version of the Edgar Wallace "locked door" mystery, it's a newspaper reporter who risks being burned to death by the killer nephew to save the innocent ward of the dead man, whereas in the 1961 version, the chararcter has moved on to being a TV interviewer. In either case, the appeal of the "How did the murderer get out?" brand of mystery had seen its day long before either of these movies were produced. The original was Britain's first talking picture using sound-on-disc, a system soon to be replaced by sound-on-film.

The Colleen Brawn *see* **Little Accident**

173 College Scandal

Based on a story by Beulah Marix Dix and Bertram Millhauser. Story: The scandal in question consists of the murder of two male students at a college just prior to the production of an annual campus show. Suspense is developed as the students, acting the parts of detectives, attempt to locate the killer before he or she can carry out the avowed plan of killing the dead boy's remaining roommate.

Paramount, 1935 (original). Director: Elliott Nugent; screenwriter: Frank Partos. Cast: Arline Judge (Sally Dunlap), Kent Taylor (Seth Dunlap), Wendy Barrie (Julie Fresnei), William Frawley (Police Chief Magoun), Benny Baker (Cuffie Lewis), William Benedict, Mary Nash, Edward Nugent, Willaim Stack.

• ***Sweater Girl*** (sequel). Paramount, 1942. Director: William Clemens; screenwriter: Eve Greene. Cast: Eddie Bracken (Jack Mitchell), June Preisser (Susan Lawrence), Phillip Terry (Martin Lawrence), Nils Asther (Prof. Henri Menard), Frieda Inescort (Mrs. Menard), Betty Rhodes, Kenneth Howell, Johnnie Johnson, William Henry, Ella Neal, Minerva Urecal.

It's difficult to decide how to classify these films. In one respect, they are light college comedies, the familiar "Hey, Why Don't We Put on a Show" films done so well by Mickey Rooney and Judy Garland. Then too, they are murder mysteries, containing just enough suspense to make them credible and enough false clues to put off audiences from finding the villain until the end of the picture. In the sequel, it's a little difficult to feel any concern for Eddie Bracken, the third boy marked to die, as he cracks wise and goes through musical numbers with June Preisser. The exposure of the murderer is effected when the college show goes on and after a wild chase on stage, Bracken is saved.

174 The College Widow

Based on the play by George Ade. Story: President Witherspoon of winless Atwater College is informed that unless he can induce some good football players to come to the school, he will be canned. His beautiful daughter, Jane, uses her personal charm and several ruses to draw noted athletes from neighboring schools to Atwater. Billy Bolton, son of a financial magnate, falls for Jane, and to prove himself, registers under an assumed name and works his way through school, showing both academic and athletic prowess. Through the jealousy of another girl, Billy learns how Jane is getting athletes for her father's school, and persuades the other jocks not to play in the big game. Jane finds them all at a notorious roadhouse and after explaining she was only trying to save her father's job, they return in time for Billy to be the hero of the victory in the football game.

• ***The College Widow*** (remake). Warner Bros., 1927. Silent. Director: Archie Mayo; screenwriters: Paul Schofield and Peter Milne. Cast: Dolores Costello (Jane Witherspoon), William Collier, Jr. (Billy Bolton), Charles Hill Marles (President Witherspoon), Douglas Gerrard (Prof. Jelicoe), Anders Randolf, Robert Ryan, Summer Getchell, Big Boy Williams.

• ***Fair Co-Ed*** (remake). MGM, 1927. Silent. Director: Sam Wood; screenwriter: Bryon Morgan. Cast: Marion Davies (Marion), John Mack Brown (Bob Dixon), Jane Winton (Betty), Thelma Hill (Rose), Gene Stone (Herbert).

• ***Freshman Love*** (remake). Warner Bros., 1936. Director: William McGann; screenwriters: Earl Felton and George Bricker. Cast: Frank McHugh (Coach Hammond), Patricia Ellis (Joan Simpkins), Warren Hull (Bob Wilson), George E. Stone (E. Prendergast Biddle), Joe Cawthorn, Mary Treen, Henry O'Neill.

The College Widow was an amusing play and the screen versions, which included a silent production by Lubin Films in 1915, were enjoyed by audiences looking for a few laughs, without expecting much more. *Fair Co-Ed,* based on another play by George Ade with that name, is pretty much the same story. Only this time, Marion Davies is induced to try college when she meets the girls' basketball coach. She joins the team and becomes the star player, also scoring with the coach. About the only thing new in *Freshman Love* is that the sport has been changed from football to rowing. Patricia Ellis is the lass that's the attraction for the muscular guys that the coach needs in order to put a winning crew in the water. Coxswain George E. Stone sets the stroking cadence with a jazz beat. The music and dancing numbers are weak and the casting is not the best. Everything happens as anticipated.

Collegiate ***see*** **The Charm School**

Color Me Dead ***see*** **D.O.A.**

The Color of Money ***see*** **The Hustler**

Colorado Territory ***see*** **High Sierra**

Come Back Charleston Blue ***see*** **Cotton Comes to Harlem**

175 Come Out of the Kitchen

Based on a story by Alice Duer Miller. Story: Claudia Dangerfield, daughter of an aristocratic but impoverished Virginia family, is able, with the help of her brothers and sisters, to raise enough money to send her ill father to New York to be treated by a specialist, but not enough to maintain her father and mother while in the city. They arrange to rent out their Southern home to Burton Crane for the needed funds, but his insistence that the price include servants forces Claudia and her siblings to pose as domestics. Claudia is to be the cook, but being unable to cook, she sneaks in a black mammy to perform the chores. By this time Burton has fallen in love with Claudia and believes she is hiding a lover. As one would suspect, everything works out alright in the end.

Paramount Pictures, 1919 (original). Silent. Director: J.S. Robertson; screenwriter: Clara Beranger. Cast: Marguerite Clark (Claudia Dangerfield), Frances Kaye (Elizabeth Dangerfield), Bradley Barker (Paul Dangerfield), Albert M. Hackett (Charles Dangerfield), Mary Kitson (Mrs. Dangerfield), George Stevens (Mr. Dangerfield), Eugene O'Brien (Burton Crane).

• ***Honey*** (remake). Paramount Pictures, 1930. Director: Wesley Ruggles; screenwriter: Herman J. Mankiewicz. Cast: Nancy Carroll (Olivia Dangerfield), Stanley Smith (Burton Crane), Skeets Gallagher (Charles Dangerfield), Lillian Roth (Cora Faulkner), Harry Green (J. William Burnstein), Mitzi Green (Doris), Zasu Pitts (Mayme).

• ***Come Out of the Pantry*** (remake). British and Dominions, 1935. Director: Jack Raymond; screenwriter: Arthur Parker. Cast: Jack Buchanan (Lord Robert Brent), Fay Wray (Hilda), James Carew (Mr. Beach-Howard), Olive Blakeney (Mrs. Beach-Howard), Fred Emery (Lord Axminister), Kate Cutler (Lady Axminister).

• ***Spring in Park Lane*** (remake). British Lion, 1948. Director: Herbert Wilcox; screenwriter: Nicholas Phipps. Cast: Anna Neagle (Judy Howard), Michael Wilding (Richard), Tom Walls (Joshua Howard), Peter Graves (Basil Maitland), Marjorie Fielding (Mildred Howard), Nicholas Phipps (Marquis of Borechester).

These comedies were each light and enjoyable with at least one delightful role per picture. In the original, Marguerite Clark was praised by critics for looking like she was really enjoying herself. Nancy Carroll, a very pretty lady but not well remembered today, was also a fine comedienne. The first remake also featured the W. Frank Horling and Sam Coslow song, "Sing You Sinners." In the third film, Jack Buchanan was very good as an English lord who, because he has lost his money, becomes a footman in the home of a millionaire. In the 1948 production, Michael Wilding demonstrated his comedy talents as the younger son of a noble family, who in order to raise money for a trip home, becomes a footman in a Park Lane mansion. Here he discovers Anna Neagle, working as a secretary, and it's love at first sight.

Come Out of the Pantry *see* **Come Out of the Kitchen**

176 Common Clay

Based on the play by Cleves Kinkead. Story: A common bargirl, Ellen Neal, trying to better herself, secures a position as a maid in the Fullerton house. She attracts the attention of the son of the house, Hugh Fullerton. She doesn't play too hard to get and soon has his baby, much to the chagrin of the family. Will he make an honest woman out of this social inferior? Remember in this period, illegitimate children were considered the fault of the woman and good servants weren't too difficult to find.

Fox Film Corporation, 1930 (original). Director: Victor Fleming; screenwriter: Jules Furthman. Cast: Constance Bennett (Ellen Neal), Lew Ayres (Hugh Fullerton), Tully Marshall (W.H. Yates), Matty Kemp (Bud Coakley), Beryl Mercer (Mrs. Neal), Purnell B. Pratt (Richard Fullerton), Ada Williams (Anne Fullerton), Hale Hamilton, Charles McNaughton, Genevieve Blinn.

• ***Private Number*** (remake). Twentieth Century–Fox, 1936. Director: Roy Del Ruth; screenwriters: Gene Markey and William Counselman. Cast: Robert Taylor (Richard Winfield), Loretta Young (Ellen Neal), Patsy Kelly (Gracie), Basil Rathbone (Wroxton), Marjorie Gateson (Mrs. Winfield), Paul Harvey (Perry Winfield), Joe Lewis, Jane Darwell, Monroe Owlsey, George Irving.

Fans enjoyed Constance Bennett so much in *Common Clay*, that she was then fed a steady diet of similiar roles for the next couple of years. In the remake, things are cleaned up, with maid Loretta Young wed to wealthy Robert Taylor, who is trying to keep the marriage a secret. As a story of class conflicts, these films don't have much to say. They seem to say opposites attract, but not always to everybody's satisfaction.

Le Comte de Monte Cristo *see* **The Count of Monte Cristo**

177 Conan the Barbarian

Based on characters created by Robert E. Howard. Story: In the Hyborean Age, a prehistoric, mythical time created by Robert E. Howard, a band of barbarians slaughter all members of a village save the boy Conan, who is doomed to spend his life going round in circles on the Wheel of Pain. Other than being a monotonous existence, this allows the boy to build up tremendous muscles and strength as he grows to manhood. One day he escapes, and sets out to seek those who had murdered his parents. During his travels, he teams up with various unusual individuals including a wizard with magical powers and an almost indecently clad beauty who can ride and fight almost as well as he can. Ultimately, he takes his revenge at the Mountain of Power, where he dispatches the leader of the tribe that enslaved him by whacking off the head of his cruel adversary.

Dino de Laurentiis/Pressman, 1981 (original). Director: John Milius; screenwriters: John Milius and Oliver Stone. Cast: Arnold Schwarzenegger (Conan), James Earl Jones (Thulsa Doom), Max Von Sydow (King Orsic), Sandahl Bergman (Valerie), Ben Davidson (Rexor), Mako (The Wizard), Tracey Walter (Malak), Gerry Lopez, Sven Olo Thorson, Valerie Quennessen.

• ***Conan the Destroyer*** (sequel). de Laurentiis/Pressman, 1984. Director: Richard Fleischer; screenwriter: Stanley Mann. Cast: Arnold Schwarzenegger (Conan), Grace Jones (Zula), Wilt Chamberlain (Bomboata), Mako (Wizard), Tracey Walter (Malak), Sarah Douglas (Queen), Olivia D'Abo (Princess).

These absurd sword and sorcery films are no doubt good fun for those who seek movies which feature a blend of nudity, profanity, sex and violence, while at the same time telling an unbelievably brutal, raunchy, sexist story. In the sequel, Conan is conned into escorting a virgin princess, who doesn't seem anxious to stay that way, on a perilous trip to find a sacred stone. Along for the ride is ex-professional basketball star Wilt Chamberlain (an ex-professional football player, Ben Davidson, appeared in the original; perhaps we can hope to see Reggie Jackson in the next film in the series) and androgynous rock singer Grace Jones. One hesitates to describe productions that cost $19 million each as rubbish, but that's the word that best seems to describe these half-witted and often unpleasant tales of nonsense.

Conan the Destroyer *see* **Conan the Barbarian**

The Concorde—Airport '79 *see* **Airport**

178 Coney Island

Based on an original screenplay by George Seaton. Story: At the turn of the century, Eddie Johnson and Joe Rocco are a pair of friendly, rival saloon owners on New York's Coney Island. They pull elaborate scams to out-do each other and only get really serious about their rivalry when they both want the same girl, singer and dancer Kate Farley. Other than that the story doesn't really matter in this musical comedy showcase for the girl with the great gams.

Twentieth Century–Fox, 1939 (original). Director: Walter Lang; screenwriter: George Seaton. Cast: Betty Grable (Kate Farley), George Montgomery (Eddie Johnson), Cesar Romero (Joe Rocco), Charles Winninger (Finnegan), Phil Silvers, Matt Briggs, Paul Hurst, Frank Orth, Phyllis Kennedy.

• ***Wabash Avenue*** (remake). Twentieth Century–Fox, 1950. Director: Henry Koster; screenwriters: Harry Turgend and Charles Lederer. Cast: Betty Grable (Ruby Summers), Victor Mature (Andy Clark), Phil Harris (Uncle Mike), Reginald Gardiner (English Eddie), James Barton, Brian Kelley, Margaret Hamilton.

The remake merely changes the setting as the plot, what there is of one, is again the friendly rivarly of two men, which only gets serious when they both want the same brassy entertainer. Here, there's not even any suspense as to who will wind up with the girl. Mature is the leading man–type, Phil Harris, more of a comedy-relief character actor. In the original, Gable sings "Cuddle Up a Little Closer" by Leo Robin and Ralph Rainger. In the remake, 26 oldies are featured, with the highlights being Grable doing "I Wish I Could Shimmy Like My Sister Kate." Of the supporting cast, Silvers and Winninger steal the show in *Coney Island* and James Barton, as an Irish drunk who sings "Harrigan," almost does the same in *Wabash Avenue.*

Conflict *see* **The Abysmal Brute**

Congo Maisie *see* **Red Dust**

Will Rogers as Sir Boss and William Farnum as King Arthur are in search of a joust in A Connecticut Yankee *(Fox Film Corp., 1931).*

179 A Connecticut Yankee

Based on the novel *A Connecticut Yankee in King Arthur's Court* by Mark Twain. Story: When Connecticut's handyman, Hank Martin, awakens after a blow on the head, he finds himself transported back in time to the days of the court of King Arthur. Armed with his modern expertise, he is believed by the residents of Camelot to be a wizard. This does not sit well with the court's magician, Merlin, who demands that Hank be burned at the stake as a witch. Hank saves himself from this fiery fate by consulting an almanac which he always carries and notes that an eclipse of the sun is imminent. He warns his captors that he will blot out the sun and when the event conveniently occurs, King Arthur pleads with Hank to dispel the darkness. This accomplished, Hank is dubbed Sir Boss, applies some Yankee know-how to the court, defeats the greatest fighter in a joust, outwits evil Queen Morgan Le Fay and falls for lovely Alisane, la Careloise, whom he calls "Sandy." After another blow to the head, he awakens to find himself back in Connecticut and discovers that many of his neighbors were characters in his Camelot excursion, including his "Sandy" who confesses her love for him.

Fox Films, 1921 (original). Silent. Director: Emmett J. Flynn; screenwriter: Bernard McConville. Cast: Harry Myers (Martin Cavendish/the Yankee), Pauline Starke (Betty/Alisande, la Careloise/Sandy), Rosemary Theby (Lady

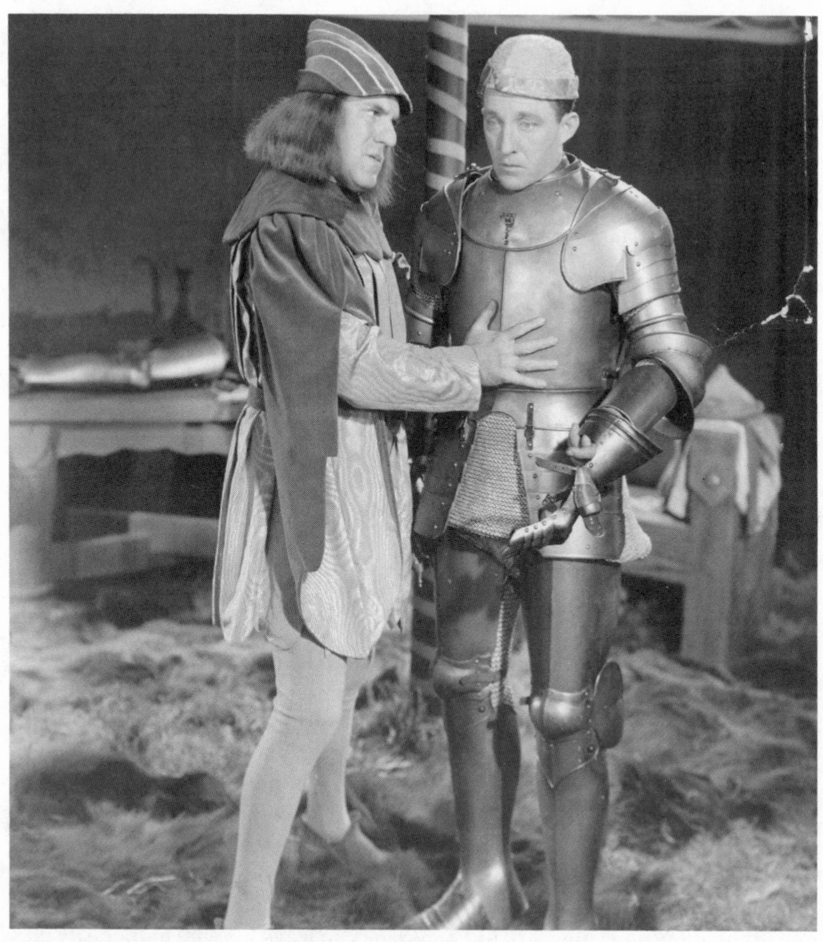

William Bendix prepares Bing Crosby (as Sir Boss) for battle in the 1949 Paramount production of A Connecticut Yankee in King Arthur's Court.

Gordon/Queen Morgan Le Fay), Charles Clary (Arthur/King Arthur), William V. Mong (Marvin/Merlin), George Seigmann, Wilfrid McDonald, Louise Lovely.

• ***A Connecticut Yankee*** (remake). Fox Films, 1931. Director: David Butler; screenwriter: William Counselman. Cast: Will Rogers (Hank/Sir Boss), William Farnum (Arthur/King Arthur), Myrna Loy (Queen Morgan Le Fay), Maureen O'Sullivan (Alisande), Frank Albertson, Brandon Hurst, Mitchell Harris.

• ***A Connecticut Yankee in King Arthur's Court*** (remake). Paramount Pictures, 1949. Director: Tay Garnett; screenwriter: Edmund Beloin. Cast: Bing Crosby (Hank Martin/Sir Boss), Cedric Hardwicke (King Arthur), Rhonda Fleming (Alisande), Virginia Field (Morgan Le Fay), Murvyn Vye (Merlin), William Bendix, Henry Wilcoxon, Richard Webb.

The 1921 film version of the Mark Twain story starring Harry Myers in the title role was the inspiration for the very successful 1927 Broadway musical starring William Gargan as Hank Martin, with songs by Richard Rodgers and Lorenz Hart. Fox Pictures produced a sound version in 1931 starring the ever-popular Will Rogers as the clever Yankee. Rogers as usual played himself, but for the part he had this was the perfect approach even if he didn't sound much like someone from Connecticut. Myrna Loy made a delectably evil Morgan Le Fay and cowboy star William Farnum was remarkably good as King Arthur.

In 1949, Paramount Pictures turned out a musical remake with a very relaxed Bing Crosby in the leading role. Crosby's light touch was most effective and his comedy touches were of such a nature that one would not have been surprised if Bob Hope and Dorothy Lamour had shown up somewhere in the picture. Cedric Hardwicke played Arthur as an ancient with ever-present sniffles. William Bendix was along for the ride to act as a foil for Crosby and Rhonda Fleming was dreamingly beautiful. The songs by James Van Heusen and Johnny Burke included "If You Stub Your Toe on the Moon," "Twixt Myself and Me" and the most successful melody, "Busy Doing Nothing."

A Connecticut Yankee in King Arthur's Court *see* **A Connecticut Yankee**

180 The Constant Nymph

Based on the novel by Margaret Kennedy and the play by Margaret Kennedy and Basil Dean. Story: A slightly mad composer and his four daughters, all half-sisters, live a carefree life. One of the daughters, the delicate Tessa, has an undying passion for young composer Lewis Dodd. When the girl's father dies, they find their future being decided by an influential uncle and his socially prominent daughter, Florence. To Tessa's dismay Dodd marries Florence, but the expectation that his career will now take off is misguided. He feels stifled in his wife's society setting. Meanwhile Tessa, unhappy away at school, runs away to him and together they write a composition. Dodd now realizes that he loves this young and ailing girl, but before he can leave his wife for her, she dies of a heart condition while listening to the first broadcast of their work.

• ***The Constant Nymph*** (remake). British Gaumont, 1934. Director: Basil Dean; screenwriter: Dorothy Farnum. Cast: Brian Aherne (Lewis Dodd), Victoria Hopper (Tessa), Peggy Blythe (Lina), Jane Baxter (Toni), Jane Cornell (Kate), Beryl Laverick (Susan), Lyn Harding (Sanger), Mary Clare (Linda), Leonora Corbett (Florence), Fritz Schultz (Jacob Birnbaum).

• ***The Constant Nymph*** (remake). Warner Bros., 1943. Director: Edmund Goulding; screenwriter: Kathryn Scola. Cast: Charles Boyer (Lewis Dodd), Joan Fontaine (Tessa Sanger), Alexis Smith (Florence Creighton), Brenda Marshall (Toni), Charles Coburn (Charles Creighton), Dame May Whitty (Lady Longborough), Peter Lorre (Fritz Bercovy), Joyce Reynolds (Paula), Jean Muir (Kate), Montagu Love (Albert Sanger).

The Constant Nymph was first filmed in England as a silent in 1928. The 1934 filming of the story of a sickly, sensitive girl, for whom the composer realizes his love too late, was described by *Variety* as "soft, delicate, fragile and meandering, beautifully directed . . . a high class picture." The 1943 remake owed a great deal of its success to the brilliant work of composer and pianist Erich Wolfgang Korngold's music, which is the work supposedly written by Charles Boyer and Joan Fontaine, as Dodd and Tessa. Korngold later published the main piece as "Tomorrow," a tone poem for contralto, woman's choir and orchestra, with author Margaret Kennedy supplying the lyrics. The performances by Boyer and Fontaine were excellent, but the production drags, suggesting that more cutting was needed.

Convicted *see* **The Criminal Code**

Cool Breeze *see* **The Asphalt Jungle**

181 Cornered

Based on the play by Mitchell Dodson and Zelda Sears. Story: Two thieves, discovering that their accomplice, Mary Brennan, is an exact double for heiress Margaret Waring, set her up in the Waring home while Margaret is absent. Margaret returns as the crooks are robbing her safe and is shot. She survives and through some clever police detection the identity of the true heiress is discovered.

Warner Bros., 1924 (original). Silent. Director: William Beaudine; screenwriter: Hope Loring. Cast: Marie Prevost (Mary Brennan/Margaret Waring), Rockliffe Fellower (Jerry, the Gent), Raymond Hatton (Nick, the Dope), John Roche (George Wells), Cissy Fitzgerald, Vera Lewis, George Pearce, Bartine Burkett, Billy Fletcher, Ruth Dwyer.

• ***Road to Paradise*** (remake). Warner Bros., 1930. Director: William Beaudine; screenwriter: F. Hugh Herbert. Cast: Loretta Young (Margaret Waring/Mary Brennan), Jack Muthall (George Wells), Raymond Hatton (Nick), George Barraud (Jerry the Gent), Kathryn Williams, Fred Kelsey, Purnell Pratt, Ben Hendricks, Jr., Dot Farley, Winter Hall, Georgette Rhodes.

In 1924, a performer playing two roles with both appearing on the screen at the same time was still a novelty. The film about a "Hell's Kitchen" girl impersonating an heiress was predictable but entertaining. The remake was described by one critic as "hogwash." It turns out that the two girls who look so much alike are actually identical twins separated since childhood. Loretta Young, as always, is good to look at.

182 The Corsican Brothers

Based on the novel by Alexandre Dumas. Story: Born Siamese twins of Corsican nobility, Mario and Lucien are separated by an operation, and survive a vendetta attack which kills their parents and other relatives. One child is taken to Paris, where he is raised by a wealthy family; the other is reared by a poor peasant of the region. Twenty-one years later the twins meet and are informed of what had happened to their family. Swearing to avenge their parents' death, the two boys separate to confuse the enemy by making widely distanced attacks on the forces of the villain Colonna. The brothers feel each other's emotions and pain. When one is wounded the other suffers. When one falls in love with Isabelle, the other also feels the love for her. Everything is put right by the end: vengeance is taken, honor restored, the poor brother killed, thus opening up the way for the other with Isabelle.

• ***The Corsican Brothers*** (remake). United Artists, 1941. Director: Gregory Ratoff; screenwriters: George Bruce, Howard Estabrook. Cast: Douglas Fairbanks, Jr. (Mario/ Lucien), Ruth Warrick (Isabelle), Akim Tamiroff (Colonna), J. Carrol Naish (Lorenzo), H.B. Warner (Dr. Paoli), John Emery (Tomasso), Henry Wilcoxon, Gloria Holden, Walter Kingsford, Nana Bryant, Pedro de Cordoba, Veda Ann Borg.

• ***The Bandits of Corsica*** (remake). United Artists, 1953. Director: Ray Nazarro; screenwriter: Richard Schayer. Cast: Richard Greene (Mario/Carlos/ Lucien), Paula Raymond (Christina), Raymond Burr (Jonatto), Dona Drake (Zelda), Raymond Greenleaf (Paoli), Lee Van Cleef (Nerva), Frank Puglia (Riggo), Nesto Paiva, Peter Mamakos, Paul Cavanaugh, Peter Brocco.

Other film versions of the Dumas story were made in 1897, 1902, 1908, 1912, 1915, 1917, 1919, 1938, 1954 and 1960. In 1969, Warner Bros. produced a spoof of the story starring Donald Sutherland and Gene Wilder, each playing identical twins who get mixed up with the intrigue of the court of Louis XVI of France. The 1941 picture demonstrated that Junior could be every bit as dashing as his famous dad, Douglas Fairbanks, Sr. It was a fine swashbuckler, very appealing to youngsters of the time who preferred plenty of swordplay and noble deaths to love and kisses.

In the 1953 remake, Richard Greene is Mario, leader of a group trying to overthrow tyrannical Raymond Burr. He also plays his jealous twin brother, Carlos, who experiences all the joys and pains of his sibling, a consequence of their Siamese-twin birth and medical separation. The pair work together to rid the country of Burr at which point Carlos, who has fallen in love with Mario's fiancée, Paula Raymond, attempts to kill his brother but is killed himself.

183 Cotton Comes to Harlem

Based on the novel by Chester Himes. Story: Gravedigger Jones and Coffin Ed Johnson are two unorthodox black police detectives who are trying to put away a charismatic black preacher, the Reverend Deke O'Malley, who is conning the citizens of Harlem with his promises of a move back to Africa. The fuzz, O'Malley and some bad white dudes are all after a bale of cotton stuffed with money—but dear old Uncle Budd gets there first.

United Artists, 1970 (original). Director: Ossie Davis; screenwriters: Ossie Davis and Arnold Perl. Cast: Godfrey Cambridge (Gravedigger Jones), Raymond St. Jacques (Coffin Ed Johnson), Calvin Lockhart (Rev. Deke O'Malley), Judy Pace (Iris), Redd Foxx (Uncle Budd), John Anderson (Bryce), Emily Yancy (Mabel), J.D. Cannon, Mabel Robinson, Dick Sabol, Theodore Wilson.

• ***Come Back Charleston Blue*** (sequel). Warner Bros., 1972. Director: Mark Warren; screenwriters: Peggy Elliot and Bontche Schweig, based on the novel *The Heat's On* by Chester Himes. Cast: Godfrey Cambridge (Gravedigger Jones), Raymond St. Jacques (Coffin Ed Johnson), Peter DeAnda (Joe), Janelle

Allen (Carol), Maxwell Glanville (Casper), Minnie Gentry, Dick Sabol, Leonardo Cimino, Percy Rodrigues, Toney Brealond, Tim Pelt.

Cambridge and St. Jacques are excellent as the two black cops, tough, smart and on occasion funny. The stories lend themselves to introducing some interesting characters with only the white guys a complete turn-off. In the sequel, Coffin Ed and Gravedigger investigate the case of a long-dead mobster who seems to be still bent on taking revenge.

184 Counsel's Opinion

Based on a play by Gilbert Wakefield. Story: It's an interesting comedy about a young barrister who allows a lady-in-distress to use his hotel room for a night. The next day he is asked to represent a friend who wishes a divorce from his adulterous wife for having spent that same night in the same hotel in a room of an unknown man. To meet her own ends, the lady in question allows the barrister to believe she and the wife are one and the same. After some amusing but predictable episodes it turns out she's a widow whom the barrister is free to marry.

London Films/Paramount, 1933 (original). Director: Allan Dwan; screenwriters: Dorothy Greenhill and Arthur Wimperes. Cast: Henry Kendall (Logan), Binnie Barnes (Leslie), Cyril Maude (Willock), Harry Tate (Taxi Driver), Laurence Grossmith (Lord Rockburn), Frances Lister (James Gonan), Mary Charles, Margaret Baird.

• ***The Divorce of Lady X*** (remake). Korda/United Artists, 1938. Director: Tim Whelan; screenwriter: Robert E. Sherwood and Lajos Biro. Cast: Merle Oberon (Leslie Steele), Laurence Olivier (Everard Logan), Binnie Barnes (Lady Mere), Ralph Richardson (Lord Mere), Morton Selten, J.H. Roberts, Gertrude Musgrave, Gus McNaughton.

Binnie Barnes, who played the mysterious lady in the first version, was bumped to the role of the real adulterous wife by Merle Oberon in the remake, with Laurence Olivier taking on the role of the young barrister, played by Henry Kendall in the 1933 film. The performances in both versions are very good, very English, with perhaps the most outstanding work coming from young Ralph Richardson as the cheated husband in the 1938 screening. Neither film will make any all-time favorite lists but they did offer some amusing entertainment of a time when an unmarried couple sharing a hotel room was considered scandalous.

185 The Count of Monte Cristo

Based on the novel by Alexandre Dumas, père. Story: Edmond Dantes, a nineteenth-century French naval officer, is unjustly accused by magistrate Villefort, Baron Danglers and King's-attorney Fernand de Montcerf of conspiring to bring Napoleon Bonaparte back to power. He is convicted of the crime and sentenced to life imprisonment in the impenetrable Chateau d'If. After 17 years of this cruel imprisonment, Dantes escapes by sewing himself into the burial sack of deceased fellow-prisoner Abbe Faria, cutting himself out of the sack when it and he are thrown into the sea. Using a map given him by the

Sidney Blackmer doesn't recognize Robert Donat as the officer that he helped frame and sentenced to life in prison, years earlier, but he can tell the Count of Monte Cristo isn't as fond of him as he is of his wife, Elissa Landi, center. The Count of Monte Cristo *(United Artists, 1934).*

Abbe, Dantes locates a great treasure hidden years ago on the island of Monte Cristo. Dantes assumes the position of the Count of Monte Cristo and seeks revenge on the men who had betrayed him. In Paris, he discovers his former fiancée, Mercedes, believing him dead, has married Fernand de Montcerf. Using his new power, wealth and influence Dantes destroys his adversaries, kills de Montcerf in a duel, and reveals his identity to Mercedes who confesses that young Captain de Montcerf is actually Dantes' son.

• ***Monte Cristo*** (remake). Selig Polyscope Company, 1912. Silent. Director and screenwriter: Colin Campbell. Cast: Hobart Bosworth (Edmond Dantes), William T. Santschi (Baron Danglers), Eugenie Besserer (Mercedes), Al E. Garcia (Fernand de Montcerf), Roy Watson (Villefort), Fred Huntley (Abbe Faria), Bessie Eyton, George Hernandez, Nicholas Cogley.

• ***Monte Cristo*** (remake). Fox Films, 1922. Silent. Director: Emmett J. Flynn; screenwriter: Bernard McConville. Cast: John Gilbert (Edmond Dantes), Estelle Taylor (Mercedes), Robert McKim (Villefort), Albert Prisco (Danglers), Ralph Cloninger (Fernand Montcerf), Renee Adoree, Maude George, Spottieswoode Aitken.

• ***The Count of Monte Cristo*** (remake). Reliance Pictures. Director:

Both George Sanders and Joan Bennett look suspiciously at Louis Hayward, appearing in the title role of The Son of Monte Cristo *(United Artists, 1940).*

Rowland V. Lee; screenwriters: Phillip Dunne, Dan Totherch and Rowland V. Lee. Cast: Robert Donat (Edmond Dantes), Elissa Landi (Mercedes), Louis Calhern (Villefort), Sidney Blackmer (Mondergo), Raymond Walburn (Danglars), O.P. Heggie (Abbe Faria), William Farnum, Lawrence Grant, Luis Alberni, Irene Hervey.

• ***The Son of Monte Cristo*** (sequel). United Artists, 1940. Director: Rowland V. Lee; screenwriter: George Bruce. Cast: Louis Hayward (Count of Monte Cristo), Joan Bennett (Grand Duchess Zona), George Sanders (Gurko Lanen), Florence Bates (Mathilde), Lionel Royce, Montagu Love, Ian MacWolfe, Clayton Moore.

• ***The Return of Monte Cristo*** (sequel). Columbia Pictures, 1947. Director: Henry Levin; screenwriters: George Bruce and Alfred Neuman. Cast: Louis Hayward (Edmond Dantes), Barbara Britton (Angele Picard), George Macready (Henri de la Roche), Una O'Connor (Miss Beedle), Henry Stephenson (Professor Duval), Steven Geray (Bombelles), Ray Collins, Ludwig Donath, Ivan Triesault.

• ***Le Comte de Monte Cristo*** (remake). French Film, 1953. Director: Robert Vernay; screenwriters: Georges Neveux and Robert Vernay. Cast: Jean Marais (Edmond Dantes), Lia Amanda (Mercedes Herera), Jacques Castelot (Villefort), Roger Pigaut (de Morcerf), Gualtiero Tumiati (Abbe Faria), Danile Ivernel, Folco Lulli, Paolo Stoppa, Daniel Cauchy.

• ***The Story of the Comte of Monte Cristo*** (remake). Les Films, France, 1961. Director: Claude Autant-Lara; screenwriter: Jean Halain. Cast: Louis Jourdan (Edmond Dantes), Yvonne Furneaux (Mercedes), Bernard Dheran (Villefort), Claudine Coster (Haydee), Franco Silva (Mario), Pierre Mondy (Caderhouse), Jean Martinelli, Henri Guisol, Marie Mergey, Yves Roldano.

Other films based on the Dumas characters were made by Selig Films in 1908; in Italy in 1908, 1911 and 1915; by Powers film in 1911; by Famous Players in 1913 with James O'Neill successfully re-creating his stage role as Dantes; in France in 1917 with Leon Mathot in the leading role; 1929 with Jean Angelo as Dantes and Lil Dagover as Mercedes; 1943, starring Pierre Richard; and in 1948, 1954, and 1968. In 1932, there was a German production, called *Der Grafin Von Monte Cristo.* Mexico's version, called *El Conde de Monte Cristo,* was released in 1943 with Arturo de Cordova as Dantes. The British chipped in with *The Secret of Monte Cristo* in 1960 and a production with the original title in 1971. The name of Monte Cristo was used to sell numerous other pictures which had little to do with the original story or characters, such as *A Modern Monte Cristo, Monte Cristo's Revenge, Sword of Monte Cristo* and *The Wife of Monte Cristo.* It's worth noting that Richard Chamberlain was an impressive Edmond Dantes in the 1975 television production.

For its time, the 1912 production was an expensive undertaking, costing $20,000, which more than earned back its investment. The 1922 spectacular with screen idol John Gilbert also impressed both audiences and critics, being judged a stirring adventure story true to the original values of the Dumas novel. In 1934, Robert Donat made the role of Dantes his own and all future performances as the Count of Monte Cristo must be judged in comparison to his stellar and exciting interpretation. Seen today, it is no less impressive than at the time of its original release.

Rowland V. Lee, who directed the Donat version, was brought back to try his magic with dashing Louis Hayward in the role as the count's son in 1940 in a filming with an original story by George Bruce. Trying to recapture the success of this venture, Curt Siodmak and Arnold Phillips were commissioned by Columbia Pictures to provide an original story vehicle for Hayward in the 1947 production *The Return of Monte Cristo.* It is the rehashing that one might expect of a venture so-named.

The French productions of *Le Comte de Mont-Cristo* in 1942 with Pierre Richard-Willm as Dantes and in 1953 with Jean Marais in the leading role were quite popular, but the 1961 screening using the title *The Story of the Comte of Monte Cristo* and the performance of Louis Jourdan as the count was compared unfavorably to the 1934 production and Donat's masterful portrayal. Actually, Jourdan wasn't that bad, but it's difficult to play up to a legendary performance so nostalgically recalled.

186 The Countess of Monte Cristo

Based on the story by Walter Fleisher. Story: In this comedy, Janet Krueger is an extra in a Viennese film studio, having difficulty keeping her head above water. She steals the auto and clothes assigned her for a movie scene, and, almost kidnapping girlfriend Mimi, drives off to a luxurious summer resort, where she registers as the Countess of Monte Cristo. She attracts the attention of two debonair jewel thieves, Rumowski and the Baron, who make a play for her and help her with expenses. By the end of the picture, these two are caught by the police and the girls return home.

Universal Pictures, 1934 (original). Director: Karl Freund; screenwriters: Karen De Wolf and Gene Lewis. Cast: Fay Wray (Janet Krueger), Paul Lukas (Rumowski), Reginald Owen (the Baron), Patsy Kelly (Mimi), Paul Page, John Sheehan, Carmel Myers, Robert McWade, Frank Reicher, Richard Tucker.

• ***The Countess of Monte Cristo*** (remake). Universal Pictures, 1948. Director: Frederick de Cordova; screenwriter: William Bowers. Cast: Sonja Henie (Karen), Olga San Juan (Jenny), Dorothy Hart (Peg Manning), Michael Kirby (Paul von Cram), Arthur Treacher, Hugh French, Freddie Trenkler, John James.

Most of the success of the first film is due to the comical talent of Patsy Kelly as the "Countess of Monte Cristo's" maid. It was the first movie in which she was given a major part, and she made the most of her opportunity. In the remake, Norwegian barmaids Henie and San Juan get extra roles at Oslo studios and check in at a swanky hotel as the countess and her maid. Naturally, there are numerous opportunities for the blade star to show her skill on skates. It wasn't one of Henie's best features, but then none of her movies were really very good. The story had been filmed once before in 1932.

187 The Country Beyond

Based on the novel by James Oliver Curwood. Story: Roger McKay is sought by Sgt. Cassidy of the Northwest Mounted Police for stealing from a trading post in order to feed some starving Indians. While hiding out, he meets and falls in love with Valencia, a backwoods girl, whom Roger believes is guilty of having murdered a white trapper. He takes blame for the supposed crime while Valencia travels to New York and becomes a successful dancer on Broadway. Learning of McKay's sacrifice, she returns to him in the Northwest. He is cleared when the wife of the murdered man confesses to the crime, and the lovers are happily reunited.

Fox Film Corporation, 1926 (original). Silent. Director and screenwriter: Irving Cummings. Cast: Olive Borden (Valencia), Ralph Graves (Roger McKay), Gertrude Astor (Mrs. Andrews), J. Farrell MacDonald (Sgt. Cassidy), Evelyn Selbie, Fred Kohler.

• ***The Country Beyond*** (remake). Twentieth Century–Fox, 1936. Director: Eugene Forde; screenwriters: Lemar Trotti and Adele Comandini. Cast: Rochelle Hudson (Jean Alison), Paul Kelly (Sgt. Cassidy), Robert Kent (Col. Robert King), Alan Hale (Jim Alison), Alan Dinehart (Ray Jennings), Andrew Tombes, Claudia Coleman, Matt McHugh, Holmes Herbert.

Neither version of the story had much excitement or action. The directors were unable to build any real suspense and everything that happened was easily predicted. In the remake, the producers couldn't quite decide what type of movie they wished to make. The first part is played for laughs and then it becomes deadly serious. Without any transformation or merging of these two approaches, the film is a mish-mash.

188 Courage

Based on the play by Tom Barry. Story: It's the sad tale of a poor widow, Mary Colbrook, with seven children to bring up. Six of them are eventually turned against their mother by the sister of the widow's husband. The remaining loyal child, Bill, ingratiates himself with a neighboring spinster who leaves him her fortune, allowing him to ease his mother's burden. The prodigal children come home when they learn of their brother's good fortune.

Warner Bros., 1930 (original). Director: Archie Mayo; screenwriter: Walter Anthony. Cast: Belle Bennett (Mary Colbrook), Marion Dixon (Muriel Colbrook), Leon Janney (Bill Colbrook), Rex Bell (Lynn Willard), Richard Tucker (James Rudlin), Carter de Haven, Jr., Blanche Frederici, Charlotte Henry, Dorothy Ward, Bryon Sage, Don Marion.

• ***My Bill*** (remake). Warner Bros., 1938. Director: John Farrow; screenwriters: Vincent Sherman and Robertson White. Cast: Kay Francis (Mary Colbrook), Bonita Granville (Gwen Colbrook), Anita Louise (Muriel Colbrook), Bobby Jordan (Reginald Colbrook), Dickie Moore (Bill Colbrook), John Litel, Bernice Pilot, Maurice Murphy, Elisabeth Risdon.

The performances in *Courage* are nothing special, although Belle Bennett as the widow tries hard. It was the youngsters who played her children that let the production down. Leon Janney as the ever-loyal Bill was something of a pain. Worse yet was Dickie Moore in the title role in the remake. He talked to Kay Francis more as if she were his sweetheart than his mom. In *My Bill*, the number of children were reduced to four, this time all legitimate. Kay Francis dressed a bit too well for a woman in desperate straits.

189 Cousin Kate

Based on the play by Hubert Henry Davies. Story: Amy Spencer is engaged to an agnostic artist and nature worshipper, Heath Desmond. A minister, John Bartlett, who is in love with Amy, influences her to break up with Heath. The families call in Cousin Kate Curtis, a novelist who herself is considered "unconventional" to see if she can patch things up. Not knowing each other, Heath and Kate meet on a train and apparently fall in love. The couple take refuge in Heath's house during a storm and when Amy arrives, Kate insists that she was only indulging in a harmless flirtation. But when Bartlett arrives and convinces Amy to marry him, Kate is happy to have her chance with Heath.

Vitagraph, 1920 (original). Silent. Director: Sidney Drew; screenwriter: L. Case Russell. Cast: Alice Joyce (Kate Curtis), Gilbert Emery (Heath Desmond), Beth Martin (Amy Spencer), Leslie Austin (Rev. James Bartlett), Freddie Verdi, Francis Miller, Henry Hallam.

• ***Strickly Modern*** (remake). Warner Bros., 1930. Director: William A. Seiter; screenwriter: Roy Harris. Cast: Dorothy Mackaill (Kate), Sidney Blackmer (Heath Desmond), Julianne Johnston (Amy Spencer), Warner Richmond (Bartlett), Micky Bennett, Katherine Clare Wood, Lottie Williams.

The story of the films is amusing and the performers acquit themselves rather well. In the remake, Warner Richmond advises Julianne Johnston to tell her prospective husband, Sidney Blackmer, that there will be no painting of nudes on Sunday and no passion in their marriage. Consequently, he leaves her at the altar and disappears, surfacing in the life of Dorothy Mackaill, the novelist cousin of Johnston who is more modern in her thinking.

Cowboy in Manhattan *see* **You're a Sweetheart**

190 Cradle Snatchers

Based on the play by Russell Medcraft and Norma Mitchell. Story: Three middle-aged matrons, Susan Martin, Ethel Drake and Kitty Ladd, tired of being ignored by their husbands and suspicious of their fidelity, hire three college boys, Henry Winton, Joe Valley and Oscar Nordholm, to spend a weekend with them at one of their homes. Their innocent plot to make their husbands jealous is complicated when the boys decide to earn their keep. Arriving with three young women at the cocktail party (uninhibitedly being enjoyed by the three wives and the college lads), the husbands find their wives considerably in dishabille. All ends well as the college boys find the husbands' girlfriends more to their liking and the husbands, now properly jealous, take note of their wives, what the women had sought all along.

Fox Films, 1927 (original). Silent: Director: Howard Hawks; screenwriter: Sarah Y. Mason. Cast: Louise Fazenda (Susan Martin), Ethel Wales (Ethel Drake), Dorothy Phillips (Kitty Ladd), Nick Stuart (Henry Winton), Joseph Striker (Joe Valley), Arthur Lake (Oscar Nordholm), J. Farrell MacDonald (George Martin), Franklin Pangborn (Howard Drake), William B. Davidson (Roy Ladd).

• ***Why Leave Home?*** (remake). Fox Films, 1929. Director: Raymond Cannon; screenwriter: Robert S. Carr. Cast: Sue Carol (Mary), Dixie Lee (Billie), Jean Baker (Jackie), Nick Stuart (Dick), Richard Keene (Jose), Walter Catlett (Elmer), Ilka Chase (Ethel), Dot Farley (Susan), Laura Hamilton (Maude), Gordon De Main (Roy), Jed Prouty (George), David Rollins (Oscar).

• ***Let's Face It!*** (remake). Paramount Pictures, 1943. Director: Sidney Lanfield; screenwriter: Harry Tugend. Cast: Bob Hope (Jerry Walker), Betty Hutton (Winnie Potter), Eve Arden (Maggie Watson), Phyllis Povah (Nancy Collister), ZaSu Pitts (Cornelia Figeson), Dona Drake (Muriel McGillicuddy), Cully Richards, Marjorie Weaver, Raymond Walburn.

The 1927 silent film based on the racy 1925 stage play starring Mary Boland, Edna May Oliver and Margaret Dale as the three philandering wives, and Humphrey Bogart as one of the college boys, was considered every bit as rowdy as was the fun-filled musical-talkie remake of 1929, called *Why Leave Home?* Songs in the latter version by Sidney Mitchell, Archie Gotter and Con Conrad, including "Look What You've Done to Me" and "Old Soldiers Never Die," did not become standards. In 1941, the musical *Let's Face It* based on the play *Cradle Snatchers,* with a book by the original authors, and Herbert and Dorothy Fields, starring Danny Kaye with music by Cole Porter and Sylvia Fine, opened

Rosalind Russell and Dorothy Wilson play out a scene before the cameras in Craig's Wife *(Columbia, 1934).*

on Broadway. Two years later, Paramount brought out their version of the hit with Bob Hope in the leading role. It turned out to be a box-office smash, but seeing it today, one must wonder why. The Cole Porter musical numbers that were kept from the Broadway production were not up to his usual standards and those written by Sylvia Fine for her husband, Danny Kaye, had been dumped.

191 Craig's Wife

Based on the play by George Kelly. Story: It's a triangular love-story, involving Harriet and Walter Craig, and "her" house. Harriet's self-centeredness and obsession with her possessions has succeeded in discouraging visits from friends and neighbors. Walter's love for his wife has blinded him to her faults but she can't fool wise old Aunt Irene who accuses Harriet of loving not Walter but her house. Walter finally sees through Harriet's pretensions and revolts, showing his rebellion by smashing one of his wife's prize figurines, defiantly smoking in the living room and packing up, leaving Harriet alone with her only love, the house.

Pathe Pictures, 1928. Director: William C. DeMille; screenwriter: Clara Beranger. Cast: Irene Rich (Harriet Craig), Warner Baxter (Walter Craig), Mabel Van Buren (Mrs. Frazier), Virginia Bradford (Ethel Landreth), Jane Keckley (Irene Austen), George Irving, Lilyan Tashman, Ethel Wales.

Joan Crawford adjusts Wendell Corey's tie in Harriet Craig *(Columbia, 1950).*

• ***Craig's Wife*** (remake). Columbia Pictures, 1936. Director: Dorothy Arzner; screenwriter: Mary C. McCall, Jr. Cast: Rosalind Russell (Harriet Craig), John Boles (Walter Craig), Billie Burke (Mrs. Frazier), Dorothy Wilson (Ethel Landreth), Alma Kruger (Irene Austen), Thomas Mitchell, Elisabeth Risdon, Nydia Westman.

• ***Harriet Craig*** (remake). Columbia Pictures, 1950. Director: Vincent Sherman; screenwriters: Anne Froelich and James Gunn. Cast: Joan Crawford (Harriet Craig), Wendell Corey (Walter Craig), Lucile Watson (Celia Fenwick), Fiona O'Sheil (Mrs. Frazier), K.T. Stevens (Clare Raymond), Patric Mitchell, William Bishop, Allyn Joslyn.

Of the three film Harriet Craigs, Joan Crawford was the most type-cast and least enjoyable. Joan's bitchiness shouldn't have taken any half way intelligent husband so long to see through. Rosalind Russell, on the other hand wasn't so blatantly disinterested in her husband. In each case, audiences were rooting for poor old Walter to get wise to this dame and put her straight. The three actors portraying Walter all came across as decent men, expecting very little from their wife and getting it.

192 Crime and Punishment

Based on the novel by Fyodor Dostoyevsky. Story: Law student Roidon Raskolnikoff kills an old pawnbroker and her sister with a hatchet and steals their money. At first he is able to justify the crime to himself, rationalizing that he has dispatched useless and vile creatures who deserved death. However, when an innocent man is arrested and accused of the crime, Raskolnikoff is tortured by remorse and guilt. Magistrate Porfiri Petrovitch is certain that Raskolnikoff is guilty of the crime but despite his repeated questioning he does not have the evidence to prove his case. Finally, Raskolnikoff is convinced by a former prostitute, Sonia, who has gotten religion, to confess. Cleansed and relieved by revealing his terrible secret, he is at peace with himself, ready to accept his fate. When he is sentenced to Siberia, Sonia goes with him.

• ***Crime and Punishment*** (remake). Pathe-Arrow Pictures, 1917. Silent: Director: Lawrence McGill. Cast: Derwent Hall-Caine (Roidon Raskolnikoff), Marguerite Courtot (Sonia), Carl Gerard (Petrovitch), Lydia Knott, Cherrie Coleman, Sidney Bracey.

• ***Crime et Chatiment*** (remake). Compagnie Generale de Production Cinematographie, 1935. Director: Pierre Chenal; screenwriters: Pierre Chenal, Christin Stengel and Vladimir Strichevski. Cast: Pierre Blanchar (Roidon Raskolnikov), Harry Baur (Porfiri Petrovitch), Madeleine Ozeray (Sonia), Marcelle Geniat (Madame Raskolnikov), Alexandre Rignault, Catherine Hessling, Marcel Delaitre, Daniel Gilbert, Magdalaine Berubet.

• ***Crime and Punishment*** (remake). Columbia Pictures, 1935. Director: Josef Von Sternberg; screenwriters: Constance Garnett, S.L. Kauren and Joseph Anthony. Cast: Peter Lorre (Roderick Raskolnikov), Edward Arnold (Inspector Porfiry), Marian Marsh (Sonya), Tala Birell (Antonya), Elisabeth Risdon (Mrs. Raskolnikov), Mrs. Patrick Campbell (The Pawnbroker), Douglass Dumbrille, Thurston Hall, Gene Lockhart, Robert Allen, Nana Bryant.

• ***Fear*** (remake). Monogram Pictures, 1946. Director: Anthony Zeisler; screenwriters: Dennis Cooper and Anthony Zeisler. Cast: Peter Cookson (Larry Crain), Warren William (Captain Burke), Anne Gwynne (Eileen), Nestor Paiva (Schaefer), James Cardwell, William Moss, Francis Pierlot, Almira Sessions, Darren McGavin.

• ***Crime and Punishment U.S.A.*** (remake). Allied Artists, 1959. Director: Denis Sanders; screenwriter: Walter Newman. Cast: George Hamilton (Robert Cole), Frank Silvera (Inspector Porter), Mary Murphy (Sally), John Harding (Swanson), Marian Seldes (Debbie), Wayne Heffley, Toni Merrill, Lew Brown, Eve McVeagh.

Other filmings of *Crime and Punishment* were made in Russia in 1910, 1913, 1922, and 1969; in Germany in 1923 as *Raskolnikov* featuring former members of the Moscow Art Theatre; in the United States in 1929 and 1948; in Sweden in 1945; in France in 1956 as *A Most Dangerous Sin* and in 1959 as *Pickpocket*, and in Egypt as *Sonya and the Madman* in 1977.

The five reeler produced in 1917 was given faint praise by critics who believed that the performances of the main characters were less than needed for such a powerful story. Speaking of the 1935 French film, *Variety* said, "There's a real picture in this Dostoyevsky book, and the French have proved it." As for the Columbia effort of the same year, starring Peter Lorre as the tortured murderer, *Variety* felt that it would take a lot of selling to capture audiences' interest. The film and Lorre's performance are now more fondly remembered. Monogram's 68-minute feature had the student killing his professor and being taunted into making a confession by a detective. In the Allied Artists production of 1959, it's back to a student murdering a pawnbroker in a rather disappointing updating of the story, hurt by its obviously low budget.

The Crime Doctor *see* **The Perfect Crime**

Crime et Chatiment *see* **Crime and Punishment**

193 The Crime of Dr. Hallett

Based on a story by Lester Cole and Carl Dreher. Story: Park Avenue doctor Philip Saunders leaves his lucrative practice and socialite wife, Claire, behind and joins two medical researchers, Dr. Paul Hallet and Dr. Jack Murray in the jungles of Sumatra, in a search for a toxin against red fever. The old pros snub the newcomer, assigning him only menial tasks. Saunders works secretively and alone, infects himself with the others' toxin and proves it's valueless by dying. The other two researchers, feeling rather bad by the turn of events, decide to continue Saunders' research, financing it by forging the dead man's traveler's checks, with Hallet assuming his identity. A new assistant, Dr. Mary Reynolds, arrives and falls in love with Saunders (that is, Hallet). The next to arrive is Saunders' wife who is about to blow the whistle on the forgers, when she develops the fever and is saved by the efforts of the physicians, using the results of her dead husband's research.

Universal Pictures, 1938 (original). Director: S. Sylvan Simon; screenwriters: Lester Cole and Brown Holmes. Cast: Ralph Bellamy (Dr. Paul Hallet), Josephine Hutchinson (Dr. Mary Reynolds), William Gargan (Dr. Jack Murray), Barbara Read (Claire Saunders), John King (Dr. Philip Saunders).

• ***Strange Conquest*** (remake). Universal Pictures, 1946. Director: John Rawlins; screenwriter: Roy Chanslor. Cast: Jane Wyatt (Dr. Mary Palmer), Lowell Gilmore (Dr. Paul Harris), Julie Bishop (Virginia Sommers), Pete Cookson (William Sommers), Milburn Stone (Bert Morrow).

It's an implausible story with sophomoric dialog, adequately directed and acted, but contains nothing to suggest that a remake was necessary. If anything the second version was even sillier and less impressive. Except for Jane Wyatt, the cast consisted of no-names, even considering this was to be the second feature in double bills. If it was a stormy night and one was trapped in a hotel room in a strange city, either film if shown on TV might prove a better time-filler than solitaire.

Crimes at the Dark House *see* **The Woman in White**

Criminal at Large *see* **The Frightened Lady**

194 The Criminal Code

Based on the play by Martin Flavin. Story: When former district attorney Brady becomes warden of a prison, he discovers one of the cons to be a man he had sentenced for manslaughter, believing all along that had he had a better lawyer, he would not have been convicted. The con, Robert Graham, falls in love with the warden's daughter, Mary. The warden tries to make things a bit easier for Graham, but the yard captain, Gleason, torments the innocent young man. Graham's chances for parole are jeopardized when he is a witness to the killing of a stoolie and refuses to break the prison code of silence. He finally wins his freedom and Mary, when his cell-mate Galloway confesses to the killing of both the stoolie and Gleason.

Columbia Pictures, 1931 (original). Director: Howard Hawks; screenwriter: Fred Niblo, Jr.. Cast: Walter Huston (Warden Brady), Phillips Holmes (Frank Graham), Constance Cummings (Mary Brady), De Witt Jennings (Gleason), Boris Karloff (Galloway), Mary Doran, John Sheehan, Clark Marshall.

• ***Penitentiary*** (remake). Columbia Pictures, 1938. Directors: Fred Niblo, Jr., and Seton I. Miller. Cast: Walter Connolly (Warden Matthews), John Howard (William Jordan), Jean Parker (Elizabeth Matthews), Robert Barrat (Grady), Boris Karloff, Marc Lawrence, Arthur Hohl, Paul Fix, Marjorie Main, Edward Van Sloan, Ann Doran.

• ***Convicted*** (remake). Columbia Pictures, 1950. Director: Henry Levin; screenwriters: William Bowers, Fred Niblo, Jr., and Seton I. Miller. Cast: Glenn Ford (Joe Hufford), Broderick Crawford (George Knowland), Millard Mitchell (Malloby), Dorothy Malone (Kay Knowland), Carl Benton Reid (Capt. Douglas), Frank Faylen, Will Geer, Martha Stewart, Henry O'Neill, Douglas Kennedy, Ed Begley.

The 1938 version was almost a word for word, situation for situation remake of the 1931 piece. The films differ from the stage play, having a happy ending. Originally, the young con was driven to murder his tormentor, but in the films, another con conveniently handles the chore. Boris Karloff and Millard Mitchell both handled this role very nicely in the first two films. Huston was excellent as the warden in the first version but Connolly did not impress in the remake. In the third version of this masculine soap opera, Ford is believable as the young man wrongly in prison, who nevertheless won't inform on a murderer, even if it means the end of his hope for parole. Broderick Crawford is well-cast as the gruff but kindly ex–D.A. who wants to give Ford a break. None of the women in the three movies are very important to the story.

195 The Crimson Circle

Based on the novel by Edgar Wallace. Story: Inspector Parr, with the assistance of Derrick Yale, a private detective who is smarter than he lets on, investigates the murder of three prominent businessmen, all killed after being threatened by a criminal mastermind who works under the sign of a crimson circle. He arrests Thalia Drummond, an associate of criminal Felix Marl. When Marl is found dead, he allows Thalia to get away and trails her and unmasks the murderer.

Kinema Club, Great Britain, 1922 (original). Silent: Director: George Ridgwell; screenwriter: Patrick L. Mannock. Cast: Madge Stuart (Thalia Drummond), Rex Davis (Jack Beardmore), Fred Groves (Inspector Parr), Clifton Boyne (Derrick Yale), Robert English (Felix Marl), Eva Moore, Lawford Davidson, Sydney Paxton, Norma Walley.

• ***The Crimson Circle*** (remake). BIFD, Great Britain, 1929. Director: Friedrich Zelnik; screenwriter: Edgar Wallace. Cast: Stewart Rome (Inspector Parr), Lya Mara (Thalia), John Castle, Louis Lerch, Albert Steinruck, Hans Marlow, Otto Wallburg.

• ***The Crimson Circle*** (remake). Wainwright, Great Britain, 1936. Director: Reginald Denham; screenwriter: Howard Irving Young. Cast: Hugh Wakefield (Derrick Yale), Alfred Drayton (Inspector Parr), Noah Beery (Felix Marl), June Duprez (Sylvia Howard), Niall MacGinnis, Renee Gadd, Basil Gill, Paul Blake, Gordon McLeod.

These three versions of the Edgar Wallace novel are fine examples of "the guilty party is the one you would least suspect" sub-genre. There were German productions of the story in 1928 and 1959, under the title *Der Rote Kreis.*

The Crimson Pirate *see* **The Black Pirate**

196 The Crooner

Based on a story by Rian James. Story: Teddy Taylor, the crooner, is a popular singer completely devoid of charm. He's swell-headed and impossible, believing his singing talent forgives him for any behavior, no matter whom it may hurt. Among those responsible for the success of his career who feel the bite of his selfish personality are his manager, Peter, and his girl, Judy. There's not much story in this character study of a big-headed lout.

Warner Bros., 1932 (original). Director: Lloyd Bacon; screenwriter: Charles Kerrigan. Cast: David Manners (Teddy Taylor), Ann Dvorak (Judy), Ken Murray (Peter), Shelia Terry, William Janney, Eddie Nugent, J. Carroll Naish, Claire Dodd, Betty Gillette, Guy Kibbee, William Halligan, Teddy Joyce.

• ***Mr. Dodd Takes the Air*** (remake). Warner Bros., 1937. Director: Alfred E. Green; screenwriter: Clarence Buddington Kelland from an original story by William Wister Haines and Elaine Ryan. Cast: Kenny Baker (Claude Dodd), Alice Brady (Mme. Moro), Jane Wyman (Marjorie Day), Henry O'Neill (Gateway), Ferris Taylor, Frank McHugh, Gertrude Michael, Harry Davenport.

These two films demonstrate how a studio would recycle an idea for a motion picture, even if it wasn't a very good idea. If the first makes the crooner to be a talented loser, lacking in humility, the second will make him a sweet, innocent and naive young man. In the latter, Kenny Baker is a lad from the sticks whose soothing baritone voice is changed into a crooning tenor when a doctor tampers with his vocal chords to cure the young man's bronchitis. This crooner, for whom the ladies go ape, is also an inventor, whose radio gadget is saved from the clutches of crooks by the quick thinking of a stenographer, who also gets the boy. In the first picture, a burlesque of the Vallee-Columbo-Crosby clan, some say that David Manners was punished by the studio by giving him this part in his last contracted film with Warners. He certainly never made it big anywhere else. The real star of the show was Ken Murray as the manager. Dvorak was in the uncomfortable position of attempting to be credible as the girl who loves a real heel.

Cross My Heart ***see*** **True Confessions**

Crossed Swords ***see*** **The Prince and the Pauper**

Crossroads ***see*** **Carrefour**

197 The Crowd

Based on characters created by King Vidor. Story: Mary and John Sims marry after their first date. After five years and two children, dreamer John, who works as a clerk, has not distinguished himself. He wins $500 in a slogan contest, which brightens their lives briefly, but when their younger child dies, the marriage starts falling apart. He loses his job, becomes a door-to-door salesman and Mary, at the urging of her family, leaves him. John is so despondent that he is considering suicide, which only concern for his son prevents. In a happy ending (not to Vidor's liking), Mary returns to him and he gets a job with an advertising firm because of his talent for slogans.

MGM, 1928 (original). Silent: Director and screenwriter: King Vidor. Cast: Eleanor Boardman (Mary), James Murray (John Sims), Bert Roach (Bert), Estelle Clark (Jane), Daniel G. Tomlinson, Dell Henderson, Lucy Beaumont, Freddie Burke Frederick.

• ***Our Daily Bread*** (remake). United Artists, 1933. Director and screenwriter: King Vidor. Cast: Karen Morley (Mary), Tom Keane (John), John Qualen (Chris), Barbara Pepper (Sally), Addison Richards (Louie).

In these two films, Vidor attempts to take a realistic look at the hardships ordinary people suffered because of economic depressions and their aftermath. In the second picture, Tom Keane and others take up squatter rights on an abandoned farm and despite great odds and natural disasters, make a go of it. The second is not really a remake or a sequel to the first, but the two films are included because they constitute a continuing story that the director wished to seriously tell about real economic problems.

198 The Crowd Roars

Based on a story by Howard Hawks. Story: It's the all-too-familiar yarn of a cocky, macho boozer with a yen for speed who accidently causes the death of a friend, hits the skids and is given the opportunity to redeem himself. This time the setting is auto racing. Hot shot driver Joe Greer becomes involved in a dispute over two women, Anne and Lee, with his kid brother Eddie. To teach the latter a thing or two about racing, he takes some unnecessary risks in a race, which causes the death of his friend and fellow driver, Spud. Joe goes on a binge and is out of racing until he is forced to substitute for his injured brother at the Memorial Day race. Would you believe, he wins?

Warner Bros., 1932 (original). Director and screenwriter: Howard Hawks. Cast: James Cagney (Joe Greer), Joan Blondell (Anne), Ann Dvorak (Lee), Eric Linden (Eddie Greer), Guy Kibbee (Dad Greer), Frank McHugh (Spud).

• ***Indianapolis Speedway*** (remake). Warner Bros., 1939. Director: Lloyd Bacon; screenwriters: Sig Herzig and Wally Klein. Cast: Pat O'Brien (Joe Greer), Ann Sheridan (Frankie Merrick), John Payne (Eddie Greer), Gale Page (Lee Mason), Frank McHugh (Spud Connors), Grace Stafford, John Ridgeley.

The 1932 feature has some excellent footage of actual races, while the remake's round and round racing scenes easily take up half the film's length. Cagney made this kind of film so often, no doubt he could do it in his sleep. It's a tribute to his professionalism that it doesn't look it. The second picture is unusual in that dear old dependable, level-headed Pat O'Brien has the Cagney role. He just isn't convincing as someone who is irresponsible and causes the death of his friend, Spud, once again played by Frank McHugh.

199 The Crowd Roars

Based on a story by George Bruce. Story: It's the familiar story of the boxing game where only the fighters have any humanity. Tommy McCoy is an exciting young boxer, surrounded by his drunken braggart of a father, a bookmaker, and a dishonest fight manager (Jim Caighn), who successfully operates on the principle that smart gamblers are the biggest suckers, and the obligatory girl, Sheila, who loves the pug, even if she doesn't quite approve of the rotten business in which he is involved.

MGM, 1937 (original). Director: Richard Thorpe; screenwriters: Thomas Lennon, George Bruce and George Oppenheimer. Cast: Robert Taylor (Tommy McCoy), Edward Arnold (Jim Caighn), Frank Morgan (Brian McCoy), Maureen O'Sullivan (Sheila Carson), William Gargan, Lionel Stander, Jane Wyman, Nat Pendleton.

• ***Killer McCoy*** (remake). MGM, 1947. Director: Roy Rowland; screenwriter: Frederick Hazlett Brennan. Cast: Mickey Rooney (Tommy McCoy), Brian Donlevy (Jim Caighn), Ann Blyth (Sheila Carson), James Dunn (Brian McCoy), Tom Tully, Sam Levene, Mickey Knox, Walter Sande, Gloria Holden.

In the original, the manipulators of crooked boxing matches are shown up as gangsters and gunmen. This would become a familiar theme in the many dramatizations of the fight game. This entry into the sub-genre is short on anything new and exciting, even for the time. In the remake, Rooney, after many years of playing kids, is finally allowed an adult role. He and his alcoholic father, James Dunn, are a song and dance team performing as an opening act for the barnstorming lightweight champion. Through this association, Rooney moves into the ring, accidently kills his friend, the champ, and then ties himself up with gambler Brian Donlevy. He falls in love with the gambler's daughter, played by Ann Blyth, and after a particularly tough ring match, quits the racket to marry her. Rooney's performance is as would be expected. Donlevy is the only one who gives any zing to his acting.

200 Cry the Beloved Country

Based on the novel by Alan Paton. Story: Steven Kumalo, a poor, black South African minister, learns that his son Absalom has murdered the son of his wealthy white neighbor, James Jarvis. The deceased had been working for racial understanding and harmony, and his father offers his friendship to the priest, whose own son is sentenced to hang.

London Films, Great Britain, 1952 (original). Director: Zoltan Korda; screenwriter: Alan Paton. Cast: Canada Lee (Stephen Kumalo), Charles Carson (James Jarvis), Sidney Poitier (Rev. Maimangu), Edric Connor (John Kumalo), Joyce Carey (Margaret Jarvis), Lionel Ngakare (Absalom), Geoffrey Keen, Vivien Clinton, Michael Goodliffe, Albertina Temba.

• ***Lost in the Stars*** (remake). American Film Theatre, 1974. Director: Daniel Mann; screenwriter: Alfred Hayes. Cast: Brock Peters (Stephen Kumalo), Melba Moore (Irina), Raymond St. Jacques (John Kumalo), Clifton Davis (Absalom), Paul Rogers (James Jarvis), Pauline Myers, Paula Kelly, H.B. Barnum, III, Ji-Tu Cumbuka, Alan Weeks, John Williams, Ivor Barry.

This very moving story with its somewhat simplistic attitudes towards racial harmony in South Africa suffered from a few indifferent performances, but basically it made audiences shed tears for the stupidity of those who insist on seeing people differently because of their color. The suffering of the two fathers, both to senselessly lose sons, is most touching. The remake is one of a series of films based on plays, originally sold only on a subscription basis. This particular example did not translate well to the screen, although some of the performances, particularly that of Brock Peters, are noteworthy.

Curly Top *see* **Daddy Long Legs**

201 Cyrano de Bergerac

Based on the play by Edmond Rostand. Story: Cyrano de Bergerac is noted for his swordsmanship, his poetry and wit, and his great peninsula of a nose. He secretly loves Roxanne, but when she confesses her passion for Christian, Cyrano decides that her happiness is more important than his. He finds that Christian is something of a tongue-tied oaf, so Cyrano supplies the romantic words Christian is to say to Roxanne. Later Christian is killed in battle and Cyrano is given the opportunity to speak of his love to Roxanne as he is dying. She understands that it was Cyrano all along whose words filled her with such love for Christian.

United Artists, 1950 (original). Director: Michael Gordon; screenwriter: Brian Hooker. Cast: Jose Ferrer (Cyrano de Bergerac), Mala Powers (Roxanne), William Prince (Christian), Morris Carnovsky (Le Bret), Ralph Clanton (De Guiche), Lloyd Corrigan, Virginia Farmer, Edgar Barrier, Elena Verdugo, Albert Cavens.

• ***Roxanne*** (remake). Columbia Pictures, 1987. Director: Fred Schepisi; screenwriter: Steve Martin. Cast: Steve Martin (C.D. Bales), Daryl Hannah (Roxanne), Rick Rossovich (Chris), Shelley Duvall (Dixie), John Kopleas (Chuck), Fred Willard, Max Alexander, Michael J. Pollard, Steve Mittleman.

Jose Ferrer won an Academy Award for his stirring performance of the ski slope–nosed swordsman, but the other leading performers, Mala Powers and William Prince, were clearly out of their league in this stagey production. In the 1987 modern remake, Steve Martin, a Washington state fire chief, has a prodigious nose and a yen for beautiful astronomer Daryl Hannah, but she cares for tongue-tied firefighter Rick Rossovitch. Martin helps the latter by writing love letters that land Daryl in the wrong man's bed. But not for long; screenwriter Martin gave the movie a happy ending for actor Martin.

D

202 Daddy Long Legs

Based on the novel by Jean Webster. Story: In a Cinderella-like romance, Judy Abbott, an orphan at an asylum where children are reared by charity minus kindness, grows up and falls in love with her guardian, Jervis Pendleton, eventually marrying him.

First National Pictures, 1919 (original). Silent: Director: Marshall Neilan; screenwriter: uncredited. Cast: Mary Pickford (Judy Abbott), Milia Davenport (Mrs. Lippert), Miss Percy Haswell (Miss Pritchard), Fay Lemport (Angelina Wyckoff), Mahlon Hamilton (Jervis Pendleton), Lillian Langdon (Mrs. Pendleton), Betty Bouton, Audry Chapman, Marshall A. Neilan, Carrie Clarke Warde.

• ***Daddy Long Legs*** (remake). Fox Film Corporation, 1931. Director: Alfred Santell; screenwriters: Sonya Levien and S.N. Behrman. Cast: Janet Gaynor (Judy Abbott), Warner Baxter (Jervis Pendleton), Una Merkel (Sally McBride), John Arledge (Jimmy McBride), Claude Gillingwater (Riggs), Kathlyn Williams (Mrs. Pendleton), Louise Closser Hale (Miss Pritchard), Elizabeth Patterson, Kendall McComas, Shelia Mannors, Edwin Maxwell, Effie Ellstar.

• ***Curly Top*** (remake). Fox Film Corp., 1935. Director: Irving Cummings; screenwriters: Patterson McNutt and Arthur Beckhard. Cast: Shirley Temple (Elizabeth Blair), John Boles (Edward Morgan), Rochelle Hudson (Mary Blair), Jane Darwell (Mrs. Denham), Rafaela Ottiano (Mrs. Higgins), Esther Dale, Etienne Girardot, Arthur Treacher, Maurice Murphy.

• ***Daddy Long Legs*** (remake). Twentieth Century–Fox, 1955. Director: Jean Negulesco; screenwriters: Phoebe and Henry Ephron. Cast: Fred Astaire (Jervis Pendleton), Leslie Caron (June), Terry Moore (Linda), Thelma Ritter (Miss Pritchard), Fred Clark (Griggs), Charlotte Austin (Sally), Larry Keating, Kathryn Givney, Kelly Brown, Sara Shane, Numa Lapeyre, Ann Codce.

As anything Mary Pickford did was just fine with her fans, including prolonging her childhood by what often seemed like an extra generation, she was well received as the orphan who grows up and picks off her benefactor as her

Shirley Temple uses the top of John Boles' piano as her dance floor in Curly Top *(1935, Fox Film Corp.), a remake of the often-filmed* Daddy Long Legs.

husband (another sign of not wanting to grow up, perhaps). Janet Gaynor, early sound's answer to "America's Sweetheart," Mary Pickford was equally praised for her ability to play the appealing little girl and still be believable as a woman who wins the heart of Warner Baxter. The Shirley Temple vehicle, a disguised version of the story, finally had a child playing the child orphan whose life-of-the-party personality doesn't sit well with the sourpuss orphanage workers. Shirley sings Ray Henderson's "Animal Crackers in My Soup" and "When I Grow Up," while John Boles chips in with "It's All So New to Me" and the title song. The 1955 film was not among the late Fred Astaire's best ventures. The entire production was clumsy and uninspiring. Still, watching Astaire dance is always a pleasure and the Academy Award–nominated Johnny Mercer song, "Something's Got to Give," was the picture's high point.

203 Daddy's Gone A-Hunting

Based on the play by Zoe Akins. Story: Julian persuades his wife, Edith, to take a menial position in order to finance his artistic studies abroad. When he returns, he is filled with bohemian attitudes and desires. Edith soon realizes that his love for her has waned. Her only joy is her daughter and her friendship with Greenough, who wishes to marry her. Julian is more than willing to step aside for the other man, but later he comes to understand what he has lost and paints a picture which he calls "Realization," which brings him international recognition and acclaim. When his daughter is hurt in an accident he arrives at her bedside in time to see her die. Afterwards, he and Edith decide to try life together again.

MGM, 1925 (original). Silent. Director: Frank Borzage; screenwriter: Kenneth B. Clarke. Cast: Alice Joyce (Edith), Percy Marmont (Julian), Virginia Marshall (Janet), Helena D'Algy (Olga), Holmes Herbert (Greenough), Ford Sterling, Edythe Chapman.

• ***Women Love Once*** (remake). Paramount Pictures, 1931. Director: Edward Goodman; screenwriter: Zoe Akins. Cast: Paul Lukas (Julien Fields), Eleanor Boardman (Helen Fields), Juliette Compton (Hester Dahlgren), Geoffrey Kerr (Allen Greenough), Judith Wood (Olga), Marilyn Knowlden (Janet Fields).

These films are just too, too sad. For purposes of plot development, the poor kid isn't allowed to die quickly after being hit by a car but is made to linger in her agony, increasing that of the audience. Such is not drama; rather it is a cheap shot to the viewers' heartstrings. Both films deal with decrepit material and are peopled by performers who are nowhere near their best.

204 Damaged Goods

Based on the play by Eugene Brieux. Story: Prior to his marriage to a prominent society belle, George Dumont contracts syphilis from a prostitute. Later, recognizing the symptoms of the disease, he goes to a specialist who advises him not to marry for two years while he is under treatment. George's impatience and circumstances lead him to a hasty marriage after being assured by a quack that he is cured. When his child is born, symptoms of the disease are noticed and the frantic father is driven to desperation by his feelings of guilt and hopelessness.

American Mutual, 1915 (original). Director: Richard Bennett; screenwriter: Eugene Brieux. Cast: Richard Bennett (George Dumont), Adrienne Morrison (Prostitute), Maud Milton (Mrs. Dumont), Olive Templeton (Henriette Locke), Josephine Ditt, Jacqueline Moore, Florence Short, Lewis Bennison, John Steppling, William Bertram, George Ferguson.

• ***Damaged Goods*** (remake). Woolf & Freedman, Great Britain, 1919. Silent: Director: Alexander Butler; screenwriter: Eugene Brieux. Cast: Campbell Gullan (George Dumont), Henriette Louches (Marjorie Day), J. Fisher White (Doctor), James Lindsay (Rouvenal), Joan Vivian Reese (Edith Wray), Bassett Roe, Annie Esmond, Winifred Dennis.

• ***Damaged Goods*** (remake). Grand National Pictures, 1937. Director: Phil Stone; screenwriter: Upton Sinclair. Cast: Pedro de Cordova (Dr. Walker), Phyllis Barry (Margie), Douglas Walton (George), Arletta Duncan (Henrietta), Ferdinand Munier, Esther Dale, Clarence Wilson, Greta Myer, Frank Melton, Gretchen Thomas.

When the play and the movie based on it were first staged, there was a conflict between those who felt the entire subject of "social diseases" should not be the subject of entertainment, while others believed that the dangers of ignorance and indifference made it absolutely necessary that everyone see the effects of syphilis on the innocent and guilty alike. The argument is somewhat reminiscent of today's controversy over AIDS and how much should be done or discussed about the disease. Things were even worse in 1937 when the bluenoses and censors had more power to prevent scenes in movies or whole films from being seen. In bringing the story up to date, Upton Sinclair transforms the work into entertainment, thus missing much of the stunning impact of the almost-documentary previous piece.

La Dame aux Camelia *see* **Camille**

Damn Yankees *see* **Faust**

Damon des Meers *see* **Moby Dick**

Dance, Charlie, Dance *see* **The Butter and Egg Man**

The Dance of Life *see* **Burlesque**

Dance Pretty Lady *see* **The Ballet Girl**

205 The Dancers

Based on the novel by Hubert Parsons and the play by Gerald Du Maurier and Viola Tree. Story: Unable to make a living in London, Tony moves to South America, where he becomes the owner of a saloon and dancehall. One of the dancers, Maxine, falls in love with him, but he remains true to the memory of his childhood sweetheart, Una. Meanwhile back in London, Una makes the rounds of wild parties and has an affair with an admirer. When Tony unexpectedly comes into an inheritance and title, he returns to England and becomes immediately engaged to Una. She keeps her indiscretion a secret until the eve of their wedding. Tony forgives her but it's too late, she has taken poison and dies. Tony returns to South America and Maxine.

Fox Film Corporation, 1925 (original). Silent: Director: Emmett J. Flynn; screenwriter: Edmund Goulding. Cast: George O'Brien (Tony), Alma Rubens (Maxine), Madge Bellamy (Una), Templar Saxe (Fothering), Joan Standing, Alice Hollister, Freeman Wood, Walter McGrail, Noble Johnson, Tippy Grey. • ***The Dancers*** (remake). Fox Film Corporation, 1930. Director: Chandler Sprague; screenwriter: Edwin Burke. Cast: Lois Moran (Diana), Phillips Holmes (Tony), Walter Bryon (Berwin), Mae Clarke (Maxine), Tyrell Davis, Mrs. Patrick Campbell.

The rather silly story did not prevent audiences from enjoying the silent film or prevent Fox from making a sound version in 1930, changing the setting from South America to Canada. The remake was also one of the few opportunities to see the great stage star Mrs. Patrick Campbell on the screen.

206 Dancing in the Dark

Based on *The Band Wagon* by George S. Kaufman, Howard Dietz and

Arthur Schwartz. Story: One-time famous actor Emery Slade, now a has-been, is given a job as a talent scout for 20th Century–Fox. The only reason that he is offered the assignment is that he is the close friend of the father of a Broadway singing star the studio is hot to sign. He is sent to New York with studio press representative Bill Davis to get the girl's name on a contract, but he double-crosses the studio by signing Julie, an unknown, instead. Julie, who just happens to be Slade's daughter by a woman he deserted before her birth, falls in love with Davis, who wants to marry her, but she puts him off because of her ambitions for a show business career. The three are fired, but they triumph over studio bureaucracy by inserting Julie's screen test into a newsreel played at a big Hollywood premiere. She's a hit and all ends happily for the trio.

Twentieth Century–Fox, 1949 (original). Director: Irving Reis; screenwriter: Mary C. McCall, Jr. Cast: William Powell (Emery Slade), Mark Stevens (Bill Davis), Betsy Drake (Julie), Adolphe Menjou (Crossman), Randy Stuart (Rosalie), Lloyd Corrigan, Hope Emerson, Walter Catlett, Don Beddoe, Helen Wescott.

• ***The Band Wagon*** (remake). MGM, 1953. Director: Vincente Minnelli; screenwriters: Betty Comden and Adolph Green. Cast: Fred Astaire (Tony Hunter), Cyd Charisse (Gaby Gerard), Oscar Levant (Lester Marton), Nanette Fabray (Lily Marton), Jack Buchanan (Jeffrey Cordova), James Mitchell, Robert Gist.

The first production is an amusing drama with music and the second is a musical-comedy with drama. Both backstage yarns are good fun, giving two extremely talented performers, Powell and Astaire, chances to show they hadn't lost any of their charm. Songs in the original by Arthur Schwartz and Howard Dietz included the title song, "Something to Remember You By," and "New Sun in the Sky."

In the remake, Astaire plays a dancing film star; Tony Hunter, an actor whose pictures of late have been flops. He has been talked into appearing in a Broadway show written by two old friends, Lily and Lester Marton. The show is to be directed by a Broadway genius, Jeffrey Cordova, who has never been involved with a musical comedy before. He turns the simple Marton story into a version of the Faustian legend and nearly ruins it. After the out-of-town opening where the production has laid an egg, Tony takes over, returning the show to its original premise and with the help of the Martons, lovely dancer Gaby Gerard, and the now cooperative Cordova, turns it into a Broadway hit.

The film incorporates twelve wonderful songs from various Broadway musicals including "Dancing in the Dark" from *Band Wagon,* "A Shine on Your Shoes" from *Flying Colors,* "I Guess I'll Have to Change My Plans" from *The Little Show,* "Triplets" from *Between the Devil,* and "Louisiana Hayride" from *Colors.* In addition, Schwartz and Dietz came up with an imaginative modern jazz ballet, "Girl Hunt," danced by Astaire and Charisse, and a rousing "That's Entertainment" performed by Astaire, Buchanan, Levant and Fabray. Everyone is in top form, but none more so than Buchanan with his brilliant comical performance. Astaire is still an old smoothy, Charisse shows one of the best pair of legs ever to grace a talented dancer, Levant is his usual hilarious complaining self and Fabray is as peppy a performer as you could ever hope to see.

207 Dangerous

Based on an original screenplay by Laird Doyle. Story: Joyce Heath is a once-famed actress, down on her luck and soused, when she meets wealthy architect Don Bellows. He takes her home with him, sobers her up and falls in love with her. He breaks his engagement to society girl Gail Armitage and invests his money in a show meant to be a come-back for Joyce. This seems a foolish thing to do, as she has a history of being a jinx for both shows and men. Her record remains unbroken as she ruins him like all the rest, and an almost forgotten husband shows up. He is conveniently killed in an automobile crash. To make amends for all the trouble she has caused, rehabilitated Joyce severs her relationship with Don, who goes back to Gail.

Warner Bros., 1935 (original). Director: Alfred E. Green; screenwriter: Laird Doyle. Cast: Bette Davis (Joyce Heath), Franchot Tone (Don Bellows), Margaret Lindsay (Gail Armitage), Alison Skipworth, John Eldredge, Dick Foran.

• ***Singapore Woman*** (remake). Warner Bros., 1941. Director: Jean Negulesco; screenwriter: Laird Doyle. Cast: Brenda Marshall (Vicki Moore), David Bruce (David Ritchie), Virginia Field (Claire Weston), Jerome Cowan, Rose Hobart, Richard Ainley, Dorothy Tree.

Bette Davis won her first Academy Award for her performance as the alcoholic actress on the skids who is reformed, but it is believed that the award was meant as a consolation prize for her having failed to win the previous year with a far superior performance as the sluttish Mildred Rogers in *Of Human Bondage.* This romantic triangle story had its good points, mostly because of the presence of Miss Davis. Everyone else in the picture was so much extra baggage although the performances of the other two leading players were intelligently handled.

In the "B" remake, David Bruce plays a rubber plantation owner who falls for a dipsomaniac, Brenda Marshall, who has the reputation of being a jinxed woman. Her rehabilitation is accomplished rather quickly after she has been brought to Bruce's home, but considering the rushed production of recycled Warner Bros.' films, this is an entertaining movie.

208 Dangerous Paradise

Based on the novel *Victory* by Joseph Conrad. Story: Alma, a member of an all-female orchestra playing at a hotel in Sourabaya in the Dutch East Indies, is frightened by the advances of the orchestra's leader, Zangiacomo, and the hotel owner, Schomberg. She stows away on the boat of Heyst, who had been kind to her at the hotel. When he finds her, he grudgingly allows her to go with him to his retreat on a remote island where he has lived since the end of an unhappy love affair. Meanwhile Zangiacomo and Schomberg fight over Alma, with the orchestra leader being killed. Schomberg is taken prisoner by three desperados, Mr. Jones, Ricardo and Pedro. To divert them, Schomberg tells them tales of gold on Heyst's island. This ploy doesn't work as they loot the hotel and kill the owner before setting out for the island, where in a final desperate confrontation with Heyst, Pedro and Ricardo are killed and Alma is wounded. The events have the startling effect on Heyst of reawakening the desire once again to care for another person.

• ***Dangerous Paradise*** (remake). Paramount–Famous Lasky, 1930. Director: William Wellman; screenwriters: William Slavens McNutt and Grover Jones. Cast: Nancy Carroll (Alma), Richard Arlen (Heyst), Warner Oland (Schomberg), Gustav von Seyffertitz (Mr. Jones), Francis McDonald (Ricardo), George Kotsonaros (Pedro), Clarence H. Wilson (Zangiacomo), Dorthea Wolbert, Evelyn Selbie, Willie Fung, Wong Wing, Lillian Worth.

• ***Victory*** (remake). Paramount Pictures, 1940. Director: John Cromwell; screenwriter: John Balderston. Cast: Fredric March (Hendrik Heyst), Betty Field (Alma), Sir Cedric Hardwicke (Mr. Jones), Jerome Cowan (Ricardo), Sig Rumann (Mr. Schomberg), Margaret Wycherly, Fritz Feld, Lionel Royce, Rafaela Ottiano, Chester Gan.

It is probably better to say that these two films, and one made in 1919, called *Victory*, are suggested by the Joseph Conrad novel. Each in its own way is a major deviation from the novelist's complex story of a Dutch East Indies recluse and the girl he is forced to protect from a gang of cutthroats. Of the performers who portrayed Heyst, Fredric March is probably the most effective in registering the transformation from a physical coward to a man of strength, both physical and mental. Cedric Hardwicke was singled out for praise by critics for his interpretation of the main villain of the piece, but director Cromwell maintained that his failure to capture the essence of the Conrad story was because Hardwicke's performance was lacking. Both Nancy Carroll and Betty Field are quite good as the girl all the men crave.

209 The Dark Angel

Based on the play by Guy Bolton, written under the nom de plume of H.B. Trevelyan. Story: The plans of Captain Alan Trent and Kitty Vane to marry are frustrated by their being unable to obtain a marriage license in time when he is unexpectedly ordered back to the front in World War I. Trent is blinded in battle and taken prisoner by the Germans. When he is reported dead, his friend, Captain Shannon, discreetly pays court to Kitty to ease her pain and loneliness. After the war, Shannon discovers Trent trying to make a living by writing children's stories. Even though by now Shannon has fallen in love with Kitty, he reports to her that Trent is alive. She goes to him and he attempts to hide his blindness from her, telling her that his feelings have changed and he feels their engagement should be considered terminated. She sees through this and convinces him that she still loves him and wants to marry him, blind or not.

Goldwyn Productions/First National Pictures, 1925 (original). Silent: Director: George Fitzmaurice; screenwriter: Frances Marion. Cast: Ronald Colman (Capt. Alan Trent), Vilma Banky (Kitty Vane), Wyndham Standing (Capt. Gerald Shannon), Frank Elliott, Charles Lane, Helen Jerome Eddy.

• ***The Dark Angel*** (remake). Goldwyn Productions/United Artists, 1935. Director: Sidney Franklin; screenwriters: Lillian Hellman and Mordaunt Shairp.

Cast: Fredric March (Alan Trent), Merle Oberon (Kitty Vane), Herbert Marshall (Gerald Shannon), Janet Beecher, John Halliday, Henrietta Crosman, Freida Inescourt.

Those who have hankies, prepare to use them now. These films, particularly the remake, are excellent tearjerkers. Merle Oberon and Fredric March have grown up together from childhood. On the night before he must join his troops in World War I, she becomes his bride without benefit of clergy because they cannot secure a marriage license in time. Both Oberon and Herbert Marshall later berate themselves for sending March to his doom when he is reported dead in battle. Instead he has been blinded and taken prisoner by the Germans. After the war, not wishing to be a burden to Oberon, he removes himself to a remote part of England where he writes children's stories under a nom de plume. When he is discovered alive, and Oberon informs him that she is coming to him, March carefully rehearses every step in his familiar rooms so as to conceal his blindness and give force to his intention of maintaining he no longer cares for her. March is masterful portraying a blind man acting as if he had sight. The blind author's performance is almost perfect, but a slight slip gives him away. The film tells the story with feeling and good taste. For her performance, Merle Oberon was nominated for an Academy Award, but did not win. Richard Day, the art director, did win an Oscar.

210 Dark Hazard

Based on the novel *Lady Luck* by W.R. Burnett. Story: Gambler Jim Turner, whose fortunes are tied to the skills of the horses he picks, is married to a puritanical woman who dominates him and does not approve of his activities. When she leaves him to return to a more respectable ex-sweetheart, Turner is able to pick up again with Valerie, a rough and ready race track frequenter who shares his interest in horses, dog racing and gambling.

Warner Bros./First National, 1934 (original). Director: Al Green; screenwriters: Ralph Block and Brown Holmes. Cast: Edward G. Robinson (Jim Turner), Genevieve Tobin (Marge Mayhew), Glenda Farrell (Valerie), Robert Barrat, Gordon Westcott, Hobart Cavanaugh, George Meeker, Henry B. Walthall.

• ***Wine, Women and Horses*** (remake). Warner Bros., 1937. Director: Louis King; screenwriter: Roy Chanslor. Cast: Barton MacLane (Jim Turner), Ann Sheridan (Valerie), Dick Purcell (George Mayhew), Peggy Bates (Marjorie Mayhew), Walter Canell, Lottie Williams, Kenneth Harlan, Eugene Jackson.

None of the characters in either version of the story are people one would like to know. They are each a sum total of their defects and as such are a repellant bunch. In the remake, the role is at least a nice change of pace for MacLane, who usually plays menacing heavies. In neither case is it believable that the gambler character and the righteous little lady from the sticks could stand each other for a moment, let alone make the mistake of getting married.

The Dark Past *see* **Blind Alley**

211 The Dark Swan

Based on Ernest Pascal's story. Story: Eve and Cornelia Quinn are as different as sisters can be. Eve is a shallow but attractive vamp while Cornelia is a quiet, thoughtful girl. The man that Cornelia loves, Lewis Dike, is taken in by Eve and marries her, but her vamping doesn't stop with a wedding ring. Lewis learns of her affair with Wilfred Meadows, but his attempts to reason with his wife get him nowhere. As Cornelia is about to sail for Europe, Lewis meets her at the dock, confesses that he made a mistake in marrying Eve and that he wishes to marry Cornelia as soon as he can divorce Eve. She doesn't give him an affirmative answer, but promises to meet with him after her trip.

Warner Bros., 1924 (original). Silent: Director: Millard Webb; screenwriter: Fred Jackson. Cast: Marie Prevost (Eve Quinn), Monte Blue (Lewis Dike), Helene Chadwick (Cornelia Quinn), John Patrick (Wilfrid Meadows), Lilyan Tashman, Vera Lewis, Carlton Miller, Mary MacLaren, Arthur Rankin.

• ***Wedding Rings*** (remake). First National Pictures, 1929. Director: William Beaudine; screenwriter: Ray Harris. Cast: H.B. Warner (Lewis Dike), Lois Wilson (Cornelia Quinn), Olive Borden (Eve Quinn), Hallam Cooley (Wilfred Meadows), James Ford, Kathlyn Williams, Aileen Manning.

The story of a girl who marries a man only because she boasted that she could take anyone away from her quiet sister seems a bit far-fetched, but then we suppose that not all sisters are looking out for each other's happiness. One does wonder why the poor simp who marries the flirtatious girl hadn't noticed her habit of leading men on and then dropping them as soon as her conquests are hooked.

212 Dark Victory

Based on the play by George Brewer, Jr., and Bertram Bloch. Story: Party girl Judith Traherne suffers from almost unbearable headaches. Brain specialist Dr. Frederick Steele diagnoses it as a brain tumor and performs what appears to be a successful operation. By this time, Steele is in love with Judith and he confides to his nurse, Ann King, that the tumor will grow back. Judith learns that she has but a short time to live and although she initially rejects Steele's marriage proposal, she relents. After their wedding, they retire to his Connecticut farm where they are blissfully happy. But while he is away at a medical convention that she insisted he attend, and with Ann visiting her, she discovers she is losing her eyesight, the condition she has been warned marks that the end is near. With Ann at her side, she retreats to her bed to await death convinced that the few brief months that she has had with Steele have been a lifetime of happiness and that she has proven victorious over both the dark and death.

Warner Bros., 1939 (original). Director: Edmund Goulding; screenwriter: Casey Robinson. Cast: Bette Davis (Judith Traherne), George Brent (Dr. Frederick Steele), Geraldine Fitzgerald (Ann King), Humphrey Bogart (Michael O'Leary), Ronald Reagan (Alec Hamlin), Henry Travers, Cora Weatherspoon, Dorothy Peterson, Herbert Rawlinson.

• ***Stolen Hours*** (remake). United Artists, 1963. Director: Daniel M. Petrie; screenwriters: Jessamyn West and Joseph Hayes. Cast: Susan Hayward (Laura

Pember), Michael Craig (John Carmody), Diane Baker (Ellen Pember), Edward Judd (Mike Bannermann), Paul Rogers (Eric MacKenzie), Robert Bacon, Paul Stassino.

Bette Davis' death scene in *Dark Victory* is one of the most moving ever filmed and convinced audiences that she really had won out over darkness. Geraldine Fitzgerald's performance almost matched that of the great Bette. George Brent, a stalwart performer accustomed to being in the shadow of his female co-stars, gave an admirable interpretation as the doctor who deeply loves his doomed wife. Humphrey Bogart, another in love with Miss Davis, adopted a horrible Irish accident in his role as the horse trainer on the Trahernes' Long Island estate. Ronald Reagan served as one of many rejected suitors. The supporting performers, particularly Henry Travers and Cora Weatherspoon, were excellent.

In the remake, Susan Hayward, who by this time was assuming more and more the roles of head-strong women on a collision course with tragedy that Bette Davis handled so marvelously, reprised the Davis role in a version of *Dark Victory*, here called *Stolen Hours*. It appeared that her fatal malady had tired her to such a point that she was unable to match Davis' spirited performance: whereas Davis was triumphant, Hayward merely died.

The Darling of Paris *see* **The Hunchback of Notre Dame**

213 Daughters Courageous

Based on the play *Fly Away Home* by Dorothy Bennett and Irving White. Story: In this Enoch Arden–like story, long-missing husband Jim Masters returns to his wife and four daughters whom he had abandoned twenty years before. His arrival on the scene corresponds to his wife's decision to marry again to a man who is the complete opposite of her first husband, down-to-earth home-body Sam Sloane. His daughters are not exactly pleased to see their dad, as they good-naturedly scheme to make his stay uncomfortable so he will hit the road again. His appearance does serve a useful purpose, however. Daughter Buff has eyes for a cynical youth, named Gabriel Lopez, who like dear old dad is basically a nomad at heart. Mother and father together make the rather wise point that marriage to Gabriel might well see Buff ending up like her mother. In the end, Masters and Lopez set off together, leaving the family in more stable hands.

Warner Bros., 1939 (original). Director: Michael Curtiz; screenwriters: Julius J. and Philip G. Epstein. Cast: John Garfield (Gabriel Lopez), Claude Rains (Jim Masters), Fay Bainter (Nan Masters), Donald Crisp (Sam Sloane), Priscilla Lane (Buff Masters), Rosemary Lane (Trinka Masters), Lola Lane (Linda Masters), Gale Page (Cora Masters), Jeffrey Lynn, May Robson, Frank McHugh, Dick Foran.

• ***Always in My Heart*** (remake). Warner Bros., 1942. Director: Jo Graham; screenwriter: Adele Commandini. Cast: Kay Francis (Marjorie Scott), Walter Huston (Mackenzie Scott), Gloria Warren (Victoria Scott), Patty Hale (Booley),

Frankie Thomas (Martin Scott), Sidney Blackmer (Philip Ames), Una O'Connor, Armida, Frank Puglia, Russell Arms.

Having killed off John Garfield's character in 1938's extremely popular *Four Daughters,* the producers brought together that film's director and cast to have another go at it, with the performers playing different but similar roles in a story that has some of the same qualities as the earlier piece. It's never made quite clear why the father of the story left his family in the first place, except to note that he's quite a rover. It's an entertaining story with pleasant performances all around, particularly from Fay Bainter as the mother, who seems to rather enjoy having two men compete for her favor.

In the remake, Walter Huston as the father has a very good reason for being long absent from his wife and two children. This outstanding musician has been wrongly convicted and given a life imprisonment sentence. His wife has divorced him, at his urging, even though she still loves him. Daughter Gloria Warren has inherited her father's musical ability, having a beautiful singing voice. Mother Kay Francis is being wooed by rich Sidney Blackmer who attempts to win the children's favor by showering them with luxuries. The father is pardoned when his innocence is established, but doesn't reveal himself to his ex-wife. Instead he tracks down Gloria and helps her with her singing. After a series of predictable episodes, he declares his true identity and gets together again with his wife and family. The film was meant to be a showcase for Warren, who was to be groomed as a rival for Deanna Durbin, but she never caught on with the public, which was growing tired of sweet young girls with operatic voices.

David and Catriona *see* **Kidnapped**

214 David Copperfield

Based on the novel by Charles Dickens. Story: David Copperfield is born six months after the death of his father. His gentle mother remarries and he is disliked immensely by his stepfather, Mr. Murdstone, who sends the boy off to London to make something of himself. David's mother later dies in childbirth. David stays with Mr. Micawber and his huge family but when Micawber is sent to debtor's prison, David runs away to Dover and takes up residence with his Aunt Betsey and her bizarre friend Mr. Dick. These two see to it that David gets a proper schooling and chase Murdstone away when he comes to claim the lad. As an adult, David is an author in love with sickly Dora Spenlow who soon dies. He is unaware of the love of Agnes Wickfield, daughter of the man who provided him with lodging while he was in college. Wickfield enlists the aid of David when the former discovers that he has been cheated by a business associate, Uriah Heep. With the help of Micawber, David is able to defeat Heep and restore to Wickfield what is his. David by now reciprocates the love of Agnes and asks her to become his wife.

• ***David Copperfield*** (remake). Hepworth, Great Britain, 1913. Silent. Director and screenwriter: Thomas Bentley. Cast: Kenneth Ware (David Copperfield), Eric Desmond (David as a child), Len Bethel (David as a youth), Alma

Taylor (Dora Spenlow), H. Collins (Wilkins Micawber), Jack Hulcup (Uriah Heep), Jamie Darling (Daniel Peggotty), Edna May (Little Emily as a child), Amy Verity (Little Emily), Cecil Mannering (Steerforth), Ella Fineberg (Agnes Wickfield), Johnny Butt (Mr. Murdstone), Miss Hartcourt (Betsey Trotwood), Miss West, Shiel Porter, Tom Arnold, Harry Royston, Marie de Solla.

• ***David Copperfield*** (remake). MGM, 1935. Director: George Cukor; screenwriter: Howard Estabrook. Cast: W.C. Fields (Micawber), Freddie Bartholomew (David Copperfield as a child), Frank Lawton (David Copperfield as a man), Elizabeth Allan (Mrs. Copperfield), Jessie Ralph (Nurse Peggotty), Lionel Barrymore (Dan Peggotty), Basil Rathbone (Mr. Murdstone), Edna May Oliver (Betsey Trotwood), Lennox Pawle (Mr. Dick), Maureen O'Sullivan (Dora), Marilyn Knowlden (Agnes as a child), Madge Evans (Agnes as an adult), Fay Chaldecott (Little Emily as a child), Florine McKinney (Little Emily older), Roland Young (Uriah Heep), John Buckler (Ham), Hugh Williams (Steerforth), Lewis Stone (Mr. Wickfield), Elsa Lanchester, Jean Cadell, Violet Kemble-Cooper, Una O'Connor, Ivan Simpson, Herbert Mundin, Harry Beresford, Hugh Walpole, Arthur Treacher.

• ***David Copperfield*** (remake). Omnibus, Great Britain, 1969. Director: Delbert Mann; screenwriter: Jack Pulman. Cast: Richard Attenborough (Mr. Tungay), Cyril Cusack (Barkis), Edith Evans (Betsy Trotwood), Pamela Franklin (Dora), Susan Hampshire (Agnes Wickfield), Wendy Hiller (Mrs. Micawber), Ron Moody (Uriah Heep), Laurence Olivier (Mr. Creakle), Robin Phillips (David Copperfield), Michael Redgrave (Mr. Peggotty), Ralph Richardson (Micawber), Emlyn Williams (Mr. Dick), Isobel Black (Clara Copperfield), Sinead Cusack (Emily), James Donald (Mr. Murdstone), Allison Mackenzie (David as a child), James Hayter, Megs Jenkins, Anna Massey, Nicholas Pennell, Corin Redgrave, Liam Redmond.

Dickens' story has also been filmed in 1912, 1913, 1922, 1923 and 1973. Of the various versions the 1935 Hollywood production is most memorable not so much because of the script but because of the fine assemblage of players, each of whom gave wonderful renditions of their parts. Most deserving of praise are Freddie Bartholomew as young David, W.C. Fields who brings Micawber to life, Edna May Oliver as a marvelously funny and righteous Aunt Betsey, Lionel Barrymore as Dan Peggotty, Roland Young as a perfect Uriah Heep and Lennox Pawle as a splendid Mr. Dick. The 1970 version had a wonderful cast of English actors and actresses but their cameo roles seemed precisely that and they did not uniformly create believable and delightful characters as did those in the 1935 masterpiece. In this piece at least, Hollywood showed England how to successfully film a Dickens work, one not written to be dramatized.

215 David Harum

Based on the novel by Edward Noyes Westcott. Story: In this homey comedy, small town banker David Harum, a bachelor, epigramist and a number one horse trader, makes a series of deals with the stingy, hard-bitten, ursury-exacting church deacon. In a secondary conflict, Harum's city-bred, woman-disillusioned bank teller is pursued by a daughter of a comfortably wealthy family, who is having trouble getting the boy to propose because of his pride and poverty. Everything works out because of a trotting race.

Famous Players/Paramount Pictures, 1915 (original). Silent. Director: George Melford; screenwriter: uncredited. Cast: William H. Crane (David Harum), Kate Meeks (Aunt Polly), May Allison (Mary Blake), Harold Lockwood (John Lenox), Hal Clarendon (Chet Timson), Guy Nichols (Deacon Perkins).

• ***David Harum*** (remake). Fox Film Corp., 1934. Director: James Cruze; screenwriter: Walter Woods. Cast: Will Rogers (David Harum), Louise Dresser (Aunt Polly), Evelyn Venable (Ann), Kent Taylor (John), Stepin Fetchit (Sylvester), Noah Beery (Woolsey), Charles Middleton (Deacon), Roger Imhoff, Frank Melton, Sarah Padden, Lillian Stuart.

David Harum was a role almost tailor-made for Will Rogers, and the team of Evelyn Venable and Kent Taylor as the young lovers were fine for those that like their romances simple, sentimental and old-fashioned. The homespun jokes may not stack up to the ribald and bathroom humor of many of today's stand-up comedians, but they are unlikely to offend anyone except those who may shudder at the stereotype antics of Stepin Fetchit.

216 Dawn Patrol

Based on the story "Flight Commander" by John Monk Saunders. Story: Major Brand, the squadron leader of the 59th British Squadron in France during World War I, is torn between his responsibility to inflict as much damage on the enemy as possible and the sure knowledge that each time he sends out his squadron on a dawn patrol, he is sending mere boys to certain death. Among the more experienced members of his squadron are Dick Courtney and Douglas Scott, close friends and drinking buddies. These two do not appreciate Brand's dilemma and merely consider some of his orders to be ludicrous. After a time, Brand is relieved of duties and Courtney is named squadron leader. He soon experiences the same doubts that had haunted Brand. When Scott's younger brother arrives as a replacement and is sent on a mission from which he never returns, the elder Scott blames Courtney. When a dangerous one-man mission is required, Scott demands the assignment. Courtney, who finds command more strainful than risking one's life on a mission, gets Scott drunk and takes his place. The mission is successful but Courtney is killed and now Scott is given the assignment as squadron leader.

Warner Bros., 1930 (original). Director: Howard Hawks; screenwriters: Dan Totherou, Howard Hawks and Seton I. Miller. Cast: Richard Barthelmess (Dick Courtney), Douglas Fairbanks, Jr. (Douglas Scott), Neil Hamilton (Major Brand), William Janney (Gordon Scott), James Finlayson, Clyde Cook, Gardner James, Edmond Breon, Frank McHugh.

• ***Dawn Patrol*** (remake). Warner Bros., 1938. Director: Edmund Goulding; screenwriters: Seton I. Miller and Dan Totherou. Cast: Errol Flynn (Courtney), David Niven (Scott), Basil Rathbone (Major Brand), Donald Crisp (Phipps), Melville Cooper, Barry Fitzgerald, Michael Brooke, Morton Lowrey, Peter Willes, Carl Esmond.

These powerful air dramas are quite effective in showing that combat can be

Douglas Fairbanks, Jr., takes exception to Richard Barthelmess' orders which will send the former's kid brother (William Janney, center) into the air against the Germans in The Dawn Patrol *(Warner Bros., 1930).*

devastating to those who must make the decisions of life and death as well for those who must take the risks in the air. It's one thing to risk your own life but quite another to demand that others sacrifice theirs for a cause no matter how important it may seem to be. In each film, the three central characters, Courtney, Scott, and Brand, are thoughtfully played by the actors assigned to the roles. In each case the transformation of Courtney from a carefree pilot with no illusions about his chances of ultimate survival to the troubled man who must agonize over sending others to their deaths is quite moving. A mere boy becomes a man, and the process is almost too painful to bear. Both Barthelmess and Flynn handle the chore with great professionalism. The role of Scott as an outwardly cocky young man who can find humor in almost any circumstance is well handled by both Fairbanks and Niven. Neil Hamilton and Basil Rathbone as Major Brand are merely superb as men who must implement orders given by those who do not have to directly deal with the risks, the consequences and the young men affected.

Dead End Kids on Dress Parade *see* **Shipmates Forever**

Dead Man's Shoes *see* **Carrefour**

David Niven and Errol Flynn contemplate their next mission in The Dawn Patrol *(Warner Bros., 1938).*

Dead Men Don't Wear Plaid *see* **The Maltese Falcon**

Deadlier Than the Male *see* **Bulldog Drummond**

Dear Brat *see* **Dear Ruth**

217 Dear Ruth

Based on the play by Norman Krasna. Story: Lt. William Seacroft has a two-day leave and an urge to see the girl, Ruth Wilkins, with whom he has been exchanging some very romantic letters. When he arrives, Ruth doesn't know who he is or what he's talking about. Seems that kid sister Miriam has been doing the writing, having sent Bill her older sister's picture. There's a lot of fun and naturally, the romance between Bill and Ruth takes off after a short time.

Paramount Pictures, 1947 (original). Director: William Russell; screenwriter: Arthur Sheekman. Cast: Joan Caulfield (Ruth Wilkins), William Holden (Lt. William Seacroft), Edward Arnold (Judge Harry Wilkins), Mary Phillips (Mrs. Edith Wilkins), Mona Freeman (Miriam Wilkins), Billy De Wolfe, Kenny O'Morrison, Virginia Welles, Marietta Canty.

- ***Dear Wife*** (sequel). Paramount Pictures, 1949. Director: Richard Haydn;

screenwriters: Arthur Sheekman and N. Richard Nash. Cast: William Holden (Bill Seacroft), Joan Caulfield (Ruth Seacroft), Billy De Wolfe (Albert Kummer), Mona Freeman (Miriam Wilkins), Edward Arnold (Judge Wilkins), Arleen Whelan, Mary Phillips, Harry Von Zell, Raymond Roe, Elizabeth Fraser.

• ***Dear Brat*** (sequel). Paramount Pictures, 1951. Director: William A. Seiter; screenwriter: Devery Freeman. Cast: Mona Freeman (Miriam), Billy De Wolfe (Albert), Edward Arnold (Senator Wilkins), Lyle Bettger (Baxter), Mary Phillips, Natalie Wood, William Reynolds, Frank Cady, Lillian Randolph, Irene Winston.

In the first sequel, Holden and Caulfield, now man and wife, must deal with the family problems caused by Holden being snagged into running for a state senatorship against his father-in-law, Edward Arnold. Things get a bit thin in the third reincarnation with Holden and Caulfield among the missing. That leaves it up to Mona Freeman to bear the brunt of this attempt to carry on the wholesome family humor of the first two films, and things are a bit tough for her. All aglow with the desire to further social reform, she brings to her home as gardener Lyle Bettger, an embittered man who had been sentenced to jail by her father when he was a judge. The complications that arise seem forced and everyone knew it was time to write finis to this family feature.

Dear Wife ***see*** **Dear Ruth**

Death Drums Along the River ***see*** **Sanders of the River**

218 Death Wish

Based on the novel by Brian Garfield. Story: When successful Manhattan architect Paul Kersey's wife is murdered and his daughter left in a catatonic state after being brutally raped, he becomes a one-man vigilante squad, intent on ridding New York of some of its vermin. He goes looking to be mugged, so that he can calmly turn on his attackers and cold-bloodedly blow them away. He becomes something of a cult hero while the police try to track him down. His activities seemingly reduce the incidence of muggings and other violent street crimes as those engaged in such activities fear encountering him. Eventually, Inspector Frank Ochoa apprehends Kersey, but neither the inspector nor the higher-ups in the police or city administration wish to prosecute this media hero. They settle for him getting out of town.

Dino de Laurentiis/Paramount, 1974 (original). Director: Michael Winner; screenwriter: Wendell Mayes. Cast: Charles Bronson (Paul Kersey), Hope Lange (Joanna Kersey), Vincent Gardenia (Inspector Frank Ochra), Kathleen Tolan, Steven Keats, William Redfield, Stuart Margolin, Stephen Elliot.

• ***Death Wish II*** (sequel). Golan/Globus, 1981. Director: Michael Winner; screenwriter: David Engelbach. Cast: Charles Bronson, Jill Ireland, Vincent Gardenia, J.D. Cannon, Anthony Franciosa.

Audiences seemed to take vicarious satisfaction in the actions of a man who strikes back when violence ruins his comfortable existence. It's understandable if not defendable that a man who had lost his wife and seen his daughter turned into a vegetable might court revenge, even to take it against those who had nothing to do with the crime that affected him, but clearly were guilty of similar offenses. The knowledge that city streets and even locked apartments are not safe from the intrusion of violence and that authorities seem unable to do anything about it, makes the easy solution of vigilante activity appealing if not legal, moral or even practical. In the remake, Bronson is up to his old tricks but now it is Los Angeles that he is attempting to clean up. In 1985, in *Death Wish 3*, he is back at the old stand, dealing with a gang of punks who are terrorizing his neighborhood. Each of the succeeding films depends more on repellant violence while sacrificing story quality. *Death Wish IV* arrived in 1986.

Death Wish II *see* **Death Wish**

Death Wish III *see* **Death Wish**

Death Wish IV *see* **Death Wish**

219 Decameron Nights

Based on the stories by Giovanni Boccaccio. Story: The bawdy stories by Boccaccio which have been filmed, depend on the production. In the 1924 silent, Saladin's disguised son loves an amnesiac Moslem princess. In the 1953 version, there are three tales woven around Boccaccio's wooing of Fiametta. The first, "Paganino the Pirate," deals with an elderly husband who prefers astrology to intimacy with his young wife, so she allows herself to be kidnapped by a handsome pirate to get the job done. The second, "Wager for Virtue," has a merchant losing faith in his wife's faithfulness due to circumstantial evidence provided by a rogue who has goaded the man into betting on his wife's virtue. The final story, "The Doctor's Daughter," is of a wife spurned by her husband, because he married her only at the command of his king.

• ***Decameron Nights*** (remake). Graham-Wilcox Productions, Great Britain, 1924. Silent. Director: Herbert Wilcox; screenwriters: Herbert Wilcox and Noel Rhys. Cast: Lionel Barrymore (Saladin), Ivy Duke (Perdita), Werner Krauss (Soldan), Bernhard Goetzke (Torello), Randle Ayrton (Ricciardo), Xenia Desni, Jameson Thomas, Hannah Ralph, Albert Steinruck.

• ***Decameron Nights*** (remake). Eros/RKO, 1952. Director: Hugh Fregonese; screenwriter: George Oppenheimer. Cast: Louis Jourdan (Boccaccio/Paganino/Guilo/Bertrando), Joan Fontaine (Fiametta/Bartolomea/Ginevra/Isabella), Binnie Barnes (Contessa/Countess/Nerina/Witch), Joan Collins (Pampinea/Maria), Godfrey Tearle (Ricciardo/Bernabo), Mara Lane, Eliot Makeham, Meinhart Maur, Noel Purcell, Marjorie Rhodes.

Boccaccio's saucy tales were also filmed in 1912, 1922, 1924, 1928, 1936 and 1972. In 1971, Pier Paolo Pasolini directed an octet of the stories with the director, as Giotto, linking them up. His production, starring Franco Citti, Ninetto Davali, Angela Luce, Patrizia Capparelli, Jovan Jovanovic, Silvano Magnano and others, was more earthy than the previous works, reflecting the times and the more permissive atmosphere in Italy. The 1952 version wasn't even titillating, leaving one uninformed as to why the Decamerons had such a naughty reputation. Adding to the production's problems was a very poor Technicolor print.

Deception *see* **Jealously**

Demetrius and the Gladiators *see* **The Robe**

Le Dernier Tourant *see* **The Postman Always Rings Twice**

Desdemona *see* **Othello**

Desdemona's Room *see* **Othello**

The Desert Hawk *see* **Arabian Nights**

Designing Woman *see* **Woman of the Year**

The Devil and Daniel Webster *see* **Faust**

220 Devil's Mate

Based on a story by Leonard Fields and David Silverstein. Story: In this mystery yarn, the first murder is of a kid being led to his execution in the electric chair. Although there's another murder and another attempted murder, it's hard to improve on the first for originality. The only ones who don't know the identity of the murderer early in the film are the dumb detectives and reporters.

Monogram Pictures, 1933 (original). Director: Phil Rosen; screenwriters: Leonard Fields and David Silverstein. Cast: Peggy Shannon (Nancy Weaver), Preston Foster (Inspector O'Brien), Ray Walker (Natural), Hobart Cavanaugh (Parkhurst), Barbara Barondess (Gwen), Paul Porcasi, Harold Waldridge, Jason Robards, Bryant Washburn, Harry Holman.

• ***I Killed That Man*** (remake). Monogram Pictures, 1942. Director: Phil Rosen; screenwriter: Harry Bancroft. Cast: Ricardo Cortez (Phillips), Joan Woodbury (Geri), Iris Adrian (Verne Drake), George Pembroke (King), Herbert Rawlinson (Warden), Pat Gleason, Ralf Harolde, Jack Mulhall, Vince Barnett.

The first piece is a dim mystery melodrama and the remake falls off from that standard. Many of the films coming from Monogram Studios were made with no pretense of having any cinematic value, but the producers knew there was a market out there for stories that weren't too taxing. These two are perfect examples of the secret of that particular success.

Dhanwan *see* **The Hunchback of Notre Dame**

221 Diary of a Chambermaid

Based on a novel by Octave Mirbeau. Story: Celestine, an opportunistic chambermaid, causes sexual frustration for members of two nineteenth-century French provincial households. Her admirers include the weak master of the house, M. Lanlaire, who is completely dominated by his wife; an eccentric aging ex-soldier, Captain Manger, who lives next door; his menacing valet, Joseph, and the wastel son of her mistress. Eventually, Celestine finds love and wealth but not before the valet kills his employer.

United Artists, 1946 (original). Director: Jean Renoir; screenwriter: Burgess Meredith. Cast: Paulette Goddard (Celestine), Burgess Meredith (Captain Manger), Hurd Hatfield (Georges Lanlaire), Francis Lederer (Joseph), Judith Anderson (Mme. Lanlaire), Reginald Owen (M. Lanlaire), Florence Bates, Irene Ryan, Almira Sessins.

• ***Diary of a Chambermaid*** (remake). Speva Films, 1964. Director: Luis Bunuel; screenwriter: Luis Bunuel and Jean Claude Carriere. Cast: Jeanne Moreau (Celestine), Michel Piccoli (M. Montiel), George Geret (Joseph), Francois Lugagne (Mme. Montiel), Daniel Ivernel (Captain Manger), Jean Ozenne (M. Rebour).

Goddard as a blonde arouses all kinds of emotions in her snooty household. She comes across a bit more innocently than does Jeanne Moreau in the remake. The first production of this romantic melodrama doesn't seem certain of where it is going. The dark humor and social comment are only partially successful. Meredith, who produced this film for his then-wife Goddard, is quite good as is Irene Ryan as a timid scullery maid. The other performers handle their chores adequately if not outstandingly. Bunuel uses the remake to comment on the changing French social structure before World War I, resulting in an interesting but not particularly successful effort. While the camera work by Lucien Andriot and the art work by Eugene Loarie in the first production is most effective, the visual quality of the remake is unattractive.

222 Dick Tracy

Based on the comic strip created by Chester Gould. Story: Jut-jawed Dick Tracy must deal with denizens of the underworld headed up by a disfigured criminal named Splitface.

RKO, 1945 (original). Director: William Berke; screenwriter: Eric Taylor. Cast: Morgan Conway (Dick Tracy), Mike Mazurki (Splitface), Jane Greer, Anne Jeffreys, Lyle Latell, Joseph Crehan, Trevor Bardette.

• ***Dick Tracy Meets Gruesome*** (sequel). RKO, 1947. Director: John Rawlins; screenwriter: uncredited. Cast: Ralph Byrd (Dick Tracy), Boris Karloff (Gruesome), Anne Gwynne, Edward Ashley, June Clayworth.

Other RKO sequels included *Dick Tracy Meets Cueball* and *Dick Tracy's Dilemma.* In addition, Ralph Byrd appeared in a number of Republic serials as the celebrated sleuth. Unfortunately for Byrd, he became so identified with the role that he found it difficult to find other parts. Besides Byrd, Boris Karloff, with his usual fine style, is eminently watchable as Gruesome in the 1947 feature.

Dick Tracy Meets Gruesome *see* **Dick Tracy**

Did You Hear the One About the Traveling Sales-Lady? *see* **The First Traveling Saleslady**

Dirtie Gertie from Harlem *see* **Sadie Thompson**

223 Dirty Harry

Based on a story by Harry Julian Fink and R.M. Fink. Story: A psychotic sniper, Scorpio, is terrorizing San Francisco. The killer sends a letter to the mayor, threatening to continue the mayhem unless he is paid $100,000. Harry Callahan is chosen to deliver the money. After bouncing Harry all over the city with elaborate telephone instructions, the sniper and the cop come face to face. Harry is told to throw away his gun and when he does, he receives a series of kicks to the head and body by the madman. Harry pulls out a stiletto and stabs Scorpio in the leg. The killer limps off without the money. Harry checks the local emergency wards of hospitals until at one he learns that a man answering Scorpio's description was treated for a leg wound and released. Harry is told the man claimed to be employed at Kezar Stadium. Going there, Harry encounters Scorpio, shoots him in the leg and takes him in. Much to Harry's chagrin, Scorpio is released because Harry did not honor the killer's constitutional rights. Angered, Harry begins to trail Scorpio. When the latter hijacks a school bus and holds a boy as hostage, Harry, a crack shot, shoots Scorpio in the shoulder, allowing the child to get away. When Scorpio makes a play for his gun, Harry blows him away.

Malpaso Company, 1971 (original). Director: Don Siegel; screenwriters: Harry Julien Fink, R.M. Fink and Dean Riesner. Cast: Clint Eastwood (Harry Callahan), Harry Guardino (Bressler), Reni Santoni (Chico), Andy Robinson (Scorpio), John Larch (Chief), John Vernon (Mayor), John Mitchum, Mae Mercer.

• ***Magnum Force*** (sequel). Malpaso Company, 1973. Director: Ted Post; screenwriters: John Millus and Michael Cimino. Cast: Clint Eastwood (Harry Callahan), Hal Holbrook (Lt. Briggs), Mitchell Ryan (McCoy), David Soul (Davis), Felton Perry (Early Smith), Robert Ulrich, Kip Niven, Tim Matheson.

Eastwood's character is nicknamed "Dirty Harry" because he always pulls the "dirtiest" assignments. Eastwood seems perfectly cast as the tough, uncompromising cop who hates criminals, particularly killers. He carries a .44 magnum revolver which can blow a person's head clear off. The film and the three other productions in the series are clearly produced to appeal to those who feel criminals are coddled by judicial decisions and restraints placed on police methods. *Magnum Force,* which is not a sequel in the usual sense, carries on this theme; only this time Harry has to combat a squad of rookie motorcycle cops acting as vigilantes, intent on ridding the streets of San Francisco of criminal vermin by executing them. Some critics claimed that the violence of the "Dirty Harry" movies was a substitute for explicit sex which could not be shown on the screen. This observation seemed to have some merit in the two films that followed, *The Enforcer* in 1976 and *Sudden Impact* in 1983. The latter is best remembered for Harry's classic line, "Go ahead, make my day," as a crook tries to decide if he should risk trying to out-shoot the cop. These films, if anything, featured even more violence and gun justice dished out by Harry Callahan than did the first two.

Dive Bomber ***see*** **Submarine D-1**

The Divorce of Lady X ***see*** **Counsel's Opinion**

224 The Dixie Merchant

Based on the novel *The Chicken-Wagon Family* by John Barry Benefield. Story: When easygoing J.P. Fippany loses his backwoods Louisiana home, he takes to the road with his wife Josephine and daughter Aida in a chickenwagon. The wagon is wrecked in a collision with Jimmy Pickett's car. The latter falls in love with Aida, but because of a misunderstanding about the Fippanys' racehorse, Marseillaise, Josephine and her daughter leave J.P. to live with relatives. Most unhappy at these turn of events, Fippany sells the horse to Jimmy's father, sends the purchase price to his wife and disappears. Meanwhile, Jimmy locates Aida and convinces her that he loves her. Fippany reappears in time to ride Marseillaise to victory in an important race and then is reconciled with his family.

Fox Film Corp., 1926 (original). Silent. Director: Frank Borzage; screenwriter: Kenneth B. Clarke. Cast: J. Farrell MacDonald (Jean Paul Fippany), Madge Bellamy (Aida Fippany), Jack Mulhall (Jimmy Pickett), Claire McDowell (Josephine Fippany), Harvey Clarke, Edward Martindel, Evelyn Arden, Onest Conly, Paul Panzer.

• ***Chicken Wagon Family*** (remake). Twentieth Century–Fox, 1939. Director: Herbert I. Leeds; screenwriter: Viola Brothers Shore. Cast: Jane Withers (Addie Fippany), Leo Carrillo (J.P.B. Fippany), Marjorie Weaver (Cecile), Spring Byington (Josephine), Kane Richmond, Hobart Cavanaugh, Hamilton McFadden, Inez Palange.

In the silent film, J. Farrell MacDonald was the leading performer, so he carried the action and eventually put things right for all concerned. In the remake, the star is young Jane Withers, and as the youngest member of a family of Cajuns who makes a trip to New York City in a chickenwagon pulled by mules, she must constantly be on the alert or Papa Leo Carrillo will gamble away all of the family's money. It's not among Jane's better pictures and no one in the cast sounds good trying to speak a jumbled French dialect meant to pass for Cajun.

225 D.O.A.

Based on a story by Russell Rouse and Clarence Green. Story: Frank Bigelow is slipped deadly luminous poison in a drink while he is making the rounds of San Francisco flesh spots. He learns from a doctor that there is nothing that can be done; he'll be dead within a couple of days. He spends this time tracking down his murderer, whom he kills, and as he finishes telling his story to the police, he drops down dead, marked D.O.A.—"Dead on Arrival."

United Artists, 1949 (original). Director: Rudolph Mate; screenwriters: Russell Rouse and Clarence Green. Cast: Edmond O'Brien (Frank Bigelow), Pamela Britton (Paula Gibson), Luther Adler (Majak), Beverly Campbell (Miss Foster), Lynn Baggett (Mrs. Phillips), William Ching, Henry Hart, Neville Brand, Laurette Luez, Jesse Kirkpatrick.

• ***Color Me Dead*** (remake). Goldsworthy, Australia, 1969. Director: Eddie Davis; screenwriters: Russell Rouse and Clarence Green. Cast: Tom Tryon (Frank Bigelow), Carolyn Jones (Paula Gibson), Rick Jason (Bradley Taylor), Patricia Connolly (Maria Rakubian), Tony Ward (Halliday), Penny Sugg (Miss Foster), Reginald Gilliam, Margot Reid, Peter Sumner, Michael Lawrence, Sandy Harbott.

The remake is almost identical to the original, with Tom Tryon being slipped radioactive poisoning because he notarized a phony uranium deal. His murderer tries to shoot him and attempts two more poisonings but Tom gets his own murderer, before dying. In 1987, Dennis Quaid appears in a disappointing remake of D.O.A.

Docks of New Orleans *see* **Mr. Wong, Detective**

Dr. Black and Mr. Hyde *see* **Dr. Jekyll and Mr. Hyde**

Doctor Faustus *see* **Faust**

Dr. Jekyll *see* **Dr. Jekyll and Mr. Hyde**

226 Dr. Jekyll and Mr. Hyde

Based on the novel by Robert Louis Stevenson. Story: Decent, dedicated London physician and scientist Dr. Henry Jekyll has discovered a formula that totally changes a person's personality. When he experiments on himself, the formula transforms him into a person who calls himself Mr. Hyde and is opposite to Jekyll in every way possible. Whereas Jekyll is handsome, Hyde is hideous; Jekyll kind and sensitive, Hyde beastly and violent. Jekyll is engaged to a beautiful socialite, but Hyde takes up with a poor prostitute that Jekyll had once befriended in an innocent and humanitarian way. Jekyll discovers that he can no longer control the transformations and that the evil Hyde is becoming dominant. When Hyde kills his unfortunate mistress in a rage, the police are after him. Depending on the version of the story filmed, Hyde is killed by the authorities and as he dies, the person of Jekyll reappears, or in a last great effort to control his evil alter ego, Jekyll commits suicide, thus killing both himself and Hyde.

• ***Dr. Jeckyll and Mr. Hyde*** (remake). Paramount-Artcraft Pictures, 1920. Silent. Director: John Stewart Robertson; screenwriter: Clara S. Beranger. Cast: John Barrymore (Dr. Jekyll/ Mr. Hyde), Martha Mansfield (Millicent

The shadow of Mr. Hyde threatens Ingrid Bergman, Spencer Tracy and Lana Turner in the 1941 MGM version of Dr. Jekyll and Mr. Hyde. *The Robert Louis Stevenson tale has been filmed many times with earlier productions starring John Barrymore in 1920 and Fredric March in 1931.*

Carew), Brandon Hurst (Sir George Carew), Charles Lane (Richard Landon), Nita Naldi (Therese), Cecil Clovelly (Edward Enfield), George Stevens, Louis Wolheim, J. Malcolm Dunn.

• ***Dr. Jekyll and Mr. Hyde*** (remake). Paramount Pictures, 1931. Director: Rouben Mamoulian; screenwriters: Samuel Hoffenstein and Percy Heath. Cast: Fredric March (Dr. Jekyll/Mr. Hyde), Rose Hobart (Muriel Carew), Miriam

Hopkins (Ivy Pearson), Holmes Herbert (Dr. Lanyon), Halliwell Hobbes (Brigadier General Carew), Edgar Norton, Arnold Lucy, Eric Wilton, Tempe Pigott.

• ***Dr. Jekyll and Mr. Hyde*** (remake). MGM, 1941. Director: Victor Fleming; screenwriter: John Lee Mahin. Cast: Spencer Tracy (Dr. Jekyll/Mr. Hyde), Ingrid Bergman (Ivy Pearson), Lana Turner (Betrix Emery), Donald Crisp (Sir Charles Emery), Barton MacLane (Sam Higgins), C. Aubrey Smith, Peter Godfrey, Sara Allgood, Frederic Worlock, Ian Hunter, Frances Robinson.

• ***The Son of Dr. Jekyll*** (sequel). Columbia Pictures, 1951. Director: Seymour Friedman; screenwriters: Mortimer Braus and Jack Pollexfen. Cast: Louis Hayward (Edward Jekyll), Jody Lawrence (Lynn), Alexander Knox (Curtis Landon), Lester Matthews (John Utterson), Gavin Muir, Paul Cavanaugh, Rhys Williams.

• ***The Two Faces of Dr. Jekyll*** (U.S. release: ***House of Fright***) (remake). Hammer Films, 1961. Director: Terence Fisher; screenwriter: Wolf Mankowitz. Cast: Paul Massie (Dr. Jekyll/Mr. Hyde), Dawn Addams (Kitty), Christopher Lee (Paul Allen), David Kossoff (Litauer), Francis De Wolff, Norman Marla.

• ***The Nutty Professor*** (remake). Paramount Pictures, 1963. Director: Jerry Lewis; screenwriters: Bill Raymond and Jerry Lewis. Cast: Jerry Lewis (Prof. Julius F. Kelp/Buddy Love), Stella Stevens (Stella Purdy), Del Moore (Dr. Hamius R. Warfield), Kathleen Freeman (Millie Lemmon), Howard Morris, Elvira Allman, Med Flory.

• ***Doctor Jekyll and Sister Hyde*** (sequel). Hammer Films, 1971. Director: Roy Ward Baker; screenwriter: Brian Clemens. Cast: Ralph Bates (Dr. Jekyll), Martine Bestick (Sister Hyde), Gerald Sim (Professor Robertson), Lewis Fiander (Howard), Dorothy Alison (Mrs. Spencer), Neil Wilson, Ivor Dean.

• ***I, Monster*** (a.k.a. ***The Man With Two Heads***) (remake). British Lions–Amicus Pictures, 1971. Director: Stephen Weeks; screenwriter: Milton Subotsky. Cast: Christopher Lee (Dr. Charles Marlowe/Edward Blake), Peter Cushing (Utterson), Susan Jameson (Diane), Mike Raven (Enfield), Richard Hurndall (Lanyon), George Merritt, Marjie Lawrence, Kenneth J. Warren.

Other versions of the Stevenson story, *The Strange Case of Dr Jekyll and Mr. Hyde,* were produced in 1908 by Selig Polyscope; in Denmark in 1910; in England in 1910 as *The Duality of Man;* in Norway in 1910; by Thanhouser Pictures in 1912; in 1913 by Universal under the name *IMP*, produced by Kineto-Kinemacolor Pictures; in 1920 by Pioneer Pictures with Sheldon Lewis in the dual roles; and in Germany in 1920 as *Der Januskopf* with Conrad Veidt as Dr. Warren and Mr. O'Connor. In the sound era, Argentina produced *Hombre y la Bestia* in 1950; Italy released *Dr. Jekyll* in 1951 and *My Friend Jekyll* in 1960; and Universal gave audiences the comedy *Abbott and Costello Meet Dr. Jekyll and Mr. Hyde* in 1953. In addition, the Indian film *Shada Kalo* was released in 1953; Great Britain produced a version called *The Ugly Duckling* in 1959 and *Heckyl and Mr. Hype* in 1980 with Oliver Reed as an ugly scientist tranformed by a formula into a handsome sadist; France came out with *La Testament du Docteur Cordelier* in 1961; and Mexico checked in with *Pact with the Devil* in 1968. There were also two independent American exploitation productions,

Adult Version of Dr. Jekyll and Mr. Hyde in 1972 and *Dr. Black and Mr. Hyde* in 1976.

John Barrymore in 1920 created an intense Dr. Jekyll and a terrifying Mr. Hyde in his highly successful effort to bring this psychological drama to the screen. Most critics find Fredric March's portrayal of a man who had discovered the way to separate the good and evil parts of his personality the most satisfying, with Miriam Hopkins' seductive performance making it understandable that a decent man might lust in his heart for her and have this desire boil over in the heat of a repressed part of one's self. The 1941 version's atmosphere and staging had the proper feeling for the piece and the era in which it was set but Spencer Tracy's decision not to depend on make-up in his appearances as Hyde made him appear more ill than mad. Ingrid Bergman's performance as the poor prostitute wasn't too bad but paled in comparison with that of Hopkins. Lana Turner, like Rose Hobart before her, didn't seem like the kind of girl who could interest a man so that he wouldn't have to turn to sluttish barmaids.

In *The Son of Dr. Jekyll,* the producers ignored the fact that in all previous filmings of the story, Jekyll died before he could marry his patient fiancée. Could it be that the good doctor wasn't as pure as we were led to believe? The two Hammer Films productions, as was that company's practice, emphasized the horror aspects of the story rather than those of a psychological nature. One supposes if a personality switch is to result in a man becoming a woman, the attractive Martine Beswick is not too bad a choice. Since all of Jerry Lewis' characters are weird if not insane, it's difficult to get too excited about his version although one must admit the film was a notch or two higher in quality than his usual productions. About the best that one can say about the adequate production *I, Monster* is that Christopher Lee was the tallest Dr. Jekyll and Mr. Hyde, even though his characters didn't go by those names.

Doctor Jekyll and Sister Hyde *see* **Dr. Jekyll and Mr. Hyde**

227 Dr. Strangelove

Based on the novel *Red Alert* by Peter George. Story: When General Jack D. Ripper, commander of the U.S. Air Force base at Burpelson, goes off the deep end and orders a B-52 atomic bomb attack on Russia, the President of the United States and others must find a way to recall the planes. President Muffley, despite the hysterical advice of General Buck Turgidson to take advantage of the situation, orders the army to attack Burpelson Air Base. Ripper kills himself rather than be captured, but his R.A.F. aide, Group Captain Lionel Mandrake, figures out the code that must precede any message to the planes before they will respond to orders to return. All seems well until it is noted that one air wing is not responding because their equipment had been damaged. The president learns from the Soviet ambassador that the Russians have a doomsday device, which will destroy the world if there is even one atomic bomb dropped on their territory. Desperate, the president turns to his crippled ex–Nazi advisor, Dr.

Strangelove, who calculates that humanity can survive if a select few take to underground shelters and remain there for about 100 years.

Columbia Pictures, 1964 (original). Director: Stanley Kubrick; screenwriters: Kubrick, Terry Southern and Peter George. Cast: Peter Sellers (Group Captain Lionel Mandrake/President Muffley/Dr. Strangelove), George C. Scott (General Buck Turgidson), Sterling Hayden (General Jack D. Ripper), Keenan Wynn (Col. Bat Guano), Slim Pickens (Maj. T.J. "King" Kong), Peter Bull, Tracy Reed, James Earl Jones, Jack Creley, Frank Berry, Shane Rimmer.

• ***Fail Safe*** (remake). Columbia Pictures, 1964. Director: Sidney Lumet; screenwriter: Walter Berstein, based on the novel of the same name by Eugene Burdick and Harvey Wheeler. Cast: Henry Fonda (The President), Dan O'Herlihy (General Black), Walter Matthau (Groeteschele), Frank Overton (Gen. Bogan), Edward Binns (Col. Grady), Fritz Weaver (Col. Cascio), Larry Hagman (Buck), William Hansen, Russell Hardie, Russell Collins, Sorrell Booke, Nancy Berg.

The first film, released in January 1964, subtitled *Or, How I Learned to Stop Worrying and Love the Bomb,* was a tongue-in-cheek, whistling-in-the-dark farce. The second feature, released in October 1964, took matters more seriously. When an emergency arises, bombers from Strategic Air Command head for their fail-safe points. When matters are cleared up, all return except one air wing, which didn't get the message because of an electronic glich. They fly past their fail-safe point headed for Moscow where they will drop atomic bombs. The president of the United States and his cabinet attempt to find a way to avert the impending disaster, with Fonda as the president talking on the red phone to the Russian premier. Finally when it is clear that Moscow is doomed, Fonda orders an atomic bomb dropped on New York as evidence of good faith with the Soviet leader. He is aware that the first lady is that day visiting the Big Apple.

228 Dr. Syn

Based on the novel by Russell Thorndyke. Story: In the nineteenth century, the vicar of Dymchurch parish church, Dr. Syn, is in reality the pirate Clegg, believed hanged some 20 years earlier. His parishioners are his accomplices in smuggling. When the revenue agents come hunting him, he destroys all evidence against him, marries his daughter to the squire's son and escapes to continue his life of crime.

Gaumont, Great Britain, 1937 (original). Director: Roy William Neill; screenwriters: Michael Hogan and Roger Burford. Cast: George Arliss (Dr. Syn), John Loder (Denis Cobtree), Margaret Lockwood (Imogene), Roy Emerton (Capt. Howard Collyer), Graham Moffatt (Jerry Jack), Frederick Burtwell, George Merritt, Athole Stewart, Wally Patch, Meinhart Maur.

• ***Captain Clegg*** (remake). Hammer/Universal, Great Britain, 1962. Director: Peter Graham Scott; screenwriters: Barbara S. Harper and Anthony Hinds. Cast: Peter Cushing (Dr. Blyss), Yvonne Romain (Imogene), Patrick Allen (Capt. Collier), Oliver Reed (Harry Crabtree), Michael Ripper (Mipps), Martin Benson, David Lodge, Daphne Anderson, Derek Francis, Milton Reid.

• ***Dr. Syn—Alias the Scarecrow*** (remake). Walt Disney, Great Britain, 1963. Director: James Neilson; screenwriter: Robert Westerby. Cast: Patrick McGoohan (Dr. Syn), George Cole (Sexton Mipps), Tony Britton (Simon Bates), Michael Hordern (Sir Thomas Banks), Geoffrey Keen (General Pugh), Kay Walsh (Mrs. Waggett), Eric Pohlman, Patrick Wymark, Alan Dobie, Sean Scully.

By the time Patrick McGoohan assumed the role, the village vicar and smuggler had grown much younger and therefore wasn't strapped with a daughter that he had to marry off. The first version of the story is the most exciting and well-handled.

Dr. Syn—Alias the Scarecrow *see* **Dr. Syn**

229 A Dog of Flanders

Based on the novel by *Ouida*. Story: It's the dull story of a Dutch lad, Nello, his noble dog, the boy's love for Maria, his rival for her (Pieter), a drawing contest—and isn't that enough excitement for you?

RKO Radio Pictures, 1935 (original). Director: Edward Sloman; screenwriter: Ainsworth Morgan. Cast: Frankie Thomas (Nello), Helen Parrish (Maria), O.P. Heggie (Jehan), Richard Quine (Pieter), Christian Rub, De Witt Jennings, Ann Shoemaker.

• ***A Dog of Flanders*** (remake). Twentieth Century–Fox, 1959. Director: James B. Clark; screenwriter: Ted Sherman. Cast: David Ladd, Donald Crisp, Theodore Bikel, Max Croiset, Monique Ahrens.

Metro had done a silent version of this idyllic tale of a boy and his dog. Jackie Coogan was the star in that version of the old-fashioned tearjerker. There was also a short version of the story in 1914. Things didn't get much better in the 1959 version. The experience may have been what inspired Alan Ladd's son, David, to consider joining brother Alan Jr. in running studios—not appearing before the camera.

230 A Doll's House

Based on the play by Henrik Ibsen. Story: Nora Helmer is treated as a child by her husband, Torvald. When he becomes ill, Nora forges the signature of her wealthy father. A clerk, Nils Krogstad, who has been dismissed from her husband's bank, learns of this and threatens her with exposure unless she convinces her husband to reinstate him to his position. Nora seeks help from her friend, terminally ill and cynical Dr. Rank, but despite his love for her, he is of no assistance. With the help of Kristine Linden, Krogstad is convinced to withdraw his accusation against Nora, but her deed is discovered by her husband. He berates her for her action, treating her even more like a child than before. Finally realizing that she is not a companion or wife to her husband but merely a "toy" or "doll" in his house, Nora packs her bags and leaves his home, slamming the door with a resounding bang behind her.

• ***A Doll's House*** (remake). Universal Pictures, 1917. Silent. Director and screenwriter: Joseph De Grasse. Cast: Dorothy Phillips (Nora Helmer),

William Stowell (Torvald Helmer), Lon Chaney (Nils Krogstad), Miriam Shelby (Mrs. Linden), Sidney Dean (Dr. Rank).

• ***A Doll's House*** (remake). Paramount Pictures, 1918. Silent. Director and screenwriter: Maurice Tourneur. Cast: Elsie Ferguson (Nora), Holmes E. Herbert (Torvald), Alexander K. Shannon (Nils Krogstad), Warren Cook (Dr. Rank), Ethel Grey Terry (Mrs. Linden).

• ***A Doll's House*** (remake). United Artists, 1922. Silent. Director: Charles Bryant; screenwriter: Peter M. Winters. Cast: Alla Nazimova (Nora), Alan Hale (Torvald), Wedgewood Nowell (Krogstad), Nigel De Brulier (Dr. Rank), Florence Fisher (Mrs. Linden).

• ***A Doll's House*** (remake). Paramount Pictures, 1973. Director: Patrick Garland; screenwriter: Christopher Hampton. Cast: Claire Bloom (Nora), Anthony Hopkins (Torvald), Denholm Elliott (Krogstad), Ralph Richardson (Dr. Rank), Anna Massey (Kristine Linde).

• ***A Doll's House*** (remake). Tomorroe Entertainment/World Film, 1973. Director: Joseph Losey; screenwriter: David Mercer. Cast: Jane Fonda (Nora), David Warner (Torvald), Edward Fox (Krogstad), Trevor Howard (Dr. Rank), Delphine Syrig (Kristine Linde).

Other film productions of the Ibsen classic occurred in 1911 by Thanhouser Pictures; an independent American production in 1915; a Russian version called *Her Sacrifice* in 1917; German productions in 1922 and 1944, entitled *Nora;* and an Argentinian filming in 1943, called *Casa de Munecas.*

Each of the filmings of Ibsen's feminist play of a young woman finally resisting her husband's dominance has suffered some panning by critics and has not played well in Peoria. The critics usually compared the production and emoting unfavorably with that seen on the legitimate stage. Perhaps for this reason, the 1922 production starring Nazimova fared the best with the critics, as she had quite successfully played the role of Nora on the stage. Of the two 1973 productions, the one with Claire Bloom was found by most critics to be superior to the Jane Fonda interpretation. The former was considered to be well-staged and performed, while the latter was too solemn and the casting of Miss Fonda was questioned. The reason for two productions in the same year, no doubt, was a result of the women's liberation movement, which was in full swing in 1973.

231 Don Juan

Based on the poem by George Gordon Byron. Story: In a prologue, Don Jose, learning of his wife's infidelity, seals her lover alive in his hiding place and drives her from the castle. Becoming a libertine, he is stabbed by his last mistress and on his deathbed implores his son to take everything from women, but give them nothing. Ten years later, Don Juan has become famous as a lover and is pursued by many women, including Lucretia Borgia, who invites him to a ball. They don't hit it off well, which causes Lucretia to hate Adriana, the daughter of the Duke, Della Varnesse, who has taken Don Juan's fancy. Lucretia plots to marry her off to Donati and poison her father. Don Juan thwarts this scheme and wins the love of Adriana. The Borgia declare war on the Della Varnese, promising to end it only if Adriana will marry Donati. Don Juan kills the latter in a duel, escapes, and after a series of battles rescues Adriana.

• ***Don Juan*** (remake). Warner Bros., 1926. Silent. Director: Alan Crosland; screenwriter: Bess Meredyth. Cast: John Barrymore (Don Juan/Don Jose), Mary Astor (Adriana Della Varnese), Estelle Taylor (Lucretia Borgia), Montagu Love (Donati), Warner Oland (Caesar Borgia), Helene Costello (Rena), Myrna Loy (Maia), Josef Swickard (Duke Della Varnese), Willard Louis, Jane Winton, John Roche, June Marlowe, Yvonne Day, Philippe De Lacey.

• ***Adventures of Don Juan*** (remake). Warner Bros., 1948. Director: Vincent Sherman; screenwriters: George Oppenheimer, Harry Kurnitz and Herbert Dalmas. Cast: Errol Flynn (Don Juan), Viveca Lindfors (Queen Margaret), Robert Douglas (Duke de Lorca), Alan Hale (Leporello), Romney Brent (King Phillip III), Ann Rutherford (Donna Elena), Robert Warwick (Count De Polan), Jerry Austin, Douglas Kennedy, Jeanne Shepherd, Mary Stuart.

The story of the man who lets his lust run wild has been filmed many times, including 1905, 1907, 1911, 1922, 1926, 1928, 1950, 1954, 1956, 1967, 1970 and 1973. The best of the lot starred John Barrymore in Warner Bros.' first full-length experiment with sound. There was a musical sound track and sound effects but no spoken dialogue. Barrymore cut a very dashing figure as he pursued numerous women, and avoided their men-folk and the strong will of Lucretia Borgia. The film was a great financial success, even though critics had mixed feelings about its overall quality. In the remake, Errol Flynn so much lived as if he were Don Juan off the screen that at 39 the ravages of his self-destructive life made it very difficult for director Vincent Sherman to put together a picture that would portray the dashing swashbuckler as a still handsome and vigorous man. There was hardly any story of note; Flynn saved the king and queen from the schemes of the unsavory Robert Douglas. Considering the role he was playing, Flynn was almost celibate, pledging his undying love and devotion to Viveca Lindfors, a woman he could not have. It wasn't one of Flynn's best, and it marked the beginning of his decline as a major star.

232 Don Quixote

Based on the novel *The Life and Achievements of Don Quixote de La Mancha* by Miguel de Cervantes. Story: An aging gentleman from a village in the Spanish province of La Mancha is obsessed with the romantic tales of knights errant. With his senses rattled by these stories and his advanced time in life, he brings forth an ancient and rusted suit of armour and with an old sword, sets out astride a sway-backed horse, Roziante, to spend the rest of his life as a knight dedicated to protecting the weak and performing noble deeds. He imagines a sluttish tavern wench, Aldonza, to be the maiden Dulcinea del Toboso to whom he will dedicate his triumphs and his noble life. He acquires the service of slow-witted Sancho Panza as his squire. He unsuccessfully tilts with windmills, which he imagines to be some horrible giants, and has a series of other misadventures, each more bizarre than the one before. Nothing discourages Quixote, who has in jest been dubbed "the Knight of the Woeful

Countenance." Despite the ridicule heaped on him by all who encounter him, Don Quixote does not see himself as either a comical figure or a madman as he pursues his quest to be the most chivalrous of knights, all for the glory and honor of his beloved Dulcinea.

• ***Don Quixote*** (remake). Triangle–Fine Arts Pictures, 1915. Silent. Director: Edward Dillon; screenwriter: Chester Withey. Cast: De Wolf Hopper (Don Quixote), Fay Tincher (Aldonza-Dulcinea), Max Davidson (Sancho Panza), Rhea Mitchell, Julia Faye, Chester Withey, George Walsh, Carl Stockdale, William Brown, Monte Blue, Edward Dillon.

• ***Don Quixote*** (remake). Nelson-Vandor/United Artists, 1933. Director: G.W. Pabst; screenwriters: Paul Morand, Alexandre Arnoux and John Farrow. Cast: Feodor Chaliapin (Don Quixote), Renee Valliers (Aldonza/Dulcinea), George Robey (Sancho Panza), Emily Fitzroy, Miles Mander, Sidney Fox, Lydia Sherwood, Wally Patch, Frank Stanmore, Donnio, Oscar Asche.

• ***Don Quixote*** (remake). Azteca Films, Spain, 1948. Director and screenwriter: Rafael Gil. Cast: Rafael Rivelles (Don Quixote), Juan Calvo (Sancho Panza), Nani Fernandez (Dorotea), Manolo Moran, Fernando Rey, Sara Montiel, Guillermo Marin, Juan Espantaleon, Guillermina Grin, Manuel Requena.

• ***Don Quixote*** (remake). Continental Films, 1973. Directors: Rudolf Nureyev and Robert Helpmann. Cast: Robert Helpmann (Don Quixote), Ray Powell (Sancho Panza), Rudolf Nureyev (Basilio), Francia Croese (Lorenzo), Lucette Aldous (Kitri), Colin Peasley, Kelvin Coe.

• ***Man of La Mancha*** (remake). United Artists, 1973. Director: Arthur Hiller; screenwriter: Dale Wasserman. Cast: Peter O'Toole (Don Quixote/Miguel de Cervantes), Sophia Loren (Aldonzo), James Coco (Sancho Panza), Harry Andrews, John Castle, Brian Blessed, Ian Richardson, Julie Gregg, Rosalie Crutchley, Gino Conforti, Marne Maitland.

Other films based on the character Don Quixote were produced in France in 1903, 1908, 1913, and 1933. Spanish versions were released in 1908 and 1962, the latter being called *Dulcinea.* The British produced *The Passionate Friends* in 1923. In addition, there was a German version in 1933; a Mexican production in 1955; Italian films in 1956 and 1968; a Russian version in 1957, a Yugoslavian picture in 1961, a joint French-German-Italian production, *Dulcinea del Toboso* in 1967, and an Australian version in 1973. Knockdowns of the story included *The Girl from La Mancha* and *Amorous Adventures of Don Quixote and Sancho Panza.* Horst Buchholz appeared as Cervantes in 1967's *Le Avventure e gli Amori de Miguel Cervantes,* directed by Vincent Sherman.

None of the screen versions of the story of Don Quixote were favorably received by critics. Each was found to fail to breathe life into the marvelous Cervantes characters. The blame usually was shared equally by the director and the performer impersonating the knight-errant. Either the mood was not reminiscent of the novel or the pace was too slow or perhaps too hectic. The actors were either too hammy or did not portray the character in a way to induce sympathy from the audience. Playing the gentle lunatic proved a monumental task, which was not completely mastered by great actors like De Wolf Hopper or opera stars such as Feodor Chaliapin. Orson Welles directed a production in Mexico in 1955, starring Francisco Reiguera as Quixote and Akim Tamiroff as Sancho, but the project was abandoned. In 1973, Rudolf Nureyev directed and appeared in a colorful spectacle, the ballet *Don Quixote.*

The 1973 musical production, based on the huge Broadway success *Man of La Mancha* with music by Mitch Leigh and lyrics by Joe Dalton, featured international stars Peter O'Toole and Sophia Loren, who were believed capable of acting even if they could not sing. In this box-office failure, they seemed unable to do either. Even the stirring songs "Man of La Mancha," "The Quest (The Impossible Dream)" and "Dulcinea" were not enough to make this filming of Cervantes and fellow prisoners of the Spanish Inquisition work, with their interpretation of the story.

233 The Doomed Battalion

Based on a story by Luis Trenker. Story: It's the melodramatic tale of the effects of World War I on a young Austrian, Florian Di Mai, his wife, Maria, and an Italian mountaineer, Arthur Franchini, whom Florian once guided up a mountain. When war is declared, the Italian finds himself billetted in the Di Mais' home.

Universal Pictures, 1932 (original). Director: Cyril Gardner; screenwriter: Luis Trenker. Cast: Tala Birell (Maria Di Mai), Luis Trenker (Florian Di Mai), Victor Varconi (Arthur Franchini), Albert Conti, Gustave Von Seyffertitz, C. Henry Gordon, Gibson Gowland, Henry Armetta, Ferdinand Gottschalk.

• ***Ski Patrol*** (remake). Universal Pictures, 1940. Director: Lew Landers; screenwriter: Paul Hutson. Cast: Luli Deste (Julia Engel), Philip Dorn (Viktor Ryder), Samuel S. Hinds (Per Vallgren), Stanley Fields (Birger Simberg), Edward Norris (Paavo Luuki), Hardie Albright, Kathryn Adams, John Qualen, John Arledge, John Ellis, Henry Brandon, Reed Hadley.

The Doomed Battalion is a gripping story with director Gardner getting the best from his cast. The remake, an unofficial reworking of the 1932 film, tells how several Olympic skiers react when Finnish troops are forced to defend a mountain being mined by the Russians.

Dorothy and the Scarecrow of Oz ***see*** **The Wizard of Oz**

234 The Double Event

Based on the play by Sidney Blow and Douglas Hoare. Story: Country cleric's daughter Dot Martingale becomes a bookie's partner to make good her father's losses and finds she likes the business. Her fiancé, Capt. Dennison, finds it necessary to bankrupt the bookmaker to get her to give up the gambling racket and marry him.

Astra Films, Great Britain, 1921 (original). Silent. Director and screenwriter: Kenelm Foss. Cast: Mary Odette (Dot Martingale), Roy Travers (Capt. Dennison), Lionelle Howard (Charles Martingale), Tom Coventry (Angus McWeir), Roy Byford, Beatie Olna, James McWilliams, Louie Freear, Sidney Wood, Julie Kean.

• ***The Double Event*** (remake). Triumph, Great Britain, 1934. Director and screenwriter: Howard Gordon. Cast: Jane Baxter (Evelyn Martingale), Ruth Taylor (Aunt Laura), O.B. Clarence (Rev. Martingale), Alexander Field (Charlie Weir), Bernard Lee (Dennison), Sebastian Smith (Uncle James).

The two films are agreeable comedies with no great moral to tell, but do provide an enjoyable hour's entertainment for those with nothing better to do. For James Bond fans, seeing "M," i.e. Bernard Lee when he was a young romantic lead, should prove interesting.

A Double Life ***see*** **Othello**

235 Doubting Thomas

Based on the play *The Torch Bearers* by George Kelly. Story: It's 78 minutes of Will Rogers horse sense with a little help from a few others in the cast who appear as members of what passes for the society folk of a small town who decide to put on an amateur variety show. The best thing about the acts is Rogers' sarcastic comments about them. The great humorist has his own spot on the stage in which he dresses as a crooner, complete with blonde locks, riding breeches, exaggerated make up and a very satirical song.

Fox Film Corp., 1935 (original). Director: David Butler; screenwriters: William Conselman and Bartlett Cormack. Cast: Will Rogers (Thomas Brown), Billie Burke (Paula Brown), Alison Skipworth (Mrs. Pampinelli), Sterling Holloway (Spindler), Andrew Tombes (Hossefrosse), Gail Patrick (Florence McCrickett), Frances Grant, Frank Albertson, John Qualen, Johnny Arthur.

• ***Too Busy to Work*** (remake). Twentieth Century–Fox, 1939. Director: Otto Brower; screenwriter: Robert Ellis. Cast: Jed Prouty (John Jones), Spring Byington (Mrs. John Jones), Ken Howell (Jack Jones), George Ernest (Roger Jones), June Carlson (Lucy Jones), Florence Roberts (Granny Jones), Billy Mahan (Bobby Jones), Joan Davis (Lolly), Chick Chandler, Marjorie Gateson, Andrew Tombes, Marvin Stephens, Irving Bacon.

The remake is based not only on George Kelly's *The Torch Bearers* but also on *Your Uncle Dudley* by Howard Lindsay and Bertrand Robinson. Both plays were old hat by the time Hollywood got around to filming them. This Jones family comedy deals with the females of the family deciding it's time to teach father a lesson. It seems he's been neglecting his drugstore business to carry on his duties as mayor. Mrs. Jones and his daughters neglect their domestic chores to become involved with an amateur variety show. Joan Davis joins the family as a cousin and breathes some new comedy life into this situation comedy series about a midwestern family.

236 The Dove

Based on the play by Willard Mack. Story: Wealthy caballero Don Jose frames gambler Johnny Powell for murder, because they both love dancehall girl Dolores, known as "The Dove." She agrees to marry Don Jose if he will clear Powell. On the eve of their wedding Powell comes back to get Dolores and after an unsuccessful escape, Don Jose plans to have both of them shot, but is dissuaded by an angry crowd and is forced to set the lovers free.

United Artists, 1927 (original). Silent. Director: Roland West; screenwriters: Roland West, Wallace Smith and Willard Mack. Cast: Norma Talmadge (Dolores), Noah Beery (Don Jose), Gilbert Roland (Johnny Powell), Eddie Borden, Harry Myers.

• ***Girl of the Rio*** (remake). RKO, 1932. Director: Herbert Brenon; screenwriter: Elizabeth Meehan. Cast: Dolores Del Rio (Dolores), Leo Carrillo (Don Jose), Norman Foster (Johnny Powell), Ralph Ince, Lucille Gleason, Edna Murphy.

• ***The Girl and the Gambler*** (remake). RKO, 1939. Director: Lew Landers; screenwriters: Joseph A. Fields and Clarence Upson Young. Cast: Leo Carrillo (El Rayo), Tim Holt (Johnny Powell), Steffi Duna (Dolores), Donald McBride, Edward Raquello, Chris-Pin Martin, Paul Fix, Julian Rivero.

The two remakes are less serious than the first version with Leo Carrillo as the Mexican badman in a stereotype that should not sit well with our good neighbors south of the Rio Grande. The United States should be willing to accept more illegal aliens from Mexico just to make up for the way that these people have been portrayed in American movies. The first film was a romantic melodrama which had some stage success in the 1920s. The two remakes are just nondescript westerns, although Dolores Del Rio's beauty made quite an impression in the 1932 picture.

The Dover Road *see* **The Little Adventuress**

Down to Earth *see* **Here Comes Mr. Jordan**

237 Dragnet

Based on the radio and TV show created by Jack Webb. Story: Based on a real-life case, Sgt. Joe Friday and his partner, Officer Frank Smith, ploddingly track down the killer whose crime is committed before the main title credits are shown. The chief suspect dies of a cancerous ulcer just when Friday and Smith have the evidence to convict him.

Warner Bros., 1954 (original). Director: Jack Webb; screenwriter: Richard L. Breen. Cast: Jack Webb (Sgt. Joe Friday), Ben Alexander (Officer Frank Smith), Richard Boone (Captain Hamilton), Ann Robinson (Grace Downey), Stacy Harris (Max Troy), Virginia Gregg, Victor Perrin, Georgia Ellis, James Griffith, Dick Cathcart, Malcolm Atterbury, Willard Sage.

• ***Dragnet*** (remake). Universal Pictures, 1987. Director: Tom Mankiewicz; screenwriters: Mankiewicz, Dan Aykroyd and Alan Zweibel. Cast: Dan Aykroyd (Joe Friday), Tom Hanks (Pep Streebeck), Harry Morgan (Frank Gannon), Christopher Plummer (Rev. Whirley), Dabney Coleman (Jerry Caesar), Elizabeth Ashley (Jane Kirkpatrick), Alexandra Pauk (The Virgin Connie Swail), Jack O'Halloran (Emil Muzz).

In the remake, Dan Aykroyd's performance is a tribute to Jack Webb's creation of a cop who believes in every law he enforces. As Webb's nephew,

Aykroyd is marvelous. Unfortunately, the plot of the film and the other performers don't measure up to Dan's work. Poor Tom Hanks is almost a straight man for the straight-talking Aykroyd. Harry Morgan as Webb's ex-partner is now the captain. Christopher Plummer is a crooked preacher, Elizabeth Ashley, a crooked police commissioner and Dabney Coleman, a lisping Hugh Heffner–like girlie magazine publisher.

Dream of Old Scrooge *see* **A Christmas Carol**

Dreaming Lips *see* **Melo**

238 Drifting

Based on the play by John Colton and Daisy H. Andrews. Story: American Cassie Cook and her accomplice, Jules Repin, are smuggling opium from China. Their activities are under the surveillance of Captain Arthur Jarvis, a government official, posing as a mining engineer. Repin attempts to kill Jarvis, but Cassie, who has fallen in love with the captain, prevents the murder and reforms.

Universal Jewel Pictures, 1923 (original). Silent. Director and screenwriter: Tod Browning. Cast: Priscilla Dean (Cassie Cook/Lucille Preston), Matt Moore (Captain Arthur Jarvis), Wallace Beery (Jules Repin), J. Farrell MacDonald (Murphy), Rose Dione (Madame Polly Voo), Edna Tichenor, William V. Mong, Anna May Wong.

• ***Shanghai Lady*** (remake). Universal Pictures, 1929. Director: John S. Robertson; screenwriter: Houston Branch. Cast: Mary Nolan (Cassie Cook), James Murray ("Badlands" McKinney), Lydia Yeamans (Polly Voo), Wheeler Oakman (Repen), Anders Randolf, Yola D'Avril, Mona Rico, Jimmy Leong, Irma Lowe.

The story of the remake has Cassie Cook as a girl thrown out of a Chinese "teahouse," who decides to become refined and find a Caucasian to take care of her. Meanwhile, McKinney, a derelict, is tricked by Chinese detective Repen into admitting that he is an escaped convict. He gets away by boarding a train, where he meets Cassie. Both believe the other to be respectable and fall in love. When Repen catches up with them, McKinney offers to surrender himself if Repen will keep his past from Cassie. A mandarin recognizes the detective as a man who had dishonored his daughter and kills him, giving Cassie and McKinney the chance to declare their love, confess their past and sail to America for a new life.

The Drowning Pool *see* **Harper**

Drum *see* **Mandingo**

Drummond *see* **Bulldog Drummond**

The Duality of Man *see* **Dr. Jekyll and Mr. Hyde**

Dulcinea *see* **Don Quixote**

Dulcinea Del Toboso *see* **Don Quixote**

239 Dust Be My Destiny

Based on a book by Jerome Odium. Story: Joe Bell has been made hard and cynical by a prison stretch for a crime which he did not commit. He is picked up as a vagrant in a small southern town and sentenced to the country work farm. There he falls in love with Mabel, who lives on the farm with her stepfather, one of the prison officials. After a fight with the older man, the pair hit a freight out of town and get married. They discover that the stepfather has been killed and Joe is wanted for the crime. The film boils down to the pair's continuous flight, hotly pursued by the authorities. Tired of running, Mabel turns Joe in to stand trial and surprise, surprise, the verdict is not guilty, allowing the pair to start a real life together.

Warner Bros., 1939 (original). Director: Lewis Seiler; screenwriter: Robert Rossen. Cast: John Garfield (Joe Bell), Priscilla Lane (Mabel), Alan Hale (Mike Leonard), Frank McHugh (Caruthers), Billy Halop (Hank), Bobby Jordan, Charley Grapewin, Henry Armetta, Stanley Ridges, John Litel, Moroni Olsen.

• ***I Was Framed*** (remake). Warner Bros., 1942. Director: D. Ross Lederman; screenwriter: Robert E. Kent. Cast: Michael Ames (Ken Marshall), Julie Bishop (Ruth Marshall), Regis Toomey (Bob Leeds), Patty Hale (Penny Marshall), John Harmon, Aldrich Bowker, Roland Drew, Oscar O'Shen, Wade Boteler.

Criminal melodramas about men wrongly sentenced to prison abounded in the 30s and this one with Garfield is about average for level of action and suspense. Garfield and Lane are quite good as the young lovers, but the pace is rather slow. In the remake, Michael Ames plays a reporter framed and jailed by the crooked governor he is about to expose. He escapes, and accompanied by his wife, takes refuge in a small town where an old doctor gets Ames a job on the local newspaper. All goes well until some five years later when a former cellmate recognizes him and attempts to blackmail the reporter. But while this is happening one of the gang who had earlier framed the reporter talks, vindicating him, and all ends well. Ames is certainly no actor and the efforts at suspense in the piece are completely unsuccessful.

E

240 Early to Bed

Based on a story by Hans Szekeley and Robert Liebmann. Story: It's the charming comedy of two young people who share the same room, he sleeping there by night, she by day. They do not see each other at the room and become resentful of each other. When they meet away from their mutual sleeping quarters, sure enough they fall in love.

UFA/Woolf and Freedman, Great Britain/Germany, 1933 (original). Director:

Ludwig Berger; screenwriter: Robert Stevenson. Cast: Sonnie Hale (Helmut), Heather Angel (Grete), Edmund Gwenn (Kruger), Fernand Graavey (Carl), Donald Calthrop (Peschke), Lady Tree, Athene Seyler, Gillian Sand, Leslie Perrins, Lewis Shaw.

• ***Rafter Romance*** (remake). RKO, 1936. Director: William Seiter; screenwriter: Glenn Tryon, based on a novel by John Wells. Cast: Ginger Rogers (Mary Carroll), Norman Foster (Jack Bacon), George Sidney (Max Eckbaum), Robert Benchley (Hubbell), Laura Hope Crews, Guinn Williams.

• ***Living on Love*** (remake). RKO Radio, 1937. Director: Lew Landers; screenwriter: Franklin Coen. Cast: James Dunn (Gary), Whitney Bourne (Mary), Joan Woodbury (Edith), Solly Ward (Eli), Tom Kennedy, Franklin Pangborn, Kenneth Terrell, James Fawcett, Chester Clute, Evelyn Carrington, Etta McDaniels.

The two American remakes of the bilingual 1933 production list a different source but perhaps novelist John Wells was influenced by the work of Szekeley and Liebmann, because the stories and their developments are very much the same. The idea of a young couple sharing the same bed but not at the same time, must have seemed a good way to thumb one's nose at the Hays Office, but not for any more than an hour and then only as the second feature of double bills.

241 Earthbound

Based on a story by Basil King. Story: A husband has been shot by a former sweetheart, now the wife of a scientist friend he had been financing. Once dead, his ghost talks his way through the rest of the film, without anyone seeing or hearing him, except for a churchman-philosopher. It seems the spirit cannot be at rest or leave this earth until the right person takes the blame for his death.

Goldwyn, 1920 (original). Silent. Director: T. Hayes; screenwriter: uncredited. Cast: Wyndham Standing (Nicholas Desborough), Naomi Childers (Caroline Desborough), Billie Cotton (Connie Desborough), Mahlon Hamilton (Jim Rittenshaw), Flora Revalles (Daisy Rittenshaw), Alec B. Francis (Dr. Roger Galloway), Lawson Butt, Kate Lester.

• ***Earthbound*** (remake). Twentieth Century–Fox, 1940. Director: Irving Pichel; screenwriters: John Howard Lawson and Samuel G. Engel. Cast: Warner Baxter (Nick Desborough), Andrea Leeds (Ellen Desborough), Lynn Bari (Linda Reynolds), Charley Grapewin (Mr. Whimser), Henry Wilcoxon (Jeffrey Reynolds), Elizabeth Patterson (Becky Tilden), Russell Hicks, Christian Rub, Ian Wolfe.

This ghostly whodunit was no great shakes when produced as a silent. In the remake it served as just one further rung downward for the fading career of Warner Baxter. It's an implausible story that few cared about either time.

242 East Is West

Based on the play by Samuel Shipman and John B. Hymer. Story: Ming Toy, the eldest daughter of Hop Toy, is rescued from the auction block by Billy

Benson and is sent to the United States in the care of Lo Sang Kee. On her arrival in Chinatown, she attracts the interest of the powerful Charley Yong. When he demands to make Ming Toy his property, she is once again rescued by Benson, resulting in a chase. Billy takes her to his home and confesses his love for the girl. Charley Yong backs out of the picture when it is revealed that Ming Toy was kidnapped from a Caucasian couple when she was a baby.

First National Pictures, 1922 (original). Silent. Director: Sidney Franklin; screenwriter: Francis Marion. Cast: Constance Talmadge (Ming Toy), Edmund Burns (Billy Benson), E.A. Warren (Lo Sang Kee), Warner Oland (Charley Yong), Frank Lanning (Hop Toy), Nick De Ruiz, Nigel Barrie, Lilian Lawrence, Winter Hall.

• ***East Is West*** (remake). Universal Pictures, 1930. Director: Monta Bell; screenwriter: Tom Reed. Cast: Lupe Velez (Ming Toy), Lew Ayres (Billy Benson), Edward G. Robinson (Charlie Yong), E. Alyn Warren (Lo Sang Kee), Mary Forbes, Tetsu Komai, Edgar Norton, Charles Middleton.

These films allowed the motion picture industry to explore the topic of miscegenation and have a way out of it as well. This touchy subject as well as white slavery intrigued audiences, who enjoyed the shocking goings on of a strange race, even if no Asian actors had featured roles. The plot of the remake of the romantic drama is essentially the same as the silent version. Neither Velez, the fiery Mexican performer, or Robinson were very convincing as Orientals.

243 East Lynne

Based on the novel by Mrs. Henry Wood. Story: Lady Isabel leads a life of bliss at her family estate, East Lynne, until she grows to suspect her husband, Archibald Carlyle, of infidelity with Barbara Hare, who has come to the estate to seek Archibald's legal advice. Vulnerable, she succumbs to the persuasion of Francis Levison to leave her husband and marry him. When Levison abandons Isabel and their daughter, she sets out for East Lynne to ask Archibald's forgiveness but is seriously injured in a train wreck. Finally arriving at East Lynne, Isabel dies before learning that Archibald, believing her to be dead, has married Barbara Hare.

• ***East Lynne*** (remake). Ballin Productions, 1921. Silent. Director and screenwriter: Hugo Ballin. Cast: Edward Earle (Archibald Carlyle), Mabel Ballin (Isabel), Gladys Coburn (Barbara Hare), Henry G. Sell (Francis Levison), Gilbert Rooney, Nellie Parker, Doris Sheerin.

• ***East Lynne*** (remake). Fox Film Corporation, 1926. Silent. Director: Emmett Flynn; screenwriters: Leonore J. Coffee and Emmett Flynn. Cast: Alma Rubens (Lady Isabel), Edmund Lowe (Archibald Carlyle), Lou Tellegen (Francis Levison), Marjorie Daw (Barbara Hare), Frank Kenan, Leslie Fenton, Paul Panzer, Belle Bennett.

• ***East Lynne*** (remake). Fox Film Corporation, 1931. Director: Frank Lloyd; screenwriters: Bradley King and Tom Barry. Cast: Ann Harding (Isabel), Clive Brook (Archibald Carlyle), Conrad Nagel (Francis Levison), Cecilia Loftus (Barbara Hare), O.P. Heggie, Beryl Mercer, Flora Sheffield.

Mrs. Henry Wood's novel was first filmed in 1916 by Fox Film Corporation with Theda Bara starring as Lady Isabel. In 1931, Gaumont-Welsh-Pearson made the slapstick army farce *East Lynne on the Western Front* in which war rookies, played by the likes of Herbert Mundin, Wilfrid Lawson, Mark Daly and Harold French, produced a version of *East Lynne* to relieve boredom.

The story of *East Lynne* changes slightly in each of the succeeding film productions. In the first remake, Carlyle buys the debt-ridden estate of Lord Mount-Severn and persuades the late lord's daughter, Isabel, to marry him. When a villager is murdered, Richard Hare, the brother of Barbara (a former sweetheart of Archibald's), is accused of the crime. When Barbara meets Archibald privately to seek help for her brother, Levison convinces Isabel that the two are lovers, and she runs off with Levison to the continent. He soon abandons her, and Isabel returns to England. Archibald marries Barbara because it has been reported that Isabel had been killed in an automobile accident. One of Isabel's children becomes ill, and disguised as a nurse, she goes to him and saves his life. Isabel then becomes ill and dies, being recognized by Archibald, who keeps her secret.

In the 1931 version starring the queen of the weepies, Ann Harding, Isabel is unjustly divorced by her husband and later loses both her lover and her sight. The film was nominated for an Academy Award for Best Picture but did not win. *Variety* described the film as having "the elemental appeal of dramatic hokum."

244 Easy Come, Easy Go

Based on the play by Owen Davis. Story: Honest young Robert Parker, temporarily out of work, innocently becomes the accomplice of veteran thief Jim Bailey. When Parker learns the truth, he attempts to shield Bailey and at the same time return a stolen payroll to its rightful owner, the president of the robbed bank, with whose daughter he is in love.

Paramount, 1928 (original). Silent. Director: Frank Tuttle; screenwriter: Florence Ryerson. Cast: Richard Dix (Robert Parker), Nancy Carroll (Babs Quayle), Charles Sellon (Jim Bailey), Frank Currier (Mr. Quayle), George Kent, Charles J. Frank, Joseph J. Franz.

• ***Only Saps Work*** (remake). Paramount, 1930. Directors: Cyril Gardner and Edwin H. Knopf; screenwriters: Sam Mintz, Percy Heath and Joseph L. Mankiewicz. Cast: Leon Errol (James Wilson), Richard Arlen (Lawrence Payne), Mary Brian (Barbara Tanner), Stuart Erwin (Oscar), Anderson Lawler, Charles Grapewin.

The two filmings of the play by Owen Davis are almost as uninteresting as the description of the story. Things are not to be taken too seriously, but the humor is modest and the episodes all too familiar. In the remake, Richard Arlen plays the innocent young man who unwittingly becomes Leon Errol's accomplice in a bank robbery. To put the authorities off his trail, Errol assumes the role of a detective investigating the very crime he has committed. Arlen has to go through a number of subterfuges himself to put things right and end up with the female of the piece, Mary Brian. In the original, cute Nancy Carroll has the unenviable assignment of standing around looking sweet while Richard Dix and Charles Sellon get in and out of trouble with the law.

Easy to Wed ***see*** **Libeled Lady**

245 Ebb Tide

Based on the story by Robert Louis Stevenson and Lloyd Osbourne. Story: Three beachcombers, Thorbecke, Robert Herrick, and Huish, are commissioned to take a small-pox infested ship away from the island which it endangers. Learning that the ship's cargo is champagne, the three conspire to take the ship to Peru instead of its destination of Australia and there sell the ship and its cargo. Aboard the ship is Faith Wishart, daughter of the captain who had died. She finally wins Herrick over to her side, only because she's better looking than his drinking buddies. All plans are changed by a typhoon which forces them to land at an uncharted island and vie with a psychopathic religious fanatic, Attwater, who kills Thorbecke and Huish. This has the effect of allowing Herrick and Faith to go their own way with the ship and its cargo.

• ***Ebb Tide*** (remake). Paramount Pictures, 1937. Director: James Hugan; screenwriter: Bertram Millhauser. Cast: Oscar Homolka (Capt. Thorbecke), Frances Farmer (Faith Wishart), Ray Milland (Robert Herrick), Lloyd Nolan (Attwater), Barry Fitzgerald (Huish), David Torrence, Lina Basquette, Charles Judels.

• ***Adventure Island*** (remake). Paramount Pictures, 1947. Director: Peter Stewart; screenwriter: Maxwell Shane. Cast: Rory Calhoun (Mr. Herrick), Rhonda Fleming (Faith Wishart), Paul Kelly (Capt. Lochlin), John Abbott (Mr. Huish), Alan Napier (Mr. Atwater).

The story was first filmed by Selig in 1915 and then in 1922 by Paramount with Lila Lee, James Kirkwood, Raymond Hatton, George Fawcett and Noah Beery. It was also produced in 1932 and 1962. In *Ebb Tide,* Homolka made his Hollywood screen debut. He, Fitzgerald and Milland were excellent as the three rum-swilling, no-good bums. Such cannot be said about the cast of the 1947 remake, *Adventure Island.* As the story dealt with men of relative brutality and criminal activity, Milland comes off as the "hero" of the first piece, but that's only by comparing him to Homolka, Fitzgerald and Nolan. The producers of the 1947 film seemed to believe that their hero really had to be a good guy.

246 The Egg and I

Based on the book by Betty MacDonald. Story: Bob MacDonald snatches wife Betty out of a Boston finishing school and sets her down in the Pacific Northwest on a poultry farm. Betty knows nothing of housekeeping and even less about working a farm. They have no indoor plumbing or electricity but they do have neighbors, the Kettles, who seem to raise as many children as chickens. Ma Kettle does all the work while Pa Kettle finds ways to fill his time doing nothing.

Universal Pictures, 1947 (original). Director: Chester Erskine; screenwriters: Erskine and Fred F. Finklehoffe. Cast: Claudette Colbert (Betty MacDonald), Fred MacMurray (Bob MacDonald), Marjorie Main (Ma Kettle), Louise

Allbritton (Harriet Putman), Percy Kilbride (Pa Kettle), Richard Long (Tom Kettle), Billy House, Ida Moore, Donald McBride, Samuel S. Hinds, Esther Dale.

• ***Ma and Pa Kettle*** (sequel). Universal-International, 1949. Director: Charles Lamont; screenwriters: Herbert Margolis and Louis Morheim. Cast: Marjorie Main (Ma Kettle), Percy Kilbride (Pa Kettle), Richard Long (Tom Kettle), Meg Randall (Kim Parker), Patricia Alphin, Esther Dale, Barry Kelley, Harry Antrim.

The original film was based on a very successful book by Betty MacDonald, but the public took not so much to Claudette Colbert and Fred MacMurray as they did to Marjorie Main and Percy Kilbride as Ma and Pa Kettle. Eager to please, the studio came out with a series of eight Kettle movies with titles such as *Ma and Pa Kettle at the Fair* (1952), *Ma and Pa Kettle at Waikiki* (1955) and *Ma and Pa Kettle Go to Town* (1950).

247 Eight Girls in a Boat

Based on a story by Helmut Brandis. Story: It's the touching story of the problems of an unmarried college student who is pregnant and contemplating suicide. In spite of the loving friendship of her friends and classmates, she reluctantly goes back home to her father to have the child.

• ***Acht Maedles im Boot*** (original). Fanal Production/Terra, Germany, 1932. Director: Ehrich Waschneck; screenwriter: Franz Winterstein. Cast: Theodor Loos (David), Karin Hardt (Christa), Helmuth Kionka (Storm), Heinz Goedecke, Ali Ghito, Martha Ziegler, Hedwig Schroeder, Katja Bennefeld, Hedie Helsig, Dora Thalmer, Sabine Peters, Gunni Dreyer, Hedi Kirchner.

• ***Eight Girls in a Boat*** (remake). Paramount Pictures, 1934. Director: Richard Wallace; screenwriter: Lewis Foster. Cast: Dorothy Wilson (Christa Storm), Douglass Montgomery (David Perrin), Kay Johnson (Hanna), Barbara Barondess (Pickles), Ferike Boros (Frau Krueger), Walter Connolly (Storm), James Bush, Colin Campbell, Peggy Montgomery, Margaret Marquis, Marjorie Cavalier, Virginia Hall, Kay Hammond.

The German version of the story was released in the United States to follow up on the popularity of *Mädchen in Uniform,* shown the year before. The octet in the title is the female crew of a racing shell at a Switzerland finishing school. When one of its number gets pregnant, the boy wishes to do the honorable thing, but her father will not hear of it. The other girls decide to underwrite the baby and become a bit resentful when a change in the parental attitude suggests a marriage and a happy ending. None of this happens before the mother-to-be gives serious thought to suicide and is dissuaded by the argument that the baby deserves a chance at life. Both films are pleasant and did well at the box office, even though the casts were not well known.

Elizabeth and Essex ***see*** **The Private Life of Henry VIII**

The Elusive Pimpernel ***see*** **The Scarlet Pimpernel**

Emergency Wedding *see* **You Belong to Me**

248 Emil and the Detectives

Based on the novel by Erich Knestner. Story: Emil is sent by train from the country to the city to visit his grandmother. His mother gives him spending money, which he pins to his inside pocket. On his journey he meets a man who steals his cash. Arriving in Berlin, he follows the man and enlists the aid of other children in his quest to regain his money. When the number of children gets too large, they elect five of their number to act as detectives to work with Emil. The juvenile vice squad finally lands their man. Emil is given 1000 marks as a reward and he flies home to be greeted by the town band and the mayor.

• ***Emil and the Detectives*** (remake). Wainwright/Gaumont, Great Britain, 1935. Director: Milton Rosner; screenwriters: Cyrus Brooks and Margaret Carter. Cast: George Hayes (The Man), Mary Glynne (Mrs. Blake), John Williams (Emil Blake), Clare Greet (Grandmother), George Merritt, Marion Foster, Donald Pittman, Bobby Rietti.

• ***Emil and the Detectives*** (remake). Walt Disney/Buena Vista, 1964. Director: Peter Tewksberry; screenwriter: A.J. Carothers. Cast: Walter Slezak (The Baron), Bryan Russell (Emil), Roger Mobley (Gustav), Heinz Schubert (Grundeis), Peter Ehrlich (Muller), Cindy Cassell, Elsa Wagner, Wolfgang Volz, Eva-Ingeborg Scholz.

This charming children's crime comedy-drama was also produced in 1923, 1937 and 1954. The 1931 German UFA production's screenplay was written by the soon-to-be-great comedy director Billy Wilder. Even the Disney studio restrained themselves and gave audiences a film mostly free of its usual cutesy approach to family fare. The kids were taken seriously and were neither loveable little tykes nor wise beyond their years. They just wanted to get Emil's money back.

The Empire Strikes Back *see* **Star Wars**

249 The Enchanted Cottage

Based on a play by Arthur Wing Pinero. Story: Coming home shell-shocked and disfigured by the war, Oliver Bashforth, bitter and disillusioned, breaks off his engagement and marries unattractive and plain Laura Pennington. Their home is to be an isolated cottage on his family's estate. When the couple enter the cottage after their wedding, they are astonished to discover that they are no longer broken and ugly. He is no longer a cripple and she has been transformed into a beauty. They share their news with blind Major Hillgrove but when they invite family and friends to the cottage to see the miracle, they quickly discover in these people's eyes that they are unchanged. Wise Major Hillgrove helps them realize that seen through the eyes of love they are perfect. With this understanding they are content and happily await the birth of what they are sure will be a beautiful child.

Inspiration Pictures, 1924 (original). Silent. Director: John S. Robertson; screenwriter: Josephine Lovett. Cast: May McAvoy (Laura Pennington), Richard Barthelmess (Oliver Bashforth), Holmes E. Herbert (Major Hillgrove),

Ethel Wright, Alfred Hickman, Ida Waterman, Marion Coakley, Florence Short, Harry Allen.

RKO, 1945. Director: John Cromwell; screenwriters: De Witt Bodeen and Herman J. Mankiewicz. Cast: Dorothy McGuire (Laura Pennington), Robert Young (Oliver Bradford), Herbert Marshall (John Hillgrove), Mildred Natwick, Spring Byington, Richard Gaines, Hillary Brooke, Alec Englander.

Critics sneered at Pinero's work but the film versions were well received by the public. Movie audiences see the transformation take place, something which cannot be achieved on the stage, and this gave the story a bit of magic. Both pairs of performers portraying the lovers were quite good as were Holmes Herbert and Herbert Marshall as their wise friend. Audiences of both films were familiar with the crippling injuries and disfigurements of wars and the fact that these two people could still find happiness and hope was taken as a reassuring sign. There is a kind of beauty to the stories and their presentations if one is not too much of a cynic.

250 The Enforcer

Based on an original screenplay by Martin Rackin. Story: District attorney Martin Ferguson's chief witness against Albert Mendoza, Joe Rico, has just fallen to his death, leaving the D.A. with the option of releasing Mendoza the next day or finding some other witness that can tie the man to the organization of murder for profit that he heads up. Throughout the night, Ferguson and his assistant Sgt. Whitlow sift through the testimony and evidence that they have gathered in the case for that one thing which will send Mendoza to the chair. After some fascinating flashbacks which detail the rise and activities of Mendoza's Murder, Inc., Ferguson finds that the one killing Mendoza handled himself was witnessed by a barber and his young daughter. Over the years, the gang had killed the barber and his daughter, or did they? Seems they had killed the girl's roommate and what brings this fact to Ferguson's attention is testimony about the color of the witness's eyes. The dead girl has the wrong color. Unfortunately, Mendoza catches on to this fact at about the same time Ferguson does and through his lawyer sends out some of his boys to get the job done correctly. It's then a case of who will get to the frightened girl first, her executioners or the police.

Warners, 1951 (original). Director: Bretaigne Windust; screenwriter: Martin Rackin. Cast: Humphrey Bogart (Martin Ferguson), Zero Mostel ("Big Babe" Lazich), Ted De Corsia (Joseph Rico), Everett Sloane (Albert Mendoza), Roy Roberts (Capt. Frank Nelson), Lawrence Tolan ("Duke" Tiano), King Donovan (Sgt. Whitlow), Robert Steele (Herman), Pat Joiner, Don Beddoe, Tito Vuolo, John Kellogg, Jack Lambert, Adelaide Klein, Susan Cabot, Mario Siletti.

• ***Murder, Inc.*** (remake). Twentieth Century–Fox, 1960. Director: Burt Balaban and Stuart Rosenberg; screenwriters: Irve Tunick and Mel Barr, from book *Murder, Inc.* by Burton Turkus and Sid Feder. Cast: Stuart Whitman (Joey), May Britt (Eadie), Henry Morgan (Turkus), Peter Falk (Reles), David J. Stewart (Lepke), Simon Oakland (Tobin), Warren Fennerty (Bug), Joseph Bernard (Mendy Weiss), Eli Mintz (Joe Rosen), Vince Gardenia (Laslo), Joseph

Elic (Alpert), Howard I. Smith (Anastasia), Helen Waters, Lou Polan, Joseph Campanella, Leon B. Stevens, Dorothy Stinnette.

• ***Lepke*** (remake). Warner Bros., 1975. Director: Menahem Golan; screenwriters: Wesley Lau and Tamar Hoffs. Cast: Tony Curtis (Lepke Buchalter), Anjanette Comer (Lepke's wife), Milton Berle (Lepke's father-in-law), Michael Callan, Warren Berlinger, Gianni Russo, Vic Tayback, Mary Wilcox.

Each of the three films deals in its own way with that part of organized crime known as Murder, Inc., founded and operated by Lepke Buchalter until his execution in the electric chair in 1944. The best of the three was the semifictional account starring Humphrey Bogart and Everett Sloane. Since the film didn't name names, it was able to make the piece more melodrama than biopic. It was the least violent of the three but perhaps the most shocking. The second feature details the "facts" about Albert Anastasia, Lepke and their number-one killer, Abe Reles, played by Peter Falk, of all persons. Their story is seen through the eyes of an almost-innocent young couple, Stuart Whitman and May Britt, kept in line as accomplices of the ring through beatings and threats. The final entry, with Tony Curtis starring as the notorious Jewish gangster and racket mastermind, is too cliché-filled to be of much interest, save to those who enjoy plenty of explicit violence.

The Enforcer (1976) *see* **Dirty Harry**

Enemi-in No Semushi *see* **The Hunchback of Notre Dame**

Ensign Pulver *see* **Mr. Roberts**

Enter Arsene Lupin *see* **Arsene Lupin**

251 Enter Madame

Based on the play by Gilda Varesi and Dolly Byrne. Story: Millionaire Gerald Fitzgerald wearies of being humbled by the experience of being married to glamorous opera prima donna Lisa Della Robbia. He asks for a divorce so he may marry homebody Flora Preston. Lisa agrees, even though she still loves her husband. After the divorce becomes finalized, Lisa invites Gerald and Flora to dinner, at which she exerts the charm and exuberance that won his heart in the first place. Gerald realizes he still loves and wants her even if he must bear the rigors of her various tours.

Zierler Photoplay Corporation/Metro Pictures, 1922 (original). Silent. Director: Wallace Worsley; screenwriter: Frank Beresford. Cast: Clara Kimball Young (Lisa Della Robbia), Elliott Dexter (Gerald Fitzgerald), Louise Dresser (Flora Preston), Arthur Rankin, Mary Jane Sanderson, Lionel Belmore, Wedgewood Nowell, Rosita Marstini, George Kuwa.

• ***Enter Madame*** (remake). Paramount Pictures, 1935. Director: Elliott Nugent; screenwriters: Charles Brackett and Gladys Lehman. Cast: Elissa Landi (Lisa Della Robbia), Cary Grant (Gerald Fitzgerald), Sharon Lynn (Flora

Preston), Frank Albertson, Cecilia Parker, Adrian Rosley, Lynne Overman, Paul Porcasi, Wilfred Hari.

The humor of the screenplay was considered subtle and sophisticated for its time. Clara Kimball Young was praised by critics for her appealing performance as the prima donna. The remake was given an elaborate operatic background with Nina Koshetz dubing Elissa Landi's singing chores. Grant gets into the swing of things by joining in the singing of the Anvil Chorus. The film isn't a good opera story and it's not the funniest of comedies, but as a farce it rates a look.

252 Enter the Dragon

Based on a screenplay by Michael Allin. Story: If you like Chinese kung fu movies and spoofs, this film will fill the bill. There's plenty of violence, as the strong Oriental hero overcomes the various villains who wish to split open his head with their hands and feet but get this treatment instead.

Warner Bros./Concord, Hong Kong, 1973 (original). Director: Robert Clouse; screenwriter: Michael Allin. Cast: Bruce Lee, John Saxon, Shih Kien, Jim Kelly, Bob Wall, Ahna Capri, Yang Tse, Angela Mao.

• ***Return of the Dragon*** (sequel). Concord, Hong Kong, 1973. Director and screenwriter: Bruce Lee. Cast: Bruce Lee, Chuck Norris, Nora Miao.

The second film was made prior to the first mentioned but released later. It is superior, containing more comedy and action. Bruce Lee was a superb acrobat if not a great actor, the latter ability not being something required in such films. The intent is to allow fans to vicariously maim, and all the grunting, springing and hitting with painful sound effects is worth seeing once—perhaps only once.

253 L'Equipage

Based on the novel by Joseph Kessel. Story: Mme. Maury, wife of a World War I aviator, falls in love with the latter's young friend and fellow pilot, Capitaine Thelis. Torn between his love for the wife and his friendship for the husband, Thelis's conflict is resolved when he is killed in a dogfight.

• ***L'Equipage*** (remake). Pathe-Natan Production, France, 1935. Director: Anatole Litvak; screenwriter: Joseph Kessel and Anatole Litvak. Cast: Annabella (Mme. Maury), Charles Varnel (Maury), Jean Murat (Capitaine Thelis), Jean-Pierre Aumont (Jean Herbillon), Suzanne Despres, Serge Grave.

• ***The Woman I Love*** (remake). RKO Radio, 1937. Director: Anatole Litvak; screenwriter: Mary Borden. Cast: Paul Muni (Maury), Miriam Hopkins (Denise), Louis Hayward (Jean), Colin Clive (Captain), Minor Watson, Elizabeth Risdon, Paul Guilfole, Wally Albright, Mady Christians.

L'Equipage was first filmed as a silent in France in 1927. The 1935 version was released in the United States under the name of *Flight Into Darkness.* While the latter film convinced Hollywood to bring both Annabelle and Anatole Litvak to this country to make movies, RKO's version in 1937, even with Litvak directing and Paul Muni borrowed from Warner Bros. and Louis Hayward from Universal, didn't result in a film that excited the public. The love triangle interspersed with the World War I adventures of a French flying squadron lost money, in part because of the uninspired screenplay and the listless performances the three leading actors gave.

254 Escape

Based on the play by John Galsworthy. Story: A perfect English gentleman is sentenced to five years in prison for manslaughter for killing a policeman in a row over a streetwalker. Not liking to be treated roughly, he escapes and the remainder of the story deals with his attempt to get away from the Dartmoor moors and the help and hindrances of the people he meets along the way. His recapture takes place in a village church.

ATP/RKO, 1930 (original). Director and screenwriter: Basil Dean. Cast: Gerald Du Maurier, Edna Best, Madeleine Carroll, Gordon Harker, Horace Hodges, Mabel Poulton, Lewis Casson, Ian Hunter, Felix Aylmer.

• ***Escape*** (remake). Twentieth Century–Fox, 1948. Director: Joseph L. Mankiewicz; screenwriter: Phillip Dunne. Cast: Rex Harrison, Peggy Cummings, William Hartnell, Norman Wooland, Jill Esmond, Frederick Piper, Marjorie Rhodes, Betty Ann Davies, Cyril Cusack, Frank Pettingell.

The first film production of the Galsworthy play was a box-office failure that didn't even recapture its costs. The producer's attempt to draw a simile between fox hunting and the hunted prisoner could have been done better. The fine cast couldn't do much with the stilted material. In the remake, Rex Harrison is an ex–RAF squadron leader, sentenced to three years' imprisonment for manslaughter. He escapes from Dartmoor and with the help of Peggy Cummings, who has fallen in love with him, eludes the police until at last he surrenders rather than allow a person to lie to the authorities. If anything this version is even less interesting than the first. Everything is so predictable.

Escape from Crime ***see*** **The Picture Snatcher**

Escape in the Desert ***see*** **The Petrified Forest**

255 Escape Me Never

Based on the play by Margaret Kennedy. Story: Gemma is an unmarried mother who marries a composer, Sebastian, who loves another. She herself is smitten by Sebastian's brother, Caryl. She's figuratively kicked around by her musician husband, but does nothing about it. This romantic weepie is a study of moods and morbidity.

B and D Productions, Great Britian, 1935 (original). Director: Pul Czinner; screenwriters: Carl Zuckmyer and R.J. Cullen. Cast: Elizabeth Bergner (Gemma), Hugh Sinclair (Sebastian), Griffith Jones (Caryl), Leon Quartermaine, Irene Vanbrugh, Penelope Dudley-Ward, Lyn Harding, Rosalinde Fuller.

• ***Escape Me Never*** (remake). Warner Bros., 1947. Director: Peter Godfrey; screenwriters: Thomas Williamson and Lenore Coffee. Cast: Errol Flynn (Sebastian), Ida Lupino (Gemma), Eleanor Parker (Fornella), Gig Young

(Caryl), Reginald Denny, Isobel Elsom, Albert Basserman, Helene Thimig, Frank Puglia.

Elizabeth Bergner's character is not sympathetically developed in this well-produced film, but it's probably her most memorable performance and won her an Academy Award nomination for Best Actress, the Oscar going to Bette Davis for *Dangerous.* The setting for this interesting if not totally satisfying movie is Venice, the Italian Alps, and finally, London.

In the remake, Flynn seems miscast as a composer, an occupation too sedentary for a man used to action roles. Ida Lupino is a widow waif with a baby, taken in off the streets by Flynn. However, the parents of wealthy Eleanor Parker believe that it is her fiancé, Gig Young, who has been living with the unfortunate girl. The two brothers and Lupino set off for the Alps to find Parker and explain everything. Flynn meets Parker and makes a pitch for her before knowing who she is. Despite his interest in Parker, Flynn marries Lupino. From then on this muddled mess deals with how Flynn writes a ballet, mistreats Lupino, chases after Parker, arrives at a rendezvous with her when Lupino's baby dies, and finally realizes what a heel he has been. In the end he and Lupino are reunited as are Parker and Young. The movie is not a great "woman's picture" but the score by Erich Wolfgang Korngold commands attention.

256 Escape to Witch Mountain

Based on the novel by Alexander Key. Story: Two orphans, Tia and Tony, have extraordinary psychic powers which evil millionaire Aristotle Bolt wishes to use for his own purposes. As they come from another planet, he proves no match for them in the long run.

Buena Vista, 1975 (original). Director: John Hough; screenwriter: Robert Malcolm Young. Cast: Eddie Albert (Jason), Ray Milland (Aristotle Bolt), Donald Pleasence (Deranian), Kim Richards (Tia), Ike Eisenmann (Tony), Walter Barnes, Reta Shaw, Denver Pyle, Alfred Ryder.

• ***Return from Witch Mountain*** (sequel). Buena Vista, 1978. Director: John Hough; screenwriter: Malcolm Marmorstein. Cast: Bette Davis (Letha), Christopher Lee (Victor), Kim Richards (Tia), Ike Eisenmann (Tony), Jack Soo (Mr. Yokomoto), Christian Juttner, Dick Bakalyan, Anthony James.

In the sequel to these better-than-average Disney movies, the brother and sister from outer space return to earth for a vacation and run afoul of Bette Davis and Christopher Lee, who wish to exploit the powers of the children. The special effects for these two pictures are rather good.

Esmerelda ***see*** **The Hunchback of Notre Dame**

Eve Knew Her Apples ***see*** **It Happened One Night**

257 Evelyn Prentice

Based on the novel by W.E. Woodward. Story: Evelyn Prentice discovers that her prominent criminal lawyer husband, John, has had an affair with Nancy

Harrison, while away on one of his frequent business trips. She seeks solace with poet Lawrence Kennard, exchanging letters with him, but after a few innocent meetings, she breaks off their friendship and takes John back. Kennard threatens to show her letters to John unless she pays him $15,000. She picks up a handy pistol and demands that he return her letters. He strikes her, the gun goes off, and Kennard falls to the floor. Evelyn rushes out just as Kennard's mistress, Judith Wilson, arrives. Judith is found alone with Kennard's body and is arrested. Grief stricken, Evelyn convinces John to defend Judith. During the trial, Evelyn loses control and shouts out her guilt. However, John, by using clever cross-examination, brings out that the shot that killed Kennard was actually fired by Judith. John and Evelyn reconcile, and with their daughter, set off on a postponed European vacation.

MGM, 1934 (original). Director: William K. Howard; screenwriter: Leonore Coffee. Cast: Myrna Loy (Evelyn Prentice), William Powell (John Prentice), Harvey Stephens (Lawrence Kennard), Isabel Jewel (Judith Wilson), Rosalind Russell (Nancy Harrison), Una Merkel, Henry Wadsworth, Edward Brophy, Jesse Ralph, Cora Sue Collins, Frank Conroy.

• ***Stronger Than Desire*** (remake). MGM, 1939. Director: Leslie Fenton; screenwriters: David Hertz and William Ludwig. Cast: Walter Pidgeon (Tyler Flagg), Virginia Bruce (Elizabeth Flagg), Ann Dvorak (Eva McLain), Lee Bowman (Michael McLain), Rita Johnson, Ilka Chase, Ann Todd, Richard Lane, Paul Stanton, Donald Douglas.

The original filming of the psychological novel was agreeable, although predictable, except the surprise ending. It was a new experience for audiences to see Myrna Loy and William Powell taking marriage serious, with Powell as a man whose romantic peccadillos drive his wife to challenge the double standards with an obvious gigolo, almost resulting in her becoming a murderer. The remake, with the exception of Pidgeon, has a much weaker cast, and in their hands the oft-told story doesn't work as well. Bruce plays the wife neglected by busy husband Pidgeon, the former innocently becoming involved with suave blackmailer Bowman, whom she shoots in a scuffle. Dvorak plays Bowman's wife who is put on trial for his murder. While the verdict for the wife is not guilty, the verdict on the movie is guilty of not delivering as much as was promised.

258 Every Which Way But Loose

Based on an original screenplay by Jeremy Joe Kronsberg. Story: A Los Angeles truck driver, Phil Beddoe, makes extra money as a bare-knuckled barroom bawler. In one of his fights he wins an orangutan, who becomes his traveling companion and best friend. Beddoe chases after singer Lynn Halsey-Taylor, while he is being chased by a motorcycle gang and a cop. There is no particular story line in this easygoing, likeable star-vehicle.

Malpaso Company, 1978 (original). Director: James Fargo; screenwriter: Jeremy Joe Kronsberg. Cast: Clint Eastwood (Phil Beddoe), Sondra Locke (Lynn Halsey-Taylor), Geoffrey Lewis (Orville), Beverly D'Angelo (Echo), Ruth Gordon (Ma), Walter Barnes.

• ***Any Which Way You Can*** (sequel). Warner Bros., 1980. Director: Buddy Van Horn; screenwriter: Stanford Sherman. Cast: Clint Eastwood (Phil Beddoe), Sondra Locke (Lynn Halsey-Taylor), Geoffrey Lewis (Orville), William Smith (Jack Willson), Harry Guardino (James Beekman), Ruth Gordon (Ma), Michael Cavanaugh, Barry Corbin, Roy Jenson, Bill McKinley.

Critics found both of these films clumsy and stupid but the he-man appeal of Eastwood, the monkey business of the orangutan, the crazy charm of Ruth Gordon and the attractiveness of Locke ensured that they were box-office successes. If you like bare-knuckle brawls, car chases and crashes these films are for you. Of the two, the sequel is the funnier, and ends with a spectacular bare-knuckles fist fight.

Everybody Does It *see* **Wife, Husband and Friend**

Everybody's Old Man *see* **The Working Man**

Ex-Bad Boy *see* **The Whole Town's Talking**

Excalibur *see* **Knights of the Round Table**

Ex-Lady *see* **Illicit**

The Expert *see* **Welcome Home**

Expose Me Lovely *see* **Farewell My Lovely**

259 The Exorcist

Based on the novel by William Peter Blatty. Story: Twelve-year-old Regan MacNeil becomes possessed by a devil. Her mother, Chris, consults Father Damien, a priest and psychologist who calls in Father Merrin to perform an exorcism when a series of grueling medical tests do no good. The exorcism itself is chilling. When it appears the exorcism will fail, Father Damien, who has lost his faith, calls upon the demon to enter his body and leave that of the child.

Warner Bros., 1973 (original). Director: William Friedkin; screenwriter: William Peter Blatty. Cast: Ellen Burstyn (Chris MacNeil), Linda Blair (Regan MacNeil), Jason Miller (Father Damien Karras), Max Von Sydow (Father Merrin), Lee J. Cobb (Lt. Kinderman), Jack MacGowran, Kitty Winn, Rev. William O'Malley.

• ***Exorcist II: The Heretic*** (sequel). Warner Bros., 1977. Director: John Boorman; screenwriter: William Goodhart. Cast: Linda Blair (Regan MacNeil), Richard Burton (Father Lamont), Louise Fletcher (Doctor Gene Tuskin), Max Von Sydow (Father Merrin), Kitty Winn, Paul Henreid, James Earl Jones, Ned Beatty.

One supposes that these films should be assigned to the horror genre, but the great popularity of the pictures and the fact that many critics and commentators saw deeper meaning in the possession of the child and the spiritual conflicts of Father Damien, commends it for inclusion in this volume. Regan's demon, who causes her to urinate in public, vomit on a priest and masturbate with a crucifix, attracted millions who would normally never consider seeing a horror movie. The voice of the demon is supplied by Mercedes McCambridge, although she was not given screen credit. In the more ridiculous sequel, Father Lamont, rather well played by Richard Burton (who is investigating the death of the exorcist who had aided Regan), discovers that her demon is alive and well and living in Africa. The prestige attached to these movies is probably not deserved, at least not if one is looking for some significant message. Rather, what makes the films work are an intriguing story and a bit of imaginative but shocking special effects.

Exorcist II: The Heretic *see* **The Exorcist**

260 The Exterminator

Based on an original screenplay by James Glickenhaus. Story: An ex–Vietnam veteran goes berserk when his close friend is crippled by a street gang. He takes the law in his own hands when the courts are unable to punish the guilty parties. He tracks down and wipes out the gang. He becomes a media hero and the police look the other way as he wages his one-man vigilante assault against criminal scum.

Interstar Corporation, 1980 (original). Director and screenwriter: James Glickenhaus. Cast: Robert Ginty, Christopher George, Samantha Eggar, Steve James, Tony DiBendetto.

• ***Exterminator 2*** (sequel). Cannon, 1984. Director: Mark Buntzman; screenwriters: Buntzman and William Sachs. Cast: Robert Ginty, Deborah Geffner, Mario Van Pebbles, Frankie Faison.

These films make the *Death Wish* series look like public service documentaries. They are violent fantasies which might appeal to those of extreme right political views who see no inconsistences in breaking the law to punish lawbreakers. In the sequel, Vietnam vet Robert Ginty employs a flamethrower to eliminate punks. These are not for the squeamish—or movie lovers.

Exterminator 2 *see* **The Exterminator**

261 Eyes in the Night

Based on the novel *Odor of Violets* by Bayard Kendrick. Story: Norma Lawry attempts to prevent her stepdaughter, Barbara, from marrying Paul Gerenti, a phony stock company actor, to whom the former was once engaged. Gerenti is found dead in his apartment and Barbara accuses Norma of the murder. Blind detective Duncan Maclain is called upon to solve the crime. He stumbles onto a nest of Nazi agents whom Barbara has innocently brought into her home. The latter nearly kill her father, Stephen, a scientist, to get at his secrets. Maclain puts everything right before the fade-out.

MGM, 1942 (original). Director: Fred Zinnemann; screenwriters: Guy Trosper and Howard Emmett Rogers. Cast: Edward Arnold (Duncan Maclain), Ann Harding (Norma Lawry), Reginald Denny (Stephen Lawry), John Emery (Paul Gerenti), Donna Reed (Barbara Lawry), Stanley Ridges, Horace McNally.

• ***The Hidden Eye*** (remake). MGM, 1945. Director: Richard Thorp; screenwriters: George Harmon Coxe and Harry Ruskin. Cast: Edward Arnold (Duncan Maclain), Frances Rafferty (Jean Hampton), Paul Langston (Barry Gifford), Ray Collins (Phillip Treadway), Bill Phillips, Thomas Jackson, Morris Ankrum.

The espionage-murder melodrama becomes just another cops and robbers battle before the end. It contained plenty of suspense for a "B" film. In the second film, the whodunit aspects are not as well developed. Most of the interest in the feature goes to the seeing-eye dog, Friday, who solves three murders and prevents a fourth. In the finale, Arnold takes on the villain in hand-to-hand combat, winning because of his special training to overcome the handicap of blindness.

F

262 The Face at the Window

Based on the novel by F. Brooke Warren. Story: Now get this. Dead Paris detective Bentick is revived so that he can track down a bank robber, who turns out to be a chevalier.

British Actors, Great Britain, 1920 (original). Silent. Director: Wilfred Noy; screenwriter: Adrian Brunel. Cast: C. Aubrey Smith (Bentick), Gladys Jennings (Marie de Brisson), Jack Hobbs (Lucien Cartwright), Charles Quartermaine (Lucien Degradoff), Ben Field, Sir Simon Stuart, Kathleen Vaughan, Kinsey Peile.

• ***The Face at the Window*** (remake). Real Art/Radio, Great Britain, 1932. Director: Leslie Hiscott; screenwriters: H. Fowler Mear. Cast: Raymond Massey (Paul le Gros), Isla Bevan (Marie de Breson), Claude Hulbert (Peter Pomeroy), Eric Maturin (Count Fournal), Henry Mollison, A. Bromley Davenpoert, Harold Meade, Dennis Wyndham.

• ***The Face at the Window*** (remake). Pennant/British Lion, Great Britain, 1939. Director: George King; screenwriters: A.R. Rawlinson and Randall Faye. Cast: Tod Slaughter (Chevalier del Gardo), Marjorie Taylor (Cecile de Brisson), John Warwick (Lucien Cortier), Leonard Henry (Gaston), Aubrey Mallalieu (de Brisson), Robert Adair (Insp. Guffert), Wallace Evenett, Kay Lewis, Margaret Yarde, Harry Terry.

In the first remake, Raymond Massey is a famous French detective who pretends that one of the victims of a series of bank robberies, in which the nightwatchman is murdered by poison, is not dead. This helps him expose a maniacal count as the killer. In the third version, in Paris of 1880, the "wolf" stabs his victims while they are looking at a hideous face at their window. Bank clerk John Warwick is suspected but the villain turns out to be his rival for Marjorie

Taylor, Tod Slaughter, with his monstrous half-brother (Harry Terry, the "face").

Fail-Safe *see* **Dr. Strangelove**

Fair Co-Ed *see* **The College Widow**

263 The Faithful Heart

Based on the play by Monckton Hoffe. Story: Naval officer Waverley Ango is forced to leave the girl he loves, Blackie Anderway, when he is suddenly recalled to his ship. They lose touch with each other and years later he is about to marry socialite Diana Oughterson, when his illegitimate daughter shows up at his door looking for his help, as her mother is now dead. When Oughterson cannot accept the idea of this girl, Ango breaks off the engagement and goes away with his daughter.

British Super/Jury, Great Britain, 1922 (original). Silent. Director: Fred Paul; screenwriter: Walter Summers. Cast: Owen Nares (Waverly Ango), Lilian Hall Davis (Blackie Anderway/Her Daughter), Cathleen Nesbitt (Diana Oughterson), A.B. Imeson (Maj. Lestrade), Ruth Maitland, Cyril Raymond, Victor Tandy.

• ***The Faithful Heart*** (remake). Gainsborough Pictures, Great Britain, 1932. Director: Victor Saville; screenwriters: Angus Macphail, Robert Stevenson, Lajos Biro and Victor Saville. Cast: Herbert Marshall (Waverley Ango), Edna Best (Blackie/Her Daughter), Anne Grey (Diana Oughterson), Athole Stewart (Sir Gilbert Oughterson), Lawrence Hanray, Mignon O'Dogherty, Griffith Jones.

As romances go, this one is nothing special. There's not enough tear-jerking to make it a legitimate "woman's picture." Marshall and Best give credible performances in the remake, but nothing to rave about.

The Falcon Takes Over *see* **Farewell, My Lovely**

264 A Family Affair

Based on the play *Skidding* by Aurania Rouveyrol. Story: It's wholesome family fare about an honest, small-town judge, who is a loving father to daughters Marian and Joan and son Andy, the latter getting the biggest laughs.

MGM, 1937 (original). Director: George B. Seitz; screenwriter: Kay Van Riper. Cast: Lionel Barrymore (Judge Hardy), Cecilia Parker (Marian Hardy), Eric Linden (Wayne Trent), Mickey Rooney (Andy Hardy), Charley Grapewin (Frank Redmond), Spring Byington (Mrs. Hardy), Julie Hayden (Joan Hardy), Sara Haden (Aunt Milly), Allen Vincent, Margaret Marquis, Selmer Jackson, Harlan Briggs.

• ***You're Only Young Once*** (sequel). MGM, 1938. Director: George B. Seitz; screenwriter: Kay Van Riper. Cast: Lewis Stone (Judge Hardy), Cecilia Parker (Marian), Mickey Rooney (Andrew), Fay Holden (Mrs. Hardy), Frank Craven

(Redmond), Ann Rutherford (Polly), Eleanor Lynn (Jerry Lane), Ted Pearson, Sara Haden, Charles Judels, Selmer Jackson.

Critics and reviewers didn't see much in the first of what would prove to be the Andy Hardy series, but the public fell in love with Mickey Rooney as Judge Hardy's troubled but respectful son. In all there would be 16 films in the series with titles such as *Out West with the Hardys* (1938), *Judge Hardy's Children* (1938), *Andy Hardy Gets Spring Fever* (1939), *Andy Hardy's Private Secretary* (1941), *Andy Hardy's Blonde Trouble* (1944) and *Andy Hardy Comes Home* (1958). The public loved the fact that at least once in every movie when Andy had yet again gotten in over his head, he would visit his father in the latter's study and receive and follow some kindly advice from the loving Judge. In some of the movies, Judy Garland or Lana Turner showed up to become Rooney's romantic interest, a role that Ann Rutherford as Polly filled as well.

265 The Family Upstairs

Based on the play by Harry Delf. Story: Louise Heller, quiet and refined, is taunted by her family for not having a sweetheart. Finally, bank teller Charles Grant falls in love with her but the romance appears ruined when, upon visiting her family, he is put off by their talk of the luxury to which Louise is accustomed. When Charles departs she accuses her family of spoiling her chance for happiness and impulsively runs off to Coney Island. Charles, who had seen through the family's pretense, follows her. She meets two boys who work in her office and when Charles tries to talk to her they believe he's a masher and clobber him. The beating has the happy result of reuniting the young couple.

Fox Pictures, 1926 (original). Silent. Director and screenwriter: John Blystone. Cast: Virginia Valli (Louise Heller), Allan Simpson (Charles Grant), J. Farrell MacDonald (Joe Heller), Jacqueline Wells (Annabelle Heller), Lilian Elliott, Edward Piel, Jr., Dot Farley.

• ***Harmony at Home*** (remake). Fox Pictures, 1929. Director: William MacFadden; screenwriters: Edwin Burke and Elliott Lester. Cast: William Collier, Sr., Marguerite Churchill (Louise), Rex Bell (Charles), Dixie Lee, Charlotte Henry, Charles Eaton, Elizabeth Patterson, Dot Farley.

• ***Stop, Look and Love*** (remake). Twentieth Century–Fox, 1939. Director: Otto Brower; screenwriters: Harold Tarshia and Sada Cowan. Cast: Jean Rogers (Louise Heller), William Frawley (Joe Heller), Robert Kellard (Dick Grant), Eddie Collins, Minna Gombell, Cora Sue Collins, Jay Ward, Roger McGee.

For what they were, these proved to be amusing and diverting pictures of family life in which the father is taken advantage of by his family with the exception of one daughter, whose hopes for a beau are generally sabotaged by her mother's eagerness and pretenses. In each case the girl finally gets the boy but not without experiencing some problems, although they seem of a routine nature.

The Fan *see* **Lady Windemere's Fan**

Fancy Pants *see* **Ruggles of Red Gap**

266 Fanny

Based on the trilogy of stories by Marcel Pagnol. Story: Fanny loves Marius, son of Marseilles dock-side cafe owner Cesar. Marius also loves Fanny but he loves the sea more. He sets out to become a sailor, leaving Fanny behind and pregnant. Her mother encourages Fanny to accept the offer of marriage of rich widower Honore Panisse. Fanny explains her predicament and Panisse is delighted. He always wanted a son and looks forward to fatherhood. Cesar, protecting the interests of his son, tells Fanny she should wait until Marius returns in two years, when he will then marry her. Explaining she is with child, Cesar withdraws his objection of her marriage to Panisse, but negotiates that the child, his grandson, will be named Cesar-Marius Panisse. Honore and Fanny marry and have a son. Later Marius returns, still in love with Fanny, learns of her marriage and child and suspects the son may be his. He goes to Fanny, declares his love, which she acknowledges is how she feels as well. Panisse and Cesar appear. Marius demands Fanny and his son. Fanny tells Marius the boy is not morally his as Panisse has been the father the boy needed and the husband she needed. Cesar orders his son to leave. He does and Fanny cries inconsolably.

Les Films Marcel, France, 1932 (original). Director: Marc Allegret; screenwriter: Marcel Pagnol. Cast: Raimu (Cesar), Orane Demazis (Fanny), Pierre Fresnay (Marius), Fernand Charpin (Honore Panisse), Alida Roufe, Robert Vattien, Auguste Mouries, Milly Mathis, Maupi, Edouard Delmont.

• ***Port of Seven Seas*** (remake). MGM, 1938. Director: James Whale; screenwriter: Preston Sturges. Cast: Wallace Beery, Frank Morgan, Maureen O'Sullivan, John Beal, Jessie Ralph, Cora Witherspoon.

• ***Fanny*** (remake). Warners, 1961. Director: Joshua Logan; screenwriter: Julius J. Epstein. Cast: Charles Boyer (Cesar), Maurice Chevalier (Honore Panisse), Leslie Caron (Fanny), Horst Buchholz (Marius), Georgette Anys, Salvatore Baccaloni, Lionel Jeffries, Raymond Bussieres, Victor Francen.

The 1932 film was the second chapter in Pagnol's masterful trilogy, preceded by *Marius* in 1931 and followed by *Cesar* in 1936. The first film deals with Marius' decision to give up his sweetheart, Fanny, and go to sea. The final installment deals with Marius returning twenty years after he leaves Fanny and his son with Panisse, to be reunited with his family. The 1938 film is a moderately successful Hollywood attempt to film Pagnol's trilogy in one film. The 1961 production is another attempt to do the same thing, somewhat better because the leading performers are French, and pretty fair French actors and actresses at that. If one has the opportunity, the Pagnol trilogy is still the best bet.

Fantasy . . . 3 *see* The Wizard of Oz

267 Far from the Madding Crowd

Based on the novel by Thomas Hardy. Story: In England in the 1870s, headstrong Bathsheba Everdene inherits her uncle's farm in Weatherbury and in so doing achieves the independence she always sought. She hires Gabriel Oak, a former suitor, to be her shepherd. Ignoring Gabriel's love, Bathsheba impulsively sends a valentine to gentleman farmer William Boldwood who misinterprets and proposes to her. She promises to give his offer some consideration but instead falls for dashing cavalry officer Frank Troy, who has refused to do the right thing by Fanny Robin, a maidservant pregnant with his child. Bathsheba foolishly marries Troy, who promptly gambles away most of her money and upsets all the farmhands. When Troy learns that Fanny has died in childbirth, he is filled with remorse. Swearing that he never loved Bathsheba, he walks into the ocean and disappears. Bathsheba agrees to marry Boldwood as soon as Troy is pronounced legally dead, but the latter shows up again and suddenly crazed Boldwood kills him and is sent to prison. Gabriel informs Bathsheba that he plans to emigrate to America. Realizing that she really loves and needs him, she persuades Gabriel to remain as her husband.

• ***Far From the Madding Crowd*** (remake). Turner Films/Ideal, Great Britain, 1915. Silent. Director and screenwriter: Larry Trimble. Cast: Florence Turner (Bathsheba Everdene), Henry Edwards (Gabriel Oak), Malcolm Cherry (William Boldwood), Campbell Gullan (Frank Troy), Marion Grey (Fanny Robin), Dorothy Rowan, John MacAndrews, Johnny Butt.

• ***Far from the Madding Crowd*** (remake). Vic Films/MGM, Great Britain, 1967. Director: John Schlesinger; screenwriter: Frederic Raphael. Cast: Julie Christie (Bathsheba Everdene), Terence Stamp (Frank Troy), Peter Finch (William Boldwood), Alan Bates (Gabriel Oak), Prunella Ransome (Fanny Robin), Fiona Walker, Alison Leggatt, Paul Dawkins, Julian Somers, John Barrett, Freddie Jones.

The location scenes for the remake were shot in Wiltshire and Dorset, England, and some critics felt that this was the best the movie had to offer—whereas the story itself and the acting paled by consideration. Hardy's novel has also been brought to the screen in 1911 and 1916.

268 Farewell, My Lovely

Based on the novel by Raymond Chandler. Story: Private Eye Philip Marlowe is hired by ex-con Moose Malloy to find his missing girl, Velma. While making this search, Marlowe is also hired to accompany a man who is ransoming stolen jewels. His client is killed and Marlowe is knocked out. When he comes to, he is hired by Mrs. Grayle, the owner of the stolen jewels, to find the murderer. He is beaten and drugged, but finally realizes that his two cases are related, that in fact Mrs. Grayle and Velma are one and the same person. He arranges a meeting with all involved parties at which Moose, Mrs. Grayle and her husband all shoot each other as Marlowe reviews their past and respective responsibilities for the stolen jewels and the murder.

• ***The Falcon Takes Over*** (original). RKO, 1942. Director: Irving Reis; screenwriters: Lynn Root and Frank Fenton. Cast: George Sanders (Falcon), Lynn Bari (Ann), James Gleason (O'Hara), Allen Jenkins (Goldy), Helen Gilbert (Diana), Ward Bond (Moose Malloy), Edward Gargan (Bates), Anne Revere, George Cleveland, Harry Shannon, Hans Conreid.

• ***Murder, My Sweet*** (remake). RKO, 1944. Director: Edward Dmytryk; screenwriter: John Paxon. Cast: Dick Powell (Philip Marlowe), Claire Trevor

(Mrs. Grayle), Mike Mazurki (Moose Malloy), Anne Shirley (Ann Grayle), Otto Kruger (Amthor), Miles Mander (Mr. Grayle), Douglas Walton, Don Douglas, Ralf Harolde, Esther Howard.

• ***Farewell, My Lovely*** (remake). Avco Embassy, 1975. Director: Dick Richards; screenwriter: David Zalag Goodman. Cast: Robert Mitchum (Philip Marlowe), Charlotte Rampling (Helen Grayle/Velma), John Ireland (Lt. Nulty), Sylvia Miles (Mrs. Florian), Jack O'Halloran (Moose Malloy), Jim Thompson (Mr. Grayle), Kate Murtaugh (Amthor), John O'Leary, Harry Dean Stanton, Sylvester Stallone.

In 1976, a pornographic version of the Raymond Chandler story, *Expose Me, Lovely*, was produced by Armand Weston. The first filming of the classic private eye story did not feature Philip Marlowe, but rather the debonair Falcon, created by Michael Arlen. This was passably entertaining but its production values and acting are what one would expect of a cheaply made B picture.

In 1944, Dick Powell appeared as Marlowe, in what is surely one of the quintessential *noir* films. In such a film, chaos is the norm, the antihero interjects himself into a dreary situation with no truly on-the-up-and-up characters, resolves one problem, and allows things to move back into the usual blackness. Powell was excellent as the detective who didn't expect much from clients, friends or strangers and thus was never disappointed. In 1975, Robert Mitchum added his sleepy interpretation of a man just doing the job for which he's paid, not trying to better the world, or accomplish anything noble. His performance was on a par with Powell's but the others in his cast didn't impress as much as those in the earlier version. Amthor this time was played by a woman, Kate Murtaugh, and she was as gross and vile as could be imagined.

269 A Farewell to Arms

Based on the novel by Ernest Hemingway. Story: In World War I, a wounded ambulance driver, Lieutenant Frederic Henry, falls in love with English nurse Catherine Barkley. The officer's close friend, Italian major Dr. Rinaldi, also loves Catherine and is unappreciative of the competition. Despite a desire to have Henry out of the way, Dr. Rinaldi remembers his Hippocratic oath and performs a successful operation on Henry's shattered leg and sends him to a Milanese hospital to be nursed back to health by Catherine. They are able to spend a few idyllic days together and then are once again separated by the war. They meet again amidst a chaotic army retreat at Caporetto. Catherine dies after delivering their son by cesarean section.

Paramount, 1932 (original). Director: Frank Borzage; screenwriter: Benjamin Glazer. Cast: Helen Hayes (Catherine Barkley), Gary Cooper (Lieutenant Frederic Henry), Adolphe Menjou (Major Rinaldi), Mary Phillips (Helen Ferguson), Blanche Frederici, Jack La Rue, Henry Armetta, George Humbert.

• ***Force of Arms*** (remake). Warner Bros., 1951. Director: Michael Curtiz; screenwriter: Richard Tregaskis, based on his story "Italian Story." Cast: William Holden (Peterson), Nancy Olson (Eleanor), Frank Lovejoy (Major

Blackford), Gene Evans (McFee), Dick Wesson, Paul Picerni, Katherine Warren.

• ***A Farewell to Arms*** (remake). Twentieth Century–Fox, 1957. Director: Charles Vidor; screenwriter: Ben Hecht. Cast: Jennifer Jones (Catherine Barkley), Rock Hudson (Lt. Frederic Henry), Vittoria De Sica (Major Alessandro Rinaldi), Mercedes McCambridge (Miss Van Campen), Elaine Strich, Oscar Homolka, Alberto Sordi.

The original is a lovely romantic story, although the acting styles of Hayes and Cooper seem a bit dated today. It was nominated for but did not win the Academy Award for Best Picture; however, an Oscar was presented to Charles Lang for his impressive photography. The 1957 remake, the last film produced by David O. Selznick, can charitably be described as overblown and boring. The performances by Jones and Hudson were just too precious to be appealing. On the other hand, De Sica was nominated for an Oscar for his performance as the doctor, but the award went to Red Buttons for his work in *Sayonara. Force of Arms* is merely a routine variation on the Hemingway story, with Holden as a soldier who falls for nurse Olson, during the Italian campaign. For those who like those kind of things, the battle sequences are quite exciting.

270 The Farmer Takes a Wife

Based on the play by Max Gordon and the book *Rome Haul* by Walter D. Edmonds. Story: Erie Canal barge cook Molly Larkins believes that physical prowess is all that matters in a man and that all farmers are cowards. Naturally, she falls for Dan Harrow, who drives a canal team so he can earn enough money for the purchase of a farm. He almost loses her when she believes he's afraid to face canal toughie Klore. But Dan settles this ruffian's hash and he and Molly retire to the life of farmers.

Twentieth Century–Fox, 1935 (original). Director: Victor Fleming; screenwriter: Edwin Burke and Oscar Bradley. Cast: Janet Gaynor (Molly Larkins), Henry Fonda (Dan Harrow), Charles Bickford (Jotham Klore), Slim Summerville, Andy Devine, Roger Imhof, Jane Withers, Margaret Hamilton.

• ***The Farmer Takes a Wife*** (remake). Twentieth Century–Fox, 1953. Director: Henry Levin; screenwriters: Walter Bullock, Sally Benson and Joseph Fields. Cast: Betty Grable (Molly), Dale Robertson (Dan Harrow), Thelma Ritter (Lucy Cashdollar), John Carroll (Jotham Klore), Eddie Foy, Jr., Charlotte Austin, Kathleen Crowley.

The first film is like a slow trip down the Erie Canal, the remake is like the return trip, even slower. There's a lot of local color but not much of a story and the addition of forgettable tunes by Harold Arlen and Dorothy Fields, such as "Somethin' Real Special" and "When the Sun Warms Up on Me" doesn't help the remake. Betty Grable had been away from films for a time when she made *Farmer;* she should have waited for a better return vehicle.

Fast and Loose *see* **The Best People**

Father Brown *see* **Father Brown, Detective**

271 Father Brown, Detective

Based on *The Blue Cross* by G.K. Chesterton. Story: Father Brown owns a diamond cross which thief Flambeau is determined to steal. His plan is to hand the diamonds over to a beautiful blonde, Evelyn Fischer, he has just met. Flambeau also robs her uncle, Sir Leopold Fischer. Father Brown redeems the thief spiritually before turning him over to the police.

Paramount Pictures, 1935 (original). Director: Edward Sedgwick; screenwriter: Harry Myers and C. Gardner Sullivan. Cast: Walter Connolly (Father Brown), Paul Lukas (Flambeau), Gertrude Michael (Evelyn Fischer), Robert Loraine (Inspector Valentine), Halliwell Hobbes (Sir Leopold Fischer), Una O'Connor, E.E. Clive.

• ***Father Brown*** (remake). Facet/Columbia Pictures, Great Britain, 1954. Director: Robert Hamer; screenwriter: Thelma Schnee. Cast: Alec Guinness (Father Brown), Joan Greenwood (Lady Warren), Peter Finch (Gustave Flambeau), Cecil Parker (The Bishop), Bernard Lee (Inspector Valentine), Sidney James, Gerard Oury, Ernest Thesiger, Ernest Clark, Everley Gregg, Austin Trevor.

In the remake, Alec Guinness as the priest-detective is on his way to a congress in Rome with a priceless cross, but is tricked by master of disguise Flambeau who steals the cross. Father Brown gets wealthy Lady Warren to risk a valuable chess set to flush out Flambeau. It does and he gets away with it as well. The priest tracks the thief to a chateau in Burgundy and not only recovers the stolen cross and chess set, but far more importantly in his eyes, he saves Flambeau's immortal soul. Both pictures are gentle, humorous pieces, depending upon the nice interplay between priest and thief for their appeal.

Father Is a Prince *see* **Big Hearted Herbert**

272 Father of the Bride

Based on the novel by Edward Streeter. Story: When Kay Banks announces to her parents, Stanley and Ellie, that she plans to marry Buckley Dunstan, Stanley can't recall what the young man looks like, since his daughter is extremely beautiful and has had many suitors. As the date for the wedding approaches, his confusion is nothing compared to the new experience of being the father of the bride. There is the meeting with young Buckley, then a dinner party with the groom's equally bewildered parents, followed by showers, meetings with caterers, the minister and so forth. Also the cost of such an undertaking is more than Stanley had ever imagined. When the day is almost upon the Banks and everything is in readiness, Kay announces the wedding is off. This is almost too much for Stanley, but fortunately, the young couple settle their imagined differences. The day of the wedding arrives and, although not without its hectic moments, the ceremony goes off with nary a hitch. Stanley and Ellie return home, feeling much, much older.

MGM, 1950 (original). Director: Vincente Minnelli; screenwriter: Frances Goodrich and Albert Hackett. Cast: Spencer Tracy (Stanley Banks), Joan Bennett (Ellie Banks), Elizabeth Taylor (Kay Banks), Don Taylor (Buckley

Spencer Tracy and daughter Elizabeth Taylor share late night confidences and a snack in Father of the Bride *(MGM, 1950).*

Dunstan), Billie Burke (Mrs. Doris Dunstan), Leo G. Carroll (Mr. Massoula), Moroni Olsen (Herbert Dunstan), Melville Cooper, Taylor Holmes, Paul Harvey, Rusty Tamblyn.

• ***Father's Little Dividend*** (sequel). MGM, 1951. Director: Vincente Minnelli; screenwriters: Albert Hackett and Frances Goodrich. Cast: Spencer Tracy (Stanley Banks), Joan Bennett (Ellie Banks), Elizabeth Taylor (Kay Dunstan), Don Taylor (Buckley Dunstan), Billie Burke (Doris Dunstan), Moroni Olsen (Herbert Dunstan), Frank Faylen, Marietta Canty, Rusty Tamblyn, Tom Irish, Hayden Rorke.

These are amusing family life pictures with likeable performances from all of the participants. Tracy was nominated for an Academy Award in the original. The picture and the screenwriters were also nominated with the honors going, respectively, to Jose Ferrer for *Cyrano De Bergerac,* 20th Century–Fox's *All About Eve* and Joseph L. Mankiewicz for the screenplay award. The sequel allows us to follow the Banks and Dunstan families when Kay and Buckley have a son. It's not quite as enjoyable but Tracy is still outstanding as an often exasperated father and grandfather, but clearly a man who loves his children and his daughter's child. Elizabeth Taylor is smashingly lovely in both films and Joan Bennett's beauty also enriches the productions.

Father's Little Dividend *see* **Father of the Bride**

Soon to be grandfathers, Moroni Olsen and Spencer Tracy sit while Joan Bennett, Elizabeth Taylor and Billie Burke stand to hear Don Taylor's toast in Father's Little Dividend *(MGM, 1951).*

273 Father's Son

Based on the novel *Old Fathers and Young Sons* by Booth Tarkington. Story: Bill Emory is a mischievious youngster who continuously and often unwittingly misbehaves. His father can't or won't understand the boy. The kid's pranks eventually split the family, his mother being more tolerant of the child, believing her husband to be too stern. The boy decides to run away from home but is brought back by a sympathetic doctor who helps the lad reconcile with his dad and put the family back together again.

First National, 1930 (original). Director: William Beaudine; screenwriter: Hope Loring. Cast: Leon Janney (Bill Emory), Lewis Stone (William Emory), Irene Rich (Ruth Emory), John Halliday (Dr. Franklin).

• ***Father's Son*** (remake). Warner Bros., 1941. Director: D. Ross Lederman; screenwriter: Fred Niblo, Jr. Cast: John Litel (William Emory), Frieda Inescort (Ruth Emory), Billy Dawson (Bill Emory), Christian Rub (Lunk Nelson), Bernice Pilot, Phillip Hurlie, Sammy McKim, Sonny Bupp, Scotty Beckett.

The original was pleasant entertainment which appealed to certain small town and country audiences who found amusement in the boy's behavior and shed a tear or two when he decided to run away. It would be a few years before Lewis Stone would become the wise and understanding Judge Hardy. The remake was cut to 57 minutes, making it barely feature length and it looked like more cutting was called for. It was blessed with a "Who are they?" cast and the homespun humor missed more often than it hit the target.

274 Faust

Based on legend and plays by Christopher Marlowe and Johann Goethe. Story: Dr. Faustus sells his soul to the devil, Mephistophles, in exchange for a rich, full life.

• ***Faust*** (remake). UFA, Germany, 1926. Silent. Director: F.W. Murnau; screenwriter: Hans Kyser. Cast: Emil Jannings (Faust), Gosta Ekman (Mephistophles), Camilia Horn (Marguerite), Yvette Guilbert, William Dieterle.

• ***All that Money Can Buy (The Devil and Daniel Webster)*** (remake). RKO, 1941. Director: William Dieterle; screenwriter: Dan Totheroh, based on the short story by Stephen Vincent Benét and the play by Benét and Douglas Moore. Cast: Edward Arnold (Daniel Webster), Walter Huston (Mr. Scratch), James Craig (Jabez Stone), Jane Darwell (Ma Stone), Anne Shirley (Mary Simpson), Simone Simon (Belle Dee), Gene Lockhart (Squire Slossum), John Qualen (Miser Stevens), H.B. Warner, Frank Conlan, Jeff Corey, George Cleveland.

• ***La Beaute du Diable*** (remake). AYJM, Italy/France, 1949. Director: Rene Clair; screenwriters: Clair and Armand Salacrou. Cast: Michel Simon, Gerald Philipe, Raymond Cordy, Nicole Besnard, Gaton Modot, Paolo Stoppa.

• ***Alias Nick Beal*** (remake). Paramount Pictures, 1949. Director: John Farrow; screenwriter: Jonathan Latimer, based on an original story by Mindret Lord. Cast: Ray Milland (Nick Beal), Audrey Totter (Donna Allen), Thomas Mitchell (Joseph Foster), George Macready (Rev. Thomas Garfield), Fred Clark (Frankie Faulkner), Geraldine Wall (Martha Foster), Henry O'Neill, Darryl Hickman, Nestor Paiva, King Donovan.

• ***Marguerite de la Nuit*** (remake). SNEG/Gaumont Actualties/Cino del Duca; France/Italy, 1955. Director: Claude Autant-Lara; screenwriters: Ghislaine Autant-Lara and Gabriel Arout. Cast: Michele Morgan, Yves Montand, Jean-Francois Calve, Massimo Girotti.

• ***Damn Yankees*** (remake). Warner Bros., 1958. Directors: George Abbott and Stanley Donen; screenwriter: George Abbott, based on the musical comedy by Abbott and Douglas Wallop and the novel *The Year the Yankees Lost the Pennant.* Cast: Gwen Verdon (Lola), Tab Hunter (Joe Hardy), Ray Walston (Mr. Applegate), Russ Brown (Van Buren), Shannon Bolin (Meg Boyd), Robert Shafer (Joe Boyd), Jimmie Komack, Nathaniel Frey, Jean Stapleton, Rae Allen, Albert Linville, Bob Fosse.

• ***Faust*** (remake). Kalmar, Inc., 1964. Director and screenwriter: Michael Suman. Cast: Robert Towner (Faust), Judy Peters (Margaret), Roban Cody (Bolus).

• ***Doctor Faustus*** (remake). Columbia Pictures, Great Britain, 1967. Directors: Richard Burton and Nevill Goghill; screenwriter: Nevill Coghill. Cast: Richard Burton (Doctor Faustus), Elizabeth Taylor (Helen of Troy), Andreas Teuber (Mephistophles), Ian Marter, Elizabeth O'Donovan, David McIntosh, Jeremy Eccles, Ram Chopra, Richard Carwardine.

• ***Bedazzled*** (remake). Twentieth Century–Fox, Great Britain, 1968.

Director: Stanley Donen; screenwriter: Peter Cook. Cast: Peter Cook, Dudley Moore, Michael Bates, Raquel Welch, Eleanor Bron.

• ***Hammersmith Is Out*** (remake). Cinerama/Crean, 1972. Director: Peter Ustinov; screenwriter: Stanford Whitmore. Cast: Elizabeth Taylor (Jimmy Jean Jackson), Richard Burton (Hammersmith), Peter Ustinov (Doctor), Beau Bridges (Billy Breedlove), Leon Ames, Leon Akin, John Schuck, George Raft.

These are just a sampling of the many movies based on the legends of the German conjurer Johann Faust who lived circa 1488–1541. Besides the work of Marlowe and Goethe, there have been musical films based on Charles Gounod's opera and even a Czechoslovakian puppet version. The first straight version was produced in 1905. The best of the silent productions of the story is the stylish 1926 version directed by Murnau. There have been other modernized versions in 1963, 1964, 1966 and even a 1967 Spanish version, *Faustina,* in which the sex of the soul-seller has been changed.

In the Stephen Vincent Benét story, New Hampshire farmer Jabez Stone is down on his luck when he swears he would sell his soul for success. Immediately, Mr. Scratch appears and takes him up on the proposition, offering Stone seven years of prosperity for a nothing thing called his soul. Jabez prospers and becomes miserly, but at the end of the seven years, he appeals to his neighbor, the great orator and U.S. congressman Daniel Webster, to get him out of his deal. Webster demands a trial before a judge and jury of Americans. Mr. Scratch obliges and brings forth from hell scourges of the earth, but Americans all, to hear the case and decide Stone's fate. Webster's eloquence defeats Mr. Scratch's prosecution and Jabez's covenant with the devil is broken. The film is a pure delight with wonderful performances by Walter Huston as the wiley, likely devil; Edward Arnold as the righteous Webster; James Craig, in the best role of his career, as the farmer; Simone Simon as the tempestuous Belle sent by Mr. Scratch to further Stone's slide into degradation; and John Qualen as Miser Stevens, who had preceeded Stone in bargaining with Mr. Scratch.

In the Rene Clair film (1949), the protagonists agree to exchange places. In *Alias Nick Beal,* district attorney Thomas Mitchell makes a deal with devil Ray Milland to obtain incriminating information illegally in order to convict a criminal. The conviction leads to his election as the governor, by which time he has compromised everything that he once held dear. He finally realizes that he cannot continue his dishonest ways and resigns, and beats Milland out of his soul. In the 1955 French-Italian film, an octogenarian makes a pact with the devil for the return of his lost youth.

Damn Yankees is a baseball musical version of the Faustian legend. Middle-aged Washington Senators fan Joe Boyd swears he would sell his soul to help the Senators win the pennant and beat those "Damn Yankees." Suddenly Mr. Applegate appears to change Joe into a strapping youth called Joe Hardy with unbelievable baseball talents. After he is signed by the Senators, his feats on the field turn the American League doormats into a contender. Joe had negotiated an escape clause with Applegate, allowing him to revert to his old self with no penalty up until a certain date. Seeing that Joe misses his wife and might exercise his option, Mr. Applegate calls on his assistant, Lola, a several-hundred-year-old hag whom he has transformed into a beautiful, seductive redhead to vamp Joe and take his mind off calling off their deal. Joe resists Lola and although the time of exercising the escape clause passes, Joe gets transformed back to his old self and returns to his wife, just after helping the Senators clinch the pennant and defeat the Yankees. The songs in this fun romp by Richard Adler and Jerry Ross include "Heart," "Shoeless Joe from Hannibal, Mo," "Whatever Lola Wants" and "Those Were the Good Old Days."

The 1964 picture by Michael Suman is a dreadful fantasy satirizing Goethe's *Faust,* with a modern illusionist taunted by his psychiatrist into doing a trick he cannot explain. Richard Burton gives us his version of Marlowe's Faust who sells his soul for power and the fulfillment of his desires, best represented by Elizabeth Taylor as beautiful Helen of Troy. In *Bedazzled,* Peter Cook is an affable British devil who grants Dudley Moore's every wish—literally. Some of the stunts are amusing, others fall flat. Burton is back in a comedy about insane Hammersmith who believes that he is the devil and persuades male nurse Beau Bridges to help him escape from the asylum. Together they turn waitress Elizabeth Taylor into a movie star.

Faustina *see* **Faust**

Fear *see* **Crime and Punishment**

Fiddlers Three *see* **Sailor's Three**

The Fiend Who Walked the West *see* **Kiss of Death**

275 The Fighting Coward

Based on the novel *Magnolia* by Booth Tarkington. Story: Southerner Tom Rumford, raised by Quaker relatives in the North, has been taught not to fight. Most everyone believes him a coward when he refuses to take part in a duel with Major Patterson, a rival for the favor of Tom's cousin Elvira. He secretly takes lessons in the use of swords and guns from General Jackson, disguises himself, and using the name of Colonel Blake, cows bully Captain Blackie and takes his revenge on Major Patterson without actually resorting to weapons. Tom wins the love of Elvira's sister Lucy, who had always admired his convictions, when he explains his actions were all a bluff.

Paramount Pictures, 1924 (original). Silent. Director: James Cruze; screenwriter: Walter Woods. Cast: Ernest Torrence (General Orlando Jackson), Cullen Landis (Tom Rumford), Mary Astor (Lucy), Noah Beery (Captain Blackie), Phyllis Haver (Elvira), C. Raymond Nye, Richard R. Neill, Carmen Phillips.

• ***River of Romance*** (remake). Paramount Pictures, 1929. Talkie and silent versions. Director: Richard Wallace; screenwriter: Ethel Doherty. Cast: Charles "Buddy" Rogers (Tom Rumford/Col. Blake), Mary Brian (Lucy Jeffers), June Collier (Elvira Jeffers), Henry B. Walthall (General Jeff Rumford),

Wallace Beery (General Orlando Jackson), Fred Kohler (Captain Blackie), Natalie Kingston, Walter McGrail.

• ***Mississippi*** (remake). Paramount Pictures, 1935. Director: Edward Sutherland; screenwriters: Claude Binyon, Herbert Fields, Francis Martin and Jack Cunningham. Cast: Bing Crosby (Tom Grayson), W.C. Fields (Commodore Jackson), Joan Bennett (Lucy Rumford), Gail Patrick (Elvira Rumford), Queenie Smith, Claude Gillingwater, John Miljan, Ed Pawley, Fred Kohler, Sr., King Baggott.

The story of a man who refuses to fight because of his convictions has been a popular theme in American movies, finding expression in such diverse films as *The Quiet Man, Friendly Persuasion* and *Sergeant York*. The three films based on Tarkington's book certainly don't rank with the latter trio of outstanding films, either in story or how they handle the conflict. Still, they were enjoyable, hokey pieces, with casts of performers adequate if predictable in their assigned roles. In the first, Noah Beery makes a nice bully and Ernest Torrence is fine in the role of General Jackson. In the first remake, Rogers struggled manfully with both his conscience and his performance, both of which defeated him, but Wallace Beery gave his usual credible if hammy performance. Bing Crosby with his slicked down hair and mustache looked like a dandy but the tunes by Richard Rodgers and Lorenz Hart weren't. Any merit the film has is due to the presence of W.C. Fields, who supplied most of the laughs.

The File of the Golden Goose *see* **T-Men**

Fille d'Amour *see* **Camille**

Fire Over England *see* **The Private Life of Henry VIII**

276 Fires of Fate

Based on the novel *Tragedy of the Korosko* by Arthur Conan Doyle and the play by Lewis Waller. Story: Colonel Egerton, with only a year to live, goes to Egypt and falls in love with Dorinne Adams, but because he is doomed, does not speak his piece. When his party, on a trek in the desert, is attacked by Bedouins led by an Arab prince, he saves Dorinne and lets her know of his love and prognosis.

Gaumont-Westminster, Great Britain, 1923 (original). Silent. Director: Tom Terriss; screenwriter: Alicia Ramsey. Cast: Wanda Hawley (Dorinne Adams), Nigel Barrie (Col. Egerton), Pedro de Corboba (Prince Ibrahim), Stewart Rome (Rev. Samuel Roden), Edith Craig, Percy Standing, Arthur Cullin, Douglas Munro, Cyril Smith.

• ***Fires of Fate*** (remake). BIP/Wardour, Great Britain, 1932. Director: Norman Walker; screenwriter: Dion Titheradge. Cast: Lester Matthews (Lt. Col. Egerton), Dorothy Bartlam (Kay Byrne), Kathleen O'Regan (Nora Belmont), Donald Calthrop (Sir William Royden), Jack Raine (Filbert Frayne), Garry Marsh, Clifford Hetherley, Jean Cadell, Hubert Harben, Arthur Chesney.

In the remake, Lester Matthews' bravery does not go unrewarded. In saving the woman he loves from the desert bandits, he receives a blow to the head that cures him. Now isn't that a kick in the head?

First a Girl *see* **Viktor und Viktoria**

277 First Blood

Based on the novel by David Marell. Story: Rambo is a returned Vietnam vet, a Green Beret, skilled in jungle warfare. He gets in trouble with the police of a small California community and declares war on the forces of the law. He and the cops stalk each other through the forests of the Pacific Northwest, with him finally facing his old Green Beret commander, Trautman. Rambo becomes a single-man army who wipes out the police station, a hardware store and blows up a gasoline station, before being taken.

Carolco, 1982 (original). Director: Ted Kotcheff; screenwriters: Michael Kazall, William Sackheim and Sylvester Stallone. Cast: Sylvester Stallone (John Rambo), Richard Crenna (Trautman), Brian Dennehy (Chief Teasle), David Caruso (Mitch).

• ***Rambo: First Blood Part II*** (sequel). Carolco, 1985. Director: George P. Cosmatos; screenwriters: Sylvester Stallone and James Cameron. Cast: Sylvester Stallone (Rambo), Richard Crenna (Trautman), Charles Napier (Murdock), Steven Berkoff (Podovsky), Julia Nickson (Co), Martin Kove, George Kee Cheung.

Stallone, the superbly trained fighting machine, is breaking rocks on a chain gang for his little temper tantrum in the original picture, where he wiped out half a town and enough people to put him high up on the list of mass killers. He is visited by Richard Crenna who has a mission for him. He is to be parachuted into Southeast Asia to scout out a suspected POW compound holding Americans captive. This is just up Sylvester's alley and he single-handedly smashes the enemy and rescues some of the MIAs. Both movies made political statements about the Vietnam War and this country's willingness to win it, but they are fairly simplistic statements, and mostly the movies are an excuse to show off Stallone's muscles, his grunting acting style and plenty of vicarious violence.

278 The First Traveling Saleslady

Based on an original screenplay by Stephen Longstreet and Devery Freeman. Story: Rose Gillray goes broke selling steel corset stays with the questionable help of scatterbrained chorus girl Molly Wade. She moves on to selling barbed wire to Texas ranchers who consider the new product dangerous. The state's biggest cattle baron, Joel Kingdom, intends either to stop her or marry her. But she ends up with admirer Charles Masters, instead. He's a cross-country auto driver who has followed her west.

RKO, 1956 (original). Director: Arthur Lubin; screenwriters: Stephen Longstreet and Devery Freeman. Cast: Ginger Rogers (Rose Gillray), Barry Nelson (Charles Masters), Carol Channing (Molly Wade), David Brian (James Carter),

James Arness (Joel Kingdom), Clint Eastwood (Jack Rice), Robert Simon, Frank Wilcox.

• ***Did You Hear the One About the Traveling Saleslady?*** (remake). Universal Pictures, 1968. Director: Don Weis; screenwriter: John Fenton Murray. Cast: Phyllis Diller (Agatha Knabenshu), Bob Denver (Bertram), Joe Flynn (Shelton), Eileen Wesson (Jeanine), Jeanette Nolan, Paul Reed, Bob Hastings, David Hartman.

The original, in its limited way, is a minor feminist statement, featuring Rogers as a businesswoman who isn't afraid to enter a man's territory and sell a product that refined young ladies shouldn't know anything about. The remake with Phyllis Diller is merely an excuse for the zany comedian to bring her TV and night-club routines to the big screen. A little of Phyllis goes a long way for most movie audiences. Her product is player-pianos and she's assisted by small-town inventor Bob Denver.

279 The First Year

Based on the play by Frank Craven. Story: Tom Tucker and Grace Livingston wed and move to a small town. Grace, who is more ambitious for Tom than he is for himself, becomes discontented with their lot and susceptible to the advances of her former suitor, Dick Loring. Meanwhile, Tom invites the principals of a deal he is working on with a railroad company to his home for dinner. The evening is a disaster: The maid is inexperienced and clumsy, Grace lets slip an unfortunate remark and Loring shows up to put in his two cents. Grace, feeling the deal has been ruined, goes home to her mother. But she had underestimated her husband. While she is gone he wraps up the deal with his guests, Mr. and Mrs. Barstow, and then goes after his wife. They are reconciled and Tom learns he is to be a father.

Fox Pictures, 1926 (original). Silent. Director: Frank Borzage; screenwriter: Frances Marion. Cast: Matt Moore (Tom Tucker), Kathryn Perry (Grace Livingston), John Patrick (Dick Loring), Frank Currier (Dr. Livingston), J. Farrell MacDonald (Mr. Barstow), Frank Cooley, Virginia Madison, Carolynne Snowden.

• ***The First Year*** (remake). Fox Pictures, 1932. Director: William K. Howard; screenwriter: Lynn Starling. Cast: Janet Gaynor (Grace Livingston), Charles Farrell (Tommy Tucker), Minna Gombell (Mrs. Barstow), Leila Bennett (Hattie), Dudley Digges (Dr. Myron Anderson), George Meeker (Dick Loring), Henry Kolker (Pete Barstow), Robert McQuade, Maude Eburne.

These homespun family comedy-melodramas were very popular with audiences in country and small towns, particularly the remake with the team of Gaynor and Farrell, who had scored so highly in several silent films. They reminded ordinary people of themselves and their actions were more to be trusted and admired than those of more sophisticated and glamorous stars. The period of adjustment to marriage in the first year has been brought to the screen many times. In fact, *Period of Adjustment* is the title of just such a film made in 1962 with Jane Fonda and Jim Hutton, as the young couple who learned the lesson that you always marry a stranger.

280 Five Came Back

Based on a story by Richard Carroll. Story: A passenger plane crashes in a South American jungle. It can be repaired enough to carry only five passengers. The survivors of the crash must decide who will live and who will be left to the native headhunters of the region. The personalities of the characters, including a detective, an anarchist, a gangster and scientists, are thrillingly revealed.

RKO, 1939 (original). Director: John Farrow; screenwriters: Jerry Cady, Dalton Trumbo and Nathaniel West. Cast: Chester Morris (Bill), Lucille Ball (Peggy), Wendy Barrie (Alice), John Carradine (Crimp), Allen Jenkins (Pete), Joseph Calleia (Vasquez), C. Aubrey Smith (Prof. Spengler), Kent Taylor (Joe), Patric Knowles (Judson Ellis), Elisabeth Risdon (Martha), Casey Johnson (Tommy), Dick Hogan (Larry).

• ***Back from Eternity*** (remake). RKO, 1956. Director: John Farrow; screenwriter: Jonathan Latimer. Cast: Robert Ryan (Bill), Anita Ekberg (Rena), Rod Steiger (Vasquez), Phyllis Kirk (Louise), Keith Andres (Joe), Gene Barry (Ellis), Fred Clark (Crimp), Beulah Bondi (Martha), Cameron Prud'homme (Henry), Jesse White (Pete), Adele Mara (Maria), John Provost (Tommy).

This is one of those "B" pictures that really worked. The director and screenwriters had a fine cast of second-feature actors with which to work, and produced a first rate adventure story. The remake had a superior production and a reasonably good cast but the dated story did not prove to be as grippingly told this time around. Both versions are worth a late night look on TV.

281 5-Star Final

Based on the play by Louis Weitzenkorn. Story: Randall is the cynical editor of a muckraking New York tabloid. He runs a series of articles on a 20-year-old murder case. The woman in the case, Nancy Voorhees Townsend, who had been acquitted, is now happily married to Michael Townsend. The publicity is too much for her so she commits suicide, followed quickly by her husband also taking his life. Daughter Jenny arrives at the newsroom with a gun in her bag, demanding to know why they had killed her parents. She cannot use her weapon and Randall, who had been growing conscience-stricken about the type of news he was forced to print, tells off the publisher and quits.

Warner Bros./First National, 1931 (original). Director: Mervyn Le Roy; screenwriter: Bryon Morgan. Cast: Edward G. Robinson (Randall), H.B. Warner (Michael Townsend), Marian Marsh (Jenny Townsend), Francis Starr (Nancy Voorhees Townsend), Anthony Bushnell, George E. Stone, Ona Munson, Boris Karloff, Robert Elliott, Aline McMahon.

• ***Two Against the World (One Fatal Hour)*** (remake). Warner Bros., 1936. Director: William McGann; screenwriter: Michael Jacoby. Cast: Humphrey Bogart (Sherry Scott), Beverly Roberts (Alma Ross), Linda Perry (Edith Carstairs), Henry O'Neill (Jim Carstairs), Helen MacKellar (Martha Carstairs), Caryle Moore, Jr., Claire Dodd, Hobart Cavanaugh, Harry Hayden.

The 1931 argument against the kind of trash that is published in tabloid newspapers has done nothing to curb their taste for incredible and shocking stories, nor dampened the public's desire to devour it. The film is still, after more than fifty years, a powerful piece of melodrama with wonderful performances from Robinson, Warner, Starr and Marsh. A bit of obvious symbolism is employed in the picture. Robinson is often seen washing his hands, and the more his conscience bothers him, the more he washes his hands. Of course, when he quits, he washes them vigorously. The remake transferred the story to a radio station with Bogart as its crusading manager who doesn't want to air the muckraking stories. Unfortunately neither the actors nor the director were able to recapture the excitement of the original, producing instead a drab, ordinary film.

282 The Flag Lieutenant

Based on the play by W.P. Drury and Leo Tovar. Story: Lt. Dick Lascelles is branded a coward after saving a beleaguered fort from the Bashi Bazouks, and letting his friend Major Thesisger, who has lost his memory, take the credit. All is ultimately resolved and both officers are treated as heroes.

Barker/Jury, Great Britain, 1919 (original). Silent. Director: Percy Nash; screenwriters: W.P. Drury and Leo Tovar. Cast: Ivy Close (Lady Hermione Wynne), George Wynn (Lt. Dicky Lascelles), Dorothy Fane (Mrs. Cameron), Ernest Wallace (Major Thesisger), Frank Adai, Wallace Bosco.

• ***The Flag Lieutenant*** (remake). Astra-National, Great Britain, 1926. Silent. Director: Maurice Elvey; screenwriter: Patrick L. Mannock. Cast: Henry Edwards (Lt. Dicky Lascelles), Lillian Oldland (Sybil Wynne), Dorothy Seacombe (Mrs. Cameron), Fred Raynham (Maj. Thesisger), Fewlass Llewellyn, Hayford Hobbs, Forrester Harvey, Humbertson Wright.

• ***Further Adventures of the Flag Lieutenant*** (sequel). Neo-Art Productions, Great Britain, 1927. Silent. Director: W.P. Kellino; screenwriter: George A. Cooper. Cast: Henry Edwards (Lt. Dicky Lascelles), Isabel Jeans (Pauline), Lillian Oldland (Sybil Wynne), Lyn Harding (The Sinister Influence), Fred Raynham (Colonel William Thesisger), Fewlass Llewellyn, Albert Egbert.

• ***The Flag Lieutenant*** (remake). British & Dominion, Great Britain, 1932. Director: Henry Edwards; screenwriter: Joan Wentworth Wood. Cast: Henry Edwards (Lt. Dicky Lascelles), Anna Neagle (Hermione Wynne), Joyce Bland (Mrs. Cameron), Peter Gawthorne (Maj. Thesisger), Louis Goodrich, Sam Livesey, Michael Hogan, O.B. Clarence, Abraham Soafer, Peter Northcote, Tully Comber.

The story of *The Flag Lieutenant* may seem pretty routine to our readers, but for Henry Edwards, between stage appearances and three movies, it was almost a career, and probably his best role in either medium. In the 1927 sequel, the extroverted Dicky Lascelles escapes from spies in Shanghai and recovers stolen plans.

283 Flame of New Orleans

Based on an original screenplay by Norman Krasna. Story: European adventuress Claire Ledeux arrives in New Orleans, determined to grab off a wealthy husband. A likely candidate appears in the person of one Giraud, who proposes marriage, but a tough ship captain, Robert, captures Claire's attention. Once this much is established, the remainder of the film deals with how she finally makes the decision to dump her potential bankroll for the poor but exciting younger man.

Universal Pictures, 1941 (original). Director: Rene Clair; screenwriter: Norman Krasna. Cast: Marlene Dietrich (Claire Ledeux), Bruce Cabot (Robert), Roland Young (Giraud), Mischa Auer, Andy Devine, Frank Jenks, Eddie Quillan, Laura Hope Crews, Franklin Pangborn, Melville Cooper, Anne Revere.

• ***Scarlet Angel*** (remake). Universal Pictures, 1952. Director: Sidney Salkow; screenwriter: Oscar Brodney. Cast: Yvonne De Carlo (Roxy McClanahan), Rock Hudson (Frank Truscott), Reginald Denny (Malcolm), Whitfield Connor, Bodil Miller, Amanda Blake, Henry O'Neill, Maude Wallace.

Apparently exiled director Clair hoped to make a sophisticated farce but something got lost in the translation. It's a lightweight entry with flimsy material, having only occasionally amusing by-plays between the principals. Dietrich almost held a patent on shady lady roles, but this wasn't one of her better efforts. Still, it was superior to that made by De Carlo in the very similar second film. Yvonne pawns herself off as the widow of the scion of a wealthy San Francisco family and almost carries it off until her seafaring lover, Hudson, shows up. She eventually gives up wealth and position to be with him. The situations are stock and the dialog trite, but the two leading players look good.

284 The Flaw

Based on a story by Brandon Fleming. Story: James Kelver devises what he believes to be a perfect crime. He is so proud of the scheme that he explains the whole thing to one of his intended victims, lawyer John Millway, after having administered poison to the latter. But Millway points out the flaw in Kelver's plan, and uses the rest of the would-be murderer's plot to turn the tables, eliminate the villain, and save his own life.

Heale/Paramount Pictures, Great Britain, 1933 (original). Director: Norman Walker; screenwriter: Brandon Fleming. Cast: Henry Kendall (John Millway), Eric Mauturin (James Kelver), Phyllis Clare (Laura Kelver), Eve Gray, Douglas Payne, Sydney Seaward, Vera Gerald.

• ***The Flaw*** (remake). Cybex/Renown, Great Britain, 1955. Director: Terence Fisher; screenwriter: Brandon Fleming. Cast: John Bentley (Paul Oliveri), Donald Houston (John Millway), Rona Anderson (Monica Oliveri), Tonia Berne, Doris Yorke, J. Trevor Davies, Cecilia Cavendish.

In the remake, the mastermind of the supposedly perfect crime is a racing car driver who plans to murder his heiress wife and get her money. His plot involves poisoning her lawyer, who loves her. It sounds more interesting than it plays. The three leads in the remake are wasted in a mediocre production.

285 The Fleet's In

Based on the play *Sailor Beware* by Kenyon Nicholson and Charles Robinson. Story: The original idea of the play is having a bunch of sailors bet on whether one of their number, a self-styled lady killer, can "score" with a hardboiled dame who hangs around the Roseland Dance Hall. The success of the mission will be proven by bringing back a certain "trophy," a designated personal item of the lady in question. Naturally the whole plot backfires as the gob and the gal fall in love, and her learning of the bet almost ruins everything. The various versions of the play brought to the screen have cleaned up the story, with the object of the bet being less intimate. The girl also gets transformed. Sometimes she's a wise but innocent young miss, then she may be sweet and girlish, whose accessibility is due to reserve rather than toughness. And in one case the characteristics of the sailor and girl are scrambled.

Paramount Pictures, 1928 (original). Silent. Director: Malcolm St. Clair; screenwriters: Monte Brice and J. Walter Ruben. Cast: Clara Bow (Peaches Deane), James Hall (Eddie Briggs), Jack Oakie (Searchlight Doyle), Bodil Rosing, Eddie Dunn, Jean Laverty, Dan Wolheim, Richard Carle, Joseph Girard.

• ***Lady Be Careful*** (remake). Paramount Pictures, 1936. Director: J.T. Reed; screenwriters: Dorothy Parker, Alan Campbell and Harry Ruskin. Cast: Lew Ayres (Dud Dynamite), Mary Carlisle (Billie), Larry Crabbe (Jake), Benny Baker (Barney), Grant Withers, Jack Chapin, Josephine McKim, Wilma Francis.

• ***The Fleet's In*** (remake). Paramount Pictures, 1942. Director: Victor Schertzinger; screenwriters: Walter De Long and Sid Silvers. Cast: Dorothy Lamour, William Holden, Eddie Bracken, Betty Hutton, Cass Daley, Gil Lamb, Leif Erickson, Betty Jane Rhodes.

• ***Sailor Beware*** (remake). Paramount Pictures, 1951. Director: Hal Walker; screenwriters: James Allardice and Martin Rackin. Cast: Dean Martin, Jerry Lewis, Corinne Calvet, Marion Marshall, Robert Strauss, Leif Erickson, Don Wilson, Skip Homeier, Dan Barton, Mike Mahoney, Mary Treen.

Winning a lady's favor is a popular movie theme. Censors have required that the favor be chaste if the seeker is successful and denied if it is more intimate. In the original, Clara Bow portrayed a hardboiled dame, not so fresh and certainly not innocent, with James Briggs out for all he could get to win his bet. Mary Carlisle was very sweet and innocent, so when Lew Ayres captured her beauty-contest sash, which was to be the proof of his victory with the girl, it was obtained accidently, not because his objective was achieved. In 1942, all the sailor was after from Dorothy Lamour was a kiss, and in 1951, Jerry Lewis, his usual bungling self, was out to get a date with sultry Corinne Calvet. Each of the films was in its own way entertaining but certainly nothing of great cinematic importance. The 1942 version had the best songs, including the Victor Schertzinger and Johnny Mercer tunes "Arthur Murray Taught Me Dancing in a Hurry," "Somebody Else's Moon" and "Tangerine." The 1951 film's songs included Mack Davis and Jerry Livingston's "Never Before," "Sailor's Polka" and "Today, Tomorrow, Forever."

The Flesh of the Orchid *see* **No Orchids for Miss Blandish**

Flight Into Darkness *see* **L'Equipage**

286 The Flirt

Based on a novel by Booth Tarkington. Story: Selfish, spoiled and flirtatious Cora Madison is engaged to Richard Lindley but is attracted to Val Corliss, who has arrived in the girl's small town to promote oil stock. When Cora's father, a prominent local businessman, refuses to endorse Val's cause, the gullible Cora is induced to forge her father's name on papers that enable Val to sell many shares. When Corliss absconds with the funds, Mr. Madison takes the blame. Cora loses her sweetheart, Lindley, to her simple and kind sister, Laura. Corliss is caught and Cora settles down with a new beau, Wade Trumbull.

Universal Pictures, 1922 (original). Silent. Director: Hobart Henley; screenwriter: A.P. Younger. Cast: George Nichols (Papa Madison), Lydia Knott (Mama Madison), Eileen Perry (Cora Madison), Helen Jerome Eddy (Laura Madison), Lloyd Whitlock (Valentine Corliss), Edward Hearn (Richard Lindley), Bert Roach (Wade Trumbull), Buddy Messenger, Harold Goodwin.

• ***Bad Sister*** (remake). Universal Pictures, 1931. Director: Hobart Henley; screenwriters: Tom Reed and Raymond L. Schrock. Cast: Conrad Nagel (Dick Lindley), Sidney Fox (Marianne), Bette Davis (Laura), Zasu Pitts (Minnie), Charles Winninger (Mr. Madison), Humphrey Bogart (Val Corliss), Emma Dunn, Slim Summerville, Bert Roach.

The first film version of *The Flirt* was produced in 1916 by Bluebird Films, presented as a five-part serial. It featured Marie Walcamp as Cora, Grace Benham as Laura, Ogden Crane as Mr. Madison and Juan de la Cruz as Val Corliss. The 1948 production of *Bad Sister* had no relation to the films of this entry.

These were pleasant small-town films with some light humor and romance as well as the unsavory Val Corliss as the menace silly Cora couldn't see through until it was too late. In the remake, Sidney Fox was the "bad" sister, here called Marianne. Bette Davis in her first movie played the sister, Laura, who got Marianne's beau, the man she secretly loved. Critics praised Davis for her performance as a sweet, simple girl, the very essence of repression. This would not be the kind of role for which Davis would become famous. Humphrey Bogart, in one of his first films, is a city slicker who fleeces the local citizens with the unwitting help of a girl too full of herself to be a good judge of others.

287 The Flying Fifty-Five

Based on the novel by Edgar Wallace. Story: Reggie Cambray, after a row with his father, Lord Fountwell, takes a job as a stableboy and rides Stella Barrington's horse when a crooked knight, Sir Jacques Gregory, injures her jockey. He wins the race and the girl, of course.

Stoll/EB, Great Britain, 1925 (original). Silent. Director and screenwriter: A.E. Coleby. Cast: Lionelle Howard (Reggie Cambray), Stephanie Stephens (Stella Barrington), Brian B. Lemon (Lord Fountwell), Lionel d'Aragon (Sir Jacques Gregory), Frank Perfitt, Bert Darley, Adeline Hayden Coffin.

• ***The Flying Fifty-Five*** (remake). Admiral/RKO, Great Britain, 1939. Director: Reginald Denham; screenwriters: Victor Greene and Vernon Clancey. Cast:

Derrick de Marney (Bill Urquhart), Nancy Burne (Stella Barrington), Marius Goring (Charles Barrington), John Warwick (Jebson), Peter Gawthorne (Jonas Urquhart), D.A. Clark-Smith (Jacques Gregory), Amy Veness, Ronald Shiner, Billy Bray, Francesca Bahrle.

Aside from stripping the various characters of their titles the remake of this dull racetrack yarn is about the same as the original. These are merely two more routine entries in the list of the many movies made from the writings of prolific Edgar Wallace.

288 The Flying Squad

Based on the novel by Edgar Wallace. Story: Inspector Bradley, of Scotland Yard's Flying Squad of detectives, poses as a murdered Jew to trick smuggler Mark McGill into a confession that he's the killer.

British Lion/Warner Bros., Great Britain, 1929 (original). Silent. Director: Arthur Maude; screenwriter: Kathleen Hayden. Cast: Dorothy Bartlam (Ann Perryman), Wyndham Standing (Mark McGill), Donald Calthrop (Sederman), John Longden (Inspector John Bradley), Eugenie Prescott, Henry Vibart, John Nedgnol, Laurence Ireland, Bryan Edgar Wallace, Carol Reed.

• ***The Flying Squad*** (remake). British Lion, Great Britain, 1932. Director: F.W. Kramer; screenwriter: Bryan Edgar Wallace. Cast: Harold Huth (Mark McGill), Carol Goodner (Ann Perryman), Edward Chapman (Sederman), Campbell Gullan (Tiser), Harry Wilcoxon (Insp. Bradley), Abraham Sofaer, Joseph Cunningham.

• ***The Flying Squad*** (remake). APBC, Great Britain, 1940. Director: Herbert Brenon; screenwriter: Doreen Montgomery. Cast: Sebastian Shaw (Insp. Bradley), Phyllis Brooks (Ann Perryman), Jack Hawkins (Mark McGill), Basil Radford (Sederman), Ludwig Stossel (Li Yoseph), Manning Whiley, Cyril Smith, Henry Oscar, Kynaston Reeves.

The role of Inspector Bradley moved center stage over the three productions of the Edgar Wallace work. In the first remake, the smuggler leads the heroine to believe that the Inspector may in fact be the one responsible for her brother's death. In the third version, the girl goes undercover in the smuggler's gang to help Inspector Bradley get his man. None of the productions is much to cheer about.

Follow the Fleet *see* **Shore Leave**

289 Fog Over Frisco

Based on a novel by George Dyer. Story: Reckless society girl Ariene Bradford becomes enmeshed in a stolen securities ring run by a crude racketeer. Her half-sister, Val, tries to defend her sibling's reputation but is unable to prevent Ariene from being murdered.

Warner Bros., 1934 (original). Director: William Dieterle; screenwriters: Robert N. Lee and Eugene Solow. Cast: Bette Davis (Ariene Bradford), Donald Woods (Tony), Margaret Lindsay (Val), Lyle Talbot (Spencer), Hugh Herbert, Arthur Bryon, Robert Bryan, Henry O'Neill, Irving Pichel.

• ***Spy Ship*** (remake). Warner Bros., 1942. Director: B. Reaves Eason; screenwriter: Robert E. Kent. Cast: Craig Stevens (Ward Prescott), Irene Manning (Pamela Mitchell), Marie Wrixon (Sue Mitchell), Michael Ames (Gordon Morrel), Peter Whitney, John Maxwell, William Forrest, Roland Drew.

The 1934 film is noted more for its fast-paced cinematic style, dissolves, wipes, and quick takes than plot. It's an adequate whodunnit, but since Davis is killed off early, audiences don't have much opportunity to judge her performance as the San Francisco heiress who goes astray. In the second-feature remake, Irene Manning is an unsavory American fifth columnist, whose selling of secrets to the enemy is halted halfway through the picture, when she is killed. Another film, also based on a novel by George Dyer *(Caught in the Fog)*, examines another girl gone wrong, but this one has her surviving and finding happiness. It was released in 1928, with some talking sequences, and is the story of several thieves posing as servants or visitors to a wealthy woman's Florida home, where they hope to steal her jewelry.

290 Fool's Paradise

Based on the story "Laurels and the Lady" by Leonard Merrick. Story: Ex-serviceman Arthur Phelps, suffering from an eye injury, falls in love with French dancer Rosa Duchene in a Mexican border town. He also encounters another dancer, Poll Patchouck, who is interested in him. When he rejects her advances, she gives him an exploding cigar which blows up in his face, leaving him blind. Later he hears Poll imitating Rosa's voice and believes she is his beloved. Poll is determined to atone for her cruelty and begs Phelps to marry her. Believing she is Rosa, he consents. Poll takes him to a surgeon who restores his sight. Seeing he has been tricked, he leaves Poll to find Rosa. His search takes him to Siam, where Rosa is living with a prince. Unable to decide which of the two men she loves, Rosa throws her glove into a pit of crocodiles, promising herself to whomever retrieves it. The prince is almost killed in the attempt to get the glove but is saved by Phelps, who refuses his prize. He leaves Rosa and returns to Poll.

Paramount Pictures, 1921 (original). Silent. Director: Cecil B. De Mille; screenwriters: Beulah Marie Dix and Sada Cowan. Cast: Dorothy Dalton (Poll Patchouk), Mildred Harris (Rosa Duchene), Conrad Nagel (Arthur Phelps), John Davidson (Prince Talaat-Noi), Theodore Kosloff, Julia Faye, Clarence Burton.

• ***The Magnificent Lie*** (remake). Paramount Pictures, 1931. Director: Berthold Viertel; screenwriter: Samuel Raphaelson. Cast: Ruth Chatterton (Poll), Ralph Bellamy (Bill), Francoise Rosay (Rosa Duchene), Stuart Erwin (Elmer), Sam Hardy, Charles Boyer, Tyler Brooke.

The story in the remake is altered to ensure that the picture is a star vehicle for Ruth Chatterton. Bellamy plays a young man who, during World War I, falls in love with France's foremost and rapidly aging actress, Rosay, when she stops to talk to him in a field hospital. Thirteen years later, he still holds to his dream and when the celebrated artiste visits New Orleans with her troupe, he attends her performance but loses his failing eyesight. By a series of circumstances, wise cafe singer Chatterton impersonates the French star. From then on it's the routine romantic story of the girl finally falling in love with the man she's fooling, the restoration of his sight and his discovery of the deception and their eventual reconciliation, with the actress finally forgotten. The stories are rather convoluted and contrived but the films experienced considerable popularity because of the female leads.

291 For Love or Money

Based on a story by Julian Blaustein, Daniel Taradash and Bernard Feins. Story: A bookie pays off a bet of $50,000 but sends some of his boys to get it back. They pull a mailroom con to get the money delivered by the U.S. Post Office but the envelope ends up in the hands of a secretary. Delighted with the windfall, she quits her job and goes on a spending spree, using $44,000 in eight hours. Meanwhile the bookie doesn't believe the story his collectors tell and gives them 36 hours to come up with the jack or else. This leads to a merry chase, a hunt for a man who will lend the money, and a string of comical situations.

Universal Pictures, 1939 (original). Director: Albert Rogell; screenwriters: Charles Grayson and Arthur Horman. Cast: June Lane (Susan), Robert Kent (Frazier), Ed Brophy (Sleeper), Etienne Girardot (Poindexter), Richard Lane (Foster), Addison Richards, Ed Gargan, Horace MacMahon.

• ***For Love or Money*** (remake). Eagle-Lion Pictures, 1948. Director: Charles Barton; screenwriters: John Grant and Howard Harris. Cast: Lou Costello (Homer), Bud Abbott (Ted Higgins), Cathy Downs (Carol), Joseph Calleia (Mike Craig), Leon Errol (McBride), Mike Mazurki, Jack Overman, Fritz Feld.

In the original, Robert Kent and Ed Brophy were quite funny as the duo caught short when June Lane gets the money they stole for their boss. In the remake, Abbott and Costello are window washers who are hired by a crooked bookie, Joseph Calleia, to recover the money he lost in a bet. Cathy Downs is okay as the girl who spends the loot as fast as she can. Among the vaudeville routines done by Bud and Lou is "You Can't Be Here," in which Bud attempts to convince Lou that he's somewhere else.

For the Love of Benji *see* **Benji**

Force 10 from Navarone *see* **The Guns of Navarone**

Forever *see* **Peter Ibbetson**

Force of Arms *see* **A Farewell to Arms**

Forgotten Commandments *see* **The Ten Commandments**

292 Forgotten Faces

Based on the story *Whiff of Heliotrope* by Richard Washburn Child. Story:

When Heliotrope Harry Harlow catches his wife, Lilly, making love to another man, he kills his rival. Before surrendering to the police, he leaves his infant daugther on the doorsteps of a wealthy couple who take the child in and raise it as their own. Years later, Lilly discovers the whereabouts of the child, now called Alice Deane, and cruelly visits Harry in prison to inform him that she is going to see the girl and make trouble for her. Fortunately, before this can occur, Harry is paroled and takes a job as a butler in the Deane home to protect Alice from her mother, without letting her know that he is her father. Harry is able to prevent Lilly from seeing Alice until, in anger, she mortally wounds him and is taken away by the law. Harry dies contented, knowing that he has prevented his daughter from coming under the evil influence of her mother.

• ***Forgotten Faces*** (remake). Paramount/Famous Lasky, 1928. Silent. Director: Victor Schertzinger; screenwriter: Howard Estabrook. Cast: Clive Brook (Heliotrope Harry Harlow), Mary Brian (Alice Deane), Olga Baclanova (Lilly Harlow), William Powell (Froggy), Fred Kohler, Jack Luden.

• ***Forgotten Faces*** (remake). Paramount Pictures, 1936. Director: E.A. DuPont; screenwriters: Marguerite Roberts, Robert Yost and Brian Marlow. Cast: Herbert Marshall (Harry Ashton), Gertrude Michael (Cleo Ashton), James Burke (Sgt. Donovan), Robert Cummings (Clinton Faraday), Jane Rhodes (Sally McBride), Robert Gleckler, Alonzo Price, Arthur Hohl, Pierre Watkin.

Richard Washburn Child's story was first filmed as *Heliotrope* in 1920 with Frederick Burton as Heliotrope Harry and lastly by Warner Bros. as *A Gentleman After Dark* in 1942 with Brian Donlevy as the man who has to stop his wife from ruining the life of their child. The best cast, direction and production was the 1928 version. That was also probably the last time audiences would find the story credible. Clive Brook was certainly believable as a man who accepted the fact that his life was past and didn't mind sacrificing it to protect his daughter from his dissolute wife.

Fortunes of Captain Blood *see* **Captain Blood**

293 Forty Little Mothers (Le Mioche)

Based on the story *Monsieur Petiot* by Jean Guitton. Story: Honest, loveable and financially unsuccessful professor Prosper Martin finds a foundling dumped on his doorstep. Instead of turning the child over to an orphanage, he takes the boy with him to a new job as a teacher in a swank finishing school with strict regulations regarding the morals and behavior of its teachers. His problem is how to keep both his job and the cute little moppet. His rebellious students find out about baby Pierrot and plan to expose Prosper, but he makes an emotional appeal to them about what it means to be a foundling in the world and apparently strikes a maternal chord with the girls, who proceed to take turns mothering the child.

• ***Le Mioche*** (original). National Pictures, France, 1938. Director: Leonide Moguy; screenwriter: Jean Guitton. Cast: Lucien Baroux (Prosper Martin), Little Phillipe (Baby Pierrot), Madeleine Robinson, Gabrielle Dorziat, Pauline Carton, Jean Perier.

• ***Forty Little Mothers*** (remake). MGM, 1940. Director: Busby Berkeley; screenwriters: Dorothy Yost and Ernest Pagano. Cast: Eddie Cantor (Gilbert Jordon Thompson), Judith Anderson (Mme. Granville), Rita Johnson (Marion Edwards), Bonita Granville (Doris), Ralph Morgan (Judge Joseph M. Williams), Diana Lewis, Nydia Westman, Margaret Early, Martha O'Driscoll, Charlotte Munier, Louise Seidel, Baby Quintavilla.

The French film was most touching and frequently hilarious especially when the girls stage a sit-down strike after the officials of the school announce that the professor is to be fired because of baby Pierrot. The remake has Eddie Cantor as a professor who saves a woman from committing suicide, gets her a job and takes the woman's baby with him to the all-girls school where he teaches. The students help him hide the baby until it can be returned to its mother. Songs by Charles Tobias and Nat Simon include "Little Curly Hair in a High Chair" which Cantor uses as a lullably on several occasions in the film.

294 Four Daughters

Based on the short story "Sister Act" by Fannie Hurst. Story: The tale deals with the loves of the four talented Lemp sisters, daughters of a professor of music. Of the suitors, one is a successful small-town businessman, another a florist's clerk, a third a composer. Finally there is a newcomer, a disillusioned fatalist, Mickey Borden. He interferes with the youngest girl's romance, marries her and when he realizes that he can't make her happy, kills himself. Just as in *Little Women*, the girls and their men gather for a wind-up sentimental get-together and one feels they will always be close.

Warner Bros., 1938 (original). Director: Michael Curtiz; screenwriters: Julius J. Epstein and Leonore Coffee. Cast: Claude Rains (Adam Lemp), Priscilla Lane (Ann Lemp), Rosemary Lane (Kay Lemp), Lola Lane (Thea Lemp), Gale Page (Emma Lemp), John Garfield (Mickey Borden), Jeffrey Lynn (Felix Deitz), May Robson (Aunt Etta), Frank McHugh, Dick Foran, Vera Lewis, Tom Dugan, Eddie Albert.

• ***Four Wives*** (sequel). Warner Bros., 1939. Director: Michael Curtiz; screenwriters: Julius J. Epstein, Philip G. Epstein, and Maurice Hanline. Cast: Claude Rains (Adam Lemp), Priscilla Lane (Ann Lemp), Rosemary Lane (Kay Lemp), Lola Lane (Thea Kemp), Gale Page (Emma Lemp), Jeffrey Lynn (Felix Deitz), May Robson (Aunt Etta), Frank McHugh, Dick Foran, Eddie Albert, Henry O'Neill, Vera Lewis.

• ***Four Mothers*** (sequel). Warner Bros., 1941. Director: William Keighley; screenwriter: Stephen Morehouse Avery. Cast: Claude Rains (Adam Lemp), Priscilla Lane (Ann Lemp Deitz), Rosemary Lane (Kay Lemp Forrest), Lola Lane (Thea Lemp Crowley), Gale Page (Emma Lemp Talbot), Jeffrey Lynn (Felix Deitz), Eddie Albert (Clint Forrest), May Robson (Aunt Etta), Frank McHugh (Ben Crowley), Dick Foran (Ernest Talbot).

• ***Young at Heart*** (remake). Warner Bros., 1954. Director: Gordon Douglas; screenwriters: Julius J. Epstein and Leonore Coffee. Cast: Doris Day (Laurie Tuttle), Frank Sinatra (Barney Sloan), Gig Young (Alex Burke), Ethel

Doris Day, Elizabeth Fraser and Ethel Barrymore admire Dorothy Malone's diamond ring in Young at Heart *(Warner Bros., 1954), a remake of* Four Daughters *(Warner Bros., 1938).*

Barrymore (Aunt Jessie), Dorothy Malone (Fran Tuttle), Robert Keith, Elizabeth Fraser, Alan Hale, Jr., Lonny Chapman, Frank Ferguson, Marjorie Bennett.

The three sentimental family stories were quite popular with audiences just prior to World War II. In the first, James Garfield as the cynical, slum-kid suitor made such an outstanding impression that in the sequel, *Four Wives,* he was discussed frequently and even was seen in some split-screen scenes. It was because of his impact that he and almost everyone else in the original film were brought together for a production of *Daughters Courageous.* Although none of the characters were the same, and the story was different, it certainly is a pseudo-sequel. The two real sequels merely followed the four daughters as they became brides and mothers. The stories weren't much, nor were they meant to be more than a wholesome look at loving families. The remake of *Four Daughters,* with Doris Day and Frank Sinatra, cut the number of daughters to three and didn't require Frank as the Garfield-like character to commit suicide. It was a modest success with a very popular title song.

Four Jacks and a Jill *see* **Street Girl**

295 The Four Feathers

Based on the novel by Alfred Edward Woodley Mason. Story: When Harry Faversham, a British regimental officer, resigns his commission to marry Ethne Eustace, at the time his regiment is sent to active duty in the Sudan, each of his three friends, Durrance, Trench and Castelton, believing him a coward, send him a token of this, a white feather. Hardest of all, however, is the fact that Ethne also gives him a white feather. Determined to redeem himself and learning that Trench is imprisoned in a native fortress, Harry disguises himself as a mute native and goes to free his former friend. He is successful but not before being sold as a slave and killing the slave trader. He leads Trench to safety, assisted by troops led by Durrance. When the outpost is besieged by native troops, a relief column headed by Castleton saves the day and Harry proves his bravery by killing a native chieftain. Harry returns the three feathers to his friends and returns to England to turn Ethne's feather over to her. All four comrades are decorated and Harry's courage is never questioned again.

• ***The Four Feathers*** (remake). Paramount/Famous Lasky, 1929. Directors: Merian C. Cooper, Ernest B. Schoedsack and Lothar Mendes; screenwriter: Howard Estabrook. Cast: Richard Arlen (Harry Faversham), Fay Wray (Ethne Eustace), Clive Brook (Lt. Durrance), William Powell (Capt. Trench), Theodore von Eltz (Lt. Castleton), Noah Beery, Zack Williams, Noble Johnson, Harold Hightower.

• ***The Four Feathers*** (remake). London Films-Korda/United Artists, Great Britain, 1939. Director: Zoltan Korda; screenwriter: R.C. Sherriff. Cast: John Clements (Harry Faversham), Ralph Richardson (Capt. John Durrance), C. Aubrey Smith (General Burroughs), June Duprez (Ethne Burroughs), Allan Jeayes (General Faversham), Jack Allen (Lt. Willoughby), Donald Gray, Frederick Culley, Clive Baxter, Archibald Baxter, Derek Elphinstone.

This marvelous adventure story of a man believed to be a coward because he questions the wisdom of war, has also been filmed in 1915, 1918, 1921 as silents, and in 1956 as *Storm Over the Nile* with Anthony Steel as Faversham. This film used most of the stock footage of the 1939 film, but that is the only way in which it compares favorably with the Korda masterpiece. Another British version of questionable quality was released in Britain in 1977.

The 1929 film was very good, but the Alexander and Zoltan Korda production is a rarity, an action-adventure film which is highly dramatic and is blessed with marvelous performances from a superb cast. John Clements deserved his knighthood for this role alone and Ralph Richardson as his blinded friend who doesn't realize that he is being rescued by a man he branded a coward is a wonderful ham. The battle scenes are spectacular and the Technicolor photography is top rate. In a year of dozens of great films, *Four Feathers* ranks near the top.

296 The Four Horsemen of the Apocalypse

Based on the novel by Vincente Blasco Ibanez. Story: When wealthy Argentine cattle owner Madariaga dies, his estate is divided and all his family move

Bit player Rudolph Valentino was picked to appear in The Four Horsemen of the Apocalypse *(Metro, 1921) and the rest, as they say, is history. Here he's demonstrating his smoldering presence dancing the tango.*

to Europe, the von Hartrotts to Germany and the Desnoyers to France. The old man's favorite grandson, Julio Desnoyers, purchases a castle on the Marne, where he entertains and paints. He falls in love with Marguerite Laurier, a woman married to a jurist. When World War I comes, Marguerite joins the Red Cross and her husband enlists in the French army and is blinded. Seeing her husband thus, Marguerite decides to resist Julio's attentions, to care for her spouse. Spurred on by the words of a stranger, who invokes the images of the Four Horsemen of the Apocalypse—War, Conquest, Famine and Death—Julio enlists, distinguishes himself for bravery and is killed by his own cousin, an officer in the German army.

Metro Pictures, 1921 (original). Silent. Director: Rex Ingram; screenwriter: June Mathis. Cast: Rudolph Valentino (Julio Desnoyers), Alice Terry (Marguerite Laurier), Pomeroy Cannon (Madariaga, the Centaur), Josef Swickard (Marcelo Desnoyers), Alan Hale (Karl von Hartrott), Bridgetta Clark (Dona Lusia), Jean Hersholt (Professor von Hartrott), Wallace Beery (Lt. Col. von Richthoffen), Brinsley Shaw, Mabel Van Buren, Nigel de Brulier, Bowditch Turner, John Sainpolis, Mark Fenton, Virginia Warwick, Derek Ghent, Stuart Holmes, Henry Klaus.

Glenn Ford gives a rather wimpy imitation of Valentino in the 1962 MGM remake of The Four Horsemen of the Apocalypse.

• ***The Four Horsemen of the Apocalypse*** (remake). MGM, 1962. Director: Vincente Minnelli; screenwriters: Robert Ardrey and John Gay. Cast: Glenn Ford (Julio Desnoyers), Ingrid Thulin (Marguerite Laurier), Charles Boyer (Marcello Desnoyers), Lee J. Cobb (Julio Madariaga), Paul Henreid (Etienne Laurier), Paul Lukas (Karl von Hartrott), Yvette Mimieux (Chi-Chi Desnoyers), Karlheinz Bohm (Heinrich von Hartrott), Harriet MacGibbon, Kathryn Givney, Marcel Hillaire, George Dolenz, Stephen Bekassy.

The silent antiwar film had Rudolph Valentino and that seemed enough. By the time the picture was remade, the assignment of Glenn Ford to the role of Julio allowed audiences to concentrate on Ibanez's story and decide that it was dull! Ford, who succeeded in some roles by being a bit laid back, here almost slept through his part. No flashing eyes and flaring nostrils for our boy Glenn; his plan to seduce Marguerite seemed to be based on first boring her so she would fall asleep. The other male performers to counteract Ford's performance appear to have banded together in a contest to see who could most overplay their role, with the winner being Lee J. Cobb, but fortunately he wasn't around for very long. The story is just about the same, but since this is World War II, Ford had to act for the Resistance, since the Germans occupied France. In this version, war was not only hell—it was a bore.

297 Four Just Men

Based on the novel by Edgar Wallace. Story: The Four Just Men (sometimes called The Secret Four) band together to oppose anyone they suspect of being foreign plotters against England and its interests. They suspect that a member of Parliament is a traitor. One of the four is killed gathering evidence, but the other three rally round the flag, avenge their fallen comrade by killing the MP and exposing his plot to stop all movements of ships and troops eastward by blocking the Suez Canal.

Stoll, Great Britain, 1921 (original). Silent. Director and screenwriter: George Ridgwell. Cast: Cecil Humphreys (Manfred), Teddy Arundell (Insp. Falmouth), C.H. Croker-King (Thery), C. Tilson-Chowne (Sir Philip Ramon), Owen Roughwood (Poiccard), George Bellamy (Gonsalez), Robert Vallis.

• ***Four Just Men*** (remake). Ealing-Caped, Great Britain, 1939. Director: Walter Forde; screenwriters: Roland Pertwee, Angus MacPhail and Sergei Nolbandov. Cast: Hugh Sinclair (Humphrey Mansfield), Griffith Jones (James Brodie), Francis L. Sullivan (Leon Poiccard), Frank Lawton (Terry), Anna Lee (Ann Lodge), Basil Sydney (Frank Snell), Alan Napier (Sir Hamar Ryman), Lydia Sherwood, Edward Chapman, George Merritt, Garry Marsh, Ellaline Teriss.

These four jingoistic patriots do not consider that laws apply to them in the carrying out of their responsibility to look out for the interests of Great Britain. When the story was used as a basis for a TV series, the four were required to work within the law, which seriously interfered with their noble work.

Four Mothers *see* **Four Daughters**

Four Musketeers *see* **The Three Musketeers**

298 Four Sons

Based on the short story "Grandma Bernie Learns Her Letters" by Ida Alexa Ross Wylie. Story: In Bavaria at the time of World War I, widow Bernie has four sons, three of whom die in battle. The fourth, Joseph, emigrates to America with his mother, sets himself up in the delicatessen business and marries Annabelle. There's not much to the story; it is more a character study of a mother who must face the tragedy of the loss of her sons in a war she doesn't understand.

Fox Film Corporation, 1928 (original). Silent. Director: John Ford; screenwriter: Philip Klein. Cast: Margaret Mann (Mother Bernie), James Hall (Joseph Bernie), Francis X. Bushman, Jr. (Franz Bernie), Charles Morton (Johann Bernie), George Meeker (Andreas Bernie), June Collyer (Annabelle), Earle Foxe, Albert Gran, August Tollaire, Jack Pennick.

• ***Four Sons*** (remake). Twentieth Century–Fox, 1940. Director: Archie Mayo; screenwriter: John Howard Lawson. Cast: Eugenie Leontovich (Frau Bernie), Don Ameche (Chris Bernie), Mary Beth Hughes (Anna), Alan Curtis (Karl Bernie), George Ernest (Fritz Bernie), Robert Lowery (Joseph Bernie), Lionel Royce, Sig Rumann, Ludwig Stossel, Christian Rub, Torben Meyer.

Both films detail the initial excitement of young men going to war despite a mother's instinctive knowledge that wars only kill, never solve problems. In the remake, to add to the agony of the mother, the sons are not even on the same side of the question. The story has been moved to Czechoslovakia, with her sons split over the Nazi cause and the resistance movement in the occupied country. These are antiwar movies but their message is not delivered in the most effective or dramatic way.

299 Four Walls

Based on the play by Dana Burnet and George Abbott. Story: When Benny Horowitz, a New York East Side gang leader, kills another gang boss in self defense, he is sentenced to prison on a manslaughter charge. After serving his term, he decides to go straight and takes a job working in a garage. His former girlfriend, Freida, wants to start up with him again, but although he still loves her, he takes up with plain Bertha, who had befriended his mother while Benny was in the pen. Later at a party, attended by Benny, the new gangleader, Monk, is killed in a fall, and the police detective who had arrested Benny before suspects him of foul play again. Eventually, Benny is cleared and he offers to share his life with Freida.

MGM, 1928 (original). Director: William Nigh; screenwriter: Alice D.G. Miller. Cast: John Gilbert (Benny Horowitz), Joan Crawford (Freida), Vera Gordon (Mrs. Horowitz), Carmel Myers (Bertha), Robert O'Connor (Sullivan), Louis Natheaux (Monk), Jack Byron (Duke Roma).

• ***Straight Is the Way*** (remake). MGM, 1934. Director: Paul Sloane; screenwriter: Bernard Schubert. Cast: Franchot Tone (Benny), May Robson (Mrs. Horowitz), Karen Morley (Bertha), Gladys George (Shirley), Nat Pendleton (Skippy), Jack LaRue (Monk), Raymond Hamilton, William Bakewell.

In the remake, Franchot Tone is a New York Jewish lad, who upon release from prison, promises his mother he will go straight. His ex-girlfriend, Shirley, is the moll of an Italian gang leader, Monk. Gladys George plays the former as cheap as she is able and Jack LaRue is menacing as the latter. Tone must kill LaRue before he can walk the straight and narrow with Karen Morley as the girl who has loved him since childhood.

Four Wives *see* **Four Daughters**

300 Francis Joins the WACS

Based on the character "Francis" created by David Stern and a story by Devery Freeman. Story: Bank clerk Peter Stirling and his talking mule, Francis, are mistakenly assigned to a WAC unit. The ensuing humorous situations are predictable and as usual in the films of this series, Francis is the brightest character in the picture.

Universal Pictures, 1954 (original). Director: Arthur Lubin; screenwriters: Devery Freeman, James B. Allardice and Herbert Baker. Cast: Donald O'Connor (Peter Stirling), Chill Wills (voice of Francis, the talking mule/General Kaye), Julia Adams (Captain Parker), Mamie Van Doren (Corporal Bunky Hilstrom), Lynn Bari (Major Louise Simpson), Zasu Pitts, Joan Shawlee, Allison Hayes.

• ***The Sergeant Was a Lady*** (remake). Universal Pictures, 1961. Director and screenwriter: Bernard Glasser. Cast: Martin West (Corporal Gale Willard), Venetia Stevenson (Sergeant Judy Fraser), Bill Williams (Colonel House), Catherine McLeod (Major Hay), Roy Engle, Gregg Martell.

The popularity of the "Francis the Talking Mule" films may be surprising to today's audiences. The situations were predictable and the humor wasn't much, sort of the level of many TV situation comedies. Donald O'Connor and Francis could have been replaced by Abbott and Costello without any noticeable difference, except Francis was made out to be brighter than Bud. The second film is not credited as a remake, but the story is much the same, sans a mule. It's not even worth watching on late night TV.

Frankie and Johnnie *see* **Her Man**

301 Freckles

Based on the novel by Gene Stratton Porter. Story: Freckles, a handicapped orphan, gets a job at McLean's lumber camp as a guard in the Limberlost forest. The job is not easy, because the forest is infested with desperate criminals intent on getting McLean's lumber any way they can. The leader of the gang, Wessner, tries to bribe Freckles to let him steal some trees. Instead Freckles gives Wessner a beating. Freckles falls in love with a beautiful girl whom he calls the "Bird Woman" and the "Swamp Angel," but because of the differences in their social status, he feels he's not worthy of her. She is of a different mind and tells him she loves him.

• ***Freckles*** (remake). FBO Pictures, 1928. Silent. Director: Leo Meehan; screenwriter: Dorothy Yost. Cast: John Fox, Jr. (Freckles), Gene Stratton Porter (Angel), Hobart Bosworth (McLean), Eulalie Jensen (Bird Woman/Swamp Angel), Billy Scott (Wessner), Lafe McKee (Duncan).

• ***Freckles*** (remake). RKO, 1935. Directors: Edward Killy and William Hamilton; screenwriter: Dorothy Yost. Cast: Tom Brown (Freckles), Virginia Weidler (Laurie Lou), Carol Stone (Mary Arden), Lumsden Hare (James McLean), James Bush, Dorothy Peterson, Addison Richards, Dick Alexander.

• ***Freckles Comes Home*** (sequel). Monogram Pictures, 1942. Director: Jean Yarborough; screenwriter: Edward Kelso. Cast: Johnny Downs (Freckles),

Gale Storm (Jane), Mantan Moreland (Jeff), Bradley Page (Quigley), Betty Blythe (Mrs. Potter), Marvin Stephens, Walter Sande, Max Hoffman, Jr.

The sentimental Gene Stratton Porter story of the handicapped orphan who falls in love with the daughter of his timber-baron boss and proves himself a hero when he prevents crooks from stealing timber has also been filmed in 1912, 1917 and 1960, the latter a 20th Century–Fox production starring Martin West as the freckled-faced, shy young man. Porter's novel reportedly has sold over two million copies. This story, like all the others he wrote, deals with the life of country folk, strong on personal virtues and as dependable as the day is long. In the sequel, *Freckles Comes Home,* the lad comes home from college to his small town, where he is forced to outsmart a slick, crooked promoter and a big-town gunman. There's no mention as to what may have happened to the "Swamp Angel."

Freckles Comes Home *see* **Freckles**

302 Free and Easy

Based on a story by Richard Schayer. Story: Elmer Butts, the befuddled manager of Kansas beauty contest winner Elvira, takes her and her mother to Hollywood to get the girl a screen test. When Elmer crashes the MGM studio gate, a wild chase through the sound stages and back lots ensues. He runs into numerous stars and movie personalities such as Lionel Barrymore, Karl Dane and Dorothy Sebastin as he tries to escape the pursuing studio cops. Ultimately Elmer is given a job as an extra, and after a series of comic complications wins a studio contract for himself. Elvira, meanwhile, has fallen in love with screen hero Larry, and settles for a screen-star husband rather than a screen career.

MGM, 1930 (original). Director: Edward Sedgwick; screenwriter: Richard Schayer. Cast: Buster Keaton (Elmer Butts), Anita Page (Elvira), Trixie Friganza (Ma), Fred Niblo, Edgar Dearing, Gwen Lee, John Miljan, Lionel Barrymore.

• ***Pick a Star*** (remake). MGM, 1937. Director: Edward Sedgwick; screenwriters: Richard Flourney, A.V. Jones and Tom Dugan. Cast: Patsy Kelly (Nelie Moore), Jack Haley (Joe Jenkins), Rosina Lawrence (Cecilia Moore), Mischa Auer (Rinaldo Lopez), Stan Laurel, Oliver Hardy, Charles Halton, Lydi Roberti.

Free and Easy was simultaneously shot in Spanish and French for foreign markets. It was funny in parts, but Keaton's days as a big star were numbered and the best feature of the movie is the fascinating glimpse of behind the scenes of a major motion picture studio. The remake is a rowdy comedy about two starstruck sisters (Kelly and Lawrence) hoping for fame and fortune in Hollywood. Mischa Auer steals the show as a tempermental star. Laurel and Hardy play themselves, stars that Kelly and Lawrence encounter at the studio.

Free and Easy (1941) *see* **But the Flesh Is Weak**

Free, Blonde and 21 *see* **Hotel for Women**

303 The French Connection

Based on the book by Robin Moore. Story: Noticing that Sal Boca lives extravagantly despite the fact that his small cafe brings in only $7,000 a year, New York detectives Jimmy Doyle and Buddy Russo put a tail on Boca. They discover that his cafe is a "front" for a drug syndicate importing heroin from abroad. The boss of this deal is Weinstock, who is awaiting a large shipment from France. The French drug kingpin Alain Charnier has hired singing star Devereaux to smuggle the drugs in through the performer's Lincoln Continental. Doyle learns of Charnier from the underworld grapevine and trails him. The latter orders his accomplice Pierre to get rid of Doyle. But after a tremendous chase involving Pierre in an out-of-control elevated train and Doyle in hot pursuit in a car, the Frenchman is shot and killed by the New York cop. When the drug deal is being made, Doyle, Russo, a squad of cops and federal agents engage in a gunfight with the criminals, killing Boca, and capturing Weinstock, but Charnier escapes.

Twentieth Century–Fox, 1971 (original). Director: William Friedkin; screenwriter: Ernest Tidyman. Cast: Gene Hackman (Jimmy Doyle), Roy Scheider (Buddy Russo), Fernando Rey (Alain Charnier), Tony LoBianco (Sal Boca), Marcel Bozzuffi (Pierre), Harold Gary (Weinstock), Frederic De Pasquale (Devereaux), Arlene Faber, Ann Rebbot, Eddie Egan, Sonny Grosso.

• ***The French Connection II*** (sequel). Twentieth Century–Fox, 1975. Director: John Frankenheimer; screenwriters: Robert Dillon, Laurie Dillon and Alexander Jacobs. Cast: Gene Hackman (Jimmy Doyle), Fernando Rey (Alain Charnier), Bernard Fresson, Jean-Pierre Castaldi.

The French Connection, a lively semidocumentary based on the real exploits of New York cop Eddie Egan, won Academy Awards for Best Picture, Best Actor (Hackman), Best Director (Friedkin) and Best Screenplay (Tidyman). Roy Scheider was nominated for Best Supporting Actor and Owen Roizman for best photography, but they did not win. The film captures the harsh reality of cops and criminals facing off against each other in the drug traffic business. The real cops that Hackman and Scheider were portraying, Eddie "Popeye" Egan and Sonny Russo, had featured roles in the film.

The sequel has Doyle going to Marseilles to track down the elusive drug king Chardier. Somehow this film just doesn't work. Hackman is still interesting and Rey remains the sophisticated criminal mastermind but the plot is almost pointless and the film lacks the intensity, originality, suspense and thrills of the original. One also grows weary of the constant bad language, which neither shocks nor helps define the characters. There are admittedly a few good action sequences in the movie, but between them is boredom.

The French Connection II *see* **The French Connection**

304 French Leave

Based on the play by Reginald Berkeley. Story: Dorothy Glenister, the wife of army captain Harry Glenister, bribes a French farmwoman to allow Dorothy to pose as the woman's daughter, in order to be near her husband during World War I. Harry has to keep her identity secret and both a fellow officer and a general fall in love with Dorothy before she comes under suspicion of being a German spy.

D&H Productions/Sterling, Great Britain, 1930 (original). Director: Jack Raymond; screenwriters: Reginald Berkeley and W.P. Lipscomb. Cast: Madeleine Carroll (Dorothy Glenister), Sydney Howard (Cpl. Sykes), Arthur Chesney (General Root), Haddon Mason (Capt. Harry Glenister), Henry Kendall, George de Warfax, May Agate, George Owen.

• ***French Leave*** (remake). Welwyn/Pathe, Great Britain, 1937. Director: Norman Lee; screenwriter: Vernon Clancey. Cast: Betty Lynne (Dorothy Glenister), Edmond Breon (Col. Root), John Longden (Lt. Glenister), Arthur Hambling (Cpl. Sykes), Frederick Burtwell, Michael Morel, Margaret Yarde.

Beautiful Madeleine Carroll was the best thing about the 1930 farce, and in the remake Betty Lynne does a good job as the actress posing as a French farmwoman's neice so she can be near her husband. As she and her husband must pretend they are just friends, other officers, including the commanding officer, Edmond Breon, see her as fair game and pay her court. She is briefly believed to be a spy, but when the real spy is caught her masquerade is exposed. Breon, being a good sport, sends her to Paris—with her husband as escort.

305 The Freshman

Based on an original screenplay by Sam Taylor, John Grey, Ted Wilde and Tim Wheelan. Story: Harold Lamb, eager to be a big man on the campus, falls short in all of his attempts. When he has the chance to be the hero of the big football game, he stops five yards short of the winning touchdown when he mistakes a factory's whistle for that of the referee. However, he recovers from the lost opportunity and becomes the star of the victory after all.

Harold Lloyd Corp./Pathe Exchange, 1925 (original). Silent. Director: Sam Taylor; screenwriters: Sam Taylor, John Grey, Ted Wilde and Tim Wheelan. Cast: Harold Lloyd (Harold Lamb), Jobyna Ralston (Peggy), Brooks Benedict, James Anderson, Hazel Keener, Joseph Harrington, Pat Harmon.

• ***The Sin of Harold Diddlebock*** (sequel). United Artists, 1947. Director and screenwriter: Preston Sturges. Cast: Harold Lloyd (Harold Diddlebock), Frances Hamsden (Miss Otis), Jimmy Conlin (Wormy), Raymond Walburn (J.E. Waggleberry), Franklin Pangborn (Formfit Franklin), Margaret Hamilton, Arline Judge, Al Bridge, Edgar Kennedy, Frank Moran, Torben Meyer, Jack Norton.

The Sin of Harold Diddlebock, also known as *Mad Wednesday*, was the last film made by Harold Lloyd and his first in nine years. Neither his personality, appearance nor comedy had changed in those intervening years. The film is a sequel to *The Freshman*, with Preston Sturges touching up the hilarious football game of the silent flick and then proceeding to follow Harold's life thereafter (the fact that he now has a different name is not explained). Harold is offered a job by alumnus Raymond Walburn, which our boy takes and finds himself stuck in a minor bookkeeper's position in an advertising agency for 22 years. Walburn, who hadn't thought of Lloyd in all that time, takes notice of him once again to fire him. Lloyd takes his first drink and in an intoxicated state makes a bet on a long shot that comes in, starts throwing his money around, buys a circus, which he later sells for a huge profit, and marries the seventh in a series of sisters he's been courting for the last 22 years. No Lloyd picture would be complete without our hero dangling from some precarious height and those expecting this will not be disappointed. Lloyd's usual trademark is included. It's an old-fashioned type of humor, but still funny if one isn't too sophisticated to laugh at the antics and the slick Preston Sturges dialog.

Freshman Love *see* **The College Widow**

306 Friendly Enemies

Based on the play by Samuel Shipman and Aaron Hoffman. Story: German immigrants Carl Pfeiffer and Henry Block are divided when the United States enters World War I. The former feels some loyalty to the old country while the latter sees himself as 100 percent American. Carl's son William enlists in the Army, further concerning Pfeiffer. He allows himself to be talked into contributing some money to the German cause by German agent Miller, who uses the money to sabotage the troop ship carrying William. The latter erroneously is reported as having been killed. Carl and Henry track down Miller with the help of Secret Service agent Hilda Schwartz. Miller is arrested, William shows up safe and sound, and Carl is now completely loyal to his adopted land.

Belasco Productions/Producers Distributing Corp., 1925 (original). Silent. Director: George Melford; screenwriter: Alfred A. Cohn. Cast: Lew Fields (Carl Pfeiffer), Joe Weber (Henry Block), Virginia Brown Faire (June Block), Jack Mulhall (William Pfeiffer), Stuart Holmes (Miller), Lucille Lee Stewart (Hilda Schwartz), Eugenie Besserer, Nora Hayden, Jules Hanft.

• ***Friendly Enemies*** (remake). United Artists, 1942. Director: Allan Dwan; screenwriter: Adelaide Heilbron. Cast: Charles Winninger (Karl Pfeiffer), Charlie Ruggles (Henry Block), James Craig (William Pfeiffer), Nancy Kelly (June Block), Otto Kruger (Anton Miller), Ilka Gruning, Greta Meyer, Addison Richards, Charles Lane, John Piffle, Ruth Holly.

The remake switches the time of the story from 1918 to 1942, but other than that there is little change in the script of this comic melodrama about two German immigrants who fight about most everything, but most particularly about relative loyalities to the United States and Germany. In this case, it is Winninger who is sympathetic to the German cause, with Ruggles as all–American as Jack Armstrong. One can remember how during the Second World War, neighbors with German names or even German-sounding names were frequently suspected of disloyalty and were shunned. But at least they didn't end up in detention camps like the Japanese-Americans.

307 The Frightened Lady

Based on the play *Criminal at Large* by Edgar Wallace and his novel *The Case of the Frightened Lady.* Story: Inspector Tanner is called in to investigate a series of strangulations at Marks Priory, the ancestral home of the Lebanon family. He finds Lady Lebanon to be quite un-cooperative, while on the other hand her son, Lord Lebanon, seems eager to help the Scotland Yard detective. In researching the family, Tanner becomes aware that madness runs in this noble family at every generation. When Lady Lebanon prevents her son from strangling his fiancée, Ilsa, the inspector is able to get a confession from the young man about the other murders.

• ***The Frightened Lady (Criminal at Large***—U.S.) (original). Gainsborough-British Lion, 1932. Director: T. Hayes Hunter; screenwriters: Angus MacPhail and Bryan Edgar Wallace. Cast: Cathleen Nesbitt (Lady Lebanon), Emlyn Williams (Lord Lebanon), Norman McKinnell (Inspector Tanner), Gordon Harker (Sgt. Totty), Belle Chrystal (Ilsa Crane), Cyril Raymond, Finlay Currie.

• ***The Case of the Frightened Lady*** (remake). Pennant Pictures, 1940. Director: George King; screenwriter: Edward Dryhurst. Cast: Marius Goring (Lord Lebanon), Helen Haye (Lady Lebanon), Penelope Dudley Ward (Ilsa Crane), George Merritt (Inspector Tanner), Ronald Shiner, Patrick Barr, Felix Aylmer.

For its time this was quite a lively murder mystery, with the madness of both Emlyn Williams and Marius Goring rather apparent, particularly because both were rather good at portraying characters not quite right. Cathleen Nesbitt and Helen Haye were both fine as the mothers trying to protect the last of the Lebanons. McKinnell and Merritt were all one could want in a clever Scotland Yard detective.

308 The Frog

Based on the play by Ian Hay and the novel by Edgar Wallace, called *The Fellowship of the Frog.* Story: When a powerful criminal organization which calls itself the Fellowship of the Frog terrorizes the country with robberies, fires and murders, Captain Gordon and Sergeant Elk of the CID take on the case, with the latter being responsible for unmasking the Frog himself.

Wilcox/GFD, Great Britain, 1937 (original). Director: Jack Raymond; screenwriters: Ian Hay and Gerald Elliott. Cast: Gordon Harker (Sgt. Elk), Carol Godner (Lola Bassano), Noah Beery (Joshua Broad), Jack Hawkins (Captain Gordon), Richard Ainley (Ray Bennett), Felix Aylmer (John Bennett), Vivian Gaye, Esme Percy, Cyril Smith, Gordon McLeod, Julien Mitchell.

• ***The Return of the Frog*** (sequel). Imperator, Great Britain, 1938. Director: Maurice Elvey; screenwriters: Ian Hay and Gerald Elliott. Cast: Gordon Harker (Insp. Elk), Una O'Connor (Mum Oaks), Rene Ray (Lila), Hartley Power (Sandford), Cyril Smith (Maggs), Charles Lefeaux (Golly Oaks), Charles Carson, George Hayes, Aubrey Mallalieu, Meinhart Maur.

In the sequel, a number of murders in London's dockland causes Inspector Elk to suspect that a gang known as the Fellowship of the Frog has found a new leader. In this adventure thriller, the good inspector survives attempts on his own life, including poisoning and bombing, to unmask the new Frog.

Rosalind Russell eavesdrops on the conversation between ex-hubby Cary Grant (left) and Frank Jenks in His Girl Friday *(Columbia, 1940), the fast-paced remake of the comedy classic* The Front Page *(United Artists, 1931).*

309 The Front Page

Based on the play by Ben Hecht and Charles MacArthur. Story: Ace reporter Hildy Johnson, intent on quitting his job, getting married and moving to New York, is conned by his Chicago editor, Walter Burns, to cover one last big story, the midnight execution of Earl Williams for the killing of a policeman. Williams escapes when the bungling sheriff insists that the condemned man reenact his crime for a doctor, giving the desperate man his own loaded pistol. Williams takes refuge in the press room and is hidden in a rolltop desk by Hildy, who has come to believe the man's innocence after hearing the tearful story of Williams' and former prostitute, girl friend, Mollie Malloy. Burns arrives in answer to Hildy's call, intent on moving the desk to his newspaper office to ensure his paper will have an exclusive. Meanwhile the governor has ordered a reprieve for Williams, but the messenger is bribed by the mayor, up for reelection on his stand against crime, to not deliver the governor's stay-of-execution. When the other reporters and the sheriff and his men enter the press room, they become suspicious that Williams may be in the desk. Mollie tries to distract everyone by jumping out of a window. The messenger returns and in a drunken state tells how he had been bribed by the mayor. Having saved an innocent man's life, Hildy is at last free to leave with his fiancée, Peggy Grant. As a wedding present, Burns gives Hildy his solid gold watch. When Hildy boards the train to New York, Burns demands that a police officer arrest Johnson, because, as he says, "The son-of-a-bitch stole my watch!"

United Artists, 1931 (original). Director: Lewis Milestone; screenwriter: Bartlett Cormack. Cast: Pat O'Brien (Hildy Johnson), Adolphe Menjou (Walter Burns), Mary Brian (Peggy Grant), George E. Stone (Earl Williams), Mae Clark (Molly Malloy), Edward Everett Horton, Walter Catlett, Phil Tead, Frank McHugh, Matt Moore, Eugene Strong, Fred Howard, Spencer Charters, Clarence H. Wilson, James Gordon, Slim Summerville.

• ***His Girl Friday*** (remake). Columbia Pictures, 1940. Director: Howard Hawks; screenwriter: Charles Lederer. Cast: Rosalind Russell (Hildy Johnson), Cary Grant (Walter Burns), Ralph Bellamy (Bruce Baldwin), John Qualen (Earl Williams), Helen Mack (Mollie Malloy), Ernest Truex, Frank Jenks, Porter Hall, Cliff Edwards, Roscoe Karns, Regis Toomey, Abner Biberman, Gene Lockhart, Frank Orth, Alma Kruger, Clarence Kolb, Billy Gilbert.

• ***The Front Page*** (remake). Universal Pictures, 1974. Director: Billy Wilder; screenwriters: Billy Wilder and I.A.L. Diamond. Cast: Jack Lemmon (Hildy Johnson), Walter Matthau (Walter Burns), Susan Sarandon (Peggy Grant), Austin Pendleton (Earl Williams), Carol Burnett (Molly Malloy), David Wayne, Charles Durning, Lou Frizzell, Noam Pilik, Dick O'Neill, Allen Garfield, Herb Edelman, Vincent Gardenia, Harold Gould, Paul Benedict.

One of the fastest-paced comedies ever filmed, the 1940 version is the most enjoyable, because of the almost perfect interplay between Russell and Grant. Each version has a gag a minute, with lines racing from the mouths of performers almost faster than the speed of sound. Perhaps the most amazing thing about the initial screening is how it demonstrated what could be done with a sound picture only a little over three years after the first talkie. O'Brien and Menjou complemented each other very nicely, but the film would not have been such a hit had it not been for the delightful performances of the many excellent character actors in support. The same compliment can be given to the cast of *His Girl Friday,* although not so much so for the 1974 remake. In the 1931 production, George E. Stone is perfect as the doomed man who recognizes an opportunity when he sees one. Edward Everett Horton was still patenting his soon-to-be-familiar fussy little man act and Mae Clarke was properly hysterical as the girl who had love for one of the few men who had ever treated her with kindness.

In 1940, Ralph Bellamy was just right as the patient but confused fiancé of Russell, ever trusting, even of Grant, who had been Russell's first husband. John Qualen turned in one of his better performances as the frightened condemned man hiding in a rolltop desk. Porter Hall, Roscoe Karns and others were delightfully cynical as reporters to whom an execution is just another story. In a small bit as the messenger, Billy Gilbert came off very well. In the 1974 production, Lemmon and Matthau were good in their roles, but somehow things didn't seem as funny as they had in the two earlier versions. Austin Pendleton's Earl Williams was okay but Carol Burnett as his girlfriend might have been doing one of her zany skits from her TV show rather than acting as a frightened and hysterical woman really wanting to save her man.

La Fuerza Del Desco *see* **Of Human Bondage**

Funeral in Berlin *see* **The Ipcress File**

Further Adventures of the Flag Lieutenant *see* **The Flag Lieutenant**

Further Adventures of the Wilderness Family *see* **The Adventures of the Wilderness Family**

Further Up the Creek *see* **Up the Creek**

G

Il Gabbiano *see* **The Seagull**

The Gables Mystery *see* **Man at Six**

Gaby *see* **Waterloo Bridge**

310 Gallant Lady

Based on the story by Gilbert Emery and Franc Rhodes. Story: It's a mother-love soap opera about an unmarried woman, Sally, who, when her lover is killed, is forced to give up her baby for adoption. In one of the coincidences so familiar to movies, she runs into her son five years later. The boy, called Deedy, immediately takes to her, without knowing that she is his real mother. Meanwhile the adoptive father, Phillip Lawrence, has become a widower and plans to marry Cynthia, whom the child dislikes. Solution, anyone?

Twentieth Century–Fox/United Artists, 1934 (original). Director: Gregory La Cava; screenwriter: Sam Mintz. Cast: Ann Harding (Sally), Clive Brook (Dan), Otto Kruger (Phillip Lawrence), Tulio Carminati (Mario), Dickie Moore (Deedy), Janet Beecher (Maria), Betty Lawford (Cynthia).

• ***Always Goodbye*** (remake). Twentieth Century–Fox, 1938. Director: Sidney Lanfield; screenwriters: Kathryn Scola and Edith Skouras. Cast: Barbara Stanwyck (Margot Weston), Herbert Marshall (Jim Howard), Ian Hunter (Phillip Marshall), Cesar Romero (Count Giovanni Corini), Lynn Bari (Jessica Reid), Binnie Barnes (Harriet Martin), John Russell (Roddy).

Ann Harding made a living portraying sacrificing women and she seemed just the type to put duty to others ahead of her own happiness. On the other hand, Barbara Stanwyck was more the kind of tough dame who looked and acted like she could take care of herself and a little thing like an illegitimate child wouldn't stand in her way. Each of these two fine actresses, as different as they were, made more out of the thin story than the authors could have hoped for. Clive Brook and Herbert Marshall as the lady's doctor friend who loved her but did not stand in the way of her marriage to her son's adoptive father also gave expert performances.

The Gambler *see* **The Great Sinner**

Gambling House *see* **Mr. Lucky**

Gambling on the High Seas *see* **Special Agent**

311 The Garden of Allah

Based on the novel by Robert Hitchens. Story: It's the ridiculous tale of Father Adrian, who has joined a Trappist monastery in Algeria, taking vows of silence, poverty, constant prayer and chastity, the last of which at least becomes more than he can bear. He accidently knocks a girl unconscious and when she revives, finds himself in her embrace. His sin is reported and he is to do penance. Instead, forgetting himself, he leaves the monastery, assumes his secular name, Androvsky, and at an oasis meets and falls in love with Domini Enfilden, a girl seeking God. They marry and go into the desert, where Androvsky recalls his identity, announces that he is a Trappist monk and returns to the monastery—but not, apparently, before breaking his vow of chastity, as she has their son.

• ***The Garden of Allah*** (remake). MGM, 1927. Silent. Director: Rex Ingram; screenwriter: Willis Goldbeck. Cast: Alice Terry (Domini Enfilden), Ivan Petrovich (Father Adrian/Boris Androvsky), Marcel Vibert (Count Anteoni), H.H. Wright, Madame Poquerette, Armand Dutertre.

• ***The Garden of Allah*** (remake). United Artists, 1936. Director: Richard Boleslawski; screenwriter: W.P. Lipscomb. Cast: Marlene Dietrich (Domini Enfilden), Charles Boyer (Boris Androvsky), Basil Rathbone (Count Anteoni), C. Aubrey Smith (Father Roubier), Tilly Losch, Joseph Schildkraut, John Carradine, Alan Marshal, Lucille Watson.

The story was first filmed by Selznick Pictures in 1916. It's such an unusual story that even as improbable as it is, it is appealing, particularly the remake with Dietrich and Boyer. Both overacted horribly but somehow looked good doing it. It was the last film directed by Boleslawski, who died shortly after it was completed. The remake is worth staying up late to watch on TV for the teaming of Dietrich and Boyer, certainly not for the story or even their acting.

312 Gaslight

Based on the play *Angel Street* by Patrick Hamilton. Story: The story begins in the 1860s in a house in London's Pimlico Square, where an old lady is brutally murdered. Years later, a Scotland Yard detective who had handled the still unsolved case recognizes the new tenant of the house as the slain woman's nephew. The latter, who is the murderer, has returned for the jewels for which he had killed and which he believes are hidden somewhere in the house. He is trying to slowly drive his young wife mad because she has innocently discovered his true identity. The detective is able to prevent this from occurring just at the moment when the nephew has finally located the jewels.

• ***Gaslight (Angel Street)*** (original). British National, 1940. Director: Thorold

Dickinson; screenwriters: A.R. Rawlinson and Bridget Boland. Cast: Anton Walbrook (Paul Mallen), Diana Wynyard (Bella Mallen), Frank Pettingell (Detective Rough), Cathleen Cordell (Nancy), Robert Newton (Vincent Ullswater).

• ***Gaslight*** (remake). MGM, 1944. Director: George Cukor; screenwriters: John Van Druten, Walter Reisch and John L. Balderston. Cast: Charles Boyer (Gregory Anton), Ingrid Bergman (Paula Alquist), Joseph Cotten (Brian Cameron), Dame May Whitty (Miss Thwaites), Angela Lansbury (Nancy).

Although seemingly a mystery film, each production of *Gaslight* is actually a superbly directed psychological study of a cold, methodical attempt to drive a woman mad. In both films, the villain cleverly plays on the doubts and fears of a not unintelligent woman until she reaches the point when she not only believes her mind is gone, but in point of fact it nearly is. Both Walbrook and Boyer as the husband are desperately searching for the jewels hidden by their victim before she was murdered. These searches only add to the wife's suspicion that she is going crazy. She hears noises emanating from the room above her bedroom where the murder victim's furniture and possessions are stored and she sees the flame of the gaslight flicker, not realizing that it is caused by her husband in the room above seeking the jewels. When the wife discovers her husband's plan, with the help of the detective, her courage returns and she is able to turn the tables on her tormentor. In Walbrook's case, he is the one seen to be insane. Boyer acts a bit more restrained on being unmasked but it's clear that his sanity is marginal.

The rights to the British version of this classic Victorian melodrama were purchased by MGM and it was withheld from theaters for years to protect the remake from any unwanted competition. When the British production was re-released, it was with the title *Angel Street.* Wynyard gave one of her most memorable performances as the wife who was being methodically driven mad. For her part, Ingrid Bergman won a greatly deserved Academy Award for Best Actress of the year. Walbrook is outstanding as the sadistic fiend whose very voice is enough to put his wife into a panic. Boyer feigns great concern for his wife's fragile health, all the better to play on her self-doubts and make her believe that she not only is forgetful but guilty of petty thefts.

Pettingell as Rough is outstanding as he pulls Wynyard back to a world of sanity. When Walbrook leaves her alone after telling her, "You will die, raving, in an asylum," she murmurs to herself that her suspicions of her husband must have been a dream. Appearing at the door, Pentingell yells, "Was I part of this curious dream?" Cotten's appearance occurs later in the remake and he has really very little to do, except like the cavalry, arrive in the nick of time to save Bergman from her own fears and the very real dangers from her husband. One other performance which was top flight was that of Angela Lansbury, in the 1944 movie, as the maid Nancy who makes no secret of her contempt for her mistress and her interest in the master.

Gator *see* **White Lightning**

The Gaunt Stranger *see* **The Ringer**

313 The Gazebo

Based on the play by Alec Coppel from a story by Myra and Alec Coppel. Story: When TV mystery writer Elliott Nash becomes the victim of a blackmailer, he takes a shot at a shadowy figure in his home and buries the body in his garden at the spot where a gazebo is to be erected. When he later learns that the real blackmailer has been murdered he wonders who he's killed. It wouldn't be fair to answer that question here.

MGM, 1959 (original). Director: George Marshall; screenwriters: Aaron and Lawrence Weingarten. Cast: Glenn Ford (Elliott Nash), Debbie Reynolds (Nell Nash), Carl Reiner (Harlow Edison), John McGiver (Sam Thorpe), Mabel Albertson (Mrs. Chandler), Doro Merande (Matilda), Bert Freed, Martin Landau, Robert Ellenstein, Herman the Pigeon.

• ***Jo (The Gazebo)*** (remake). Trianon Leo/MGM, France, 1971. Director: Jean Girault; screenwriters: Claude Magnier and Jacques Vilfridi. Cast: Louis De Funes (Antoine), Claude Gensac (Sylvie), Michael Galabru (Tonelotti), Bernard Blier (Inspector), Guy Trejan, Jacques Freboist, Yvonne Clech, Freddy Mayne.

The black comedy was surprisingly appealing with both Glenn Ford and Debbie Reynolds handling the comedy quite well. However, John McGiver and Doro Merande steal the show with their droll performances. The French remake is nothing special, just more of the fun of Louis De Funes accidently killing his blackmailer and finding that the body won't stay put.

314 The General

Based on Andrew's Raid during the American Civil War. Story: Johnnie Gray, a young railroad engineer, is in Georgia when the Civil War breaks out. He tries to enlist in the Confederate Army but is refused because his job is considered more important. His girl, Annabelle Lee, is en route to visit her father when the train on which she is traveling is stolen by a group of Union raiders. Johnnie gives chase in another locomotive, which takes him behind Union army lines. There he rescues Annabelle and with the stolen train, The General, they return—this time with Union troops in pursuit. He arrives safely in the South, informs the Confederate commander of the Union plans, and when this results in a victory for the South, Johnnie is commissioned a lieutenant and wins his Annabelle Lee.

Keaton/United Artists, 1927 (original). Silent. Director and screenwriter: Buster Keaton. Cast: Buster Keaton (Johnnie Gray), Glen Cavender (Capt. Anderson), Jim Farley (Gen. Thatcher), Marion Mack (Annabelle Lee), Frederick Vroom, Charles Smith, Frank Barnes, Joseph Keaton, Mike Donlin, Tom Nawn.

• ***The Great Locomotive Chase*** (remake). Walt Disney Studios, 1956. Director: Francis D. Lyon; screenwriter: Lawrence E. Watkin. Cast: Fess Parker (James J. Andrews), Jeffrey Hunter (William A. Fuller), Jeff York (William Campbell), John Lupton (William Pittenger), Eddie Firestone, Kenneth Tobey, Claude Jarman, Jr.

The Keaton film is a silent comedy classic. Even viewed today it is a hysterical example of sight humor. Keaton with his constant sad, straight face goes about the rescuing of his lady fair and The General with great seriousness, but his exploits in dismantling the train to get wood for the engine are among the great comedy moments of movie history. He's the whole show, although Marion Mack as Annabelle is a perfect foil for "the Great Stone Face."

In the Disney remake, things are taken a great deal more seriously. When James J. Andrews and his Union raiders steal a train behind Confederate lines and head north, they have not counted on the persistence of a young conductor, William A. Fuller, who gives chase, and ultimately gets back the train. Andrews' raiders are captured one by one, and Andrews himself is executed as a spy. It's a good adventure yarn with plenty of excitement.

315 Gentle Julia

Based on the novel by Booth Tarkington. Story: It's the all too familiar tale of an attractive hometown girl, Julia, who has many suitors, but is lured to the big city by an older man. When she learns that he is already married, she returns home to wed her devoted sweetheart, Noble Dill.

Fox Film Corporation, 1924 (original). Silent. Director: Rowland W. Lee; screenwriter: Donald W. Lee. Cast: Bessie Love (Julia), Harold Goodwin (Noble Dill), Frank Elliott (Randolph Crum), Charles K. French, Clyde Benson, Harry Dickinson, Jack Rollins, Frances Grant.

• ***Gentle Julia*** (remake). Twentieth Century–Fox, 1936. Director: John Blystone; screenwriter: Lamar Trotti. Cast: Jane Withers (Florence Atwater), Tom Brown (Noble Dill), Marsha Hunt (Julia Atwater), Jackie Searl (Herbert Atwater), Francis Ford (Mr. Tubbs), George Meeker (Mr. Crum), Maurice Murphy, Harry Holman.

This is the kind of story in which audiences only need to hear the names of the characters to sort out the good guys from the bad. Noble Dill was noble. Randolph Crum was indeed. In the remake, the studio beefed up the part of Julia's sister in order to make it their young star's (Jane Withers) picture. Jane helps straighten out the love lives of her friends, and in particular Julia who becomes involved with a charming scoundrel and almost loses her bashful newspaper beau.

A Gentleman After Dark *see* **Forgotten Faces**

Gentlemen Marry Brunettes *see* **Gentlemen Prefer Blondes**

316 Gentlemen Prefer Blondes

Based on the novel by Anita Loos. Story: Blonde gold-digger Lorelei Lee books passage on an ocean liner for herself and friend Dorothy Shaw. She has paid for the trip with money borrowed from button king Gus Eisman. Lorelei sets her sights on America's richest bachelor, Henry Spofford, who is making the crossing to investigate immoral activities of American tourists in Paris. While he is seasick in his cabin, Lorelei amuses herself with Sir Francis

Beckman, whom she induces to lend her his wife's diamond tiara. In Paris, Lorelei lures Spofford to her hotel room, then hides him in her closet when his mother, their lawyer, the Beekmans and Gus Eisman all arrive at once demanding to know what's going on. Lorelei, with Dorothy's help, resolves the situation and on the trip back to America, marries Spofford.

Paramount Pictures, 1928 (original). Silent. Director: Malcolm St. Clair; screenwriters: Anita Loos and John Emerson. Cast: Ruth Taylor (Lorelei Lee), Alice White (Dorothy Shaw), Ford Sterling (Gus Eisman), Holmes Herbert (Henry Spofford), Mack Swain (Francis Beekman), Emily Fitzroy (Lady Beekman), Trixie Friganza (Mrs. Spofford), Blanche Frederici (Miss Chapman).

• ***Gentlemen Prefer Blondes*** (remake). Twentieth Century–Fox, 1953. Director: Howard Hawks; screenwriter: Charles Lederer. Cast: Jane Russell (Dorothy), Marilyn Monroe (Lorelei), Charles Coburn (Sir Francis Beekman), Elliott Reid (Malone), Tommy Noonan (Gus Esmond), George Winslow (Henry Spofford III), Marcel Dalio, Taylor Holmes.

• ***Gentlemen Marry Brunettes*** (sequel). United Artists, 1955. Director: Richard Sale; screenwriters: Mary Loos and Richard Sale. Cast: Jane Russell (Bonnie Jones/Mimi Jones), Jeanne Crain (Connie Jones/Mitzi Jones), Alan Young (Charles Biddle/Mrs. Biddle/Mr. Biddle, Sr.), Scott Brady (David Action), Rudy Vallee (himself), Guy Middleton, Eric Pohlman, Ferdy Mayne.

Anita Loos' novel about the exploits of the gold-digging blonde, Lorelei Lee, was very popular, as was the silent screen version, although the story is really nothing special. The appeal was the attitude of Lorelei. She was out to get what she wanted and the only thing she had to barter with was herself, and she had no qualms about using her bait. She wasn't looking for love; she wanted the real thing, money.

In 1953, Lorelei as impersonated by Marilyn Monroe was excused for this crass attitude by being made none too bright. She wasn't really only mercenary, just a simple girl in need of a good man to look after her and teach her about love—sure! This casting cost the movie the sly humor of the stage production. The level of the humor in the film is illustrated by the conversation of two sailors when Monroe and Russell boarded the ship. One sailor asks the other whom he would save if the ship floundered. The other, older and more experienced, eyeing the girls' spectacular superstructures, allowed that neither of the two would ever sink. The most popular songs in the film, written by Jule Styne and Leo Robin, were "Diamonds Are a Girl's Best Friend" and "Two Little Girls from Little Rock."

In the sequel, two performers, Russell and Crain, accept an invitation to perform in Paris where their mothers were all the rage both on and off the stage during the Roaring Twenties. It's a dismal piece and the musical numbers by Herbert Spencer and Earle Hagen were quickly forgettable.

Geronimo *see* **The Lives of a Bengal Lancer**

Gert and Daisy Clean Up *see* **Gert and Daisy's Weekend**

317 Gert and Daisy's Weekend

Based on a screenplay by Maclean Rogers, Kathleen Butler and H.F. Maltby. Story: Cockney sisters Gert and Daisy are put in charge of evacuee children, who wreck Lady Plumtree's manor but also unmask jewel thieves.

Butcher, Great Britain, 1941 (original). Director: Maclean Rogers; screenwriters: Rogers, Butler and Maltby. Cast: Elsie Waters (Gert), Doris Waters (Daisy), Iris Vandeleur (Ma Butler), John Slater (Jack Densham), Elizabeth Hunt (Maisie Butler), Wally Patch, Anne Esmond, Aubrey Mallalieu, Gerald Rex, Johnny Schofield.

• ***Gert and Daisy Clean Up*** (sequel). Butcher, Great Britain, 1942. Director: Maclean Rogers; screenwriters: Kathleen Butler and H.B. Maltby. Cast: Elsie Waters (Gert), Doris Waters (Daisy), Iris Vandeleur (Ma Butler), Elizabeth Hunt (Hettie), Joss Ambler, Ralph Michael, Tonie Edgar Bruce, Douglas Stewart, Harry Herbert, Angela Glynne, Uriel Porter.

In the sequel to this pretty wild comedy, Gert and Daisy expose a black marketeer who is trying to corner the canned fruit market in the area. It's a farce with the two cockney girls going all out, if you like that sort of thing.

318 Get Carter

Based on the novel *Jack's Return Home* by Ted Lewis. Story: It's a brutal British crime melodrama about small-time hood Jack Carter, who searches Newcastle for those responsible for his brother's death. He kills the killers but then is killed himself by a sniper. Throw in a little sex and you've got the idea.

MGM, Great Britain, 1971 (original). Director and screenwriter: Mike Hodges. Cast: Michael Caine (Jack Carter), Ian Hendry (Eric Paice), Britt Ekland (Anna Fletcher), John Osborne (Cyril Kinnear), Tony Beckley (Peter), George Sewell, Geraldine Moffatt, Dorothy White, Rosemarie Dunham, Petra Markham.

• ***Hit Man*** (remake). MGM, 1972. Director and screenwriter: George Armitage. Cast: Bernie Casey (Tyrone), Pamela Grier (Gozelda), Lisa Moore (Laural), Bhetty Waldron (Ivelle), Sam Laws (Sherwood), Candy All, Don Diamond, Edmund Cambridge, Bob Harris, Rudy Challenger, Tracy Ann King.

The remake is just a black version of the same story. Both films owe a great deal to Raymond Chandler and the *film noir* movies of the late 40s and early 50s, but the producers do not seem to have learned the lesson well.

The Get-Away *see* **Public Hero #1**

319 Getting Gertie's Garter

Based on the play by Avery Hopwood and Wilson Collinson. Story: Gertie Darling is given a diamond-studded garter by an admirer, Ken Walrick. When both become engaged to others, Gertie seeks to return the garter but as would be expected, this is easier said than done. The laughs are frequent as Gertie, her asinine fiancé, Ken, his jealous fiancée, a philanderer, his wife, an amicable bachelor, an aunt and a knowing butler all become involved with the retrieval of the incriminating item of leg wear.

Producers Distributing Corporation, 1927 (original). Silent. Director: E. Mason Hopper; screenwriter: F. McGrew Willis. Cast: Marie Prevost (Gertie Darling), Charles Ray (Ken Walrick), Harry Myers (Jimmy Felton), Fritzi Ridgeway (Barbara Felton), Franklin Pangborn (Algy Brooks), Sally Rand, William Orlamond.

• ***Getting Gertie's Garter*** (remake). United Artists, 1945. Director: Allan Dwan; screenwriters: Allan Dwan and Karen De Wolf. Cast: Dennis O'Keefe (Ken), Marie McDonald (Gertie), Barry Sullivan (Ted), Sheila Ryan, Binnie Barnes, J. Carrol Naish, Jerome Cowan.

These films were produced at a time when it was possible to show naughtiness on the screen without anyone taking all their clothes off. The suggestive humor was based on the premise that engaged partners of both sexes expected that their intended had never been "involved" with anyone before them. Nowadays such an idea would seem ludicrous if it were incorporated into a theme of a movie. In the remake, Marie "The Body" McDonald as always looked good, but her acting abilities seemed inversely proportional to her beauty. Dennis O'Keefe, a likeable performer, seemed defeated by the material. Only Binnie Barnes came off in a favorable light. By 1945, the idea of the film just wasn't amusing enough.

320 The Ghost Breakers

Based on the play by Paul Dickey and Charles W. Goddard. Story: Escaping from a Kentucky mountain-family feud, Warren Jarvis meets Maria Theresa and agrees to help her rid her father's castle of ghosts and find a treasure thought to be hidden there. They discover that the "ghosts" have been hired by Duke D'Alva, a neighbor of Maria who hoped to find the treasure and get her to marry him. Warren settles for half that action when no gold is found in the now de-ghosted castle.

Paramount Pictures, 1922 (original). Silent. Director: Alfred E. Green; screenwriter: Walter De Leon. Cast: Wallace Reid (Warren Jarvis), Lila Lee (Maria Theresa), Arthur Carewe (Duke D'Alva), Walter Hien, J. Farrell MacDonald, Frances Raymond, Snitz Edwards.

• ***The Ghost Breakers*** (remake). Paramount Pictures, 1940. Director: George Marshall; screenwriter: Walter De Leon. Cast: Bob Hope (Larry Lawrence), Paulette Goddard (Mary Carter), Anthony Quinn (Ramon), Paul Lukas, Richard Carlson, Willie Best, Pedro de Cordoba, Virginia Brissac, Noble Johnson.

• ***Scared Stiff*** (remake). Paramount Pictures, 1953. Director: George Marshall; screenwriters: Herbert Baker and Walter De Leon. Cast: Dean Martin (Larry Todd), Jerry Lewis (Myron Mertz), Lizabeth Scott (Mary Carroll), Carmen Miranda, George Dolenz, Dorothy Malone, William Ching, Paul Marion, Jack Lambert.

Dickey and Goddard's light comedy was best presented on the screen with the Hope and Paulette Goddard version. Bob is a crime-beat radio commentator who becomes involved with a murder, is hidden from the police by Goddard in her trunk and goes with her to Cuba to rid her inherited island home of real and put-on things that go bump in the night. Bob is not quite the snook that would become his trademark in later pictures and so his attempts at heroics and romancing the beautiful Goddard seem more believable. Willie Best is excellent as Hope's man who rises above the usually sniveling black servant stereotype common to many films of the era. In the 1953 version, the thriller element is played down to take advantage of the comedy aspects. The profitable film has Martin as the one who helps rid a girl's inherited mansion of ghosts. Lewis has an expanded Willie Best role. Seen today, it's just barely tolerable.

321 The Ghost Train

Based on the play by Arnold Ridley. Story: In this comedy-thriller, detective Teddy Deakin poses as a "silly ass" to uncover gun runners using an abandoned railway line and to expose the stationmaster, Saul Hodgkin, as the ringleader of the gang.

Gainsborough, Great Britain, 1927 (original). Silent. Director: Geza M. Bolvary; screenwriter: uncredited. Cast: Guy Newall (Teddy Deakin), Ilse Bois (Miss Bourne), Louis Ralph (Saul Hodgkin), Anna Jennings (Peggy Murdock), John Manners (Charles Murdock), Agnes Korolenko, Ernest Verebes, Rosa Walter.

• ***The Ghost Train*** (remake). Gainsborough, Great Britain, 1931. Director: Walter Forde; screenwriters: Angus Macphail and Lajos Biro. Cast: Jack Hulbert (Teddy Deakin), Cicely Courtneidge (Miss Bourne), Donald Calthrop (Saul Hodgkin), Ann Todd (Peggy Murdock), Cyril Raymond (Richard Winthrop), Angela Baddeley (Julia Price), Allan Jeayes, Henry Caine, Tracy Holmes, Carol Coombe.

• ***The Ghost Train*** (remake). Gainsborough, Great Britain, 1941. Director: Walter Forde; screenwriters: Marriott Edgar, Val Guest and J.O.C. Orton. Cast: Arthur Askey (Tommy Gander), Richard Murdoch (Teddy Deakin), Kathleen Harrison (Miss Bourne), Morland Graham (Dr. Sterling), Linden Travers (Julie Price), Peter Murray Hill, Carole Lynn, Herbert Lomas, Raymond Huntley, Betty Jardine, Stuart Latham.

The best of the three versions of the comedy-thriller about passengers stranded at a haunted station in Cornwall was the 1931 production. Jack Hulbert was perfection and an absolute delight as the detective who is much smarter than he lets on. Others in the cast who gave well of their talents include Cicely Courtneidge and Donald Calthrop. The 1941 film was an adequate remake with the lead being split into two characters, the better of the two being Arthur Askey, who with the help of Richard Murdoch routs a gang of fifth columnists running arms.

The Gift of Love *see* **Sentimental Journey**

322 Gigi

Based on the novel by Colette. Story: Sixteen-year-old Gigi is raised by her grandmother and aunt to become a courtesan. Bored Parisian Gaston finds the company of the young girl delightful, but when he becomes aware that she has grown to be a desirable woman, he must make a decision about his future relationship with her—as a protector or husband.

UGCF, France, 1949 (original). Director: Jacqueline Andy; screenwriter: Pierre Laroche. Cast: Yvonne De Bray (Mme. Alvarez), Gaby Morlay (Alicia), Danielle Delmore (Gigi), Frank Villard (Gaston), Jean Tissier.

• ***Gigi*** (remake). MGM, 1958. Director: Vincente Minnelli; screenwriter: Alan Jay Lerner. Cast: Leslie Caron (Gigi), Maurice Chevalier (Honore Lachaille), Louis Jourdan (Gaston Lachaille), Hermione Gingold (Madame Alvarez), Isabel Jeans (Aunt Alicia), Eva Gabor (Liane d'Exelmans), Jacques Bergerac, Monique Van Vooren, John Abbott.

Alan Jay Lerner and Vincente Minnelli softened the story of a girl being raised to become a courtesan, making Gigi into a precocious adolescent who grows into a beautiful young woman who wants and gets marriage to Gaston. The musical won nine Academy Awards, including Best Picture, Best Director, Best Screenplay and Best Song (the title number). Other outstanding Lerner and Frederick Loewe songs included "Thank Heaven for Little Girls," sung by Chevalier, "The Night They Invented Champagne," featuring Caron, Jourdan and Gingold, and the pure delight "I Remember It Well," marvelously performed by Chevalier and Gingold. The film was a beautiful marriage of color, story, music and period with memorable performances from Caron, Chevalier, Gingold and Jourdan.

323 The Gilded Lily

Based on a story by Melville Baker and Jack Kirkland. Story: Lillian Drake, a Broadway cafe hostess, has many admirers, including wealthy man-about-town Creighton Howard, and small-town boy Frank Thompson. Despite his mother's objections and some misgivings on Lillian's part, she marries Frank. She gives up her job, hoping for the quiet life. All goes well until Frank starts drinking. He encourages her to resume her career and she does. Creighton comes back into her life and when Frank takes a shot at his rival, the marriage is ended. But Lillian's single existence is to be brief as Creighton introduces her to his mother as his fiancée.

Famous Players/Paramount Pictures, 1921 (original). Silent. Director: Robert Z. Leonard; screenwriter: Clara Beranger. Cast: Mae Murray (Lillian Drake), Lowell Sherman (Creighton Howard), Jason Robards (Frank Thompson), Charles Gerard, Leonora Ottinger.

• ***The Gilded Lily*** (remake). Paramount Pictures, 1935. Director: Wesley Ruggles; screenwriter: Charles Binyon. Cast: Claudette Colbert (Marilyn David), Fred MacMurray (Pete Dawes), Ray Milland (Charles Gray/Granville), C. Aubrey Smith (Lord Granville), Eddie Craven, Luis Alberni, Donald Meek.

The silent feature, with its story of a popular girl torn between choosing for her husband a rich sophisticate or an average guy almost turned out badly for the heroine, but she got a second chance. In the remake, things go the other way around. Colbert and MacMurray spend a lot of time on a bench in front of the New York Public Library discussing anything that comes to mind, no matter how trivial. Although he loves her, she's looking for someone a bit more ambitious and successful than this newspaper reporter. She finds him in Ray Milland, a titled and wealthy Englishman. Through a misunderstanding, Colbert turns down Milland's proposal as well as MacMurray's. Angered, Fred writes an article about her, referring to her as "The No Girl." The publicity gets her booked into a nightclub as a singer and dancer. Although she's not very good at either, her charm wins over the audience and she is a success. She renews her relationship with Milland but after mulling it over for awhile, chooses genteel poverty with MacMurray to riches with Milland. This was the first of nine films that Colbert and MacMurray would make together between 1935 and 1949, and is usually considered to be their best collaboration. The film was rated as one of the year's ten best by most critics.

The Girl and the Gambler *see* **The Dove**

The Girl from Avenue A *see* **The Brat**

Girl from Havana *see* **The Leathernecks Have Landed**

324 The Girl from Leningrad

Based on the screenplay by Serge Mikhailov and Mikhail Rosenberg and the novel by Maurice Clark and Victor Trivas. Story: Its the story of the courage, dedication and patriotism of the Soviet volunteer Red Cross nurses during the siege of Leningrad by the Germans in 1941.

Lenfilm Studios/Artinko, 1941 (original). Director: Victor Eisimont; screenwriters: Serge Mikhailov and Mikhail Rosenberg. Cast: Zoya Fyodorova (Natasha), Maria Kapustina (Tamara), Tatiana Aloyshina (Zina), Elena Melentyeva (Shura), Alexander Abrikosov (Lt. Sergei Korovin), Konstantin Adashevsky (Field Doctor Katner), Yuri Tolubeyev, Boris Blinov, Vasil Abramov, Oleg Zrakov, Olga Fyodorina.

• ***Three Russian Girls*** (remake). United Artists, 1944. Director: Fedor Ozep and Henry Kesler; screenwriters: Aben Kandel and Dan James. Cast: Anna Sten (Natasha), Kent Smith (John Hill), Mimi Forsythe (Tamara), Alexander Granach (Major Braginski), Kathy Frye (Chijik), Paul Guilfoyle, Kane Richmond, Mannart Kippen, Jack Gardner, Marcia Lenack, Marry Herriot.

Both films are effective propaganda pieces made during World War II, dramatic in bringing the reality of war home to audiences. The nurses were brave, their work was exhausting, nerve-wracking and horrible. The films are not great art but for what they were intended to be, they succeeded. The performances ran from amateurish to most impressive.

The Girl from Tenth Avenue *see* **The Outcast**

325 A Girl in Every Port

Based on an original story by Howard Hawks. Story: Sailor Spike Madden discovers that another sailor has been making time with the girls that he calls his own in his various ports of call. When he catches up with the other sailor, called Salami, they become fast friends, and the latter saves Spike from making a mistaken commitment to French gold-digger Marie.

Fox Film Corporation, 1926 (original). Silent. Director: Howard Hawks; screenwriters: Howard Hawks and Seton I. Miller. Cast: Victor McLaglen (Spike Madden), Louise Brooks (Marie), Robert Armstey (Salami), Maria Casajuana, Frances McDonald, Natalie Joyce, Dorothy Mathews, Elena Jurado, Leila Hyams.

• ***Goldie*** (remake). Fox Film Corporation, 1931. Director: Benjamin Stoloff; screenwriters: Howard Hawks and Seton I. Miller. Cast: Spencer Tracy (Bill), Warren Hymer (Spike), Jean Harlow (Goldie), Lina Basquette, Maria Alba, Eleanor Hunt, Leila Karnelly, Ivan Linow, Jesse De Vorska, Eddie Kane.

It's quite a feat to make a movie screenplay out of the legend that sailors have girls in every port, but Howard Hawks was able to pull it off, most entertainingly. In the remake, Hymer finds that the girls he goes with in various ports are all identically tattooed. Determined to meet the man who made the tattoos his mark of conquest, he finally catches up with Tracy, and they become fast friends. Whey Hymer thinks he's in love with gold-digger Jean Harlow, Tracy tries to warn him about her, but Hymer won't listen. His eyes are opened when he discover's Bill's tattoo on Goldie. He's not angry with Bill, as he realizes his buddy was just trying to protect him. Even in this early film, Tracy demonstrated the charm which would endear him to audiences for the next thirty-some years.

The Girl Most Likely ***see*** **Tom, Dick and Harry**

The Girl of La Mancha ***see*** **Don Quixote**

326 The Girl of the Golden West

Based on the play by David Belasco. Story: The Girl, owner of the Polka Saloon in Cloudy Mountain, Colorado, falls in love with Ramerrez, whom she later learns is a bandit. When a snowstorm forces Ramerrez to spend the night with the Girl, jealous dancer Nina Micheltorena reveals his identity and whereabouts to Sheriff Jack Rance, who also loves the Girl. When Ramerrez tries to escape, he is shot, and the Girl hides him, but drops of his blood prove to the sheriff that she is lying when she denies knowing where he is. Ramerrez wins his freedom and the Girl in a poker game with Rance. Aroused by Nina, a mob is about to lynch Ramerrez when Rance explains his bargain and restores the bandit to the Girl.

First National Pictures, 1923 (original). Silent. Director: Edwin Carewe; screenwriter: Adelaide Heilbron. Cast: Sylvia Breamer (the Girl), J. Warren Kerrigan (Ramerrez), Russell Simpson (Jack Rance), Rosemary Theby (Nina

Micheltorena), Wilfrid Lucas, Nelson McDowell, Charles McHugh, Hector V. Sarno.

• ***The Girl of the Golden West*** (remake). First National Pictures, 1930. Director: John Francis Dillon; screenwriter: Waldemar Young. Cast: Ann Harding (Minnie), James Rennie (Dick Johnson), Harry Bannister (Jack Rance), Ben Hendricks, Jr., J. Farrell MacDonald, George Cooper, Johnny Walker, Richard Carlyle, Arthur Stone.

• ***The Girl of the Golden West*** (remake). MGM, 1938. Director: Robert Z. Leonard; screenwriters: Isabel Dawn and Boyce De Gaw. Cast: Jeanette MacDonald (Mary Robbins), Nelson Eddy (Ramerez/Lt. Johnson), Walter Pidgeon (Jack Rance), Leo Carrillo, Buddy Ebsen, Leonard Penn, Priscilla Lawson, Bob Murphy, Olin Howland.

The talkie remake of the Belasco play was almost identical to the 1905 stage production and as such the film seemed unnecessarily confining and artificial. The MacDonald-Eddy musical was perhaps the pair's least successful collaboration. Neither of the two were any great shakes as actors and when faced with making a go of this creaky plot, their thespian shortcomings were all the more evident. It didn't help that the one thing they did well—sing—was handicapped by a forgettable score by Sigmund Romberg and Gus Kahn, including "Senorita," "The Mariachi," "Dance with Me My Love" and the best of the lot, "Who Are We to Say."

327 Girl of the Limberlost

Based on the novel by Gene Stratton Porter. Story: Katherine Comstock is a young backwoods girl in Indiana who must overcome the hatred of her mother, who erroneously believes the girl is responsible for the death of her father.

• ***Girl of the Limberlost*** (remake). Monogram Pictures, 1934. Director: Christy Cabanne; screenwriter: Adele Comandini. Cast: Louise Dresser (Elinora Comstock), Ralph Morgan (Wesley Stinton), Marian Marsh (Katherine Comstock), H.B. Walthall (Dr. Amon), GiGi Parrish, Helen Jerome Eddy, Betty Blythe, Barbara Bedford, Robert Ellis.

• ***Romance of the Limberlost*** (remake). Monogram Pictures, 1938. Director: William Nigh; screenwriter: Marion Orth. Cast: Jean Parker (Laurie), Eric Linden (Wayne), Marjorie Main (Nora), Edward Pawley (Carson), Betty Blythe, Sarah Padden, George Cleveland, Hollis Jewell.

• ***The Girl of the Limberlost*** (remake). Columbia Pictures, 1945. Director: Melchor G. Ferrer; screenwriter: Erna Lazarus. Cast: Ruth Nelson (Kate Comstock), Dorinda Clifton (Elinora Comstock), Loren Tindall (Pete Reed), Gloria Holden (Miss Nelson), Ernest Cossart, Vanessa Brown, James Bell.

These are fine examples of wholesome family pictures, but why do wholesome families have to be so dull? These three productions are tearful rehashes of the sentimental old story first filmed in 1924. Well, at least the swamp girl completed her high school education.

Girl of the Rio *see* **The Dove**

Girls About Town *see* **The Gold Diggers**

328 Girl's Dormitory

Based on the play by Ladislaus Fodor. Story: Dr. Stephen Dominick, head of a girl's private finishing school in Europe, falls in love with Marie Claudel, one of the students. The two plan to announce their engagement until Marie learns that one of the teachers, Anna Mathe, is also in love with Stephen. Marie steps aside to give Stephen the opportunity to marry the older woman. But Stephen knows who he wants and goes after Marie when she walks out of his life.

Twentieth Century–Fox, 1936 (original). Director: Irving Cummings; screenwriter: Gene Markey. Cast: Herbert Marshall (Dr. Stephen Dominick), Ruth Chatterton (Prof. Anna Mathe), Simone Simon (Marie Claudel), Constance Collier (Prof. Augusta Wimmer), J. Edward Bromberg (Dr. Spindler), Tyrone Power, Jr. (Count Vallais), Dixie Dunbar, John Qualen, Shirley Deane, Frank Reicher.

• ***A Very Young Lady*** (remake). Twentieth Century–Fox, 1941. Director: Harold Schuster; screenwriters: Ladislaus Fodor and Elaine Ryan. Cast: Jane Withers (Kitty Russell), Nancy Kelly (Alice Carter), John Sutton (Dr. Meredith), Janet Beecher (Miss Steele), Richard Clayton (Tom Brighton), June Carlson, Charles Halton, Cecil Kellaway, Marilyn Kinsley.

As originally written, the headmaster turns to his assistant who has loved him for years when the young girl nobly gives him up so the older woman can have him. At the last moment the producers decided to reunite the teacher with his young love, believing her gesture was sufficient box-office sacrifice, and besides audiences were used to seeing Ruth Chatterton suffer. The performances of the three principals were quite acceptable, with the lovely Simon's accent most charming. Nowadays the only thing this film is remembered for is that it introduced young Tyrone Power, Jr., to the screen. In the remake, studios, taking note of the fact that Jane Withers was growing up, adapted the story so Jane could have a puppy love for John Sutton, the head of the private school she attends. She gets over her crush, but not before one of her imaginative love letters almost gets everyone into hot water.

329 The Glass Key

Based on the novel by Dashiell Hammett. Story: It's the improbable but enjoyable tale of Ed Beaumont, a henchman of political boss Paul Madvig, who proves that his boss is not guilty of killing his daughter's boyfriend, Taylor Henry, son of a senator; that in fact it was the senator who killed his own son.

Paramount Pictures, 1935 (original). Director: Frank Tuttle; screenwriters: Kathryn Scola and Kubec Glasmon. Cast: George Raft (Ed Beaumont), Claire Dodd (Janet Henry), Edward Arnold (Paul Madvig), Rosalind Keith (Opal Madvig), Ray Milland (Taylor Henry), Charles Richman (Senator Henry), Robert Gleckler, Guinn Williams, Tammany Young, Henry Tyler.

• ***The Glass Key*** (remake). Paramount Pictures, 1942. Director: Stuart

Brian Donlevy appears to be giving a lecture to Alan Ladd as the peek-a-boo girl Veronica Lake looks on in the 1942 Paramount version of The Glass Key, *first filmed in 1935 by the same studio.*

Heisler; screenwriter: Jonathan Latimer. Cast: Brian Donlevy (Paul Madvig), Veronica Lake (Janet Henry), Alan Ladd (Ed Beaumont), Bonita Granville (Opal Madvig), Richard Denning (Taylor Henry), Joseph Calleia (Nick Varna), William Bendix, Frances Gifford, Donald McBride, Margaret Hayes, Moroni Olsen, Eddie Marr.

Both George Raft and Alan Ladd impressed in these two filmings of the Dashiell Hammett mystery, with the remake refurbished to overcome some of the script problems with the first, namely a general lack of motivation for behavior. The three main performers in the remake were coming off personal triumphs, Ladd and Veronica Lake in *This Gun for Hire* and Brian Donlevy in *Wake Island.* Lake was at the peak of her come-hither era and most men in the audiences wished she would flash the look at them. Ladd exploded on the screen as the strong, silent type, whose antisocial behavior was just part of a job. Donlevy had delighted audiences as a political boss in *The Great McGinty,* and seeing him in this film was just like more of the same.

330 Glorious Betsy

Based on the play by Rida Johnson Young. Story: While visiting Baltimore incognito, Jerome Bonaparte meets and wins the love of Elizabeth Patterson, a society girl. After they are married, he reveals that he is the brother of Napoleon Bonaparte. The Emperor is outraged and, refusing to allow her to land in France, has the marriage annulled, sending Betsy back to Baltimore. On the eve of his arranged wedding to the Princess of Wurtemberg, Jerome escapes and returns to Betsy shortly after the birth of their child.

Warner Bros., 1928 (original). Silent. Director: Alan Crosland; screenwriter: Anthony Coldeway. Cast: Dolores Costello (Betsy Patterson), Conrad Nagel (Jerome Bonaparte), John Miljan (Preston), Marc McDermott (Col. Patterson), Pasquale Amato (Napoleon Bonaparte), Michael Varitch, Andre De Sequrola, Clarissa Selwynne, Betty Blythe.

• ***Hearts Divided*** (remake). Warner Bros., 1936. Director: Frank Borzage; screenwriters: Laird Doyle and Casey Robinson. Cast: Marion Davies (Betsy Patterson), Dick Powell (Jerome Bonaparte), Charles Ruggles (Henry Ruggles), Claude Rains (Napoleon Bonaparte), Edward Everett Horton, Arthur Treacher, Henry Stephenson, Clara Blandick, John Larkin.

The silent was a very popular period piece at the time of its release. The remake had a fine cast and even some musical numbers, but not unlike the Emperor of France, the story became their Waterloo. It is hard to decide precisely what type of movie the producers hoped to make; what resulted was a disappointment.

331 The Godfather

Based on the novel by Mario Puzo. Story: The story of a Mafia family opens in 1945 at the New York estate of aging Don Vito Corleone on the day of his daughter's marriage. In attendance are the Don's three sons, Sonny, Fredo and the youngest, Michael, just returned from World War II. Shortly after the wedding, the Corleones meet with their archrivals, the Tattaglias, who propose that the two mobs join together and control the growing drug trade. Corleone, despite his criminal ventures, draws the line at this. Because of his stand he is later shot but survives the attack. When Michael discovers the identity of the gunmen, he offers to kill them, even though it was intended that he would not enter into the family business. After completing this assignment, Michael goes to Italy until the heat is off. He returns after a "peace conference" between the recovered Don and the other gang leaders. The peace doesn't last long, as the Don's heir apparent as the Godfather, Sonny, is shot to death. Soon after this the Don suffers a fatal heart attack and Michael assumes the leadership of his father's criminal empire.

Alfran Productions/Paramount Pictures, 1972 (original). Director: Francis Ford Coppola; screenwriters: Mario Puzo and Francis Ford Coppola. Cast: Marlon Brando (Don Vito Corleone), Al Pacino (Michael Corleone), James Caan (Sonny Corleone), Richard Castellano (Clemenza), Robert Duvall (Tom Hagen), Diane Keaton (Kay Adams), Sterling Hayden (Captain McClusky), John Marley (Jack Woltz), Richard Conti (Barzini), Abe Vigoda (Tessio), Al Lettieri (Sollozzo), John Cazale (Fredo Corleone), Talia Shire (Connie Corleone (Rizzi), Morgana King, Al Martino, Lenny Montana, Rudy Bond, John Martino, Salvatore Corsitto, Richard Bright, Alex Rocco, Tony Giorgio.

• ***The Godfather, Part II*** (sequel). Coppola/Paramount Pictures, 1974. Director: Francis Ford Coppola; screenwriters: Francis Ford Coppola and Mario Puzo. Cast: Al Pacino (Michael Corleone), Robert Duvall (Tom Hagen), Diane Keaton (Kay Corleone), Robert De Niro (Vito Corleone), John Cazale (Fredo Corleone), Talia Shire (Connie Corleone Rizzi), Lee Strasberg (Hyman Roth), Morgana King (Mama Corleone), Troy Donahue (Merle Johnson), Abe Vigoda (Tessio), Gianni Russo (Carlo), James Caan (Sonny Corleone), Harry Dean Stanton, Roger Corman, Michael Gazzo, G.D. Spradlin, Richard Bright, Gaston Moschin, Tom Rosqui, Frank Sivero, B. Kirby, Jr., Francesco De Sapio, Mariana Hill, Leopoldo Trieste, Dominic Chianese, Giuseppe Sillato, Mario Cotone.

One of the most popular pictures of all time, *The Godfather* captured the Academy Award for Best Picture, Best Director, Best Actor (Brando), and Best Screenplay. In addition, Caan, Duvall and Pacino were all nominated for but did not win the Best Supporting Actor Award. The sequel was equally popular and won Academy Awards for Best Picture, Best Director, Best Screenplay, Art and Set Direction, Best Original Dramatic Score, and Best Supporting Actor (De Niro). Pacino, who was superb, was nominated for Best Actor but did not win, and of course, Michael V. Gazzo and Lee Strasberg lost out for the Best Supporting Actor award to De Niro. In addition, Talia Shire was nominated for but did not win the Best Supporting Actress Award.

As difficult as it might have seemed at the time, the sequel was actually a better picture than the tremendous first film. In it audiences are given glimpses not only of the further deterioration of a basically decent man, Pacino, into a heartless and ruthless gang leader, who saw it as his duty to have both his brother and brother-in-law killed because of their betrayals, but also the story of how the family came to prominence in the crime world, established by flashbacks to a young Don Vito Corleone, played beautifully by Robert De Niro.

Taken together these two films, the first running 175 minutes and the second, 200, give audiences a chilling and thrilling look into a criminal kingdom that exists around them. The Corleones are presented as amoral characters when it comes to their business, in which murder and corruption of elected and appointed officials are merely good business practices. The performances, down to the smallest roles, are splendid, with the leading performers at the top of their form. Everything about the films, from the music, the sets, the color, the feeling for the period, as well as the acting, is nearly perfect. The genius behind all of this success is, clearly, director Coppola, whose work ranks with the best ever brought to the screen.

The Godfather, Part II *see* **The Godfather**

332 God's Country and the Woman

Based on the novel by James Oliver Curwood. Story: A married woman with a grown-up daughter is forcibly dishonored by a villain while her husband is away for a year. As a result she has the cad's child. Her grown-up daughter agrees to pretend the baby is hers when her father comes home, alleging that she was married but her husband had died. Then she meets "Mr. Right" and the story is amended to her husband lived, but before dear old dad can get home to be fed the story, the villain coveting the girl kidnaps her and threatens to reveal all. Everything is resolved before the fade-out but getting there seemed interminable to critics.

Vitagraph, 1916 (original). Silent. Director: Rollin B. Sturgeon; screenwriter: James Oliver Curwood. Cast: William Duncan (Phillip Weyman), Nell Shipman (Josephine Adare), George Holt (Arnold Lang), William Bainbridge (John Adare), Nell Clark Keller (Miriam Adare), Edgar Keller (Jean Corisset), George Kunkel (Thoreau).

• ***God's Country and the Woman*** (remake). Warner Bros., 1937. Director: William Keighley; screenwriters: Peter Milne and Charles Belden. Cast: George Brent (Steve Russett), Beverly Roberts (Jo Barton), Barton MacLane (Bullhead), Robert Barrat (Jefferson Russett), Alan Hale (Bjorn Skalka), Joseph King, El Brendel, Joseph Crehan, Addison Richards.

It's a hackneyed, incredible story and the remake had terrible Technicolor. Bette Davis was originally assigned the Beverly Roberts role but she wisely fled to England rather than appear in this stinker.

333 The Go-Getter

Based on the story by Peter B. Kyne. Story: It's a comedy about Bill Peck, just out of a hospital where he spent two years recovering from war wounds, which cost him a leg. He is determined to overcome his handicap and make a success of himself as a salesman with Cappy Rick's lumber yard. He goes through a series of comical situations before winning a management position and the love of Mary Skinner.

Cosmopolitan Productions/Paramount Pictures, 1923 (original). Silent. Director: E.H. Griffith; screenwriters: William J. MacMillan and Dr. William V. Healey. Cast: T. Roy Barnes (Bill Peck), Seena Owen (Mary Skinner), William Norris (Cappy Ricks), Tom Lewis (Charles Skinner), Louis Wolheim (Daniel Silver), Fred Huntley, John Carr, Frank Currier, William J. Sorrelle.

• ***The Go-Getter*** (remake). Warner Bros., 1937. Director: Busby Berkeley; screenwriter: Delmer Daves. Cast: George Brent (Bill Austin), Anita Louise (Margaret Ricks), Charles Winninger (Cappy Ricks), John Eldridge (Lloyd Skinner), Henry O'Neill (Commander Tisdale), Joseph Crehan, Willard Robertson, Herbert Rawlinson, Ed Gargan.

These stories of a crippled man making good as a go-getting salesman for a lumber yard are lightweight comedies with stories bordering on the ridiculous. For instance, at one point in the remake, George Brent supposedly dives off an ocean liner and swims to the shore 14 miles away. We believe in hiring the handicapped, but this may be a bit too much of a test for anyone. Besides Brent, Charles Winninger as the soft-hearted owner of the lumberyard is winning, while the love interest Anita Louise seems to be mimicking Bette Davis.

334 Going My Way

Based on a story by Leo McCarey. Story: Father Chuck O'Malley, a young priest, is sent to a New York slum parish by the bishop, seemingly to assist aging pastor Father Fitzgibbon, as his curate. Actually, he is to succeed the elderly priest who is no longer able to perform all of his duties. Initially, Father Fitzgibbon disapproves of the methods of the young cleric and resents his presence, but as time passes, their gentle sparring turns to genuine respect and affection.

Paramount Pictures, 1944 (original). Director: Leo McCarey; screenwriters: Frank Butler and Frank Cavett. Cast: Bing Crosby (Father Chuck O'Malley), Barry Fitzgerald (Father Fitzgibbon), Frank McHugh (Father Timothy O'Dowd), Rise Stevens (Genevieve Linden), Jean Heather (Carol James), James Brown, Gene Lockhart, Porter Hall, Fortunio Bonanova, Carl "Alfalfa" Switzer.

• ***The Bells of St. Mary's*** (sequel). RKO, 1945. Director: Leo McCarey; screenwriter: Dudley Nichols. Cast: Bing Crosby (Father O'Malley), Ingrid Bergman (Sister Benedict), Henry Travers (Horace Bogardus), Joan Carroll (Patsy), William Gargan, Martha Sleeper, Dickie Tyler, Ruth Donnelly, Rhys Williams, Una O'Connor.

Bing Crosby's easygoing nature was never more in evidence or popular as in his appearances as the charming priest, Father O'Malley. In the original, he won the Academy Award as Best Actor, with Barry Fitzgerald, having the unusual distinction of having been nominated for both Best Actor and Best Supporting Actor, winning the latter. Also an Academy Award winner was the picture itself, director Leo McCarey, and the Jimmy Van Heusen and Johnny Burke song "Swinging on a Star."

In the sequel, Crosby as Father O'Malley is made the pastor of a church and has his run-ins with the principal of the Catholic school, Sister Benedict, played lovingly by Ingrid Bergman. She believes in strict standards and the power of prayer. She gently but firmly counters Crosby's interference in her school and prays that ill-tempered, miserly old Horace Bogardus will donate his new building to replace her crumbling school. Between her prayers and the priest's persuasiveness, she gets her school, but like Moses will not be allowed to see the promised land because her health requires that she be sent away from the city.

The picture, McCarey, Crosby and Bergman each were nominated for Academy Awards, but none won. For products of Catholic parishes and schools the films are nostalgic, for others they are rather sweet without being sugary glimpses into a period and way of life, much changed today.

Going Places *see* **The Hottentot**

Going Wild *see* **The Aviator**

335 The Gold Diggers

Based on a play by Avery Hopwood. Story: An assortment of Broadway chorus girls are less interested in becoming stars on the Great White Way than in snagging a millionaire who will take care of their needs and desire for material things. The wealthiest and most disapproving target becomes the first to succumb to the charms of one of the girls, offering more than the usual proposition, and instead marries her. The plot's not the thing in these escapist movies. Rather, it's the chance to see some pretty girls, often in abbreviated costumes, frankly and with frankness snaring handsome, wealthy men.

Warner Bros., 1923 (original). Silent. Director: Harry Beaumont; screenwriter: Grant Carpenter. Cast: Hope Hampton (Jerry La Mar), Wyndham Standing (Stephen Lee), Louise Fazenda (Mabel Munroe), Gertrude Short (Topsy St. John), Alec B. Francis (James Blake), Arita Gillman (Eleanor Montgomery), Peggy Brown (Trixie Andrews), Anne Cornwall (Violet Dayne), Louise Beaudet (Cissie Gray).

• ***Gold Diggers of Broadway*** (remake). Warner Bros., 1929. Director: Roy Del Ruth; screenwriter: Robert Lord. Cast: Nancy Welford (Jerry), Conway Tearle (Stephen Lee), Winnie Lightner (Mabel), Ann Pennington (Ann Collins), Lilyan Tashman (Eleanor Montgomery), William Bakewell (Wally Saunders), Nick Lucas (Nick), Helen Foster (Violet Dayne), Albert Gran (James Blake), Gertrude Short (Topsy St. John).

• ***Gold Diggers of 1933*** (remake). Warner Bros., 1933. Director: Mervyn LeRoy; screenwriters: Edwin Gelsey and James Seymour. Cast: Ruby Keeler (Polly Parker), Dick Powell (Brad Roberts), Joan Blondell (Carol King), Warren William (J. Lawrence Bradford), Aline MacMahon (Trixie Lorraine), Guy Kibbee (Faneuil H. Peabody), Ned Sparks (Barney Hopkins), Ginger Rogers (Fay Fortune).

• ***Painting the Clouds with Sunshine*** (remake). Warner Bros., 1951. Director: David Butler; screenwriters: Harry Clark, Roland Kibbee and Peter Milne. Cast: Virginia Mayo (Carol), Dennis Morgan (Vince Nichols), S.Z. Sakall (Felix Hoff), Gene Nelson (Ted Lansing), Lucille Norman (Abby), Virginia Gibson (June), Wallace Ford (Sammy Parks), Tom Conway (Bennington).

Gold Diggers of 1935, *Gold Diggers of 1937*, and *Gold Diggers in Paris* (1938), although neither remakes or sequels in the true sense of the words, hewed pretty closely to the formula of show girls seeking rich husbands which proved so popular in the earlier productions. Other films with a similar theme, although supposedly based on completely different sources, included *Girls About Town* (1931), *The Greeks Had a Word for Them* (1932), *Three Blind Mice* (1938), *Moon Over Miami* (1941), *Three Little Girls in Blue* (1946), and *How to Marry a Millionaire* (1953).

The *Gold Diggers* remakes were musicals, with bouncy songs, slightly naughty, but spectacular dance sequences and suggestive lyrics. The songs by Al Dubin and Joe Burke in the 1929 picture included "The Song of the Gold Diggers," "Keeping the Wolf from My Door," "Painting the Clouds with Sunshine" and "Tip-Toe Through the Tulips." In 1933, the Harry Warren and Al Dubin songs, staged and directed with great imagination and creativity by Busby Berkeley, included "Pettin' in the Park," "My Forgotten Man," "The Shadow Waltz" and "We're in the Money." In the latter, Ginger Rogers sings a chorus in pig Latin. In the 1951 film, the songs featured included the title number by Dubin and Burke, Rodgers and Hart's "With a Song in My Heart," "Birth of the Blues" by Buddy De Sylva, Lew Brown and Ray Henderson, and "Jealousy" by Vera Bloom and Jacob Gade. Each in their own way were fun movies, particularly those of the '30s, that helped audiences briefly forget the trials of the Depression.

Gold Diggers in Paris *see* **The Gold Diggers**

Gold Diggers of Broadway *see* **The Gold Diggers**

Gold Diggers of 1933 *see* **The Gold Diggers**

Gold Diggers of 1935 *see* **The Gold Diggers**

Gold Diggers of 1937 *see* **The Gold Diggers**

The Golden Blade *see* **The Arabian Nights**

The Golden Voyage of Sinbad *see* **Sinbad the Sailor**

Goldie *see* **A Girl in Every Port**

336 Good and Naughty

Based on the play *Naughty Cinderella* by Rene Peter and Henri Falk. Story: Germaine Morris, considered rather plain, is in love with interior decorator Gerald Gray, who is having an affair with Claire Fenton, the wife of a wealthy broker. When Claire invites Gerald on a yachting trip to Florida, his friend Bunny West invites showgirl Chouchou Rouselle along to pose as Gerald's fiancée, but Germaine is determined to have this role and turns herself into a beauty. In Florida, she's pursued by all the men, prompting a quarrel between Claire and Gerald. Thomas Fenton, hoping to catch his wife with some man so he can divorce her, suggests that he take Germaine, and Claire and Gerald go off together. A third country is heard from, when "Bad News" Smith, the showgirl's admirer, also tries to claim Germaine. Gerald gives him a beating, effects a reconciliation between the Fentons and proposes to a happy Germaine.

Paramount Pictures, 1926 (original). Silent. Director: Malcolm St. Clair; screenwriter: Pierre Collings. Cast: Pola Negri (Germaine Morris), Tom Moore (Gerald Gray), Ford Sterling (Bunny West), Miss Du Pont (Claire Fenton), Stuart Holmes (Thomas Fenton), Marie Mosquini (Chouchou Rouselle), Warren Richmond ("Bad News" Smith).

• ***This Is the Night*** (remake). Paramount Pictures, 1932. Director: Frank Tuttle; screenwriter: George Marion, Jr. Cast: Lily Damita (Germaine), Charles Ruggles (Bunny West), Roland Young (Gerald Grey), Thelma Todd

(Claire), Cary Grant (Stephen), Irving Bacon (Jacques), Claire Dodd (Chou-Chou).

These bedroom farces were fairly enjoyable, dealing as they did with infidelity, mistaken identity, marriage, love, betrayal and nudity. Negri almost handles the latter, when she appears in Moore's room in a revealing negligee. The remake is notable for being Cary Grant's first featured role. He's an Olympic javelin thrower who throws a lovely tantrum when he discovers that his wife, Todd, is having an affair. Lily Damita is appealing as the object of fascination of all the males. In this version the locale has been switched to Paris and Venice where the complications multiply and the situations get more and more compromising.

337 The Good Companions

Based on a play by J.B. Priestley and Edward Knonblock. Story: Dissatisfied with their lives, inarticulate Yorksman Jess Oakroyd and schoolmaster Indigo Jolifant desert their responsibilities and join a troupe of traveling amateur players, featuring Susie Dean. When they become stranded, the group (called the Dinky-Doos) is rescued by a spinster, Miss Trant, who gives them money and a new name, The Good Companions. Newly christened, they experience modest success as they travel through the provinces, until a rival producer sics a group of toughs on them, setting fire to their theater. Now forced to disband, the members at least have the satisfaction of knowing that they had an adventure. Indigo experiences success as a composer and Susie as a singer of his songs, while Oakroyd emigrates to Canada to live out his remaining days with a married daughter.

Gaumont-British Productions, 1933 (original). Director: Victor Saville; screenwriters: W.P. Lipscomb, Angus Macphail and Ian Dalrymple. Cast: Jessie Matthews (Susie Dean), John Gielgud (Indigo Jolifant), Edmund Gwenn (Jess Oakroyd), Mary Glynne (Miss Trant), Jack Hawkins, Dennis Hoey, Viola Compton, Finlay Currie, George Zucco, Frank Pettingell.

• ***The Good Companions*** (remake). A.B.P.C./Pathe Productions, 1957. Director: J. Lee Thompson; screenwriters: T.J. Morrison, J.L. Hodgson and John Whiting. Cast: Janette Scott (Susie Dean), John Fraser (Indigo Jolifant), Eric Portman (Jess Oakroyd), Celia Johnson (Miss Trant), Alec McCowen, John Salew, Mona Washbourne, Hugh Griffith, Joyce Grenfell, Anthony Newley, Rachel Roberts.

Jessie Matthews, a vivacious singer and dancer, was one of the most popular British performers of the thirties and *The Good Companions* was among her biggest hits. She had a lovely face and curvaceous body to accompany her musical talents. These two productions of the musical melodrama are not great theater but they do nicely demonstrate a period in show business, perhaps peculiar to England, whose day has passed, of the traveling amateur troupes. The songs are no great shakes and the need for a remake is questionable, particularly when it was decided to update it and add modern songs. It had an old-fashioned story line in 1933 and this fact and the stale dialog did not allow for the remake to be well-received, even in England.

338 The Good Fairy

Based on the play by Ferenc Molnar and the English adaptation by Jane Hinton. Story: It's a whimsical comedy about naive, unworldly Luisa (Lu) Ginglebusher, fresh from an asylum, who becomes an usherette in a Budapest theater. She is convinced that she was born to bring good luck and happiness to all and is to be everyone's good fairy. She's so innocent that various men wish to protect her, always with the result that she turns their lives upside down. She rejects the jewels of a businessman, Konrad, asking in return for her company only that he conduct all his business through lawyer Max Sporum, to whom she claims to be married. She has never met Max, having chosen his name at random from a telephone book. When she runs off with a waiter named Detlaff, Konrad informs the highly ethical lawyer of his wife's behavior. The lawyer naturally insists that he is not married to Lu, the truth costing him Konrad's business. But nothing daunts the innocently amoral Lu.

Universal Pictures, 1935 (original). Director: William Wyler; screenwriter: Preston Sturges. Cast: Margaret Sullavan (Luisa Ginglebusher), Herbert Marshall (Dr. Max Sporum), Frank Morgan (Konrad), Reginald Owen (Detlaff), Alan Hale, Beulah Bondi, Cesar Romero, Hugh O'Connell, Eric Blore, Luis Alberni.

• ***I'll Be Yours*** (remake). Universal Pictures, 1947. Director: William A. Seiter; screenwriter: Preston Sturges. Cast: Deanna Durbin (Louise Ginglebusher), Tom Drake (George Prescott), William Bendix (Wechsberg), Adolphe Menjou (J. Conrad Nelson), Walter Catlett, Franklin Pangborn.

Preston Sturges' screenplay of the Molnar comedy consists of a lot of near slapstick horseplay which makes for some entertaining sequences. Margaret Sullavan portrays the charming but rather strange young woman with surety. Frank Morgan, as Konrad, her benefactor, is bombastic and implausible but most enjoyable. Herbert Marshall's role offers no challenge but Reginald Owen as the waiter is given the opportunity to demonstrate his considerable ability. One result of the film is that Sullavan and director Wyler were married on its completion, although they did not initially get along well on the set.

The remake was meant to help Durbin's sagging career, but it didn't. The fantasy of the Molnar play was now completely absent, and even though Preston Sturges once again did the screenplay, the piece did not possess the charm of the Sullavan version. Miss Durbin, as would be expected, sang prettily, her numbers including "Granada" and "It's Dream Time."

339 Good News

Based on the play by Laurence Schwab, Lew Brown, Frank Mandel and B.G. De Sylva. Story: It's a typical 1920s college story, where football is king and the star player, Tommy, is in danger of flunking, thus being unable to play in Tait College's big game. To the rescue comes shy, plain and bright Connie, who secretly loves the lug and would like to take him away from the campus vamp, Patricia. Tommy isn't as dumb as he seems and Connie is not as plain as she thinks. Love blossoms during the tutoring.

MGM, 1930 (original). Director: Nick Grinde; screenwriters: Frances Marion and Joe Farnham. Cast: Mary Lawlor (Connie), Stanley Smith (Tommy), Bessie Love (Babe), Cliff Edwards (Kearney), Gus Shy (Bobbie), Lola Lane (Patricia), Thomas Jackson, Delmer Daves, Billy Taft.

• ***Good News*** (remake). MGM, 1947. Director: Charles Walters; screenwriters: Betty Comden and Adolph Green. Cast: June Allyson (Connie Lane), Peter Lawford (Tommy Marlowe), Patricia Marshall (Pat McClellan), Joan McCracken (Babe Doolittle), Ray McDonald, Mel Torme, Robert Strickland, Donald McBride.

The plot to these pictures is just enough to keep audiences interested. The viewers of the '30s who didn't attend college found '20s fraternity and sorority life, football heroes and pretty coeds good fun. By the 1947 production, a new generation enjoyed the songs by B.G. De Sylva, Lew Brown and Ray Henderson, which included "Just Imagine," "The Best Things in Life Are Free," "French Lesson," "Pass That Peace Pipe," and the lively "Varsity Drag" of the finale. For all the fine music and splendid young talent, the film was just average entertainment.

The Good Old Soak *see* **The Old Soak**

340 Goodbye Again

Based on the play by George Haight and Alan Scott. Story: A famous novelist rekindles his affair with old flame Julie, much to the disappointment and disapproval of his jealous and smitten secretary, Anne. The latter, amusingly, finds ways to protect her interests.

Warner Bros., 1933 (original). Director: Michael Curtiz; screenwriter: Ben Markson. Cast: Joan Blondell (Anne), Genevieve Tobin (Julie), Warren William (the Novelist), Helen Chandler (Elizabeth), Ruth Donnelly, Wallace Ford, Hugh Herbert, Hobart Cavanaugh.

• ***Honeymoon for Three*** (remake). Warner Bros., 1941. Director: Lloyd Bacon; screenwriters: Earl Baldwin, Julius J. Epstein and Philip G. Epstein. Cast: Ann Sheridan (Anne Rogers), George Brent (Kenneth Bixby), Charlie Ruggles (Harvey Wilson), Osa Massen (Julie Wilson), Jane Wyman (Elizabeth Clochessy), William T. Orr, Lee Patrick.

These are two short second features meant to be vehicles for the leading female performers. Joan Blondell was supposed to be the lead in the original, but the one who got the most laughs was Hugh Herbert. In the remake, Ann Sheridan, secretary-fiancée to writer George Brent, has to deal with a rekindled romance between her man and Osa Massen. It's a flat piece, with only infrequent and predictable humor.

Goodbye Broadway *see* **The Shannons of Broadway**

341 Goodbye, Mr. Chips

Based on the novel by James Hilton. Story: Aged Charles Chipping, affectionately referred to as Mr. Chips, recalls his days at Brookfield, a boys' public school, from 1870 to 1928. Earlier he had much trouble with the lads who did

Greer Garson and Robert Donat look lovingly at each other as Paul von Henreid and others toast the couple's marriage in Goodbye, Mr. Chips *(MGM, 1939).*

not like his stern and unapproachable manner. This was changed when he met and married his beloved Katherine who helped humanize the pedagogue, to a point that he was named headmaster. She dies in childbirth and he plods along sorrowfully without her. He remembers "all my boys . . ." as he dies.

MGM-British, Great Britain, 1939 (original). Director: Sam Wood; screenwriters: Eric Maschwitz, R.C. Sheriff and Claudine West. Cast: Robert Donat (Charles Edward Chipping), Greer Garson (Katherine Ellis), Terry Kilburn (John/Peter Colley), John Mills (Peter Colley), Paul von Henreid (Max Staefel), Judith Furse (Flora), Lyn Harding (Dr. Wetherby), Milton Rosmer, Frederick Leister, Louise Hampton, Austin Trevor, David Tree.

• ***Goodbye, Mr. Chips*** (remake). APJAC/MGM, Great Britain, 1969. Director: Herbert Ross; screenwriter: Terence Rattigan. Cast: Peter O'Toole (Arthur Chipping), Petula Clark (Katherine), Michael Redgrave (the Headmaster), George Baker (Lord Sutterwick), Sian Phillips (Ursula Mossbank), Michael Bryant (Max Staefel), Jack Hedley, Alison Leggatt, Clinton Greyn, Barbara Couper, Michael Culver.

Despite stiff competition in a year of many great performances, Robert Donat won the Academy Award for his superb portrayal of the shy schoolmaster. The film was nominated for Best Picture, Best Script, Best Director and Best Actress. The elaborate musical remake was a disappointment and

Peter O'Toole (center) takes his eyes off his tea to look admiringly at his wife Petula Clark in the 1969 MGM *musical remake of* Goodbye, Mr. Chips.

although Peter O'Toole was nominated for a Best Actor Oscar, his performance paled compared to that of Donat. The story is updated to make Katherine a singer in an English music hall and her return to Chips not setting at all well with the school's chief benefactor, but he is forced to back down from threatening to have Chips removed when Pet Clark as Katherine invites the man's ex-mistress to the Founder's Day celebration. Clark is killed by a German bomb after entertaining troops, before O'Toole can inform her that he has been named headmaster in the final year of World War II. Songs by Leslie Bricusse include "Where Did My Childhood Go?," "And the Sky Smiled," "When I Am Older," "Schooldays" and "You and I."

342 The Goose Woman

Based on a story by Rex Beach. Story: When internationally known opera star Marie de Nardi gives birth to an illegitimate son, her career is ruined. Bitter, she turns to drink and lives with the boy in a tumbledown shack, tending geese for a livelihood. Blaming the boy for her downfall, she gives him neither love nor affection. When he is grown, Gerald becomes engaged to a local actress, Hazel Woods. Out of spite, Marie, who has lived all these years as Mary Holmes, tells Gerald of his illegitimacy and how he is the cause of her ruined life. When a millionaire, Amos Ethridge, who backs the local theater company, is murdered, Mary fabricates a story about the murder which pushes her center stage once again as a key witness. However, the circumstances of her story seem to implicate Gerald in the murder. At last showing some concern for her son, she changes her testimony. A doorman confesses to the murder, which he committed because Amos had seduced so many stage-struck young girls, and he wished to protect Hazel from a similar fate.

Universal Pictures, 1925 (original). Silent. Director: Clarence Brown; screenwriter: Melville Brown. Cast: Louise Dresser (Mary Holmes/Marie de Nardi), Jack Pickford (Gerald Holmes), Constance Bennett (Hazel Woods), Marc MacDermott (Amos Ethridge), James O. Barrows, Spottiswoode Aitken, George Cooper, Gustav von Seyffertitz, George Nichols.

• ***The Past of Mary Holmes*** (remake). RKO, 1933. Directors: Harlan Thompson and Slvako Vorkapich; screenwriters: Edward Marion Dix and Edward Doherty. Cast: Helen MacKellar (Mary Holmes), Eric Linden (Geoffrey Holmes), Jean Arthur (Joan Hoyt), Skeets Galagher (Pratt), Ivan Simpson (Jacob Riggs), Clay Clement, Franklin Parker, Eddie Nugent, Roscoe Ates, J. Carroll Naish.

It's an interesting story, well handled in the silent film, with Dresser excellent in the lead. The performers in the remake, particularly Helen McKellar and Eric Linden, simply overact and nothing seems natural. In this version, the mother's only pleasures are guzzling gin and raking her son over the coals when she loses her operatic voice and career, because she hadn't practiced safe sex and found herself with child.

Der Grafin Von Monte Cristo *see* **The Count of Monte Cristo**

343 The Gorilla

Based on the play by Ralph Spence. Story: Two incompetent detectives, Garrity and Mulligan, are assigned to protect a prominent zoologist from an attack by a mysterious gorilla who has been killing indiscriminately. It's decided that one should pose as a gorilla to attract the real thing, but then the phony and the killer ape can't be told apart.

• ***The Gorilla*** (remake). Warner Bros., 1931. Director: Bryan Foy; screenwriter: Ralph Spence. Cast: Lila Lee (Alice Denby), Joe Frisco (Garrity), Harry Gribbon (Mulligan), Walter Pidgeon (Arthur Mardsen), Purnell Pratt, Edwin Maxwell, Roscoe Karns.

• ***The Gorilla*** (remake). Twentieth Century–Fox, 1939. Director: Allan Dwan; screenwriters: Rian James and Sid Silvera. Cast: Jimmy Ritz (Garrity), Harry Ritz (Harrigan), Al Ritz (Mulligan), Anita Louise (Norma Denby), Patsy Kelly (Kitty), Lionel Atwill (Walter Stevens), Bela Lugosi (Peters), Joseph Calleia, Edward Norris, Wally Vernon, Paul Harvey, Art Miles.

The Gorilla was first filmed by First National as a silent comedy in 1927. Frisco and Gribbon are good for a few wild laughs, but one should keep their eye on Walter Pidgeon if interested in the mystery aspect of the screwball movie. In the remake, the story is reworked to serve as a vehicle for the zany Ritz Brothers. Those who appreciated the crazy humor of this trio and the comic antics of Patsy Kelly will find the movie a scream. Otherwise, it's just a lot of people running around yelling and getting in each other's way. The plot has very little logic to it but with the Ritz Brothers, none should be expected. Atwill, Lugosi and Calleia provide a nice trio of suspects for the mastermind behind the gorilla's killings.

344 The Grand Duchess and the Waiter

Based on the play by Alfred Savoir. Story: Millionaire Alfred Durant becomes infatuated with a Russian refugee in Paris, the Grand Duchess Zenia. When he can't get to meet her, he disguises himself as a waiter. Zenia hires him for her personal staff but gives him only menial assignments. Despite herself she falls for his presumptuous manner, but when he reveals his true identity, she leaves Paris. Months later, Albert finds her, now with her funds gone, living in a humble inn. When he proposes she accepts his offer of marriage.

Famous Players/Paramount Pictures, 1926 (original). Silent. Director: Malcolm St. Clair; screenwriter: Pierre Collings. Cast: Adolphe Menjou (Albert Durant), Florence Vidor (Grand Duchess Zenia), Lawrence Grant (Grand Duke Peter), Andre Beranger (Grand Duke Paul), Dot Farley, Barbara Pierce, Brandon Hurst, William Courtright.

• ***His Tiger Lady*** (remake). Famous Players/Paramount Pictures, 1928. Silent. Director: Hobart Henley; screenwriter: Ernest Vajda. Cast: Adolphe Menjou (Henri), Evelyn Brent (The Tiger Lady), Rose Dione (Madame Duval), Emil Chautard, Mario Carillo, Leonardo De Vesa, Jules Rancourt.

• ***Here Is My Heart*** (remake). Paramount Pictures, 1934. Director: Frank Tuttle; screenwriters: Edwin Justus Mayer and Harlan Thompson. Cast: Bing Crosby (J. Paul Jones), Kitty Carlisle (Princess Alexandra), Roland Young (Prince Nickolas), Alison Skipworth (Countess Rostova), Reginald Owen (Prince Vladimir), William Frawley, Cecilia Parker, Marian Mansfield, Charles E. Arnt, Akim Tamiroff.

Debonair Adolphe Menjou was in top form in the thinly plotted *The Grand Duchess and the Waiter.* The title tells the whole story, but in this case the plot isn't the thing, it is the delightful performances of all the participants. In 1927, Menjou came back with *Service for Ladies,* which again found him as a headwaiter in a ritzy Paris hotel who goes ga-ga over an American heiress, played by Menjou's then wife, Kathryn Carver. In *His Tiger Lady,* Menjou plays a phony rajah and enters a tiger's cage to interest a beautiful and naughty duchess, played by Evelyn Brent. Finally, Bing Crosby poses as a waiter to be close to princess Kitty Carlisle. But we're not fooled into thinking he's a singing waiter, even when he croons the Ralph Rainger and Leo Robin songs "June in January" and "With Every Breath I Take."

345 Grand Hotel

Based on the novel *Menschen im Hotel* by Vicki Baum. Story: It's the story of various Berlin hotel guests and how their lives become intertwined. These include a world-weary ballerina, a penniless baron, a timid, dying clerk and a boorish business tycoon who tries to set up a brief affair with one of the hotel's stenographers. The ballerina and the baron share a brief romantic idyll that ends tragically when he is beaten to death during a robbery attempt by the businessman. The clerk finally finds the courage to confront his hated boss and the stenographer goes off with him.

MGM, 1932 (original). Director: Edmund Goulding; screenwriter: William A. Drake. Cast: Greta Garbo (Grusinskaya), John Barrymore (Baron Felix von Geigern), Joan Crawford (Flaemmchen), Wallace Beery (Preysing), Lionel Barrymore (Otto Kringelein), Lewis Stone (Dr. Otternschlag), Jean Hersholt (Senf), Ferdinand Gottschalk, Tully Marshall, Sam McDaniel, Robert McWade, Purnell B. Pratt, Rafaela Ottiano.

• ***Weekend at the Waldorf*** (remake). MGM. Director: Robert Z. Leonard; screenwriters: Sam and Bella Spewack. Cast: Ginger Rogers (Irene Malvern), Lana Turner (Bunny Smith), Walter Pidgeon (Chip Collyer), Van Johnson (Capt. James Hollis), Edward Arnold (Martin X. Edley), Phyllis Thaxter, Keenan Wynn, Robert Benchley, Leon Ames, Lina Romay, Samuel S. Hinds.

Even though somewhat dated, *Grant Hotel* has remained a film favorite for over five decades. It's not that the story is so outstanding, nor that the distinguished cast is at their best, for they are not. It's because of the kind of magic that motion pictures can sometimes achieve, making the whole greater than the sum of its parts. The love scene between Garbo and John Barrymore is so lovingly photographed that audiences can feel the emotions of the two people and it hurts so good. Crawford looks good and in many ways seems the most natural actor among the lot. Beery with his phony German accent is just doing one of his two acts. He could either play a crude, unlikeable bully, or a sweet, unaffected (and usually boozy) nice guy. Here he's in the former posture. Lionel Barrymore plays his role for audience sympathy and gets it. It's a grand film but one can't help noticing that the comment made by the hotel director, played by Lewis Stone, at the end of the film, has some truth to it: "People Come. People Go. Nothing Ever Happens."

The remake has no particular movie magic and the thinness of the material is much more apparent as it details the stories of various guests at New York's then-largest hotel during the Second World War. No performance stands out and none is extremely bad. It's just a routine all-star picture, with twisted stories similar to those in *Grand Hotel.*

346 The Great Adventure

Based on the play by Arnold Bennett and his novel *Buried Alive.* Story: Priam Farll, the greatest painter of his day, fed up with publicity, finds the anonymity he seeks by assuming the identity of his deceased valet, Henry Leek, who's body is mistakingly identified by the coroner as being Priam's. He is thrown out of Westminster Abbey, during his "own" pomp and circumstance funeral, for creating a disturbance. Injured, he is nursed by a young widow, Alice Challice, whom he eventually marries to get her meager inheritance, but he grows to love her. He continues to paint, but must contend with Leek's widow who demands he care for her and "their" children. He is saved by a dealer who knows his work and breaks the news to the world that Farll is still alive. Priam now happily accepts the recognition his work brings, content to settle down to married bliss with Alice.

• ***The Great Adventure*** (remake). First National Pictures, 1921. Silent. Director: Kenneth Webb; screenwriter: Dorothy Farnum. Cast: Lionel Barrymore (Priam Farll), Doris Rankin (Alice Challice), Thomas Brandon (Henry Leek), Ivo Dawson, Octavia Broske, Arthur Rankin, Paul Kelly, Charles Land, Jed Prouty.

• ***His Double Life*** (remake). Paramount Pictures, 1933. Directors: William C. De Mille and Arthur Hopkins; screenwriters: Clara Beranger and Arthur Hopkins. Cast: Roland Young (Priam Farll), Lillian Gish (Alice Challice), Montagu Love (Duncan Farll), Lumsden Hare, Lucy Beaumont, Charles Richman, Philip Tonge.

• ***Holy Matrimony*** (remake). Twentieth Century–Fox, 1943. Director: John Stahl; screenwriter: Nunnally Johnson. Cast: Monty Woolley (Priam Farll), Gracie Fields (Alice Challice), Laird Cregar (Clive Oxford), Una O'Connor, Alan Mowbray, Melville Cooper, Franklin Pangborn, Eric Blore, Ethel Griffies.

The Great Adventure was first filmed in England in 1915, with Henry Ainley portraying the publicity-shy painter, Ilam Carve (the name used in the Bennett play and novel). The comical aspects of the story grew with each production, climaxing with the grand performance by Monty Woolley and the offbeat casting of English Music Hall star Gracie Fields. These two were so good together that they were reunited in 1945 in *Molly and Me.*

In the 1933 production, the best thing critics could think to say about it was that it was an "extremely nice" picture, which of course is faint praise. They were also pleased to have Lillian Gish back on the screen, after years away appearing on the stage. Lionel Barrymore, in the second silent version, was enjoyable as the painter who initially benefited from having his valet's death be mistaken for his, but found after marrying Alice, that the valet's wife believed him to be her long-missing husband.

347 The Great Divide

Based on the play by William Vaughn Moody. Story: Ruth Jordan finds herself in a desperate situation. She is alone in a wilderness cabin with three drunken brutes who are arguing over which one will have her. Trying to make the best of this bad situation, Ruth appeals to the least despicable of the three, Stephen Ghent, to save her from the other two. He does and then drags her off to the next town, where he forces her to marry him. During the three-day ride to Ghent's gold mine, Ghent roughly makes love with his bride when the mood strikes him. Later, Ruth is rescued by her brother and taken to the latter's ranch to recover from her ordeal. Ghent, who has decided he loves Ruth, tries to get her back, but she won't see him. When her illness becomes desperate, Ghent goes for a doctor and when on the return trip the doctor's horse is injured, Ghent gives up his mount, placing himself in peril from a flood. Ruth has a son, and hearing of Ghent's performance decides she loves him also, and the two are reunited.

• ***The Great Divide*** (remake). MGM, 1925. Director: Reginald Barker;

screenwriter: Benjamin Glazer. Cast: Alice Terry (Ruth Jordan), Conway Tearle (Stephen Ghent), Wallace Beery (Dutch), Huntley Gordon (Philip Jordan), Allan Forest (Dr. Winthrop Newbury), George Cooper, Zasu Pitts, William Orlamond.

• ***The Great Divide*** (remake). First National Pictures, 1929. Director: Reginald Barker; screenwriter: Fred Myton. Cast: Dorothy Mackaill (Ruth Jordan), Ian Keith (Stephen Ghent), Myrna Loy (Manuella), Lucien Littlefield (Texas Tommy), Creighton Hale (Edgar Blossom), George Fawcett, Claude Gillingwater, Roy Stewart.

• ***Woman Hungry*** (remake). First National Pictures, 1931. Director: Clarence Badger; screenwriter: Howard Estabrook. Cast: Lila Lee (Judith Temple), Sidney Blackmer (Geoffrey Brand), Raymond Hatton (Joac), Fred Kohler (Kampen), Kenneth Thomson (Leonard Temple), Olive Tell, David Newell, J. Farrell MacDonald, Ton Dugan, Blanche Frederici.

These melodramas tell the unlikely story of a woman being brutalized by a man, married against her will or kidnapped, and later deciding that she liked this cave-man treatment, calling it love. While no doubt there are women who might fit this picture, surely they are just a wee bit sick. In the 1929 movie, Dorothy Mackaill is the one who gets the rough treatment from Ian Keith but she has a rival in the person of Myrna Loy, in one of her many half-caste portrayals. The 1931 movie goes back to the 1923 plot. The story was also filmed in 1915.

348 The Great Gatsby

Based on the novel by F. Scott Fitzgerald. Story: One summer night in 1917 in Louisville, young officer Jay Gatsby falls in love with Daisy Fay. They are separated when he must leave for the war, but not before Jay pledges to raise himself to a social standing and wealth which will make him worthy of her love. Daisy does not wait for Jay and with pressure from her parents, marries wealthy Tom Buchanan. When Jay reappears on the scene nine years later, he has kept his promise, having through some mysterious association with Charles Wolf come to possess great wealth and own a fabulous Long Island estate. Meanwhile, Buchanan is having an affair with Myrtle Wilson, a garage-keeper's wife. At a party hosted by Gatsby, Daisy confesses she still loves him. Tom charges Gatsby with making love to his wife and having made his money from bootlegging. Meanwhile, Myrtle's husband angrily accuses her of infidelity, although with whom he is not certain. She dashes into the road and is hit and killed by Gatsby's roadster, supposedly carrying him and Daisy away to a new life together. Although Daisy was driving, Gatsby nobly accepts responsibility. Alone in his house, Jay is gunned down by Wilson, who believes him not only to be the man who killed his wife, but her lover as well.

Paramount Pictures, 1926 (original). Silent. Director: Herbert Brenson; screenwriter: Becky Gardiner. Cast: Warner Baxter (Jay Gatsby), Lois Nelson (Daisy Buchanan), Neil Hamilton (Nick Carraway), Georgia Hale (Myrtle Wilson), Hale Hamilton (Tom Buchanan), William Powell (George Wilson), George Nash (Charles Wolf), Carmelita Geraghty (Jordan Baker).

• ***The Great Gatsby*** (remake). Paramount Pictures, 1949. Director: Elliott Nugent; screenwriters: Cyril Hume and Richard Maibaum. Cast: Alan Ladd (Jay Gatsby), Betty Field (Daisy Buchanan), Barry Sullivan (Tom Buchanan), MacDonald Carey (Nick Carraway), Shelley Winters (Myrtle Wilson), Howard Da Silva (George Wilson), Ruth Hussey (Jordan Baker), Henry Hull (Dan Cody), Carole Mathews (Ella Cody), Ed Begley (Myron Lupus).

• ***The Great Gatsby*** (remake). Paramount Pictures, 1974. Director: Jack Clayton; screenwriter: Francis Ford Coppola. Cast: Robert Redford (Jay Gatsby), Mia Farrow (Daisy Buchanan), Sam Waterston (Nick Carraway), Bruce Dern (Tom Buchanan), Karen Black (Myrtle Wilson), Scott Wilson (George Wilson), Lois Chiles (Jordan Baker), Howard Da Silva (Meyer Wolfsheim).

Of the three filmings of Fitzgerald's bittersweet romantic tragedy, the one starring Alan Ladd came off the best. It seemed best at capturing the period of the piece and Ladd was the most successful at making plausible the devotion of a man who can't get over his love for a shallow and selfish girl. Baxter is too dark and brooding to be taken seriously as the essentially romantic man driven to prove himself worthy of the socialite, who had chosen security with a man who cares but little for her, over an uncertain life with a man who adores her. Robert Redford looked the part, but he sounded uncomfortable with his lines, made all the more difficult to deliver to Mia Farrow, who seemed intent on portraying Daisy as some ethereal numbskull to whom love is imported shirts, sweaters and shoes. In the latter film, the best performance was given by Sam Waterston as the narrator, Nick Carraway. He at least seemed to be flesh and blood and not some one-dimensional caricature. The only other enjoyable feature of the movie was the song "What'll I Do," hauntingly played while Jay is showing off his possessions to a nauseatingly flighty Daisy.

349 The Great Gay Road

Based on the novel by Tom Gallon. Story: Sir Crispin Vickrey hires gentleman tramp Hilary Kite to pose as the former's lost son and marry his neice, who loves a younger man.

Broadwest, Great Britain, 1920 (original). Silent. Director and screenwriter: Norman MacDonald. Cast: Stewart Rome (Hilary Kite), Pauline Johnson (Nancy), John Stuart (Rodney Foster), Ernest Spaulding (Crook Perkins), A. Bromley Davenport (Sir Crispin Vickrey), Ralph Forster, Helena Lessington.

• ***The Great Gay Road*** (remake). Stoll/Butcher, Great Britain, 1931. Director: Sinclair Hill; screenwriter: Leslie Howard Gordon. Cast: Stewart Rome (Hilary Kite), Frank Stanmore (Crook Perkins), Kate Cutler (Aunt Jessie), Arthur Hardy (Sir Crispin), Pat Paterson (Nancy), Billy Milton, Hugh E. Wright, Frederick Lloyd, Ethel Warwick, Wally Patch.

In the remake, Stewart Rome, repeating the role he played eleven years earlier, is a gentleman tramp who returns to the home he left 20 years earlier and resumes his place in the family. He falls in love with his cousin, Pat Paterson (the "Great Lover" Charles Boyer's wife of 40 plus years), and his father

The cast of The Great Gatsby *(Paramount, 1949) line up for a publicity photo. From left to right, they are: Barry Sullivan (Tom Buchanan), Betty Field (Daisy Buchanan), Alan Ladd (Jay Gatsby), Ruth Hussey (Jordan Baker), Macdonald Carey (Nick Carraway) and Howard Da Silva (Wilson).*

wishes they would marry, but she's already engaged so he hits the road again.

350 The Great Impersonation

Based on the novel by E. Phillips Oppenheim. Story: When Sir Everard Dominey and his almost identical Oxford classmate, Baron Leopold von Ragastein, meet again several years later in German West Africa during World War I, von Ragastein is the military commandant and Dominey has left England after being suspected of murdering a man. Von Ragastein plots to have Dominey poisoned, and assuming Dominey's identity, proceeds to England to spy for Germany. There von Ragastein renews acquaintances with German contact Princess Eiderstrom, with whom he once had an affair. She resents the attention von Ragastein pays to Rosamund, Dominey's mentally ill wife. The princess, together with another spy, Schmidt, remind him of his obligations to Germany, but it turns out that Dominey is actually Dominey, having foiled von Ragastein's plot back in Africa and posed as von Ragastein posing as himself to ferret out German spies such as the Princess and Schmidt, who are promptly arrested. Dominey is happily reunited with Rosamund, who is much better, thank you.

Famous Players–Lasky/Paramount Pictures, 1921 (original). Silent. Director: George Melford; screenwriter: Monte M. Katterjohn. Cast: James Kirkwood

The cast from The Great Gatsby *(Paramount, 1974) in character are (left to right) Tom Buchanan (Bruce Dern), Nick Carraway (Sam Waterston), Daisy Buchanan (Mia Farrow), and Jay Gatsby (Robert Redford).*

(Sir Everard Dominey/Leopold von Ragastein), Ann Forrest (Rosamund Dominey), Winter Hall (Duke of Oxford), Truly Shattuck (Duchess of Oxford), Fontaine La Rue (Princess Eiderstrom), Alan Hale (Gustave Seimann), William Burgess (Dr. Hugo Schmidt), Bertram Johns, Cecil Holland, Tempe Piggot.

• ***The Great Impersonation*** (remake). Universal Pictures, 1935. Director: Alan Crosland; screenwriters: Frank Wead and Eve Greene. Cast: Edmund Lowe (Everard Dominey/Leopold von Ragenstein), Valerie Hobson (Eleanor Dominey), Wera Engles (Princess Stephanie), Lumsden Hare (Duke Henry), Spring Byington (Duchess Caroline), Frank Reicher (Dr. Schmidt), Henry Mollison, Brandon Hurst, Leonard Mudie.

• ***The Great Impersonation*** (remake). Universal Pictures, 1942. Director:

John Rawlins; screenwriter: W. Scott Darling. Cast: Ralph Bellamy (Sir Edward Dominey/Baron von Ragenstein), Evelyn Ankers (Muriel), Aubrey Mather (Sir Ronald), Edward Norris (Bardinet), Karen Verne (Baroness Stephanie), Henry Daniell (Seaman), Ludwig Stossel (Dr. Schmidt), Mary Forbes, Rex Evans, Charles Coleman.

Neither of the Universal remakes of the story were any great shakes in their attempt to portray English lords and ladies, or German aristocrats acting as spies. More often than not the performers forget their accents and for Edmund Lowe and Ralph Bellamy, who had to struggle with recalling which accent they were to employ at a particular point in the movie, it became just too much. The silent film didn't have this problem, of course, so James Kirkwood could concentrate on the convoluted story. Continuity also didn't seem to note that the characters in the latter films were supposed to be in the 1914 period, but the characters dressed in whatever was handy at the time and sometimes drove in automobiles that would have set the folks of the World War I era on their ears.

The Great Locomotive Chase *see* **The General**

The Great O'Malley *see* **The Making of O'Malley**

The Great St. Trinian's Train Robbery *see* **Belles of St. Trinian's**

351 The Great Sinner

Based on the novel *The Possessed* by Fydor Dostoyevsky. Story: Writer Fedja meets and falls in love with Pauline Ostrovsky on a train headed for Paris. She is addicted to gambling as is her father. Fedja reasons that he will go to the gaming tables, win enough to pay off her father's debts and everything will be hunky-dory. Initially his luck at the casinos in Weisbaden is incredible but when it turns sour, he disintegrates into a wastrel to whom gambling is the only thing in life.

MGM, 1949 (original). Director: Robert Siodmak; screenwriters: Ladislas Fodor and Christopher Isherwood. Cast: Gregory Peck (Fedja), Ava Gardner (Pauline Ostrovsky), Melvyn Douglas (Armand de Glasse), Walter Huston (General Ostrovsky), Ethel Barrymore (Grandmother), Frank Morgan (Aristide Pitard), Agnes Moorehead, Frederick Ledebur, Ludwig Donath, Curt Bois.

• ***The Gambler*** (remake). Paramount Pictures, 1974. Director: Karel Reisz; screenwriter: James Toback. Cast: James Caan (Alex Freed), Paul Sorvino (Hips), Lauren Hutton (Billie), Morris Carnovsky (A.R. Lowenthal), Jacqueline Brookes (Naomi Freed), Burt Young (Carmine), Carmine Caridi, Stuart Margolin, Vic Tayback.

Those familiar with the Dostoyevsky novel will note that the producers have taken many liberties with his work. Perhaps that's why neither production gives him any credit. Each shows how gambling can destroy lives. In the first movie, Frank Morgan is a gambler reduced to thievery and eventual suicide because of his addiction. Even Ethel Barrymore is destroyed by one last—and fatal—

fling at the tables. In the remake, Caan is a college professor, heavily in debt to gamblers, who borrows the money from his mother to pay what he owes. Instead, he blows it all at Las Vegas and gets deeper in trouble with the underworld. Don't bet what you can't afford to lose is advice neither Peck nor Caan would accept.

352 The Great White Way

Based on the story "Cain and Mabel" by Harry Charles Witwer. Story: Press agent Jack Murray, trying to kill two birds with one stone, romantically links the names of his only two clients, prizefighter Joe Cain and follies dancer Mabel Vandergrift. Things work out so well the two actually fall in love, but Brock Morton, jealous owner of Mabel's show, threatens to pull his backing unless Mabel breaks up with Joe. To save the show and their love, Joe buys out Morton by agreeing to meet the British boxing champion. Joe wins the bout, Mabel's show is saved and the two can make their future plans together.

Cosmopoliton Corp./Goldwyn, 1924 (original). Silent. Director: E. Mason Hopper; screenwriters: L. Dayle and Luther Reed. Cast: Anita Stewart (Mabel Vandergrift), Oscar Shaw (Joe Cain), T. Roy Barnes (Jack Murray), Tom Lewis, Dore Davidson, Hal Forde, Ned Wayburn, G.L. "Tex" Rickard, Harry Watson, Olin Howard.

• ***Cain and Mabel*** (remake). Cosmopolitan/Warner Bros., 1936. Director: Lloyd Bacon; screenwriter: Laird Dayle. Cast: Marion Davies (Mabel O'Dare), Clark Gable (Larry Cain), Allen Jenkins (Dodo), Roscoe Karns (Reilly), Walter Catlett (Jake Sherman), David Carlyle (Ronny Cauldwell), Hobart Cavanaugh, Ruth Donnelly, Pert Kelton, William Collier, Sr.

These comedy-dramas nicely blend show business and the fight world, with many celebrities of each appearing as themselves in the silent version. The 1936 piece has Marion Davies and Clark Gable pleasantly handling the comedy aspects of the story of a contrived romance between a prizefighter and a show girl that develops into the real thing.

The Greeks Had a Word for Them *see* **The Gold Diggers**

353 The Green Goddess

Based on the play by William Archer. Story: Major Crespin, his wife and Dr. Traherne flee a Hindu uprising but their plane crashes at a distant kingdom where they are taken prisoner by the Rajah of Rukh, who informs them that they will be killed in retaliation for the approaching execution of the Rajah's three brothers by the British. Crespin is able to send a radio message for help before being shot by the Rajah. British pilots arrive in time to rescue Mrs. Crespin and Dr. Traherne.

Distinctive Productions/Goldwyn-Cosmopolitan, 1923 (original). Silent. Director: Sidney Olcott; screenwriter: Forrest Halsey. Cast: George Arliss (Rajah of Rukh), Alice Joyce (Lucilla Crespin), David Powell (Dr. Traherne), Harry T. Morey (Major Crespin), Jetta Goudal, Ivan Simpson, William Worthington.

• ***The Green Goddess*** (remake). Warner Bros., 1930. Director: Alfred Green; screenwriter: Julien Josephson. Cast: George Arliss (The Rajah), H.B. Warner (Crespin), Alice Joyce (Lucilla Crespin), Ralph Forbes (Dr. Traherne), David Tearle, Reginald Sheffield, Nigel De Brulier, Betty Boyd, Ivan Simpson.

• ***Adventures in Iraq*** (remake). Warner Bros., 1943. Director: D. Ross Lederman; screenwriters: George B. Rilson and Robert E. Kent. Cast: John Loder (George Torrence), Ruth Ford (Tess Torrence), Warren Douglas (Doug Everett), Paul Cavanaugh (Sheik Ahmid Bel Nor), Barry Bernard, Peggy Carson.

The fine star and character actor George Arliss repeated his silent role in the 1930 remake, with the plot remaining essentially the same. In the 1943 film, the play was produced as an indifferent adventure yarn with a roster of little-talent B actors and actresses, who fall into the hands of some Nazi-Arabs. The updating didn't do a thing for the film.

354 Greetings

Based on a screenplay by Brian De Palma and Charles Hirsch. Story: In trying to cope with contemporary society, three young New Yorkers, Paul Shaw, Lloyd Clay, and Jon Rubin, are respectively trying to avoid the draft, solve the John F. Kennedy assassination and persuade young women to disrobe to suit their peeping Tom fixation.

West End Films/Sigma III, 1968 (original). Director: Brian De Palma; screenwriters: Charles Hirsch and DePalma. Cast: Jonathan Warden (Paul Shaw), Robert De Niro (Jon Rubin), Gerritt Graham (Lloyd Clay), Richard Hamilton, Megan McCormick, Bettina Kugen, Jack Cowley, Jane Lee Salmons, Ashley Oliver, Melvin Marguiles, Cynthia Peltz, Peter Maloney, Ruth Alda.

• ***Hi, Mom!*** (sequel). West End Films/Sigma III, 1970. Director: Brian De Palma; screenwriters: De Palma and Charles Hirsch. Cast: Robert De Niro (Jon Rubin), Charles Durnham (Superintendent), Allen Garfield (Joe Banner), Jennifer Salt (Judy Bishop), Gerritt Graham (Gerrit Wood), Nelson Peltz, Hector Valentin Lino, Jr., Carole Leverett.

In the sequel to the antiestablishment film, Robert De Niro, employed by pornographic filmmaker Allen Garfield, trains his camera on the windows of a high rise. Among his subjects are a revolutionary, a playboy, a middle-class family, and a trio of girls, one of whom, Jennifer Salt, he decides to seduce. During their lovemaking, his camera tips, falls and fails to capture the special moment, thus ending his career as a blue movie photographer. The film moves on to other equally uninteresting episodes in his life. The films are nothing to praise, but both De Palma and De Niro show the promise on which they will later deliver.

Greyfriar's Bobby *see* **Challenge to Lassie**

Greystoke, the Legend of Tarzan *see* **Tarzan of the Apes**

The Grissom Gang *see* **No Orchids for Miss Blandish**

Guadalcanal Diary *see* **The Lost Patrol**

355 The Guardsman

Based on the play *Der Leibgardist* by Ferenc Molnar. Story: An actor is jealous and suspicious of his actress-wife of six months and so to test her, he sends passionate love letters and flowers to her, supposedly from a Russian Cossack guardsman inflamed by her beauty and talent. When the wife arranges a rendezvous with her unknown admirer, the actor impersonates his creation and attempts to make love to her. With things going too well, he reveals himself to his wife, who claims she knew all along that the guardsman and her husband were one and the same. Believing his performance to have been perfect, the actor is forever perplexed. Did she or didn't she really know?

MGM, 1931 (original). Director: Sidney Franklin; screenwriters: Ernest Vajda and Claudine West. Cast: Alfred Lunt (the Actor), Lynn Fontanne (the Actress), Roland Young, Maude Eburne, Zasu Pitts, Herman Bing, Ann Dvorak.

• ***The Chocolate Soldier*** (remake). MGM, 1941. Director: Roy Del Ruth; screenwriters: Leonard Lee and Keith Winter, based on Molnar's play and Oscar Strauss' operetta *Der Tapfere Soldat (The Chocolate Soldier)*. Cast: Nelson Eddy (the Actor, Karl Lang/Vasili Vasilovich Varonofsky), Rise Stevens (Maria Lanyi), Nigel Bruce, Florence Bates, Dorothy Gilmore, Nydia Westman, Max Barwyn.

This frothy sex farce of marital infidelity was performed by Lunt and Fontanne consistent with the high standards that they had developed with their numerous stage triumphs. Both the National Board of Review and *The Film Daily* named it among their ten best pictures of the year. But Lunt and Fontanne decided this medium was not to be for them, as they repeatedly turned down offers to appear together in other films. *The Guardsman* was remade as a musical when MGM was unable to gain George Bernard Shaw's permission to use his play *The Arms and the Man* which was the libretto for the operetta *The Chocolate Soldier* by Oscar Strauss. Undaunted, the studio combined the music of Strauss and the story of *The Guardsman* and called the result *The Chocolate Soldier*. Despite the obstacles, the musical was successful because of the fine performances by Rise Stevens and Nelson Eddy. Songs in the film included "My Hero," "The Chocolate Soldier Man," "Song of the Flea" and "While My Lady Sleeps."

Guilty As Charged *see* **Guilty As Hell**

356 The Greene Murder Case

Based on the novel by S.S. Van Dine. Story: Erudite amateur detective Philo Vance quizzes nine suspects after the murder of eccentric millionaire Chester Greene in his New York mansion. Before he can solve the case, two more of the Greene family are murdered when the least suspected falls to his or her death while committing yet another murder.

Paramount Pictures, 1929 (original). Director: Frank Tuttle; screenwriter: Louise Long. Cast: William Powell (Philo Vance), Florence Elderidge (Shelia

Greene), Ulrich Haupt (Dr. Von Blon), Jean Arthur (Ada Greene), Eugene Pallette (Sgt. Heath), E.H. Calvert (John F.X. Markham), Gertrude Norman (Mrs. Tobias Greene), Lowell Drew, Morgan Farley, Brandon Hurst.

• ***Night of Mystery*** (remake). Paramount Pictures, 1937. Director: E.A. DuPont; screenwriters: Frank Partos and Gladys Unger. Cast: Grant Richards (Philo Vance), Roscoe Karns (Sgt. Heath), Helen Burgess (Ada Greene), Ruth Coleman (Sibella), Elizabeth Patterson (Mrs. Greene), Harvey Stephens, June Martel, Purnell Pratt, Colin Tapley, James Bush, Ivan Simpson.

William Powell is highly professional as the likeable amateur detective, but by the time of the remake with Grant Richards, audiences expected more of their murder mysteries than merely piling up bodies and finally settling on the least likely suspect as the murderer. The remake is definitely "B" caliber material and hardly worth a 66-minute investment.

Gribouille *see* **Heart of Paris**

357 Guilty As Hell

Based on the play *Riddle Me This* by Daniel N. Rubin. Story: Dr. Tindall has planned the perfect crime. He puts on rubber gloves, strangles his faithless wife, sets a trap for her lover, establishes an ironclad alibi, and sits back to watch the law finish the job on the cheating couple. He almost gets away with it, if it were not for the combined actions of reporter Russell Kirk, who is hot for the suspect's sister, and police detective McKinley.

Paramount Pictures, 1932 (original). Director: Earle Kenton; screenwriters: Arthur Kober and Frank Partos. Cast: Edmund Lowe (Russell Kirk), Victor McLaglen (Detective McKinley), Richard Arlen (Frank Marsh), Ralph Ince (Jack Reed), Adrienne Ames (Vera Marsh), Henry Stephenson (Dr. Tindall), Elizabeth Patterson, Noel Francis, Arnold Lucy, Willard Robertson.

• ***Night Club Scandal*** (remake). Paramount Pictures, 1937. Director: Ralph Murphy; screenwriter: Lillie Howard. Cast: John Barrymore (Dr. Ernest Tindall), Lynne Overman (Russell Kirk), Louise Campbell (Vera Marsh), Charles Bickford (Capt. McKinley), Harvey Stephens (Frank Marsh), J. Carrol Naish (Jack Reed), Evelyn Brent, Elizabeth Patterson, Cecil Cunningham.

Variety was concerned that the "hell" in the title of the first film would hurt business. It was released in Great Britain as *Guilty As Charged.* It's not a whodunit, because the audience sees the doctor strangle his wife. The suspense comes as Victor McLaglen and Edmund Lowe piece together a circumstantial evidence case against Richard Arlen, the unfortunate lover of the murdered woman, but get on the right track just in time to save an innocent man from the electric chair. In the remake, John Barrymore's looks had faded as had his ability to remember lines, but he still was a stylish performer as the doctor who strangles his wife and gives himself an almost airtight alibi and arranges for his wife's lover to take the blame for her murder. If he didn't have to kill a nightclub owner and racketeer who knew his secret, he might have gotten away with murder. Charles Bickford as the investigating detective is so dumb, it's a wonder he can find his badge. Lynne Overman, as the reporter, stumbles over rather than deduces the truth.

358 Gulliver's Travels

Based on the novel by Jonathan Swift. Story: Of course Swift's story about Gulliver in the lands of Lilliput and Blefuscu is a satire, but over the years the targets of his wit have been forgotten and the tale has become basically a story for children. In Lilliput, he is a giant who is captured by his tiny hosts, but he ultimately plays peacemaker and cupid for them.

• ***Gulliver's Travels*** (remake). Paramount Pictures, 1939. Director: David Fleischer. Animated. Cast: Lanny Ross and Jessica Dragonette (voices).

• ***The Three Worlds of Gulliver*** (remake). Columbia, U.S./Spain, 1960. Director: Jack Sher; screenwriters: Arthur Ross and Jack Sher. Cast: Kerwin Mathews (Gulliver), Basil Sydney, Mary Ellis, Jo Murrow, June Thornburn, Gregorie Aslan.

• ***Gulliver's Travels*** (remake). EMI, Great Britain, 1977. Director: Peter Hunt; screenwriter: Don Black. Cast: Richard Harris (Gulliver), Catherine Schell, Norman Shelley, voices of Meredith Edwards, Julian Glover, Murray Melvin.

Swift's tale was also filmed in 1902, 1903, 1905, 1923, 1933, 1935, 1960, 1965, 1970 and 1978. The 1939 piece is Paramount's answer to Walt Disney, but their animated full-length feature can't compare to the master's *Snow White and the Seven Dwarfs* (1937). The Ralph Rainger and Leo Robin song "Faithful Forever" was nominated for an Academy Award, but "All's Well" is a better piece. The special effects of the 1960 picture are quite good and the film is fine for those who like stories made for children. In the 1977 version only Gulliver is human with all others animated. The music by Michel Legrand is extremely forgettable.

The Gun Runners *see* **To Have and Have Not**

359 Gunga Din

Based on a story by Ben Hecht and Charles MacArthur, and the poem by Rudyard Kipling. Story: It's the rousing adventure yarn of three sergeants stationed at India's northern boundary in Victorian times. The three fun-loving brawlers are Cutter, a Cockney always on the trail of a possible fortune, MacChesney, the prototype regular army Irishman, and the educated Ballantine, who threatens to break up the trio by leaving the service to marry pretty Emmy Stubbins and enter the tea business. Following the three like a faithful dog is a native water carrier, the bhisti Gunga Din, who dreams of becoming a soldier like his heroes.

Just as Ballantine is making his choice of romance over comradeship, the regiment becomes aware of the resurgence of the cult of Thugee, whose members are sworn to commit murder to honor their god Kali. They carry small pickaxes with which they dig the graves of their intended victims, whom they strangle with lengths of cloth. Cutter, in search of treasure with Gunga Din,

Douglas Fairbanks, Jr., Cary Grant and Victor McLaglen take up the "white man's burden" and send a lot of Indians to their death in Gunga Din *(RKO, 1939).*

walks in on a mass prayer session of the sect. He sends Din to get help. MacChesney tricks Ballentine into accompanying him on a rescue mission. They are able to take the Guru hostage but the latter throws himself into a pit of poisonous snakes so his followers will continue with their plan to ambush an approaching regiment. Din saves the day with a bugle call that alerts the regiment to the danger, but is killed. The Thugee are routed and Din is given a full military funeral accompanied by Kipling's famous line, "You're a better man than I am, Gunga Din!"

RKO Pictures, 1939 (original). Director: George Stevens; screenwriters: Joel Sayre, Fred Guiol and William Faulkner. Cast: Cary Grant (Cutter), Victor McLaglen (MacChesney), Douglas Fairbanks, Jr. (Ballantine), Sam Jaffe

Dean Martin, Peter Lawford and Frank Sinatra pause for a moment's reflection before taking up the "white man's burden" and sending a lot of Indians to their death in Sergeants 3 *(United Artists, 1962).*

(Gunga Din), Eduardo Ciannelli (Guru), Joan Fontaine (Emmy Stebbins), Montagu Love, Robert Coote, Abner Biberman.

• ***Soldiers Three*** (remake). MGM, 1951. Director: Tay Garnett; screenwriters: Marguerite Roberts, Tom Reed and Malcolm Stuart Boyland. Cast: Stewart Granger (Pvt. Archie Ackroyd), Walter Pidgeon (Col. Brunswick), David Niven (Capt. Pindenny), Robert Newton (Pvt. Jack Sykes), Cyril Cusak (Pvt. Dennis Malloy), Greta Gynt, Frank Allenby, Robert Coote, Dan O'Herlihy, Michael Ansara.

• ***Sergeants 3*** (remake). United Artists, 1962. Director: John Sturges; screenwriter: W.R. Burnett. Cast: Frank Sinatra (First Sgt. Mike Merry), Dean Martin (Sgt. Chip Deal), Sammy Davis, Jr. (Jonah Williams), Peter Lawford (Sgt. Larry

Barrett), Henry Silva (Mountain Hawk), Joey Bishop, Buddy Lester, Ruta Lee.

There was an independent production based on the story of Gunga Din made in 1964, called *The Last Blast.* Nothing more need be said about this unnecessary and uninteresting remake.

Although Gunga Din is a sympathetic character, so is Uncle Tom, and critics in India rightly grew tired of seeing their people portrayed as fanatics and savages, especially when the British were the imperialists. The white man's burden of the movie was not the only lesson of *Gunga Din;* grown men enjoyed the riotous life of fighting and carousing together, with women as only spoiled things to be enjoyed between battles.

The 1951 movie is a Gunga Din–like film without a Gunga Din. It consists mainly of the comical adventure antics of three soldiers, Granger, Newton and Cusak in India, about the same time as in the previous story. It's an insubstantial film not on a par with its predecessor.

In the cavalry and Indians remake *(Sergeants 3),* macho actors such as Frank Sinatra and Dean Martin were right in step as men who fought the redman and could captivate anything in skirts. Davis as the westernized Gunga Din was considerably more savvy than his noble but ignorant predecessor but his position vis-à-vis the brave Indian fighters Sinatra, Martin, and Lawford was clearly inferior. Henry Silva was as menancing as Eduardo Cianelli, but the latter was a better actor and at least could point to a cause that forgave his murderous activities.

If one can ignore the racist and sexist aspects of the films and most people have, *Gunga Din* will be found to be an exciting and winning adventure yarn filled with humor and heroics, several enjoyable if immature characters, a lovely villain and the touching humanity of the title character. The other two movies, however, are pieces of fluff, lacking in the charm of the original. The Sinatra-Martin-Lawford-Davis picture is just a continuation of the antics of the "Rat Pack" started in *Ocean's Eleven* (1960).

360 The Guns of Navarone

Based on the novel by Alistair MacLean. Story: In 1943, an Allied force is trapped on the island of Kheros in the Aegean Sea. The only escape route is through a narrow channel dominated by two huge German guns buried deep in the rocks of Navarone. Since the guns are impregnable against air or sea attack, a small guerilla team is sent in to destroy the guns. Along the way, they discover that one of their members is a traitor who is informing the Germans of their plans. This one is killed and with some additional loss of life of other members of their party, they are successful in blowing up the guns.

Columbia Pictures, 1961 (original). Director: J. Lee Thompson; screenwriter: Carl Foreman. Cast: Gregory Peck (Mallory), David Niven (Miller), Anthony Quinn (Andrea), Stanley Baker (Brown), Anthony Quayle (Franklin), Irene Papas (Maria), Gia Scala (Anna), James Darren (Pappadimos), James Robertson Justice, Richard Harris, Bryan Forbes, Allan Cuthbertson.

• ***Force 10 from Navarone*** (sequel). American International, Great Britain,

1978. Director: Guy Hamilton; screenwriters: Robin Chapman and Carl Foreman. Cast: Robert Shaw (Mallory), Harrison Ford (Barnsby), Edward Fox (Miller), Barbara Bach (Maritza), Franco Nero (Lescover), Carl Weathers (Weaver), Richard Kiel (Drazac), Angus MacInnes, Michael Byrne, Alan Badel, Christopher Malcolm.

What makes the second film a sequel to the first is that some of the survivors of the assault on the guns of Navarone are sent to Yugoslavia to blow up a bridge that is important to the Germans. It's a routine war melodrama but with plenty of action, intrigue and plot twists.

Gypsy Colt *see* **Lassie Come Home**

H

361 Hail the Conquering Hero

Based on a screenplay by Preston Sturges. Story: Woodrow Truesmith, medically discharged from the U.S. Marines after only one month of service because of hay fever, keeps up the myth that he is not only a gyrene but one who has seen plenty of action. He is befriended by six real marines, who dress him up in a uniform, place their decorations on his chest and take him home. He is greeted as a hero. In gratitude for all he has done, the town pays off his mother's mortgage on her home, and plans to build a statue of Woodrow and his father, who had been a marine killed in World War I. They even offer him the mayoral nomination. In the end he confesses that he is a phony but not before he has endeared himself to his community and all is forgiven and he is still treated as a hero.

Paramount Pictures, 1944 (original). Director and screenwriter: Preston Sturges. Cast: Eddie Bracken (Woodrow Truesmith), Ella Raines (Libby), Bill Edwards (Forest Noble), Raymond Walburn (Mayor Noble), William Demarest (Sergeant), Jimmie Dundee (Corporal), Georgia Caine (Mrs. Truesmith), Alan Bridge, James Damore, Freddie Steele, Stephen Gregory, Len Hendry, Esther Howard.

• ***The Reluctant Astronaut*** (remake). Universal Pictures, 1967. Director: Edward J. Montagne; screenwriters: Jim Fritzell and Everett Greenbaum, based on an idea by Don Knotts. Cast: Don Knotts (Roy Fleming), Leslie Nielsen (Maj. Fred Gifford), Joan Freeman (Ellie Jackson), Jesse White (Donelli), Jeanette Nolan (Mrs. Fleming), Arthur O'Connell (Buck Fleming), Frank McGrath, Joan Shawlee, Guy Raymond, Nydia Westman, Paul Hartman, Robert F. Simon.

Eddie Bracken might have had a longer and more successful career had Preston Sturges lived to write and direct more vehicles for the comic. The 1944 piece is still funny and is filled with more human interest than *The Miracle of Morgan's Creek*, the other major collaboration between Sturges and Bracken. The remake, while giving no credit to Sturges, is certainly a logical extension of his piece. Don Knotts, a timid man terrified of heights, learns that he has been accepted in the astronaut training program, after his father entered his name as an applicant. When he arrives at the space center, he finds that he has been accepted as a janitor. This doesn't jibe with the hero's send-off that he received when he left home for Houston, so he lets the home folks think what they will. His father and two cronies arrive for a visit, and Don pretends he is an astronaut, with disastrous results. He loses his job as a janitor, but is soon called back when the United States decides to prove their space capsule is superior to the Russians and can be handled by the least qualified astronaut around—a perfect description of Knotts. Somehow he carries it off and lands back on earth a national hero.

Half a Sinner *see* **Alias the Deacon**

Half a Sixpence *see* **Kipps**

362 Hamlet

Based on the play by William Shakespeare. Story: Shakespeare's complex tragedy is the story of the brooding Prince of Denmark, Hamlet, who learns that his father was murdered by his uncle, Claudius, who has since become king and married Hamlet's mother, Gertrude. The young prince agonizes over how to avenge his father. He must also decide what to do about the Lady Ophelia, who is surely a bit mad.

• ***Hamlet*** (remake). Two Cities Films, 1948. Director: Laurence Olivier; screenwriters: Laurence Olivier and Alan Dent. Cast: Laurence Olivier (Hamlet), Basil Sydney (Claudius), Eileen Herlie (Gertrude), Jean Simmons (Ophelia), Felix Aylmer (Polonius), Terence Morgan (Laertes), Harcourt Williams (First Player), Patrick Troughton (Player King), Tony Tarver (Player Queen), Peter Cushing (Osric), Stanley Holloway (Gravedigger), Russell Thorndyke, John Laurie, Esmond Knight, Anthony Quayle, Niall MacGinnis, John Gielgud (voice only), Norman Wooland.

• ***Hamlet*** (remake). Columbia Pictures, 1969. Director: Tony Richardson; screenwriter: William Shakespeare. Cast: Nicol Williamson (Hamlet), Gordon Jackson (Horatio), Anthony Hopkins (Claudius), Judy Parfitt (Gertrude), Mark Dignam (Polonius), Michael Pennington (Laertes), Marianne Faithful (Ophelia), Ben Aris, Clive Graham, Peter Gate, John Carney, Richard Everett, Roger Livesey, Robin Chadwick, Ian Colier, Michael Elphick.

Hamlet has been brought to the screen many times, including silent versions in 1900, 1904, 1905, each year from 1907 through 1917, 1919, 1920, 1922, 1927 and 1928. Sound versions and Hamlet-like films were produced in 1935, 1945, 1952, 1953, 1959, 1960, 1962, 1964, 1965, 1967, 1968, 1972, 1973, 1976, 1977 and 1978.

It is generally accepted that the definitive Hamlet thus far is Olivier's version in 1948. For his outstanding performance, Sir Larry won the Academy Award as Best Actor and the film itself won the Oscar for Best Picture. Oscars were also given to Roger K. Furse and Carmen Dillon for Art and Set Direction, respectively, and to Furse for Costume Design. Other nonwinning nominees for Academy Awards were Olivier for the screenplay, Jean Simmons for Best

Actress and William Walton for Best Musical Score. It's a compelling production, beautifully photographed in black and white, even if perhaps too much film is spent on looking down gloomy corridors. Olivier's renditions of Shakespeare's familiar speeches are inspiring. The performances of Basil Sydney, Eileen Herlie, Jean Simmons, Felix Aylmer and Stanley Holloway are each deserving of admiring praise. It must be reported that some critics found the film cold and marred by injudicious text-cutting.

Producer Neil Hortley and Tony Richardson give William Shakespeare sole credit for the screenplay of their version of *Hamlet,* so we suppose that they are claiming that their production is a more faithful translation of the play to the screen. This may be so, but it does not make it the better film. Although Williamson gives an excellent impersonation of the brooding prince, many others in the cast seem merely along for the ride. It would be too obvious to comment on Marianne Faithful's performance as Ophelia by making a pun on her last name, so we will let it pass. Of the other film versions of the play, the 1964 Russian production based on a translation by Boris Pasternak and directed by Grigori Kozintsev impresses with its strong acting and interesting photography.

Hammer the Toff *see* **Salute the Toff**

Hammersmith Is Out *see* **Faust**

Hands of the Ripper *see* **The Lodger**

363 Handy Andy

Based on the play *Merry Andrew* by Lewis Beach. Story: It's a star vehicle for Will Rogers as a midwestern druggist whose wife forces him to retire to further her social ambitions. There's plenty of crackerbarrel philosophy thrown around.

Fox Film Corporation, 1934 (original). Director: David Butler; screenwriters: William Counselman and Henry Johnson. Cast: Will Rogers (Andrew Yates), Peggy Wood (Ernestine Yates), Conchita Montenegro (Fleurette), Mary Carlisle (Janice Yates), Roger Imhof (Doc Burmeister), Robert Taylor (Lloyd Burmeister), Paul Harvey, Grace Goodall, Gregory Gaye.

• ***Young As You Feel*** (remake). Twentieth Century–Fox, 1940. Director: Malcolm St. Clair; screenwriters: Joseph Hoffman and Stanley Rauh. Cast: Jed Prouty (John Jones), Spring Byington (Mrs. Jones), Joan Valerie (Bonnie), Russell Gleason (Herbert), Ken Howell (Jack), George Ernest, June Carlson, Florence Roberts, Billy Mahan, Helen Erickson, George Givot.

Will Rogers films were usually predictable, with the homespun comedian merely playing himself, but they were inevitably popular with a large number of fans of this unique man. The stories seldom were very much, as is the case in this entry, but audiences enjoyed hearing Rogers talk and liked the fact that he was able to resolve problems mostly because of his persuasiveness. The remake was the sixteenth in the long-running Jones Family saga. The Jones films were nothing special, but they had their loyal fans who felt comfortable with the comings and goings of familiar people in situations bordering on the ordinary. In this version, the Joneses have to go to New York to save son Jack from a scheming crook. There's very little action and only modest adventure, but such movies served their purposes before TV.

364 The Happy Ending

Based on the play by Ian Hay. Story: Wastrel Denis Craddock, who has roamed the world for years, tries to return to his family, but his wife Mildred has brought up their children to believe that he died a hero, and she sees no reason to burst that bubble.

Gaumont, Great Britain, 1925 (original). Silent. Director: George A. Cooper; screenwriter: P.L. Mannock. Cast: Fay Compton (Mildred Craddock), Jack Buchanan (Captain Dale Conway), Joan Barry (Molly Craddock), Jack Hobbs (Denis Craddock), Gladys Jennings (Joan Craddock), Eric Lewis, Donald Searle, Drusilla Wills, Pat Doyle, A.G. Poulton, Benita Hume, Doris Mansell.

• ***The Happy Ending*** (remake). Gaumont, Great Britain, 1931. Director: Millard Webb; screenwriter: H. Fowler Mear. Cast: Anne Grey (Mildred Craddock), Benita Hume (Yvonne), George Barraud (Denis Craddock), Alf Goddard (Alf), Cyril Raymond (Anthony Fenwick), Daphne Courtenay, Alfred Drayton, Irene Russell.

These films should not be confused with the movie of the same name produced in 1969, starring Jean Simmons as a middle-aged woman who is bored and disillusioned with her marriage of 16 years to John Forsythe. The title of the films under consideration is misleading: the husband's unsuccessful attempt to return to his wife ends with him dying in a hospital.

Happy Is the Bride *see* **Quiet Wedding**

Harmony At Home *see* **The Family Upstairs**

365 Harold Teen

Based on the comic strip character by Carl Ed. Story: Farmboy Harold Teen moves to the city to attend high school where he becomes involved with a variety of extracurricular activities, including football and dramatics. He convinces his classmates to put on a western movie rather than a class play. Part of the script calls for blowing up a dam, which just happens to cut off water to Harold's country homestead. After the explosion, Harold goes on the lam, but returns in time to be a hero in a football game.

First National Pictures, 1928 (original). Silent. Director: Mervyn LeRoy; screenwriter: Tom J. Geraghty. Cast: Arthur Lake (Harold Teen), Mary Brian (Lillums Lovewell), Lucien Littlefield (Dad Jenks), Jack Duffy (Grandpop Teen), Alice White (Giggles Dewberry), Jack Egan, Hedda Hopper, Ben Hall, William Bakewell, Lincoln Stedman, Fred Kelsey, Jane Keckley.

• ***Harold Teen*** (remake). Warner Bros., 1934. Director: Murray Roth;

screenwriters: Paul C. Smith and Al Cohn. Cast: Hal LeRoy (Harold), Rochelle Hudson (Lillums), Patricia Ellis (Mimi), Guy Kibbee (Pa Lovewell), Hugh Herbert, Hobart Cavanaugh, Chic Chandler, Eddie Tamblyn, Douglas Dumbrille, Clara Blandick.

The comic strip "Harold Teen" had a long run of popularity in daily newspapers, with the 1920s being its high point. These two movies based on the character are no better or worse than dozens of others dealing with high school life and pulling out the victory in a sporting event at the last moment. Arthur Lake would move on to greater success as another comic strip character, Dagwood Bumstead, in the long-lived *Blondie* series. In the second film, Hal LeRoy as Harold Teen works for a newspaper and hobnobs with bankers and other town leaders. Whatever happened to Hal LeRoy?

366 Harper

Based on the novel *The Moving Target* by Ross McDonald. Story: Private eye Lew Harper is asked by lawyer friend Albert Graves to investigate the disappearance of the millionaire husband of Elaine Sampson, a bitter cripple. Harper also meets Elaine's spoiled stepdaughter, Miranda, and their handsome pilot, Alan Taggert. In no time at all, Harper is playing up to plump alcoholic ex-starlet Fay Estabrook, questioning Betty Fraley, a drug-addicted singer, and visiting a religious fanatic, Claude, on a mountaintop site given to him by the missing man. All of these people are red herrings however, as Harper finds Sampson's body and the murderer is none other than lawyer Albert Graves who hated the deceased and loved his daughter Miranda.

Warner Bros., 1966 (original). Director: Jack Smight; screenwriter: William Goldman. Cast: Paul Newman (Lew Harper), Lauren Bacall (Mrs. Sampson), Julie Harris (Betty Fraley), Arthur Hill (Albert Graves), Pamela Tiffin (Miranda Sampson), Robert Wagner (Alan Taggert), Robert Webber (Dwight Troy), Shelley Winters (Fay Estabrook), Janet Leigh (Susan Harper), Harold Gould, Roy Jenson, Strother Martin, Martin West, Jacqueline De Witt.

• ***The Drowning Pool*** (sequel). Warner Bros., 1975. Director: Stuart Rosenberg; screenwriters: Tracy Keenan Wynn, Lorenzo Semple, Jr., and Walter Hill. Cast: Paul Newman (Harper), Joanne Woodward (Iris Devereux), Carol Browne, Tony Franciosa, Murray Hamilton, Gail Strickland, Richard Jaeckel.

In the dreary sequel, Newman goes to New Orleans to help former lover Woodward out of a jam, and ends up investigating a murder. The title refers to an actual pool in which one of the villains sticks Newman and Carol Browne and then turns on the water. As they are fairly securely tied, the baddie is counting on them drowning. No such luck, they escape so this less-than-gripping mystery can continue.

367 The Harrad Experiment

Based on the novel by Robert H. Rimmer. Story: Rimmer's novel dealt with the sociological premise that the world would be a far better place if people spent most of their time making love—or more precisely screwing, since love didn't seem to have much to do with it. In describing how an experiment with this philosophy was incorporated into the curriculum of a college, Rimmer did not titillate, nor cater to prurient interests—he bored his readers with repeated descriptions of sexual coupling and how happy it made everybody, and wasn't this going to make everything just wonderful? The film version is not quite as good as the book and a whole lot less interesting. It's enough to get people to swear off sex.

Cinerama, 1973 (original). Director: Ted Post; screenwriter: Ted Cassedy. Cast: James Whitmore (Philip), Tippi Hedren (Margaret), Don Johnson (Stanley), B. Kirby, Jr. (Harry), Laurie Walters (Sheila), Victoria Thompson (Beth), Elliot Street, Sharon Taggart, Robert Middleton, Billy Sands, Melody Patterson.

• ***Harrad Summer*** (sequel). Cinerama, 1974. Director: Steven Hillard Stern; screenwriter: Morth Thaw. Cast: Robert Reiser (Stanley), Laurie Walters (Sheila), Richard Doran (Harry), Victoria Thompson, Emaline Henry, Bill Dana.

Having not completely turned off all the college students to sex, in the equally boring sequel the participants in a sexual EST–like training discover they can apply their knowledge in their daily lives living in "straight" society. It's not a question as to whether the premise is ludicrous, as much as who cares.

Harrad Summer *see* **The Harrad Experiment**

Harriet Craig *see* **Craig's Wife**

368 The Harvester

Based on the novel by Gene Stratton Porter. Story: David Langston, who harvests medicinal herbs found in forests, comes across Ruth during one of his treks and finds her to perfectly match his notion of the ideal girl for him. They meet several times and David tells Ruth of his love for her, but she is overcome by shyness. David convinces her to marry him but she shrinks from his advances. He shows great patience and understanding and when she becomes deathly ill, he sends for Dr. Harmon, who Ruth had once promised to marry. As Harmon cares for Ruth, she perceives that he is actually in love with the nurse and when she recovers she happily returns to David, who had left her, feeling that he had failed her.

R-C Pictures/F.B.O., 1927 (original). Silent. Director: Leo Meehan; screenwriter: Dorothy Yost. Cast: Orville Caldwell (David Langston), Natalie Kingston (Ruth), Will R. Walling (Henry Jamison), Edward Hearn (Dr. Harmon), Jay Hunt, Lola Todd, Fanny Midgley.

• ***The Harvester*** (remake). Republic Pictures, 1936. Director: Joseph Stanley; screenwriters: Gertrude Orr, Homer Cory, Robert Lee Johnson and. Elizabeth Meehan. Cast: Alice Brady (Mrs. Biddle), Russell Hardie (David Langston), Ann Rutherford (Ruth Jameson), Frank Craven (Mr. Biddle), Cora

Sue Collins (Naomi Jameson), Emma Dunn, Eddie Nugent, Joyce Compton, Roy Atwell, Spencer Charters.

These tributes to rural life are mildly interesting domestic melodramas with adequate if not outstanding performances. In the second version of the Gene Stratton Porter story, Alice Brady plays an ambitious mother who pushes young farmer Russell Hardie into becoming engaged to her daughter, Ann Rutherford.

369 Hawaii

Based on the novel by James A. Michener. Story: A shipload of stern New England missionaries and their newly acquired wives sail for Hawaii to carry the word of God to the heathens. The sternest and most unbending of these is Abner Hale. His good wife, Jerusha, had been expected to wait for the return of sea captain Rafer Hoxworth to marry her, but duty was put ahead of personal happiness. In Hawaii, the Hales are royally received by the Queen, Malama. Jerusha easily makes friends with the natives but Abner is so sanctimonious that he refuses to make any concessions and rigidly imposes his will on the pleasure and peace-loving people. Other white men arrive at the islands and a measles epidemic succeeds in decimating the Hawaiians. Jerusha dies after having given birth to three sons and working unstintingly with and for her taskmaster husband, who is ultimately relieved of his ministry by the hierarchy of the church. Although somewhat mellowed in his old age, Abner feels righteous in the fact that he was unlike many others who had made that voyage so many years before. It was said of these missionaries-turned-entrepreneurs that "they came to Hawaii to do good, and they did well."

United Artists, 1966 (original). Director: George Roy Hill; screenwriters: Dalton Trumbo and Daniel Taradash. Cast: Julie Andrews (Jerusha Bromley), Max von Sydow (Abner Hale), Richard Harris (Rafer Hoxworth), Jocelyne La Garde (Malama), Manu Tupou (Keoki), Ted Nobriga (Kelolo), Elizabeth Logue (Noelani), Carroll O'Connor, Elizabeth Cole, Diane Sherry, Heather Menzies, Torin Thatcher, Gene Hackman, John Cullum, Lou Antonio.

• ***The Hawaiians*** (sequel). United Artists, 1970. Director: Tom Gries; screenwriter: James R. Webb. Cast: Charlton Heston (Whip Hoxworth), Geraldine Chaplin (Purity Hoxworth), John Philip Law (Noel Hoxworth), Tina Chen (Nyuk Tsin), Alec McCowen (Micah Hale), Mako (Mun Ki), Don Knight, Miko Mayama, Virginia Ann Lee, Naomi Stevens, Harry Townes, Khigh Dhiegh, Keye Luke, James Gregory, Lyle Bettger.

Michener's epic novel was long enough and contained enough history of the Hawaiian Islands to provide material for several more movies, but when the producers of the sequel squeezed so many of the author's interesting characters together in various selfish struggles for control of the islands, audiences yawned. Whereas they sat through the three-hour first movie because of the interesting conflict between the native Hawaiians and the "ugly New Englanders," it was just too much to expect that they would invest another two hours watching Charlton Heston act like a prejudiced Moses, who instead of parting the Red Sea, drills for water that allows him to irrigate the previously barren land and make a fortune.

The Hawaiians *see* **Hawaii**

370 He Couldn't Take It

Story by Dore Schary. Story: This film was produced with the intention of playing it only in small towns and the country where it was believed any entertainment, no matter how feeble, would be welcomed. Here Jimmy Case is a pugnacious ne'er-do-well trying to find some means of employment which will keep him in the bucks without being too strainful. He tries prizefighting, bus driving and work as a process server. Eleanor Rogers is a naive, gullible girl who can't even see the most obvious passes made by her boss, a crooked lawyer, who Jimmy Case links with the underworld. The plot is just enough to handle the action, which is meant to be featured.

Monogram Pictures, 1934 (original). Director: William Nigh; screenwriter: Dore Schary. Cast: Ray Walker (Jimmy Case), Virginia Cherrill (Eleanor Rogers), George E. Stone (Sammy Kohn), Stanley Fields (Sweet Sue), Dorothy Granger (Grace Clarice), Jane Darwell, Paul Porcasi, Donald Douglas, Astrid Allwyn.

• ***Here Comes Kelly*** (remake). Monogram Pictures, 1943. Director: William Beaudine; screenwriter: Charles R. Marion. Cast: Eddie Quillan (Jimmy Kelly), Joan Woodbury (Margie), Maxie Rosenbloom (Trixie Bell), Armida (Carmencita), Sidney Miller (Sammy Cohn), Mary Gordon, Ian Keith.

The second film's story is credited to Jeb Aschery, but it's sufficiently reminiscent of *He Couldn't Take It* to consider it an unofficial remake. Eddie Quillan, a cocky Irishman, can't hold a job because of his tendency to engage in fistfights. He gets in trouble with his girl, his mother, the law, becomes a process server and gets drafted into the army. Tain't much here, don't you know.

He Hired the Boss *see* **The Ten Dollar Raise**

371 Heart of Paris (Gribouille)

Based on an original screenplay by Marcel Achard. Story: An elderly idealist and dreamer, Camille Morestan, takes pity on friendless beauty Natalie Roguin, who has just been acquitted by a jury on which Camille served of murdering her lover. He invites her to stay in his home. His fatherly interest in Natalie is misinterpreted by his son Claude and her presence in a middle-class home disrupts everyone's life with almost tragic consequences.

Tri-National, France, 1939 (original). Director: Marc Allegret; screenwriters: H.G. Lustig, A. Thiraud and M. Kelber. Cast: Raimu (Camille Morestan), Jeanne Provost (Louise Morestan), Michele Morgan (Natalie Roguin), Gilbert Gil (Claude Morestan), Jean Worms, Carette, Marcel Andre, Jacques Gretillat.

• ***The Lady in Question*** (remake). Columbia Pictures, 1940. Director: Charles Vidor; screenwriter: Lewis Meltzer. Cast: Brian Aherne (Andre

Morestan), Rita Hayworth (Natalie Roguin), Glenn Ford (Pierre Morestan), Irene Rich (Michele Morestan), George Coulouris, Lloyd Corrigan, Evelyn Keyes, Edward Norris, Curt Bois, Frank Reicher.

The remake sticks pretty close to the French picture with Brian Aherne assuming Raimu's role and Rita Hayworth appearing as the defendant in a murder trial who, after being acquitted, is taken into Aherne's home without his family knowing of her past. Keeping his wife and children from discovering the problems she's seen keeps Aherne and Hayworth hopping. When Aherne's son, played by Glenn Ford, falls in love with Hayworth and finds out about her past, he dips into his father's strongbox to get money for their elopement. Everything turns out alright before the fade out.

372 Hearts in Exile

Based on the novel by John Oxenham. Story: Hope Ivanovna, who devotes her life to helping the poor, has many suitors. Among them are Serge Palma, a wealthy young man, poor student Paul Pavloff, and Count Nicolai, a Russian nobleman. She marries Serge, who agrees to put his money at her disposal for her charity work. Count Nicolai, intent on having Hope at any cost, arranges for her husband to be sent to Siberia for 15 years as a nihilist. He also has Paul sent away for five years. The two men meet on their way to exile and because Paul loves Hope, he offers to exchange places with Serge and accept the longer sentence. Meanwhile Count Nicolai presses his advantage, but Hope will not have him. Instead she goes to Siberia to be with her husband and is of course put with Paul, who has assumed Serge's identity. They live together rather than give away the exchange. When Serge escapes and comes to get Paul, he finds that his wife is in love with Paul. In the attempted escape by the trio, Serge is killed, leaving Paul and Hope together to live happily ever after.

World Film, 1915 (original). Silent. Director: James Young; screenwriter: Owen Davis. Cast: Clara Kimball Young (Hope Ivanovna), Vernon Steele (Paul Pavloff), Claude Fleming (Serge Palma), Montagu Love (Count Nicolai), Fred Truesdell, Paul McAllister, Bert Sharkey, Miss Selwynne.

• ***Hearts in Exile*** (remake). Warner Bros., 1929. Vitaphone. Silent. Director: Michael Curtiz; screenwriter: Harvey Gates. Cast: Dolores Costello (Vera Ivanovna), Grant Withers (Paul Pavloff), James Kirkwood (Baron Serge Palma), George Fawcett (Dmitri Ivanov), David Torrence, Olive Tell, Lee Moran, Tom Dugan, Rose Dione, William Irving, Carrie Daumery.

In the remake, the Count was eliminated and a baby who died in Siberia was added. Miss Costello, the daughter of a Moscow fishmonger, marries James Kirkwood when her student lover, Grant Withers, tells her he is not ready to settle down. Before long the three find themselves in Siberia, Costello with Withers who has taken Kirkwood's identity so the latter's exile from Costello will be less, and Kirkwood in another part of the province. Costello's child dies of exposure and when Kirkwood shows up and sees how much in love Costello and Withers are, he shoots himself during their escape attempt. Then, depending on which ending is used, the couple are either recaptured and sent back to finish out the exile, or remain free and live happily ever after.

373 Heat Lightning

Based on the play by Leon Abrams and George Abbott. Story: Olga, the mechanic-proprietress of an auto camp on the edge of a Southern California desert, becomes involved with murderers George and Jeff, the former once being her lover. When George tries to do her in, she plugs him.

Warner Bros., 1934. Director: Mervyn LeRoy; screenwriters: Brown Holmes and Warren Duff. Cast: Aline MacMahon (Olga), Preston Foster (George), Lyle Talbot (Jeff), Ann Dvorak (Myra), Glenda Farrell (Mrs. Tifton), Frank McHugh, Ruth Donnelly, Theodore Newton.

• ***Highways West*** (remake). Warner Bros., 1941. Director: William McGann; screenwriters: Allen Rivkin, Charles Kenyon and Kenneth Gamet. Cast: Brenda Marshall (Claire Foster), Arthur Kennedy (George Foster), Olympe Bradna (Myra Abbott), William Lundigan (Dave Warren), Slim Summerville (Gramps), Willie Best (Wellington), Frank Wilcox, John Ridgely, Dorothy Tree.

Aline MacMahon appeared miscast in the original, but she tried valiantly to bring some life to her part, which is more than can be said for others in the cast. In the remake, Brenda Marshall plays a wife who discovers her seemingly respectable husband is actually a gunman. Apparently, she's none too astute because Kennedy kills a bank teller early in the movie and for the rest of the film he's on the lam from the police, but most of the time she still thinks he's a traveling salesman. Guess she was too busy looking out for farmers' daughters to notice pursuing cops.

Heaven Can Wait *see* **Here Comes Mr. Jordan**

Heckyl and Mr. Hype *see* **Dr. Jekyll and Mr. Hyde**

374 Hedda Gabler

Based on the play by Henrik Ibsen. Story: Selfish Hedda Gabler, bored with her husband, Professor George Tesman, learns that a former suitor, alcoholic author Eilert Lovborg, has been reformed with the help of Hedda's former schoolmate, Thea Elvsted, and is writing again. Jealous and anxious to avenge herself on her old lover, Hedda entices Lovborg to jump off the wagon and she then burns his latest manuscript. Ever helpful, she supplies Eilert with pistols with which he commits suicide. Learning of the circumstances of the man's death, libertine Judge Brack offers to trade his silence for Hedda's favors. Unwilling to be controlled by anyone, Hedda turns the pistols on herself.

World Pictures, 1917 (original). Director: Frank Powell; screenwriter: Alfred Hickman. Cast: Nance O'Neill (Hedda Gabler), Aubrey Beattie (George Tesman), Einar Linden (Eilert Lovborg), Alfred Hickman (Judge Brack), Ruth Bryon (Thea Elvsted), Lillian Paige (Aunt Julia), Edith Campbell Walker (Mlle. Diana).

• ***Hedda Gabler*** (remake). Brut Productions, 1975. Director and screenwriter: Trevor Nunn. Cast: Glenda Jackson (Hedda Gabler), Peter Eyre (George Tesman), Patrick Stewart (Eilert Lovborg), Timothy West (Judge

Brack), Jennie Linden (Thea Elvsted), Constance Capman (Aunt Julie), Pam St. Clement (Bertha).

Hedda Gabler was also produced in Italy in 1919 and 1923 and in Germany in 1924. In 1917 critics weren't sure that the picture should be seen by mixed audiences because of the nature of the subject matter. They had no need to worry; the film did not do much at the box office. The 1975 Royal Shakespeare Company's stage production filming won Glenda Jackson an Academy Award nomination but generally the offering was considered flat and Miss Jackson's sarcastic performance anything but award-worthy.

Heliotrope *see* **Forgotten Faces**

Hell Up in Harlem *see* **Black Caesar**

Hello, Dolly *see* **The Matchmaker**

Hello Sweetheart *see* **The Butter and Egg Man**

Her Cardboard Lover *see* **The Cardboard Lover**

Her Husband Lies *see* **Street of Chance**

375 Her Man

Based on the folk song "Frankie and Johnnie." Story: "Frankie and Johnnie were lovers!/ Oh, Lordy, how they could love!/ They swore to be true to each other,/ Just as true as the stars above,/ He was her man, but he done her wrong."

Pathe Pictures, 1930 (original). Director: Tay Garnett; screenwriters: Thomas Buckingham, Howard Higgin and Tay Garnett. Cast: Helen Twelvetrees (Frankie), Ricardo Cortez (Johnnie), Marjorie Rambeau (Annie), Phillips Holmes (Dan), Thelma Todd (Nelly), James Gleason (Steve), Franklin Pangborn, Harry Sweet.

• ***Cafe Hostess*** (remake). Columbia Pictures, 1940. Director: Sidney Salkow; screenwriter: Harold Shumate. Cast: Preston Foster (Dan Walters), Ann Dvorak (Jo), Douglas Fowley (Eddie Morgan), Wynne Gibson (Annie), Arthur Loft (Steve Mason), Bruce Bennett, Eddie Acuff, Bradley Page, Linda Winters.

• ***Frankie and Johnnie*** (remake). United Artists, 1966. Director: Frederick de Cordova; screenwriter: Alex Gotlieb, story by Nat Perrin. Cast: Elvis Presley (Johnnie), Donna Douglas (Frankie), Harry Morgan (Cully), Sue Ann Langdon (Mitzi), Nancy Kovack (Nellie Bly), Audrey Christie, Robert Strauss, Anthony Eisley.

In the first movie based on the folk song, things are given a French apache setting. A second version, filmed by RKO in 1935, followed the song fairly closely, and Frankie with a "rat-a-tat-tat" shot Johnnie dead. The third version, without Frankie and Johnnie, tells a very similiar story of a young sailor, Foster, who falls for a nightclub hostess (Dvorak) and strays a bit. Finally, it wouldn't do to kill off Elvis Presley, so as a Mississippi gambler, he only temporarily strays from Donna Douglas to Nancy Kovack, in the hope of improving his luck. Sure enough, Elvis rocks out a new version of the title song.

376 Her Sister from Paris

Based on the play *Maskerade* by Ludwig Fulda. Story: When celebrated author Joseph Weyringer loses interest in his wife, Helen, she tells her troubles to her sister, Lola, a famous dancer and vamp. Lola suggests that Helen assume her identity and return to her husband. Both Joseph and his friend Robert fall in love with "Lola," with Joseph attempting to seduce her. "Lola" asserts that she will give herself to him, as soon as he confesses that he had been a rotten husband to Helen. Joseph is all too happy to make such a confession and then Helen reveals that he had been making love to his own wife. Shocked but pleased to learn that he still loves his wife and she has picked up some new ideas about love from her sister, Joseph and Helen reconcile.

First National Pictures, 1925 (original). Silent. Director: Sidney Franklin; screenwriter: Hans Kraly. Cast: Constance Talmadge (Helen Weyringer/Lola), Ronald Colman (Joseph Weyringer), George K. Arthur (Robert Well), Margaret Mann (Bertha).

• ***Moulin Rouge*** (remake). United Artists, 1934. Director: Sidney Lanfield; screenwriter: Henry Lehrman. Cast: Constance Bennett (Helen), Franchot Tone (Douglas), Tulio Carminati (Le Maire), Helen Westley (Mrs. Morris), Andrew Tombres, Russ Brown.

• ***Two-Faced Woman*** (remake). MGM, 1941. Director: George Cukor; screenwriters: S.N. Behrman, Salka Viertel and George Oppenheimer. Cast: Greta Garbo (Karin Borg), Melvyn Douglas (Larry Blake), Constance Bennett (Griselda Vaughn), Roland Young (O.O. Miller), Robert Sterling, Ruth Gordon, George B. Huntley, Jr.

The original production is a light, sophisticated comedy, especially tailored to the talents of its star, Constance Talmadge. The second film, while based on a book by Miriam Young, tells a very similiar story. In it, Constance Bennett, the wife of a songwriter, impersonates her own sister in order to revitalize her marriage and singing career. The third film of this entry finds Melvyn Douglas on a ski vacation where he meets and marries ski instructor Garbo. His ex-flame, Constance Bennett, plots to get Douglas back, and when Garbo sees Bennett, she fears that she can't compete with the glamorous Constance. Garbo impersonates her own twin, a gay and wordly-wise woman. Douglas sees through the trick and tries to get Garbo to expose herself. When they make love, she believes that her plan has backfired until Douglas proves he knew she was his wife all along. Garbo, incredibly beautiful at only 37, decided to call it quits after this movie, and if it wasn't as good as some of her classic films, it was amusing and entertaining, even arousing the concerns of some bluenoses at the time because of its "immorality."

Her Wedding Night *see* **Miss Bluebeard**

Warren Beatty entertains Julie Christie in the 1978 Paramount production of Heaven Can Wait, *a remake of* Here Comes Mr. Jordan *(Columbia, 1941), and* not *of* Heaven Can Wait *(20th Century–Fox, 1943).*

Herbie Goes Bananas *see* **The Love Bug**

Herbie Goes to Monte Carlo *see* **The Love Bug**

Herbie Rides Again *see* **The Love Bug**

377 Here Comes Mr. Jordan

Based on the play *Heaven Can Wait* by Harry Segall. Story: When the private plane carrying heavyweight boxing contender Joe Pendleton appears about to crash, Heavenly Messenger #7013 impetuously collects the man's soul, only to discover that Joe was supposed to survive and live an additional 50 years. The Messenger's superior, Mr. Jordan, takes responsibility for rectifying the error. Unfortunately, Pendleton's manager, Max Corkle, had arranged to have Joe's body cremated. Now it's up to Mr. Jordan to find a substitute. After rejecting several possibilities, Joe agrees to take over the body of millionaire playboy Farnsworth, recently murdered by his wife, Julia, and her lover, Tony Abbott. His reappearance is quite a shock to Julia and Tony as is Farnsworth's sudden interest in taking up the sport of boxing. Pendleton, now Farnsworth, calls on his old manager, Max, to help him get a title fight. While in training he meets and falls for Bette Logan. The Farnsworth body doesn't work out as Julia and Tony revise their plan to do away with Joe's host. Fortunately, the death of another boxer provides a more suitable home for Pendleton's soul. After Mr. Jordan leaves, Joe has no memory of what has occurred, except when he encounters Bette, they both feel like they had known each other before and it looks like love will win out over Joe's unfortunate luck with bodies.

Columbia Pictures, 1941 (original). Director: Alexander Hall; screenwriters: Sidney Buchman and Seton I. Miller. Cast: Robert Montgomery (Joe Pendleton), Claude Rains (Mr. Jordan), Evelyn Keyes (Bette Logan), Rita Johnson (Julia Farnsworth), Edward Everett Horton (Heavenly Messenger #7013), James Gleason (Max Corkle), John Emery (Tony Abbott), Donald McBride, Don Costello, Halliwell Hobbes, Benny Williams.

• ***Angel on My Shoulder*** (remake). United Artists, 1946. Director: Archie Mayo; screenwriters: Harry Segall and Roland Kibbee. Cast: Paul Muni (Eddie Kagle), Anne Baxter (Barbara Foster), Claude Rains (Nick), Onslow Stevens (Dr. Higgins), George Cleveland (Albert), Erskine Sanford, Hardie Albright, James Flavin.

• ***Down to Earth*** (remake). Columbia Pictures, 1947. Director: Alexander Hall; screenwriters: Edwin Blum and Don Hartman. Cast: Rita Hayworth (Terpsichore), Larry Parks (Danny Miller), Marc Platt (Eddie), Roland Culver (Mr. Jordan), James Gleason (Max Corkle), Edward Everett Horton (Messenger #7013), Adele Jergens (Georgia Evans), George Macready (Joe Mannion), William Frawley, James Burke, Lucien Littlefield, Jean Donahue, Kathleen O'Malley.

• ***Heaven Can Wait*** (remake). Paramount Pictures, 1978. Directors: Warren Beatty and Buck Henry; screenwriters: Elaine May and Warren Beatty. Cast: Warren Beatty (Joe Pendleton), James Mason (Mr. Jordan), Julie Christie (Betty Logan), Jack Warden (Max Corkle), Charles Grodin (Tony Abbott), Dyan Cannon (Julia Farnsworth), Vincent Gardenia (Krim), Buck Henry (the Escort), Joseph Mahler, Hamilton Camp, Arthur Malet, Stephanie Farcy.

What makes the original filming of the Segall play work is the earnest performance of Robert Montgomery, giving one of the most memorable and enjoyable portrayals of his career. Although the plot is sheer nonsense, the comic devices of the piece of whimsy are delightful. Claude Rains is perfection as the heavenly bureaucrat bailing out his incompetent assistant, bunglingly played by Edward Everett Horton. James Gleason as Max Corkle is also in excellent form, knowing his Joe is back when he hears Farnsworth play his fighter's saxophone, badly as usual.

In *Angel on My Shoulder,* Claude Rains works for heaven's competitors. He is a devil who plops a dead gangster, Paul Muni, into the body of a crime-busting judge, henceforth to act as the devil's agent. The gangster double-crosses his satantic master. In *Down to Earth,* several of the characters in *Here Comes Mr. Jordan* are part of the story of the muse Terpsichore, played by Rita Hayworth, who comes down to earth to help Broadway producer Larry Parks fix his new show in which she is to be featured.

Finally, Warren Beatty's remake of *Here Comes Mr. Jordan,* with Segall's original title, transforms Joe Pendleton from a boxer to a quarterback for the Los Angeles Rams. Other than this switch of setting, things are much as they were before, with Beatty effective as Joe and James Mason as the ever-helpful Mr. Jordan. Fine comical performances are given by Dyan Cannon and Charles Grodin as the conniving murderers and Jack Warden as the hard-nosed but sentimental football trainer.

378 Here Comes the Groom

Based on a story by Richard Flournoy. Story: A goofy bachelor, Mike Scanlon, involved in a robbery, escapes on a train and is picked up by Patricia Randolph, who is in desperate need of a husband and she insists that Scanlon will fit the bill. They then become entangled in the theft of Patricia's mother's jewels.

Paramount Pictures, 1934 (original). Director: Edward Sedgwick; screenwriters: Leonard Praskins and Casey Robinson. Cast: Jack Haley (Mike Scanlon), Mary Boland (Mrs. Widden), Patricia Ellis (Patricia Randolph), Neil Hamilton (Jim), Isabel Jewell, Lawrence Gray, Sidney Toler, E.H. Calvert, James Burtis.

• ***Here Comes the Groom*** (remake). Paramount Pictures, 1951. Director: Frank Capra; screenwriters: Virginia Van Upp, Liam O'Brien and Myles Connelly, based on a story by Robert Riskin and Liam O'Brien. Cast: Bing Crosby (Pete), Jane Wyman (Emmadel Jones), Alexis Smith (Winifred Stanley), Franchot Tone (Wilbur Stanley), James Barton, Robert Keith, Jacques Gencel, Beverly Washburn, Connie Gilchrist.

The second film is not a true remake of the first, but the basic conflict is the same. In the first, a woman needs a husband, any husband, quickly; in the second, carefree newspaperman Crosby discovers that he must be married within a week if he is to be allowed to adopt two French war ophans. Apparently, the kids have some real appeal for Bing, because he sets about to reclaim his ex-long-suffering fiancée, Jane Wyman, who is now being rushed by rich lawyer Franchot Tone. The charm of the kids and Bing are too much, and Jane agrees to marry Crosby, leaving Tone to find consolation with Alexis Smith. Perhaps the best thing about this inferior Frank Capra film is the Academy Award–winning song "In the Cool Cool Cool of the Evening" by Jay Livingston and Ray Evans.

Here Is My Heart *see* **The Grand Duchess and the Waiter**

379 The Hero

Based on the play by Gilbert Emery. Story: Oswald Lowe is welcomed by his hometown as a war hero. He enjoys recounting his exploits whenever he can get anyone to listen. The thing is, he's really a heel. He moves in with his brother Andrew and soon is not only making love to Martha, the maid, but also finds Andrew's wife, Hester, receptive to his charms. After stealing money entrusted to Andrew by his church, Oswald is on his way out of town when he spots a fire in a school and rescues several children, being seriously burned in the process. When Andrew offers his own skin for grafting to Oswald's, the latter directs Hester to return the money he has stolen.

Preferred Pictures, 1922 (original). Silent. Director: Louis J. Gasnier; screenwriter: Eve Unser. Cast: Gaston Glass (Oswald Lane), Barbara La Marr (Hester Lane), John Saimpolis (Andrew Lane), Martha Mattox (Sarah Lane), Frankie Lee (Andy Lane), Doris Pawn (Martha), David Butler, Ethel Shannon.

• ***Swell Guy*** (remake). Universal International, 1946. Director: Frank Tuttle; screenwriter: Richard Brooks. Cast: Sonny Tufts (Jim Duncan), Ann Blyth (Marian Tyler), Ruth Warrick (Ann Duncan), William Gargan (Martin Duncan), John Litel (Arthur Tyler), Thomas Gomez, Millard Mitchell, Mary Nash.

In the remake, one of the world's least talented actors and most charming men, Sonny Tufts, is a returning war correspondent who comes home to a hero's welcome but soon proves to be nothing but a heel.

Hers to Hold *see* **Three Smart Girls**

Hi, Beautiful *see* **Love in a Bungalow**

Hi, Mom *see* **Greetings**

380 Hi, Nellie

Based on a story by Roy Chanslor. Story: In this comedy thriller, rebellious newspaper managing editor Brad is demoted to Advice-to-the-Lovelorn editor, but regains his former position when in his new role he solves the case of the kidnapping and murder of a banker.

Warner Bros., 1934. Director: Mervyn LeRoy; screenwriters: Aben Finkel and Sidney Sutherland. Cast: Paul Muni (Brad), Glenda Farrell (Gerry), Douglass Dumbrille (Harvey Dawes), Robert Barrat (Brownell), Ned Sparks, Hobart Cavanaugh, Pat Wing, Edward Ellis, George Meeker.

• ***Love Is on the Air*** (remake). Warner Bros., 1937. Director: Nick Grinde; screenwriter: Morton Grant. Cast: Ronald Reagan (Andy McLeod), Eddie Acuff (Dunk Glover), Robert Barrat (J.D. Harrington), Raymond Hatton (Weston), Willard Parker (Lee Quimby), Spec O'Donnell, Tommy Bupp, Jack Mower, June Travis, Ben Welden.

• ***You Can't Escape Forever*** (remake). Warner Bros., 1942. Director: Jo Graham; screenwriters: Fred Niblo, Jr. and Hector Chevigny. Cast: George Brent (Steve "Mitch" Mitchell), Brenda Marshall (Laurie Abbott), Gene Lockhart (Carl Robelink), Roscoe Karns (Mac McTurk), Edward Ciannelli (Boss Greer), Paul Harvey (Major Turner), Edith Barrett, Harry Hayden, Charles Halton, Don DeFore.

Ironically, in the first remake, Ronald Reagan, a crusading radio reporter and commentator, gets bounced from his job for exposing politicians who have betrayed their public trust by protecting mobsters and Ron's dishonest sponsor. He is shifted to handling the Kiddie Klub, but wins his job back by proving his case against his sponsor, linking him to criminals. In the third film, George Brent engagingly plays the managing editor who gets put into the newspaper's doghouse position, the Advice to the Lovelorn, when he turns down a chance to acquire a document from an eccentric which purports to expose a crime syndicate. Brent wins back his position by infiltrating the syndicate and bringing it to its knees.

The Hidden Eye *see* **Eyes in the Night**

381 Hide-Out

Based on the story by Mauri Grashin. Story: Lucky Wilson is an affable muscle man forced to flee New York City for a hideout in Connecticut where he meets the farmer's daughter, Pauline. There love grows in an idyllic setting. In the end, he is captured by cops MacCarthy and Britt, but they allow as he'll be back with Pauline after serving about eighteen months.

Metro Pictures, 1934 (original). Director: W.S. Van Dyke; screenwriters: Frances Goodrich and Albert Hackett. Cast: Robert Montgomery (Lucky Wilson), Maureen O'Sullivan (Pauline), Edward Arnold (MacCarthy), Elizabeth Patterson (Ma Miller), Whitford Kane (Pa Miller), Mickey Rooney (Willie), C. Henry Gordon, Muriel Evans, Edward Brophy, Henry Armetta, Herman Bing, Louise Henry, Harold Huber.

• ***I'll Wait for You*** (remake). MGM, 1941. Director: Robert B. Sinclair; screenwriter: Guy Trosper. Cast: Robert Sterling (Lucky Wilson), Marsha Hunt (Pauline Miller), Virginia Weidler (Lizzie Miller), Paul Kelly (Lt. McFarley), Fay Holden (Mrs. Miller), Henry Travers (Mr. Miller), Don Costello, Carol Hughes, Reed Hadley, Ben Weldon.

Mickey Rooney just about stole the show in the 1934 picture, but Robert Montgomery seemed miscast and Edward Arnold was wasted in the part of the detective. The remake of this formula story gave "B" players Robert Sterling and Marsha Hunt some experience in leading roles. What the film gave audiences is not clear. There was nothing unusual in either the acting, script or direction to recommend the movie.

382 High Pressure

Based on the play *Hot Money* by Abem Kandel. Story: Gar Evans is a high-powered con artist who believes there's a fortune to be made in artificial rubber and forms the Golden Gate Artificial Rubber Company, but when Doctor Rudolph, the inventor of the process, can't be found, he finds himself in serious but amusing trouble with some mean gangsters.

Warner Bros., 1932 (original). Director: Mervyn LeRoy; screenwriter: Joseph Jackson. Cast: William Powell (Gar Evans), Evelyn Brent (Francine), George Sidney (Ginsberg), Guy Kibbee (Clifford Gray), Evelyn Knapp (Helen), Harry Beresford (Doctor Rudolph), John Wray, Frank McHugh, Polly Walters.

• ***Hot Money*** (remake). Warner Bros., 1936. Director: William McGann; screenwriter: William Jacobs. Cast: Ross Alexander (Chick Randall), Beverly Roberts (Grace Lane), Joseph Cawthorn (Max Dourfuss), Paul Graetz (Doctor David), Andrew Tombes, Harry Burns, Ed Conrad, Anne Nagel, Frank Orth, Cy Kendall.

High Pressure is an entertaining comedy, made so by the disarming charm of its star, William Powell. He could sell snow to Eskimos. In the remake, Ross Alexander is also supposed to be an engaging con man who plans to drive the oil companies out of business by inventing a gasoline substitute. Unfortunately, Alexander is no Powell and the film doesn't come off as well as the original.

383 High Sierra

Based on the novel by W.R. Burnett. Story: Roy Earle, an ex-con, is planning one last big heist before he retires. He's stuck with two inexperienced accomplices, Babe and Red, who are constantly fighting over a girl, Marie, whom they have brought along. Marie finds Roy much more interesting than the two boys, but Earle has his heart set on a young crippled girl, Velma, for whose successful operation he has paid. Velma thinks Roy's too old and gratitude is not love. Disappointed but not crushed, Roy and his gang set out to rob a plush hotel with the help of an inside man. Everything goes wrong, with the two young men killed in a car crash and Roy and Marie forced to take it on the lam. Unable to get any help from his old criminal friends, Roy is eventually trapped in the Sierras and gunned down like a dog, with only Marie and a stray mongrel that he has befriended to mourn him.

Warner Bros., 1941 (original). Director: Raoul Walsh; screenwriters: John Huston and W.R. Burnett. Cast: Humphrey Bogart (Roy Earle), Ida Lupino (Marie), Alan Curtis (Babe), Arthur Kennedy (Red), Joan Leslie (Velma), Henry Hull (Doc Banton), Henry Travers (Pa), Barton MacLane, Donald McBride, Paul Harvey, Isabel Jewel, Willie Best, Cornel Wilde.

• ***Colorado Territory*** (remake). Warner Bros., 1949. Director: Raoul Walsh; screenwriters: John Twist and Edmund North. Cast: Joel McCrea (Wes McQueen), Virginia Mayo (Colorado Carson), Dorothy Malone (Julie Ann), Henry Hull (Winslow), John Archer (Reno Blake), James Mitchum (Duke Harris), Morris Ankrum, Basil Ruysdael, Frank Puglia, Ian Wolfe, Harry Woods.

• ***I Died a Thousand Times*** (remake). Warner Bros., 1955. Director: Stuart Heisler; screenwriter: W.R. Burnett. Cast: Jack Palance (Roy Earle), Shelley Winters (Marie), Lori Nelson (Velma), Lee Marvin (Babe), Gonzales Gonzales (Chico), Lon Chaney, Jr. (Big Mac), Perry Lopez, Richard Davalos, Olive Carey, Ralph Moody, James Millican.

Roy Earle was just one of several good roles that Bogart got because George Raft turned them down. Bogie was very effective as the aging criminal who showed he had a spark of decency when he helped a migrant family and their crippled daughter. On the other hand, he would kill if it seemed necessary and during the manhunt he was referred to as "Mad Dog" Earle, not without justification. Ida Lupino was a very appealing Marie, a girl who hitched her wagon to a falling criminal star. Of the other performers, the only one to impress was Henry Travers as Velma's grandfather, a man who only knew Earle as a good man. The remakes were about as would be expected. The 1949 version cast Joel McCrea as a western outlaw, who was too far gone to go straight, and is pursued by a posse which guns him down. In 1955, Jack Palance reprised the role of Roy Earle and gave a satisfactory if not outstanding performance. The same cannot be said of others in the cast, all of whom could have benefited from some acting lessons.

High Society *see* **The Philadelphia Story**

Highways West *see* **Heat Lightning**

Hillbilly Blitzkrieg *see* **Private Snuffy Smith**

384 Hindle Wakes

Based on the play by Stanley Houghton. Story: It's the tale of independently minded Fanny Hawthorne in a Lancashire mill town who leaves home rather than marry the mill owner's son, with whom she spent a holiday.

Diamond-Super/Royal, Great Britain, 1918 (original). Silent. Director: Maurice Elvey; screenwriter: Eliot Stannard. Cast: Norman McKinnel (Nat Jeffcoate), Colette O'Neil (Fanny Hawthorne), Hayford Hobbs (Alan Jeffcoate), Ada King (Mrs. Hawthorne), Edward O'Neill (Chris Hawthorne), Margaret Bannerman, Frank Dane, Dolly Tree.

• ***Hindle Wakes*** (remake). Gaumont, Great Britain, 1927. Silent. Director: Maurice Elvey; screenwriter: Stanley Houghton. Cast: Estelle Brody (Fanny Hawthorne), John Stuart (Alan Jeffcoate), Norman McKinnel (Nat Jeffcoate), Marie Ault (Mrs. Hawthorne), Humberston Wright (Chris Hawthorne), Gladys Jennings, Irene Rooke, Peggy Carlisle, Arthur Chesney, Alf Goddard.

• ***Hindle Wakes*** (remake). Gaumont, Great Britain, 1931. Director: Victor Saville; screenwriters: Victor Saville and Angus Macphail. Cast: Sybil Thorndike (Mrs. Hawthorne), John Stuart (Alan Jeffcoate), Norman McKinnel (Nat Jeffcoate), Edmund Gwenn (Chris Hawthorne), Belle Chrystal (Fanny Hawthorne), Mary Clare, Muriel Angelius, A.G. Poulton, Ruth Peterson.

• ***Hindle Wakes*** (remake). Monarch, Great Britain, 1952. Director: Arthur Crabtree; screenwriter: John Baines. Cast: Lisa Daniely (Jenny Hawthorne), Leslie Dwyer (Chris Hawthorne), Brian Worth (Alan Jeffcoate), Sandra Dorne (Mary Hollins), Ronald Adam (Nat Jeffcoate), Joan Hickson (Mrs. Hawthorne), Michael Medwin, Mary Clare, Bill Travers, Beatrice Varley, Tim Turner, Diana Hope.

In the last of the four versions of the Stanley Houghton play (the third being probably the best), mill girls Lisa Daniely and Sandra Dorne go to Blackpool from their hometown of Hindle for the Wakes Week holiday. While there Lisa meets the mill owner's son, Brian Worth, and they go off for a week together. When her parents find out, they insist that the two get married but she doesn't love him and refuses to do so.

His Captive Woman *see* **The Woman God Changed**

His Double Life *see* **The Great Adventure**

His Girl Friday *see* **The Front Page**

385 His Grace Give Notice

Based on the novel by Lady Trowbridge. Story: Butler George Barwick falls in love with the daughter of the house where he is employed. When later he inherits a dukedom, he stays in service long enough to save her from eloping with a married cad.

Stoll, Great Britain, 1924 (original). Silent. Director: W.P. Kellino; screenwriter: Lydia Hayward. Cast: Nora Swinburne (Cynthia Bannock), Henry Victor (George Barwick), John Stuart (Joseph Longley), Eric Bransby Williams (Ted Burlington), Mary Brough, Gladys Hamer, Phyllis Lytton, Knighton Small.

• ***His Grace Give Notice*** (remake). Real Art/Radio, Great Britain, 1933. Director: George A. Cooper; screenwriter: H. Fowler Mear. Cast: Arthur Margetson (George Barwick), Viola Keats (Barbara Rannock), S. Victor Stanley (James Roper), Barry Livesey (Ted Burlington), Ben Welden (Michael Collier), Edgar Norfolk, Dick Francis, Lawrence Hanray, Charles Groves, O.B. Clarence, Gertrude Sterroll.

Margetson gives the best performance in these two romantic comedies about a butler who inherits a title but stays on to woo the daughter of the house.

386 His Majesty, Bunker Bean

Based on the novel *Bunker Bean* by Harry Leon Wilson and the play by Lee Wilson Dodd. Story: Mousy clerk Bunker Bean is convinced by a phony clairvoyant that he is the reincarnation of an Egyptian king, Ram Tah. Bean agrees to pay Professor Balthasar $5,000 for a phony mummy, whose body he believes his spirit once occupied. With new confidence in his worth, he becomes engaged to Marie Breede. When Bean's dog tears the mummy apart, showing it to be a fake, Bean's self esteem plummets once again but he has enough gumption to fight his rival for Marie and wins. With renewed confidence, he prepares to marry Marie.

• ***His Majesty, Bunker Bean*** (remake). Warner Bros., 1925. Silent. Director: Harry Beaumont; screenwriter: Julien Josephsen. Cast: Matt Moore (Bunker Bean), Dorothy Devore (Marie Breede), David Butler (Bud Matthews), Helen Dunbar (Mrs. Breede), Frank Leigh (Prof. Balthasar), Nora Cecil, Henry Barrows, Gertrude Claire.

• ***Bunker Bean*** (remake). RKO, 1936. Directors: William Hamilton and Edward Killy; screenwriters: Edmund North, James Gow and Dorothy Yost. Cast: Owen Davis, Jr. (Bunker Bean), Louise Latimer (Mary Kent), Robert McWade (J.C. Kent), Lucille Ball (Miss Kelly), Berton Churchill (Prof. Balthasar), Jessie Ralph, Edward Nugent, Hedda Hopper, Pierre Watkin, Charles Arnt.

The real star of these two films and the 1918 silent made by Paramount Pictures is an inferiority complex. In both cases the timid clerk gains confidence when he is told by a crystal-ball gazer that he is the reincarnation of both Napoleon and an Egyptian king. Armed with this information the worm turns and wins the love of the boss's daughter, much to the chagrin of the boss. Both Matt Moore and Owen Davis, Jr., look the part of a man who would believe a fortune teller and be taken in by a phony Egyptologist.

His Majesty, The Scarecrow of Oz *see* **The Wizard of Oz**

His Night Out *see* **Oh, Doctor!**

His Tiger Lady *see* **The Grand Duchess and the Waiter**

Hit Man *see* **Get Carter**

Hit the Deck *see* **Shore Leave**

387 Hobson's Choice

Based on the play by Harold Brighouse. Story: Henry Hobson, a Lancaster bootmaker with three daughters, has very definite views on parental duty and privilege. Basically, he subscribes to the theory that women are there to serve his every want. When his eldest, Maggie, sets her cap for his apprentice, Will Mossup, Hobson meets his match, as she drives Will to success as a competitor to her father.

Master, Great Britain, 1920 (original). Silent. Director: Percy Nash; screenwriter: W.C. Rowden. Cast: Joe Nightingale (Will Mossup), Joan Ritz (Maggie Hobson), Arthur Pitt (Henry Hobson), Joan Cockram (Vickey Hobson), Phyllis Birkett (Alice Hobson), Charles Heslop, Ada King, Mary Byron, Louis Rihil.

• ***Hobson's Choice*** (remake). BIP, Great Britain, 1931. Director: Thomas Bentley; screenwriter: Frank Launder. Cast: Viola Lyel (Maggie Hobson), James Harcourt (Hobson), Frank Pettingell (Will Mossup), Belle Chrystal (Vicky Hobson), Joan Maude (Alice Hobson), Jay Laurier, Amy Veness, Reginald Bach, Basil Moss.

• ***Hobson's Choice*** (remake). London/BLPA, Great Britain, 1954. Director: David Lean; screenwriters: David Lean, Wynyard Browne and Norman Spencer. Cast: Charles Laughton (Henry Hobson), John Mills (Willie Mossup), Brenda de Banzie (Maggie Hobson), Daphne Anderson (Alice Hobson), Prudnella Scales (Vicky Hobson), Richard Wattis, Derek Blomfield, Helen Haye, Joseph Tomelty.

In this lovely struggle between an unstoppable force and an immovable object (that is, Maggie Hobson vs. her father, Henry), it is the audience that is the victor. The most frequently seen version is the last with Charles Laughton and Brenda de Banzie as the tyrannical father and his strong-willed daughter. It beautifully catches the mood of turn-of-the-century England when dictators in homes were common. John Mills is particularly good as the good-natured but none-too-bright Willie, who merely trades one master for another with hardly any noticeable benefit. Laughton is a roaring lion, playing a bit above form to be sure, but perfectly delightful despite his hamminess. Brenda de Banzie never had a better film role and she makes the most of her part, proclaiming her independence and turning around to give her "dear old dad" his comeuppance.

Hold That Blonde *see* **Paths to Paradise**

388 Holiday

Based on the play by Philip Barry. Story: When wealthy and sophisticated Julia Seton meets Johnny Case, she brings him home to her family, introducing him as her fiancé. Case is a poor lawyer with not a great deal of ambition. He is greeted with friendly tolerance by the elder Seton and his other children, Linda and Ned. Seton agrees to give an engagement party for the couple. About the only friends of Johnny's asked to the party are Nick and Susan Potter. Linda, not caring for her sister's society games, has a private party herself in the old playroom, where Johnny, Ned, Nick and Susan join her. Johnny reveals that he has invested his money in the stock market and plans to quit work so he can explore a bit of the world. Old man Seton and Julia are furious at this lack of responsibility, but Linda, who has come to love Johnny, sides with him. The engagement between Johnny and Julia is off, and Case prepares to go to Europe with the Potters. Proud of his assertion of independence, Linda joins Johnny aboard the steamer.

Pathe Exchange, 1930 (original). Director: Edward H. Griffith; screenwriter: Horace Jackson. Cast: Ann Harding (Linda Seton), Mary Astor (Julia Seton), Robert Ames (Johnny Case), Edward Everett Horton (Nick Potter), Hedda Hopper (Susan Potter), Monroe Owsley (Ned Seton), William Holden (Edward Seton), Elizabeth Forrester, Mabel Forest, Creighton Hale.

• ***Holiday*** (remake). Columbia Pictures, 1938. Director: George Cukor; screenwriters: Donald Ogden Stewart and Sidney Buchman. Cast: Katharine Hepburn (Linda Seton), Cary Grant (Johnny Case), Doris Nolan (Julia Seton), Lew Ayres (Ned Seton), Edward Everett Horton (Nick Potter), Ruth Donnelly (Susan Potter), Henry Kolker (Edward Seton), Binnie Barnes, Jean Dixon, Henry Daniell.

While the 1930 production of the Philip Barry play was well received by both critics and audiences, with Ann Harding and writer Horace Jackson receiving Academy Award nominations, the 1938 version was simply spectacular. Somehow the second production took basically the same story, same lines, same settings, even the same actors—in the case of Edward Everett Horton—and made it all seem so fresh and new. It is an elegant film, full of bright humor, pathos and love. The film must be numbered among the career best of Katharine Hepburn, Cary Grant, Lew Ayres, Edward Everett Horton and Ruth Donnelly. Despite the high praise which has been heaped on the film and its performers both at the time of its release and since, it had no Academy Award nomination.

Holy Matrimony *see* **The Great Adventure**

Hombre y la Bestia *see* **Dr. Jekyll and Mr. Hyde**

389 The Home Towners

Based on the play by George M. Cohan. Story: When Vic Arnold, a middle-aged Manhattan millionaire, invites his boyhood chum, P.H. Bancroft, of South Bend, Indiana, to come to New York to be his best man for his marriage to Beth

Calhoun, a girl half his age, Bancroft suspects the girl's motives. He becomes more concerned that Beth is a gold digger when he discovers that Arnold has advanced $200,000 to Beth's father. Bancroft insults Beth in front of her parents and she breaks off the engagement. Reasoning that a real gold digger wouldn't be put off by a mere insult, Bancroft decides that he has misjudged the girl's motivation and so gets the two together again and this time, as their best man, "forever holds his peace."

Warner Bros., 1928. Director: Bryan Foy; screenwriters: Addison Burkhart and Murray Roth. Cast: Richard Bennett (Vic Arnold), Doris Kenyon (Beth Calhoun), Robert McWade (P.H. Bancroft), Robert Edeson (Mr. Calhoun), Gladys Brockwell, John Miljan, Vera Lewis, Stanley Taylor, James T. Mack.

• ***Times Square Playboy*** (remake). Warner Bros., 1936. Director: William McGann; screenwriter: Roy Chanslor. Cast: Warren William (Vic Arnold), June Travis (Beth Calhoun), Barton MacLane (Casey), Gene Lockhart (P.H. Bancroft), Kathleen Lockhart (Lottie Bancroft), Dick Purcell, Craig Reynolds.

The Home Towners, a very early talkie, didn't suffer from all of the difficulties of the new advance in filmmaking that beset many other movies of the time. The remake is more of the same with Warren William as a wealthy stockbroker, whose friend Gene Lockhart interferes when William announces his intent to marry poor girl June Travis. The story was also brought to the screen in 1940 for Warner Bros. as *Ladies Must Live* with Wayne Morris, Priscilla Lane and Roscoe Karns.

Honey ***see*** **Come Out of the Kitchen**

Honeymoon for Three ***see*** **Goodbye Again**

The Honeymoon's Over ***see*** **Six Cylinder Love**

Hoopla ***see*** **The Barker**

390 The Hoosier Schoolmaster

Based on the novel by Edward Eggleston. Story: When Ralph Hartsook returns from the Civil War, he settles in a small Indiana community and becomes its schoolmaster. He resides in the home of wealthy Jack Means, who hopes Ralph will marry his daughter, Mirandy. Instead, Ralph falls in love with Hannah Thompson, a 20-year-old orphan who works as a servant in the Means home. The area is infested with a gang of night riders who pull a series of robberies. First to be suspected is war veteran John Pearson, who is almost lynched. Then Ralph becomes a suspect and is brought to trial, where he successfully defends himself. It comes out that political boss Pete Jones and physician Dr. Small are the leaders of the gang of robbers. Freed, Ralph marries Hannah.

Whitman Bennett Productions/Hodkinson, 1924 (original). Silent. Director: Oliver L. Sellers; screenwriter: Eve Stuyvesant. Cast: Henry Hull (Ralph Hartsook), Jane Thomas (Hannah Thompson), Frank Dane (Dr. Small), Arthur

Ludwig (Pete Jones), Walter Plam (Old Jack Means), Dorothy Allen (Mirandy), Frank Andrews (John Pearson), Mary Foy, Nat Pendleton, G.W. Hall.

• ***The Hoosier Schoolmaster*** (remake). Trem Carr/Monogram Pictures, 1935. Director: Lewis D. Collins; screenwriter: Charles Logue. Cast: Norman Foster (Ralph), Charlotte Henry (Hannah), Dorothy Libarie (Martha), Sarah Padden (Sarah), Otis Harlan (Hawkins), Russell Simpson (Dr. Small), William V. Mong, Fred Kohler, Wallace Reid, Jr.

Neither production is memorable, but both are fair entertainment for the times in which they were produced. They would hold little appeal today. In the sequel, Norman Foster once again demonstrates his limitations as an actor, giving a rather stilted performance in the title role.

Hot Money ***see*** **High Pressure**

391 Hotel for Women

Based on a story by Elsa Maxwell and Kathryn Scola. Story: Marcia Bromley goes from Syracuse to New York City to see her boyfriend, Jeff Buchanan. Now a successful architect, Jeff has no time for her. She moves into a hotel for women and with the encouragement of the other guests, becomes a top model, which brings Jeff back on the run, but by now he has a lot of competition.

Twentieth Century–Fox, 1939 (original). Director: Gregory Ratoff; screenwriters: Kathryn Scola and Darrell Ware. Cast: Ann Sothern (Eileen Connelly), Linda Darnell (Marcia Bromley), James Ellison (Jeff Buchanan), Jean Rogers (Nancy Prescott), Lynn Bari (Barbara Hunter), June Gale (Joan Mitchell), Joyce Compton (Emeline Thomas), Elsa Maxwell (herself), John Halliday, Katharine Aldridge, Alan Dinehart, Sidney Blackmer.

• ***Free, Blonde and 21*** (sequel). Twentieth Century–Fox, 1940. Director: Ricardo Cortez; screenwriter: Frances Hyland. Cast: Lynn Bari (Carol), Mary Beth Hughes (Jerry), Joan Davis (Nellie), Henry Wilcoxon (Dr. Mayberry), Robert Lowery (Dr. Stephen Greig), Alan Baxter (Mickey), Katharine Aldridge, Helen Ericson, Chick Chandler, Joan Valerie, Elise Knox.

Sixteen-year-old Linda Darnell made quite a smash in her first film, with her remarkable dark beauty. Elsa Maxwell, co-creator of the story, appeared as a guest of the hotel for women, dispensing advice to the girls, whether requested or not. The second film, a sort of a sequel, told the story of some more guests of a New York hotel for women, concentrating on glib blonde Mary Beth Hughes, whose cheating of men winds her up in jail, and Lynn Bari as a hard-working artist who ends up with a millionaire.

392 Hotel Imperial

Based on the play *Szinmu Negy Felvonasban* by Lajos Biro. Story: After riding into a frontier town, Lt. Paul Almasy discovers that it is occupied by the Russians. In the ensuing battle between his Hungarian Hussars and the enemy, he is hurt, but drags himself to the nearby Hotel Imperial. The remaining servants, Anna, Elias, and Anton, carry him to a bedroom where he sleeps. The next morning, Anna convinces him to pose as a waiter while they find a way for him to escape. Anna is desired by Russian General Juschkiewitsch, whose advances she accepts to ensure Paul's escape. Meanwhile, Tabakowitsch, a Russian spy, arrives at the hotel, and orders Paul to draw his bath. Learning that Tabakowitsch has plans for routing the Hungarian forces, Paul kills him. Anna makes the death appear to be a suicide but the general suspects otherwise and has Paul investigated. Before the General can dispose of Paul and Anna, the Hungarians retake the town, and the couple, now in love, are reunited.

Famous Players–Lasky/Paramount Pictures, 1927 (original). Silent. Director: Mauritz Stiller; screenwriter: Jules Furthman. Cast: Pola Negri (Anna Sedlak), James Hall (Paul Almasy), George Siegmann (General Juschkiewitsch), Max Davidson (Elias Butterman), Michael Vavitch (Tabakowitsch), Otto Fries (Anton Klinak), Nicholas Soussanin, Golden Wadhams.

• ***Hotel Imperial*** (remake). Paramount Pictures, 1939. Director: Robert Florey; screenwriters: Gilbert Gabriel and Robert Thoeren. Cast: Isa Miranda (Anna), Ray Milland (Lt. Nemassy), Reginald Owen (General Videnko), Gene Lockhart (Elias), J. Carroll Naish (Kurpin), Curt Bois (Anton), Henry Victor, Albert Dekker.

Pola Negri gave perhaps her best Hollywood performance as the earthy chambermaid who falls in love with a fugitive Hungarian officer, but must also endure the advances of a Russian general who has an ever-present firing squad ready to bend people to his will. The remake was a weak sister, which had been first started in 1936 with Marlene Dietrich in the role of Anna. When she bowed out, she was replaced by Margaret Sullavan, who promptly broke her arm. The film was then shelved until Paramount signed Italian star Isa Miranda for the part. She didn't click and made only one more Hollywood picture before returning to Europe. Ray Milland as the fugitive officer and Reginald Owen as the Russian general didn't seem to know what was expected of them—even to the extent of sometimes forgetting that this was meant to be serious drama. Well, at least the remake simplified the names of the Russians.

393 The Hottentot

Based on the play by William Collier and Victor Mapes. Story: Peggy Fairfax mistakes Sam Harrington, who has a fear of horses, for a famous steeplechase rider. She prevails on him to ride the high-spirited Hottentot, from which he is thrown. His excuse for the accident is accepted by Peggy and she offers him her horse to ride in a steeplechase. He declines, disappointing her greatly. To please Peggy, he buys Hottentot as a gift for her, overcomes his fear, and rides the horse to victory.

First National Pictures, 1922 (original). Silent. Directors: James W. Horne and Del Andrews; screenwriter: Del Andrews. Cast: Douglas MacLean (Sam Harrington), Madge Bellamy (Peggy Fairfax), Lila Leslie, Martin Best, Truly Shattuck, Raymond Hatton.

Warner Bros., 1929. Director: Roy Del Ruth; screenwriter: Harvey Thew. Cast: Edward Everett Horton (Sam Harrington), Patsy Ruth Miller (Peggy Fairfax), Douglas Gerard, Edward Earle, Stanley Taylor, Gladys Brockwell.

• ***Going Places*** (remake). Warner Bros., 1938. Director: Ray Enright;

screenwriters: Jerry Wald, Sig Herzig and Maurice Leo. Cast: Dick Powell (Pete Mason), Anita Louise (Peggy), Ronald Reagan, Louis Armstrong, Allen Jenkins, Walter Catlett.

The 1929 remake of *The Hottentot* was merely a sound repeat of the 1922 version with Edward Everett Horton somewhat more amusing in the improbable story than Douglas MacLean. In the 1938 production, Dick Powell, who wasn't much of a comedian, didn't fare as well. He didn't even get to sing the hit song "Jeepers Creepers" by Harry Warren and Johnny Mercer, which was nominated for an Academy Award. That honor went to Louis Armstrong. Movies like this may have convinced Powell to give up musical comedy and try some dramatic roles.

394 The Hound of the Baskervilles

Based on the story by Arthur Conan Doyle. Story: Sir Henry Baskerville's evil ancestor, Sir Hugo, killed his wife and her faithful dog, causing the hound to haunt the area and take revenge on Hugo's ancestors throughout the years. Sherlock Holmes, ably abetted by Dr. Watson, solves the mystery and demonstrates that at least at the present the threat comes from some live menace, not a long-dead mutt.

- ***Der Hund Von Baskerville*** (original). Vitascope/Greenbaum Film, Germany, 1914 and 1915. Silent. Director: Rudolph Meinert; screenwriter: Richard Oswald. Cast: Alwin Neuss (Sherlock Holmes), Friedich Kuehne (Stapleton), Erwin Fichtner (Lord Henry), Hanni Weisse, Andreas Van Horn, Tatjana Irrah, Hilde Borke.
- ***Hound of the Baskervilles*** (remake). Gainsborough/First Division, England, 1932. Director: V.G. Gundrey; screenwriter: Edgar Wallace. Cast: Robert Rendel (Sherlock Holmes), Fred Lloyd (Dr. Watson), Elizabeth Vaughn (Laura Lyons), John Stuart (Sir Henry), Reginald Bach (Stapleton), Heather Angel (Beryl).
- ***The Hound of the Baskervilles*** (remake). Twentieth Century–Fox, 1939. Director: Sidney Lanfield; screenwriter: Ernest Pascal. Cast: Basil Rathbone (Sherlock Holmes), Nigel Bruce (Dr. Watson), Richard Greene (Sir Henry), Morton Lowry (John Stapleton), John Carradine (Barryman), Lionel Atwill (Dr. James Mortimer), Wendy Barrie (Beryl Stapleton), Ralph Forbes, Barlowe Borland, Meryl Mercer.
- ***The Hound of the Baskervilles*** (remake). United Artists/Hammer Films, 1959. Director: Terence Fisher; screenwriter: Peter Bryan. Cast: Peter Cushing (Sherlock Holmes), Andre Morell (Doctor Watson), Christopher Lee (Sir Henry), Marla Landi (Cecile), David Oxley (Sir Hugo), Miles Malleson, Francis De Wolff, Ewen Solon, John Le Mesurier.
- ***The Hound of the Baskervilles*** (remake). Michael White Ltd./Hemdale, 1978. Director: Paul Morrissey; screenwriters: Peter Cook, Dudley Moore and Paul Morrissey. Cast: Peter Cook (Sherlock Holmes), Dudley Moore (Dr. Watson/Mrs. Ada Holmes/Mr. Spiggot), Denholm Elliott (Stapleton), Dana Gillespie (Beryl Stapleton), Terry-Thomas, Max Wall, Irene Handl, Kenneth Williams, Jessie Matthews, Joan Greenwood.

Other film versions were made in France in 1915, in Germany in 1917 and 1929, in Great Britain in 1921, 1934 and 1941, and By Film Booking Offices in 1922. The first screening in Germany was a four-part feature by Josef Greenbaum, who produced the first two parts for Vitagraph and the second two for his own company. Vitagraph then released its own part three, but no one had cleared the rights with Conan Doyle. In the 1932 movie, the producers painted the poor hound with phosphorescent paint but this didn't help the film rise above its mediocre acting, sets and photography.

The 1939 movie was the first of 14 films starring Rathbone as Holmes and Bruce as Watson. For most people who have not seen William Gillette on the stage, Rathbone is the definitive Holmes. There's no doubt in this film and the second in the series, *The Adventures of Sherlock Holmes,* also released in 1939, that Basil was an ideal choice for the famous sleuth. In this film, Nigel Bruce, although certainly no genius, had not yet become the bungling, almost senile silly ass which he would play when the series moved to Universal Pictures.

Peter Cushing and Andre Morell are quite good as Holmes and Watson, as they seek the truth behind the mystery of the Baskervilles' hound. The Hammer production is rich in period, made with high standards. Cook and Moore attempt to make a farce of the story and with the exception of a few sequences, it's not funny. No doubt we can look forward to many additional attempts to film Holmes, Watson and the damned hound.

The Hour of 13 *see* **Mystery of Mr. X**

House of Bamboo *see* **The Street with No Name**

House of Women *see* **Caged**

The House on 92nd Street *see* **The Street with No Name**

House Without a Key *see* **The Chinese Parrot**

How to Be Very, Very Popular *see* **She Loves Me Not**

How to Marry a Millionaire *see* **The Gold Diggers** *and* **Three Blind Mice**

395 Huckleberry Finn

Based on the novel by Mark Twain. Story: Huckleberry Finn, who can't stand schools or dressing up, disappears when his father shows up demanding money from the maiden aunts who are raising him. He meets escaped slave Jim, with whom he makes his way down the Mississippi on a raft. Jim is sent back to face a false charge of murdering Finn when the latter is recovering from a rattlesnake bite. Finn dashes upriver in time to save Jim from a lynching.

• ***Huckleberry Finn*** (remake). Paramount, 1931. Director: Norman Taurog; screenwriter: Grover Jones. Cast: Jackie Coogan (Tom Sawyer), Mitzi Green (Becky Thatcher), Junior Durkin (Huckleberry Finn), Jackie Searl (Sid

The great black actor Rex Ingram, as Jim, shares a watermelon with Mickey Rooney in The Adventures of Huckleberry Finn *(MGM, 1939).*

Sawyer), Clarence Muse (Jim), Clara Blandick (Aunt Polly), Jane Darwell, Eugene Pallette, Oscar Apfel, Warner Richmond.

• ***Huckleberry Finn*** (remake). MGM, 1939. Mickey Rooney (Huckleberry Finn), Walter Connolly (the "King"), William Frawley (the "Duke"), Rex Ingram (Jim), Lynne Carver (Mary Jane), Jo Ann Sayers, Minor Watson, Elizabeth Risdon, Victor Kilian, Clara Blandick.

• ***Huckleberry Finn*** (remake). MGM, 1960. Director: Michael Curtiz; screenwriter: James Lee. Cast: Eddie Hodges (Huckleberry Finn), Archie Moore (Jim), Tony Randall, Neville Brand, Judy Canova, Buster Keaton, Andy Devine.

• ***Huckleberry Finn*** (remake). United Artists, 1974. Director: J. Lee Thompson; screenwriters: Robert B. and Richard M. Sherman. Cast: Jeff East (Huck Finn), Paul Winfield (Jim), Harvey Korman (King), David Wayne (Duke), Arthur O'Connell (Col. Grangerford), Gary Merrill (Pap), Natalie Trundy, Lucille Benson, Kim O'Brien, Jean Fay.

Huckleberry Finn was also filmed by Paramount in 1920 and in Russia in 1974 as *Lost Boy.* The best Huck was surely Mickey Rooney, and the only time that Hollywood was able to turn the wonderful story into a box-office loser was in 1974. The best Jim was the great black actor Rex Ingram, who always made the most of the limited roles offered to him. He provided Jim with all the dignity

Eddie Hodges and ex-light heavyweight champion Archie Moore, as Jim, share adventures in the 1960 MGM version of The Adventures of Huckleberry Finn.

that Twain had given his character. It is a shame that some misguided individuals have taken the erroneous view that Huckleberry Finn is a racist story. It would seem that they have completely missed Twain's point. The ex-boxer Archie Moore couldn't match Ingram's performance and poor Paul Winfield, a fine actor, was stuck in a bland version of the famous story in 1974. Other filmings of the story are bound to follow for future generations. It's timeless entertainment.

Huis Clos *see* **No Exit**

396 The Hunchback of Notre Dame

Based on Victor Hugo's novel "Notre-Dame de Paris." Story: Quasimodo, the deformed and deaf bell ringer of the Cathedral of Notre Dame in Paris during the reign of Louis XI, is befriended by gypsy girl Esmerelda while being given public punishment that he did not deserve. He returns the favor when Esmerelda is framed for murder and witchcraft by the chief magistrate, Frollo, who blames her for his passion for her. As she is about to be executed in front of Notre Dame, Quasimodo swings down from his perch in the belfry and demands sanctuary for her within the Cathedral. Fearing the nobles will take her from the church and carry out the execution, Clopin, the king of thieves, sets siege to the cathedral to rescue her. Misunderstanding their intentions, Quasimodo defends the girl, furiously throwing building stones and boiling oil on those below, killing many. He also is forced to kill his mentor, Frollo, who has come to get the girl. Depending on the version of the story, Quasimodo, who loves the girl, is also killed or left sadly with his bells as Esmerelda is reunited with her lover, the poet Gringoire.

• ***Esmerelda*** (original). French Gaumont Films, 1905. Director and screenwriter: Mme. Alice Blache. Cast: Henry Vorins (Quasimodo), Denise Becker (Esmerelda).

• ***The Darling of Paris*** (remake). Fox Films, 1917. Silent. Director and screenwriter: J. Gordon Edwards. Cast: Theda Bara (Esmerelda), Glenn White (Quasimodo), Walter Frallo (Claude Frollo), Herbert Heyes (Captain Phoebus), Alice Gale (Gypsy Queen), John Webb Dillon (Clopin), Louis Dean (Gringoire).

• ***The Hunchback of Notre Dame*** (remake). Universal Pictures, 1923. Silent. Director: Wallace Worsley; screenwriter: Edward T. Lowe, Jr. Cast: Lon Chaney (Quasimodo), Patsy Ruth Miller (Esmerelda), Ernest Torrence (Clopin), Norman Kerry (Phoebus), Raymond Hatton (Gringiore), Brandon Hurst (Jehan Follo), Nigel De Brulier (Dom Claude Frollo), Tully Marshall (Louis XI), Kate Lester, Gladys Blackwell, Eulalie Jensen, Winifred Bryson, Harry Van Meter.

• ***The Hunchback of Notre Dame*** (remake). RKO Pictures, 1939. Director: William Dieterle; screenwriters: Sonya Levien and Bruno Frank. Cast: Charles Laughton (Quasimodo), Maureen O'Hara (Esmerelda), Thomas Mitchell (Clopin), Sir Cedric Hardwicke (Jehan Frollo), Walter Hamden (Claude Frollo), Edmond O'Brien (Gringiore), Alan Marshal (Phoebus), Harry Davenport (Louis XI), Katherine Alexander, Arthur Hohl, Rod La Rocque, George Zucco, Etienne Girardot, Minna Gombell.

• ***The Hunchback of Notre Dame*** (remake). Allied Artists, 1957. Director: Jean Delannoy; screenwriters: Jean Aurenche and Jacques Prevert. Cast: Anthony Quinn (Quasimodo), Gina Lollobrigida (Esmerelda), Jean Danet (Phoebus), Alain Cluny (Claude Frollo), Phillippi Clay (Clopin), Robert Hirsch (Gringiore), Danielle Dumont, Roger Blin, Marianne Oswald, Jean Tissier.

Opposite, top: *Lon Chaney as Quasimodo carries Patsy Ruth Miller, as the gypsy girl Esmerelda, while Eulalie Jensen rages from a dungeon window in* The Hunchback of Notre Dame *(Universal, 1923)*. Bottom: *Gypsy girl Esmerelda, played by Maureen O'Hara, dances in the 1939 RKO production of* The Hunchback of Notre Dame.

Other movies telling the story of the bell ringer and the gypsy were *Esmerelda* in 1906 in England; *Notre-Dame De Paris* in France and Italy in 1911; *Notre Dame* in 1913 in France; *Enmei-in No Semushi* in Japan in 1925; and in India, *Dhanwan* in 1937, and *Badshah Dampati* in 1953.

The best versions of the Dumas story are the stunning silent, starring the incomparable Lon Chaney with his riveting performance as the pitiful bell ringer, and the 1939 masterpiece with Charles Laughton giving one of the most moving and memorable portrayals of his distinguished career. Others in this remarkable remake deserving of considerable praise include Thomas Mitchell as the king of thieves, Cedric Hardwicke as the possessed villain who blames the object for his sin of lust, and Harry Davenport as a kindly King Louis XI. The 1957 picture with Anthony Quinn and Gina Lollobrigida suffers in comparison to the previous works, not because it is poorly done nor the performances bad, but rather that it had an almost impossible act to follow.

Der Hund Von Baskervilles *see* **The Hound of the Baskervilles**

397 The Hurricane

Based on the novel by Charles Nordhoff and James N. Hall. Story: Terangi and Marama are a young South Sea islands native couple, carefree and happy. When Terangi is sentenced to a prison term in Tahiti for a misunderstanding, he can't stand being penned up and separated from Marama so he escapes. This results in a longer sentence, as does his next escape. Finally he kills a cruel guard and now the unbending governor orders him shot on sight. Fortunately or unfortunately, depending on your point of view, a great typhoon hits the islands and the young couple is finally able to escape their tormentors.

Goldwyn/United Artists, 1937 (original). Directors: John Ford and Stuart Heisler; screenwriters: Dudley Nichols and Oliver N.P. Garrett. Cast: Dorothy Lamour (Marama), Jon Hall (Terangi), Mary Astor (Mrs. De Laage), C. Aubrey Smith (Father Paul), Thomas Mitchell (Dr. Kersaint), Raymond Massey (Governor De Laage), John Carradine, Jerome Cowan, Al Kikume, Kuulei De Clercq, Mamo Clark.

• ***The Hurricane*** (remake). Dino De Laurentiis Productions, 1979. Director: Jan Troell; screenwriter: Lorenzo Semple, Jr. Cast: Jason Robards (Captain Bruckner), Mia Farrow (Charlotte Bruckner), Max Von Sydow (Doctor Bascomb), Trevor Howard (Father Malone), Dayton Ka'ne (Matangi), Timothy Bottoms (Jack Strang), James Keach, Arlirau Tekurarere, Willie Myers.

This tropical island melodrama compounds the problem the South Sea natives had with their European masters by treating them as simple children who can't possibly understand why they are punished when bad. Other than this "white man's burden" mentality, the original is an enjoyable and exciting film of innocence betrayed. Hall is athletic and a fine example of the European's notion of a noble savage while Lamour continues her crusade to make the sarong one of the more sensuous pieces of apparel ever seen on the screen.

The remake fails at almost every level—acting, dialogue, production and even the big storm. Mia Farrow has this thing for poor unfortunate Dayton

Ka'ne who is an even worse actor than Jon Hall. A lot of talent is wasted on a story which was creaky the first time around.

398 The Hustler

Based on the novel by Walter Tevis. Story: "Fast Eddie" Felson, a brash pool shark, arrives in New York with his partner, Charlie Burns, to challenge Minnesota Fats, the undisputed pool champ in the country. The two men play pool for 36 hours. At first everything goes Eddie's way, but then, filled with too much liquor and conceit, he loses everything. Beaten and broken, he picks up alcoholic cripple Sarah Packard at an all-night coffeeshop and goes home with her. To bring in some money for the two of them, Eddie goes around to different pool halls and hustles the locals. At one place, his arrogance gets both of his thumbs broken. When he recovers he throws in with cold-blooded gambler Bert Gordon, who agrees to arrange big time matches for 70 percent of the profits. Sarah accompanies Eddie and Bert to Louisville where Eddie makes a big score against a wealthy billiards player. Tragically, Bert's insistence on total domination of Eddie and anything that is Eddie's, including Sarah, causes her to slash her wrists and die. Realizing that his ego has once again got in the way of his chance for happiness, Eddie again challenges Minnesota Fats, wins big and refuses to give any cut to Bert, defiantly walking out of the pool hall.

Twentieth Century–Fox, 1961 (original). Director: Robert Rossen; screenwriters: Sidney Carroll and Rossen. Cast: Paul Newman (Eddie Felson), Jackie Gleason (Minnesota Fats), Piper Laurie (Sarah Packard), George C. Scott (Bert Gordon), Myron McCormick (Charlie Burns), Murray Hamilton, Michael Constantine, Stefan Gierasch.

• ***The Color of Money*** (sequel). Touchstone, 1986. Director: Martin Scorsese; screenwriter: Richard Price. Cast: Paul Newman (Eddie Felson), Tom Cruise (Vince), Helen Shaver (Janelle/Carmen), Mary Elizabeth Mastrantonio, Bill Cobbs, Forest Whitaker, John Turturro.

The 1986 film is described by Newman and Scorsese as a follow-up rather than a sequel, but whatever it is, Paul Newman finally won his elusive Oscar by re-creating a role which won him a nomination in 1961. At that time, the film was nominated for Best Picture, Rossen was up for Best Director, and Sidney Carroll for Best Script, while Piper Laurie, Jackie Gleason and George C. Scott were given acting nominations. The only award gathered in was for Eugen Schufftan's moody photography. In the 1986 film, Newman, 25 years later, is a liquor salesman who bankrolls pool hotshots as a hobby. In Tom Cruise, he sees himself as an arrogant, unbeatable pool shark. Newman trains Cruise, treating him almost like a race horse so that he can be a winner in the big time in Atlantic City.

I

399 I Am a Camera

Based on the "Berlin" stories by Christopher Isherwood and the play by John

Van Druten. Story: In Berlin of 1932, tutor Christopher Isherwood platonically shares his lodgings with Sally Bowles, a singer and dancer in a third-rate cabaret. They encourage an affair between two Jews, Natalie Landauer and Fritz Wendel. Sally and Christopher's relationship is in turn fostered by wealthy Clive, who becomes Sally's lover but eventually deserts them with the coming to power of the Nazis. Sally and Christopher also separate but meet again twenty years later when she publishes her memoirs.

Remus/United Artists, Great Britain, 1955 (original). Director: Henry Cornelius; screenwriter: John Collier. Cast: Julie Harris (Sally Bowles), Laurence Harvey (Christopher Isherwood), Shelley Winters (Natalie Landauer), Ron Randall (Clive), Lea Seidl (Frau Schneider), Anton Diffring (Fritz Wendel), Jean Gargoet, Frederick Valk, Tutte Lemkow, Patrick McGoohan, Stanley Maxted.

• ***Cabaret*** (remake). Allied Artists, 1973. Director: Bob Fosse; screenwriter: Jay Presson Allen. Cast: Liza Minnelli (Sally Bowles), Michael York (Brian Roberts), Joel Grey (Master of Ceremonies), Helmut Griem (Baron Max von Heune), Fritz Wepper (Fritz Wendel), Marisa Berenson (Natalia Landauer), Elisabeth Neumann-Vietrel, Sigrid von Richthofen, Helen Vita.

Some critics threw up their hands when Liza Minnelli and Joel Grey walked off with Academy Awards for their performances in—of all things—a musical, but fans didn't seem to mind. Liza with a Z came across both innocently appealing and degenerate at the same time, quite an accomplishment. Grey is just marvelous as the M.C. of the Kit Kat Klub, never seen out of character. He seemed to sum up in his leering, almost maniacal grins and suggestive chatter the acceptance of the evil and debasement that Germans had to the rise of the Nazi party and its anti–Semitism. The stylized dancing of director and choreographer Bob Fosse was spectacular, as was the music of John Kander and Fred Ebb, including the title song, "Money, Money," "Maybe This Time," "Wilkommen," "Mein Herr" and the chilling "Tomorrow Belongs to Me." The story is another thing. Liza shares her British lover York with her homosexual German lover Griem, considers having the baby she's carrying, but then aborts it because it would interfere with her affairs. Oh well, you can't have everything.

400 I Am a Criminal

Based on an original idea by Harrison Jacobs. Story: Newsboy Bobby is used by a racketeer, Brad MacArthur, whom the ten-year-old greatly admires, to beat a manslaughter rap. As the picture develops, Brad and the other tough guys in the neighborhood come to love the little tyke. Bobby provides another service for Brad when he thwarts the plans of the racketeer's erstwhile girlfriend, Linda, to take him to the cleaners.

Monogram Pictures, 1938 (original). Director: William Nigh; screenwriter: John Krafft. Cast: John Carroll (Brad MacArthur), Kay Linaker (Linda), Craig Reynolds (Clint Reynolds), Martin Spellman (Bobby), Lester Matthews, Mary Kornman, May Beatty, Robert Fiske.

• ***Smart Guy*** (remake). Monogram Pictures, 1943. Director: Lambert

Hillyer; screenwriters: Charles R. Marion and John W. Krafft. Cast: Rick Vallin (Johnny), Bobby Larson (Bobby), Veda Ann Borg (Lee), Wanda McKay (Jean), Jack LaRue (Taylor), Mary Gordon, Paul McVey, Addison Richards.

Both films are B productions following a strict formula of bringing them in cheaply and quickly. Despite the haste in making the pictures, both move slowly. In the remake, Rick Vallin is the racketeer who adopts newsboy Bobby Larson to get favorable publicity to beat a manslaughter rap—but the kid gets to him, teaching the mobster some important moral lessons.

401 I Cover the Waterfront

Based on the novel by Max Miller. Story: San Diego newspaperman Joe Miller suspects fisherman Eli Kirk of smuggling illegal Chinese aliens into the country. To get more information for his planned expose, he romances Eli's daughter, Julie, but he falls in love with her. Eli is wounded in a fracas with the Coast Guard and shoots Joe. But instead of making his escape, Eli takes Joe to a doctor at Julie's pleading for the life of the man she loves. Eli dies of his wounds but Joe recovers and marries Julie.

United Artists, 1933 (original). Director: James Cruze; screenwriter: Wells Root. Cast: Claudette Colbert (Julie Kirk), Ben Lyon (Joe Miller), Ernest Torrence (Eli Kirk), Hobart Cavanaugh, Purnell Pratt, Harry Beresford, Maurice Black.

• ***Secret of Deep Harbor*** (remake). United Artists, 1961. Director: Edward L. Cahn; screenwriters: Owen Harris and Wells Root. Cast: Ron Foster (Skip Hanlon), Barry Kelley (Milo Fowler), Merry Anders (Janey Fowler), Norman Alden, James Seay, Grant Richards, Ralph Manza, Billie Bird, Elaine Walker.

While the plot's not hot, the performance of the three leading actors made *I Cover the Waterfront* a tough, picturesque melodrama. The B remake with unknown performers, who mostly stayed that way, converts the story to one of a young gangster, Foster, who falls for the daughter, Anders, of a rival syndicate boss, Kelley. By this time, the theme and plot had been done to death both in movies and on TV.

I Died a Thousand Times ***see*** **High Sierra**

I Killed That Man ***see*** **Devil's Mate**

I Married a Doctor ***see*** **Main Street**

I, Monster ***see*** **Dr. Jekyll and Mr. Hyde**

402 I the Jury

Based on the novel by Mickey Spillane. Story: When amputee Jack Williams is shot to death, his best friend, private detective Mike Hammer, swears vengeance. His suspects include Myrna, a former heroin addict and Jack's fiancée; psychiatrist Charlotte Manning; the beautiful but love-starved Bellamy twins; and George Kalecki, a fight promoter turned art collector. While making his investigation, using illegal tactics, Hammer stumbles over a large number of corpses and killings. Finally the clues lead to Mike's own fiancée, Charlotte, who wanted to take over Kalecki's narcotics organization. As Mike explains to Charlotte how he knows she is the killer, she seductively and slowly partially undresses. She embraces him, but before she can reach for a hidden gun, Mike shoots and kills her.

Parklane Productions, 1953 (original). Director and screenwriter: Harry Essex. Cast: Biff Elliot (Mike Hammer), Preston Foster (Capt. Pat Chambers), Peggie Castle (Charlotte Manning), Margaret Sheridan (Velda), Alan Reed (George Kalecki), Frances Osborne (Myrna), Tani Seitz (Mary Bellamy), Dran Seitz (Esther Bellamy), Robert Swanger (Jack Williams), Robert Cunningham, Elisha Cook, Jr., Paul Dubov, Mary Anderson, John Qualen.

• ***I the Jury*** (remake). American Cinema, 1982. Director: Richard T. Heffron; screenwriter: Larry Cohen. Cast: Armand Assante (Mike Hammer), Barbara Carrera (Dr. Charlotte Bennett), Alan King (Charles Kalecki), Luarene London (Velda), Geoffrey Lewis (Jor), Paul Sorvino (Det. Pat Chambers), Judson Scott, Barry Snider, Julia Barr, Jessica James.

Mickey Spillane's novel *I the Jury* was a book passed around a great deal by connoisseurs of good smut. Such books just naturally fell open to the hot spots with certain passages underlined and judged with marginal comments. The book had everything to please a prurient heart: promiscuous, sexy women and cold-blooded violence and sadism, and that's just on the part of the good guys. The film had to be a disappointment, even had it been given better production values and a name cast. No one could get away with putting on the screen what adolescent and post-adolescent males imagined as they read the book. Surprise, surprise, in twenty years, producers were willing to try anything—and there's the rub for the remake. By the time it was released, the exploitation movies had made explicit violence and sex so common—so very common—that few found the Spillane story anything more than old-hat material.

403 I Wake Up Screaming

Based on the novel by Steve Fisher. Story: Beautiful Vicky Lynn is murdered and the chief suspect is Frankie Christopher, who has been grooming Vicky for stardom in films. Her sister Jill demands that the police do something about Vicky's death and they assign detective Ed Cornell to the case. Cornell dogs his prey and promises to get him, but it turns out he is the murderer, having idolized Vicky from afar and unwilling to share her with the world.

Twentieth Century–Fox, 1941. Director: H. Bruce Humberstone; screenwriter: Dwight Taylor. Cast: Betty Grable (Jill Lynn), Victor Mature (Frankie Christopher), Carole Landis (Vicky Lynn), Laird Cregar (Ed Cornell), William Gargan (Jerry MacDonald), Alan Mowbray, Allyn Joslyn, Elisha Cook, Jr., Chick Chandler.

• ***Vicki*** (remake). Twentieth Century–Fox, 1953. Director: Harry Horner; screenwriter: Dwight Taylor. Cast: Jeanne Crain (Jill), Jean Peters (Vicki), Elliott Reid (Steve), Richard Boone (Cornell), Casey Adams (Larry Evans), Alex D'Arcy (Robin Ray), Carl Betz, Aaron Spelling, Roy Engel, Parley Baer, Stuart Randall.

Originally, *I Wake Up Screaming* was released as *Hot Spot*. It is a classy suspense movie with a memorable performance by the very fine character actor Laird Cregar. There are few changes in the remake, which features Jean Peters as the witness promoted into becoming a model by publicist Elliott Reid. When Peters is murdered, the police assign detective Richard Boone to the case. His judgement is clouded by his obsessive love for the dead girl. He hounds the publicist unfairly. The publicist and Jeanne Crain, the dead girl's sister, are forced to unmask the killer themselves.

I Was Framed *see* **Dust Be My Destiny**

I'd Give My Life *see* **The Noose**

I'd Rather Be Rich *see* **It Started With Eve**

404 Idle Rich

Based on the play *White Collars* by Edith Ellis. Story: When millionaire William Van Luyn marries stenographer Joan Thayer, he offers her family the benefits that his money can provide. In a reverse snobbery, they haughtily refuse his kind offer. Joan insists that he move in with her family and share the virtues and discomforts of their simple home life. Believing that money means nothing to Joan and his family, he makes plans to give his away. At this his in-laws have a quick change of heart about accepting the benefits of his fortune.

MGM, 1929 (original). Director: William De Mille; screenwriter: Clara Beranger. Cast: Conrad Nagel (William Van Luyn), Bessie Love (Helen Thayer), Leila Hyams (Joan Thayer), Robert Ober, James Neill, Edythe Chapman, Paul Kruger.

• ***Rich Man, Poor Girl*** (remake). MGM. Director: Reinhold Schunzel; screenwriters: Joseph A. Field and Jerome Chodorov. Cast: Robert Young (Bill Harrison), Lew Ayres (Henry Thayer), Ruth Hussey (Joan Thayer), Lana Turner, Rita Johnson.

These are unexciting comedy-dramas of a proletariat family and the tribulations of a poor millionaire who becomes involved with them. The theme that money can't buy happiness is much better handled in Frank Capra's *You Can't Take It with You* (1938). The most notable thing about the remake is that Lew Ayres had rejoined the studio where he had begun his career nine years earlier, co-starring with Greta Garbo in *The Kiss*.

405 If I Were King

Based on the play by Justin Huntley McCarthy. Story: It tells the tale of fourteenth-century French poet and rascal Francois Villon, who matches wits with Louis XI and rouses the people to thwart the planned take-over by the Duke of Burgundy and other nobles.

• ***If I Were King*** (remake). Fox Film Corp., 1920. Silent. Director: J. Gordon Edwards; screenwriter: E. Lloyd Sheldon. Cast: William Farnum (Francois

Villon), Betty Ross Clarke (Katherine), Fritz Leiber (Louis XI), Walter Law (Thibault), Henry Carvill (Tristan), Claude Payton (Montigney), V.V. Clogg, Harold Clairmont, Renita Johnston.

• ***The Beloved Rogue*** (remake). United Artists, 1927. Silent. Director: Alan Crosland; screenwriter: Paul Bern. Cast: John Barrymore (Francois Villon), Conrad Veidt (Louis XI), Marceline Day (Charlotte de Vauxcelles), Henry Victor (Thibault), Lawson Butt (John, Duke of Burgundy), Mack Swain, Slim Summerville, Otto Matieson, Rose Dione, Bertram Grassby, Lucy Beaumont.

• ***The Vagabond King*** (remake). Paramount Pictures, 1930. Director: Ludwig Berger; screenwriter: Herman J. Mankiewicz, based on the operetta by William H. Post, Brian Hooker and Rudolf Friml. Cast: Dennis King (Francois Villon), Jeanette MacDonald (Katherine), O.P. Heggie (Louis XI), Lillian Roth (Huguette), Warner Oland (Thibault), Lawford Davidson, Arthur Stone, Thomas Ricketts.

• ***If I Were King*** (remake). Paramount Pictures, 1938. Director: Frank Lloyd; screenwriter: Preston Sturges. Cast: Ronald Colman (Francois Villon), Basil Rathbone (Louis XI), Frances Dee (Katherine de Vaucelles), Ellen Drew (Hugette), C.V. France (Father Villon), Henry Wilcoxon (Captain of the Watch), Heather Thatcher (Queen), Stanley Ridges (Rene de Montigny), Bruce Lester, Walter Kingsford, Alma Lloyd, Sidney Toler, Colin Tapley, Ralph Forbes.

• ***The Vagabond King*** (remake). Paramount Pictures, 1956. Director: Michael Curtiz; screenwriters: Ken Englund and Noel Langley. Cast: Kathryn Grayson (Catherine de Vaucelles), Oreste (Francois Villon), Rita Moreno (Hugette), Cedric Hardwicke (Tristan), Walter Hampden (Louis XI), Leslie Nielsen (Thibault), William Prince (Rene), Jack Lord, Billy Vine, Harry McNaughton, Florence Sunstrom.

The life and exploits of Francois Villon have been nicely handled on the screen with earlier versions appearing in 1915 and 1918. For straight adventure and acting, it's hard to beat the combination of Ronald Colman and Basil Rathbone in 1938. With Preston Sturges providing the screenplay, the wit of these two friendly adversaries is made a most important aspect of the story. John Barrymore and William Farnum made impressive vagabonds, but the two silent pieces don't stack up with the moody 1938 piece. Of the musical versions of the story, Dennis King wins out over Oreste. The Rudolf Friml songs include "Hugette Waltz," "Love for Sale," "Love Me Tonight," "Only a Rose," "Some Day," "Song of the Vagabonds" and the title number.

406 If Winter Comes

Based on the novel by A.S.M. Hutchinson. Story: Mark Sabre hires Effie Bright to be a companion for his snobbish wife, Mabel, while he is away at war. When he returns, Effie, who has been dismissed by Mabel, comes to him with her baby seeking his help. He takes Effie and the baby in, causing Mabel to leave him and himself to be ostracized. When Effie kills her baby and commits suicide, Mark suffers a nervous breakdown at a coroner's examination, conducted on the basis of untrue and circumstantial evidence. Sabre is rescued when his former sweetheart, Nona, comes to his aid.

Fox Film Corporation, 1923 (original). Silent. Director: Harry Millarde; screenwriter: Paul Sloane. Cast: Percy Marmont (Mark Sabre), Gladys Leslie (Effie Bright), Margaret Fielding (Mabel), Leslie King (Nona), Arthur Metcalfe, Sidney Herbert, Wallace Kolb, William Riley, Raymond Bloomer, Russell Sedgwick.

• ***If Winter Comes*** (remake). MGM, 1948. Director: Victor Saville; screenwriters: Marguerite Roberts and Arthur Wimperis. Cast: Walter Pidgeon (Mark Sabre), Deborah Kerr (Nona Tybar), Angela Lansbury (Mabel Sabre), Janet Leigh (Effie Bright), Binnie Barnes, Dame May Whitty, Rene Ray, Virginia Keiley, Reginald Owen.

When the novel was published, thousands of readers cried at this unconvincing romantic nonsense of an idealistic man, unhappily married, who finds himself at the mercy of village gossip when he takes in an unfortunate girl and her child. Millions more cried when the silent film was released in 1923. By 1948, audiences had no more tears left for the artificial production, yawning instead.

I'll Be Yours *see* **The Good Fairy**

I'll Never Forget You *see* **Berkeley Square**

407 I'll Tell the World

Based on a story by Lincoln Warberg and Lt. Commander Frank Wead. Story: This second feature revolves around the antics of a brash young reporter, Stanley Brown, who writes about a lost dirigible, then discovers that it is part of a plot to overthow the government of a mythical country.

Universal Pictures, 1934 (original). Director: Edward Sedgwick; screenwriters: Dale Van Every and Ralph Spence. Cast: Lee Tracy (Stanley Brown), Gloria Stuart (Jane Hamilton), Roger Pryor (William S. Briggs), Onslow Stevens (Prince Michael), Alec B. Francis (Grand Duke Ferdinand), Herman Bing, Willard Robertson, Hugh Enfield, Dorothy Granger, Leon Waycoff (Ames).

• ***I'll Tell the World*** (remake). Universal Pictures, 1945. Director: Leslie Goodwins; screenwriters: Henry Blankett and Lester Kline. Cast: Lee Tracy (Gabriel Patton), Brenda Joyce (Lorna Gray), Raymond Walburn (H.I. Bailey), June Preisser (Madge Bailey), Thomas Gomez (J.B. Kindell), Howard Freeman, Lorin Raker, Janet Shaw, Pierre Watkin, Peter Potter, Gene Rodgers.

These movies are most noted for the fast-paced talking of their star, Lee Tracy. In the remake, now with a new identity, Tracy is a sports announcer on the radio who decides the best way to get his small station recognized is to organize a lonely-hearts program.

I'll Wait for You *see* **Hide-out**

Illegal *see* **The Mouthpiece**

408 Illicit

Based on the play by Edith Fitzgerald and Robert Riskin. Story: Anne Vincent is living with her wealthy boyfriend, Dick Ives. His father persuades them to marry but Anne finds that married life is not particularly glamorous, and when her husband finds female interests away from home, she walks out on him. However, they get together again before the fade-out.

Warner Bros., 1931 (original). Director: Archie Mayo; screenwriters: Edith Fitzgerald and Robert Riskin. Cast: Barbara Stanwyck (Anne Vincent), James Rennie (Dick Ives), Charles Butterworth (Georgie), Joan Blondell (Dukie), Ricardo Cortez (Prince Raines), Natalie Moorhead, Claude Gillingwater.

• ***Ex-Lady*** (remake). Warner Bros., 1933. Director: Robert Florey; screenwriter: David Boehm. Cast: Bette Davis (Helen Bauer), Gene Raymond (Don Peterson), Frank McHugh (Hugo Van Hugh), Monroe Owsley (Nick Malvyn), Claire Dodd (Iris Van Hugh), Kay Strozzi, Ferdinand Gottschalk.

Living together sans marriage was a daring topic in pre–women's liberation days. It was also a dangerous practice, what with so many laws on the books making the practice illegal. Even so, critics were not upset by the theme of Barbara Stanwyck's first film for Warner Bros. They just didn't care for its development or production. Audiences, on the other hand, were less critical and the film prospered. *Ex-Lady* just beat the strict standards of the Legion of Decency which went in effect in 1934, allowing Bette Davis not only to initially prefer cohabitation to marriage with her ad-writer boyfriend, played by Gene Raymond, but also to appear *en dishabille* in her boudoir scenes. Despite this allure, neither critics nor audiences were impressed with this version of the story.

409 Imitation of Life

Based on the novel by Fannie Hurst. Story: Widowed Bea Pullman goes in business with her black housekeeper, Delilah, and makes a fortune with the latter's pancake recipe. Their lives are both nearly destroyed when Bea finds herself in competition with her daughter, Jessie, for the love of Stephen Archer, while Delilah's daughter, Peola, meets tragedy when she breaks with her mother and because of her light skin, attempts to pass for white.

Universal Pictures, 1934. Director: John M. Stahl; screenwriter: William Hurlburt. Cast: Claudette Colbert (Bea Pullman), Warren William (Stephen Archer), Louise Beavers (Aunt Delilah), Ned Sparks (Elmer), Rochelle Hudson (Jessie Pullman at eighteen), Fredi Washington (Peola Johnson at nineteen), Baby Jane, Sebie Hendricks, Dorothy Black, Alan Hale.

• ***Imitation of Life*** (remake). Universal Pictures, 1959. Director: Douglas Sirk; screenwriters: Eleanore Griffin and Allan Scott. Cast: Lana Turner (Lora Meredith), John Gavin (Steve Archer), Robert Alda (Allen Loomis), Sandra Dee (Susie Meredith), Susan Kohner (Sara Jane Johnson), Juanita Moore (Annie Johnson), Terry Burhan, Karen Dicker, Troy Donahue, Dan O'Herlihy, Mahalia Jackson.

These tearjerkers have ranked high in the so-called women's picture category. The performances of the leading actors in both versions are quite good, with both Kohner and Moore being nominated for but not winning the Best Supporting Actress Academy Award. The first version was nominated for the Best Picture award but did not win. Parents who have ever been alienated from a child, even for a little while, will no doubt feel the plucking of the heart strings in these moving soap opera melodramas. Tears come to many when in the second version, Sara Jane, who has refused to acknowledge her mother, breaks down at the latter's funeral. Bring two handkerchiefs.

The Immortal Sergeant *see* **The Lost Patrol**

Imp *see* **Dr. Jekyll and Mr. Hyde**

In Like Flint *see* **Our Man Flint**

410 In Old Kentucky

Based on the play by Charles T. Dazey. Story: Gambler and alcoholic Jimmy Brierly returns to his now poverty-stricken family of horsebreeders in Kentucky after World War I. By coincidence, a famous racehorse that Jimmy rode during the war is repurchased. Jimmy trains the horse and enters it in the Kentucky Derby, which the horse wins, thus resurrecting the family's fortunes.

• ***In Old Kentucky*** (remake). MGM, 1927. Silent. Director: John M. Stahl; screenwriter: A.P. Younger. Cast: James Murray (Jimmy Brierly), Helene Costello (Nancy Holden), Wesley Barry (Skippy Lowry), Dorothy Cummings (Mrs. Brierly), Edward Martindel (Mr. Brierly), Harvey Clark, Stepin Fetchit, Carolynne Snowden, Nick Cogley.

• ***In Old Kentucky*** (remake). Twentieth Century–Fox, 1935. Director: George Marshall; screenwriters: Sam Hellman and Gladys Lehman. Cast: Will Rogers (Steve Tapley), Dorothy Wilson (Nancy Martingale), Russell Hardie (Lee Andrews), Charles Sellon (Ezra Martingale), Louise Henry, Esther Dale, Alan Dinehart, Charles Richman, Bill Robinson.

In Old Kentucky was the last film made by Will Rogers and critics and fans alike felt it was among his best. The story had not changed from the 1927 film or for that matter, not markedly from the 1920 silent version by First National Pictures. However, with Rogers, the comedy aspects of the story are effectively emphasized, making it a far more enjoyable picture. Besides Rogers, the film also highlights the dancing talents of the legendary Bill "Bojangles" Robinson. Adding to the fun are Charles Sellon as a slap-happy grandpa who delights in taking pot shots at the opposition any chance he gets.

In the Good Old Summertime *see* **The Shop Around the Corner**

411 In the Heat of the Night

Based on the novel by John Ball. Story: Virgil Tibbs, a black man waiting for a train in a small Mississippi town, finds himself arrested and suspected of the killing of a white man. When Police Chief Bill Gillespie demands that the "boy"

Warren William, Louise Beavers and Claudette Colbert beam in one of the rare happy scenes in the classic "women's picture," Imitation of Life *(Universal, 1934).*

identify himself, Tibbs pulls out his badge. He's a police detective from the North and an expert on homicides. Before long Tibbs and Gillespie have formed an uneasy alliance to solve the murder case.

United Artists, 1967 (original). Director: Norman Jewison; screenwriter: Stirling Silliphant. Cast: Sidney Poitier (Virgil Tibbs), Rod Steiger (Police Chief Bill Gillespie), Warren Oates (Deputy Sam Wood), Lee Grant (Mrs. Leslie Colbert), James Patterson (Purdy), Quentin Dean (Delores Purdy), Larry Gates, William Schallert, Beah Richards, Scott Wilson.

• ***They Call Me Mr. Tibbs*** (sequel). United Artists, 1970. Director: Gordon Douglas; screenwriter: Alan R. Trustman. Cast: Sidney Poitier (Virgil Tibbs), Martin Landau (Rev. Logan Sharpe), Barbara McNair (Valerie Tibbs), Anthony Zerbe (Rice Weedon), Jeff Corey (Capt. Marden), David Sheiner, Juano Hernandez, Norma Crane, Edward Asner.

• ***The Organization*** (sequel). United Artists, 1971. Director: Don Medford; screenwriter: James R. Webb. Cast: Sidney Poitier (Virgil Tibbs), Barbara McNair (Valerie Tibbs), Sheree North (Gloria Morgan), Gerald O'Loughlin (Lt. Jack Pecora), Raul Julia (Juan Mendoza), Ron O'Neal, Lani Miyazaki, Allen Garfield, Bernie Hamilton.

In the Heat of the Night was given high marks for intelligently dealing with prejudices on both sides of the black and white question, but the story itself is a nothing mystery, with the culprit as obvious to all as was the fact that a grudging respect would develop between Poitier and Steiger. Rod won an

Before he became ambassador to Mexico, John Gavin romanced Lana Turner in this 1959 Universal remake of Imitation of Life.

Oscar for his southern police chief, but it wasn't the best performance of the year and not even one of his best.

In the first sequel, Poitier is back in his home territory investigating the murder of a girl, of which his friend, Martin Landau, a priest, may be guilty. It's not a very good movie but better than the truly dull third movie featuring Lt. Virgil Tibbs battling drug dealers in San Francisco.

412 In the Next Room

Based on the novel *The Mystery of the Boule Cabinet* by Burton Egbert Stevenson and the play by Eleanor Robson Belmont and Harriet Ford. Story: When police are called to the house of Mr. Vantine, he refuses to admit them. Reporter Jimmy Godfrey, engaged to Vantine's niece, is brought in to gain them entry. They unpack an antique cabinet and find a woman in a hypnotic trance. This is closely followed by the son of the former owner of the cabinet falling dead; a police detective being slugged unconscious; Mr. Vantine getting a light knock to the noggin; his niece being kidnapped and taken to a wine cellar, from where she is rescued by a one-legged butler; the mysterious woman reviving to reveal that she and her partner had planned to smuggle diamonds into the house but that he had been poisoned; and finally that the cabinet had been sent to the wrong address. Then the reporter and detective get to work unraveling the mystery—or is.it the script?

First National Pictures, 1930 (original). Director: Edward Cline; screenwriter: Harvey Gates. Cast: Jack Mulhall (James Godfrey), Alice Day (Lorna), Robert O'Connor (Det. Tim Morel), John St. Polis (Philip Vantine), Claude Allister (Parks, the butler), Aggie Herring (Mrs. O'Connor), De Witt Jennings, Webster Campbell, Lucien Prival.

• ***The Case of the Black Parrot*** (remake). First National Pictures, 1941. Director: Noel M. Smith; screenwriter: Robert E. Kent. Cast: William Lundigan (Jim Moore), Maris Wrixon (Sandy Vantine), Eddie Foy, Jr. (Tripod Daniels), Paul Cavanaugh (Max Armand), Lull Deste (Madame de Charriere), Charles Waldron (Paul Vantine), Joseph Crehan, Emory Parnell, Phyllis Barry.

Those among the readers who aren't too sure they understand the plot of this film from the description given above can rest assured that seeing the movie won't make it any more comprehensible. The first version not only had the convoluted story but also suffered badly from use of the Vitaphone sound method. Things get somewhat better in the remake. William Lundigan is a newspaperman looking for an international criminal known as "The Black Parrot." On a ship on its way to America, Lundigan and his photographer buddy, Eddie Foy, Jr., encounter Maris Wrixon traveling with her uncle, Charles Waldron, who has purchased a rare cabinet which he has in his cabin. When during a false submarine alert, the cabinet is entered by persons unknown, Lundigan is sure it is the work of "The Black Parrot." He's even more convinced when two mysterious murders occur aboard the ship. Lundigan solves the mystery and gets the culprit.

In the Wake of the Bounty *see* **Mutiny on the Bounty**

413 The Incomparable Bellairs

Based on the play *The Bath Comedy* by Agnes and Egerton Castle. Story: In eighteenth-century England, flirt Kitty Bellairs is on a coach en route to Bath to spend the summer with her sister and her husband. They are robbed by a highwayman who returns Kitty's valuables, taking only kisses and embraces. Kitty enchants the people of Bath, receiving a heartfelt poem from a shy nobleman and a pledge of allegiance and love from the highwayman. In the end the nobleman has to banish the highwayman to win sweet Kitty Bellairs.

London Films, Great Britain, 1914 (original). Silent. Director: Harold Shaw; screenwriter: Bannister Merwin. Cast: Edna Flugrath (Kitty Bellairs), Gregory Scott (Jernigan), Mercy Hatton (Rachel Page), Wyndham Guise (Dennis O'Hara), Lewis Gilbert (Stafford), Christine Rayner (Lydia), Wallace Bosco (Lord Manderville), Hubert Willis (Captain Spencer), Florence Wood (Lady Dere-Stanmer).

• ***Sweet Kitty Bellairs*** (remake). Silent. Paramount Pictures, 1916. Director: James Young; screenwriter: David Belasco. Cast: MacMurray (Kitty Bellairs), Joseph King (Sir Jasper), James Neil (Col. Villiers), Tom Forman (Lt. Vernay), Belle Bennett (Lady Julia), Lucille Young (Lady Barbara Flyte), Lucille Lavarney (Lady Maria), Horace B. Carpenter (Capt. Spicer), Robert Gray (Capt. O'Hara).

• ***Sweet Kitty Bellairs*** (remake). Warner Bros., 1930. Director: Alfred E. Green; screenwriter: J. Grubb Alexander. Cast: Claudia Dell (Kitty Bellairs),

Ernest Torrence (Sir Jasper Standish), Walter Pidgeon (Lord Vernay), Perry Askam (Captain O'Hara), June Collyer (Julia Standish), Lionel Belmore (Col. Villiers), Arthur Carew (Capt. Spicer), Flora Finch, Douglas Gerrard, Christine Yves.

By the time the story was brought to the United States and staged by David Belasco, it was old hat and neither the silent nor the sound version received much praise. Claudia Dell, in the 1930 film, did look like a quite nice little flirt.

Indiana Jones and the Temple of Doom *see* **Raiders of the Lost Ark**

Indianapolis Speedway *see* **The Crowd Roars (1932)**

414 The Informer

Based on the novel by Liam O'Flaherty. Story: In Ireland of 1920, IRA man Gypo Nolan is taunted by a prostitute he fancies, because he doesn't have the price of the passage so they may emigrate to the United States. When a reward is offered for information leading to the arrest of Gypo's friend Frankie McPhillip, Gypo provides the British with the whereabouts of the Irish rebel leader. Brutish and slow-witted Gypo is fairly easily identified by other IRA members as the Judas, and they kill him, but not before he asks for and receives forgiveness from Frankie's mother.

British International, Great Britain, 1929 (original). Director: Arthur Robinson; screenwriters: Benn W. Levy and Rolfe E. Vanto. Cast: Lars Hansen (Gypo Nolan), Lya de Putti (Katie Fox), Warwick Ward (Dan Gallagher), Carl Harbord (Francis McPhillip), Dennis Wyndham (Murphy), Janice Adair (Bessie), Daisy Campbell (Mrs. McPhillip), Craighall Sherry, Ellen Pollock, Johnny Butt.

• ***The Informer*** (remake). RKO/Radio, 1935. Director: John Ford; screenwriter: Dudley Nichols. Cast: Victor McLaglen (Gypo Nolan), Heather Angel (Mary McPhillip), Preston Foster (Dan Gallagher), Margot Grahame (Katie Madden), Wallace Ford (Frankie McPhillip), Una O'Connor (Mrs. McPhillip), J.M. Kerrigan (Terry), Joseph Sauers (Bartly Mulholland), Neil Fitzgerald, Donald Meek, D'Arcy Corrigan, Gaylord Pendleton, Francis Ford, May Boley, Grixelda Harvey, Dennis O'Dea, Jack Mulhall.

• ***Uptight*** (remake). Paramount Pictures, 1968. Director: Jules Dassin; screenwriters: Dassin, Ruby Dee and Julian Mayfield. Cast: Raymond St. Jacques (B.G.), Ruby Dee (Laurie), Frank Silvera (Kyle), Roscoe Lee Browne (Clarence), Julian Mayfield (Tank), Janet MacLachlan (Jeannie), Ji-Tu Chumbuka (Rick), Max Julie, John Wesley Rodgers, Richard Anthony Williams, Robert DoQui.

Lars Hansen was an odd choice for the lead in a film about Irishmen and don't think critics didn't complain that this fine Swedish actor was out of place in an early British talkie. The John Ford piece is a marvelous, moody picture, winning Academy Awards for the director, for Victor McLaglen as Best Actor, Dudley Nichols for Best Screenplay and Max Steiner for Best Score. The movie was also nominated for Best Picture of the Year. The production was most impressive and McLaglen seemed perfect as the slow thinking traitor who finds it hard to understand why he must die for being responsible for his friend's death. But when the realization does sink in, he doesn't want to die until he's received forgiveness from his victim's mother. The 1968 black version of the story has Julian Mayfield in the Gypo Nolan role, as an unemployed steelworker who is expelled from a black militant group for unreliability, after which he turns in one of his friends for a police award. He spends the money too freely and is tracked down and killed by others in the group.

415 The Innocents

Based on the story *The Turn of the Screw* by Henry James and the play by William Archibald. Story: In Victorian times, Miss Giddens, the governess of two orphans at a wealthy English country estate, soon discovers that there is something strange and eerie about these seemingly angelic youngsters. From the motherly housekeeper, Mrs. Grose, Miss Giddens learns that the previous governess, Miss Jewell, and a servant, Peter Quint, had a passionate but doomed love affair. Believing that the dead lovers are intent on possessing the souls of the children, Miss Giddens tries to protect them, but with chilling results.

Twentieth Century–Fox, 1961 (original). Director: Jack Clayton; screenwriters: William Archibald and Truman Capote. Cast: Deborah Kerr (Miss Giddens), Martin Stephens (Miles), Pamela Franklin (Flora), Megs Jenkins (Mrs. Grose), Michael Redgrave (Uncle), Peter Wyngarde (Peter Quint), Clytie Jessop (Miss Jessel).

• ***The Nightcomers*** (prequel). Schmitar/Kastner-Kanter-Ladd, 1972. Director: Michael Winner; screenwriter: Michael Hastings. Cast: Marlon Brando (Peter Quint), Stephanie Beacham (Margaret Jessel), Thord Hird (Mrs. Grose), Harry Andrews (the Guardian), Verna Harvey (Flora), Christopher Ellis (Miles), Anna Palk (the New Governess).

In the tension-filled production of Henry James' gothic ghost story, Deborah Kerr is excellent as the compassionate governess with Martin Stephens and Pamela Franklin very convincing as the possessed children. In a prequel to *The Innocents, The Nightcomers* tells how the children came to be possessed by Peter Quint and Miss Jessel. This film did not capture the feeling of the period as had the original. It is rather an unpleasant film with an unconvincing plot.

416 Inquest

Based on the play by Michael Barringer. Story: A year after the death of her husband, seemingly from a weak heart, Margaret Hamilton finds herself in trouble, when his body is exhumed and he is found to have been shot. The coroner seems biased against her, but young Norman Dennison, king's counsel, comes to her defense and establishes her innocence.

Majestic-New Era, Great Britain, 1931 (original). Director: G.B. Samuelson; screenwriter: Michael Barringer. Cast: Mary Glynne (Margaret Hamilton),

Campbell Gullan (Norman Dennison, KC), Sydney Morgan (Coroner), Haddon Mason (Richard Hanning), G.H. Mulcaster, Lena Halliday, Peter Coleman, Reginald Tippett.

• ***Inquest*** (remake). Charter/Grand National, Great Britain, 1939. Director: Roy Boulting; screenwriter: Francis Miller. Cast: Elizabeth Allan (Margaret Hamilton), Herbert Lomas (Mr. Knight), Hay Petrie (Stephen Neale, KC), Barbara Everest, Olive Sloane, Philip Friend, Harold Anstruther, Malcolm Morley.

These standard courtroom mystery features adequately maintain the tension. In the remake, Elizabeth Allen is suspected of doing in her husband when a revolver is found in her attic and weed killer in the kitchen. Local coroner Herbert Lomas is convinced she's guilty but Hay Petrie, by clever deduction, arrives at the surprising truth.

Inspector General ***see*** **The Pink Panther**

417 The Inspector General

Based on the novel by Nicolai Gogol. Story: A small town in a rural part of old Russia is burdened with stupid, worthless political leeches. They learn that the Czar is sending an inspector general and plan to put on a good front to impress the official. They mistake a traveling dandy as the official and for a few days the rogue lives the part to the hilt. He departs just before the town officials wise up, but not before duping them out of a chest full of rubles, given as bribes. At this moment the real inspector general's arrival is announced.

Garrison Films/Meissner Films, Czechoslovakia, 1931 (original). Director: Mac Fric; screenwriters: V. Solin, V. Menger and Prof. Mathesius. Cast: Vlasta Burian (the Inspector General), T. Tregl (Josef), J. Marvan (the Mayor), Z. Baldova (the Mayor's Wife), T. Crosslichtova, J. Rovensky, Fr. Hlavaty, Fr. Czerny.

• ***The Inspector General*** (remake). Warner Bros., 1949. Director: Henry Koster; screenwriters: Philip Rapp and Harry Kurnitz. Cast: Danny Kaye (Georgi), Walter Slezak (Yakov), Barbara Bates (Leza), Elsa Lanchester (Maria), Gene Lockhart (the Mayor), Alan Hale (Kovatch), Walter Catlett (Col. Castine), Rhys Williams (Inspector General), Benny Baker, Norman Leavitt, Sam Hearn, Lew Hearn.

In the remake, Kaye is an illiterate buffoon, mistaken for the Czar's inspector general. Kaye is at his best in the musical numbers with his wife, Sylvia Fine, and Johnny Mercer, including "Onward, Onward," "Lonely Hearts," "Soliloquy for Three Heads," "Happy Times" and the title song. Walter Slezak, Gene Lockhart, Alan Hale, Elsa Lanchester, and Walter Catlett are as nice a group of venial, incompetent and stupid village officials that could ever infest an unfortunate town. It's not classic Kaye, but still worth the investment of a couple of hours to watch.

418 Interference

Based on the play by Roland Pertwee and Harold Dearden. Story: Reported killed in action, Philip Voaze assumes a new identity in London. Voaze's former mistress, Deborah Kane, recognizes him and attempts to blackmail his wife, Lady Marley, who had remarried. Learning from his wife's husband, eminent physician Sir John Marley, that he is terminally ill with heart disease, Voaze poisons Deborah, destroys all evidence connecting him to Lady Marley and turns himself into the authorities for the murder.

Paramount Pictures, 1928 (original). Silent and talking versions. Directors: Lothar Mendes and Roy J. Pomeroy; screenwriter: Hope Loring. Cast: Clive Brook (Sir John Marley), Doris Kenyon (Faith Marley), William Powell (Philip Voaze), Evelyn Brent (Deborah Kane), Tom Ricketts, Brandon Hurst, Louis Payne, Donald Stuart.

• ***Without Regret*** (remake). Paramount Pictures, 1935. Director: Harold Young; screenwriters: Charles Brackett and Doris Anderson. Cast: Paul Cavanaugh (Sir Robert Godfrey), Elissa Landi (Jennifer Gage), Frances Drake (Mona Gould), Kent Taylor (Steven Paradine), Gilbert Emery (Inspector Hayes), David Niven (Bill Gage), Colin Tapley, Marina Schubert, Joseph North, Tetsui Komai.

Interference was Paramount's first all-dialogue feature, directed by troubleshooter Roy Pomeroy after being first completed as a silent film, directed by Lothar Mendes. It was presented as a mystery as to whom had murdered the blackmailing adventuress, with both Lady Marley's present and former husband being suspected of the crime. Since it was to be the first talkie, the producers barely allowed any silent moments. The remake about the unintentional bigamy, blackmail and murder was clobbered by reviewers as a dull picture with barely adequate performances.

Interlude ***see*** **When Tomorrow Comes**

International Squadron ***see*** **Ceiling Zero**

International Velvet ***see*** **National Velvet**

419 Internes Can't Take Money

Based on a magazine story by Max Brand. Story: Young intern Jimmie Kildare becomes involved with Janet Haley, which gets him in dutch with the underworld, as the two frantically search for Janet's missing three-year-old daughter. A suave crook named Innis offers to sell them information about the child but later tries to jack up the price to include Janet herself. Kildare, with but crude instruments available, saves the life of racketeer Hanlon, but rejects the latter's offer of $1000 for his effort. Kildare believes it is contrary to his medical ethics to take the money (where does one go to find such a physician?) Janet pleads with him to take the money because it's precisely the sum that Innis demands for his information about the child. Kildare's ethics remain unblemished and the child is returned to her mother.

Paramount Pictures, 1937. Director: Alfred Santell; screenwriters: Rian James and Theodore Reeves. Cast: Barbara Stanwyck (Janet Haley), Joel McCrea

(Jimmie Kildare), Lloyd Nolan (Hanlon), Stanley Ridges (Innis), Gaylord Pendleton, Lee Bowman, Irving Bacon, Barry Macollum, Pierre Watkin.

• ***Young Dr. Kildare*** (remake). MGM, 1938. Director: Harold S. Bucquet; screenwriters: Harry Ruskin and Willis Goldbeck. Cast: Lew Ayres (Dr. James Kildare), Lionel Barrymore (Dr. Leonard Gillespie), Lynne Carver (Alice Raymond), Nat Pendleton (Wayman), Jo Ann Sayers (Barbara Chanler), Samuel S. Hinds (Dr. Steve Kildare), Emma Dunn, Walter Kingsford, Truman Bradley, Monty Woolley, Pierre Watkin, Nella Walker.

The second movie has nothing to do with the first, other than both feature Dr. James Kildare. The MGM film launched a series of fifteen movies, the first nine of which had Lew Ayres as the gallant young doctor. When Ayres declared himself a conscientious objector during World War II, he was written out of the series and the films then concentrated on Lionel Barrymore as crusty old Dr. Gillespie with Van Johnson coming in as a young doctor to supply some romantic interest.

420 The Interns

Based on the novel by Richard Frede. Story: A team of new young doctors are assigned to a major city hospital, where they must deal with birth, abortion, sudden death, drugs, women's liberation—not to mention the problems of the patients as well. It's another one of those tales supporting the premise that one learns more the first year on the job than all that was digested during the many years of study. Naturally, there must be the crusty but concerned older doctor with whom the interns and their new fangled ways conflict.

Columbia, 1962 (original). Director: David Swift; screenwriters: Walter Newman and David Swift. Cast: Michael Callan (Doctor Considine), Cliff Robertson (Doctor John Paul Otis), James MacArthur (Doctor Lew Worship), Nick Adams (Doctor Sid Lackland), Suzy Parker (Liza Cardigan), Haya Harareet (Mado), Anne Helm (Mildred), Stephanie Powers (Gloria), Buddy Ebsen (Doctor Sidney Wohl), Telly Savalas (Doctor Riccio), Katherine Bard, Kay Stevens.

• ***The New Interns*** (sequel). Columbia, 1964. Director: John Rich; screenwriter: Wilton Schiller. Cast: Barbara Eden (Laura Rogers), Telly Savalas (Doctor Riccio), George Segal (Doctor Tony Parelli), Kay Stevens (Didi Loomis), Inger Stevens (Nancy), Jimmy Mathers (Freddie), Michael Vandever, George Furth, Ellie Wood, Lee Patrick, Greg Morris, Adam Williams.

In *The New Interns,* a predictable sequel to the first, changes are made to some of the staff, keeping the predictable medical pathos which TV fans of the various medical series came to love.

421 The Invisible Menace

Based on the play by Ralph Spencer Zink. Story: It's an undistinguished mystery story of murder at an army post. Boris Karloff in the role of Jevries is predictably scary but the mystery, setting and other performances are not worth recalling.

Warner Bros., 1938 (original). Director: John Farrow; screenwriter: Crane Wilbur. Cast: Boris Karloff (Jevries), Marie Wilson (Sally), Eddie Craven (Eddie Pratt), Eddie Acuff (Corporal Sanger), Regis Toomey (Lt. Matthews), Henry Kolker, Cy Kendall, Charles Trowbridge, Frank Faylen.

• ***Murder on the Waterfront*** (remake). Warner Bros., 1943. Director: B. Reaves Eason; screenwriter: Robert E. Kent. Cast: Warren Douglas (Joe Davis), Joan Winfield (Gloria), John Loder (Lt. Com. Holbrook), Ruth Ford (Lana Shane), Bill Crago, Bill Kennedy, William B. Davidson, Don Costello, James Flavin.

Changing the setting from an army camp to a navy yard didn't improve this nothing mystery. The remake was concerned with the murder of the inventor of a device which would protect weapons against high temperatures. Mercifully, the no-name stinker only ran 48 minutes. It made the 38 model look high-class. The earlier film at least had Karloff, who if his performances weren't always very good, they were seldom very bad. Unfortunately the same cannot be said of Marie Wilson, who was disastrous as one-half of the love interest.

422 The Ipcress File

Based on the novel by Len Deighton. Story: Harry Palmer, member of the British civil intelligence unit, is assigned to the case of the disappearance of scientist Dr. Radcliffe. The latter is among a number of scientists who have been disappearing lately. After dealing with a crook, Bluejay, who deals in recovering stolen things for a price, the death of an associate who apparently has figured out what is going on and an attempt to brainwash him, Harry unmasks the head of his unit as a traitor behind the disappearances.

Rank/Universal Pictures, Great Britain, 1965 (original). Director: Sidney J. Furie; screenwriter: Bill Canaway. Cast: Michael Caine (Harry Palmer), Nigel Green (Dalby), Guy Doleman (Ross), Sue Lloyd (Jean), Gordon Jackson (Carswell), Aubrey Richards (Radcliffe), Frank Gatliff (Bluejay), Thomas Baptiste, Oliver McGreevy, Freda Bamford, David Glover.

• ***Funeral in Berlin*** (sequel). Lowndes/Paramount Pictures, Great Britain, 1966. Director: Peter Medak; screenwriter: Evan Jones, based on the novel of the same name by Len Deighton. Cast: Michael Caine (Harry Palmer), Eva Renzi (Samantha Steel), Paul Hubschmid (Johnny Vulkan), Oscar Homolka (Col. Stok), Guy Doleman (Ross), Rachel Gurney, Hugh Burden, Thomas Holtzmann, Gunter Meisner.

• ***Billion Dollar Brain*** (sequel). Lowndes/United Artists, Great Britain, 1967. Director: Ken Russell; screenwriter: John McGrath, based on the novel of the same name by Len Deighton. Cast: Michael Caine (Harry Palmer), Karl Malden (Leo Newbegin), Ed Begley (General Midwinter), Oscar Homolka (Col. Stok), Francoise Dorleac (Anya), Guy Coleman (Ross), Vladek Sheybal, Milo Sperber, Mark Elwes, Sidney Caine.

In the first sequel of the story of a working-class James Bond, Michael Caine is coerced into becoming a British spy and sent to Berlin to arrange for the defection of Oscar Homolka, the Soviet officer in charge of the Berlin Wall security. Along the way Caine gets involved with Eva Renzi, an Israeli agent tracking down a Nazi war criminal. The two plots dovetail when it is discovered that Homolka's defection is a phony, intent on eliminating Gunter Meisner, who could identify the war criminal Paul Hubschmid. In the final installment, Caine quits British intelligence to run a private detective agency, but he gets blackmailed to work for the agency again to infiltrate a zealous anticommunist group financed by a Texas billionaire. Seems this group has some eggs which are growing a deadly virus that is to be used against the Soviets. With some help from the Russian security people, Caine is able to thwart their plans.

423 The Iron Man

Based on the novel by W.R. Burnett. Story: It's the prize-fighting yarn of Kid Mason, a young boxer, his manager, Regan, a beautiful but capricious blonde, Rose Mason, and their struggle for dominance over the Kid. She's only really interested in her husband when he's on the top, otherwise she turns to old beau Lewis for excitement.

Universal Pictures, 1931 (original). Director: Tod Browning; screenwriter: Francis Edward Faragoh. Cast: Lew Ayres (Young Mason), Robert Armstrong (Regan), Jean Harlow (Rose Mason), John Miljan (Lewis), Eddie Dillon, Mike Donlin, Morrie Cohan, Mary Doran, Mildred Van Dorn, Ned Sparks.

• ***Some Blondes Are Dangerous*** (remake). Universal Pictures, 1937. Director: Milton Carruth; screenwriters: W.R. Burnett and Lester Cole. Cast: William Gargan (George Regan), Dorothy Kent (Rose Whitney), Nan Grey (Judy Williams), Noah Beery, Jr. (Bud Mason), Roland Drew (Paul Lewis), Polly Rowles, John Butler, Lew Kelly, Eddie Roberts, Ed Stanley.

• ***Iron Man*** (remake). Universal Pictures, 1951. Director: Joseph Pevney; screenwriters: George Zuckerman and Borden Chase. Cast: Jeff Chandler (Coke Mason), Evelyn Keyes (Rose Mason), Stephen McNally (George Mason), Joyce Holden (Tiny), Rock Hudson (Speed O'Keefe), Jim Backus (Max Watkins), Jim Arness, Steve Martin, Doris Cole, Mushy Callahan.

Hollywood has had a long love affair with the notion that a good boxer can be brought to his knees by the wrong kind of woman. These three pictures supply exhibits A, B, and C in the persons of Jean Harlow, Dorothy Kent and Evelyn Keyes. The poor saps don't have a chance. In the 1937 version, chump Noah Beery, Jr., becomes champ but he's knocked for a loop by his unfaithful new love, loses the big fight and returns to the "good" girl who was waiting for him. In the 1951 production, Jeff Chandler is a coal miner who becomes a killer in the ring, even though outside of it, he's a nice guy.

424 The Iron Mask

Based on the novel by Alexandre Dumas. Story: Anne of Austria, wife of Louis XIII of France gives birth to twins. Cardinal Richelieu, learning of this, smuggles one of the boys out of the palace and sends him to Spain. Constance, present at the birth, is kidnapped by Rochefort; her lover, D'Artagnan, rushes to her rescue but she is killed. D'Artagnan is ordered to guard the little prince and Rochefort raises the second twin as pretender to the throne. Years later, Rochefort smuggles the pretender into the palace and kidnaps Louis XIV.

D'Artagnan and the Three Musketeers, Athos, Porthos and Aramis, rescue the king but at the cost of all four of their lives. Reinstated on his throne, Louis XIV orders that the pretender spend the rest of his life imprisoned, and wear an iron mask.

Elton Corp./United Artists, 1929 (original). Silent and sound. Director: Allan Dwan; screenwriters: Lotta Woods and Elton Thomas. Cast: Douglas Fairbanks (D'Artagnan), Leon Barry (Athos), Stanley J. Sanford (Porthos), Gino Corrado (Aramis), Belle Bennett (Queen Mother), Marguerite De La Motta (Constance), Dorothy Revier (Milady de Winter), Vera Lewis (Madame Peronne), Rolfe Sedan (Louis XIII), William Bakewell (Louis XIV/his twin), Gordon Thorpe (the Young Prince/his twin), Nigel De Brulier (Cardinal Richelieu), Ullrich Haupt (Rochefort).

• ***The Man in the Iron Mask*** (remake). United Artists, 1939. Director: James Whale; screenwriter: George Bruce. Cast: Louis Hayward (Louis XIV/ Philippe, his twin), Joan Bennett (Maria Theresa), Warren William (D'Artagnan), Joseph Schildkraut (Fouquet), Alan Hale (Porthos), Miles Mander (Aramis), Bert Roach (Athos), Walter Kingsford (Colbert), Marian Martin, Montagu Love, Doris Kenyon, Albert Dekker, William Boyle.

• ***The Lady in the Iron Mask*** (remake). Twentieth Century–Fox, 1952. Director: Ralph Murphy; screenwriters: Jack Pollexen and Aubrey Wisberg. Cast: Louis Hayward (D'Artagnan), Patricia Medina (Princess Anne/Princess Louise), Alan Hale, Jr. (Porthos), Judd Holdren (Aramis), Steve Brodie (Athos), John Sutton (Duke of Valdac), Hal Gerard (Philip of Spain), Lester Matthews (Prime Minister).

In like vein, *Prisoner of the Iron Mask* and *Behind the Iron Mask* were filmed in 1961 and 1977, respectively. The Douglas Fairbanks film was a spirited star vehicle and despite a few talking sequences the last of the big silent costume films. In the remake the focus is away from D'Artagnan and to the twin of Louis XIV, Philippe, who is thrown into the Bastille and fitted with a devilish iron mask. Whereas in the earlier picture, the pretender twin was the bad guy, in the remake, Louis XIV gets his comeuppance for being such a rotten fellow by being forced to replace his brother behind the iron mask, and Philippe takes his place with almost no one the wiser, save D'Artagnan and the Three Musketeers, who this time help the usurper. It's a fine adventure yarn with plenty of swashbuckling excitement. Louis Hayward was at his best as the two brothers. In *The Lady in the Iron Mask*, Hayward returns, this time as D'Artagnan, who together with his resurrected musketeer buddies, rescues a French princess who has been kidnapped by the evil powers that be and fitted with a grotesque iron mask so that her twin sister can take her place. Patricia Medina handles her double role quite adequately and John Sutton makes a properly urbane heavy who usually looks like he smells something bad and talks like he tasted it.

425 The Iron Stair

Based on the novel by *Rita*. Story: George Gale impersonates his twin brother, Geoffrey, a cleric, and forges checks, allowing Geoffrey to go to prison for his crimes. Geoffrey breaks out to prove his innocence and George takes his place.

Stoll, Great Britain, 1920 (original). Silent. Director and screenwriter: F. Martin Thornton. Cast: Reginald Fox (Geoffrey/George Gale), Madge Stuart (Renee Jessup), Frank Petley (Andrew Jessup), H. Agar Lyons, J. Edwards Barber.

• ***The Iron Stair*** (remake). Real Art/Radio, Great Britain, 1933. Director: Leslie Hiscott; screenwriter: H. Fowler Mear. Cast: Henry Kendall (Geoffrey/George Gale), Dorothy Boyd (Eva Marshall), Michael Hogan (Pat Derringham), Michael Sherbrooke (Benjamin Marks), Steffi Duna (Elsa Damond), A. Bromley Davenport, S. Victor Stanley, Charles Groves, Charles Paton, John Turnbull.

The plot of this thriller is a bit complicated but most can get through it. In the remake, George impersonates his twin brother, Geoffrey, forges checks and lets Geoffrey take the rap. Geoffrey escapes from prison to clear himself, but the same night George is killed in a fall. With some help from George's mistress, Elsa, Geoffrey is able to prove his innocence.

426 Is Zat So?

Based on a play by James Gleason and Richard Taber. Story: Hap Hurley is a wisecracking fight manager who plans to make a champion out of Ed "Chick" Cowan. Low on funds, the two join the staff of a young millionaire, G. Clinton Blackburn. Eventually, Chick wins the championship and he and Hap get the girls of their choices, and prove that Blackburn's brother-in-law is a crook.

Fox Film Corp., 1927 (original). Silent. Director: Alfred E. Green; screenwriter: Philip Klein. Cast: George O'Brien (Ed "Chick" Cowan), Edmund Lowe (Hap Hurley), Kathryn Perry (Marie Mestretti), Cyril Chadwick (Robert Parker), Doris Lloyd (Sue Parker), Dione Ellis (Florence Hanley), Douglas Fairbanks, Jr. (G. Clinton Blackburn), Richard Maitland, Philippe De Lacey, Jack Herrick.

• ***Two Fisted*** (remake). Paramount Pictures, 1935. Director: James Cruze; screenwriters: Sam Hellman, Francis Martin and Eddie Moran. Cast: Lee Tracy (Hay Hurley), Roscoe Karns (Chick Moran), Grace Bradley (Marie), Kent Taylor (Clint Blackburn), Gail Patrick (Sue Parker), Gordon Westcott, G.P. Huntley, Jr., Billy Lee, John Indrisano.

The humor of farces about a prizefighter and his manager who enter service in the home of a millionaire depend on the popularity of the leading characters and their familiar routines. Lee Tracy is supposed to be fast-talking and Karns something of a know-it-all, who doesn't. There's nothing innovative in either movie because all concerned knew precisely what they were creating—a fast-moving piece with time-tested routines and lines to get the expected laughs.

Island of Lost Men *see* **White Woman**

The Island of Lost Souls *see* **White Woman**

Isle of Fury *see* **The Narrow Corner**

Istanbul *see* **Singapore**

It Ain't Hay *see* **Princess O'Hara**

427 It Happened One Night

Based on a story "Night Bus" by Samuel Hopkins Adams. Story: When her father, Alexander Andrews, opposes her marriage to King Westley, heiress Ellie Andrews takes flight from Florida to be with her fiancé in New York. This is a big news item and when out-of-work reporter Peter Warne spots her boarding a bus, he sees an opportunity to get a scoop and his job back. Their escapades as they travel north, with no money, trying to elude the authorities and no doubt the constant proximity of two rather sexy individuals, leads them to overcome their initial dislike of each other and fall in love. Through a misunderstanding at the end of their journey, each feels the other wasn't serious about their affection. By this time, Mr. Andrews, still believing Westley isn't the man his daughter needs, relents and agrees to hold a wedding for her. Ellie, no longer so eager to marry King, is resigned to it because she made such a fuss and is afraid to appear the fool. Peter arrives at the Andrews estate demanding payment for his "expenses" in escorting Ellie. Her father, expecting a demand for some large sum to kill the scandalous story, is pleasantly surprised when Peter only insists on the modest out-of-pocket expenses he incurred. Andrews puts two and two together, and believing that Peter is just what Ellie needs in a husband, helps the two escape the wedding. They end up in a motor lodge in which they spend one innocent but titillating night on their flight north.

Columbia Pictures, 1934 (original). Director: Frank Capra; screenwriters: Robert Riskin and Frank Capra. Cast: Clark Gable (Peter Warne), Claudette Colbert (Ellie Andrews), Walter Connolly (Alexander Andrews), Jameson Thomas (King Westley), Roscoe Karns, Ward Bond, Alan Hale, Eddie Chandler, Wallis Clark, Arthur Hoyt, Blanche Frederici.

• ***Eve Knew Her Apples*** (remake). Columbia Pictures, 1945. Director: Will Jason; screenwriter: E. Elwin Moran. Cast: Ann Miller (Eve Porter), William Wright (Ward Williams), Robert Williams (Steve Ormand), Ray Walker, Charles D. Brown, John Eldredge, Eddie Bruce.

• ***The Runaround*** (remake). Universal Pictures, 1946. Director: Charles Lamont; screenwriters: Arthur T. Herman and Sam Hellman. Cast: Rod Cameron (Kildane), Ella Raines (Penelope), Broderick Crawford (Louis Prentice), Frank McHugh, Samuel S. Hinds, Joan Fulton, George Cleveland, Joe Sawyer, Nana Bryant.

• ***You Can't Run Away From It*** (remake). Columbia, 1956. Director: Dick Powell; screenwriters: Claude Binyon and Robert Riskin. Cast: June Allyson (Ellie Andrews), Jack Lemmon (Pete Warne), Charles Bickford, Jim Backus, Stubby Kaye, Paul Gilbert, Allyn Joslyn.

It Happened One Night is one of the most honored pictures ever made. It won the big five Academy Awards: Best Picture, Best Director, Best Actor, Best Actress and Best Screenplay. Neither Gable nor Colbert wanted to do the picture, both being loaned to Columbia by their home studio. Of course, Gable wasn't sure he wanted to portray Rhett Butler in *Gone with the Wind*, either, so it's a good thing that others made his casting decisions. After more than fifty years, the film is as delightful, funny and sexy as ever. The scene in the motor lodge where Gable and Colbert take refuge is a classic. When Gable undressed and was seen not to wear an undershirt it knocked that industry for a loop, as other men decided to emulate the king. It is a very suggestive scene, more so than most of the nude grapplings between hero and heroine now common on the screen. They didn't even touch each other; it was enough to know that these two who wanted each other were separated only by a blanket, "the wall of Jericho" that Gable had hung across the room. Equally as hilarious and at the same time sexy was the hitchhiking episode. After all of Gable's techniques for getting a car to stop and pick them up, Colbert merely straightened her stockings and every man in the audience knew he'd be glad to stop for her.

The remakes, disguised and otherwise, couldn't capture the magic of the combination of the story, the two stars, Frank Capra and Robert Riskin's screenplay. The performers in the four other movies lacked the charm of Gable and Colbert. The directors didn't have the style. In the second feature, Ann Miller is a radio singer who runs away from the pressures of her career and fans, meets itinerant newspaper reporter William Wright, and falls in love. The next film has two detectives, Cameron and Crawford, chasing after runaway heiress Raines, hoping to get a $15,000 reward. The whole thing is a ruse set up by the father. Ho-hum! The fourth movie is just a flat remake of *It Happened One Night*. Neither Allyson nor Lemmon had the kind of authority to make the film a successful comical romance. Instead they tried for a romantic comedy. The difference makes all the difference.

428 It Pays to Advertise

Based on a play by Roi Cooper Mergrue and Walter Hackett. Story: Pampered playboy Rodney Martin, angered by the little regard with which he is held by his soap-manufacturer father, Cyrus Martin, joins Ambrose Peale to compete with his Pa in manufacturing soap. Peale's advertising program for the proposed new soap is a grand success. Unfortunately there are no funds left to actually produce the soap. To prevent yet another competitor from buying the rights to the nationally known but nonexistent product, Cyrus settles a small fortune on his son and Peale so he may manufacture the soap. Happily, Rodney also wins the hand of his dad's secretary, Mary Grayson.

Paramount Artcraft Pictures, 1919 (original). Silent. Director: Donald Crisp; screenwriter: Elmer Harris. Cast: Bryant Washburn (Rodney Martin), Lois Wilson (Mary Grayson), Walter Hiers (Ambrose Peale), Frank Currier (Cyrus Martin), Julia Faye (Comtesse de Beaurien).

• ***It Pays to Advertise*** (remake). Paramount, 1931. Director: Frank Tuttle; screenwriters: Arthur Kobler and Ethel Doherty. Cast: Norman Foster (Rodney Martin), Carole Lombard (Mary Grayson), Skeets Gallagher (Ambrose Peale), Eugene Pallette (Cyrus Martin), Helen Johnson (Countess de Beaurien), Lucien Littlefield, Louise Brooks, Morgan Wallace.

Neither film is anything to get excited about. The story is trite and the acting is bombastic. Advertising as a film theme has only been handled well once, in *The Hucksters,* which is also a story about a nasty soap manufacturer. The remake is perhaps most notable for featuring Louise Brooks in a minor role, perhaps as punishment for deserting Hollywood to star in German films such as *Pandora's Box.*

429 It Started with Eve

Based on the story "Almost an Angel" by Hans Kraly. Story: Jonathan Reynolds is on his deathbed and his last request is to meet his son Jonathan Jr.'s fiancée. Since she's not readily available, Junior conscripts hat-check girl Anne Terry to pinch hit. The old man is delighted with Anne, but he doesn't pass out of the picture; in fact he recovers nicely. The complications arise when Junior's real fiancée, Gloria Pennington, shows up. You just know everything will be satisfactorily resolved before the fade out.

Universal Pictures, 1941 (original). Director: Henry Koster; screenwriters: Norman Krasna and Leo Townsend. Cast: Deanna Durbin (Anne Terry), Charles Laughton (Jonathan Reynolds), Robert Cummings (Jonathan Reynolds, Jr.), Guy Kibbee (Bishop), Margaret Tallichet (Gloria Pennington), Catherine Doucet, Walter Catlett, Charles Coleman, Leonard Elliott, Irving Bacon.

• ***I'd Rather be Rich*** (remake). Universal Pictures, 1964. Director: Jack Smith; screenwriters: Oscar Brodney, Norman Krasna and Leo Townsend. Cast: Sandra Dee (Cynthia Dulaine), Robert Goulet (Paul Benton), Andy Williams (Warren Palmer), Maurice Chevalier (Grandpa Philip Dulaine), Hermione Gingold (Nurse Grimshaw), Gene Raymond, Charles Ruggles, Laurie Main.

Charles Laughton was very appealing as the old man who didn't die once he met his son's supposed fiancée. Deanna Durbin had time to sing Vincente Valverde's "Clavlitos" and "Going Home" by Anton Dvorak. In the remake, it's Sandra Dee having to scrape up a fiancé in the person of Robert Goulet to satisfy the dying wish of grandfather Maurice Chevalier, who also survived to complicate matters. Andy Williams, in the role of the real fiancé, loses Sandra but sings Gus Khan and Isham Jones' "It Had to Be You."

430 It's a Date

Based on a story by Jane Hall, Frederick Kohner and Ralph Block. Story: Pamela Drake is the daughter of Broadway musical star Georgia Drake. Attending a summer stock school while her mother is vacationing in Hawaii, Pamela is picked to play the lead in a fall show originally intended for none other than dear old mom. Pamela takes a ship to Honolulu, intending to get some coaching in the part from mother. On the ship she meets millionaire John Arlen. When they arrive and Pamela discovers that she is a rival to her mother for the role, she tries to step aside and have a romance with Arlen. Instead, he goes for Mom and Pamela scores in the show.

Universal Pictures, 1940 (original). Director: William Seiter; screenwriter: Norman Krasna. Cast: Deanna Durbin (Pamela Drake), Kay Francis (Georgia

Drake), Walter Pidgeon (John Arlen), Eugene Pallette (Governor Allen), Henry Stephenson (Captain Andrew), Cecilia Loftus, Samuel S. Hinds, S.Z. Sakall, Lewis Howard, Fritz Feld.

• ***Nancy Goes to Rio*** (remake). MGM, 1950. Director: Robert Z. Leonard; screenwriter: Sidney Sheldon. Cast: Jane Powell (Nancy Barklay), Ann Sothern (Francis Elliott), Barry Sullivan (Paul Berten), Carmen Miranda (Marina Rodrigues), Louis Calhern (Gregory Elliott), Scotty Beckett, Fortunio Bonanova, Glenn Anders, Nella Walker, Hans Conreid, Frank Fontaine.

Deanna Durbin's seventh film under the production of Joe Pasternek was a breezy treat for her fans. She sings four songs: "Love Is All," "Ave Maria," "Musetta's Street Song" and "Loch Lomond." Her voice was at its peak and for those who enjoy wholesome fun, this picture is bound to hit the target. The same thing can be said of the 1950 remake with Jane Powell as the ambitious youngster who finds herself in competition with her actress mother, played by Ann Sothern. Powell, Sothern, and Louis Calhern as grandfather, happily give out with the old favorite "Shine on Harvest Moon," while Sothern scores nicely with "Time and Time Again," Carmen Miranda burns up the screen with "Yipsee-I-O" and "Cha Bomm Pa Pa," and Powell delights with "Magic in the Moonlight" and "Musetta's Waltz."

It's a Dog's Life ***see*** **Almost Human**

It's a Gift ***see*** **It's the Old Army Game**

It's in the Bag ***see*** **Keep Your Seats, Please**

431 It's the Old Army Game

Based on the play by Joseph McEvoy. Story: There is no plot to speak of, this being instead just a string of wonderful gags and situations involving a small-town pharmacist, his family, and various others who wander in and out of his business establishment. Describing what happens cannot possibly capture the comical genius of W.C. Fields. It must be seen to be appreciated.

Famous Players–Lasky/Paramount Pictures, 1926 (original). Silent. Director: Edward Sutherland; screenwriters: Tom J. Geraghty and J. Clarkson Miller. Cast: W.C. Fields (Elmer Pettywillie), Louise Brooks (Mildred Marshall), Blanche Ring (Tessie Overholt), William Gaxton (George Parker), Mary Foy (Sarah Panacoast), Mickey Bennett, Josephine Dunn, Jack Luden.

• ***It's a Gift*** (remake). Paramount Pictures, 1935. Director: Norman McLeod; screenwriters: Henry Sharp, Charles Burke and J.P. McEvoy. Cast: W.C. Fields (Harold Bissonette), Baby LeRoy (Baby Dunk), Kathleen Howard (Amelia Bissonette), Jean Rouverol (Mildred Bissonette), Tammany Young, Tom Bupp, Diana Lewis, Kulian Madison, T. Roy Barnes.

In the remake, practically a comedy monologue for Fields, the best bit has him trying to get to sleep at night on his porch, only to be frustrated by his wife, telephone, neighbors and the milk man. Later in the film, Fields buys an orange grove in California, sight and site unseen. When he and his family drive to their purchase, they discover it to be a bit of desert between other groves. Things work out when it turns out that Fields' land is vital to the construction of a race track. He ends up with a real orange grove and $40,000 in cash.

432 Ivanhoe

Based on the novel by Sir Walter Scott. Story: In 1190, in return for saving wealthy Jewish merchant Issac from robbers, Saxon knight Wilfrid of Ivanhoe is promised the rest of the money he needs to ransom King Richard the Lion-hearted from the Austrians. Opposing Ivanhoe in his quest to free his king is Prince John and his supporters, Sir Brian Bois-de-Guilbert and Sir Hugh de Bracy, who arrange for Ivanhoe and Issac's daughter, Rebecca, who has come to love the dashing knight, to be held by their Norman followers. The two are rescued by Ivanhoe's Saxon friends, Sir Brian and Sir Hugh are killed, Richard is ransomed and Ivanhoe weds his love, Rowena, leaving the saddened Rebecca to return to her people.

• ***Ivanhoe*** (remake). Independent Motion Pictures, Great Britain, 1913. Silent. Director and screenwriter: Herbert Brenon. Cast: King Baggot (Ivanhoe), Leah Baird (Rebecca), Evelyn Hope (Lady Rowena), Herbert Brenn (Issac), Wallace Widdecombe (Sir Brian), Jack Bates (Sir Reginald), Wallace Bosco (Cedric), George Courtney (Prince John), Arthur Scott-Craven (King Richard), W. Thomas (Robin Hood), H. Holles (Friar Tuck), W. Calvert, A.J. Charlwood.

• ***Ivanhoe*** (remake). Zenith Films, Great Britain, 1913. Silent. Director and screenwriter: Leedham Bantock. Cast: Lauderdale Maitland (Ivanhoe), Edith Bracewell (Rebecca), Nancy Bevington (Lady Rowena), Hubert Carter (Issac), Henry Lonsdale (Sir Brian), Austin Milroy (Front de Boeuf).

• ***Ivanhoe*** (remake). MGM British, Great Britain, 1952. Director: Richard Thorpe; screenwriters: Aeneas Mackenzie and Noel Langley. Cast: Robert Taylor (Ivanhoe), Elizabeth Taylor (Rebecca), Joan Fontaine (Rowena), George Sanders (Sir Brian Bois-de-Guilbert), Robert Douglas (Sir Hugh de Bracy), Finlay Currie (Cedric), Felix Aylmer (Isaac of York), Francis de Wolff (Front-de-Boeuf), Norman Woodland (King Richard), Guy Rolfe (Prince John), Basil Sydney, Harold Warrender, Patric Holt, Sebastian Cabot, Megs Jenkins, Valentine Dyall.

The derring-do of Ivanhoe and his romances with Rebecca and Lady Rowena was also filmed in 1911, 1912 and 1964. The 1952 spectacular was a rouser in terms of action but the acting was really quite terrible. The three main performers, Robert Taylor, Elizabeth Taylor, and Joan Fontaine, each looked right for their parts, but unfortunately they were given lines to speak, and the lines were frequently stinkers, almost laughably inappropriate. Perhaps that is why Bob, Liz and Joan delivered them as if they were reading a grocery list. One final complaint, with all due respect to Joan Fontaine, her beauty and charm, it's not credible that Robert Taylor would have chosen the dull and unexciting woman she portrayed over Liz, who shared adventures with him, cured his wounds and was then in the bloom of her loveliness, unless perhaps he was prejudiced against Jews.

J

Jack the Ripper *see* **The Lodger**

433 Jailbreak

Based on the story "Murder in Sing Sing" by Jonathan Finn. Story: In this prison whodunit, convict Ed Slayden is accused of murdering fellow con Big Mike Eagan, his sworn enemy. But of course, he's innocent, even if he does look like he's mimicking Jimmy Cagney. With the help of Detective Captain Roarke, reporter Ken Williams, posing as a prisoner, solves the crime and wins female reporter Jane Rogers, who seems to like to hang out at penitentiaries.

Warner Bros., 1936. Director: Nick Grinde; screenwriters: Robert Andrews and Joseph Hoffman. Cast: June Travis (Jane Rogers), Craig Reynolds (Ken Williams), Barton MacLane (Detective Captain Roarke), Richard Purcell (Ed Slayden), Joseph King (Big Mike Eagan), Addison Richards, George E. Stone, Eddie Acuff, Joseph Crehan, Mary Treen, Henry Hull.

• ***Murder in the Big House*** (remake). Warner Bros., 1942. Director: B. Reeves Eason; screenwriters: Raymond L. Schrock and Jerry Chodorov. Cast: Faye Emerson (Gladys Wayne), Van Johnson (Bert Bell), George Meeker (Scoop Conner), Frank Wilcox (Randall), Michael Ames (Dapper Dan Malloy), Roland Drew, Ruth Ford, Joseph Crehan, William Gould, Douglas Wood, John Maxwell.

In the remake, Van Johnson, then virtually an unknown, portrays a cub reporter who becomes suspicious when Michael Ames, just prior to making the walk of his last mile to his execution, is electrocuted in his cell by a bolt of lightning. With the help of veteran reporter George Meeker and female scribe Faye Emerson, he uncovers a plot to eliminate Ames before he could squeal. This film, which was reissued in 1945 as *Born for Trouble,* will not rank highly in the annals of prison movies.

434 Jane Eyre

Based on the novel by Charlotte Bronte. Story: Jane Eyre, an orphan, is sent away to school for ten years by her benefactor and aunt, Mrs. Reed. To escape her depressing existence under the stern tutelage of Mr. Brocklehurst, she obtains a position in the home of Fairfax Rochester as companion for Adele, Rochester's ward. Love blossoms and Jane happily accepts Rochester's proposal of marriage. During the wedding, a man named Mason interrupts the ceremony, declaring that Rochester already has a wife, a madwoman, kept in isolation and guarded by an alcoholic, Grace Poole. Pleading that for all intents and purposes his wife has been dead for years, Rochester is unable to prevent Jane from leaving him. She takes up residence in the home of a young clergyman, St. John Rivers, who comes to love her and proposes marriage. Meanwhile, the mad wife escapes and sets fire to the house, destroying it, killing herself and leaving Rochester blind. Jane arrives to find Rochester praying for her return. A specialist restores his sight and finally the two are able to marry.

• ***Jane Eyre*** (remake). Thanhauser Pictures, 1910. Silent. Director and screenwriter: Theodore Marston. Cast: Irma Taylor (Jane Eyre), Frank Crane (Rochester), Amelia Barleon, Alphonse Ethier, William Garwood.

• ***Jane Eyre*** (remake). W.W. Hodkinson Corporation, 1921. Silent. Director and screenwriter: Hugo Ballin. Cast: Mabel Ballin (Jane Eyre), Norman Trevor (Fairfax Rochester), Crauford Kent (St. John Rivers), Emily Fitzroy (Grace Poole), John Webb Dillon (Mason), Stephen Carr, Louis Grisel, Vernie Atherton, Elizabeth Aeriens.

• ***Jane Eyre*** (remake). Monogram Pictures, 1934. Director: Christy Cabanne; screenwriter: Adele Comandini. Cast: Virginia Bruce (Jane Eyre), Colin Clive (Rochester), Aileen Pringle (Blanche Ingram), Jameson Thomas (Charles Craig), Beryl Mercer (Mrs. Fairfax), Lionel Belmore (Lord Ingram), Joan Standing, David Torrence, Edith Fellows, Desmond Roberts, Ethel Griffies.

• ***Jane Eyre*** (remake). Twentieth Century–Fox, 1944. Director: Robert Stevenson; screenwriters: Aldous Huxley, John Houseman and Robert Stevenson. Cast: Orson Welles (Edward Rochester), Joan Fontaine (Jane Eyre), Margaret O'Brien (Adele Varens), Peggy Ann Garner (Jane, as a child), John Sutton (Dr. Rivers), Sara Allgood (Bessie), Henry Daniell (Brocklehurst), Agnes Moorehead (Mrs. Reed), Aubrey Mather (Colonel Dent), Edith Barrett (Mrs. Fairfax), Barbara Everest, Hilary Brooke, Ethel Griffies, Mae Marsh, Eily Maylon, Mary Forbes, Thomas London, John Abbott, Ronald Harris, Elizabeth Taylor.

• ***Jane Eyre*** (remake). British Lion Films, 1970. Director: Delbert Mann; screenwriter: Jack Pulman. Cast: George C. Scott (Rochester), Susannah York (Jane Eyre), Ian Bannen (Rev. St. John Rivers), Jack Hawkins (Mr. Brocklehurst), Nyree Dawn Porter (Blanche Ingram), Rachel Kempson (Mrs. Fairfax), Kenneth Griffith (Mason), Peter Copley, Michele Dotrice, Kara Wilson, Jean Marsh, Rosalyn Landor.

The first filming of *Jane Eyre*, produced by Thanhauser, was a one-reel feature, with barely time to give the gist of the Bronte story. Other versions appeared in Italy in 1909 and a Universal Pictures two-reeler in 1914 with Ethel Grandin as Jane Eyre and Irving Cummings as Rochester. In 1914 Blinkhorn Photoplays Corporation produced a four-reeler starring Alberta Ray as Jane Eyre, followed in 1915 by Biograph's three-reeler with Louise Vale in the title role. In 1918, Select Pictures starred Alice Brady as Jane and Elliott Dexter as Rochester in *Woman and Wife*. Finally, 20th Century–Fox's *Three Sisters of the Moors* presented Molly Lamount, Lynne Roberts and Heather Angel as Charlotte, Emily and Anne Brontz, respectively, in which the story of the three Victorian authors' famous novels are discussed.

The 1934 feature produced by Monogram Pictures, one of the poverty-row studios, was a 62-minute piece of tedium. Things were only slightly better in the 20th Century–Fox film, in which Orson Welles seemed strangely miscast. His playing generates no sympathy from audiences, making Rochester a rather unpleasant man who seems only slightly less mad than his deranged wife. Joan Fontaine was much better as the adult Jane and Peggy Ann Garner played her as a strong-willed youngster. Others in the cast who were excellent included Henry Daniell as the self-righteous Brocklehurst and Agnes Moorehead as the no-nonsense Mrs. Reed. The British Lion feature found its proper place as a TV special, its only U.S. release. Neither Susannah York nor George C. Scott seemed up to the demands of their parts.

Der Januskopf *see* **Dr. Jekyll and Mr. Hyde**

435 Jaws

Based on the novel by Peter Benchley. Story: Several people are killed in shark attacks at the resort community of Amity Island. Fearing bad publicity, the mayor has local fishermen hunt the killer and when they capture a medium-size shark, he declares that the area is now completely safe. Ichthyologist Roy Hooper's investigation convinces him that the attacks are the work of a great white shark. After another attack, Police Chief Brody agrees and the two men hold a town meeting to decide what to do. A rugged fisherman named Quint agrees to hunt the shark for a large fee with the help of Hooper and Chief Brody. The rest of the movie is the tale of how these three struggle to capture or kill the 28-foot beast, an ordeal that Quint does not survive.

Universal Pictures, 1975 (original). Director: Steven Spielberg; screenwriters: Peter Benchley and Carl Gottlieb. Cast: Roy Scheider (Chief Brody), Robert Shaw (Quint), Richard Dreyfuss (Roy Hooper), Loraine Gary (Ellen Brody), Murray Hamilton (Mayor Vaughn), Carl Gottlieb, Jeffrey C. Kramer, Susan Backlinie, Jonathan Filley, Ted Grossman, Chris Rebello.

• ***Jaws II*** (sequel). Univeral Pictures, 1978. Director: Jeannot Szwarc; screenwriters: Carl Gottlieb and Howard Sacker. Cast: Roy Scheider (Brody), Loraine Gary (Ellen Brody), Murray Hamilton (Mayor Vaughn), Joseph Mascolo (Peterson), Jeffrey Kramer, Ann Dusenberry, Mark Gruner, Collin Wilcox.

A sequel to *Jaws* was inevitable. This exploitation film took in more money than any other. While having some suspenseful and truly frightening sequences the movie was much too talkative. The sequel suffered from the need to repeat shark attacks and shark hunts—so what else is new? Still, with Roy Scheider back to sound the alarm, it was immensely more exciting and interesting than 1983's *Jaws 3-D* with Dennis Quaid, Bess Armstrong and Louis Gossett, Jr., in which a great white shark gets loose inside a Florida theme park. To demonstrate that producers believe that the public can't get too much of a bad thing, Michael Caine appeared in *Jaws 4: The Revenge* in 1987, but then nowadays Caine seems willing to appear in just about anything offered to him. With his talent, one could wish that he would be more selective.

Jaws II *see* **Jaws**

Jaws 3-D *see* **Jaws**

Al Jolson, Eugenie Besserer and May McAvoy strike some very serious poses in the first "talkie," The Jazz Singer *(Warner Bros., 1927).*

Jaws 4: The Revenge *see* **Jaws**

436 The Jazz Singer

Based on the story "The Day of Atonement" and the play of the same name by Samson Raphaelson. Story: Jakie Rabinowitz, son of Cantor Rabinowitz, of a long line of Cantors, has become Jack Robin, a jazz singer. He meets a gentile girl, Mary Dale, a leading vaudeville star who arranges for him to get an audition with a New York impresario, remarking, "You sing jazz, but it's different—there's a tear in it." Jack is looking forward to returning to New York in order to see his beloved mother. As for his father, the Cantor maintains that he has no son. Jack's big chance and the opening of his Broadway show occurs on the night of the beginning of Yom Kippur. His mother arrives at the theater and tells her son that his father is dying and there is no one to sing at the synagogue that night. Despite the warnings of his producers that his career will be ruined, Jack Robin becomes Jakie Rabinowitz for one last time, and as his father listens from his deathbed, sings "Kol Nidre." The Cantor's last words are, "Mama, we have our son again." Despite the predictions, Robin's show opens the next night and is a huge success with him singing in black-face, "I'd walk a million miles for one of your smiles, My Mammy" with his mother weeping in the audience.

The great Miss Peggy Lee and Danny Thomas swing it hot in the 1953 Warner Bros. remake of The Jazz Singer

Warner Bros., 1927 (original). Director: Alan Crosland; screenwriter: Alfred A. Cohn. Cast: Al Jolson (Jakie Rabinowitz/Jack Robin), Bobby Gordon (Jakie, as a boy), May McAvoy (Mary Dale), Warner Oland (Cantor Rabinowitz), Eugenie Besserer (Sara Raboniwitz), Cantor Josef Rosenblatt (himself).

• ***The Jazz Singer*** (remake). Warner Bros., 1953. Director: Michael Curtiz; screenwriters: Frank Davis, Leonard Seler and Peggy Lee. Cast: Danny Thomas (Jerry Golding), Peggy Lee (Judy Lane), Mildred Dunnock (Mrs. Golding), Eduard Franz (Cantor David Golding), Alex Gerry, Tom Tully, Allyn Joslyn.

• ***The Jazz Singer*** (remake). EMI, 1980. Director: Richard Fleischer; screenwriters: Herbert Baker and Stephen H. Foreman. Cast: Neil Diamond, Laurence Olivier, Lucie Arnaz, Catlin Adams, Sully Boyar.

Not a great film but certainly a movie milestone, *The Jazz Singer*, the now familiar story of a man torn between the demands of his family and boyhood religion and his own musical ambitions, will always be remembered as the film that began the sound era. It wasn't Jolson's first film and it wasn't the first time that the Vitaphone method of synchronizing talking and singing with actors on the screen was given public exposure. But it was the first time the two had been combined and Jolson's popularity, the sentimental but moving story and sound were a combination that just couldn't be beat.

Bobby Gordon, not Jolson, had the honor of being the first person heard in this major production, when as the young Jakie he is seen singing popular songs in a cafe. The film is only a part-talkie with more titles than dialogue dominating the production. The first line by Jolson is his famous, "Wait a minute, wait a minute, you ain't heard nothing yet" just before he bursts into a stirring rendition of "Toot Toot Tootsie." The film was given a special Academy Award for "the pioneer picture, which has revolutionized the industry." Jolson also sings "My Gal Sal," "Waiting for the Robert E. Lee," "Dirty Hands, Dirty Faces" and "Mother O'Mine."

In the well-made remake of the overly-sentimental story, Danny Thomas correctly decided not to try to recapture Jolson's style, instead bringing his own personality to the role and looking good doing it. Peggy Lee, the self-proclaimed "greatest female singer," almost convinces audiences that she deserves the title, especially when she sings "Lover" and "Just One of Those Things." Thomas pipes in with "Four Leaf Clover," "Birth of the Blues" and "Just to Be with You." When called upon, Thomas performs nobly in chanting the Yom Kipper "Kol Nidre" service. The film is well done but there's nothing really new to it.

The 1980 remake starring Neil Diamond as the Cantor's son was a real bust, when it became apparent that the pop-folk ballad singer was not an actor. More embarrassing was the appearance of the great actor Laurence Olivier as the Cantor. He acted as a second-rate shylock rather than a devoted man of God.

An interesting sidelight of the filming of *The Jazz Singer* was that the Vitaphone technique of using a sound disc to give the motion pictures sound was short lived. It was doomed to ultimate abandonment because there was the constant threat that the film and the disc might lose synchronization during the course of projection. It was discarded in 1931 when sound-on-film systems proved more reliable and clearly superior. Another interesting note: George Jessel, who had appeared on Broadway in the stage production of the story, was originally slotted for the title role, but for reasons never made clear was replaced by Jolson. Warner Bros. publicized the film as Jolson's own story and Samson Raphaelson, who had written the original story, admitted that he was inspired by seeing Jolson in a similar role on Broadway.

437 Jealousy

Based on the play by Louis Verneuil. Story: Yvonne, the wife of poor artist Pierre, goes to her former lover, Rigaud, when the young couple experience financial difficulties. She finds him murdered. Suspicion falls upon Clement, but Pierre confesses he killed the man, confident that he will get off with a light sentence because Rigaud ruined young girls.

Paramount/Famous Lasky Corp., 1929 (original). Director: Jean De Limur; screenwriters: Eugene Walter, Garnett Fort and John D. Williams. Cast: Jeanne Eagels (Yvonne), Fredric March (Pierre), Halliwell Hobbes (Rigaud), Blanche Le Clair (Renee), Henry Daniell (Clement), Hilda Moore, Carlotta Coerr.

• ***Deception*** (remake). Warner Bros., 1946. Director: Irving Rapper; screenwriters: John Collier and Joseph Than. Cast: Bette Davis (Christine Radcliffe), Paul Henreid (Karel Novak), Claude Rains (Alexander Hollenius), John Abbott (Bertram Gribble), Benson Fong (the Manservant), Richard Walsh, Suzi Crandall, Richard Erdman.

In the remake, composer Paul Henreid goes off the wall when he discovers that his wife, Bette Davis, had formerly been the mistress of famous musician Claude Rains. The title refers to her deception in attempting to prevent her husband from learning of this former relationship. This time it's Miss Davis who removes her ex-lover from the scene, while listening to Henreid play one of Rains' compositions.

438 Jeannie

Based on the play by Aimee Stuart. Story: When Scottish lass Jeannie McLean comes into a bit of money from a modest inheritance, she takes a holiday in Vienna, where she meets a gigolo Austrian, Count Erich. When her funds are gone, so is the Count, and she moves on to London to become a housemaid.

General Film, 1941 (original). Director: Harold French; screenwriters: Tansa and Marcel Hellman. Cast: Barbara Mullen (Jeannie McLean), Wilfrid Lawson (James McLean), Gus McNaughton (Angus Whitelaw), Phyllis Stanley (Mrs. Whitelaw), Michael Redgrave (Stanley Smith), Albert Lieven (Count Erich), Percy Walsh, Kay Hammond, Edward Chapman, Hilda Bailey, Marjorie Fielding.

• ***Let's Be Happy*** (remake). Associated British-Pathe, 1957. Director: Henry Levin; screenwriter: Marcel Hellman. Cast: Vera-Ellen (Jeannie McLean), Tony Martin (Stanley Smith), Robert Fleming (Lord James MacNarin), Zena Marshall (Helene), Helen Horton (Sadie Whitelaw), Beckett Hould (Rev. MacDonald), Alfred Burke, Vernon Greeves, Richard Molinas, Paul Young.

Jeannie is a mildly amusing little comedy as is the musical remake with Vera-Ellen as a Vermont heiress who, while touring Scotland, is rushed by a Scottish lord, Robert Fleming, but goes home to marry an American salesman, Tony Martin. The music by Nicholas Brodsky has deservedly been forgotten.

The Jewel of the Nile *see* **Romancing the Stone**

Jigsaw *see* **Mirage**

439 Jim the Penman

Based on the play by Charles Lawrence Young. Story: In order to save the father of Nina Bronson, the woman he loves, bank cashier James Ralston forges a check in the name of Baron Hartfield. When the latter discovers the fraud, he promises Ralston immunity if Jim will aid the Baron's gang of swindlers. Jim further uses his talent for forgery to compose letters which break off Nina's engagement with Louis Percival, and allow Jim to marry her and prosper. In a scheme to ruin Percival, Jim is exposed by his wife. In remorse, he traps the Baron and his gang on a yacht, sinks it and dies with them.

• ***Jim the Penman*** (remake). First National Pictures, 1921. Silent. Director: Kenneth Webb; screenwriter: Dorothy Farnum. Cast: Lionel Barrymore (James Ralston), Doris Rankin (Nina Bronson), Anders Randolf (Baron Hartfield), Douglas MacPherson (Louis Percival), Gladys Leslie, Charles Coghlan, James Laffey, Ned Burton.

• ***Jim the Penman*** (remake). New Realm Pictures, Great Britain, 1947. Director: Frank Chisnell; screenwriters: Terry Sanford and Edward Eve. Cast: Mark Dignam (James T. Saward), Beatrice Kane (Amy), Campbell Singer (Sutro), Alec Ross (Insp. Atwell), George Street (Sir George), Daphne Maddox, Theodore Tree, Colin Gordon.

Paramount made a silent film of the story in 1915 and there was a French version in 1926. The remake is a documentary-style thriller about a nineteenth-century barrister who becomes the greatest forger of all time. He is finally tracked down by a private investigator.

Jo *see* **The Gazebo**

440 Joan of Arc

Based on the life of the saint and plays by George Bernard Shaw and Maxwell Anderson. Story: Joan of Arc, a simple peasant girl, is told by voices of angels to make the Dauphin king of France and drive the British out of her country. She accomplishes the first and has a major victory at Orleans, but is betrayed to the British where she is tried by a church court as a heretic and when she refuses to renounce her voices or confess her sins, she is burned at the stake.

• ***Joan of Arc*** (remake). RKO, 1948. Director: Victor Fleming; screenwriters: Maxwell Anderson and Andrew Solt. Cast: Ingrid Bergman (Jeanne d'Arc), Jose Ferrer (the Dauphin, Charles VII), Gene Lockhart (Georges de la Tremouille), George Coulouris (Sir Robert), George Zucco (Constable of Clervaux), John Ireland (Captain Jean de la Boussao), Francis L. Sullivan (Count Bishop of Beauvais), J. Carrol Naish (Count of Luxemborg), Sheppard Strudwick (Father Massieu), John Emery (Jean, Duke d'Alencon), Cecil Kellaway (Inquisitor of Rouen), Selena Royle, Robert Barrat, James Lydon, Rand Brooks, Roman Bohnen, Irene Rich, Nestor Paiva, Richard Derr, Ray Teal, Nicholas Joy, Richard Ney, Vincent Donahue, Leif Erickson, Henry Brandon, Morris Ankrum, Hurd Hatfield, Dennis Hoey, Alan Napier.

• ***Saint Joan*** (remake). Wheel/United Artists, Great Britain, 1957. Director: Otto Preminger; screenwriter: Graham Greene. Cast: Jean Seberg (Joan of Arc), Richard Widmark (Charles VII, the Dauphin), Richard Todd (Dunois),

Anton Walbrook (Cauchon, Bishop of Beauvais), John Gielgud (Earl of Warwick), Felix Aylmer (the Inquisitor), Harry Andrews (John de Stogumber), Barry Jones (de Courcelles), Finlay Currie (Archbishop of Rheims), Bernard Miles (Master executioner), Patrick Barr (Captain La Hire), Kenneth Haigh, Archie Duncan, Margot Grahame, Francis de Wolff, David Oxley, Sydney Bromley.

Other film versions of the life of Joan of Arc include the 1918 production *Joan the Woman* with Geraldine Farrar; the Carl Dreyer 1928 silent masterpiece *The Passion of Joan of Arc* with the title role memorably played by Falconetti in her only screen appearance; Simone Genevois in the 1930 Marco de Gastyne–directed *Saint Joan the Maid;* the 1935 German production with Angela Salloker and 1962's *The Trial of Joan of Arc* with Florence Carrez.

Critics were not kind to either Ingrid Bergman or Jean Seberg for their performances as the Maid of Orleans. Bergman seemed too mentally tortured, causing her to overact, according to several reviews. She was also seen as much too worldly-acting to be the simple girl from Lorraine. Still, she and Jose Ferrer received Academy Award nominations and fans found her performance touching and were sympathetic to her portrayal. As for Seberg, she won the role in a major talent search, and critics didn't believe that was the way one should cast a most demanding role. Considering that it was her first appearance in a movie, she did remarkably well, but it may have hurt her chances to have a long, successful Hollywood career as she was given few chances in the United States to develop her acting talents and was forced, partially on personal grounds, to move to France to find decent roles.

Joan the Woman *see* **Joan of Arc**

Joe Macbeth *see* **Macbeth**

441 John Halifax, Gentleman

Based on the novel by Elizabeth Craik. Story: In 1790, wanderer John Halifax saves a crippled boy and as a reward is given a job with the boy's father's mill. Because of his diligence, in a few years John is a partner. He marries a disowned heiress, incurring the hatred of the nobleman for whom she was a ward. Throughout his life he proves a good and fair employer and man, always remaining true to his class.

Samuelson/Moss, Great Britain, 1915 (original). Silent. Director: George Pearson; screenwriter: James L. Pollitt. Cast: Fred Paul (John Halifax), Peggy Hyland (Ursula March), Harry Paulo (Abel Fletcher), Lafayette Ranney (Phineas Fletcher), Edna Maude, Charles Bennett, Bertram Burleigh.

• ***John Halifax, Gentleman*** (remake). King/MGM, Great Britain, 1938. Director: George King; screenwriter: A.R. Rawlinson. Cast: John Warwick (John Halifax), Nancy Burne (Ursula March), Ralph Michael (Phineas Fletcher), D.J. Williams (Abel Fletcher), Brian Buchel, Billy Bray, Elsie Wagstaffe, Roddy McDowall.

It's a plodding period piece with many missed opportunities to be a good yarn. However, it seems that the writers and directors always chose the least interesting path when they came to a fork in the story.

442 Johnny Dark

Based on a screenplay by Franklin Coen. Story: Engineer Johnny Dark steals the new sports car he has designed and enters a border-to-border (Canada to Mexico) race. He wins despite some stiff competition from former buddy Duke Benson. He also wins cute little Liz Fielding.

Universal Pictures, 1954 (original). Director: George Sherman; screenwriter: Franklin Coen. Cast: Tony Curtis (Johnny Dark), Piper Laurie (Liz Fielding), Don Taylor (Duke Benson), Paul Kelly (Jim Scott), Ilka Chase (Abbie Binns), Sidney Blackmer, Ruth Hampton, Russell Johnson, Joseph Sawyer.

• ***The Lively Set*** (remake). Universal Pictures, 1964. Director: Jack Arnold; screenwriters: Mel Goldberg and William Wood. Cast: James Darren (Casey Owens), Pamela Tiffin (Eadie Manning), Doug McClure (Chuch Manning), Joanie Somers (Doreen Gray), Marilyn Maxwell (Marge Owens), Charles Drake, Carole Wells, Greg Morris, Peter Mann.

The slim scripts for these two films weren't helped much by the performers. The big race at the end of each film is the high point of both movies. In the remake, James Darren is a college student who prefers cars to studies and girls—well, all except Pamela Tiffin, that is. Songs in this routine musical comedy include "If You Love Him" and "Casey, Wake Up" by Bobby Darin.

Johnny Trouble *see* **Someone to Remember**

Journey Back to Oz *see* **The Wizard of Oz**

443 Journey Into Fear

Based on the novel by Eric Ambler. Story: An attempt is made on the life of American naval ordnance engineer Graham by Nazi agents as he is returning to the United States from Istanbul. Col. Haki, the head of the Turkish secret police, takes charge and changes Graham's route from train to boat in order to throw off the trailing Nazis. His wife Stephanie is left to ride the train by herself, but aboard ship Graham finds himself surrounded by Germans. Graham makes some accommodations with the Nazis but has to effect his escape before being reunited with his wife and allowed to continue his trip.

RKO, 1942 (original). Director: Norman Foster (with help from Orson Welles); screenwriter: Orson Welles. Cast: Joseph Cotten (Graham), Dolores Del Rio (Josette), Ruth Warwick (Stephanie), Agnes Moorehead (Mme. Mathews), Jack Durant (Gogo), Orson Welles (Col. Haki), Everett Sloane (Kopeikin), Eustace Wyatt, Frank Readick, Edgar Barrier, Jack Moss, Stefan Schnabel, Hans Conreid.

• ***Journey Into Fear*** (remake). Canadian Film, 1975. Director: Delbert Mann; screenwriter: uncredited. Cast: Sam Waterson, Zero Mostel, Yvette Mimieux, Scott Marlowe, Ian McShane, Joseph Wiseman, Shelley Winters, Stanley Holloway, Donald Pleasence, Vincent Price.

Welles' 1942 piece was muddled enough but the Canadian remake, despite an impressive cast, is almost completely at loose ends. The earlier piece, for all of its confusing characters, still holds one's attention and builds suspense and tension. The remake pales by comparison.

444 Journey's End

Based on the play by Robert Cedric Sheriff. Story: Captain Stanhope, who has become an alcoholic in order to stand his many years of fighting in World War I, is idolized by young second lieutenant Raleigh. This admiration is stretched to the breaking point when Stanhope drowns his pain in drink during a raid on German trenches in which many men are killed. The rift between Stanhope and Raleigh is ultimately resolved, with both developing a better understanding of each other and themselves.

Gainsborough/Tiffany, 1930 (original). Director: James Whale; screenwriter: Joseph Moncure March. Cast: Colin Clive (Captain Stanhope), David Manners (Lt. Raleigh), Ian MacLaren (Lt. Osborne), Anthony Bushell (Lt. Hibbert), Thomas Whiteley (Sgt. Major), Charles Mason, Jack Pitcairn, Billy Bevan, Warner Klinger.

• ***Aces High*** (remake). EMI Films, 1976. Director: Jack Gold; screenwriter: Howard Barker. Cast: Malcolm McDowell (Gresham), Christopher Plummer (Sinclair), Simon Ward (Crawford), Peter Firth (Croft), John Gielgud (Headmaster), Trevor Howard (Lt. Col. Silkin), Richard Johnson (Col. Lyle), Ray Milland (Brigadier Whale), David Wood, Elliott Cooper, Jeanne Patou.

Journey's End was one of the first sound films to deal with war. It provided an interesting examination of the tensions in the trenches in World War I. The acting and the directing was uninspired, but Colin Clive and James Whale may have been saving themselves for their next collaboration, *Frankenstein.* The 1976 remake transferred the story to the air war and the stress young pilots of World War I faced in their daily jaunts into the sky. As such it resembled *The Dawn Patrol,* but was not nearly as interesting.

Jubal *see* **Othello**

Judge Hardy's Children *see* **A Family Affair**

445 Judge Priest

Based on short stories by Irvin S. Cobb. Story: In 1890 Kentucky, Jerome Priest, the lawyer nephew of folksy Judge Priest, wants to marry schoolteacher Ellie May Gillespie. His mother feels a better match would be the daughter of the judge's chief political rival. It is discovered in Judge Priest's courtroom that the local blacksmith, Bob Gillis, on trial for assault in defending Ellie May's good name, is actually her father and a Civil War hero. This makes Ellie May more acceptable in the eyes of Jerome Priest's mother.

Fox Film Corporation, 1934 (original). Director: John Ford; screenwriters: Dudley Nichols and Lamarr Trotti. Cast: Will Rogers (Judge Priest), Tom Brown (Jerome Priest), Anita Louise (Ellie May Gillespie), Henry B. Walthall

(Rev. Ashby Brand), David Landau (Bob Gillis), Rochelle Hudson (Virginia Maydew), Berton Churchill, Francis Ford, Stephin Fetchit.

• ***The Sun Shines Bright*** (remake). Republic Pictures, 1953. Director: John Ford; screenwriter: Laurence Stallings. Cast: Charles Winninger (Judge William Pittman Priest), Arleen Whelan (Lucy Lee Lake), John Russell (Ashby Corwin), Stepin Fetchit (Jeff Poindexter), Russell Simpson (Dr. Lewt Lake), Ludwig Stossel, Grant Withers, Milburn Stone, Dorothy Jordan.

Will Rogers' movies were merely meant to be a vehicle for the star's homey and humorous talents. Those looking for an example of the man's work, could do worse than to examine this movie. In the remake, Charles Winninger, a very different type of performer, effectively tackles the role of a judge who faces a tough reelection bid, and wins despite preventing the lynching of an innocent black and leading the funeral procession of a prostitute. Both films lovingly evoke feelings of time gone by and are really quite splendid.

446 Julius Caesar

Based on the play by William Shakespeare. Story: In this Shakespeare dramatization of the death of Julius Caesar, senators including Brutus, Cassius and Casca fear that Caesar will proclaim himself king and that the populace will accept it. They decide that Caesar must die and on the Ides of March, they stab him repeatedly until he dies in the Senate anteroom. Brutus addresses the people and at least momentarily convinces them that the assassins had performed a patriotic service. This lasts until Caesar's friend, Mark Antony, is allowed to address the people, with his famous "Friends, Romans, Countrymen" speech turning the tide against the killers. From then on it is a battle between the forces of the assassins and those following Mark Antony and Octavius to see who will succeed Caesar. Antony's troops prevail and Brutus throws himself on his sword.

• ***Julius Caesar*** (remake). MGM, 1953. Director and screenwriter: Joseph L. Mankiewicz. Cast: Louis Calhern (Julius Caesar), Marlon Brando (Mark Antony), James Mason (Brutus), John Gielgud (Cassius), Greer Garson (Calpurnia), Edmond O'Brien (Casca), Deborah Kerr (Portia), Morgan Farley (Artemidorus), Douglas Watson (Octavius), Douglas Dumbrille, John Doucette, George Macready, Michael Pate, Richard Hale, Alan Napier, William Cottrell, John Hardy, John Hoyt, Tom Powers, Jack Raine, Ian Wolfe.

• ***Julius Caesar*** (remake). AIP, 1970. Director: Stuart Burge; screenwriter: Robert Furnival. Cast: Charlton Heston (Mark Antony), Jason Robards (Brutus), John Gielgud (Julius Caesar), Robert Vaughn (Casca), Richard Chamberlain (Octavius), Diana Rigg (Portia), Jill Bennett (Calpurnia), Christopher Lee (Artemidorus), Alan Browning, Norman Bowler, Andrew Crawford, David Dodimead, Peter Eyre, Edward Finn, Derek Godfrey.

Shakespeare's drama was also brought to the screen in 1907, 1908, 1909, 1911, 1914, 1918, 1922, 1926, 1949, 1960 and 1969. The assassination of Julius Caesar showed up in several other films, notably in the two versions of *Cleopatra.*

The 1953 production was a mixed bag, with several very impressive performances, notably from Calhern, Brando (although a bit hammy), and Mason, but many others in the cast, such as Edmond O'Brien and Greer Garson, seemed to be reading their speeches from cue cards. The 1970 version was miserably miscast. Heston, apparently believing that he could never fail in a period piece, did. John Gielgud moved up smartly from his fine performance as Cassius in the 1953 piece to the title character. Jason Robards looked like he wanted to play Al Capone. Robert Vaughn and Richard Chamberlain were plainly out of their league, but they can always boast that once they played Shakespeare, but both they and the Bard lost.

447 June Moon

Based on the play by Ring Lardner and George S. Kaufman. Story: Fred Stevens gives up his job as a shipping clerk to move to Tin Pan Alley to become a songwriter. He teams up with Paul Sears, collaborating on the song "June Moon," which becomes an instant hit. His overnight success causes him to turn his attention from home-town girlfriend Edna Baker to blonde and glamorous Eileen Fletcher. The latter soon helps him squander his royalties on her. When they are all gone, so is she. Sadder but wiser, he returns to the waiting arms of ever faithful Edna.

Paramount Pictures, 1931 (original). Director: Edward Sutherland; screenwriters: Keene Thompson and Joseph Mankiewicz. Cast: Jack Oakie (Fred Stevens), Frances Dee (Edna Baker), Wynne Gibson (Lucille Sears), Harry Akst (Maxie Schwartz), June MacCloy (Eileen Fletcher), Sam Hardy, Ethel Sutherland, Frank Darien.

• ***Blonde Trouble*** (remake). Paramount Pictures, 1937. Director: George Archainbaud; screenwriter: Lillie Hayward. Cast: Johnny Downs (Fred Stevens), Eleanore Whitney (Edna Baker), Helen Flint (Lucille Sears), Benny Baker (Maxie), Terry Walker (Eileen Fletcher), William Demarest (Paul Sears), John Patterson, El Brendel, Barlowe Borland, Kitty McHugh, Lynne Overman.

The play on which these films was based had been a smash on Broadway in 1929, and the hilarity and satricial bite were carried over to the screen. Jack Oakie was a hit in his first starring role, with Harry Akst, June MacCloy, Wynne Gibson and Sam Hart as Tin Pan Alley characters cracking wise with fine one-liners. The remake was more of the same, only this time it was the likes of William Demarest, El Brendel and Lynne Overman supplying the merriment.

448 Jungle Book

Based on the story by Rudyard Kipling. Story: Mowgli, an adolescent who has the unique talent of being able to converse with the animals in the jungle near his Indian village, prevents the getaway of three thieves.

United Artists, 1942 (original). Director: Zoltan Korda; screenwriter: Laurence Stallings. Cast: Sabu (Mowgli), Joseph Calleia (Buideo), John Qualen (the Barber), Frank Puglia (the Pundit), Rosemary De Camp (Messua), Patricia O'Rourke (Mahala), Ralph Byrd (Durga), John Mather (Rao), Faith Brook, Noble Johnson.

• ***Jungle Book*** (remake). Walt Disney, 1967. Director: Wolfgang Reitherman; screenwriters: Larry Clemmons, Ralph Wright, Ken Anderson and Vance Gerry. Cast: the voices of: George Sanders (Shere Khan the Tiger), Phil Harris (Baloo the Bear), Sebastian Cabot (Bagheera the Panther), Louis Prima (King Louie of the Apes), Sterling Holloway (Kaa the Snake), J. Pat O'Malley (Colonel Hathi the Elephant), Bruce Reitherman (Mowgli the Man Cub), Verna Felton, Clint Howard, Chad Stuart, Tim Hudson, John Abbott, Ben Wright, Darleen Carr.

The Disney animated musical tells the story of an Indian boy baby, Mowgli, abandoned in the jungle and raised by a wolf family as just another cub. Ten years later, when it is learned that Shere Khan the Tiger is returning, the wolves fear for Mowgli's safety and decide he must return to the world of men. Mowgli is reluctant and protesting as Bagheera the Panther escorts him through the jungle. The two encounter numerous dangers, but ultimately Mowgli has to face the Tiger and with the help of his animal friends sends that one running with a burning branch tied to its tail. The song "The Bare Necessities" by Terry Gilkyson was nominated for an Academy Award.

K

449 The Karate Kid

Based on a screenplay by Robert Mark Kamen. Story: In this heartwarming story, Daniel is a very put-upon adolescent, new to California and very much an outsider. He joins a karate club and with the help of Miyagi develops enough skill to defeat the bullies who had been making his life miserable.

Columbia Pictures, 1984. Director: John G. Avildsen; screenwriter: Robert Mark Kamen. Cast: Ralph Macchio (Daniel), Noriyuki "Pat" Morita (Miyagi), Elisabeth Shue (Ali), Martin Kove (Kreese), Randee Heller (Lucille), William Zabka, Ron Thomas, Rob Garrison, Chad McQueen.

• ***The Karate Kid, Part 2*** (sequel). Columbia Pictures, 1986. Director: John G. Avildsen; screenwriter: Robert Mark Kamen. Cast: Ralph Macchio (Daniel), Noriyuki "Pat" Morita (Miyagi), Danny Kamekona, Nobu McCarthy, Tamlyn Yomita, Yuji Okumoto, Martin Kove, William Zabka.

These films, which owe a great deal to the "Rocky" series for inspiration, provoke the desire in audiences to cheer at the climactic scene when the young hero banishes the bad guys, each worthy of a loud hiss. The sequel begins shortly after Macchio's victory in the original. Morita receives word that his father is dying in Okinawa. Taking Macchio with him he heads for home, where he encounters an old enemy and an old love. Macchio also makes an enemy and a lovely friend. It's more of the same, but done well enough so that audiences do not grow tired of the premise and its production.

The Karate Kid, Part 2 *see* **The Karate Kid**

450 Kathleen Mavourneen

Based on an old Irish song and the novel by Clara Mulholland. Story: Kathleen Mavourneen is an Irish colleen who is desired by the squire. Plotting to make her his, he informs her parents that they will be evicted unless they pay what they owe. As the price of letting them alone he tells Kathleen that he will accept her in marriage. Meanwhile her lover is working frantically to come up with the money which will prevent this unhappy state of affairs. Sure and he comes through in the nick of time.

Fox Film Corp., 1919 (original). Silent. Director: Charles J. Brabin; screenwriter: uncredited. Cast: Theda Bara (Kathleen Mavourneen), Edward O'Connor (Kathleen's Father), Jennie Dickerson (Kathleen's Mother), Raymond McKee (Terence O'More), Marc McDermott (the Squire of Traise), Marcia Harris, Henry Hallam, Harry Gripp, Morgan Thorpe.

• ***Kathleen Mavourneen*** (remake). Welwyn/Argyle British, Great Britain, 1937. Director: Norman Lee; screenwriters: Marjorie Deans and John Glen. Cast: Sally O'Neil (Kathleen O'Moore), Tom Burke (Mike Rooney), Sara Allgood (Mary Ellen O'Dwyer), Jack Daly (Dennis O'Dwyer), Talbot O'Farrell (Dan Milligan), Denis O'Neil, Fred Duprez, Pat Noonan, Jeanne Stuart, John Forbes-Robertson.

In the remake Kathleen, a waitress in Liverpool, has to earn enough for her brother and sister as well as herself. Singing stevedore Mike Rooney, who loves her, pays for them to go to their aunt's farm in Ireland. Their aunt tries unsuccessfully to put the children in an orphanage. Kathleen falls in love with a wealthy landowner and Mike returns to England for a singing career.

451 Keep Your Seats, Please

Based on the play *The Twelve Chairs* by Elie Ilf and Eugene Petrov. Story: An eccentric old lady has hidden a fortune in jewels in one of a set of twelve antique chairs and her nephew George Withers has to chase all over the country to track down the one containing his inheritance. He is abetted by his girl, Flo, and hampered by an unscrupulous lawyer, Drayton.

• ***Keep Your Seats, Please*** (remake). Associated Talking Pictures, Great Britain, 1936. Director: Monty Banks; screenwriters: Tom Geraghty, Ian Hay and Anthony Kimmins. Cast: George Formby (George Withers), Florence Desmond (Flo), Gus McNaughton (Max), Alastair Sim (Drayton), Harry Tate, Enid Stamp Taylor, Hal Gordon, Tom Payne, Clifford Heatherley, Fiona Stuart, Fred Culpitt.

• ***It's in the Bag*** (remake). United Artists, 1945. Director: Richard Wallace; screenwriters: Jay Dratler and Alma Reville, from a story by Morris Ryskind. Cast: Fred Allen (Fred Floogle), Jack Benny (himself), William Bendix (himself), Binnie Barnes (Eve Floogle), Robert Benchley (Parker), Jerry Colonna, John Carradine, Gloria Pope, William Terry, Minerva Pious, Dickie Tyler.

• ***The Twelve Chairs*** (remake). UMC, 1970. Director and screenwriter: Mel Brooks. Cast: Ron Moody (Vorobyaninov), Frank Langella (Ostap Bender), Dom Deluise (Father Fyodor), Mel Brooks (Tikon), Bridget Brice, Robert Bernal, David Lander, Andreas Voutsinas, Vlada Petric, Diana Coupland.

The play by Ilf and Petrov was first filmed in Russia during the silent era, although the exact year is uncertain. It was once again filmed in the U.S.S.R. in 1971. In the 1945 disguised remake, flea circus operator Fred Allen learns that he has inherited twelve million dollars from a granduncle and then discovers that the money has disappeared. The majority of the picture is taken up with tracking down chairs in which some of the money has been hidden. The Mel Brooks piece doesn't rank with his better known farces and remakes of movie classics. Neither Moody nor Langella can be too proud that this film is listed in their credits. They don't get the jewels hidden in the chair, but do develop a beggar partnership based on Moody's ability to draw a crowd faking epilepsy.

452 The Keeper of the Bees

Based on the novel by Gene Stratton Porter. Story: World War I hero James Lewis MacFarlane learns that he has but a year to live because of a wound sustained in the war that will not heal. He leaves the government hospital and is befriended by Michael Worthington, the Bee Master, who is himself fatally ill and soon dies. MacFarlane inherits half of Worthington's estate and apiary. James marries a girl about to drown herself because she is to bear an illegitimate child. Soon afterwards she disappears, leaving a note signed "Alice Louise MacFarlane." With the aid of a neighbor, Margaret Cameron, MacFarlane regains his health. At about that time, he is informed that his wife has given birth to a son. When he arrives at the hospital, the woman identified as Mrs. MacFarlane is not the one he married. The new mother soon dies, and Molly Cameron, daughter of his helpful neighbor, appears. She's the girl he married. She confesses that she married James to get a wedding certificate with her sister's name on it, so she would not have her child out of wedlock. All ends well, as Molly and James marry this time for love.

Gene Stratton Porter Productions, 1925 (original). Silent. Director and screewriter: James Leo Meehan. Cast: Robert Frazer (James Lewis MacFarlane), Josef Swickard (Michael Worthingon), Martha Mattox (Margaret Cameron), Clara Bow (Alice Louise Cameron), Alyce Mills (Molly Cameron), Gene Stratton, Joe Coppa, Ainse Charland, Billy Osborne.

• ***The Keeper of the Bees*** (remake). Monogram Pictures, 1935. Director: Christy Cabanne; screenwriter: Adele Buffington and George Waggner. Cast: Neil Hamilton (Jamie), Betty Furness (Molly), Emma Dunn (Margaret), Edith Fellowes (Scout), Hobart Bosworth (the Bee Master), Helen Jerome Eddy, Marion Schilling, James Burtis.

The Gene Stratton Porter chestnut was last produced for Columbia Pictures in 1947. Porter's stories had an appreciative audience in the sticks for years, but even these unsophisticates finally grew tired of his Victorian stories. In the remake Betty Furness plays the unwed mother-to-be, who, fearful of shaming her family, goes away to find a man, in this case Neil Hamilton, who will go through with a phony wedding ceremony to give her child a father.

453 Keeping Company

Based on an original story by Herman J. Mankiewicz. Story: Real estate broker Harry C. Thomas' eldest of three daughters, Mary, becomes engaged to Ted Foster, and despite some troubles with his ex-girlfriend Anastasia Atherton, they marry. As often happens, things do not run smoothly during the period of adjustment, and despite lots of advice from family and friends the couple separate and contemplate divorce before resolving their differences.

MGM, 1941 (original). Director: S. Sylvan Simon; screenwriters: Harry Ruskin, James H. Hill and Adrian Scott. Cast: Frank Morgan (Harry C. Thomas), Ann Rutherford (Mary Thomas), John Shelton (Ted Foster), Irene Rich (Mrs. Thomas), Gene Lockhart (Mr. Hellman), Virginia Weidler (Harriet Thomas), Virginia Grey (Anastasia Atherton), Dan Dailey, Jr., Gloria De Haven.

• ***This Time for Keeps*** (remake). MGM, 1942. Director: Charles Reisner; screenwriters: Muriel Roy Bolton, Rian James and Harry Ruskin. Cast: Ann Rutherford (Katherine White), Robert Sterling (Lee White), Guy Kibbee (Harry Bryant), Irene Rich (Mrs. Bryant), Virginia Weidler (Harriet Bryant), Henry O'Neill.

Keeping Company was intended to be the first of a series dealing with the lives and loves of the three Thomas girls, but nothing came of the plan. The second film is not a sequel, just another attempt at making the story idea work—it didn't succeed, either. In it, Ann Rutherford marries Robert Sterling, who is talked into going to work for his father-in-law, Guy Kibbee. The latter refuses to allow his son-in-law the right to exercise initiative. The result is a strained marriage, but it all works out. Unfortunately, few people cared.

454 The Kennel Murder Case

Based on the novel by S.S. Van Dine. Story: The title does not refer to the person killed. Rather it is a kennel club on Long Island to which various characters in the story belong, including two murdered brothers. Philo Vance is a dog fancier detective who unravels the mystery and exposes the culprit.

Warner Bros., 1933 (original). Director: Michael Curtiz; screenwriters: Robert N. Lee and Peter Milne. Cast: William Powell (Philo Vance), Mary Astor (Hilda Lake), Eugene Pallette (Heath), Ralph Morgan (Raymond Werde), Helen Vinson (Doris Delafield), Jack LaRue (Eduardo Grassi), Paul Cavanaugh (Sir Bruce McDonald), Robert Barrat, Arthur Hohl, Etienne Girardot.

• ***Calling Philo Vance*** (remake). Warner Bros., 1940. Director: William Clemens; screenwriter: Tom Reed. Cast: James Stephenson (Philo Vance), Margot Stevenson (Hilda), Henry O'Neill (Markham), Edward Brophy (Ryan), Ralph Forbes (Tom MacDonald), Donald Douglas (Philip Wrede), Martin Kosleck, Sheila Bromley, James Conlon, Edward Raquello, Creighton Hale, Harry Strang.

The Philo Vance stories were quite successful in their screen presentations, none more so than *The Kennel Murder Case* starring William Powell as the bright detective, and superbly directed by Michael Curtiz. The remake suffered precisely because it had a lesser star and an inferior director. James Stephenson, who during his career gave a few notable performances, especially so in *The Letter*, just didn't seem to have star quality and found himself relegated to increasingly less important roles in poorly financed productions.

Variety called the second picture "as exciting as the solution of a problem in mathematics." As one of your authors is a mathematician, this criticism seems unnecessarily double-edged and misguided.

455 Kick In

Based on the play by Willard Mack. Story: Molly Hewes encourages her ex-convict husband, Chick, to go straight but the task is made difficult by suspicious police, who feel he is behind the theft of a diamond necklace. Chick is offered immunity from prosecution if he will turn in the thief, who turns out to be Molly's drug-addicted brother. Chick and pregnant Molly are arrested as accomplices but Molly's impassionate plea convinces Commissioner Garvey that the young couple are innocent and releases them to begin a new life of peace and dignity.

Pathe-Astra Films, 1917 (original). Silent. Director and screenwriter: George Fitzmaurice. Cast: William Courtenay (Chick Hewes), Mollie King (Molly), John Boyle (Commissioner Garvey), Robert Clugston, Richard Tucker, Suzanne Willia.

• ***Kick In*** (remake). Paramount Pictures, 1922. Silent. Director: George Fitzmaurice; screenwriter: Quida Bergere. Cast: Bert Lytell (Chick Hewes), Betty Compson (Molly Brandon), May McAvoy (Myrtle Sylvester), Gareth Hughes, Kathleen Clifford, Robert Agnew, Walter Long, John Miltern, Mayme Kelso, Jed Prouty.

• ***Kick In*** (remake). Paramount Pictures, 1931. Director: Richard Wallace; screenwriter: Bartlett Cormack. Cast: Regis Toomey (Chick Hewes), Clara Bow (Molly), Wynne Gibson (Myrtle Sylvester), Juliette Compton, Leslie Fenton, James Murray, Donald Crisp.

This underworld drama was filmed three times, without making much change in the story or much impression on the public. John Barrymore had appeared as Chick Hewes on Broadway in 1914. In the last working of the story, Clara Bow, looking somewhat overweight and no longer the "it girl," was nevertheless effective as the young wife struggling to help her husband reform. It was her last picture for Paramount.

The Kid from Brooklyn *see* **The Milky Way**

456 Kid Galahad

Based on a story by Francis Wallace. Story: Querulous fight manager Nick Donati turns a bellhop into a prizefighter, billed as Kid Galahad. Nick maneuvers his boxer through a string of bouts, always with the notion of paying off a grudge that he holds against Turkey Morgan, another fight manager who uses dishonest means to advance the careers of his fighters. Nick's mistress, Fluff, and his convent-bred sister, Marie, both fall in love with the Kid. As a sort of a switch for fight movies, the boxer doesn't die in the final reel, but the manager does.

Warner Bros., 1937 (original). Director: Michael Curtiz; screenwriter: Seton I. Miller. Cast: Edward G. Robinson (Nick Donati), Bette Davis (Fluff),

Humphrey Bogart (Turkey Morgan), Wayne Morris (Kid Galahad), Jane Bryan (Marie), Harry Carey, William Hande, Soledad Jiminez, Joe Cunningham, Ben Welden.

• ***The Wagons Roll at Night*** (remake). Warner Bros., 1941. Director: Ray Enright; screenwriters: Fred Niblo, Jr. and Barry Trivers. Cast: Humphrey Bogart (Nick Coster), Sylvia Sidney (Flo Lorraine), Eddie Albert (Matt Varney), Joan Leslie (Mary Coster), Sig Rumann, Cliff Clark, Charley Foy.

• ***Kid Galahad*** (remake). United Artists, 1962. Director: Phil Karlson; screenwriter: William Fay. Cast: Elvis Presley (Walter Gulick), Gig Young (Wally Grogan), Lola Albright (Dolly Fletcher), Joan Blackman (Rose Grogan), Charles Bronson (Lew Nyack), Ned Glass, Robert Emhardt, David Lewis.

So as not to confuse it with the Elvis Presley film, the 1937 production's title has been changed to *The Battling Bellhop* for its release to television. Presley's film wasn't the only one to have a song; the 1937 picture featured "The Moon Is in Tears, Tonight" by M.K. Jerome and Jack Scholl. In the first remake of a story of heartless exploitation of an innocent, the setting is changed, having Humphrey Bogart as a tough carnival operator who hires grocery clerk Eddie Albert, who has a way with animals, as his lion tamer. Bogart doesn't seem too annoyed when his girl, Sylvia Sidney, as the show's fortune teller, takes an interest in Albert, but when the latter becomes involved with Humphrey's sister, played by Joan Leslie, Bogie decides to literally feed Albert to the lions. Facing a losing battle with a mad lion, Albert is almost a goner when Bogie relents, enters the cage, saves Albert and is himself killed by the animal. The Presley vehicle is about of average quality for the rock 'n' roll king's movie career. None of the songs from the movie found their way into Presley's all-time hits list, although as with everything he sung, they sold well. Taking a role as a boxer must have meant that Elvis forgot that he once said, "I wanted to be a singer, because I didn't want to sweat."

457 Kidnapped

Based on the novel by Robert Louis Stevenson. Story: A young Scotsman, David Balfour, is cheated out of his inheritance by his wicked uncle. He has many exciting escapades with the likes of adventurer and outlaw Alan Breck on the way to reclaiming his rightful place. These include a kidnapping, being sold into slavery, sailing and fighting with pirates, and becoming a patriot while fighting King George's redcoats during a Highland rebellion. Not all of the same action is included in the three movies mentioned below, but this is sort of a composite story.

• ***Kidnapped*** Twentieth Century–Fox, 1938. Director: Alfred L. Werker; screenwriters: Sonya Levien, Richard Sherman and Walter Ferris. Cast: Warner Baxter (Alan Breck), Freddie Bartholomew (David Balfour), Arleen Whelan (Jean MacDonald), C. Aubrey Smith (Duke of Argyle), Reginald Owen (Captain Hoseason), John Carradine (Gordon), Nigel Bruce, Miles Mander, Ralph Forbes, H.B. Warner, Arthur Hohl, E.E. Clive, Halliwell Hobbes, Montagu Love.

• ***Kidnapped*** (remake). Walt Disney/Buena Vista, 1960. Director and screenwriter: Robert Stevenson. Cast: Peter Finch (Alan Breck Stewart), James MacArthur (David Balfour), Bernard Lee (Captain Hoseason), Niall MacGinnis (Shaun), John Laurie (Uncle Ebenezer), Finlay Currie (Cluny MacPherson), Peter O'Toole (Robin Oig MacGregor), Miles Malleson, Oliver Johnston, Duncan MacRea, John Pike.

• ***Kidnapped*** (remake). American International Pictures, England, 1971. Director: Delbert Mann; screenwriter: Jack Pulman. Cast: Michael Caine (Alan Breck), Trevor Howard (Lord Advocate-Lord Grant), Jack Hawkins (Captain Hoseason), Donald Pleasence (Ebenezer Balfour), Gordon Jackson (Charles Stewart), Vivien Heilbron (Catriona), Lawrence Douglas (David Balfour), Freddie Jones, Jack Watson, Andrew McCullough, Eric Woodburn, Roger Booth.

The Stevenson story was also filmed in 1917 by Edison Studios; in East Germany, as *Achsuuse Unterm Galgen,* in 1969; in Great Britain in 1971 as *David and Catriona;* and an independently produced version in 1973. The 1938 version was probably the most exciting and with Bartholomew as the youngster sold into slavery by his wicked uncle, the most altered of the stories. The Disney version is the most faithful to the book and Finch is quite good as the outlaw who befriends David Balfour. The 1971 version incorporated portions of Stevenson's novel *Catriona* and had a fine British cast, but still didn't come off as very exciting.

458 Kiki

Based on the play by Andre Picard as adapted by David Belasco. Story: Kiki, a Parisian gamine who lives by her wits, becomes a chorus girl and pursues Victor Renel, the theater manager and sweetheart of Paulette, the star of the show. Despite Paulette's attempts to humiliate and ruin Kiki, the latter gets her man.

Talmadge Productions/First National Pictures, 1926 (original). Silent. Director: Clarence Brown; screenwriter: Hans Kraly. Cast: Norman Talmadge (Kiki), Ronald Colman (Renel), Gertrude Astor (Paulette), Marc MacDermott, George K. Arthur, William Orlamond, Erwin Connelly, Frankie Darro.

• ***Kiki*** (remake). United Artists, 1931. Director and screenwriter: Sam Taylor. Cast: Mary Pickford (Kiki), Reginald Denny (Victor Randall), Joseph Cawthorn (Alfred Rapp), Margaret Livingston (Paulette Vaile), Phil Tead, Fred Walton.

This comedy-drama of two women fighting over a man is an uninspired and uninteresting trifle which not even the performance of a Norma Talmadge or a Mary Pickford can make otherwise. In the remake, tomboyish Mary Pickford sets her cap for divorced Reginald Denny, but his ex, Margaret Livingston, is particular about who he takes up with.

Killer McCoy ***see*** **The Crowd Roars (1937)**

459 The Killers

Based on a story by Ernest Hemingway. Story: The film begins with Ole

"Swede" Anderson waiting patiently in a sleazy hotel room for two assassins to kill him. They do and audiences learn why he made no effort to protect himself as insurance agent Riordan tracks down the events leading up to the killing. Seems Swede had gotten involved in a robbery because a girl, Kitty Collins, is made to look like a traitor within the caper, and is killed to cover up for the real informer.

Universal Pictures, 1946. Director: Robert Siodmak; screenwriter: Anthony Veiller. Cast: Burt Lancaster (Ole "Swede" Anderson), Ava Gardner (Kitty Collins), Edmond O'Brien (Riordan), Albert Dekker (Colfax), Sam Levene (Lt. Lubinsky), Charles D. Brown, Donald McBride, Phil Brown, Charles McGraw, John Miljan, William Conrad, Queenie Smith, Garry Owen.

• ***The Killers*** (remake). Universal Pictures, 1964. Director: Donald Siegal; screenwriter: Gene L. Coon. Cast: Lee Marvin (Charlie), Angie Dickinson (Sheila Farr), John Cassavetes (Johnny North), Ronald Reagan (Browning), Clu Gulager, Claude Atkins, Norman Fell, Virginia Christine, Don Haggerty, Robert Phillips.

Burt Lancaster was impressive in his movie debut as a man resigned to the fact that he is going to be killed and knowing there is nothing he can do about it. The film is a quasi-*film noir,* in which fate deals the Swede a tough hand, and by the end of the movie most of the criminals involved in the robbery are dead. Don Siegel, who directed the remake, was considered for the job with the first production, but was not available. His version was intended as a TV movie but because of its violence was released in the theaters. Ronald Reagan, in his last film role, was the chief villain.

460 Kind Lady

Based on the story "The Silver Casket" by Hugh Walpole and the play *Kind Lady* by Edward Chodorov. Story: A con man, Henry Abbott, insinuates himself and his criminal friends into the London townhouse of wealthy spinster Mary Herries when his supposedly sick wife faints at the doorstep, is invited in and is pronounced unfit to be moved by an accomplice posing as a doctor. The Abbotts take over the house, dismissing Miss Herries' servants and systematically selling off her art collection and furnishings, while holding her a prisoner in her own home. The Abbotts convince Miss Herries' friends that she has turned senile. But Miss Herries fights off the effects of the drugs they are using to control her, gets word out of her captivity, and sees her tormentors taken away by the authorities.

MGM, 1935 (original). Director: George B. Seitz; screenwriter: Bernard Schubert. Cast: Aline MacMahon (Mary Herries), Basil Rathbone (Henry Abbott), Mary Carlisle (Phyllis), Frank Albertson (Peter), Dudley Digges (Mr. Edwards), Doris Lloyd, Nola Luxford, Murray Kinnell, Eily Malyon, Justine Chase, Barbara Shields.

• ***Kind Lady*** (remake). MGM, 1951. Director: John Sturges; screenwriters: Edward Chodorov, Jerry Davis and Charles Bennett. Cast: Ethel Barrymore (Mary Herries), Maurice Evans (Henry Elcott), Angela Lansbury (Mrs. Edwards), Keenan Wynn (Mr. Edwards), Betsy Blair (Ada Elcott), John Williams

(Mr. Foster), Doris Lloyd, John O'Malley, Henri Letondal, Moyna Macgill, Barry Bernard.

Once the premise of the story is established, the films move rather slowly to the climax. The suspense and the suffering of the imprisoned woman is at times nerve-twisting, with both Aline MacMahon and Ethel Barrymore effective as the spinster who's strong will allows her to finally triumph over her captors. Rathbone and Evans as the head con artists are adequate but not outstanding in portraying the cruel but inventive schemer.

King Arthur Was a Gentleman *see* **Knights of the Round Table**

King of the Khyber Rifles *see* **The Black Watch**

King of the Lumberjacks *see* **Tiger Shark**

461 King Solomon's Mines

Based on the novel by H. Rider Haggard. Story: Kathy O'Brien goes searching for her father, who has been lost since he left on an expedition to locate King Solomon's mines. She takes up with a native porter, Umbopa, and a party of white big-game hunters led by Allan Quartermaine. Discarding their wagons and abandoned by their native crew, they struggle through wastelands and deserts until they reach a tribe, who mistake them for white gods. The chief of the tribe, usurper of Umbopa's rightful position, plots with a witch doctor to kill them, but their knowledge of an imminent eclipse of the sun proves that their magic is superior. The deposed king rallies other tribes against them, but the hunters prevail in a pitched battle. Their troubles are not over, as the witch doctor traps them at Solomon's mines as a volcano's eruption threatens to overrun them. The ever resourceful Umbopa leads them to safety and reclaims his throne.

Gaumont-British Productions, 1937 (original). Director and screenwriter: Robert Stevenson. Cast: Paul Robeson (Umbopa), Cedric Hardwicke (Allan Quartermaine), Roland Young (Commander Good), John Loder (Henry Curtis), Anna Lee (Kathy O'Brien), Makubalo Hlubi (Kapsie), Ecce Homo Toto (Infadoos), Robert Adams, Frederick Leister, Alf Goddard, Arthur Sinclair.

• ***King Solomon's Mines*** (remake). MGM, 1950. Directors: Compton Bennett and Andrew Morton; screenwriter: Helen Deutsch. Cast: Deborah Kerr (Elizabeth Curtis), Stewart Granger (Allan Quartermain), Richard Carlson (John Goode), Hugo Haas (Smith), Lowell Gilmore (Eric Masters), Kimursi (Khiva), Siriaque (Umbopa), Sekaryongo, Baziga.

• ***Watusi*** (remake). MGM, 1959. Director: Kurt Neumann; screenwriter: James Clavell. Cast: George Montgomery (Harry Quartermain), Taina Elg (Erica Neuler), David Farrar (Rick Cobb), Rex Ingram (Umbopa), Dan Seymour (Mohamet), Robert Goodwin, Anthony M. Davis, Paul Thompson, Harold Dyrenforth.

Richard Chamberlain appears as Alan Quartermain in a 1985 production of *King Solomon's Mines*. The 1937 version of the adventure novel remains the best, with a strong cast headed by the massive and formidable Paul Robeson and the solemn Sir Cedric Hardwicke. The final reel still ranks as among the best action footage. The 1950 film is beautifully photographed, winning an Academy Award for Best Cinematography for Robert Surtees, but the picture itself didn't deserve the Best Picture nomination it received. Apparently the voters agreed. It was only the third motion picture to be shot entirely on location in Africa, and was Stewart Granger's first Hollywood movie. *Watusi* was cursed with a poor cast, unimaginative director, and a screenplay by James Clavell, which may have convinced him to concentrate on writing adventure novels rather than adapting them.

The King's Pirate *see* **Against All Flags**

462 Kipps

Based on the novel by H.G. Wells. Story: When Kipps, an illiterate, unpopular draper's assistant, inherits a fortune, he finds instant love and friends as he crashes high society. Set in Victorian England, the film examines British class consciousness with all of its peculiarities.

• ***Kipps*** (remake). Twentieth Century–Fox, Great Britain, 1941. Director: Carol Reed; screenwriter: Sidney Gilliat. Cast: Michael Redgrave (Kipps), Diana Wynyard (Helen Walshingham), Arthur Riscoe (Chitterlow), Phyllis Calvert (Ann Pornick), Helen Haye, Lloyd Pearson, Edward Rigby, MacKenzie Ward, Hermione Baddeley, Betty Ann Davies.

• ***The Remarkable Mr. Kipps*** (remake). Twentieth Century–Fox, Great Britain, 1942. Director: Carol Reed; screenwriter: Sidney Gilliat. Cast: Michael Redgrave (Kipps as a man), Philip Frost (Kipps as a boy), Diana Wynyard (Helen Walshingham), Phyllis Calvert (Ann Pornick as a woman), Diana Calderwood (Ann Pornick as a girl), Arthur Riscoe (Chitterlow), Max Adrian, Helen Haye, Michael Wilding, Lloyd Pearson, Edward Rigby, MacKenzie Ward, Hermione Baddeley, Betty Ann Davies.

• ***Half a Sixpence*** (remake). Paramount Pictures, Great Britain, 1967. Director: George Sidney; screenwriter: Beverley Cross. Cast: Tommy Steele (Arthur Kipps), Julia Foster (Ann), Cyril Richard (Chitterlow), Penelope Horner (Helen), Grover Dale (Pearce), Elaine Taylor (Kate), Hilton Edwards, Julia Sutton, Leslie Meadows, Sheila Falconer, Pamela Brown.

The 1942 film is merely an 86-minute version of the 1941 picture which had a running time of 112 minutes, considered much too long at the time for American theaters, particularly considering the subject—an unpopular British hick who comes into money and almost marries the snooty Helen Walshingham before coming to his senses and running off with his old love, Ann Pornick. The 1967 musical remake didn't score that well with American audiences. While Tommy Steele's performance was admired, the movie itself was considered overly long and short on memorable musical numbers. *Kipps* was also produced for the screen in a 1920 silent in Great Britain.

Richard Carlson (left), Deborah Kerr and Stewart Granger light the way through a cave in search of treasure in the 1950 MGM production of King Solomon's Mines. *The original was filmed in 1937 by Gainsborough, starring Cedric Hardwicke and Paul Robeson.*

463 Kismet

Based on the play by Edward Knoblock. Story: Hajj, a Baghdad street poet, a charming and conniving rascal, is arrested for stealing, but released by the wicked Wazir, when the former agrees to kill the young Caliph Abdallah. Hajj bungles the attempted assassination and is thrown into a dungeon with an old enemy, Sheik Jawan. Hajj strangles Jawan and escapes in the latter's clothing. He discovers that his daughter, Marsinah, has been put into the Wazir's harem. He rescues her, and drowns the Wazir. The Caliph, who had disguised himself as a gardener and fallen in love with Marsinah, reveals his true identity, makes plans to marry her and reluctantly banishes his future father-in-law for his crimes. Feigning plans to visit Mecca, Hajj returns to his usual stand in front of the Mosque and resumes his beggar's ways, trying to sell his poems.

Zenith Films, England, 1914 (original). Silent. Director and screenwriter: Leedham Bantock. Cast: Oscar Asche (Hajj), Lily Brayton (Marsinah), Herbert Grimwood (Wazir), Frederick Worlock (Caliph Abdallah), Caleb Porter (Sheik Jawan), Suzanne Sheldon, Bessie Major, H.R. Hignett, Arthur Grenville.

• ***Kismet*** (remake). Robertson-Cole, 1920. Silent. Director and screenwriter: Louis Gasnier. Cast: Otis Skinner (Hajj), Elinor Fair (Marsinah), Leon

Barry (Caliph Abdallah), Rosemary Theby (Kut-Al-Kulub), Marguerite Comont (Nargis), Herschall Mayall (Jawan), Hamilton Revelle (Wazir Mansur), Cornelia Otis Skinner (Miskah), Fred Lancaster, Nicholas Dunaew, Sidney Smith, Sam Kaufman.

• ***Kismet*** (remake). First National Pictures, 1930. Director: John Francis Dillon (German version director: William Dieterle; screenwriter: Howard Estabrook. Cast: Otis Skinner (Hajj), Loretta Young (Marsinah), David Manners (Caliph Abdallah), Sidney Blackmer (Wazir Mansur), Mary Duncan (Zeleekha), Montagu Love, Ford Sterling, Theodore von Eltz, John St. Polis, Edmund Breese, Blanche Frederici.

• ***Kismet*** (remake). MGM, 1944. Director: William Dieterle; screenwriter: John Meehan. Cast: Ronald Colman (Hafiz), Marlene Dietrich (Jamilla), James Craig (Caliph), Joy Ann Page (Marsinah), Edward Arnold (Grand Vizar Mansur), Hugh Herbert (Feisal), Florence Bates, Robert Warwick, Harry Davenport, Hobart Cavanaugh, Victor Killian, Barry Macollum.

• ***Kismet*** (remake). MGM, 1955. Director: Vincente Minnelli; screenwriter: Charles Lederer. Cast: Howard Keel (Hajj), Ann Blyth (Marsinah), Vic Damone (the Caliph), Dolores Gray (Lalume), Monty Woolley (Omar), Sebastian Cabot (Wazir), Jay C. Flippen (Jawan), Mike Mazurki, Jack Elam, Ted De Corsica, Julie Robinson.

Kismet was also produced in France in 1919 and in Germany in 1930. Oscar Asche, who originated the role of Hajj on the London stage in 1911, appeared in the first film version, followed by two flawless portrayals by Otis Skinner who had originated the role of Hajj on Broadway in 1911. Ronald Colman appeared as the wily begger in the 1944 Technicolor picture, with Marlene Dietrich as the lovely gold body-painted Jamilla and Edward Arnold as a grand scheming Vizar. In 1953, a musical version of *Kismet* opened on Broadway, followed two years later by a screen version. The team of Robert Wright and George Forrest adapted the music of Russian composer Alexander Borodin to the story, resulting in beautiful songs such as, "Stranger in Paradise," "And This Is My Beloved," "Baubles, Bangles and Beads" and "Not Since Nineveh." The roles of the poet-begger, his daughter, the caliph, the wazir and his sexy wife were played quite entertainingly by Howard Keel, Ann Blyth, Vic Damone, Sebastian Cabot and Dolores Gray, respectively. It's kitsch, but great kitsch.

464 Kiss and Tell

Based on the play by F. Hugh Herbert. Story: Corliss Archer's brother, an Army lieutenant posted overseas, has secretly married his neighborhood sweetheart but wishes to keep it quiet, because the two families are feuding for some forgotten reason. The wife is pregnant and because Corliss is so tied to the secret, she allows herself to be thought of as the one with child, going so far as naming her next-door boyfriend the prospective father. The resolution of this heavy problem for a sixteen year old leads to some very funny moments.

Columbia Pictures, 1945 (original). Director: Richard Wallace; screenwriter: F. Hugh Herbert. Cast: Shirley Temple (Corliss Archer), Jerome Courtland

(Dexter Franklin), Walter Abel (Mr. Archer), Katharine Alexander (Mrs. Archer), Robert Benchley (Uncle George), Tom Tully (Mr. Pringle), Mary Phillips (Mrs. Pringle), Darryl Hickman, Scott McKay, Porter Hall, Edna Holland.

• ***A Kiss for Corliss*** (sequel). United Artists, 1949. Director: Richard Wallace; screenwriter: Howard Dimsdale. Cast: Shirley Temple (Corliss Archer), David Niven (Kenneth Marquis), Tom Tully (Harry Archer), Darryl Hickman (Dexter Franklin), Virginia Welles, Robert Ellis, Richard Gaines, Kathryn Cord.

Shirley Temple, appearing as Corliss Archer in these two films, continued to have difficulty making the adjustment from child star to adult actress. After the sequel she retired from movies. Most of the other actors gave performances bordering on caricatures. There was some fun in the pictures but it may not be the kind of humor that will appeal to today's audiences, used to teenage movies whose laughs are derived from their sexual exploits, explicitly depicted.

465 The Kiss Before the Mirror

Based on the play by Ladislas Fodor. Story: In Vienna, lawyer Dr. Paul Held defends Dr. Walter Bernsdorf who has killed his wife, Lucie, when he discovered her with another man. Held soon discovers that his own wife, Maria, is similarly cuckolding him.

Universal Pictures, 1933 (original). Director: James Whale; screenwriter: William Anthony McGuire. Cast: Nancy Carroll (Maria Held), Frank Morgan (Dr. Paul Held), Paul Lukas (Dr. Walter Bernsdorf), Gloria Stuart (Lucie Bernsdorf), Jean Dixon, Charles Grapewin, Walter Pidgeon, Donald Cook, Allen Connor.

• ***Wives Under Suspicion*** (remake). Universal Pictures, 1938. Director: James Whale; screenwriter: Myles Connolly. Cast: Warren William (Jim Stowell), Gail Patrick (Lucy Stowell), Ralph Morgan (Shaw McAllen), William Lundigan (Phil), Constance Moore (Elizabeth), Cecil Cunningham, Jonathan Hale, Lillian Yarbo, Milburn Stone, Anthony Hughes.

It takes real talent to completely miscast a movie as is done with *The Kiss Before the Mirror*. Even if there had been a permutation of the central characters it would have been better. At least Morgan and Lukas should have exchanged roles. In the remake, District Attorney Warren William is prosecuting a love-triangle murder case, only to discover that there's a lot of that going around, even in his own home.

A Kiss for Corliss *see* **Kiss and Tell**

466 A Kiss in the Dark

Based on the play *Aren't We All* by Frederick Lonsdale. Story: Walter Grenham, who has a weakness for the ladies, marries Janet Livingstone, promising to be ever faithful. However, they plan to travel to New York in the company of married couple Betty and Johnny King. Somehow, Betty and Walter get left behind in Havana. Walter flies to Key West where he overtakes Janet and convinces her that nothing happened while he and Betty were stranded. Meanwhile, Betty goes to New York where she finds Johnny in the arms of a chorus girl. Walter comes along and gets the couple straightened out and prepares to settle down to wedded bliss.

Famous Players–Lasky/Paramount Pictures, 1925 (original). Silent. Director: Frank Tuttle; screenwriter: Townsend Martin. Cast: Adolphe Menjou (Walter Grenham), Aileen Pringle (Janet Livingstone), Lillian Rich (Betty King), Kenneth MacKenna (Johnny King), Ann Pennington, Kitty Kelly.

• ***Aren't We All?*** (remake). Paramount Pictures, Great Britain, 1932. Directors: Harry Lachman and Rudolph Mate; screenwriter: Basil Mason. Cast: Gertrude Lawrence (Margot), Hugh Wakefield (Willie), Owen Nares (Von Elsen), Marie Lohr (Lady Frinton), Rita Page, Renee Gadd, Aubrey Mather, Emily Fitzroy.

The remake, despite Gertrude Lawrence's efforts, doesn't hold up well. This conversation piece is almost killed by the level of the conversation. There's not much plot, and if the characters don't deliver amusing lines to each other, audiences have every right to question why the films are called comedies.

Kiss Me Again *see* **Mademoiselle Modiste**

Kiss Me Kate *see* **The Taming of the Shrew**

467 Kiss of Death

Based on a story by Eleanor Lipsky. Story: Nick Bianco is a small-time hood sent to prison for a crime that he committed with others. He resists the D.A.'s urging to inform on his cohorts because they have promised to take care of his wife and children. On the trip to the slammer, he is cuffed to notorious criminal Tommy Udo, a psychotic killer. When Nick learns that his wife has been driven to suicide by his buddies and that his two kids have been put in an orphanage, he agrees with D.A. D'Angelo to finger Udo for a murder in return for parole and protection from Udo's gang. He meets and falls in love with Nettie and is planning a new life with her and his kids when he learns that Udo has been acquitted and is free. Realizing that the cruel, sick mind of Udo will want to hurt him first through Nettie and the kids, Nick deliberately sets himself up as a target for the killer's bullets in order to deliver him to the police.

Twentieth Century–Fox, 1947 (original). Director: Henry Hathaway; screenwriters: Ben Hecht and Charles Lederer. Cast: Victor Mature (Nick Bianco), Brian Donlevy (D'Angelo), Coleen Gray (Nettie), Richard Widmark (Tommy Udo), Taylor Holmes (Earl Howser), Howard Smith, Karl Malden, Anthony Ross, Mildred Dunnock, Millard Mitchell, Temple Texas, J. Scott Smart, Jay Jostyn.

• ***The Fiend Who Walked the West*** (remake). Twentieth Century–Fox, 1958. Director: Gordon Douglas; screenwriters: Harry Brown and Phillip Yordan. Cast: Hugh O'Brien (Hardy), Robert Evans (Felix Griffin), Dolores Michaels (May), Linda Cristal (Ellen Hardy), Stephen McNally (Emmett),

Edward Andrews, Ron Ely, Ken Scott, Emile Meyer, Gregory Morton, Shari Lee Bernath.

Few actors have made a more impressive movie debut than did Richard Widmark in his portrayal of the maniacal Tommy Udo. To make the effect even more menacing, Widmark shaved off his eyebrows for the role. This, together with his skeletal face, his smile that did not include his eyes, his crackle that passed for a laugh and his sudden changes of personality and moods, made him foreboding, indeed. The presence of Widmark had a salutory effect on Mature. He gave one of his best and most controlled performances of his career as the protagonist of this brilliant *film noir.*

The western remake is another story. It's not a good picture but compared to exploitation films that would come later it was something to behold. The fiend in question is Robert Evans, who among other things feeds ground glass to one of his victims, breaks a girl's neck, shoots an arrow through an old lady, scares a pregnant woman into a miscarriage, mistreats his girlfriend in assorted cruel ways and finally gets his comeuppance at the hands of Hugh O'Brien, a former cellmate of Evans. There isn't much rhyme or reason to this "horror" western and it can't touch the original for interest or performances.

Kisses for Breakfast *see* **The Matrimonial Bed**

468 Kissing Cup's Race

Based on the poem by Campbell Rae Brown. Story: Impoverished Lord Hilhoxton is forced to sell off his stable of horses, but he keeps one back, Kissing Cup, in hopes that it will win a big race and restore his fortune. Despite the shenanigans of his crooked rival, it does.

Hopson/Butcher, Great Britain, 1920 (original). Silent. Director: Walter West; screenwriters: J. Bertram Brown and Benedict James. Cast: Violet Hopson (Constance Medley), Gregory Scott (Lord Hilhoxton), Clive Brook (Lord Rattlington), Arthur Walcott (John Wood), Philip Hewland, Adeline Hayden Coffin, Joe Plant.

• ***Kissing Cup's Race*** (remake). Butcher, Great Britain, 1930. Director: Castleton Knight; screenwriters: Knight and Blanche Metcalfe. Cast: Stewart Rome (Lord Rattlington), Madeleine Carroll (Lady Mollie Adair), John Stuart (Lord Jimmy Hilhoxton), Richard Cooper (Rollo Adai), Chili Boucher, Moore Marriott, J. Fisher White, James Knight, Gladys Hamer, Wally Patch.

The best thing about the dull remake of the dull silent is the beauty and studied inanimation of Madeleine Carroll. Her exquisite features cover up many sins in a poor movie, and this one is poverty-stricken.

469 Klondike

Based on an original screenplay by Tristam Tupper. Story: The loss of a patient on the operating table badly damages the confidence of surgeon Dr. Cromwell. He leaves his practice and flys off to the far north where his plane crashes and he is nursed back to health, physically and spiritually, by a trading post operator.

Monogram Pictures, 1932 (original). Director: Phil Rosen; screenwriter: Tristam Tupper. Cast: Lyle Talbot (Dr. Cromwell), Frank Hawks (Donald Evans), Thelma Todd (Klondike), H.B. Walthall (Mark Armstrong), Jason Robards, Ethel Wales, Tully Marshall, Pat O'Malley, Priscilla Dean.

• ***Klondike Fury*** (remake). Monogram Pictures, 1942. Director: William K. Howard; screenwriter: Tristam Tupper. Cast: Edmund Lowe (Dr. John Mandre), Lucille Fairbanks (Peg), Bill Henry (Jim Armstrong), Ralph Morgan (Dr. Brady), Mary Forbes (Mrs. Langston), Jean Brook, Vince Barnett, Clyde Cook.

The story has been brought to the screen as a lot of talk and not much action, but all in all, the films are not too bad, considering that they were made at a studio which never invested much money in their productions. The key to the salvation of the surgeon in this story is that as he's recovering from his plane crash in the far north, he is faced with performing the same operation whose failure caused him to lose confidence in his ability. This time he comes through with flying colors.

Klondike Fury *see* **Klondike**

470 Knights of the Round Table

Based on "Le Morte d'Arthur" by Sir Thomas Malory. Story: It's the familiar tale of the brave knight, Lancelot, who comes to Camelot to serve at the Round Table of King Arthur, with tragedy following when he falls in love with Arthur's queen, Guinevere.

MGM, 1953 (original). Director: Richard Thorpe; screenwriters: Talbot Jennings, Jan Lustig and Noel Langley. Cast: Robert Taylor (Lancelot), Ava Gardner (Guinevere), Mel Ferrer (King Arthur), Anne Crawford (Morgan Le Fay), Stanley Baker (Modred), Felix Aylmer (Merlin), Maureen Swanson, Gabriel Woolf, Anthony Forwood, Robert Urquhart, Niall MacGinnis, Ann Hanslip.

• ***Lancelot and Guinevere*** (remake). Emblem Productions, 1963. Director: Cornel Wilde; screenwriters: Richard Schayer and Jefferson Pascal. Cast: Cornel Wilde (Lancelot), Jean Wallace (Guinevere), Brian Aherne (King Arthur), George Baker (Sir Gawaine), Archie Duncan (Sir Lamorak), Adrienne Corri (Lady Vivian), Michael Meacham (Sir Modred), Ian Gregory, Mark Dignam, Reginald Beckwith, John Barrie.

• ***The Sword and the Stone*** (remake). Walt Disney, 1963. Director: Wolfgang Reitherman; screenwriter: Bill Peet, based on the novel *The Once and Future King* by T.H. White. Animated.

• ***Camelot*** (remake). Warner Bros., 1967. Director: Joshua Logan; screenwriter: Alan Jay Lerner, based on the Broadway musical by Alan Jay Lerner and Frederick Loewe. Cast: Richard Harris (King Arthur), Vanessa Redgrave (Guinevere), Franco Nero (Lancelot), David Hemmings (Modred), Laurence Naismith (Merlin), Lionel Jeffries, Pierre Olaf, Estelle Winwood.

• ***Excalibur*** (remake). Warner Bros., 1981. Director: John Boorman; screenwriter: Rospo Pallenberg and John Boorman. Cast: Nigel Terry, Helen Mirren, Nicol Williamson, Nicholas Clay, Cherie Lunghi, Paul Geoffrey.

The character of King Arthur has shown up in other films, notably in *A Connecticut Yankee in King Arthur's Court.* Arthur's sword, Excalibur, figured prominently in *King Arthur Was a Gentleman* (1942), in which a soldier becomes a hero when he is led to believe that he has Arthur's legendary weapon. The 1953 and 1963 films made Lancelot and his love for Guinevere the center of the story. Robert Taylor filled all the requirements for a brave knight and Ava Gardner looked like the kind of woman who could cause a man to forget chivalry and his leige. Cornel Wilde's version was surprisingly good, being an independent production when studios still called the shots. Brian Aherne made a very sympathetic and understanding Arthur. Jean Wallace, wife to Wilde, was passably good as Guinevere.

The Disney animated story borrows its plot from T.H. White's delightful novel *The Once and Future King,* concentrating on the legend of how a young boy named Wart becomes King Arthur when he successfully pulls the sword from the stone. He is then given an amazing education at the hands of Merlin. It's not one of the Disney studio's better productions and even the animation doesn't seem up to the usual high standards.

The musical *Camelot* takes up where Disney left off with White's version of the legendary English king. It tells of the marriage of Arthur and Guinevere, his founding of the Knights of the Round Table, the arrival of Lancelot (who would become his best friend and the one to steal the love of his queen), and the arrival of Arthur's bastard son, Modred, who would wittingly be the catalyst for ending Arthur's dreams for Camelot and his order of chivalry. Despite some fine songs by Lerner and Loewe, including "The Merry Month of May," "If Ever I Would Leave You," "C'est Moi," "Take Me to the Fair" and the title song, the film is disappointing. It drags at numerous spots, and the acting of the three principle performers is one-dimensional. Still the film is better than the lengthy and dull *Excalibur,* which examines Arthur's relationship with Merlin, Uther Pendragon, the Holy Grail and the Lady of the Lake. At times it looks like a Conan the Barbarian clone, with enough gore to delight those for whom a movie's not a movie unless someone gets chopped up into little pieces and blood gushes all over the screen.

Kongo *see* **West of Zanzibar (1929)**

En Kvinnas Ansikte *see* **A Woman's Face**

L

471 Laddie

Based on the book by Gene Stratton Porter. Story: Laddie, son of an Ohio pioneer family, the Stantons, falls in love with Pamela Pryor, daughter of a neighboring aristocratic English family. The Pryor family has a condescending attitude towards the Stantons and have no interest in a matrimonial merger. Through the efforts of little sister, who knows of the love of Laddie and Pamela, the two secretly communicate. Meanwhile, Shelley Stanton falls in love with city lawyer Robert Paget, and when he leaves her under mysterious circumstances, she comes home brokenhearted. The Pryors are also suffering as they learn of a disgrace brought upon the family by a son back in London. It turns out that Paget is in fact this banished son. After a strained crisis, Pryor forgives his son, accepts Laddie and the two couples are happily united.

First National, 1926. Silent. Director: James Leo Meehan; screenwriter: Jeanette Porter Meehan. Cast: John Bowers (Laddie), Bess Flowers (Pamela Pryor), Theodore Von Eltz (Robert Paget), Eugenia Gilbert (Shelley Stanton), David Torrence, Eulalie Jensen, Arthur Clayton, Fannie Midgley, Aggie Herring, Gene Stratton, John Fox, Jr.

• ***Laddie*** (remake). RKO Pictures, 1935. Director: George Stevens; screenwriters: Ray Harris and Dorothy Yost. Cast: John Beal (Laddie), Gloria Stuart (Pamela Pryor), Virginia Weidler (Little Sister), Charlotte Henry (Shelley Stanton), Donald Crisp, Gloria Shea, Willard Robertson, Dorothy Peterson, Jenny Butler, Grady Sutton, Greta Meyer, Mary Forbes.

• ***Laddie*** (remake). RKO Pictures, 1940. Director: Jack Hively; screenwriters: Bert Granet and Jerry Cady. Cast: Tim Holt (Laddie), Nan Grey (Margie), Mischa Auer (Gomez), Edgar Kennedy (Chauncey), Allen Jenkins (Kenneth), Eddie Quilian (Joe), Wally Vernon, Joy Hodges, Richard Lane, Emmet Vogan, Pauline Heddon.

The story of Laddie and his family, lacking in modern appeal even in 1935, belongs to generations long ago. All versions lack punch and conflict, and the hominess of the story is not sufficient to thrill audiences. Critics in the big cities allowed as how the films might do well in the "hinterlands," a rather insulting and uninformed opinion of the intelligence and taste of the less sophisticated inhabitants of small towns and rural areas. The producers did not invest much in the projects, either in terms of talent or staging, so any return on these saccharine sentimental pieces would probably turn a profit.

472 Ladies in Retirement

Based on the play by Edward Percy and Reginald Denham and a tale in H.B. Irving's *French Crime and Criminals.* Story: Ellen Creed is the companion-housekeeper of Leonora Fiske, a former actress, now living on a substantial pension from a former lover. Forced to bring her two half-crazy sisters, Emily and Louisa, into the household, Ellen is briefly at a loss for what to do, when they get on Leonora's nerves and the latter insists they leave. To save them from being sent to a mental institution, Ellen strangles her employer and proceeds to take over the house. When a renegade relative of the deceased, Albert Feather, arrives at the manse, he gradually suspects the truth, and tricks Ellen into making a confession. She makes a break for it, but realizing she is trapped, makes arrangements for her sisters' care and surrenders to the police.

Columbia Pictures, 1941 (original). Director: Charles Vidor; screenwriters: Reginald Denham and Edward Percy. Cast: Ida Lupino (Ellen Creed), Isobel Elsom (Leonora Fiske), Louis Hayward (Albert Feather), Edith Barrett (Louise

Creed), Elsa Lanchester (Emily Creed), Evelyn Ankers, Emma Dunn, Queenie Leonard, Clyde Cook.

• ***The Mad Room*** (remake). Columbia Pictures, 1969. Director: Bernard Girard; screenwriter: Bernard Gerard and A.Z. Martin. Cast: Stella Stevens (Ellen Hardy), Shelley Winters (Mrs. Armstrong), Skip Ward (Sam Aller), Carol Cole (Chris), Steven Darden, Beverly Garland, Michael Burns, Barbara Sammeth.

Some critics of the time doubted that the sordid combination of a murderess and two mentally deranged sisters would be the kind of story that would appeal to audiences. The remake almost made the reviewer's point, being a rather nauseating and brutal telling of essentially the same story. Of course, by today's standards it was still a bit tame for that segment of moviegoers who like their blood and gore in ever-gushing color. In the original, Ida Lupino's performance was considered "a sterling reading of the principal role" and Edith Barrett and Elsa Lanchester were something special as the unbalanced sisters. On the other hand, Stella Stevens and the rest of the cast in the remake acted merely tasteless.

Ladies Must Live *see* **The Home Towners**

473 Ladies of Leisure

Based on the play *Ladies of the Evening* by David Belasco. Story: Wealthy artist Jerry Strong and party girl Kay Arnold meet, after both have escaped from disappointing parties. Struck by her beauty, he tells her he wishes to paint her. At his studio, the air is filled with romance and promise of passion, although each spends the night in separate rooms. By morning, her vulnerability and his tension leads first to an argument and then to the realization that they are in love. Jerry's family objects to the match, but a dramatic rescue after Kay's attemped suicide reunites them.

Columbia Pictures, 1930 (original). Director: Frank Capra; screenwriter: Jo Swerling. Cast: Barbara Stanwyck (Kay Arnold), Ralph Graves (Jerry Strange), Lowell Sherman (Bill Standish), Marie Prevost (Dot Lamar), Nance O'Neal (Mrs. Strange), George Fawcett (Mr. Strange), Johnnie Walker (Charlie), Juliette Compton (Claire Collins).

• ***Women of Glamour*** (remake). Columbia Pictures, 1937. Director: Gordon Wiles; screenwriters: Lynn Starling and Mary McCall, Jr. Cast: Virginia Bruce (Gloria Hudson), Melvyn Douglas (Dick Stark), Reginald Denny (Fritz Eagen), Leona Maricle (Carol Coulter), Pert Kelton (Fan La Roque), Thurston Hall (Mr. Stark), Mary Forbes (Mrs. Stark).

Ladies of Leisure is most important for being the picture that made a star of Barbara Stanwyck. It's not one of Frank Capra's better pictures, but it does have some effective moments, notably in a daring scene of great sensitivity. Stanwyck undresses in silhouette before the artist's big studio window, while he is seen through another window getting ready for bed as well. The second film is the usual B remake of a studio property, meant to fill the second half of a double bill, with the expectation that not too many in the audience will recognize that they had seen it somewhere before, or care. In it wealthy Melvyn Douglas is loved by two women, one Leona Maricle, a socialite, and the other, show girl Virginia Bruce. In such films the hero always chooses the right girl after some initial confusion as to who she is.

474 Ladies of the Big House

Based on the play by Ernst Booth. Story: Kathleen and Standish McNeil are framed for murder. They are imprisoned in the same penitentiary with Standish sentenced to be executed. Kathleen is determined to save her man and proposes to join in a jailbreak for that end. While visiting him along with the rest of the female inmates who have husbands in the same prison, she outlines her plans. The film has a happy ending with a dramatic finale with justice triumphing.

Paramount Pictures, 1931 (original). Director: Marion Goring; screenwriter: Louis Weitzenkorn. Cast: Sylvia Sidney (Kathleen Storm), Gene Raymond (Standish McNeil), Wynne Gibson (Susie Thompson), Rockliffe Fellowes (Martin Doremus), Earle Foxe, Frank Sheridan, Edna Bennett, Fritzi Ridgeway, Louise Beavers.

• ***Women Without Names*** (remake). Paramount Pictures, 1940. Director: Robert Florey; screenwriters: William R. Lipman and Horace McCoy. Cast: Ellen Drew (Joyce King), Robert Paige (Fred MacNeil), Judith Barrett (Peggy Athens), John Miljan (John Martin), Fay Helm, John McGuire, Louise Beavers, James Seay.

Variety described *Ladies of the Big House* as "a picture with intense human appeal that abundantly compensates for its depressing atmosphere of a jail." Sylvia Sidney is the fragile type of actress who is perfect for the sympathetic role of a young girl who innocently becomes enmeshed in a criminal conspiracy. Gene Raymond, who had few decent roles, plays the condemned man with restrained simplicity. In the B remake, Ellen Drew draws the assignment as the wrongly convicted girl, desperate to save her innocent husband from execution. Fortunately she meets Judith Barrett in prison, whose last minute confession saves the day.

475 Ladies of the Jury

Based on the play by John Frederick Ballard. Story: This comedy is set mostly in a jury room, where the case of attractive young widow Mrs. Gordon, up for the murder of her husband, is being considered. Members of the jury stand 11 to 1 for conviction when wealthy Mrs. Crane goes into action, getting them to all change their mind after they visit the sight of the murder and discover the plot of the dead man's nephew and the house maid.

RKO Pictures, 1932 (original). Director: Lowell Sherman; screenwriter: Frederick Ballard. Cast: Edna May Oliver (Mrs. Crane), Ken Murray (Wayne Dazy), Roscoe Ates (Andrew MacKaig), Kitty Kelly (Mayme Mister), Guinn Williams (Steve Bromm), Jill Esmond (Mrs. Gordon), Kate Price, C.D. Clark, Cora Weatherspoon.

• ***We're on the Jury*** (remake). RKO Pictures, 1937. Director: Ben Holmes;

screenwriter: Franklin Coen. Cast: Victor Moore (J. Clarence Beaver), Helen Broderick (Mrs. Dean), Phillip Huston (Steve), Louise Latimer (Mrs. Clyde), Vinton Haworth (M. Williams), Robert McWade (Judge Prime), Maxine Jennings, Frank M. Thomas, Colleen Clare, Billy Gilbert, Charles Lane, Charles Middleton.

It's a trite tale and no competition for Henry Fonda's masterful film *12 Angry Men* in which one juror finally convinces the others that the guilt of a youngster accused of killing his father had not been proven. Oliver and Murray are quite enjoyable handling most of the comedy, but without any name leading performers it did only modestly at the box office. In the remake, Helen Broderick is the hold-out for acquittal in a murder case, who convinces the other jurors to change their mind about who's guilty. Victor Moore does his usual fine job as a moderately befuddled but kindly old man.

476 The Lady

Based on the play by Martin Brown. Story: Leonard St. Aubyns is immediately disinherited by his wealthy father when he marries Polly Pearl, a singer in a second-rate English music hall. Leonard soon squanders his small stake at Monte Carlo and dies, reducing Polly to singing in a waterfront dive in Marseilles to support herself and her young son. The elder St. Aubyns wishes to take her son from her, so she entrusts the boy to an acquaintance who takes the child to England. When Polly follows, she cannot locate her son. Years pass and Polly, now the owner of a cafe in Le Havre, witnesses a British soldier accidently killing a drunken friend. Polly discovers that the soldier is her son and attempts to take the blame for the killing. The boy will not hear of it and escapes the authorities, embarking for America, without knowing that Polly is his mother.

First National Pictures, 1925 (original). Silent. Director: Frank Borzage; screenwriter: Frances Marion. Cast: Norma Talmadge (Polly Pearl), Wallace MacDonald (Leonard St. Aubyns), Brandon Hurst (Mr. St. Aubyns), Alf Goulding (Tom Robinson), Doris Lloyd, Walter Long, George Hackathorne, Marc MacDermott.

• ***The Secret of Madame Blanche*** (remake). MGM, 1933. Director: Charles Brabin; screenwriters: Frances Goodrich and Albert Hackett. Cast: Irene Dunne (Sally), Lionel Atwill (Aubrey St. John), Phillips Holmes (Leonard St. John), Una Merkel (Ella), Douglas Walton, C. Henry Gordon, Jean Parker, Mitchell Lewis.

These films are among the many which dealt with the tale of a poor woman who has somehow been separated from a child whom she encounters again when he or she is an adult. Many in the audience, particularly the ladies, enjoyed a good cry when faced with this popular mother-child separation theme. Irene Dunne, who was quite at home as a put-upon woman, is excellent as the female who lives from the 1890s to World War I, dreaming of her missing child, and at least in this version is reunited with her son.

477 Lady and Gent

Based on a story by Grover Jones and William Slavens McNutt. Story: It's a sentimental story built around a rough and tumble prize-fighting dummy, Slag Bailey, and a heart of gold nightclub hostess, Puff Rogers, who look after the orphaned child of Bailey's manager, when the latter dies.

Paramount Pictures, 1932 (original). Director: Stephen Roberts; screenwriters: Grover Jones and William Slavens McNutt. Cast: George Bancroft (Slag Bailey), Wynne Gibson (Puff Rogers), Charles Starrett (Ted Streaver), James Gleason (Pin Streaver), John Wayne, Morgan Wallace, James Crane.

• ***Unmarried*** (remake). Paramount Pictures, 1939. Director: Kurt Neumann; screenwriter: Lillie Hayward and Brian Marlow. Cast: Helen Twelvetrees (Pat Rogers), Buck Jones (Slag Bailey), Donald O'Connor (Ted Streaver at 12), John Hartley (Ted Streaver), Robert Armstrong (Pins Streaver), Sidney Blackmer.

No doubt inspired by the success of *Min and Bill* (1930), Paramount wished to bring out their own version of two calloused city dwellers who have taken their relationship for granted for many years until called upon to exert some responsibility to others. Slag and Puff finally demonstrate great humanity beneath their gruff and uneducated exterior. They almost succeed in producing the hoped-for sentimental comedy, but the picture unhappily tapers off before the forced and labored ending. The remake was even less successful in capturing the mood sought as the cast was definitely inferior, as were the production values.

Lady Be Careful *see* **The Fleet's In**

478 Lady Chatterly's Lover

Based on the novel by D.H. Lawrence. Story: Constance, the wife of a crippled and impotent mine owner, has an affair with Mellors, her husband's coarse gamekeeper, to satisfy her spouse's desire for a child.

Cohen-Seat/Columbia, France, 1956 (original). Director: Marc Allegret; screenwriters: Joseph Kessel, Marc Allegret, Gaston Bonheur and Philippe Rothschilde. Cast: Danielle Darrieux (Constance), Leo Genn (Clifford), Erno Crisa (Mellors), Jacqueline Noelle, Berthe Tissen, Jeanine Crispin.

• ***Young Lady Chatterly*** (remake). Pro International, 1977. Director: Alan Roberts; screenwriter: Steve Michaels. Cast: Harlee McBride (Cynthia Chatterly), Peter Ratray (Paul), William Beckley (Philip), Ann Michelle, Joi Staton.

• ***Lady Chatterly's Lover*** (remake). Cannon/Producteurs Associes, France, 1981. Director: Just Jaeckin; screenwriters: Christopher Wicking and Just Jaeckin. Cast: Sylvia Kristel (Constance), Nicholas Clay (Clifford), Shane Briant (Mellors), Ann Mitchell, Elizabeth Spriggs.

One might think that Lawrence's classic erotic novel would be impossible to film and seeing these attempts, this opinion would still prevail. The first effort is tame, ludicrous, and almost completely without cinematic interest. The second is a soft-core porn story of a girl who inherits the Chatterly estate, who upon reading her infamous ancestor's diary is inspired to emulate her with the servants. The 1981 version also has some soft-porn moments but except for sexual athletics, holds no interest. It is probably fair to say that the real Lawrence story is yet to be filmed, awaiting someone who can find a way to make the daring material interesting on the screen.

479 The Lady Eve

Based on an original screenplay by Preston Sturges. Story: Traveling on a luxury ocean liner, dull and naive millionaire Charles Pike, wary of girls because he believes they are all after his money, is spotted by Jean Harrington, who is after his money. She travels with her card-sharp father, Colonel Harrington, preying on rich men attracted by her and fleeced by her father. To meet Charles, she trips him, uses all of her feminine wiles and gets him to fall in love with her. Her scheme is figured out by Charles' viligant bodyguard, Muggsy, and Pike reads Jean out of his life. Bent on revenge, Jean assumes the identity of the Lady Eve, and shows up at Pike's home. The dummy doesn't recognize her as the same dame, and falls for her again. They marry and on their wedding night, Jean, now in love with the sap, admits her past errors and sins. As the list grows and grows, Charles walks away from her in disgust. Sometime later, on another ocean liner, Jean trips Charles again and this time he's glad to see her, sorry for past misunderstandings and so thoroughly confused, he goes on with their marriage.

Paramount Pictures, 1940 (original). Director and screenwriter: Preston Sturges. Cast: Barbara Stanwyck (Jean Eve), Henry Fonda (Charles Pike), Charles Coburn (Col. Harrington), Eugene Pallette (Mr. Pike), William Demarest (Muggsy), Eric Blore, Melville Cooper, Martha O'Driscoll, Janet Beecher.

• ***The Birds and the Bees*** (remake). Paramount Pictures, 1956. Director: Norman Taurog; screenwriters: Sidney Sheldon and Preston Sturges. Cast: George Gobel (George Hamilton), Mitzi Gaynor (Jean Harris), David Niven (Col. Harris), Reginald Gardiner (Gerald), Fred Clark (Mr. Hamilton), Harry Bellaver, Hans Conreid, Margery Maude, Clinton Sundberg.

The Lady Eve is a delightfully spicy and sexy comedy, with Stanwyck enticingly wicked as the shady lady and Fonda marvelous as the wealthy dope who finally lucks out enough to earn her love. The others in the cast were just right for their parts. Charles Coburn gave his daughter loving advice on her behavior, allowing that it was acceptable to be crooked but not to be coarse. William Demarest was at his best as the ever suspicious guardian of the poor rich simpleton and Eugene Pallette was a riot as Charles' always outraged and ignored father.

The remake was dragged down by the casting of George Gobel in a leading role. He looked and acted as a simpleton alright, but he didn't have the ability to carry off the romantic angles of the plot. Mitzi Gaynor is a pale shadow of the magnificent Ms. Stanwyck and Niven couldn't carry the whole show by himself. Then too, the production didn't have the benefit of the comical genius of writer-director Preston Sturges, even though the film was based in part on his original screenplay.

480 Lady for a Day

Based on the short story "Madame La Gimp" by Damon Runyon. Story:

David Niven, George Gobel and Mitzi Gaynor appear in The Birds and the Bees *(Paramount, 1956), a disappointing remake of the sparkling comedy* The Lady Eve *(Paramount, 1941), which had starred Barbara Stanwyck, Henry Fonda and Charles Coburn.*

Apple Annie sells apples in Times Square, where local gangster Dave the Dude considers it lucky to buy from her. Annie's illegitimate daughter, Louise, ignorant of her mother's circumstances, is engaged to Carlos, the son of a wealthy Spanish count, who wishes to check on the social status of his son's fiancée. Dude and other characters of the street pitch in and set Annie up as a real society lady, completely fooling the count, his son and her daughter.

Columbia Pictures, 1933 (original). Director: Frank Capra; screenwriter: Robert Riskin. Cast: Warren William (Dave the Dude), May Robson (Apple Annie), Glenda Farrell (Missouri Martin), Guy Kibbee (Judge Blake), Ned Sparks (Happy), Jean Parker (Louise), Barry Norton, Walter Connolly.

• ***Pocketful of Miracles*** (remake). United Artists, 1961. Director: Frank Capra; screenwriters: Hal Kanter and Harry Tugend. Cast: Glenn Ford (Dave the Dude), Bette Davis (Apple Annie), Hope Lange (Queenie Martin), Arthur O'Connell (Count Romero), Peter Falk (Joy Boy), Thomas Mitchell (Judge Blake), Peter Mann (Carlos), Ann-Margret (Louise).

Lady for a Day was given four Academy Award nominations, for Best Picture, Best Director, Best Actress and Best Screenplay, but came away empty handed. It is a charming sentimental picture, capturing a real feeling for the Damon Runyan characters. Capra's 1961 remake didn't have the same magic touch. Reportedly, the friction between Davis and Ford, caused by his demanding special treatment for his then lady-fair, Hope Lange, didn't help.

Lady in Cement ***see*** **Tony Rome**

481 The Lady in Ermine

Based on the operetta by Rudolph Schanzer and Ernst Welish. Story: In 1810 as the Austrian army invades Italy, Countess Marianna Beltrami marries Count Adrian Murillo before he leaves for the front. When the Austrians arrive, handsome General Dostal makes his headquarters at the Countess' castle and immediately vies for her affection with the Austrian Crown Prince, a member of his staff. Count Murillo breaks through the Austrian lines and returns to the castle. He is discovered and ordered shot as a spy. The Countess tells of a similar invasion by the French, years before, when her grandmother saved her husband by appearing before a general wearing only an ermine coat. The drunken Austrian general dreams of a similar visit by the Countess and believing it to be real, sets the Count free.

First National, 1927 (original). Silent. Director: James Flood; screenwriter: Benjamin Glazer. Cast: Corinne Griffith (Countess Mariana Beltrami), Einar Hansen (Count Adrian Murillo), Ward Crane (Archduke Stephen), Francis X. Bushman (General Dostal), Jane Keckley (Mariana's maid).

• ***Bride of the Regiment*** (remake). First National, 1930. Director: John Francis Dillon; screenwriter: Humphrey Pearson. Cast: Vivienne Segal (Countess Anna-Marie), Allan Prior (Count Adrian Beltrami), Walter Pidgeon (Colonel Vultow), Louisa Fazenda (Teresa), Myrna Loy (Sophie), Lupino Lane (Sprotti), Ford Sterling, Harry Cording, Claude Fleming, Herbert Clark.

• ***That Lady in Ermine*** (remake). Twentieth Century–Fox, 1948. Director: Ernst Lubitsch; screenwriter: Samson Raphaelson. Cast: Betty Grable (Francesca/Angelina), Douglas Fairbanks, Jr. (Colonel/Duke), Cesar Romero (Marco), Walter Abel (Major Horvath), Reginald Gardiner, Harry Davenport, Virginia Campbell, Edmund MacDonald.

Hollywood was never daunted in making silent films of musicals, even though usually the stories by themselves were rather silly and meaningless. Such was the case with *The Lady in Ermine.* Without the music of Rudolph Schanzer and Ernst Welish, the film seemed lacking in substance, and indeed it was. On the other hand, the presence of the music, as was the case in the first remake, was no guarantee of wonderful theater. However, by all reports the

Technicolor talkie film was well-liked by audiences of the day. Sadly, no color prints survive by which to judge the production. The second remake was interrupted by the death of director Ernst Lubitsch, with Otto Preminger finishing the project, refusing to take any credit for the film, so as to honor Lubitsch. The tongue-in-cheek fairy tale was unusual for Betty Grable, in that there were no production numbers as such in which to show off her singing, dancing and great legs. The songs by Leo Robin and Frederick Hollander, including "This Is the Moment" and "The Melody Must Be Right," were nothing special.

The Lady in Question *see* **Heart of Paris**

The Lady in the Iron Mask *see* **The Iron Mask**

A Lady to Love *see* **The Secret Hour**

482 Lady Windemere's Fan

Based on the play by Oscar Wilde. Story: In this comedy, Lady Windemere suspects that her husband, Lord Windemere, is involved with Mrs. Erlynne. The loss of Lady Windemere's fan almost causes scandal, but the Lord and Lady are reconciled. The audience, but not Lady Windemere, learns that Mrs. Erlynne is her mother who follows her daughter around to keep her out of trouble with her numerous admirers.

• ***Lady Windemere's Fan*** (remake). Warner Bros., 1925. Silent. Director: Ernst Lubitsch; screenwriter: Julien Josephson. Cast: Ronald Colman (Lord Darlington), Irene Rich (Mrs. Erlynne), May McAvoy (Lady Windemere), Bert Lytell (Lord Windemere), Edward Martindel, Helen Dunbar, Carrie Daumery, Billie Bennett.

• ***The Fan*** (remake). Twentieth Century–Fox, 1949. Director: Otto Preminger; screenwriters: Walter Reisch, Dorothy Parker and Ross Evans. Cast: Jeanne Crain (Lady Windemere), Madeleine Carroll (Mrs. Erlynne), George Sanders (Lord Darlington), Richard Greene (Lord Windemere), Martita Hunt, John Sutton.

The teaming of the great wit of Oscar Wilde and the comical genius of Ernst Lubitsch resulted in the latter's best silent film. Lubitsch has changed the setting of the play to the twenties and perhaps in no other film is the meaning of "the Lubitsch Touch" better illustrated. Besides the excellent directing, the cast distinguishes itself, particularly so in the cases of Ronald Colman and Irene Rich. The remake is a reasonably good piece with George Sanders walking away with the acting honors. Wilde's play was also filmed in Russia in 1913, in Great Britain in 1916, in the United States in 1919, in Germany in 1935, in Mexico in 1944, and in Argentina as *Story of a Wicked Woman* in 1948.

Lancelot and Guinevere *see* **Knights of the Round Table**

Land of Oz *see* **The Wizard of Oz**

483 The Land That Time Forgot

Based on the novel by Edgar Rice Burroughs. Story: In 1916, survivors of a torpedoed supply ship find themselves on a hitherto undiscovered island where dinosaurs still live. The British fight with the Germans for control of the island, which in the end is destroyed by a volcano.

American International Pictures, 1975 (original). Director: Kevin Connor; screenwriters: James Cawthorn and Michael Moorcock. Cast: Doug McClure (Bowen Tyler), John McEnery (Captain Von Schoenvorts), Susan Penhaligon (Lisa Clayton), Keith Barron (Bradley), Anthony Ainley, Godfrey James, Bobby Farr.

• ***The People That Time Forgot*** (sequel). American International Pictures, 1977. Director: Kevin Connor; screenwriter: Patrick Tilley. Cast: Patrick Wayne (Ben McBride), Doug McClure (Bowen Tyler), Sarah Douglas (Charly), Dana Gillespie (Ajor), Thorley Walters, Shane Rimmer.

These adventure yarns, with casts of no-names, appealed to some children but they were no great shakes with older viewers. In the sequel, Wayne, seeking marooned World War I naval hero McClure, discovers a land in the Arctic filled with prehistoric animals, cavemen and volcanoes. Burroughs should have stuck to the Tarzan legend.

484 Lassie Come Home

Based on the novel by Eric Knight. Story: The setting is Yorkshire, England, where Joe Carraclough's poor father is forced to sell the boy's pet collie to the Duke of Rudling, who takes the reluctant dog to his estate in Scotland. Lassie escapes and sets out for home. Before being finally reunited with her young master, the animal must travel hundreds of miles through storms and across rivers, escape from the local dog wardens and outsmart a couple of crooks.

MGM, 1943 (original). Director: Fred McLeod Wilcox; screenwriter: Hugo Butler. Cast: Lassie, Roddy McDowall (Joe Carraclough), Donald Crisp (Sam Carraclough), Edmund Gwenn (Rowlie), Dame May Whitty (Dolly), Nigel Bruce (Duke of Rudling), Elsa Lanchester (Mrs. Carraclough), Elizabeth Taylor (Priscilla), Ben Webster, J. Patrick O'Malley, Alec Craig.

• ***Gypsy Colt*** (remake). MGM, 1954. Director: Andrew Marton; screenwriter: Martin Berkeley. Cast: Donna Corcoran (Meg MacWade), Ward Bond (Frank MacWade), Frances Dee (Em MacWade), Larry Keating (Wade Y. Gerald), Lee Van Cleef (Hank), Bobby Hyatt (Phil Gerald), Nacho Galindo, Rodolfo Hoyas, Jr.

Lassie Come Home proved to be a sleeper hit in 1943 and started a career for the dog's trainer that outlasted ten or more collies (all male) portraying the brave and intelligent animal in several other films and for many years on television. Having been successful in telling the story of a boy and his dog in Great Britain, producers felt it might just work one more time with an American farmer forced to sell his daughter's colt. The remake was a nice sentimental piece for children but didn't have the impact of the dog version of the story.

485 The Last Mile

Based on the play by John Wexley. Story: Condemned men on death row watch one of their numbers walk the last mile to the electric chair. "Killer" John Mears, swearing he won't make the same stroll, strangles a sadistic prison guard and sets the others free from their cells. He commands the prison for a long period of horror and violence until, realizing he can't escape, he walks into a hail of machine gun bullets, content that at least he didn't have to make the trip down the last mile to the hot seat. Before this occurs, it is established that one of the condemned men, Richard Walters, is innocent and will be reprieved.

World-Wide Pictures, 1932 (original). Director: Sam Bischoff; screenwriter: Seton I. Miller. Cast: Preston Foster (John Mears), Howard Phillips (Richard Walters), George E. Stone (Berg), Noel Madison (D'Amoro), Alan Roscoe, Paul Fix, Al Hill, Daniel L. Haynes, Frank Sheridan, Alec B. Francis, Edward Van Sloan.

• ***The Last Mile*** (remake). United Artists, 1959. Director: Howard W. Koch; screenwriter: Seton I. Miller. Cast: Mickey Rooney (John Mears), Clifford Davis (Richard Walters), John Seven (D'Amoro), Michael Constantine (Eddie Werner), Harry Millard, John Vari, Frank Conroy, Frank Overton, Leon Janney, Donald Barry, Alan Bunce.

The 1932 film toned down the grim realism of the stage version, but some critics still felt it wasn't enough to make the movie appropriate fare for women to see. One change from the stage version was making Richard Walters an innocent young man who earned his freedom. On stage, he had cold-bloodedly murdered his girlfriend and was executed. For the time, the acting was excellent, but would seem too frantic by today's standards. The remake with Mickey Rooney as "Killer" Mears was even more hysterical and somber, although surprisingly entertaining. Rooney's portrayal is well done if one can keep from thinking of Andy Hardy.

486 The Last of Mrs. Cheyney

Based on the play by Frederick Lonsdale. Story: Mrs. Fay Cheyney, an adventuress posing as a wealthy Australian widow, is invited for a weekend at the country home of Mrs. Webley. Actually she is there to steal Mrs. Webley's valuable pearl necklace. She is abetted in this plan by Charles, acting as her servant, who is the mastermind of the plot, having trained a former salesgirl to act like a lady for purposes just such as this. Fay, finding how well she is received by the society set and having fallen in love with Mrs. Welbey's nephew, Lord Arthur Dilling, is reluctant to carry out the theft but finally is persuaded by Charles. She is caught with the necklace by Dilling, who offers his silence if she will spend the night with him. Stealing is one thing, but fornication is another, so Fay calls together Mrs. Welbey and her guests and confesses, leaving her fate up to them. One of their number, Lord Elton, admits that he had sent a letter to Mrs. Cheyney proposing marriage but also included juicy secrets about each of those now present. The group decides to buy Fay off but she tears up both the letter and their check. They now welcome her back into their society as the future Lady Dilling.

MGM, 1929. Director: Sidney Franklin; screenwriters: Hans Kraly and Claudine West. Cast: Norma Shearer (Mrs. Fay Cheyney), Basil Rathbone (Lord Arthur Dilling), Hedda Hopper (Lady Maria Frinton), George Barraud (Charles), Herbert Bunston (Lord Elton), Maude Turner (Mrs. Webley), Cyril Cadwick, Moon Carroll, Madeleine Seymour, George K. Arthur, Finch Smiles.

• ***The Last of Mrs. Cheyney*** (remake). MGM, 1937. Director: Richard Boleslawski; screenwriter: Samson Raphaelson. Cast: Joan Crawford (Fay Cheyney), Robert Montgomery (Lord Arthur Dilling), Aileen Pringle (Lady Maria Frinton), William Powell (Charles), Frank Morgan (Lord Kelton), Nigel Bruce, Jesse Ralph, Melville Cooper, Ralph Forbes, Benita Hume, Colleen Clare, Wallis Clark.

• ***The Law and the Lady*** (remake). MGM, 1951. Director: Edwin H. Knopf; screenwriters: Leonard Spigelgass and Karl Tunberg. Cast: Greer Garson (Jane Hoskins), Michael Wilding (Nigel Duxbury), Fernando Lamas (Juan Dinas), Marjorie Main (Mrs. Wortin), Hayden Roarke (Tracy Collins), Margalo Gillmore, Ralph Dumke, Phyliss Stanley, Rhys Williams, Natalie Schafer, Soledad Jiminez.

The 1929 film was the first MGM production released with a soundtrack. Until that time, talkies had been recorded on discs. Norma Shearer was just fine as the woman of selective principles as was Basil Rathbone as the cad who hoped to take advantage of what he had on her, but had to finally resort to marriage. The remake with Joan Crawford in the title role did not prove as successful as the Shearer picture, although Crawford showed more talent for comedy than had Shearer. The revised version of the story with Greer Garson as the larcenous lady fared even worse. It got what it deserved, as it was a weary and dreary simplification of the plot. Michael Wilding made his Hollywood debut in the film, but hardly anyone noticed or cared.

487 The Last Outpost

Based on a story by F. Britten Austin. Story: The central conflict has Michael Andrews and John Stevenson, two British co-fighters in the Mesopotamian campaign of World War I, in love with the same woman, nurse Rosemary Haydon. She's the wife of Stevenson, who has saved Andrews' life. Naturally, Stevenson drops out of the picture long enough for the two lovers to feel that he's a goner and that they are free to share their love. No such luck, he shows up again.

Paramount Pictures, 1935 (original). Director: Charles Barton; screenwriter: Phillip MacDonald. Cast: Cary Grant (Michael Andrews), Claude Rains (John Stevenson), Gertrude Michael (Rosemary Haydon), Kathleen Burke. Colin Tapley, Jameson Thomas, Margaret Swope, Billy Bevan, Nick Shald.

• ***The Last Outpost*** (remake). Paramount Pictures, 1951. Director: Lewis R. Foster; screenwriters: Geoffrey Homes, George Worthing Yates and Winston Miller. Cast: Ronald Reagan (Vance Britton), Rhonda Fleming (Julie McCloud), Bruce Bennett (Jeb Britton), Bill Williams, Noah Beery, Jr., Peter Hansen, Hugh Beaumont.

If the story of the first movie wasn't old and predictable at the time of its release, it is now and not even Cary Grant and Claude Rains can make it palatable. A lot of natives get machine-gunned while the Rover Boys are travelling all over Africa in their pursuit of glory and Miss Michael. The remake doesn't credit Austin for its story, but although the setting has been changed to the early nineteenth-century West and skirmishes between the blue and the grey in the American Civil War, the plot is about the same. Ronald Reagan and Bruce Bennett are brothers who love the same woman, Rhonda Fleming. In this one a group of Confederate guerrillas save a Union post from massacre, and a lot of Indians bite the dust. There's a message here, we think—"color is thicker than water."

Last Remake of Beau Geste *see* **Beau Geste**

The Law and the Lady *see* **The Last of Mrs. Cheyney**

Law of the Tropics *see* **Oil for the Lamps of China**

Law of the Underworld *see* **The Pay Off**

488 Lawful Larceny

Based on the play by Samuel Simpson. Story: While his wife is on a vacation in Europe, Andrew Dorsey loses so much money to Vivian Hepburn, owner of a shady gambling house, and her silent partner, Guy Tarlow, that Vivian convinces him to give her one of his firm's checks to cover his loss. When Marion Dorsey arrives home, Andrew confesses to her what he has done. Determined to get the check back, Marion poses as a wealthy widow, vamps Tarlow and gets him to rob Vivian's safe so the two of them can elope. Marion then steals everything in the safe, later giving all its contents back to the irate Vivian, save the check from her husband and the money he lost.

Famous Players/Paramount Pictures, 1923 (original). Silent. Director: Allan Dwan; screenwriter: John Lynch. Cast: Hope Hampton (Marion Dorsey), Conrad Nagel (Andrew Dorsey), Nita Naldi (Vivian Hepburn), Lew Cody (Guy Tarlow), Russell Griffin, Yvonne Hughes, Dolores Costello, Gilda Gray.

• ***Lawful Larceny*** (remake). RKO, 1930. Director: Lowell Sherman; screenwriter: Jane Murfin. Cast: Bebe Daniels (Marion Dorsey), Kenneth Thomson (Andrew Dorsey), Lowell Sherman (Guy Tarlow), Olive Tell (Vivian Hepburn), Purnell B. Pratt, Lou Payne, Bert Roach, Maude Turner Gordon, Helene Millard, Charles Coleman.

Now, Marion Dorsey is a most resourceful and understanding wife. She not only knows how to deal with shady ladies who have vamped her weak husband, she can turn on the smouldering looks herself when it's called for. If there had been a sequel to either of these movies, one would bet that Andrew Dorsey would be made to pay for his indiscretions by his strong-willed wife.

489 The Leathernecks Have Landed

Based on a story by Wellyn Totman and James Green. Story: In this war film, a group of American marines crush a Chinese rebellion while in the process of protecting an oil and mining company in China.

Republic Pictures, 1936 (original). Director: Howard Bretherton; screenwriter: Seton I. Miller. Cast: Lew Ayres (Woody Davis), Isabel Jewel (Brooklyn), Jimmy Ellison ("Mac" MacDonald), James Burke (Corrigan), J. Carroll Naish (Brenov), Clay Clement, Maynard Holmes, Ward Bond, Paul Porcasi, Claude King.

• ***Girl from Havana*** (remake). Republic Pictures, 1940. Director: Lew Landers; screenwriter: Karl Brown. Cast: Dennis O'Keefe (Woody Davis), Claire Carlton (Havana), Victory Jory (Tex Moore), Steffi Duna (Chita), Gordon Jones (Tubby Waters), Bradley Page, Addison Richards, Abner Biberman.

Republic Pictures couldn't afford too many scripts, so they merely recycled the ones they had, changing the setting and showing basically the same plot, even in sequels. The movies were quickly shot with little concern for production values and usually returned a fair profit. In the second film, O'Keefe, one of the best of the "B" heroes, and Jory are two friends interested in the same girl, Claire Carlton, with Dennis winning her after Victor gets involved with a gun-running outfit. In both films, Americans are throwing their weight around in somebody else's country, wiping out rebels, who today would probably be described as freedom fighters.

490 The Leavenworth Case

Based on the novel by Anna Katharine Green. Story: Eleanor Leavenworth is about to be arrested for the death of her rich bachelor uncle. However, every other member of the Leavenworth household seems to have had both motive and opportunity for doing the uncle in. Raymond, an attorney in love with Eleanor, solves the mystery and gets a confession from the real culprit, who falls to his death trying to escape.

Bennett Productions/Vitagraph, 1923 (original). Silent. Director: Charles Giblyn; screenwriter: Eve Stuyvesant. Cast: Seena Owen (Eleanor Leavenworth), Martha Mansfield (Mary Leavenworth), Wilfred Lytell (Anderson), Bradley Barker (Raymond), Paul Doucet, William Walcott, Francis Miller Grant, Fred Miller.

• ***The Leavenworth Case*** (remake). Republic Pictures, 1936. Director: Lewis D. Collins; screenwriters: Albert DeMond and Sidney Sutherland. Cast: Donald Cook (Dr. Harwell), Jean Rouverol (Eleanor), Norman Foster (Bob), Erin O'Brien-Moore (Gloria), Maude Eburne (Phoebe), Warren Hymer, Frank Sheridan, Gavin Gordon, Clay Clement, Ian Wolfe, Peggy Stratford, Archie Robbins.

Anna Katharine Green wrote this mystery melodrama in 1878 and neither production did much to update the story or characterization. Each was a hastily made feature with indifferent casts and sloppy direction. The plot uses the now disregarded plot device of making the murderer the least suspected member of the cast. However, this means the audiences spot the killer almost immediately. No one in the remake made much of an impression with their performances; each was content to wait their turn to deliver some inane line.

491 The Legend of Nigger Charley

Based on a screenplay by Larry G. Spangler and Martin Goldman. Story: In this tale of slavery told from the black perspective, Nigger Charley is an escaped slave who takes it upon himself to emancipate his friends and other slaves held in bondage in the South.

Paramount Pictures, 1972 (original). Director: Martin Goldman; screenwriters: Martin Goldman and Larry G. Spangler. Cast: Fred Williamson (Nigger Charley), D'Urville Martin (Toby), Don Pedro Colley (Joshua), Gertrude Jeanette (Theo), Marcia McBroom (Julia), Alan Gifford (Hill Carter), John Ryan, Will Hussung, Mill Moor, Thomas Anderson, Jerry Gatlin.

• ***The Soul of Nigger Charley*** (sequel). Paramount Pictures, 1973. Director: Larry G. Spangler; screenwriter: Harold Stone. Cast: Fred Williamson (Charley), D'Urville Martin (Toby), Denise Nichols (Elena), Pedro Armendariz, Jr. (Sandoval), Kirk Calloway (Marcellus), George Allen, Kevin Hagen, Michael Cameron, Johnny Greenwood, James Garbo, Nai Bonet.

The movie industry discovered there was money to be made by featuring a black performer as a strong black character. Although Fred Williamson isn't much of an actor, he was adequate for what was expected of him. It was at least refreshing to see a black man who wasn't content to remain a slave after so many Hollywood movies featuring darkies who seemed quite content to serve the "massa." These are not good films and certainly don't make up for the years and years in which black actors could find no film roles other than faithful or comical servants, but it proved that blacks had just as much right as whites to star in inferior films.

492 The Lemon Drop Kid

Based on a story by Damon Runyan. Story: Wally Brooks, known as the Lemon Drop Kid because of his addiction for the candy, is a race track tout and incompetent con man who gets into trouble with a dangerous mobster when he can't come up with the money for a gambling debt. Besides the crooks, he's pursued by the law, but with the help of a small-town girl, Alice Deering, and other street people, he comes out of everything smelling like a rose.

Paramount Pictures, 1934 (original). Director: Marshall Nellan; screenwriters: Howard Green and J.P. McEvoy. Cast: Lee Tracy (Wally Brooks), Helen Mack (Alice Deering), William Frawley (the Professor), Minna Gombell (Maizie), Baby Leroy, Robert McWade, Henry B. Walthall, Clarence H. Wilson.

• ***The Lemon Drop Kid*** (remake). Paramount Pictures, 1951. Director: Sidney Lanfield; screenwriters: Edmund Hartmann and Robert O'Brien. Cast: Bob Hope (Lemon Drop Kid), Marilyn Maxwell (Brainey Baxter), Lloyd Nolan (Charlie), Jane Darwell (Nellie Thursday), Andrea King (Stella), Fred Clark (Moose Moran), Jay C. Flippen (Straight Flush), William Frawley (Gloomy Willie).

Lee Tracy's fast paced speech and unusual voice made him an ideal Damon Runyan character, but Hope was a better Lemon Drop Kid. Ski-nose tries his best to be a heartless schemer, raising money with a cast of street Santas for an old folks home, which he intends to use to pay off his debt to Moose Moran or be killed. He does the right thing despite himself. As the girl who loves him even though she know's he's apt to disappoint her, Marilyn Maxwell is a bit too refined. A better choice for the role would have been a character like Lucille Ball played in another Runyan story starring Hope, *Sorrowful Jones* (1949). That girl had no illusions about the kind of loveable louse her man was.

493 Lena Rivers

Based on the novel by Mary Jane Holmes. Story: Lena Rivers is an orphaned girl shuttled from relative to relative, always being resented and mistreated until she finally settles down next door to her own father without the fact being known to either. Before the fade-out, however, they are reunited and she marries her father's stepson.

Chord Pictures/Arrow Pictures, 1925 (original). Silent. Director: William Bennett; screenwriter: Dana Rush. Cast: Earle Williams (Henry Rivers Grahame), Johnny Walker (Durward Belmont), Gladys Hulette (Lena Rivers), Edna Murphy (Carrie Nichols), Marcia Harris, Doris Rankin, Irma Harrison, Frank Sheridan.

• ***Lena Rivers*** (remake). Tiffany Pictures/Educational Pictures, 1932. Director: Phil Rosen; screenwriters: Stuart Anthony and Warren B. Duff. Cast: Charlotte Henry (Lena Rivers), Beryl Mercer (Grandmother), James Kirkwood (Graham), Morgan Galloway (Durrie Graham), Joyce Compton (Caroline), Betty Blythe, John St. Polis, Russell Simpson.

These were the sentimental kind of pictures of an unfortunate orphan who must endure much loneliness and misery before happiness comes her way. Such themes don't work anymore, unless the orphan is someone like E.T., left behind by his parents when their spaceship left earth without him. The story of the trials and tribulations of innocent Lena Rivers was first filmed in 1914.

Lepke *see* **The Enforcer**

Let's Be Happy *see* **Jeannie**

Let's Do It Again *see* **The Awful Truth**

Let's Face It *see* **Cradle Snatchers**

494 Let's Fall in Love

Based on a screenplay by Herbert Fields. Story: When a somewhat mad movie director's tempermental star disappears, he passes off a circus attendant as a glamorous foreign star. Of course after the usual problems they fall in love and she turns out to be a success on the screen.

Columbia Pictures, 1934 (original). Director: David Burton; screenwriter:

Herbert Fields. Cast: Edmund Lowe (Ken), Ann Sothern (Jean), Miriam Jordon (Gerry), Gregory Ratoff (Max), Tala Birell, Arthur Jarrett, Marjorie Gateson, Greta Meyer.

Columbia Pictures, 1949. Director: Douglas Sirk; screenwriter: Karen De Wolf. Cast: Dorothy Lamour (Mary O'Leary), Don Ameche (John Gayle), Janis Carter (Louisa Gayle), Willard Parker (Douglas Hyde), Adele Jergens, Jeanne Manet, Frank Ferguson, Myron Healey.

The 67-minute original is still too long. It's just another of many predictable, quickly shot films in which mistaken or hidden identities are milked for all the laughs possible. In this case the cow is dry. The remake is no great shakes either. Dorothy Lamour, the carnival dancer turned French movie star, is always a pleasure to look at, but this treat is not enough to sustain one for 80 predictable minutes of rather tedious and not very funny material.

495 The Letter

Based on the play by W. Somerset Maugham. Story: Unhappy with her life stranded on a rubber plantation in the East Indies, Leslie Crosbie takes Geoffrey Hammond as a lover. When Geoffrey falls in love with a Chinese woman, Leslie shoots and kills him. Placed on trial for her life, she is able to convince both her husband and the court that she had killed defending her honor. However, the Chinese woman has an incriminating letter Leslie had written to Hammond, which the Crosbies must pay for to recover, bankrupting them. Now Leslie faces a loveless future and no money with which to start over.

Paramount Pictures, 1929 (original). Director: Jean De Limur; screenwriter: Garrett Fort. Cast: Jeanne Eagels (Leslie Crosbie), O.P. Heggie (Howard Joyce), Reginald Owen (Robert Crosbie), Tamaki Yoshiwara (Ong Chi Seng), Herbert Marshall (Geoffrey Hammond), Lady Tsen Mei (Li-Ti), Kenneth Thompson (John Withers).

• ***The Letter*** (remake). Warner Bros., 1940. Director: William Wyler; screenwriter: Howard Koch. Cast: Bette Davis (Leslie Crosbie), Herbert Marshall (Robert Crosbie), Freida Inescort (Dorothy Joyce), James Stephenson (Howard Joyce), Gale Sondergaard (Mrs. Hammond), Victor Sen Yung (Ong Chi Seng), Bruce Lister, Elizabeth Earl, Cecil Kellaway, Willie Fung, Doris Lloyd.

• ***The Unfaithful*** (remake). Warner Bros., 1947. Director: Vincent Sherman; screenwriters: David Goodis and James Gunn. Cast: Ann Sheridan (Chris Hunter), Lew Ayres (Larry Hannaford), Zachary Scott (Bob Hunter), Eve Arden (Paula), Jerome Cowan, Steven Geray, John Hoyt, Peggy Knudsen, Marta Mitrovich, Douglas Kennedy.

In addition to those mentioned above, a French version of the 1929 piece, called *La Lettre,* was released in 1930, as well as the Spanish, *La Carta,* and the German, *Weib im Dschungel.*

Jeanne Eagels made her talking film debut with the film and Herbert Marshall, his U.S. debut as the lover. In the 1940 picture, he portrayed the understanding and deceived husband. Bette Davis gave a marvelous performance, beginning with the opening scene where she is seen pumping holes into her lover with calm intensity. The moral times being what they were, a few changes had to be made in the remake. The Chinese woman, played with great stoical patience by Gale Sondergaard, was actually the dead man's wife and she was to provide the fatal punishment for Davis that the court chose not to inflict. Giving the performance of his career was James Stephenson as the conscience-stricken lawyer who knew buying the incriminating letter was wrong but still the only way to save the life of his friend's wife. He joined Bette and director Wyler as nominees for Academy Awards but like the picture itself none won any Oscars. Still the picture was one of the best of the year and is still engrossing entertainment.

Warner Bros. updated and revised the story in it's *The Unfaithful,* but did not produce a film that could be compared for quality, drama and acting to the previous works. Ann Sheridan, whose talent as an actress was often underappreciated, was excellent as the unfaithful wife. However, others in the cast were merely adequate.

La Lettre ***see*** **The Letter**

496 Libeled Lady

Based on a story by Wallace Sullivan. Story: In this definitive screwball comedy, newspaper reporter Warren Haggerty falsely accuses socialite Connie Allenbury of having an affair with a married man, thus breaking up his marriage. Connie's father sues the paper and the newspaperman. Warren hires a friend, Bill Chandler, to marry the reporter's own fiancée, Gladys, and then make a play for Connie. If Bill can start an affair with the socialite, Warren figures it will weaken her position in the suit. His plan goes awry when Bill and Connie fall in love and his "wife," Gladys, also decides she wants Bill. The sorting out of this love quadrangle is good, crazy fun.

MGM, 1936 (original). Director: Jack Conway; screenwriter: Howard Emmett Rogers. Cast: Jean Harlow (Gladys), Myrna Loy (Connie Allenbury), Spencer Tracy (Warren Haggerty), William Powell (Bill Chandler), Walter Connelly (Mr. Allenbury), Charley Grapewin, Cora Witherspoon, E.E. Clive.

• ***Easy to Wed*** (remake). MGM, 1946. Director: Edward Buzzell; screenwriter: Dorothy Kingsley. Cast: Van Johnson (Bill Stevens Chandler), Esther Williams (Connie Allenbury), Lucille Ball (Gladys Benton), Keenan Wynn (Warren Haggerty), Cecil Kellaway (J.B. Allenbury), Carlos Ramirez, Ben Blue, Ethel Smith, June Lockhart, Grant Mitchell, Josephine Whittell.

For the younger set who have heard TV's *Moonlighting* described as a screwball comedy reminiscent of the 30s, this is the type of film which is being referred to. To have a screwball comedy, there must be a cast of characters, with crazy and improbable romantic problems, which they take quite seriously while acting as zanily as possible. Audiences enjoy watching the characters get in and out of sexual and love-oriented difficulties. In the original, Harlow, Loy, Powell and Tracy really were in high gear all through the nonsensical but delightful comedy. The remake had a sort of second team, who, although they tried very hard, couldn't quite score the laughs and looniness of the original. Lucille Ball and Keenan Wynn were equipped to handle the roles, but Van Johnson had played too many bland young juveniles and Esther Williams was only at ease when wet, to be comfortable in their roles.

497 Licensed to Kill

Based on a story by Lindsay Shonteff and Howard Griffiths. Story: British secret agent Charles Vine is assigned the dangerous job of protecting Swedish scientist Henrik Jacobsen, who has invented an anti-gravity machine, the sale of which he is negotiating with the British government. Russian agents wish to prevent the sale and would rather the scientist was dead than have the British get their hands on the machine. Although many attempts are made on the scientist's life, Vine always manages to save him.

Alistair Film/Embassy, Great Britain, 1965 (original). Director: Lindsay Shonteff; screenwriters: Howard Griffiths and Lindsay Shonteff. Cast: Tom Adams (Charles Vine), Karel Stepanek (Henrik Jacobsen), Veronica Hurst (Julia Lindberg), Peter Bull (Masterman), John Arnatt (Rockwell), Francis De Wolff, Felix Felton, George Pastell, Judy Huxtable.

• ***Where the Bullets Fly*** (sequel). Puck Films/Embassy, Great Britain, 1966. Director: John Gilling; screenwriter: Michael Pittock. Cast: Tom Adams (Charles Vine), Dawn Addams (Felicity "Fiz" Moonlight), Sidney James (Mortician), Wilfrid Brambell (Guard), Joe Baker (Minister), Tim Barrett, Michael Ripper, Suzan Farmer, Heidi Erich, Julie Martin, Maggie Kimberley.

When the original film was released in the United States it was given the title *The Second Best Secret Agent in the Whole Wide World*—just in case someone might mistake Charles Vine for 007, we suspect. In the sequel, Vine saves England from disaster by disguising himself as a woman and eliminating enemy agents who intend to fire off a guided missile aimed at the houses of Parliament. And that's only the beginning of this dull, "tain't funny, McGee" action melodrama. Always go for number one is our advice to viewers.

Licensed to Love and Kill *see* **No. 1 of the Secret Service**

Lt. Robin Crusoe, U.S.N. *see* **Robinson Crusoe**

Life at the Top *see* **Room at the Top**

498 Life Begins

Based on the play by Mary McDougal Axelson. Story: The story is set in a maternity ward of a hospital and the audience is treated to the drama that unfolds in a typical night. Patients include Grace Sutton, a young girl suffering from a difficult delivery, and Florette, a nightclub entertainer anxious to get her birthing over with so she can get back to her job.

First National/Warner Bros., 1932 (original). Directors: James Flood and Elliott Nugent; screenwriter: Earl Baldwin. Cast: Loretta Young (Grace Sutton), Eric Linden (Jed Sutton), Aline MacMahon (Miss Bowers), Glenda Farrell

(Florette), Dorothy Peterson, Vivienne Osborne, Frank McHugh, Gilbert Roland, Hale Hamilton, Herbert Mundin, Clara Blandick.

• ***A Child Is Born*** (remake). Warner Bros., 1940. Director: Lloyd Bacon; screenwriter: Robert Rossen. Cast: Geraldine Fitzgerald (Grace Sutton), Jeffrey Lynn (Jed Sutton), Gladys George (Florette), Gale Page (Miss Bowers), Spring Byington (Mrs. West), Johnnie Davis, Henry O'Neill, John Litel, Gloria Holden, Nanette Fabares.

A French version of the first film was released simultaneously. Critics considered it a "splendid woman's picture" with the unstated assumption, we suppose, that men would not find it interesting. However, the subject matter should also appeal to men who have ever had to pace anxiously in a waiting room while their wife gave birth. The remake is also adequate entertainment, but both are rather tame for audiences who have spent years fascinated by TV hospital shows. None of the performances are anything special, but all are satisfactory for what is expected.

499 The Life of Jimmy Dolan

Based on the play *The Sucker* by Bertram Milhauser and Beulah Marie Dix. Story: After winning the championship, boxer Jimmy Dolan gets stewed and accidently kills a reporter. His manager, in attempting a getaway after crossing Dolan, is killed in a car crash and burned beyond recognition. The police, with the exception of one old cop, believe that the body is that of Dolan, and consider the case of the reporter's death to be closed. Dolan scrams without funds or his championship and assumes the name of Jack Dougherty. He's taken in at a children's health farm run by Peggy and her aunt. When it appears that the women are to lose the farm, Dolan, now Dougherty, arranges to appear in a bout where he takes a beating for five rounds, at $500 per round, to save the place. The old cop recognizes him and follows Jimmy to the farm to arrest him, but seeing how he has straightened out, lets him go.

Warner Bros., 1933 (original). Director: Archie Mayo; screenwriters: David Boehm and Erwin Gelsey. Cast: Douglas Fairbanks, Jr. (Jimmy Dolan), Loretta Young (Peggy), Aline McMahon (the Aunt), Guy Kibbee (Phlaxter), Lyle Talbot (Doc Woods), Fifi Dorsay, Shirley Grey, George Meeker.

• ***They Made Me a Criminal*** (remake). Warner Bros., 1939. Director: Busby Berkeley; screenwriter: Sig Herzig. Cast: John Garfield (Johnnie), Billy Halop (Tommy), Bobby Jordan (Angel), Leo Gorcey (Spit), Huntz Hall (Dippy), Gabriel Hall (T.B.), Bernard Punsley (Milt), Claude Rains (Det. Phelan), Ann Sheridan (Goldie), May Robson (Grandma), Gloria Dickson, Robert Gleckler, John Ridgely, Barbara Pepper, Ward Bond.

The remake was John Garfield's second picture and first starring role. In this improbable but compelling film, he is a cynical boxer who, after winning the middleweight championship, sobers up from his post-fight celebration to read in the paper that he supposedly was killed in a crash after killing a reporter. He bums his way to Arizona where he makes a home on a fruit ranch, becomes a hero to the Dead End Kids, who had been sent from New York's slums to be regenerated, and falls in love with the sister of one of them. From then on it's just a question of how Garfield will get back on top without having to face a murder rap.

500 Life with the Lyons

Based on the radio series. Story: Looking forward to moving into their new home, the Lyons create so much chaos that the landlord refuses to sign the lease. Trying to persuade him, they create one disaster after another before all is settled at the end of the film.

Hammer, Great Britain, 1954 (original). Director: Val Guest; screenwriters: Guest and Robert Dunbar. Cast: Bebe Daniels (Bebe Lyon), Ben Lyon (himself), Barbara Lyon (herself), Richard Lyon (himself), Horace Percival (Mr. Wimple), Molly Weir, Hugh Morton, Arthur Hill, Doris Rogers, Gwen Lewis, Belinda Lee.

• ***The Lyons in Paris*** (sequel). Hammer, Great Britain, 1955. Director and screenwriter: Val Guest. Cast: Bebe Daniels (Bebe Lyon), Ben Lyon (himself), Barbara Lyon (herself), Richard Lyon (himself), Reginald Beckwith (Captain le Grand), Martine Alexis (Fifi le Fleur), Pierre Dudan, Dino Galvani, Horace Percival, Molly Weir, Doris Rogers, Gwen Lewis, Hugh Morton.

When their American film careers came to an end in the middle thirties, Bebe Daniels and her husband, Ben Lyon, moved to England where, during World War II and after, they had two of the most popular radio shows on the air. These movies are just film versions of some of their family humor. Bebe Daniels was an excellent comedienne, but this kind of fun—an English version of Lucille Ball and Desi Arnaz—may not be everybody's cup of tea. In the sequel the Lyons children suspect that their father is having an affair with Martine Alexis. While on holiday in Paris the family's complications include Ben facing a duel and both he and his son Richard becoming involved with Alexis.

501 The Light That Failed

Based on the novel by Rudyard Kipling. Story: Dick Heldar, an artist who has become famous for his wartime sketches, returns to London and his childhood sweetheart, Maisie Wells, who encourages him to paint his masterpiece. He chooses street urchin Bessie Broke for his model, but, blaming Dick for separating her from her lover, Torpenhow, she lets on to Maisie that she is Dick's mistress. Dick finishes the painting before his failing eyesight—caused by a battle wound—completely leaves him. Still angry, Bessie destroys the painting, but later confesses to Maisie that she had made up the story about her and Dick being lovers, and Maisie hurries to Dick to care for him.

• ***The Light That Failed*** (remake). Famous Players/Paramount Pictures, 1923. Director: George Melford; screenwriters: F. McGrew Willis and Jack Cunningham. Cast: Jacqueline Logan (Bessie Broke), Percy Marmont (Dick Heldar), David Torrence (Torpenhow), Sigrid Holmquist (Maisie Wells), Mabel Van Buren, Luke Cosgrave, Peggy Schaffer.

• ***The Light That Failed*** (remake). Paramount Pictures, 1939. Director: William A. Wellman; screenwriter: Robert Carson. Cast: Ronald Colman (Dick Heldar), Walter Huston (Torpenhow), Muriel Angelus (Maisie), Ida Lupino

(Bessie Broke), Dudley Digges, Ernest Cossart, Ferlike Boros, Pedro de Cordova, Colin Tapley.

The Kipling story was first filmed by Pathe in 1916. Not much is remembered about the 1923 silent because of the 1939 Ronald Colman star feature. In it he struggles valiantly to finish his masterpiece before going blind, not counting on the nastiness of Ida Lupino, who handles her role as the unhappy model quite well. It's a nicely made feature, but not very exciting. Colman's voice, of course, is always a treat, as in his line to Lupino: "Laugh, you little fool, laugh . . . for I'm giving you something you've never had before . . . a soul . . . on canvas!"

502 Lightnin'

Based on a book by Frank Bacon and the play by Winchell Smith and Frank Bacon. Story: Storyteller and easygoing Civil War veteran "Lightnin'" Bill Jones and his wife run a hotel on the California-Nevada line with the boundary being painted on the lobby floor to make it easier for guests who are seeking a divorce in Nevada or running from the law. Young lawyer John Marvin moves in after being innocently involved with a shady real estate deal pulled by Thomas and Hammond. These two persuade Mrs. Jones to sell them the hotel but Bill won't agree to the deal. The crooks convince Mrs. Jones to file for divorce from Bill, but when the case comes to court he exposes the land grabbers. He and his wife are reconciled and Marvin settles down with Bill's stepdaughter, Millie.

Fox Film Corporation, 1925 (original). Silent. Director: John Ford; screenwriter: Frances Marion. Cast: Jay Hunt (Lightnin' Bill Jones), J. Farrell MacDonald (Jude Townsend), Madge Bellamy (Millie), Wallace MacDonald (John Marvin), Ethel Clayton (Margaret Davis), Edythe Chapman (Mrs. Bill Jones), Brandon Hurst (Everett Hammond), Richard Travis (Raymond Thomas).

• ***Lightnin'*** (remake). Fox Film Corporation, 1930. Director: Henry King; screenwriters: S.N. Behrman and Sonya Levien. Cast: Will Rogers (Lightnin' Bill Jones), Louise Dresser (Mrs. Jones), Joel McCrea (John Marvin), Helen Cohan (Millie Jones), Jason Robards (Raymond Thomas), J.M. Kerrigan (Lemuel Townsend), Walter Percival (Everett Hammond).

The original was a faithful transcription of the play with a fine performance from Jay Hunt in the title role. The remake was an archetypal Will Rogers vehicle of a man wiser than he appears. It had high production values and was Rogers' first big talkie hit.

503 Lights Out

Based on the play by Paul Dickey and Mann Page. Story: Two notorious crooks, "Hairpin" Annie and Sea Bass, rob a screenwriter, Egbert Winslow, and then convince him to write a screenplay about the underworld with their help. Sea Bass considers it an opportunity to expose a rival, "High-Shine" Joe. Bass so describes Joe and his activities that when the movie is made and Joe sees it, he recognizes himself and heads for the studio intent on killing Egbert. However, the police arrive in time to save him.

R-C Pictures/F.B.O., 1923 (original). Silent. Director: Al Santell; screenwriter: Rex Taylor. Cast: Ruth Stonehouse ("Hairpin" Annie), Walter McGrail

(Sea Bass), Theodore von Eltz (Egbert Winslow), Ben Deely ("High-Shine" Joe), Marie Astaire, Hank Mann, Ben Hewlett, Mabel Van Buren.

• ***Crashing Hollywood*** (remake). RKO, 1937. Director: Lew Landers; screenwriters: Paul Yawitz and Gladys Atwater. Cast: Lee Tracy (Michael), Joan Woodbury (Barbara), Paul Guilfoyle (Horman), Lee Patrick (Goldie), Richard Lane (Wells), Bradley Page, Tom Kennedy, George Irving, Frank M. Thomas, Jack Carson.

These crook melodramas are nothing special, but filled a second bill as needed. In the remake, Lee Tracy collaborates with ex-convict Paul Guilfoyle on a screenplay about a bank robbery based on the one for which the con was framed. When the movie comes out it gives the police some leads to criminals and gangsters descend on Hollywood to put a stop to realistic crime stories.

504 Li'l Abner

Based on the comic strip by Al Capp. Story: There was even less plot in the film than in Al Capp's comic strips. The screenwriters attempted to tie together the antics of the inhabitants of Dogpatch with Abner's continual efforts to elude Daisy Mae's marriage traps, including the Sadie Hawkins' Day race.

Vogue Productions/RKO, 1940 (original). Director: Albert S. Rogell; screenwriters: Charles Kerr and Tyler Johnson. Cast: Granville Owen (Li'l Abner), Martha O'Driscoll (Daisy Mae), Mona Ray (Mammy Yokum), Johnnie Morris (Pappy Yokum), Buster Keaton (Lonesome Polecat), Billie Seward (Cousin Delightful), Kay Sutton (Wendy Wilecat), Maude Eburne (Granny Scraggs), Edgar Kennedy (Cornelius Cornpone), Charles A. Post (Earthquake McGoon), Bud Jamison (Hairless Joe), Dick Elliot (Marryin' Sam), Johnny Arthur, Lucien Littlefield, Frank Wilder, Chester Conklin.

Paramount/Panama-Frank, 1959. Director and screenwriters: Norman Panama and Melvin Frank. Cast: Peter Palmer (Li'l Abner), Leslie Parrish (Daisy Mae), Stella Stevens (Appassionata von Climax), Howard St. John (General Bullmoose), Stubby Kaye (Marryin' Sam), Julie Newmar (Stupefyin' Jones), Robert Strauss (Romeo Scragg), Billie Hayes (Mammy Yokum), Joe E. Marks (Pappy Yokum), Bern Hoffman (Earthquake McGoon), Al Nestor (Evil Eye Fleagle), Carmen Alvarez (Moonbeam McSwine), William Lanteau, Alan Carney, Joe E. Morris, Ted Thurston, Stanley Simmonds, Joe Ploski.

The first effort to bring Al Capp's illiterate hillbilly to the screen was a hodgepodge of comic strip–length bits featuring actors and actresses hired because of their resemblance to the characters they were impersonating. It wouldn't even have played big in Dogpatch. The 1959 musical was a remake of the Broadway smash with songs by Gene De Paul and Johnny Mercer, the best of which was "Jubilation T. Cornpone" shouted out by Stubby Kaye and the entire cast. The dancing, the singing and the girls in their abbreviated costumes all looked good and Peter Palmer, who repeated his Broadway role as the country bumpkin, captured the essence of Li'l Abner, an accomplishment of no great consequence—but one which gave the young man his one big career opportunity. Just for the record, the story of the film dealt with the government decision to use Dogpatch for an atomic bomb test, because it was the most expendable spot in the country.

505 Lilies of the Field

Based on the play by William Hurlbut. Story: Walter Harker, who loves another woman, finds an opportunity to divorce his wife, Mildred. He remarries and takes custody of their child, Rose. Mildred gets a job as a model and plenty of propositions, but she has no intentions of going that route. She finally accepts the marriage proposal of wealthy Louis Willing, when he proves his love by helping her regain custody of Rose.

First National Pictures, 1924 (original). Silent. Director: John Francis Dillon; screenwriter: Marion Fairfax. Cast: Corinne Griffith (Mildred Harker), Conway Tearle (Louis Willing), Alma Bennett (Doris), Sylvia Breamer (Vera), Myrtle Stedman (Mazie), Crauford Kent (Walter Harker), Charles Murray, Phyllis Haver, Cissy Fitzgerald, Edith Ransom, Charles Gerrard, Dorothy Brock.

• ***Lilies of the Field*** (remake). First National Pictures, 1930. Director: Alexander Korda; screenwriter: John F. Goodrich. Cast: Corinne Griffith (Mildred Harker), Ralph Forbes (Ted Willing), John Loder (Walter Harker), Eve Southern (Pink), Jean Barry (Gertie), Tyler Brooke (Bert Miller), Freeman Wood, Ann Schaeffer, Clarissa Selwynne.

Griffith re-created her silent role in the remake. This time, after being framed by her husband in divorce proceedings and losing the custody of her child, she takes up residence in a cheap hotel and becomes a show girl, where she meets a group of gold-digging "lilies." Ted Willing, a wealthy man, becomes her admirer but she refuses financial help from him. When she learns that her child has forgotten her, she accepts Ted's proposal. At a party she is informed that the child is dead. Grief-stricken, she goes crazy and is arrested for disorderly conduct, but Ted comes to her rescue and she finds comfort in his arms.

506 Liliom

Based on the play by Ferenc Molnar. Story: Liliom is a swaggering, hot-tempered Budapest barker for a carousel owned by his mistress, Mrs. Muskrat. He meets and impulsively marries sweet young Julie. Mrs. Muskrat fires him and, without a job, Liliom frequently beats his wife. But when he learns that she is going to have a baby, he seeks support for his family, joining in a scheme of a shady friend to attempt the robbery of a bank messenger. Liliom is killed in the bungled attempt. After 16 years in purgatory, he is allowed one day back on earth to do a good deed for his family. On his way back to earth, he steals a star for his daughter, but when she refuses it he strikes her, his temper as bad as ever. The girl tells her mother that she felt no pain when the strange man struck her. Remembering, Julie says, "There are times when a slap becomes a caress." Liliom is returned to purgatory.

• ***A Trip to Paradise*** (original). Metro Pictures, 1921. Silent. Director: Maxwell Karger; screenwriter: June Mathis. Cast: Bert Lytell (Curley Flynn),

Virginia Valli (Nora O'Brien), Brinsley Shaw (Meek), Unice Vin Moore (Widow Boland), Victory Bateman, Eve Gordon.

• ***Liliom*** (remake). Fox Film Corporation, 1930. Director: Frank Borzage; screenwriter: S.N. Behrman. Cast: Charles Farrell (Liliom), Rose Hobart (Julie), Estelle Taylor (Madame Muskrat), Lee Tracy (Buzzard), James Marcus, H.B. Warner, Guinn Williams, Mildred Van Dorn, Lillian Elliott, Walter Abel.

• ***Liliom*** (remake). Fox Europa Films, 1934. Director: Fritz Lang; screenwriter: Robert Leiberman. Cast: Charles Boyer (Liliom), Madeleine Ozeray (Julie), Florelle (Madame Muskrat), Mimi Funes (Marie), Pierre Alcover (Alfred), Alexandre Rignault, Roland Toutain, Henry Richard, Mila Parley.

• ***Carousel*** (remake). Twentieth Century–Fox, 1956. Director: Henry King; screenwriters: Phoebe and Henry Ephron. Cast: Gordon MacRae (Billy Bigelow), Shirley Jones (Julie Jordon), Cameron Mitchell (Jigger), Barbara Ruick (Carrie), Robert Rounseville (Mr. Snow), Audrey Christie (Mrs. Mullin), Claramae Turner (Cousin Nettie), Gene Lockhart (Star Keeper), Susan Luckey (Louise).

The ingeniously staged fantasy was filmed on four occasions, first with a changed title and characters but still the story of the dumb and quick-tempered carousel barker who has strange ways of showing his love for a shy and sensitive girl. In 1930, the role seemed a bit too complex for Charles Farrell, who usually played wholesome one-dimensional men, but his popularity ensured decent box-office receipts. Charles Boyer was more at home with the role in the French version. The musical *Carousel,* based on Rodgers and Hammerstein's Broadway hit, contained the lovely music and was nicely photographed but it is clear for all to see that there's not much to the story. Among the delightful songs in the film are "Carousel Waltz," "If I Loved You," "June Is Bustin' Out All Over," "Soliloquy," "What's the Use of Wond'rin" and "You'll Never Walk Alone."

507 The Lily of Killarney

Based on the play "The Colleen Bawn" by Dion Boucicault and the operetta by Charles Benedict. Story: A poor landowner, Hardress Creegan, in love with a peasant girl, Eily O'Connor, who is kidnapped by a notorious smuggler, Myles na Coppaleen, mortgages his estate to Sir James, who shortly threatens to foreclose. Creegan rescues the girl and keeps his land when his horse beats Sir James' in a big race.

• ***The Lily of Killarney (Tense Moments from Opera, Series)*** (original). Gaumont, Great Britain, 1922. Silent. Director: Challis Sanderson; screenwriter: Frank Miller. Cast: Betty Farquhar (Eily O'Connor), Bertram Burleigh (Hardress Creegan), Booth Conway (Myles na Coppaleen), Miriam Merry, Alec Hunter.

• ***The Colleen Bawn*** (remake). Stoll, Great Britain, 1924. Silent. Director: W.P. Kellino; screenwriter: Eliot Stannard. Cast: Henry Victor (Hardress Creegan), Colette Brettell (Eily O'Connor), Stewart Rome (Myles na

Coppaleen), Gladys Jennings, Clive Currie, Marie Ault, Marguerite Leigh, Aubrey Fitzgerald, Dave O'Toole.

• ***Lily of Killarney*** (remake). BIP, Great Britain, 1929. Director and screenwriter: George Ridgwell. Cast: Cecil Landeau (Hardress Cregan), Pamela Parr (Eily O'Connor), Dennis Wyndham (Myles na Coppaleen), Barbara Gott, Gillian Dean, H. Fisher White, Edward O'Neill, Wilfred Shine, Henry Wilson.

• ***Lily of Killarney*** (remake). Twickenham, Great Britain, 1934. Director and screenwriter: Maurice Elvey. Cast: John Garrick (Sir Patrick Cregan), Gina Malo (Eileen O'Connor), Stanley Holloway (Father O'Flynn), Leslie Perrins (Sir James Corrigan), Dennis Hoey (Myles na Coppaleen), Sara Allgood, Dorothy Boyd, D.J. Williams, Hughes Macklin, Pamela May, A. Bromley Davenport.

The original story was the tale of a poor aristocrat who hires a halfwit (in a later version, a dwarf) to drown his secret wife so he can wed an heiress. By the 1934 production, this villain is transformed into a hero whose rival frames him for murder when his peasant lover is kidnapped by a smuggler.

508 Lily of the Dust

Based on the novel *Das Hohe Lied* by Hermann Sudermann and the play *The Song of Songs* by Edward Brewster Sheldon. Story: Lily Czepanek, working in a bookstore, meets young German officer Richard von Prell, who falls in love with her, but she marries an older man, Colonel von Mertzbach. This does not end her affair with Prell, and when Mertzbach learns of their continuing relationship, he wounds the young man in a duel, and throws the baggage out. She then takes up with Karl Dehnecke, until Prell comes back into the picture. His uncle and guardian doesn't think much of Lily, refusing to accept her as a niece-in-law, so Lily returns to Dehnecke.

• ***Lily of the Dust*** (remake). Famous Players/Paramount Pictures, 1923. Silent. Director: Dimitri Buchowetski; screenwriter: Paul Bern. Cast: Pola Negri (Lily Czepanek), Ben Lyon (Richard von Prell), Noah Beery (Colonel von Mertzbach), Raymond Griffith (Karl Dehnecke), Jeanette Daudet, William J. Kelly.

• ***Song of Songs*** (remake). Paramount Pictures, 1933. Director: Rouben Mamoulian; screenwriters: Leo Birinski and Samuel Hoffenstein. Cast: Marlene Dietrich (Lily Czepanek), Brian Aherne (Waldow), Lionel Atwill (Baron von Mertzbach), Alison Skipworth (Mrs. Rasmussen), Hardie Albright (Walter von Prell), Helen Freeman, Morgan Wallace, Hans Schumm.

The story was first filmed in 1918 as *Lily Czepanek*, starring Elsie Ferguson. These stories of innocent young girls who move from one lover to another are no great shakes. Even Dietrich couldn't inject much interest into the story of a German peasant girl who goes to Berlin to live with her aunt, falls in love with a sculptor, and makes the mistake of marrying a jealous baron.

509 The Limping Man

Based on the play *Creeping Shadows* by Will Scott. Story: This melodrama-whodunit is the story of good and bad twin brothers, mistaken identities, thieves after a valuable painting, a scientific criminologist, a silly-ass colonel, a couple of guys from Chicago out to get the man who "done" their sisters wrong, an old house with the usual furtive butler, creaking doors, secret panels, and a limping killer sniper. It's the usual chatty British mystery, finally unraveled by the brilliant work of the criminologist.

• ***The Limping Man*** (remake). Pathe British, 1936. Director and screenwriter: Walter Summers. Cast: Francis L. Sullivan (Theodore Disher), Hugh Wakefield (Col. Paget), Iris Hoey (Mrs. Paget), Patricia Hilliard (Gloria Paget), Ronald Cochran (Philip Nash), Harry Hutchinson, Leslie Perrins, Judy Kelly, Frank Atkinson, Arthur Brander, Syd Crossley.

• ***The Limping Man*** (remake). Lippert Pictures, 1953. Director: Charles De Lautour; screenwriters: Ian Stuart and Reginald Long. Cast: Lloyd Bridges (Frank Prior), Moira Lister (Pauline French), Alan Whestley (Insp. Braddock), Leslie Phillips (Cameron), Helen Cordet (Helene Castle), Andre Van Gyseghem, Rachel Roberts, Irisia Cooper.

Will Scott's play was first produced for the screen in 1931, using his original title. In the 1936 version, Ronald Cochran inherits Monk's Revel and is dogged by a limping man who has mistaken Cochran for his evil twin brother. Eventually the brother is bumped off and it's up to Francis L. Sullivan to solve the mystery. In the remake, Lloyd Bridges is an American who has returned to England to take up his wartime romance with actress Moira Lister. As he leaves his plane, a man he is talking to is killed by a limping sniper. The murdered man, who had been blackmailing Lister, later proves to be very much alive. Just as he is about to kill Frank, the latter wakes up. This unnecessary device spoils the otherwise competent thriller.

510 Little Accident

Based on the novel by Floyd Dell and the play *An Unmarried Father* by Floyd Dell and Thomas Mitchell. Story: Norman Overbeck postpones his second marriage when he discovers that his first wife is having a baby. She wishes to put the child up for adoption but Norman opposes the plan and kidnaps the child to care for it himself.

Universal Pictures, 1930 (original). Director: William James Craft screenwriters: Gene Towne and Gladys Lehman. Cast: Douglas Fairbanks, Jr. (Norman), Anita Page (Isabel), Sally Blane (Madge), Zasu Pitts (Monica), Joan Marsh (Doris), Roscoe Karns, Slim Summerville, Henry Armetta, Myrtle Stedman.

• ***Little Accident*** (remake). Paramount Pictures, 1939. Director: Charles Lamont; screenwriters: Paul Yawitz and Eve Greene. Cast: Hugh Herbert (Herbert Peterson), Florence Rice (Alice Peterson), Richard Carlson (Perry Allerton), Ernest Truex (Tabby Moran), Joy Hodges (Joan Huston), Fritz Feld, Kathleen Howard, Baby Sandy, Howard Hickman, Edgar Kennedy.

• ***Casanova Brown*** (remake). International Pictures/RKO, 1944. Director: Sam Wood; screenwriter: Nunnally Johnson. Cast: Gary Cooper (Casanova Q. Brown), Teresa Wright (Isabel Drury), Frank Morgan (Mr. Ferris), Anita Louise (Madge Ferris), Patricia Collins (Mrs. Drury), Edmond Breon, Jill Esmond.

Learning that your ex has just given birth to your child the day before your second wedding should be enough to give one pause, but this light-hearted comedy isn't as amusing as the producers hoped. The baby seems unperturbed by being passed around among so many different people, but it surely upsets the adults. The 1939 remake has little in common with the original, save that a baby is passed around among various people when abandoned in a newsroom. In 1944, the producers return to the original story with Cooper playing the bewildered new father who ends up with no help from either his ex-wife or his fiancée. Viewers in a light-hearted mood might find any one of these movies smile-producing, but not memorable comedies.

511 The Little Adventuress

Based on A.A. Milne's play *The Dover Road.* Story: A man and his wife each decide to have an extramarital affair on the French Riviera. On their way to Calais, both straying couples seek lodging at the house of a rich eccentric whose home is on the Dover Road. His hobby is to kidnap philandering couples, making sure they are not making a mistake. He persuades them to test their love before continuing their journeys. Their experience causes the fire of passion to burn out and the married couple are deserted by their respective paramours just as another straying couple arrives.

Producers Distributing Corporation, 1927 (original). Silent. Director: William C. DeMille; screenwriter: Clara Beranger. Cast: Vera Reynolds (Helen Davis), Victor Varconi (George Le Fuente), Phyllis Haver (Victoria Stoddard), Theodore Kosloff (Antonio Russo), Robert Ober (Leonard Stoddard), Fred Walton (Dominick).

• ***Where Sinners Meet (The Dover Road)*** (remake). RKO, 1934. Director: J. Walter Ruben; screenwriter: H.W. Hannemann. Cast: Clive Brook (Mr. Latimer), Diana Wynyard (Anne), Billie Burke (Eustasia), Reginald Owen (Leonard), Alan Mowbray (Nicholas), Gilbert Emery (Dominic).

It has been reported that Milne was displeased with the 1927 film version of his work and that he particularly objected to the decision to give it a title considered more suggestive. It and the 1934 movie are very stagey pieces, neither of which was very successful at the box office. Whimsy, unless done extremely well, doesn't seem to attract huge audiences.

512 The Little Foxes

Based on the play by Lillian Hellman. Story: The Hubbard family is a group of post–Civil War schemers who will stop at nothing to get what they want and outwit each other. Brothers Ben and Oscar Hubbard offer their beautiful, bitchy sister, Regina Hubbard Giddens, one-third interest in a questionable cotton mill scheme if she will advance them $75,000 of her terminally ill husband's funds. Horace Giddens refuses the loan, so Oscar orders his snivelling son, Leo, who works in Giddens' bank, to steal bonds from Horace's safety deposit box. Horace discovered the theft but because of his wife does not expose her brothers. Regina's violent outburts of telling Horace how much she despises him causes the man to have a heart attack, but she won't get his medicine which might save his life. His death is followed by Regina demanding a third of the brothers' deal or she will tell about the theft of the bonds. Ben is able to check her by correctly guessing the events of Horace's death.

RKO, 1941 (original). Director: William Wyler; screenwriter: Lillian Hellman. Cast: Bette Davis (Regina Hubbard Giddens), Herbert Marshall (Horace Giddens), Charles Dingle (Benjamin Hubbard), Dan Duryea (Leo Hubbard), Patricia Colling (Birdie Hubbard), Carl Benton Reid (Oscar Hubbard), Teresa Wright (Alexandra Giddens), Richard Carlson (David Hewitt), Jessica Grayson, John Marriott, Russell Hicks, Lucien Littlefield, Virginia Brissac.

• ***Another Part of the Forest*** (prequel). Universal-International Pictures, 1948. Director: Michael Gordon; screenwriter: Vladimir Pozner. Cast: Fredric March (Marcus Hubbard), Ann Blyth (Regina Hubbard), Edmond O'Brien (Ben Hubbard), Florence Eldredge (Lavinia Hubbard), Dan Duryea (Oscar Hubbard), John Dall, Dona Drake, Betsy Blair, Fritz Leiber, Whit Bissell, Don Beddoe.

In the 1941 film, Lilian Hellman (screenplay), William Wyler (directing), Meredith Willson (music), and Bette Davis, Teresa Wright and Patrice Colling (as performers) were all nominated for Academy Awards, but none won. It's a superb film from a brilliant play, with everyone in the cast doing themselves proud, but none more so than Davis and Duryea. The second film is a prequel of the first, telling how the Hubbards got that way, apparently from dear old dad, Marcus Hubbard, nicely played by Fredric March. Dan Duryea, the son in *The Little Foxes*, is cast as his father in the prequel. It's an absorbing film, but not quite as stylish as the original.

The Little Gypsy *see* **The Little Minister**

513 Little Lord Fauntleroy

Based on the novel by Frances Hodgson Burnett. Story: Cedric lives with his mother, the widow of the third son of the Earl of Dorincourt, in mean poverty in New York City during the 1880s. The Earl, now without heirs, arranges to have the boy brought to England to become Lord Fauntleroy, but his mother is forced to live away from the castle, because the Earl never approved of her marriage to his son. Cedric charms the Earl, but complications arise when a solicitor appears with a woman who claims that the Earl's eldest son, Bevis, fathered her child, and he should inherit the title. When this news reaches New York, Cedric's old friends journey to England to expose the woman as a fraud. Cedric's mother is then invited to stay at the castle, and the three live happily together.

• ***Little Lord Fauntleroy*** (remake). Pickford Co./United Artists, 1921. Silent. Directors: Alfred E. Green and Jack Pickford; screenwriter: Bernard McConville. Cast: Mary Pickford (Cedric-Little Lord Fauntleroy/Dearest, Cedric's mother), Claude Gillingwater (the Earl of Dorincourt), Joseph Dowling (Haversham), Hames Marcus (Hobbs), Kate Price (Mrs. McGinty), Fred Malatesta (Fred), Rose Dione, Frances Marion.

• ***Little Lord Fauntleroy*** (remake). United Artists, 1936. Director: John

Cromwell; screenwriter: Hugh Walpole. Cast: C. Aubrey Smith (Earl of Dorincourt), Freddie Bartholomew (Ceddie), Dolores Costello Barrymore (Dearest/Mrs. Errol), Henry Stephenson (Haversham), Guy Kibbee (Mr. Hobbs), Mickey Rooney (Dick), Eric Alden (Ben), Jackie Searl, Reginald Barlow, Ivan Simpson, E.E. Clive, Constance Collier.

Little Lord Fauntleroy was also filmed in 1914 in Britain and in a made-for-TV movie in 1980, featuring Ricky Schroder as Ceddie and Alec Guinness as the Earl. It's a sticky, sentimental story with the behavior of Ceddie making one question the Earl's judgement. Both versions mentioned in this entry were made to feature their leading performer. Mary Pickford was so popular that she could have portrayed the Earl and found an audience. Freddie Bartholomew had a strange fascination for audiences in the '30s. Still, the film is enjoyable and C. Aubrey Smith is a delightful old coot.

514 Little Men

Based on the novel by Louisa May Alcott. Story: Jo and her professor, Bhaer, run the Plumfield School for Boys. When street urchins Dan and Nat arrive, they fight with everyone, set the dormitory afire and are accused of stealing.

Mascot Pictures, 1935 (original). Director: Phil Rosen; screenwriter: Gertrude Orr. Cast: Ralph Morgan (Professor Bhaer), Erin O'Brien-Moore (Jo March Bhaer), Junior Durkin (Franz), Cora Sue Collins (Daisy), Frankie Darro (Dan), David Durand (Nat), Phyllis Fraser, Dickie Moore, Tad Alexander, Buster Phelps.

• ***Little Men*** (remake). RKO, 1940. Director: Norman Z. MacLeod; screenwriter: Mary Kelly. Cast: Kay Francis (Jo), Jack Oakie (Willie), George Bancroft (Major Burdle), Jimmy Lydon (Dan), Ann Gillis (Nan), Charles Esmond (Professor), Richard Nichols, Casey Johnson, Francesca Santoro, Johnny Burke, Lillian Randolph.

The novel *Little Men* was inferior to Alcott's *Little Women* and the same can be said of the movie adaptations. Of course the cast for the two versions can't match that assembled for the Katharine Hepburn version of *Little Women.* Those who had not read Miss Alcott's novels but had seen the movie of the lives of the March sisters and enjoyed it, may have gone to the theater hoping for another treat with the sequel but most came away disappointed. The two film versions were teary, insignificant stories with nothing memorable about them.

515 The Little Minister

Based on the play by James Barrie. Story: Young Presbyterian minister Gavin Dishart has earned a reputation as a man who can resist all temptations. He numbers among his flock a group of suspicious and rebellious villagers. One evening while on an errand to convince armed, striking weavers not to resist the soldiers sent to disperse them, he encounters a Gypsy girl, Babbie, who had come to the woods to warn the weavers of the advance of the soldiers. When the latter arrive, they threaten to arrest the Gypsy, but she declares that she is the wife of "the little minister." Gavin does not dispute the claim, and in these parts, silence legalizes the marriage. After this the girl and the minister meet frequently and fall in love. When the captain of the soldiers announces that the girl and Dishart are legally married, the shocked parishioners are prepared to have the minister recalled, but it is discovered that Babbie is actually Lady Barbara, daughter of Lord Rintoul, and this makes everything alright.

Vitagraph Company, 1913 (original). Silent. Director and screenwriter: James Young. Cast: Clara Kimball Young (Babbie), James Young (Gavin Dishart), Herbert L. Barry, William V. Ranous, Charles Eldridge, William Shea, Richard Leslie.

• ***The Little Minister*** (remake). Neptune Pictures, England, 1915. Silent. Director and screenwriter: Perry Nash. Cast: Joan Ritz (Babbie), Gregory Scott (Gavin Dishart), Douglas Payne, Harry Vibart, May Whitty, Fay Davis, Frank Tennant, Brian Daly.

• ***The Little Gypsy*** (remake). Fox Pictures, 1915. Silent. Director: Oscar C. Apfel and Mary Murillo; screenwriter: Walter Dare. Cast: Dorothy Bernard (Babbie), Thurlow Bergen (Gavin Dishart), Julia Hurley, Raymond Murray, W.J. Herbert.

• ***The Little Minister*** (remake). Paramount Pictures, 1921. Silent. Director: Penrhyn Stanlaws; screenwriter: Edfrid Bingham. Cast: Betty Compson (Babbie), George Hackathorne (Gavin Dishart), Edwin Stevens, Nigel Barrie, Guy Oliver.

• ***The Little Minister*** (remake). Vitagraph Company, 1922. Silent. Director: David Smith; screenwriters: C. Graham Baker and Harry Dittmar. Cast: Alice Calhoun (Babbie), James Morrison (Gavin Dishart), Henry Herbert, Alberta Lee, William McCall, Dorthea Wolbert, Maud Emery.

• ***The Little Minister*** (remake). RKO Pictures, 1934. Director: Richard Wallace; screenwriters: Jane Murfin, Sarah Y. Mason, Victor Heerman, Mortimer Offner and Jack Wagner. Cast: Katharine Hepburn (Babbie), John Beal (Gavin Dishart), Frank Conroy, Alan Hale, Donald Crisp, Mary Gordon, Dorothy Stickney.

The whimsical play was popular in its various silent movie productions, but the talkie is one of the movies that made Hollywood believe that Katharine Hepburn was box-office poison. Apparently it was one thing to read the title frames of the silent films but quite another to listen to the cloying Scottish dialog, especially as delivered by a Bryn Mawr–bred lass. Actually, most critics found Hepburn's performance charming, but audiences didn't agree. John Beal, never much of an actor, didn't help much, and the rest of the cast were no great shakes, but it's the story itself that outstayed its welcome.

Little Miss Big *see* **Three Kids and a Queen**

516 Little Miss Marker

Based on a story by Damon Runyon. Story: Bookmaker Sorrowful Jones reluctantly accepts a man's five-year-old daughter as a marker on a $20 bet. He has reason to be sorrowful when the father is killed by disgruntled mobsters and Jones finds himself the unwilling guardian of the kid. Marky, as the child comes to be called, has just learned the story of King Arthur and dubs the

Adolphe Menjou is a gambler who has taken Shirley Temple as a marker for a bet and is stuck with her when her father is killed in Little Miss Marker *(Paramount, 1934).*

various unsavory characters she meets through Jones, knights of the Round Table. Parsimonious pagan Jones finds himself falling for the little tyke, and at least by his standards, mending his ways. It looks like Jones and his gal, Bangles Carson, will become permanent King Arthur and Queen Guinevere for Marky.

Paramount Pictures, 1934 (original). Director: Alexander Hall; screenwriters: William R. Lipman, Sam Hellman and Gladys Lehman. Cast: Adolphe Menjou (Sorrowful Jones), Dorothy Dell (Bangles Carson), Charles Bickford (Big Steve), Shirley Temple (Miss Marker), Lynne Overman (Regret), Frank McGlynn, Sr., Willie Best, Gary Owen.

• ***Sorrowful Jones*** (remake). Paramount Pictures, 1949. Director: Sidney

Bob Hope, William Demarest, Mary Jayne Saunders and Lucille Ball line up for this publicity pose for Sorrowful Jones *(Paramount, 1949), a remake of* Little Miss Marker.

Lanfield; screenwriters: Melville Shavelson, Edmund Hartman and Jack Rose. Cast: Bob Hope (Sorrowful Jones), Lucille Ball (Gladys O'Neill), William Demarest (Regret), Bruce Cabot (Big Steve Holloway), Mary Jane Saunders (Martha Jane Smith/Miss Marker), Thomas Gomez, Houseley Stevenson.

• ***Forty Pounds of Trouble*** (remake). Universal Pictures, 1962. Director: Norman Jewison; screenwriter: Marion Hargrove. Cast: Tony Curtis (Steve McCluskey), Suzanne Pleshette (Chris Lockwood), Claire Wilcox (Penny Piper), Larry Storch, Howard Morris, Edward Andrews, Phil Silvers.

• ***Little Miss Marker*** (remake). Universal Pictures, 1980. Director: Walter Bernstein; screenwriter: Bernstein. Cast: Walter Matthau, Julie Andrews, Tony Curtis, Bob Newhart, Sara Stimson, Lee Grant, Brian Dennehy.

Five-year-old Shirley Temple walked away with the 1934 production, although Adolphe Menjou more than held his own in the action area. He just wasn't as cute as the little dimpled-one. Temple's spontaneity is a joy to behold. Menjou seemed more a Damon Runyon character than did Bob Hope in the 1949 remake. Ski-nose was perfecting his character of a wise-cracking, frightened boy full of hot air. He would pull this pose out of his bag of tricks in many movies in the years that followed. The 1962 piece doesn't give credit to Runyon, but it's clearly modeled on the earlier work. Tony Curtis is the manager of a gambling casino who not only must contend with the efforts of his ex-wife's detective to collect long overdue alimony payments, but he gets stuck with an orphaned six-year-old girl. It's standard stuff with a fun, climactic chase through Disneyland. The 1980 remake allows Walter Matthau to be his usual acerbic self, but the production is flat and the storyline is just too old-hat for the 80s.

Little Miss Nobody *see* **Blue Skies**

517 Little Old New York

Based on the play by Rida Johnson Young. Story: Patrick O'Day sails for New York from Ireland to claim a fortune left to him, but dies en route. Under these circumstances, the fortune is supposed to revert to a stepson, Larry Delavan. Patrick's sister, Patricia, disguises herself as her brother, gets the inheritance and becomes friends with Larry when she helps him finance Robert Fulton's steamboat venture. During a riot, Patricia reveals her true identity. She and Larry fall in love, marry and return to Ireland.

Goldwyn/Cosmopolitan Distributing Corporation, 1923. Silent. Director: Sidney Olcott; screenwriter: Luther Reed. Cast: Marion Davies (Patricia O'Day), Stephen Carr (Patrick O'Day), J.M. Kerrigan (John O'Day), Harrison Ford (Larry Delavan), Courtney Foote (Robert Fulton), Mahlon Hamilton (Washington Irving), Norval Keedwell, George Barraud, Sam Hardy, Andrew Dillon.

• ***Little Old New York*** (remake). Twentieth Century–Fox, 1940. Director: Henry King; screenwriter: Harry Tugend. Cast: Alice Faye (Pat O'Day), Fred MacMurray (Charles Browne), Richard Greene (Robert Fulton), Brenda Joyce (Harriet Livingston), Andy Devine ("Commodore"), Henry Stephenson, Fritz Feld, Ward Bond, Clarence Hummel Wilson, Robert Middlemass, Roger Imhof, Theodore von Eltz.

These are two nineteenth-century name-dropping features, with the likes of Washington Irving, Cornelius Vanderbilt and Jacob Astor appearing on the scene in the story of the scheme to finance and build Robert Fulton's steamboat. In the remake, Fulton also must take time out to convince Pat O'Day, played by Alice Faye, that it is she he loves, not the daughter of his main backer.

518 Little Orphan Annie

Based on the comic strip by Harold Gray. Story: A spunky little orphan Annie, and her buddy Mickey endure a number of harrowing adventures before finding happiness with rich and lovable Daddy Warbucks.

• ***Little Orphan Annie*** (remake). RKO, 1932. Director: John Robertson; screenwriters: Wanda Tuchock and Tom McNamara. Cast: Mitzi Green (Annie), Buster Phelps (Mickey), May Robson (Mrs. Stewart), Kate Lawson (Mrs. Burgh), Matt Moore (Dr. Griffiths), Edgar Kennedy (Daddy Warbucks), Sidney Bracey (Butler).

• ***Little Orphan Annie*** (remake). Paramount Pictures, 1938. Director: Ben Holmes; screenwriters: Budd Schulberg, Samuel Ornitz and Endre Bohem.

Cast: Ann Gillis (Annie), J.M. Kerrigan (Daddy Warbucks), J. Farrell MacDonald, Robert Kent, Ben Welden, June Travis, James Burke, Ian MacLaren.

• ***Annie*** (remake). Columbia, 1982. Director: John Huston; screenwriter: Carol Sobieski. Cast: Albert Finney (Daddy Warbucks), Carol Burnett (Miss Hannigan), Bernadette Peters (Lily), Ann Reinking (Grace Farrell), Tim Curry (Rooster), Aileen Quinn (Annie), Geoffrey Holder (Punjab), Roger Minami (the Asp), Edward Herrmann, Lois DeBanzie, Peter Marshall.

America's Oliver Twist, *Little Orphan Annie* was first filmed by Pioneer Studios in 1919. None of the films about the mop-headed little girl, her dog, Sandy, and her fairy godfather, Daddy Warbucks, held much interest. In the 1938 version, Annie becomes involved in the fight game in the person of a Golden Gloves hopeful. The 1982 musical, based on the Broadway hit, couldn't quite decide what it was trying to be—melodrama, musical, or comedy. It failed on all three counts. The best parts of the movie were the dancing of leggy Ann Reinking and Aileen Quinn's rendition of "Tomorrow" by Martin Charnin and Charles Strouse.

519 Little Shepherd of Kingdom Come

Based on the novel by John William Fox. Story: Chad, an orphan from Kentucky, is adopted by Major Buford, who conceals his belief that the boy is his nephew. When the Civil War breaks out, Chad joins the Union Army, losing the affection of his foster father and his sweetheart, Margaret Dean. Chad, now a captain, passes through the town of his birth and becomes reacquainted with childhood sweetheart Melissa Turner, and they fall in love again. After the war he declines an offer to take over the estate of the deceased Major Buford and stays with Melissa.

• ***Little Shepherd of Kingdom Come*** (remake). First National Pictures, 1928. Silent. Director: Alfred Santell; screenwriter: Bess Meredyth. Cast: Richard Barthelmess (Chad Buford), Molly O'Day (Melissa Turner), Nelson McDowell (Old Joel Turner), Martha Mattox (Maw Turner), Claude Gillingwater (Major Buford), Doris Dawson (Margaret Dean), Victor Potel, Mark Hamilton, William Bertram.

• ***Little Shepherd of Kingdom Come*** (remake). Twentieth Century–Fox, 1961. Director: Andrew V. McLaglen; screenwriter: Barre Lyndon. Cast: Jimmie Rodgers (Chad), Luana Patten (Melissa Turner), Chill Wills (Major Buford), Linda Hutchins (Margaret Dean), Robert Dix (Caleb Turner), George Kennedy (Nathan Dillon), Kenny Miller, Neil Hamilton, Shirley O'Hara.

MGM had a 1920 silent film version of the story of the young man from Kingdom Come, Kentucky, who loses the affection of his Confederate benefactor and his sweetheart when he joins the Union Army during the Civil War. The 1961 picture with Jimmie Rodgers did not distinguish itself but it was fairly faithful to the earlier version. That could be the problem.

520 Little Shop of Horrors

Based on a story by Charles B. Griffith. Story: Seymour Krelboin, who lives with his always sick and complaining mother, works in Gravis Mushnik's florist shop. Seymour develops a new plant by combining a butterworth and a Venus fly trap and names it Audrey Jr. after Mushnik's daughter, who loves Seymour. The plant looks sickly and about to die until Seymour accidently pricks his finger and his blood flows into the plant, which screams "Feeed Me!" When Seymour accidently kills a tramp, he feeds it to Audrey Jr. and the plant grows larger. Later, when Seymour's sadistic dentist attempts to treat him without using novocaine, Seymour kills him and Audrey Jr.'s pleas for food are met. Ultimately Seymour tries to destroy his creation but becomes just another meal for the ravenous plant.

Filmgroup, 1960 (original). Director: Roger Corman; screenwriter: Charles B. Griffith. Cast: Jonathan Haze (Seymour Krelboin), Jackie Joseph (Audrey), Mel Welles (Gravis Mushnik), Jack Nicholson (Wilbur Force), Dick Miller (Fouch), Myrtle Vail (Winifred Krelboin), Leola Wendorff (Mrs. Shiva).

• ***Little Shop of Horrors*** (remake). Pinewood Studios, 1987. Director and screenwriter: Frank Oz. Cast: Rick Moranis (Seymour Krelboin), Ellen Greene (Audrey), Steve Martin (Orin Scrivello), Bill Murray (Denton), John Candy (Weird Wink Wilkenson), Vincent Gardenia (Mushnik), Tichina Arnold, Tisha Campbell, Michelle Weeks.

The original movie was shot in two days and one night and has become a cult favorite. The musical remake is of the skid-row florist shop assistant who creates a new plant that believes his master has good taste—make that tastes good. Rick Moranis is hilarious as Seymour who has the hots for Ellen Greene of the spectacular cleavage, but she bares her soul among other things for sadistic dentist and motorcycle biker Steve Martin. Others in the cast include Bill Murray, who just loves the plain inflicted on him by dentist Martin, and John Candy as a two-ton, wacky disk jockey who interviews Seymour and his bloodthirsty green friend. The voice of Audrey Jr. is Levi Stubbs, lead singer of the Four Tops. He had a hit with his rendition of "Feed Me!" Other songs include "Mean Green Mother," "Da Doc," "Downtown" and "Grow For Me."

521 Little Women

Based on the novel by Louisa May Alcott and the play by Marian De Forest. Story: The Reverend Jonathan March's four daughters, Meg, Jo, Beth and Amy, are, each in their own way, strong-willed young women. Growing up in Concord, Massachusetts, at the time of the Civil War, they endure the crises of their father's serious illness as a chaplain for the Union Army, Beth's death of scarlet fever, and the musical chair-like reassignments of Jo's various beaus. Aspiring musician Laurie, rejected by Jo, settles on the temptestuous Amy and his tutor, John Brooke, marries Meg. Jo, the writer and most forthright of the girls, wins the love of shy Professor Bhaer. After the war the remaining members of the family, now augmented by Meg's twins, share a heart-warming Christmas.

Moss Pictures, England, 1917 (original). Silent. Directors: Alexander Butler and G.B. Samuelson. Cast: Ruby Miller (Jo), Mary Lincoln (Meg), Muriel Myers (Beth), Daisy Bussell (Amy), Minna Grey (Marmee), Florence Nelson (Aunt March), Bert Darley (Rev. March), Roy Travers (John Brook), Windham Guise (Prof. Bhaer), Milton Rosmer (Laurie).

• ***Little Women*** (remake). Paramount-Artcraft Pictures, 1918. Silent. Director: Harley Knoles; screenwriter: George Kelson. Cast: Dorothy Bernard (Jo), Isabel Lamon (Meg), Lillian Hall (Beth), Florence Finn (Amy), Kate Lester (Marmee), Julia Hurley (Aunt March), George Nelson (Rev. March), Conrad Nagel (Laurie), Henry Hull (John Brooke), Lynn Hammond (Prof. Bhaer).

• ***Little Women*** (remake). RKO Pictures, 1933. Director: George Cukor; screenwriters: Sarah Y. Mason and Victor Heerman. Cast: Katharine Hepburn (Jo), Frances Dee (Meg), Jean Parker (Beth), Joan Bennett (Amy), Spring Byington (Marmee), Edna May Oliver (Aunt March), Samuel S. Hinds (Mr. March), Douglass Montgomery (Laurie), John Davis Lodge (John Brooke), Paul Lukas (Prof. Bhaer).

• ***Little Women*** (remake). MGM, 1949. Director: Mervyn LeRoy; screenwriters: Victor Heerman, Andrew Salt and Sarah Y. Mason. Cast: June Allyson (Jo), Janet Leigh (Meg), Margaret O'Brien (Beth), Elizabeth Taylor (Amy), Mary Astor (Marmee), Lucille Watson (Aunt March), Leon Ames (Mr. March), Peter Lawford (Laurie), Richard Stapley (John Brooke), Rossano Brazzi (Prof. Bhaer).

Louisa May Alcott's sentimental story plays lovingly on the viewer's emotions in the four film versions. The characters are filled with life and what happens to them matters to audiences. Tears shed upon Beth's death are sincerely felt. The young women, their parents, aunt and the men in their lives are fine roles which have been well-played by the various actors assigned to them. By far the best of the screen versions is the lavish 1933 production used by RKO as a vehicle for its new young star, Katharine Hepburn. Kate is marvelous as the enthusiastic young Jo. No less impressive were Frances Dee, Jean Parker and Joan Bennett as her sisters. Even more memorable were Spring Byington as the mother, Marmee, and Edna May Oliver as their autocratic maiden aunt. Samuel S. Hinds gave a fine performance as the father and as the suitors, Douglass Montgomery, John Davis Lodge and Paul Lukas were adequate to their tasks. The 1949 remake, while not as spectacular, still was able to pull both a smile and a tear from audiences at the appropriate times. June Allyson, although not as effective as Hepburn, gave one of her better performances and Margaret O'Brien was quite wonderful as the doomed Beth.

The Lively Set *see* **Johnny Dark**

522 The Lives of a Bengal Lancer

Based on the novel by Frances Yeats Brown. Story: Of two new officers assigned to the 41st Regiment of Bengal Lancers stationed in the dangerous open country of Northwest India, one, Lt. Stone, is the son of the commanding officer, Colonel Stone, who treats his son coldly. Young Stone and Lt. Forsythe are put in the charge of experienced frontier fighter Lt. MacGregor. News reaches the Lancers that Mohammed Khan is putting together a coalition of tribes to fight the British. Lt. Stone is kidnapped by alluring Russian spy Tania and taken to the Khan's mountain stronghold. Colonel Stone refuses to send aid, but Forsythe and MacGregor, disguised as pilgrims, gain entry to the fort,

are discovered and taken prisoner. All three of the officers are tortured and Stone finally gives the Khan the information he is seeking. The three break loose and Stone redeems himself by killing the Khan; MacGregor is killed blowing up the Khan's arsenal. The film ends with Colonel Stone awarding the Distinguished Service Order to Forsythe and his son, and pinning MacGregor's medal on the saddle of his horse.

Paramount Pictures, 1935 (original). Director: Henry Hathaway; screenwriters: Waldemar Young, John L. Balderston and Achmed Abdullah. Cast: Gary Cooper (Lt. MacGregor), Franchot Tone (Lt. Forsythe), Richard Cromwell (Lt. Stone), Sir Guy Standing (Colonel Stone), C. Aubrey Smith (Major Hamilton), Monte Blue (Hamzulia Khan), Kathleen Burke (Tania), Douglass Dumbrille (Mohammed Khan), Colin Tapley, Akim Tamiroff, Jameson Thomas, Noble Johnson.

• ***Geronimo*** (remake). Paramount Pictures, 1939. Director and screenwriter: Paul H. Sloane. Cast: Preston Foster (Captain Starrett), Ellen Drew (Alice Hamilton), Andy Devine (Sneezer), Gene Lockhart (Gillespie), William Henry (Lt. Steele), Ralph Morgan (General Steele), Pierre Watkin (Colonel White), Chief Thunder Cloud (Geronimo), Marjorie Gateson, Kitty Kelly, Monte Blue, Joseph Crehan.

The Cooper movie was a dandy adventure yarn, with plenty of action, two handsome heroes, a beautiful spy, a cowardly son, a martinent of a father and a vicious villain. The western remake is another matter, although it did surprisingly well at the box office. The script meticulously transfers the story of *Lives of a Bengal Lancer* to the Old West, using stock footage from several other western hits. The story basically deals with Preston Foster's efforts to stop an Indian war. As in *Lancer*, the Indians are bloody savages, turning on the white man for no apparent reason. Chief Thunder Cloud is very good in his brief appearance in the title role.

Living It Up *see* **Nothing Sacred**

Living on Love *see* **Early to Bed**

The Locked Door *see* **The Sign on the Door**

523 The Lodger

Based on the novel by Marie Belloc Lowndes. Story: Hitchcock's first English film is a variant on the "Jack the Ripper" story. Mrs. Bunting comes to believe that her handsome young lodger, who goes on nocturnal outings carrying a suspicious looking black bag, is the sex maniac who specializes in murdering young girls like her daughter Daisy, who has blonde curls. In fact, he is an

Opposite, top: *The* Little Women *(RKO, 1933) are, from left to right, Meg (Frances Dee), Beth (Jean Parker), Jo (Katharine Hepburn) and Amy (Joan Bennett).* Bottom: *MGM's* Little Women *(1949) are, from left to right, Amy (Elizabeth Taylor), Meg (Janet Leigh), Jo (June Allyson) and Beth (Margaret O'Brien).*

innocent man who is tracking the murderer of his sister. This, however, is not revealed until decent citizens decide he is the guilty party and he is almost torn limb from limb by an angry mob.

Gainsborough Productions, 1926 (original). Silent. Director: Alfred Hitchcock; screenwriters: Hitchcock and Eliot Stannard. Cast: Ivor Novello (the Lodger), June, Lady Inverclyde (Daisy Bunting), Marie Ault (Mrs. Bunting), Arthur Chesny (Mr. Bunting), Malcolm Keen (Joe Betts).

• ***The Lodger*** (remake). Twentieth Century–Fox, 1944. Director: John Brahm; screenwriter: Barre Lyndon. Cast: Merle Oberon (Kitty Langley), George Sanders (John Warwick), Laird Cregar (the Lodger), Sir Cedric Hardwicke (Robert Burton), Sara Allgood (Ellen Burton), Audrey Mather, Queenie Leonard, Doris Lloyd, David Clyde.

• ***Jack the Ripper*** (remake). Regal Films International/Mid-Century Films, Great Britain, 1959. Directors: Robert Baker and Monty Berman; screenwriter: Jimmy Sanster, from an original story by Peter Hammond and Colin Craig. Cast: Lee Patterson (Sam Lowry), Eddie Byrne (Inspector O'Neill), Betty McDowell (Anne Ford), Ewen Solon (Sir David Rogers), John Le Mesurier (Dr. Tranter), George Rose (Clarke), Philip Leaver, Barbara Burke, Anne Sharpe, Denis Shaw.

• ***Hands of the Ripper*** (remake). Universal Pictures, Great Britain, 1971. Director: Peter Sasdy; screenwriter: L.W. Davidson, based on a story by Edward Spencer Shaw. Cast: Eric Porter (Dr. Pritchard), Angharad Rees (Anna), Jane Merrow (Laura), Keith Bell (Michael), Derek Godfrey (Dysart), Dora Bryan, Marjorie Lawrence, Marjorie Rhodes, Norman Bird.

Films based on the Jack the Ripper legend also included *The Lodger (The Phantom Fiend)* in 1932 with Ivor Novello once again the lodger, only this time guilty of the crimes; *Room to Let* in 1950 in Great Britain; 20th Century–Fox's 1953 film *Man in the Attic;* and the 1965 British production, *A Study in Terror,* in which Sherlock Holmes discovers the identity of Jack the Ripper.

The two best productions of this theme occurred in the suspenseful Hitchcock movie and the 1944 version, starring the magnificent character actor Laird Cregar as the lodger. He's a bible-quoting zealot who butchers five prostitutes and terrorizes a music hall star, played by Merle Oberon. He is caught by Scotland Yard's finest, George Sanders, in an exciting finish. The best thing about the average 1959 film was the scenes of the workings of Scotland Yard. The 1971 thriller has Jack the Ripper killing his wife, vanishing and returning years later to force his daughter to supernaturally commit vicious murders.

Long John Silver *see* **Treasure Island**

524 The Longest Day

Based on the book by Cornelius Ryan. Story: It's an all-star cast appearing in a documentary-like film about the Allied invasion of Normandy on D-Day, the sixth of June, 1944. It tells of the build-up for the invasion in England and the heavy fighting on the beaches of France.

Twentieth Century–Fox, 1962 (original). Directors: Ken Annakin, Andrew

Marton and Bernhard Wicki; screenwriters: Cornelius Ryan, Romain Gary, James Jones, David Purcell and Jack Sedden. Cast: John Wayne (Ben Vandervoort), Robert Mitchum (Brig. Gen. Norman Cota), Robert Ryan (Brig. Gen. James M. Gavin), Richard Beymer (Pvt. Dutch Schultz), Red Buttons (Pvt. John Steele), Henry Fonda (Brig. Gen. Theodore Roosevelt), Mel Ferrer (Maj. Gen. Robert Haines), Jeffrey Hunter (Sgt. Fuller), Eddie Albert (Col. Tom Newton), Edmond O'Brien (General Raymond O. Barton), Peter Lawford (Lord Lovat), Sean Connery (Pvt. Flanagan), Curt Jurgens (Maj. Gen. Blumentritt), Gerte Frobe (Sgt. Kaffee Klatsch), Rod Steiger, Robert Wagner, Paul Anka, Fabian Forte, Tommy Sands, Sal Mineo, Roddy McDowall, Stuart Whitman, Steve Forest, Tom Tryon, Ray Danton, Mark Damon, Richard Burton, Richard Todd, Christopher Lee.

• ***Up from the Beach*** (sequel). Twentieth Century–Fox, 1965. Director: Robert Parrish; screenwriter: Howard Clewes, based on the novel *Epitaph for an Enemy* by George Barr. Cast: Cliff Robertson (Sgt. Edward Baxter), Red Buttons (Pfc. Harry Devine), Irina Demick (Lili Rolland), Marius Goring (German Commandant), Slim Pickens (Artillery Colonel), James Robertson Justice (British Beachmaster), Broderick Crawford (U.S. MP Major), George Chamarat, Francoise Rosay, Raymond Bussieres, Fernand Ledoux, Louise Chevalier, German Delbat, Paula Dehedy, Gabriel Gobin, Charles Bouilland, Georges Adet, Pierre Moncorbier.

It's an exciting war spectacular which jumps around from one star performer, in an almost cameo role, to another. It's sometimes difficult to keep up with precisely what's happening but nevertheless, considering what it is, it is good entertainment. The sequel picks up the troops after they break away from the Normandy beach, concentrating on a squad of soldiers, led by Cliff Robertson, that liberates a French village, held by the Germans, ready for a last-ditch effort.

525 Lord Jim

Based on the novel by Joseph Conrad. Story: Jim, first mate of a ship carrying Moslem pilgrims, deserts his post when the craft hits a derelict. He loses his seaman's certificate and enters into a life of dissipation. Several years later he arrives in Patusan, and becomes a respected friend and advisor of the natives. Later, three of his ex-shipmates, now pirates, show up, and are befriended by Jim. When they kill the rajah's son, according to the law, Jim's life must be forfeited. He is executed, dying in the arms of a native girl, Jewell, with whom he has fallen in love.

Famous Players/Paramount Pictures, 1925 (original). Silent. Director: Victor Fleming; screenwriter: George C. Hull. Cast: Percy Marmont (Lord Jim), Shirley Mason (Jewell), Noah Beery (Captain Brown), Raymond Hatton (Cornelius), Joseph Dowling (Stein), George Margill (Dain Waris), Nick De Ruiz (Sultan), J. Gunnis Davis, Jules Cowles, Duke Kahanamoku.

• ***Lord Jim*** (remake). Columbia–Keep Films, 1965. Director and screenwriter: Richard Brooks. Cast: Peter O'Toole (Lord Jim), James Mason (Gentleman Brown), Curt Jurgens (Cornelius), Jack Hawkins (Marlow), Eli Wallach (the General), Paul Lukas (Stein), Dahlia Lavi (the Girl), Akim Tamiroff (Schomberg), Ichizo Llami, Tatsuo Saito, Andrew Keir, Jack MacGowran, Eric Young, Noel Purcell.

It's a rambling story of a senstive young seaman, who after one moment of cowardice, spends the rest of his life with remorse and an urge to redeem himself. He helps enslaved natives, is raped by a tribal chief, and finally sacrifices his life, almost with a sense of relief. The performance of Peter O'Toole in the remake is such that he does not engender much sympathy. Jim is a rather boring character. The best acting and most interesting character is provided by James Mason.

526 Lost Horizon

Based on the novel by James Hilton. Story: Robert Conway, a world-weary British consul, his brother and a group of Americans are aboard the last plane to escape a revolution in Baskul, China. Their regular pilot has been replaced by a mysterious Oriental and after a long flight, with their destination unknown to them, the plane crash lands in the Himalayas, killing the pilot. They are soon joined by a group of natives who lead them on a treacherous journey until they begin to descend into a valley and get their first glimpse of the beautiful Shangri-La. It is a Utopian world, where illness is almost unknown and life is long and pleasant. It turns out that they were not brought to the place by accident. The ancient High Lama, finally dying, wishes Conway to take his place. Conway is tempted, enjoying the serenity of the place after all the hate and war he has had to deal with, and particularly when he meets the beautiful young Sondra. Conway's younger brother George is not as enthralled and is anxious to leave and take with him a lovely young girl, Maria. In fact Maria is considerably older than she looks, and when George finally convinces Conway to make the dangerous trek back to "civilization," she disintegrates into an ancient, wrinkled woman and dies. George is killed in an avalanche and Conway succeeds in making his way back to Shangri-La, back to Sondra, and back to his new destiny as High-Lama.

Columbia Pictures, 1937 (original). Director: Frank Capra; screenwriter: Robert Riskin. Cast: Ronald Colman (Robert Conway), Jane Wyatt (Sondra), Edward Everett Horton (Alexander B. Lovett), Margo (Maria), John Howard (George Conway), Thomas Mitchell (Henry Barnard), Isabel Jewell (Gloria Stone), H.B Warner (Chang), Sam Jaffe (High Lama).

• ***Lost Horizon*** (remake). Columbia Pictures, 1973. Director: Charles Jarrott; screenwriter: Larry Kramer. Cast: Peter Finch (Richard Conway), Liv Ullman (Catherine), Michael York (George Conway), Olivia Hussey (Maria), Bobby Van (Harry Lovett), Charles Boyer (High Lama), John Gielgud (Chang), Sally Kellerman (Sally Hughes), George Kennedy (Sam Cornelius).

The 1937 film *Lost Horizon* is one of the best-loved of Hollywood movies. At the time of its release, people were delighted to imagine a place of peace, prosperity and health after years of surviving the Depression. Today, it can be appreciated for its elaborate and imaginative production, its marvelous cast, the never-dull story and the magic of the direction by Frank Capra and the

Upfront from left to right are Ronald Colman, John Howard, Isobel Jewell and Thomas Mitchell (with Edward Everett Horton just behind him) as they catch first sight of Shangri-La in Lost Horizon *(Columbia, 1937).*

sensational screenplay by Robert Riskin. Ronald Colman's beautiful voice and noble demeanor suggest that he just might be the right man to lead the world to everlasting peace. Sam Jaffe's brief appearance as the aged High Lama is both eerie and commanding. H.B Warner as the wise and kind Chang proves once again why he is one of the best character actors in the business. Horton and Mitchell, included for comedy relief with their interchanges, become more and more loveable as their attachment for Shangri-La grows. Margo's transformation from a young beauty to a dying old hag is a triumph of makeup and camera work. Jane Wyatt made a very attractive extra inducement for Colman to remain in Paradise.

The musical remake suffered as much from the nostalgia held for the original as for its faults. Surely the cast was good enough and several, notably Peter Finch, Charles Boyer and John Gielgud, were quite good, but those old enough were secretly comparing them to Colman, Jaffe and Warner and found them wanting. Younger generations didn't find the story or the Burt Bacharach and Hal David songs, such as "The World Is a Circle," "Living Things, Growing Things" and "Question Me an Answer" very tuneful.

Lost in the Stars *see* **Cry the Beloved Country**

527 A Lost Lady

Based on the novel by Willa Cather. Story: Beautiful, spoiled Marian Forester, bored with her much older husband, runs off with Frank Ellinger, who promises to marry her when she is divorced. Marian learns that her wealthy husband has lost all his money trying to save a bank, so she returns to him out of loyalty. When she hears that Ellinger has decided not to wait for her and is planning to marry another woman, Marian attempts to go to him, but is delayed by a storm, and ends up at the home of an admirer, Neil Herbert, from where she calls Ellinger and is firmly rejected. A bit later, her husband dies and she takes to drink. Neil takes her in until he finds that she is cheating on him with yet another man. Years later, Neil finds that she is happily married to a South American millionaire.

Warner Bros., 1924. Silent. Director: Harry Beaumont; screenwriter: Dorothy Farnum. Cast: Irene Rich (Marian Forrester), Matt Moore (Neil Herbert), June Marlowe (Constance Ogden), John Roche (Frank Ellinger), Victor Potel (Ivy Peters), George Fawcett (Captain Forrester), Eva Gordon, Nanette Valone.

Warner Bros., 1934. Director: Alfred E. Green; screenwriters: Gene Markey and Kathryn Scola. Cast: Barbara Stanwyck (Marian Ormsby), Frank Morgan (Daniel Forrester), Ricardo Cortez (Ellinger), Lyle Talbot (Neil), Phillip Reed (Ned), Hobart Cavanaugh (Robert), Rafaela Ottiana, Henry Kolker, Edward McWade, Walter Walker, Samuel Hinds.

Marian Forrester is a girl who seems to know what she doesn't want, but isn't too sure of what she does want. The first film was hampered by too many flashbacks. Neither fans nor critics enjoyed the Barbara Stanwyck vehicle about a girl who loves three different men in three different ways. The producers decided to give the film a happier ending than provided by author Willa Cather, but hardly anyone cared.

The Lost Man *see* **Odd Man Out**

528 The Lost Patrol

Based on the story "Patrol" by Philip MacDonald. Story: The action takes place in the Mesopotamian desert during the British campaign against the Arabs in 1917. After suffering in the desert, a patrol, lost when their commanding officer is killed, reaches an oasis where one by one they are killed by the Arabs until only the sergeant is left as relief finally arrives.

Michael York, Peter Finch, George Kennedy, Sally Kellerman and Bobby Van are amazed by Shangri-La in the 1973 Columbia musical remake of Lost Horizon.

• ***The Lost Patrol*** (remake). RKO, 1934. Director: John Ford; screenwriter: Dudley Nichols. Cast: Victor McLaglen (Sergeant), Boris Karloff (Sanders), Wallace Ford (Morelli), Reginald Denny (Brown), J.M. Kerrigan (Quincannon), Billy Bevan, Alan Hale, Brandon Hurst, Douglas Walton, Sammy Stein, Howard Wilson, Paul Hanson.

• ***The Thirteen*** (remake). Mosfilm, 1937. Director: Mikhail Romm; screenwriters: Ivan Prut and Mikhail Romm. Cast: Ivan Novoseltsev (the Commander), Helen Kuzmina (his wife), Alexei Chistiakov (the Geologist), Arsen Fait (Lt. Colonel), Olya Kuznetsov, Andrei Dolinin, Pyoir Masokha.

• ***Sahara*** (remake). Columbia Pictures, 1943. Director: Zoltan Korda; screenwriters: John Howard Lawson and Zoltan Korda. Cast: Humphrey Bogart (Sgt. Joe Gunn), Bruce Bennett (Waco Hoyt), Lloyd Bridges (Fred Clarkson),

Rex Ingram (Tarabul), J. Carroll Naish (Giuseppe), Dan Duryea (Jimmy Doyle), Richard Nugent (Capt. Jason Halliday), Patrick O'Moore, Louis T. Mercier, Carl Harbord, Guy Kingsford, Kurt Krueger, John Wengraf, Hans Schumm.

This very suspenseful if depressing subject for a movie has a small group of people being killed off one by one. The theme has been successfully developed in murder whodunnits like *And Then There Were None.* Another popular setting for this plot technique is to follow the fate of a group of fighting men in combat. The film we have chosen to feature as the first in this entry is certainly not the first of its kind to have been made. In fact, *The Lost Patrol* itself was produced as a silent in Great Britain in 1929, with Cyril McLaglen, Victor's brother, in the same starring role. The Russian film *The Thirteen,* follows a small band of Soviet cavalrymen on its way home through a desert. They take refuge in a desert stronghold and send one of their number for help. The remaining are in a desperate battle with a much superior enemy and one by one are killed until only one is left when a rescue column arrives.

Sahara is just one example of World War II pictures of this sub-genre which could be featured. *Bataan, Wake Island, Guadalcanal Diary* and *The Immortal Sergeant* also could fill the bill. Each of these films show the helplessness of the position of a brave and dedicated group of men willing to die for their country. In such films, the producers ordinarily attempt to round up characters of various nationalities, religions and even races, to show how patriotic and united young American fighting men are.

No matter how they started out, each man about to die becomes like Nathan Hale before his bullet hits him. In *Sahara,* the Americans are a bit more resourceful and several survive, by getting the Germans attacking their desert position to believe that they have water, when in fact neither side does. Finally, the Germans surrender to get some water, and are they ever surprised. This last story was followed very closely in *The Last of the Comanches,* a 1953 film from Columbia Pictures starring Broderick Crawford, Barbara Hale, Lloyd Bridges and Martin Milner. In it, survivors of an Indian raid take refuge in an abandoned mission and play the same trick on the Comanches that Humphrey Bogart and his North Africa comrades did on the Germans.

Love *see* **Anna Karenina**

529 Love Affair

Based on an original story by Mildred Cram and Leo McCarey. Story: In this Cinderella-like film, Michael and Terry meet aboard a ship and their flirtation turns to something more serious. However, both are engaged to marry, but neither are too thrilled with their respective choices. They agree to meet again in six months at the top of the Empire State Building to see if the feelings have lasted. At the appointed time, Terry is hit by a car on her way to Michael, and when she doesn't arrive, Michael decides her feelings for him have cooled and she has married her fiancé. Later, when they meet by chance, he learns the truth and they are reunited.

RKO, 1939 (original). Director: Leo McCarey; screenwriters: Delmer Daves and Donald Ogden Stewart. Cast: Irene Dunne (Terry MacKay), Charles Boyer (Michael Marna), Maria Ouspenskaya (Grandmother Janou), Lee Bowman (Ken Bradley), Astrid Allwyn (Lois Clarke), Maurice Moscovich, Scotty Beckett, Jean Brodel (Joan Leslie), Leyland Hodgson.

• ***An Affair to Remember*** (remake). Twentieth Century–Fox, 1957. Director: Leo McCarey; screenwriters: Delmer Daves and Leo McCarey. Cast: Cary Grant (Nickie Ferrante), Deborah Kerr (Terry McKay), Cathleen Nesbitt (Grandmother Janou), Richard Denning (Kenneth), Neva Patterson (Lois), Robert Q. Lewis, Charles Watts, Fortunio Bonanova, Walter Woolf King.

This comedy-melodrama is full of wonderful surprises as the two stars give outstanding performances, filled with warmth, sincerity and charm. It was nominated for an Academy Award for Best Picture; Maria Ouspenskaya, the delightful little character actress and drama teacher, was nominated for the Best Supporting Actress award; and Mildred Cram and Leo McCarey were nominated for Best Original Story. None won. Adding to the pleasure of the film were the Harold Arlen and Ted Koehler songs, "Wishing" and "Sing My Heart."

In the remake, ex-nightclub singer Deborah Kerr falls in love with wealthy Cary Grant, whom she meets on an ocean liner. Although both are engaged to others, they agree to meet in six months atop the Empire State Building, after having straightened out their personal lives. Kerr is hit by an automobile on the way to the rendezvous and is crippled. When Grant locates her, he declares that her handicap does not deter his love. The picture was nominated for three Academy Awards, but did not win any. The nominees were Milton Krasner for Best Photography, Hugo Friedhofer for Best Score and the title song, by Harry Warren, Harold Adamson and Leo McCarey, for Best Song.

Love and the Devil *see* **The Night Watch**

Love Begins at Twenty *see* **Broken Dishes**

530 The Love Bug

Based on a story by Gordon Buford. Story: Jim Douglas is an unsuccessful racing driver until he buys a Volkswagon with a mind of its own, which he calls Herbie. Entering Herbie in races, Davis wins with ease, and believes that it is because he's such a good driver. He finally comes to understand the value of the little car when in one race Herbie literally splits in two, coming in both first and third.

Walt Disney/Buena Vista, 1969 (original). Director: Robert Stevenson; screenwriters: Bill Walsh and Don DaGradi. Cast: Dean Jones (Jim Douglas), Michelle Lee (Carole Bennett), David Tomlinson (Peter Thorndyke), Buddy Hackett (Tennessee Steinmetz), Joe E. Ross, Barry Kelley, Joe Flynn, Benson Fong.

• ***Herbie Rides Again*** (sequel). Buena Vista, 1974. Director: Robert Stevenson; screenwriter: Bill Walsh. Cast: Helen Hayes (Mrs. Steinmetz), Ken Berry

Cary Grant and Deborah Kerr seek some spiritual guidance in An Affair to Remember *(20th Century–Fox, 1957), a remake of* Love Affair *(RKO, 1939).*

(Willoughby Whitfield), Stefanie Powers (Nicole), John McIntire, Keenan Wynn, Huntz Hall, Ivor Barry, Dan Tobin, Vito Scotti.

• ***Herbie Goes to Monte Carlo*** (sequel). Buena Vista, 1977. Director: Vincent McEveety; screenwriters: Arthur Alsberg and Don Nelson. Cast: Dean Jones (Jim Douglas), Don Knotts (Wheely Applegate), Julie Sommars (Diane Darcy), Jacques Marvin (Inspector Bouchet), Roy Kinnear, Bernard Fox, Eric Braeden.

The Love Bug was one of Disney's biggest hits. The first sequel was okay as Herbie helps Helen Hayes, who is trying to save her house from being torn down to make room for a skyscraper. In the second sequel, Herbie enters a Monte Carlo rally and thwarts a band of thieves. In 1980, yet another Love Bug film was released, called *Herbie Goes Bananas*, but there's not much pep left in the little car when Charles Martin Smith and Stephen W. Burns take Herbie to South America.

531 Love 'Em and Leave 'Em

Based on the play by John Van Alstyne Weaver and George Abbott. Story: While Mame Walsh is away on vacation, her younger sister, Janie, flirts with Mame's sweetheart, Bill Billingsley. At a surprise party Mame arranges for Bill, at which she plans to announce their engagement, she catches him smooching with Janie. Mame announces she's going to adopt her sister's attitude of "Love 'em and leave 'em" from then on. She begins a flirtation with Lem Woodruff, a petty crook and gambler. Meanwhile, Janie has embezzled some money to cover her losses from betting on the horses, and her supervisor threatens to prosecute. So Janie shifts the blame to Mame. However, the girls finally get everything straightened out and Mame takes Bill back.

Famous Players/Paramount Pictures, 1926 (original). Silent. Director: Frank Tuttle; screenwriter: Townsend Martin. Cast: Evelyn Brent (Mame Walsh), Lawrence Gray (Bill Billingsley), Louise Brooks (Janie Walsh), Osgood Perkins (Lem Woodruff), Jack Egan, Marcia Harris, Edward Garvey, Vera Sisson, Joseph McClunn.

• ***The Saturday Night Kid*** (remake). Famous Players/Paramount Pictures, 1929. Director: Edward Sutherland; screenwriter: Ethel Doherty. Cast: Clara Bow (Mame), James Hall (Bill), Jean Arthur (Janie), Charles Sellon (Lem Woodruff), Ethel Wales, Frank Ross, Edna May Oliver, Hyman Meyer, Eddie Dunn, Leone Lane, Jean Harlow.

These romantic comedies about the problems a flirtatious and irresponsible younger sister causes her sibling are pleasant diversions and little else. The various actresses who portrayed Mame and Janie looked the parts and seemed to be enjoying themselves. The remake had a young Jean Harlow in a small part, but the role didn't make her a star.

532 Love from a Stranger

Based on the short story "Philomel Cottage" by Agatha Christie and the play by Frank Vosper. Story: Carol Howard falls in love with and marries suave stranger Gerald Lovell without learning very much about him. Unwittingly, she signs away her fortune to him, believing she is merely agreeing to a mortgage transfer. But before long, Carol suspects that her husband may be a maniac who marries women for their money and then murders them.

Trafalgar Films, Great Britain, 1937 (original). Director: Rowland V. Lee; screenwriter: Frances Marion. Cast: Ann Harding (Carol Howard), Basil Rathbone (Gerald Lovell), Binnie Hale (Kate Meadows), Bruce Seton, Jean Cadell, Bryan Powley, Joan Hickson, Donald Calthrop, Eugene Leahy.

• ***Love from a Stranger*** (remake). Eagle-Lion Productions, Great Britain, 1947. Director: Richard Whorf; screenwriter: Philip MacDonald. Cast: Sylvia Sidney (Cecily Harrington), John Hodiak (Manuel Cortez), John Howard (Nigel Lawrence), Ann Richards (Navis Wilson), Isobel Elsom, Ernest Cossart, Anita Sharpe-Bolster.

Basil Rathbone is superb in this Bluebeard-like story. He doesn't rant and rave, but displays his madness quite subtly and effectively. Ann Harding is convincing as the latest victim of the fanatical villain—she suffers a paralytic stroke because of his treachery. In the remake, the villain meets his end when he is run over by a team of rampaging horses, after a climactic fist fight between Sylvia Sidney's maniacal husband, John Hodiak, and her devoted suitor, detective John Howard. Hodiak's behavior from the first should have aroused Sidney's suspicions that he wasn't quite right, but apparently she was too much in love to notice.

533 Love in a Bungalow

Based on the story by Eleanor Griffin and William Rankin. Story: Mary and Jeff win a contest for the perfect "Married Couple." Unfortunately, they aren't married. Technicalities, technicalities.

Universal Pictures, 1937 (original). Director: Raymond B. McCarey; screenwriters: Austin Parker, Karen De Wolf and James Millhauser. Cast: Nan Grey (Mary), Kent Taylor (Jeff), Louise Beavers (Millie), Jack Smart (Babcock), Minerva Urecal (Mrs. Kester), Hobart Cavanaugh (Mr. Kester), Richard Carle, Marjorie Main, Margaret McWade, Arthur Hoyt, Florence Lake.

• ***Hi, Beautiful*** (remake). Universal Pictures, 1944. Director: Leslie Goodwins; screenwriter: Dick Irving Hyland. Cast: Martha O'Driscoll (Patty Callahan), Noah Beery, Jr. (Jeff), Hattie McDaniel (Millie), Walter Catlett (Bisbee), Tim Ryan (Babcock), Florence Lake (Mrs. Bisbee), Grady Sutton, Lou Lubin.

These are examples of a studio's quickly produced "B" pictures to keep some of their less important contract players earning their keep. Both films run a little over an hour, but the stories are so contrived and the acting so hurried that they seem longer. These films are so maddening, because even children in the audience realize that the conflict which fuels the story is nonsense and easily resolved if only the characters had any sense.

Love in a Wood *see* **As You Like It**

Love in the Rough *see* **Spring Fever**

Love Is in the Air *see* **Hi, Nellie**

534 Love Is News

Based on an original story by William R. Lipman and Frederick Stephani. Story: Tony Gateson is a young and beautiful heiress who has grown weary of constantly being written about by newspaper reporters who consider everything she does fair game for stories that will appeal to ordinary folks who live rather dull and uneventful lives. She turns the tables on at least one reporter, Steve Leyton, whom she considers the worst offender, by announcing that the two are engaged. Now he becomes newsworthy and becomes the butt of jokes by the other reporters. The newshound doesn't like it, but as one might expect, the story ultimately turns out to be prophetic.

Twentieth Century–Fox, 1937 (original). Director: Tay Garnett; screenwriters: Harry Tugend and Jack Yellen. Cast: Tyrone Power (Steve Leyton), Loretta Young (Tony Gateson), Don Ameche (Martin Canavan), Slim

Summerville (Judge Hart), Dudley Digges, Walter Catlett, George Sanders, Jane Darwell, Stepin Fetchit, Pauline Moore, Elisha Cook, Jr.

• ***Sweet Rosie O'Grady*** (remake). Twentieth Century–Fox, 1943. Director: Irving Cummings; screenwriter: Ken Englund. Cast: Betty Grable (Madeleine Marlowe), Robert Young (Sam Magee), Adolphe Menjou (Thomas Moran), Reginald Gardiner (Duke of Trippingham), Virginia Grey (Edna), Phil Regan, Sig Rumann, Alan Dinehart, Hobart Cavanaugh, Frank Orth.

• ***That Wonderful Urge*** (remake). Twentieth Century–Fox, 1948. Director: Robert Sinclair; screenwriter: Jay Dratler. Cast: Tyrone Power (Thomas Jefferson Tyler), Gene Tierney (Sara), Reginald Gardiner (Andre), Arleen Whelan (Jessica), Lucile Watson (Aunt Cornelia Farley), Gene Lockhart (the Judge), Lloyd Gough, Porter Hall, Richard Gaines, Taylor Holmes, Chill Wills.

In the first remake, Robert Young is an 1880s *Police Gazette* reporter who exposes the snooty musical comedy star Madeleine Marlowe as the ex–Rosie O'Grady, former burlesque queen and singer at Flugleman's Brooklyn Beer Garden. This costs Betty Grable, who stars in the title role, an English duke but she eventually settles for the reporter. Betty's songs include an oldtime melody of "My Heart Tells Me," "Country Fair" and "The Wishing Waltz." In the third film of this entry, Power is once again a cynical reporter given the assignment of assassinating the character of heiress Gene Tierney. She turns the tables on him, making him the laughingstock of the nation. In the final scene, of course, these two adversaries fall into a very nice clinch.

535 Love Story

Based on an original screenplay by Erich Segal. Story: While at Harvard, Oliver Barrett IV falls in love with Jenny Cavilleri, a student at Radcliffe. After graduation, Oliver and Jenny marry and Oliver Barrett III cuts off Oliver IV financially as he had promised he would do if his son married below his class. Now forced to work his way through law school, Oliver takes odd jobs and Jenny works as a voice coach for a boys' choir. Despite the new experience of scrimping for a millionaire's son, the two are incredibly happy together, and Oliver graduates third in his class. Now that Oliver has found a good paying job with a future, the two try to have a child, with no luck. When they undergo physicals to determine what's wrong, it's discovered that Jenny is dying of a rare disease. They spend their remaining time together and he lies down next to her in her hospital bed when she dies.

Paramount Pictures, 1970 (original). Director: Arthur Hiller; screenwriter: Erich Segal. Cast: Ali MacGraw (Jenny Cavilleri), Ryan O'Neal (Oliver Barrett IV), Ray Milland (Oliver Barrett III), John Marley (Phil Cavilleri), Russell Nype, Katherine Balfour, Sydney Walker, Robert Modica, Tommy Lee Jones.

• ***Oliver's Story*** (sequel). Paramount Pictures, 1978. Director: John Korty; screenwriters: John Korty and Erich Segal. Cast: Ryan O'Neal (Oliver Barrett), Candice Bergen (Marcie Bonwit), Nicola Pagett (Joanna Stone), Edward Binns (Phil Cavilleri), Benson Fong, Charles Haid, Kenneth McMillan, Ray Milland, Josef Sommar, Sully Boyar, Swoosie Kurtz, Meg Mundy.

It's impossible to criticize this movie, even though the story and the sentiments are trite and the acting of the two leading players is generally poor. It was such a big success at the time. Everyone was seeing the movie, reading Erich Segal's quickly released novella from his screenplay and crying their eyes out over this tragic couple. Personally, our favorite comment on the impact of the movie was the response one woman gave when asked if she cried when she saw the movie. "I sure did," she said, "Ray Milland is bald." The sequel shows how Jenny's death placed Oliver into a state of depression but as the old saying goes, "time heals all wounds," and Candice Bergen didn't hurt either.

Love That Brute *see* **Tall, Dark and Handsome**

The Loves and Times of Scaramouche *see* **Scaramouche**

The Loves of Camille *see* **Camille**

536 The Luck of the Navy

Based on the play by Clifford Mills. Story: Spy Mrs. Peel has her son, Louis, steal the submarine plans of Admiral Maybridge. These are then smuggled aboard an enemy vessel and an exciting high seas chase is on.

Graham-Wilcox, Great Britain, 1927 (original). Silent. Director: Fred Paul; screenwriter: Dion Clayton Calthrop. Cast: Evelyn Laye (Cynthia Eden), Henry Victor (Lt. Clive Stanton), Hayford Hobbs (Louis Peel), Robert Cunningham (Admiral Maybridge), Norma Whalley (Mrs. Peel), H. Agar Lyons, William Freshman.

• ***The Luck of the Navy*** (remake). Associated British Pictures, Great Britain, 1938. Director: Norman Lee; screenwriter: Clifford Grey. Cast: Geoffrey Toone (Cmdr. Clive Stanton), Judy Kelly (Cynthia Maybridge), Kenneth Kent (Prof. Suvaroff), Albert Burdon (Noakes), Clifford Evans (Lt. Peel), John Wood (Lt. Wing Eden), Edmond Breon (Admiral Maybridge), Marguerite Allan, Leslie Perrins.

In the remake, spies led by a "crippled" Professor Suvaroff pose as guests of the admiral in order to steal secret orders. These are smuggled aboard an enemy Q-ship, but Commander Clive Stanton pursues it in his destroyer and blows it out of the water.

Lucky Partner *see* **Bonne Chance**

The Lyons in Paris *see* **Life with the Lyons**

Lydia *see* **Un Carnet du Bal**

M

537 M

Based on a screenplay by Thea von Harbou. Story: "M" is the sign of recognition of a child's murderer who is sought by both the police and the underworld of a German city. The criminal element enter the quest for the person who is terrorizing the city, because the constant police raids looking for the murderer is bad for their business. After a thrilling chase the murderer is caught by the mobster organizations when a blind man who was a "witness" to the abduction of one child, hears the killer whistling the same tune, "In the Halls of the Mountain King," and chalks the letter "M" on the back of his coat. The underworld then puts the murderer on trial before their own members.

Nerofilm Production, Germany, 1931 (original). Director: Fritz Lang; screenwriter: Thea von Harbou. Cast: Peter Lorre (the Murderer), Ellen Widman, Inge Landgut, Gustaf Gruendgens, Otto Wernicke, Fritz Gnass, Fritz Odemar.

• ***M*** (remake). Columbia Pictures, 1951. Director: Joseph Losey; screenwriter: Norman Reilly Raine. Cast: David Wayne (M), Howard Da Silva (Carney), Martin Gabel (Marshall), Luther Adler, Steve Brodie, Glenn Anders, Norman Lloyd.

Without a doubt a film classic, this melodrama of a psychopathic killer of children is unforgettable and the performance of Peter Lorre as the crazed murderer stalked like a trapped animal is simply superb. The pace is just about perfect and the visual images will forever stay in the memories of viewers. The remake doesn't fare as well. The location has been moved from Germany to some place in the United States, probably California. David Wayne is a child murderer whose activities are interfering with the criminal business headed by Martin Gabel. Although the police are on Wayne's trail, it is the mobsters who find him and put him on trial before a court of beggars and underworld characters. He even has a defense lawyer, in the person of Luther Adler. The high point of the film is Wayne pleading his own case, explaining his warped mind. The police arrive just in time to prevent his summary execution. Both films are suspenseful, but the original is a brilliantly staged and visually exciting, high-tension exploration of the social implications to all of a child killer on the loose, particularly to the killer himself, while the remake is often merely morbid and gruesome. The story was also used as the basis of the 1965 film *The Vampire of Dusseldorf*.

Ma and Pa Kettle *see* **The Egg and I**

Ma and Pa Kettle at the Fair *see* **The Egg and I**

Ma and Pa Kettle at Waikiki *see* **The Egg and I**

Ma and Pa Kettle Go to Town *see* **The Egg and I**

538 Macbeth

Based on the play by William Shakespeare. Story: Three witches predict that Scottish Thane Macbeth will become king, but as he notes, "Duncan still lives." Goaded on by his ambitious wife, Macbeth disposes of this obstacle and soon afterward his wife goes mad, not being able to deal with their crime. Macbeth finds that it isn't easy to keep a usurped throne and he is defeated in battle by Macduff, who makes Duncan's son Malcolm king.

• ***Macbeth*** (remake). Reliance Films, 1916. Silent. Director: John Emerson. Cast: Herbert Tree (Macbeth), Constance Collier (Lady Macbeth), Spottiswoode Aitken (Duncan), Wilfred Lucas (Macduff), Ralph Lewis (Banquo), L. de Nowskowski (Malcolm), Bessie Buskirk, Jack Conway, Seymour Hastings.

• ***Macbeth*** (remake). Republic Pictures, 1948. Director: Orson Welles. Cast: Orson Welles (Macbeth), Jeanette Nolan (Lady Macbeth), Dan O'Herlihy (Macduff), Roddy McDowall (Malcolm), Edgar Barrier (Banquo), Erskine Sanford (Duncan), Alan Napier, John Dierkes, Keene Curtis, Peggy Webber.

• ***Joe Macbeth*** (remake). Columbia Pictures, 1955. Director: Ken Hughes; screenwriter: Philip Yordan. Cast: Paul Douglas (Joe Macbeth), Ruth Roman (Lily), Bonar Colleano (Lennie), Gregoire Aslan (Duce), Sidney James (Banky), Nicholas Stuart (Duffy), Robert Arden, Minerva Pious, Harry Green, Bill Nagy.

• ***Macbeth*** (remake). British Lion, Great Britain, 1961. Director: George Schaefer. Cast: Maurice Evans (Macbeth), Judith Anderson (Lady Macbeth), Michael Horden (Banquo), Ian Bannen (Macduff), Felix Aylmer (Doctor), Malcolm Keen (Duncan), Jeremy Brett (Malcolm), Megs Jenkins, Barry Warren, Charles Carson, George Rose.

• ***Macbeth*** (remake). Playboy/Caliban, Great Britain, 1972. Director: Roman Polanski; screenwriters: Polanski and Kenneth Tynan. Cast: Jon Finch (Macbeth), Francesca Annis (Lady Macbeth), Martin Shaw (Banquo), Nicholas Selby (Duncan), John Stride (Ross), Stephan Chase (Malcolm), Terence Bayler (Macduff), Paul Shelley, Andrew Laurence, Frank Wylie, Bernard Ardhard, Brian Purchase.

Shakespeare's twenty-seventh of his thirty-seven dramas also reached the screen in 1905, 1908, 1909, 1910, 1911, 1912, 1913, 1917, 1920, 1922, 1946, 1950, 1952, 1958, 1960 and 1962. The 1958 production was the Japanese version, *Throne of Blood,* directed by Akira Kurosawa and starring Toshiro Mifune and Isuzu Yamada in the Macbeth and Lady Macbeth–like roles. Reviewers of the 1916 silent questioned if Shakespeare's play could be successful on the screen, as it was the Bard's language that has kept his work popular over the centuries. The Orson Welles production was done on a shoestring and it showed in the paper-mache sets. The great one's performance was uneven and Jeanette Nolan was not up to the role of Lady Macbeth, but still it was a film shown in schools across the country to high school students studying *Macbeth.*

The 1955 analogy is of a modern gangster, Paul Douglas, egged on by his wife, Ruth Roman, for supremacy in the underworld. They eliminate the kingpin and his wife, but in turn suffer the expected downfall at the hands of the couple's son. The two British productions of 1961 and 1972 are technically well done but especially in the case of the Roman Polanski version, far from what Shakespeare might have envisioned.

539 McFadden's Flats

Based on the play *McFadden's Row of Flats* by Gus Hill. Story: One of Dan

McFadden's closest friends is barber Jock McTavish, and the admiration continues into the next generation as Jock's son, Sandy, falls in love with Dan's daughter, Mary Ellen. Having prospered as a contractor, Dan, to the dismay of Sandy, sends Mary Ellen away to a finishing school. The two friends argue more frequently as Dan's ambition to complete an apartment building grows. Overextending himself, Dan is in deep financial straits, but Jock bails him out, and the two friends are harmonious again as their children plan to marry.

First National Pictures, 1927 (original). Silent. Director: Richard Wallace; screenwriter: Charles Logue. Cast: Charles Murray (Dan McFadden), Chester Conklin (Jock McTavish), Edna Murphy (Mary Ellen McFadden), Larry Kent (Sandy McTavish), Aggie Herring, De Witt Jennings, Cissy Fitzgerald, Dorothy Dwan, Freeman Wood, Dot Farley.

• ***McFadden's Flats*** (remake). Paramount Pictures, 1935. Director: Ralph Murphy; screenwriter: Arthur Caesar. Cast: Walter C. Kelly (Dan McFadden), Andy Clyde (Jock McTavish), Richard Cromwell (Sandy McTavish), Betty Furness (Molly McFadden), Jane Darwell, George Barbier, Phyllis Brooks, Howard Wilson.

The remake of the story about two old codgers, who alternate between friendship and feuding as their children fall in love, has some expert clowning from Walter C. Kelly and Andy Clyde, even though the material seemed and was old in 1935. Both films stereotype the Irish and the Scots, but then that was par for the course at the time and saved on character development efforts.

540 McHale's Navy

Based on a story by Si Rogers and the television series of the same name. Story: It's a 99-minute version of the then popular television series consisting of just about the same antics. McHale and his zany crew of PT-73 continue to outwit Captain Binghampton and romance some French gals while now and then fighting the Japanese in World War II.

Universal Pictures, 1964 (original). Director: Edward J. Montague; screenwriters: Frank Gill, Jr. and G. Carleton Brown. Cast: Ernest Borgnine (Lt. Commander Quinton McHale), Joe Flynn (Capt. Wallace Binghampton), Jean Willes (Margot Monet), Tim Conway (Ensign Charles Parker), Claudine Longet (Andrea Bouchard), Carl Ballentine, Gary Vinson, Billy Sands, Edson Stroll.

• ***McHale's Navy Joins the Army*** (sequel). Universal Pictures, 1965. Director and screenwriter: Edward J. Montague. Cast: Joe Flynn (Capt. Wallace Binghampton), Tim Conway (Ensign Charles Parker), Gary Vinson (Christy Christopher), Bob Hastings, Billy Sands, Edson Stroll, John Wright.

On the small screen, *McHale's Navy* was moderately popular. It should have been satisfied with its limited success. On the big screen, it made Abbott and Costello movies look cerebral. Tim Conway, who would become a fine comedian later on TV's *The Carol Burnett Show,* was here still only polishing his craft. Joe Flynn as the put-upon Captain Binghampton maintained his high-decibel unhappiness every time he was on camera, and that was too often. Ernest Borgnine looked bored with the whole thing and wisely did not appear in the sequel, when the PT crew finds themselves in Europe, mixed up with a Soviet merchant ship.

McHale's Navy Joins the Army *see* **McHale's Navy**

541 Macon County Line

Based on a story by Max Baer. Story: Based on a true story, three hell-raisers in a Louisiana town are so unwelcome that they are falsely accused of murder. Much bloodshed occurs before the surprise ending.

American International, 1974 (original). Director: Richard Compton; screenwriters: Max Baer and Richard Compton. Cast: Alan Vint (Chris Dixon), Jesse Vint (Wayne Dixon), Cheryl Waters (Jenny), Max Baer (Deputy Reed Morgan), Geoffrey Lewis (Hamp), Joan Blackman (Carol Morgan), Sam Gilman, Timothy Scott.

• ***Return to Macon County*** (sequel). American International, 1975. Director and screenwriter: Richard Compton. Cast: Nick Nolte (Bo Hollinger), Don Johnson (Harley McKay), Robin Mattson (Junell), Robert Viharo (Sgt. Whittaker), Eugene Daniels (Tom), Matt Greene, Devon Ericson, Ron Prather, Philip Crews, Laura Sayer.

See what happens as a result of the Clampetts (TV's "The Beverly Hillbillies") sending Jethro to school all the way up to fifth grade? He comes up with a Southern redneck story, filled with blood and guts. Ah, Max, ignorance is bliss. It's hard to believe that there were enough drive-in movies still around in the mid-'70s to justify making these features. In the unintentionally funny sequel, two shiftless youths pick up a waitress and make the mistake of wandering into Macon County where they encounter a maniacal sheriff.

Mad About Men *see* **Miranda**

542 Mad About Music

Based on a story by Marcello Burke and Frederick Kolmer. Story: Gloria Harkinson's vain Hollywood actress mother, Gwen Taylor, keeps the teenager well-hidden in a boarding school in Switzerland, so as to maintain her own image of youthfulness. Gloria invents an adventurous father for herself and boasts of his exploits to her schoolmates and teachers. When it's put up or shut up time, Gloria recruits Richard Todd to impersonate her fantasy parent, which he does to perfection.

Universal Pictures, 1938 (original). Director: Norman Taurog; screenwriters: Bruce Manning and Felix Jackson. Cast: Deanna Durbin (Gloria Harkinson), Herbert Marshall (Richard Todd), Arthur Treacher (Tripps), Gail Patrick (Gwen Taylor), William Frawley (Dusty Rhodes), Jackie Moran (Tommy), Helen Parrish, Marcia Mae Jones, Christian Rub, Charles Peck.

• ***The Toy Tiger*** (remake). Universal Pictures, 1956. Director: Jerry Hopper; screenwriter: Ted Sherdeman. Cast: Jeff Chandler (Rick Todd), Laraine Day (Gwen Taylor), Tim Hovey (Timmie Harkinson), Cecil Kellaway (James),

Richard Haydn (John), David Janssen, Judson Pratt, Jacqueline de Witt, Mary Field.

Mad About Music was Deanna Durbin's third feature and first where she got top billing. The film's story is nonsense but between the sweetness of Deanna and the polish of Herbert Marshall, audiences didn't seem to mind. The star sang "I Love to Whistle" by Harold Adamson and Jimmy McHugh, and Gounod's "Ave Maria" with the Vienna Boy's Choir.

The remake reworked the story, having scene-stealing Tim Hovey as a lonely, fatherless kid who cons executive Jeff Chandler into pretending he's the lad's father. When Chandler meets Hovey's mother, played by Laraine Day, the chances of a nice family trio by the end of the picture seems a certainty. It's not much, but if one likes cute kids, Hovey may be just the thing.

Mad Wednesday *see* **The Freshman**

The Mad Room *see* **Ladies in Retirement**

543 Madame Bovary

Based on the novel by Gustave Flaubert. Young and beautiful Emma Bovary finds life in a small, provincial French town and marriage to poor and uninteresting Dr. Charles Bovary intolerable. She seeks excitement through affairs, squanders her husband's savings, loses the affection of her child and with nothing left to live for commits suicide by taking arsenic.

• ***Unholy Love*** (original). First Division/Allied Pictures, 1932. Director: Albert Ray; screenwriter: Frances Hyland. Cast: Joyce Compton (Sheila Bailey), Lila Lee (Jane Bardford), H.B. Warner (Dr. Gregory), Beryl Mercer (Mrs. Cawley), Lyle Talbot (Jerry Gregory), Ivan Lebedoff, Jason Robards, Sr., Kathlyn Williams, Frances Rich, Richard Carlyle.

• ***Madame Bovary*** (remake). CIE Films, France, 1934. Director and screenwriter: Jean Renoir. Cast: Valentine Tessier (Emma Bovary), Pierre Renoir (Charles Bovary), Fernand Fabre (Rodolphe), Alice Tissot (Mrs. Bovary), Pierre Larquey (Hippolyte), Daniel Lecourtois, Helena Manson, Max Dearly.

• ***Madame Bovary*** (remake). Casion Film Exchange, Germany, 1937. Director and screenwriter: Gerhard Lamprecht. Cast: Pola Negri (Emma Bovary), Albert Waecher (Charles Bovary), Werner Scheff (Rodolphe).

• ***Madame Bovary*** (remake). MGM, 1949. Director: Vincente Minnelli; screenwriter: Robert Ardrey. Cast: Jennifer Jones (Emma Bovary), James Mason (Gustave Flaubert), Van Heflin (Charles Bovary), Louis Jourdan (Rodolphe Boulanger), Christopher Kent (Leon Dupuis), Gene Lockhart (J. Homais), Frank Allenby, Gladys Cooper, John Abbott, Henry Morgan, George Zucco.

Other filmings of the scandalous behavior of Emma Bovary were made in Argentina in 1947 and a West German–Italian production, *Madame Bovary (Play the Game Or Leave the Bed)*, in 1969.

As the subject matter of Flaubert's novel had outraged people in every country in which it appeared, movie producers were very cautious in their productions, which usually resulted in making adultery and suicide boring. MGM went so far as to frame the story with the trial of Flaubert for corrupting public morals. This device of a story within a story may have satisfied moralists but it did not make for good cinema. At least Jennifer Jones fit the description of the unfaithful wife, young and beautiful. Pola Negri was nearly forty when she made her attempt to portray the vixen. None of the productions seemed to care why this particular young woman so casually threw off prevailing moral standards. Was she brave, stupid, uncaring, ahead of her time? Was she only doing what many other wives stuck in a dull marriage wished to do but did not have the courage? The movies don't supply any credible answers.

544 Madame Butterfly

Based on the play by David Belasco. Story: Cho-Cho-San is a simple Japanese girl who has an affair with American naval officer Lt. Pinkerton, who crams an entire married life into his six weeks' shore leave. He then abandons her. She has their child but she commits suicide when she finally realizes he is married and is never coming back to her.

• ***Madame Butterfly*** (remake). Paramount Pictures, 1915. Silent. Director: Marshal Nelian; screenwriter: uncredited. Cast: Mary Pickford (Cho-Cho-San/Madame Butterfly), Marshal Nelian (Lt. Pinkerton), Olive West (Suzuki), Jane Hall (Adelaide), Lawrence Wood, Caroline Harris, M.W. Rale, N.T. Carleton, David Burton, Frank Eekum.

• ***The Toll of the Sea*** (remake). Metro, 1922. Silent. Director: Chester M. Franklin; screenwriter: Frances Marion. Cast: Anna May Wong (Lotus Flower), Kenneth Harlan (Allen Carver), Beatrice Bentley (Barbara Carver), Baby Marion, Etta Lee, Ming Young.

• ***Madame Butterfly*** (remake). Paramount Pictures, 1932. Director: Marion Gering; screenwriters: Josephine Lovett and Joseph Mancure March. Cast: Sylvia Sidney (Cho-Cho-San), Cary Grant (Lt. Pinkerton), Charles Ruggles (Lt. Barton), Sandor Kallay (Goro), Irving Pichel (Yomadori), Helen Jerome Eddy, Edmund Breeze, Judith Vosselli, Louise Carter.

The story of Madame Butterfly was also filmed in 1910, 1919, 1939 and 1970. The 1922 film supposedly tells of a different tragic love affair between an Oriental girl and an American, but despite the setting being China, the desertion by the man and the suicide of the girl seem very familiar. Sylvia Sidney, despite her use of pidgin English, was appealing in the 1932 film but Cary Grant was stiff as a board.

545 Madame Spy

Based on the novel by *Under False Flags* by Max Kimmich. Story: This implausible romantic melodrama has Maria, the Russian wife of German Captain Franck, as an agent known only as B-24. Her husband, working for the Austrian Secret Police, is on the trail of this same spy, B-24.

• ***Madame Spy*** (remake). Universal Pictures, 1934. Director: Karl Freund; screenwriters: Johannes Brandt, Joseph Than, Max Kimmich and William Hurlburt. Cast: Fay Wray (Maria), Nils Asther (Captain Franck), Edward

Arnold (Schultz), John Miljan (Weber), David Torrence (Seefeldt), Douglas Walton (Karl), Oscar Apfel, Vince Barnett, Robert Ellis, Mabel Marden, Noah Beery, Sr., Rollo Lloyd.

• ***Madame Spy*** (remake). Universal Pictures, 1942. Director: Roy William Neill; screenwriters: Lynn Riggs and Upson Young. Cast: Constance Bennett (Joan Bannister), Don Porter (David Bannister), John Litel (Peter), Edward S. Brophy (Mike Reese), John Eldredge (Carl Gordon), Nana Bryant (Alicia Rolf), Selmer Jackson, Edmund MacDonald, Jimmy Conlin, Nino Pipitone, Cliff Clark.

Max Kimmich's story was first filmed in Germany in 1932 as *Unter Falschen Flaggen.* For the 1942 film the plot was similar, although based on an original story by Upson Young. In it, Constance Bennett is an attractive, newly married wife suspected of being a Nazi agent. Actually, she's an American counter-espionage operator. That's about all there is to this 63-minute, ordinary movie.

546 Madame X

Based on the play by Alexandre Bisson. Story: Jacqueline leaves her husband, Floriot, for another man. When her son becomes ill, she returns to care for him, but her husband refuses to allow it. Thus begins her path of degradation. Years later, she becomes involved with a cardsharp, Laroque. When they return to France, this unworthy lout decides because of her name, he can gain a handsome sum by blackmail. Jacqueline shoots the cad and in her subsequent trial, she is defended by her now-grown son, Raymond, who does not know she is his mother. Rather than let her son learn of her degrading life, she confesses to the killing, still using an assumed identity. For him, she remains Madame X.

• ***Madame X*** (remake). MGM, 1929. Director: Lionel Barrymore; screenwriter: Willard Mack. Cast: Ruth Chatterton (Jacqueline), Lewis Stone (Floriot), Raymond Hackett (Raymond), Holmes Herbert (Noel), Eugenie Besserer (Rose), Ullrich Haupt (Laroque), John P. Edington, Mitchell Lewis, Sidney Toler.

• ***Madame X*** (remake). MGM, 1937. Director: Sam Wood; screenwriter: John Meehan. Cast: Gladys George (Jacqueline Fleuriot), John Beal (Raymond Fleuriot), Warren William (Bernard Fleuriot), Reginald Owen (Maurice Dourel), William Henry, Henry Daniell, Phillip Reed, Lynne Carver, Emma Dunn, Ruth Hussey.

• ***Madame X*** (remake). Universal Pictures, 1966. Director: David Lowell Rich; screenwriter: Jean Holloway. Cast: Lana Turner (Holly Parker), John Forsythe (Clay Anderson), Constance Bennett (Estelle Anderson), Ricardo Montalban (Phil Benton), Burgess Meredith (Dan Sullivan), Keir Dullea (Clay Anderson, Jr.), John Van Dreelan, Virginia Grey, Warren Stevens.

The story of the woman who paid and paid for her sins was also filmed in 1909 with Jane Harding, in 1916 with Dorothy Donnelly and in 1920 with Pauline Frederick. Other sound versions were made in 1931, 1948 and 1960. Both Lionel Barrymore and Ruth Chatterton were nominated for Academy Awards for their work on the early talkie, but neither won. The 1937 picture with Gladys George was a competent remake with a fine cast. The Lana Turner

John Forsythe brags to his wife (Lana Turner) about some of his ancestors, pictured in the background, in the 1966 Universal remake of Madame X.

attempt was the most elaborate production and the least satisfying. Turner was wooden and the men in her life, including Keir Dullea as the unsuspecting son, seemed to move through their parts as if in a trance. Besides the sadness of the plot and the production, fans were sad that this would be the beautiful Constance Bennett's last film, her death coming shortly after its completion.

Mademoiselle Fifi *see* **The Woman Disputed**

547 Mademoiselle Modiste

Based on the comic opera by Henry Martyn Blossom and Victor Herbert. Story: Hat dealer Hiram Bent from St. Louis visits the salon of Madame Claire of Paris to see her new line. The saleswoman is Fifi, who makes a rather large

Ruth Chatterton is in the dock, defended against a murder charge by Raymond Hackett, the son she lost years and years ago, in Madame X *(MGM, 1929).*

sale and wins Hiram's admiration for her business sense. While delivering a hat to the fiancée of Etienne Du Beauvray, Fifi complains to an officer, who is none other than Du Beauvray himself, about his horse destroying the hat. This is the beginning of a romance between Fifi and Etienne, with his former fiancée soon forgotten. Then, still impressed by her sales ability, Hiram Bent buys out Madame Claire, and establishes Fifi as "Mademoiselle Modiste." Suspicious of Bent's intentions, Etienne challenges him to a duel but the misunderstanding is cleared up and Fifi is reunited with Etienne.

Corinne Griffith Productions/First National Pictures, 1926 (original). Silent. Director: Robert Z. Leonard; screenwriter: Adelaide Heilbron. Cast: Corinne Griffith (Fifi), Norman Kerry (Etienne), Willard Louis (Hiram Bent), Dorothy Cumming (Marianne), Rose Dione (Madame Claire).

• ***Kiss Me Again*** (remake). First National Pictures, 1931. Director: William Seiter; screenwriter: Henry Blossom. Cast: Bernice Claire (Fifi), Walter Pidgeon (Paul de St. Cyr), Edward Everett Horton (Rene), Claude Gillingwater (Count de St. Cyr), Frank McHugh (Francois), Judith Voselli, June Collyer.

The remake puts the Victor Herbert music back into the story, including "I Want What I Want When I Want It" and the lovely title song. The screening of a stage musical and accounting for the difference in the two mediums has long been a problem for the motion picture industry, and it certainly wasn't even considered in filming this old-fashioned operetta. It's quaint but it's not very entertaining.

548 Madonna of the Streets

Based on the play *The Ragged Messenger* by William Babington Maxwell. Story: When the Reverend John Morton inherits his uncle's fortune, the latter's mistress, Mary Carlson, feeling the money is rightly hers, shows up, uses her wiles on the innocent clergyman, and is soon his wife. To her dismay, Morton spends the money on charitable works. When he learns Mary's true identity and the fact that she has been unfaithful to him, he sends her away. Years later, they are reunited when she appears at a home for fallen women that he is dedicating.

First National Pictures, 1924 (original). Silent. Director: Edwin Carewe; screenwriter: Frank Griffin. Cast: Nazimova (Mary Carlson/Mary Ainsleigh), Milton Sills (Rev. John Morton), Claude Gillingwater (Lord Patrington), Courtenay Foote, Wallace Beery, Anders Randolf, Tom Kennedy, John T. Murray.

• ***Madonna of the Streets*** (remake). Columbia Pictures, 1930. Director: John S. Robertson; screenwriter: Jo Swerling. Cast: Evelyn Brent (May Fisher), Robert Ames (Peter Morton), Ivan Linow (Slumguillion), Josephine Dunn (Marion), Edwards Davis, Zack Williams, Ed Brody, Richard Tucker.

In the remake, Evelyn Brent is shocked to learn that on his death her millionaire lover has left all his money to his nephew, Robert Ames, who runs a mission on San Francisco's Barbary Coast. She takes a post as Ames' assistant, working closely at his side—a bit too close, decides Ames' fiancée, played by Josephine Dunn. Brent falls in love with Ames, and refuses to respond when he advertises for his uncle's mistress so he can turn the inheritance over to her. The couple are married, but when her true identity comes out Ames, feeling betrayed, sends her away, only to ask her to come back when she saves his life.

The Magic Cloak of Oz *see* **The Wizard of Oz**

The Magnificent Ambersons *see* **Pampered Youth**

The Magnificent Lie *see* **Fool's Paradise**

549 Magnificent Obsession

Based on the novel by Lloyd C. Douglas. Story: When playboy Bobby Merrick's drunken and wastrel ways cause the blindness of Helen Hudson, he develops a "magnificent obsession" to redeem himself and restore Helen's sight. He dedicates himself to six years of study, becoming a brilliant eye specialist and cures the woman he has also come to love.

Universal Pictures, 1935 (original). Director: John M. Stahl; screenwriters: George O'Neill, Sarah T. Mason and Victor Heerman. Cast: Irene Dunne (Helen Hudson), Robert Taylor (Bobby Merrick), Charles Butterworth (Tommy Masterson), Betty Furness (Joyce Hudson), Sara Haden (Nancy Ashford), Ralph Morgan, Henry Armetta, Gilbert Emery, Arthur Hoyt, Lowell Durham, Alan Davis.

• ***Magnificent Obsession*** (remake). Universal Pictures, 1954. Director: Douglas Sirk; screenwriter: Robert Blees. Cast: Jane Wyman (Helen Phillips), Rock Hudson (Bob Merrick), Barbara Rush (Joyce Phillips), Agnes Moorehead (Nancy Ashford), Otto Kruger (Randolph), Gregg Palmer, Sara Shane, Paul Cavanaugh, Judy Nugent, George Lynn, Richard H. Cutting.

Talk about wringing out the emotions. These films leave no tear unshed with a premise that is difficult to accept. Everyone, after Merrick's miraculous transformation brought on by the woman's blindness, is so damn good and self-sacrificing that one's reaction might not be a sniffle but a snicker. The directors of these two films are so skillful at hiding the fact that the story is dishonest and without sufficient complexity to be considered a classic woman's picture that they certainly drew in the audiences at the time of their releases. Jane Wyman was even nominated for an Academy Award for her performance, but did not win. Rock Hudson and Robert Taylor were good enough for what was expected of them, and that wasn't much.

Magnum Force *see* **Dirty Harry**

Magoo at Sea *see* **Moby Dick**

550 Main Street

Based on the novel by Sinclair Lewis. Story: Carol Milford, an intelligent, artistic girl, moves from a big city to Gopher Prairie to marry Dr. Will Kennicott,

Robert Taylor, sans moustache, Betty Furness and Charles Butterworth look plenty worried in this scene from the weeper Magnificent Obsession *(Universal, 1935).*

one of the town's leading lights. Feeling the locals are boobs and Gopher Prairie to be the end of the world as far as culture is concerned, Carol tries to do something about the condition she deplores. The townspeople don't respond to her leadership, believing she's putting on airs. The only person who seems to share her views is Erik Valborg. Despite his entreaties, she refuses his offer of love and escape from the hick town. When he leaves without her, Carol is denounced as the cause of Erik's waywardness. Will defends his wife and shames the townspeople for spreading malicious gossip about her. Carol sees her husband and the townspeople in a new light and vows to accept life in Gopher Prairie.

Warner Bros., 1923 (original). Silent. Director: Harry Beaumont; screenwriter: Julien Josephson. Cast: Florence Vidor (Carol Milford), Monte Blue (Dr. Will Kennicott), Robert Gordon (Erik Valborg), Harry Myers (Dave Dyer), Noah Beery (Adolph Valborg), Alan Hale (Miles Bjornstram), Louise Fazenda (Bea Sorenson), Anne Schaefer, Josephine Crowell, Otis Harlan, Gordon Griffith, Lon Poff, J.P. Lockney.

• ***I Married a Doctor*** (remake). Warner Bros., 1936. Director: Archie Mayo; screenwriter: Casey Robinson. Cast: Pat O'Brien (Dr. William P. Kennicott), Josephine Hutchinson (Carol Kennicott), Ross Alexander (Erik Valborg), Guy Kibbee (Samuel Clark), Louise Fazenda (Bea Sorenson), Olin Howland (Dave Dyer), Margaret Irving, Alma Lloyd, Grace Stafford, Ray Mayer.

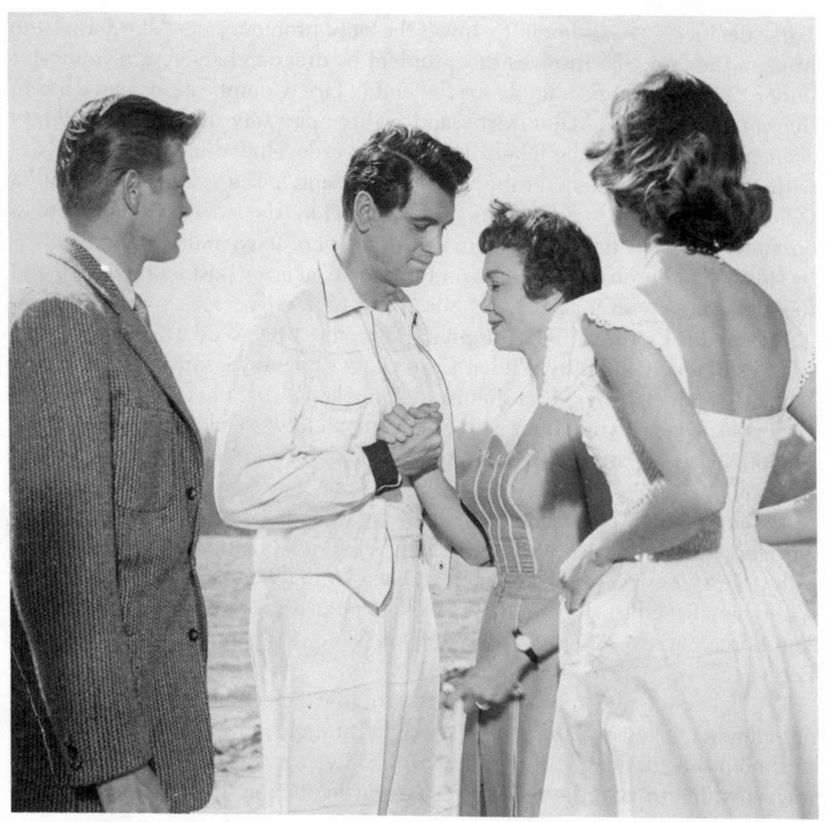

Rock Hudson reassuringly holds Jane Wyman's hand tightly in the 1954 Universal remake of Magnificent Obsession.

Sinclair Lewis' novel *Main Street* made better reading than viewing. The initial attempt to film it has a good cast but the production is tiresome. The casting in the remake is questionable, although critics of the time found much to praise in the work of Pat O'Brien as the hardworking, level-headed midwestern doctor and Josephine as his big city, liberal-thinking wife. This disparity in opinion of quality can be explained by noting that often the circumstances of when one sees a performance must be factored in, when judging its value. What is safe to say about the remake is that director Mayo has done a credible job in bringing to the screen a popular novel. Why the name was changed is not so clear.

551 The Major and the Minor

Based on a story by Fannie Kilbourne and the play by Edward Charles Carpenter. Story: Susan Applegate, disillusioned by her lack of success in New

York, decides to head home to Iowa, the only problem being she hasn't the price of the fare. She resolves this problem by dressing herself as a youngster under 12 in order to be eligible for the child's fare. Complications place her in the compartment of Major Kirby and a three-day stay over at the military academy for boys that he heads. Here our overdeveloped moppet is pursued with enthusiasm by some of the young cadets and Susan is also able to pull a Cinderella-like ploy to grab Kirby's interest. Before she leaves, Susan is able to circumvent Kirby's fiancée's plan to keep him out of active military service. Kirby stops off at Susan's Iowa home on the way to an army post on the coast, and the glass slipper, so to speak, fits Susan just perfectly.

Paramount Pictures, 1942 (original). Director: Billy Wilder; screenwriters: Charles Brackett and Billy Wilder. Cast: Ginger Rogers (Susan Applegate), Ray Milland (Major Kirby), Rita Johnson (Pamela Hill), Robert Benchley (Mr. Osborne), Diana Lynn (Lucy Hill), Edward Fielding (Colonel Hill), Frankie Thomas (Cadet Osborne), Raymond Roe, Charles Smith, Larry Nunn, Billy Dawson.

• ***You're Never Too Young*** (remake). Paramount Pictures, 1955. Director: Norman Taurog; screenwriter: Sydney Sheldon. Cast: Dean Martin (Bob Miles), Jerry Lewis (Wilbur Hoolick), Diana Lynn (Nancy Collins), Nina Foch (Gretchen Brendin), Raymond Burr (Noonan), Mitzi McCall (Skeets), Veda Ann Borg, Margery Maude, Romo Vincent, Nancy Kulp, Milton Frome, Donna Percy.

The 1942 comedy is a light and fluffy yarn in which Ginge never really looks pre-adolescent and Milland should see right through her pose—for that matter, so should the conductor. It didn't matter; it was fun and as the nation was at war, anything to take the mind off what was happening to sons, fathers, boyfriends, etc., was welcomed.

In the Martin and Lewis feature, Jerry is a barber's apprentice who unwittingly obtains a stolen diamond. As he runs from the jewel thief, he disguises himself as an 11 year old in an outlandish sailor's suit and shares a cabin with pretty Diana Lynn on a train which takes them to a girl's school where she is employed. Jerry, as the youngster, has to fight off the advances of the aggressive bobby-soxers. You can bet that Dean Martin is not too far from this action, acting as Lewis' competition for Diana Lynn. There's a very funny climax with Lewis on water skis and Dean driving a motor boat that gets high marks among movie chase scenes.

Make Me a Star *see* **Merton of the Movies**

552 The Making of O'Malley

Based on the short story by Gerald Beaumont. Story: Patrolman Jim O'Malley is a stickler for the letter of the law. He is assigned to duty near a grade school where he becomes a favorite with the children and he develops a yen for beautiful teacher Lucille Thayer. He arranges for an operation that cures little lame Margie. Jim discovers the hideout of a gang of bootleggers and arrests all but the ringleader Herbert Browne, who escapes. Later, at a party held by

Lucille, he spots Browne, only to discover that the crook is her fiancée. Rather than hurt Lucille, Jim allows Browne to get away and for this dereliction of duty he is thrown off the force in disgrace. Danny the Dude (Margie's father whom Jim had sent to prison) learns of O'Malley's kindness to his daughter, exposes Browne and Jim's sacrifice becomes known. He is reinstated to the force with full honors and wins Lucille's love.

First National Pictures, 1925 (original). Silent. Director: Lambert Hillyer; screenwriter: Eugene Clifford. Cast: Milton Sills (Jim O'Malley), Dorothy Mackaill (Lucille Thayer), Helen Rowland (Margie), Warner Richmond (Danny the Dude), Thomas Carrigan (Herbert Browne), Julia Hurley, Claude King, Allen Brander, Charles Graham, Jack De Lacey.

• ***The Great O'Malley*** (sequel). Warner Bros., 1937. Director: William Dieterle; screenwriters: Milton Krims and Tom Reed. Cast: Pat O'Brien (Patrick O'Malley), Sybil Jason (Barbara Phillips), Humphrey Bogart (John Phillips), Freida Inescourt (Mrs. Phillips), Ann Sheridan (Judy Nolan), Donald Crisp (Capt. Cromwell), Henry O'Neill, Mary Gordon, Michael Colcord, Frank Sheridan, Lillian Harmer, Delmar Watson, Frank Reicher.

In the sequel, Pat O'Brien is a tough Irish cop, don't you know. But his heart is softened by a wee crippled tyke, played by Sybil Jason. The child's father is Bogart, a criminal who later is shot by O'Brien, despite the fact that the latter is responsible for getting a surgeon to cure the child. Ann Sheridan plays the school teacher in this version of the Gerald Beaumont story.

Male and Female ***see*** **The Admirable Crichton**

553 The Male Animal

Based on the play by James Thurber and Elliott Nugent. Story: Shy, timid Tommy Turner's quiet academic life as an English professor is interrupted by two events. The first is the imminent arrival of his wife Ellen's former sweetheart, Joe Ferguson, an ex-college football star. The second is the flak caused by student newspaper editor Michael Barnes' proposal to read executed anarchist Vanzetti's farewell letter to his daughter aloud to Tommy's class. At a football game, Tommy and Michael drink a great deal and together muse on the male animal's role in love and life. After the game, Tommy challenges Ferguson to a fight, which doesn't occur and Michael reads the letter which proves to be non-inflammatory. Ellen tells her husband that she loves only him and things revert to normal in the halls of ivy.

Warner Bros., 1942 (original). Director: Elliott Nugent; screenwriters: Julius and Philip Epstein, and Stephen Morehouse Avery. Cast: Henry Fonda (Tommy Turner), Olivia de Havilland (Ellen Turner), Jack Carson (Joe Ferguson), Herbert Anderson (Michael Barnes), Don De Fore, Joan Leslie, Ivan Simpson, Minna Phillips, Eugene Pallette, Regina Wallace, Bobby Barnes, Hattie McDaniel, Jean Ames, Frank Mayo.

• ***She's Working Her Way Through College*** (remake). Warner Bros., 1952. Director: Bruce Humberstone; screenwriter: Peter Milne. Cast: Ronald Reagan (John Palmer), Virginia Mayo (Angela Gardner), Gene Nelson (Don

Weston), Don De Fore (Shep Slade), Phyllis Thaxter (Helen Palmer), Patrice Wymore, Roland Winters, Raymond Greenleaf, Norman Bartold, Amanda Randolph, George Meader, Eve Miller.

The Male Animal is a pleasant enough little comedy, but it doesn't catch either Fonda or de Havilland at their best. After all the things that have happened on college campuses since 1942, today's audiences may wonder what's all the fuss. Academic freedom is regularly denied by proponents of causes from both the left and the right, usually with the feeble argument that some messages are too dangerous to be spoken or heard. This, then, is what is of lasting merit in the Thurber and Nugent work.

The remake has Virginia Mayo as a burlesque queen attending college and arousing too many males, including professor Ronald Reagan. The freedom of expression which some wish denied here is the girl's occupation away from the school. The premise is sound—a student should be judged by what they do in the classroom, not by how the tuition is raised—assuming the means are legal. Unfortunately, the musical remake is not a civil libertarian's dream. The acting, production and songs by Sammy Cahn and Vernon Duke are weak.

554 The Maltese Falcon

Based on the novel by Dashiell Hammett. Story: "The things that dreams are made of" is how private eye Sam Spade describes the priceless Maltese Falcon, a jewel-encased statue which was to have been a present to a king during the times of the Crusades, but never reached its destination and its ownership has been in dispute ever since. Spade is brought into the centuries-old case by a beautiful woman full of curves and lies. This leads to involvement with the "Fat Man," Kasper Gutman, and other assorted baddies. In the process of bringing the guilty to justice and discovering that this particular version of the falcon, which has cost four men their lives, is made of lead, Spade jokes, fights, falls in love and then "sends his love over" to the police because she's also a murderer.

Warner Bros., 1931 (original). Director: Roy Del Ruth; screenwriters: Maude Fulton, Lucien Hubbard and Brown Holmes. Cast: Bebe Daniels (Ruth Wonderly), Ricardo Cortez (Sam Spade), Dudley Digges (Kasper Gutman), Una Merkel (Effie Perine), Robert Elliott (Dundy), Thelma Todd (Iva), Otto Matieson (Cairo), Oscar Apfel (D.A.), Walter Long (Archer), Dwight Frye (Wilmer), J. Farrell McDonald (Polhaus), A. Borgato (Captain Jacobi).

• ***Satan Met a Lady*** (remake). Warner Bros., 1936. Director: William Dieterle; screenwriter: Brown Holmes. Cast: Bette Davis (Valerie Purvis), Warren William (Ted Shane), Alison Skipworth (Madame Barabbas), Arthur

Opposite, top: *Sam Spade (Humphrey Bogart, left), Joel Cairo (Peter Lorre), Brigid O'Shaughnessy (Mary Astor), and Kasper Gutman (Sydney Greenstreet) examine the black bird in* The Maltese Falcon *(Warner Bros., 1941) before discovering it to be a fake.* Bottom: *Lee Patrick (left), Signe Hasso, Lionel Stander, George Segal and Stephanie Audran line up behind a midget Nazi in the spoof sequel to* The Maltese Falcon, The Black Bird *(Columbia, 1975).*

Treacher (Anthony Travers), Winifred Shaw (Astrid Ames), Marie Wilson (Miss Burgatroyd), Porter Hall, Olin Howland, Charles Wilson, Maynard Holmes, Barbara Blane.

• ***The Maltese Falcon*** (remake). Warner Bros., 1941. Director and screenwriter: John Huston. Cast: Humphrey Bogart (Sam Spade), Mary Astor (Brigid O'Shaughnessy), Gladys George (Iva Archer), Peter Lorre (Joel Cairo), Barton Maclane (Lt. Dundy), Lee Patrick (Effie Perine), Sydney Greenstreet (Kasper Gutman), Ward Bond (Det. Tom Polhaus), Jerome Cowan (Miles Archer), Elisha Cook, Jr. (Wilmer Cook), James Burke, Frank Richman, John Hamilton, Walter Huston.

In 1975, Columbia Pictures produced a spoofy sequel to *The Maltese Falcon* called *The Black Bird* with George Segal appearing as Sam Spade, Jr. In this witless film, he has to contend with crooks still after the falcon. For nostalgia purposes, Lee Patrick as Effie and Elisha Cook, Jr., as Wilmer of the 1941 classic, are featured. Not content with one failure, in 1978 Columbia brought out *The Cheap Detective* starring Peter Falk in a Bogart-like portrayal of private eye Lou Peckinpaugh. This desperate farce attempted to incorporate bits of several of Bogie's big hits, including *The Maltese Falcon, Casablanca,* and *The Big Sleep.* In 1982, Steve Martin, a comedian of questionable talent and appeal, appeared in *Dead Men Don't Wear Plaid* which ripped off a whole series of classic movies, including *The Maltese Falcon,* by having Martin play to film clips from the various movies. It was a real yawn—only reminding one that people once made movies, not a mere collage of pieces of film.

The Dashiell Hammett story combines comedy, mystery, drama and burlesque all in one delightful yarn. The characters from Spade to Wilmer the gunsel are pure delights. The dialog, even in the Bogart piece, is sometimes inspired, sometimes claptrap. The characters are inconsistent, constantly changing in their attitudes towards each other, and not the least bit predictable. Because the 1941 film is considered to be the definitive private eye piece, audiences nowadays seldom have the opportunity to see the 1931 piece or the much altered 1936 remake. In the case of the latter, this is hardly a loss, for all the changes were for the worse. However, the first version of the story of the bejewelled bird holds more that a mere historical interest. It was one of the best of the early talkies and was in fact a good picture with fine performances by the entire cast. Having been overshadowed by John Huston's masterpiece should not condemn the earlier version to the vault of forgotten films—but it has.

Much has been written about the 1941 film. Most movie buffs know that Bogart got the role only when others like George Raft turned it down, and that it propelled him to the position of an important star. It's also fairly common knowledge that the film was John Huston's first film as director, that his father, Walter, made a brief uncredited appearance as a dying man, and that Sidney Greenstreet made his film debut at the age of 62 as the marvelous villain Kasper Gutman. The film was nominated for the Academy Award, Huston was nominated for Best Writer and Greenstreet for Best Supporting Actor, but none won. Having viewed the film recently in its colorized version, your authors are convinced that if God had wanted the film to be done in color, John

Huston would have done it that way. As critic Francis Wyndham said, years ago: "admirable photography of the sort in which black and white gives full value to every detail, every flicker of panic." It's a film worth seeing time and again, enjoying it every time.

Mame *see* **Auntie Mame**

555 Man at Six

Based on the play by Jack Celestin and Jack De Leon. Story: Sybil Vane, an insurance investigator, unmasks a colleague as an international jewel thief who poses as a woman and kills his victims.

BIP/Wardour, Great Britain, 1931 (original). Director: Harry Hughes; screenwriters: Harry Hughes and Victor Kendall. Cast: Anne Grey (Sybil Vane), Lester Matthews (Campbell Edwards), Gerald Rawlinson (Frank Pine), John Turnbull (Inspector Dawford), Kenneth Kove, Charles Farrell, Arthur Stratton.

• ***The Gables Mystery*** (remake). Welwyn/MGM, 1938. Director: Harry Hughes; screenwriters: Victor Kendall and Harry Hughes. Cast: Antoinette Cellier (Helen Vane), Francis L. Sullivan (Power), Leslie Perrins (Inspector Lloyd), Derek Gorst (Frank Rider), Jerry Verno, Aubrey Mallalieu, Sidney King, Laura Wright.

The movie wasn't all that exciting the first time, and seven years didn't add any thrills to this rather routine and boring tale of a girl detective who wins a battle of wits with an elusive international jewel thief.

A Man for All Seasons *see* **The Private Life of Henry VIII**

Man Friday *see* **Robinson Crusoe**

556 The Man in Half Moon Street

Based on the play by Barre Lyndon and his novel *The Man Who Could Cheat Death.* Story: Young scientist Julian Karell, a man in his nineties, has discovered a surgical procedure which keeps him young. Every ten years, Dr. Kurt Van Bruecken performs an operation replacing some of Julian's parts with those of young men Karell has murdered for just this purpose. Finally Van Bruecken can stand his complicity no longer and refuses to operate. Karell kills him and kidnaps the fiancée of another surgeon to force him to carry on the life-saving procedures. The latter agrees to the ransom demand but only pretends to perform the operation. Karell reverts quickly to his real age and dies in a fire as the police rescue the surgeon and his fiancée.

Paramount Pictures, 1944 (original). Director: Ralph Murphy; screenwriter: Charles Kenyon. Cast: Nils Asther (Julian Karell), Helen Walker (Eve Brandon), Reinhold Schunzel (Dr. Kurt Van Bruecken), Paul Cavanaugh (Dr. Henry Latimer), Edmond Breon, Morton Lowry, Brandon Hurst, Aminta Dyne.

• ***The Man Who Could Cheat Death*** (remake). Hammer Cadogan Films, England, 1959. Director: Terence Fisher; screenwriter: Jimmy Sanster. Cast: Anton Diffring (Dr. Georges Bonner), Christopher Lee (Pierre), Hazel Court

(Janine), Arnold Marle (Dr. Ludwig Weisz), Delphi Lawrence, Francis de Wolf.

The first filming of Barre's play and novel was given a literal interpretation, thereby losing what modest dramatic impact the work possessed. The reviews were unkind, but accurate—it was a meaningless potboiler lacking a meaningful point of view, unlike *The Picture of Dorian Gray,* which also featured a man who had found the secret of staying young. The Hammer remake played the story as a straight horror picture and it was only moderately enjoyable even for Hammer fanatics.

557 The Man in Possession

Based on the play by H.M. Harwood. Story: Raymond Dabney, a charming but not too responsible member of a very proper British family, takes a position as the bailiff's man in the home of bankrupt Crystal Wetherby, without knowing she is engaged to his stuffy brother, Claude. To protect Crystal's pride, Raymond poses as the woman's butler, and it is in this position that he is functioning when his family comes to pay a call on Crystal. The Dabneys are not amused with Raymond's job as a servant. All ends well, except for Claude, when Raymond and Crystal realize that they are in love, and move to the continent for a new start in life.

MGM, 1931 (original). Director: Sam Wood; screenwriters: Sarah Y. Mason and P.G. Wodehouse. Cast: Robert Montgomery (Raymond Dabney), Irene Purcell (Crystal Wetherby), Charlotte Greenwood (Clara), C. Aubrey Smith (Mr. Dabney), Beryl Mercer (Mrs. Dabney), Reginald Owen (Claude Dabney).

• ***Personal Property*** (remake). MGM, 1937. Director: W.S. Van Dyke; screenwriters: Ernst Vajda and Hugh Mills. Cast: Robert Taylor (Raymond Dabney), Jean Harlow (Crystal Wetherby), Una O'Connor (Clara), E.E. Clive (Mr. Dabney), Henrietta Crosman (Mrs. Dabney), Reginald Owen (Claude Dabney).

The 1931 film cleverly got around some of the strictures of the Hays Office on sex, but not often enough to make it top-flight sexual comedy. Robert Montgomery ran away with the acting honors, his stage-trained speaking voice a great improvement over that of many performers who had not fared well with the advent of sound. The remake, with Taylor and Harlow, had the box-office ammunition, and although it wasn't a bomb, it also wasn't of high caliber. Sorry about that.

Man in the Attic *see* **The Lodger**

Man of La Mancha *see* **Don Quixote**

A Man to Remember *see* **One Man's Journey**

558 The Man Who Came Back

Based on a story by John Fleming Wilson and the play of the same name by Jules Eckert Goodman. Story: When Henry Potter is banished from his home by his father for his renegade ways, Marcelle, who loves him, also leaves home. They meet later in Shanghai where she has become a morphine addict. Because their love still burns brightly, they are able to overcome their bad habits, regain their self respect and reconcile Henry with his father.

Fox Film Corp., 1924 (original). Silent. Director: Emmett Flynn; screenwriter: Edmund Goulding. Cast: George O'Brien (Henry Potter), Dorothy Mackaill (Marcelle), Ralph Lewis (Thomas Potter), Cyril Chadwick, Emily Fitzroy, Harvey Clark, Edward Piel, David Kirby.

• ***The Man Who Came Back*** (remake). Fox Film Corp., 1930. Director: Raoul Walsh; screenwriter: E.J. Burke. Cast: Janet Gaynor (Angie), Charles Farrell (Stephen Randolph), Kenneth McKenna (Capt. Trevelyan), William Holden, Mary Forbes, Ulrich Haupt.

What began as a gripping melodrama in the first film became a typical sweetness and light picture with Janet Gaynor and Charles Farrell in the remake. Gaynor is a heavy drug user and Farrell partial to strong drink, but they blissfully and with seemingly no great trouble overcome these addictions, so that he can be a prodigal son to his stern father. Surprise, dear old dad isn't all that bad, after all. He had been plotting for years to get these two together and share in his great wealth. Perhaps if he had let them in on his plan, they wouldn't have ended up in opium dens. But then the whole story as produced in this version is inane. Apparently, it was believed that the public so dearly loved the pairing of Gaynor and Farrell that they would swallow anything. Sad to say, this estimation of the public's taste was accurate.

559 The Man Who Changed His Name

Based on the play by Edgar Wallace. Story: Faithless wife Nita Clive mistakenly believes her husband Selby is a murderer. He goes along with the misunderstanding to prevent her from running off with her lover.

British Lion, Great Britain, 1928 (original). Director: A.V. Bramble; screenwriter: Kathleen Hayden. Cast: Stewart Rome (Selby Clive), Betty Faire (Nita Clive), James Raglan (Frank O'Ryan), Ben Field (Sir Ralph Whitcombe), Wallace Bosco, Douglas Payne.

Real Art/Universal Pictures, Great Britain, 1934. Director: Henry Edwards; screenwriter: H. Fowler Mear. Cast: Lyn Harding (Selby Clive), Betty Stockfield (Nita Clive), Leslie Perrins (Frank Ryan), Ben Welden (Jerry Muller), Arthur Mather (Sir Ralph Whitcombe), Richard Dolman, Stanley Vine.

Lyn Harding, in the remake, is quite good as the millionaire who poses as a murderer to prevent his wife leaving him. Otherwise it's an unexceptional picture.

The Man Who Could Cheat Death *see* **The Man in the Half Moon Street**

The Man Who Dared *see* **Star Witness**

560 The Man Who Knew Too Much

Based on the screenplay by Edwin Greenwood, Emlyn Williams and A.R. Rawlinson. Story: While dancing with Jill Lawrence, a British Secret Service agent is shot. With his dying breath, he implores Jill to secure a message hidden in a brush in his room. Bob Lawrence, Jill's husband, recovers the hidden message but before he can do anything about it, he receives a shocking communication. His daughter has been kidnapped and will be killed if he talks. The Lawrences go to London in search of their daughter, but will tell the police nothing of what they know. Finally Bob traces a telephone call and locates the gang's hiding place. Although taken prisoner, he manages to smuggle a message to his wife that a famous statesman is to be assassinated that very night at Albert Hall. Jill goes to the concert and manages to foil the shooting. This is followed by a raid on the gang's headquarters and the rescue of Bob and his daughter.

Gaumont, Great Britain, 1934 (original). Director: Alfred Hitchcock; screenwriters: Edwin Greenwood, Emlyn Williams and A.R. Rawlinson. Cast: Leslie Banks (Bob Lawrence), Edna Best (Jill Lawrence), Peter Lorre (Abbott), Nova Pilbeam (Betty Lawrence), Frank Vosper (Levine), Hugh Wakefield (Clive), Pierre Fresnay (Louis Bernard), Cicely Oates, D.A. Clarke-Smith, George Curzon, Henry Oscar.

• ***The Man Who Knew Too Much*** (remake). Paramount Pictures, 1956. Director: Alfred Hitchcock; screenwriters: John Michael Hayes and Angus MacPhail. Cast: James Stewart (Ben McKenna), Doris Day (Jo McKenna), Brenda de Banzie (Mrs. Drayton), Bernard Miles (Mr. Drayton), Ralph Truman (Buchanan), Daniel Gelin (Louis Bernard), Mogens Wieth, Alan Mowbray, Hillary Brooke, Christopher Olsen, Reggie Nalder, Richard Wattis.

The remake changed the sex of the missing child, the location of the kidnapping, and the killing of the Secret Service agent, but other than this and the use of Technicolor, the story is just about the same. Audiences were "treated" to Doris Day singing the Academy Award–winning song "Que Sera Sera." It was a bad year for original movie songs. The 1934 film was among Hitchcock's first movie thrillers to involve exotic settings for his characters' chase after their "McGuffin." While Banks and Best were not box-office names in the United States, as were Stewart and Day, the former made a more believable couple and Peter Lorre was a masterful villain, much more so than Bernard Miles, usually appearing as a nice, trustworthy chap.

561 The Man Who Lost Himself

Based on the novel by H. DeVere Stockpile. Story: The Earl of Rochester, something of a no-good, meets his double in London, a broke American named Victor Jones. The Earl gets Jones drunk and delivers him to the former's home where Jones is put to bed. When he awakens the next morning, Jones reads in the newspapers that Jones has committed suicide, and at breakfast a note from the Earl is handed him, telling him to take the Earl's place in the world. Jones redeems the family's fortune, falls in love with Rochester's wife and when he attempts to tell the truth, is put into the hands of a trio of alienists who declare the Earl daffy.

Jimmy Stewart strikes a fearful pose in the 1956 Paramount remake of Alfred Hitchcock's 1935 Gaumont British film The Man Who Knew Too Much. *Maybe he's afraid that co-star and wife Doris Day will break into another chorus of "Que Sera Sera."*

Selznick, 1920 (original). Silent. Director: Clarence Badger; screenwriter: uncredited. Cast: William Faversham (Victor Jones/Earl of Rochester), Hedda Hopper (Countess of Rochester), Violet Reed (Lady Plinlimon), Radcliffe Steele (Sir Patrick Spence), Claude Payton, Mathilde Brundage, Emily Fitzroy, Downing Clarke.

• ***The Man Who Lost Himself*** (remake). Universal Pictures, 1941. Director: Edward Ludwig; screenwriter: Eddie Moran. Cast: Brian Aherne (John Evans/Malcolm Scott), Kay Francis (Adrienne Scott), Henry Stephenson (Frederick Collins), S.Z. Sakall (Paul), Nils Asther (Peter Ransome), Sig Ruman, Dorothy Tree, Janet Beecher, Marc Lawrence.

In the remake, Brian Aherne assumes the dual role of a Puerto Rican planter and a rich but eccentric drunken millionaire. The pair meet at a nightclub, and the planter is dropped off at the other's home after a wild night together. The drunken millionaire is killed in an automobile accident and identified as the planter. Aherne takes the rest of the picture trying to straighten out identities but the lure of the deceased's wife, Kay Francis, makes things all the more difficult.

562 The Man Who Played God

Based on the play *The Silent Voice* by Jules Eckert. Story: At the height of his career, wealthy musician John Arden loses his hearing as a result of an explosion. He becomes morose, cynical and suicidal, putting his young wife's (Marjorie) devotion to a major test, particularly since she loved Philip Stevens when she agreed to marry Arden because of her admiration for his talent. At the urging of a friend, Arden learns lip reading and amuses himself by studying people in Central Park through binoculars. Discovering several in dire need he turns to philanthrophy, but it's also by this means of eavesdropping that he learns of the feelings between his wife and Stevens. He offers to release her from her obligations to him, but she refuses, choosing to stay with a man she is proud to call her husband. Shortly thereafter, he recovers his hearing in a fall.

United Artists, 1922 (original). Silent. Director: Harmon Wright. Cast: George Arliss (John Arden), Ann Forrest (Marjorie Blaine), Edward Earle (Philip Stevens), Ivan Sampson, Effie Shannon, Miriam Battista, Mickey Bennett, Mary Astor, Pierre Gendron, Marjorie Seddon, J.D. Walsh.

• ***The Man Who Played God*** (remake). Warner Bros., 1932. Directors: John Adolfi; screenwriters: Julien Josephson and Maude Howell. Cast: George Arliss (Montgomery Royale), Bette Davis (Grace), Donald Cook (Harold), Violet Heming (Mildred), Ivan Simpson, Louise Closser Hale, Raymond Milland, Dorothy Libaire, Charles Evans.

• ***Sincerely Yours*** (remake). Warner Bros., 1955. Director: Gordon Douglas; screenwriter: Irving Wallace. Cast: Liberace (Anthony Warren), Joanne Dru (Marion Moore), Dorothy Malone (Linda Curtis), Alex Nicol (Howard Ferguson), William Demarest (Sam Dunne), Lori Nelson (Sarah Cosgrove), Lurene Tuttle, Richard Eyer, James Bell, Herbert Heyes, Ian Wolfe.

In the remake, concert pianist George Arliss' career is finished when an anarchist's bomb explodes and deafens him. He is befriended by Bette Davis, with whom he falls deeply in love, but steps aside for another man, when he discovers that although she loves the other and not him, she is willing to sacrifice her happiness to live with him. Apparently the producers and Arliss agreed that he had aged to such a point in ten years that he shouldn't get the girl. The 1955 film starring Liberace as a pianist who has lost his hearing was a major bomb for Warners. Perhaps all those middle-age to elderly women who just loved the boy with the candelabra didn't go to movies or more likely, they only wanted to hear him play, not attempt to act. He was no George Arliss—of that you can be certain.

563 The Man Who Reclaimed His Head

Based on the play by Jean Bart (pseudonym for Marie Antoinette Sarlabous). Story: Brilliant writer Paul Verin lives in poverty with his beautiful wife, Adele. He is hired by a publisher, Henri Dumont, to write anti-war editorials and stories. Dumont takes a fancy to Adele, and so to get Paul out of the way, sends him on many dangerous missions. Paul returns home unexpectedly and discovers Dumont making advances at his wife. Although Dumont's love is unrequited, Paul goes mad and kills him.

Universal Pictures, 1934 (original). Director: Edward Ludwig; screenwriters: Jean Bart and Samuel Ornitz. Cast: Claude Rains (Paul Verin), Joan Bennett (Adele Verin), Lionel Atwill (Henri Dumont), Baby Jane Quigley (Linette Verin), Henry O'Neil, Wallace Ford, Lawrence Grant, William B. Davidson.

• ***Strange Confession*** (remake). Universal Pictures, 1945. Director: Jack Hoffman; screenwriter: M. Coates Webster. Cast: Lon Chaney, Jr. (Jeff Carter), Brenda Joyce (Mary Carter), J. Carroll Naish (Roger Graham), Milburn Stone (Stevens), Lloyd Bridges, Addison Richards, Mary Gordon, Jack Norton, Gregory Muradian.

The melodramatic *The Man Who Reclaimed His Head* had a fine cast but a confused script. The weak remake, a radio "Inner Sanctum" mystery, starred Lon Chaney, Jr., as a chemist who murders his drug-peddling boss, J. Carroll Naish. He gets his lawyer friend, Milburn Stone, to defend him. Brenda Joyce appears as Chaney's wife and the trigger to his murderous rage.

The Man Who Talked Too Much *see* **The Mouthpiece**

The Man Who Wouldn't Talk *see* **The Valiant**

564 Man, Woman and Sin

Based on a story by Monta Bell. Story: Reporter Al Whitcomb falls in love with society editor Vera Worth, without knowing that she is being kept by the newspaper's owner. While visiting Vera, Al kills the owner in self-defense and to protect her reputation, Vera perjures herself at his trial, but later changes her story, allowing Whitcomb to go free.

MGM, 1927. Silent. Director: Monta Bell; screenwriter: Alice D.G. Miller. Cast: John Gilbert (Al Whitcomb), Jeanne Eagels (Vera Worth), Gladys Brockwell, Marc MacDermott, Philip Anderson, Hayden Stevenson, Charles K. French, Aileen Manning.

• ***Up for Murder*** (remake). Universal Pictures, 1931. Director and screenwriter: Monta Bell. Cast: Lew Ayres (Robert Marshall), Genevieve Tobin (Myra Deane), Purnell B. Pratt (William Winter), Richard Tucker, Frank McHugh, Louise Beavers, Frederick Burt.

The remake is just about the same as the silent version, except now, when cub reporter Lew Ayres kills Genevieve Tobin's rich lover, he sullenly gives himself up but won't give any explanation of what happened because he's trying to protect Tobin's good name. She eventually saves him by giving testimony in his trial. If the stories here don't sound too interesting, just remember that at this time people didn't have television for stinkers like this to be shown as part of some indifferent series.

565 Mandingo

Based on the novel by Kyle Onstott and the play by Jack Kirkland. Story: Unlike *Gone with the Wind*, things are not so docile and bucolic on a slave breeding plantation in Louisiana during the 1840s. Blacks are treated like animals, but it's as forbidden sex objects that they appeal most to refined young white ladies. Conversely, the passionate, everything-goes sex attitudes of the black girls drive the white massas nearly mad with desire. It's trash but well-produced trash, and if one feels like rolling around in sexual depravity and brutality for 126 minutes, one could do a lot worse than this movie and its sequel.

Paramount Pictures, 1975 (original). Director: Richard Fleischer; screenwriter: Norman Wexler. Cast: James Mason (Maxwell), Susan George (Blanche), Perry King (Hammond), Richard Ward (Agamemnon), Brenda Sykes (Ellen), Ken Norton (Mede), Lillian Hayman, Roy Poole, Ji-Tu Cumbuka, Paul Benedict.

• ***Drum*** (sequel). United Artists, 1976. Director: Steve Carver; screenwriter: Norman Wexler. Cast: Warren Oates (Hammond), Isela Vega (Marianna), Ken Norton (Drum), Pam Grier (Regine), Yaphet Kotto (Blaise), John Colicos (Bernard), Fiona Lewis (Agusta), Paula Kelly (Rachel), Royal Dano, Lillian Hayman.

In the sequel, ex-boxer Ken Norton plays the son of his character in *Mandingo*. He's also the son of the white woman who was the death of his father when it was discovered she was pregnant with a black man's child. The mother and her slave, who pretends to be Norton's mother, move to New Orleans where they open a brothel, where Norton gets a fine sexual education from the "ladies" and the clients.

Manhattan Heartbeat *see* **Bad Girl**

566 Manhattan Melodrama

Based on a story by Arthur Caesar. Story: Two Irish slum boys are adopted by Poppa Rosen, who had lost his own son in the 1904 SS *Slocum* disaster. As they grow up, one, Jim, becomes the district attorney and the other, Blackie, a gangster. Eventually, the D.A. must send his boyhood chum to the electric chair for killing a man intent on killing Jim. The D.A. successfully argues before the jury that as the Volstead Act has been repealed, there is no reason to see the outlaw as some glorious Robin Hood, giving the people what they want.

Cosmopolitan/MGM, 1934 (original). Director: W.S. Van Dyke; screenwriters: Oliver H.P. Garrett and Joseph L. Mankiewicz. Cast: Clark Gable (Blackie), William Powell (Jim), Myrna Loy (Eleanor), Mickey Rooney (Blackie as a boy), Jimmy Butler (Jim as a boy), Leo Carrillo (Father Joe), Nat Pendleton (Spud), George Sidney (Poppa Rosen), Isabell Jewell, Muriel Evans, Thomas Jackson, Shirley Ross.

• ***Northwest Rangers*** (remake). MGM, 1942. Director: Joe Newman;

screenwriters: Gordon Kahn and David Lang. Cast: James Craig (Frank "Blackie" Marshall), William Lundigan (James Kevin Gardiner), Patricia Dane (Jean Avery), John Carradine (Martin Caswell), Jack Holt (Duncan Frazier), Keenan Wynn (Slip O'Mara), Grant Withers, Darryl Hickman, Drew Roddy.

The story of *Manhattan Melodrama* is a bit old-hat now, but it won an Academy Award for Arthur Caesar for original story at the time. Another interesting note about the film is that it was the one that John Dillinger saw with the "Lady in Red" at the Biograph Theater in Chicago, just before he was gunned down in a hail of bullets from the guns of FBI men. In the remake, two boys, Darryl Hickman and Drew Roddy, are left homeless by an Indian raid in Canada. They are taken care of by the Mounties. One boy, played by William Lundigan, grows up to be a Mountie and the other matures into a notorious gambler (James Craig). The latter not only loses his girl, Patricia Dane, to his boyhood chum, but is tracked down by Lundigan and brought to justice after he has murdered two men. The film is nothing to get excited about but isn't a bad recycling of *Manhattan Melodrama*.

Manpower ***see*** **Tiger Shark**

567 Manslaughter

Based on the novel by Alice Duer Miller. Story: Rich and reckless Lydia Thorne is unsympathetic when Evans, her maid, is jailed for stealing her jewels. District Attorney O'Bannon tries to make Lydia see the error of her own ways when her automobile driving causes the death of a motorcycle cop. Lydia's resentment and rebuff of O'Bannon, who has come to love her, causes him to turn to drink. In prison, Lydia reforms and realizes that she loves O'Bannon. When she is released she joins with Evans to run a soup kitchen for unfortunates. A chance meeting with O'Bannon gets him back on track. He rebounds so well that he considers running for governor, but withdraws his candidacy to marry Lydia when he realizes that her record would damage his campaign.

Famous Players/Paramount Pictures, 1922 (original). Silent. Director: Cecil B. De Mille; screenwriter: Jeanie Macpherson. Cast: Thomas Meighan (Daniel O'Bannon), Leatrice Joy (Lydia Thorne), Lois Wilson (Evans), John Miltern, George Fawcett, Julia Faye, Edythe Chapman, Jack Mower, Dorothy Cumming, Casson Ferguson.

Manslaughter (remake). Paramount-Publix Corporation, 1930. Director and screenwriter: George Abbott. Cast: Claudette Colbert (Lydia Thorne), Fredric March (Dan O'Bannon), Emma Dunn (Miss Bennett), Natalie Moorhead (Eleanor), Richard Tucker, Hilda Vaughn, G. Pat Collins, Gaylord Pendleton, Stanley Fields, Arnold Lucy.

Cecil B. De Mille was able to work a Roman orgy sequence into the film in Lydia Thorne's pre-reformation period. The picture was a success as was the remake with Claudette Colbert and Fredric March. George Abbott nicely updated the Alice Duer Miller story. Colbert did some of her best dramatic work, particularly in the courtroom and prison scenes.

568 Mantrap

Based on the novel by Sinclair Lewis. Story: Bachelor New York lawyer Ralph Prescott has developed a low opinion of women from handling so many of their divorce cases. To escape them he goes on a camping trip to Mantrap Landing deep in a Canadian woods. At a trading post, he meets woodsman Joe Easter and his wife, Alvena. She's bored with her life and her husband and she comes on strongly with Ralph, begging him to take her with him when he leaves. He does, although reluctantly. The pair is stranded when their canoe is stolen. They are rescued by a pilot on the way to fight a forest fire. During the trip, Alvena, a natural and unashamed coquette, flirts outrageously with the flyer. Joe arrives and is willing to give Alvena a divorce to marry whomever she pleases, but she decides to stay with Joe, who accepts her flirting ways.

Famous Players–Lasky/Paramount Pictures, 1926 (original). Silent. Director: Victor Fleming; screenwriters: Adelaide Heilbron and Ethel Doherty. Cast: Ernest Torrence (Joe Easter), Clara Bow (Alvena), Percy Marmont (Ralph Prescott), Eugene Pallette (E. Wesson Woodbury), Tom Kennedy (Curly Evans), Josephine Crowell, William Orlamond, Charles Stevens.

• ***Untamed*** (remake). Paramount Pictures, 1940. Director: George Archainbaud; screenwriters: Frederick Hazlitt Brennan and Frank Butler. Cast: Ray Milland (Dr. William Crawford), Patricia Morison (Alvena Easter), Akim Tamiroff (Joe Easter), William Frawley (Les Woodbury), Jane Darwell (Mrs. Maggie Moriarty), Esther Dale, J.M. Kerrigan, Eily Malyon, Fay Helm.

Many critics credited Clara Bow's fine performance in *Mantrap* to the fact that at the time she was carrying on a torrid romance with director Victor Fleming. She did look cute and cuddly even in the simple clothes one wears in the backwoods of Canada. In the remake, Ray Milland is a surgeon who heads for the Canadian woods, hoping to cure himself of a drinking problem. Patricia Morison, the wife of guide Akim Tamiroff, falls in love with Milland during her husband's absence. Milland is required to use his medical skills during an epidemic. He and Morison must trek through a snowstorm to get medicine and have to be rescued by Tamiroff, who conveniently freezes to death, allowing the lovers to be together. It's a none-too convincing soap opera with none-too impressive acting by the three leading performers.

Marguerite de la Nuit *see* **Faust**

Marius *see* **Fanny**

Le Marraine De Charley *see* **Charley's Aunt**

569 The Marriage Circle

Based on the play *Nuir ein Traum* by Lothar Goldschmidt. Story: When Professor Stock's wife, Mizzi, begins a flirtation with Dr. Franz Braun, the husband of her best friend, Charlotte, the professor sees this as his chance to finally divorce the wife he does not love. Into this romantic merry-go-round comes Dr. Mueller, Braun's partner, who admires Charlotte. She in turn doesn't take

Mueller very seriously, nor does Franz encourage Mizzi, so in the end Mueller and Mizzi turn to each other for affection.

Warner Bros., 1924 (original). Silent. Director: Ernst Lubitsch; screenwriter: Paul Bern. Cast: Florence Vidor (Charlotte Braun), Monte Blue (Dr. Franz Braun), Marie Prevost (Mizzi Stock), Creighton Hale (Dr. Gustav Mueller), Adolphe Menjou (Professor Josef Stock), Harry Myers, Dale Fuller.

• ***One Hour With You*** (remake). Paramount Pictures, 1932. Director: Ernst Lubitsch; screenwriter: Samson Raphaelson. Cast: Maurice Chevalier (Dr. Andre Bertier), Jeanette MacDonald (Colette Bertier), Genevieve Tobin (Mitzi Olivier), Charles Ruggles (Adolph), Roland Young (Prof. Olivier), George Barbier, Josephine Dunn, Richard Carle, Charles Judels, Barbara Leonard.

Both versions of this comedy of manners had the "Lubitsch Touch." In the musical remake of a sick marriage trying to take a bite out of a healthy one, Maurice Chevalier had hoped that his leading ladies would be Kay Francis and Carole Lombard, for both of whom he had romantic yearnings. Whether these two ladies would have done a better job than Jeanette MacDonald and Genevieve Tobin can never be decided, but the latter two seem just perfect for this risque comedy. The movement from song lyrics to simple dialog is often handled so smoothly that the transition is hardly noticed. The Oscar Strauss, Leo Robin and Richard A. Whiting songs in the joyful movie included "Three Times a Day," a doctor's prescription with perhaps a double-meaning (make that a triple-meaning), "What Would You Do," "We Will Always Be Sweethearts" and the title song. Everything about the picture is appealing, including the lovely boudoir and ballroom sets.

Mary of Scotland *see* **The Private Life of Henry VIII**

Mary, Queen of Scots *see* **The Private Life of Henry VIII**

M*A*S*H *see* **Battle Circus**

Masquerade in Mexico *see* **Midnight**

570 The Masquerader

Based on the novel by Katherine Cecil Thurston and the play by John Hunter Booth. Story: Distinguished Member of Parliament John Chilcote has, through excessive indulgence, nearly ruined his career. He convinces his exact double and cousin, newspaperman John Loder, to change places with him and redeem his fading political career. Chilcote's wife, Eve, comes to love the cousin more that she ever did her husband, but it's immoral, isn't it? This question becomes moot when Chilcote dies.

Tully Productions/First National Pictures, 1922 (original). Silent. Director: James Young; screenwriter: Richard Walton. Cast: Guy Bates Post (John Chilcote/John Loder), Ruth Sinclair (Eve Chilcote), Edward M. Kimball, Herbert Standing, Lawson Butt, Marcia Manon, Barbara Tennant.

• ***The Masquerader*** (remake). Goldwyn Productions/United Artists, 1933.

The main characters of The Matchmaker *(Paramount, 1958) pose for a publicity shot. From left to right: Wallace Ford, Paul Ford, Shirley Booth, Perry Wilson, Anthony Perkins, Shirley MacLaine and Robert Morse.*

Director: Richard Wallace; screenwriter: Howard Estabrook. Cast: Ronald Colman (John Chilcote/John Loder), Elissa Landi (Eve Chilcote), Juliette Compton (Lady Joyce), Halliwell Hobbes, David Torrence, Creighton Hale, Helen Jerome Eddy, Eric Wilton.

The book on which these movies and the play that preceded them are based was a best seller for over a generation beginning in 1905. On seeing either film, one might conclude that the plot is trite and incredibly predictable. This is true from the perspective of having seen elements of the plot and characterizations used in so many other movies and television shows. At one time this material was fresh and new, but even with Ronald Colman, the material is not the sort which can stand the test of time. It's cinematic value was most definitely higher in its time.

571 The Matchmaker

Based on the story *The Merchant of Yonkers* and the play *The Matchmaker* by Thornton Wilder. Story: Dolly Levi, a widowed Jewish matchmaker, has been hired by wealthy Yonkers grain merchant Horace Vandergelder to find him a bride. Dolly has her cap set for Horace herself, and his announcement that he plans to marry milliner Irene Molloy sends her into a frenzied action.

Miscast Barbra Streisand dances with Tommy Tune and ensemble in the musical remake of The Matchmaker, Hello, Dolly! *(20th Century–Fox, 1969).*

She sends Horace's two clerks, Cornelius and Barnaby, into New York to Irene's shop, and the hoped-for happens: Cornelius and Irene fall in love. Horace discovered Cornelius hiding in Irene's shop, and in accordance with Dolly's plan, calls off the engagement. That night all the central characters are at a fancy New York restaurant, and since he's the only one that can afford it, Horace ends up with the check. He fires Cornelius and Barnaby, but the next day he finds his two ex-clerks and Dolly have opened a rival grain store across the street. Ultimately, Horace gives in, takes Cornelius into the business as a partner, makes Barnaby head clerk, and proposes to Dolly, who accepts as does Irene to a like proposal from Cornelius.

Paramount Pictures, 1958 (original). Director: Joseph Anthony; screenwriter: John Michael Hayes. Cast: Shirley Booth (Dolly Levi), Paul Ford (Horace Vandergelder), Anthony Perkins (Cornelius Hackl), Shirley MacLaine (Irene Molloy), Robert Morse (Barnaby), Wallace Ford, Perry Wilson.

• ***Hello, Dolly!*** (remake). Twentieth Century–Fox, 1969. Director: Gene Kelly; screenwriter: Ernest Lehman. Cast: Barbra Streisand (Dolly Levi), Walter Matthau (Horace Vandergelder), Michael Crawford (Cornelius Hackl), Louis Armstrong (Orchestra Leader), Marianna McAndrew (Irene Molloy), E.J. Peaker (Minnie Fay), Danny Locklin (Barnaby), Joyce Ames, Tommy Tune, Judy Knaiz, David Hurst, Fritz Feld.

The original version of the Thornton Wilder play was perfectly delightful, with everyone in the cast performing at the top of his or her game. The wide-eyed wonderment of the young people and the always in control Shirley Booth charmed audiences. Paul Ford, still a bit of the flustered Colonel from his Sergeant Bilko days, was nevertheless wonderfully bombastic, selfish and short-sighted. Nevertheless, he allowed some brief glimmer of redeeming qualities to be seen, suggesting that he might have more to offer to a poor widow than money.

The musical remake had been a huge Broadway success with Carol Channing and David Burns in the lead roles and these two were ideal for them. Not so, Streisand and Matthau. Streisand seemed to be trying to combine aspects of Mae West and Sophie Tucker in her interpretation of Dolly, and did not come across the least bit believable. Matthau was of such a sour disposition that it is almost impossible to believe any woman, no matter how desperate, would have him, let alone pursue him. The production scenes were lavish and the Jerry Herman songs were fun, but the piece doesn't have the charm of the simple black and white 1958 movie.

572 The Matrimonial Bed

Based on the play by Yves Mirande and Andre Mouezy-Eon, adapted from the French by Edward Seymour Hicks. Story: After a railway accident, Adolphe Noblet loses his memory for five years. His wife, Juliette, believing she is a widow, has remarried to Gustave Corton by whom she has had a child. A new servant in the Corton household, on seeing a picture of her mistress' late husband, observes how much he reminds her of a hairdresser named Leopold Trebel. The latter is invited to dinner, and all are amazed at the resemblance to Adolphe. Complications arise when Dr. Friedland hypnotizes Leopold, who remembers that he is Adolphe, but not his life as Leopold. Shortly thereafter, his "wife" Suzanne Trebel arrives, and although he does not recognize her or the four children she claims are his, he agrees to go off with her and live his life as Leopold.

Warner Bros., 1930 (original). Director: Michael Curtiz; screenwriters: Harvey Thew and Seymour Hicks. Cast: Frank Fay (Adolphe Noblet/Leopold Trebel), Lilyan Tashman (Sylvaine), James Gleason (Gustave Corton), Beryl Mercer (Corinne), Marion Bryon (Marianne), Vivian Oakland (Suzanne Trebel), Florence Eldredge (Juliette), Arthur Edmund Carew (Dr. Friedland).

• ***Kisses for Breakfast*** (remake). Warner Bros., 1941. Director: Lewis Seiler; screenwriter: Kenneth Gamet. Cast: Dennis Morgan (Rodney Trask), Jane Wyatt (Laura Anders), Shirley Ross (Juliet Mardsen), Lee Patrick (Betty Trent), Jerome Cowan (Lucius Lorimer), Una O'Connor (Ellie), Barnett Parker, Romaine Callender, Lucia Carroll, Cornel Wilde, Willie Best, Louise Beavers, Clarence Muse.

The remake is a pleasant farce in which Dennis Morgan, a newly married husband of Shirley Ross, gets amnesia when struck during a fight; the only thing he remembers is the address of his bride's cousin, Jane Wyatt, which he finds in his coat. Hoping to find out who he is he goes south to see Wyatt, but she doesn't know him. However, he stays around and helps her keep her plantation, during which time the two fall in love and marry. When Wyatt wants to show off her new husband to her cousin Ross, the two travel north and—well, almost anyone can predict the rest of the story.

573 Maybe It's Love

Based on the play by Maxwell Anderson. Story: It's a humdrum family comedy about Bobby Halevy, a private secretary to Adolphe Mengle, Sr., who's in love with Rims O'Neill, a fellow office worker. Along comes Adolphe Mengle, Jr., the son of the boss, who tries to win Bobby from Rims. She won't go for it, but Junior manages to make Rims jealous enough to call things off between himself and Bobby. Of course they get back together and get married. Soon after the honeymoon, Rims gets fired, tells off his in-laws, and Bobby moves out and goes back to work. Rims is despondent, but wins back his wife once again.

Warner Bros., 1935. Director: William McGann; screenwriters: Jerry Wald, Harry Sauber, Lawrence Hazard and Daniel Reed. Cast: Gloria Stuart (Bobby Halevy), Ross Alexander (Rims O'Neill), Frank McHugh (Willie Sands), Helen Lowell (Mrs. Halevy), Phillip Reed (Adolphe Mengle, Jr.), Joseph Cawthorn (Adolphe Mengle, Sr.), Joseph Cawthers, Ruth Donnelly, Dorothy Dare, Henry Travers.

• ***Saturday's Children*** (remake). Warner Bros., 1940. Director: Vincent Sherman; screenwriters: Julius J. and Philip G. Epstein. Cast: John Garfield (Rims Rosson), Claude Rains (Mr. Halevy), Lee Patrick (Florris Sands), George Tobias (Herbie Smith), Anne Shirley (Bobby Halevy), Roscoe Karns, Dennie Moore.

These melodramas contain just enough humor to salvage them. The story of the on-again, off-again relationship of a young couple seems to suggest that this pattern will continue once the film is completed and if we visited the characters in a sequel a few years down the road in their lives, we would find them splits for keeps. In the remake, John Garfield plays a slow-thinking inventor of impractical devices who is tricked into marriage and then finds the struggle to make ends meet very difficult. Anne Shirley is very good as the romantic girl and wife. An interesting note—Olivia de Havilland was suspended when she refused this role, the first battle in her war to win decent roles for herself.

574 Mayerling

Based on the novel *Idyl's End* by Claude Anet, the novel *The Archduke* by Michael Arnold, the play *The Masque of Kings* by Maxwell Anderson and historical documentation. Story: Crown Prince Rudolph of Austria-Hungary rebels against the despotic rule of his father, Emperor Franz-Josef, appealing directly to the Pope to annul his arranged marriage to Stephanie of Belgium. Rudolph meets and falls in love with beautiful 17-year-old Baroness Marie Vetsera with whom he has a scandalous love affair. They meet at the Hapsburg's hunting lodge, Mayerling, in the Vienna woods. Convinced that they will not be allowed a future together, they enter into a suicide pact. Rudolph kills his mistress and then shoots himself.

• ***Mayerling*** (remake). Pax Films, France, 1936. Director: Anatole Litvak; screenwriters: Joseph Kessel and Irma Von Cube. Cast: Charles Boyer (Archduke Rudolph of Austria), Danielle Darrieux (Marie Vetsera), Suzie Prim (Countess Larisch), Jean Dax (Emperor Franz-Joseph), Gabrielle Dorziat (Empress Elizabeth), Jean Debucourt (Count Taafe), Marthe Regnier, Andre Dubosc, Wladimir Sokoloff, Rene Bergeron, Yolande Laffon, Gina Manes.

• ***Le Secret de Mayerling*** (remake). Codo Cinema, France, 1949. Director: Jean Delannoy; screenwriter: Jacques Remy. Cast: Jean Marais (Rodolphe), Dominique Blanchar (Maria Vetsera), Claude Farrell (Comtese Larisch), Jean Debucourt (Emperor Francois-Joseph), Silvia Montfort (Archduchesse Stephanie), Michel Vitold, Jane Marken, Marguerite Jamois, Jacques Dacqmine.

• ***Mayerling*** (remake). Les Films Corona/Winchester Film Productions/ MGM, Great Britain, 1968. Director and screenwriter: Terence Young. Cast: Omar Sharif (Crown Prince Rudolf), Catherine Deneuve (Maria Vetsera), Genevieve Page (Countess Larisch), James Mason (Emperor Franz-Joseph), Ava Gardner (Empress Elizabeth), James Robertson Justice (Edward, Prince of Wales), Andrea Parisy (Crown Princess Stephanie), Ivan Desny, Charles Millot, Maurice Teynac, Roger Pigaut, Fabienne Dali.

The tragic story of doomed royal love was also filmed in Russia in 1915, in Germany as *Tragodie im Hause Habsburg* in 1924, and as *Die Vetsera* in 1928. There was a French production, *Mayerling to Sarajevo,* in 1940 and an Austrian film, *Mayerling,* in 1958. The work of Charles Boyer and Danielle Darrieux as the doomed imperial lovers in the 1936 version is handled with great delicacy and has been highly praised by critics of all countries. The 1949 picture depicted Rodolphe as a sick and neurotic individual desperately seeking someone with whom to form a suicide pact and the adoring Marie Vetsera fills the bill. The 1968 film is a great disappointment, translating the great romantic story into a tedious love affair. Some of the individual supporting performances were fine—for instance, Ava Gardner as the Empress Elizabeth, but the two leading performers, Omar Sharif and Catherine Deneuve, were sadly miscast.

Mayerling to Sarajevo *see* **Mayerling**

575 Maytime

Based on the play by Rida Johnson Young and Cyrus Wood and the musical comedy by Rida Johnson Young and Sigmund Romberg. Story: Ottlie Van Zandt, the beautiful daughter of a wealthy colonel, loves Richard, the son of her father's gardener, but is forced to marry her cousin, Claude, instead. Richard leaves before the wedding, vowing to make his fortune and come back to marry Ottlie. He succeeds on the first point, but because Ottlie is already married, he takes Alice Tremaine as wife. Years later, Ottlie, now a widow, has been evicted from her house. Richard buys it back for her. Two generations pass and a new Ottlie, granddaughter of the first, lives in the house where she teaches dancing. She develops a friendship with Richard Wayne, the wealthy grandson of the former gardener's son. This blossoms into love and the two marry, something their loving grandparents of long ago were never privileged to do.

B.P. Schulberg Productions/Preferred Pictures, 1923 (original). Silent. Director: Louis Gasnier; screenwriter: Olga Printzlau. Cast: Ethel Shannon (Ottlie Van Zandt/Ottlie the granddaughter), Harrison Ford (Richard Wayne/Richard the grandson), Clara Bow (Alice Tremaine), Wallace MacDonald (Claude Van Zandt), Josef Swickard (Colonel Van Zandt), William Norris, Martha Mattox, Betty Francisco, Robert McKim.

• ***Maytime*** (remake). MGM, 1937. Director: Robert Z. Leonard; screenwriter: Noel Langley. Cast: Jeanette MacDonald (Marcia Morrison/Marcia Mornay), Nelson Eddy (Paul Allison), John Barrymore (Nicolai Nazaroff), Herman Bing (Archipenco), Tom Brown (Kip), Lynn Carver, Rafaela Ottiano, Charles Judels, Paul Porcasi, Sig Rumann, Walter Kingsford.

The remake is the film version of the Sigmund Romberg operetta, based on the Rida Johnson Young play. At a 1906 May Day festival, kindly old Jeanette MacDonald consoles an unhappy young girl who must choose between her love and her dancing career. MacDonald relates her own story as a famous opera star who married her teacher and mentor, John Barrymore, out of a sense of obligation and then met the man of her dreams, Nelson Eddy. They separate, but years later appear together in an opera and the feelings are just as strong as ever. Mad with jealousy, Barrymore shoots and kills Eddy. Not to worry—by the end of the movie, MacDonald goes to her reward and finds the spirit of Eddy waiting for her. We can only speculate as to where Barrymore is residing.

Some of the scenes in the operetta, such as the lavish ball at the court of Louis Napoleon, the opera sequences, and the lovely May Day country fair are as fine as have ever been seen on a screen. It's a radiant film which is able to overcome the acting defects of MacDonald and Eddy. The best Romberg song is the beautiful and moving "Will You Remember," the only song remaining from the original stage presentation.

576 Me and My Gal

Based on a story by Philip Klein and Barry Connors. Story: Happy-go-lucky New York waterfront cop Dan flirts with a waitress, Sally, in a cheap beanery and learns that her sister Helen is implicated in a robbery pulled off by a crook, Johnnie, that Dan has been trailing. Dan captures the crook, clears the sister, and uses the reward money for a Bermuda honeymoon with Sally.

Fox Film Corporation, 1932 (original). Director: Raoul Walsh; screenwriters: Barry Connors and Philip Klein. Cast: Spencer Tracy (Dan), Joan Bennett (Helen), Marion Burns (Sally), George Walsh (Johnnie), J. Farrell MacDonald, Noel Madison, Henry B. Walthall, Bert Hanlon.

• ***Pier 13*** (remake). Twentieth Century–Fox, 1940. Director: Eugene Forde; screenwriters: Stanley Rauh and Clark Andrews. Cast: Lynn Bari (Sally Kelly), Lloyd Nolan (Danny Dolan), Joan Valerie (Helen Kelly), Douglas Fowley (Johnnie Hale), Chick Chandler, Oscar O'Shea, Michael Morris, Louis Jean Heydt.

An early Spencer Tracy movie, *Me and My Gal* is pleasant but not very taxing entertainment. Tracy's star quality was apparent even then. The remake with Lloyd Nolan is just more of the same. No stars but no boos either.

Mean Streets *see* **Who's That Knocking At My Door**

577 The Meanest Man in the World

Based on the play by George M. Cohan. Story: Soft-hearted lawyer Richard Clark is tired of deadbeats and decides it's time to get tough with those who owe him money. He starts his new collection policy with one "J. Hudson," who turns out to be Jane Hudson, a very attractive girl. Her property is in danger of appropriation by dishonest oil speculators. Jane joins Clark in raising enough money to finance their own oil drilling operation. Of course, they fall in love in the process.

Paramount Pictures, 1923 (original). Silent. Director: Edward F. Cline; screenwriter: Austin McHugh. Cast: Bert Lytell (Richard Clark), Blanche Sweet (Jane Hudson), Bryant Washburn (Ned Stevens), Maryon Aye, Lincoln Steadman, Helen Lynch, Ward Crane, Frances Raymond, Carl Stockdale.

• ***The Meanest Man in the World*** (remake). Twentieth Century–Fox, 1942. Director: Sidney Lanfield; screenwriters: George Seaton and Allan House. Cast: Jack Benny (Richard Clark), Priscilla Lane (Janie Brown), Eddie "Rochester" Anderson (Sufro), Edmund Gwenn (Frederick P. Leggitt), Matt Briggs, Anne Revere, Margaret Seddon, Helene Reynolds.

The story of a man deciding to get tough with those who are in debt to him is not much of a premise for a successful movie, even when the man is Jack Benny, playing his usual tight-with-money personage. Jack plays a small-town lawyer with a strong sense of justice and a love of humankind but not much business sense. His valet, Rochester, suggests that he get mean. When he does, business picks up, but his girl, Priscilla Lane, doesn't like the new man. She walks out on him, but her father brings the two together again. It's not Benny at his best, but it has a few amusing moments.

Men Are Like That *see* **The Show Off**

Men Are Not Gods *see* **Othello**

Men of Boy's Town *see* **Boy's Town**

Men of Sherwood Forest *see* **Robin Hood**

578 Meatballs

Based on an original screenplay by Janis Allen, Len Blum, Dan Goldberg and Harold Ramis. Story: In this sophomoric *Animal House*–like tale of the antics of campers and counselors alike at a summer camp, Tripper, who provides a crazy role model for the youngsters, takes the time to know and help one lonely boy, Rudy, teaching him to like himself and win the respect of fellow campers.

Paramount Pictures, Canada, 1979 (original). Director: Ivan Reitman; screenwriters: Allen, Blum, Goldberg and Ramis. Cast: Bill Murray (Tripper), Chris Makepeace (Rudy), Harvey Atkin (Morty), Russ Banham (Crockett), Ron Barry (Lance), Jack Blum (Spaz), Matt Craven (Hardware), Kristine DeBell (A.L.), Norma Dell 'Agnese (Brenda), Cindy Girling (Wendy), Todd Hoffman, Keith Wright, Kate Lynch, Margot Pinvidic, Sarah Torgov.

• ***Meatballs, Part Two*** (sequel). Paramount Pictures, 1984. Director and screenwriter: Ken Weiderhorn. Cast: Richard Mulligan (Giddy), Kim Richards (Cheryl), John Mengatti (Flash), Misty Rowe (Fanny), Archie Hahn (Jamie), Tammy Taylor (Nancy), Ralph Seymour, Hamilton Camp, John Larroquette, Paul Reubens.

The success of the first picture rests solely on the fact that Bill Murray is a very funny—make that strange—individual. He carried the whole movie, with a little help from some attractive young girls and an appealing Chris Makepeace. The sequel had only the cute girl campers and an alien. Not enough.

Meatballs, Part Two ***see*** **Meatballs**

Meet Me Tonight ***see*** **Tonight at 8:30**

579 Meet the Girls

Based on the screenplay by Marguerite Roberts. Story: A pair of small-time entertainers lose their job in Honolulu, lose their money for passage home to San Francisco, become stowaways on a ship, get involved with jewel thieves, and eventually resolve their predicament.

Twentieth Century–Fox, 1938. Director: Eugene Forde; screenwriter: Marguerite Roberts. Cast: Lynn Bari (Terry), June Lang (Judy), Robert Allen, Ruthe Donnelly, Gene Lockhart, Wally Vernon, Eric Rhodes, Constance Romanoff, Jack Norton.

• ***Pardon Our Nerve*** (sequel). Twentieth Century–Fox, 1939. Director: Bruce Humberstone; screenwriters: Robert Ellis and Helen Logan. Based on a story by Hilda Stone and Betty Reinhardt. Cast: Lynn Bari (Terry), June Lang (Judy), Quinn Williams (Samson Smith), Michael Whalen, Edward Brophy, John Miljan, Theodore von Eltz.

These two inconsequential comedies were put together in the hope that the team of Bari and Lang might develop a following. They didn't. The second film has the girls as gold diggers who go through several money making schemes until they hit upon promoting a prizefighter named Samson Smith. He wins his fights because of the tricks the girls pull—until certain people realize what they're up to.

580 Melo

Based on the play by Henry Bernstein. Story: The wife of an orchestra violinist falls in love with a visiting concert violinist and ultimately commits suicide rather than choose between them.

French Film, 1932 (original). Director and screenwriter: Paul Czinner. Cast: Gaby Morlay (the Wife), Victor Francen (the Husband), Pierre Blanchard (the Concert Violinist).

• ***Dreaming Lips*** (remake). Trafalgar Film/United Artists, 1937. Director: Paul Czinner; screenwriter: Carl Mayer. Cast: Elisabeth Bergner (Gaby), Raymond Massey (Miguel de Vayo), Romney Brent (Peter), Joyce Bland (Christine), Sydney Fairbrother, Felix Aylmer, Fisher White.

Melo was also filmed as *Der Traumende Mund* in Germany in 1952 and released by Distributor's Corporation of America as *Dreaming Lips* in 1958. The story of a happily married woman who suddenly finds herself attracted to a dashing stranger has been told many times, but it doesn't always end with the wife solving her dilemma by making certain nobody wins. The films appealed to a very select audience and would seem to have in some way inspired the Dudley Moore comedy *Unfaithfully Yours* (1984), in which he is an orchestra conductor who suspects his wife, Nastassia Kinski, of being unfaithful with a visiting soloist. He concocts an elaborate plan to murder her and put the blame on her lover. It doesn't work.

581 Merely Mary Ann

Based on the story by Israel Zangwill. Story: A young composer and a girl meet and move into a cottage in the country where he works on his music and she keeps the house for him. When she comes into a large inheritance, they separate, but meet again at the premiere of his opera—and love wins out over fame and fortune.

Artcraft, 1916 (original). Silent. Director: John G. Adolfi; screenwriter: Israel Zangwill. Cast: Vivian Martin (Mary Ann), Harry Hillard (John), Laura Lyman, Isabel O'Madigan, Sidney Bracey, Niles Welch.

• ***Merely Mary Ann*** (remake). Fox Film Corp., 1931. Director: Henry King; screenwriter: Jules Furthman. Cast: Janet Gaynor (Mary Ann), Charles Farrell (John Lonsdale), Beryl Mercer (Mrs. Leadbatter), J.M. Kerrigan, Arnold Lucy, Lorna Balfour, Tom Whitely, G.P. Huntley, Jr.

The story was also filmed by Fox in 1920 with Shirley Mason in the title role as a wistful slave in a London lodging house. As audiences adored "America's Sweethearts," Gaynor and Farrell, the fact that the plot was almost nonexistent did not hurt the 1931 film at the box office.

Merrily We Live *see* **What a Man**

The Merry Men of Sherwood *see* **Robin Hood**

582 The Merry Widow

Based on the operetta by Franz Lehar. Story: Prince Danilo and Crown Prince Mirko of the kingdom of Monteblanco vie for the affection of Sally O'Hara, a follies girl on tour. Sally favors Danilo and accepts a dinner meeting with him, where he does his best to seduce her. Mirko discovers them in a compromising situtation, and Danilo, realizing his love for the girl, announces his intention to marry Sally. The king and queen of Monteblanco prevent the marriage and Sally, believing that Danilo was trifling with her affections, spitefully marries Baron Sadoja, the richest man in the kingdom. The wedding night proves too exciting for the aged Baron, who dies before even consummating the marriage. Sally moves to Paris, where she becomes known as the "Merry Widow." Mirko goes to her with the intention of getting her to marry him and return her fortune to the kingdom. Danilo accompanies Mirko to Paris and to further torment him, Sally agrees to marry Mirko. Danilo strikes Mirko, resulting in a duel, where Danilo deliberately allows Mirko to wound him because he believes that Sally really loves the crown prince. However he discovers that Sally still loves him, and when the king dies and the crown prince is assassinated, Danilo becomes king with Sally as his queen.

• ***The Merry Widow*** (remake). MGM, 1925. Silent. Director: Erich von Stroheim; screenwriters: Erich von Stroheim and Benjamin Glazer. Cast: Mae Murray (Sally O'Hara), John Gilbert (Prince Danilo), Roy D'Arcy (Crown Prince Mirko), Josephine Crowell (Queen Milena), George Fawcett (King Nikita), Tully Marshall (Baron Sadoja), Albert Conti, Sidney Bracy, Don Ryan, Hughie Mack, Ida Moore.

• ***The Merry Widow*** (remake). MGM, 1934. Director: Ernst Lubitsch; screenwriters: Ernst Lubitsch and Samson Raphaelson. Cast: Maurice Chevalier (Captain Danilo), Jeanette MacDonald (Sonia), Edward Everett Horton (Ambassador Popoff), Una Merkel (Queen Dolores), George Barbier (King Achmed), Minna Gombell, Sterling Holloway, Donald Meek.

• ***The Merry Widow*** (remake). MGM, 1952. Director: Curtis Bernhardt; screenwriters: Sonya Levien and William Ludwig. Cast: Lana Turner (Crystal Radek), Fernando Lamas (Count Danilo), Una Merkel (Kitty Riley), Richard Haydn (Baron Popoff), Thomas Gomez (King of Marsovia), John Abbott, Marcel Dalio, King Donovan, Robert Coote.

The Merry Widow has also been filmed in France (1913), in an Austrian-French production (1962) and in France as *La Vevue Joyeuse* (1934). In addition, Alma Rubens and Wallace Reid appeared in a two-reeler for Essanay in 1912.

The extravagances of von Stroheim in 1925 almost drove studio head Irving Thalberg around the bend. His star, Mae Murray, referred to the director as "the dirty hun" and accused him of being a madman intent on making a filthy picture. As she said, "All the business of a dirty old man kissing girls' feet and drooling over a closet of woman's clothes! It's repulsive!"

MGM was happy to have the opportunity to film the story with sound in 1934 and use the Franz Lehar music, including "Vilia," "Maxims," "Girls, Girls, Girls" and "The Merry Widow Waltz." There was no question of the choice for Danilo— everyone agreed on Maurice Chevalier; but there were differences as to who should portray the widow. Joan Crawford pleaded for the assignment, but Louis B. Mayer, wouldn't hear of it, preferring Gracie Moore instead. Director Lubitsch, however, felt she was too heavy for the role and his preference was Jeanette MacDonald, who soon became the choice of the studio heads, as well. It is a charming production with both Chevalier and MacDonald delightful as they spar suggestively when he tries to seduce her.

For the 1952 version, Paul Francis Webster was hired to write new lyrics for the Lehar songs and Trudy Erwin was employed to dub for Lana Turner's singing voice. In this version, Turner is an American millionaire, who on returning to Marshovia, the country of her late husband's birth, meets and falls in love with

Count Danilo. Their romance is briefly interrupted when she discovers that he was assigned the job of getting her to fall in love with him by the king of Marshovia, who wanted her to keep her fortune in his kingdom. Turner and Lamas are appealing together, until they open their mouths and speak. It is an expensive production done in bad taste.

583 Merton of the Movies

Based on the novel *Merton* by Harry Leon Wilson and the play by George S. Kaufman and Marc Connelly. Story: When he is fired as a clerk in a small village general store, star-struck Merton Gill goes to Hollywood with hopes of becoming a movie actor. He is befriended by slapstick comedy actress "Flips" Montague. After numerous setbacks and complications, he gets a part in a burlesque of his idol, Harold Parmalee, which he mistakes as a serious drama. His acting is seen as a new type of dead-pan comedy and he is offered a contract with "Flips" as his leading lady, both on and off the screen.

Famous Players/Paramount Pictures, 1924 (original). Silent. Director: James Cruze; screenwriter: Walter Woods. Cast: Glenn Hunter (Merton Gill), Viola Dane (Sally "Flips" Montague), Elliott Roth (Harold Parmalee), Charles Sellor, Sadie Gordon, DeWitt Jennings, Charles Ogle, Ethel Wales.

• ***Make Me a Star*** (remake). Paramount Pictures, 1932. Director: William Beaudine; screenwriters: Sam Mintz, Walter De Leon and Arthur Kober. Cast: Stuart Erwin (Merton Gill), Joan Blondell ("Flips" Montague), Zasu Pitts (Mrs. Scudder), Ben Turpin (Ben), Charles Sellon, Florence Roberts, Helen Jerome Eddy, Arthur Hoyt, Dink Templeton, Ruth Donnelly, Sam Hardy.

• ***Merton of the Movies*** (remake). 1947. Director: Robert Alton; screenwriters: George Wells and Lou Breslow. Cast: Red Skelton (Merton Gill), Virginia O'Brien (Phyllis Montague), Gloria Grahame (Beulah Baxter), Leon Ames (Lawrence Rupert), Alan Mowbray, Charles D. Brown, Hugo Haas, Harry Hayden.

In the 1924 version of the film, Glenn Hunter successfully re-created his Broadway role as the young man with stars in his eyes. Hunter played the role with great sincerity and the production was a hit with both critics and audiences. The 1932 movie with Stu Erwin was even funnier, with Merton playing a western burlesque as if it were a serious John Ford piece. Joan Blondell is a delight as the very helpful "Flips" and the rest of the cast pitches in to make the film a comical success. The time-tested story was made again in 1947 with the great clown Red Skelton in the title role, but by this time audiences and critics didn't seem to get the joke. It wasn't the kind of thing that could bring out Skelton's true comical genius and with a little luck, we have seen the end of the tale of *Merton of the Movies.*

584 Michael O'Halloran

Based on the novel by Gene Stratton Porter. Story: Orphan newsboy Michael O'Halloran adopts little crippled "Peaches" when her grandmother's death leaves her alone. Through a chance encounter with lawyer Douglas Bruce, the children meet the Hardings, a farm couple who take Michael and Peaches to the country to live. The healthy life on the farm renews Peaches' strength and she is soon walking again. Among the children's other acquaintances are the Minturns, a wealthy young couple whose marriage breaks up when the wife neglects her children for society life. She ultimately realizes her error, devotes herself to hospital work, and is reunited with her husband while bird-calling in the woods.

Hodkinson Corporation, 1923 (original). Silent. Director and screenwriter: James Meehan. Cast: Virginia True Boardman (Michael O'Halloran), Ethelyn Irving (Peaches), Irene Rich (Nellie Minturn), Charles Clary (James Minturn), Charles Hill Mailes (Peter Harding), Claire McDowell (Nancy Harding), William Boyd (Douglas Bruce).

• ***Any Man's Wife (Michael O'Halloran)*** (remake). Republic Pictures, 1937. Director: Karl Brown; screenwriter: Adele Buffington. Cast: Wynne Gibson (Grace Minturn), Warren Hull (Dr. Douglas Bruce), Jackie Moran (Michael O'Halloran), Charlene Wyatt (Lily O'Halloran), Sidney Blackmer (Jim Minturn), Hope Manning, G.P. Huntley, Jr., Robert Greig, Helen Lowell.

• ***Michael O'Halloran*** (remake). Monogram Pictures, 1948. Director: John Rawlins; screenwriter: Emma Lazarus. Cast: Scotty Beckett (Michael), Allene Roberts (Lily), Tommy Cook (Joey), Isabell Jewell (Mrs. Nelson), Charles Arnt (Doctor Bruce), Jonathan Hale, Gladys Burke, Roy Gordon, Florence Aver.

Gene Stratton Porter's sentimental story of a poor boy and his little crippled friend is interwoven with the marital problems of the wealthy Minturns in the silent production. By the first remake, the melodramatic domestic tragedy concentrates on Michael and his crippled sister, Lily, surviving the agony of a broken home, with Grace Minturn playing mother. In the third version, Michael helps mentally ill Lily (now that's modernization for you) realize the value of life. The story is archaic and the acting is unbelievably overemotional. The characters just don't ring true.

585 Middle Watch

Based on the play by Ian Hay and Stephen King-Hall. Story: It's a comedy about two young ladies who come aboard a ship as the guests of a couple of officers and are forced to stay the night when the picketboat breaks down. The unexpected visit of the admiral causes the crew to scramble to hide the girls. This finally fails but the arrival of the admiral's jealous wife saves everyone's skin.

British Independent Productions, 1930 (original). Director: Norman Walker; screenwriters: Norman Walker and Frank Launder. Cast: Owen Nares, Jacqueline Logan, Jack Raine, Dodo Watts, Frederick Volpe, Muriel Asked, Phyllis Loring.

• ***Middle Watch*** (remake). Associated British Productions, 1939. Director: Thomas Bentley; screenwriters: Clifford Grey and J. Lee Thompson. Cast: Jack Buchanan, Greta Gynt, Kay Walsh, Fred Emney, Leslie Fuller, Jean Gillie, Martita Hunt, David Hutcheson.

• ***Girls at Sea*** (remake). Associated British Productions, 1958. Director: Gilbert Gunn; screenwriters: T.J. Morrison and Gilbert Gunn. Cast: Michael Horden (the Admiral), Guy Rolfe (the Captain), Ronald Shiner (Marine Ogg),

Fabia Drake (Admiral's wife), Anne Kimbell, Nadine Tallier, Mary Steele, Alan White, Richard Coleman, Lionel Jeffries.

If one is in the proper frame of mind, these inventive comedies are good fun. If not, one may wonder why the stage version was such a smash hit and why it was filmed three times. The films are unevenly produced with the middle one being the least enjoyable. In the last version, Michael Horden, a fine comical gentleman, is rather good as a disapproving admiral who is ultimately blamed for everything by his suspicious wife. The fact that no one is guilty of any real improper behavior is more for lack of opportunity than morality.

586 Midnight

Based on a story by Edwin Justus Mayer and Franz Schulz. Story: Stranded in Paris, gold-digging American adventuress Eve Peabody is hired by aristocrat Georges Flammarion to seduce the gigolo Jacques Picot, who is paying too much attention to the aristocrat's wife, Helene. This gets Eve into European royal society but she eventually falls in love with a poor taxi driver, Tibor Czerny.

Paramount Pictures, 1939 (original). Director: Mitchell Leisen; screenwriters: Charles Brackett and Billy Wilder. Cast: Claudette Colbert (Eve Peabody), Don Ameche (Tibor Czerny), John Barrymore (Georges Flammarion), Francis Lederer (Jacques Picot), Mary Astor (Helene Flammarion), Elaine Barrie, Hedda Hopper, Rex O'Malley, Monty Woolley, Armand Katz.

• ***Masquerade in Mexico*** (remake). Paramount Pictures, 1945. Director: Mitchell Leisen; screenwriter: Karl Tunberg. Cast: Dorothy Lamour (Angel O'Reilly), Arturo de Cordova (Manolo Segovia), Patric Knowles (Thomas Grant), Ann Dvorak (Helen Grant), George Riquad, Natalie Schafer, Mikhail Rasumny.

Midnight is a smart, sophisticated comedy with sparkling performances from an excellent cast. Critics have described it as one of the best comedies of the thirties. The reviews of the remake were not so positive. It can't be the story since it has Patric Knowles convincing Dorothy Lamour to masquerade as a countess in order to lure Arturo de Cordova away from his wife, Ann Dvorak. It can't be the director, because Leisen's back at the old stand for the remake. That leaves changing fashions and the rest of cast. Who'll bet on the cast?

587 Midnight Warning

Based on a story by Norman Battle. Story: A detective investigates an attempted murder in a hotel whose management is attempting to hide the fact that one of its guests has died of bubonic plague.

Mayfair Films, Great Britain, 1933 (original). Director: Spencer G. Bennett; screenwriter: J.T. Neville. Cast: William Boyd, Claudia Dell, Huntley Gordon, John Harron, Hooper Atchley, Lloyd Whitlock, Phillips Smalley, Lloyd Ingraham.

• ***So Long At the Fair*** (remake). Sydney Box/GFD, 1950. Directors: Terence Fisher and Anthony Darnborough; screenwriters: Anthony Thorne and Hugh Mills. Cast: Jean Simmons (Vicky Barton), Dick Bogarde (George Hathaway),

David Tomlinson (Johnny Barton), Marcel Poncin (Narcisse), Cathleen Nesbitt (Madame Merve), Honor Blackman, Betty Warren, Eugene Deckers, Andre Morell, Austin Trevor, Felix Aylmer.

The story of these movies is intriguing. When one of a hotel's guests contracts bubonic plague, the owners, fearing the effect on their business, try desperately to hide the fact, denying that the man was ever a guest, even going so far as to disguise the room that he had stayed in, making it appear that it never existed. In the second version, Jean Simmons is the sister of the man who becomes ill, and his disappearance while they are visiting the Paris Exhibition of 1889 causes her sanity to be questioned by everyone except a painter, Dirk Bogarde, who had met her with her brother shortly before he disappeared. The reason for the disappearance becomes known to the audience at the same time Simmons and Bogarde learn of it.

588 Midshipman Easy

Based on the novel by Frederick Marryat. Story: Argumentative boy Jack Easy wants a life at sea. A family friend arranges for him to be appointed to the position of midshipman in the navy. His independent spirit ensures him many adventures, including fighting Spanish privateers, rescuing a lady and finding a treasure.

Ideal, Great Britain, 1915 (original). Silent. Director: Maurice Elvey; screenwriter: Eliot Stannard. Cast: Compton Coutts (Jack Easy), Elizabeth Risdon (Don's daughter), Fred Groves (Don Sylvo), A.V. Bramble (Mesty).

• ***Midshipman Easy*** (remake). Associated Talking Pictures, Great Britain, 1935. Director: Carol Reed; screenwriter: Anthony Kimmins. Cast: Hughie Green (Jack Easy), Margaret Lockwood (Donna Agnes), Harry Tate (Mr. Biggs), W. Robert Adams (Mesty), Roger Livesey (Capt. Wilson), Dennis Wyndham (Don Silvio), Leis Casson, Tom Gill, Frederick Burtwell, Desmond Tester, Dorothy Holmes-Gore.

These juvenile adventure stories probably wouldn't score high marks with today's youngsters, but at the time of their release, they were like the siren's call, to many, of a youth who would go down to the sea in ships.

589 A Midsummer Night's Dream

Based on the play by William Shakespeare. Story: The problems of two pairs of lovers are sorted out with the "assistance" of fairies at midnight in the woods of Athens.

• ***A Midsummer Night's Dream*** (remake). Warner Bros., 1935. Directors: Max Reinhardt and William Dieterle; screenwriters: Charles Kenyon and Mary McCall. Cast: James Cagney (Bottom), Joe E. Brown (Flute), Hugh Herbert (Snout), Victor Jory (Oberon), Olivia de Havilland (Hermia), Ross Alexander (Demetrius), Verre Teasdale (Hippolyta), Dick Powell (Lysander), Jean Muir (Helena), Ian Hunter (Theseus), Anita Louise (Titania), Mickey Rooney (Puck), Frank McHugh (Quince), Grant Mitchell (Egeus), Nini Theilade, Dewey Robinson, Hobart Cavanaugh, Otis Harlan, Arthur Treacher, Billy Barty.

• ***A Midsummer Night's Dream*** (remake). Columbia Pictures, 1966.

Directors: George Balanchine and Dan Eriksen; screenwriters: William Shakespeare, with the ballet conceived by George Balanchine. Cast: Susan Farrell (Titania), Edward Villella (Oberon), Arthur Mitchell (Puck), Patricia McBride (Hermia), Nicholas Magallanes (Lysander), Mimi Paul (Helena), Roland Varquez (Demetrius), Jacques D'Amboise, Allegra Kent, Francisco Monican, Gloria Gourin, Richard Rapp.

• ***A Midsummer Night's Dream*** (remake). Eagle Films, 1969. Director: Peter Hall; screenwriter: William Shakespeare. Cast: Derek Godfrey (Theseus), Barbara Jefford (Hippolyta), Hugh Sullivan (Philostrate), Nicholas Selby (Egeus), David Warner (Lysander), Michael Jayston (Demetrius), Diana Rigg (Helena), Helen Mirra (Hermia), Ian Richardson (Oberon), Judi Dench (Titania), Ian Holm (Puck), Paul Rogers (Bottom), Sebastian Shaw (Quince), Bill Travers (Snout), John Normington (Flute), Clive Swift (Snug), Donald Eccles (Starveling).

Silent versions of *A Midsummer Night's Dream* were filmed in 1909, 1910, 1912, 1913, 1917, 1925 and in 1929. In addition to those mentioned above, sound productions included the 1959 Czechoslovakian puppet version directed by Jiri Trinka, and a 1967 movie by Columbia Pictures. The Max Reinhardt production is the most well-known, not because it was the best version of Shakespeare's play, but because of its all-star Hollywood cast. Performers like James Cagney, Joe E. Brown, and Mickey Rooney seemed merely to be adapting their usual portrayals to unusual material. The lovers were at best wimpy, acting as if they weren't certain that their behavior was appropriate for the play. For the most part their fears were well-founded. The film has been highly praised in some corners as a Hollywood classic and in others dismissed as a travesty. The truth lies somewhere between these views. It's not great theater and it's not a bad movie. It's just an entertaining romp, with a mixed bag of performances.

The balletic staging of Shakespeare's fantastical comedy about love among humans and forest spirits, with music by Felix Mendlessohn, was in many ways a lovely piece, with beautiful dancing and decent camera work, even though these weren't able to overcome the fact that what is seen is merely the filming of a ballet, not a movie with a developing story. The 1969 version of the comedy was billed as "realistic" and a faithful following of the Bard's script, but despite a fine, well-spoken cast drawn from the Royal Shakespeare Company, many viewers began to squirm in their seats long before the play was concluded.

590 The Milky Way

Based on the play by Lynn Root and Harry Clark. Story: Burleigh Sullivan, a timid milkman, is deluded into believing that he is a great prizefighter. It seems that as a put-upon youth he learned to be extremely good at ducking. One night, Burleigh becomes involved in a street brawl. He ducks and when he raises his head, he finds himself standing over the reigning middleweight boxing champion, who never saw the horse that kicked him in the chin. No one else saw it either, all believing that Burleigh had floored the champ with a mighty punch. To redeem his fighter, the manager of the champion, Gabby Sloan, concocts a plan of providing the milkman with a series of set-up fights, and after an impressive string of these fixed matches, put him in the ring with the champion, who will then destroy Burleigh. Is it really necessary to go on?

Paramount Pictures, 1936 (original). Director: Leo McCarey; screenwriters: Grover Jones, Frank Butler and Richard Connell. Cast: Harold Lloyd (Burleigh Sullivan), Adolphe Menjou (Gabby Sloan), Verree Teasdale (Ann Westley), Helen Mack (Mae Sullivan), William Gargan (Speed MacFarland), George Barbier (Wilbur Austin), Dorothy Wilson, Lionel Stander, Charles Lane.

• ***The Kid from Brooklyn*** (remake). RKO, 1946. Director: Norman Z. McLeod; screenwriters: Don Hartman and Melville Shavelson. Cast: Danny Kaye (Burleigh Sullivan), Virginia Mayo (Polly Pringle), Vera-Ellen (Susie Sullivan), Steve Cochran (Speed MacFarland), Eve Arden (Ann Westley), Walter Abel (Gabby Sloan), Fay Bainter, Clarence Kolb, Victor Cutler, Charles Cane, Jerome Cowan, Don Wilson, Knox Manning, Johnny Downs, the Goldwyn Girls.

Lloyd's comedy is a frolicsome piece with many signs of the comedian's old silent film genius. The supporting cast is excellent, particularly Menjou as the gum-chewing manager and Lionel Stander as the illiterate, ice-cream loving trainer. In the repeat, Danny Kaye portrays the meek milkman who accidently fells a champion boxer and finds himself with a new career in the ring. It's certainly not Kaye at his best, but with his almost-repertoire company of Virginia Mayo, Vera Ellen and Steve Cochran, the film has some splendid moments.

Million Dollar Duck *see* **Mr. Drake's Duck**

The Millionaire *see* **The Ruling Passion**

The Mind of Mr. Reeder *see* **Mr. Reeder in Room 13**

The Miniver Story *see* **Mrs. Miniver**

Le Mioche *see* **Forty Little Mothers**

591 The Miracle Man

Based on the short story by Frank L. Packard and the play by George M. Cohan. Story: Tom Burke, Rose and the Frog are three con artists who plan to use a faith healer, the Patriarch, to bilk money from the gullible public. When the faith healer performs a real miracle, all three amend their ways.

Mayflower/Artcraft/Paramount Pictures, 1919 (original). Silent. Director and screenwriter: George Loane Tucker. Cast: Thomas Meighan (Tom Burke), Betty Compson (Rose), Lon Chaney (the Frog), Joseph J. Dowling (the Patriarch), J.M. Dumont (the Dope), W. Lawson Butt, Elinor Fair.

• ***The Miracle Man*** (remake). Paramount Pictures, 1932. Director: Norman McLeod; screenwriters: Waldemar Young and Samuel Hoffenstein. Cast: Sylvia Sidney (Helen Smith), John Madison (Chester Morris), Irving Pichel (Henry Holmes), John Wray (the Frog), Robert Coogan (Bobbie), Hobart Bosworth (the Patriarch), Boris Karloff, Ned Sparks, Lloyd Hughes, Virginia Bruce, Florine McKinney.

The silent film was among the most highly praised and successful films of its era. It made stars out of Thomas Meighan, Betty Compson and the incredible Lon Chaney. The latter, known respectfully as "the Man of a Thousand Faces" gave one of the most memorable character performances in the history of motion pictures. The remake was a faithful adaptation of the silent classic and had fine performances from a decent cast, with John Wray doing a good job as the Frog, but it didn't have the power of the original. The nature of the story made it more effective to be told with the faces of the performers rather than to hear their words.

592 The Miracle of Morgan's Creek

Based on a screenplay by Preston Sturges. Story: Dimwitted, stuttering, boy-crazy, jitterbugging Trudy Kockenlocker, daughter of the town constable, finds herself pregnant, but because she was drunk at the time, she doesn't know which soldier is the father. She thinks she was with a "Sergeant Ratsky-Atsky." She and her precocious sister, Emmy, concoct a scheme to marry Trudy to Norval Jones, a beleaguered draft rejectee.

Paramount Pictures, 1944 (original). Director and screenwriter: Preston Sturges. Cast: Betty Hutton (Trudy Kockenlocker), Eddie Bracken (Norval Jones), Diana Lynn (Emmy Kockenlocker), William Demarest (Officer Kockenlocker), Brian Donlevy (Governor McGinty), Akim Tamiroff (the Boss), Georgia Caine, Emory Parnell, Almira Sessions, J. Farrell MacDonald, Jimmy Conlin, Bryon Foulger, Jack Norton, Bobby Watson, Porter Hall.

• ***Rock-a-Bye Baby*** (remake). 1958. Director and screenwriter: Frank Tashlin. Cast: Jerry Lewis (Clayton Poole), Marilyn Maxwell (Carla Naples), Connie Stevens (Sandy Naples), Salvatore Baccaloni (Salvatore Naples), Reginald Gardiner (Henry Herman), Hans Conreid, Ida Moore, Gary Lewis, Judy Franklin.

Preston Sturges was not only a great comic director but also a great writer of comic material. In *The Miracle of Morgan's Creek*, he took on the censors and the prevailing portrayal of the girl back home during the war years. Bluenoses didn't see any humor in an unmarried girl being pregnant, particularly if she had no idea which man was responsible. Movies of the time might hint that a young loving couple went all the way just prior to the boy being shipped off to the war, but no one was supposed to laugh at the beauty of their true feelings for each other. Girls who were crazy for anything in uniform didn't get the guys and they certainly didn't get a baby. A lesser writer and director might have not been able to pull it off and get away with thumbing his nose at both the Hays Office and the sentimental notions people liked to hold about their youngsters. But Sturges' madcap comedy not only survived the furor with the censors, he produced a first class comical masterpiece. The cast, headed by Betty Hutton, Eddie Bracken and Diana Lynn, was superb.

And then we have *Rock-a-Bye Baby*. This tasteless remake doesn't even give credit to Sturges, but perhaps that's just as well for the master's reputation. In this version, film star Marilyn Maxwell asks her devoted admirer, Jerry Lewis, to mind her triplets by a secret marriage. In complying, Jerry disrupts the shooting of a Cecil B. De Mille–type production of a Hollywood religious epic. In comparing this film to the Sturges picture, one notices that the characters are unsympathetic, unlike the Kockenlockers, whom one really cares for.

593 The Mirage

Based on the play by Edwin Selwyn. Story: Leaving her small hometown and sweetheart, Irene Martin goes to New York hoping to become an opera singer. She is able to secure a job in a show on the Knickerbocker Roof, where she meets wealthy Henry Galt, who asks her to a party. The next day, Irene receives some roses and money from Galt, payment for entertaining his guests. Outraged that Galt would mistake her for a girl who sold her company, she goes to him to return the money. He explains that he often hires chorus girls to entertain at his parties but only to enjoy themselves with his male guests, nothing more, and works out an arrangement for Irene to serve as a hostess at his various soirées. She handles the assignment with aloofness and Galt comes to love her. Enter Irene's hometown sweetheart, Al Manning, who believes the worst about Irene and her work with Galt. Deciding if she's that kind of girl, she should be for him as well, he tries to "force his attentions on her." When these are repelled, Al tells Irene's mother that her daughter is a fallen woman. Galt, recognizing that he has compromised Irene, asks her to marry him. Believing he's only trying to be gallant, she refuses, but when he declares his love for her she agrees.

Regal Pictures, 1924 (original). Silent. Director: George Archainbaud. Cast: Florence Vidor (Irene Martin), Clive Brook (Henry Galt), Alan Roscoe (Al Manning), Vola Vale, Myrtle Vane, Charlotte Stevens.

• ***Possessed*** (remake). MGM, 1931. Director: Clarence Brown; screenwriter: Lenore Coffee. Cast: Joan Crawford (Marian), Clark Gable (Mark Whitney), Wallace Ford (Al Manning), Skeets Gallagher, Frank Conroy, Marjorie White, John Miljan, Clara Blandick.

In the remake, Joan Crawford is not so lily pure as was Florence Vidor. She's Clark Gable's mistress and they live together, openly. Even coming at the end of the Roaring Twenties, such behavior was pretty daring and this film no doubt contributed to the pressure on the studios to clean up their act and adopt some stringent production codes. By today's relaxed standards, neither story is shocking, merely a bit quaint.

594 Mirage

Based on the novel *Fallen Angels* by Howard Fast. Story: David suddenly finds that he can't remember the past two years of his life. He goes so far as to hire a private investigator and a psychiatrist to help him discover who he is, what has happened to him and why he can't remember any part of his past life. It slowly becomes clear that there are those who don't wish him to regain his memory. Ultimately he learns that during a New York blackout, he was present when an executive fell or was pushed to his death from a window high in a skyscraper and the shock cost him his memory.

Universal Pictures, 1965. Director: Edward Dmytryk; screenwriter: Peter Stone. Cast: Gregory Peck (David), Diane Baker (Sheila), Walter Matthau (Ted Caselle), Kevin McCarthy (Josephson), Jack Weston (Lester), Leif Erickson, Walter Abel, George Kennedy, Robert H. Harris, Anne Seymour.

• ***Jigsaw*** (remake). Universal Pictures, 1968. Director: James Goldstone; screenwriter: Quentin Werty. Cast: Harry Guardino (Arthur Belding), Bradford Dillman (Jonathan Fields), Hope Lange (Helen Atterbury), Pat Hingle (Lew Haley), Diana Hyland (Sarah), Victor Jory, Paul Stewart, Susan Saint James.

Mirage is a rather slow moving film but nevertheless enjoyable, with Peck effectively showing how frightening it is not to remember anything about one's earlier life. The process of getting his memory back is interestingly presented. *Jigsaw* resorts to the more trendy problem of LSD-induced hallucinations of a man trying to remember what happened to him. Unfortunately, the potential suspense of the movie is ruined because this is a mystery only to the main character. The audience is made aware of much too much early in the movie and everything else is just for shock appeal as the hero puts the pieces together.

595 Miranda

Based on the play by Peter Blackmore. Story: While spending a fishing holiday alone in Cornwall, a prominent British physician, Paul Marten, is dragged out of his boat and taken to the bottom of the sea by a lovely mermaid, Miranda. After surviving this, he takes her to London disguised as an invalid. The expected comical situations of keeping her identity secret and what to do about a rather unnatural love take up the remaining running time of the film.

Gainsborough-Box Productions, 1948 (original). Director: Ken Annakin; screenwriter: Peter Blackmore. Cast: Glynis Johns (Miranda), Googie Withers (Claire Marten), Griffith Jones (Paul Marten), John McCallum (Nigel), Margaret Rutherford (Nurse Cary), David Tomlinson, Yvonne Owen, Sonia Holm.

• ***Mad About Men*** (sequel). General Film Distributors, 1954. Director: Ralph Thomas; screenwriter: Peter Blackmore. Cast: Glynis Johns (Miranda/Caroline), Anne Crawford (Barbara), Donald Sinden (Jeff), Margaret Rutherford (Nurse Cary), Dora Bryan (Berengaria), Nicholas Phipps, Peter Martyn.

These two films were quite successful, even though the humor was predictable. Glynis Johns was fetching as the mermaid and Margaret Rutherford scored high marks as the comical Nurse Cary. In the sequel, Miranda persuades her on-land double to go on vacation so she can take her place and have some romantic adventures. 1948 was a good year for mermaids, as Universal Pictures tried to cash-in on the success of *Miranda* by releasing its own funny film, *Mr. Peabody and the Mermaid* starring William Powell and Ann Blyth as the title characters, respectively. It wasn't among the highlights of the careers of either of the stars. In 1984, Ron Howard directed a surprise hit, *Splash!*, with Daryl Hannah as a delectable blonde mermaid who finds her legs every now and then, usually just in time to make love to Tom Hanks. With this last film, one would think that the motion picture industry has about exhausted all of the jokes that can be made about a mermaid and a man, but we'll just have to wait and see what the tide washes up in the future.

596 The Misadventures of Merlin Jones

Based on a story by Bill Walsh. Story: Merlin Jones is a brainy student who develops the ability to read minds. He mentally eavesdrops on a judge, and discovers his honor is plotting a robbery. But the police won't believe Merlin when he reports what he has uncovered. It's just as well. Seems the judge writes mysteries and he was just preparing a new story. Merlin's other interest is hypnotism, once again with the judge as his guinea pig. His experiment causes the judge to break into a college's lab and steal a chimpanzee who seems smarter than anyone else in this silly movie.

Disney/Buena Vista, 1963 (original). Director: Robert Stevenson; screenwriters: Tom and Helen August. Cast: Tommy Kirk (Merlin Jones), Annette Funicello (Jennifer), Leon Ames (Judge Holmsby), Stuart Erwin, Alan Hewitt, Connie Gilchrist.

• ***The Monkey's Uncle*** (sequel). Disney/Buena Vista, 1966. Director: Robert Stevenson; screenwriters: Tom and Helen August. Cast: Tommy Kirk (Merlin Jones), Annette Funicello (Jennifer), Leon Ames (Judge Holmsby), Frank Faylen, Arthur O'Connell, Leon Tyler, Norman Grabowksi, Alan Hewitt.

Disney movies are meant to be wholesome family fare, but must wholesome and family be equated with inane and boring? The Disney people produced these films to guarantee that they would fill the time frames of the Disney television show. Both have two separate stories, taking up about half of each movie. The sequel is a better movie but that's meant as faint praise and is only offered for the sequence that deals with Merlin's invention of a flying machine. It is designed to satisfy a rich man's desire to see a man fly, after which he promises to give the college ten million dollars. Merlin flies, but the benefactor proves to be a nut escaped from a funny farm to which he is promptly returned.

597 Les Miserables

Based on the novel by Victor Hugo. Story: Jean Valjean is sentenced to the galleys at Toulon for stealing a loaf of bread to feed the starving family of his sister. After many long years of hard labor he escapes, and the bitter man is befriended by Bishop Bienvenu from whom he steals silver candlesticks. Caught with the loot, he is brought back to the Bishop, who tells the gendarmes that he had given the candlesticks to the man as a present. This act of kindness restores Valjean's faith in mankind. He makes a success of himself under a new identity, adopts Cosette, the daughter of a dying prostitute (Fantine) he had tried to help, and is even elected mayor of a small French town. His secret is uncovered by relentless police inspector Javert, and he is forced to flee with Cosette to Paris. Here Cosette falls in love with revolutionary young student Marius. Javert by this time is a police official in Paris and recognizes Valjean and is off in pursuit of him once again. When Marius is wounded in a street riot, Valjean risks his own capture to rescue the young man, carrying him from the scene of the riot through the sewers, closely followed by Javert. Finally, compassion for Valjean conflicts with Javert's insistence on strict adherence to the law. Unable to resolve his confused feelings, Javert allows Valjean to escape and drowns himself in the Seine.

• ***Les Miserables*** (remake). Fox Film Corporation, 1917. Silent. Director and screenwriter: Frank Lloyd. Cast: William Farnum (Jean Valjean), Hardee Kirkland (Javert), Jewell Carmen (Cosette), George Moss (the Bishop), Harry Springler (Marius), Sonia Markova (Fantine), Dorothy Bernard, Edward Elkas, Mina Ross.

• ***Les Miserables*** (remake). Films de France, 1926. Silent. Director and screenwriter: Henri Fascourt. Cast: Gabriel Gabrio (Jean Valjean), Jean Toulout (Javert), Paul Jorge (Msgr. Myriel), Sandra Milowanoff (Fantine/Cosette), Nivette Saillard, Paul Guide, Clara Narcey-Roche, M.G. Saillard, Renee Carl, M. Rozet.

• ***Les Miserables*** (remake). Pathe-Nathan Productions, France, 1934. Director: Raymond Bernard; screenwriters: Andre Lang and Raymond Bernard. Cast: Harry Baur (Jean Valjean), Charles Vanel (Javert), Josseline Gael (Fantine/Cosette), Henry Krauss (Msgr. Myriel), Jean Servais (Marius), Charles Dullin, Emile Genevois, Marguerite Moreno, Gaby Triquet.

• ***Les Miserables*** (remake). United Artists, 1935. Director: Richard Boleslawski; screenwriter: W.P. Lipscomb. Cast: Fredric March (Jean Valjean), Charles Laughton (Javert), Cedric Hardwicke (Bishop Bienvenu), Rochelle Hudson (Cosette), John Beal (Marius), Florence Eldridge (Fantine), Frances Drake, Jesse Ralph, Ferdinand Gottschalk, Jane Kerr, Eily Malyon, Marilyn Knowlden.

• ***Les Miserables*** (remake). Twentieth Century–Fox, 1952. Director: Lewis Milestone; screenwriter: Richard Murphy. Cast: Michael Rennie (Jean Valjean), Robert Newton (Javert), Debra Paget (Cosette), Edmund Gwenn (the Bishop), Sylvia Sidney (Fantine), Cameron Mitchell (Marius), Elsa Lanchester, James Robinson Justice, Joseph Wiseman, Rhys Williams, Florence Bates, Merry Anders.

Other versions of *Les Miserables* were filmed in France in 1906, 1911, 1933, 1952 and 1957; in the United States in 1909, 1910, 1925, 1927, and 1929; in Great Britain in 1912; in Japan in 1929 and 1950; in Russia in 1937; in Mexico in 1943; in India in 1955 and in Turkey in 1967.

Hugo's magnificent story was perhaps most successfully filmed in 1935 with Fredric March as Jean Valjean and Charles Laughton as Inspector Javert. It was a lavish production, and the performances were outstanding. The expression that comes across March's face when he realizes that the Bishop, beautifully played by Cedric Hardwicke, is not going to have him sent back to the galleys, but rather give him a new start in life, is magnificent. Both March and Laughton give one of their most memorable performances. Others in the cast were also excellent, making the production first-rate all around.

The 1952 remake with Michael Rennie and Robert Newton in the leading roles was somewhat disappointing. It's not that the story wasn't told in a way to bring tears to audiences and get the adrenaline flowing as Javert closed in on Valjean, but something important seemed to be missing. The transformation of Valjean, from a bitter, almost animal-like man to one who helped others and showed his decency in many ways, wasn't as well developed as in the United Artists version. Also, Newton's conflict seemed more the obsession of a seriously mentally ill man, rather than a dedicated civil servant who didn't know how to factor compassion into the equation of life that he had so willingly written.

598 Miss Bluebeard

Based on the play *Little Miss Bluebeard* by Avery Hopwood and *Der Gatte des Frauleins* by Gabor Dregely. Story: Larry Charters, a composer of popular songs, has friend Bob Hawley impersonate him so he can have a little peace and quiet while on vacation and not be hounded by admiring female fans. As the pair travel through France, Bob meets French actress Colette on a train. Accidently left behind in a small village, Bob and Colette go to the mayor's house in search of lodging. The mayor, who is drunk, thinks they wish to be married and he performs the ceremony, marrying Colette to Bob in Larry's name. When the two arrive in Paris, Larry meets his new and unexpected wife. Larry falls in love with Colette and arranges for her to stay with him, but she insists that the arrangement be as his wife in name only until it can be straightened out as to who really is her husband. Meanwhile, Bob becomes engaged to Gloria, one of Colette's friends. Finally, Colette and Larry decide that they love each other and just to be on the safe side, they should marry or remarry, whatever the case may be.

Famous Players/Paramount Pictures, 1925 (original). Silent. Director: Frank Tuttle; screenwriter: Townsend Martin. Cast: Bebe Daniels (Colette Girard), Robert Frazer (Larry Charters), Kenneth MacKenna (Bob Hawley), Raymond Griffith (the Mayor), Martha Madison (Lulu), Diana Kane (Gloria Harding), Lawrence D'Orsay, Florence Billings, Ivan Simpson.

• ***Her Wedding Night*** (remake). Paramount-Publix Corp., 1930. Director: Frank Tuttle; screenwriters: Henry Myers and Avery Hopwood. Cast: Clara Bow (Norma Martin), Ralph Forbes (Larry Charters), Charles Ruggles (Bertie Bird), Skeets Gallagher (Bob Hawley), Geneva Mitchell (Gloria Marshall), Rosita Moreno (Lulu), Natalie Kingston, Wilson Benge, Lillian Elliott.

These bedroom farces were fine fun with winning performances from all of the principals, particularly Raymond Griffith and Charley Ruggles, who impersonated the intoxicated mayor in the two pictures. As is usually the case in these mixed-up identity plots, the complications only occur to the participants. All difficulties could be resolved in more sane ways that those chosen, but then there would be no movie, would there?

Miss Brewster's Millions *see* **Brewster's Millions**

599 Miss Pinkerton

Based on the novel by Mary Roberts Rinehart. Story: It's a conventional murder mystery about a courageous nurse, Miss Adams, who searches for clues in the gloomy corridors of a dreary old house. The audience is kept guessing about who killed Herbert Wynne. Was it the butler? The housekeeper? The demonic doctor?

First National Pictures, 1932 (original). Director: Lloyd Bacon; screenwriters: Nevin Busch and Lillian Hayward. Cast: Joan Blondell (Miss Adams), George Brent (Patten), Mae Madison (Nurse), John Wray (Hugo), Ruth Hall (Paula Brent), Alan Lane (Herbert Wynne), C. Henry Gordon, Donald Dilloway, Elizabeth Patterson, Blanche Frederici.

• ***The Nurse's Secret*** (remake). First National/Warner Bros., 1941. Director: Noel M. Smith; screenwriter: Anthony Coldeway. Cast: Lee Patrick (Ruth Adams), Regis Toomey (Inspector Tom Patten), Julie Bishop (Florence Lents), Ann Edmonds (Paula Brent), George Campeau (Charles Elliott), Clara Blandick (Juliet Mitchell), Charles D. Waldron, Charles Trowbridge, Leonard Muse, Virginia Brissac, Frank Reicher, Georgia Caine.

These whodunnits have the grace not to make it easy on the viewers to spot the murderer. Many suspects will benefit from the death and enough false clues keep the audience guessing as to the identity of the villain. The acting isn't anything special, but the films are a satisfactory hour's diversion. In the remake, Lee Patrick is a nurse assigned to an ailing dowager and Regis Toomey appears as a police inspector who must solve a murder that occurred in the old lady's house. The main suspects are Ann Edmonds, George Campeau, Clara Blandick and Leonard Muse.

Miss Robin Hood *see* **Robin Hood**

Miss Sadie Thompson *see* **Sadie Thompson**

The Missing Guest *see* **The Secret of the Blue Room**

600 Missing in Action

Based on a screenplay by Arthur Silver, Larry Levison and Steve Bing. Story: Colonel James Braddock is a one-man army whose mission is to free the other Americans who shared with him the Vietnam prison from which he escaped.

Cannon Group, 1984 (original). Director: Joseph Zito; screenwriters: Arthur Silver, Larry Levison and Steve Bing. Cast: Chuck Norris (Col. James Braddock), M. Emmet Walsh, Leonore Kasdorf, James Hong.

• ***Missing in Action 2: The Beginning*** (sequel). Cannon Group, 1985. Director: Lance Hool; screenwriter: Larry Levison, Arthur Silver and Steve Bing. Cast: Chuck Norris (Col. Braddock), Soon-Teck Oh (Col. Yin), Steven Williams (Nester), Bennett Ohta (Col. Ho), Cosie Costa, Joe Michael Terry, John Wesley, David Chung.

Karate star Chuck Norris almost succeeds in making these violent films enjoyable. The sequel of the surprise hit of 1984 is actually a prequel (well, actually it's the same movie as far as story and action is concerned), showing how Norris escaped from a Vietnam prison after ten years of torture.

Missing in Action 2: The Beginning *see* **Missing in Action**

Missing Witnesses *see* **Bureau of Missing Persons**

Mississippi *see* **The Fighting Coward**

601 The Mississippi Gambler

Based on a story by Karl Brown and Leonard Fields. Story: Handsome Jack Morgan is a gambler who plies his trade on the Mississippi riverboats. He wins a large amount of money from Junius Blackburn, which doesn't belong to the latter. Junius' daughter Lucy had shown Morgan a locket which she says she will one day give to the man she loves. Jealous of Morgan's obvious interest in the lovely Lucy, one of his earlier conquests, Suzette, denounces Morgan to Lucy, claiming that he is a cheat and has obtained her father's money dishonestly. Lucy demands that Morgan return the winnings but he refuses. However, he offers Lucy the chance of winning the money in a card game with her putting herself up as the matching bet. In desperation she agrees. Morgan pretends to lose, and returns the money. When Lucy learns that he had the winning hand, she sends her locket to him.

Universal Pictures, 1929 (original). Part talkie. Director: Reginald Barker; screenwriter: Edward T. Lowe, Jr. Cast: Joseph Schildkraut (Jack Morgan), Joan Bennett (Lucy Blackburn), Carmelita Geraghty (Suzette Richards), Alec B. Francis (Junius Blackburn), Otis Harlan, William Welsh.

• ***The Mississippi Gambler*** (remake). Universal Pictures, 1953. Director: Rudolph Mate; screenwriter: Seton I. Miller. Cast: Tyrone Power (Mark Fallon), Piper Laurie (Angelique Duroux), Julia Adams (Ann Conant), John McIntire (Kansas John Polly), Paul Cavanaugh (Edmund Duroux), John Baer (Laurent Duroux), Ralph Dumke (Caldwell), Ron Randall, Robert Warwick, William Reynolds, Guy Williams.

Of the two, the earlier one makes the most sense. In the second film, Tyrone Power is an honest riverboat gambler who meets fiery southern belle Piper Laurie when he cleans out her brother in a card game. He continues his negative wooing of Piper in New Orleans, where because of him, her brother is branded a coward, then later killed, once again with Power the indirect instrument. To make matters worse, Piper's father is killed in a duel, defending the honor of Power and Julia Adams, a girl that Ty has befriended after her brother had killed himself because of card losses. Things don't look too good for the romance when Piper marries banker Ron Randall, but the latter turns out to be a scoundrel who absconds with some funds and leaves the way open for Ty and Piper to end the movie in a happy embrace. The moral is clear: "Don't gamble more that you can afford to lose." It might also be, "true love doesn't run smoothly" or some other equally snappy maxim. The film looked better than it was.

Mr. Belvedere Goes to College *see* **Sitting Pretty**

Mr. Belvedere Rings the Bell *see* **Sitting Pretty**

Mr. Billion *see* **Mr. Deeds Goes to Town**

602 Mr. Deeds Goes to Town

Based on the novel *Opera Hat* by Clarence Budington Kelland. Story: Guileless young poet Longfellow Deeds' quiet small-town life is disrupted when he inherits a fortune. Encouraged by friends, he moves to New York, where opportunists take advantage of his naiveté. Particularly galling to Deeds is to discover that a girl, Babe Bennett, he has met and felt cared for him is actually a newspaper reporter who has been writing stories about him, making fun of his innocence. He decides to give away all of the money which has not brought him happiness, and this intention gets him thrown into a sanity hearing. With the help of Babe, who now has come to love the sweet and simple young man, he proves he's not any crazier than anyone else.

Columbia Pictures, 1936 (original). Director: Frank Capra; screenwriter: Robert Riskin. Cast: Gary Cooper (Longfellow Deeds), Jean Arthur (Babe Bennett), George Bancroft (Mac Wade), Lionel Stander (Cornelius Cobb), Margaret McWade (Amy Faulkner), Margaret Seddon (Jane Faulkner), Douglas Dumbrille (John Cedar), Raymond Walburn, Margaret Matzenauer, H.B. Warner.

• ***Mr. Billion*** (remake). Twentieth Century–Fox, 1977. Director: Jonathan Kaplan; screenwriters: Ken Friedman and Jonathan Kaplan. Cast: Terence Hill (Guido Falcone), Valerie Perrine (Rosi Jones), Jackie Gleason (John Cutler), Slim Pickens (Duane Hawkins), William Redfield (Leopold Lacy), Chill Wills (Colonel Clayton T. Winkle), Dick Miller, R.G. Armstrong, Dave Cass.

Frank Capra won an Academy Award for Best Director for *Mr. Deeds Goes to Town,* while the picture, Cooper and screenwriter Riskin were nominated for awards but did not win. Capra's comedies were always generously laced with social commentary, depicting the plight of an innocent up against corruption in the world, and after a struggle, winning. This film has been given much praise but it's not Capra at his best, even though it is entertaining. Things drag every once in awhile and a review of Capra filmography will probably lead one to the conclusion that James Stewart was more ideally suited to be a Capra hero than was Gary Cooper. The disguised remake, *Mr. Billion,* is a moderately enjoyable old-fashioned comedy-adventure about an Italian mechanic who inherits a fortune, and while on his way to San Francisco to claim it, encounters a wide assortment of con artists, phonies and crooks who wish to take it from him.

603 Mr. Drake's Duck

Based on the radio play by Ian Messiter. Story: It's a satire about a newlywed couple, Don and Penny Drake, who settle on a British farm, only to find that one of their ducks lays uranium eggs. This puts the Drakes in conflict with the military, who declare the farm restricted territory in the name of national security.

Angel-Fairbanks/Eros, 1951 (original). Director and screenwriter: Val Guest. Cast: Douglas Fairbanks, Jr. (Don Drake), Yolande Donlan (Penny Drake), Howard Marion-Crawford, Reginald Beckwith, Wilfrid Hyde-White, John Boxer, Jon Pertwee, Peter Butterworth, Tom Gill, A.E. Matthews.

• ***Million Dollar Duck*** (remake). Disney/Buena Vista, 1971. Director: Vincent McEveety; screenwriter: Roswell Rogers; based on a story by Ted Key. Cast: Dean Jones (Professor Albert Dooley), Sandy Duncan (Kate), Joe Flynn, Tony Roberts, James Gregory, Lee Harcourt Montgomery.

The first version of the amazing poultry story gives several fine British character actors an opportunity to strut their stuff. They made the production mildly amusing. The Disney film gives no credit to the Val Guest–directed movie, but the story is more than vaguely familiar. In this one, a duck lays eggs with golden yolks, which raises the interest both of the government and a band of crooks.

604 Mr. Lucky

Based on the short story "Bundles for Freedom" by Milton Holmes. Story: During World War II roguish gambling ship owner Joe Adams, known as Mr. Lucky, plans to use a war-relief organization as a front for his illegal activities. But after associating with the dedicated ladies running the Bundles for Britain operation, particularly Dorothy Bryant, he develops some patriotism and turns on his associates who wish to continue with the original plan.

RKO Pictures, 1943 (original). Director: H.C. Potter; screenwriters: Milton Holmes and Adrian Scott. Cast: Cary Grant (Joe Adams), Laraine Day (Dorothy Bryant), Charles Bickford (Hard Swede), Gladys Cooper (Captain Steadman), Alan Carney (Crunk), Henry Stephenson, Paul Stewart, Kay Johnson.

• ***Gambling House*** (remake). RKO Pictures, 1950. Director: Ted Tetzlaff; screenwriters: Marvin Borowsky and Allen Rivkin, based on a story by Erwin Gelsey. Cast: Victor Mature (Marc Fury), Terry Moore (Lynn Warren), William Bendix (Joe Farrow), Zachary A. Charles (Willie), Basil Ruysdael, Donald Randolph, Damian O'Flynn, Cleo Moore, Ann Doran.

These two films, based on different stories, are paired because both deal with the theme of a gambler who finally comes to a realization of what his country means to him. Both Grant's and Mature's characters have taken advantage of being in America, until with the help of a loving woman, they come to see that they have some obligations also. Mature portrays a gambler who is blamed for a murder committed by William Bendix. Although he is able to clear himself, it comes out that he was born in Italy, and he is faced with deportation as an undesirable alien. Social worker Terry Moore helps him convince the hearing judge that he loves his adopted country and deserves the chance to become a citizen. Neither film is successful cinematically. Neither Grant nor Mature seem to be sure of what they are doing. In the first film, audiences are sometimes hard pressed to decide if the film is a comedy or a drama and it ends up being neither. There's no doubt of the intended format in the second film; it's heavy melodrama all the way with a happy ending.

Mr. Moto on Danger Island *see* **Murder in Trinidad**

Mr. Music *see* **Accent on Youth**

Mr. Peabody and the Mermaid *see* **Miranda**

Mister Quilp *see* **The Old Curiosity Shop**

605 Mr. Reeder in Room 13

Based on the novel *Room 13* by Edgar Wallace. Story: Mr. Reeder, a Bank of England detective, is on the trail of a counterfeit gang. He enlists the aid of a Foreign Office employee, Johnny Gray, who serves three years in prison trying to become part of the counterfeit ring. On his release, he finds his girl has married the gang leader. Her father, whose ex-partner was the crime chief's equally crooked father, takes a macabre revenge, while Reeder has to save Gray from being hanged by the rest of the gang.

Associated British Productions, 1938 (original). Director: Norman Lee; screenwriters: Doreen Montgomery, Victor Kendall and Elizabeth Meehan. Cast: Gibb McLaughlin (Mr. Reeder), Peter M. Hill (Johnny Gray), Sally Gray, Leslie Perrins.

• ***The Mind of Mr. Reeder*** (sequel). Grand National Pictures, 1939. Director: Jack Raymond; screenwriters: Bryan Wallace, Marjorie Gaffney and Michael Hogan. Cast: Will Fyffe (Mr. Reeder), John Warwick (Bracher), Romily Lunge (Inspector Gaylor), George Curzon, Chili Bouchier.

Novelist Edgar Wallace's works were filmed many times. Between 1960 and 1963, Greenwood Productions turned out 47 second features, supposedly based on the author's work. Mr. Reeder, detective for the Bank of England, was just one of many of the creations of the prolific writer. In the sequel, Mr. Reeder trails a gang of forgers to a nightclub run by Bracher, and finds a printing press in the cellar. Inspector Gaylor is shot trying to arrest Bracher and fragments of glass lead Reeder to suspect a Mr. Welford, whose wife is Bracher's mistress, of being involved with the forgery ring. Reeder tricks Welford into confessing and Bracher is killed in a gun battle with the police.

Mr. Robinson Crusoe *see* **Robinson Crusoe**

606 Mr. Roberts

Based on the novel by Thomas Heggen and the play by Heggen and Joshua Logan. Story: Lieutenant j.g. Doug Roberts is an executive officer on a supply ship in the Pacific during World War II who wants to be transferred to a fighting ship. His captain, an insensitive pig, won't hear of it, because Doug does his job so well and makes it possible for the captain to ignore the men of the ship and keep on good terms with the higher ups. Among Doug's friends are Doc, the ship's medical officer, and Ensign Frank Pulver, the number-one goldbrick. Trying to ensure shore leave for the men of the ship, Doug is forced to promise the captain that he will make no further requests for a transfer. The men believe that the depressed Doug has gone over to the captain and turn on him. Eventually, this misconception is cleared up and Doug gets transferred to a battleship where he is killed in a Japanese raid. The film ends with Ensign Pulver, finally having screwed up his courage, confronting the captain and assuming Doug's role as the protector of the men.

Warner Bros., 1955 (original). Directors: John Ford and Mervyn LeRoy; screenwriters: Frank Nugent and Joshua Logan. Cast: Henry Fonda (Lt. Doug Roberts), James Cagney (the Captain), William Powell (Doc), Jack Lemmon (Ensign Frank Pulver), Betsy Palmer (Lt. Ann Girard), Ward Bond, Martin Milner, Nick Adams, Ken Curtis.

• ***Ensign Pulver*** (sequel). Warner Bros., 1964. Director: Joshua Logan; screenwriters: Joshua Logan and Peter S. Fiebleman. Cast: Robert Walker, Jr. (Ensign Pulver), Burl Ives (the Captain), Walter Matthau (Doc), Tommy Sands (Bruno), Millie Perkins (Scotty), Kay Medford, Larry Hagman, Gerald O'Laughlin.

Of the two films, the first is perhaps the more disappointing. It has a first rate cast and a story which was a big success on the stage, with its star, Henry Fonda, repeating his Broadway role. With all this going for it, it should have been a better film. Even though it was nominated for a Best Picture Academy Award, the story stumbled along in too many places, with several characters, including the captain, being one-dimensional stereotypes. Fonda was effective as the weary and bored executive officer, but was not totally believable. William Powell, in his last film appearance, didn't have much to do and so he didn't. The high point of the film was Jack Lemmon as Pulver, a role for which he won a deserved Academy Award. When he was in the picture, the film worked. When he wasn't it dragged. The sequel was merely meant to be a mindless comedy and as such it did not disappoint. Even though it included every possible cliché, audiences had not been deceived into believing that it was to be fresh and new. One can recommend *Mr. Roberts* as a moderately entertaining film and wish that it had been as good as it seemed on the stage. No doubt the rift between Fonda and director Ford, which almost came to blows, contributed to the problems with the film.

607 Mr. Smith Goes to Washington

Based on a screen story by Lewis B. Foster. Story: When the junior senator of a certain state dies, the governor appoints innocent and idealistic Jefferson Smith to fill out the term, because it is believed that he can be easily controlled by the crooked political boss, Jim Taylor, through the person of the state's senior senator, Joseph Paine. When he arrives in Washington, Smith is in awe and his naiveté and sincere patriotism is laughable to the seasoned politicians and "seen-it-all" newspapermen. Clarissa Saunders is planted in his office as an administrative assistant to make sure he doesn't do anything. However, he is encouraged by Senator Paine to draft some innocuous bill for the experience. Smith gets very excited about the prospect and with the help of Saunders, who is falling for him, prepares a bill that would create a boy's camp at the spot that the crooked political bosses of his state plan for their own dishonest purposes.

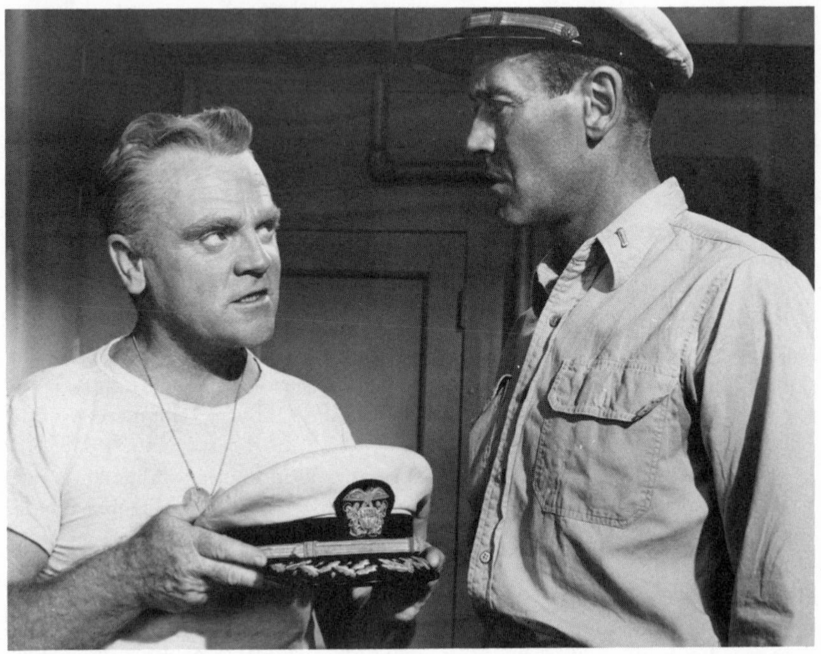

James Cagney shows Henry Fonda the commander's cap he hopes to earn in Mister Roberts *(Warner Bros., 1955).*

With Paine's help, they are able to make it appear that Smith's bill is intended to line his pockets, rather than theirs. To combat his enemies and buy time for the arrival of evidence that will expose the real crooks, Smith puts on a filibuster in the Senate chamber. Exhausted and ready to collapse, he turns his comments to Senator Paine, reminding the older man of his own youthful idealism, which apparently had gone sour over the years. So effective are Smith's words that Paine confesses all, clearing Smith of all wrongdoing and then attempts to commit suicide. Smith is a hero and wins Saunders in the bargain.

Columbia Pictures, 1939 (original). Director: Frank Capra; screenwriter: Sidney Buchman. Cast: James Stewart (Jefferson Smith), Jean Arthur (Saunders), Claude Rains (Senator Joseph Paine), Edward Arnold (Jim Taylor), Guy Kibbee (Hubert Hopper), Thomas Mitchell (Dix Moore), Eugene Pallette (Chick McCann), Beulah Bondi (Ma Smith), H.B. Warner (Senator Fuller), Harry Carey (President of the Senate), Astrid Allywn, Ruth Donnelly, Grant Mitchell, Porter Hall, Pierre Watkin, Charles Lane.

• ***Billy Jack Goes to Washington*** (remake). Taylor-Laughlin Distribution Co., 1977. Director: T.C. Frank; screenwriters: T.C. Frank and Teresa Cristina. Cast: Tom Laughlin (Billy Jack), Delores Taylor (Jean Roberts), E.G. Marshall (Senator Joseph Paine), Teresa Laughlin, Sam Wanamaker, Lucie Arnaz, Dick Gautier, Pat O'Brien.

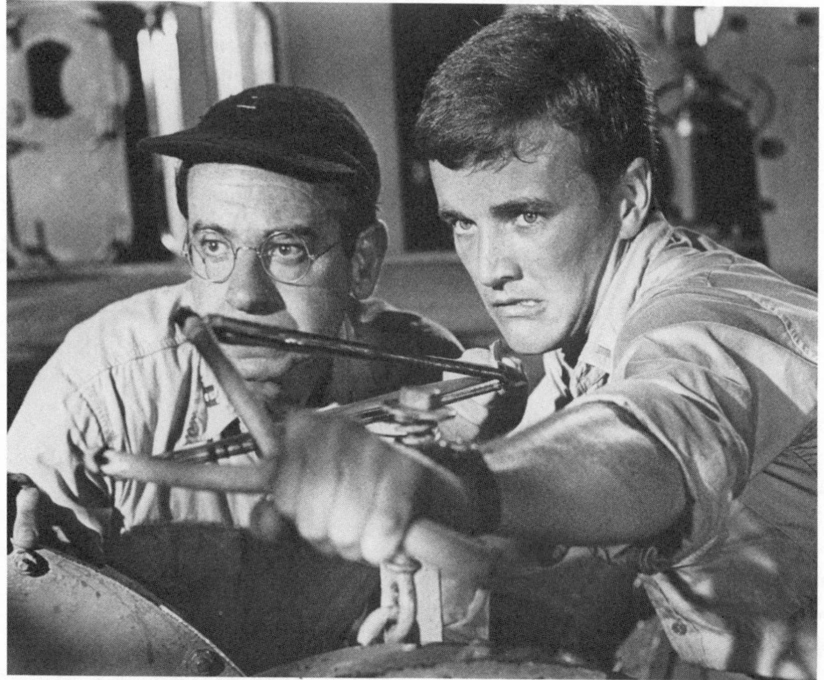

Could Ensign Pulver, played by Robert Walker, Jr., be aiming at the captain in Ensign Pulver *(Warner Bros., 1964) the sequel to* Mister Roberts? *Walter Matthau, as Doc, hopes not.*

Nominated for six Academy Awards, *Mr. Smith Goes to Washington* won only the Oscar for Best Original Story by Lewis R. Foster; one must remember however, that 1939 was perhaps the year with the most great movies of any year in motion picture history, including *Destry Rides Again, The Four Feathers, Gone with the Wind, Goodbye, Mr. Chips, Gunga Din, The Hunchback of Notre Dame, Intermezzo, Ninotchka, Of Mice and Men, Stagecoach, The Wizard of Oz* and *Wuthering Heights.*

The film is classic Capra, directing Stewart to perfection as the very good man, innocently surrounded by wolves who no longer see themselves as servants of the people, but manipulators of the populace for their own comfort and profit. It is a message that more politicians should hear, but each year we have abundant examples that they have not learned its lesson. Capra was able to manipulate the audience's emotions to fever pitch with his populist theories. Stewart embodies the notion that one good man can overcome hundreds of evil ones, because he has right on his side. Sadly, it may not be so. Of the others in the cast, one fondly remembers Claude Rains as the corrupt senator who perhaps once was a Jefferson Smith–like politician and still had enough of a conscience to do the right thing when the proper nerve was probed. Harry Carey as the President of the Senate was also a delight, portraying a wise man who could not be rushed into a negative judgement of Smith, and intended to see that the young senator got every opportunity to use the rules of the Senate to protect himself. Jean Arthur was fine as the hard-nosed realist who hated to see what was happening to her naive young boyfriend.

The remake was produced by Frank Capra, Jr., featuring Billy Jack, the idealistic native American Vietnam veteran who fights for the rights of the weak and powerless. He succeeds with much less naiveté to thwart the crooked plans of politicians to use a nuclear power plant for their own financial gain. Even many who would agree with Tom Laughlin's stand on various issues would find it hard to compare this film favorably to the original. Billy Jack doesn't have Jefferson Smith's appeal. Whereas Smith comes across as one who wants to correct, not change the system, Billy Jack appears to wish to throw out the baby with the bath water, and in doing so loses sympathy for his overdeveloped sense of self-righteousness.

Mr. Topaze *see* **Topaze**

608 Mr. Wong, Detective

Based on a story by Hugh Wiley. Story: In this first of the Mr. Wong series, starring Boris Karloff, the Chinese detective is faced with discovering a poison-gas killer. The latter dispatches his victims by means by glass bombs which explode when specific sounds are made.

Monogram Pictures, 1938 (original). Director: William Nigh; screenwriter: Houston Branch. Cast: Boris Karloff (Mr. Wong), Grant Withers (Capt. Street), Maxine Jennings (Myra), Evelyn Brent (Olga), Lucien Prival (Mohl), William Gould, John Hamilton, Tchin, John St. Polis, Hooper Atchley.

• ***Docks of New Orleans*** (remake). Monogram Pictures, 1948. Director: Derwin Abrahams; screenwriter: W. Scott Darling. Cast: Roland Winters (Charlie Chan), Victor Sen Yung (Tommy), Mantan Moreland (Birmingham), John Galludet (Capt. McNally), Virginia Dale (Rene), Boyd Irwin, Carol Forman, Howard Negley, Douglas Fowley.

Mr. Wong was not a particularly interesting detective and Roland Winters was not the best choice for Charlie Chan. Both films rested on accepted stereotypes about the Chinese and in the Chan film, two non-white races were badly represented, with Mantan Moreland as the almost obligatory frightened black in any mystery story of the time. The Wong movies took things rather seriously, whereas the Chan movies injected a healthy ration of humor—racist, usually—into the crime-solving proceedings. In the remake, Chan investigates several killings and the theft of a shipment of chemicals in New Orleans. Although the cops are baffled, Charlie figures it all out in just under 67 minutes.

609 Mr. Wong in Chinatown

Based on a story by Hugh Wiley. Story: A Chinese princess who has set out to buy a million dollars' worth of airplanes for the Chinese government is murdered in San Francisco's Chinatown. Each in their own way, reporter Bobby Logan, Inspector Street, and detective Mr. Wong, seek to unravel the mystery. Most of the action takes place aboard a Pacific freighter, although Princess Lin Hwa gets hers in Wong's apartment. Her death and that of two others is achieved by the means of a poisoned blow-dart.

Monogram Pictures, 1939 (original). Director: William Nigh; screenwriter: Scott Darling. Cast: Boris Karloff (James Lee Wong), Grant Withers (Inspector Street), Marjorie Reynolds (Bobby Logan), Peter Gordon Lynn (Capt. Jackson), Lotus Long (Princess Lin Hwa), William Royle, Huntley Gordon, James Flavin, Richard Loo, Bessie Loo, Lee Tong Foo.

• ***The Chinese Ring*** (remake). Monogram Pictures, 1947. Director: William Beaudine; screenwriter: W. Scott Darling. Cast: Roland Winters (Charlie Chan), Warren Douglas (Sgt. Davidson), Victor Sen Yung (Tommy), Mantan Moreland (Birmingham), Philip Ahn (Capt. Kong), Louise Currie (Peggy Cartwright), Jean Wong (Princess Mei Ling), Bryon Fougler, Thayer Roberts, Chabing, George L. Spaulding.

Other than the personality differences associated with the two Chinese detectives, the scripts for the two films are almost identical. In the remake, Roland Winters, taking over the identity of Charlie Chan, is able to pin the murder of a Chinese princess on a bank manager, who was trying to cut himself into the princess' fortune. Chan is ably assisted by his son Tommy, played by Victor Sen Yung and chauffeur (the always frightened Birmingham), played by Mantan Moreland.

610 Moby Dick

Based on the novel by Herman Melville. Story: Young seaman Ishmael and harpooner Queequeg sign aboard the whaler *Pequod,* out of New Bedford, Massachusetts, despite the warnings of an old sailor named Elijah who tells them that the ship's captain, Ahab, is mad in his obsession to kill the great white whale, Moby Dick, which had earlier caused him to lose his leg. When the *Pequod* sails, Ahab tells the men that the real mission of the voyage is to seek and destroy Moby Dick. Ahab's personality is so strong that the men are inspired by his intensity and promise to keep a weather-eye out for the white beast. In their quest, they ignore other smaller whales and the appeal of the captain of the *Rachel,* who seeks their help in searching for his son, lost at sea. Queequeg foresees his death and has the ship's carpenter make him a coffin. Moby Dick is sighted and in his fury, Ahab leaps on the whale's back with a harpoon and repeatedly stabs it, but Moby Dick takes him under the water and drowns the obsessed captain. When it surfaces, the beast attacks the *Pequod,* sinking it and sending everyone to a watery grave, save Ishmael, who survives by clinging to Queequeg's floating coffin. He is picked up by the *Rachel.*

• ***The Sea Beast*** (original). Warner Bros., 1926. Silent. Director: Millard Webb; screenwriter: Bess Meredyth. Cast: John Barrymore (Ahab Ceeley), Dolores Costello (Esther Harper), George O'Brien (Derek Ceeley), Mike Donlin (Flask), Sam Baker (Queequeg), Sam Allen, Frank Nelson, Mathilde Comont, James Barrows, Vadim Uraneff, Sojin, Frank Hagney.

• ***Moby Dick*** (remake). Warner Bros., 1930. Director: Lloyd Bacon; screenwriter: J. Grubb Alexander. Cast: John Barrymore (Captain Ahab), Joan

Bennett (Faith Mapple), Lloyd Hughes (Derek Ceeley), May Boley (Whale Oil Rosie), Walter Long (Stubbs), Tom O'Brien (Starbuck), Nigel De Brulier, Noble Johnson, William Walling, Virginia Sale, Jack Curtis, John Ince.

• ***Moby Dick*** (remake). Moulin Productions/Houston, 1956. Director: John Huston; screenwriters: Ray Bradbury and John Huston. Cast: Gregory Peck (Captain Ahab), Richard Basehart (Ishmael), Leo Genn (Starbuck), Harry Andrews (Stubbs), Friedrich Ledebur (Queequeg), Bernard Miles (Manxman), Mervyn Jones (Peleg), Orson Welles (Father Mapple), Noel Purcell, Eddie Connor, Joseph Tomelety, Royal Dano, Seamus Kelly, Philip Stainton, James Robertson Justice, Tamba Allenby, Francis DeWolff, Ted Howard, Tom Clegg.

A German version of the 1930 production was released in 1931 as *Der Damon des Meers* and UPA produced an animated Mr. Magoo feature in 1964 called *Magoo at Sea.* The 1926 silent merely used the Melville classic as background for a love story between John Barrymore and Dolores Costello, who would soon become his wife. Somehow the great sea story got lost in this production although the love scenes were red hot. In 1930, Barrymore came back with his love interest now being Joan Bennett, but this version did bring back most of the Melville characters. The production was far superior to the silent picture. In 1956, John Huston, who had wanted to cast his father Walter as Ahab, settled for Gregory Peck when his distinguished acting father died. This version was the most faithful to the Melville work and although it suffered from certain excesses, was an enjoyable adventure yarn, with Peck, perhaps, a bit too maniacal. Richard Basehart was splendid as the narrator, Ishmael, and the various supporting players, particularly Friedrich Ledebur as Queequeg, were excellent.

A Modern Monte Cristo ***see*** **The Count of Monte Cristo**

A Modern Salome ***see*** **Salome**

Mogambo ***see*** **Red Dust**

The Monkey's Uncle ***see*** **The Misadventures of Merlin Jones**

611 Monsieur Beaucaire

Based on the novel by Booth Tarkington. Story: The Duc de Chartres is banished from France by King Louis XV for refusing to marry Princess Henriette, because even though he loves her, he is stung by her taunts. In England, he poses as the French Ambassador's barber, Monsieur Beaucaire. He mingles with British society and becomes fascinated by Lady Mary. However, when he is exposed, he seeks the king's pardon and upon receiving it returns to France to the love of Princess Henriette.

• ***Monsieur Beaucaire*** (remake). Famous Players/Paramount Pictures, 1924. Silent. Director: Sidney Olcott; screenwriter: Forest Halsey. Cast: Rudolph Valentino (Duc de Chartres/Monsieur Beaucaire), Bebe Daniels (Princess Henriette), Lowell Sherman (King Louis XV), Lois Wilson (Queen Marie), Doris Kenyon (Lady Mary), Paulette Duval, John Davidson, Oswald Yorke, Flora Finch, Louis Waller.

• ***Monte Carlo*** (remake). Paramount Pictures, 1930. Director: Ernst Lubitsch; screenwriter: Ernest Vadja; based on a novel by Hans Mueller. Cast: Jack Buchanan (Count Rudolph Falliere), Jeanette MacDonald (Countess Vera Von Conti), Zasu Pitts (Maria), Claude Allister (Prince Otto Von Seibenhelm), Tyler Brooks, Edgar Norton, John Roche, Albert Conti, Helen Garden.

• ***Monsieur Beaucaire*** (remake). Paramount Pictures, 1946. Director: George Marshall; screenwriters: Melvin Frank and Norman Panama. Cast: Bob Hope (Monsieur Beaucaire), Joan Caulfield (Mimi), Patric Knowles (Duc de Chartres), Marjorie Reynolds (Princess Maria of Spain), Cecil Kellaway (Count D'Armand), Joseph Schildkraut (Don Francisco), Reginald Owen (King Louis XV), Constance Collier, Hillary Brooke, Fortunio Bonanova.

Rudolph Valentino was such an idol of the ladies that his material hardly seemed to matter, as long as his passionate good looks and burning glances at the females were featured. *Monte Carlo* is not a remake of *Monsieur Beaucaire,* although the story is similar and a reference to Tarkington's work is made in the film. Buchanan, a wealthy and handsome count visiting Monte Carlo, sees the impoverished Countess Vera (Jeanette MacDonald) losing heavily at roulette but all his attempts to meet her are frustrated. By accident, he meets her hairdresser and arranges to pass himself off as the ladies' new hairdresser, hoping to reveal his love for her. After a series of expected complications, true love triumphs. Musical numbers by Leo Robin and Richard Whiting include "Beyond the Blue Horizon." In the 1946 version, Bob Hope, who is the barber Monsieur Beaucaire, is compelled to impersonate the Duc de Chartres and marry a Spanish princess but instead he falls for a chambermaid, Mimi, and the real Duc decides to take the plunge into marriage with Spanish royalty. *Monsieur Beaucaire* was filmed twice before as silents in 1905 and 1909.

Monte Carlo *see* **Monsieur Beaucaire**

Monte Cristo *see* **The Count of Monte Cristo**

Monte Cristo's Revenge *see* **The Count of Monte Cristo**

Moon Over Miami *see* **The Gold Diggers** and **Three Blind Mice**

The Moor *see* **Othello**

612 Morals

Based on the play "The Morals of Marcus Ordeyne" by William John Locke. Story: Anxious to avoid an odious marriage, Carlotta escapes from the Turkish harem where she has been reared. She goes to London with an English adventurer. When he is killed, she is left destitute and begs for protection from Sir Marcus Ordeyne. He takes her home out of pity but later falls in love with her and plans marriage. Divorcee Judith Mainwaring, who has her own interest in Marcus, tells Carlotta that he only intends to marry her to avoid scandal. Carlotta runs away with Pasquale, a friend of Marcus. Later, Judith encounters

Carlotta in Paris and confesses that Marcus really loves the girl and is searching for her. Carlotta returns to her benefactor.

• ***Morals*** (remake). Realart/Paramount Pictures, 1921. Silent. Director: William D. Taylor; screenwriter: Julia Crawford Ivers. Cast: May McAvoy (Carlotta), William P. Carleton (Sir Marcus Ordeyne), Kathlyn Williams (Judith Mainwaring), William Lawrence (Sebastian Pasquale), Marian Skinner, Nicholas De Ruiz, Stanke Patterson.

• ***The Morals of Marcus*** (remake). Realart/Gaumont Studios, 1935. Director: Miles Mander; screenwriters: Guy Bolton and Miles Mander. Cast: Lupe Velez (Carlotta), Ian Hunter (Sir Marcus Ordeyne), Adrianne Allen (Judith), Noel Madison (Tony Pasquali), J.H. Roberts, H.F. Maltby, D.J. Williams, Arnold Lucy.

William John Locke's story was first filmed by Edison Studios in 1915. Despite the serious-sounding plot, it's meant to be a comedy, albeit a slow-paced one, about archaeologist and confirmed bachelor Marcus who takes pity on the half-caste Carlotta. There's little to choose between the two actresses who played Carlotta, although Lupe Velez was more at home with exotic creature roles.

The Morals of Marcus *see* **Morals**

More American Graffiti *see* **American Graffiti**

613 The More the Merrier

Based on an original story by Robert Russell and Frank Ross. Story: Bachelor girl Connie Milligan reluctantly rents half of her Washington apartment to an elderly businessman, Benjamin Dingle, during the height of the housing-bed shortage during World War II. Dingle turns around and rents half of his half to young aviation expert Joe Carter. As one would expect there are numerous privacy problems to overcome, as Dingle acts as an over-aged cupid to the two young people.

Columbia Pictures, 1943 (original). Director: George Stevens; screenwriters: Robert Russell, Frank Ross, Richard Flournoy and Lewis R. Foster. Cast: Jean Arthur (Connie Milligan), Joel McCrea (Joe Carter), Charles Coburn (Benjamin Dingle), Richard Gaines, Bruce Bennett, Frank Sully, Stanley Clements.

• ***Walk, Don't Run*** (remake). Columbia Pictures, 1966. Director: Charles Walters; screenwriter: Sol Saks. Cast: Cary Grant (William Rutland), Samantha Eggar (Christine Easton), Jim Hutton (Steve Davis), John Standing, Miiko Taka, Ted Hartley, Ben Astar, George Takei.

Charles Coburn stole the show in the 1943 film and walked off with the Best Supporting Actor Academy Award. The film was nominated for Best Picture of the Year. Other nominations went to George Stevens for direction, Jean Arthur for Best Actress, Ross and Russell for Best Original Story, and Flournoy, Foster, Russell and Ross for their screenplay. The film was a big hit and many shared the views of Bosley Crowther who described it as "As warm and refreshing a ray of sunshine as we've had in a very late spring." In the remake, Grant is an

English industrialist in Tokyo at the time of the Olympic Games, finding himself without a room. He cons his way into sharing lodgings with Samantha Eggar, and then gives shelter to Jim Hutton, a member of the U.S. walking team. He's not as interesting a cupid as was Coburn, but he does manage to get the young people together. Grant never made another movie. Perhaps he should have retired after his penultimate film, *Father Goose* (1964). Neither Eggar or Hutton demonstrated much talent for the comical implications of the plot, as Arthur and McCrea had so delightfully done in the original.

614 Morning Glory

Based on the play by Zoe Atkins. Story: Eva Lovelace is a garrulous New Englander who arrives in New York with a burning ambition to become a stage star. She gets her chance when blonde star Rita Vernon chooses to hold out for more money just prior to the opening of her new show. Producer Louis Easton fires his star and sends Eva on in her place, and the rest, as the saying goes, in history: Eva is triumphant.

RKO, 1933 (original). Director: Lowell Sherman; screenwriter: Howard J. Grant. Cast: Katharine Hepburn (Eva Lovelace), Adolphe Menjou (Louis Easton), Douglas Fairbanks, Jr. (Joseph Sheridan), C. Aubrey Smith (Robert Harley Hedges), Mary Duncan (Rita Vernon), Tyler Brooke, Richard Carle, Geneva Mitchell, Don Alvarado.

• ***Stage Struck*** (remake). RKO/Buena Vista, 1958. Director: Sidney Lumet; screenwriters: Ruth and Augustus Goetz. Cast: Henry Fonda (Lewis Easton), Susan Strasberg (Eva Lovelace), Joan Greenwood (Rita Vernon), Herbert Marshall (Robert Hedges), Christopher Plummer (Joe Sheridan), Daniel Ocko, Pat Harrington, Frank Campanella.

The role of Eva Lovelace fit garrulous New Englander Katharine Hepburn perfectly. She was RKO's up and coming young star and they couldn't have been more pleased when her performance as the ambitious actress won Kate her first Academy Award. The movie is all Hepburn's and the love triangle involving her, Menjou, and Fairbanks as a writer, seemed almost an afterthought.

In the remake, Susan Strasberg is a starry-eyed small-town girl who arrives in New York with the confidence that she is that one in a million who can become a great actress. She becomes romantically involved with producer Fonda and playwright Plummer, but gets her break when the show's intransigent star, Greenwood, tries to get more money for her work. Strasberg goes on and her success is such that she no longer feels a need for romance with either man in her life. The theater is so much more fascinating.

A Most Dangerous Sin *see* **Crime and Punishment**

615 Mother Carey's Chickens

Based on the novel by Kate Douglas Wiggin. Story: It's the homespun tale of the love of four children for their widowed mother. The husband and father had gone away to war, never to return. The survivors must endure the efforts of others to dispossess the family of the house that they had acquired and

Jean Arthur, Joel McCrea and Charles Coburn discuss the shower schedule in The More the Merrier *(Columbia, 1943).*

renovated, with the intention that it would be their home as long as they would be together. Despite the loss of the father and the near loss of the house the story is not a tearjerker, in fact it has many joyful and amusing sequences.

RKO, 1938 (original). Director: Rowland V. Lee; screenwriter: Gertrude Purcell. Cast: Anne Shirley (Nancy), Ruby Keeler (Kitty), James Ellison (Ralph), Fay Bainter (Mrs. Carey), Walter Brennan (Popham), Frank Albertson (Tom), Alma Kruger (Bertha), Donnie Dunagan (Peter), Jackie Moran (Gilbert), Margaret Hamilton (Mrs. Fuller), Ralph Morgan (Capt. Carey), Phyllis Kennedy, Harvey Clark, Lucille Ward, George Irving.

• ***Summer Magic*** (remake). Disney/Buena Vista, 1963. Director: James Neilson; screenwriter: Sally Benson. Cast: Hayley Mills (Nancy Carey), Burl Ives (Osh Popham), Dorothy McGuire (Margaret Carey), Deborah Walley (Cousin Julia), Eddie Hodges (Gilly Carey), Jimmy Mathers (Peter Carey), Michael Pollard (Digby Popham), Wendy Turner (Lallie Joy), Una Merkel (Maria Popham), Peter Brown, Jim Stacey, O.Z. Whitehead.

The story of the trials and tribulations of an American family in a small town of the 1890s is pleasant enough if one is content with observing a loving family dealing with their daily problems, under the wise guidance of a widowed mother. The Disney remake plays the story a wee bit too cutesy for some tastes, but it still isn't too bad—or too good.

Cary Grant, Jim Hutton and Samantha Eggar seek assistance from Miiko Taka (left) in Walk, Don't Run *(Columbia, 1966), the remake of* The More the Merrier.

Moulin Rouge *see* **Her Sister from Paris**

Mountain Family Robinson *see* **The Adventures of the Wilderness Family**

The Mouse on the Moon *see* **The Mouse That Roared**

616 The Mouse that Roared

Based on the novel by Leonard Wibberley. Story: Faced with a collapsing economy, Prime Minister Montjoy of the Duchy of Grand Fenwick convinces its ruler, Grand Duchess Gloriana, to send twenty men, armed with crossbows and led by game warden Tully, to invade the United States. The plan is to lose the war quickly and then have the tiny Duchy's economy subsidized by the conquering Americans. Things go awry when Tully and his men arrive during a practice atomic preparation alert and the bowmen accidently capture the ultimate weapon, the Q-bomb.

Columbia Pictures, 1959 (original). Director: Jack Arnold; screenwriters: Roger MacDougall and Stanley Mann. Cast: Peter Sellers (Grand Duchess Gloriana/Prime Minister Count "Bobo" Montjoy/Tully/Bascombe), Jean Seberg (Helen Kokintz), David Kossoff (Professor Kokintz), William Hartnell (Will Buckley), Timothy Bateson, Monty Landis, Harold Krasket, Leo McKern, Colin Gordon.

• ***The Mouse on the Moon*** (sequel). United Artists, 1963. Director: Richard Lester; screenwriter: Michael Pertwee. Cast: Margaret Rutherford (Grand Duchess Gloriana), Bernard Cribbins (Vincent), Ron Moody (Mountjoy), David Kossoff (Kopintz), Terry-Thomas (Spender), June Ritchie (Cynthia), Roddy McMillan, John Le Mesurier, John Phillips, Tom Aldredge.

The success of the comedy is due to the multi-talented Sellers, who is able to make each of his four characters come alive, which is more than can be said for most of the other performers. The film has a few lively moments but is of no great consequence. Even less can be said for the sequel. Without Sellers it's just a flat piece with very few amusing moments. In this one, the prime minister of the smallest country in the world has the U.S. and the U.S.S.R. competing with one another in helping Grand Fenwick develop its space program. Accidently, the tiny Duchy becomes the first to place a man on the moon.

617 The Mouthpiece

Based on the play by Frank J. Collins. Story: Stylish prosecuting attorney Vincent Day persuades a jury to convict an innocent man and send him to the electric chair. As a result, Vincent suffers a moral collapse and turns to a life of defending mobsters and embezzlers in a series of sensational trials.

Warner Bros., 1932. Directors: James Flood and Elliott Nugent; screenwriter: Earl Baldwin. Cast: Warren William (Vincent Day), Celia Fox (Celia), Aline MacMahon (Miss Hickey), William Janney (John), John Wray (Barton), Ralph Ince (J.B.), Mae Madison, Morgan Wallace, Guy Kibbee, Stanley Fields.

• ***The Man Who Talked Too Much*** (remake). Warner Bros., 1940. Director: Vincent Sherman; screenwriter: Frank J. Collins. Cast: George Brent (Stephen Forbes), Virginia Bruce (Joan Reed), Brenda Marshall (Celia Farraday), Richard Barthelmess (J.B. Roscoe), William Lundigan (Johnny Forbes), George Tobias, John Litel, Henry Armetta, David Bruce.

• ***Illegal*** (remake). Warner Bros., 1955. Director: Lewis Allen; screenwriters: W.R. Burnett and James R. Webb. Cast: Edward G. Robinson (Victor Scott), Nina Foch (Ellen Miles), Hugh Marlowe (Ray Borden), Jayne Mansfield (Angel O'Hara), Albert Dekker (Frank Garland), Howard St. John, Ellen Corby, Edward Platt.

The Mouthpiece is a powerful drama, reportedly based on certain incidents in the life of a celebrated New York lawyer. In the original, the directors are able to expose the corrupt legal system of the underworld. In the first remake, Brent is the lawyer who mistakenly sends an innocent kid to the chair and out of remorse and out of money, defends gangster Barthelmess to get the funds to send his brother, Lundigan, to school. The gangster frames Lundigan for murder but Brent is able to save him just before he is to be executed. In the second remake, Robinson, in a so-so performance, turns to defending gangsters after sending an innocent man to his death, but reforms just before he dies defending Nina Foch, a victimized wife. Civil libertarians may well object to the notion of these films that gangsters shouldn't be defended by competent lawyers. Not to worry, it's the crooked legal practices which the producers expose.

Move Over Darling *see* **My Favorite Wife** and **Too Many Husbands**

618 Mrs. Miniver

Based on the novel by Jan Struther. Story: It's the story of a supposedly typical British village family, the Minivers (Kay, Clem and their children), and how they coped during World War II, surviving German attacks and the loss of loved ones. At one point, Mrs. Miniver captures a young German pilot and hides his gun behind a dresser at the same time her husband is rescuing British troops from the beaches of Dunkirk. Through it all, the family, led by the example of Kay, maintains their courage, hope and sense of familial love, aided by a strong spiritual belief and sincere patriotism.

MGM, 1942 (original). Director: William Wyler; screenwriters: Arthur Wimperis, George Froeschel, James Hilton and Claudine West. Cast: Greer Garson (Kay Miniver), Walter Pidgeon (Clem Miniver), Teresa Wright (Carol Beldon), Dame May Whitty (Lady Beldon), Henry Travers (Mr. Ballard), Henry Wilcoxon (Vicar), Richard Ney (Vin Miniver), Miles Mander, Rhys Williams, Helmut Dantine, Mary Field, Ben Webster.

• ***The Miniver Story*** (sequel). MGM, 1950. Director: H.C. Potter; screenwriters: Ronald Miller and George Froeschel. Cast: Greer Garson (Kay Miniver), Walter Pidgeon (Clem Miniver), John Hodiak (Spike), Leo Genn (Steve Brunswick), Cathy O'Donnell (Judy Miniver), Henry Wilcoxon (Vicar), Reginald Owen, Anthony Bouchel, Richard Gale, Peter Finch, William Fox.

The Academy awards presented to *Mrs. Miniver* were for Best Picture, Best Director (Wyler), Best Actress (Garson), Best Supporting Actress (Wright), Best Screenplay (Froeschel, Hilton, West and Wimperis) and Best Cinematography (Joseph Ruttenberg). In addition, Walter Pidgeon was nominated for Best Actor, Henry Travers for Best Supporting Actor and Dame May Whitty for Best Supporting Actress.

Mrs. Miniver at the time of its release was both a huge critical and box-office success. It was a tremendous morale booster for Americans then in the war. Franklin D. Roosevelt told Wyler that it lessened the political opposition to increasing aid to Britain. Since that time, revisionists have downgraded the movie, complaining that it is unrealistic and too sentimental. The appeal of a particular movie is often a function of the conditions at the time of its release. This is particularly true of this film. Those who did not experience it at the time this country was at war may be excused for finding it not quite to their liking. But for those who lived at a time when the outcome of the war was in doubt, this movie, precisely as filmed, was reassuring to people who appreciated and needed the reassurance. It was probably correct to reject the notion that the film is a classic with long-lasting values, but it is cinematic snobbery to suggest that its merits are minimal. The acting and the production values are top-notch, and if the story is too sentimentally uplifting for some, one can only mourn the loss of belief that people can be good and kind in the face of adversity.

It is much fairer to criticize the sequel, the glum telling of the Miniver family in postwar England. Kay visits her doctor at the close of the war and learns that she does not have long to live. She bravely keeps the news from her family, concentrating rather on helping her daughter with her romantic problems, and dies on her daughter's wedding day. While the bravery of one facing death by cancer or death by war is equally valuable as a story line, this film turns it in to a rather typical soap opera. It's not that we don't admire Kay's courage, but with no hope left to her, here we feel realism would be welcomed.

619 Mrs. Wiggs of the Cabbage Patch

Based on the novel by Alice Hegan Rice. Story: Mrs. Wiggs is the Pollyanna mother of a brood of kids that she rears alone in their shantytown home. Nothing seems to change Mrs. Wiggs' rosy-colored view of life, not even when one of the children dies. About halfway through this look at poverty, Mr. Stubbins arrives in the community and commences a romance with Miss Hazy. As handled by W.C. Fields and Zasu Pitts, these scenes are as funny as those with the uncomplaining Mrs. Wiggs, with all her suffering, are sad.

• ***Mrs. Wiggs of the Cabbage Patch*** (remake). Paramount Pictures, 1934. Director: Norman Taurog; screenwriters: William Slaven McNutt and Jane Storm. Cast: Pauline Lord (Mrs. Wiggs), W.C. Fields (Mr. Stubbins), Zasu Pitts (Miss Hazy), Evelyn Venable (Lucy Olcott), Kent Taylor (Bob Redding), Charles Middleton, Donald Meek, Jimmy Butler.

• ***Mrs. Wiggs of the Cabbage Patch*** (remake). Paramount Pictures, 1942. Director: Ralph Murphy; screenwriters: Doris Anderson, William Slavens McNutt and Jane Storm. Cast: Fay Bainter (Mrs. Elvira Wiggs), Carolyn Lee (Europena Wiggs), Hugh Herbert (Mr. Marcus Throckmorton), Vera Vague (Miss Tabitha Hazy), John Archer (Dr. Robert Redmond), Barbara Britton (Asia Wiggs), Moroni Olsen, Carl Switzer, Mary Thomas.

Paramount also filmed the story in 1919 with an earlier silent having appeared in 1914. The 1942 film stuck pretty close to the '34 version of Mrs. Wiggs, her brood of five children living in poverty on the wrong side of the tracks, and Miss Hazy, here played by the zany Vera Vague of radio fame, as the neighboring spinster who chooses a husband, Hugh Herbert, from a matrimonial catalogue. It's still a tearjerker with moments of humor that don't seem to interfere with the story of a courageous and deliberately optimistic woman.

620 Murder Goes to College

Based on the novel by Kurt Steele. Story: When a college professor is murdered, newspaperman Sim Perkins and private operator Hank Hyer team up in a series of wild escapades before solving the puzzling case. The duo is constantly in hot water, first with the police, next from a numbers racketeer and finally from the growing list of suspects.

Paramount Pictures, 1937 (original). Director: Charles Reisner; screenwriters: Brian Marlow, Robert Wyler and Eddie Welch. Cast: Roscoe Karns (Sim Perkins), Marsha Hunt (Nora Barry), Lynne Overman (Hank Hyer), Astrid Allwyn (Greta Barry), Harvey Stephens (Paul Broderick), Larry Crabbe (Strike Belno), Earl Foxe, Anthony Nace, John Indrisano, Barlow Borland, Charles Wilson.

• ***Partners in Crime*** (sequel). Paramount Pictures, 1937. Director: Ralph

Murray; screenwriter: Garnett Weston. Cast: Lynne Overman (Hank Hyer), Roscoe Karns (Sim Perkins), Muriel Hutchinson (Odette La Vin), Anthony Quinn (Nivholas Mazaney), Inez Courtney (Lillian Tate), Lucien Littlefield, Charles Halton, Charles Wilsòn, June Brewster, Esther Howard.

In these two lightweight comedy-mysteries, Roscoe Karns and Lynne Overman get in some pretty good wisecracking, but not enough to warrant sitting through the two cockeyed movies. In the original, underrated actress Astrid Allwyn, who usually played a tough, not very pure broad, does a nice job as the showgirl married to the college professor who gets bumped off. In the sequel, Overman gets involved in crooked mayoral politics, convincing reporter buddy Karns to run for the office on a reform ticket. He wins, but just as the two are celebrating the triumph of good government, Karns is disqualified.

Murder in the Big House *see* **Jailbreak**

Murder in the Blue Room *see* **The Secret of the Blue Room**

Murder in the Private Car *see* **Red Lights**

621 Murder in Trinidad

Based on the novel by John W. Vandercook. Story: Before Nigel Bruce became Dr. John Watson to Basil Rathbone's Sherlock Holmes, he appears in this film as super-detective Bertram Lynch, who, like Holmes, works quietly, using his intelligence to solve crimes. He never gets excited as he modestly goes through the chore of solving a case of the stabbing death of three people in Trinidad. The villains include diamond smugglers and Lynch must also contend with a dangerous swamp, filled with crocodiles and quicksand.

Fox Film Corp., 1934. Director: Louis King; screenwriter: Seton I. Miller. Cast: Nigel Bruce (Bertram Lynch), Heather Angel (Joan Cassell), Victor Jory (Howard Sutter), Murray Kinnell (Major Bruce Cassell), Douglas Walton (Gregory Bronson), J. Carroll Naish (Duval), Claude King, Pat Somerset.

• ***Mr. Moto in Danger Island*** (remake). Twentieth Century–Fox, 1939. Director: Herbert I. Leeds; screenwriter: Peter Milne, based on a character created by J.P. Marquand. Cast: Peter Lorre (Mr. Moto), Jean Hersholt (Sutter), Amanda Duff (Joan Castle), Warren Hymer (Twister McGurk), Richard Lane, Leon Ames, Douglas Dumbrille, Charles D. Brown, Paul Harvey.

• ***The Caribbean Mystery*** (remake). Twentieth Century–Fox, 1945. Director: Robert Webb; screenwriters: Jack Andrews and Leonard Praskins. Cast: James Dunn (Mr. Smith), Sheila Ryan (Mrs. Jean Gilbert), Edward Ryan (Gerald McCracken), Jackie Paley (Linda Lane), Reed Hadley, Roy Roberts, Richard Shaw.

In the first remake, Mr. Moto is on the island of Puerto Rico, asked by the U.S. government to look into diamond smuggling after a previous investigator has been killed. Guilt points in many directions, but the clever Mr. Moto knows where to look last to uncover the murderous villains, but not before engaging in fist fights, motorboat chases and some gunplay. This was the last produced

Ian Wolfe whispers in Charles Laughton's ear as Stanley Fields, Clark Gable and Dudley Digges pay attention to punishment in Mutiny on the Bounty *(MGM, 1935).*

Mr. Moto film, although it was released ahead of its predecessor, *Mr. Moto Takes a Vacation.* In the final film, James Dunn is a Brooklyn detective who arrives at a Caribbean island in search of a murderer and encounters quicksand, swamps, alligators and dead bodies before he gets his man.

Murder, Inc. *see* **The Enforcer**

Murder My Sweet *see* **Farewell My Lovely**

Murder on the Waterfront *see* **The Invisible Menace**

622 Mutiny on the Bounty

Based on the novel by Charles Nordhoff and James Norman Hall. Story: Based on a true incident that took place in 1787 aboard the HMS *Bounty,* the film tells the story of the cruelty of Captain Bligh in his treatment of the seamen under his command on a voyage to the South Seas. He has men flogged and keel-hauled for minor infractions. There is a brief respite from his brutal behavior when the ship reaches Tahiti, where the contrast between the life on the *Bounty* and the paradise-like existence of the natives plants the seeds of mutiny in the minds of some of the men, including one of Bligh's officers,

Trevor Howard's face, as Captain Bligh, shows the contempt he has for Fletcher Christian, played by a happy-looking Marlon Brando, in the 1961 MGM remake of Mutiny on the Bounty. *Reportedly, Howard held Brando in the same high regard as did Bligh for Christian.*

Fletcher Christian. When things get even worse on the return passage, Christian takes command of the ship and sets Bligh adrift in a longboat with some of the loyal seamen. While Christian and the rest of the mutineers are making plans for where to spend the rest of their lives, Bligh courageously takes his small craft thousands of miles before being rescued. He returns in another British ship to capture the mutineers, successfully locating some, but never finding Christian and a few others who settled on uninhabited Pitcairn Island.

• ***Mutiny on the Bounty*** (remake). MGM, 1935. Director: Frank Lloyd; screenwriters: Talbot Jennings, Jules Furthman and Carey Wilson. Cast: Charles Laughton (Captain William Bligh), Clark Gable (Fletcher Christian), Franchot Tone (Roger Byam), Dudley Digges (Bacchus), Henry Stephenson (Sir Joseph Banks), Donald Crisp (Burkitt), Eddie Quillan (Ellison), Movita (Tehanni), Ian Wolfe, Spring Byington, DeWitt Jennings, Stanley Fields (Muspratt), Dick Winslow, Pat Flaherty, Lionel Belmore, Herbert Mundin, David Torrence (Lord Hood).

• ***Mutiny on the Bounty*** (remake). MGM, 1961. Director: Lewis Milestone; screenwriter: Charles Lederer. Cast: Marlon Brando (Fletcher Christian), Trevor Howard (Captain Bligh), Richard Harris (John Mills), Hugh Griffith

(Smith), Richard Haydn (Brown), Tarita (Maimiti), Percy Herbert, Duncan Lamont, Gordon Jackson, Chips Rafferty, Noel Purcell, Frank Silvera.

• ***The Bounty*** (remake). Orion Pictures, 1984. Director: Roger Donaldson; screenwriter: Robert Bolt; based on the book *Captain Bligh and Mr. Christian*. Cast: Mel Gibson (Fletcher Christian), Anthony Hopkins (Lt. William Bligh), Laurence Olivier (Admiral Hood), Edward Fox (Captain Greetham), Daniel Day-Lewis, Bernard Hill, Philip Davis, Liam Neeson, Wi Kuki Kaa, Tevait Vernette.

The story of the mutiny aboard the Bounty was first filmed in Australia in 1916, followed by the Australian film *In the Wake of the Bounty*, in 1933, starring a very young but dashing Errol Flynn as mutineer Fletcher Christian. The magnificent 1935 adventure film won the Academy Award for Best Picture. Frank Lloyd was nominated for Best Director, Furthman, Jennings and Wilson for Best Screenplay, and Laughton, Gable and Tone were each nominated for Best Actor. All were beaten out by the director, John Ford, the screenwriter, Dudley Nichols, and the actor, Victor McLaglen, of *The Informer*.

Among the most memorable things about this exciting movie are the brave words spoken at various times by members of the cast. Perhaps the best being Laughton, as Bligh, defiantly telling Christian, "Casting me adrift 3,500 miles from a port of call! You're sending me to my doom, eh? Well, you're wrong, Christian, I'll take this boat, as she floats, to England if I must. I'll live to see you—all of you—hanging from the highest yardarm in the British fleet."

The 1961 version won Academy Award nominations for Best Picture, Best Cinematography, Best Musical Score (Bronislau Kaper) and Best Song ("Follow Me") by Kaper and Paul Francis Webster. Although entertaining and not without excitement, the film did not compare favorably in the minds of those who had been thrilled by the 1935 production. Trevor Howard made a fine Bligh, but Marlon Brando chose to ensure that no one could accuse him of imitating the strong masculine performance of Clark Gable, by adopting the pose of a foppish, almost effeminate Fletcher Christian. His voice was, to say the least, annoying, certainly not that of a man a crew might feel comfortable in following in a mutiny.

The 1984 film was told mostly from the memory of Captain Bligh in a court martial that threatened his career. He and Christian had been close friends. There was even a hint of latent homosexuality between the two. Both Mel Gibson as Christian and Anthony Hopkins as Bligh gave sensitive performances, but somehow the picture seems to drag and does not capture the excitement of the Gable-Laughton film.

My Bill *see* **Courage**

My Fair Lady *see* **Pygmalion**

623 My Favorite Wife

Based on a story by Sam Spewack, Bella Spewack and Leo McCarey. Story: On the day that Nick Arden has his wife Ellen, missing for seven years,

Thelma Ritter has raised James Garner's eyebrows with the news that his long-missing first wife is alive, while second wife Polly Bergen just raises her eyes to heaven in Move Over Darling *(20th Century–Fox, 1963), an inferior remake of* My Favorite Wife *(RKO, 1940).*

declared legally dead, he marries Bianca. Also on that day, Ellen returns to civilization after being rescued from an island whose only other occupant was a sailor named Burkett. Ellen shows up at Nick and Bianca's honeymoon hotel, putting something of a pall on the occasion. While Nick tries to decide who he is married to and more importantly to whom he wants to be married, he learns about Burkett and accuses Ellen of having had an affair with the handsome castaway. After many comical complications and misunderstandings, Nick and Ellen get back together.

RKO, 1940 (original). Director: Garson Kanin; screenwriters: Sam and Bella Spewack. Cast: Irene Dunne (Ellen Arden), Cary Grant (Nick Arden), Randolph Scott (Burkett), Gail Patrick (Bianca), Ann Shoemaker (Ma Arden), Scotty Beckett, Donald McBride, Mary Lou Harrington, Granville Bates, Pedro de Cordova.

• ***Move Over Darling*** (remake). Twentieth Century–Fox, 1963. Director: Michael Gordon; screenwriters: Hal Kanter and Jack Shea. Cast: Doris Day (Ellen Wagstaff Arden), James Garner (Nick Arden), Polly Bergen (Bianca Steele Arden), Chuck Connors (Stephen "Adam" Burkett), Thelma Ritter (Grace Arden), Fred Clark, Don Knotts, Elliott Reid, Edgar Buchanan, John Astin, Pat Harrington, Jr.

Other films that touched on the same theme include *Too Many Husbands* (1940) with Jean Arthur an unwitting bigamist when her long-missing first husband shows up after she has remarried. This was remade as *Three for the Show* in 1955 with Betty Grable, the gal with one husband too many. Best of all with this theme was the 1940 version with Grant mugging delightfully, Dunne showing great comedy talent, Scott as someone most women would be happy to be marooned on an island with, and Lee Patrick. She made a comfortable living as a beautiful woman who never got the man, getting off some nice lady-like cracks at her "husband" and his indecision.

The Doris Day remake told basically the same story, but by this time, it had been done so many times in one disguised form or another, that it lacked freshness. It also had a cast that wasn't nearly as talented as in the original. Doris Day made several enjoyable movies; this just wasn't one of them. James Garner has a great deal of charm but he wasn't given much opportunity to display it here. Polly Bergen is certainly a poor woman's Lee Patrick and ex–Dodger and Cub first baseman Chuck Connors made more whiffs than hits in his movie career. Give him an E-3.

624 My Friend Flicka

Based on the novel by Mary O'Hara. Story: Ken McLaughlin's prayers are answered when his father gives him a wild filly of his own. Though Rob McLaughlin warns his won that the horse is "loco," Ken's patience and kindness result in the animal being a good companion for the youngster.

Twentieth Century–Fox, 1943 (original). Director: Harold Schuster; screenwriters: Lillie Hayward and Francis Edwards Faragoh. Cast: Roddy McDowall (Ken McLaughlin), Preston Foster (Rob McLaughlin), Rita Johnson (Nell), James Bell, Jeff Corey, Diana Hale, Arthur Loft.

• ***Thunderhead, Son of Flicka*** (sequel). Twentieth Century–Fox, 1945. Director: Louis King; screenwriters: Dwight Cummins and Dorothy Yost. Cast: Roddy McDowall (Ken McLaughlin), Preston Foster (Rob McLaughlin), Rita Johnson (Nell), James Bell, Diana Hale, Carleton Young, Ralph Sanford, Robert Filmer, Alan Bridge.

My Friend Flicka is a winning boy-and-horse picture, one of the most popular films of 1943. McDowall gives a sensitive performance and the horse is excellent. In the sequel, Ken works with Flicka's white colt in the hopes of making him a racehorse. The photography in both films is spectacular.

625 My Friend Irma

Based on the radio series by Cy Howard. Story: It's the slapstick saga of the adventures of dumb blonde Irma Peterson, her brighter roommate, Jane Stacy, and the men in their lives. In this one, Irma finally wises up to the shenanigans of her conman boyfriend Al, and takes up with soda-jerk Richard Rhinelander. Although it wasn't intended that way, the real stars of the film were Dean Martin and Jerry Lewis in their movie debut.

Paramount Pictures, 1949. Director: George Marshall; screenwriters: Cy Howard and Parke Levy. Cast: Marie Wilson (Irma Peterson), Diana Lynn

(Jane Stacy), John Lund (Al), Don Defoe (Richard Rhinelander), Dean Martin (Steve Laird), Jerry Lewis (Seymour), Hans Conreid (Prof. Kropotkin), Kathryn Givney, Percy Helton, Erno Verebes, Gloria Gordon, Margaret Field.

• ***My Friend Irma Goes West*** (sequel). Paramount Pictures, 1950. Director: Hal Walker; screenwriters: Cy Howard and Parke Levy. Cast: Marie Wilson (Irma), John Lund (Al), Diana Lynn (Jane), Dean Martin (Steve), Jerry Lewis (Seymour), Corinne Calvet, Lloyd Corrigan.

My Friend Irma was a highly popular radio comedy which later transferred with somewhat less success to television. The films now are mainly known for introducing the comedy team of Martin and Lewis to movie audiences, which would be a gold mine for the studio for the next 16 years. Their parts are considerably built up in the sequel. They are offered Hollywood contracts and take Irma along with them to the coast, with some funny moments on their train trip.

626 My Lady Friends

Based on the novel *His Lady Friends* by May Eddington, the play by Emil Nyitray and Frank Mandel and the musical comedy by Frank Mandel and Otto Harbach. Story: Wealthy Bible publisher Jimmy Smith is a model husband who enjoys sharing his happiness and money with attractive women. His frugal wife, Sue, dismisses the suggestions of her friend Lucille Early that her husband is unfaithful. She is more concerned with their ward, Nanette's, romantic interest in Tom Trainor. When three of Jimmy's female friends, Winnie, Betty, and Flora, arrive at his house at the same time, he enlists the help of Billy Early to entertain them. Lucille decides that her husband is a philanderer and leaves him. Meanwhile, Nanette's escapades in Atlantic City have turned off Tom Trainor. When Jimmy explains that his only interest in life is to make everyone happy, all the warring couples get back together because they wish to be happy, too.

First National Pictures, 1921 (original). Silent. Director: Lloyd Ingraham; screenwriter: Rex Taylor. Cast: Carter De Haven (James Smith), Mrs. Carter De Haven (Catherine Smith), Thomas G. Lingham (Edward Early), Helen Raymond (Lucille Early), Lincoln Stedman (Tom Trainor), Helen Lynch (Eva Johns), May Wallace, Hazel Howell, Clara Morris, Ruth Ashby.

• ***No, No, Nanette*** (remake). 1930. Director: Clarence Badger; screenwriters: Beatrice Van and Howard Emmett Rogers. Cast: Bernice Claire (Nanette), Alexander Gray (Tom Trainor), Louise Fazenda (Sue Smith), Lucien Littlefield (Jim Smith), Lilyan Tashman (Lucille Early), Bert Roach (Bill Early), Zasu Pitts, Mildred Harris, Jocelyn Lee, Henry Stockridge.

• ***No, No, Nanette*** (remake). RKO, 1940. Director: Herbert Wilcox; screenwriter: Ken Englund. Cast: Anna Neagle (Nanette), Richard Carlson (Tom Trainor), Helen Broderick (Sue Smith), Roland Young (Jimmy Smith), Victor Mature, Zasu Pitts, Eve Arden, Tamara, Dorothea Kent, Aubrey Mather, Mary Gordon, Russell Hicks, Benny Rubin, Billy Gilbert.

• ***Tea for Two*** (remake). Warner Bros., 1950. Director: David Butler; screenwriter: Harry Clark. Cast: Doris Day (Nanette Carter), Gordon MacRae

(Jimmy Smith), Gene Nelson (Tommy Trainor), Eve Arden (Pauline Hastings), Patrice Wymore (Beatrice Darcy), S.Z. Sakall (J. Maxwell Bloomhaus), Billy De Wolfe (Larry Blair), Bill Goodwin (William Early), Crauford Kent, Virginia Gibson, Mary Eleanor Donahue, Elizabeth Flourney, Johnny McGovern.

As the story moved from novel to play to musical comedy to movies, the role of Nanette advanced and that of the Bible publisher and his desire to make everyone happy, particularly pretty young women, declined. The songs by Vincent Youmans, Irving Caesar and Otto Harbach for *No, No, Nanette* included the title number, "Dance of the Wooden Soldiers," "Dancing to Heaven" and "As Long as I Have You." Neither version of the Broadway musical met with much success and some critics were so unkind as to suggest that Herbert Wilcox and his wife and star, Anna Neagle, had set back musical comedy by many years. The 1950 production had the title song, "Tea for Two," and Doris Day as a girl who is promised $25,000 by her uncle (Sakall) for her new musical show if she can answer no to every question for 24 hours. As did the protagonist of *Nothing But the Truth,* who had to tell the absolute truth for 24 hours to win a bet, Doris found this stipulation causing many problems, embarrassments and romantic complications.

627 My Lips Betray

Based on the play by Attila Orbok. Story: It was the then-popular theme of a commoner in love with royalty. In this film, King Rupert prefers a revolution with a pretty waitress, Lilli, at his side, to his throne with an ugly princess in an arranged marriage.

Fox Film Corporation, 1933 (original). Director: John Blystone; screenwriters: Hans Kraly and Jane Storm. Cast: Lillian Harvey (Lilli), John Boles (King Rupert), El Brendel (Stigmat), Irene Browne (Queen Mother), Maude Eburne, Henry Stephenson, Herman Bing.

• ***Thin Ice*** (remake). Twentieth Century–Fox, 1937. Director: Sidney Lanfield; screenwriters: Boris Ingster and Milton Sperling. Cast: Sonja Henie (Lili Heiser), Tyrone Power (Prince Rudolph), Arthur Treacher (Nottingham), Raymond Walburn (Uncle Dornik), Joan Davis (Orchestra Leader), Sig Rumann, Alan Hale, Leah Ray, Melville Cooper, Maurice Cass, George Girot.

Thin describes the plot of both these films. Nevertheless, the remake, Sonia Henie's second film, was among the biggest money-makers of the year of its release. The Olympic ice-skating champ portrays a Swiss hotel ski instructor who falls in love with Tyrone Power, without knowing that he is a prince about to marry a princess. Sonia is given ample opportunity to display her artistry on ice.

628 My Man Godfrey

Based on the novel by Eric Hatch. Story: This top-notch screwball comedy is the story of Godfrey, a former socialite who has dropped out and become a bum. While on a scavenger hunt, of which one item is a forgotten man, Irene Bullock brings Godfrey into her crazy family, hiring him as a butler. Godfrey adjusts quite well to the role, attempting to bring some kind of order to the chaotic lifestyle of the Bullock family. Irene falls in love with Godfrey and although he resists her loony charms because of a previously unhappy love affair, he ultimately decides she needs him to take care of her.

Universal Pictures, 1936 (original). Director: Gregory La Cava; screenwriters: Morrie Ryskind and Eric Hatch. Cast: William Powell (Godfrey Parke), Carole Lombard (Irene Bullock), Alice Brady (Angelica Bullock), Gail Patrick (Cornelia Bullock), Eugene Pallette (Alexander Bullock), Mischa Auer (Carlo), Alan Mowbray, Jean Dixon, Robert Light, Pat Flaherty, Robert Perry, Franklin Pangborn.

• ***My Man Godfrey*** (remake). Universal Pictures, 1957. Director: Henry Koster; screenwriters: Everett Freeman, Pierre Bernels and William Bowers. Cast: June Allyson (Irene), David Niven (Godfrey), Jessie Royce Landis (Angelica), Robert Keith (Mr. Bullock), Eva Gabor (Francesca), Jay Robinson (Vincent), Martha Hyer (Cordelia), Jeff Donnell, Herbert Anderson, Eric Sinclair, Dabbs Greer, Fred Essler.

The classic crazy comedy was completely blanked in the Academy Award sweepstakes, although it received nominations for Best Director, Best Actor (Powell), Best Actress (Lombard), Best Supporting Actor (Auer), Best Supporting Actress (Brady), and Best Screenplay (Hatch and Ryskind). As many in the country were still suffering the effects of the Great Depression, audiences took perverse delight in laughing at the wealthy, and there wasn't a more amusing family around than the Bullocks, each of whom seemed like they had fallen from their highchairs too many times when children. Even their guests were crazy, with Auer being only the most outstanding example. He delighted audiences with his gorilla impersonations. Compared to these nuts, hobo Powell appeared the sanest of men.

The 1957 remake suffered not just because screwball comedies were no longer the vogue but because the cast was incredibly wrong for their roles. Allyson had spent most of her career playing sensible girls who got her men because they admired her brains and spirit. She just wasn't comfortable or believable as a scatterbrained lovely. Niven might have been able to pull off his impersonation but he seemed to sense it just wasn't going to work. In the original, it was the supporting players that made the picture so special. In the remake, the performers in these roles continually dropped the ball. Cinemascope added to the things that are wrong with this picture. All the wide screen did was to magnify the picture's defects.

629 My Old Dutch

Based on the play by Albert Chevalier and Arthur Shirley. Story: Sal Gratton, a London "coster" girl (one who sells vegetables, fruit, fish, or other goods from a wheelbarrow or outdoor stall) marries costermonger Joe Brown. Following the birth of their son, Herbert, she suddenly comes into a fortune. The parents decide to raise their son ignorant of his parentage so that he may become a gentleman. When he graduates from the university, Herbert becomes a notorious and losing gambler. Diana, his snobbish fiancée, dismisses him and upon learning of his parents, he returns, penniless, to Sal and Joe. During World War I he matures and is reunited with Diana in a hospital. Returning to London, he finds that his parents have been evicted and sent to the poorhouse. He rescues them and they are invited to live with him and his new wife, Diana.

• ***My Old Dutch*** (remake). Universal Pictures, 1926. Silent. Director and screenwriter: Lawrence Trimble. Cast: May McAvoy (Sal Gratton), Pat O'Malley (Joe Brown), Cullen Landis (Herbert Brown), Jane Winton (Lady Diana Crowes), Jean Hersholt, Agnes Steele, Patsy O'Byrne, Edgar Kennedy.

• ***My Old Dutch*** (remake). Gainsborough/Gaumont-British, 1934. Director: Sinclair Hill; screenwriters: Marjorie Gaffney, Mary Murillo, Michael Hogan and Bryan Edgar Wallace. Cast: Betty Balfour (Lil), Gordon Harker (Ernie), Michael Hogan (Bert), Florrie Forde (Aunt Bertha), Mickey Brantford, Glennis Lorimer.

The sentimental melodrama was also filmed in 1911, 1915 and 1917, the middle one starring the co-author of the play on which it was based, singer Albert Chevalier, with Florence Turner and Henry Edwards. The 1934 movie had very little to do with the other versions, being the story of a cockney girl and boy who get married, rear a son, see him go off to war, and marry a sweet girl the night before heading for the front, where he is killed. As might be expected, the young wife is pregnant, and when she has a baby, her wealthy father wishes to take the child from her in-laws. It's very sad—the circumstances, as well.

630 My Sister Eileen

Based on the play by Joseph Fields and Jerome Chodorov and the short stories of Ruth McKinney. Story: Two Ohio sisters, Ruth and Eileen Sherwood, come to New York to seek love and success. Ruth is the sensible one, while Eileen attracts men no matter where she goes, because of her innocent sexuality. They live in a seedy Greenwich Village basement apartment, surrounded by some zany characters. Ruth does her best to protect the not-so-bright Eileen from predatory men, and finds herself the object of affection of publisher Robert Baker.

Columbia Pictures, 1942 (original). Director: Alexander Hall; screenwriters: Joseph Fields and Jerome Chodorov. Cast: Rosalind Russell (Ruth Sherwood), Brian Aherne (Robert Baker), Janet Blair (Eileen Sherwood), George Tobias (Appopolous), Allyn Joslyn (Chic Clark), Elizabeth Patterson (Grandma Sherwood), Grant Mitchell, Richard Quine, June Havoc, Gordon Jones, Donald McBride.

• ***My Sister Eileen*** (remake). Columbia Pictures, 1955. Director: Richard Quine; screenwriters: Blake Edwards and Richard Quine. Cast: Janet Leigh (Eileen Sherwood), Betty Garrett (Ruth Sherwood), Jack Lemmon (Bob Baker), Robert Fosse (Frank Lippencott), Kurt Kasznar (Appopolous), Richard York, Lucy Marlow, Tommy Rall, Barbara Brown, Horace MacMahon, Henry Slate, Hal March, Alberto Morin.

Opposite, top: *William Powell appears as Godfrey Parke in the zany comedy* My Man Godfrey *(Universal, 1936).* Bottom: *Heiress June Allyson helps butler David Niven polish the silver in the 1957 Universal remake of* My Man Godfrey.

The high jinks of Rosalind Russell, who was nominated for an Academy Award, and Janet Blair as her knock-out of a sister, are entertaining but not of much lasting interest. Brian Aherne did a nice job in one of his few comedy roles. The remake was a musical, with songs such as "Give Me a Band and My Baby" and "It's Bigger Than You and Me" by Jule Styne and Leo Robin, but not to be confused with "Wonderful Town," a Broadway musical of 1953, also based on *My Sister Eileen.* Janet Leigh made a luscious Eileen and Betty Garrett was a reasonably funny Ruth. Jack Lemmon took over the Brian Aherne role but did not particularly distinguish himself. The funniest sequence in the movie occurs when a group of Brazilian naval cadets follow Eileen home, and congo through the girls' small apartment.

631 My Wife's Family

Based on the play by Fred Duprez. Story: Peggy Gay mistakes a piano hidden in a summer house for her husband Jack's illegitimate baby. No, they don't look alike. She hears about the one and thinks it's the other, don't you see?

British International, Great Britain, 1931 (original). Director: Monty Banks; screenwriters: Fred Duprez and Val Valentine. Cast: Gene Gerrard (Jack Gay), Muriel Angelus (Peggy Gay), Jimmy Godden (Doc Knott), Amy Veness (Arabella Nagg), Charles Paton (Noah Nagg), Dodo Watts, Tom Helmore, Molly Lamont, Ellen Pollock.

• ***My Wife's Family*** (remake). Camden/Pathe, Great Britain, 1941. Director: Walter C. Mycroft; screenwriters: Norman Lee and Clifford Grey. Cast: Charlie Clapham (Doc Knott), John Warwick (Jack Gay), Patricia Roc (Peggy Gay), Wylie Watson (Noah Bagshott), Chili Bouchier (Rosa Latour), Peggy Bryan, Margaret Scudamore, Leslie Fuller, David Tomlinson, Joan Greenwood.

• ***My Wife's Family*** (remake). Forth Films, Great Britain, 1956. Director: Gilbert Gunn; screenwriters: Gunn and Talbot Rothwell. Cast: Ronald Shiner (Doc Knott), Ted Ray (Jack Gay), Greta Gynt (Gloria Marsh), Robertson Hare (Noah Parker), Fabia Drake (Arabella Parker), Diane Hart (Stella Gay), Zena Marshall, Benny Lee, Jessica Cairns, Jimmy Mageean, Gilbert Harding.

The remakes rely on old jokes, that don't play very well, about infidelity, bastards, pianos, in-laws, crooks, glamorous actresses, etc. The cast consistently overplays—all three of them.

632 Mystery of Mr. X

Based on the novel *Mystery of the Dead Police* by Philip MacDonald. Story: Mr. X sets out to kill 15 London bobbies, one for each year he served in prison. His count has reached eight when gentleman crook Revel, who has stolen a

Opposite, top: *George Tobias points out the plush surroundings of a Greenwich village basement apartment to Janet Blair and Rosalind Russell, two sisters, just recently arrived from Ohio, intent on making their mark in New York, in* My Sister Eileen *(Columbia, 1942).* Bottom: *Betty Garrett and Janet Leigh appear to be telling landlord Kurt Kasznar about all the things wrong with their apartment in the 1955 Columbia remake of* My Sister Eileen.

valuable diamond, not only returns it but makes the apprehension of the maniacal Mr. X his top priority. He almost single-handedly succeeds when in mortal combat he overcomes the mysterious cop-killer.

• MGM, 1934, (original). Director: Edgar Selwyn; screenwriter: Philip MacDonald. Cast: Robert Montgomery (Nick Revel), Elizabeth Allen (Jane Frenshaw), Lewis Stone (Connor), Ralph Forbes (Marche), Henry Stephenson (Frenshaw), Leonard Mudie (Mr. X), Forrester Harvey, Ivan Simpson, Alex B. Francis, Charles Irwin.

• ***The Hour of 13*** (remake). MGM, Great Britain, 1952. Director: Harold French; screenwriters: Leon Gordon and Howard Emmett Rogers. Cast: Peter Lawford (Nicholas Revel), Dawn Addams (Jane Frenshaw), Roland Culver (Connor), Derek Bond (Sir Christopher Lenhurst), Leslie Dwyer (Ernie Perker), Richard Shaw (the Terror), Michael Hordern, Colin Gordon, Heather Thatcher, Jack McNaughton, Campbell Cotts.

The setting of the story is 1890 London, and the combination of a Raffles-like gentleman jewel thief with a mad killer on the loose makes both versions of the Philip MacDonald mystery thriller good chase pictures. Lawford, like Montgomery, was capable of being quite charming, and he doesn't disappoint in the remake. The photography and sets for the movies greatly enhance the suspense and foreboding nature of the story. Either version should be a nice rainy afternoon diversion for thriller fans.

N

633 Nana

Based on the novel by Emile Zola. Story: The high life and subsequent degradation of a Parisian courtesan, Nana, whose sexual allure turns men into her slaves, is told here. The film concentrates on her affairs with three nobles, particularly Count Muffat. She drives two of them to suicide but finally dies of smallpox in the arms of Muffat.

• ***Nana*** (remake). Films-Renoir, 1926. Silent. Director: Jean Renoir; screenwriter: Pierre Lestringuez. Cast: Catherine Hessling (Nana), Werner Krauss (Count Muffat), Jean Angelo (Count de Vandeuvres), Raymond Guerin-Catelain (Georges Hugon), Valeska Gert, Pierre Philippe, Claude Moore, Jacqueline Forzane, Harbacher, Nita Romani, Jacqueline Ford, Pierre Champagne.

• ***Nana*** (remake). United Artists, 1934. Director: Dorothy Arzner; screenwriters: Willard Mack and H.W. Gribble. Cast: Anna Sten (Nana), Phillips Holmes (Lt. George Muffat), Lionel Atwill (Colonel Andre Muffat), Richard Bennett (Greiner), Mae Clark (Satin), Muriel Kirkland, Reginald Owen, Jessie Ralph, Lawrence Grant.

• ***Nana*** (remake). Roitfield, 1955. Director: Christian Jacques; screenwriter: Henri Jeanson, Jean Ferry, Albert Valentin and Christian Jacques. Cast: Martine Carol (Nana), Charles Boyer (Count Muffat), Jacques Castelot (Vandeuvres), Elisa Cegani (Sabine, Countess Muffat), Noel Roquevert (Steiner),

Walter Chiari, Jean Debucourt, Marguerite Pierry, Pierre Palau, Paul Frankeur.

• ***Nana*** (remake). Distinction Films, Sweden, 1971. Director and screenwriter: Mac Ahlberg. Cast: Anna Gael (Nana), Gillian Hills (Tina), Lars Lunoe (Count Haupt), Keve Hjelm, Gerard Berner.

Nana was also produced in 1912, 1913, 1923 and 1944. The 1926 version has been described as director Jean Renoir's finest silent film. For the 1934 movie, Samuel Goldwyn imported Anna Sten from Europe, intent on making her an international star. He said she "is better than Garbo, sexier than Dietrich and a finer actress than Norma Shearer." With such a build up, it wasn't too surprising that she found it difficult to live up to her billing. Her accent was not as pleasing to audiences as were Garbo's and Dietrich's, and after two more films she went back to Europe without the star status Goldwyn had sought for her.

Nana died in many different ways in her various film lives. Besides the smallpox of the Renoir piece, she committed suicide in 1934, and was strangled by her jealous count in the 1955 French production. The 1971 Swedish film was given an X rating as it dealt a bit too explicitly with prostitution, sex and sexuality, nudity and pornography.

Nancy Goes to Rio ***see*** **It's a Date**

634 The Narrow Corner

Based on the story by W. Somerset Maugham. Story: Very little happens in this story of a young murderer who flees to a remote South Pacific island, but finds he can't escape his fate.

Warner Bros., 1933 (original). Director: Alfred E. Green; screenwriter: Robert Presnell. Cast: Douglas Fairbanks, Jr. (Fred), Patricia Ellis (Louise), Dudley Digges (Dr. Saunders), Ralph Bellamy (Eric), Arthur Kohl, Henry Kolker, Willie Fung, Reginald Owen, William V. Mong, Joseph Swickard.

• ***Isle of Fury*** (remake). Warner Bros., 1936. Director: Frank MacDonald; screenwriters: Robert Andrews and William Jacobs. Cast: Humphrey Bogart (Val Stevens), Margaret Lindsay (Lucille Gordon), Donald Woods (Eric Blake), Paul Graetz (Capt. Deever), Gordon Hart, E.E. Clive, George Regas, Sidney Bracy, Tetsu Komai, Miki Morita, Houseley Stevenson, Sr.

The Maugham story had little feminine interest, but the producers couldn't allow that, so they drew attention away from the interplay of four men, including one, Fairbanks, who was on the run from a murder charge in Australia, by building up Patricia Ellis' role as the former fiancée of Ralph Bellamy, with whom Fairbanks falls in love.

The remake will never become one of the Bogart cult films. It has been reported that Bogart denied ever having made the film. Perhaps he just wished he hadn't. It's 60 minutes of pure tedium as Bogie, a fugitive from justice, seeks refuge on a South Sea island and finds the love of a good woman, Margaret Lindsay.

635 The Narrow Street

Based on the novel by Edwin Bateman Morris. Story: Simon Haldane, who gets no respect, is stunned to find a strange girl in his bedroom one morning, but he is up to the task of sending for a doctor to treat the girl's chill. She is forced to stay overnight, causing Simon's co-workers at the Faulkner Iron Works to believe that Simon is married to this girl, Doris, and so all come to visit Simon to get a look at her. Briefly, Doris' head is turned by the self-assurance of salesman Ray Wyeth, but Simon summons up enough courage to win Doris for himself. He even wins a promotion in an office shakeup. He has some bad moments when he learns that Doris' father is his employer, but this time she takes charge and all ends well.

Warner Bros., 1924 (original). Silent. Director: William Beaudine; screenwriter: Julien Josephson. Cast: Matt Moore (Simon Haldane), Dorothy Devore (Doris), David Butler (Ray Wyeth), George Pearce (Edgar Deems), Russell Simpson (Garvey), Gertrude Short, Joe Butterworth, Kate Toncray, Tempe Pigott.

• ***Wide Open*** (remake). Warner Bros., 1930. Director: Archie Mayo; screenwriter: James A. Starr. Cast: Edward Everett Horton (Simon Haldane), Patsy Ruth Miller (Julia Faulkner/Doris), Louise Fazenda (Agatha Hathaway), Vera Lewis, T. Roy Barnes, E.J. Radcliffe, Louise Beavers, Edna Murphy, Frank Beal.

The motivation of some of the characters in these two films is a little hard to understand and the happy coincidences even more difficult to believe, but these movies were not meant to be exercises in logic, rather farces that demonstrated the two stars' (Matt Moore and Edward Everett Horton) talents in portraying the timid bachelor who would have likely stayed that way had not a woman taken the initiative and gone after him.

National Lampoon's European Vacation ***see*** **National Lampoon's Vacation**

636 National Lampoon's Vacation

Based on an original screenplay by John Hughes. Story: Clark Griswold plans to drive his family, consisting of wife, Ellen, and children, Audrey and Rusty, from Chicago to California's amusement park, Walleyworld, during their vacation. While visiting some relatives along the way, he finds that he is to deliver his wife's aunt to her other children. The aunt dies, Clark has a running flirtation with a blonde in a Ferrari, he almost totals his car, and after numerous other complications which break up ten-year-olds, arrives only to find Walleyworld closed. He gets a gun and forces the guards to open the park for his family so their trip won't be a total waste.

Warner Bros., 1983 (original). Director: Harold Ramis; screenwriter: John Hughes. Cast: Chevy Chase (Clark Griswold), Beverly D'Angelo (Ellen Griswold), Dana Barron (Audrey Griswold), Anthony Michael Hall (Rusty Griswold), Randy Quaid (Cousin Eddie), Imogene Coca (Aunt Edna), John Candy, Eddie Bracken, Christine Brinkley, James Keach, Eugene Levy, Brian Doyle-Murray.

• ***National Lampoon's European Vacation*** (sequel). 1986. Director: Amy Heckerling; screenwriters: John Hughes and Robert Klane. Cast: Chevy Chase (Clark Griswold), Beverly D'Angelo (Ellen Griswold), Dana Hill (Audrey Griswold), Jason Lively (Rusty Griswold), John Astin, Eric Idle, William Zabka, Robbie Coltrane.

From the people who gave you *Animal House* comes a sometimes amusing farce about a loony father who dearly believes in family togetherness, and is not easily disturbed when things go wrong. The first film has a certain amount of irreverent freshness to it. By the time of the sequel, the formula became weary. It wasn't that Chase and his dumb family were going to play the ugly Americans and have numerous disasters which they would survive without breaking stride that was bothersome, but that one could see the mix-ups coming a country ahead.

637 National Velvet

Based on the novel by Enid Bagnold. Story: In an English seacoast village, 12-year-old Velvet Brown wins a horse in a raffle and with the help of Mi Taylor, a former jockey, she prepares to race the horse, called "The Pie" at the Grand National Steeplechases, with herself as the rider.

MGM, 1944 (original). Director: Clarence Brown; screenwriters: Theodore Reeves and Helen Deutsch. Cast: Mickey Rooney (Mi Taylor), Elizabeth Taylor (Velvet Brown), Donald Crisp (Mr. Brown), Anne Revere (Mrs. Brown), Angela Lansbury (Edwina Brown), "Butch" Jenkins (Donald Brown), Juanita Quigley, Reginald Owen, Terry Kilburn, Alec Craig, Arthur Shields, Dennis Hoey, Arthur Treacher.

• ***International Velvet*** (sequel). MGM, 1978. Director and screenwriter: Bryan Forbes. Cast: Tatum O'Neal (Sarah Brown), Christopher Plummer (John Seaton), Anthony Hopkins (Captain Johnson), Nanette Newman (Velvet Brown), Peter Barkworth, Dinsdale Landen, Sarah Bullen, Jeffrey Bryon, Richard Warwick, Daniel Abineri, Jason White.

Ann Revere won the Best Supporting Actress Academy Award for her portrayal of Velvet's mother and film editor Robert J. Kern also won an Oscar. Clarence Brown was nominated for Best Director and Leonard Smith for Best Color Cinematography. This most beloved of all racing horse movies was sentimental without being sickeningly sweet. Elizabeth Taylor was such a lovely youngster, that there was little doubt she would grow to the beauty she did become. The *New York World Telegram* described her performance as "burning eagerness tempered with sweet fragile charm." The sequel takes place 25 years after Velvet Brown won the Grand National. She helps her orphaned niece, who has a similar love for horses, train to become a member of the British Olympic riding team. Unfortunately, the film has none of the charm of the original.

Navjawan ***see*** **The Hunchback of Notre Dame**

638 The Nervous Wreck

Based on a story by E.J. Rath and the play by Owen Davis. Story: Henry

Williams, a hypochondriac, convinces himself that he has a fatal illness. He sets out for Arizona and a better climate, stops at a ranch owned by Jud Morgan and his daughter, Sally, and decides to stay. While taking Sally across the desert to the train station, he runs out of gas. In a series of misadventures, he holds up a car brandishing a monkey wrench to get fuel, is forced to take a job as a waiter at the ranch of Jerome Underwood, the man he held up, is pursued by the sheriff and Sally's father and after a climactic chase, tumbles down a mountain-side with Sally, survives, decides he is cured and marries Sally.

Producers Distributing Corporation, 1926 (original). Silent. Director: Scott Sidney; screenwriter: F. McGrew Willis. Cast: Harrison Ford (Henry Williams), Phyllis Haver (Sally Morgan), Mack Swain (Jerome Underwood), Hobart Bosworth (Jud Morgan), Paul Nicholson, Vera Steadman, Charles Gerrard, Clarence Burton.

• ***Whoopee!*** (remake). United Artists, 1930. Director: Thornton Freeland; screenwriter: William Counselman; based on the musical comedy by Walter Donaldson, Gus Khan and William Anthony McGuire. Cast: Eddie Cantor (Henry Williams), Eleanor Hunt (Sally Morgan), Paul Gregory (Wanenis), John Rutherford (Sheriff Bob Wells), Ethel Shutta (Mary Custer), Spencer Charters (Jerome Underwood), Chief Caupolican, Albert Hackett, Walter Law, William H. Philbrick.

• ***Up in Arms*** (remake). RKO, 1944. Director: Elliott Nugent; screenwriters: Don Hartman, Allen Boretz and Robert Pirosh. Cast: Danny Kaye (Danny Weems), Dinah Shore (Virginia), Dana Andrews (Joe), Constance Dowling (Mary Morgan), Louis Calhern (Colonel Ashley), George Mathews (Blackie), Benny Baker (Butterball), Elisha Cook, Jr., Lyle Talbot, Walter Catlett, George Meeker.

The Harrison Ford of *The Nervous Wreck* is no relation to the actor who portrays Indiana Jones. The little comedy did not really come into its own until Eddie Cantor got his hands on it, first on Broadway and then on the screen, making him a movie star. Another significant fact about the movie was the introduction of Busby Berkeley to screen audiences. Cantor is the hypochondriac who finds himself on an Arizona ranch, populated by cowboys, Indians and a bevy of beautiful chorus girls. He sings his most successful song, "Making Whoopee," and at the center of Berkeley's first abstract pattern of dancers is teen-age Betty Grable. Other songs included "My Baby Just Cares for Me" and "The Song of the Setting Sun."

In 1944, Danny Kaye appears as the hypochondriac, but rather than landing at a ranch in Arizona, this elevator boy in a building full of doctors is drafted in the Army along with his very good friend, Dana Andrews, the girl of his dreams, Constance Dowling, and the girl who eventually gets him, Dinah Shore. This was Kaye's cinematic debut and the motion picture industry had never seen anyone like him before. His most famous number in the picture is "Manic-Depressive Picture Presents," penned by Sylvia Fine, soon to be Mrs. Kaye, and Max Liebman. Kaye delights audiences with this breathless paean to movie credits. Other songs include "Melody in 4F" by Fine and Liebman and "All Out for Freedom" by Ted Koehler and Harold Arlen.

Nevada Smith *see* The Carpetbaggers

639 Never Say Die

Based on the play by William H. Post and William Collier. Story: When physicians mistake the buzzing of a bee for heart murmurs, they erroneously give wealthy Jack Woodbury just three months to live. His friend, Hector Walters, seeing a way to make some money from an inheritance, convinces his own fiancée, Violet Stevenson, to marry Jack. At the appointed time, Jack doesn't die and Violet finds that she has fallen in love with him.

Associated Exhibitors/MacLean Productions, 1924 (original). Silent. Director: George J. Crone; screenwriters: Raymond Cannon, Raymond Griffith and Wade Boteler. Cast: Douglas MacLean (Jack Woodbury), Lillian Rich (Violet Stevenson), Hallam Cooley (Hector Walters), Helen Ferguson, Lucien Littlefield, Tom O'Brien.

• ***Never Say Die*** (remake). Paramount Pictures, 1939. Director: Elliott Nugent; screenwriters: Don Hartman, Frank Butler and Preston Sturges. Cast: Martha Raye (Mickey Hawkins), Bob Hope (John Kidley), Andy Devine (Henry Munch), Alan Mowbray (Prince Smirnov), Gale Sondergaard (Juno), Sig Rumann, Ernest Cossart, Paul Harvey.

Both versions of the comedy are predictable pieces with the Hope version being done just shortly before he became a star. He's a millionaire hypochondriac who believes he's dying and marries Martha Raye, so she will inherit his money. It has some bright moments, but on the whole, it's nothing special.

640 Never the Twain Shall Meet

Based on the novel by Peter Bernard Kyne. Story: Dan Pritchard falls in love with beautiful Tamea, a South Sea island queen, when she is left in his care in San Francisco by her French sea captain father. After exploring the delights of American civilization, the couple return to her island. After awhile, Dan grows bored with the life, starts drinking heavily, and ultimately deserts her and returns to the mainland.

MGM, 1925 (original). Silent. Director: Maurice Tourneur; screenwriter: Eugene Mullin. Cast: Anita Stewart (Tamea), Bert Lytell (Dan Pritchard), Huntley Gordon (Mark Mellenger), Justine Johnstone (Maisie Morrison), George Steigman, Lionel Belmore, Emily Fitzroy, Florence Turner, William Norris.

• ***Never the Twain Shall Meet*** (remake). MGM, 1931. Director: W.S. Van Dyke; screenwriter: Edwin Justys Mayer. Cast: Leslie Howard (Dan), Conchita Montenegro (Tamea), C. Aubrey Smith (Mr. Pritchard), Karen Morley (Maisie), Mitchell Lewis, Hale Hamilton, Clyde Cook, Bob Gilbert.

These films seem to suggest that people of different cultures may find it impossible to give up their own ways and adopt those of another, even if they are in love. Everyone likes the familar, we suppose. The film was no better with Leslie Howard as the San Francisco importer who falls in love with a Polynesian maiden left in his care by her dying sea captain father.

The New Interns *see* **The Interns**

Night Club Scandal *see* **Guilty As Hell**

641 Night Must Fall

Based on the play by Emlyn Williams. Story: A charming young bellboy, Danny, who is really a psychopathic murderer, ingratiates himself with rich old Mrs. Bramson, and then murders her. Despite her attraction to Danny, Mrs. Bramson's companion, Olivia Grayne, suspects Danny of the crime. When she confronts him, he confesses and is arrested before he can kill her.

MGM, 1937 (original). Director: Richard Thorpe; screenwriter: John Van Druten. Cast: Robert Montgomery (Danny), Rosalind Russell (Olivia Grayne), Dame May Whitty (Mrs. Bramson), Alan Marshal (Justin), Kathleen Harrison, Merle Tottenham, Matthew Boulton, Eily Malyon.

• ***Night Must Fall*** (remake). MGM, 1964. Director: Karel Reisz; screenwriter: Clive Exton. Cast: Albert Finney (Danny), Susan Hampshire (Olivia), Mona Washbourne (Mrs. Bramson), Sheila Hancock (Dora), Michael Medwin, Joe Gladwin, Martin Wyldeck.

This taut, suspenseful piece, a change of pace for Robert Montgomery, who until this time had played sophisticated playboys, was one of the biggest hits of the year. Montgomery was nominated for an Academy Award as was 72-year-old Dame May Whitty in her screen debut. Neither won. The remake was a rather dreary thriller about axe-wielding Albert Finney, his invalid victim, Mona Washbourne, and Susan Hampshire, who had very mixed feelings about the strange young man. Finney was wooden and couldn't match Montgomery for appearing both charming and sinister.

Night of Mystery *see* **The Greene Murder Case**

A Night to Remember *see* **Titantic!**

642 The Night Watch

Based on the play by Claude Farrere and Lucienne Nepoty. Story: French Commander Corlaix and his wife, Yvonne, hold a shipboard dinner for his officers. Afterward, Lt. D'Artelle convinces Yvonne to go with him to his cabin. War is declared and Corlaix orders his ship into battle, not knowing his wife is still aboard. The ship is sunk by a torpedo and Corlaix is court-martialed for incompetence. Seems the Admiralty Court believes that his mind wasn't on his job, as he was busy shooting one of his own officers. Yvonne gives testimony that compromises her but proves that her husband had adhered to duty. Realizing her love for him, Corlaix forgives Yvonne for her indiscretion.

First National Pictures, 1928 (original). Sound effects and musical score. Director: Alexander Korda; screenwriter: Lajos Biro. Cast: Billie Dove (Yvonne), Paul Lukas (Cmdr. Corlaix), Donald Reed (D'Artelle), Nicholas Soussanin, Nicholas Bela, George Periolat, William Tooker, Gus Partos, Anita Garvin.

• ***The Woman from Monte Carlo*** (remake). First National Pictures, 1932. Director: Michael Curtiz; screenwriter: Harvey Threw. Cast: Lil Dagover (Yvonne), Walter Huston (Corlaix), Warren William (D'Artelle), John Wray, Robert Warwick.

If the story sounds familiar, it's because the plot of a married woman being found in another man's bedroom and then having to disgrace herself by telling about it to save her husband has been incorporated into several movies, including another one directed by Alexander Korda in 1929, called *Love and the Devil.* The 1932 remake was glamorous German actress Lil Dagover's first American film, but did nothing for her Hollywood career. Come to think of it, it didn't do much for those of Walter Huston and Warren William, either.

The Nightcomer *see* **The Innocents**

Nikki, Wild Dog of the North *see* **Northern Patrol**

643 1984

Based on the novel by George Orwell. Story: In this futuristic tale, Winston Smith works in the Ministry of Truth, where his job is to re-write history to meet the prevailing teachings of the all-powerful authority "Big Brother." Among the things forbidden to party members such as Smith are love and sex. Despite this prohibition, he falls in love with Julia. He is ultimately betrayed by a party official, O'Connor, who had seemed to befriend him and he must endure re-programming, resulting in the loss of his love and his freedom to think independently.

Holiday/Associated British Pathe, 1956 (original). Director: Michael Anderson; screenwriters: William P. Templeton and Ralph Bettinson. Cast: Edmond O'Brien (Winston Smith), Michael Redgrave (O'Connor), Jan Sterling (Julia), David Kossoff, Mervyn Johns, Donald Pleasence, Carol Wolveridge, Ernest Clark, Patrick Allen.

• ***1984*** (remake). Umbrella/Atlantic Releasing Corporation, 1984. Director and screenwriter: Michael Radford. Cast: John Hurt (Winston Smith), Richard Burton (O'Brien), Suzanna Hamilton (Julia), Cyril Cusack (Charrington), Gregor Fisher, James Walker.

With Europe as the fascist state of Oceania, ruled by Big Brother, Edmond O'Brien as Winston Smith questions only in his mind the notions of Doublethink, the thought police, the anti-sex league and blind obedience to a dictator. Through junkshop owner David Kossoff, he feels he has found a sanctuary from constant observation, in a grungy room that he rents. When he reveals his feelings to Julia, this becomes their trysting place. But it was all a setup by O'Connor who then goes about the task of brainwashing the unfortunate Smith. In the remake, the settings are even more dismal and the lovemaking more explicit, but this didn't make it succeed anymore than did the earlier version in bringing to the screen a literary piece that dealt more with thoughts than action. Although both movies made valiant efforts, neither was able to depict the horror of a totalitarian regime that controls even one's thoughts. Perhaps

Greta Garbo and Melvyn Douglas take in the sights of Paris in Ninotchka *(MGM, 1939).*

audiences had seen more compelling documentations of dehumanizing futures on television news shows.

644 Ninotchka

Based on a screen story by Melchior Lengyel. Story: Ninotchka is a Russian envoy sent to Paris to determine why three emissaries, Iranoff, Buljanoff, and Kopalski, had not completed their assignment to sell some crown jewels. Seems that the three had been seduced by the good life in the City of Lights, and are living it up in good capitalistic style in the most expensive hotel in Paris. Ninotchka herself falls for the charms of Count Leon d'Algout, who shows her the sights and breaks through her frigid bureaucratic facade.

MGM, 1939 (original). Director: Ernst Lubitsch; screenwriters: Charles Brackett, Billy Wilder and Walter Reisch. Cast: Greta Garbo (Ninotchka), Melvyn Douglas (Count Leon d'Algout), Ina Claire (Grand Duchess Swana), Sig Rumann (Iranoff), Felix Bressart (Buljanoff), Alexander Granach (Kopalski), Bela Lugosi, Gregory Gayle, Richard Carle, Edwin Maxwell, George Tobias, Dorothy Adams.

• ***Silk Stockings*** (remake). MGM, 1957. Director: Rouben Mamoulian; screenwriters: Leonard Gershe and Leonard Spigelgass. Cast: Fred Astaire (Steve Canfield), Cyd Charisse (Ninotchka), Janis Paige (Peggy Dayton),

Fred Astaire and lovely Cyd Charisse are just about to dance in Silk Stockings, *the 1957 MGM musical remake of* Ninotchka.

George Tobias (Vassili Markovitch), Peter Lorre (Brankov), Jules Munschin (Bibinski), Joseph Buloff (Ivanov), Wim Sonneveld.

Ninotchka gathered four Academy Award nominations (Best Picture, Best Actress, Best Original Story and Best Screenplay) but came away empty-handed. No matter, the Lubitsch magic worked to perfection with this trite story and it still delights audiences when seen today. The comedy and the sexy snuggling of Garbo and Douglas are superb and no one could doubt that Ninotchka would soon be agreeing with Leon's message in the following interchange: (Douglas) "It's midnight. Look at the clock. One hand has met the other hand. They kiss. Isn't that wonderful?" (Garbo) "That's the way clocks work. What's wonderful about it?" (Douglas) "But, Ninotchka, it's midnight. One half of Paris is making love to the other half."

The musical remake made the plot even more corny. Fred Astaire is a movie producer who wishes to use the music of a defecting Russian composer, and three Russian emissaries have been sent to Paris to get him to come back home and write songs about tractors and factories. When Astaire introduces them to some beauties and the Parisian night life, they forget their mission until special envoy Cyd Charisse shows up. Astaire romances her and she finds that she also likes a life in which she can wear sexy underwear and silk stockings. Charisse is a great dancer, but not an actor, so it's not surprising that she's at her best in a scene in her hotel room where she dances around the room doing sort of a reverse strip tease as she sexily dresses in pretty things. The Cole Porter songs included "All of You" and "Fated to Be Mated," danced by Astaire and Charisse; "Stereophonic Sound," performed by Janis Paige and Astaire, and the title song, danced bewitchingly by Charisse.

645 No Exit

Based on the play by Paul Bowles, translated from Jean-Paul Sarte's play *Huis Clos*. Story: Cowardly former Nazi collaborator Garcin has been executed as a traitor and his assignment in hell is a bricked-in room with no exit. His only companions in the room are beautiful, bitchy Estelle, who has murdered her illegitimate child and bitter Inez, a lesbian who has destroyed her cousin's marriage and died with her in a suicide pact. The three are sentenced to spend eternity together acting as their own torturers, supporting Garcin's observation that "Hell is other people."

• ***Huis Clos*** (original). Mondial Films/Mareau, 1954. Director: Jacqueline Audry; screenwriter: Pierre Laroche. Cast: Arletty (Inez), Franck Villard (Garcin), Gaby Sylvia (Estelle), Yves Deniaud, Renaud-Mary, Danielle Delmore, Suzanne Dehily, Claude Nicot, Paul Frankeur, Jean Debcourt, Isabell Pia.

• ***No Exit*** (remake). Zenith Pictures, 1962. Director: Tad Danielski; screenwriter: George Tabori. Cast: Viveca Lindfors (Inez), Morgan Sterne (Garcin), Rita Gam (Estelle), Ben Piazza, Susan Mayo, Orlando Sacha, Manuel Rosen, Mirtha Miller, Miguel A. Irate, Elsa Dorian, Mario Horna, Carlos Brown.

Although filmed in France in 1954, it wasn't until 1958 that *Huis Clos* was allowed to be released in England because of censor problems. The second version was filmed in Argentina and won the German Film Festival Award. It included flashbacks of the lives of the three inhabitants of the bricked-in hellish room. Both films are quite grim.

646 No Orchids for Miss Blandish

Based on the novel by James Hadley Chase. Story: Heiress Barbara Blandish is kidnapped by small-time crooks who beat her fiancé to death. She is stolen from them by the even tougher Grissom gang and she falls for their psychopathic leader, Slim Grissom. The police track her to the gang's hideout and Slim is killed in a shoot-out.

Alliance/Tudor/Renown, 1948 (original). Director and screenwriter: St. John L. Clowes. Cast: Jack La Rue (Slim Grissom), Linden Travers (Barbara Blandish), Hugh McDermott (Fenner), Walter Crisham (Eddie), Leslie Bradley

(Bailey), Zoe Gail, Charles Goldner, MacDonald Parke, Percy Marmont, Lilly Molner.

• ***The Grissom Gang*** (remake). Cinerama, 1971. Director: Robert Aldrich; screenwriter: Leon Griffiths. Cast: Kim Darby (Barbara Blandish), Scott Wilson (Slim Grissom), Tony Musante (Eddie Hagan), Irene Dailey (Ma Grissom), Robert Lansing (Dave Fenner), Connie Stevens (Anna Borg), Joey Faye, Don Keefer, Ralph Waite.

• ***The Flesh of the Orchid*** (remake). Twentieth Century–Fox/Lira, 1975. Director: Patrice Chereau; screenwriter: Patrice Chereau and Jean-Claude Carriere. Cast: Charlotte Rampling (Claire), Bruno Cremer (Louis), Edwige Feuillere (Aunt), Simone Signoret (Lady Vamos), Hughes Quester, Alida Valli, Hans Christian Blech, Francois Simon.

The British version of the American gangster film is really a delightfully awful film. It's so bad that it might have qualified for a cult film if only enough people had actually sat through it. In the remake, a New York heiress, Darby, is kidnapped in 1931 by a gang of small-time hoods led by a homicidal old lady, Ma Grissom, and her psychotic son, Slim. It's almost as bad as the original, with much emphasis on unnecessary violence. The final film in this troika of poor taste concerns Charlotte Rampling as an heiress committed to an asylum by her aunt. She escapes, and with the aid of a young man is able to see that the injustice is corrected.

647 The Noose

Based on the play by Willard Mack and H.H. Van Loan. Story: A gambler has placed his son in a reform school to toughen him. When the youngster is released the gambler tells him that his mother is now married to the state's governor and he plans to embarrass his ex-wife by publicly announcing her previous marriage. To prevent this, the boy shoots and kills his father. He is arrested, tried and sentenced to die, but steadfastly refuses to discuss his motives for the killing. The governor's wife expresses interest in the case and saves her son's life, without realizing their relationship, by begging her husband to pardon the boy.

First National Pictures, 1928 (original). Silent. Director: John Francis Dillon; screenwriters: H.H. Van Loan and Willard Mack. Cast: Richard Barthelmess (Nickie Elkins), Montagu Love (Buck Gordon), Robert O'Connor (Jim Conley), Jay Eaton (Tommy), Lina Basquette (Dot), Thelma Todd (Phyllis), Ed Brady (Seth McMillan), Fred Warren, Charles Giblyn, Alice Joyce, William Walling, Robert T. Haines.

• ***I'd Give My Life*** (remake). Paramount Pictures, 1936. Director: Edwin L. Marin; screenwriters: George O'Neill and Ben Ryan. Cast: Sir Guy Standing (Gov. Bancroft), Frances Drake (Mary Reyburn), Tom Brown (Nickie Elkins), Janet Beecher (Mrs. Bancroft), Robert Gleckler, Helen Lowell, Paul Hurst, Charles C. Wilson, Charles Richman.

Neither film should have taken as long as it did as the only really dramatic parts are the last 20 minutes or so when the fate of the young convicted killer is in doubt. There's nothing like an impending execution to build tension.

Neither cast is outstanding but they handle their chores as journeymen. These are gloomy tales.

648 Northern Patrol

Based on the novel *Nomads of the North* by James Oliver Curwood. Story: Mountie Rod Webb and his dog come across the body of a young trapper, whose death appears to be a suicide, but further investigation undercovers a theft and a motive for the young man's death.

• ***Northern Patrol*** (remake). Allied Artists, 1953. Director: Rex Bailey; screenwriter: Warren Douglas. Cast: Kirby Grant (Corporal Rod Webb), Chinock (himself), Marion Carr (Quebec Kid), Bill Phipps, Claudie Drake, Dale Van Sickle, Gloria Talbot, Richard Walsh.

• ***Nikki, Wild Dog of the North*** (remake). Disney/Buena Vista, 1961. Directors: Jack Couffer and Don Haldane; screenwriter: Winston Hibbler. Cast: Jean Coutu (Andre Dupas), Emile Genest (Jacques Lebeau), Uriel Luft (Makoki), Robert Rivard, Nikki, Neewa.

The story was also filmed in 1920 under its original title, *Nomads of the North*, by First National. The 1953 picture should be a challenge to movie buffs to find some place where it is still shown. Even late night television has its standards. Other than Gloria Talbot, only the dog looks familiar. The Disney movie treats its story as a documentary, although the subject matter is fiction, and comes up with a picture that will appeal to dog and bear fans. Nikki the dog adopts a bear-cub, Neewa, whose mother is murdered by a killer-bear. Much like Sidney Poitier and Tony Curtis in *The Defiant Ones* (1958) they are tied together and have to make a long trek together, learning that they need each other. Nikki has the usual adventures required in these films—lose a good master, be treated cruelly by another, live to see the latter get his, and be reunited with the good master.

Northwest Rangers *see* Manhattan Melodrama

649 Not So Dusty

Based on a story by Wally Patch and Frank Atkinson. Story: Two dustmen (garbage collectors), Dusty Grey and Nobby Clark, find a valuable first edition among books thrown out as rubbish. Various parties are happy to take the piece off their hands, including some crooks. To complicate matters a fake copy of the book comes into play before Dusty and Nobby get their just deserts.

GS Enterprises/Radio, Great Britain, 1936 (original). Director: Maclean Rogers; screenwriters: Kathleen Butler and H.F. Maltby. Cast: Wally Patch (Dusty Grey), Gus McNaughton (Nobby Clark), Muriel George (Mrs. Clark), Phil Ray (Dan Stevens), Johnny Singer, Isobel Scaife, Ethel Griffies, Raymond Lovell.

• ***Not So Dusty*** (remake). Jarwell/Eros, Great Britain, 1956. Director and screenwriter: Maclean Rogers. Cast: Joy Nichols (Lobelia), Bill Owen (Dusty), Leslie Dwyer (Nobby Clark), Roddy Hughes (Mr. Layton), Harold Berens

(Driver), Ellen Pollock (Agatha), Wally Patch, Dudley Nichols, William Simons, Totti Trueman Taylor, Bill Shine.

Some may find that English subtitles would help them enjoy these cockney comedies. In the remake, the two dustmen are given the rare book for performing a good deed and the donor's sneaky sister, Ellen Pollock, is intent on getting the property back, but the boys are able to sell it to a wealthy man who will appreciate it.

650 Nothing but the Truth

Based on the novel by Frederic Isham and the play by James Montgomery. Story: To win a $10,000 bet, Robert Bennett, a junior partner in a brokerage firm, agrees not to tell a lie during a 24-hour period. He wins the bet but gets himself, his friends and his employer in a whole lot of trouble. After the 24-hour period is over, he tells a series of convincing lies to make everything right again.

• ***Nothing but the Truth*** (remake). Famous Players/Paramount Pictures, 1929. Director: Victor Schertzinger; screenwriter: John McGowan. Cast: Richard Dix (Robert Bennett), Berton Churchill (E.M. Burke), Louis John Bartels (Frank Connelly), Ned Sparks (Clarence Van Dyke), Wynne Gibson, Helen Kane, Dorothy Hall, Madeline Grey, Nancy Ryan.

• ***Nothing but the Truth*** (remake). Paramount Pictures, 1941. Director: Elliott Nugent; screenwriters: Don Hartman and Ken Englund. Cast: Bob Hope (Steve Bennett), Paulette Goddard (Gwen Saunders), Edward Arnold (T.T. Rayston), Leif Erikson (Tommy Van Deusen), Glen Anders (Dick Donnelly), Helen Vinson, Grant Mitchell, Willie Best, Clarence Rolb, Catherine Doucet, Mary Forbes, Rose Hobart.

The story was first filmed in 1920 by Metro starring Taylor Holmes as Bennett. The 1929 comedy also produced a hit song for Helen Kane, "Do Something," written by Bud Green and Sammy Stept. The Hope film has Ski-nose being given $10,000 by Paulette Goddard with instructions to double it within three days, but he gets into a passle of trouble when he places the money on a bet that he can tell only the truth for 24 hours. The complications take place aboard a lavish houseboat where he finds telling the absolute truth to be difficult and embarrassing.

651 Nothing Sacred

Based on the short story "Letter to the Editor" by James H. Street. Story: Dr. Enoch Downer erroneously diagnoses New England girl Hazel Flagg as suffering from a fatal dose of radium poisoning. The story of her tragedy is picked up by the New York newspapers and reporter Wally Cook convinces his editor, Oliver Stone, that hers would be a great human interest story. She is brought to New York and given the royal treatment by the Big Apple. Unfortunately, it becomes rather embarrassing for all concerned when she doesn't die.

Selznick/United Artists, 1937 (original). Director: William A. Wellman; screenwriter: Ben Hecht. Cast: Carole Lombard (Hazel Flagg), Fredric March (Wally Cook), Charles Winninger (Dr. Enoch Downer), Walter Connolly

(Oliver Stone), Sig Rumann, Frank Fay, Maxie Rosenblum, Alex Schoenberg, Monty Woolley, Aileen Pringle.

• ***Living It Up*** (remake). Paramount Pictures, 1954. Director: Norman Taurog; screenwriters: Jack Rose and Melville Shavelson; based on the musical *Hazel Flagg*, the book by Ben Hecht, music by Jule Styne and lyrics by Bob Hilliard. Cast: Dean Martin (Steve), Jerry Lewis (Homer), Janet Leigh (Wally Cook), Edward Arnold (the Mayor), Fred Clark (Oliver Stone), Sheree North, Sammy White, Sid Tomack.

Nothing Sacred was one of Hollywood's most biting satires, with March and Lombard really giving it to each other. One of the best lines belongs to Charles Winninger, as the Warsaw, Vermont, doctor who on first encountering reporter March, tells him, "I'll tell you briefly what I think of newspapermen. The hand of God, reaching down into the mire, couldn't elevate one of them to the depths of degradation." One of the few disappointments about this joy of a crazy comedy is that when shown on television, the Technicolor is of poor quality.

The Martin and Lewis remake changes the sexes of the characters, with Jerry as the hick who is wrongly diagnosed as dying of radioactive poisoning and Janet Leigh as the reporter who plans to give him one final big spree in the big city. Martin is the doctor who gets things wrong. The high points of the film turn out to be the boys' performances of Styne and Hilliard's "Every Street's a Boulevard in Old New York" and Martin's rendition of "How Do You Speak to an Angel."

652 Notorious Gentleman

Based on a story by Colin Clements and Florence Dyerson. Story: Lawyer Kirk Arlen believes he has committed the perfect murder when he kills Clayton Bradford and frames his fiancée, Nina Thorne, while pretending to protect her. John Barrett discovers the truth and lets out all of the scheme in the climatic courtroom scene.

Universal Pictures, 1935 (original). Director: Edward Laemmle; screenwriters: Leopold Atlas and Robert Tasker. Cast: Charles Bickford (Kirk Arlen), Sidney Blackmer (Clayton Bradford), Helen Vinson (Nina Thorne), Onslow Stevens (John Barrett), Dudley Digges, John Darrow, John Larkin, Evelyn Selbie, Alice Ardell.

• ***Smooth As Silk*** (remake). Universal Pictures, 1946. Director: Charles Barton; screenwriters: Dane Lussier and Kerry Shaw. Cast: Kent Taylor (Mark Fenton), Virginia Grey (Paula), Jane Adams (Susan), Milburn Stone (John Kimble), John Litel, Danny Morton, Charles Trowbridge, Theresa Harris, Harry Cheshire.

Both versions of this well-worn plot are quite ordinary with disappointing climaxes. In the remake, Kent Taylor, a criminal lawyer in love with Virginia Grey, plots to murder her new lover and frame her for the crime when she throws him over. None of the leading performers in either movie seem to be trying very hard, but that was par for the course for many such "B" pictures, which were always underfinanced and hurriedly shot.

Notre Dame *see* **The Hunchback of Notre Dame**

Notre Dame de Paris *see* **The Hunchback of Notre Dame**

Now I'll Tell *see* **Street of Chance**

653 The Nuisance

Based on a story by Chandler Sprague and Howard Emmett Rogers. Story: Joe Stevens is, plain and simple, an ambulance chaser with a fine record of winning big damage awards. His favorite target is a tractor company whose surface cars have been in a large number of accidents. Angered by his success at their expense, officials of the company hire pretty Dorothy Mason to get some evidence on the lawyer so they can smear him. Naturally, Joe and Dorothy fall in love and he's able to beat the company at its own game and duck disbarment, which he richly deserves.

MGM, 1933 (original). Director: Jack Conway; screenwriters: Sam Spewack and Bella Cohen. Cast: Lee Tracy (Joe Stevens), Madge Evans (Dorothy), Frank Morgan (Dr. Prescott), Charles Butterworth (Floppy), John Miljan (Calhoun), Virginia Cherrill (Miss Rutherford), David Landau, Greta Meyer, Herman Bing, Samuel S. Hinds, Syd Taylor.

• ***The Chaser*** (remake). MGM, 1938. Director: Edwin L. Marin; screenwriters: Everett Freeman, Henry Ruskin, Bella and Samuel Spewack. Cast: Dennis O'Keefe (Thomas Z. Brandon), Ann Morriss (Dorothy Mason), Lewis Stone (Dr. Prescott), Nat Pendleton (Floppy Phil), Henry O'Neill (Calhoun), Ruth Gillette, John Qualen, Robert Emmett Keane, Jack Mulhall, Irving Bacon, Pierre Watkin.

The title for the remake is better than of the original, giving more of an idea about the nature of the enterprising and rather dishonest lawyer (a redundancy, perhaps). Once again, Dennis O'Keefe, who lacked the ambition if not the talent to be a major star, gives a charming and amusing performance as the attorney with questionable ethics. The girl planted to discredit O'Keefe is Ann Morriss, about which little was known before this movie or afterwards.

654 No. 1 of the Secret Service

Based on a story by Howard Craig. Story: Agent Charles Bind, Number 1 of the Secret Service, thwarts mad millionaire Arthur Loveday, who is in league with a gang of paramilitary assassins.

Shonteff/Hemdale, Great Britain, 1978 (original). Director: Lindsay Shonteff; screenwriter: Howard Craig. Cast: Nick Henson (Charles Bind), Richard Todd (Arthur Loveday), Aimi MacDonald (Anna Hudson), Geoffrey Keen (Stockwell), Dudley Sutton, Sue Lloyd, Jon Pertwee, Milton Reid.

• ***Licensed to Love and Kill*** (sequel). Shonteff/Palm Springs, 1979. Director: Lindsay Shonteff; screenwriter: Jeremy Lee Francis. Cast: Gareth Hunt (Charles Bind), Nick Tate (Jensen Fury), Fiona Curzon (Carlotta Muff Dangerfield), Gary Hope (Senator Orchid), Geoffrey Keen (Stockwell), Jay Benedict, Don Fellows, John Arnatt, Toby Robins.

Audiences can be forgiven if they are not certain if the stories of these two movies are to be taken seriously or if they are spoofs of James Bond, Matt Helm, Derek Flint, etc. In the sequel, secret agent Charles Bind foils a plot to replace the president of the United States with a duplicate created by a mad scientist. The producers mix genres without much success.

655 Number 17

Based on the play by J. Jefferson Farjeon. Story: This comedy-thriller is the story of old Ben, "late of the Merchant Service," who with the assistance of a reformed female crook, helps the police capture a gang of jewel thieves.

W & F Films, 1928 (original). Silent. Sound added in 1929. Director and screenwriter: Geza M. Bolvary. Cast: Guy Newall (Ben), Lien Dyers, Fritz Greiner, Hertha von Walter, Carl de Vogt, Craighall Sherry, Ernst Neicher, Frederick Solm.

• ***Number 17*** (remake). Wardour Films, 1932. Director and screenwriter: Alfred Hitchcock. Cast: John Stuart (the Detective), Leon M. Lion (Ben), Anne Grey (the Girl), Garry Marsh, Donald Calthrop, Ann Casson, Barry Jones, Henry Caine, Herbert Langley.

The original was made in Germany with sound added in England. When Hitchcock remade it, he threw out most of the second half of the story, substituting an exciting race between a bus and a train. It was a lightweight Hitchcock thriller with some nice touches by the master, including a scarey empty house, quaking as passing trains roar by, with a girl left hanging by her wrists in the dark. She later is put in bondage again, this time handcuffed and nearly drowned in a sinking railroad car.

The Nurse's Secret *see* **Miss Pinkerton**

The Nutty Professor *see* **Dr. Jekyll and Mr. Hyde**

O

656 Odd Man Out

Based on the novel by F.L. Green. Story: Fresh out of prison and still very weak from the confinement, Irish rebel leader Johnny McQueen takes part in a robbery to get funds to finance the uprising, and is shot and deserted by his frightened comrades. He wanders through Belfast looking for help. He is discovered by Kathleen, the woman who loves him, but the British patrols seem to be everywhere seeking him. He is helped and hindered equally by those he meets, but his fate is sealed and Kathleen chooses to die with him rather than be captured.

J. Arthur Rank/Universal Pictures, 1947 (original). Director: Sir Carol Reed; screenwriters: F.L. Green and R.C. Sheriff. Cast: James Mason (Johnny McQueen), Kathleen Ryan (Kathleen), Robert Beatty (Dennis), Denis O'Dea (Constable), W.G. Fay (Father Tom), F.J. McCormick (Shell), Robert Newton

(Lukey), Kitty Kirwin, Elwyn Brook-Jones, Fay Compton, Beryl Measor, Cyril Cusack, Dan O'Herlihy, Roy Irving, Maureen Delaney.

• ***The Lost Man*** (remake). Universal Pictures, 1969. Director and screenwriter: Robert Alan Arthur. Cast: Sidney Poitier (Jason Higgs), Joanna Shimkus (Cathy Ellis), Al Freeman, Jr. (Dennis), Michael Tolan (Hamilton), Leon Bibb (Eddie), Richard Dysart, David Sternberg, Beverly Todd, Paul Winfield, Dolph Sweet.

Odd Man Out is an interesting character study with an outstanding performance by Mason as a man who is a victim of a far larger social and moral battle than can be rightly understood by a single IRA fighter. In the remake, Poitier promotes demonstrations by his black followers to cover up a robbery. He wants the money to take care of the children of black activists who have been jailed. When the heist goes wrong, he is pursued by the police and must go into hiding. Neither film had much to say about the movements which were so important to the leading characters.

657 Oedipus Rex

Based on the play by Sophocles. Story: The city of Thebes has been cursed by the gods and this condition will be maintained unless its king, Oedipus, finds and punishes the murderer of its previous king. Oedipus discovers that he is the guilty party, that the king was his father, and to make things worse, he has unwittingly married his own mother. In agony, he plucks out his eyes.

• ***Oedipus Rex*** (remake). Kipnis/Lesser, 1957. Director: Tyrone Guthrie; screenwriter: Sophocles, translated by W.B. Yeats. Cast: Douglas Rain (Messenger), Douglas Campbell (Oedipus), Eric House (Priest), Robert Goodier (Creon), Donald Davis (Tiresias), Eleanor Stuart (Jocasta), Barbara Franklin (Antigone), Tony van Bridge, William Hutt, Gertrude Tyas, Naomi Cameron.

• ***Oedipus the King*** (remake). Crossroads/Universal Pictures, 1968. Director: Philip Saville; screenwriters: Michael Luke and Philip Saville. Cast: Christopher Plummer (Oedipus), Orson Welles (Tiresias), Lilli Palmer (Jocasta), Richard Johnson (Creon), Cyril Cusack (Messenger), Roger Livesey, Donald Sutherland, Frederick Ledebur, Alexis Mantheakis, Demos Starenios.

The tragedy by Sophocles has also been filmed in Italy in 1909 and 1967, in France in 1912, in the United States by an independent producer in 1914, and in Canada in 1957. Both versions described above are true to the playwright's work and provide fine performances, but it is questionable if the play can really be successfully filmed. It seems to cry out for the stage, and the atmosphere that theatergoers expect.

Oedipus the King *see* **Oedipus Rex**

658 Of Human Bondage

Based on the novel by W. Somerset Maugham. Story: Clubfooted medical student Philip Carey develops an obsessive infatuation with a selfish, sluttish waitress, Mildred Rogers. She uses the sensitive young man ruthlessly, nearly destroying his career and his life in the process. His emotional enslavement,

Leslie Howard and Bette Davis appear in a rare peaceful moment in Of Human Bondage *(RKO, 1934).*

despite her apparent contempt for him, is finally broken in a climactic scene, when he summons the courage to tell her that she disgusts him. She erupts into a venomous assault on him, tearing up his apartment and destroying his precious paintings and books.

RKO, 1934 (original). Director: John Cromwell; screenwriter: Lester Cohen. Cast: Leslie Howard (Philip Carey), Bette Davis (Mildred Rogers), Frances Dee (Sally), Kay Johnson (Norah), Reginald Denny (Griffiths), Alan Hale, Reginald Sheffield, Tempe Pigott, Desmond Roberts, Reginald Owen.

• ***Of Human Bondage*** (remake). Warner Bros., 1946. Director: Edmund Goulding; screenwriter: Catherine Turney. Cast: Eleanor Parker (Mildred Rogers), Paul Henreid (Philip Carey), Edmund Gwenn (Athelny), Martin Lamont (Dunsford), Janis Paige (Sally Athelny), Patric Knowles (Griffiths), Isobel Elsom, Alexis Smith, Henry Stephenson, Richard Nugent, Eva Moore.

• ***Of Human Bondage*** (remake). MGM, 1964. Director: Ken Hughes; screenwriter: Bryan Forbes. Cast: Kim Novak (Mildred Rogers), Laurence Harvey (Philip Carey), Robert Morley (Doctor Jacobs), Siobhan McKenna (Norah Nesbitt), Roger Livesey (Thorpe Athelny), Jack Hedley (Griffiths), Nanette Newman, Ronald Lacey.

W. Somerset Maugham's classic 1915 novel was filmed in Mexico in 1955 as *La Fuerza Del Desco.*

Eleanor Parker, as waitress Mildred Rogers, plays the coquette for Paul Henreid in Of Human Bondage *(Warner Bros., 1946).*

Bette Davis used every device she could to get the part of Mildred Rogers, even accepting any assignment offered her by her home studio, Warner Bros., so that they would lend her to RKO for the film. It made her a star, as she was magnificent in an otherwise mediocre screenplay of a slattern who treated the medical student precisely as it seemed he wanted to be. For if not, reasoned many among the audience, why did he keep coming back for more?

Much has been written about how Davis was given the 1935 Oscar for Best Actress in *Dangerous* because she had been passed over for her far better performance as Mildred. Another factor in her losing in 1934 might be that the picture lost money because audiences did not join critics in appreciating her mean, peroxide-haired character. Her delivery of ravings such as the following demonstrated her great ability as an actress, but did not win her any sympathy from the folks in Peoria:

> You cad! You dirty swine! I never cared for you, not once. I was making a fool of you. I hated you. It made me sick when I had to let you kiss me. I only did it because you begged me. You hounded me. You drove me crazy. And after you kissed me, I always used to wipe my mouth—wipe my mouth—but I made up for it. For every kiss, I had to laugh.

The first remake contains a strong performance from underrated Eleanor Parker, as Mildred, with Paul Henreid sufficiently wimpy to make a passable Philip Carey. It still wasn't a movie that pulled in the audiences. Many who saw the film found it and its subject rather dull and boring, and it was still difficult for many to understand why an educated man would put up with such treatment from a little tramp. Perhaps all three movies would have been more interesting, if this question had been more satisfactorily explored. In the final version, Kim Novak figured by playing Mildred she would prove that she really was an actress, not just a girl with lavender hair and a great back. Her calculations were off and although she made a valiant effort, it is difficult to choose who was more disastrous in their role, she or Laurence Harvey.

659 Oh, Doctor!

Based on the novel by Harry Leon Wilson. Story: In this comedy, frail hypochondriac Rufus Billups, Jr., borrows money with a promise of repaying it by turning over his entire inheritance to his creditors when he comes into it in three years. Anxious to protect their investment, the three, Mr. Clinch, Mr. McIntosh and Mr. Peck, hire pretty nurse Dolores Hicks to keep an eye on Rufus. He falls for her and when he discovers that she prefers strong adventurous men, Rufus undertakes a series of dangerous stunts to prove himself to his beloved. Dolores convinces the creditors that they had better renegotiate the loan and receive only their principal and a reasonable amount of interest when the loan comes due. Rufus then descends from a flagpole where he has been sitting and gets the girl.

Universal Pictures/Jewel, 1925 (original). Silent. Director: Harry A. Pollard; screenwriter: Harvey Thew. Cast: Reginald Denny (Rufus Billups, Jr.), Mary Astor (Dolores Hicks), Otis Harlan (Mr. Clinch), William V. Mong (Mr. McIntosh), Tom Ricketts (Mr. Peck), Lucille Ward, Mike Donlin, Clarence Geldert.

• ***Oh, Doctor!*** (remake). Universal Pictures, 1937. Director: Raymond B. McCarey; screenwriters: Harry Clork and Brown Holmes. Cast: Edward Everett Horton (Edward J. Billop), Donrue Leighton (Helen Frohman), William Hall (Rodney Cummings), Eve Arden (Shirley Truman), Thurston Hall, Catherine Doucet, William Demarest, Edward Brophy, Minerva Urecal.

The 1935 Universal movie *His Night Out* has a similiar plot. In it, Edward Everett Horton plays Homer Bitts, who loses his timidity when he is told he has only three months to live. He innocently becomes involved in a robbery and traps the crooks. In the 1937 version of the novel by Harry Leon Wilson, Horton is a hypochondriac who's afraid that he'll die before he receives the inheritance which will allow him to go out in style.

660 Oh, God!

Based on the novel by Avery Corman. Story: God comes to Earth to enlist the aid of supermarket manager Jerry Landers in delivering the simple message that the world can work if people will only make the effort.

Warner Bros., 1977. Director: Carl Reiner; screenwriter: Larry Gelbart.

Cast: George Burns (God), John Denver (Jerry Landers), Teri Garr (Bobbie Landers), Donald Pleasence (Dr. Harmon), Ralph Bellamy (Sam Raven), William Daniels (George Summers), Barnard Hughes (Judge Baker), Paul Sorvino (Rev. Willie Williams), Barry Sullivan, Dinah Shore, Jeff Corey, George Furth, David Ogden Stiers, Titos Vandis.

• ***Oh God—Book Two*** (remake). Warner Bros., 1980. Director: Gilbert Cates; screenwriters: Joss Greenfield, Hal Goldman, Fred S. Fox and Melissa Miller. Cast: George Burns (God), Suzanne Pleshette (Paula), David Birney (Don), Louanne (Tracy), Hans Conreid (Dr. Barnes), Wilfrid Hyde-White (Judge Miller).

• ***Oh God, You Devil*** (remake). Warner Bros., 1984. Director: Paul Bogart; screenwriter: Andrew Bergman. Cast: George Burns (Devil), Ted Wass (Bobby Shelton), Ron Silver (Gary Fraute), Roxanne Hart (Wendy Shelton), Eugene Roche (Charlie Gray).

After his Academy Award–winning performance in *The Sunshine Boys*, George Burns launched a new career as a comedian, singer and movie star. Having the ancient Burns play the role of God was good for a laugh or two, but it was difficult to sustain the humor for 104 minutes, let alone two sequels of sorts. In the second film, Burns as God stoops to having a child, Louanne, and reminds people that he is still around. This one was not only implausible, but it didn't have many jokes. In the final film, George trades in his omnipotence for the pitchfork of the devil, who buys the soul of a struggling musician.

Oh God—Book Two *see* **Oh, God!**

Oh God, You Devil *see* **Oh, God!**

661 Oil for the Lamps of China

Based on the novel by Alice Tisdale Hobart. Story: The Atlantis Oil Company sends dedicated company man Stephen Chase to China to sell oil. While he's saving his company money, his wife loses their first child at birth. When his best friend blows a minor deal, he fires him. The list of evidence of his putting his company first goes on and on. (Can't you see it coming?) During a revolution, rebels try to steal some of the company's money. Chase risks his life, sees his assistant shot, is badly wounded himself, but he saves the money. After he has spent months in a hospital, the company demotes him. In the novel, the poor snook who believes the motto "the company always takes care of its own" finds out how empty is the phrase. In the film, the company eventually comes through. The company's not unfeeling, just its corrupt officials are, don't you know.

Cosmopolitan/Warner Bros., 1935. Director: Mervyn LeRoy; screenwriter: Laird Doyle. Cast: Pat O'Brien (Stephen Chase), Josephine Hutchinson (Hester Chase), Jean Muir (Alice), John Elderedge (Don), Lyle Talbot (Jim), Arthur Bryon, Henry O'Neill, Donald Crisp, Ronnie Cosby, Willie Fung.

• ***Law of the Tropics*** (remake). Warner Bros., 1941. Director: Ray Enright; screenwriter: Charles Grayson. Cast: Constance Bennett (Joan Madison), Jeffrey Lynn (Jim Conway), Regis Toomey (Tom Marshall), Mona Maris (Rita), Hobart Bosworth (Davis), Frank Puglia, Thomas Jackson, Paul Harvey, Craig Stevens.

Whereas the novel by Alice Hobart rode the best seller lists for over a year, the film versions failed to capture such loyalty. Pat O'Brien was splendid as the man who put loyalty to company ahead of everything else, only to discover that it wasn't to be reciprocated. In the remake, Jeffrey Lynn is a rubber tree planter who incurs the disapproval of his employers by marrying Constance Bennett, a lady with a past, when his intended turned up her nose at living in the tropics. Lynn goes to bat for his slightly tainted older wife and nearly knocks the block off the son of the rubber company's president. By this film, Bennett's career was on the downside, although she would have a few more enjoyable roles. Lynn's career never had a downside because it never had an upside.

662 Okay America

Based on a story by William Anthony McGuire. Story: Egotistical reporter Larry Wayne gets involved when the daughter of a cabinet minister is kidnapped and held for $100,000 ransom. He meets a rather sticky end.

Universal Pictures, 1932 (original). Director: Tay Garnett; screenwriter: William Anthony McGuire. Cast: Lew Ayres (Larry Wayne), Maureen O'Sullivan (Miss Barton), Louis Calhern (Mileaway Rosso), Edward Arnold (Alsotto), Walter Catlett, Alan Dinehart, Rollo Lloyd, Margaret Lindsay, Wallis Clarke, Nance O'Neill.

• ***Risky Business*** (remake). Universal Pictures, 1939. Director: Arthur Lubin; screenwriters: Charles Grayson and Maurice Wright. Cast: George Murphy (Dan Clifford), Dorothea Kent (Mary Dexter), Eduardo Cianelli (De Cann), Leon Ames (Hinge Jackson), El Brendel (Lucius), Richard Tucker, Frances Robinson, John Wray.

These dreary crime melodramas won't keep anyone up late at night watching them on television. In the remake the reporter has been transformed into radio gossip columnist George Murphy, who aids the effort to retrieve the kidnapped daughter of a movie producer.

663 The Old Curiosity Shop

Based on the novel by Charles Dickens. Story: Miserly dwarf money-lender Quilp prevents a rich man from tracking down evicted gambler Trent and his granddaughter Little Nell, who runs a curiosity shop, resulting in their deaths.

Hepworth, Great Britain, 1913 (original). Silent. Director and screenwriter: Thomas Bentley. Cast: Mai Deacon (Little Nell), Warwick Buckland (Grandfather Trent), E. Felton (Quilp), Jamie Darling (Single Gentleman), Willie West (Dick Swiveller), Billy Rex, S. May, Bert Stowe, Sydney Locklynne, Moya Nugent, R. Phillips.

• ***The Old Curiosity Shop*** (remake). Welsh/Pearson, Great Britain, 1921. Silent. Director: Thomas Bentley; screenwriter: J.A. Atkinson. Cast: Mabel Poulton (Little Nell), William Lugg (Grandfather), Hugh E. Wright (Tom Codlin), Pino Conti (Daniel Quilp), Bryan Powley (Single Gentleman), Barry Livesey, Cecil Bevan, Beatie Olna Travers, Minnie Rayner, Dennis Harvey, Dezma duMay.

• ***The Old Curiosity Shop*** (remake). British International, Great Britain,

1934. Director: Thomas Bentley; screenwriters: Margaret Kennedy and Ralph Neale. Cast: Ben Webster (Grandfather Trent), Elaine Benson (Nell Trent), Hay Petrie (Quilp), Beatrix Thompson (Mrs. Quilp), Gibb McLaughlin (Sampson Brass), Reginald Purdell (Dick Swiveller), James Harcourt (Single Gentleman), Polly Ward, J. Fisher White, Lily Long, Dick Tubb.

• ***Mister Quilp*** (remake). Reader's Digest Films/EMI, Great Britain, 1975. Director: Michael Tuchner; screenwriters: Louis Kamp and Irene Kamp. Cast: Anthony Newley (Daniel Quilp), David Hemmings (Richard Swiveller), David Warner (Sampson Brass), Michael Hordern (Grandfather), Paul Rogers (Henry Trent), Jill Bennett (Sally Brass), Sarah-Jane Varley (Nell Trent), Sarah Webb, Mona Washbourne, Yvonne Antrobus, Peter Duncan.

This is the Dickens work which has most resisted being brought successfully to the screen. None of the versions mentioned above are anything better than sloppily sentimental pieces and the 1975 musical version is simply sloppy.

Old Heidelberg ***see*** **The Student Prince of Heidelberg**

664 The Old Soak

Based on the play by Don Marquis. Story: Now retired from his garage business, Clem Hawley spends a great deal of time visiting the local bootlegger. His son, Clemmy, employed by a bank owned by his cousin Webster, makes nightly trips to New York City to see showgirl Ina Heath, whom Clemmy has believing he comes from a wealthy Long Island family. Ina pops in on Clemmy one day and is shocked by his humble background, but she stays for dinner. Meanwhile, Mrs. Hawley discovers that some valuable stock certificates are missing. Clemmy confesses that he took them and lent them to Webster, but old Clem takes the blame. Ina and Clem discover that Webster is in cahoots with the bootlegger and Clemmy is saved and reconciled with Ina.

Universal Pictures, 1926 (original). Silent. Director: Edward Sloman; screenwriter: Charles Kenyon. Cast: Jean Hersholt (Clem Hawley, Sr.), George Lewis (Clemmy Hawley), June Marlowe (Ina Heath), William V. Mong (Webster), Gertrude Astor (Sylvia De Costa), Lucy Beaumont (Mrs. Hawley), Louise Fazenda, Adda Gleason, Tom Ricketts, George Siegmann, Arnold Gregg.

• ***The Good Old Soak*** (remake). MGM, 1937. Director: J. Walter Reuben; screenwriter: A.E. Thomas. Cast: Wallace Beery (Clem Hawley), Una Merkel (Nellie), Eric Linden (Clemmie Hawley), Judith Barrett (Ina), Betty Furness (Lucy), Ted Healy, Janet Beecher, George Sidney, Robert McWade, James Bush.

These early "Father Knows Best"-like sentimental melodramas are pure hokum with the situations stock and expected. The leads as the old soaks, Jean Hersholt and Wallace Beery, did not disappoint their fans who came to expect a certain familiar performance from the two and in these films they got what they were looking for—and nothing more.

665 The Old Swimmin' Hole

Based on the poem by James Whitcomb Riley. Story: Carefree country boy Ezra spends his time fishing and hanging out at the old swimmin' hole, but he greatly admires pretty Myrtle. He attempts to impress her and passes notes to her at school, causing him the dickens of a bad time. When she finally deigns to go boat-riding with him, his rival, Skinny, takes her away from him. His disappointment isn't long however, as Esther, a long-time admirer of Ezra, offers to share her lunch with him on the riverbank.

First National Pictures, 1921 (original). Silent. Director: Joseph De Grasse; screenwriter: Bernard McConville. Cast: Charles Ray (Ezra), James Gordon (Pa), Laura La Plante (Ma), Blanche Rose (Myrtle), Marjorie Prevost (Esther), Lincoln Stedman (Skinny), Lon Poff (teacher).

• ***The Old Swimmin' Hole*** (remake). Monogram Pictures, 1941. Director: Robert McGowan; screenwriters: Gerald Breitigam and Dorothy Reid. Cast: Jacki Moran (Chris), Marcia Mae Jones (Betty), Leatrice Joy (Julie), Charles Brown (Elliott), Theodore von Eltz (Baker), George Cleveland (Harper), Dix Davis (Jimmy).

One shouldn't expect too much from a movie based on a short poem. The second film elaborated on James Whitcomb Riley's sentiments by having Jackie Moran and Marcia Mae Jones as two gangly youngsters trying to interest his mother, Leatrice Joy, in her father, Charles Brown. Hardly anyone cared if they succeeded.

Oliver! *see* **Oliver Twist**

666 Oliver Twist

Based on the novel by Charles Dickens. Story: Orphan Oliver Twist, who has the audacity to ask for more gruel at the parish workhouse to which he is assigned, is sold by the Beedle, Mr. Bumple, as an apprentice to an undertaker. After a fight with the mortician's assistant, Oliver sets off for London, where he meets the Artful Dodger. The latter introduces him to Fagin, the chief of a gang of adolescent pickpockets and thieves, and vicious criminal Bill Sykes. Arrested as a thief, Oliver is placed in the care of kindly, wealthy Mr. Brownlow, who plans to raise Oliver as his own son. Fearful that Oliver will inform on them, Fagin and Sykes kidnap the boy and return him to his job as an assistant to Sykes in his burglaries. Prostitute Nancy rebels and attempts to return Oliver to Mr. Brownlow, but is beaten to death by Bill. Pursued by an angry mob, Sykes, holding Oliver as a hostage, tries to escape but is killed. Oliver is reunited with Mr. Brownlow and discovers his benefactor is his mother's uncle.

• ***Oliver Twist*** (remake). Crystal Studios, 1912. Silent. Director: H.A. Spanuth. Cast: Nat C. Goodwin (Fagin), Vinnie Burns (Oliver Twist), Mortimer Martine (Bill Sykes), Charles Rogers (the Artful Dodger).

• ***Oliver Twist*** (remake). Paramount Pictures, 1916. Silent. Director: James Young. Cast: Marie Doro (Oliver Twist), Tully Marshall (Fagin), Hobart Bosworth (Bill Sykes), Raymond Hatton (the Artful Dodger), James Neill (Mr. Brownlow), Elsie Jane Wilson (Nancy), Harry Rattenburg, Carl Stockdale, W.S. Van Dyke.

• ***Oliver Twist*** (remake). First National Pictures, 1922. Silent. Director: Frank Lloyd; screenwriter: Harry Weil and Frank Lloyd. Cast: Jackie Coogan (Oliver Twist), Lon Chaney (Fagin), Gladys Brockwell (Nancy), George

Jack Wild and Mark Lester strike a comradely pose in Fagin's den of thieves in the musical production Oliver! *(Columbia, 1968), based on the Charles Dickens classic* Oliver Twist.

Siegmann (Bill Sykes), Edouard Trebaol (the Artful Dodger), Lionel Belmore (Mr. Brownlow), Carl Stockdale, Eddie Boland, Taylor Graves, Lewis Sargent, James Marcus, Angie Herring, Joan Standing.

• ***Oliver Twist*** (remake). Monogram Pictures, 1933. Director: William Cowen; screenwriter: Elizabeth Meehan. Cast: Dickie Moore (Oliver Twist), Irving Pichel (Fagin), William "Stage" Boyd (Bill Sykes), Doris Lloyd (Nancy), Alec B. Francis (Mr. Brownlow), Sonny Ray (the Artful Dodger), Lionel Belmore (Mr. Bumble), Barbara Kent (Rose Maylie), George B. Arthur, Clyde Cook, George Nash, Tempe Pigott, Nelson McDowall, Virginia Sale.

• ***Oliver Twist*** (remake). General Film Distributors/J. Arthur Rank Productions, 1948. Director: David Lean; screenwriters: Stanley Haynes and David Lean. Cast: John Howard Davies (Oliver Twist), Alec Guinness (Fagin), Robert Newton (Bill Sykes), Kay Walsh (Nancy), Anthony Newley (the Artful Dodger), Henry Stephenson (Mr. Brownlow), Francis L. Sullivan (Mr. Bumble), Gibb McLaughlin (Mr. Sowerberry), Kathleen Harrison (Mrs. Sowerberry), Ralph Truman, Mary Clare, Josephine Stuart, Amy Veness, Diana Dors, Frederick Lloyd.

• ***Oliver!*** (remake). Columbia Pictures, 1968. Director: Carol Reed; screenwriter: Vernon Harris. Cast: Mark Lester (Oliver Twist), Ron Moody (Fagin),

Oliver Reed (Bill Sykes), Shani Wallis (Nancy), Jack Wild (the Artful Dodger), Sheila White (Bet), Harry Secombe (Mr. Bumble), Peggy Mount (Widow Corney), Leonard Rossiter (Mr. Sowerberry), Hylda Baker (Mrs. Sowerberry), Joseph O'Connor (Mr. Brownlow), Elizabeth Knight, Kenneth Cranham, Wensley Pithey, Megs Jenkins, James Hayter, Hugh Griffith.

Dickens' Oliver Twist was also filmed in 1909 by Vitagraph Company, in 1910 by Pathe, in France and Denmark in 1910, in 1912 by Hepworth Pictures, in Germany in 1920 as *Die Deheimnisse Von London,* in 1921 by Fox Film Corporation as *Oliver Twist, Jr.*, and in the United States in 1940 by an independent producer.

The appealing story of the poor orphan Oliver Twist and the many fascinating and dangerous characters he meets, before being reunited with his loving uncle, has been successfully brought to the screen on many occasions, but none was more well-done than the 1948 British version with Alec Guinness as a marvelous Fagin and Robert Newton as a personification of evil and brutality as Bill Sykes. Showing of the film in the United States was delayed because of concerns that it contained anti–semitic messages because of the character of Fagin. This just shows what a fine performance Alec Guinness gave.

The 1968 musical is certainly the most spectacular production of the story with a strong cast, headed by Mark Lester, who makes you want to hug and protect him. Ron Moody and Jack Wild were nominated for Academy Awards for Best Actor and Best Supporting Actor but did not take them home. The picture, however, did win the Award for Best Picture, with Carol Reed winning the Best Director Award and John Green the Best Musical Score. The very enjoyable Lionel Bart songs included "Where Is Love," "Food, Glorious Food," "Consider Yourself," "As Long As He Needs Me," "Who Will Buy?" "I'd Do Anything" and the title song.

Oliver's Story ***see*** **Love Story**

667 On Approval

Based on the play by Frederick Lonsdale. Story: The comedy is about a selfish duke who is in love with a pickle maker's daughter. It's an atypical farce about "silly ass" upperclass Englishmen, which relies more on dialog than on story to amuse audiences.

British and Dominion Productions, 1930 (original). Director: Tom Walls; screenwriter: W.P. Lipscomb. Cast: Tom Walls (George, Duke of Bristol), Yvonne Arnaud (Maria), Edmund Breon, Winifred Shotter, Robertson Hare, Mary Brough.

• ***On Approval*** (remake). Gaumont-British, 1944. Director and screenwriter: Clive Brook. Cast: Clive Brook (George, Duke of Bristol), Beatrice Lillie (Maria Wislack), Googie Withers (Helen Hale), Roland Culver (Richard Halton), O.B. Clarence, Lawrence Hanray, Elliot Mason, Hay Petrie.

The Lonsdale play was considered quite daring at the turn of the century, but by the thirties it was dull and not particularly funny. There's very little action, but a lot of nonsensical and none too amusing chatter. In the remake,

Clive Brook did about everything—write, direct and star—so one might suppose he's to blame, but only if it was also his idea to remake the movie.

On Moonlight Bay *see* **Penrod**

668 On Trial

Based on the play by Elmer Rice. Story: When Robert Strickland is brought to trial on charges of killing his partner, Gerald Trask, and stealing $20,000 from the latter's safe, Strickland confesses his guilt and requests that the trial be terminated. The judge denies the request, and Mrs. Trask is put on the stand, where she relates that Strickland shot her husband and was immediately apprehended by Glover, her husband's secretary. The next day, Strickland's small daughter, Doris, is put on the stand and reveals that on the day of the killing her father had learned that his wife had spent the day with Trask. On the third day of the trial, the defense attorney locates the missing Mrs. Strickland, who takes the stand and exposes Trask as a blackmailer and lecher. The police discover that Glover has stolen the money. Strickland is found innocent of the charge of premeditated murder and is reunited with his wife and daughter.

• ***On Trial*** (remake). Warner Bros., 1928. Released both as silent and talkie. Director: Archie Mayo; screenwriters: Robert Lord and Max Pollock. Cast: Pauline Frederick (Joan Trask), Bert Lytell (Robert Strickland), Lois Wilson (May Strickland), Holmes Herbert (Gerald Trask), Vondell Darr (Doris Strickland), Johnny Arthur (Glover), Richard Tucker, Jason Robards, Franklin Pangborn.

• ***On Trial*** (remake). Warner Bros., 1939. Director: Terry Morse; screenwriter: Don Ryan. Cast: John Litel (Robert Strickland), Margaret Lindsay (Mae Strickland), Edward Norris (Arbuckle), Janet Chapman (Doris Strickland), James Stephenson (Gerald Trask), Nedda Harrigan (Joan Trask), Larry Williams (Glover), William Davidson, Earl Dwire, Gordon Hart, Charles Trowbridge.

The Elmer Rice play was first filmed by Essanay Studios in 1916. The 1928 sound version was more false start than breakthrough in the era of sound. The technique used was the soon-to-be-abandoned Vitaphone method, which not only refused to synchronize speech with lips but also gave performers some odd levels of sound and serious speech defects. The remake wasn't bad for a film based on such a creaky old story. Defense attorney Edward Norris gets no cooperation from his client John Litel, but nevertheless is able to prove that the killing of James Stephenson was justifiable homicide.

Once a Lady *see* **Three Sinners**

Once a Woman *see* **Viktor Und Viktoria**

Once You Kiss a Stranger *see* **Strangers on a Train**

One Fatal Hour *see* **5-Star Final**

One Hour With You *see* The Marriage Circle

669 One Man's Journey

Based on the story *Failure* by Katherine Haviland-Taylor. Story: Eli Watt is a doctor who returns to the rural community where he was raised to practice medicine. He not only mends bodies, but hearts as well, bringing together the pairs of lovers: Letty McGinnis and Bill Radford, and Eli's son Jimmy with Joan Stockton. His charges for curing the townspeople's ailments run to vegetables and poultry—but never mind, he's a wonderfully self-sacrificing and noble man, not looking to become rich, merely to be of service to humanity.

RKO Radio Pictures, 1933 (original). Director: John Robertson; screenwriter: Katherine Haviland-Taylor. Cast: Lionel Barrymore (Eli Watt), May Robson (Sarah Watt), Dorothy Jordan (Letty McGinnis), Joel McCrea (Jimmy Watt), Frances Dee (Joan Stockton), James Bush, David Landau, Buster Phelps.

• ***A Man to Remember*** (remake). RKO Radio Pictures, 1938. Director: Garson Kanin; screenwriter: Dalton Trumbo. Cast: Anne Shirley (Jean), Edward Ellis (Doctor Abbott), Lee Bowman (Dick), William Henry (Howard Sykes), John Wray (Johnson), Granville Bates, Harlan Briggs, Frank M. Thomas.

These films fall into the "heartwarming" category. In the first, it's all Lionel Barrymore as the decent country doctor who has no aspirations for fame and fortune, but is happy when his son, Joel McCrea, becomes a famous physician. In the remake, Edward Ellis is the small-town doctor who spends 20 years working diligently and effectively with little or no appreciation or recompense, but becomes a hero when he saves his community from an infantile paralysis (polio) epidemic. They don't make doctors like these anymore; now they're trained to view their patients and their ailments dispassionately.

670 One Million B.C.

Based on a story by Mikell Novak, George Baker and Joseph Frickert. Story: Except for the grunts and groans of the cavemen and cavewomen, this film might as well have been a silent. It's the tale of two different prehistoric tribes, the Rock people and the Shell people, plus a lot of phony looking and historically inaccurate monsters. Man seems to dispatch these giant lizards and iguanas at will, unless the director is trying to make some dramatic point and some cave person becomes a meal for these large vegetarians. The two tribes learn something about common cause and put aside their differences to work and hunt together, the better to survive. There's even a little women's lib of sorts, when Loana sees to it that women are served the roast dinosaur first, rather than fight among themselves for the leavings of the men.

United Artists, 1940 (original). Directors: Hal Roach, Sr., and Hal Roach, Jr.; screenwriters: Mikell Novak, George Baker and Joseph Frickert. Cast: Victor Mature (Tumak), Carole Landis (Loana), Lon Chaney, Jr. (Akhoba), John Hubbard (Odtao), Mamo Clark (Nupondi), Nigel de Brulier (Peytow), Mary Gale Fisher, Edgar Edwards, Inez Palange, Jacqueline Dalyk, Conrad Nagel.

• ***One Million Years B.C.*** (remake). Hammer/20th Century–Fox, Great Britain, 1966. Director: Don Chaffey; screenwriters: Mikell Novak, George Baker and Joseph Frickert. Cast: Raquel Welch (Loana), John Richardson (Tumak), Percy Herbert (Sakana), Robert Brown (Akhoba), Martine Bestwick (Nupondi), Jean Wiadon, Lisa Thomas, Malaya Nappi, William Lyon Brown.

Readers will forgive the spelling of the names in these two films. It's important to remember that they are mere transliterations taken from scratchings found on the walls of caves. Neither movie was meant to be funny—but they were. They were supposed to be scary—but they weren't. There was quite a bit of cheesecake, provided by Raquel Welch and Martine Bestwick in the remake and by Carole Landis and Victor Mature in the original. Whatever messages the producers of these films felt they were delivering seems to have been lost over the centuries.

One Million Years B.C. *see* **One Million B.C.**

One More Time *see* **Salt and Pepper**

One More Tomorrow *see* **The Animal Kingdom**

One Night in the Tropics *see* **The Reckless Age**

One Romantic Night *see* **The Swan**

671 One Stolen Night

Based on D.D. Calhoun's story *The Arab.* Story: Diantha Ebberly travels with her parents to the edge of the Sahara, where she is to meet for the first time the man she has been betrothed to since childhood, Herbert Medford. When attacked by a swarm of beggars in the marketplace, she is rescued by an "Arab" whom she meets again that night when she slips away from her parents dressed as a native. They fall in love but the girl is kidnapped by Sheik Amud, who fancies her. The "Arab" rescues her and only then is it revealed that her lover and her betrothed are one and the same.

Vitagraph Co. of America, 1923 (original). Silent. Director: Robert Ensminger; screenwriter: Bradley J. Smallen. Cast: Alice Calhoun (Diantha Ebberly), Herbert Heyes (Herbert Medford/"The Arab"), Russ Powell (Sheik Amud), Otto Hoffman, Adele Farrington, Oliver Hardy.

• ***One Stolen Night*** (remake). Warner Bros., 1929. Part-talkie. Director: Scott R. Dunlap; screenwriter: Edward T. Lowe. Cast: Betty Bronson (Jeanne), William Collier, Jr. (Bob), Mitchell Lewis (Stanton), Harry Todd, Charles Hill Marles, Nina Quartaro, Rose Dione, Otto Lederer, Angelo Rossitto.

The revelation that Diantha's fiancé and her "Arab" were the same man was telegraphed to even the most unsophisticated moviegoer. Despite this, the film was considered exciting and good entertainment for the times.

The remake of D.D. Calhoun's *The Arab* drastically changed the story. In the second version, Bob and his brother Stanton are members of a British regiment in the Sudan. When Stanton steals the commissary funds, Bob accepts the blame, deserts his post and teams up with a cheap traveling show. Here he falls

in love with Jeanne, the stooge in a whip act. When a sheik kidnaps Jeanne, Bob is ready to make the rescue but the sheik gives her back because she's too white for his tastes.

672 One Sunday Afternoon

Based on the play by James Hagan. Story: Biff Grimes, a quick-tempered, struggling dentist, gets an emergency call to extract one of Hugo Barnstead's teeth. Biff considers giving his old enemy an overdose of gas. Hugo is responsible for Biff having spent two years in prison in his youth and if that wasn't enough, Hugo eloped with Biff's sweetheart, Virginia Brush. Biff married Virginia's best friend, Amy Lind, on the rebound, although he doesn't consider Amy as attractive or exciting as Virginia. But Biff finds that Virginia has become an overbearing, shrewish woman who is making Hugo's life miserable. Realizing that he married the right girl all along, Biff removes the offending molar without incident—and without gas.

Paramount Pictures, 1933 (original). Director: Stephen Roberts; screenwriters: William Slavens McNutt and Grover Jones. Cast: Gary Cooper (Biff Grimes), Fay Wray (Virginia Brush), Neil Hamilton (Hugo Barnstead), Frances Fuller (Amy Lind), Roscoe Karns, Jane Darwell, Clara Blandick, Sam Hardy, Harry Schultz, James Burtis, A.S. Byron.

• ***The Strawberry Blonde*** (remake). Warner Bros., 1941. Director: Raoul Walsh; screenwriters: Julius J. and Philip G. Epstein. Cast: James Cagney (Biff Grimes), Rita Hayworth (Virginia Brush), Jack Carson (Hugo Barnstead), Olivia De Havilland (Amy Lind), Alan Hale, George Tobias, Una O'Connor, George Reeves, Lucille Fairbanks, Helen Lynd, Roy Gordon.

• ***One Sunday Afternoon*** (remake). Warner Bros., 1948. Director: Raoul Walsh; screenwriter: Robert L. Richards. Cast: Dennis Morgan (Biff Grimes), Janis Paige (Virginia Brush), Don De Fore (Hugo Barnstead), Dorothy Malone (Amy Lind), Ben Blue, Oscar O'Shea, Alan Hale, Jr., George Neise.

This pleasant period-piece comedy drama was presented most winningly in the 1941 James Cagney version. The four top performers seem just right and the film supplies a believable atmosphere for a very human story. The 1948 musical remake was adequate but undistinguished with songs such as "Mary, You're a Little Bit Old Fashioned" by Henry Marshall and Marion Sunshine, and "Girls Were Meant to Take Care of Boys" by Ralph Blane.

673 One Way Passage

Based on an original story by Robert Lord. Story: In this ill-fated love story, Dan Hardesty, a condemned murderer, and Joan Ames, a terminally ill woman,

Opposite, top: *Wearing well-tailored skins and a clean-shaven face, Victor Mature flares his nostrils at John Hubbard, as two unidentified cavemen to Vic's left and Nigel De Brulier and Carole Landis on his right look concerned in* One Million B.C. *(Hal Roach, 1940).* Bottom: *John Richardson points the way to spectacularly attired Raquel Welch in the grunt and groan remake* One Million Years B.C. *(Hammer/20th Century–Fox, 1966).*

meet aboard a ship and fall in love. Each learns of the other's secret, but conceal their knowledge and agree to meet on New Year's Eve, long after both will be dead.

Warner Bros., 1932. Director: Tay Garnett; screenwriters: Wilson Mizner and Joseph Jackson. Cast: William Powell (Dan Hardesty), Kay Francis (Joan Ames), Frank McHugh (Skippy), Aline MacMahon (Countess Barilhaus/Barrel House Betty), Warren Hymer (Steve Burke), Frederick Burton, Douglas Gerrard, Herbert Mundin, Roscoe Karns, Wilson Mizner.

• ***'Till We Meet Again*** (remake). Warner Bros., 1940. Director: Edmund Goulding; screenwriter: Warren Duff. Cast: Merle Oberon (Joan Ames), George Brent (Dan Hardesty), Pat O'Brien (Steve Burke), Geraldine Fitzgerald (Bonny Coburn), Binnie Barnes (Comtesse de Bresac), Frank McHugh (Rocky), Eric Blore, Henry O'Neill, George Reeves, Frank Wilcox, Doris Lloyd.

This story was amusingly satirized on the Carol Burnett television show with her and the late James Coco in the two leading roles. One can't satirize trash and these films, despite a story which in the wrong hands could have turned out abominably, were sensitively made and well-acted by both pairs of leading couples and the major supporting performers. Certainly the story is improbable, but it isn't the circumstances of their ill-fated romance that made the movies so touching; rather it was the love and happiness that the couple shared, even knowing it could not last. Better to have loved and lost than never to have loved at all, was their motto. Any tears shed for the two doomed lovers were not derived by phony sentimentality.

Only Saps Work ***see*** **Easy Come, Easy Go**

The Opening of Misty Beethoven ***see*** **Pygmalion**

The Opposite Sex ***see*** **The Women**

Orders Are Orders ***see*** **Orders Is Orders**

674 Orders Is Orders

Based on the play by Ian Hay and Anthony Armstrong. Story: A Hollywood film company takes over a British army base to make a Foreign Legion film. Director Ed Waggermeyer convinces Colonel Bellamy, the base's commanding officer, to take the lead in the film. The latter only escapes a court martial because the film is accidently destroyed.

Gaumont, Great Britain, 1933 (original). Director: Walter Forde; screenwriters: Leslie Arliss, Sidney Gilliat and James Gleason. Cast: James Gleason (Ed Waggermeyer), Charlotte Greenwood (Wanda), Cyril Maude (Col. Bellamy), Cedric Hardwicke (Brigadier), Ian Hunter (Capt. Harper), Ray Milland (Dashwood), Jane Carr, Donald Calthrop, Eliot Makeham, Hay Plumb.

• ***Orders Are Orders*** (remake). British Lion, Great Britain, 1954. Director: David Paltenghi; screenwriters: Donald Taylor, Geoffrey Orme and Eric Sykes. Cast: Brian Reece (Capt. Harper), Margot Grahame (Wanda Sinclair),

Raymond Huntley (Col. Bellamy), Sidney James (Ed Waggermeyer), Tony Hancock (Lt. Wilfred Cartroad), Peter Sellers (Pte. Goffin), Clive Morton, June Thorburn, Maureen Swanson, Peter Martyn, Bill Fraser, Edward Lexy.

Besides changing the form of "to be" in the title, the remake has the American film unit descend on a British army camp to make a science-fiction film, and the soldiers are all after the film unit's female members until a snap inspection by the divisional commander results in the expulsion of the Americans to a nearby haunted house to finish their picture. These are looney farces but not outstanding comedies.

The Organization *see* **In the Heat of the Night**

Ossessione *see* **The Postman Always Rings Twice**

675 Othello

Based on the play by William Shakespeare. Story: Othello, the Moor of Venice, and Desdemona marry against the wishes of her father. Provoked by the evil machinations of the envious and hateful Iago, Othello becomes so unfoundedly suspicious of Desdemona's fidelity that he kills his beloved wife and himself.

• ***Othello*** (remake). Mercury/Films Marceau, 1952. Director and screenwriter: Orson Welles. Cast: Orson Welles (Othello), Suzanne Cloutier (Desdemona), Michael MacLiammoir (Iago), Robert Coote (Roderigo), Michael Lawrence (Cassio), Fay Compton (Emilia), Doris Dowling (Bianca).

• ***Othello*** (remake). Mosfilm Productions, U.S.S.R., 1955. Director and screenwriter: Sergei Yutkevich. Cast: Sergei Bondarchuk (Othello), Andrei Popov (Iago), Irina Skobtseva (Desdemona), Vladimir Soshalsky (Cassio), E. Vesnik (Roderigo), A. Maximova (Emilia), E. Teterin, M. Troyanovsky, A. Kelgerer, N. Brilling, L. Ashrafova.

• ***Othello*** (remake). British Home Entertainments/Warner Bros., 1965. Director: Stuart Burge; screenwriter: William Shakespeare. Cast: Laurence Olivier (Othello), Maggie Smith (Desdemona), Frank Finlay (Iago), Derek Jacobi (Cassio), Joyce Redman (Emilia), Robert Lang (Roderigo), Anthony Nicholls (Brabantio), Roy Holder, Sheila Reid, Harry Lomax, Michael Turner, Kenneth MacKintosh, Terrence Knapp.

The Othello story has also been filmed in Italy in 1907 and 1909, in Denmark in 1908, in Sweden as *Desdemona* in 1912, in France in 1915, in Germany in 1918 and in 1922 as *The Moor,* in Great Britain in 1914, 1921, and 1923, in the U.S.S.R. in 1960 and 1967, and in the U.S. in 1910 as *Up in Desdemona's Room,* and in 1974 as *Catch My Soul.*

Othello-inspired films include *Men Are Not Gods* (1936), a British film about an actor, played by Sebastian Shaw, who plans to kill his wife, played by Miriam Hopkins, on stage, during a performance of Othello; *A Double Life* (1947), with Ronald Colman having similiar plans for Signe Hasso as he portrays the Moor; *Jubal* (1956), a Western entry, with Rod Steiger as an Iago character who prompts Ernest Borgnine as a rancher, Othello, to have a gunbattle with Glenn

Ford, whom Borgnine's promiscuous wife, Valerie French, prefers to Steiger; and *All Night Long* (1962), a jazz version with Patrick McGoohan trying to strangle his wife at an all-night party.

Orson Welles rearranged Shakespeare's play to suit himself, but as usual with his European ventures, he was underfinanced and the film is of poor technical quality with the acting a definite mixed bag. The Russian version stressed the hero's goodness corrupted by the jealous, evil Iago. For the 1965 version, based on the National Theatre production of the play, directed by John Dexter, Laurence Olivier was nominated for the Academy Award for Best Actor, while Frank Finlay, Joyce Redman and Maggie Smith were each nominated for Best Supporting Actor and Actress, respectively. None won.

Our Daily Bread *see* **The Crowd**

Our Girl Friday *see* **The Admirable Crichton**

676 Our Man Flint

Based on a story by Hal Fimberg. Story: It's a tongue-in-cheek rip-off of the James Bond series, with super-intelligent ladies man Derek Flint called upon by the American government to save the world from three mad scientists intent on taking over control of the world by regulating the planet's weather to serve their ends.

Twentieth Century–Fox, 1966 (original). Director: Daniel Mann; screenwriters: Hal Fimberg and Ben Starr. Cast: James Coburn (Derek Flint), Lee J. Cobb (Cramden), Gila Golan (Gila), Richard Mulhare (Malcolm Rodney), Benson Fong, Shelby Grant, Sigrid Valdis, Gianna Serra, Helen Funai, Michael St. Clair, Rhys Williams.

• ***In Like Flint*** (sequel). Twentieth Century–Fox, 1967. Director: Gordon Douglas; screenwriter: Hal Fimberg. Cast: James Coburn (Derek Flint), Lee J. Cobb (Cramden), Jean Hale (Lisa), Andrew Duggan (the President), Anna Lee (Elisabeth), Hanna Landy, Totty Ames, Steve Ihnat, Thomas Hason, Mary Michael, Diane Bond, Jacki Ray.

These spy spoofs seem mostly an excuse to parade a lot of scantily dressed young beauties around the premises. Coburn wasn't too bad as the clever agent, but it was sad to see the very fine actor Lee J. Cobb reduced to a burlesque part. In the sequel, Flint has to deal with the plot of Steve Ihnat and Anna Lee to substitute an actor for the president of the United States.

Out of the Storm *see* **The Wrong Road**

Out West with the Hardys *see* **A Family Affair**

677 The Outcast

Based on the play by Hubert Henry Davies. Story: Miriam is homeless and starving when she meets Geoffrey Sherwood, who is trying to overcome the grief of losing his love, Valentine, to another man. He helps Miriam and after awhile they fall in love, but then Valentine re-enters the picture, prepared to leave her new husband for Geoffrey. Her intentions change once again, and she goes back home. Miriam, believing that she will be always second in the thoughts of Geoffrey, sets off for South America. She is pursued by Geoffrey, who prevents her from committing suicide.

Famous Players/Paramount Pictures, 1922 (original). Silent. Director: Chet Withey; screenwriter: Josephine Lovett. Cast: Elsie Ferguson (Miriam), David Powell (Geoffrey Sherwood), William David (Tony Hewlitt), Mary MacLaren (Valentine Moreland), Charles Wesley, Teddy Sampson, William Powell.

• ***The Outcast*** (remake). First National Pictures, 1928. Silent. Director: William A. Seiter; screenwriter: Agnes Christine Johnson. Cast: Corinne Griffith (Miriam), James Ford (Tony), Edmund Lowe (Geoffrey), Kathryn Carver (Valentine), Louise Fazenda, Claude King, Sam Hardy, Patsy O'Bryne, Lee Moran.

• ***The Girl from Tenth Avenue*** (remake). Warner Bros., 1935. Director: Alfred E. Green; screenwriter: Charles Kenyon. Cast: Bette Davis (Miriam Brady), Ian Hunter (Geoffrey), Katherine Alexander (Valentine), Colin Clive (Moreland), Allison Skipworth, John Eldredge, Philip Reed.

The story of these films is the kind that one would find in some *True Romances* type magazine, worth 20 minutes of someone's time with nothing better to do, while sitting in a waiting room or a beauty parlor, but not the approximate one-hour running-time of the three. The story of a streetwalker, down on her luck, was first filmed in 1917. In the 1928 version Corinne Griffith, as Miriam, meets the intoxicated, disconsolate socialite Geoffrey, played by Edmund Lowe, who on a whim takes her to the wedding of the girl who threw him over for another man. Lowe rents an apartment for Griffith and she falls deeply in love with him. When the vampish ex-love tries to re-enter Lowe's life, Griffith tries to hit the streets again, but finds because of her feelings for Lowe, she can't give herself to another man. All ends well when Lowe realizes he loves the ex-whore with a heart of gold. In the 1935 picture, Ian Hunter goes on a binge when Kathleen Alexander jilts him, meets Bette Davis, and wakes up the next morning married to her. This twist doesn't make the story any more palatable. It's not Davis at her best, but the fault lies in the material.

Outcast Lady *see* **A Woman of Affairs**

The Outrage *see* **Rashomon**

678 Outside the Law

Based on a story by Tod Browning. Story: "Silent" Madden and his daughter Molly are persuaded to give up their criminal pursuits by Chang Lo, but before they can make good on their pledge, gang leader "Black Mike" Sylva frames Madden and the latter is sent to prison. Molly joins Sylva's gang, agreeing to participate in a jewel heist. When she learns that Sylva is going to set her up like he did her father, she and "Dapper Bill" take off with the loot. In a battle with the gang, Sylva is killed and Molly and Bill are caught by the cops. But Chang Lo arranges their release by returning the jewels.

Universal Pictures, 1921 (original). Silent. Director and screenwriter: Tod Browning. Cast: Priscilla Dean (Molly Madden/Silky Moll), Ralph Lewis ("Silent" Madden), Lon Chaney ("Black Mike" Sylva/Ah Wing), Wheeler Oakman ("Dapper Bill" Ballard), E.A. Warren (Chang Lo), Stanley Goethals, Melbourne MacDowall, Wilton Taylor.

• ***Outside the Law*** (remake). Universal Pictures, 1931. Director: Tod Browning; screenwriters: Tod Browning and Parret Fort. Cast: Mary Nolan (Connie), Edward G. Robinson (Cobra), Owen Moore (Fingers), Edwin Sturgis (Jake), John George (Humpy), Delmar Watson, Dewitt Jennings, Rockcliffe Fellowes.

Priscilla Dean got rave reviews for her portrayal of "Silky Moll," a society crook who couldn't quite decide whether to go straight or not. Lon Chaney stole the show in the dual role of the head crook and a Confucian priest who helps Dean learn right from wrong. In a cinematic achievement of the time, a climactic scene has his oriental character putting a slug into his criminal counterpart. The performances by Edward G. Robinson, Mary Nolan and Owen Moore in the remake were so wretched that most audiences were sorry sound had been added to the story.

679 The Outsider

Based on the play by Dorothy Brandon. Story: Leontine Sturdee, an aristocratic dancer, goes to a gypsy camp in Hungary to learn some native dances. She meets a mystic, Ragatzy, who has made some impressive cures. Leontine sustains an injury which cripples her. She refuses Ragatzy's offer of help, believing him a fraud, and returns to England, where the best physicians diagnose her case as hopeless. Ragatzy, who has fallen in love with Leontine, arrives, and this time she accepts his attempt at a cure. Initially, he fails, but as he is about to leave, she realizes that she loves the gypsy and walks to him.

Fox Film Corporation, 1926 (original). Silent. Director: Rowland V. Lee; screenwriter: Robert N. Lee. Cast: Jacqueline Logan (Leontine Sturdee), Lou Tellegen (Anton Ragatzy), Walter Pidgeon (Basil Owen), Roy Atwell, Charles Lane, Joan Standing.

• ***The Outsider*** (remake). Cinema House/MGM, 1933. Director and screenwriter: Harry Lachman. Cast: Harold Huth (Ragatzy), Joan Barry (Leontine Sturdee), Frank Lawton, Mary Clare, Norman McKinnell, Annie Esmond, Glenmore Pointin, Fewlass Llewellyn.

• ***The Outsider*** (remake). Associated British Productions, 1940. Director: Paul L. Stein; screenwriter: Dudley Leslie. Cast: Mary Maguire (Lalage Sturdee), George Sanders (Ragatzy), Barbara Blair, Peter Murray Hill, Frederick Leister, P. Kynaston Reeves.

The remakes told the moving story of an unqualified surgeon who cures cripples using electricity. He is an "outsider" as far as the established medical profession is concerned, until he takes on the case of a Harley Street specialist's crippled daughter, whose fiancé has deserted her. After a year of treatment by the osteopath, she fails to walk and her father denounces Ragatzy as a fraud. Just at this moment, her love for Ragatzy gives her the strength to walk to him.

680 Outward Bound

Based on the play by Sutton Vane. Story: The passengers aboard a mysterious, fog-shrouded ocean liner include high-strung alcoholic Tom Prior, his mother Mrs. Midget (whose identity is not known to Prior), a pair of lovers, Henry and Ann, snobbish dowager Mrs. Clivedon Banks, an obnoxious businessman, Mr. Lingley, and a dedicated missionary, the Reverend William Duke. The only apparent crew member is the steward Scrubby. The passengers slowly come to the realization that they are all dead on a trip to eternity. When they reach their destination, Thompson the Examiner comes aboard to pass judgement on the voyagers and kindly announces their fate. Henry and Ann, called "half-ways" because they had turned on the gas in their apartment in order to commit suicide, are not on the examiner's list and are left with Scrubby on the ship. Henry hears a dog barking and the breaking of glass. Slowly the picture dissolves and the couple is back in their flat. Their dog had broken a windowpane, saving their lives.

Warner Bros., 1930 (original). Director: Robert Milton; screenwriter: J. Grubb Alexander. Cast: Leslie Howard (Tom Prior), Douglas Fairbanks, Jr. (Henry), Helen Chandler (Ann), Beryl Mercer (Mrs. Midget), Alec B. Francis (Scrubby), Alison Skipworth (Mrs. Clivedon-Banks), Lionel Watts (Rev. William Duke), Montagu Love (Mr. Lingley), Dudley Digges (Thompson the Examiner).

• ***Between Two Worlds*** (remake). Warner Bros., 1944. Director: Edward A. Blatt; screenwriter: Daniel Fuchs. Cast: John Garfield (Tom Prior), Paul Henreid (Henry), Eleanor Parker (Ann), Sara Allgood (Mrs. Midget), Edmund Gwenn (Scrubby), Isobel Elsom (Mrs. Clivedon-Banks), Dennis King (Rev. William Duke), George Coulouris (Mr. Lingley), Sydney Greenstreet (Thompson the Examiner), George Tobias (Pete Musick), Faye Emerson (Maxine).

Audiences were either fascinated by the 1930 film or found it boring nonsense. There's little action and a great deal of talking, but for those in the mood for leisurely character development this is fine entertainment. Unlike the original, in the remake, audiences were aware of the state of the passengers on the ocean liner, as they had been filmed being killed in a London bombing raid. Two new characters were added to the picture: Merchant Marine Pete Musick, who thought the timing of his death was really unfair, and gold-digging Maxine, who initially insisted she wouldn't cooperate with the examiner in any way. Best acting honors in the two productions go to Alec B. Francis and Edmund Gwenn as the lovable steward, and Dudley Digges and Sydney Greenstreet as the amicable examiner.

681 Owd Bob

Based on the novel by Alfred Olivant. Story: In the Lake district of England

"Don't you see, we're all dead," Douglas Fairbanks, Jr. (right) seems to be explaining to Alex B. Francis and Helen Chandler in Outward Bound, *(Warner Bros., 1930).*

an old farmer's sheepdog is saved from being destroyed when a rival's dog is proved to be the sheep killer.

Atlantic Union, Great Britain, 1925 (original). Silent. Director: Henry Edwards; screenwriter: Hugh Maclean. Cast: J. Fisher White (Adam McAdam), Ralph Forbes (Davie McAdam), James Carew (James Moore), Yvonne Thomas (Maggie Moore), Frank Stanmore (Jim Burton), Grace Lane, Robert English.

• ***Owd Bob*** (remake). Gainsborough, Great Britain, 1938. Director: Robert Stevenson; screenwriters: Michael Hogan and J.B. Williams. Cast: Will Fyffe (Adam McAdam), John Loder (David Moore), Margaret Lockwood (Jeannie McAdam), Moore Marriott (Samuel), Graham Moffatt (Tammas), Wilfred Walter, Eliot Mason, A. Bromely Davenport, H.F. Maltby, Edmund Breon, Wally Patch, Alf Goddard.

Twentieth Century–Fox used essentially the same plot for its 1947 release *Thunder in the Valley.* In the 1938 movie, Will Fyffe is terrific as the drunken, quarrelsome old Scots shepherd, whose dog Black Wull is the rival of Owd Bob, a dog owned by newly arrived John Loder, who falls in love with Fyffe's daughter, Margaret Lockwood. Wull not only loses the sheepdog trials to Owd Bob, but is shot when it is discovered to be a sheepkiller. The sequences involving the dogs and the sheep are excellent.

Something has distracted the passengers on a vessel sailing between life and death in Between Two Worlds *(Warner Bros., 1944), a remake of* Outward Bound. *From left to right: Dennis King, Sara Allgood, John Garfield, Faye Emerson, George Tobias, Gilbert Emery and Isobel Elsom.*

Oz *see* **The Wizard of Oz**

P

Pacific Rendezvous *see* **Rendezvous**

682 Paddy-the-Next-Best-Thing

Based on the novel by Gertrude Page. Story: Impoverished Irish landowner General Adair orders his eldest daughter, Eileen, to marry Lawrence Blake, a man she does not love, so Adair may get out of debt. Her younger sister, Paddy, intervenes, making it possible for Eileen to marry the man she loves and for Paddy to marry Blake, whom she loves.

Garham-Wilcox, Great Britain, 1923 (original). Silent. Director: Graham Cutts; screenwriters: Herbert Wilcox and Eliot Stannard. Cast: Mae Marsh (Paddy Adair), Darby Foster (Lawrence Blake), Lillian Douglas (Eileen Adair), George K. Arthur (Kack O'Hara), Sir Simeon Stuart (General Adair), Nina Boucicault, Haidee Wright, Marie Wright, Marie Ault, Mildred Evelyn, Tom Coventry.

• ***Paddy-the-Next-Best-Thing*** (remake). Fox Film Corporation, 1933. Director: Harry Lachman; screenwriter: Edwin Burke. Cast: Janet Gaynor (Paddy), Warner Baxter (Lawrence Blake), Walter Connolly (Major Adair), Harvey Stephens (Jack Breen), Margaret Lindsay (Eileen), Joseph M. Kerrigan (Collins), Mary McCormack, Fiske O'Hara, Merle Tottenham.

Paddy, as played by Janet Gaynor, is a charming tomboy who proves to everyone's surprise that she's really a woman with her own designs on a man. It's a modest star comedy and unless Gaynor appeals to one, there's really not much to it.

683 The Painted Lady

Based on the story by Larry Evans. Story: After being released from prison for a crime committed by her sister, Violet can find no other way to support herself than becoming a prostitute. While on a cruise to a South Seas island, she encounters Luther Smith, a sailor on the trail of those responsible for the death of his sister. She feels unworthy of his love but later Luther rescues Violet from Captain Sutton, the man who caused Luther's sister's tragic death.

• ***The Painted Lady*** (remake). Fox Film Corporation, 1924. Silent. Director: Chester Bennett; screenwriter: Thomas Dixon, Jr. Cast: George O'Brien (Luther Smith), Dorothy Mackaill (Violet), Harry T. Morey (Captain Sutton), Lucille Hutton (Pearl Thompson), Lucille Ricksen, Margaret McWade, John Miljan, Frank Eliott.

• ***Pursued*** (remake). Fox Film Corporation, 1934. Director: Sol M. Wurtzel; screenwriters: Lester Cole and Stuart Anthony. Cast: Rosemary Ames (Mona), Victor Jory (Beauregard), Pert Kelton (Gilda), Russell Hardie (David Landeen), George Irvin, Torben Meyer.

South Sea stories of fallen women were quite popular in the twenties and thirties but there was seldom anything to distinguish them one from another. One difference was a function of the decade, not the story. In the twenties, little doubt was left as to how the girl plied her trade. In the next decade she was a "hostess or a singer or a girl down on her luck" but if the audiences believed that she peddled her body to keep herself alive, that was just in their dirty minds; the producers said no such thing. The Larry Evans *Saturday Evening Post* story was first filmed as *When a Man Sees Red* in 1917 by Fox.

684 The Painted Veil

Based on the novel by W. Somerset Maugham. Story: Katrin marries Dr. Walter Fane and goes with him to China. Because of his busy practice, he has little time for her, and when she meets attentive Jack Townsend, she has an affair with him. Fane discovers what is going on and insists that Katrin must accompany him into the interior to deal with an epidemic, unless Townsend will divorce his wife and marry Katrin. Townsend is noncommittal, so Katrin goes with her husband, where she becomes a dedicated worker. Townsend arrives just about the time that Dr. Fane is stabbed by an angry Chinese, but Katrin, realizing she still loves her husband, ignores him to care for Walter.

MGM, 1934 (original). Director: Richard Boleslavski; screenwriters: John

Meehan, Salka Viertel and Edith Fitzgerald. Cast: Greta Garbo (Katrin), Herbert Marshall (Walter Fane), George Brent (Jack Townsend), Warner Oland (General Yu), Jean Hersholt, Beulah Bondi, Katherine Alexander, Cecilia Parker, Soo Yong.

• ***The Seventh Sin*** (remake). MGM, 1957. Director: Ronald Neame; screenwriter: Karl Tunberg. Cast: Eleanor Parker (Carol Carwin), Bill Travers (Doctor Walter Carwin), George Sanders (Tim Waddington), Jean-Pierre Aumont (Paul Duvelle), Francoise Rosay, Ellen Corby, Judy Dan.

The Painted Veil wasn't one of Garbo's better movies and the remake with Eleanor Parker was even less appealing. The story was told in an old-fashioned way, almost like a silent tearjerker, but there wasn't much to waste one's tears on. Both films were confusing and slow-paced—real yawns, even though both Garbo and Parker were beautiful to see.

Painting the Clouds with Sunshine *see* **The Gold Diggers**

685 A Pair of Sixes

Based on the play by Edward Peple. Story: T. Boggs Johns and his partner George Nettleton decide to settle their constant bickering over how their pill company should be run by playing a game of poker with the loser becoming the other's servant for an entire year and the winner taking sole control of the company for the same period. The comic implications are predictable but amusing.

Essanay Studios, 1918 (original). Silent. Director: L.O. Windham; screenwriter: George K. Spoor. Cast: Taylor Holmes (T. Boggs Johns), Robert Conness (George Nettleton), Alice Mann (Florence Cole), Edna Phillips Holmes (Mrs. Nettleton), Cecil Eburne, Maude Eburne, C.E. Ashley, John Cossar, Bryon Aldenn.

• ***Queen High*** (remake). Paramount Pictures, 1930. Director: Fred Newmeyer; screenwriter: uncredited. Cast: Stanley Smith (Dick Johns), Ginger Rogers (Polly Stockwell), Charles Ruggles (T. Boggs Johns), Frank Morgan (George Nettleton), Helen Carrington, Theresa Maxwell Conover, Betty Garde.

In the musical remake, the loser of the poker game becomes the servant of his partner in the garter business for a year with no explanations to anyone. The wise-cracking between Ruggles and Morgan was a scream at the time. The best song is that sung by Ruggles, "I Love the Ladies in My Own Peculiar Way."

686 Pampered Youth

Based on the novel *The Magnificent Ambersons* by Booth Tarkington. Story: At the turn of the twentieth century, the Ambersons are the leading family of a small Indiana town, with daughter Isabel having a difficult job of choosing between two suitors, until one of them, Eugene Moran, disgraces himself in the eyes of Isabel's father, Major Amberson, by performing a drunken serenade to his lady fair. Isabel marries Wilbur Minafer, although she doesn't love him, and Eugene leaves town. As the years pass, Wilbur dies and Isabel concentrates all her attention on her son George, who grows from a spoiled brat to a shallow, self-centered man. Eugene, now a widower, returns to town with his daughter, with whom George falls in love. Despite this, George resents the attention Eugene pays to his mother and her apparent attachment to her old suitor. When Major Amberson dies, George, who has squandered the family fortune, gets his comeuppance when he is forced to swallow his pride and find a job. Hard work has a salutary effect on George and he becomes reconciled with Eugene and his daughter when the former rescues Isabel in a fire at the Amberson mansion.

Vitagraph Co. of America, 1925 (original). Silent. Director: David Smith; screenwriter: Jay Pilcher. Cast: Cullen Landis (George Minafer as a man), Ben Alexander (George Minafer as a boy), Allan Forrest (Eugene Moran), Alice Calhoun (Isabel Minafer), Emmett King (Major Amberson), Wallace MacDonald (Wilbur Minafer), Charlotte Merriam, Kathryn Adams, Aggie Herring.

• ***The Magnificent Ambersons*** (remake). RKO, 1942. Director and screenwriter: Orson Welles. Cast: Joseph Cotten (Eugene), Dolores Costello (Isabel), Anne Baxter (Lucy), Tim Holt (George), Agnes Moorehead (Fanny), Ray Collins (Jack), Erskine Sanford, Richard Bennett, Don Dillaway.

Critics of Orson Welles' *The Magnificent Ambersons* objected as much to his timing as they did to his filmmaking. Many believed that the depressing story of a spiteful and spoiled young man in an overall gloomy picture, just as the world was settling down to a world war, was much too dismal a subject for the screen at the time. While these reviews could not possibly please Welles, they were less depressing than the fact that the studio, unhappy with the overall length of the film and the downbeat ending, cut 40 minutes from the film and brought in Robert Wise to supply a more positive finish. Although Welles had every right to decry what had been done to his masterpiece, what remains is still an outstanding piece of cinema.

Once again, as in his movie *Citizen Kane,* Welles introduced new, imaginative cinematic techniques and camera angles which give the movie a magnificent visual effect. There is something obviously missing in the second half of the film, where the greatest number of cuts have been made. Here the story seems to lurch forward like an automobile in need of a tune up. Still the movie has so much to praise that these shortcomings can easily be forgiven. Each individual scene is so almost perfect, that it is like being at an exhibition of paintings at an art institute. One can wish that there was more transition from one to another, but it's difficult to fault the composition, arrangements and sequencing. The performances are impressive and memorable, not just those of Costello, Cotten, Baxter and Holt, but most especially those of Ray Collins, Agnes Moorehead, and Richard Bennett as the major. Moorehead was nominated for an Academy Award for Best Supporting Actress, Stanley Cortez for his photography and the film for Best Picture. None won. *The Magnificent Ambersons* was among the few films, *Fahrenheit 451* being another, in which the credits are all spoken, rather than printed on the film. These ended with the great one saying, "I wrote and directed the picture. My name is Orson Welles."

687 Panama Flo

Based on an original screenplay by Garrett Fort. Story: It's the absurd story of a honky-tonk girl named Flo, stranded in Panama, who is forced to keep house for McTeague or he will have her jailed for stealing his wallet. Her problems increase when a former lover, Babe, shows up. In this confusing story, McTeague, who is a real meany, turns out to be the man of her dreams and Babe, who looks like he's going to be her champion, is revealed to be a murderer.

RKO/Pathe, 1932 (original). Director: Ralph Murphy; screenwriter: Garrett Fort. Cast: Helen Twelvetrees (Flo), Robert Armstrong (Babe), Charles Bickford (McTeague), Marjorie Peterson, Maude Eburne, Paul Hurst, Ernie Adams, Relna Velez.

• ***Panama Lady*** (remake). RKO, 1939. Director: Jack Hively; screenwriter: Michael Kanin. Cast: Lucille Ball (Lucy), Allan Lane (McTeague), Steffi Duna (Cheema), Evelyn Brent (Lenore), Donald Briggs (Roy), Bernadene Hayes, Abner Biberman.

One film was enough to make of this stinker, but never underestimating the public's taste, the producers decided to see if they couldn't get away one more time with this weak hokum of a story. Feeling obliged to say something positive about this entry, one will note that the 1939 film is less dreary than the 1932 movie, probably because Lucille Ball tried so hard as the lady of the title who was practically kidnapped by an oilman and brought to his wilderness camp, after he caught her with her hand in his pocket.

Panama Lady *see* **Panama Flo**

Panama Patrol *see* **Cipher Bureau**

Paid *see* **Within the Law**

Partners in Crime *see* **Murder Goes to College**

The Passion of Joan of Arc *see* **Joan of Arc**

The Passionate Friends *see* **Don Quixote**

The Past of Mary Holmes *see* **The Goose Woman**

The Patchwork Girl of Oz *see* **The Wizard of Oz**

688 Paths to Paradise

Based on the play *The Heart of a Thief* by Paul Armstrong. Story: The Dude from Duluth, a confidence man, goes to a den in Chinatown, where Molly separates tourists from their valuables. The Dude allows her to practice her trade and then flashes a badge, claiming to be a detective who can be bought off. She gives him everything she has and the fleecer has become the fleecee.

They meet again, later, in a wealthy home, he once more posing as a detective and she as a maid. Both are after a valuable necklace. They decide to work together and after grabbing the jewelry, start off for Mexico to fence it. They are chased by every cop between San Francisco and the border, but arrive safely. Tired of this life, Molly convinces the Dude to send the necklace back to its rightful owner and the two settle down to the straight life.

Famous Players/Paramount Pictures, 1925 (original). Silent. Director: Clarence Badger; screenwriter: Keene Thompson. Cast: Betty Compson (Molly), Raymond Griffith (the Dude from Duluth), Tom Santschi, Bert Woodruff, Fred Kelsey.

• ***Hold That Blonde*** (remake). Paramount Pictures, 1945. Director: George Marshall; screenwriters: Walter DeLeon, Earl Baldwin and E. Edwin Moran. Cast: Eddie Bracken (Ogden Spencer Trulow III), Veronica Lake (Sally Martin), Albert Dekker (Inspector Callahan), Willie Best (Willie Shelby), Frank Fenton, George Zucco, Donald MacBride, Lewis L. Russell, Norma Varden.

The comedy *Paths to Paradise* was an amusing romp, as was the thin remake with Eddie Bracken as a wealthy kleptomaniac, told by his psychiatrist that romance might cure his problem. Unfortunately, his choice for this prescription is Veronica Lake, a jewel thief. There are a few funny situations in this slapstick farce before he can convince her to renounce her life of crime.

689 The Pay Off

Based on a story by Samuel Shipman. Story: It's the incredible tale of world-weary gang leader Gene Fenmore, who falls for Annabelle and then she and her fiancé, Tommy, innocently get involved in a robbery in which a man is killed. Fenmore takes the blame and goes to the electric chair to safeguard her.

RKO, 1930 (original). Director: Lowell Sherman; screenwriter: Jane Murfin. Cast: Lowell Sherman (Gene Fenmore), Marion Nixon (Annabelle), Hugh Trevor (Rocky), William Janney (Tommy), Helene Millard, George F. Marion, Walter McGrail, Robert McWade, Alan Roscoe, Lita Chevret, Bert Moorehouse.

• ***Law of the Underworld*** (remake). RKO, 1938. Director: Lew Landers; screenwriter: Bert Granet. Cast: Chester Morris (Gene Fellmore), Anne Shirley (Annabelle), Eduardo Ciannelli (Rocky), Walter Abel (Rogers), Richard Bond (Tommy), Lee Patrick, Paul Guilfoyle, Frank M. Thomas, Eddie Acuff.

The Bard has said, "The play's the thing." Well in the case of these two dull movies, the play's not much of anything. The dialog is so sloppily sentimental that audiences would like to send the whole lot of the performers to the chair, not just chivalrous gang leader Chester Morris. Although it's not saying much, Lowell Sherman's world-weary mobster was more effective than Morris' suave, sophisticated gentleman crook. Others in the casts contributed very little, but then they had very little with which to work.

690 Peacock Alley

Based on an original story by Ouida Bergere. Story: Elmer Harmon from

Pennsylvania goes to Paris, France, to sign a contract with the government. He meets dancer Cleo, who is instrumental in his getting the contract. They are married, but when they are back in his hometown, the neighbors are shocked both by Cleo's clothes and her manners. Moving to New York City, Elmer runs out of money and forges his uncle's name to a check. He is arrested and Cleo takes a theater engagement to raise money for her husband's bail. Elmer misinterprets her relationship with another performer and leaves her, but begs her to take him back when he learns the truth of the matter.

Tiffany Pictures, 1922 (original). Silent. Director: Robert Z. Leonard; screenwriter: Edmund Goulding. Cast: Mae Murray (Cleo), Monte Blue (Elmer Harmon), Edmund Lowe (Phil Garrison), W.J. Ferguson, Anders Randolph, William Tooker.

• ***Peacock Alley*** (remake). Tiffany Pictures, 1930. Director: Marcel De Sano; screenwriter: Frances Hyland. Cast: Mae Murray (Claire Tree), George Barraud (Stoddard Clayton), Jason Robards (Jim Bradbury), Richard Tucker (Martin Saunders), W.L. Thorne, Phillips Smalley, E.H. Calvert.

In the second version, Mae Murray, long in love with millionaire George Barraud, meets him at the Peacock Alley Hotel in New York. When he still refuses to marry her, she announces that she will wed her hometown sweetheart, attorney Jason Robards. The two are married the next day and take a room at the Peacock Alley, but Robards forgets to register Murray and the hotel detective orders them out, insisting that Mae had spent the night with another man the previous night. Robards is enraged and wants to confront Barraud. Murray is outraged that her new husband doesn't trust her. They separate and Mae goes back to work as a chorus girl, but on her opening night, Barraud arrives to tell her he's now ready for marriage, and she accepts his belated proposal.

691 Peck's Bad Boy

Based on the story *Peck's Bad Boy and His Pa* by George Wilbur Peck. Story: Peck's Bad Boy is a mischievous boy, whose exploits include releasing a lion from a circus cage, disguising a friend as a girl and trying to set up a date with "her" for his father so he can blackmail his Pa, putting ants in his father's pleurisy pad and causing the arrest of his sister's beau, a young doctor. After all this it's a wonder that the doctor saved the boy and his dog from being run over by a train.

First National Pictures, 1921 (original). Silent. Director and screenwriter: Sam Wood. Cast: Jackie Coogan (Peck's Bad Boy), James Corrigan (Pa), Wheeler Oakman, Doris May, Raymond Hatton, Lillian Leighton, Charles Hatton, Gloria Wood, Queenie.

• ***Peck's Bad Boy*** (remake). Fox Film Corporation, 1934. Director: Eddie Cline; screenwriters: Bernard Schubert and Marguerite Roberts. Cast: Jackie Cooper (Peck's Bad Boy), Thomas Meighan (Pa), Dorothy Peterson, Jackie Searle, O.P. Heggie, Gertrude Howard.

Peck's Bad Boy doesn't really mean any harm, he's just high-strung, curious and accident prone. However, he makes Dennis the Menace look like an angel and it's only funny because he's not a member of one's own family. Both

Jackies, Coogan and Cooper, do a nice job in this American juvenile comic classic.

692 Peg o' My Heart

Based on the play by J. Hartley Manners. Story: Peg is the daughter of a poor Irish farmer and an upperclass Englishwoman whose family has disowned her. She is sent to England to live with the snobbish Chichesters, where her only friend is Jerry, who lives on a neighboring estate. Learning that the only reason the Chichesters tolerate her is because they are paid to do so by her uncle and that her friend is really the laird of the neighboring manor, she returns, disillusioned, to Ireland. Jerry follows her, and convinces her to marry him.

Metro Pictures, 1922 (original). Silent. Director: King Vidor; screenwriter: Mary O'Hara. Cast: Laurette Taylor (Peg O'Connell), Mahlon Hamilton (Jerry), Russell Simpson (Jim O'Connell), Ethel Grey Terry (Ethel Chichester), Nigel Barrie, Lionel Belmore, Vera Lewis, Sidna Beth Ivins, D.R.O. Hatswell, Aileen O'Malley.

• ***Peg o' My Heart*** (remake). Cosmopolitan/MGM, 1933. Director: Robert Z. Leonard; screenwriters: Frances Marion and Frank R. Adams. Cast: Marion Davies (Peg), Onslow Stevens (Jerry), J. Farrell MacDonald (Pat), Juliette Compton (Ethel), Irene Browne, Tyrrell Davis, Alan Mowbray, Robert Greig.

Laurette Taylor originated the role of Peg on the Broadway stage and her success there was repeated on the screen, with the sentimental picture being quite popular. By 1933, the time for such a story seemingly had passed and few in the metropolitan areas were interested in the story of an English nobleman falling for a roguish Irish colleen, although it did decent box office in the small towns.

Penitentiary *see* The Criminal Code

693 Penrod

Based on the novel and play by Booth Tarkington. Story: Penrod Schofield, something of a troublemaker, is the president of the America's Boys Protective Association, which meets weekly to report the mistreatment of boys by parents, neighbors, policemen, etc. During a hectic summer, Penrod and his friends ruin an amateur theatrical production and scandalize the town with their antics at a cotillion. The leading citizens of the town want to do something about the mischief the gang is causing, but when the boys capture two notorious bandits, Penrod becomes a hero.

First National Pictures, 1922 (original). Silent. Director: Marshall Neilan; screenwriter: Lucita Squier. Cast: Wesley Barry (Penrod), Tully Marshall (Mr. Schofield), Claire McDowell (Mrs. Schofield), John Harron (Robert Williams), Gordon Griffith (Sam Williams), Newton Hall, Harry Griffith, Cecil Holland, Sunshine Morrison, Florence Morrison, Marjorie Daw, Clara Horton.

• ***Penrod and Sam*** (sequel). First National Pictures, 1931. Director: William Beaudine; screenwriter: Waldemar Young. Cast: Leon Janney (Penrod), Matt

Moore (Mr. Schofield), Dorothy Peterson (Mrs. Schofield), Junior Coghlan (Sam), Johnny Arthur, Zasu Pitts, Charles Sellon, Wade Boteler, Helen Beaudine.

• ***Penrod and Sam*** (sequel). First National Pictures, 1937. Director: William McGann; screenwriters: Lillie Hayward and Hugh Cummings. Cast: Billy Mauch (Penrod), Frank Craven (Mr. Schofield), Spring Byington (Mrs. Schofield), Craig Reynolds, Charles Halton, Harry Watson, Jackie Morrow, Phillip Hurlic.

• ***Penrod and His Twin Brother*** (sequel). Warner Bros., 1938. Director: William McGann; screenwriters: William Jacobs and Hugh Cummings. Cast: Billy Mauch (Penrod), Bobby Mauch (Danny), Frank Craven (Mr. Schofield), Spring Byington (Mrs. Schofield), Charles Halton, Claudia Coleman, Jackie Morrow, Phillip Hurlic, Bennie Bartlett, Bernice Pilot, John Pirrone, Billy Lechner.

• ***Penrod's Double Trouble*** (sequel). Warner Bros., 1938. Director: Lewis Seller; screenwriters: Crane Wilbur and Ernest Booth. Cast: Billy Mauch (Penrod), Bobby Mauch (Danny), Dick Purcell (Tex Boyden), Gene Lockhart (Mr. Schofield), Kathleen Lockhart (Mrs. Schofield), Hugh O'Connell (Prof. Caligostro), Charles Halton, Bernice Pilot, Jackie Morrow, Phillip Hurlic.

• ***On Moonlight Bay*** (remake). Warner Bros., 1951. Director: Roy Del Ruth; screenwriters: Jack Rose and Melville Shavelson. Cast: Doris Day (Marjorie Winfield), Gordon MacRae (Willie Sherman), Leon Ames (George Winfield), Rosemary De Camp (Mrs. Winfield), Billy Gray (Wesley Winfield), Jack Smith (Hubert Wakely), Mary Wickes, Ellen Corby, Jeffrey Stevens, Eddie Marr, Henry East.

• ***By the Light of the Silvery Moon*** (sequel). Warner Bros., 1953. Director: David Butler; screenwriters: Robert O'Brien and Irving Elinson. Cast: Doris Day (Marjorie), Gordon MacRae (William Sherman), Leon Ames (George Winfield), Rosemary De Camp (Mrs. Winfield), Billy Gray (Wesley), Mary Wickes, Russell Arms, Maria Palmer, Howard Wendell, Walter Flannery, Geraldine Wall.

Warner Bros. got a lot of mileage out of Tarkington's stories, although by the 1937 film, the author would hardly recognize them. At that point Penrod and his friends turned into junior G-men, working on the side of right, although still getting into their share of trouble. With Billy Mauch now cast as Penrod, it must have seemed a waste not to use his twin brother, Bobby, so in 1938, Penrod acquired a look-alike friend to share in his adventures, discovering the hide-out of some gangsters. By *Penrod's Double Trouble,* this look-alike had been converted into Penrod's twin brother, as the boys deal with kidnapping and the villain, Professor Caligostro.

Finally, in the two Doris Day musicals, Penrod had lost his name and his top billing, as the story revolved around his blonde tomboy sister and her romance with college man Gordon MacRae, who lives across the street. This is followed in the sequel by the complications Doris faces in marrying her returning serviceman sweetheart, who wants to delay the wedding until he can put aside some money. The musical numbers in *On Moonlight Bay* include the title song by Percy Wenrich and Edward Madden, "Till We Meet Again" by Ray Egan and Richard Whiting and "I'm Forever Blowing Bubbles" by Jean Kenbrovin and John W. Kellette. In the follow-up *By the Light of the Silvery Moon,* Day and MacRae sang such songs as "If You Were the Only Girl in the World" by Clifford Grey and Nat D. Ayer, "Ain't We Got Fun" by Gus Kahn and Richard Whiting and the title song by Gus Edwards and Edward Madden.

Penrod and His Twin Brother *see* **Penrod**

Penrod and Sam *see* **Penrod**

Penrod's Double Trouble *see* **Penrod**

694 Penthouse

Based on the novel by Arthur Somers Roche. Story: Rich lawyer Jackson Durant is able to save framed Tom Siddell from being sent to the chair for murdering Mimi Montagne, and Gertie Waxted helps him save himself from murder when he has outlived his usefulness to the underworld.

Cosmopolitan/MGM, 1933 (original). Director: W.S. Van Dyke; screenwriters: Frances Goodrich and Albert Hackett. Cast: Warner Baxter (Jackson Durant), Myrna Loy (Gertie Waxted), Charles Butterworth (Layton), Mae Clarke (Mimi Montagne), Phillips Holmes (Tom Siddell), C. Henry Gordon, Martha Sleeper, Nat Pendleton, George E. Stone, Robert Emmett O'Connor.

• *Society Lawyer* (remake). MGM, 1939. Director: Edwin L. Marin; screenwriters: Frances Goodrich, Albert Hackett, Leo Gordon and Hugo Butler. Cast: Walter Pidgeon (Christopher Durant), Virginia Bruce (Pat Abbott), Leo Carrillo (Tony Gazotti), Lee Bowman (Philip Siddell), Eduardo Ciannelli, Frances Mercer, Ann Morriss, Herbert Mundin, Frank M. Thomas, Edward S. Brophy, Tom Kennedy.

Penthouse is a witty murder comedy-drama, with some of the team that would do it so much better starting the next year with *The Thin Man.* In the second feature-remake, Pidgeon is the lawyer who successfully defends gangster Leo Carrillo, and then is somewhat embarrassed by the number of gangsters who come to him for aid.

The People That Time Forgot *see* **The Land That Time Forgot**

695 Pepe-le-Moko

Based on the novel by Detective Ashelbe (Henri La Barthe). Story: Notorious thief Pepe-le-Moko successfully hides from both the French and native Algerian police in the Casbah, but he is bored with his mistress, Ines, and wishes to return to Paris. He meets lovely Gaby being escorted around the native quarters by police inspector Slimane, who notes with interest the sparks between the two. To lure Pepe out of the Casbah, Slimane informs Maxime, the rich man who is keeping Gaby, about the blossoming romance. Maxime forbids Gaby to visit the Casbah any more. Angry, she leaves to go to her lover, but

A publicity still for Algiers *(United Artists, 1938), a remake of the Jean Gabin French film* Pepe-le-Moko, *shows Sigrid Gurie, Charles Boyer and Hedy Lamarr smiling together, something they never did in the movie.*

Slimane informs her that Pepe has been killed. She then makes plans to leave the city. When Pepe learns that Gaby is sailing that day, he decides to join her, despite the pleas of Ines. Jealous, she informs Slimane of Pepe's plans, and while Pepe is searching for Gaby on the ship, he is arrested and led away in handcuffs. He requests and is granted a final favor from his friendly adversary, Slimane, that he be allowed to watch the ship sail. He sees Gaby on deck, staring towards the Casbah, and yells out her name, but the ship's whistle drowns out his shout. Completely trapped, Pepe stabs himself as the ship sails away.

Paris Films Production, 1937 (original). Director: Julien Duvivier; screenwriters: Julien Duvivier and Henri Jeanson. Cast: Jean Gabin (Pepe-le-Moko), Mireille Balin (Gaby), Lucas Gridoux (Inspector Slimane), Line Noro (Ines), Charles Granval (Maxime), Gabriel Gabrio, Marcel Dalio, Saturnin Fabre, Fernand Charpin.

• ***Algiers*** (remake). United Artists, 1938. Director: John Cromwell; screenwriters: John Howard Lawson and James M. Cain. Cast: Charles Boyer (Pepe-le-Moko), Hedy Lamarr (Gaby), Joseph Calleia (Inspector Slimane), Sigrid Gurie (Ines), Gene Lockhart (Regis), Alan Hale, Johnny Downs, Nina Koshetz, Joan Woodbury, Claudia Dell, Robert Greig, Stanley Fields, Charles D. Brown, Ben Hall.

• ***Casbah*** (remake). Universal Pictures, 1948. Director: John Berry; screenwriters: Ladislaus Bus-Fekete and Arnold Manoff. Cast: Tony Martin (Pepe-le-Moko), Yvonne De Carlo (Ines), Peter Lorre (Slimane), Marta Toren (Gaby), Thomas Gomez (Louvaine), Hugo Haas, Douglas Dick, Katherine Durnham, Herbert Rudley, Virginia Gregg, Gene Walker, Curt Conway.

The French romantic melodrama is modeled on the American gangster film, and many would agree with Graham Greene, who said of the movie, "Perhaps there have been pictures as exciting on the thriller level . . . but I cannot remember one which has succeeded so admirably in raising the thriller to a poetic level." In the first remake, Charles Boyer definitely did not say to Hedy Lamarr, in her first American film, "Come to the Casbah"; they were already there. He did receive a nomination for an Academy Award for Best Actor, and Gene Lockhart was nominated for Best Supporting Actor for his portrayal of a snivelling informer. Neither won, but their performances, as well as those of Lamarr, Calleia and Gurie were certainly first rate. Such cannot be said of the musical version made in 1948 with nonactor Tony Martin as Pepe. It did have a couple of decent songs, namely "For Every Man There's a Woman" and "It Was Written in the Stars," by Harold Arlen and Leo Robin.

696 The Perfect Crime

Based on the novel *The Big Bow Mystery* by Israel Zangwill. Story: The world's leading criminologist, Benson, disappointed in love, becomes a recluse and ponders the "perfect crime." He finally gives into his impulses and kills one Frisbee, leaving absolutely no clues. Two things happen to upset his delight with his cleverness. First, Stella, the woman who jilted him, comes back and Trevor, a former roommate of Frisbee, is convicted on circumstantial evidence of killing the man, and is sentenced to die. His conscience bothering him, Benson confesses to the crime, thus sealing his own doom. Then he wakes up; it was all a dream.

F.B.O. Pictures, 1928 (original). Silent. Director: Bert Glennon; screenwriter: Ewart Adamson. Cast: Clive Brook (Benson), Irene Rich (Stella), Carroll Nye (Trevor), Tully Marshall (Frisbee), Ethel Wales, Gladys McConnell, Edmund Breese.

• ***The Crime Doctor*** (remake). RKO, 1934. Director: John Robertson; screenwriter: Jane Martin. Cast: Otto Kruger (Dan Gifford), Karen Morley (Andra), Nils Asther (Eric Anderson), Judith Wood (Blanche Flynn), William Frawley (Fraser), Donald Crisp, Martin Conroy, J. Farrell MacDonald, Fred Kelsey, G. Pat Collins.

• ***The Perfect Crime*** (remake). Warner Bros., 1946. Director: Don Siegel; screenwriter: Peter Milne. Cast: Sydney Greenstreet (Ex-Scotland Yard Superintendent), Peter Lorre (Victor Emmric), Joan Lorring, George Coulouris, Rosalind Ivan, Paul Cavanaugh.

Zangwill's story of a man obsessed by coming up with the perfect crime has found its way to the screen in three interesting if not totally satisfactory films. In the first remake, criminologist Otto Kruger engineers his perfect crime so as to implicate his wife's lover. In the 1946 version, Greenstreet is a disgraced superintendent of police who plots the perfect murder after being sacked from the force. Lorre is his curious friend, whose inquisitiveness almost results in his death.

Period of Adjustment *see* **The First Year**

Personal Property *see* **Man in Possession**

697 Peter Ibbetson

Based on the novel by George du Maurier and the play by John Nathan Raphael and Constance Collier. Story: Childhood sweethearts Peter Ibbetson and Mimsey meet again as adults and begin a romance. They are separated once again when Peter is convicted of murdering Colonel Ibbetson, an English rake who had adopted Peter when he was a boy. Peter is sentenced to hang, but his sentence is commuted through the influence of Mimsey, who is now the Duchess of Towers. Though he is in prison, their romance continues for 25 years as Mimsey visits him and they share dreams. When Mimsey perishes while rescuing children from a burning orphanage, her soul returns to Peter, and Peter soon joins her in death.

• ***Forever (Peter Ibbetson)*** (remake). Famous Players/Paramount Pictures, 1921. Silent. Director: George Fitzmaurice; screenwriter: Ouida Bergere. Cast: Wallace Reid (Peter Ibbetson), Elsie Ferguson (Mary "Mimsey," Duchess of Towers), Montagu Love (Colonel Ibbetson), George Fawcett (Major Duquense), Dolores Cassinelli (Dolores), Paul McAllister, Elliott Dexter, Jerome Patrick, Barbara Dean, Nell Roy Buck, Charles Eaton.

• ***Peter Ibbetson*** (remake). Paramount Pictures, 1935. Director: Henry Hathaway; screenwriters: Vincent Lawrence and Waldemar Young. Cast: Gary Cooper (Peter Ibbetson), Ann Harding (Mary, Duchess of Towers), John Halliday (Duke of Towers), Ida Lupino (Agnes), Douglas Dumbrille (Colonel Forsythe), Virginia Weidler, Dickie Moore, Doris Lloyd, Elsa Buchanan, Christian Rub, Donald Meek.

The story of the two lovers whose relationship is based on shared dreams was first filmed by Paramount Pictures in 1914. It's a peculiar romantic fantasy but it holds one's interest. In the 1935 remake, Cooper and Harding are childhood sweethearts (as children played by Dickie Moore and Virginia Weidler) who are separated and when they meet again, still have strong feelings for each other, even though she is now married to the Duke of Towers, played by John Halliday. Cooper accidently kills her husband and is sentenced to life in prison, forcing them to construct a dreamworld paradise where he and Harding can be together. When they die, they are reunited in heaven. The critics had mixed reactions to the film, ranging from calling it "A triumph of surrealist thought" (Andre Breton) to *Variety's* "Paramount hopes to sell a picture about dreams, and beauty, and love. It just isn't in the cards."

698 Peter Pan

Based on the play by James M. Barrie. Story: Peter Pan, the boy who never grew up, visits the nursery of the Darling family trying to retrieve his shadow and persuades Wendy and her two brothers, Michael and John, to accompany him to Never Never Land. The presence of Wendy raises the jealousy of Peter's personal fairy, Tinker Bell, who tries to poison Wendy. After a series of adventures, including Peter rescuing the Darling children from the pirate Captain Hook, they all decide to return home, all that is except Peter.

Lasky/Paramount Pictures, 1924 (original). Silent. Director: Herbert Brendon; screenwriter: Willis Goldbeck. Cast: Betty Bronson (Peter Pan), Ernest Torrence (Captain Hook), Cyril Chadwick (Mr. Darling), Esther Ralston (Mrs. Darling), Virginia Browne Faire (Tinker Bell), Mary Brian (Wendy), Anna May Wong (Tiger Lily), Philippe De Lacey (Michael), Jack Murphy (John), George Ali (Nana).

• ***Peter Pan*** (remake). Disney/RKO, 1953. Directors: Hamilton Luske, Clyde Geronimi and Wilfred Jackson; screenwriters: Ted Sears, Bill Peet, Joe Rinaldi, Erdman Penner, Winston Hibler, Milt Banta and Ralph Wright. Cast: voice of Bobby Driscoll (Peter Pan), voice of Kathryn Beaumont (Wendy), voice of Hans Conreid (Capt. Hook/Mr. Darling), voice of Bill Thompson (Smee), voice of Heather Angel (Mrs. Darling), voice of Candy Candido (Indian chief), voice of Paul Collins (Michael), voice of Tommy Luske (John), Tom Conway (Narrator).

Productions of James M. Barrie's delightful fantasy about an orphaned boy, Peter Pan, who wishes never to grow up, and his friend, Wendy, who is about to pass from childhood into the adult world have always been a winner, no matter what the medium, including a smash stage hit with Mary Martin as Peter. These two films were no exceptions, each very successful, both with children and their parents. The Disney animated version, while not on a par with the best work from that studio, is still head and shoulders above any competitor's attempts at telling a classic story through animation. Its charming songs included "You Can Fly, You Can Fly, You Can Fly" and "The Second Star to the Left" by Sammy Cahn and Sammy Fain, and "Never Smile at a Crocodile" by Frank Churchill and Jack Lawrence.

699 The Petrified Forest

Based on the play by Robert E. Sherwood. Story: Disenchanted writer Alan Squier wanders into a small desert cafe in Arizona, where he takes an interest in Gabrielle Maple, a waitress with a poetic nature, who has dreams of escaping her dreary life and going to Paris. The cafe is taken over by the notorious Duke Mantee's gang and Alan, tired of his existence, convinces Duke to kill him, so Gaby will receive the only thing of value he owns, an insurance policy for which he has made her the benefactor. Duke obliges, but he is himself gunned down by the police.

Warner Bros., 1936. Director: Archie Mayo; screenwriters: Charles Kenyon and Delmer Daves. Cast: Leslie Howard (Alan Squier), Bette Davis (Gabrielle Maple), Humphrey Bogart (Duke Mantee), Genevieve Tobin (Mrs. Chisholm), Dick Foran (Boze Hertzlinger), Porter Hall (Jason Maple), Charley Grapewin (Gramp Maple), Paul Harvey (Mr. Chisholm), Joseph Sawyer, Eddie Acuff, Adrian Morris, Nina Compana, Slim Thompson, Gus Leonard.

• ***Escape in the Desert*** (remake). Warner Bros., 1945. Director: Edward A. Blatt; screenwriters: Thomas Job and Marvin Borowsky. Cast: Jean Sullivan (Jane), Philip Dorn (Philip Artveld), Irene Manning (Mrs. Lora Tedder), Helmut Dantine (Captain Becker), Alan Hale (Dr. Orville Tedder), Samuel S. Hinds, Bill Kennedy, Kurt Krueger, Rudolph Anders, Hans Schumm, Blayney Lewis.

The motion picture adaptation of Robert E. Sherwood's play has received a great deal more praise than it probably deserves. It's a very stagey piece with a great deal more talk than action, and the talk is not particularly profound or interesting. Leslie Howard, for all his talent, plays the bored traveller a bit too boringly. Bette Davis' performance is satisfactory but not outstanding. Humphrey Bogart, who had played the role of Duke Mantee on Broadway with Leslie Howard as Squier, was cast in the movie at the insistance of Howard, and did get a great deal of recognition in the role. Although it did not, as is commonly believed, make him a star, he was offered more interesting roles after his portrayal of Mantee. He had made quite a few movies and stage appearances as a second romantic lead, prior to this appearance. His real break in movies came when he filled in for George Raft who turned down roles such as *High Sierra* (1941) and *The Maltese Falcon* (1941).

The remake, which is only remembered because it is a slightly disguised version of *The Petrified Forest*, is the story of a group of escaped Nazi prisoners of war, on their way to Mexico, who take over a small desert inn, terrorizing the patrons and owners. The hero of the piece, Philip Dorn, is a Dutch flier hitchhiking his way across America. This melodrama has next to nothing to say about anything of significance.

Pettigrew's Girl *see* **The Shopworn Angel**

700 Peyton Place

Based on the novel by Grace Metalious. Story: The sleepy little Eastern town of Peyton Place is a hotbed of sexual activity, perversions and frustrations. The central characters are Constance MacKenzie, a frigid divorcee, her repressed and alienated daughter, Alison, sexy high school tramp Betty Anderson, rich, confused Rodney Harrington, Norman Page, whose sexual identity is not certain, poor put-upon Selena Cross, the object of her pappy Lucas' desire, and other assorted town folks with not-too-well-kept secrets, mostly dealing with their sexual preferences. The climactic event in the film is Selena Cross's trial for killing her incestuous stepfather.

Twentieth Century–Fox, 1957 (original). Director: Mark Robson; screenwriter: John Michael Hayes. Cast: Lana Turner (Constance MacKenzie), Hope Lange (Selena Cross), Lee Phillips (Michael Rossi), Lloyd Nolan (Dr. Swain), Arthur Kennedy (Lucas Cross), Russ Tamblyn (Norman Page), Diana Varsi (Alison MacKenzie), Terry Moore (Betty Anderson), Barry Coe (Rodney Harrington), Betty Field, David Nelson, Leon Ames, Bill Lundmark, Mildred Dunnock, Lorne Greene.

• ***Return to Peyton Place*** (sequel). Twentieth Century–Fox, 1961. Director:

A party guest's joke meets with mixed reactions from the young people of Peyton Place *(20th Century–Fox, 1957). Note in particular Barry Coe, center, Diane Varsi and Terry Moore to his left, and Russ Tamblyn in the back.*

Jose Ferrer; screenwriter: Ronald Alexander. Cast: Carol Lynley (Alison MacKenzie), Jeff Chandler (Lewis Jackman), Eleanor Parker (Connie), Mary Astor (Roberta Carter), Robert Sterling (Mike Rossi), Luciana Paluzzi (Raffaella), Tuesday Weld (Selena Cross), Brett Halsey, Gunnar Hellstrom, Kenneth MacDonald, Bob Crane.

Viewers of television series such as *Dallas, Falcon Crest,* and *The Colbys* may wonder what all the fuss was about. These movies are tame in their subject matter, compared to what is portrayed on prime time TV soap operas today. But when Grace Metalious' novel first came out in the fifties, it was considered scandalous and prurient, especially since it was written by a woman, who shouldn't be thinking these things, let alone writing about them. Nevertheless, the book became a best-seller, as everyone felt compelled to read what they were condemning as pornography.

The films themselves were watered-downed adaptations with not much of the passion and sexual excitement of the novel. The casting ran from adequate in the cases of Arthur Kennedy, Russ Tamblyn and Hope Lange to horrible in the cases of Lee Phillips, Terry Moore and Barry Coe. About in the middle fell Lana Turner and Diana Varsi. Nevertheless, the film received nine Academy Award nominations, for Best Picture, Best Director, Best Actress (Turner), Best

Left to right: *Tuesday Weld, Carol Lynley, Brett Halsey and Jeff Chandler seem to be discussing their dates in this scene from* Return to Peyton Place *(20th Century–Fox, 1961).*

Supporting Actor (Kennedy and Tamblyn), Best Supporting Actress (Lange and Varsi), Best Screenplay (John Michael Hayes) and Best Cinematography (William Mellor), and in a rarity came away without a single Oscar.

The sequel, not surprisingly, garnered no award nominations, being merely a continuation of the gossipy but not too interesting story of the lives of some of the characters encountered in the original. *Peyton Place* had a popular (if not critical) and successful run on television in the sixties, giving experience and exposure to some young performers who would go on to movie careers of varying success. These included Mia Farrow, Ryan O'Neal, and Barbara Parkins.

The Phantom Fiend *see* **The Lodger**

The Phantom Killer *see* **The Sphinx**

701 The Philadelphia Story

Based on the play by Donald Ogden Stewart. Story: Rich, beautiful society woman Tracy Lord is about to be married for the second time. Scandal-sheet publisher Sidney Kidd threatens to run a damaging expose of the exploits of Tracy's father, Seth Lord, unless he is given an exclusive on the wedding. He arranges through Tracy's former husband, C.K. Dexter Haven, to have writer Mike Connor and photographer Liz Imbrie cover the wedding. Tracy, a strong-willed but unforgiving type, finds the interruption, by her ex and the magazine employees, of her careful plans to marry self-made and ambitious George Kittredge, most perplexing and confusing. Her resolve that Kittredge is the perfect man for her is compromised by her attraction to Mike Connor and her lingering feelings for Dexter. Events of the weekend of the wedding prove to her that she had chosen the right man the first time and she remarries Dexter.

MGM, 1940 (original). Director: George Cukor; screenwriter: Donald Ogden Stewart. Cast: Katharine Hepburn (Tracy Lord), Cary Grant (C.K. Dexter Haven), James Stewart (Macaulay "Mike" Connor), Ruth Hussey (Liz Imbrie), John Howard (George Kittredge), Roland Young (Uncle Willie), Virginia Weidler (Dinah Lord), Henry Daniell (Sidney Lord), John Halliday (Seth Lord), Mary Nash (Margaret Lord), Lionel Pape, Rex Evans, Lee Phelps, Dorothy Fay.

• ***High Society*** (remake). MGM, 1956. Director: Charles Walters; screenwriter: John Patrick. Cast: Grace Kelly (Tracy Lord), Bing Crosby (C.K. Dexter Haven), Frank Sinatra (Mike Connor), Celeste Holm (Liz Imbrie), John Lund (George Kittredge), Louis Calhern (Uncle Willie), Sidney Blackmer (Seth Lord), Louis Armstrong (himself), Margalo Gilmore (Mrs. Lord), Lydia Reed (Caroline Lord), Gordon Richards, Richard Garrick.

Certainly one of Hollywood's brightest comedies, *The Philadelphia Story* was blessed with a superb cast, each giving marvelously entertaining portrayals. Katharine Hepburn had originated the role of Tracy Lord on Broadway and wisely acquired the movie rights to the play. She was perfection as the stuffy heiress who learned a little humility and more importantly, something about herself.

Tracy Lord had to endure comments such as the following from her ex-husband: "You'll never be a first-class human being or a first-class woman until you've learned to have some regard for human frailty. It's a pity your own foot can't slip a little sometime, but your sense of divinity wouldn't allow that. This goddess must and shall remain intact," and the following stinging rebuke from her erring father: "You have a good mind, Tracy. You have a pretty face, a fine disciplined body that does what you tell it to do. You have everything it takes to make a lovely woman—except the one essential: an understanding heart. Without it, you might just as well be made of bronze." Tracy does slip, believing that while intoxicated she had gone to bed with Mike Connor, and she also finds that she has an understanding heart, almost unused.

Opposite, top: *Katharine Hepburn remarries her ex-husband, Cary Grant, at the end of* The Philadelphia Story. *Looking almost as shocked as the bride and groom are Jimmy Stewart and Ruth Hussey (between Jimmy and Cary). Less impressed with the ceremonies is father of the bride, John Halliday, behind and to the left of Stewart.* Bottom: *Frank Sinatra recovers from a sock on the jaw, delivered by Bing Crosby, to save Frank from a worse beating at the hands of John Lund in* High Society *(MGM, 1956), the musical remake of* The Philadelphia Story.

The film received six Academy Award nominations: Best Picture, Best Director, Best Actress, Best Actor, Best Supporting Actress and Best Screenplay, but only Jimmy Stewart took home an Oscar.

The musical remake, while not as magical as the original, was at least entertaining and contained much of the dialogue of the original. The setting had been moved from Philadelphia to Newport, Rhode Island, but the plot is essentially the same, with ex-husband Crosby returning home from the Newport Jazz festival at the same time his ex, Grace Kelly, whom he still loves, is on the verge of marrying John Lund. Her father's philandering forces her to accept coverage of her wedding by writer Frank Sinatra and photographer Celeste Holm for the scandal magazine *Spy*. The Cole Porter songs included, "Now You Have Jazz" featuring Crosby and Louie Armstrong, "Who Wants to Be a Millionaire?" sung by Sinatra and Holm, and the million-selling hit "True Love" sung by Crosby with Kelly helping out.

Pick a Star *see* **Free and Easy**

Pickpocket *see* **Crime and Punishment**

702 The Pickwick Papers

Based on the novel by Charles Dickens. Story: Mr. Pickwick, jovial chairman of the Pickwick Club, sets out on a tour of England with fellow club members Tupman, Winkle and Snodgrass. They meet one Jingle, who gets them into all kinds of scrapes, including a phony breach-of-promise suit against Mr. Pickwick which causes him to be thrown into debtor's prison. But all ends well in this happy Dickens classic.

• ***The Pickwick Papers*** (remake). Vitgraph Co., Great Britain, 1913. Silent. Director and screenwriter: Larry Trimble. Cast: John Bunny (Samuel Pickwick), James Pryor (Mr. Tupman), Sidney Hunt (Mr. Snodgrass), Fred Hornby (Mr. Winkle), Arthur Ricketts (Mr. Jingle), H.P. Owen (Sam Weller), George Temple (the fat boy), Minnie Rayner (Mrs. Budger), Arthur White (Dr. Slammer).

• ***The Adventures of Mr. Pickwick*** (remake). Ideal, Great Britain, 1921. Silent. Director: Thomas Bentley; screenwriters: Eliot Stannard and E.A. Baughan. Cast: Fred Volpe (Samuel Pickwick), Mary Brough (Mrs. Bardell), Bransby Williams (Sgt. Buzfuz), Ernest Thesiger (Mr. Jingle), Kathleen Vaughan (Arabella Allen), Joyce Dearsley (Isabella Wardle), Arthur Cleave (Mr. Winkle), Athene Seyler (Rachel Wardle), John Kelt (Mr. Snodgrass), Hubert Woodward, Norman Page, Thomas Weguelin, Townsend Whitley, Harry Gilbey, John E. Zecchini.

• ***The Pickwick Papers*** (remake). Renown, Great Britain, 1952. Director and screenwriter: Noel Langley. Cast: James Hayter (Samuel Pickwick), Nigel Patrick (Mr. Jingle), James Donald (Mr. Winkle), Kathleen Harrison (Rachel Warde), Hermione Baddeley (Martha Bardell), Joyce Grenfell (Mrs. Leo Hunter), Hermione Gingold (Miss Tompkins), Donald Wolfit (Sgt. Buzfuz), Harry Fowler (Sam Weller), Alexander Gauge (Tracy Tupman), Lionel Murton (Augustus Snodgrass), Sam Costa, George Robey, Mary Merrall, Athene Seyler.

The Dickens story appeared on screen in 1900, 1914 and 1970 as well. The 1952 film struck a nice note and a mood that seemed properly Dickensian, with James Hayter a splendid Pickwick. The other performers in the very large cast handled their roles quite nicely and seemed to enter into the spirit of the piece, making the movie on the whole thoroughly enjoyable.

703 The Picture of Dorian Gray

Based on the novel by Oscar Wilde. Story: Dorian Gray is vain about his good looks and youthful appearance. To maintain these while living a life of debauchery encouraged by millionaire Lord Henry Wotton, Gray sells his soul. As he continues his sexual excesses with numerous lovers, prostitutes and wives of friends, his youthful appearance and vigor remains constant over the years, but his portrait, painted by Basil Hallward, continuously changes, showing the effects of Gray's hedonistic living. Angered by the gross appearance of his portrait, Gray kills the artist and slashes his likeness. As he stabs the painting, he feels the fatal blow. The portrait reverts to the original youthful Gray, while Dorian, as he is dying, slowly changes into the appearance of the once grotesque portrait.

• ***The Picture of Dorian Gray*** (remake). New York Motion Picture Company, 1913. Silent. Director: Phillips Smalley. Cast: Wallace Reid (Dorian Gray), Lois Weber (Sibyl Vane), Phillips Smalley (Lord Henry Wotton).

• ***The Picture of Dorian Gray*** (remake). Barker-Neptune Pictures, 1916. Silent. Director: Fred W. Durrant; screenwriter: Rowland Talbot. Cast: Henry Victor (Dorian Gray), Jack Jordan (Lord Henry Wotton), Pat O'Malley (Sybil Vane), Sydney Bland (Basil Hallward), A.B. Imeson (Satan), Douglas Cox, Dorothy Fane, Miriam Ferris.

• ***The Picture of Dorian Gray*** (remake). MGM, 1945. Director and screenwriter: Albert Lewin. Cast: Hurd Hatfield (Dorian Gray), George Sanders (Lord Henry Wotton), Angela Lansbury (Sybil Vane), Peter Lawford (David Stone), Donna Reed (Gladys Hallward), Lionel Gilmore (Basil Hallward), Richard Fraser, Douglas Walton, Morton Lowry, Miles Mander, Lydia Bilbrook, Mary Forbes, Robert Grigg.

"If only the picture could change and I could be always what I am now. For that, I would give anything. Yes, there's nothing in the world I wouldn't give. I'd give my soul for that." With these words, Dorian Gray sealed his fate in this Dr. Jekyll and Mr. Hyde–like story, which was also filmed in Denmark in 1910 and 1913; in Russia in 1915 and by Thanhauser Pictures in the United States the same year; in Great Britain in 1916; in Germany and Hungary in 1917; and in the United States in 1970 as *The Secret of Dorian Gray;* again in 1975 with the original title and in 1978 as *Take Off.*

The 1945 film won an Academy Award for Harry Standing for Best Photography and a nomination for Angela Lansbury as Best Actress. The star of the show, however, was George Sanders, who not only had the best lines, but delivered them in his famous haughty and condescending way, making for a splendid characterization. Hurt Hatfield was also excellent as the Victorian gentleman whose portrait showed the ravages of his horrid lifestyle. Hatfield had few good roles in films, this being his best. Some have suggested that his good looks were too much of the Tyrone Power type and only one such star was needed. It was good to see Hatfield in the role of the old grandfather in the 1986 production of *Crimes of the Heart.*

704 Picture Snatcher

Based on a story by Danny Ahearn. Story: Danny is a reformed hoodlum, just released from prison, who joins a scurillous tabloid called the *New York Graphic-News.* He specializes in getting sensationalist pictures such as the electrocution of a female murderer at Sing Sing, using a camera fastened around his ankle. His behavior outrages everyone save his editor and Patricia, the girl he loves, although her father, an honest cop, does take a shot at him.

Warner Bros., 1933 (original). Director: Lloyd Bacon; screenwriters: Allen Rivkin and P.J. Wolfson. Cast: James Cagney (Danny), Patricia Ellis (Patricia), Alice White (Alison), Ralph Bellamy (McLean), Robert E. O'Connor (Casey Nolan), George Pat Collins, Tom Wilson, Ralf Harolde, Robert Barrat.

• ***Escape from Crime*** (remake). Warner Bros., 1942. Director: D. Ross Lederman; screenwriter: Raymond L. Schrock. Cast: Richard Travis (Red O'Hara), Julie Bishop (Molly O'Hara), Jackie C. Gleason, Frank Wilcox, Rex Williams.

Cagney played Cagney in the original; tough, pugnacious and sarcastic. Other than Jimmy the only other performer to show any spark was Alice White as a sob-sister reporter. The remake was a real no-name film, meant for the second end of a double bill at a children's matinee. Richard Travis was the ex-con who gets a job with a newspaper as a photographer and wins a pardon for his past crimes when his work puts away his former gang. Jackie Gleason had a role as a convict in the picture about a picture taker.

Pier 13 ***see*** **Me and My Gal**

Pimpernel Smith ***see*** **The Scarlet Pimpernel**

705 The Pink Panther

Based on a screenplay by Maurice Richlin and Blake Edwards. Story: Sir Charles Lytton, who in reality is the famous jewel thief the Phantom, plans to steal the priceless Pink Panther ruby owned by beautiful Princess Dala. Inspector Clouseau has been chasing the Phantom for 15 years without becoming aware that his wife is Lytton's mistress and accomplice. After a series of enjoyable pratfalls, chases and hiding of lovers by Simone Clouseau, the Pink Panther is stolen, not by Sir Charles but by Dala herself, because she fears that the revolutionaries who have taken over her country will be sustained in their claim to the jewel. Nevertheless, Sir Charles is brought to trial as the Phantom, but Simone and Dala conspire to have Inspector Clouseau himself believed to be the Phantom.

United Artists, 1964 (original). Director: Blake Edwards; screenwriters: Edwards and Maurice Richlin. Cast: David Niven (Sir Charles Lytton), Peter

Sellers (Inspector Jacques Clouseau), Capucine (Simone Clouseau), Robert Wagner (George Lytton), Claudia Cardinale (Princess Dala), Fran Jeffries, Brenda De Banzie, James Lamphier, Colin Gordon, John Le Mesurier, Guy Thomajan.

• ***A Shot in the Dark*** (sequel). United Artists, 1964. Director: Blake Edwards; screenwriters: Edwards and William Peter Blatty. Cast: Peter Sellers (Inspector Clouseau), Elke Sommer (Maria Gambrelli), George Sanders (Benjamin Ballon), Herbert Lom (Chief Inspector Charles Dreyfus), Tracy Reed, Graham Stark, Andre Maranne, Douglas Wilmer, Martin Benson.

• ***Inspector Clouseau*** (sequel). United Artists, 1968. Director: Bud Yorkin; screenwriters: Tom and Frank Waldman. Cast: Alan Arkin (Inspector Clouseau), Delia Boccardo (Lisa Morrel), Frank Finlay (Superintendent Weaver), Patrick Cargill (Sir Charles Braithwaite), Beryl Reid, Barry Foster, Clive Francis.

• ***The Return of the Pink Panther*** (sequel). United Artists, 1974. Director: Blake Edwards; screenwriters: Edwards and Frank Waldman. Cast: Peter Sellers (Inspector Clouseau), Christopher Plummer (Sir Charles Litton), Catherine Schell (Claudia Litton), Herbert Lom (Chief Inspector Dreyfus), Burt Kwouk (Cato), Peter Arne, Gregorie Aslan, Peter Jeffrey, David Lodge, Eric Pohlmann, Andre Maranne.

• ***The Pink Panther Strikes Again*** (sequel). United Artists, 1976. Director: Blake Edwards; screenwriters: Edwards and Frank Waldman. Cast: Peter Sellers (Inspector Clouseau), Herbert Lom (Dreyfus), Colin Blakely (Alec Drummond), Leonard Rossiter (Quinlan), Lesley-Anne Down (Olga), Burt Kwouk, Andre Maranne, Marne Maitland, Richard Vernon.

• ***Revenge of the Pink Panther*** (sequel). United Artists, 1978. Director: Blake Edwards; screenwriters: Edwards, Ron Clark and Frank Waldman. Cast: Peter Sellers (Inspector Clouseau), Herbert Lom (Dreyfus), Dyan Cannon (Simone Legree), Robert Webber (Douvier), Burt Kwouk, Paul Stewart, Robert Loggia, Graham Stark, Sue Lloyd.

Like the "Thin Man" series, the title of the first film in "The Pink Panther" series was carried on into the others, even though it had nothing to do with the new plots or characters. Unlike many films that inspired a number of sequels, the quality of the pictures did not suffer until Blake Edwards unwisely decided to release *The Trail of the Pink Panther*, using some outtakes of Sellers from previous films with additional footage of the likes of David Niven, Capucine and Herbert Lom. The result was not a memorial to the late, great comic actor, but a mishmash in poor taste. Of the sequels, the best seems to be the 1974 film in which the Pink Panther is once again stolen and bungling Inspector Clouseau is brought in to solve the case. Sellers has by now perfected his role as an insufferable ass who does not realize what a ridiculous figure he is, and because of his unwavering confidence in his brilliance, charm and deductive skills, his reactions to anything that goes wrong—which is just about everything—are priceless.

The Pink Panther Strikes Again *see* **The Pink Panther**

A Place in the Sun *see* **An American Tragedy**

Platinum High School *see* **Bad Day at Black Rock**

Play the Game *see* **Leave the Bed**

The Pleasure Seekers *see* **Three Coins in the Fountain**

Le Plombier Amoureux *see* **The Cardboard Lover**

Pocketful of Miracles *see* **Lady for a Day**

706 The Pointing Finger

Based on the novel by *Rita.* Story: Captain Jasper Mallory has his half brother kidnapped so that he himself will become the heir to an earldom. Complications arise and things go wrong with his plot.

Stoll, Great Britain, 1922 (original). Silent. Director: George Ridgwell; screenwriter: Paul Rooff. Cast: Milton Rosmer (Lord Rollestone/Earl Edensore), Madge Stuart (Lady Susan Silchester), J.R. Tozer (Captain Jasper Mallory), Teddy Arundell, Irene Rooke, James English, Norman Whalley, Gibb McLaughlin.

• ***The Pointing Finger*** (remake). Real Art/Radio, Great Britain, 1933. Director: George Pearson; screenwriter: H. Fowler Mear. Cast: John Stuart (Lord Rollestone), Viola Keats (Lady Mary Stuart), Leslie Perrins (Hon. James Malloy), Michael Hogan, A. Bromley Davenport, Henrietta Watson, D.J. Williams, Clare Greet.

In the remake of this melodrama, Leslie Perrins is the scoundrel who plans to have his cousin John Stuart disposed of, so he will inherit the earldom, but you don't really think he's going to get away with it, now, do you?

707 Police Academy

Based on a screenplay by Neal Israel, Pat Proft and Hugh Wilson. Story: When the mayor of an American city lifts all eligibility requirements for admission to the police academy, the new class consists of losers of every stripe. The officer in charge of them does his best to get them to drop out, but as would be expected in dreary material like this they become heroes when called upon to act as real cops.

Maslansky/Ladd/Warners, 1984 (original). Director: Hugh Wilson; screenwriters: Neal Israel, Pat Proft and Hugh Wilson. Cast: Steve Guttenberg (Carey Mahoney), Kim Cattrall (Karen Thompson), G.W. Bailey (Lt. Harris), Bubba Smith (Moses Hightower), Georgina Spelvin (Hooker), George Gaynes, Donovan Scott, Michael Winslow, Andrew Rubin, David Graf.

• ***Police Academy 2: Their First Assignment*** (sequel). Warner Bros., 1985. Director: Jerry Paris; screenwriters: Barry Blaustein and David Sheffield. Cast: Steve Guttenberg (Carey Mahoney), Bubba Smith (Hightower), David Graf (Tackleberry), Michael Winslow (Larvell Jones), Bruce Mahler (Doug Fackler),

Marion Ramsey (Laverne Hooks), Colleen Camp (Kirkland), Howard Hesseman (Pete Lassard), Art Metrano (Lt. Mauser), George Gaynes, Bob Goldthwait, Julie Brown, Peter Van Norden.

Not satisfied with one inept sequel to the story about inept cops, the producers came out with *Police Academy III: Back in Training* in 1986. Whereas the first film was moderately amusing in places and the second produced a chuckle or two, the third has all the humor of a mass funeral. The group of misfit cops rally around their muddle-headed mentor, George Gaynes, when the governor proposes to close one of the state's two police academies. The other is headed by nasty Art Metrano.

Police Academy 2: Their First Assignment *see* **Police Academy**

Police Academy III: Back in Training *see* **Police Academy**

708 Polly of the Circus

Based on the play by Margaret Mayo. Story: Polly, a bareback rider with a circus, falls in love with the local minister when she is injured trying a difficult trick. The congregation doesn't approve of circus people and besides, the deacon's daughter has her cap set for the minister. In addition to resolving this little triangle, the picture deals with the love of another circus member for Polly, and a horse named Bingo that wins a bit of money for her, just in time.

Goldwyn, 1917 (original). Silent. Director: Laurence Trimble; screenwriter: Margaret Mayo. Cast: Mae Marsh (Polly), Vernon Steele (Rev. John Douglas), Charles Eldridge (Toby, the Clown), Wellington Playter (Big Jim), George Trimble (Barker), Lucille Laverne (Mandy), Dick Lee (Hasty), Charles Riegel (Deacon Strong), Lucille Satterthwaite, J.B. Hollis, Helen Salinger, Isabel Vernon, Viola Compton.

• ***Polly of the Circus*** (remake). Metro, 1932. Director: Alfred Santell; screenwriter: Carey Wilson. Cast: Marion Davies (Polly), Clark Gable (Rev. John Hartley), C. Aubrey Smith (Rev. James Northcott), Raymond Hatton (Downey), David Landau (Beef), Ruth Selwyn (Mitzi), Maude Eburne, Little Billy, Guinn Williams, Clark Marshall.

The silent film was the first production of Samuel Goldwyn and was well received by both critics and audiences. The remake has young preacher Clark Gable marrying circus trapeze artist Marion Davies, but losing his church and parishioners. This leads Davies to consider suicide to free him, by missing the bar in her act when she does a dangerous somersault. Gable looks uncomfortable in a role which is clearly not for him.

Poppy *see* **Sally of the Sawdust**

709 Pollyanna

Based on the novel by Eleanor H. Potter. Story: When she loses her father, motherless Pollyanna comes to live in the home of a wealthy maiden aunt,

Polly. The little girl has been taught by her Dad always to find things to be glad about. Gradually her cheerful nature wins over everyone in the village. The wealthy man who loved her mother will do anything Pollyanna wants, including adopting her little orphaned boy friend. He's the first on hand to help when she is injured trying to save a child in an automobile accident. This reunites Aunt Polly with the doctor, a former suitor. When the girl recovers and finds she can walk again, everybody's happy.

United Artists, 1920 (original). Silent. Director: Paul Powell; screenwriter: uncredited. Cast: Mary Pickford (Pollyanna), J. Wharton James (Rev. Whittier), Katherine Griffith (Aunt Polly Harrington), William Courtleigh (John Pendleton), Herbert Prior (Dr. Chilton), Jerome Eddy (Nancy), George Berrell (Tom), Howard Ralston (Jimmie Bean).

• ***Pollyanna*** (remake). Disney/Buena Vista, 1960. Director and screenwriter: David Swift. Cast: Jane Wyman (Aunt Polly), Richard Egan (Dr. Edmond Chilton), Hayley Mills (Pollyanna), Karl Malden (Rev. Paul Ford), Nancy Olson (Nancy Furman), Adolphe Menjou (Mr. Pendergast), Donald Crisp (Mayor Karl Warren), Agnes Moorehead (Mrs. Snow), Kevin Corcoran (Jimmy Bean), James Drury, Reta Shaw, Leora Dana.

The remake of the Mary Pickford feature was a personal triumph for little Hayley Mills, who makes the tale of the perpetually good-natured and optimistic 12-year-old girl almost palatable. Unfortunately, the sticky sweet concoction is whipped up by the Disney people, who rely too much on cuteness and sentimentality.

710 Porky's

Based on a story by Bob Clark. Story: Basically it's a vulgar and ghastly look at a Florida high school nerd of the early fifties who is trying to get laid. In the process he and his friends wreck a brothel in the next county owned by a pig of a man called Porky. Our lad finally achieves his quest with the local "good time was had by all" girl. Tha-a-a-a-t's all, folks.

Astral Bellvue Pathe, Canada, 1981 (original). Director and screenwriter: Bob Clark. Cast: Dan Monahan, Kim Cattrall, Mark Herrier, Wyatt Knight, Roger Wilson, Scott Columby, Art Hindle, Wayne Maunder, Alex Karras, Nancy Parsons, Susan Clark.

• ***Porky's II: The Next Day*** (sequel). Astral Bellvue Pathe, Canada, 1983. Director and screenwriter: Bob Clark. Cast: Dan Monahan, Wyatt Knight, Mark Herrier, Roger Wilson, Kaki Hunter, Scott Columby, Nancy Parsons, Edward Winter.

• ***Porky's Revenge*** (sequel). Astral Bellvue Pathe, Canada, 1985. Director and screenwriter: James Komack. Cast: Dan Monahan, Wyatt Knight, Tony Ganios, Mark Herrier, Kaki Hunter, Scott Columby.

How can one adequately describe the stupidity of these three movies? Some might suggest that one can't argue with success: the films made money—a lot of money. But that's sad too. How gullible can the public be? Pretty gullible! In the first sequel, the same bunch of raunchy boys thwart the plans of a prejudiced redneck preacher and his followers from closing down a Shakespeare festival. In the final (we hope) film, Porky is back with a floating brothel and the boys decide if they can't make use of its services then they should wreck it as well. It's depressing to think that these films might accurately portray the male adolescent of some period in time. It's not that one objects to their preoccupation with sex, that's probably natural. It's just that in trying to make it dirty, they've only succeeded in making it dull.

Porky's Revenge *see* **Porky's**

Porky's II: The Next Day *see* **Porky's**

Port of Seven Seas *see* **Fanny**

711 The Poseidon Adventure

Based on the novel by Paul Gallico. Story: The tale begins aboard the ocean liner *Poseidon* during a New Year's Eve party. A huge tidal wave capsizes the ship, and surviving passengers who were on the upper decks now find themselves trapped at the "bottom" of the sinking hulk. Their only chance is to climb "up" to the bottom. The little party that sets out on this adventure is decimated one by one as they bicker among themselves, trying to figure out who among them has the right idea about what they should do. They die cowardly, stupidly and courageously, and a few reach the promised land.

Twentieth Century–Fox, 1972 (original). Director: Ronald Neame; screenwriters: Wendell Mayes and Stirling Silliphant. Cast: Gene Hackman (Rev. Frank Scott), Ernest Borgnine (Rogo), Red Buttons (Martin), Carol Lynley (Nonnie), Roddy McDowall (Acres), Stella Stevens (Linda Rogo), Shelley Winters (Belle Rosen), Jack Albertson, Leslie Nielson, Pamela Sue Martin.

• ***Beyond the Poseidon Adventure*** (sequel). Warner Bros., 1979. Director: Irwin Allen; screenwriter: Nelson Gidding. Cast: Michael Caine (Mike Turner), Sally Field (Celeste Whitman), Telly Savalas (Capt. Svevo Stefan), Peter Boyle (Frank Mazzetti), Jack Warden (Harold Meredith), Shirley Knight, Shirley Jones, Karl Malden, Slim Pickens, Veronica Hamel.

As implausible as it was (theoretically, tidal waves should not be able to capsize a ship), the soap-opera disaster film held one's interest. As for the sequel, it's amazing that so many otherwise talented actors and actresses would all come up with their career-worst performance in the same picture. To top that coincidence is the story. The first to reach the upside down ship are there to plunder, not rescue the passengers.

Possessed *see* **The Mirage**

712 The Postman Always Rings Twice

Based on the novel by James M. Cain. Story: Drifter Frank Chambers stops at a roadside cafe and gas station and accepts Nick Smith's kind offer of a job. He's even happier he accepted when he sees Nick's young sexy wife, Cora. She's bored with her older husband and her life. Sparks fly between the two, but for awhile they play it cool. When they can no longer resist their passion, they decide that Nick has to be killed so that Cora can get his money and the cafe. Their first attempt to bump him off is unsuccessful, but ultimately they get it accomplished with Cora driving, Nick getting drunk next to her and Frank striking from the back seat. The two are put on trial for the murder, but get off due to a clever ploy by their attorney. While still feeling the hots for each other, they no longer trust each other after their behavior at their trial. Cora is killed in an automobile accident and Frank is convicted of murdering her, although he is not legally responsible. He goes to his execution in the sure knowledge that he is paying for his crime against Nick, not for killing the woman he loved.

• ***The Postman Always Rings Twice*** (remake). MGM, 1946. Director: Tay Garnett; screenwriters: Harry Ruskin and Niven Busch. Cast: Lana Turner (Cora Smith), John Garfield (Frank Chambers), Cecil Kellaway (Nick Smith), Hume Cronyn (Arthur Keats), Audrey Totter (Madge Garland), Leon Ames (District Attorney Kyle Sackett), Alan Redd, Jeff York, Charles Williams, Cameron Grant, Wally Cassell.

• ***The Postman Always Rings Twice*** (remake). Northstar International, 1981. Director: Bob Rafelson; screenwriter: David Mamet. Cast: Jack Nicholson (Frank Chambers), Jessica Lange (Cora Papadakis), John Colicos (Nick Papadakis), Michael Lerner (Katz), John P. Ryan (Kennedy), Anjelica Huston (Madge).

The James M. Cain story was also filmed in France in 1939 as *Le Dernier Tourant* and in Italy in 1942 as *Ossessione.* The first version appears to have been made hoping to be another *Double Indemnity,* but it took too many switches and turns getting to its climax to be much of a threat for the superior *film noir.* Garfield gave Turner some hot looks and Lana was a cool goddess who warmed up John, but in the 1981 film, Nicholson and Lange fornicated on a table where everyone could see. Both films are about equally interesting, with the greater explicitness of the latter not making for better melodrama.

713 The Prince and the Pauper

Based on the novel by Mark Twain. Story: In Tudor England, young Edward VI trades places with street urchin Tom Canty, his exact double. The boys not only exchange roles but dangers as well. There are schemers in the court plotting to prevent Edward from assuming the throne, and those in town, including Tom's beastly father, who would kill him for not being a productive criminal. The boys' champion is Miles Hendon, who finally gets things straightened out and sees to it that the villains get their just deserts.

• ***The Prince and the Pauper*** (remake). Warner Bros., 1937. Director: William Keighley; screenwriter: Laird Doyle. Cast: Errol Flynn (Miles Hendon), Billy and Bobby Mauch (Edward VI/Tom), Claude Rains (Duke of Norfold), Montagu Love, Barton MacLane, Henry Stephenson, Alan Hale, Eric Portman, Lionel Pape, Halliwell Hobbes.

• ***Crossed Swords*** (remake). International Films, 1977. Director: Richard Fleischer; screenwriter: George MacDonald Fraser. Cast: Oliver Reed (Miles Hendon), Raquel Welch (Lady Edith), Mark Lester (Edward/Tom), Ernest

Borgnine (John Canty), George C. Scott, Rex Harrison, Charlton Heston, David Hemmings.

The Twain story was also filmed in 1909, 1915, 1920, 1922, 1923, 1943, 1962, 1966, 1968, 1972 and 1977. The Flynn version was one of the charming Irishman's least enjoyable swashbucklers. It lacks credibility and there's not enough excitement to overcome the ho-hum story. The remake had several big names in almost cameo roles but this didn't do much for the production. It wasn't interesting enough to make a good adventure yarn. The Mauch twins and Mark Lester were fine as Edward and his double, but their characters are difficult to care much about.

The Prince of Thieves *see* **Robin Hood**

714 Princess O'Hara

Based on a story by Damon Runyan. Story: Vic Toledo tries to help the four children of a taxi driver who was killed. One of the four, nicknamed Princess O'Hara, "steals" a racehorse and is threatened with a long jail stretch, but the horse wins the big race and somehow or other the charges get lost, as the authorities are too busy with more menacing criminals.

Universal Pictures, 1935 (original). Director: David Burton; screenwriters: Doris Malloy and Harry Clark. Cast: Jean Parker (Princess O'Hara), Chester Morris (Vic Toledo), Leon Errol (Last Card Louie), Vince Barnett (Fingers), Henry Armetta (Spidoni), Verna Hillie, Ralph Remley, Dorothy Gray.

• ***It Ain't Hay*** (remake). Universal Pictures, 1943. Director: Earle C. Kenton; screenwriters: Allen Boretz and John Grant. Cast: Bud Abbott (Grover), Lou Costello (Wilbur Hoolihan), Grace McDonald (Kitty McClain), Cecil Kellaway (King O'Hara), Patsy O'Connor (Peggy, Princess O'Hara), Eugene Pallette, Leighton Noble, Shemp Howard, Samuel S. Hinds, Eddie Quillan.

The story is not one of Damon Runyan's best. The remake is not among Abbott and Costello's best. These comedies have little going for them today, although the remake is still shown on those TV stations which make it a practice of running Abbott and Costello films for the kiddies. Costello attempts to find a horse to replace the one that used to pull Cecil Kellaway's hack. Hearing of one to be given away at the racetrack, he and Abbott pick up the wrong nag. The one they spirit away turns out to be a champion racehorse. The boys go through some absurd antics before Lou finds himself as a jockey in the big race. It could have been funnier. The songs by Harry Revel and Paul Webster include "Hang Your Troubles on a Rainbow."

The Prisoner of the Iron Mask *see* **The Iron Mask**

715 The Prisoner of Zenda

Based on the novel by Anthony Hope and the play by Edward Rose. Story: While vacationing in Ruritania, Rudolf Rassendyll is convinced by Colonel Sapt and Fritz von Tarlenheim to impersonate his cousin and look-alike, Rudolf, shortly to be crowned king of the realm. Rudolf has been drugged by his

Douglas Fairbanks, Jr., explains that he's wise to C. Aubrey Smith's plan to pass off visiting Englishman Ronald Colman as the kidnapped king-to-be of Ruritania in The Prisoner of Zenda *(United Artists, 1937). David Niven gives Doug an "if looks could kill" stare.*

half-brother Michael, Duke of Strelsau, who aspires to the throne and his co-conspirator, Rupert of Hentzau, to prevent the coronation. Sapt has hidden Rudolf at his hunting lodge and drills Rassendyll so he can stand in for his cousin at the ceremonies. Rassendyll falls in love with Rudolf's future queen, Princess Flavia, and she reciprocates, thinking only that her future husband's feelings towards her have changed significantly and for the better. Rudolf is kidnapped from his hunting lodge and is held prisoner in Michael's castle at Zenda. With the aid of Michael's jealous mistress, Antoinette De Mauban, Rassendyll gains access to the castle as Rupert of Hentzau kills Michael in a jealous rage over Antoinette. Rupert deals with Rassendyll, but as Sapt and his soldiers arrive, the sly Rupert escapes. Rassendyll and Flavia realize that their love is impossible as she must marry Rudolf. They part and Rassendyll returns to England.

Famous Players, 1913 (original). Silent. Directors: Edwin S. Porter and Daniel Frohman. Cast: James K. Hackett (Rudolf Rassendyll/King Rudolf V), Beatrice Beckley (Princess Flavia), David Torrence (Duke Michael), Frazer Coulter (Col. Sapt), C.R. Randall (Fritz von Tarlenheim), Walter Hale (Rupert of Henzau), Minna Gale Haynes (Antoinette de Mauban), Frank Shannon, Charles Green, Tom Callahan, Sydney Barrington.

Jane Greer tends wounded Stewart Granger with loving care as James Mason looks on arrogantly in the 1952 MGM *remake of* The Prisoner of Zenda.

• ***The Prisoner of Zenda*** (remake). Metro Pictures, 1922. Director: Rex Ingram; screenwriter: Mary O'Hara. Cast: Lewis Stone (Rudolf Rassendyll/King Rudolf V), Alice Terry (Princess Flavia), Robert Edeson (Col. Sapt), Stuart Holmes (Duke Michael of Strelsau), Ramon Samanyagos (Rupert of Hentzau), Barbara La Marr (Antoinette de Mauban), Malcolm McGregor (Count von Tarlenheim), Edward Connelly, Lois Lee.

• ***The Prisoner of Zenda*** (remake). United Artists, 1937. Directors: John Cromwell and W.S. Van Dyke; screenwriters: John Balderstone, Wells Root and Donald Ogden Stewart. Cast: Ronald Colman (Rudolf Rassendyll/King Rudolf V), Madeleine Carroll (Princess Flavia), Douglas Fairbanks, Jr. (Rupert of Hentzau), Mary Astor (Antoinette de Mauban), Raymond Massey ("Black Michael," Duke of Streslau), C. Aubrey Smith (Col. Sapt), David Niven (Fritz von Tarlenheim), Eleanor Wesselhoeft, Montagu Love, William von Brincken.

• ***The Prisoner of Zenda*** (remake). MGM, 1952. Director: Richard Thorpe; screenwriters: John Balderstone and Noel Langley. Cast: Stewart Granger (Rudolf Rassendyll/King Rudolf V), Deborah Kerr (Princess Flavia), James Mason (Rupert of Hentzau), Jane Greer (Antoinette de Mauban), Louis Calhern (Col. Sapt), Robert Douglas (Michael of Streslau), Robert Coote (Fritz von Tarlenheim), Tom Browne, Eric Alden, Stephen Roberts, Lewis Stone.

• ***The Prisoner of Zenda*** (remake). Universal Pictures, 1979. Director:

Richard Quine; screenwriters: Dick Clement and Ian La Frenais. Cast: Peter Sellers (Rudolf IV/Rudolf V/Syd), Lynne Frederick (Princess Flavia), Lionel Jeffries (Col. Sapt), Elke Sommer (the Countess), Gregory Sierra (the Count), Jeremy Kemp (Duke Michael), Catherine Schell (Antoinette), Simon Williams (Fritz), Stuart Wilson (Rupert of Hentzau), Norman Rossington, John Laurie.

The Prisoner of Zenda is a marvelous action film, most brilliantly brought to the screen with the 1937 production starring an incomparable Ronald Colman and a splendid supporting cast, most notably C. Aubrey Smith as Col. Sapt, Douglas Fairbanks, Jr., as Rupert of Hentzau and Mary Astor as Antoinette. The production was so ideal that the 1952 remake repeated it almost frame for frame and speech for speech, and still fell short of the earlier masterpiece. Although Stewart Granger was quite good in the 1952 movie, it was James Mason who walked off with acting honors. In the 1922 production, Rupert of Hentzau was played by a relative unknown, Ramon Samanyagos, soon to become more familiar as Ramon Novarro. The Peter Sellers farce in 1979 was not as adventurous as the earlier films and not as funny as most Sellers features, thus becoming a run of the mill movie, not likely to be long remembered by any who saw it.

716 The Private Life of Henry VIII

Based on the screenplay by Lajos Biro and Arthur Wimperis. Story: The film depicts the British monarch's personal relationship with five of his six wives, but does not bother with his first, Katherine of Aragon, whom he divorced to marry Anne Boleyn, hoping she would give him a male heir. Instead she produced Elizabeth, a greater monarch than her father. Henry had broken with Rome over his insistence that a divorce from Katherine be granted. He formed the Church of England with the monarch as its head. Anne was beheaded, possibly because she was unfaithful, but more likely so Henry could marry Jane Seymour, who would give him a male heir, although she dies in childbirth. He moves on to Katherine Howard, but she's also accused of being unfaithful and disposed of. Anne of Cleves and Henry agree to disagree and part. His final marital fling is with Katherine Parr, who henpecks him in his old age.

London Films, Great Britain, 1933 (original). Director: Alexander Korda; screenwriters: Lajos Biro and Arthur Wimperis. Cast: Charles Laughton (Henry VIII), Robert Donat (Thomas Culpepper), Franklin Dyall (Thomas Cromwell), Miles Mander (Worthesly), Lawrence Hanray (Archbishop Cranmer), William Austin (Duke of Cleves), John Loder (Peynell), Merle Oberon (Anne Boleyn), Wendy Barrie (Jane Seymour), Elsa Lanchester (Anne of Cleves), Binnie Barnes (Katherine Howard), Evelyn Gregg (Katherine Parr).

• ***A Man for All Seasons*** (remake). Columbia/Highland, Great Britain, 1966. Director: Fred Zinnemann; screenwriter: Robert Bolt, based on his play. Cast: Paul Scofield (Sir Thomas More), Wendy Hiller (Alice More), Robert Shaw (King Henry VIII), Leo McKern (Thomas Cromwell), Orson Welles (Cardinal Wolsey), Susannah York (Margaret More), Nigel Davenport (Duke of Norfolk), John Hurt (Richard Rich), Corin Redgrave, Vanessa Redgrave.

• ***Anne of the Thousand Days*** (remake). Universal Pictures, Great Britain,

1969. Director: Charles Jarrott; screenwriters: John Hale and Bridget Boland, based on the play by Maxwell Anderson. Cast: Richard Burton (King Henry VIII), Genevieve Bujold (Anne Boleyn), Irene Papas (Queen Katherine), Anthony Quayle (Cardinal Wolsey), John Colicos (Thomas Cromwell), Michael Hordern, Katharine Blake, Peter Jeffrey, Joseph O'Connor, William Squire.

Charles Laughton showed up as Henry VIII again in 1953 in *Young Bess,* a rather boring tale of the times in the life of Elizabeth of England just prior to Henry's death and her ascension to the throne. Jean Simmons appeared as Bess. Elizabeth herself has been portrayed in numerous films, including *Fire Over England* and *The Sea Hawk* with Flora Robson, and *Elizabeth and Essex* and *The Virgin Queen* with Bette Davis doing the honors. Henry's grandniece, Mary Stuart, Queen of Scots, has been portrayed by Katharine Hepburn in *Mary of Scotland* and by Vanessa Redgrave in *Mary Queen of Scots* with Glenda Jackson as Elizabeth.

Laughton won an Academy Award for his stunning portrayal of the king of great appetites, with sex and food leading the way, in the 1934 picture, which itself received an Oscar nomination. Paul Scofield won an Oscar for his portrayal of a man who attempted to keep his head by keeping his tongue when Henry divorced Katherine to marry Anne Boleyn in *A Man for All Seasons.* The picture was named Best Movie of the year by the Motion Picture Academy. Burton and Bujold were nominated for Oscars for the 1969 picture, which also was nominated for Best Picture, even though it seems rather dull.

The Private Life of Sherlock Holmes ***see*** **Sherlock Holmes**

717 Private Lives

Based on the play by Noel Coward. Story: This sitting-room comedy tells of a divorced couple, Amanda and Elyot, who desert their new spouses the night of their honeymoons to start over again. There's no action to speak of but the Noel Coward dialog is smart, sophisticated and witty.

MGM, 1931 (original). Director: Sidney Franklin; screenwriters: Hans Kraly and Richard Schayer. Cast: Norma Shearer (Amanda), Robert Montgomery (Elyot), Reginald Denny (Victor), Una Merkel (Sibyl), Jean Hersholt (Oscar).

• ***Les Amants Terribles (The Terrible Lovers)*** (remake). Pathe Consortium. Cinema/Paris Cine Production, 1936. Director and screenwriter: Marc Allegret. Cast: Gaby Morlay (Annette Fournier), Maris Glery (Lucie), Andre Luguel (Daniel Fournier), Henri Guisol (Victor Lambert).

Variety was convinced that the 1931 film would not appeal to men, adding that to entice men to join their wives in the theaters to see the film, the studios had made certain there were glimpses of Norma Shearer in her boudoir, dressed enticingly. We are certain that many "real" men found the Coward comedy good fun, even though no one got killed, Bob Montgomery was somewhat neurotic (read "weak") and Norma Shearer was a bric-a-brac smashing clotheshorse.

Private Number ***see*** **Common Clay**

718 Private Snuffy Smith

Based on the cartoon strip by Billy De Beck. Story: Hillbilly Snuffy Smith is drafted in the army and finds his sergeant to be a revenuer who had been on his trail for years. Snuffy also successfully deals with a fifth-column plot in this inconsequential comedy.

Monogram Pictures, 1942 (original). Director: Edward Cline; screenwriter: Billy De Beck. Cast: Bud Duncan (Snuffy Smith), Edgar Kennedy (Sgt. Cooper), Sarah Padden (Loweezy), Doris Linden (Cindy), Andraia Palmer, J. Farrell MacDonald, Pat McVeigh, Frank Austin, Jimmy Dodd.

• ***Hillbilly Blitzkeig*** (sequel). Monogram Pictures, 1942. Director and screenwriter: Roy Mack. Cast: Bud Duncan (Snuffy Smith), Cliff Nazarro (Barney Google), Edgar Kennedy (Sgt. Gatling), Doris Linden (Julie James), Lucien Littlefield, Alan Baldwin, Nicolle Andre, Jimmy Dodd.

Some studios spare no expense when producing a movie. With these films as evidence it would seem that Monogram encountered no expenses—the talent is poor, the story is poor, the directing is poor, the photography and scenery are poor, etc. In the sequel of this two-part motion picture fiasco, Edgar Kennedy as a sergeant and Bud Duncan as Snuffy Smith are assigned to guard an important rocket invention that foreign spies try to steal. The only humor in the piece is provided by a race between Barney Google's horse Spark Plug and a mule—and it's only mildly amusing.

719 Public Enemy's Wife

Based on a story by P.J. Wolfson. Story: G-man Lee Laird falls for Judith Maroc, the ex-wife of a gangster. She has spent three years in prison for a crime she didn't commit, and despite her husband's warning about what will happen to her if she ever hitches up with anyone else, she divorces the lifer and takes up with a playboy, Thomas Duncan McKay. Initially, Judith has no use for Laird, but comes to admire and love him. Interspersed with the scenes building the romance, Laird and his partner Gene Ferguson have plenty of time to shoot it out with the mobsters.

Warner Bros., 1936 (original). Director: Nick Grinde; screenwriters: Abem Finkel and Harold Buckley. Cast: Pat O'Brien (Lee Laird), Margaret Lindsay (Judith Maroc), Robert Armstrong (Gene Ferguson), Cesar Romero (Gene Maroc), Dick Foran (Thomas Duncan McKay), Joseph King, Richard Purcell.

• ***Bullets for O'Hara*** (remake). Warner Bros., 1941. Director: William K. Howard; screenwriter: Raymond Schrock. Cast: Joan Perry (Patricia Van Dyne), Roger Pryor (Mike O'Hara), Anthony Quinn (Tony Van Dyne), Maris Wrixon (Elaine Standish), Dick Purcell, Hobart Bosworth, Richard Ainley.

O'Brien pleased audiences with his portrayal of the clever Fed. Margaret Lindsay and Robert Armstrong handled their roles quite well, and Cesar Romero was adequate as the dangerous husband. In the 50-minute remake, Roger Pryor is a detective, determined to put criminal Anthony Quinn out of business. Incredibly, he arranges to have Quinn's wife, Joan Perry, acquitted of complicity in her husband's crimes. Thankful, Perry agrees to divorce her husband, start a phony romance with Pryor and even go through with a wedding ceremony, all to draw her ex out of hiding. It works, and Quinn gets his just deserts.

Pure Hell at St. Trinian's *see* **Belles of St. Trinian's**

720 Public Hero No. 1

Based on a story by J. Walter Rubin and Wells Root. Story: Sonny and Jeff, two cons, plot and carry out a successful prison break. However, it develops that Jeff is actually a G-man planted in the prison to gain Sonny's confidence, hoping the latter will lead him to the hideout of the notorious Purple Gang, which is precisely what he does.

MGM, 1935 (original). Director: J. Walter Ruben; screenwriters: Ruben and Wells Root. Cast: Lionel Barrymore (Doctor), Jean Arthur (Theresa), Chester Morris (Jeff Crane), Joseph Calleia (Sonny), Paul Kelly (Duff), Lewis Stone, Sam Baker, Paul Hurst, George E. Stone.

• ***The Get-Away*** (remake). MGM, 1941. Director: Edward Buzzell; screenwriters: Wells Root and W.R. Burnett. Cast: Robert Sterling (Jeff Crane), Charles Winninger (Dr. Joseph Glass), Donna Reed (Maria Theresa O'Reilly), Henry O'Neill (Warden Alcott), Dan Dailey, Jr. (Sonny Black), Don Douglas, Ernest Whitman, Grant Withers, Chester Gan.

One wonders if the G-men of these movies aren't guilty of entrapment—but then, these movies were made before the days in which the Supreme Court took notice of the rights of those allegedly guilty of a crime. In the original, Lionel Barrymore plays a dipsomaniac physician who might have been a great surgeon if he could have laid off the booze. Now he's reduced to patching up criminals. G-man Morris even donates blood to keep Calleia alive, during an operation by Barrymore. In the remake, Charles Winninger also makes the most of the good character role of the drunken doctor. Robert Sterling is the Fed who wins the confidence of mobster Dan Dailey, but almost blows everything by falling in love with the latter's sister, played by Donna Reed.

Pursued *see* **The Painted Lady**

721 Pygmalion

Based on the play by George Bernard Shaw. Story: Phonetics professor Henry Higgins, who brags that he can pass off a Cockney flower girl as a duchess within three months by teaching her how to speak the English language correctly, is challenged by Colonel Pickering to do so. With Eliza Doolittle in tow, Higgins sets about to prove he knows of what he speaks. The painful transformation completed, Eliza is a smashing success at the Ambassador's Ball, causing Higgins and Pickering to be most self-congratulatory about their accomplishments, totally ignoring Eliza's contributions in the experiment. Unable to return to live with her father, dustman Alfred Doolittle, because he has been forced to adopt middle class morality and marry his current mistress due to Higgins' meddling in his life, Eliza turns to Mrs. Higgins and Freddie Eynsford-Hill for comfort. Higgins, finally recognizing that Eliza

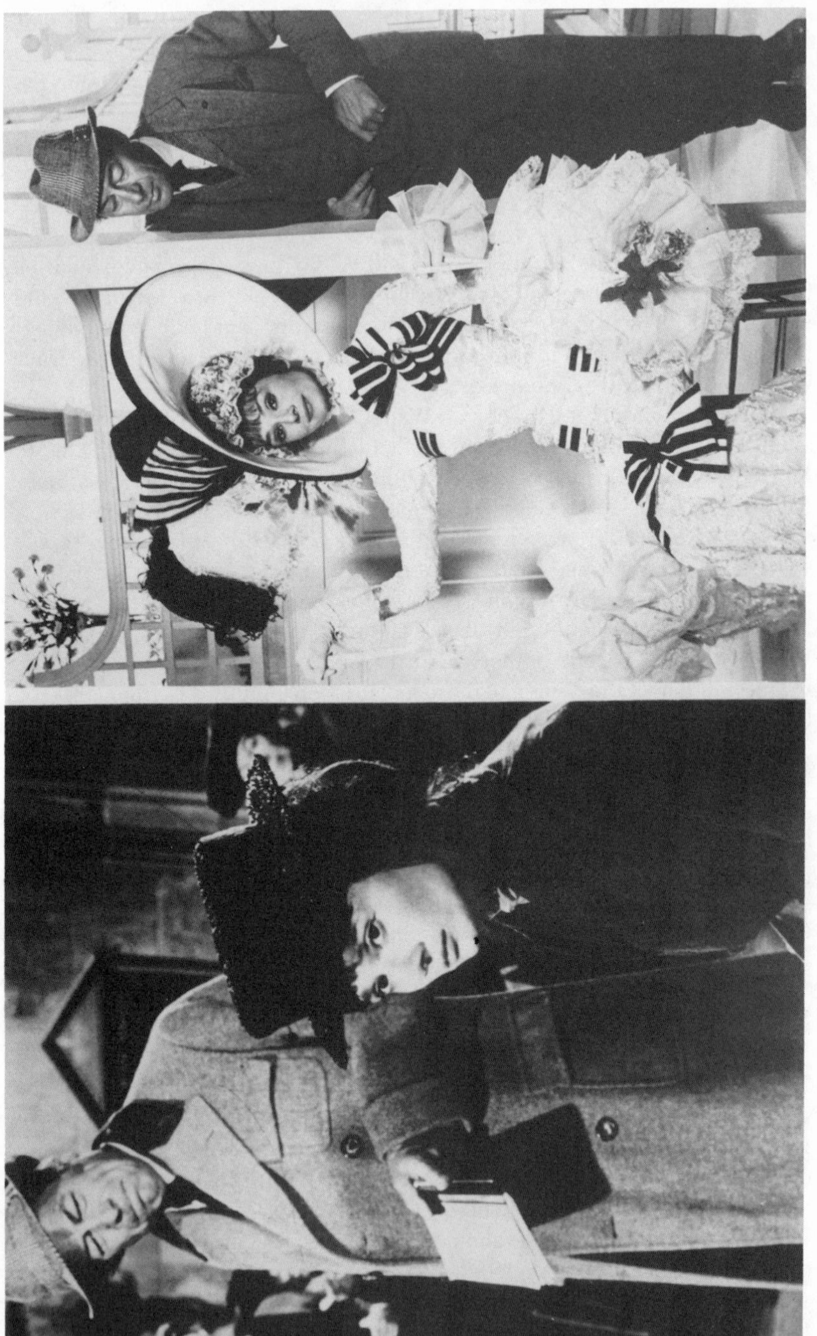

Not only has Leslie Howard succeeded in making Wendy Hiller look like a duchess in Pygmalion *(MGM, 1938), but he has taught her to speak like one as well.*

has become an important part of his life, is delighted when she shakes off Freddie's marriage proposal and returns to him. His treatment of her has not changed however, as he bellows for her to find his slippers.

• ***Pygmalion*** (remake). MGM, 1938. Director: Anthony Asquith; screenwriters: George Bernard Shaw, W.P. Lipscomb and Cecil Lewis. Cast: Leslie Howard (Henry Higgins), Wendy Hiller (Eliza Doolittle), Wilfrid Lawson (Alfred Doolittle), Scott Sunderland (Col. Pickering), David Tree (Freddie Eynsford-Hill), Everley Gregg (Mrs. Eynsford-Hill), Marie Lohr (Mrs. Higgins),

Opposite: *In before and after pictures, Rex Harrison looks sourly at flower girl Audrey Hepburn on the left, while at the right his glance at her at the Ascot races is more appreciative.* My Fair Lady *(Warner Bros., 1964).*

Jean Cadell (Mrs. Pearce), Lueen MacGrath (Clara Hill), Esme Percy (Count Aristid Karpathy), Violet Vanbruth, O.B. Clarence, Irene Browne.

• ***My Fair Lady*** (remake). Warner Bros., 1964. Director: George Cukor; screenwriter: Alan Jay Lerner. Cast: Rex Harrison (Henry Higgins), Audrey Hepburn (Eliza Doolittle), Stanley Holloway (Alfred P. Doolittle), Wilfrid Hyde-White (Col. Hugh Pickering), Gladys Cooper (Mrs. Higgins), Jeremy Britt (Freddy Eynsford-Hill), Theodore Bikel (Zoltan Karpathy), Isobel Elsom (Mrs. Eynsford-Hill), Mona Washbourne (Mrs. Pearce), John Alderson, Henry Daniell, Clive Halliday, Olive Reeves Smith, John McLiam.

Pygmalion was also filmed in Germany in 1935, in Holland in 1936, and there have been many movies with this same theme, transformed to a new setting. One such film is *The Opening of Misty Beethoven,* produced in 1975.

It's hard to choose between the 1938 black and white production nominated as Best Picture of the Year and the glorious color musical of 1964 which won the distinction, so why bother? Each should be among any serious collection of all-time best motion pictures. Leslie Howard and Rex Harrison were both superb as Henry Higgins; both were nominated for the Academy Award for Best Actor, with Harrison winning. Equally so were Wilfrid Lawson and Stanley Holloway as Alfred Doolittle, with Holloway being nominated for but not winning an Oscar for Best Supporting Actor. Wendy Hiller, nominated for Best Actress, and Audrey Hepburn both impressed as Eliza Doolittle, despite the non-issue as to whether the latter should have had the role made so popular by Julie Andrews on Broadway. It was not exactly a precedent that Hollywood chose to cast someone other that the Broadway star in the film version of a musical comedy. The teaming of Audrey Hepburn's acting with Marni Nixon's voice more than made up for the missing Andrews, who won that year's Academy Award for *Mary Poppins.* Songs by Alan Jay Lerner and Frederick Loewe included "Why Can't the English," "Wouldn't It be Loverly," "With a Little Bit of Luck," "The Rain in Spain," "I Could Have Danced All Night," "On the Street Where You Live," "Get Me to the Church on Time" and "I've Grown Accustomed to Her Face."

Q

722 Quality Street

Based on the play by Sir James Barrie. Story: When Dr. Valentine Brown returns from the Napoleonic Wars after a ten-year stay, he does not recognize his former sweetheart, Phoebe Throssel, who has drifted into spinsterhood with faded beauty. Determined to get the man she has waited so long for, Phoebe masquerades as her frivolous non-existent niece, Livvy, and completely captivates Valentine and wins his love once again when she reveals her true identity.

MGM, 1927 (original). Silent. Director: Sidney Franklin; screenwriters: Hans Kraly and Albert Lewin. Cast: Marion Davies (Phoebe Throssel), Conrad Nagel

(Dr. Valentine Brown), Helen Jerome Eddy (Susan Throssel), Flora Finch (Mary Willoughby), Kate Price, Margaret Seddon, Marcelle Corday.

RKO, 1937. Director: George Stevens; screenwriters: Mortimer Offner and Allan Scott. Cast: Katharine Hepburn (Phoebe Throssel), Franchot Tone (Dr. Valentine Brown), Fay Bainter (Susan Throssel), Estelle Winwood, Cora Witherspoon, Helena Grant, Florence Lake, Bonita Granville.

Whimsy is very difficult to film but those responsible for these two productions worked at the task very hard and, though not completely successful, one can at least applaud their effort. It's a bit hard to understand why Marion Davies, a fine comedienne, was miscast as Phoebe, a role not in her repertoire. Hepburn doesn't really look like a woman who has lost her beauty despite all of her nervous movements of hands, mouth and lips, and Franchot Tone doesn't seem the sort one would wait ten years for; he's not that impressive a catch. All in all, these movies don't earn many stars for quality.

Queen High *see* **A Pair of Sixes**

723 The Queen Was in the Parlour

Based on the play by Noel Coward. Story: Widowed princess Nadya falls in love with a commoner, Sabieri, in Paris. But she is called home to Ruitania to take her throne and marry a prince. Is suicide the only way out?

Gainsborough, Great Britain, 1927 (original). Silent. Director and screenwriter: Graham Cutts. Cast: Lili Damita (Nadya), Paul Richter (Sabieri), Harry Leichke (Prince Keri), Rosa Richards (Zana), Trude Hesterberg (Grand Duchess Emilie).

• ***Tonight Is Ours*** (remake). Paramount Pictures, 1933. Director: Stuart Walker; screenwriter: Edwin Justus Mayer. Cast: Claudette Colbert (Nadya), Fredric March (Sabien Pastal), Alison Skipworth (Grand Duchess Emilie), Paul Cavanaugh (Prince Keri), Arthur Byron, Ethel Griffies, Clay Clemont, Warburton Gamble.

Fans drawn to the theaters by the names of Colbert, March and Coward were mostly disappointed in the talky, slowly developing comedy remake. The performers did what they were asked but the screenplay and the dialogue is lacklustre.

724 Quiet Wedding

Based on the play by Esther McCracken. Story: Bride-to-be Janet Royd and her fiancé, Dallas Chaytor, are almost driven around the bend by their friends' and relatives' advice and interference as their wedding day approaches. The strain begins to tell on the lovers and in order to settle the upheaval between them, the couple go off to spend the night before the nuptials together.

Soskins Productions/Paramount Pictures, Great Britain, 1941 (original). Director: Anthony Asquith; screenwriters: Terrence Rattigan and A. de Grunwald. Cast: Margaret Lockwood (Janet Royd), Derek Farr (Dallas Chaytor), Marjorie Fielding (Mildred Royd), A.E. Matthews (Arthur Royd), Athene

Seyler, Jean Cadell, Margaretta Scott, David Tomlinson, Sidney King, Peggy Ashcroft, Frank Cellier.

• ***Happy Is the Bride*** (remake). British Lion, 1958. Director: Roy Boulting; screenwriters: Jeffrey Dell and Roy Boulting. Cast: Ian Carmichael (David Chaytor), Janette Scott (Janet Royd), Cecil Parker (Arthur Royd), Terry-Thomas (Policeman), Joyce Grenfell (Aunt Florence), Eric Barker, Edith Sharpe, Elvi Hale, Richard Bennett, John Le Mesurier.

The remake is just as amicable and inconsequential as the original film version of the successful stage production, but both are pleasant 90-minute diversions. Ian Carmichael and Janette Scott hope to have a quiet wedding, but they did not reckon with the delight of their families and the resulting interference with the young couple's plans. This results in their first fight and to resolve their differences, they disappear together on the eve of their wedding. The next day, their trip to the altar is almost shelved when they find themselves arrested for a traffic offense, but they make it just in the nick of time.

R

725 The Racket

Based on the play by Bartlett Cormack. Story: Despite warnings, bootlegger Nick Scarsi transports liquor and is captured by the police. Through the intervention of powerful politician Burr McIntosh, who needs the votes controlled by the Scarsi gang, Nick is set free. When Nick later murders a patrolman, police captain McQuigg, long an enemy of Nick, captures and kills the bootlegger when he tries to escape.

Paramount Pictures, 1928 (original). Silent. Director: Lewis Milestone; screenwriters: Harry Behn and Del Andrews. Cast: Thomas Meighan (Captain McQuigg), Marie Prevost (Helen Hayes), Louis Wolheim (Nick Scarsi), George Stone (Joe Scarsi), John Darrow, Skeets Gallagher, Lee Moran, Lucien Prival, Tony Marlo.

• ***The Racket*** (remake). RKO, 1951. Director: John Cromwell; screenwriters: William Wister Haines and W.R. Burnett. Cast: Robert Mitchum (Captain McQuigg), Lizabeth Scott (Irene), Robert Ryan (Nick), William Talman (Johnson), Ray Collins (Welch), Joyce MacKenzie, Robert Hutton, Virginia Huston, William Conrad, Don Porter.

These films tell the story of the fight between a good cop and a big-city mobster. There are no shadings here; it's good versus evil. In the remake Robert Mitchum is the honest police captain and Robert Ryan, the racketeer. Mitchum must not only deal with the scum in the rackets but the crooked politicians who aid and abet them, here portrayed by Ray Collins and William Conrad. Feminine interest is kept to a minimum and is supplied by Lizabeth Scott, who sings "A Lovely Way to Spend an Evening."

726 Raffles

Based on stories by E.W. Hornung. Story: Raffles, a clever, suave safecracker who has successfully eluded Scotland Yard for years, falls hopelessly in love with Lady Gwen and decides to give up his life of crime. When his close friend, Bunny, attempts suicide in desperation over his debts, Raffles decides to pull one last job. Lady Melrose, who is quite taken by the handsome Raffles, supplies an opportunity when she invites him for a weekend at her house. Also present is Inspector MacKenzie, who has learned that burglars are planning to steal Lady Melrose's fabulous diamond necklace. Using this information to his advantage, Raffles takes off with the necklace and is followed by MacKenzie to London where he admits to being an amateur cracksman, but escapes with plans to meet Lady Gwen in Paris.

• ***Raffles, the Amateur Cracksman*** (remake). Universal Pictures, 1925. Silent. Director: King Baggot; screenwriter: Harvey Thew. Cast: House Peters (Raffles), Miss Du Pont (Gwendolyn Amersteth), Hedda Hopper (Mrs. Clarice Vidal), Frederick Esmelton (Captain Bedford), Walter Long (Crawshay), Winter Hall, Kate Lester, Freeman Wood.

• ***Raffles*** (remake). United Artists, 1930. Directors: Harry D'Abbadie D'Arrast and George Fitzmaurice; screenwriter: Sidney Howard: Cast: Ronald Colman (Raffles), Kay Francis (Gwen), Bramwell Fletcher (Bunny Manners), Frances Drake (Ethel), David Torrence (MacKenzie), Alison Skipworth (Lady Melrose), Frederick Kerr, John Rogers, Wilson Benge.

• ***Raffles*** (remake). United Artists, 1939. Director: Sam Wood; screenwriter: John Van Druten. Cast: David Niven (Raffles), Olivia de Havilland (Gwen), Dame May Whitty (Lady Melrose), Dudley Digges (MacKenzie), Douglas Walton (Bunny), Lionel Pape (Lord Melrose), E.E. Clive, Peter Godfrey, Margaret Seddon, Gilbert Emery.

The stories of the amateur cracksman Raffles were also filmed in 1905, 1910, 1914, 1917, 1920, 1921, 1932 and 1960. Each time the gentleman safecracker's role was assigned to a sophisticated and suave actor such as Ronald Colman or David Niven. The stories aren't much but these performers have made Raffles an interesting, intelligent and amusing character. Additional adventures of Raffles include his thwarting jewel thieves intent on stealing a valuable necklace during an ocean voyage. Raffles now steals only to protect others or if he feels his ability is being challenged. Then he must prove his skill by lifting valuable pieces right under the noses of the police, just to prove that he can get away with it.

727 Raiders of the Lost Ark

Based on a story by George Lucas. Story: Indiana Jones is an archaeologist whose obsessive search for the Ark which contains the original Ten Commandments puts him in competition with an old nemesis, Belloq, who is working for the Nazis, and reunites him with an old love, Marion Ravenswood. He is as dashing as an Errol Flynn hero ever was, but just as unconvinced of the wisdom of taking risks for others as was a Humphrey Bogart character.

Paramount Pictures, 1981 (original). Director: Steven Spielberg; screenwriter: Lawrence Kasdan. Cast: Harrison Ford (Indiana Jones), Karen Allen (Marion Ravenswood), Paul Freeman (Belloq), John Rhys-Davies (Sallah), Wolf

Kahler (Dietrich), Ronald Lacey (Toht), Denholm Elliott (Marcus Brody), Anthony Higgins, Alfred Molina, Vic Tablian.

• ***Indiana Jones and the Temple of Doom*** (sequel). Paramount Pictures, 1984. Director: Steven Spielberg; screenwriters: Willard Huyck and Gloria Katz. Cast: Harrison Ford (Indiana Jones), Kate Capshaw (Willie Scott), Ke Huy Quan (Short Round), Amrish Puri (Mola Ram), Rosham Seth (Chattar Lal), Philip Stone, Ray Chiao, David Yip, Ric Young.

Raiders is a spectacularly entertaining film. It not only can give one the fright of one's life when least expected, but it's all done with great good humor and style. Indiana Jones is a brave man, ready to enter where angels fear to tread, but he's no fool. If he has to abandon pretty little Karen Allen to make his escape or further his quest for the Ark, then so be it. He can't stand snakes, but when he finds himself and Karen in a pit filled with them, he realizes now is not the time to give in to one's phobias. His tenacity and resilence is amazing, but he does bruise and he's often obviously in pain. It's just not going to stop him, that's all. George Lucas claimed to be saluting the wonderful adventure serials of his youth, but they weren't as wonderful as this extraordinary movie.

Having praised the original, the second, a sort of prequel to the first, taking place some years earlier in Indiana Jones' life, is a great disappointment. It falls far short of what audiences hoped might be found in another telling of the exciting life of Indy. Instead, it was one long chase movie, stopping only long enough to disgust with brutality and horror as Ford, his half-pint partner, Ke Huy Quan, and buxomy but brainless Kate Chapshaw search for the sacred Sankara stone in India. It lacked the humor, surprise and delight of the original. Unlike *Raiders,* the villains were never made three-dimensional. We feared them, hated them, but didn't know them. Ford looked rather bored with the whole thing, probably hoping to move on to less physically taxing roles.

Rain ***see*** **Sadie Thompson**

728 The Rains Came

Based on the novel by Louis Bromfield. Story: Tom Ransome, the wastrel son of a good British family, has been drinking his life away in Ranchipur, India, for years. His close friend is Doctor Major Rama Safti, who has no time for romantic dalliances as he dedicates himself to his medical duties. Things change when Lady Edwina Esketh shows up. She is visiting the Maharajah with her boorish husband, Lord Albert. These and other British parasites are put to the test when a major flood devastates the region.

Twentieth Century–Fox, 1939 (original). Director: Clarence Brown; screenwriters: Philip Dunne and Julien Josephson. Cast: Myrna Loy (Lady Edwina Esketh), Tyrone Power (Major Rama Safti), George Brent (Tom Ransome), Brenda Joyce (Fern Simon), Nigel Bruce (Lord Albert Esketh), Maria Ouspenskaya (Maharani), Joseph Schildkraut (Mr. Bannerjee), Mary Nash, Jane Darwell, Marjorie Rambeau.

• ***The Rains of Ranchipur*** (remake). Twentieth Century–Fox, 1955.

Director: Jean Negulesco; screenwriter: Merle Miller. Cast: Lana Turner (Edwina), Richard Burton (Dr. Safi), Fred MacMurray (Tom Ransome), Joan Caulfield (Fern), Michael Rennie (Lord Esketh), Eugenie Leontovich (Maharani), Gladys Hurlout, Madge Kennedy, Carlo Arizzo, Beatrice Kraft, King Calder.

The original was an absorbing disaster spectacular with a monsoon causing cruel devastation. The development of the relationships of the characters is not merely a vamper until the rains come; all the characters in their own peculiar way are interesting if not always admirable. The remake is a different story. Lana Turner is a dull temptress and Richard Burton just too mystical as the good Indian doctor. Fred MacMurray, as the disillusioned drunk, is in the wrong picture and Michael Rennie still looks like he came from another planet rather than from dear old England.

The Rains of Ranchipur *see* **The Rains Came**

Rambo: First Blood II *see* **First Blood**

729 Rashomon

Based on the novel *In the Forest* by Ryunosuke Akutagawa. Story: A woodcutter and a Buddhist priest take shelter from a storm in the ruined gatehouse of the once-great Rashomon Gate of Kyoto, where they tell a wigmaker of a crime committed in a nearby forest. A bandit attacked a samurai, tied him up, raped the man's wife before his eyes and then killed the husband. In court, the bandit admits to having killed the husband in a fair duel after the wife had disappeared. The wife testifies that the bandit had raped her and that she was so ashamed of her submission to him, she pleaded with her husband to kill her after the bandit had left. When he angrily refused she fainted and awoke to find her dagger protruding from her husband's chest. A medium conjures up the spirit of the husband who admits he committed suicide after his raped wife left with the bandit. The woodcutter tells the others that he witnessed the crime and saw the wife encourage the bandit to kill her husband, but not wanting to get involved, did not come forth with his story.

Daiei Production, Japan, 1950 (original). Director: Akira Kurosawa; screenwriters: Akira Kurosawa and Shinobu Hashimoto. Cast: Toshiro Mifune (Tajomaru, the Bandit), Masayuki Mori (Takehiro, the Samurai), Machiko Kyo (Masago, the Wife), Takashi Shimura (the Woodcutter), Minoru Chiaki (the Priest), Kichijiro Ueda (the Wigmaker), Daisuke Kato, Fumiko Homma.

• ***The Outrage*** (remake). MGM, 1964. Director: Martin Ritt; screenwriter: Michael Kanin. Cast: Paul Newman (Juan Carrasco), Laurence Harvey (the Husband), Claire Bloom (the Wife), Edward G. Robinson (Con Man), William Shatner (the Preacher), Howard Da Silva, Albert Salmi, Thomas Chalmers, Paul Fix.

When *Rashomon* won the Grand Prix at the Venice International Film Festival in 1951, it opened the Western world to Japanese cinema and the special genius of director Akira Kurosawa. Speaking of this film, the director says, "Human beings are unable to be honest about themselves. They cannot talk about themselves without embellishing. This script portrays such human beings—the kind who cannot survive without lies to make them feel they are better people than they really are. . . . Egotism is a sin the human being carries with him from birth; it is the most difficult to redeem. . . ."

As *Rashomon* is so magnificent, one may question the need to film a remake, set in the American West, starring Paul Newman as a Mexican bandit. While it is true that Martin Ritt's picture can not stand up to Kurosawa's, it did offer the viewers who might not attend the original, perhaps because they don't like to read translations of dialogue, an opportunity to consider some of the questions about truth raised in the story. It's appropriate to complain that some of the performers tended to overact, but the story of conflicting views of a murder is still interesting.

Raskolnikov *see* **Crime and Punishment**

730 The Rat

Based on the play by Ivor Novello and Constance Collier. Story: Pierre Boucheron, a Parisian apache, dancer and thief known as "the Rat," milks money from rich ladies, but is reformed by the love of the orphaned daughter, Odile Etrange, of another criminal. When she is arrested for murder (but in actuality killed someone in self-defense) he confesses, but an old love, Zeile de Chaumet, perjures herself to save him.

Gainsborough, Great Britain, 1925 (original). Silent. Director and screenwriter: Graham Cutts. Cast: Ivor Novello (Pierre Boucheron), Mae Marsh (Odile Etrange), Isobel Jeans (Zeile de Chaumet), Robert Scholtz (Herman Stetz), James Lindsay (Inspector Caillard), Marie Ault, Julie Suedo, Hugh Brook, Esme Fitzgibbons, Lambart Glasby, Iris Grey.

• ***The Triumph of the Rat*** (sequel). Gainsborough, Great Britain, 1926. Silent. Director: Graham Cutts; screenwriters: Graham Cutts, Reginald Fogwell and Roland Pertwee. Cast: Ivor Novello (Pierre Boucheron), Isobel Jeans (Zeile de Chaumet), Nina Vanna (Comtesse Madeleine), Julie Suedo (Mou-Mou), Marie Ault, Lewin Mannering, Mrs. Hayden Coffin, Charles Dormer, Gabriel Rosca.

• ***The Return of the Rat*** (sequel). Gainsborough, Great Britain, 1929. Director: Graham Cutts; screenwriters: Edgar C. Middleton, A. Neil Lyons and Angus McPhail. Cast: Ivor Novello (Pierre Boucheron), Isabel Jeans (Zeile de Chaumet), Mabel Poulton (Lisette), Bernard Nedell (Henri), Marie Ault, Gordon Harker, Scott Kelly, Harry Terry.

• ***The Rat*** (remake). Imperator/Radio, Great Britain, 1937. Director: Jack Raymond; screenwriters: Hans Rameau, Marjorie Gaffney, Miles Malleson and Romney Brent. Cast: Ruth Chatterton (Zeile de Chaumet), Anton Walbrook (Jean Boucheron), Rene Ray (Odile Verdier), Beatrix Lehmann (Marguerite), Mary Clare (Mere Colline), Felix Aylmer, Hugh Miller, Gordon McLeod.

In this list the second and third movies are sequels to the first. Ivor Novello, who with Constance Collier created the characters, had a nice run as the apache dancer who can't quite permanently reform. In the first sequel, he bets he can win Nina Vanna in a month's time and makes the mistake of falling in love with her. In the second sequel, he deserts the underworld to marry Isabel Jeans, but it doesn't work out and he returns to his old hangouts and falls in love with barmaid Mabel Poulton. In addition, he is challenged to a duel by his wife's lover. The final film is an unsuccessful attempt to resuscitate the series with Anton Walbrook as "the Rat."

731 The Razor's Edge

Based on the novel by W. Somerset Maugham. Story: After World War I, volunteer ambulance driver Larry Darrell postpones his marriage to Isabel Bradley because he wants to spend some time in Paris finding himself. When he doesn't find himself among the bohemian dropouts, he takes a passage to India, where he briefly becomes a contemplative monk. He leaves this life to return to Paris where he tries to save Sophie, a young woman swept up in drugs and alcohol after her husband and child are killed in an automobile accident. He's unable to do so and turns to Isabel with all he has really learned: nothing really matters.

Twentieth Century–Fox, 1946 (original). Director: Edmund Goulding; screenwriter: Lamar Trotti. Cast: Tyrone Power (Larry Darrell), Gene Tierney (Isabel Bradley), John Payne (Gray Maturin), Anne Baxter (Sophie), Clifton Webb (Elliott Templeton), Herbert Marshall (W. Somerset Maugham), Lucille Watson (Louise Bradley), Frank Latimore, Elsa Lanchester, Fritz Kortner, John Wengraf, Cecil Humphreys.

• ***The Razor's Edge*** (remake). Columbia, 1984. Director: John Byrum; screenwriters: Byrum and Bill Murray. Cast: Bill Murray (Larry Denholm), Theresa Russell (Sophie), Catherine Hicks (Isabel), Denholm Elliott (Templeton), James Keach (Gray Maturin), Brian Doyle-Murray (Piedmont), Peter Vaughan, Faith Brook.

According to Maugham, the source for his title is the Oriental proverb, "The sharp edge of a razor is difficult to pass over; thus the wise say that the path to salvation is hard." Anne Baxter won an Oscar for Best Supporting Actress in the 1946 production, which was nominated for Best Picture and Best Supporting Actor (Clifton Webb). No awards have been given to the remake, although it would be unfair to say it was a bad picture; it is just an unusual choice for a remake and a vehicle for comic Bill Murray. Audiences can be forgiven for wondering when his shy little grin will break out and he will do something outrageous—but he doesn't, and his attempt to convey spirituality just doesn't work.

732 Rebecca of Sunnybrook Farm

Based on the novel by Kate Douglas Wiggin. Story: This sweet story of a Pollyanna-like girl, Rebecca, deals with her efforts to win over her dour, rich aunt, Miranda, convince an atheist, Zion Simpson, to marry his common-law wife, and get Dr. Ladd involved in community work. Little Miss Fix-it has a busy time, as there is so much good to do, and so little time.

• ***Rebecca of Sunnybrook Farm*** (remake). Fox Film Corporation, 1932. Directors: Alfred Santell; screenwriters: S.N. Behrman and Sonya Levien. Cast:

Marian Nixon (Rebecca), Ralph Bellamy (Dr. Ladd), Mae Marsh (Aunt Jane), Louise Closser Hale (Aunt Miranda), Alphonz Ethier (Mr. Cobb), Sarah Padden (Mrs. Cobb), Alan Hale (Mr. Simpson), Eula Guy (Mrs. Simpson), Charlotte Henry, Claire McDowell, Ronald Harris, Willis Marks.

• ***Rebecca of Sunnybrook Farm*** (remake). Twentieth Century–Fox, 1939. Director: Allan Dwan; screenwriters: Karl Tunberg and Don Ettinlinger. Cast: Shirley Temple (Rebecca), Randolph Scott (Anthony Kent), Jack Haley (Orville Smithers), Gloria Stuart (Gwen Warren), Phyllis Brooks (Lola Lee), Helen Westley (Aunt Miranda Wilkins), Slim Summerville (Homer Busby), Bill Robinson (Aloysius), J. Edward Bromberg, Alan Dinehart, Dixie Dunbar.

The first of the saccharine Rebeccas was "America's Sweetheart," Mary Pickford. The 1932 version was to star Janet Gaynor as Rebecca and Charles Farrell as Dr. Ladd, but this fell through, and the teaming of Marian Nixon and Ralph Bellamy probably was just as good, or bad, depending on how much sweetness one can tolerate. The 1939 production starring Shirley Temple had more going for it, as the little curly-haired one could be forgiven for seeing everything as black and white and having easy solutions for all problems. Actually, the film doesn't resemble the original story much, but the "little child shall lead them" theme is still presented with a heavy hand. The best and certainly most memorable part of the film is her famous tap dancing on stairs with Bill "Bojangles" Robinson. Shirley's songs include "An Old Straw Hat" by Mack Gordon and Harry Revel and "Come Get Your Happiness" by Sam Pokrass and Jack Yellan.

733 The Reckless Age

Based on the story *Love Insurance* by Earl Derr Biggers. Story: When Lord Harrowby takes out an insurance policy against losing his wealthy bride-to-be, Cynthia Meyrick, the insurance company sends confidential agent Dick Minot to the wedding proceedings to protect their investment. Naturally, he falls in love with Cynthia and after a series of comical situations wins her and loses big for his company.

• ***The Reckless Age*** (remake). Universal Pictures, 1924. Silent. Director: Harry Pollard; screenwriter: Rex Taylor. Cast: Reginald Denny (Dick Minot), Ruth Dwyer (Cynthia Meyrick), John Steppling (Spencer Meyrick), William Austin (Lord Harrowby), May Wallace, Tom McGuire, Fred Malatesta, Henry A. Barrows.

• ***One Night in the Tropics*** (remake). Universal Pictures, 1940. Director: A. Edward Sutherland; screenwriters: Gertrude Purcell and Charles Grayson. Cast: Allan Jones (Jim), Nancy Kelly (Cynthia), Bud Abbott (himself), Lou Costello (himself), Robert Cummings (Steve), Mary Boland, William Frawley, Peggy Moran, Leo Carrillo, Don Alvarado.

One Night in the Tropics was the first film for Bud Abbott and Lou Costello and the only one in which they appeared in supporting roles. Critics and audiences noted that the only thing saving this film was the periodic appearances of these vaudevillain clowns, featuring several of their routines from radio and the stage in six specialty numbers. Aside from that the movie picks

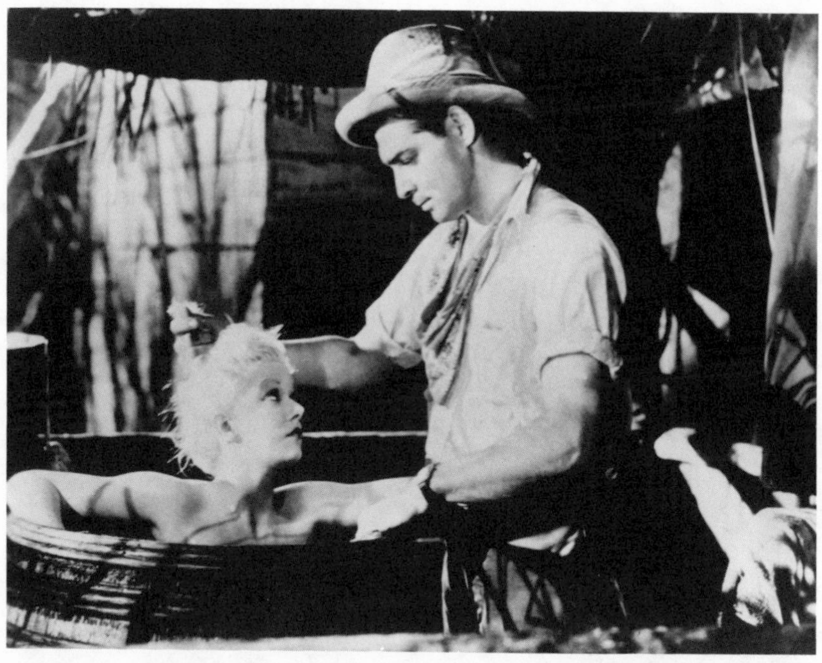

Perhaps Clark Gable plans to give Jean Harlow a shampoo in this famous bathing scene from Red Dust *(MGM, 1932).*

up the thread of the Biggers story, first filmed under its original title, *Love Insurance,* in 1919. In the 1940 remake, Allan Jones sells pal Robert Cummings a policy against not marrying Nancy Kelly, only to fall for the gal himself.

734 Red Dust

Based on the play by Wilson Collinson. Story: Dennis Carson is the boss of a rubber plantation in Indochina with two women on his hands. One is Vantine, a fallen woman with the proverbial "heart of gold." The other is Barbara Willis, wife of the new engineer, Gary Willis. Carson makes a play for Barbara, and she's more interested than she would like to admit. Carson realizes that she's the wrong gal for him, and sends her and her husband back to a more civilized existence, leaving Vantine as a more appropriate woman for his life-style.

Metro Productions, 1932 (original). Director: Victor Fleming; screenwriter: John Mahin. Cast: Clark Gable (Dennis Morgan), Jean Harlow (Vantine), Gene Raymond (Gary Willis), Mary Astor (Barbara Willis), Donald Crisp, Tully Marshall, Forrester Harvey, Willie Fung.

• ***Congo Maisie*** (remake). MGM, 1940. Director: Henry C. Potter; screenwriter: Mary C. McCall, Jr. Cast: Ann Sothern (Maisie Ravier), John Carroll (Dr. Michael Shane), Rita Johnson (Kay McWade), Shepperd Strudwick (Dr. John McWade), J.M. Kerrigan (Capt. Finch), E.E. Clive, Everett Brown, Tom Fadden, Lionel Pape.

In a remake of Red Dust, *a much more mature Clark Gable leads the way with Donald Sinden, Ava Gardner and Philip Stainton close behind in* Mogambo *(MGM, 1953).*

• ***Mogambo*** (remake). MGM, 1953. Director: John Ford; screenwriter: John Lee Mahin. Cast: Clark Gable (Victor Marswell), Ava Gardner (Eloise Y. Kelly), Grace Kelly (Linda Nordley), Donald Sinden (Donald Nordley), Philip Stainton, Eric Pohlmann, Laurence Naismith, Denis O'Dea.

Jean Harlow's shower scene in *Red Dust* raised the jungle's heat as well as Clark Gable's temperature. For her age, she gave a surprisingly mature performance. Gable, a old hand at having women crazy about him, was wonderfully natural. Mary Astor, as the heretofore innocent girl, almost sacrifices her marriage when she feels a passion which she doesn't understand, but is just a trifle too hysterical to be effective. Gene Raymond is too much of a wimpy strawman to have any chance in a comparison with Gable. The two may be back together at the end but Astor will never completely get Gable out of her mind.

In *Congo Maisie,* Ann Sothern, stranded in a West African settlement, stows away on a steamer and ends up in a rubber plantation hospital, run by Shepperd Strudwick. She prevents John Carroll from following through on his romantic inclinations towards Strudwick's wife, Rita Johnson, and saves the group from a native attack.

Gable repeats his *Red Dust* role in *Mogambo.* This time he is a big-game hunter in Africa, pursued by Ava Gardner, a stranded prostitute, and Grace Kelly, the wife of Donald Sinden, who has hired Gable as their guide. Kelly cooly plays the role of a wife looking for some excitement with the macho Mr. Gable. She becomes flustered when she discovers that Gable won't play the affair by her rules. Ava Gardner, looking like a sleek jungle cat, is clearly a better match for the man who takes his pleasures wherever and whenever he finds them.

735 Red Head

Based on the novel by Vera Brown. Story: Dale Carter is an artist's model innocently dragged into an accidental death case. Because of her looks, the papers won't let the story die. Playboy Ted Brown, who has had his support cut off by his father, gets the smart idea of marrying the girl and shaking down the old man to buy her off. The only thing is the old man won't be shaken down and in fact offers Dale money to reform his son. She does and Ted blows his top when he discovers that his old man was just as underhanded as he was. He leaves Dale but comes back when he discovers she had refused the payment and in fact really loves him.

Monogram Pictures, 1934 (original). Director: Melville Brown; screenwriter: Betty Burbridge. Cast: Bruce Cabot (Ted Brown), Grace Bradley (Dale Carter), Regis Toomey (Scoop), Berton Churchill (Mr. Brown).

• ***Redhead*** (remake). Monogram Pictures, 1941. Director: Edward Cahn; screenwriters: Conrad Seiler and Dorothy Reid. Cast: June Lang (Dale Carter), Johnny Downs (Ted Brown), Eric Blore (Digby), Frank Jacquet (T.H. Brown), Weldon Heyburn, Anna Chandler, Harry Burns.

Here are two films which have almost nothing going for them: The novel on which they are based has too little dramatic content, the script has strange senses of priorities, the directors are short on subtlety, and the performers in the leads aren't leading performers. It's difficult to find anything interesting about these characters, even though Bradley and Lang fill the bill as beautiful young women.

736 Red Lights

Based on the play *The Rear Car* by Edward E. Rose. Story: Railroad tycoon Luke Carson learns that his daughter Ruth, who was kidnapped as a child and never heard from again, has been located, now an adult, living in Los Angeles. Mr. Carson takes a train west to be reunited with her, where he finds that she is being menaced by mysterious shrouded figures. Ruth's fiancé, John Blake, brings in Sheridan Scott, a "crime deflector," who in theory eliminates the criminal before a crime is committed. Scott does succeed in solving the mystery, and everyone is happy at the end.

Goldwyn Pictures, 1923 (original). Silent. Director: Clarence G. Badger; screenwriters: Carey Wilson and Alice D.G. Miller. Cast: Marie Prevost (Ruth Carson), Raymond Griffith (Sheridan Scott), Johnnie Walker (John Blake), William Worthington (Luke Carson), Alice Lake (Norah O'Neill), Dagmar Godowsky, Frank Elliott, Lionel Belmore, Jean Hersholt, George Reed.

• ***Murder in the Private Car*** (remake). MGM, 1934. Director: Harry Beaumont; screenwriters: Ralph Spence, Edgar Allan Woolf, Al Bosaberg and Harvey

Thew. Cast: Charlie Ruggles (Scott), Una Merkel (Georgia), Mary Carlisle (Ruth), Russell Hardie (Blake), Porter Hall (Murray), Willard Robertson, Berton Churchill, Cliff Thompson, Snowflake.

Edward E. Rose's mystery melodrama was transformed into a comedy murder mystery in the remake with Charlie Ruggles as a screwy amateur detective supplying most of the humor. This time, the once-kidnapped girl is traveling eastward in a private railroad car to be with her wealthy father. She and her small party of friends must cope with murders, attempted murders, an escaped ape, and the railroad car loaded with explosives, rolling backwards down a steep incline towards an oncoming express.

737 The Redeeming Sin

Based on a story by L.V. Jefferson. Story: Parisian apache dancer Joan falls in love with sculptor Paul Dubois and asks him to make her a lady. He does, and reciprocates her love. All is well until Joan sees Paul with another woman and in a rage enlists Lupin, a leader of a gang of thieves, to steal a string of pearls from Paul's mother and kill him. Paul is stabbed but survives. Then Joan discovers that the other woman was Paul's sister. She repents, arranges for the return of the pearls and when she sees Paul in church, the two are reunited.

Vitagraph Co. of America, 1925 (original). Silent. Director: J. Stuart Blackton. Cast: Nazimova (Joan), Lou Tellegen (Lupin), Carl Miller (Paul Dubois), Otis Harlan (Papa Chuchu), Rosita Marstini (Mere Michi), William Dunn, Rose Tapley.

• ***The Redeeming Sin*** (remake). Warner Bros., 1929. Part-talkie. Director: Joe Jackson; screenwriter: Harvey Gates. Cast: Dolores Costello (Joan Billaire), Conrad Nagel (Dr. Raoul de Boise), Philippe De Lacy (Petit), George E. Stone, Lionel Belmore, Warner Richmond, Nina Quartero.

Apparently the apache dancer had not quite reformed when the sculptor helped her become a lady. One wonders if years later, should he happen to notice a pretty face, if she'll hire another hit man to punish him for his infidelity. In the remake, Joan becomes romantically involved with a doctor she once tried to shoot. These are dangerous women to know.

Redhead *see* **Red Head**

The Reluctant Astronaut *see* **Hail the Conquering Hero**

The Remarkable Mr. Kipps *see* **Kipps**

738 Rendezvous

Based on the novel *American Black Chamber* by Herbert O. Yardley. Story: Bill Gordon, the puzzle editor of a Washington newspaper, enlists in the army to fight during World War I. The day before he is to leave, he meets Joel Carter, and falls in love with her. Her uncle is an Under-Secretary of War and at her request, he arranges for Bill to be assigned to the Cipher Bureau to decode messages and break enemy codes. He's indignant but makes rapid progress in his assignment, and alienates Joel when he pays a bit too much attention to Olivia, a Russian spy. He's able to smash a German spy ring with his quick wit and now feels that he should be allowed to head for the real fighting, but he's sent back to the Bureau to deal with more conspiracies.

MGM, 1935 (original). Director: William K. Howard; screenwriters: Bella and Sam Spewack. Cast: William Powell (Bill Gordon), Rosalind Russell (Joel Carter), Binnie Barnes (Olivia), Lionel Atwill (William Brennan), Hugh Romero (Nickolajeff), Samuel S. Hinds, Henry Stephenson, Frank Reicher, Charles Grapewin.

• ***Pacific Rendezvous*** (remake). MGM, 1942. Director: George Sidney; screenwriters: Harry Kurnitz, P.J. Wolfson and George Oppenheimer. Cast: Lee Bowman (Lt. Bill Gordon), Jean Rogers (Elaine Carter), Mona Maris (Olivia Kerlov), Carl Esmond (Andre Leemuth), Paul Cavanaugh (Commander Brennan), Blanche Yurka, Russell Hicks.

The first film was a fun comedy melodrama with Powell and Russell working well enough together to be favorably compared to the teaming of Powell and Myrna Loy in the *Thin Man* series. The remake is a flimsy effort with Lee Bowman as a code expert who falls in love with a scatterbrain, Jean Rogers, becomes involved with Russian spy Mona Maris, and puts a crimp into the plans of a German espionage gang.

Reserved for Ladies *see* **Service for Ladies**

739 Resurrection

Based on the novel by Leo Tolstoy. Story: While spending the summer in a rural district, Prince Dimitri of St. Petersburg has an affair with orphaned peasant girl Katusha. When her aunt discovers that she is pregnant with Dimitri's child, the girl is thrown out in disgrace. The child dies and poor Katusha is reduced to prostitution. She is falsely accused of poisoning and robbing a merchant. Dimitri is summoned to be on the jury at her trial, feels responsible for her situation and offers to marry her. She refuses and although innocent of the crime, she bravely accepts her banishment to Siberia, content that she is loved.

• ***Resurrection*** (remake). United Artists, 1927. Silent. Director: Edwin Carewe; screenwriter: Finis Fox. Cast: Rod La Rocque (Prince Dimitri Nekhludoff), Dolores Del Rio (Katusha Maslova), Marc McDermott (Major Schoenblock), Lucy Beaumont (Aunt Sophya), Vera Lewis, Clarissa Selwynne, Eve Southern, Count Ilya Tolstoy.

• ***Resurrection*** (remake). Universal Pictures, 1931. Director: Edwin Carewe; screenwriter: Finis Fox. Cast: John Boles (Prince Dmitri Nekhludoff), Lupe Velez (Katusha Maslova), Nance O'Neil (Princess Marya), William Keighley (Major Schoenblock), Rose Tapley, Michael Mark, Sylvia Nadina, George Irving, Edward Cecil, Mary Forman.

Tolstoy's story of a woman wronged and redeemed by love was first filmed in 1918 by Paramount Pictures. In 1963, the U.S.S.R. produced a 2½ hour version of the work. The productions are uneven in presenting the story and the acting is not uniformly appropriate. The two Katushas, Dolores Del Rio and Lupe Velez, do generate a great deal of sympathy for their characters, but their leading men, Rod La Rocque and John Boles, often seem uncomfortable as Russian aristocrats. The scenic shots are frequently more interesting than the plot.

Return from Witch Mountain *see* **Escape to Witch Mountain**

The Return of Jimmy Valentine *see* **Alias Jimmy Valentine**

The Return of Monte Cristo *see* **The Count of Monte Cristo**

740 The Return of Peter Grimm

Based on the play by David Belasco. Story: Peter Grimm coaxes his ward Catherine into an engagement with his nephew, Frederick, and then dies. Despite loving another man, Catherine marries Frederick and when he proves to be a rascal, old Peter's spirit comes back to straighten the young man out.

Fox Film Corporation, 1926 (original). Silent. Director: Victor Schertzinger; screenwriter: Bradley King. Cast: Alec B. Francis (Peter Grimm), John Roche (Frederick Grimm), Janet Gaynor (Catherine), Richard Walling (James Hartman), John St. Polis, Lionel Belmore, Elizabeth Patterson, Bodil Rosing, Mickey McBan.

• ***The Return of Peter Grimm*** (remake). RKO, 1935. Director: George Nicholls, Jr.; screenwriter: Francis Faragoh. Cast: Lionel Barrymore (Peter Grimm), Helen Mack (Catherine), Edward Ellis (Dr. MacPerson), Donald Meek (Mr. Bartholomey), Allen Vincent (Frederick), George Breakston, James Bush, Ethel Griffies, Lucien Littlefield.

These somber fantasies were very old fashioned, even when first released. As a spook story, neither is very satisfactory and the story is quite implausible even without the spiritualism. Why Catherine would allow herself to be talked into marrying a man she doesn't love is hard to understand. She's not coerced anyway, just anxious to please old Peter Grimm on his deathbed. Even the exceptional ability of Lionel Barrymore isn't enough to make the story work.

The Return of Sherlock Holmes *see* **Sherlock Holmes**

Return of the Dragon *see* **Enter the Dragon**

The Return of the Frog *see* **The Frog**

Return of the Jedi *see* **Star Wars**

The Return of the Pink Panther *see* **The Pink Panther**

Return of the Rat *see* **The Rat**

Return of the Scarlet Pimpernel *see* **The Scarlet Pimpernel**

Return of the Terror *see* **The Terror**

Return to Macon County *see* **Macon County**

Return to Peyton Place *see* **Peyton Place**

741 Revenge of the Nerds

Based on a story by Tim Metcalfe, Miguel Tejada-Flores, Steve Zacharias and Jeff Buhai. Story: When no one else will have them or have anything to do with them, geeky college freshmen—nerds to the jocks and college cuties—band together and form their own fraternity affiliated with an all-black Greek society, Lambda Lambda Lambda. This results in all-out war between the two groups, but with their superior intelligence the nerds outsmart their muscle-bound adversaries and prove to the girls that they have something going for them—what, one can only wonder.

Twentieth Century–Fox, 1984. Director: Jeff Kanew; screenwriters: Tim Metcalfe, Miguel Tejada-Flores, Steve Zacharias and Jeff Buhai. Cast: Robert Carradine (Lewis), Anthony Edwards (Gilbert), Curtis Armstrong (Booger), Larry B. Scott (Lamar), Julie Montgomery, Ted McGinley, Michelle Meyrink, Bernie Casey, James Cromwell.

• ***Revenge of the Nerds II: Nerds in Paradise*** (sequel). Twentieth Century–Fox, 1987. Director: Joe Roth; screenwriters: Dan Guntzelman and Steve Marshall. Cast: Robert Carradine (Lewis), Curtis Armstrong (Booger), Larry B. Scott (Lamar), Timothy Busfield (Poindexter), Courtney Thorne-Smith (Sunny), Andrew Cassese (Wormser), Donald Gibb, Bradley Whitford, Ed Lauter, Priscilla Lopez.

Some viewers may take exception with college students being divided into two groups, the brawny and beautiful on one side and the bright and godawful twerps on the other. Still, since more people can identify with those who were not campus VIPs, there is a natural bias toward these poor excuses for preppies who put their ingenuity to work to win the right to their turf on the campus. In the sequel, the Tri-Lambs, just as disgusting and horribly dressed as ever, attend an intrafraternity council meeting in Fort Lauderdale, where they are once again shunned by everyone, including the hotel at which they are scheduled to stay. Led by Robert Carradine, the head nerd, they end up in the world's worst dump. They sing a rap number about nerd pride which is the best thing about the movie, and that's being kind.

Revenge of the Nerds II: Nerds in Paradise *see* **Revenge of the Nerds**

Revenge of the Pink Panther *see* **The Pink Panther**

The Ribald Tales of Robin Hood *see* **Robin Hood**

Rich Man, Poor Man *see* **The Idle Rich**

742 Richard III

Based on the play by William Shakespeare. Story: During the reign of England's Edward IV, everyone at court is involved in some kind of intrigue, but none more so that Edward's brother Richard, Duke of Gloucester, who has a long-range scheme to become king. One by one he eliminates those who stand between him and the throne. Once king, he is confronted with the threat of exiled Henry Tudor, who successfully seizes the throne by defeating Richard's forces at Bosworth.

• ***Tower of London*** (remake). Universal Pictures, 1939. Director: Rowland V. Lee; screenwriter: Tobert N. Lee. Cast: Basil Rathbone (Richard, Duke of Gloucester), Boris Karloff (Mord), Barbara O'Neil (Queen Elizabeth), Ian Hunter (King Edward IV), Vincent Price (Duke of Clarence), Nan Grey (Lady Alice Barton), Ernest Cossart (Tom Clink), John Sutton (John Wyatt), Leo G. Carroll (Lord Hastings), Miles Mander, Rose Hobart.

• ***Richard III*** (remake). London Films, Great Britain, 1955. Director: Laurence Olivier; screenwriter: Alan Dent. Cast: Laurence Olivier (Richard III), Cedric Hardwicke (Edward IV), Ralph Richardson (Buckingham), John Gielgud (Clarence), Mary Kerridge (Queen Elizabeth), Claire Bloom (Lady Anne), Pamela Brown (Jane Shore), Stanley Baker (Henry Tudor), Nicholas Hannen, Andrew Cruickshank, Clive Morton, Helen Haye, John Phillips.

The story of the schemes of Richard "Crouchback" to become King Richard III of England has appeared on the screen in 1908, 1911, 1913 and 1922. In 1964, United Artists released a remake of *Tower of London* with Vincent Price having graduated from the role of. Clarence, drowned in his own favorite wine, to the cruel, hunchbacked Richard. Basil Rathbone and Boris Karloff, together in the first version of this movie, reminded one of their earlier collaboration in *The Son of Frankenstein.* In this version, Karloff serves Rathbone as a sinister torturer and executioner. The 1955 film, blessed with a cast consisting of the cream of British actors, is a splendid piece, made even more interesting by the asides that Olivier as Richard delivers from time to time directly to the audience to keep them aware of the intrigue and the hunchback's motivation and future plans. Shakespeare's poetry is impeccably delivered in this most fascinating and exciting drama.

743 The Richest Girl in the World

Based on a screenplay by Norman Krasna. Story: Dorothy Hunter is a wealthy girl seeking a man who will love her for herself and not be primarily concerned with her money. She has to resort to a bit of deception before she discovers that Tony Travers fits the bill nicely.

RKO, 1934 (original). Director: William A. Seiter; screenwriter: Norman Krasna. Cast: Miriam Hopkins (Dorothy Hunter), Henry Stephenson (John), Joel McCrea (Tony Travers), Fay Wray (Sylvia), Reginald Denny (Phillip), George Meeker, Burr McIntosh, Edgar Norton, Wade Boteler.

• ***Bride by Mistake*** (sequel). RKO, 1944. Director: Richard Wallace;

screenwriters: Phoebe and Henry Ephron. Cast: Alan Marshal (Tony), Laraine Day (Norah), Marsha Hunt (Sylvia), Allyn Joslyn (Phil Vernon), Edgar Buchanan (Connors), Michael St. Angel, Marc Cramer, William Post, Jr., Bruce Edwards.

Miriam Hopkins is convincing as the heiress who knows she's found her true love when Joel McCrea, slightly drunk, cradles his head in her lap and babbles nonsense. It's sweet romantic claptrap but everyone is pulling their weight so well that it works. In the sequel, Marsha Hunt impersonates wealthy Laraine Day, because of the latter's shyness. Laraine thinks Alan Marshal is just about right for her, but he sets his sights on Hunt, whom he believes has the money. When Marsha turns him down because she's already got Allyn Joslyn, Marshal settles for Day, and on the wedding night discovers she's the one with the money. He briefly takes the news badly, but when Laraine appears in a revealing negligee, he forgets what's bothering him.

Riding High *see* **Broadway Bill**

744 The Right of Way

Based on the novel by Sir Gilbert Parker. Story: Brilliant and insolent lawyer Charlie Steele does his best work when drunk. He enters into a cold-blooded marriage, believing in neither love nor God. Five years later he catches his brother-in-law embezzling and mortgages his last piece of property to clear his connection with the crook and heads north. There, amidst a drunken brawl, he falls into a river and is believed dead. However, he survives, having merely lost his memory. When he regains it, he learns that his wife has re-married and he is believed to be the embezzler. He does not return to clear matters up, but instead falls in love with a backwoods girl he cannot marry. He gets religion shortly before he is killed in a fight.

Metro Productions, 1915 (original). Silent. Director: G. Rolfe; screenwriter: Gilbert Parker. Cast: William Faversham (Charlie Steele), Jane Grey (Rosalie), Edward Brennan (Joe Portugaise), Henry Bergman (Trudel), Harold DeBecker (Billy Wantage).

• ***The Right of Way*** (remake). First National Pictures, 1931. Director: Frank Lloyd; screenwriter: Francis E. Faragoh. Cast: Conrad Nagel (Charles Steele), Loretta Young (Rosalie Evantural), Fred Kohler (Joseph Portugaise), William Janney (Billy Wantage), Snitz Edwards, George Pierce, Halliwell Hobbes, Olive Tell, Brandon Hurst.

The story of the monocled dandy was also produced in 1920 with Bert Lytell in the lead. Everything about the remake, except Loretta Young's beautiful face, looks careless and the dialogue makes one yearn for titles.

The Right to be Happy *see* **A Christmas Carol**

The Right to Live *see* **The Sacred Flame**

Right to the Heart *see* **Woman Power**

745 The Ringer

Based on the novel *The Gaunt Stranger* by Edgar Wallace. Story: A criminal master of disguise returns to England to kill his former partner and the police can do nothing to prevent it because no one knows what he looks like without one of his disguises.

British Lion, Great Britain, 1928 (original). Silent. Director: Arthur Maude; screenwriter: Edgar Wallace. Cast: Leslie Faber (Dr. Lomond), Annette Benson (Cora Ann Milton), Lawson Butt (Maurice Meister), Nigel Barrie (Insp. Wembury), Hayford Hobbs (Insp. Bliss), John Hamilton, Muriel Angelus, Charles Emerald, Esther Rhodes.

• ***The Ringer*** (remake). Gainsborough-British Lion, Great Britain, 1931. Director: Walter Forde; screenwriters: Angus MacPhail and Robert Stevenson. Cast: Gordon Harker (Sam Hackett), Franklin Dyall (Maurice Meister), John Longden (Insp. Wembury), Carol Goodner (Cora Ann Milton), Patrick Curwen (Dr. Lomond), Dorothy Bartlam, Esmond Knight, Henry Hallett, Arthur Stratton, Kathleen Joyce.

• ***The Gaunt Stranger*** (remake). Ealing, Great Britain, 1938. Director: Walter Forde; screenwriter: Sidney Gilliat. Cast: Sonnie Hale (Sam Hackett), Wilfrid Lawson (Maurice Meister), Louise Henry (Cora Ann Milton), Patrick Barr (Insp. Alan Wembury), Alexander Knox (Dr. Anthony Lomond), John Longden (Insp. Bliss), Peter Croft, Patricia Roc, George Merritt, Arthur Hambling, John Turnbull.

The 1931 talkie has the classic line "The Ringer has been seen in Deptford!" Of course no one knows what the Ringer looks like without his disguises. In the remakes, secret passages and suspects are in great numbers, but despite all the police effort to save Maurice Meister, the killer gets him with a sword stick and escapes.

Risky Business *see* **Okay America**

River of Romance *see* **The Fighting Coward**

746 River's End

Based on the novel by James Oliver Curwood. Story: Mountie Conniston goes into the North Country searching for Keith, who is wanted for murder. He gets his man, but on the trip south, Conniston dies. The latter's guide suggests that Keith should impersonate Conniston because the resemblance between the two is uncanny. Keith finds that his impersonation is unnecessary when he arrives at his destination, because he has been cleared of the crime. However, he finds Miriam, Conniston's girlfriend, to be most lovely and if anything more deeply in love with him than she was with the deceased. But Miriam is informed by a former jealous suitor, Martin, that Conniston is already married. Keith is forced to confess to his deception, without going into all of the details, and is flogged by the Mounties. As he leaves town, he finds Miriam waiting for him in a boat.

• ***River's End*** (remake). Warner Bros., 1930. Director: Michael Curtiz;

screenwriter: Charles Kenyon. Cast: Charles Bickford (Keith/Conniston), Evelyn Knapp (Miriam), J. Farrell MacDonald (O'Toole), Zasu Pitts (Louise), Walter McGrail (Martin), David Torrence, Junior Coughlin, Tom Santschi.

• ***River's End*** (remake). Warner Bros., 1940. Director: Ray Enright; screenwriters: Barry Trivers and Bertram Milhauser. Cast: Dennis Morgan (John Keith/Sgt. Conniston), George Tobias (Andy Dijon), Elizabeth Earl (Linda Conniston), Victor Jory (Norman Talbot), James Stephenson (Inspector McDowell), Steffi Duna, Edward Pawley.

James Oliver Curwood's story of the Canadian woods country and the Mounties was first filmed in 1920 by First National Pictures. In the 1940 film, Dennis Morgan plays the duel role of an innocent man convicted of murder and the Mountie who goes to get him. When the Mountie dies, Morgan assumes his identity because they look just alike, and through a series of almost absurd circumstances, clears himself. George Tobias provides some nice comic relief in the melodrama.

The Road Back *see* **All Quiet on the Western Front**

The Road to Paradise *see* **Cornered**

747 Rob Roy

Based on the novel by Sir Walter Scott. Story: Scottish rebel Rob Roy MacGregor fights against King George I and the injustice of English rule in Scotland.

United Films, Great Britain, 1911 (original). Silent. Director and screenwriter: Arthur Vivian. Cast: John Clyde (Rob Roy MacGregor), Theor Henries (Helen MacGregor), Durward Lely (Francis Osbaldistone), W.G. Robb (the Baillie), George Hunter (the Dougal Craitur).

• ***Rob Roy*** (remake). Gaumont-Westminister, Great Britain, 1922. Silent. Director: W.P. Kellino; screenwriter: Alicia Ramsey. Cast: David Hawthorne (Rob Roy MacGregor), Gladys Jennings (Helen Campbell), Sir Simeon Stuart (Duke of Montrose), Wallace Bosco (James Grahame), Alec Hunter (the Dougal Creatur), Eva Llewellyn (Mother MacGregor), Tom Morriss (Sandy the Biter), Roy Kellino (Ronald MacGregor).

• ***Rob Roy the Highland Rogue*** (remake). Walt Disney/RKO, Great Britain, 1953. Director: Harold French; screenwriter: Lawrence E. Watkin. Cast: Richard Todd (Rob Roy MacGregor), Glynis Johns (Helen Mary), James Robertson Justice (Duke of Argyll), Michael Gough (Duke of Montrose), Finlay Currie (Hamish McPherson), Jean Taylor Smith, Geoffrey Kean, Archie Duncan.

The 1911 film was Britain's first three-reel movie and proved quite successful. The tale of one of the clan leaders who refuses to accept defeat the hands of the British and rebels against the king plays like an American western combined with a Robin Hood in kilts. The Disney movie might have been better if it had been an animated feature. Richard Todd and others could have had some life pumped into them.

Rob Roy, The Highland Rogue *see* **Rob Roy**

748 The Robe

Based on the novel by Lloyd C. Douglas. Story: Arrogant young tribune Marcellius Gallio is in charge of the crucifixion of Jesus Christ. The experiences and the clutching of Christ's robe at the moment of the latter's death has a profound effect on him. His muscular and moody slave, Demetrius, is also affected by the event. Gallio's spiritual encounter and his love for lovely Roman maid Diana, who is a Christian, causes him to lose more than favor with the mad emperor Caligula, who demands the robe be brought to him, believing it to possess godly powers. By the end of the film Marcellius and Diana go happily together to their death, anticipating being with Jesus in heaven.

Twentieth Century–Fox, 1953 (original). Director: Henry Koster; screenwriter: Philip Dunne from an adaptation of the novel by Gina Kaus. Cast: Richard Burton (Marcellius Gallio), Jean Simmons (Diana), Victor Mature (Demetrius), Jay Robinson (Caligula), Dean Jagger (Justus), Peter Rennie (Peter), Richard Boone (Pontius Pilate), Torin Thatcher (Senator Gallio).

• ***Demetrius and the Gladiators*** (sequel). Twentieth Century–Fox, 1954. Director: Delmer Daves; screenwriter: Philip Dunne. Cast: Victor Mature (Demetrius), Susan Hayward (Messalina), Michael Rennie (Peter), Jay Robinson (Caligula), Debra Paget (Lucia), Anne Bancroft (Paula), Barry Jones (Claudius).

The Robe and its sequel were both shown in CinemaScope on giant 68′ × 24′ screens, which was great for panoramic action scenes but did nothing for intimate moments between two lovers. Burton's performance suggested that his experience at the crucifixion had affected him more physically than spiritually, as he looked deathly ill and ready to have a fit whenever he hears a familiar phrase that takes his mind back to the execution. Victor Mature on the other hand merely demonstrates the strength of his coversion by flaring his famous nostrils, almost frighteningly in giant closeups, and looking like he has a slight stomach ache. Jay Robinson portrays Emperor Caligula at the top of his shriek and as usual, Michael Rennie as Peter looks otherworldly, something like an early-day Mr. Spock. Jean Simmons is lovely, but is only allowed to mouth banalities. Not to be outdone by the histrionics of those in the original, Susan Hayward as the ever raunchy Messalina shouts, shrieks and pouts with the best of them in the sequel.

The story of the sequel is simple enough. Demetrius, having found God in the original picture, loses him when Debra Paget goes into a catatonic state after being assaulted by some rowdies. Old Demetrius can't understand why God would allow this to happen to one so good and pure. Not waiting for an answer, he jumps into the arena as an honored gladiator and the bed of Messalina as stud. By the end of the picture Roman soldiers have dispatched mad old Caligula, replacing him with his Uncle Claudius, Messalina gets her comeuppance, Paget comes out of the trance, and in gratitude, Mature resumes his Christian faith.

Robin and Marian *see* **Robin Hood**

749 Robin Hood

Based on the legend. Story: The Sheriff of Nottingham illegally strips Robert of Huntington of his title, land and properties, giving them to Sir Guy of Gisbourne. Robert is forced to take to the woods of Sherwood Forest with a band of merry men who rob from the rich and give to the poor. Robert takes the new name of Robin Hood. Betrayed by one of his own men, Robin is captured by the Sheriff of Nottingham and sentenced to be executed after watching his beloved Maid Marian Fitzwalter married to Sir Guy. Three of Robin's men, Friar Tuck, Little John, and Will Scarlett, interrupt the ceremony, bringing a pardon for Robin from King Richard the Lion-Hearted, who has just arrived back in England from the Crusades. Robert's title and properties are restored to him as is Maid Marian.

• ***Robin Hood*** (remake). United Artists, 1922. Silent. Director: Allan Dwan; screenwriter: Lotta Woods, based on a story by Elton Thomas. Cast: Douglas Fairbanks (Robin Hood/The Earl of Huntington), Enid Bennett (Maid Marian Fitzwalter), William Lowery (Sheriff of Nottingham), Willard Louis (Friar Tuck), Alan Hale (Little John), Maine Geary (Will Scarlet), Lloyd Talman (Alan-a-Dale), Wallace Beery (Richard the Lion-Hearted), Sam De Grasse (Prince John), Billie Bennett, Merrill McCormick, Wilson Benge, Paul Dickey.

• ***The Adventures of Robin Hood*** (remake). First National Pictures, 1938. Directors: Michael Curtiz and William Keighley; screenwriters: Norman Reilly Raine and Seton I. Miller. Cast: Errol Flynn (Robin Hood/Sir Robert of Locksley), Olivia de Havilland (Maid Marian), Basil Rathbone (Sir Guy of Gisbourne), Claude Rains (Prince John), Patric Knowles (Will Scarlet), Eugene Pallette (Friar Tuck), Alan Hale (Little John), Melville Cooper (Sheriff of Nottingham), Ian Hunter (King Richard the Lion-Hearted), Montagu Love, Herbert Mundin, Una O'Connor, Leonard Wiley, Robert Warwick, Colin Kenney.

• ***The Bandit of Sherwood Forest*** (remake). Columbia Pictures, 1946. Directors: George Sherman and Henry Levin; screenwriters: Wilfrid H. Petitt and Melvin Levy, based on Paul A. Castleton's novel *Son of Robin Hood*. Cast: Cornel Wilde (Robert of Nottingham), Anita Louise (Lady Catherine Maitland), Edgar Buchanan (Friar Tuck), Henry Daniell (the Regent), John Abbott (Will Scarlet), Lloyd Corrigan (Sheriff of Nottingham), Jill Esmond (Queen Mother), George Macready (Fritz-Herbert), Russell Hicks (Robin Hood), Ray Teal (Little John), Leslie Denison, Ian Wolfe, Maurice R. Tauzin.

• ***The Prince of Thieves*** (remake). Columbia Pictures, 1948. Director: Howard Bretherton; screenwriter: Maurice Tombragel, based on a story by Alexandre Dumas. Cast: Jon Hall (Robin Hood), Patricia Morison (Lady Marian), Adele Jergens (Lady Christabel), Alan Mowbray (Friar Tuck), Michael Duane (Sir Allan Claire), H.B. Warner (Gilbert Hend), Lowell Gilmore, Gavin Muir, Robin Raymond, Lewis L. Russell, Walter Sande.

• ***Rogues of Sherwood Forest*** (remake). Columbia Pictures, 1950. Director: Gordon Douglas; screenwriter: George Bruce. Cast: John Derek (Robin, Earl of Huntington), Diana Lynn (Lady Marianne), George Macready (King John),

Paul Cavanaugh (Sir Giles), Alan Hale (Little John), Lowell Gilmore, Billy House, William Bevan.

• ***The Story of Robin Hood*** (remake). Disney/RKO, 1952. Director: Ken Annakin; screenwriter: Lawrence E. Watkin. Cast: Richard Todd (Robin Hood), Joan Rice (Maid Marian), Peter Finch (Sheriff of Nottingham), James Hayter (Friar Tuck), James Robertson Justice (Little John), Martita Hunt (Queen Eleanor), Hubert Gregg (Prince John), Bill Owen, Reginald Tate, Elton Haytes.

• ***Men of Sherwood Forest*** (remake). Hammer Films, 1954. Director: Val Guest; screenwriter: Allan Mackinnon. Cast: Don Taylor (Robin Hood), Eileen Moore (Lady Alys), Reginald Beckwith (Friar Tuck), Patrick Holt (King Richard), Leslie Linder (Little John), Leonard Sachs (Sheriff of Nottingham), John van Eyssen, David Kingwood, Douglas Wilmer, Harold Lang.

• ***Sword of Sherwood Forest*** (remake). Hammer Films/Yeoman Films, 1960. Director: Terence Fisher; screenwriter: Alan Hackney. Cast: Richard Greene (Robin Hood), Peter Cushing (Sheriff of Nottingham), Sarah Branch (Maid Marian), Niall MacGinnis (Friar Tuck), Nigel Green (Little John), Richard Pasco, Vanda Godsell, Jack Gwillim, Edwin Richfield, Oliver Reed.

• ***Robin Hood*** (remake). Buena Vista Productions, 1973. Director: Wolfgang Reithermann; screenwriters: Larry Clemmons, Eric Cleworth, Vance Gerry, Frank Thomas and Ken Anderson. Cast: voices of: Brian Bedford (Robin Hood), Peter Ustinov (Prince John), Phil Harris (Little John), Terry-Thomas (Sir Hiss), Monica Evans (Maid Marian), Carole Shelley, Andy Devine, Roger Miller, Pat Buttram, George Lindsey, Ken Curtis.

• ***Robin and Marian*** (sequel). Columbia Pictures, 1976. Director: Richard Lester; screenwriter: James Goldman. Cast: Sean Connery (Robin Hood), Audrey Hepburn (Maid Marian), Robert Shaw (Sheriff of Nottingham), Richard Harris (King Richard), Nicol Williamson (Little John), Denholm Elliott (Will Scarlet), Ronnie Barker, Kenneth Haigh, Ian Holm, Bill Maynard.

The legend of Robin Hood was first brought to the screen in 1908 in Great Britain as *Robin Hood and His Merry Men.* Since that time other versions have been released in 1912, 1913, and Britain's 1931 *The Merry Men of Sherwood; Tales of Robin Hood* and *Miss Robin Hood* in 1952; *Son of Robin Hood* in 1959; Italy's *Triumph of Robin Hood* in 1962; Frank Sinatra's Rat Pack version in 1964, *Robin and the Seven Hoods;* another Italian version, *Robin Hood and the Pirates* in 1964; *Robin Hood* in 1966; *Challenge for Robin Hood* in Great Britain in 1968; *The Ribald Tales of Robin Hood* in 1969; two versions in 1971; Rankin-Bass' 1972 production, and finally a 1975 knock-down called *Robin Hoodnik.*

Of all the various performers on stage and screen who have portrayed Robin Hood, it is likely that most people still will associate the role primarily and most fondly with the great swashbuckler Errol Flynn and his 1938 film. Here was a handsome, charming, dashing, adventurous, humorous, loving, loyal, selfless, sharing, bright man perfectly imbuing his character with these virtues. Actually, everything about the 1938 film is memorable, from the color photography to the excellent cast headed by Flynn and Olivia de Havilland, but also blessed with the likes of Basil Rathbone, Claude Rains, Eugene Pallette, Alan Hale (who played the role of Little John in three different pictures in three different decades), Melville Cooper, Herbert Mundin, Una O'Connor and Ian Hunter.

The other filmings of the Robin Hood legend could be rated, but since everyone would compete as second best to the 1938 production, it doesn't seem worth the trouble to argue for a runner up since they are so far behind that movie in quality, entertainment value and memorability. Richard Greene and Douglas Fairbanks both made fine Robin Hoods, the former more restrained than Flynn and the latter showing all of his acrobatic skills, and are certainly worth a look if the opportunity to view them arises. The 1976 film with Sean Connery and Audrey Hepburn proposed to answer the question, What happened to Robin Hood and Marian years later after their encounters with Sir Guy Gisbourne, the Sheriff of Nottingham and Prince John? Unfortunately, one must report that they had not grown better in the ensuing years, just older and a bit on the boring side.

Robin Hood and His Merry Men *see* **Robin Hood**

Robin Hood and the Pirates *see* **Robin Hood**

Robin Hood and the Seven Hoods *see* **Robin Hood**

Robin Hoodnik *see* **Robin Hood**

750 Robinson Crusoe

Based on the novel by Daniel Defoe. Story: A man is shipwrecked in 1659 near Tobago and survives on a deserted island for a long time with no other humans except for a native he names Man Friday for the day of the week that he met him.

• ***Robinson Crusoe*** (remake). Epic Films, Great Britain, 1927. Silent. Director and screenwriter: M.A. Wetherell. Cast: M.A. Wetherell (Robinson Crusoe), Fay Compton (Sophie), Herbert Waithe (Man Friday), Reginald Fox.

• ***Mr. Robinson Crusoe*** (remake). United Artists, 1932. Director: Edward Sutherland; screenwriter: Tom Geraghty. Cast: Douglas Fairbanks (Mr. Robinson Crusoe), Maria Alba (Girl Friday), William Farnum, Earle Brown.

• ***Robinson Crusoe on Mars*** (remake). Paramount Pictures, 1964. Director: Byron Haskin; screenwriters: Ib Melchior and John C. Higgins. Cast: Paul Mantee (Cmdr. Christopher "Kit" Draper), Vic Lundin (Friday), Adam West (Col. Dan McReady).

• ***Lt. Robin Crusoe, U.S.N.*** (remake). Disney/Buena Vista, 1966. Director: Byron Paul; screenwriters: Bill Walsh and Don DaGradi. Cast: Dick Van Dyke (Lt. Robin Crusoe), Nancy Kwan (Wednesday), Akim Tamiroff (Tanamashua), Arthur Malet, Tyler McVey, Pete Renoudet, Peter Duryea, John Dennis.

• ***Man Friday*** (remake). Avco Embassy, Great Britain, 1975. Director: Jack Gold; screenwriter: Adrian Mitchell. Cast: Peter O'Toole (Crusoe), Richard Roundtree (Friday), Peter Celler (Carey), Christopher Cabot (McBain), Joel Fluellen, Sam Sebrooke, Stanley Clay.

The story of the shipwrecked sailor and his native companion has also been filmed in 1902, 1903, 1910, 1913, 1915, 1916, 1917, 1921, 1927, 1928, 1929, 1936, 1940, 1946, 1950, 1951, 1954, 1960, 1962, 1968 and 1972. Douglas Fairbanks in one of his more minor movies accepts a bet that he can survive on a deserted island for a year alone. Within four months he manages to build a house with all the comforts of home, including a radio, out of the raw materials on the island. He also meets Maria Alba, a lovely Girl Friday, who doesn't have much to say other than some unintelligible grunts, but her looks makes her a welcomed addition to any bachelor pad.

The title of the 1964 production says it all: an astronaut gets pulled into the gravitational field of Mars and has to learn to survive with the help of a pet monkey and a slave who had escaped from an alien spaceship, who naturally is given the name Friday. The Disney film has pilot Dick Van Dyke forced to parachute into the Pacific and end up on a deserted island, that is until he teams up with a chimp who had survived a space mission and a native girl he names Wednesday. For the 1975 British release, shipwrecked O'Toole finds Roundtree washed up on his island and makes the latter his slave. Roundtree begins to ask some questions and finally rebels against white supremacy. It's a fairly obvious allegory on race relations and tensions, but both O'Toole and Roundtree are quite good.

Robinson Crusoe on Mars *see* **Robinson Crusoe**

Rock-a-Bye Baby *see* **The Miracle of Morgan's Creek**

751 Rock, Pretty Baby

Based on the screenplay by Herbert Margolis and William Raynor. Story: This teenage-directed film wraps 17 rock 'n' roll numbers around the simple tale of high school senior Jimmy Daley, who wants to become a bandleader despite the objections of his physician father, who hopes his son will follow in his footsteps and choose a medical profession.

Universal Pictures, 1956 (original). Director: Richard Bartlett; screenwriters: Herbert Margolis and William Raynor. Cast: John Saxon (Jimmy Daley), Sal Mineo (Angelo "Nino" Barrato), Luana Patten (Joan Wright), Edward C. Platt (Dr. Thomas Daley, Sr.), Fay Wray (Beth Daley), Rod McKuen ("Ox" Bentley), John Wilder, Alan Reed, Jr., Douglas Fowley, Bob Courtney.

• ***Summer Love*** (sequel). Universal Pictures, 1958. Director: Charles Haas; screenwriters: William Raynor and Herbert Margolis. Cast: John Saxon (Jimmy Daley), Molly Bee (Alice), Rod McKuen (Ox Bentley), Judy Meredith (Joan Wright), Jill St. John (Erica Landis), John Wilder, George "Foghorn" Winslow, Fay Wray, Edward C. Platt, Shelley Fabares.

One can neither condemn nor praise these movies for being exactly what they were meant to be, rock concerts with a slender story to fill in the spaces between the musical numbers. These included the title song, "What's It Gonna Be," and "Rockabye Lullaby Blues" in the first film. The numbers from the sequel are even less familiar, probably even to those who attended these movies when they were teens. This time John Saxon has a gig with his group at a summer camp and can't decide between Judy Meredith and Jill St. John for his love interest.

752 Rocky

Based on an original story by Sylvester Stallone. Story: By day punk-club fighter Rocky Balboa works as an enforcer for a local loan shark, but he's basically a good guy, awkwardly in love with shy Adrian who works in a Philadelphia pet shop in the same slum neighborhood that is home to our hero. When he gets a fight, it's difficult to look at him and tell who won as he always takes a tremendous beating, but that seems to be his strength—he can take tremendous beatings. Unbelievably, the world heavyweight champion, Apollo Creed, decides to schedule a New Year's Eve fight with an unknown to prove that this is the land of opportunity. He chooses Rocky as his opponent because he likes the kid's nickname, "the Italian Stallion." It's from here on that the movie becomes special, as Rocky prepares himself with almost mystical and religious passion for his opportunity. Here's a real underdog that audiences can rally around as a poor man's hero.

Chartoff-Winkler/United Artists, 1976 (original). Director: John Avildsen; screenwriter: Sylvester Stallone. Cast: Sylvester Stallone (Rocky Balboa), Talia Shire (Adrian), Burt Young (Paulie Balboa), Carl Weathers (Apollo Creed), Burgess Meredith (Mickey), Thayer David, Joe Spinell, Jimmy Gambina, Bill Baldwin.

• ***Rocky II*** (sequel). Chartoff-Winkler/United Artists, 1979. Director and screenwriter: Sylvester Stallone. Cast: Sylvester Stallone (Rocky), Talia Shire (Adrian), Burt Young (Paulie), Carl Weathers (Apollo Creed), Burgess Meredith (Mickey), Tony Burton.

• ***Rocky III*** (sequel). Chartoff-Winkler/United Artists, 1982. Director and screenwriter: Sylvester Stallone. Cast: Sylvester Stallone (Rocky), Carl Weathers (Apollo Creed), Talia Shire (Adrian), Burt Young (Paulie), Burgess Meredith (Mickey), Ian Fried, Mr. T. (Clubber Lang), Al Silvani.

• ***Rocky IV*** (sequel). Chartoff-Winkler/United Artists, 1985. Director and screenwriter: Sylvester Stallone. Cast: Sylvester Stallone (Rocky), Talia Shire (Adrian), Burt Young (Paulie), Carl Weathers (Apollo Creed), Brigitte Nielsen (Ludmilla), Tony Burton (Duke), Dolph Lundgren (Drago), Michael Pataki, R.J. Adams.

The very poignant story of a semi-literate slob who gets his chance to show he's something captured the imagination not only of vast numbers of moviegoers, but also the voters of the Motion Picture Academy of Arts and Sciences, who elected it the Best Picture of the Year, and John G. Avildsen as Best Director. Losers in the Oscar sweepstakes were Stallone as writer and actor; Meredith, Shire and Young as actors and the film's theme song, "Gonna Fly Now," by Carol Connors, Ayn Robbins and Bill Conti.

Fans found the three sequels (so far) of Rocky to be just as exciting and inspirational. Cinematically, they had nothing much new to say about the characters—they weren't the most attractive individuals in the first place. The first sequel begins precisely where the first film ended, with his moral victory against heavyweight champion Apollo Creed. Rocky's now a celebrity and he can afford to marry Adrian, buy a car and a house. Then he starts looking for a job. He's not supposed to fight again because of damage to his eyes, but there's really nothing else he's able to do. So, like Sugar Ray Leonard, he risks going blind to fight Apollo Creed again. In the third film, Rocky is challenged by a brutal slugger who beats him in the first match, but the war doesn't end there. In *Rocky IV,* Rambo and Rocky get mixed together in some Russia-bashing, featuring a giant Communist fighting machine, Drago, who unconcernedly kills retired Apollo Creed in what was meant to be an exhibition match. It's up to Rocky to avenge his friend and wrap himself in the American flag of superiority of our animal over their animal.

Rocky II *see* **Rocky**

Rocky III *see* **Rocky**

Rocky IV *see* **Rocky**

Rogues of Sherwood Forest *see* **Robin Hood**

753 Romance

Based on the novel by Edward Brewster Sheldon. Story: When Rector Tom Armstrong learns that opera star Rita Cavallini, whom he loves, was once the mistress of wealthy Cornelius Van Tuyl, he denounces her. Then he pleads with her to spend her last night before rejoining Van Tuyl with him. She begs him not to treat her like other men have and begins praying. Armstrong comes to his senses, leaves and never sees her again.

United Artists, 1920 (original). Silent. Director: Chet Withey; screenwriter: Edward Sheldon. Cast: Doris Keane (Madame Cavallini), Basil Sidney (Tom Armstrong), Norman Trevor (Van Tuyl).

• ***Romance*** (remake). MGM, 1930. Director: Clarence Brown; screenwriters: Bess Meredyth and Edwin Justus Mayer. Cast: Greta Garbo (Rita Cavallini), Gavin Gordon (Tom Armstrong), Lewis Stone (Cornelius Van Tuyl), Elliott Nugent, Florence Lake, Clara Blandick, Henry Armetta, Mathilde Comont.

D.W. Griffith bought the picture rights to the Broadway hit with hopes of large profits, but the picture lost money; it was a stodgy production. The remake didn't have a better story, just Greta Garbo, and that made all the difference. She emotes beautifully and audiences find they really do care about this lovely opera singer and her troubles with men.

Romance of the Limberlost *see* **Girl of the Limberlost**

754 Romancing the Stone

Based on a screenplay by Diane Thomas. Story: Joan Wilder, an author of romantic thrillers, gets a frantic message from her sister in South America. Unless Joan flies to Cartagena with a treasure map showing the location of a priceless jewel, Sis will be killed. Arriving in Columbia, Joan gets tangled up with an assortment of dangerous people, each with their own plans for the jewel. These include the local police, the thugs who hold Joan's sister and a gang of mountain bandits. Joan is aided, albeit reluctantly, by hunter Jack Colton. Along the way they fall in love or at least in lust and Joan experiences some of the adventures and emotions she had been only writing about up to this time. By the fade-out, they have got the jewel, rescued the sister and seem to be making plans for the sequel.

Twentieth Century–Fox, 1984 (original). Director: Robert Zemeckis; screenwriter: Diane Thomas. Cast: Michael Douglas (Jack Colton), Kathleen Turner (Joan Wilder), Danny DeVito (Ralph), Alfonso Arau (Juan), Manuel Ojeda (Zolo), Zack Norman.

• ***The Jewel of the Nile*** (sequel). Twentieth Century–Fox, 1985. Director: Lewis Teague; screenwriters: Mark Rosenthal and Lawrence Konner. Cast: Michael Douglas (Jack Colton), Kathleen Turner (Joan Wilder), Danny DeVito (Ralph), Avner Eisenberg (Holy Man), Spiros Focas (Omar), Paul David Magid, Howard Jay Petterson.

These two films both spoof and rival *Raiders of the Lost Ark* and are most entertaining in the process. Michael Douglas proves adept at comedy as well as derring-do and Kathleen Turner, fast becoming a modern-day Carole Lombard, is a delight, showing great comical skill as well as one of the best pair of legs now seen on the screen. In the sequel, Joan is conned by Spiros Focas into writing his biography as he plans to usurp power along the Nile. Jack has to come along and rescue Joan and Avner Eisenberg, a holy man, and the jewel mentioned in the title.

Romanoff and Juliet *see* **Romeo and Juliet**

755 Rome Express

Based on the story by Clifford Grey. Story: It's a "Grand Hotel"–like drama of travelers on a train from Paris to Rome. Its passengers include criminals Zurat and Tony chasing Poole, who has double-crossed them; Mrs. Maxtred and Grant, married but not to each other; film star Asta Marvelle and her manager; philanthropist Allistair McBane and his secretary, Mills; and M. Jolif, head of the French Surete. Add to these characters a bit of murder and thievery and one has an exciting melodrama.

Gaumont-British Productions, 1933 (original). Director: Walter Forde; screenwriter: Sidney Gilliat. Cast: Esther Ralston (Asta Marvelle), Conrad Veidt (Zurat), Hugh Williams (Tony), Donald Calthrop (Poole), Joan Barry (Mrs. Maxtred), Harold Huth (Grant), Gordon Harker (Tom Bishop), Eliot Markeham (Mills), Cedric Hardwicke (Alistair McBane), Frank Vosper (M. Jolif), Muriel Aked.

• ***Sleeping Car to Trieste*** (remake). GFD/Rank/Two Cities, 1948. Director: John Paddy Carstairs; screenwriter: Allan Mackinnon. Cast: Jean Kent (Valya),

Albert Lieven (Zurta), Derrick de Marney (George Grant), Paul Dupuis (Jolif), Rona Anderson (Joan Maxted), David Tomlinson (Tom Bishop), Bonar Colleano (Sgt. West), Finley Currie (Alastair MacBain), Coco Aslan, Alan Wheatley, Hugh Burden, David Hutcheson, Claude Larue, Zena Marshall.

Espionage dramas with a transcontinental train setting have provided interesting films throughout the history of motion pictures. These two versions of the subgenre are quite excellent. The only problem with such films is that it often takes up a great deal of time to introduce all of the various characters, and during this period the suspense of the story is delayed and almost forgotten. In the remake, Jean Kent and Albert Lieven are the heavys seeking a diary containing vital political information. The film has an interesting complement of train travelers.

756 Romeo and Juliet

Based on the play by William Shakespeare. Story: In fifteenth-century Verona, Romeo and Juliet, the offsprings of feuding families, fall in love. Their romance is doomed because of the bad blood and they end up committing suicide.

• ***Romeo and Juliet*** (remake). Gaumont, Great Britain, 1908. Silent. Director and screenwriter: uncredited. Cast: Godfrey Tearle (Romeo), Mary Malone (Juliet), Gordon Bailey (Mercutio), James Annand (Tybalt).

• ***Romeo and Juliet*** (remake). MGM, 1936. Director: George Cukor; screenwriter: Talbot Jennings. Cast: Leslie Howard (Romeo), Norma Shearer (Juliet), John Barrymore (Mercutio), Basil Rathbone (Tybalt), Edna May Oliver (Nurse), Henry Kolker, C. Aubrey Smith, Violet Kemble-Cooper, Robert Warwick, Virginia Hammond, Reginald Denny, Ralph Forbes, Andy Devine, Conway Tearle.

• ***Romeo and Juliet*** (remake). Rank, Great Britain, 1954. Director and screenwriter: Renato Castellani. Cast: Laurence Harvey (Romeo), Susan Shentall (Juliet), Aldo Zollo (Mercutio), Enzo Fiermonte (Tybalt), Flora Robson (Nurse), Mervyn Johns (Friar Laurence), Sebastian Cabot, Lydia Sherwood, Giulio Garbinetti, Nietta Zocchi, Bill Travers, Norman Woodland, John Gielgud.

• ***Romanoff and Juliet*** (remake). Universal/International, 1961. Director and screenwriter: Peter Ustinov. Cast: Peter Ustinov (the General), Sandra Dee (Juliet Moulsworth), John Gavin (Igor Romanoff), Akim Tamiroff (Vadim Romanoff), Alix Talton, Rik von Nutter, John Phillips, Peter Jones.

• ***West Side Story*** (remake). United Artists, 1961. Director: Robert Wise and Jerome Robbins; screenwriter: Ernest Lehman. Cast: Natalie Wood (Maria), Richard Beymer (Tony), Russ Tamblyn (Riff), Rita Moreno (Anita), George Chakiris (Bernardo), Simon Oakland, Ned Glass, William Bramley, John Astin, Penny Santon, Tucker Smith, Tony Mordente, David Winters, Eliot Feld, Robert Banas, Susan Oakes, Jose De Vega, Jay Norman, Yvonne Othon.

• ***Romeo and Juliet*** (remake). Embassy, Great Britain, 1966. Director: Paul Czinner. Ballet: Sergei Sergevich Prokofiev. Cast: Margot Fonteyn (Juliet),

In the middle-aged version of Romeo and Juliet, *Leslie Howard reaches out for Norma Shearer in the balcony scene of the 1936 MGM production of the Shakespearean story of two star-crossed lovers.*

Rudolf Nureyev (Romeo), David Blair (Mercutio), Desmond Doyle (Tybalt), Anthony Dowell, Derek Rencher, Michael Somes, Julia Farron.

• ***Romeo and Juliet*** (remake). Paramount Pictures, Great Britain/Italy, 1968. Director: Franco Zeffirelli; screenwriters: Franco Brusati, Franco Zeffirelli and Masolino D'Amico. Cast: Leonard Whiting (Romeo), Olivia Hussey (Juliet), Michael York (Tybalt), John McEnery (Mercutio), Murray Head (Chorus), Bruce Robinson (Benvolio), Robert Bisacco (Count Paris), Pat Heywood (Nurse), Milo O'Shea (Friar Laurence), Keith Skinner, Richard Warwick, Dyson Lovell, Ugo Barbone, Paul Hardwick, Natasha Parry, Esmerelda Ruspoli, Antonio Pierfederici, Robert Stephens, Paola Tedesco, Roy Holder.

The familiar teenage love story has also been brought to the screen in 1900,

Romeo and Juliet come to a New York slum in the Leonard Bernstein and Stephen Sondheim musical, West Side Story *(United Artists, 1961), with Richard Beymer and Natalie Wood in their balcony scene.*

1911, 1912, 1914, 1916, 1917, 1919, 1921, 1924, 1942, 1943, 1948, 1951, 1954, 1955, 1964, 1969 and 1978. The 1936 Hollywood production had an excellent cast if one did not mind that the main characters were almost middle-aged. It received Academy Award nominations for Best Picture, Best Actress (Shearer) and Best Supporting Actor (Rathbone). None won. It is reported that Fredric March, Robert Donat and Robert Montgomery all turned down the assignment of playing Romeo. In 1968, Zeffirelli made the movie with Leonard Whiting and Olivia Hussey in the title roles; they were about the ages Shakespeare had in mind. It was a beautifully staged production for the most part and Hussey was incredibly lovely. Peter Ustinov's modern version of the story had the feud not only between families but between the nations of the United States and the Soviet Union.

West Side Story, a masterful piece, featured the tremendously appropriate Leonard Bernstein and Stephen Sondheim music, including "Maria," "America," "Something's Coming," "Tonight," "I Feel Pretty," 'Gee, Officer Krupke," "Somewhere," "A Boy Like That" and "Jet Song." In this modernized version, the respective warring families are two rival New York street gangs, one Puerto Rican and the other, an established Anglo gang. Maria has just recently arrived in New York from San Juan and is looked after by her brother

Bernardo, leader of the Sharks, and his girlfriend, Anita. Tony, one of the co-founders with Riff of the Jets is growing a little too old for the gang, but when passions get the best of him in a rumble he has come to stop, he stabs and kills Bernardo. He is later killed by Chino, but Maria survives. The film won the Best Picture Oscar. Other winners were Robert Wise and Jerome Robbins for direction (although the latter only staged a few dance sequences), Daniel L. Fapp for photography, Rita Moreno for Best Supporting Actress and George Chakaris for Best Supporting Actor.

El Ronde de Monte Cristo *see* **The Count of Monte Cristo**

Rookies in Burma *see* **Adventures of a Rookie**

757 Room at the Top

Based on the novel by John Braine. Story: Joe Lampton, a small-timer in the North Country, is determined to get to the top and marriage seems the best way. He puts a push on Susan Brown, daughter of a wealthy businessman, but Mr. Brown sends his daughter abroad to forget Joe. He picks up with unhappily married Alice Aisgill, but when Susan returns, Joe gets her pregnant and Mr. Brown reluctantly gives his approval to their marriage. Joe has to tell Alice that their affair is through, even though he loves her more than Susan. Alice despairingly and drunkenly crashes her car and is killed.

Remus, Great Britain, 1959 (original). Director: Jack Clayton; screenwriter: Neil Patterson. Cast: Simone Signoret (Alice Aisgill), Laurence Harvey (Joe Lampton), Heather Sears (Susan Brown), Donald Wolfit (Mr. Brown), Donald Houston (Charlie Soames), Hermione Baddeley (Elspeth), Allan Cuthbertson, Raymond Huntley, John Westbrook, Ambrosine Philpotts.

• ***Life at the Top*** (sequel). Romulus/Columbia, Great Britain, 1965. Director: Ted Kotcheff; screenwriter: Mordecai Richler. Cast: Laurence Harvey (Joe Lampton), Jean Simmons (Susan Lampton), Honor Blackman (Norah Hauxley), Michael Craig (Mark), Donald Wolfit (Abe Brown), Robert Morley (Titfield), Margaret Johnston, Allan Cuthbertson, Ambrosine Philpotts.

Simone Signoret's performance was flawless and this was recognized by the members of the Motion Picture Academy of Arts and Sciences when they awarded her an Oscar. Neil Patterson won an Oscar for his screenplay. The film was up for the Best Picture Award, Jack Clayton for Best Director, Laurence Harvey for Best Actor and Hermione Baddeley for Best Supporting Actress. Since the most compelling character was killed in the original, the sequel was bound to suffer. Laurence Harvey's character is no more sympathetic the second time around. Ten years after marrying for money and position, he and his wife are dissatisfied with each other and both have affairs, he with TV star Honor Blackman. Joe Lampton later showed up in a long-running British TV series called *Man at the Top* with Kenneth Haigh in the leading role as the belligerent, aging, ambitious man. This was followed by a very predictable film of the same name.

758 Room Service

Based on the play by John Murray and Allan Boretz. Story: This vehicle for the Marx Brothers is too structured to be counted among their comedy masterpieces. In it, Groucho is Gordon Miller (too ordinary a name for him), an impresario with no money who has holed up with his troupe of 22 in a luxury hotel where he has run up a large bill. The humor comes from the struggle of the hotel officials to evict the deadbeats while Groucho and the others fight to stay until their ship comes in.

RKO, 1938 (original). Director: William A. Seiter; screenwriter: Morrie Ryskind. Cast: Groucho Marx (Gordon Miller), Chico Marx (Harry Binelli), Harpo Marx (Faker), Lucille Ball (Christine), Ann Miller (Hilda), Frank Albertson (Leo Davis), Donald McBride (Gregory Wagner), Cliff Dunstan, Philip Loeb, Phillip Wood.

• ***Step Lively*** (remake). RKO, 1944. Director: Tom Whelan; screenwriters: Warren Duff and Peter Milne. Cast: Frank Sinatra (Glen), George Murphy (Miller), Adolphe Menjou (Wagner), Gloria De Haven (Christine), Walter Slezak (Gribble), Eugene Pallette (Jenkins), Wally Brown, Alan Carney, Grant Mitchell, Anne Jeffreys.

In the Marx Brothers version of the Murray and Boretz play, one misses the usual harp solo by Harpo and Chico's turn at the piano. The comedy is weak and contrived, so different from the zany antics usually associated with Groucho, Chico and Harpo. The best bits are provided by Donald MacBride as the hotel executive. MacBride is the master of the slow burn and bombastic behavior and here he demonstrates it beautifully. The remake with Sinatra is a pleasant little trifle with basically the same plot. Sinatra is—what else—a singer who causes bobby soxers and even older gals to swoon. His songs include "As Long As There's Music" and "Where Does Love Begin?" by Ernst Matray and Ken Darby.

Room to Let *see* **The Lodger**

Der Rote Kreis *see* **The Crimson Circle**

Roxanne *see* **Cyrano De Bergerac**

Roxie Hart *see* **Chicago**

759 Ruggles of Red Gap

Based on the novel by Harry Leon Wilson. Story: Newly rich Egbert Floud wins Ruggles, the valet of an English lord, in a poker game while he and his wife are on a visit to Europe. Returning to the western town of Red Gap, Floud introduces Ruggles as a gentleman and because of his very proper manners and behavior, he is accepted as one. When Ruggles' former master arrives for a visit, he falls in love with Kate Kenner, a girl from the other side of the tracks. His brother is summoned to break up the engagement and does so by marrying

Kate himself. Ruggles, meanwhile, opens a successful restaurant and marries Emily Judson.

• ***Ruggles of Red Gap*** (remake). Famous Players/Paramount Pictures, 1923. Silent. Director: James Cruze; screenwriters: Walter Woods and Anthony Coldeway. Cast: Edward Everett Horton (Ruggles), Ernest Torrence (Egbert Floud), Lois Wilson (Kate Kenner), Fritzi Ridgeway (Emily Judson), Charles Ogle (Jeff Tuttle), Louise Dresser (Effie Floud), Anna Lehr, William Austin, Lillian Leighton, Thomas Holding.

• ***Ruggles of Red Gap*** (remake). Paramount Pictures, 1935. Director: Leo McCarey; screenwriters: Walter DeLeon, Harlan Thompson and Humphrey Pearson. Cast: Charles Laughton (Ruggles), Mary Boland (Effie Floud), Charles Ruggles (Egbert Floud), Zasu Pitts (Mrs. Judson), Roland Young (George Vane Bassingwell), Leila Hyams (Nell Kenner), Maude Eburne (Ma Pettingwell), Lucien Littlefield, Leota Lorraine, James Burke, Dell Henderson.

• ***Fancy Pants*** (remake). Paramount, 1950. Director: George Marshall; screenwriters: Edmund Hartmann and Robert O'Brien. Cast: Bob Hope (Humphrey), Lucille Ball (Agatha Floud), Bruce Cabot (Cart Belknap), Jack Kirkwood (Mike Floud), Lea Penman (Effie Floud), Hugh French (George Van Bassingwell), Eric Blore (Sir Wimbley), Joseph Vitale, John Alexander, Norma Varden, Virginia Kelley.

The story of the English valet transported to the old West was first brought to the screen in 1918 by Essanay Studios. The most enjoyable version starred Charles Laughton as the very proper gentleman's gentleman who responds positively to the notion of a democratic society, leaves service and goes into the restaurant business. Laughton's low-key approach to his character was perfection as he gradually evolves from an inhibited servant to become his own master. It's a very funny and human picture.

Bob Hope's go at the role was out and out farce. He isn't even a gentleman's gentleman, being instead an incompetent actor who is brought in as the old family retainer when an Englishman intent on impressing Lucille Ball and her mother, played by Lea Penman, hires the cast of a failing stage play to pose as his family. Penman is so impressed, she insists on taking Hope back with her to her American West home. There he is mistaken for an English lord and runs into the animosity of Ball's suitor, Bruce Cabot. Before everything is resolved, Hope has to go hunting with Teddy Roosevelt, beautifully played by John Alexander, who made the role his in *Arsenic and Old Lace.*

760 The Ruling Passion

Based on the story *Idle Hands* by Earl Derr Biggers. Story: Multimillionaire machinist, designer and inventor James Alden is ordered to rest for six months by his physician. Unable to adjust to inactivity, on the sly he goes into partnership with young Bill Merrick, opening a garage on a new state highway. They attract a large number of customers because of their courtesy and service. Alden's daughter, Angie, discovers her father's secret life and falls in love with his partner, Merrick, who knows Alden only as John Grant. Alden gives his

blessing to the marriage of the youngster and feels refreshed by his change-of-pace rest cure.

United Artists, 1922 (original). Silent. Director: Harmon Weight; screenwriter: Forrest Halsey. Cast: George Arliss (James Alden), Doris Kenyon (Angie Alden), Edward Burns (Bill Merrick), Ida Darling (Mrs. Alden), J.W. Johnston, Ernest Hilliard, Harold Waldridge, Brian Darley.

• ***The Millionaire*** (remake). Warner Bros., 1931. Director: John Adolfi; screenwriter: Booth Tarkington. Cast: George Arliss (James Alden), Evalyn Knapp (Barbara Alden), David Manners (Bill Merrick), Florence Arliss (Mrs. Alden), Noah Beery (Peterson), J. Farrell MacDonald, Bramwell Fletcher, James Cagney.

• ***That Way With Women*** (remake). Warner Bros., 1947. Director: Frederick De Cordova; screenwriter: Leo Townsend. Cast: Dane Clark (Greg Wilson), Martha Vickers (Marcia Alden), Sydney Greenstreet (James P. Alden), Alan Hale (Herman Brinker), Craig Stevens (Carter Andrews), Barbara Brown, Don McGuire, John Ridgely.

The 1931 film had George Arliss repeating his silent success in a sound version. The film develops slowly and isn't really interesting until the director has got the business of Arliss being ordered into a six-month rest period, and his chafing at his forced inactivity, out of the way. It's not one of Arliss' best efforts, but demonstrates that he can bring to life a character role and sustain audiences' interest in a non-romantic hero. The 1947 production creaks with its age and despite a talented cast, fails to impress. The drama and the humor are in short supply in this mildly interesting movie.

The Runaround *see* **It Happened One Night**

S

Sabu and the Magic Ring *see* **The Arabian Nights**

761 The Sacred Flame

Based on the play by W. Somerset Maugham. Story: On the same day that Colonel Maurice Taylor of the Royal Flying Corps marries Stella Elburn, his back is broken in a crash, leaving him an invalid. He clings to life for three years and when his younger brother Colin returns from South America, Maurice encourages Colin to take Stella out. He does and they gradually fall in love.

Opposite, top: *Irvin S. Cobb is the center of attraction when he visits the set of* Ruggles of Red Gap, *(Paramount, 1935). Hanging on the humorist's every word are, from left to right, Leila Hyams, Charles Laughton, Zasu Pitts, Charlie Ruggles, Mary Boland, Roland Young, Maude Eburne and Lucien Littlefield.* Bottom: *Bob Hope isn't proposing to Lucille Ball in this scene from* Fancy Pants *(Paramount, 1950), a remake of* Ruggles of Red Gap. *He just has a case of indigestion brought on by his latest self-made predicament.*

When Maurice dies, Nurse Wayland accuses Colin of murdering his brother with a sleeping powder. However, Mrs. Taylor, the boys' mother, confesses that she gave her son the fatal dose because she realized that Stella was going to leave him and she didn't want to ever know of it.

Warner Bros., 1929. Director: Archie Mayo; screenwriter: Harvey Thew. Cast: Pauline Frederick (Mrs. Taylor), Conrad Nagel (Col. Maurice Taylor), William Courtenay (Major Liconda), Lila Lee (Stella Elburn), Walter Bryon (Colin Taylor), Alec B. Francis (Dr. Harvester), Dale Fuller (Nurse Wayland).

• ***The Right to Live*** (remake). Warner Bros., 1935. Director: William Keighley; screenwriter: Ralph Block. Cast: Josephine Hutchinson (Stella Trent), George Brent (Colin Trent), Colin Clive (Maurice Trent), Peggy Wood (Nurse Wayland), Henrietta Crosman (Mrs. Trent), C. Aubrey Smith (Major Liconda), Leo G. Carroll, Phyllis Coghlan.

In the first film, the very popular silent star of "women's movies," Pauline Frederick, was given first billing in this all too tragic story. In the remake, the young couple whose love is an act of disloyalty to her husband and his brother, move front and center. This story of a mercy killing was too depressing to be very popular. In the second version, Peggy Wood, as the nurse who suspects the patient she has developed an affection for has been murdered, gives the most satisfying performance.

762 Sadie Thompson

Based on the story "Rain" by W. Somerset Maugham. Story: Sadie Thompson, on the run from the police, shows up at a small hotel on a South Seas island, where she strikes up a romance with Sergeant O'Hara, a marine with whom she discusses marriage. Also staying at the hotel is tyrannical reformer Alfred Atkinson, who rails against Sadie's immorality, threatening to turn her over to the authorities. His constant harassment and preaching finally get to her and she resolves to reform. Now trusting Atkinson, she is attacked by him and raped. She reverts to her old cynical personality and plans to move on to Australia, perhaps with Sgt. O'Hara.

United Artists, 1928 (original). Silent. Director and screenwriter: Raoul Walsh. Cast: Gloria Swanson (Sadie Thompson), Lionel Barrymore (Alfred Atkinson), Raoul Walsh (Sgt. Tim O'Hara), Blanche Frederici (Mrs. Atkinson), Charles Lane, Florence Midgley, James A. Marcus, Sophia Artega, Will Stanton.

• ***Rain*** (remake). United Artists, 1932. Director: Lewis Milestone; screenwriter: Maxwell Anderson. Cast: Joan Crawford (Sadie Thompson), Walter Huston (Alfred Davidson), William Gargan (Sgt. O'Hara), Guy Kibbee (Joe

Opposite, top: *"Don't resist, I'm just trying to save your soul," is Lionel Barrymore's message to Gloria Swanson in the 1928 United Artists production of W. Somerset Maugham's* Rain, Sadie Thompson. Bottom: *Silent Walter Huston looks to heaven for help in his fight to reform South Seas tramp Joan Crawford in* Rain *(United Artists, 1932).*

Horn), Walter Catlett (Quartermaster Bates), Beulah Bondi (Mrs. Davidson), Matt Moore, Kendall Lee, Ben Hendricks, Frederic Howard.

• ***Miss Sadie Thompson*** (remake). Columbia Pictures, 1953. Director: Curtis Bernhardt; screenwriter: Harry Kleiner. Cast: Rita Hayworth (Sadie Thompson), Jose Ferrer (Alfred Davidson), Aldo Ray (Sgt. Phil O'Hara), Russell Collins (Dr. Robert MacPhail), Diosa Costello (Ameena Horn), Harry Bellaver, Wilton Graff, Peggy Converse, Henry Slate, Rudy Bond.

An adaptation of Sadie Thompson, in a black version, was produced in 1946, with the name *Dirty Gertie from Harlem,* USA. The three versions of W. Somerset Maugham's book are each of interest, with the three stars, Gloria Swanson, Joan Crawford, and Rita Hayworth, each giving their own unique interpretations of the fallen woman who proves too much of a temptation for a man claiming he is trying to redeem her. There is much to enjoy in the respective performances of Lionel Barrymore, Walter Huston and Jose Ferrer as the man whose puritanical rantings apparently mask his feelings of lust. Arguments have been forwarded that the first two versions were superior to the 3-D 1953 production, but this may reflect a bias that appreciates older movies over newer versions for no apparent cinematic reason. Each filming of the story of steamy sex, sin and salvation in the South Seas has its faults, but each does justice to the Maugham tale as well.

Sahara *see* The Lost Patrol

Sailor Beware *see* The Fleet's In

Sailor of the King *see* Brown on "Resolution"

763 Sailors Three (Three Cockeyed Sailors)

Based on a screenplay by Angus Macphail, John Dighton and Austin Melford. Story: Three British sailors stranded in a South American port on a foggy night board a German pocket battleship, which they mistake for their own ship after a drunken spree. With the help of an Austrian seaman, they capture the ship for the British.

Ealing Studios, 1940 (original). Director: Walter Forde; screenwriters: Angus Macphail, John Dighton and Austin Melford. Cast: Tommy Trinder, Michael Wilding, Claude Hulbert, Carla Lehmann, Jeanne de Casalis, James Hayter, Henry Hewitt, John Laurie, Harold Warrender, John Glyn Jones, Julien Vedey.

• ***Fiddlers Three*** (sequel). Ealing Studios, 1944. Director: Henry Watt; screenwriters: Harry Watt, Diana Morgan and Angus Macphail. Cast: Tommy Trinder, Sonnie Hale, Diana Wrecker, Frances Day, Francis L. Sullivan, Elisabeth Welch, Mary Clare, Ernest Milton, Frederick Piper, Robert Wyndham, Russell Thorndike.

In the second film Tommy Trinder and Sonnie Hale pick up a Wren, Diana Decker. When a storm breaks out they take shelter under the altar stone at Stonehenge. They are struck by lightning and transported back to ancient

Rome. At first they save their lives by making prophecies, but their luck runs out, and they are about to be thrown to the lions when lightning strikes again and they are transported back again. Both films have their moments, but they move a bit slowly.

Saint Joan *see* **Joan of Arc**

Saint Joan the Maid *see* **Joan of Arc**

764 Sal of Singapore

Based on the novel *The Sentimentalists* by Dale Collins. Story: Captain Erickson finds a baby abandoned in a lifeboat on his ship. He abducts a waterfront prostitute, Singapore Sal, to take care of the child. The reluctant surrogate mother develops an affection for the little tyke and when the baby becomes ill, she and Erickson fight for its life. The child's fever breaks as they reach San Francisco. Now Sal is reluctant to go back to her old profession, leaves the baby with Erickson and ships out with Erickson's arch rival, Captain Sunday. Erickson gives chase, boards Sunday's ship, beats up Sunday and forces him to perform a marriage ceremony between Sal and himself. Sal is not reluctant to be reunited with the captain and the baby.

Pathe Exchange, 1929 (original). Talking sequences. Director: Howard Higgin; screenwriter: Elliott Clawson. Cast: Phyllis Haver (Sal), Alan Hale (Captain Erickson), Fred Kohler (Captain Sunday), Noble Johnson, Dan Wolheim, Jules Cowles, Pat Harmon, Harold William Hill.

• ***Sal of Singapore*** (remake). Paramount Pictures, 1931. Director: Edward Sloman; screenwriters: Adelaide Heilbron and Melville Baker. Cast: Gary Cooper (Captain Sam Whalen), Claudette Colbert (Sally Clark), Averill Harris (Mate Gatson), Richard Spiro (Sammy), Douglas Dumbrille (Alisandroe), Raquel Davida, Hamtree Harrington, Sidney Easton, Joan Blair, Charlotte Wynters.

The scenarists changed the story in the sequel thusly: Cooper is a captain who finds a baby, and decides to keep the child. He sends members of his crew to find a proper lady to mother the child. Colbert, who is a witness in a blackmailing case, has been hiding out as a dancehall girl, eager to go home. She overhears the crew members interviewing prospective "mothers" and knows precisely what they are looking for. Assuming a prim and dignified mein, she lands the position. All is bliss aboard the ship until Cooper's mate, Averill Harris, recognizes Colbert and threatens to expose her unless she gives herself to him. She refuses and in an ensuing fight he falls overboard. When they dock in New York, Cooper is arrested for attempted murder, Averill having been picked up by another ship. Colbert comes to his defense at the trial, but with her secret out, Cooper will have nothing to do with her, until the baby's illness brings them together again.

765 Sally Bishop

Based on the novel by Ernest Temple Thurston. Story: Barrister John Traill takes typist Sally Bishop as his mistress for several years but abandons her for socialite Janet Hallard. He returns to Sally just in time to prevent her from taking her own life.

Gaumont, Great Britain, 1916 (original). Director and screenwriter: George Pearson. Cast: Aurele Sydney (John Traill), Marjorie Villis (Sally Bishop), Peggy Hyland (Janet Hallard), Alice de Winton, Jack Leigh, Christine Rayner, Hugh Croise, Fred Rains.

• ***Sally Bishop*** (remake). Stoll, Great Britain, 1923. Director: Maurice Elvey; screenwriter: uncredited. Cast: Marie Doro (Sally Bishop), Henry Ainley (John Traill), Florence Turner (Janet), Sydney Fairbrother, Valia, A. Bromley Davenport, Mary Dibley.

• ***Sally Bishop*** (remake). British Lion, Great Britain, 1932. Director: T. Hayes Hunter; screenwriters: John Drinkwater and G.E. Wakefield. Cast: Joan Barry (Sally Bishop), Harold Huth (John Traill), Isabel Jeans (Dolly Durlacher), Benita Hume (Evelyn Standish), Kay Hammond (Janet Hallard), Emlyn Williams, Anthony Bushell, Annie Esmond, Diana Churchill.

In the first remake, Sally threatens to expose her rich lover when he chooses to prosecute the divorce case of the socialite he wishes to marry. At least in this version she had some gumption. The 1932 version is the poor "Back Street"–like story of a typist who becomes mistress to a rich man, and after three years sees his sister maneuver him into becoming engaged to a socialite. She also finds new romance, but her wealthy lover comes back to her, begging forgiveness. Things don't always happen like that in real life. A mistress is a mistress, a wife is a wife, and it doesn't follow that the former will become the latter.

766 Sally, Irene and Mary

Based on the play by Edward Dowling and Cyrus Wood. Story: The three girls of the title are Sally, too wise in the ways of the world; Irene, lost in dreams of romance; and Mary, an innocent young Irish girl from New York's East Side. The three are chorus girls in a Broadway show. Marcus Morton, the wealthy man who keeps Sally in a luxurious apartment, falls for Mary and proposes marriage. She at first refuses, but when Jimmy Dugan, her one-time plumber sweetheart, expresses his disgust with the kind of life she's now living, Mary accepts Marcus' offer. Meanwhile, Irene, disappointed in a love affair with another millionaire, impulsively marries a college boy and shortly thereafter is killed in an automobile accident. This tragedy greatly affects Mary, who breaks off her engagement to Marcus and returns to her plumber sweetheart.

MGM, 1925 (original). Silent. Director and screenwriter: Edmund Goulding. Cast: Constance Bennett (Sally), Joan Crawford (Irene), Sally O'Neil (Mary), William Haines (Jimmy Dugan), Henry Kolker (Marcus Morton), Douglas Gilmore, Ray Howard, Kate Price, Aggie Herring, Sam De Grasse, Lillian Elliott.

• ***Sally, Irene and Mary*** (remake). Twentieth Century–Fox, 1938. Director: William A. Seiter; screenwriters: Harry Tugend and Jack Yellen. Cast: Alice Faye (Sally Day), Tony Martin (Tommy Reynolds), Fred Allen (Gabriel Green), Jimmy Durante (Jefferson Twitchell), Gregory Ratoff (Baron Zorka), Joan Davis (Irene Keene), Marjorie Weaver (Mary Stevens), Louise Hovick (Joyce

Taylor), J. Edward Bromberg, Barnett Parker, Eddie Collins, Andrew Tombes.

It's always been good Hollywood box office to show some shameful behavior of loose-living girls and then to routinely punish the worst offenders with death or disgrace, while allowing the least guilty to barely escape a similiar fate. So it is with the silent version of the Dowling and Wood play. The remake is another Hollywood cliche, a backstage show used as a vehicle for Alice Faye's song styling, singing "Who Stole the Jam," "Help Wanted—Male," "Sweet As a Song" and "I Could Use a Dream." These musical classics were penned by the teams of Walter Bullock and Harold Spina, and Mack Gordon and Harry Revel. Besides the fine to see and hear Miss Faye, Jimmy Durante and Fred Allen proved an effective comedy team.

767 Sally of the Sawdust

Based on the play *Poppy* by Dorothy Donnelly. Story: Professor Eustace McGargle is a carnival con man and loveable rogue, with a young ward named Sally. He sees a new job offer in Green Meadows as an opportunity to reunite Sally with her grandparents, the Fosters. Sally meets and falls for society scion Peyton Lennox. Sally is arrested, accused of being a front for a shell game that McGargle has perfected. The latter falls in with some bootleggers but is able to convince the judge that Sally is innocent of any wrongdoing. He also informs the judge that the girl is his honor's granddaughter.

D.W. Griffith/United Artists, 1925 (original). Silent. Director: D.W. Griffith; screenwriter: Forest Halsey. Cast: Carol Dempster (Sally), W.C. Fields (Prof. Eustace McGargle), Alfred Lunt (Peyton Lennox), Erville Alderson (Judge Foster), Effie Shannon (Mrs. Foster), Charles Hammond, Roy Applegate, Florence Fair, Marie Shotwell.

• ***Poppy*** (remake). Paramount Pictures, 1936. Director: A. Edward Sutherland; screenwriters: Waldmar Young and Virginia Van Upp. Cast: W.C. Fields (Prof. McGargle), Rochelle Hudson (Poppy), Richard Cromwell (Billy Farnsworth), Lynne Overman (Anthony Whiffen), Catherine Doucet (Countess De Puizzi), Rosalind Keith, Granville Bates, Adrian Morris, Ralph Remley.

With most W.C. Fields pictures, and that includes these two, the plot's not the thing and the action among the other characters is just an unwanted interruption of Fields' comical antics. When Fields is not in the picture, these two renditions of Dorothy Donnelly's play are merely nineteenth-century melodramas with little appeal. The romantic scenes consist of starry-eyed glances and sighs between two people who don't seem too sure what they should be doing. The only supporting characters who deserve any praise in these productions are those who properly recognize their roles as foils for the master. Into this category nicely falls Catherine Doucet in the remake.

768 Salome

Based on the play by Oscar Wilde. Story: Enraged by Jokaanan's refusal of her kiss, Salome performs the dance of the seven veils for King Herod in return for Jokaanan's head on a silver platter. Herod grants her request, but is disgusted by Salome's kissing the severed head and has her executed.

• ***Salome*** (remake). Nazimova Productions/Allied Producers and Distributors, 1922. Silent. Director: Charles Bryant; screenwriter: Peter M. Winters. Cast: Nazimova (Salome), Rose Dione (Herodias), Mitchell Lewis (Herod), Nigel De Brulier (Jokaanan), Earl Schenck, Arthur Jasmine, Frederick Peters, Louis Dumar.

• ***Salome*** (remake). Malcom Strauss Pictures, 1923. Silent. Director and screenwriter: Malcolm Strauss. Cast: Diana Allen (Salome), Vincent Coleman (Herod), Christine Winthrop (Herodias).

• ***Salome*** (remake). Columbia Pictures, 1953. Director: William Dieterle; screenwriter: Harry Kleiner, based on a story by Jesse L. Lasky, Jr. Cast: Rita Hayworth (Princess Salome), Stewart Granger (Commander Claudius), Charles Laughton (King Herod), Judith Anderson (Queen Herodias), Sir Cedric Hardwicke (Caesar Tiberius), Alan Badel (John the Baptist), Basil Sydney, Maurice Schwartz, Rex Reason.

The story of Salome was also filmed in 1902, 1908, 1909, 1913, 1918, 1922 and 1972. In 1920, MGM produced a *A Modern Salome* and in 1925 Paramount Pictures produced *Salome of the Tenements*, both adaptations of the Salome story. Nazimova played Salome as the classic vamp she was. Rita Hayworth's Salome was supposedly an innocent girl in love with Stewart Granger who was manipulated by her mother, Herodias, to dance for lustful Herod and then ask for the head of John the Baptist, who spoke against Herodias' adulterous marriage to Herod. This was one of Laughton's most annoyingly hammy films and Hayworth's dance really wasn't very exciting.

Salome of the Tenements ***see*** **Salome**

769 Salt and Pepper

Based on a screenplay by Michael Pertwee. Story: It's the far-fetched tale of two Soho gambling club owners, Charles Salt and Christopher Pepper, who become involved in a plot to overthrow the British government by a madman, Colonel Woodstock, who threatens nuclear war unless his demands are met. After a number of people are killed and the boys themselves become targets, they commandeer an ancient army tank and rout their adversaries. They are now national heroes and are knighted at Buckingham Palace.

Chrislaw/Trace-Mark/United Artists, 1968 (original). Director: Richard D. Donner; screenwriter: Michael Pertwee. Cast: Sammy Davis, Jr. (Charles Salt), Peter Lawford (Christopher Pepper), Michael Bates (Inspector Crabbe), Ilona Rodgers (Marianne Renaud), John Le Mesurier (Colonel Woodstock), Graham Stark, Ernest Clark, Jeanne Roland, Robert Dorning.

• ***One More Time*** (sequel). United Artists, 1970. Director: Jerry Lewis; screenwriter: Michael Pertwee. Cast: Sammy Davis, Jr. (Charlie Salt), Peter Lawford (Christopher Pepper/Lord Sydney Pepper), Maggie Wright (Miss Tompkins), Leslie Sands, John Wood, Sydney Arnold, Edward Evans, Percy Herbert, Bill Maynard.

The cleverest thing about these "comedies" is giving the name Salt to a black man, Sammy Davis, Jr., and Pepper to a white man, Peter Lawford. From then on it's downhill. If such shows were put on by a high school dramatic club, they would be criticized for being too sophomoric. With the production costs for these films, it's just indefensible to waste some otherwise talented individuals on such blue sky material. In the sequel, Lawford is called on to do double damage by playing not only the co-owner of a Soho nightclub, Chris Pepper, but also his wealthy brother, Sydney. When Sydney is killed, Chris takes over, at least until he and Salt find the murderer.

770 Salute the Toff

Based on the novel by John Creasy. Story: Society sleuth "the Toff" responds to an appeal from Fay to find her missing boss Draycott, finds a dead body, is attacked, and finally finds the man hiding from an insurance swindler out to kill him. The Toff, with the help of his butler and Inspector Grice, cleans up the case, saving Draycott.

Nettlefold Productions, 1951 (original). Director: Maclean Rogers; screenwriter: uncredited. Cast: John Bentley (Hon. Richard Rollison/the Toff), Tony Britton (Draycott), Carol Marsh (Fay), Valentine Dyall (Inspector Grice), Roddy Hughes, Shelagh Frase, Wally Patch, June Elvin.

• ***Hammer the Toff*** (sequel). Nettlefold Productions, 1952. Director: Maclean Rogers; screenwriter: uncredited. Cast: John Bentley (Richard Rollinson/the Toff), Patricia Dainton (Susan Lancaster), Valentine Dyall (Inspector Grice), John Robinson, Roddy Hughes, Katherine Blake, Wally Patch, Basil Dignam.

If one doesn't expect too much, these thriller-comedies are enjoyable. In the second film, the Toff meets a girl on a train and helps her prove that a Robin Hood–like crook is innocent of killing her uncle for a secret steel formula.

771 Salvation Nell

Based on a play by Edward Brewster Sheldon. Story: Working as a scrubwoman in a saloon, Nell's jealous sweetheart, Jim, kills the overly attentive saloonkeeper and is confined to prison for seven years. Nell finds a friend in a Salvation Army girl, Maggie, has a baby and then is courted by Major Williams. Although she still loves Jim she refuses to return to him after he is released from prison.

• ***Salvation Nell*** (remake). Whitman Bennett/First National, 1921. Silent. Director: Kenneth Webb; screenwriter: Dorothy Farnum. Cast: Pauline Stark (Nell Sanders), Joseph King (Jim Platt), Gypsy O'Brien (Myrtle Hawes), Edward Langford (Major Williams), Evelyn C. Carrington (Hallelujah Maggie), Charles McDonald (Sid McGovern), Matthew Bates (Al McGovern), Marie Haynes, A. Earl, William Nally, Lawrence Johnson.

• ***Salvation Nell*** (remake). Tiffany Productions, 1931. Director: James Cruze; screenwriter: Selma Stein. Cast: Ralph Graves (Jim Platt), Helen Chandler (Nell Saunders), Sally O'Neill (Myrtle), Jason Robards (Major Williams), Dewitt

Jennings (McGovern), Charlotte Walker (Maggie), Matthew Betz, Rose Dione, Wally Albright.

Salvation Nell was first filmed in 1915 by World Productions. In the remake of this melodrama the story starts in 1912, a few years before the great war discovered the Salvation Army. Nell is a poor unfortunate who is left alone to have her baby until the Salvation Army comes along to help. There's a lot being said about morality, vice and virtue in these films, but the stories are so old-fashioned and creaky that it's doubtful if the message will mean much to today's audiences.

Sanctuary *see* **The Story of Temple Drake**

772 Sanders of the River

Based on the novel by Edgar Wallace. Story: In Nigeria, African ex-convict Bosambo is given a probationary post as a local chief by British Commissioner R.G. Sanders. The Old King hates Bosambo because he wipes out the slave trade. White Sanders is away, his deputy, Ferguson, sells alcohol and weapons to the natives. The Old King sends warriors to attack Bosambo, taking him captive and killing Ferguson. Sanders comes back and straightens everything out like the good civil servant he is, rescuing Bosambo, who returns the favor by killing the Old King when the latter tries to spear Sanders. Bosambo is made new king and everybody is happy in this "white man's burden" tale.

London/United Artists, Great Britain, 1935 (original). Director: Zoltan Korda; screenwriters: Lajos Biro, Jeffrey Dell and Arthur Wimperis. Cast: Paul Robeson (Bosambo), Leslie Banks (R.G. Sanders), Nina Mae McKinney (Lilongo), Robert Cochran (Tibbets), Martin Walker (Ferguson), Tony Wane (Old King), Richard Grey, Marquis de Portago, Eric Mautin, Allan Jeayes, Charles Carson, Orlando Martins.

• ***Death Drums Along the River*** (remake). Big Ben/Hallam, Great Britain, 1963. Director: Lawrence Huntington; screenwriters: Harry Alan Towers, Nicolas Roeg, Kevin Kavanaugh and Lawrence Huntington. Cast: Richard Todd (Inspector Harry Sanders), Marianne Koch (Dr. Inge Jung), Albert Lieven (Dr. Weiss), Vivi Bach (Marlene), Walter Rilla (Dr. Schneider), Jeremy Lloyd, Robert Arden, Bill Brewer.

• ***Coast of Skeletons*** (sequel). Towers of London/British Lion, Great Britain, 1964. Director: Robert Lynn; screenwriters: Anthony Scott Veitch and Peter Welbeck. Cast: Richard Todd (Harry Sanders), Dale Robertson (A.J. Mangus), Heinz Drache (Janny von Koltze), Marianne Koch (Helga), Elga Anderson (Elizabeth von Koltze), Derek Nimmo, Gabriel Bayman, George Leech, Gordon Mulholland.

In the remake, the inspector, played by Richard Todd, is investigating a murder in a hospital and stumbles across a hidden diamond mine. In the sequel to this film, Todd investigates the scuttling of an American tycoon's diamond dredger and search for sunken gold. With all of its shortcomings, the 1935 film is far superior to the two early '60s films. They just don't hold one's interest. The earlier film captured the mystique of something—perhaps it was Africa.

Paul Robeson couldn't have been happy to see his role become that of an Uncle Tom–like black who just loves the white "massa."

Satan Met a Lady *see* **The Maltese Falcon**

773 Satan's Sister

Based on the novel *Satan* by H. DeVere Stacpoole. Story: In Jamaica a rich man, Bobby Ratcliffe, saves a captain's son, Jude Tyler, from pirates and discovers that "he" is a girl. Romance blossoms, naturally.

B.W.P. Films, Great Britain, 1925. Silent. Director and screenwriter: George Pearson. Cast: Betty Balfour (Jude Tyler), Guy Phillips (Satan Tyler), James Carew (Tyler), Frank Stanmore (Cleary), Caleb Porter, Frank Perfitt, Jed Barlow.

• ***The Truth About Spring*** (remake). Universal Pictures, Great Britain, 1965. Director: Richard Thorpe; screenwriter: James Lee Barrett. Cast: Hayley Mills (Spring Tyler), John Mills (Tommy Tyler), James MacArthur (William Ashton), Lionel Jeffries (Cark), Harry Andrews (Sellers), Niall MacGinnis, Lionel Murton, David Tomlinson.

It says something about fleeting fame to have your daughter's name appear above yours in the movie credits when you are as distinguished an actor as Sir John Mills. In the remake, Mills and his tomboy daughter Hayley are traveling in the Caribbean, when they encounter a millionaire's boat. He has young lawyer James MacArthur aboard, who accepts an invitation to stay on the Mills houseboat. He and Hayley have eyes for each other but their romance is interrupted long enough to get involved in a fruitless search for sunken treasure.

Saturday Night Kid *see* **Love 'Em and Leave 'Em**

774 Saturday's Children

Based on the play by Maxwell Anderson. Story: Ambitious stenographer Bobby Halevy marries Rims O'Neil and they settle down in a small cottage. They soon find that married life is not all loving bliss, but more often than not a never ending string of bills and minor financial crises. Bobby leaves Rims, not because she has fallen out of love but because she sincerely believes he would be better off without her. Intent on finding a lover, not a husband, she returns to work, taking up residence in a boardinghouse where gentlemen callers are not allowed. Lonely and hurt, Rims climbs the fire escape to Bobby's room and convinces her that love is necessary for a Saturday's child who must always work for a living.

First National Pictures, 1929 (original). Part talkie. Director: Gregory La Cava; screenwriter: Forrest Halsey. Cast: Corinne Griffith (Bobby Halevy), Grant Withers (Rims O'Neil), Albert Conti (Mengle), Alma Tell (Florrie), Lucien Littlefield (Willie), Charles Lane, Ann Schaeffer, Marcia Harris.

• ***Maybe It's Love*** (remake). First National Pictures, 1934. Director: William McGann; screenwriters: Jerry Wald and Harry Sauber. Cast: Gloria Stuart (Bobby Halevy), Ross Alexander (Rims O'Neil), Frank McHugh (Willie Sands),

Ruth Donnelly (Florie Sands), Phillip Reed (Adolph Mengle, Jr.), Helen Lowell, Joseph Cawthorn, Dorothy Dare, Henry Travers.

• ***Saturday's Children*** (remake). Warner Bros., 1940. Director: Vincent Sherman; screenwriters: Julius J. and Philip G. Epstein. Cast: Anne Shirley (Bobby Halevy), John Garfield (Rims Rosson), Roscoe Karns (Willie Sands), Lee Patrick (Florrie Sands), Elizabeth Risdon (Mrs. Halevy), George Tobias, Dennie Moore, Bertron Churchill, Frank Faylen.

The 1929 film suffered from poor sound technology in those sequences where the producers attempted dialog, often resulting in the words not being heard at all. The remake was met by angry complaints of some critics that the script for the Anderson play was being too often used under a variety of different titles, but this was only the second to credit the Anderson work. The 1940 film had John Garfield as an impractical inventor married to the ambitious Anne Shirley with their finances putting a freeze on their romance. It wasn't a picture to do credit to any of its participants.

Scalawag *see* **Treasure Island**

775 Scaramouche

Based on the novel by Rafael Sabatini. Story: Andre Moreau vows to fight against the aristocracy when his friend Philippe is killed in a duel with the Marquis de la Tour. Andre leads his guardians and sweetheart Aline to join a group of strolling players, becoming a celebrated clown, Scaramouche. Andre is present in the streets of Paris when the revolution breaks out and discovers that his father is none other than the Marquis de la Tour and his mother is a countess. Andre convinces the crowd to allow his mother's carriage to leave the city, while the Marquis dies a nobleman's death among the throng in the grip of revolution.

Metro, 1923 (original). Silent. Director: Rex Ingram; screenwriter: Willis Goldbeck. Cast: Ramon Novarro (Andre-Louis Moreau), Alice Terry (Aline de Kercadiou), Lewis Stone (Marquis de la Tour d'Azyr), Lloyd Ingraham (Quintin de Kercadiou), Julia Swayne Gordon (Countess Therese de Plougastel), William Humphrey, Otto Matiesen, George Siegmann, Bowditch Turner.

• ***Scaramouche*** (remake). MGM, 1952. Director: George Sidney; screenwriters: Ronald Millar and George Froeschel. Cast: Stewart Granger (Andre Moreau), Eleanor Parker (Lenore), Janet Leigh (Aline de Gavrillac), Mel Ferrer (Noel, Marquis de Maynes), Henry Wilcoxon (Chevalier de Chabrilliane), Nina Foch (Marie Antoinette), Richard Anderson, Robert Coote, Lewis Stone, Elisabeth Risdon.

A combined French, Italian and Spanish production of Scaramouche was made in 1963 and Embassy Productions brought forth *The Loves and Times of Scaramouche* in 1976. The 1923 silent with Ramon Novarro was a spectacular of ten reels in length, featuring a large and impressive cast. The 1952 version was true to the opening line of the novel on which it was based: "He was born with the gift of laughter and a sense that the world was mad." In it Granger is a fun-loving man, supported by funds from some unknown father. When the payments stop, Granger forces his contact to reveal his father's identity. He is erroneously told that he is the son of the Duc de Gavrillac, who he finds has died. He meets and falls in love with Aline de Gavrille, before learning her identity and is dismayed by the belief that she is his sister. Aline, played by Janet Leigh, is intrigued but is also being courted by Noel, Marquis de Maynes, sneeringly played by Mel Ferrer. When Ferrer kills Granger's young revolutionary friend in a duel, Granger swears to avenge the death, but first he must earn a living and learn to use a sword.

He does the first by joining a company of traveling players which includes his mistress, Leonore, and becoming the star of the show, a masked clown called Scaramouche. As for the second, since Ferrer is the best swordsman in France, Granger finds it advisable to take lessons from Ferrer's teacher, who, not too fond of the snooty nobleman, teaches Granger things he withheld from Ferrer. Eventually the expected confrontation takes place in a Paris theatre in what turns out to be the longest (six and one-half minutes of film time) and most exciting duels in cinematic history. When Granger has Ferrer at his mercy, instead of killing him, he hurls his sword into the stage floor and walks away. Later, it is explained to him why he couldn't kill his enemy. Ferrer is actually Granger's half-brother. The good news here is that Janet Leigh isn't his sister and he proceeds to marry her.

Scared Stiff *see* **The Ghost Breakers**

776 Scarface

Based on the novel by Armitage Trail. Story: Tony Camonte, known as Scarface for obvious reasons, rises from playing bodyguard for a mobster beer baron to booze chief of the entire city. Along the way he double-crosses his old boss, has him killed and even takes the man's mistress, Poppy, a girl who just loves gunmen and gunfire. She's the only one of the villians who doesn't get hers before the film is completed.

United Artists, 1932 (original). Director: Howard Hawks; screenwriter: Ben Hecht. Cast: Paul Muni (Tony Camonte), Ann Dvorak (Cesca), Karen Morley (Poppy), Osgood Perkins (Lovo), Boris Karloff (Gaffney), C. Henry Gordon (Guarino), George Raft (Rinaldo), Purnell Pratt, Vince Barnett, Ines Palange, Edwin Maxwell, Tully Marshall.

• ***Scarface*** (remake). Universal Pictures, 1983. Director: Brian De Palma; screenwriter: Oliver Stone. Cast: Al Pacino (Tony Montana), Steven Bauer (Manny Ray), Michelle Pfeiffer (Elvira), Mary Elizabeth Mastrantonio (Gina), Robert Loggia (Frank Lopez), Paul Shenar, Harris Yulin.

The original picture is clearly a *film à clef* of Chicago's Al Capone. Dvorak plays Muni's incestuous sister in what may be the most vivid gangster film of the era. George Raft made quite a splash as a coin-flipping hood, giving him a forever-associated trademark, even with those who don't know where it originated. The second film takes place in modern day Miami and Scarface is now an emigré Cuban, making good—and bad—in his new country. The detailed violence may be too much for some as might the foul language, but Pacino, as usual, gives a masterful performance as the tortured gangster.

Scarlet Angel *see* **Flame of New Orleans**

The Scarlet Daredevil *see* **The Scarlet Pimpernel**

777 The Scarlet Letter

Based on the novel by Nathaniel Hawthorne. Story: In Puritan New England, Hester, to please her father, marries Roger Pyrnne, a man she doesn't love. During her husband's frequent, long absences, she shares walks in the woods with her pastor, the Reverend Arthur Dimmesdale, and they soon fall in love. When a child is born to Hester, whom Roger maintains is not his, Hester is condemned to wear a scarlett letter A for adulturess on her breast. She refuses to divulge the name of the child's father and patiently endures the jeers and insults of the villagers, fighting to keep her child. Hester is to be further punished in the pillory and when led to the public scaffold, Dimmesdale, who has been too fearful to risk helping Hester and his daughter, confesses, collapses and dies in anguish in Hester's arms.

• ***The Scarlet Letter*** (remake). MGM, 1926. Silent. Director: Victor Seastrom; screenwriter: Frances Marion. Cast: Lillian Gish (Hester Pyrnne), Lars Hanson (the Reverend Arthur Dimmesdale), Henry B. Walthall (Roger Pyrnne), Karl Dane (Giles), William H. Hooker, Marcelle Corday, Fred Herzog, Jules Cowles, Mary Hawes, Joyce Coad, James A. Marcus.

• ***The Scarlet Letter*** (remake). Dartmoor/Majestic Pictures, 1934. Director: Robert G. Vignola; screenwriters: Leonard Fields and David Silverstein. Cast: Colleen Moore (Hester Prynne), Hardie Albright (Arthur Dimmesdale), Henry B. Walthall (Roger Chillingworth), William Farnum (Governor Billingham), Alan Hale (Bartholomew Hockins), Virginia Howell, Cora Sue Collins, William Kent.

The Nathaniel Hawthorne classic has also been filmed in 1917 and 1920 in the United States and in 1973 in Germany. Lillian Gish gave a lovely portrayal of a very fragile-looking but brave Hester. Lars Hanson played the Reverend Dimmesdale for the coward he was. The earlier film is much more satisfying than the 1934 version, in which the producers unwisely attempted to lighten up the story by supplying some extremely questionable and unnecessary comedy relief of a Miles Standish and John Alden–like development, supplied by Alan Hale and William Kent. The comedy is integrated into the story as well as could be expected but its mere presence distracts from the suspense and power of the story. As for Colleen Moore, she gave genuine dignity to her role while Hardie Albright portrays Dimmesdale with excellent restraint.

778 The Scarlet Pimpernel

Based on the novel by Baroness Orczy. Story: Foppish Sir Percy Blakeney is in reality the Scarlet Pimpernel, master of disguise and leader of a band of gentlemen who rescue French aristocrats from the French Revolution and the guillotine. Percy's supercilious manners and apparently sole interest—the latest in fashion—is a perfect cover for his activities. However, he cannot resist a slight thumbing of his nose at his adversaries by composing the doggerel: "We seek him here, we seek him there, those Frenchies seek him everywhere. Is he in heaven? Is he in hell? That demmed, elusive Pimpernel." Embarrassed by the situation, the French government sends Chauvelin to England as Ambassador to discover the identity of the Pimpernel. Chauvelin offers a bargain to Lady Blakeney: the life of her brother arrested in Paris as a French aristocrat for her help in uncovering the mystery man. Unwittingly, she helps deliver her own husband to Chauvelin's hands, but the clever Blakeney pulls off one more grand ruse and escapes with his wife, who has a new appreciation and respect for her husband.

• ***The Scarlet Pimpernel*** (remake). London Films, Great Britain, 1934. Director: Harold Young; screenwriters: Lajos Biros, S.N. Behrman, Robert Sherwood and Arthur Wimperis. Cast: Leslie Howard (Sir Percy Blakeney), Merle Oberon (Lady Blakeney), Raymond Massey (Chauvelin), Nigel Bruce (Prince of Wales), Bramwell Fletcher, Anthony Bushnell, Joan Gardner, Walter Rilla, Mabel Terry-Lewis, O.B. Clarence.

• ***The Return of the Scarlet Pimpernel*** (remake). London Films, Great Britain, 1937. Director: Hans Schwartz; screenwriters: Lajos Biros, Arthur Wimperis and Adrian Brunel. Cast: Barry Barnes (Sir Percy Blakeney), Sophie Stewart (Marguerite), Margeretta Scott (Thresia Cabarrus), James Mason (Jean Tallien), Francis Lister (Chauvelin), Anthony Bushnell, Patrick Barr, David Tree.

• ***Pimpernel Smith*** (remake). British National, Great Britain, 1941. Director: Leslie Howard; screenwriter: Anatole de Grunwald. Cast: Leslie Howard (Professor Smith), Francis L. Sullivan (Von Graum), Mary Morris (Ludmilla), Hugh Macdermott (David Maxwell), Peter Gawthorne, Raymond Huntley.

• ***The Elusive Pimpernel*** (remake). London Films, Great Britain, 1950. Directors: Michael Powell and Emeric Pressburger. Cast: David Niven (Sir Percy Blakeney), Margaret Leighton (Lady Blakeney), Cyril Cusack (Chauvelin), Jack Hawkins (Prince of Wales), David Hutcheson, Robert Coote.

The Scarlet Pimpernel was also produced for the screen in 1917 by Fox Studios, in England in 1919 as *The Elusive Pimpernel* and in 1928 by World-Wide as *The Scarlet Daredevil.* Leslie Howard was born to play Sir Percy. His perfect Mayfair accent and languid style must have been precisely what Baroness Orczy had in mind when she created her hero. Raymond Massey was equally impressive as the Pimpernel's French adversary who despite all his cleverness, saw his prize slip away and realized the penalty he faced for failure. Merle Oberon was, as usual, beautiful, but her role called for her to be little more that decorative.

Critics were not so kind in describing the 1937 film, some questioning the manliness of the male performers as well as why Alexander Korda thought a remake necessary. At the beginning of World War II, Howard was back in an updated version of the story of how an English professor and a team of his students snatched political prisoners away from the Germans. The latter were treated as far more reasonable and human adversaries than they would be for the next couple of decades. Francis L. Sullivan in the Chauvelin-like character tracks down his prey by following-up a lead of a tune that the modern Pimpernel whistles while doing his work. Sullivan also feels that he has Howard where he wants him at the end of the picture, but in a blink of an eye, the elusive Pimpernel has escaped once again.

Scarlet Street *see* **La Chienne**

779 School for Scandal

Based on the play by Richard Brinsley Sheridan. Story: A wealthy eighteenth-century man poses as a moneylender to learn which of his nephews deserves to be his heir.

Gems of Literature Series, British and Colonial, Great Britain, 1923 (original). Silent. Director: Edwin Greenwood; screenwriter: Eliot Stannard. Cast: Russell Thorndike (Sir Peter Teazle), Nina Vanna (Lady Teazle), Florence Wulff (Lady Sneerwell).

• ***School for Scandal*** (remake). British International, Great Britain, 1923. Silent. Director: Bertram Phillips; screenwriter: Frank Miller. Cast: Queenie Thomas (Lady Teazle), Frank Stanmore (Sir Peter Teazle), Basil Rathbone (Joseph Surface), John Stuart (Charles Surface), Sydney Paxton (Sir Oliver Surface), A.G. Poulton, Elsie French, Mary Brough, Jack Miller, Billie Shotter.

• ***School for Scandal*** (remake). Albion/Paramount Pictures, Great Britain, 1930. Director: Maurice Elvey; screenwriter: Jean Jay. Cast: Basil Gill (Sir Peter Teazle), Madeleine Carroll (Lady Teazle), Ian Fleming (Joseph Surface), Henry Hewitt (Charles Surface), Edgar K. Bruce (Sir Oliver Surface), Hayden Coffin, Hector Abbas, Dodo Watts, Anne Grey, John Charlton, Stanley Lathbury.

The 1930 film was one of the first in Britain to use color. Other than that innovation, there's nothing remarkable about the play-like filming of Sheridan's famous eighteenth-century farce.

Scrooge *see* **A Christmas Carol**

The Sea Beast *see* **Moby Dick**

780 The Sea Hawk

Based on the novel by Rafael Sabatini. Story: Oliver Tressilian, a wealthy baronet, is shanghaied and blamed for the death of Peter Godolphin, brother of Oliver's fiancée, Rosamund. The actual villain is Oliver's half-brother, Lionel. At sea Oliver is captured by the Spaniards and made a galley slave. He escapes to the Moors and becomes Sakr-el-Bahr or the Sea Hawk, the scourge of Christendom. When he learns that Lionel has married Rosamund, he kidnaps both of them but later surrenders to a British ship. Rosamund intercedes for his life and after Lionel is disposed of, they marry.

First National Pictures, 1924 (original). Silent. Director: Frank Lloyd;

screenwriter: J.G. Hawks. Cast: Milton Sills (Sir Oliver Tressilian/Sakr-el-Bahr, the Sea Hawk), Enid Bennett (Rosamund Godolphin), Lloyd Hughes (Lionel Tressilian), Wallace MacDonald (Peter Godolphin), Marc MacDermott (Sir John Killigrew), Wallace Beery (Jasper Leigh), Frank Currier, Medea Radzina, William Collier, Jr.

• ***The Sea Hawk*** (remake). Warner Bros., 1940. Director: Michael Curtiz; screenwriters: Howard Koch and Seton I. Miller. Cast: Errol Flynn (Geoffrey Thorpe), Brenda Marshall (Dona Maria), Claude Rains (Don Jose Alvarez de Cordoba), Donald Crisp (Sir John Burleson), Flora Robson (Queen Elizabeth), Alan Hale (Carl Pitt), Henry Daniell (Lord Wolfingham), Una O'Connor, James Stephenson, Gilbert Roland, William Lundigan.

The sound remake greatly expands the swashbuckling adventure to include a great deal of court intrigue. Errol Flynn as the major character is a dashing privateer who along with others of his ilk, called Sea Hawks, attack Spanish ships for their own profit, and apparently also to protect England. In this they are secretly encourage by Queen Elizabeth who has not yet raised the British fleet which will one day defeat the Spanish Armada. One could have hoped for more rousing adventures at sea; the best battle sequence comes early in the film and subsequent sequences never approach anything as exciting. There is an excellent duel between Flynn and the traitorious Henry Daniell. Flora Robson does a nice job as Queen Elizabeth but beyond that there's not much to praise in the acting end of the film.

781 The Sea Wolf

Based on the novel by Jack London. Story: When a ferry going from San Francisco to Oakland collides with a steamer, Humphrey Van Weyden and Maud Brewster are picked up by Captain "Wolf" Larsen and his schooner *Ghost.* Larsen is a mystic, philosopher and absolute ruler of his ship. Members of the crew have lewd plans for Maud, but Larsen takes it upon himself to protect her and decides to marry her. But as the ceremony begins, his crew mutinies and Larsen suffers one of his blind spells. The ship is set afire, and while Humphrey and Maud are rescued by another ship, Larsen refuses to quit his command and goes up in flames with the schooner.

• ***The Sea Wolf*** (remake). Producers Distributing Corp., 1926. Silent. Director: Ralph Ince; screenwriter: J. Grubb Alexander. Cast: Ralph Ince (Wolf Larsen), Claire Adams (Maud Brewster), Theodore von Eltz (Humphrey Van Weyden), Snitz Edwards, Mitchell Lewis.

• ***The Sea Wolf*** (remake). Fox Film Corp., 1930. Director: Alfred Santell; screenwriter: Ralph Block. Cast: Milton Sills (Wolf Larsen), Jane Keith (Lorna Marsh), Raymond Hackett (Allen Rand), Mitchell Harris ("Death" Larsen), Nat Pendleton, John Rogers, Harold Kinney, Sam Allen, Harry Tenbrook.

• ***The Sea Wolf*** (remake). Warner Bros., 1941. Director: Michael Curtiz; screenwriter: Robert Rossen. Cast: Edward G. Robinson (Wolf Larsen), Ida Lupino (Ruth Brewster), John Garfield (George Leach), Alexander Knox (Humphrey Van Weyden), Gene Lockhart (Dr. Prescott), Barry Fitzgerald

(Cooky), Stanley Ridges, David Bruce, Francis McDonald, Howard Da Silva, Frank Lackteen.

Wolf Larsen was also portrayed on the screen by Hobart Bosworth in 1913 and by Noah Beery in 1920. The story also showed up as a western named *Barricade* in 1950 with Raymond Massey, as *Wolf Larsen* in 1958 with Barry Sullivan and in the 1975 Italian film *Wolf of the Seven Seas* starring Chuck Connors.

Wolf Larsen's schooner is a hellship, captained by a callous and inhuman skipper who fears only his elder brother, "Death" Larsen. In the most praised version of the novel, Edward G. Robinson vividly captures the complexity of the captain who equally enjoys breaking people's spirits and having philosophical discussions when he can find someone such as Alexander Knox, whom he considers to be on an intellectual par with himself. John Garfield and Ida Lupino provide the romantic interest, both on the lam from the law, he a rebellious member of the crew, she a ferry passenger rescued by Larsen's ship when the former sinks. These four and the skill of director Curtiz make the film a standout, if a bit talky in places.

782 The Seagull

Based on the play by Anton Chekhov. Story: Nineteenth-century Russian actress Irina Arkadina has no interest in her 20-year-old son Konstantin's attempts at becoming a playwright and she ridicules his unrequited love for actress Nina. The latter loves novelist Boris Trigorin, who is Irina's lover. Nina becomes Boris' mistress, but he deserts her after the birth of their child and returns to Irina. By this time Konstantin has published but his mother is still uninterested, and Nina is unwilling to return his love, being still enamored with Trigorin. Despondent, Konstantin kills himself, much as he had once killed a seagull and given it to Nina as a prediction of his suicide.

Warner Bros., 1968 (original). Director: Sidney Lumet; screenwriter: Moura Budberg. Cast: Simone Signoret (Irina Arkadina), James Mason (Boris Trigorin), Vanessa Redgrave (Nina), David Warner (Konstantin), Harry Andrews (Sorin), Eileen Herlie (Polina), Ronald Radd, Kathleen Widdoes, Denholm Elliott.

• ***Chayka*** (remake). Mosfilm, U.S.S.R., 1971. Director and screenwriter: Yuli Karasik. Cast: Yuri Yakovlev (Boris Trigorin), Alla Demedova (Irina Arkadina), Lyudmilla Savoyeleva (Nina), Vladimir Chetverikov (Konstantin), Valentina Telchihkina.

The 1968 film is a most proficient movie with a generally fine cast, especially James Mason and Vanessa Redgrave, with David Warner right at home as the young playwright. Simone Signoret, however, was not the best choice for Irina. The Russian version of the Chekhov play had a limited release in the United States as did the 1977 Italian film *Il Gabbiano*.

The Second Best Secret Agent in the Whole Wide World *see* **Licensed to Kill**

783 Second Floor Mystery

Based on the novel *Agony Column* by Earl Derr Biggers. Story: Geoffrey West and Marian Ferguson, using the noms de plume Lord Strawberries and Lady Grapefruit, communicate through the personal columns of the *London Times.* When she advertises that she wishes to receive "exciting" letters, he obliges by sending her chapters of a lurid murder melodrama, but after awhile it seems fact is imitating fiction.

Warner Bros., 1930 (original). Director: Roy Del Ruth; screenwriter: Joseph Jackson. Cast: Grant Withers (Geoffrey West), Loretta Young (Marian Ferguson), H.B. Warner (Inspector Bray), Claire McDowell (Aunt Hattie), Sidney Bracy, Crauford Kent, John Loder, Claude King, Judith Voselli.

• ***Second Floor Mystery*** (remake). Warner Bros., 1941. Director: D. Ross Lederman; screenwriter: Fred Niblo, Jr. Cast: Keith Douglas, Lucille Fairbanks, Paul Cavanaugh, Richard Ainley, Marjorie Gateson, Gloria Holden, Lumsden Hare.

The remake is set in Hong Kong just prior to the Japanese invasion. Keith Douglas attempts to excite the girl of his dreams, Lucille Fairbanks, by inventing a murder story in which he claims to be involved. She's not only excited, she believes him. Too bad the movie didn't excite audiences.

784 The Second Mrs. Tanqueray

Based on the play by Sir Arthur Wing Pinero. Story: Despite being warned by his friends, Aubrey Tanqueray takes as his second wife Paula, a woman with a scarlet past. Her reputation causes her to be ostracized by Aubrey's friends, she fights constantly with Aubrey's daughter, Ellean, and discovers that the latter's fiancé is one of her ex-lovers. Seeing no future for herself, she commits suicide.

Ideal, Great Britian, 1916 (original). Silent. Director: Fred Paul; screenwriter: Benedict James. Cast: George Alexander (Aubrey Tanqueray), Hilda Moore (Paula), Norman Forbes (Cayley Drummle), Marie Hemingway (Ellean Tanqueray), James Lindsay (Sir George Orreyd), May Leslie Stuart, Nelson Ramsey, Mary Roarke, Roland Pertwee, Minna Grey, Bernard Vaughan.

• ***The Second Mrs. Tanqueray*** (remake). Vandyke, Great Britain, 1953. Director: Dallas Bower; screenwriter: uncredited. Cast: Pamela Brown (Paula Tanqueray), Hugh Sinclair (Aubrey Tanqueray), Ronald Ward (Cayley Drummle), Virginia McKenna (Ellean Tanqueray), Andrew Osborn (Capt. Ardale), Mary Hinton, Peter Haddon, Peter Bull, Bruce Seton.

This story of a notorious Victorian woman was also filmed in 1922. The movies are based on an antiquated play but the 1953 remake has some interest even though little was spent on the production. The screenplay was well written, but it's now almost completely outdated.

785 Second Wife

Based on the play *All the King's Men* by Fulton Oursler. Story: In this story of the difficulties of dealing with stepchildren in second marriages, widower Walter Fairchild is convinced by his wife, Florence Wendell, that for his new marriage to be successful, he must establish a new home for them and send his son, Junior, from his first marriage away to school. When Florence is expecting their child, Walter receives word that his son in Switzerland is dying and makes immediate preparations to go to the boy. Florence considers his actions inconsiderate of her feelings and tells Walter he cannot come back to her. Nevertheless Walter goes to his son, who recovers. Walter brings him back to the States and puts him in another school. Meanwhile, Florence is getting a lot of attention from Gilbert Gaylord, a former suitor, who encourages her to leave her husband. She's almost convinced but when Walter insists that she will have to give up their child, she reconsiders and is reconciled with Walter and Junior.

RKO, 1930 (original). Director: Russell Mack; screenwriters: Hugh Herbert and Bert Glennon. Cast: Conrad Nagel (Walter Fairchild), Lila Lee (Florence Wendell), Hugh Huntley (Gilbert Gaylord), Mary Carr (Mrs. Rhodes), Freddie Burke Frederick (Junior).

• ***Second Wife*** (remake). RKO, 1936. Director: Edward Killy; screenwriter: Thomas Lennon. Cast: Gertrude Michael (Virginia Howard), Walter Abel (Kenneth Carpenter), Erik Rhodes (Dave Bennett), Emma Dunn (Mrs. Brown), Lee Van Atta (Junior), Florence Fair (Mrs. Stephenson), Brenda Fowler, Frank Reicher, George Breakston.

These films don't suggest any workable solutions to the problems that new spouses can encounter when they live in the same house with children from a previous marriage. If it is true that one always marries a stranger, that goes double for the children of this stranger. The problems can be resolved but it takes a lot of work on the part of all involved as well as their goodwill. These two sluggish films dealt with everything on a superficial level. There are no surprises, no insights and no outstanding performances.

The Secret Call ***see*** **The Telephone Call**

The Secret de Mayerling ***see*** **Mayerling**

786 The Secret Hour

Based on the play *They Knew What They Wanted* by Sidney Howard. Story: Elderly fruit grower Tony sends a photograph of Joe, his foreman, to a young waitress, Amy, with whom he is corresponding. When Tony proposes marriage, Amy, having fallen in love with the photograph, accepts. An automobile accident prevents Tony from meeting Amy's train, so he sends Joe to fetch her. At this meeting, Joe falls in love with the girl who already loves him, and they secretly marry, regretting their action the next morning. Three months later, Tony, now healed from his accident, makes plans to marry Amy. She and Joe confess their secret and Tony orders them both out of the house, but later takes them back because he realizes that the mix-up was his fault.

Paramount/Famous Lasky Corp., 1928. Silent. Director and screenwriter: Rowland V. Lee. Cast: Pola Negri (Amy), Jean Hersholt (Tony), Kenneth Thomson (Joe), Christian J. Frank, George Kuwa, George Periolat.

• ***A Lady to Love*** (remake). MGM, 1930. Director: Victor Seastrom; screenwriter: Sidney Howard. Cast: Vilma Banky (Lena), Edward G. Robinson (Tony), Robert Ames (Buck), Richard Carle, Lloyd Ingraham, Anderson Lawler, Gum Chin, Henry Armetta, George Davis.

• ***They Knew What They Wanted*** (remake). RKO, 1940. Director: Garson Kanin; screenwriter: Robert Ardrey. Cast: Charles Laughton (Tony), Carole Lombard (Amy), William Gargan (Joe), Frank Fay (Father McKee), Harry Carey (the Doctor), Lee Tung-Foo, Joe Bernard, James Fox, Karl Malden, Victor Kilian.

The story of the fruit grower, his foreman and the mail-order bride was also filmed by MGM as a 1930 German-language movie with Edward G. Robinson and Vilma Banky as Tony and Mizzi, and Joseph Schildkraut playing the foreman, Buck. Sidney Howard's play was also the basis for the moving opera-like 1956 Broadway musical *The Most Happy Fella* with words and music by Frank Loesser.

This simple story is very special and touching. There are no villains, no great dramatic moments, just likeable people caught in an unlikely triangle not totally of their making. Each of the versions of the play retains a certain delightful freshness, with natural performances from the principals and those in support. The same cannot be said for the unfortunate reworking of the bittersweet story in 1957, titled *The Unholy Wife*, with Diana Dors as a woman married to a much older vineyard owner, Rod Steiger. She plans to murder him, but instead kills a friend and is ultimately sent to prison for the accidental death of her mother-in-law.

The Secret of Deep Harbor *see* **I Cover the Waterfront**

The Secret of Dorian Gray *see* **The Picture of Dorian Gray**

Secret of Madame Blanche *see* **The Lady**

Secret of Monte Cristo *see* **The Count of Monte Cristo**

787 The Secret of the Blue Room

Based on the story by Erich Phillipi. Story: To test their love for Irene von Heldorf, three suitors, Captain Walter Brink, Frank Faber, and Thomas Brandt, each agree to spend the night alone in the blue room of Robert von Heldorf's castle. The room has remained shut ever since the mysterious murder of three people in the room 20 years earlier.

Universal Pictures, 1933 (original). Director: Kurt Neumann; screenwriter: William Hurlbut. Cast: Lionel Atwill (Robert von Heldorf), Gloria Stuart (Irene von Heldorf), Paul Lukas (Captain Walter Brink), Onslow Stevens (Frank Faber), William Janney (Thomas Brandt), Robert Barrat, Muriel Kirkland, Russell Hopton, Elizabeth Patterson, Anders van Haden, James Durkin.

• ***The Missing Guest*** (remake). Universal Pictures, 1938. Director: John Rawlins; screenwriters: Charles Martin and Paul Perez. Cast: Paul Kelly (Scoop

Hanlon), Constance Moore (Stephanie Kirkland), William Lundigan (Larry Dearden), Edwin Stanley (Dr. Carroll), Selmer Jackson (Frank Baldrich), Billy Wayne, George Cooper, Patrick J. Kelly, Florence Wix.

• ***Murder in the Blue Room*** (remake). Universal Pictures, 1944. Director: Leslie Goodwins; screenwriters: I.A.L. Diamond and Stanley Davis. Cast: Anne Gwynne (Nan Kirkland), Donald Cook (Steve Randall), John Litel (Frank Baldrich), Grace McDonald (Peggy), Betty Kean (Betty), June Preisser (Jerry), Regis Toomey (Inspector McDonald), Nella Walker, Andrew Tombes, Ian Wolfe.

Although the first of the three movies was played pretty much as a straight mystery and the second was only unintentionally funny, the third remake was a mystery comedy about a haunted house with all the usual sliding panels, secret passages, fainting women and a ghost or two. In the 1938 version, reporter Paul Kelly poses as a psychic when a family reopens the mansion where a murder took place 20 years before. In the 1944 movie, even though it lasted only 61 minutes, the participants find time for five musical numbers while a man tries to solve the mystery of his wife's first husband, who was killed in the mansion's blue room. This leads to more murders.

788 Secret Service

Based on the play by William Gillette. Story: Secret Service agent Lewis K. Dumont works to bring about the capture of Richmond, Virginia, during the Civil War when the city was beleaguered by Union forces. He poses as a Southern officer and carries a dying Confederate soldier to the latter's Richmond home where he meets the lad's sister, Edith Varney. He virtually moves in with the family. By the time he has been arrested as a Northern spy and led away to prison, she's hooked and regional differences no longer seem important to her.

Paramount Pictures, 1919 (original). Silent. Director: Hugh Ford; screenwriter: William Gillette. Cast: Robert Warwick (Lewis K. Dumont), Wanda Hawley (Edith Varney), Theodore Roberts (Gen. Nelson Randolph), Edythe Chapman (Mrs. Varney), Raymond Hatton (Howard Varney), Casson Ferguson, Robert Caine, Irving Cummings, Guy Oliver, Lillian Leighton.

• *Secret Service* (remake). RKO/Radio Productions, 1931. Director: J. Walter Ruben; screenwriter: Bernard Schubert. Cast: Richard Dix (Lewis Dumont), Shirley Grey (Edith Varney), William Post, Jr. (Lt. Dumont), David Gordon (Arelsford), Fred Warren (Gen. Grant), Nance O'Neill, Virginia Sale, Florence Lake, Clarence Muse.

It must have been something to have seen the great William Gillette play the role of the Northern spy. His version was one of the greatest successes of the American stage. One gets the feeling from the films that something got lost in the media transformation. Neither picture is any great shakes in regard to story or acting.

789 Secrets

Based on the play by Rudolph Bessier and May Edgington. Story: Old Mary

Carlton, sitting up with her sick husband, John, falls asleep and dreams of her girlhood in England, her elopement with John, their life on a ranch in the United States, their return to England—rich and famous—and his infidelity. She awakens to find that he has passed the crisis and is on the road to recovery.

Schenck/First National Pictures, 1924 (original). Silent. Director: Frank Borzage; screenwriter: Francis Marion. Cast: Norma Talmadge (Mary Marlow/Mary Carlton), Eugene O'Brien (John Carlton), Patterson Dial (Susan), Winter Hall (Dr. Arbuthnot), Frank Elliott (Robert Carlton), Emily Fitzroy, Harvey Clark, Frances Feeney, Alice Day, George Cowl.

• ***Secrets*** (remake). United Artists, 1933. Director: Frank Borzage; screenwriter: Frances Marion. Cast: Mary Pickford (Mary Marlow/Mary Carlton), Leslie Howard (John Carlton), C. Aubrey Smith (Mrs. Marlow), Blanche Frederici (Mrs. Marlowe), Doris Lloyd (Susan Channing), Lyman Williams, Virginia Grey, Huntley Gordon, Ethel Clayton.

These melodramas have only moderate punch and despite the presence of Norma Talmadge and Mary Pickford, the films did not pull audiences into theaters in large numbers. The flashback approach to the story was much more a novelty at the time than now and its use drew some interest, but basically it's just the recollections of an old lady about life with her husband. Too bad we don't have his version to compare with hers. Eugene O'Brien was satisfactory as the husband in the original but Leslie Howard's fragile physique makes one believe that he would never have risked the ordeals of life in the Old West. These films will never rival Michener's *Centennial.*

790 Sentimental Journey

Based on the story "The Little Horse" by Nelia Gardner White. Story: Famous stage actress Julie has a heart condition. She falls in love with an orphan, Hitty, and adopts the child so her producer husband, Bill, won't be left alone just in case something happens to her. Well, it does, and when Julie suffers a fatal heart attack, Hitty attempts to fill the void left by the death of her foster-mother.

Twentieth Century–Fox, 1946. Director: Walter Lang; screenwriters: Samuel Hoffenstein and Elizabeth Reinhardt. Cast: John Payne (Bill), Maureen O'Hara (Julie), William Bendix (Donnelly), Cedric Hardwicke (Dr. Miller), Connie Marshall (Hitty), Glenn Langan, Mischa Auer, Kurt Krueger.

• ***The Gift of Love*** (remake). Twentieth Century–Fox, 1958. Director: Jean Negulesco; screenwriter: Luther Davis. Cast: Lauren Bacall (Julie Beck), Robert Stack (Bill Beck), Evelyn Rudie (Hitty), Lorne Greene (Grant Allan), Anne Seymour, Edward Platt, Joseph Kearns.

"Sentimental Journey" is a nifty tune, but it isn't the most appropriate background music for this tearjerker. Something more funereal is called for to set the proper mood for viewing the body—and by that we don't mean the lovely one of Maureen O'Hara. The title should have been *Sentimentality Journey.* The remake is worse because Lauren Bacall and Robert Stack are miscast as the soon-to-be-departed wife and her husband. Little Evelyn Rudie, whom Bacall hopes will be a comfort to Stack when she is gone, proves to be something of an annoyance to him while Lauren's still on earth. When Ma dies, Pa puts the kid back in an orphanage because the child lives in a fantasy world, but through some kind of ESP, he arrives just in time to save her life when she is about to be swallowed up by the Pacific Ocean.

The Sergeant Was a Lady *see* **Francis Joins the WACS**

Sergeants 3 *see* **Gunga Din**

Serpent of the Nile *see* **Cleopatra**

791 Service for Ladies

Based on the story *Head Waiter* by Ernst Vajda. Story: Albert Leroux, headwaiter at an exclusive Paris hotel, falls in love with a visiting American heiress, Elizabeth Foster, but is convinced she would not be interested in him because of his position. They meet under more romantic settings at a winter resort in the Alps and love melts the snow. As Albert leaves once again for Paris, Elizabeth's father discovers his daughter's lover's true identity. When they arrive at the Paris hotel, Albert is sacked and then given controlling interest in the hotel by the Fosters, and at last he is worthy of her love.

Paramount/Famous Players–Lasky, 1927 (original). Silent. Director: Harry D'Arst; screenwriter: Chandler Sprague. Cast: Adolphe Menjou (Albert Leroux), Kathryn Carver (Elizabeth Foster), Charles Lane (Robert Foster), Lawrence Grant (King Boris).

• ***Reserved for Ladies*** (remake). Paramount Pictures, 1932. Director: Alexander Korda; screenwriter: Ernest Vajda. Cast: Leslie Howard (Max), George Crossmith (King), Benita Hume (Countess), Elizabeth Allan (Sylvia), Morton Shelton, Anne Esmond, Ben Field.

Critics generally felt the silent version to be superior to that starring Leslie Howard, even though the latter's performance and speech were given special praise. By 1932, it was believed that audiences wouldn't buy the farfetched story of a head waiter who pals with a comical king and romances a rich young Englishwoman who believes he is a prince. Benita Hume plays a "bad girl" first seen taking a bath, whereas "good girl" Elizabeth Allan gives audiences an early peek at her in lingerie.

792 Seven Keys to Baldpate

Based on the novel by Earl Derr Biggers and the play by George M. Cohan. Story: Author William Halowell Magee's impending marriage to Mary Norton, his publisher's daughter, is in jeopardy unless he finishes his latest novel. A rival for Mary's affection, Bentley, offers Magee the use of his mountain resort, Baldpate Inn, to finish the manuscript, giving him what he says is the only key. While at the inn, Magee is interrupted by Bland, who opens the door with his own key and hides $200,000 in a safe. In rapid succession, Magee is interrupted by several others, each with their own key and each causing problems in meeting his deadline to finish the novel. Finally the sheriff comes with a seventh key and arrests everyone, leaving Magee to finish his novel, and it becomes apparent that the action that has just taken place was in the novel that Magee was writing.

• ***Seven Keys to Baldpate*** (remake). Famous Players/Paramount Pictures, 1925. Silent. Director: Fred Newmeyer; screenwriter: Frank Griffith. Cast: Douglas MacLean (William Halowell Magee), Edith Roberts (Mary Norton), Anders Randolf (J.K. Norton), Crauford Kent (Bentley), Ned Sparks (Bland), William Orlamond, Wade Boteler, Edwin Sturges, Betty Francisco, Maym Kelso, Fred Kelsey.

• ***Seven Keys to Baldpate*** (remake). RKO, 1929. Director: Reginald Barker; screenwriter: Jane Murfin. Cast: Richard Dix (William Magee), Miriam Seegar (Mary Norton), Crauford Kent (Hal Bentley), Margaret Livingston (Myra Thornhill), Joseph Allen, Lucien Littlefield, De Witt Jennings, Carleton Macy, Nella Walker.

• ***Seven Keys to Baldpate*** (remake). RKO, 1935. Directors: William Hamilton and Edward Killy; screenwriters: Wallace Smith and Anthony Veiller. Cast: Gene Raymond (Magee), Margaret Callahan (Mary), Eric Blore (Bolton), Erin O'Brien-Moore (Myra), Moroni Olsen (Cargan), Grant Mitchell, Ray Mayer, Henry Travers, Murray Alper.

By the time the story was first brought to the screen in 1915, the plot was already developing arthritic conditions. Each passing year made the play more eligible for old-age assistance but that didn't prevent more film productions, including a silent in 1917 and the last, at least for the time being, in 1947, once again by RKO. If one isn't looking for much, viewing one of the productions of *Seven Keys* won't hurt any more than many television shows that we all sit through night after night. Tip your hat to the aged—or is that the dead?

The Seven Per Cent Solution *see* **Sherlock Holmes**

793 Seven Sinners

Based on a story by Ladislaus Fodor and Laslo Vadnal. Story: Bijou Blanche, a sultry honky-tonk singer, arrives at the South Sea island of Boni-Kimba for an engagement at the Seven Sinners Cafe. She displays her charms and her implied promises so effectively that Lt. Bruce Whitney is ready to give up his naval career to marry her. Bijou realizes that it would never work out and sends him back to his first love, the sea, but not before there is a knock 'em down, tear 'em up brawl, which completely destroys the cafe.

Universal Pictures, 1940 (original). Director: Tay Garnett; screenwriter: Harry Tugend. Cast: Marlene Dietrich (Bijou Blanche), John Wayne (Lt. Bruce Whitney), Broderick Crawford (Little Ned), Mischa Auer (Sasha), Albert Dekker (Dr. Martin), Billy Gilbert (Tony), Oscar Homolka (Antro), Anna Lee, Samuel S. Hinds, Reginald Denny, Vince Barnett.

• ***South Sea Sinner*** (remake). Universal Pictures, 1950. Director: Bruce Humberstone; screenwriters: Joel Malone and Oscar Brodney. Cast: Macdonald Carey ("Jake" Davis), Shelley Winters (Coral), Helena Carter (Margaret

Landis), Luther Adler (Cognac), Frank Lovejoy (Doc), Art Smith, John Ridgely, James Flavin, Molly Lamont, Silan Chen, Liberace.

Marlene Dietrich was almost satirizing herself in this sultry tropical romance, rolling her eyes, hips and anything else to draw attention to herself. She gave her usual husky rendition of two Frank Loesser and Frederick Hollander songs, "The Man's in the Navy" and "I've Never Been in Love Before." In the remake, Shelley Winters was the girl showing her flesh to the regulars at a South Sea Island cafe, seemingly a cross between Mae West and Sadie Thompson. Her piano player was Liberace, sans sequins, who got to play a bit of Liszt Piano Concerto Number One. Shelley gave out with "It Had to Be You" by Gus Kahn and Isham Jones and "One Man Woman" by Jack Brooks and Milton Schwarzwald, among others. Her romantic interest is world-weary beach bum MacDonald Carey.

Seven Sinners (1936) *see* **The Wrecker**

794 Seventh Heaven

Based on the play by Austin Strong. Story: Chico, a Paris sewer worker, rescues Diane, who has been forced into a life of prostitution and stealing by her brutal drunken sister, Nana. Diane is saved from being arrested by Chico's claim that she is his wife. He takes her to his seventh floor, walk-up flat called his "seventh heaven." Their love is realized just as World War I breaks out, but their marriage is put off as Chico is called to arms. Diane works as a munitions worker and following the Armistice receives word that Chico is dead. However, he returns to their "seventh heaven," blinded by the war. The lovers are reunited with his appraisal, "I'm a most remarkable fellow."

Fox Film Corporation, 1927 (original). Silent. Director: Frank Borzage; screenwriter: Benjamin Glazer. Cast: Janet Gaynor (Diane), Charles Farrell (Chico), Ben Bard (Col. Brissac), David Butler (Gobin), Marie Mosquini (Madame Gobin), Albert Gran (Boul), Gladys Brockwell (Nana), Emile Chautard (Pere Chevillon), George Stone (Sewer Rat), Jessie Haslett, Brandon Hurst, Lillian West.

• ***Seventh Heaven*** (remake). Twentieth Century–Fox, 1937. Director: Henry King; screenwriter: Melville Baker. Cast: Simone Simon (Diane), James Stewart (Chico), Gale Sondergaard (Nana), John Qualen (the Sewer Rat), Victor Kilian (Gobin), Mady Christians (Marie), Thomas Beck (Brissac), Jean Hersholt (Pere Chevillon), J. Edward Bromberg (Aristide), Gregory Ratoff (Boul), Sig Rumann, Rollo Lloyd, Rafaela Ottiano.

The presentation of Janet Gaynor as the absurd waif Diane, safe and at peace in the "heaven" she shares with Charles Farrell as Chico, is one of the all-time most popular silent romances. The fame of the movie rests on the middle part of the picture when Chico and Diane come to love each other. Diane's delight in being treated kindly by someone is touchingly portrayed in little bits of pantomime. Audiences really cared about these two people and felt the delight of their growing love. Janet Gaynor's performance is particularly appealing. She invests Diane with a rare sweetness and loveliness. The pair of Gaynor and Farrell became one of the most popular love teams of all times.

The remake with James Stewart and Simone Simon was disastrous. Neither of the leads were appropriate for their parts and they seemed to know it, stumbling through the same scenes that Gaynor and Farrell invested with such beauty, dignity and passion. The story is nothing if audiences don't feel pity for the unfortunate Diane; this point seems to have been completely forgotten by the director, screenwriters and star. Another problem with the remake is the dialogue itself, unfortunately inferior in communicating the sublime feelings of Chico and Diane that in the silent version were elegantly conveyed by mere glances and little bits of action. The story was also filmed in China in 1930 as *Wild Grass.*

The Seventh Sin *see* **The Painted Veil**

The Seventh Voyage of Sinbad *see* **Sinbad the Sailor**

Shado Kalo *see* **Dr. Jekyll and Mr. Hyde**

795 Shadow of a Doubt

Based on a story by Gordon McDowell. Story: Uncle Charlie, who is actually the "Merry Widow" murderer of wealthy women and on the run from the Philadelphia police, arrives for a visit with his sister's family in a small California town. It is his adoring niece, called "Young Charlie," who begins to suspect him of having a guilty conscience about something. This is reinforced by the arrival of two Philadelphia detectives whom Uncle Charlie refuses to see and is confirmed when young Charlie is almost killed by her uncle, although it is apparently an accident. His final attempt to dispose of her results in her turning the tables on him.

Universal Pictures, 1943 (original). Director: Alfred Hitchcock; screenwriters: Thornton Wilder, Sally Benson and Alma Reville. Cast: Teresa Wright (Young Charlie), Joseph Cotten (Uncle Charlie), Macdonald Carey (Jack Graham), Patricia Collinge (Emma Newton), Henry Travers (Joseph Newton), Hume Cronyn (Herbie Hawkins), Wallace Ford, Edna May Wonicott, Charles Bates.

• ***Step Down to Terror*** (remake). Universal Pictures, 1958. Director: Harry Keller; screenwriters: Thornton Wilder, Sally Benson and Alma Reville. Cast: Charles Drake (Johnny Williams), Colleen Miller (Helen Walters), Rod Taylor (Mike Randall), Josephine Hutchinson (Mrs. Williams), Jocelyn Brando (Lily), Ricky Kellman, Ann Doran.

Hitchcock nicely caught the mood of small-town life and juxtaposed evil in the person of Joseph Cotten, and good supplied by Teresa Wright, to good advantage. The supporting cast, particularly Patricia Collinge, Henry Travers, and Hume Cronyn, nicely complemented the stars in this gripping character study. In the remake, Charles Drake returns home after being away six years to visit his devoted mother. His widowed sister-in-law, Colleen Miller, comes to believe that he is a killer and if it were not for the intervention of Rod Taylor,

the psychopath would have succeeded in adding Miss Miller to his list of victims.

Shadow of the Thin Man *see* **The Thin Man**

796 Shaft

Based on the novel by Ernest Tidyman. Story: John Shaft is a black Harlem private eye who is hired by a black gangster to rescue his daughter who has been kidnapped. Before he can complete his mission there's a lot of violence and blood-letting.

MGM, 1971 (original). Director: Gordon Parks, Sr.; screenwriters: John D.F. Black and Ernest Tidyman. Cast: Richard Roundtree (John Shaft), Moses Gunn (Bumpy Jones), Charles Cioffi (Lt. Vic Androzzi), Christopher St. John (Ben Buford), Gwenn Mitchell, Lawrence Pressman, Victor Arnold, Sherri Brewer, Rex Robbins, Camille Yarborough, Margaret Warncke.

• ***Shaft in Africa*** (sequel). MGM, 1973. Director: John Guillermin; screenwriter: Stirling Silliphant. Cast: Richard Roundtree (John Shaft), Frank Finlay (Amafi), Vonetta McGee (Aleme), Neda Arneric (Jazar), Debebe Eshetu (Wassa), Spiros Focas, Jacques Herlin, Jho Jhenkins, Willie Jonah.

• ***Shaft's Big Score*** (sequel). MGM, 1973. Director: Gordon Parks, Sr.; screenwriter: Ernest Tidyman. Cast: Richard Roundtree (John Shaft), Moses Gunn (Bumpy Jones), Drew Bundi (Willy), Joseph Mascolo (Mascola), Kathy Imrie (Rita), Wally Taylor, Julius W. Harris, Rosalind Miles, Joe Santos.

The title number of the 1971 picture won the Academy Award for Best Song. It was written and sung by Issac Hayes. The above-average crime thriller was one of the best of the black exploitation films of the '70s and Roundtree demonstrated both style and cool. In the first sequel, he is kidnapped by an Ethiopian emir who has him track down a gang of slavers. In the 1973 film, Roundtree is back in Harlem to avenge the death of a friend, which puts him in conflict with numbers racketeers.

Shaft in Africa *see* **Shaft**

Shaft's Big Score *see* **Shaft**

The Shaggy D.A. *see* **The Shaggy Dog**

797 The Shaggy Dog

Based on the novel *The Hound of Florence* by Felix Salten. Story: Wilby Daniels visits a museum and is transformed into a large shaggy dog by an ancient spell on a ring, which he accidently acquires. As a dog, Wilby looks

Opposite, top: *Charles Farrell (right) is dreaming of Janet Gaynor as David Butler and George E. Stone look on sympathetically in* Seventh Heaven *(Fox Film Corp., 1927).* Bottom: *James Stewart (right) gets advice and support from John Qualen (left), Jean Hersholt and Gregory Ratoff in* Seventh Heaven *(20th Century–Fox, 1937).*

exactly like one owned by a neighbor, Franceska Andrassy. Since Wilby's father, Wilson, is allergic to dogs, Wilby spends most of his time at the neighbors, causing a great deal of confusion as he changes back and forth from dog to human. As a dog he discovers that Franceska's father is a spy, planning to steal missile plans. Wilby makes Wilson aware of the plot and after a wild chase, Wilby as the shaggy dog saves Franceska and the spies are captured.

Buena Vista/Disney, 1959 (original). Director: Charles Barton; screenwriters: Bill Walsh and Lillie Hayward. Cast: Fred MacMurray (Wilson Daniels), Jean Hagen (Frieda Daniels), Tommy Kirk (Wilby Daniels), Annette Funicello (Allison D'Allessio), Tim Considine (Buzz Miller), Kevin Corcoran (Moochie Daniels), Cecil Kellaway (Prof. Plumcutt), Alexander Scourby (Dr. Mikhail Andrassy), Roberta Shore (Franceska Andrassy), James Westerfield, Jacques Aubuchon, Strother Martin, Forrest Lewis.

• ***The Shaggy D.A.*** (sequel). Buena Vista/Disney, 1976. Director: Robert Stevenson; screenwriter: Don Tait. Cast: Dean Jones (Wilby Daniels), Suzanne Pleshette (Betty), Tim Conway (Tim), Keenan Wynn (John Slade), Jo Anne Worley (Katrinka), Dick Van Patten (Raymond).

The first film was a low-budget comedy shot in black and white that grossed over $8,000,000 in its first release. It was the first live-action comedy made by the Disney Studios and the first film with Fred MacMurray, who would make several successful family comedies for the Mickey Mouse studio. In this one, he's a total grinning idiot who's never shown doing any work. Fred has no problem with the notion that his son, Tommy Kirk, is a dog, as if this was something that happened to people every day. In the remake, Wilby has grown into manhood—well, at least he's no longer a pup. Once again he comes into possession of the magic ring and he's turned into a shaggy dog, which slightly complicates his run for district attorney. Dean Jones, another Disney regular, is as just at ease looking the idiot as was Fred MacMurray.

Shanghai Lady *see* **Drifting**

798 The Shannons of Broadway

Based on the play by James Gleason. Story: Vaudevillians Mickey and Emma Shannon are refused accommodations in a New England hotel, so they buy it and make extensive renovations. They find that several people want the hotel because of a proposed airport to be built nearby. This proves to be a hoax, but the Shannons sell the property for a nice profit and return to the stage with a new act.

Universal Pictures, 1929 (original). Part-talkie. Director: Emmett J. Flynn; screenwriter: Agnes Christine. Cast: James Gleason (Mickey Shannon), Lucille Webster Gleason (Emma Shannon), Mary Philbin (Tessie), John Breeden (Chuck), Tom Santschi (Bradford), Harry Tyler, Gladys Crolius, Helen Mehrmann.

• ***Goodbye Broadway*** (remake). Universal Pictures, 1938. Director: Ray McCarey; screenwriters: Roy Chanslor and A. Dorian Otvos. Cast: Alice Brady (Molly Malloy), Charles Winninger (Pat Malloy), Tom Brown (Chuck

Bradford), Dorothea Kent (Jeanne Carlyle), Frank Jenks, Jed Prouty, Willie Best, Donald Meek.

James Gleason's story is so tired, it went to bed with the chickens, but that didn't prevent it from being a somewhat successful Broadway play in the late '20s and brought to the screen as a showplace for Gleason and his wife, Lucille, both delightful characters. But enough is enough. The attempt to modernize the story in the 1938 film was unsuccessful and merely demonstrated that the original appeal was the Gleasons, not the plot. The material is paper-thin and even such competent performers as Alice Brady and Charles Winninger couldn't build anything with it.

She Came, She Saw, She Conquered ***see*** **Sis Hopkins**

799 She Loves Me Not

Based on the novel by Edward Hope and the play by Howard Lindsay. Story: Princeton undergrads Paul Lawton and Buzz Jones give refuge to nightclub singer Curly Flagg, on the run after witnessing a murder. The boys disguise Curly as a man to fool the dean and his daughter, Midge, girlfriend of Paul.

Paramount Pictures, 1934 (original). Director: Elliott Nugent; screenwriter: Benjamin Glazer. Cast: Bing Crosby (Paul Lawton), Miriam Hopkins (Curly Flagg), Kitty Carlisle (Midge Mercer), Edward Nugent (Buzz Jones), Henry Stephenson (Dean Mercer), Warren Hymer, Lynne Overman, Judith Allen, George Barbier.

• ***True to the Army*** (remake). Paramount Pictures, 1942. Director: Albert S. Rogell; screenwriters: Art Arthur and Bradford Ropes. Cast: Judy Canova (Daisy Hawkins), Allan Jones (Pvt. Bill Chandler), Ann Miller (Vicki Marlow), Jerry Colonna (Pvt. Fothergill), William Demarest (Sgt. Butes), Clarence Kolb, William Wright, Edward Pawley, Edwin Miller.

• ***How to Be Very, Very Popular*** (remake). Twentieth Century–Fox, 1955. Director and screenwriter: Nunnally Johnson. Cast: Betty Grable (Stormy), Sheree North (Curly), Bob Cummings (Wedgewood), Charles Coburn (Tweed), Tommy Noonan (Eddie), Orson Bean (Toby), Fred Clark, Charlotte Austin, Alice Pearce.

The first version of the Howard Lindsay play opened in New York while the play was still running on Broadway, and New York critics, not surprisingly, preferred the stage version, feeling that Miriam Hopkins and Kitty Carlisle were miscast, although they praised the work of Bing Crosby. The songs include "Straight from the Shoulder" and "I'm Hummin'" by Mack Gordon and Harry Revel and the Leo Robin and Ralph Rainger tune "Love in Bloom," later Jack Benny's theme song, which became a million record seller for Crosby.

The remake was the studio's attempt to expose comic Judy Canova to the big time, but it didn't work. Her brand of humor had a limited appeal and her masquerading as a soldier to escape a gang of crooks on her trail didn't do much for her career. *How to Be Very, Very Popular* turned out to be Betty Grable's swan song in movies and it's a shame she couldn't have been given a better farewell vehicle. In it, she and Sheree North are two stripteasers who witness a murder and take refuge at a college. They are hidden in a fraternity by Robert Cummings and Orson Bean. The best performance from the cast comes from Charles Coburn as the college president who will graduate anyone with money.

800 The Shepherd of the Hills

Based on the novel by Harold Bell Wright. Story: When stranger David Howitt arrives in a small village in the Ozarks, the townsfolk call him the Shepherd because of his gentle and kindly ways. He actually is a man hoping to atone for the sin of his son, who years earlier had betrayed a local girl. When the area is hit with a continued drought, the villagers mock the Shepherd, who begs them to keep their faith. When the rains finally come, everyone is so relieved that even the father of the betrayed girl gives up on his thirst for vengeance when the Shepherd confesses his son's guilt.

• ***The Shepherd of the Hills*** (remake). First National Pictures, 1928. Silent. Director: Albert Rogell; screenwriter: Marin Jackson. Cast: Alec B. Francis (David Howitt, the Shepherd), Molly O'Day (Sammy Lane), John Boles (Young Matt), Matthew Betz (Wash Gibbs), Romaine Fielding, Otis Harlan, Joseph Bennett, Maurice Murphy.

• ***The Shepherd of the Hills*** (remake). Paramount Pictures, 1941. Director: Henry Hathaway; screenwriters: Grover Jones and Stuart Anthony. Cast: John Wayne (Young Matt), Betty Field (Sammy Lane), Harry Carey (David Howitt), Beulah Bondi (Aunt Mollie), James Barton (Old Matt), Samuel S. Hinds, Marjorie Main, Marc Lawrence.

Harold Bell Wright's novel, which sold more than a million copies, has been made into a movie four times. The other two were a silent in 1919 and a 1963 production. While not as popular as the novel, each film helped fill out some double bills. In 1941, Harry Carey as the Shepherd turns out to be John Wayne's father, who the Duke has vowed to kill for deserting him and his mother years ago. Perhaps the best of several fine performances is given by Marc Lawrence playing a mute.

801 Sherlock Holmes

Based on the character created by Arthur Conan Doyle and the play by Doyle and William Gillette. Story: Master detective Sherlock Holmes is persuaded by his friend Dr. John Watson to help Alice Faulkner recover some letters, written by her sister, who killed herself after being rejected by her royal lover. The letters are being used to blackmail Alice by evil criminal mastermind Professor Moriarty and his agents. Using a series of clever disguises, Holmes is able to survive several confrontations with the villains, and bring Moriarty to justice.

Essanay Pictures, 1916 (original). Silent. Director: Arthur Bertelet; screenwriter: H.S. Sheldon. Cast: William Gillette (Sherlock Holmes), Ernest Maupain (Professor Moriarty), Edward Fielding (Dr. Watson), Marjorie Kay (Alice Faulkner), Stewart Robbins, Hugh Thompson, Chester Beery, William Postance.

• ***Sherlock Holmes*** (remake). Goldwyn Pictures, 1922. Silent. Director: Albert Parker; screenwriters: Marion Fairfax and Earle Brown. Cast: John Barrymore (Sherlock Holmes), Roland Young (Dr. Watson), Carol Dempster (Alice Faulkner), Gustav von Seyffertitz (Professor Moriarty), Louis Wolheim, Peggy Bayfield, David Torrence, Lumsden Hare, Jerry Devine, Hedda Hopper, Percy Knight.

• ***The Return of Sherlock Holmes*** (remake). Paramount Pictures, 1929. Director: Basil Dean; screenwriters: Garret Fort and Basil Dean based on Conan Doyle's *The Dying Detective* and *His Last Row.* Cast: Clive Brook (Sherlock Holmes), H. Reeves-Smith (Dr. Watson), Betty Lawford (Mary Watson), Harry T. Morey (Professor Moriarty), Phillips Holmes, Charles Hay, Hubert Druce.

• ***The Adventures of Sherlock Holmes*** (remake). Twentieth Century–Fox, 1939. Director: Alfred Werker; screenwriters: Edwin Blum and William Drake. Cast: Basil Rathbone (Sherlock Holmes), Nigel Bruce (Dr. Watson), Ida Lupino (Ann Brandon), Alan Marshal (Jerrold Hunter), George Zucco (Professor Moriarty), Terry Kilburn, Henry Stephenson, E.E. Clive, Arthur Hohl, Mary Gordon.

William Gillette was not the first to portray Sherlock Holmes; that honor goes to C.H.E. Brookfield who appeared in the role in 1893 at the Royal Court Theatre in London. The next year, John Webb stepped into the role at the Theatre Royal in Glasgow, Scotland. But in 1899 at New York's Garrick Theatre, Gillette assumed the role which he would play for 36 years of his life, being also the first radio Holmes when at the age of 82 he reprised his famous role for new audiences who had never been in a theatre. His home in Connecticut, now a state park known as Gillette's Castle, is a monument both to the actor and his most famous role. Before Basil Rathbone came along, Gillette was how people believed Holmes really looked.

No fictional character has been portrayed more often in films than Sherlock Holmes and there never seems any shortage of producers and directors willing to take another shot at telling his story. Besides the 14 Holmes movies made starring Rathbone with Nigel Bruce as a somewhat befuddled Dr. Watson, other treats for the Baker Street Irregulars include *The Sleeping Cardinal* (1931) with Arthur Wonter as Holmes and Ian Fleming as Watson, *The Speckled Band* (1931) with Raymond Massey in the lead and Athole Stewart as his medical sidekick, *A Study in Scarlet* (1933) starring Reginald Owen as the master detective and Warburton Gamble as Watson, *A Study in Terror* (1965) with John Neville as Holmes and Donald Houston as Dr. Watson, *The Private Life of Sherlock Holmes* with Robert Stephens in the title role and Colin Blakely as Watson, and *The Seven-Per-Cent Solution* starring Nicol Williamson and Robert Duvall as Holmes and Watson, respectively.

Sherlock Holmes and the Spider Woman *see* **The Sign of the Four**

She's Working Her Way Through College *see* **The Male Animal**

802 Shipmates Forever

Based on a story by Delmer Daves. Story: Richard Melville rebels against the family tradition of joining the Navy. Never mind that his father's an admiral, he'd rather sing and hang around with pretty dancers like June Blackburn, than spend a lot of time away at sea. Naturally he eventually succumbs to family pressure and June's good advice.

Warner Bros., 1935 (original). Director: Frank Borzage; screenwriter: Delmer Daves. Cast: Dick Powell (Richard Melville), Ruby Keeler (June Blackburn), Lewis Stone (Admiral Melville), Ross Alexander (Sparks), Eddie Acuff, Dick Foran, John Arledge, Robert Light, Joseph King.

• ***Dead End Kids on Dress Parade*** (remake). Warner Bros., 1939. Director: William Clemens; screenwriters: Tom Reed and Charles Belden. Cast: Bobby Jordan, Huntz Hall, Leo Gorcey, Gabriel Dell, John Litel, Cissie Loftus, Aldrich Bowker, Frankie Thomas.

The second film is a disguised remake of the first. In it the Dead End Kids are students at a military school. Jordan gets into one fight after another, but redeems himself by saving the life of another cadet in a fire. Even fans of Huntz Hall and Leo Gorcey will have trouble finding something good to say about this one.

803 Shoot the Works

Based on the play *The Great Magoo* by Ben Hecht and Gene Fowler. Story: It's the love story of carnival grifters out to make a fast buck at their low level of show business. Nicky is the spieler at Hubert's museum who falls for Lily Raquel, who sticks by him in his schemes despite his selling her out twice.

Paramount Pictures, 1934 (original). Director: Wesley Ruggles; screenwriter: Howard J. Green. Cast: Jack Oakie (Nicky), Ben Bernie (Joe Davis), Dorothy Dell (Lily Raquel), Arline Judge (Jackie), Alison Skipworth (the Countess), Roscoe Karns, William Frawley, Paul Cavanaugh, Lew Cody.

• ***Some Like It Hot*** (remake). Paramount Pictures, 1939. Director: George Archainbaud; screenwriters: Lewis R. Foster and Wilkie Mahoney. Cast: Bob Hope (Nicky Nelson), Shirley Ross (Lily Raquel), Una Merkel (Flo Saunders), Gene Krupa (himself), Rufe Davis, Bernard Nedell, Frank Sully, Bernadene Hayes.

The story of these two films is mighty thin, so success or failure rested squarely on the shoulders of the leading performers. Oakie and Dell's performances are nothing to get excited about. The best thing about the film is the Mack Gordon and Harry Revel song "With My Eyes Wide Open I'm Dreaming" sung by Dorothy Dell, who was killed in a car crash soon after the film was released.

The remake didn't experience the hoped-for repeat success of the Bob Hope and Shirley Ross teaming in *The Big Broadcast of 1938* and *Thanks for the Memory.* It did have two Frank Loesser and Burton Lane songs, "The Lady's in Love with You" and the title song, both sung by Shirley Ross. Just as in the first film, Ben Bernie and his band were featured; in the remake, Gene Krupa and his swing band gave the jitterbug set something to cheer about.

804 The Shop Around the Corner

Based on the play by Nikolaus Laszlo. Story: Alfred Kralik, head clerk in a Budapest shop run by Hugo Matuschek, carries on a correspondence with a young lady who had advertised in the paper for a pen pal interested in intellectual matters. They do not reveal their identities to each other, merely referring to each others as "dear friend." Despite Kralik's objections, Matuschek hires Klara Novak as a clerk. Alfred and Klara just don't get along, clashing over even the most trivial matters. Finally when Alfred and his "dear friend" agree to a meeting, he wearing a carnation, she carrying a certain book, Alfred arrives and is shocked to discover that Klara is his unknown letter-writing friend. He throws away the carnation and greets her without revealing that he is her pen pal. She demands that he leave as she is waiting for someone, who of course never shows. Meanwhile Matuschek learns that his wife is having an affair with one of his clerks. He assumes it is Alfred and dismisses him. Later, it is learned that the guilty man is actually Ferencz Vadas. Ashamed, Hugo attempts to shoot himself but is prevented from doing so. While in the hospital, Hugo re-employs Alfred as his general manager. By now Alfred and Klara find they are in love and she is pleased when he reveals that he was her secret letter-writer.

MGM, 1940 (original). Director: Ernst Lubitsch; screenwriter: Samson Raphaelson. Cast: Margaret Sullavan (Klara Novak), James Stewart (Alfred Kralick), Frank Morgan (Hugo Matuschek), Joseph Schildkraut (Ferencz Vadas), Sara Haden, Felix Bressart, William Tracy, Inez Courtney, Sarah Edwards.

• ***In the Good Old Summertime*** (remake). MGM, 1949. Director: Robert Z. Leonard; screenwriters: Samson Raphaelson and Albert Hackett, Frances Goodrich and Ivan Tors. Cast: Judy Garland (Veronica Fisher), Van Johnson (Andrew Delby Larkin), S.Z. "Cuddles" Sakall (Otto Oberkugen), Spring Byington (Nellie Burke), Buster Keaton (Hickey), Clinton Sundberg, Marcia Van Dyke, Lillian Bronson.

Both films are true delights. The first, directed by Ernst Lubitsch, is a beguiling comedy with lovely performances from James Stewart and Margaret Sullavan. The film has an old-world charm and the supporting cast, from the hard-to-please proprietor, Frank Morgan, to the browbeaten clerk, Felix Bressart, and the heart-breaking Joseph Schildkraut, fit in perfectly.

In the charming remake, Van Johnson and Judy Garland endear themselves to audiences with their easy-going performances as the head clerk and his secret letter-writing friend. The film counts on musical nostalgia by featuring such old time favorites as "Put Your Arms Around Me Honey," "Wait Till the Sun Shines, Nellie" and the title song. The story is just about the same as the first time around, except that Sakall plays his role as the proprietor more as a childish and sometime churlish sweet old uncle than did Morgan.

805 The Shopworn Angel

Based on Dana Burnet's short story "Private Pettigrew's Girl." Story: Daisy Heath, a sophisticated New York show girl, is attracted to two men—suave man-about-town Bailey and naive army private William Tyler. She plays Tyler's infatuation with her for laughs and continues her affair with Bailey. When Bill is ordered to embark for France, he goes AWOL to tell Daisy of his love for her. At this, she decides that Bill is the man for her and they plan to marry, but halfway through the ceremony, Bill is dragged off by M.P.'s and sent off with his regiment to France. Realizing how important Bill is to her, she decides to avoid all her old contacts and wait faithfully for him to come home again to her.

• ***The Shopworn Angel*** (remake). Paramount Pictures, 1928. Silent with a sound sequence. Director: Richard Wallace; screenwriters: Howard Estabrook and Albert Shelby Le Vino. Cast: Nancy Carroll (Daisy Heath), Gary Cooper (William Tyler), Paul Lukas (Bailey), Emmett King, Mildred Washington, Roscoe Karns, Bert Woodruff.

• ***The Shopworn Angel*** (remake). MGM, 1938. Director: H.C. Potter; screenwriter: Waldo Salt. Cast: Margaret Sullavan (Daisy Heath), James Stewart (Bill Pettigrew), Walter Pidgeon (Sam Bailey), Hattie McDaniel, Nat Pendelton, Alan Curtis, Sam Levene, Eleanor Lynn, Charles D. Brown.

The story was first filmed in 1919 as *Pettigrew's Girl* with Ethel Clayton as Daisy and Monte Blue as Bill. In the 1928 silent, Cooper was perfection as the ingenuous soldier and Nancy Carroll proved that she was able to take the transition from silents to sound in stride. Near the end of the otherwise silent film, the characters began to speak and even sing, with Nancy singing "A Precious Little Thing Called Love" by Lou Davis and J.F. Coots. Miss Carroll was about as cute a film star that ever graced the screen and here she demonstrated both sensitivity and intelligence.

Margaret Sullavan and James Stewart matched Nancy Carroll and Gary Cooper's performance in the 1938 remake, poignantly appearing as a kept woman having a bitter-sweet affair with a naive soldier. The story was filmed a fourth time in 1959 as *That Kind of Woman*, with the rather unusual casting of Sophia Loren and Tab Hunter. Somehow, these two just didn't seem right for each other and the dated material came off as dull.

806 Shore Leave

Based on the play by Hubert Osborne. Story: When the fleet anchors in a New England port, "Bilge" Smith meets village dressmaker Connie Martin. She takes their flirtation seriously and Smith promises to return to her. While Smith is at sea, Connie has her father's old ship converted into a tearoom, which proves to be very successful. When the fleet returns, not knowing her Smith's first name, she sends word to the ships inviting all the Smiths to a party. Bilge Smith arrives, but initially doesn't remember Connie. Seeing how serious she is about her love for him, he proposes but when he discovers her prosperity he takes off, swearing never to be taken care of by a woman. Later she sends a message to him, saying she is now penniless. He returns to her, finds she has tricked him and prepares to leave again, when she tells him she has put the ownership of the ship-tearoom in a trust for her first child, as long as its last name is Smith. Smith decides to stay and marry Connie.

First National Pictures, 1925 (original). Silent. Director: John S. Robertson screenwriter: Josephine Lovett. Cast: Richard Barthelmess ("Bilge" Smith),

Dorothy Mackaill (Connie Martin), Ted McNamara ("Bat" Smith), Nick Long, Marie Shotwell, Arthur Metcalfe, Warren Cook, Samuel S. Hinds.

• ***Hit the Deck*** (remake). RKO, 1930. Director and screenwriter: Luther Reed. Cast: Jack Oakie (Bilge), Polly Walker (Looloo), Roger Gray (Mat), Franker Woods (Bat), Harry Sweet (Bunny), Marguerita Padula, June Clyde, Wallace MacDonald, George Overy.

• ***Follow the Fleet*** (remake). RKO, 1936. Director: Mark Sandrich; screenwriters: Dwight Taylor and Allan Scott. Cast: Fred Astaire (Bat), Ginger Rogers (Sherry), Randolph Scott (Bilge), Harriet Hillard (Connie), Astrid Allwyn, Betty Grable, Harry Beresford, Russell Hicks, Brooks Benedict.

• ***Hit the Deck*** (remake). MGM, 1955. Director: Roy Rowland; screenwriters: Sonya Levien and William Ludwig. Cast: Jane Powell (Susan Smith), Tony Martin (William F. Clark), Debbie Reynolds (Carol Pace), Walter Pidgeon (Rear Adm. Daniel Xavier Smith), Vic Damone (Rico Ferrari), Gene Raymond (Wendell Craig), Ann Miller (Ginger), Russ Tamblyn (Danny Xavier Smith), Kay Armen, J. Carrol Naish, Richard Anderson.

The first remake owes any success almost exclusively to the work of Jack Oakie, although the Vincent Youmans music, particularly "Sometimes I'm Happy," is just fine. In the 1936 version of the story of sailors and their girls, Fred Astaire and Ginger Rogers dance superbly to the enchanting "Let's Face the Music and Dance." Other less sublime musical numbers by Irving Berlin included "We Saw the Sea," "Let Yourself Go," "I'm Putting All My Eggs in One Basket," and "Get Thee Behind Me, Satan." The movie can't stack up to other Astaire and Rogers films such as *Top Hat,* since it lacked the comedy elements of the more successful collaborations. The 1955 MGM entry had a talented cast headed by darling little Jane Powell, but with the exception of the Youmans music that it reprised, it had little charm and the thin story didn't give the numerous performers anything to do while waiting for their chance to sing or dance.

Short Cut to Hell *see* **This Gun for Hire**

A Shot in the Dark *see* **The Pink Panther**

A Shot in the Dark *see* **Smart Blonde**

807 Show Girl

Based on the play by Joseph Patrick McEvoy. Story: Brooklyn-born Dixie Dugan gets her theatrical chance when producers Eppus and Kibbitizer like what they see when she poses in a bathing suit. They team her with Alvarez Romano in a nightclub dance act. Alvarez is the possessive type and one night when Dixie is visiting at the apartment of sugar-daddy millionaire Jack Milton, her partner arrives and wounds Milton with a knife. Cynical reporter Jimmy Doyle, who loves Dixie, puts the story on his newspaper's front page. Dixie is then kidnapped by Alvarez, but quickly manages to escape. Doyle persuades her to continue to be kidnapped as a publicity stunt and once again Dixie hits page one. Milton locates Dixie and in a generous gesture offers to finance a Broadway show for her written by Doyle. The show is a smash and Dixie and Jimmy marry.

First National Pictures, 1928 (original). Part talkie. Director: Alfred Santell; screenwriter: James T. O'Donohue. Cast: Alice White (Dixie Dugan), Donald Reed (Alvarez Romano), Lee Moran (Denny), Charles Delaney (Jimmy Doyle), Richard Tucker (Jack Milton), Gwen Lee, James Finlayson, Kate Price.

• ***Show Girl in Hollywood*** (sequel). First National Pictures, 1930. Director: Mervyn LeRoy; screenwriters: Harvey Thew and James A. Starr. Cast: Alice White (Dixie Dugan), Jack Mulhall (Jimmy Doyle), Blanche Sweet (Donna Harris), Ford Sterling (Sam Otis), John Miljan, Virginia Sale, Lee Shumway.

The first movie of the publicity seeking show girl contained the title song and "Buy, Buy for Baby" by Bernie Grossman and Ed Ward. Other than these musical interludes it is a silent picture. In the sequel, Dixie Dugan and Jimmy Doyle take their stuff to Hollywood where Dixie becomes a tempermental and conceited star until Jimmy straightens her out; the film ends with her movie being a big success and everyone happy.

808 The Sign of the Cross

Based on the play by Wilson Barrett. Story: Marcus Superbus, a noble Roman, is desired by Poppaea, wife of Emperor Nero, but Superbus has lost his heart to Mercia, one of a small group of Christians who have settled in Rome. The torture these people willingly sacrifice for their religion as well as his feelings for Mercia, cause Marcus to turn his back on his country and take up the Christians' cause, only to die in the lions' den with others who are condemned by Nero.

Paramount Pictures, 1914 (original). Director: Oscar Apfel; screenwriter: Wilson Barrett. Cast: William Farnum (Marcus Superbus), Rosina Henley (Mercia), Sheridan Block (Nero), Morgan Thorpe (Favius), Ethel Gray Terry (Berenice), Lila Barclay (Poppaea), Giorgini Majeroni, Ogden Child, Ethel Phillips, Charles E. Verner, Rienzi de Cordova.

• ***The Sign of the Cross*** (remake). Paramount Pictures, 1932. Director: Cecil B. De Mille; screenwriters: Walderman Young and Sidney Buchman. Cast: Fredric March (Marcus Superbus), Elissa Landi (Mercia), Claudette Colbert (Poppaea), Charles Laughton (Nero), Ian Keith (Tigellinus), Vivian Tobin (Daccia), Harry Beredford (Flavius), Ferdinand Gottschalk, Arthur Hohl, Joyzelle Joyner, Tommy Conlen, Nat Pendleton, Clarence Burton.

Charles Laughton played Nero as a "gay" emperor. Claudette Colbert's nipples showed ever so briefly in her bath of asses' milk. Fredrich March stomped around looking a bit foolish in his short tunic. Elissa Landi proved that she wasn't a major actress. And Cecil B. De Mille gave audiences just what they craved, sex, sadism and salvation. Debauchery and wild orgies are all forgiven when De Mille hits us with his moralizing. Still it's impossible not to enjoy the film and to be impressed with its genuine horror.

809 The Sign of the Four

Based on the story by Arthur Conan Doyle. Story: Sherlock Holmes clears up a mystery that involves a hidden fortune, a secret pact and a pygmy who murders his victims with a poison dart blow pipe.

Stoll Pictures, Great Britain, 1923 (original). Silent. Director and screenwriter: Maurice Elvey. Cast: Eille Norwood (Sherlock Holmes), Arthur Cullen (Dr. Watson), Isobel Elsom (Mary Morston), Norma Page (J. Small), Humberston Wright (Thaddeus Sholto), Fred Raynham (Abdullah Khan), Arthur Bell, Madame d'Esterre, Henry Wilson.

• ***The Sign of the Four*** (remake). Associated Radio-British Pictures, Great Britain, 1932. Director: Graham Cutts; screenwriter: W.P. Lipscomb. Cast: Arthur Wonter (Sherlock Holmes), Ian Hunter (Dr. Watson), Isla Bevan (Mary Morston), Claire Greet (Mrs. Hudson), Miles Malleson (Thaddeus Sholto), Graham Soutten (Jonathan Small), Gilbert Davis, Edgar Norfolk, Herbert Lomas, Roy Emerson.

• ***Sherlock Holmes and the Spider Woman*** (remake). Universal Pictures, 1944. Director: Roy William Neill; screenwriter: Bertram Millhauser. Cast: Basil Rathbone (Sherlock Holmes), Nigel Bruce (Dr. Watson), Gale Sondergaard (Andrea Spedding), Vernon Dowling (Norman Locke), Dennis Hoey (Inspector Lestrade), Alec Craig, Arthur Hohl, Mary Gordon, Teddy Infuhr.

Critics complained that the 1932 film suffered from poor lighting, making it difficult to enjoy an otherwise worthwhile production. Wonter makes a fine Holmes, with his disguises so good that he is not immediately recognized by viewers when made-up to confound the villains. The 1944 film is probably the best of the modernized Holmes stories done by Rathbone, and the credit goes to the marvelous villain Gale Sondergaard.

810 Silence

Based on the play by Max Marcin. Story: Jim Warren is awaiting execution for the murder of Harry Silvers. Through flashbacks, it is revealed that Jim discovers his marriage to Norma Drake is technically invalid and that she is pregnant. Jim plans to legalize his marriage, but Norma is arrested when she is found with some stolen money. To insure Norma's freedom, he agrees to marry a saloon owner, Millie Burke. Believing that Jim has deserted her, Norma marries Phil Powers to give her baby a father. Years later little Norma has grown up and on the eve of her wedding, Jim, accompanied by crook Silvers, confronts Phil with the girl's mother's letters, threatening blackmail. Norma shoots Silvers with Jim's gun, and he is arrested and convicted of the killing. As he is being led to his execution, Norma confesses her crime. Jim is freed and at her trial Norma is absolved.

De Mille Pictures/Producers Distributing Co., 1926 (original). Silent. Director: Rupert Julian; screenwriter: Beulah Marie Dix. Cast: Vera Reynolds (Norma Drake/Norma Powers), H.B. Warner (Jim Warren), Raymond Hatton (Harry Silvers), Rockliffe Fellowes (Phil Powers), Virginia Pearson (Millie Burke).

• ***Silence*** (remake). Paramount Pictures, 1931. Directors: Louis Gasnier and

Max Marcin; screenwriter: Max Marcin. Cast: Clive Brook (Jim Warren), Marjorie Rambeau (Mollie Burke), Peggy Shannon (Norma the daughter/Norma the sweetheart), Charles Starrett (Arthur Lawrence), Willard Robertson (Phil Powers), John Wray (Harry Silvers), Frank Sheridan, Paul Nicholson, J.M. Sullivan.

In the remake Clive Brook portrays a cockney crook in a condemned cell telling how he took the blame for his illegitimate daughter's murder of a blackmailer. The melodrama is heavy with dialog but has little action. The performances are appropriate to that which is demanded of the actors, but that is very little.

Silk Stockings *see* **Ninotchka**

Sinbad and the Eye of the Tiger *see* **Sinbad the Sailor**

811 Sinbad the Sailor

Based on a legend. Story: Sinbad the Sailor has a series of sterling adventures and romances as he explores the world looking for treasures.

• ***Sinbad the Sailor*** (remake). RKO, 1947. Director: Richard Wallace; screenwriter: John Twist. Cast: Douglas Fairbanks, Jr. (Sinbad), Maureen O'Hara (Shireen), Walter Slezak (Melik), Anthony Quinn (Emir), George Tobias (Abbu), Jane Greer (Pirouze), Mike Mazurki, Sheldon Leonard, Alan Napier, John Miljan, Barry Mitchell.

• ***Son of Sinbad*** (sequel) RKO, 1955. Director: Ted Tetzlaff; screenwriters: Aubrey Wisberg and Jack Pollexfen. Cast: Dale Robertson (Sinbad), Sally Forrest (Ameer), Lilli St. Cyr (Nerissa), Vincent Price (Omar), Mari Blanchard (Kristina), Leon Askin, Jay Novello, Nejla Ates, Kalantan, Ian MacDonald.

• ***Seventh Voyage of Sinbad*** (remake). Columbia Pictures, 1958. Director: Nathan Juran; screenwriter: Kenneth Kolb. Cast: Kerwin Mathews (Sinbad), Kathryn Grant (Parisa), Richard Ever (the Genie), Torin Thatcher (Sokurah), Alec Mango (Caliph), Danny Green, Harold Kasket, Alfred Brown, Nana de Herrera.

• ***Captain Sinbad*** (remake). MGM, 1963. Director: Bryon Haskin; screenwriters: Samuel B. West and Harry Relis. Cast: Guy Williams (Captain Sinbad), Heidi Bruhl (Princess Jana), Pedro Armendariz (El Kerim), Abraham Sofaer (Galgo), Bernie Hamilton, Helmut Schneider, Margaret Jahnen, Rolf Wanka.

• ***The Golden Voyage of Sinbad*** (sequel). Morningside/Columbia, Great Britain, 1973. Director: Gordon Hessler; screenwriter: Brian Clemens. Cast: John Philip Law (Sinbad), Caroline Munro (Margiana), Tom Baker (Koura), Douglas Wilmer (Vizier), Martin Shaw, Gregoire Aslan, Kurt Christian, Takis Emmanuel, Jon D. Garfield.

• ***Sinbad and the Eye of the Tiger*** (sequel). Columbia Pictures, 1977. Director: Sam Wanamaker; screenwriter: Beverly Cross. Cast: Patrick Wayne (Sinbad), Taryn Power (Dione), Margaret Whiting (Zenobia), Jane Seymour (Farah), Patrick Troughton (Melanthius), Kurt Christian, Nadim Sawaiha, Damien Thomas.

In addition to the above, Sinbad's adventures were also screened in 1919, 1930, 1939, 1946, 1951, 1952, 1962, 1963 and 1964. Throughout the years these escape fantasies depended more on special effects than on story. Sinbad and his men had to counter many monsters and other menancing creatures, alive or otherwise. None of the films can be described as memorable, but served their purpose as pre-television adventure stories and drive-in theater fodder.

Sincerely Yours *see* **The Man Who Played God**

812 Singapore

Based on a story by Seton I. Miller. Story: Matt Gordon returns to Singapore after World War II to continue his trade as a pearl smuggler. Through flashbacks we learn of his relationship with Linda, who apparently was killed on their wedding night in an air raid. But no, she's alive, married to another man and suffering from total amnesia. Naturally, Matt helps her regain her memory of him but in the meantime he has to deal with a gang after some pearls which he had hidden in a hotel room during the Japanese occupation.

Universal Pictures, 1947 (original). Director: John Braham; screenwriters: Seton I. Miller and Robert Thoern. Cast: Fred MacMurray (Matt Gordon), Ava Gardner (Linda), Roland Culver (Michael Van Layden), Richard Haydn (Chief Inspector Hewitt), Spring Byington (Mrs. Bellows), Porter Hall (Mr. Bellows), Thomas Gomez, George Lloyd, Maylia, Holmes Herbert.

• ***Istanbul*** (remake). Universal Pictures, 1957. Director: Joseph Pevney; screenwriters: Seton I. Miller, Barbara Gray and Richard Alan Simmons. Cast: Errol Flynn (Jim Brennan), Cornell Borchers (Stephanie Bauer/Karen Fielding), John Bentley (Inspector Nural), Torin Thatcher (Douglas Fielding), Leif Erickson (Charlie Boyle), Peggy Knudsen, Martin Benson, Nat "King" Cole, Werner Klemperer, Vladimir Sokoloff, Jan Arvan.

Outside of the stars, these two stinkers have nothing going for them. One can hardly blame MacMurray, Gardner and Flynn. They had no material to work with. In the remake, Flynn is an American pilot who had hidden a valuable bracelet in a hotel room and five years later comes back to Istanbul to recover it and is chased both by a gang of smugglers and Turkish customs officers. Cornell Borchers plays the woman he believed had burned to death on their wedding night but who has survived, married Torin Thatcher and has no recollection of her past. Besides Flynn, the only other thing worth noting is that Nat "King" Cole sings Jack Brooks' "When I Fall in Love."

Singapore Woman *see* **Dangerous**

The Sins of Harold Diddlebock *see* **The Freshman**

813 Sis Hopkins

Based on the story *She Came, She Saw, She Conquered* by Carroll Fleming and Edward P. Kidder. Story: It's the old-fashioned comedy melodrama about a rural gal who drifts to the big city and a college only to become a big-shot on campus. She has to deal with her snooty cousin but she proves that hayseeds are not necessarily air-heads.

• ***She Came, She Saw, She Conquered*** (remake). Goldwyn, 1919. Silent. Director: Clarence B. Badgar; screenwriter: uncredited. Cast: Mabel Normand (Sis Hopkins), John Bowers (Ridy Scarboro), Sam De Grasse (Vibert), Thomas Jefferson (Pa Hopkins), Nicholas Cogley, Eugenie Ford.

• ***Sis Hopkins*** (remake). Republic Pictures, 1941. Director: Joseph Santley; screenwriters: Jack Townley, Milt Gross and Edward Eliscu. Cast: Judy Canova (Sis Hopkins), Susan Hayward (Carol Hopkins), Bob Crosby (Jeff Farnsworth), Charles Butterworth (Horace Hopkins), Jerry Colonna (Professor), Katherine Alexander (Clara Hopkins), Elvia Allman, Carol Adams, Lynn Merrick, Mary Ainslee.

Rose Melville re-created her stage role as Sis Hopkins in 1916 in the film *She Came, She Saw, She Conquered.* Mabel Normand was most amusing as the girl sent to a "girl's cemetary" for "eddickashion." Judy Canova, portraying a pigtailed country bumpkin, was right at home in the musical remake role. Her favorite line is "You're tellin' I," to which her snobbish cousin Susan Hayward responds "Your syntax is irregular." Judy looks startled, quickly views herself, and asks, "Where?" Judy sings "Wait for the Wagon" and an excerpt from *La Traviata.*

814 A Sister to Assist'er

Based on the play by John le Breton. Story: Whenever landlady Mrs. McNatch asks for the rent from her tenant Mrs. May, the latter, an impoverished widow, employs some trick or another to get out of paying. When the landlady confiscates Mrs. May's trunk, she invents a rich twin sister whom she impersonates and not only gets her trunk back but a present in her marriage to a local fishmonger.

• ***A Sister to Assist'er*** (remake). Gaumont Pictures, Great Britain, 1930. Director and screenwriter: George Dewhurst. Cast: Barbara Gott (Mrs. May), Polly Emery (Mrs. McNash), Donald Stuart, Charles Paton, Maude Gill, Alec Hunter, Johnny Butt.

• ***A Sister to Assist'er*** (remake). Associated Industries/Columbia Pictures, Great Britain, 1938. Directors: Widgey R. Newman and George Dewhurst; screenwriter: George Dewhurst. Cast: Muriel George (Mrs. May), Pollie Emery (Mrs. Gretch), Charles Paton, Billy Percy, Harry Herbert, Dorothy Vernon, Dora Levis.

• ***A Sister to Assist'er*** (remake). Bruton/Trytel/Premier, Great Britain, 1948. Director and screenwriter: George Dewhurst. Cast: Muriel George (Mrs. May), Muriel Aked (Mrs. Gretch), Michael Howard.

This old stage chestnut was also filmed in 1922 and 1927 in England. Mrs. May is a cunning old dear, endearingly played by Muriel George. If one doesn't care for an old gal who has a rich imagination when it comes to finding ways not to pay the rent she doesn't have, then these creaky films will not seem amusing.

815 Sitting Pretty

Based on the novel *Belvedere* by Gwen Davenport. Story: Harry and Tacey

King, stuck with three unmanageable children, advertise for a live-in baby sitter. A surprising applicant is haughty, sneering Mr. Belvedere, who is hired with much misgivings by Harry, especially after asking about Mr. Belvedere's qualifications, to which the latter replies, "I am a genius." Belvedere takes total control of the household, insisting everything be done precisely as he says, because as he reminds the parents frequently, he's the genius, not them. Nosey neighbors, especially obnoxious Mr. Appleton, suspect that Mr. Belvedere and Tacey are having an affair. When Harry gets wind of the rumor, he becomes jealous and confronts Mr. Belvedere, who dismisses the husband's concerns as if he were dealing with the imaginings of a silly child. Belvedere's real reason for accepting the menial job becomes clear when he publishes a book, none too flattering to his employers and the neighbors. Everything is thrown in an uproar but as one would expect, a genius is able to put everything right.

Twentieth Century–Fox, 1948 (original). Director: Walter Lang; screenwriter: F. Hugh Herbert. Cast: Clifton Webb (Lynn Belvedere), Robert Young (Harry King), Maureen O'Hara (Tacey King), Richard Haydn (Mr. Appleton), Louise Albritton, Randy Stuart, Ed Begley, Larry Olsen, Roddy Macaskill, Anthony Sydes.

• ***Mr. Belvedere Goes to College*** (sequel). Twentieth Century–Fox, 1949. Director: Elliott Nugent; screenwriters: Richard Sale, Mary Loos and Mary McCall, Jr. Cast: Clifton Webb (Lynn Belvedere), Shirley Temple (Ellen Baker), Tom Drake (Bill Chase), Alan Young (Avery Brubaker), Jessie Royce Landis, Kathleen Hughes, Taylor Holmes, Alvin Greenman, Paul Harvey, Barry Kelley.

What made the original so delightful was that Mr. Belvedere is all he claims to be. He is not a braggart, merely a man who knows himself thoroughly and for whom modesty would be a sham. Clifton Webb is absolutely perfect as the fastidious baby sitter, who when splattered with oatmeal by his youngest charge, solemnly pours the bowl of gruel over the child's head, assuring the boy's parents that he has learned an object lesson which he will never forget.

In the sequel, Mr. Belvedere chooses to attend college in order to get a degree so that he may qualify for a literary award. According to him, his formal education consisted of a couple of weeks in kindergarten. This does not prevent him from answering "Everything," when asked what he can do. The story, inferior to the original, is the usual college farce with freshmen hazing and a college widow who tangles with Belvedere. Naturally, the brilliant one whizzes through the curriculum in record time, teaching his professors a thing or two in the process. Shirley Temple and Tom Drake, included for the romantic angle, have little to do but admire Belvedere's brilliance.

There was a third film featuring Belvedere, *Mrs. Belvedere Rings the Bell,* featuring Joanne Dru, Hugh Marlowe, Zero Mostel and a bunch of delightful, elderly actors. It is the weakest of the trio and no doubt why the series didn't develop further. It has Belvedere assuming the identity of a dead man and moving into an old folk's home in order to get material for a book. Belvedere seems to have mellowed, being something of a do-gooder and not the character audiences had come to love, one who spends his entire life cultivating his own self-interest and showing obvious distaste for lesser mortals. This was beautifully demonstrated in *Sitting Pretty* when he told Tacey, "Your husband has a great deal to be modest about."

816 Six Cylinder Love

Based on the play by William Anthony McGuire. Story: The happiness of two families, the Burtons and the Sterlings, in turn, is almost ruined by ownership of an expensive automobile. When both families are broke, their janitor buys the car.

Fox Film Corp., 1923 (original). Silent. Director: Elmer Clifton; screenwriter: Carl Stears Clancy. Cast: Ernest Truex (Gilbert Sterling), Florence Eldridge (Marilyn Sterling), Donald Meek (Richard Burton), Maude Hill (Geraldine Burton), Anne McKittrick (Phyllis Burton), Thomas Mitchell (Bertram Rogers), Ralph Sipperly, Berton Churchill, Harold Mann, Frank Tweed.

• ***The Honeymoon's Over*** (remake). Twentieth Century–Fox, 1939. Director: Eugene Forde; screenwriters: Hamilton McFadden, Clay Adams and Leonard Hoffman. Cast: Stuart Erwin (Donald), Marjorie Weaver (Betty), Patric Knowles (Pat), Russell Hicks (Walker), Jack Carson (Donroy), Hobart Cavanaugh (Butterfield), June Gale, E.E. Clive, Renie Riano, Harrison Greene, Lelah Tyler.

The play by William Anthony McGuire was also filmed in 1931 by Fox Film Corporation. The movie well-served the need for second-feature material. The humor in the story of fairly sensible people who go broke buying new cars and joining country clubs is modest but well-done. In the remake, poor Stu Erwin gets in trouble when he marries Marjorie Weaver, the girl who has the desk next to him at his office and she decides she wants some of the finer things in life—even if they can't afford them.

817 16 Fathoms Deep

Based on a story by Eustace L. Adams. Story: Young sponge fisherman Joe borrows money for a boat from a rival, Nick, who plans to make it impossible for Joe to repay so he won't be able to marry Rosie. She upsets this plan and Nick commits suicide, allowing Joe and Rosie to find their happiness.

Monogram Pictures, 1934 (original). Directors: Armand Schaefer and Paul Malvern; screenwriters: Norman Houston and Archie Stout. Cast: Sally O'Neil (Rosie), Creighton Chaney (Joe), George Regas (Savanis), Maurice Black (Nick), Lloyd Ingram, George Nash, Robert Kortman, Si Jenks, Russell Simpson.

• ***16 Fathoms Deep*** (remake). Monogram Pictures, 1948. Director: Irving Allen; screenwriter: Max Trell. Cast: Lon Chaney, Jr. (Dimitri), Arthur Lake (Pete), Lloyd Bridges (Douglas), Eric Feldary (Alex), Tanis Chandler (Simi), John Qualen (Athos), Ian MacDonald, Dickie Moore, Harry Cheshire, John Rieifer, Grant Means.

Creighton Chaney is the son of the great silent star Lon Chaney, and soon after the 1934 picture, he chose to identify himself as Lon Chaney, Jr. In the remake he portrays a crooked sponge dealer in competition with a boat on which ex–Navy diver Lloyd Bridges is a crewman. Arthur Lake is along to supply the comedy relief. Outside of Chaney, the nonhuman menaces include sharks and giant clams. The stories in both of these films follow predictable formulas.

Ski Patrol *see* **The Doomed Batallion**

818 Skin Deep

Based on the story *Lucky Damage* by Marc Edmund Jones. Story: When he returns from World War I, crook Bud Doyle resolves to go straight but finds it difficult to do so because "he looks like a crook." To make matters worse, his wife, Sadie, her new lover, Joe Culver, and Boss McQuarg frame Bud and he is sent to prison. He escapes, has an accident and is taken to a hospital where plastic surgery completely changes his appearance. He works with the D.A. against his wife, Culver and McQuarg, and has the satisfaction of seeing them jailed. He then marries the nurse at the hospital where his life as well as his features were changed.

Thomas Ince Corp./First National Pictures, 1922 (original). Silent. Director: Lambert Hillyer; screenwriter: LeRoy Stone. Cast: Milton Sills (Bud Doyle), Florence Vidor (Ethel Carter), Marcia Manon (Sadie Doyle), Charles Clary (James Carlson), Joe Singleton (Joe Culver), Frank Campeau (Boss McQuarg), Winter Hall, Gertrude Astor, Muriel Dana, B.H. De Lay.

• ***Skin Deep*** (remake). Warner Bros., 1929. Part-talkie. Director: Ray Enright; screenwriter: Gordon Rigby. Cast: Monte Blue (Joe Daley), Betty Compson (Sadie Rogers), Alice Day (Elsa Langdon), John Davidson (Blackie Culver), John Bowers, Davey Lee, Georgie Stone, Tully Marshall, Robert Perry.

In the remake of this crime melodrama, Joe Daley is betrayed by his two-timing wife and sentenced to five years in the pen for stealing $100,000, which he was actually returning to show the D.A. his intention to go straight. His wife, Sadie, visits him faithfully in prison, so he is unaware of her continuing deception and adultery. She convinces Joe that the D.A. has designs on her and that he should escape to avenge her "honor." He is hurt in an accident during his escape and is brought to the home of a plastic surgeon by the doctor's daughter, Elsa Langdon. With his battered appearance now completely altered, he learns of Sadie's treachery and she is killed by a bullet meant for him. Joe returns to Elsa to start a new life.

819 The Skin Game

Based on the play by John Galsworthy. Story: Rich Mrs. Hillcrist thwarts pottery manufacturer Hornblower's plans to build houses on land she feels should be left unspoiled by exposing his daughter-in-law Chloe's past.

Granger-Binger, Great Britain, 1920 (original). Silent. Director and screenwriter: B.E. Doxat-Pratt. Cast: Edmund Gwenn (Hornblower), Mary Clare (Chloe Hornblower), Helen Haye (Mrs. Hillcrist), Dawson Millward (Mr.

Hillcrist), Malcolm Keen (Charles Hillcrist), Frederick Cooper (Rolf Hornblower), Ivor Barnard, Muriel Alexander, James Dodd.

• ***The Skin Game*** (remake). BIP/Wardour, Great Britain, 1931. Director: Alfred Hitchcock; screenwriters: Alfred Hitchcock and Alma Reville. Cast: Edmund Gwenn (Hornblower), Phyllis Konstam (Chloe Hornblower), John Longden (Charles Hornblower), Frank Lawton (Rolf Hornblower), C.V. France (Mr. Hillcrist), Helen Haye (Mrs. Hillcrist), Jill Esmond (Jill Hillcrist), Edward Chapman, Ronald Frankau, Herbert Ross, Dora Gregory, R.E. Jeffrey.

Those who thought Hitchcock only directed thrillers should take note of this modest drama about a country family who uses blackmail to thwart a rich man's building plans. It's a study of class confrontation and not the best possible example of such a conflict.

Skinner Steps Out ***see*** **Skinner's Dress Suit**

Skinner's Big Idea ***see*** **Skinner's Dress Suit**

820 Skinner's Dress Suit

Based on the novel by Henry Irving Dodge. Story: Meek and humble clerk Skinner is encouraged by his wife to ask his boss for a raise. He's turned down, but rather than risk his wife's displeasure, he tells her that he got it. She immediately buys him a dress suit and starts the two on a round of social activities which leads Skinner to bankruptcy and the loss of his job. Before he can inform his wife of their reduced circumstances, she whisks him off to a society dance at a hotel where one of his most important clients, Jackson, and his wife are staying. The wife wants to go to the dance and persuades her husband to ask Skinner to invite them. Before the evening is over Skinner puts over a big deal with Jackson and is made a partner in his old company.

• ***Skinner's Dress Suit*** (remake). Universal Pictures, 1926. Silent. Director: William A. Seiter; screenwriter: Rex Taylor. Cast: Reginald Denny (Skinner), Laura La Plante (Honey Skinner), Ben Hendricks, Jr. (Perkins), E.J. Ratcliffe (McLaughlin), Arthur Lake (Tommy), Lionel Braham (Jackson), Lucille Ward (Mrs. Jackson), Hedda Hopper, Henry Barrows, Fiona Hale, William H. Strauss, Betty Morrisey.

• ***Skinner's Big Idea*** (sequel). F.B.O. Pictures, 1928. Silent. Director: Lynn Shores; screenwriter: Randolph Bartlett. Cast: Bryant Washburn (Skinner), William Orlamond (Hemingway), James Bradbury, Sr. (Carlton), Robert Dudley (Gibbs), Ole M. Ness, Charley Wellesley, Martha Sleeper, Hugh Trevor, Ethel Grey Terry.

• ***Skinner Steps Out*** (remake). Universal Pictures, 1929. Director: William James Craft; screenwriters: Matt Taylor and Albert De Mond. Cast: Glenn Tryon (Skinner), Merna Kennedy (Honey Skinner), E.J. Ratcliffe (Jackson), Burr McIntosh (McLaughlin), Lloyd Whitlock, William Welsh, Katherine Kerrigan, Frederick Lee, Jack Lipson, Edna Marion.

In the second of the three films dealing with businessman Skinner, he is a junior partner whom the senior partners, off on a vacation, tell to fire the company's three eldest employees. Instead, Skinner hires a chorus girl who rejuvenates the three, and when they accidently win a big contract for the company, the senior partners decide to keep them on. The 1929 movie is a fairly faithful remake of the 1926 silent feature, dealing with the difference a dress suit can make in a man's life. The story was first brought to the screen by Essanay in 1917.

821 Skippy

Based on Percy Crosby's newspaper cartoon strip. Story: It's a kids story, but not just for kids, showing how tough it can be to be a kid. When Skippy's shantytown pal Sooky's dog is killed, the two set about to replace the animal, including Skippy giving up his long-sought bicycle. The boys are very enterprising if not always astute with their schemes, which run from selling undrinkable lemonade to putting on a show, and stiffing the performers who were promised a cut of the profits. Finally, when really needed, some adults come through and put the finishing touches onto solving the problems the youngsters had been facing.

Paramount Pictures, 1931 (original). Director: Norman Taurog; screenwriters: Percy Crosby, Sam Mintz, Joseph L. Mankiewicz and Norman McLeod. Cast: Jackie Cooper (Skippy Skinner), Robert Coogan (Sooky Wayne), Mitzi Green (Eloise), Jackie Searl (Sidney), Willard Robertson (Dr. Herbert Skinner), Enid Bennett (Mrs. Helen Skinner), Donald Haines, Helen Jerome Eddy, Jack Clifford.

• ***Sooky*** (sequel). Paramount Pictures, 1931. Director: Norman Taurog; screenwriters: Percy Crosby, Joseph L. Mankiewicz and Norman McLeod. Cast: Jackie Cooper (Skippy), Robert Coogan (Sooky), Jackie Searl (Sidney Saunders), Willard Robertson (Dr. Skinner), Enid Bennett (Mrs. Skinner), Helen Jerome Eddy, Leigh Allen, Harry Beresford, Oscar Apfel.

Norman Taurog won the Academy Award for directing *Skippy* and the movie was nominated for Best Picture, Joseph Mankiewicz and Norman McLeod for Best Script and Jackie Cooper, for Best Actor. It and its sequel were humorous pieces, sympathetic to a believable group of appealing youngsters. In the second film, Sooky desperately wants a soldier uniform and a Sam Browne belt and the audience is made to feel that this longing is just as important as those that motivate adults to action in grown-up dramatic films.

822 Slaughter

Based on a story by Mark Hanna and Don Williams. Story: Slaughter is a black Vietnam veteran who, in tracking down the underworld group that killed his parents, lives up to his name.

American International, 1972 (original). Director: Jack Starrett; screenwriters: Mark Hanna and Don Williams. Cast: Jim Brown (Slaughter), Rip Torn, Don Gordon, Cameron Mitchell.

• ***Slaughter's Big Rip-Off*** (sequel). American International, 1973. Director: Gordon Douglas; screenwriter: Charles Johnson. Cast: Jim Brown (Slaughter), Ed MacMahon, Brock Peters, Don Stroud.

The great fullback for the Cleveland Browns never lacked for front-line support when he rushed for records in professional football. But in these movies he was a sitting duck, what with terrible scripts and supporting players who looked embarrassed to be associated with the proceedings. Oh, and one other thing—Brown can't act. In the sequel, Brown, who seems to lose a lot of people close to him, is out to get the gangsters who have killed his best friend. He does—violently.

Slaughter's Big Rip-Off *see* **Slaughter**

823 Sleepers East

Based on the novel by Frederick Nebel and the character "Michael Shayne" created by Brett Halliday. Story: Lena Karelson, an ex-con, is a surprise witness being taken to a trial by train. There are a number of individuals who would like to keep her from testifying.

Fox Film Corp., 1934 (original). Director: Kenneth MacKenna; screenwriters: Lester Cole and Ernest Palmer. Cast: Wynne Gibson (Lena Karelson), Preston Foster (Jason Everett), Mona Barrie (Ada Robillard), Harvey Stephens (Martin Knox), J. Carroll Naish, Howard Lally.

• ***Sleepers East*** (remake). Twentieth Century–Fox, 1941. Director: Eugene Forde; screenwriter: Lou Breslow. Cast: Lloyd Nolan (Michael Shayne), Lynn Bari (Kay Bentley), Mary Beth Hughes (Helen Carlsen), Louis Jean Heydt (Everett Jason), Edward Brophy, Don Costello, Ben Carter, Don Douglas, Oscar O'Shea.

In the remake of this minor and often clumsy detective story, Lloyd Nolan plays detective Michael Shayne, who must deliver surprise witness Mary Beth Hughes to San Francisco for a murder trial, and is kept busy keeping her alive on the train on which they are traveling. The "excitement" hoped for in this entry in a series of "Michael Shayne" detective movies is fairly ho-hum as the story drags along.

Sleeping Car to Trieste *see* **Rome Express**

The Sleeping Cardinal *see* **Sherlock Holmes**

824 A Slight Case of Murder

Based on the play by Damon Runyon and Howard Lindsay. Story: Twenties gang leader Remy Marco calls together his cronies to announce that because of the repeal of Prohibition, it will be necessary for them to find a legitimate business. Marco has purchased a brewery and assigns positions in his company for each member of his mob. Going straight is easier said than done, what with other crooks involving Marco and his boys in murder and the search for hidden loot. Reluctantly and with hilarious results, Marco and the others find themselves on the side of their former natural enemies, the police. Complicating matters, Marco's daughter is engaged to a wealthy, timid young man who has just joined the state troopers. Respectability comes to the family and former mobsters but not before a great round of black comedy ensues around the theme, "Who's got the corpses?"

Warner Bros., 1938 (original). Director: Lloyd Bacon; screenwriters: Earl Baldwin and Joseph Schrank. Cast: Edward G. Robinson (Remy Marco), Jane Bryan (Mary Marco), Ruth Donnelly (Nora Marco), Allen Jenkins (Mike), Willard Parker (Dick Whitewood), John Litel (Post), Edward Brophy (Lefty), Harold Huber (Guiseppe), Eric Stanley (Ritter), Paul Harvey, Bobby Jordan, Joe Downing, Margaret Hamilton, George E. Stone.

• ***Stop, You're Killing Me*** (remake). Warner Bros., 1952. Director: Roy Del Ruth; screenwriter: James O'Hanlon. Cast: Broderick Crawford (Marco), Claire Trevor (Nora), Virginia Gibson (Mary), Bill Hayes (Chance Whitelaw), Charlie Cantor (Mike), Sheldon Leonard (Lefty), Joe Vitale (Guiseppe), Howard St. John (Mahoney), Henry Morgan, Margaret Dumont, Stephen Chase, Don Beddoe.

The first version of Runyon and Lindsay's play poked fun at all the gangster movies, their characters and methods. It is a swift-paced farce, a rowdy and funny piece with all the familiar movie gangster situations developed but this time with the mobsters firmly on the side of law and order. Robinson is perfect as the retired gangster chief. Ruth Donnelly is at her wise-cracking best as Marco's wife yearning for respectability but not surprised when it didn't come easily. Jenkins, Brophy and Huber head up a fine cast of supporting actors in the roles of the reformed mobsters who were having a hard time keeping straight.

The remake with Crawford was also a fine piece but if anything suffered because it was produced too long after the films it was parodying were popular. Crawford and Trevor as his loyal wife are excellent as they find their rented vacation home in Saratoga not only filled with the former henchmen of the retired mobster but also four dead crooks and a live one searching the house for a hidden $500,000 in loot. The humor got a bit grisly as corpses are shifted around but apparently few in the audiences were offended as they laughed at the antics on the screen.

Slim *see* **Tiger Shark**

825 Slippy McGee

Based on the novel by Marie Conway Oemler. Story: Safecracker Slippy McGee is seriously injured in making his getaway after pulling a job. He is taken in by Father De Rance and is nursed back to health by Mary Virginia after his leg is amputated. Because of the kindness shown him and his growing love for Mary Virginia, he reforms, but he has to use his safecracking skills one last time to obtain some incriminating letters when George Inglesby attempts to blackmail Mary Virginia into marrying him.

Morosco Productions/First National Pictures, 1923 (original). Silent. Director: Wesley Ruggles; screenwriter: Marie Conway Oemler. Cast: Wheeler Oakman (Slippy McKee), Colleen Moore (Mary Virginia), Sam De Grasse (Father De Rance), Edmund Stevens (George Inglesby), Edith Yorke, Lloyd Whitlock, Pat O'Malley.

• ***Slippy McGee*** (remake). Republic Pictures, 1948. Director: Albert Kelley; screenwriters: Norman S. Hall and Jerry Gruskin. Cast: Donald "Red" Barry (Slippy McGee), Dale Evans (Mary Hunter), Tom Brown (Father Shanley), Harry V. Cheshire (Doctor Moore), James Seary (Thomas Eustis), Murray Alper, Dick Elliott.

The gangster melodrama's second version had a western cast in Donald "Red" Barry and Dale Evans, but it was really a fairly faithful repeat of the story of the safecracker. One difference is that his leg is merely broken, not amputated, and the menace comes from his own old gang which he liquidates as well as the blackmailer of his newly found sweetheart. Tain't much, but to those for whom television was merely a dream, it may have been the only entertainment in town.

826 Small Town Girl

Based on the novel by Ben Ames Williams. Story: Kay Brannan is the small-town girl who is picked up by playboy Bob Dakin and married during a drunken spree. His rich fiancée, Priscilla, demands that he get an annulment, but Bob decides that he prefers Kay even when he is sober, and that's about it.

MGM, 1936 (original). Director: William Wellman; screenwriters: John Lee Mahin and Edith Fitzgerald. Cast: Janet Gaynor (Kay Brannan), Robert Taylor (Bob Dakin), Binnie Barnes (Priscilla), Lewis Stone (Dr. Dakin), Andy Devine (George), Elizabeth Patterson, Frank Craven, James Stewart, Douglas Fowley, Isabell Jewell.

• ***Small Town Girl*** (remake). MGM, 1953. Director: Leslie Kardos; screenwriters: Dorothy Cooper and Dorothy Kingsley. Cast: Jane Powell (Cindy Kimbell), Farley Granger (Rick Below Livingston), Ann Miller (Lisa Bellmount), S.Z. Sakall (Eric Schlemmer), Robert Keith (Judge Gordon Kimbell), Bobby Van (Ludwig Schlemmer), Chill Wills, Billie Burke, Fay Wray, Nat King Cole, Dean Miller, William Campbell.

Small Town Girl was Janet Gaynor's first film for MGM and she became the studio's biggest attraction until Shirley Temple replaced her as the jewel in the studio's crown. However, it was her personal appeal, not the story of this picture, which made her a hit. In the musical remake, Jane Powell and Farley Granger take over for Miss Gaynor and Robert Taylor in basically the same story. What makes the version superior are the musical numbers staged by Busby Berkeley and the songs by Nicholas Brodszky and Leo Robin, including "Street Dance" impressively performed by Bobby Van, "I've Gotta Hear That Beat" nicely done by Ann Miller while showing off her shapely legs, and "The Fellow I'd Follow," sung by Jane Powell.

827 Smart Blonde

Based on a story by Frederick Nebel. Story; This is the first film in the "Torchy Blane" series, with Glenda Farrell as the newspaperwoman who helps police detective Steve McBride, played by Barton MacLane, solve murder cases. In this one, a mobster supposedly wishes to go straight so he can marry into Boston society, but it's all a ruse to cover up some murders.

Warner Bros., 1937 (original). Director: Frank MacDonald; screenwriters: Don Ryan and Kenneth Gamet. Cast: Glenda Farrell (Torchy Blane), Barton MacLane (Steve McBride), Winifred Shaw (Dolly Ireland), Craig Reynolds (Tom Carney), Addison Richards, Charlotte Winters, Jane Wyman, David Carlyle.

• ***A Shot in the Dark*** (remake). Warner Bros., 1941. Director: William McGann; screenwriter: M. Coates Webster. Cast: William Lundigan (Peter Kennedy), Nan Wynn (Dixie Waye), Ricardo Cortez (Phil Richards), Regis Toomey (Bill Ryder), Maris Wrixon, Lucia Carroll, Donald Douglas, Noel Madison.

Studios had no shame when it came to recycling stories, particularly those of marginal interest. It appears their belief was that if people stayed away in large numbers from a film under one guise, then there was a large potential market for it in another. The Torchy Blane films kept Glenda Farrell and Barton MacLane gainfully employed for awhile but the movies don't rank among the more memorable mystery-whodunit series. No doubt, they appealed to those who enjoyed seeing cops shown up by a smart-alecky newspaperwoman. The "B" remake seemed destined for theaters in communities in which even casting shadows on a wall would gather a crowd. Once again, a gang leader is quitting his nightclub business to marry a society girl, which doesn't set well with his jealous former sweetheart. It takes a couple of murders before Bill Lundigan, in the role of a newspaperman, fights in out with detective Regis Toomey to see who's the first to solve the crime.

Smart Guy ***see*** **I Am a Criminal**

828 Smilin' Through

Based on the play by Allan Langdon Martin. Story: On the very day that John Carteret is to marry Moonyeen Clare, one of her rejected suitors, Jeremiah Wayne, accidently kills her while trying to shoot John. Years later, John's niece and ward, Kathleen, announces that she is going to marry Jeremiah's son Kenneth. John forbids the marriage and orders Kathleen never to see Kenneth again. Throughout the years, as she promised dying in John's arms, Moonyeen's spirit visits him from time to time. When Kenneth returns from World War I while all the time Kathleen has faithfully waited for him, Moonyeen appears to John and pleads that he allow the young couple to have the happiness denied to them. John relents, dies and his spirit joins Moonyeen's for eternity.

First National Pictures, 1922 (original). Silent. Director: Sidney A. Franklin; screenwriters: James Ashmore Creelman and Sidney A. Franklin. Cast: Norma Talmadge (Kathleen/Moonyeen), Harrison Ford (Kenneth/Jeremiah Wayne), Wyndham Standing (John Carteret), Glenn Hunter, Grace Griswold, Miriam Battista, Eugene Lockhart, Alec B. Francis.

• ***Smilin' Through*** (remake). MGM, 1932. Director: Sidney Franklin; screenwriter: Ernst Vajda, Claudine West, Donald Ogden Stewart and James Bernard Fagan. Cast: Norma Shearer (Kathleen/Moonyeen Clare), Leslie Howard (John Carteret), Fredric March (Jeremy/Kenneth Wayne), Ralph Forbes, O.P. Heggie,

Beryl Mercer, Margaret Seddon, David Torrence, Forrester Harvey, Cora Sue Collins.

• ***Smilin' Through*** (remake). MGM, 1941. Director: Frank Borzage; screenwriters: Donald Ogden Stewart and John Balderston. Cast: Jeanette MacDonald (Kathleen/Moonyeen Clare), Brian Aherne (Sir John Carteret), Gene Raymond (Jeremy/Kenneth Wayne), Ian Hunter, Frances Robinson, Patrick O'Moore, Jackie Horner, Eric Lonsdale, Frances Carson, Ruth Rickaby, Wyndham Standing, David Clyde.

The 1932 version of the play was nominated for but did not win the Academy Award for Best Picture. It's an absorbing, sentimental and unbelievable romantic drama with fine performances by Shearer, Howard and March. The 1941 musical remake with Jeanette MacDonald as the unfortunate bride is flat despite some fine traditional songs including the title song, "There's a Long, Long Trail Awinding," "Drink to Me Only with Thine Eyes" and "Rose of Tralee."

829 Smokey and the Bandit

Based on the screenplay by James Lee Barrett, Charles Shyer and Alan Mandel. Story: It's a road film about "Bandit," who sure can drive, be it a fancy car or an 18-wheeler. For a large amount of money he agrees to race 1800 miles from Georgia to Texas and back in 28 hours, delivering a load of beer to a crazy but rich father and son, who fancy the beer, speed, and loony stunts. Along the way he picks up a runaway bride, whose potential father-in-law just happens to be a county sheriff. The chase is on.

Universal Pictures/Rastar, 1977 (original). Director: Hal Needham; screenwriter: James Lee Barrett, Charles Shyer and Alan Mandel. Cast: Burt Reynolds (Bandit), Sally Field (Carrie), Jackie Gleason (Smokey—the Sheriff), Jerry Reed, Mike Henry, Pat McCormick, Paul Williams.

• ***Smokey and the Bandit II*** (sequel). Universal Pictures/Rastar. Director: Hal Needham; screenwriter: Jerry Belson and Brock Yates. Cast: Burt Reynolds (Bandit), Sally Field (Carrie), Jackie Gleason (Smokey—the Sheriff), Jerry Reed, Dom DeLuise, Paul Williams, Pat McCormick, David Huddleston.

• ***Smokey and the Bandit III*** (sequel). Universal Pictures, 1983. Director: Dick Lowry; screenwriter: Stuart Birnbaum and David Dashev. Cast: Jackie Gleason, Jerry Reed, Mike Henry, Pat McCormick, Burt Reynolds, Dean Martin, Frank Sinatra.

These films were popular with those who like macho, good-old-boy pictures with little plot and a whole lot of reckless driving and raunchy language. Apparently, there are a lot of such people, because the films were huge successes at the box office. Burt Reynolds has a charming way about him that gives the first two chase pictures a special appeal. He only appeared briefly in the second sequel in a cameo role and hopefully that's the end of the line for the series, good buddy.

Smokey and the Bandit II *see* **Smokey and the Bandit**

Smokey and the Bandit III *see* **Smokey and the Bandit**

830 Smooth As Satin

Based on *The Chatterbox* by Bayard Veiller. Story: While posing as a maid, jewel thief Gertie Jones surprises Jimmy Hartigan rifling the safe she planned to rob. She offers to split the loot with him, an agreement acceptable to him, but the police arrive and Jimmy takes the full blame for the robbery. Gertie helps Jimmy escape and they take refuge in the country, where they are married. Deciding to go straight, they return to the city with the stolen cash, investing it with Bill Munson, who runs off with it. Jimmy is picked up by a detective and is being returned to prison when Gertie boards the train carrying Jimmy and his detective escort with the money that she had recovered from Munson. She offers it to the detective to let Jimmy go, but the proposition is refused. When the train is caught in a tunnel collapse, Gertie and Jimmy save the detective rather than escape. The detective promises to return the money to its proper owners and allows Jimmy to go free.

R-C Pictures/Booking Offices of America, 1925 (original). Silent. Director: Ralph Ince; screenwriter: Fred Kennedy Myton. Cast: Evelyn Brent (Gertie Jones), Bruce Gordon (Jimmy Hartigan), Fred Kelsey (Kersey), Fred Esmelton (Bill Munson), Mabel Van Buren, John Gough.

• ***Alias French Gertie*** (remake). RKO, 1930. Director: George Archainbaud; screenwriter: Wallace Smith. Cast: Bebe Daniels (Marie), Ben Lyon (Jimmy), Robert Emmett O'Connor (Kelcey), John Ince, Daisy Belmore, Betty Pierce.

We suppose things must have changed considerably from the '20s and early '30s, as it doesn't seem likely that today's hard-boiled detectives would let a pair of safecrackers go free to start a new life, but that's precisely what happens in both of these crime melodramas and in the remake, there isn't even the excuse that the pair saved the detective's life. He just sees some good in "Gertie the Gun" and Jimmy, and bids them to go free and reform.

Smooth As Silk *see* **Notorious Gentleman**

Snow White and the Seven Dwarfs *see* **Ball of Fire**

831 So Big

Based on the novel by Edna Ferber. Story: When her father dies after losing his fortune, Selina Peake, who had attended finishing school and toured Europe, is reduced to taking a teaching position in a high school in a Dutch community near Chicago. She eventually marries farmer Pervus DeJong, and shares his hard life with him. Her only source of pleasure is their son Dirk, whom she calls "So-Big." Pervus dies and Selina is reduced to abject poverty. The father of an old school friend, Julie Hempel, lends Selina enough money to properly farm the land, and after 18 years of hard work, Selina proudly attends the graduation of Dirk as an architect. His promising career is threatened by scandal when the husband, William Storm, of the woman with whom Dirk is having an affair threatens to name Dirk as correspondent in a divorce suit.

Barbara Stanwyck, center, has struggled all her life and it shows in her face. Here Bette Davis and George Brent show some forced admiration in So Big *(Warner Bros., 1932).*

Selina pleads with Storm, and he changes his mind, allowing Dirk to return to his true love, Dallas, and giving Selina hope of having some pleasant final days.

First National Pictures, 1924 (original). Silent. Director: Charles Brabin; screenwriter: Adelaide Heilbron. Cast: Colleen Moore (Selina Peake), Joseph De Grasse (Simeon Peake), John Bowers (Pervus DeJong), Ben Lyon (Dirk DeJong), Jean Hersholt (Aug Hempel), Charlotte Merriam (Julie Hempel), Henry Herbert (William Storm), Rosemary Theby (Paula Storm), Phyllis Haver (Dallas O'Meara), Wallace Beery, Gladys Brockwell, Dot Farley, Ford Sterling, Frankie Darro.

• ***So Big*** (remake). Warner Bros., 1932. Director: William A. Wellman;

Sterling Hayden is the farmer who Jane Wyman marries and teaches to read in So Big *(Warner Bros., 1953).*

screenwriters: J. Grubb Alexander and Robert Lord. Cast: Barbara Stanwyck (Selina Peake), George Brent (Roelf), Dickie Moore (Dirk as a boy), Bette Davis (Dallas O'Meara), Mae Madison (Julie Hempel), Hardie Albright (Dirk as a man), Robert Warwick (Simeon Peake), Earle Foxe (Pervus DeJong), Arthur Stone, Alan Hale, Dorothy Peterson, Dawn O'Day, Dick Winslow, Harry Beresford.

• ***So Big*** (remake). Warner Bros., 1953. Director: Robert Wise; screenwriter: John Twist. Cast: Jane Wyman (Selina DeJong), Sterling Hayden (Pervus DeJong), Nancy Olsen (Dallas O'Meara), Steve Forest (Dirk DeJong), Elizabeth Fraser (Julie Hempel), Martha Hyer (Paula Hempel), Richard Beymer, Walter Coy, Tommy Rettig.

The three film versions of Edna Ferber's Pulitzer Prize–winning novel won no awards, but the performances of Barbara Stanwyck and Jane Wyman were greatly admired and once again demonstrated the remarkable range of these two highly talented actresses. In the 1932 film, Bette Davis' role got her noticed but it would be untrue to say that her remarkable ability was apparent even in this early appearance. In the Jane Wyman version, Sterling Hayden was convincing in the part of the hard-working farmer husband and Richard Beymer scored as the 12-year-old, sensitive pianist befriended by Wyman.

So Long at the Fair *see* **Midnight Warning**

832 So This Is London

Based on the Arthur Goodrich's adaptation of the George M. Cohan play. Story: Hiram Draper is a cotton mill owner who distrusts and dislikes anything British. While in England on a business trip with his wife and son, Junior meets and falls in love with Elinor, an English girl. In London, Junior conspires to have his parents meet the girl's parents, Lord and Lady Worthing. In an attempt to kill the romance, Hiram decides to live up to what he believes is the English conception of an American, an uncouth, uncivilized meddler. But when Hiram meets Elinor, he decides that he may have been mistakened about everything and goes to work to right the wrong he has caused so the couple may marry.

Fox Film Corp., 1930 (original). Director: John Blystone; screenwriters: Sonya Levin and Owen Davis. Cast: Will Rogers (Hiram Draper), Irene Rich (Mrs. Hiram Draper), Frank Albertson (Junior Draper), Maureen O'Sullivan (Elinor Worthing), Lumsden Hare (Lord Percy Worthing), Mary Forbes (Lady Worthing), Bramwell Fletcher, Dorothy Christy, Ellen Woodston.

• ***So This Is London*** (remake). Twentieth Century–Fox, 1939. Director: Thornton Freeland; screenwriter: William Counselman. Cast: Alfred Drayton (Lord Worthing), Robertson Hare (Henry Honeycutt), Ethel Revnell (Dodie), Gracie West (Lix), Berton Churchill (Hiram Draper), Lily Cahill (Mrs. Draper), Carla Lehmann (Elinor Draper), Fay Compton (Lady Worthing), Stewart Granger, George Sanders, Mavis Clair, Aubrey Mallalieu.

There is a great deal of slapstick-like fun in these two films with the adaptations in each case made to fit the personalities of the leading character, in the first case Will Rogers and in the second, Alfred Drayton. In the remake, the two central characters, an American businessman and an English Lord, accept misfortune like men—they blame everything on their wives. It's somewhat dated material now, but if one can appreciate things in their historical perspective, it's possible to appreciate the enjoyment the shows brought to audiences of the time.

Society Lawyer *see* **Penthouse**

833 A Society Scandal

Based on the play *The Laughing Lady* by Alfred Sutro. Story: When Harrison Peters, an admirer of Marjorie Colbert, deliberately compromises her, Hector Colbert sues his wife for divorce with the enthusiastic support of his lawyer, Daniel Farr, who shows in many ways his disapproval of Marjorie's behavior. In winning the divorce, lawyer Farr ruins Marjorie's reputation. Later, when Farr and Marjorie meet again, she plans a revenge in kind against the lawyer, but her plans are abandoned when she falls in love with him.

Famous Players/Paramount Pictures, 1924 (original). Silent. Director: Allan Dwan; screenwriter: Forrest Halsey. Cast: Gloria Swanson (Marjorie Colbert), Rod La Rocque (David Farr), Ricardo Cortez (Harrison Peters), Allan Simpson

(Hector Colbert), Ida Waterman, Thelma Converse, Fraser Coalter, Catherine Proctor, Wilfred Donovan, Yvonne Hughes.

• ***A Society Scandal*** (remake). Paramount/Famous Lasky Corp., 1929. Director: Victor Schertzinger; screenwriters: Bartlett Cormack and Arthur Richman. Cast: Ruth Chatterton (Marjorie Lee), Clive Brook (Daniel Farr), Dan Healy (Al Brown), Nat Pendleton (James Dugan), Raymond Walburn (Hector Lee), Dorothy Hall, Hedda Harrigan, Lillian B. Tonge, Marguerite St. John.

These society melodramas did quite well in the cities but seemed too far from reality for the rest of the country. It's difficult to buy a plot involving an innocent flirtation which sparks a mean divorce led by a righteous lawyer who seemed to believe that he was on some holy crusade. Even more difficult to believe is that when the aggrieved lady has her chance to get even, she throws in the towel and declares her love for her earlier tormentor.

Soldiers Three *see* **Gunga Din**

Some Blondes Are Dangerous *see* **The Iron Man**

Some Like It Hot *see* **Shoot the Works** *and* **Viktor und Viktoria**

834 Someone at the Door

Based on the play by Dorothy and Campbell Christie. Story: Young reporter Ronald Martin pretends to have murdered his sister Sally in order to get himself arrested and have a sensational scoop when she shows up alive and healthy. Her hiding place turns out to be the hiding place of jewel thieves as well and two real murders take place before everything in this comedy is ironed out, giving Ronald a scoop he hadn't expected.

BIP/Wardour, Great Britain, 1936 (original). Director: Herbert Brenon; screenwriters: Jack Davies and Marjorie Deans. Cast: Billy Milton (Ronald Martin), Aileen Marson (Sally Martin), Noah Beery (Harry Kapel), Edward Chapman (Price), John Irwin (Bill Reid), Hermione Gingold (Mrs. Appleby), Charles Mortimer, Edward Dignon, Lawrence Hanray, Jimmy Godden.

• ***Someone at the Door*** (remake). Hammer, Great Britain, 1950. Director: Francis Searle; screenwriter: A.R. Rawlinson. Cast: Michael Medwin (Ronnie Martin), Garry Marsh (Kapel), Yvonne Owen (Sally Martin), Hugh Latimer (Bill Reid), Danny Green (Price), Campbell Singer, John Kelly.

In the remake, Ronnie and his sister Sally own a supposedly haunted house with many secret rooms. He plans to pretend to murder her while she hides in one of these rooms. He will go on trial and get a heck of a story when she reappears. Her fiancé, a medical student, provides them with a corpse, but things go awry and Ronnie is sentenced to hang.

Someone to Love *see* **The Charm School**

835 Someone to Remember

Based on a story by Ben Ames Williams. Story: Mrs. Freeman is a kindly old lady whose contract with a hotel allows her to remain living in it when a university takes it over for a men's dormitory. The lads look on her as a mother away from home and she patiently awaits the return of her own boy who had disappeared from the university some 25 years earlier. When Dan Freeman shows up to take residence in the dorm, she assumes that he is her grandson and treats him as such, giving him sound advice, keeping him on the straight and narrow and even pointing him towards a romance with Lucy Stanton. But the announcement that Dan's father is coming for a visit proves too much for Mrs. Freeman. She dies with a smile on her face in anticipation of being reunited with her son. He isn't of course, her son had died when he vanished.

Republic Pictures, 1943 (original). Director: Robert Siodmak; screenwriter: Frances Hyland. Cast: Mabel Paige (Mrs. Freeman), John Craven (Dan Freeman), Dorothy Morris (Lucy Stanton), Charles Dingle (Jim Parsons), Harry Shannon, Tom Seldel, David Bacon, Richard Crane, Russell Hicks.

• ***Johnny Trouble*** (remake). Warner Bros., 1957. Director: John H. Auer; screenwriter: Charles O'Neal and David Lord. Cast: Ethel Barrymore (Mrs. Chandler), Cecil Kellaway (Tom McKay), Carolyn Jones (Julie), Jesse White (Parsons), Rand Harper (Phil), Paul Wallace, Edward Byrnes, Edward Castagna.

Both Mabel Paige and Ethel Barrymore offer warm portrayals of the wealthy woman who insists on staying on when her hotel is converted to a men's dorm for the local university. Each is touching in her belief that the son, vanished these 27 years, will someday show up, and the proof of the soundness of this conviction is when a recalcitrant student with the same last name shows up to be treated like a grandson.

Son of Ali Baba *see* **Chu Chin Chow**

Son of Captain Blood *see* **Captain Blood**

The Son of Dr. Jekyll *see* **Dr. Jekyll and Mr. Hyde**

The Son of Flubber *see* **The Absent-Minded Professor**

836 Son of Fury

Based on the novel *Benjamin Blake* by Edison Marshall. Story: Benjamin Blake, who lives in England during the reign of King George III, undergoes great hardships and reverses in an attempt to establish his birthright, snatched from him by a scheming uncle, Sir Arthur Blake. When he succeeds, finally regaining his title and estates, he parcels these out to his servants, and returns to the tropic isle where he became rich from a fortune of pearls and found the love of an exotic native girl, Eve.

Twentieth Century–Fox, 1942 (original). Director: John Cromwell; screenwriter: Philip Dunne. Cast: Tyrone Power (Benjamin Blake), Gene Tierney (Eve), George Sanders (Sir Arthur Blake), Frances Farmer (Isabel), Roddy

McDowall (Benjamin as a boy), John Carradine (Caleb Green), Elsa Lanchester, Harry Davenport, Kay Johnson, Dudley Digges.

• ***Treasure of the Golden Condor*** (remake). Twentieth Century–Fox, 1953. Director and screenwriter: Delmer Daves. Cast: Cornel Wilde (Jean-Paul), Constance Smith (Clara), Finlay Currie (MacDougal), Walter Hampden (Pierre), Anne Bancroft (Marie), George Macready (Marquis), Fay Wray (Marquise), Leo G. Carroll, Konstantin Shayne, Louis Heminger, Tudor Owen, Gil Donaldson.

Tyrone Power comes off fairly well in this action-adventure yarn. Not only does he come out on top in a magnificent fistfight with George Sanders, but he wins the love of the dusky and sultry-looking Gene Tierney. In the remake, the action is transferred to France; Cornel Wilde, likeable as the dashing hero, joins forces with Finlay Currie to secure a map that shows the location of a fabulous Mayan treasure in Guatemala. After it is found, Wilde returns to France and proves his case against his evil uncle, George Macready, but not before he barely escapes the hangman's rope. Wilde gives away everything and travels back to Guatemala, Currie and the latter's lovely daughter, played by Constance Smith. Both films are a lot of fun, with acting taking a back seat to action.

The Son of Monte Cristo ***see*** **The Count of Monte Cristo**

The Son of Sinbad ***see*** **Sinbad the Sailor**

A Song Is Born ***see*** **Ball of Fire**

Song of Songs ***see*** **Lily of the Dust**

Song of the Thin Man ***see*** **The Thin Man**

Sonya and the Madman ***see*** **Crime and Punishment**

Sooky ***see*** **Skippy**

837 Sorrell and Son

Based on the novel by George Warwick Deeping. Story: This long, mostly sad tale of devotion, integrity and unselfishness finds Stephen Sorrell returning from World War I and finding that his wife, Dora, has deserted him and abandoned their son, Kit. Sorrell endures all kinds of deprivation and makes every sacrifice to raise his son, eventually getting him accepted at a genteel boarding school. At college, Kit is determined to become a surgeon. While in school his mother shows up, having married a rich man; she tries to win back her son with the things money can buy, but Kit rejects her. Established as a surgeon, Kit is asked by his father to hasten the latter's end in his fatal illness, completing this life of intense devotion between a man and his son.

Feature Production/United Artists, 1927 (original). Silent. Director and screenwriter: Herbert Brenon. Cast: H.B. Warner (Stephen Sorrell), Anna Q. Nilsson (Dora Sorrell), Mickey McBain (Kit as a child), Nils Asther (Kit as an adult), Carmel Myers (Flo Palfrey), Lionel Belmore (John Palfrey), Norman Trevor, Betsy Ann Hisle, Louis Wolheim, Paul McAllister, Alice Joyce, Mary Nolan.

British & Dominion Productions/United Artists, 1934. Director: Jack Raymond; screenwriter: Lydia Hayward. Cast: H.B. Warner (Stephen Sorrell), Peter Penrose (Kit as a child), Hugh Williams (Kit as an adult), Winifred Shotter (Molly), Margot Grahame (Dora), Donald Calthrop (Dr. Orange), Wally Patch, Evelyn Roberts, Hope Davy, Louis Hayward, Ruby Miller.

H.B. Warner is nearly perfect in his characterization of the father who sacrifices all for his son, in these two versions of the sentimental and sometimes stilted story. Others in the two casts do not give quite as fine impersonations of their characters. This almost "woman's story" has a man in the role of the unfortunate individual badly treated by the woman he loves, and almost equally so by others that he encounters as he dedicates himself to his son's success and happiness. The remake's transition of time is not the most satisfactory, resulting in some rather jumpy and raggedy plot developments.

838 Sounder

Based on the novel by William H. Armstrong. Story: When Nathan Lee Morgan, the father of a poor black sharecropping family in Louisiana during the Depression, steals a ham to feed his hungry family, he is put in prison. It's up to mother Rebecca Morgan to pull the family through the crisis, which she does as well as anyone can be expected to do.

Twentieth Century–Fox, 1972 (original). Director: Martin Ritt; screenwriter: Lonne Elder III. Cast: Cicely Tyson (Rebecca Morgan), Paul Winfield (Nathan Lee Morgan), Kevin Hooks (David Lee Morgan), Carmen Mathews (Mrs. Boatwright), Taj Mahal (Ike), James Best (Sheriff Young), Yvonne Jarrell, Eric Hooks, Sylvia "Kuumba" Williams, Janet MacLachlen, Teddy Airhart.

• ***Sounder: Part 2*** (sequel). Gamma III, 1976. Director: William Graham; screenwriter: Lonne Elder III. Cast: Harold Sylvester (Nathan), Ebony Wright (Rebecca), Taj Mahal (Ike), Annazette Chase (Camille), Darryl Young (David), Eric Young, Ronald Bolden, Barbara Chaney, Kuumba, Ted Airhart.

This well-made, not too exciting family movie won nominations for Best Picture, Best Screenplay, Best Actor and Best Actress, but came away empty-handed, which wasn't an injustice. The sequel badly misses Cicely Tyson and Paul Winfield. In it the sharecropper's family finds themselves involved in the building of a schoolhouse.

Sounder: Part 2 *see* **Sounder**

South Sea Sinner *see* **Seven Sinners**

839 Spawn of the North

Based on the novel by Barrett Willoughby. Story: This all-star film recounts the battle between licensed Alaskan fishermen and pirates who steal their catch from the traps they set for salmon at spawning time. Jim Kemerlee and boyhood friend Tyler Dawson find themselves on opposite sides of the war, when the latter goes over to the side of the Russian heavy, Red Skain. In a fierce night encounter, Jim shoots Tyler, but he lives long enough to make up for his defection.

Paramount Pictures, 1938 (original). Director: Henry Hathaway; screenwriter: Jules Furthman. Cast: George Raft (Tyler Dawson), Henry Fonda (Jim Kemerlee), Dorothy Lamour (Nicky Duval), Akim Tamiroff (Red Skain), John Barrymore (Windy Turlon), Louise Platt (Diane), Lynne Overman (Jackson), Fuzzy Knight, Vladimir Sokoloff, Duncan Renaldo, Richard Ung, Lee Shumway.

• ***Alaska Seas*** (remake). Paramount Pictures, 1954. Director: Jerry Hopper; screenwriter: Geoffrey Homes. Cast: Robert Ryan (Matt Kelly), Jan Sterling (Nicky), Brian Keith (Jim Kimmerly), Gene Barry (Verne Wiliams), Richard Shannon (Tom Erickson), Ralph Dumke, Ross Bagdasarian, Fay Roope, Timothy Carey.

The original story provided plenty of excitement and is still worth a viewing both for the acting and action. Fonda as the good hero, Raft as the bad hero and Tamiroff as the bad villain are all excellent. Adding fine support are Lamour, Barrymore and Overman. The remake is the difference between fresh and frozen fish. Except for Robert Ryan, everyone is miscast, and he's totally unsympathetic, not like Raft in the earlier version. He's an unscrupulous Alaskan salmon fisherman who steals his best friend Brian Keith's fiancée, Jan Sterling, and robs the man's traps. He redeems himself later when he deliberately steers another heavy's boat into a glacier to protect Keith.

840 Special Agent

Based on an idea by Martin Mooney. Story: Special investigator Bill Bradford pretends to be a newspaperman to hide the fact that he's on the trail of a mobster, Carston. There's a lot of gunplay and murder in this gangster picture.

Cosmopolitan/Warner Bros., 1935 (original). Director: William Keighley; screenwriters: Laird Boyle and Abel Finkel. Cast: Bette Davis (Julie Gardner), George Brent (Bill Bradford), Ricardo Cortez (Carston), Jack LaRue (Andrews), Henry O'Neill, Robert Strange, Joseph Crehan, J. Carroll Naish.

• ***Gambling on the High Seas*** (remake). Warner Bros., 1940. Director: George Amy; screenwriter: Robert E. Kent. Cast: Wayne Morris (Jim Carter), Jane Wyman (Laurie Ogden), Gilbert Roland (Greg Morella), John Litel, Roger Pryor, Frank Wilcox, Robert Strange, John Galludet, Frank Ferguson.

The first film was one of Bette Davis' minor efforts. As *Variety* saw it, all she did in the picture was assume different poses. Neither Brent nor Cortez were believable in their respective roles either. It was just a lot of gunplay with very little plot development. The remake, a "B" programmer, has Wayne Morris as a special investigator probing the dealings of gang boss Gilbert Roland, who has a ship-based gambling den. Jane Wyman plays Roland's secretary and Morris' love interest. It's all wrapped up in 56 minutes, with everything aimed for the climactic chase and shoot-out.

The Speckled Band *see* **Sherlock Holmes**

841 The Sphinx

Based on the story by Albert DeMond. Story: It's an acceptable murder mystery involving a deaf mute who may or may not be a mass-murderer. The twist is that he has a twin brother. The one who is truly a deaf mute provides an alibi for his brother, who not only can hear and speak but also can kill.

Monogram Pictures, 1933 (original). Director: Phil Rosen; screenwriter: Albert DeMond. Cast: Lionel Atwill (Jerome Breen), Sheila Terry (Jerry Crane), Theodore Newton (Jack Burton), Paul Hurst (Terrence Hogan), Luis Alberni, Robert Ellis, Lucien Prival, Paul Fix, Lillian Leighton.

• ***The Phantom Killer*** (remake). Monogram Pictures, 1942. Director: William Beaudine; screenwriter: Karl Brown. Cast: Dick Purcell (Edward Clark), Joan Woodbury (Barbara Mason), John Hamilton (John G. Harrison), Warren Hymer (Sgt. Corrigan), Kenneth Harlan, J. Farrell MacDonald, Mantan Moreland, Gayne Whitman.

These films were produced to balance double bills. Lionel Atwill was a fine character actor, who even when he wasn't the villain of a film, audiences suspected that he must be. In the remake, an ambitious district attorney believes a wealthy public benefactor is guilty of murder. He's known as a kindly deaf mute and when he's brought to trial, he's acquitted. The D.A. resigns, still believing his man is guilty, and is proven correct when later it's discovered the man has a twin brother who is actually a deaf mute. The two worked together; the deaf mute appearing in public, the other committing the crimes.

842 The Spiral Staircase

Based on the novel *Some Must Watch* by Ethel Lina White. Story: Because of a shock as an infant, Helen Capel, a serving girl in the old mansion of wealthy, bed-ridden Mrs. Warren, has lost her ability to speak, but she is nevertheless a happy, carefree girl. That is, until a killer begins to terrorize the region by taking the lives of young women with physical afflictions. Helen realizes that she is a likely target and soon finds herself petrified by shadows and noises as she moves around the house and garden. Suspicion falls on everyone in the household, but in the old "least-likely" ploy, the killer is revealed to be Mrs. Warren's seemingly compassionate son, Professor Warren.

RKO/Radio, 1946 (original). Director: Robert Siodmak; screenwriter: Mel Dinelli. Cast: Dorothy McGuire (Helen Capel), George Brent (Professor Warren), Ethel Barrymore (Mrs. Warren), Kent Smith (Doctor Parry), Rhonda Fleming (Blanche), Gordon Oliver (Steve Warren), Elsa Lanchester (Mrs. Oates), Sara Allgood (Nurse Barker), Rhys Williams (Mr. Oates), James Bell (Constable).

• ***The Spiral Staircase*** (remake). Raven/Columbia-Warners, Great Britain, 1975. Director: Peter Collinson; screenwriter: Allan Scott, Chris Bryant and

Mel Dinelli. Cast: Jacqueline Bisset (Helen Mallory), Christopher Plummer (Prof. Sherman), Sam Wanamaker (Lt. Fields), John Philip Law (Steven), Mildred Dunnock (Mrs. Sherman), Gayle Hunnicutt (Blanche), Sheila Brennan (Mrs. Oates), Elaine Stritch (Nurse), John Ronane (Dr. Rawley), Ronald Radd (Oates)

The setting of Ethel Lina White's novel was contemporary England, but for the 1946 film it was placed in early twentieth-century New England. Dorothy McGuire was touching as the mute in this effective thriller. In the remake, Jacqueline Bisset, an actress of lesser talents than Miss McGuire, nevertheless is convincing as the mute girl who realizes that her uncle is a mad murderer of physically handicapped women.

Spirit of Culver *see* **Tom Brown of Culver**

Splash! *see* **Miranda**

843 Sporting Blood

Based on the story *Horseflesh* by Frederick Hazlitt Brennan. Story: It's the usual yarn of a race horse passing through various hands, often being mistreated, but eventually ending up with a girl who puts the animal in shape again and enters him in the Kentucky Derby, which the colt proceeds to win.

MGM, 1930 (original). Director: Charles Brabin; screenwriters: Charles Brabin, Willard Mack and Wanda Tuchock. Cast: Clark Gable (Rid Riddell), Ernest Torrence (Jim Rellence), Madge Evans (Ruby), Lew Cody (Tip Scanlon), Marie Prevost (Angela), Harry Holman, Haliam Cooley, J. Farrell McDonald, John Larkin.

• ***Sporting Blood*** (remake). MGM, 1940. Director: S. Sylvan Simon; screenwriter: Lawrence Hazard, Albert Mannheimer and Dorothy Yost. Cast: Robert Young (Myles Vanders), Maureen O'Sullivan (Linda Lockwood), Lewis Stone (Davis Lockwood), William Gargan (Duffy), Lynne Carver, Clarence Muse, Lloyd Corrigan, George H. Reed.

Variety observed that it was too bad the 1930 film didn't have any box-office names, although they allowed how this young Clark Gable was beginning to be a hit with the females. In it, the future "King" is an unsympathetic, shady gambler who fixes races and gets in trouble with mobsters when things don't go according to plan. In the remake, Robert Young is a small-stable owner who sometimes is reduced to becoming a tout to pay expenses. He's involved in an old family feud, with Lewis Stone being his adversary; one of Stone's daughters, Lynne Carver, he pays court to and the other, Maureen O'Sullivan, he marries after their horse wins the big race, beating dear old dad's entry.

844 Spring Fever

Based on the play by Vincent Lawrence. Story: This romantic comedy features wisecracking Jack Kelly, a shipping clerk, who gains entrance to an exclusive country club and falls in love with Allie Monte. Through a series of disillusionments, Kelly keeps landing on his feet, vanquishes his rivals and wins the girl, who proves to be wealthy in her own right.

MGM, 1927 (original). Silent. Director: Edward Sedgwick; screenwriter: Albert Lewin. Cast: William Haines (Jack Kelly), Joan Crawford (Allie Monte), George K. Arthur (Eustace Tewksbury), George Fawcett (Mr. Waters), Eileen Percy, Edward Earle, Bert Woodruff, Lee Moran.

• ***Love in the Rough*** (remake). MGM, 1930. Director: Charles F. Reisner; screenwriter: Sarah Y. Mason. Cast: Robert Montgomery (Kelly), Dorothy Jordan (Marilyn), Benny Rubin (Benny), J.C. Nugent (Waters), Dorothy McNulty (Virgie), Tyrell David (Tewksbury), Harry Burns, Allan Lane, Catherine Moylan, Edward Davis.

The remake is a musical comedy with a country club setting, featuring the Dorothy Fields and Jimmy McHugh numbers "I'm Doing That Thing," "Go Home and Tell Your Mother" and "Like Kelly Can." Neither version of the Vincent Lawrence play is a keeper. The performances are flat and the story is trite. It's not likely that either will be shown any place where the average viewer might encounter them.

Spring in Park Lane *see* **Come Out of the Kitchen**

845 Square Crooks

Based on the play by James P. Judge. Story: Two young ex-cons, Eddie Ellison and Larry Scott, decide to go straight, but the latter falls off the wagon, and agrees to hold some jewelry stolen by a member of his old gang. Eddie saves his buddy from being arrested by returning the loot. The two get jobs as chauffeurs and Scott marries a telephone operator.

Fox Film Corporation, 1928 (original). Silent. Director: Lewis Seiler; screenwriter: Becky Gardiner. Cast: Robert Armstrong (Eddie Ellison), John Mack Brown (Larry Scott), Dorothy Dwan (Jane Brown), Dorothy Appleby (Kay Ellison), Eddie Sturges, Clarence Burton, Jackie Coombs, Lydia Dickson.

• ***Baby, Take a Bow*** (remake). Fox Film Corporation, 1934. Director: Harry Lachman; screenwriters: Philip Klein and E.E. Paramore. Cast: Shirley Temple (Shirley), James Dunn (Eddie Ellison), Claire Trevor (Kay Ellison), Alan Dinehart (Welch), Ray Walker (Larry Scott), Dorothy Libaire, Ralf Harolde, James Flavin, Richard Tucker, Olive Tell.

The remake of the crook melodrama concentrates on the contributions of Shirley Temple in her first star vehicle, and they are numerous in this hokey story of two ex-cons, James Dunn and Ray Walker, trying to go straight but being harassed both by their ex-criminal associates and by Alan Dinehart, a tough and unscrupulous cop who would like to send them back up the river. This property, as silly as it is, established Shirley's star in the Hollywood heavens. Shirley and Dunn combine on the title song by Bud Green and Sam Slept.

846 Squibs

Based on the play by Clifford Seyler and George Pearson. Story: Cockney spitfire Squibs Hopkins' romance with Yorkshire policeman Charlie Lee is threatened because her father is a bookie and her sister is in love with a crook.

Welsh/Pearson, Great Britain, 1921 (original). Silent. Director: George Pearson; screenwriters: Pearson and Eliot Stannard. Cast: Betty Balfour (Squibs Hopkins), Hugh E. Wright (Sam Hopkins), Fred Groves (PC Charlie Lee), Mary Brough (Mrs. Lee), Cronin Wilson (Bully Dawson), Annette Benson (Ivy Hopkins), Ambrose Manning, Tom Morriss, William Matthews.

• ***Squibs Wins the Calcutta Sweep*** (sequel). Welsh/Pearson, Great Britain. Silent. Director and screenwriter: George Pearson. Cast: Betty Balfour (Squibs), Fred Groves (PC Charlie Lee), Hugh E. Wright (Sam Hopkins), Bertram Burleigh (the Weasel), Annette Benson (Ivy), Mary Brough (Mrs. Lee), Hal Martin, Donald Searle, Tom Morriss, Sam Lewis.

• ***Squibs, MP*** (sequel). Welsh/Pearson, Great Britain, 1923. Silent. Director: George Pearson; screenwriters: Pearson, Leslie Hiscott and Will Dyson. Cast: Betty Balfour (Squibs), Hugh E. Wright (Sam Hopkins), Fred Groves (Charlie Lee), Irene Tripod, Frank Stanmore, Odette Myrtil.

• ***Squibs' Honeymoon*** (sequel). Welsh/Pearson, Great Britain, 1923. Silent. Director: George Pearson; screenwriters: Pearson, Betty Balfour and T.A. Welsh. Cast: Betty Balfour (Squibs), Hugh E. Wright (Sam Hopkins), Fred Groves (Charlie Lee), Frank Stanmore, Irene Tripod, Robert Vallis, Maurice Redmund.

• ***Squibs*** (remake). Twickenham, Great Britain, 1935. Director: Henry Edwards; screenwriters: Michael Hogan and H. Fowler Mear. Cast: Betty Balfour (Squibs Hopkins), Gordon Harker (Sam Hopkins), Stanley Holloway (PC Charlie Lee), Margaret Yarde (Mrs. Lee), Morris Harvey (Insp. Lee), Michael Shepley, Drusilla Wills, O.B. Clarence, Ronald Shiner, Thomas Weguelin.

In the first sequel, Cockney flower girl Squibs Hopkins wins £60,000 and takes her family to Paris to save her sister from a murderous husband. In the second sequel, Squibs stands for Parliament when a rival milk company accuses her fiancé, Charlie, of bribery. In the third sequel, the title just about says it all. She finally marries her Charlie and goes to Paris for her honeymoon. Oh, yes, she must pose as a man to escape capture by apaches. The 1935 film is a sound remake of portions of each of those which had gone before.

Squibs' Honeymoon *see* **Squibs**

Squibs, MP *see* **Squibs**

Squibs Wins the Calcutta Sweep *see* **Squibs**

Stage Struck *see* **Morning Glory**

Stand Up Virgin Soldiers *see* **The Virgin Soldiers**

847 A Star Is Born

Based partly on the story *What Price Hollywood?* by Adela Rogers St. John

and on an original story by Dorothy Parker, Alan Campbell and Robert Carson. Story: Esther Blodgett is a stage-struck kid who hopes to make it in the movies. She is discovered by alcoholic leading man Norman Maine, whose own career is in sharp decline. Maine convinces studio head Oliver Niles to give Esther a big build up and make her a star. They change her name to Vicki Lester, put her in a production and she becomes a smash hit. Vicki and Norman marry, but his drinking continues. As her star ascends, Norman's descends, much to the delight of several at the studio who didn't care for how he treated them when he was on top. Eventually Norman comes to believe that he is holding his wife back and he commits suicide, but at her first public appearance since his death, while accepting an award, Vicki introduces herself by saying "Hello, this is Mrs. Norman Maine."

• ***A Star Is Born*** (remake). United Artists, 1937. Director: William A. Wellman; screenwriters: Dorothy Parker, Alan Campbell and Robert Carson. Cast: Janet Gaynor (Esther Blodgett/Vicki Lester), Fredric March (Norman Maine), Adolphe Menjou (Oliver Niles), Andy Devine (Danny McGuire), May Robson (Granny), Lionel Stander (Libby), Owen Moore, Elizabeth Jenns, J.C. Nugent, Clara Blandick.

• ***A Star Is Born*** (remake). Warner Bros., 1954. Director: George Cukor; screenwriter: Moss Hart. Cast: Judy Garland (Esther Blodgett/Vicki Lester), James Mason (Norman Maine), Charles Bickford (Oliver Niles), Jack Carson (Libby), Tommy Noonan (Danny McGuire), Lucy Marlow (Lola Lavery), Amanda Blake, Irving Bacon, Hazel Shermet, James Brown, Joan Shawlee, Dub Taylor.

• ***A Star Is Born*** (remake). Warner Bros., 1975. Director: Frank Pierson; screenwriters: John Gregory Dunne, Joan Didion and Frank Pierson. Cast: Barbra Streisand (Esther Hoffman), Kris Kristofferson (John Norman Howard), Gary Busey (Bobby Ritchie), Oliver Clark (Gary Daninger), Vanetta Fields, Clyde King, Marta Heflin, M.G. Kelly, Sally Kirkland, Joanne Linville.

The first handling of the Adela Rogers St. John story was in a George Cukor–directed 1932 film entitled *What Price Hollywood?* starring Constance Bennett as a waitress who becomes a film star with the help of an alcoholic director, Lowell Sherman, who later commits suicide. The 1937 film is still considered the best movie with Hollywood as a background. It won the Academy Award for Best Original Story and for Photography. It also received Oscar nominations for Best Picture, Best Script, Best Director, Best Actress and Best Actor. In the 1954 remake, Judy Garland's top number was "The Man Who Got Away" by Harold Arlen and Ira Gershwin, although she must have felt it was the embarrassing tribute to herself, "Born in a Trunk," so lengthy that one might be forgiven for having forgotten what movie was being watched. Nevertheless, Judy, James Mason and "The Man Who Got Away" received Oscar

Opposite, top: *It's "Lights, Camera, Action" for Fredric March and Janet Gaynor in* A Star Is Born *(United Artists, 1937).* Bottom: *Everybody's ecstatic that Judy Garland is going to be a movie star in the 1954 Warner Bros. remake of* A Star Is Born. *From left to right, Jack Carson, James Mason, Garland and Charles Bickford.*

nominations. Barbra Streisand and Paul Williams' "Evergreen" won an Oscar in 1976. The story was modified to have the setting changed from the movies to the world of pop singers, with Kris Kristofferson on his way down as Barbra climbs the musical ladder of success.

848 Star Trek: The Motion Picture

Based on the television series created by Gene Roddenberry. Story: In the twenty-third century a mysterious entity known as the "Intruder" is on a collision course with Earth. Starfleet Command orders the starship U.S.S. *Enterprise,* skippered by Admiral Kirk, to investigate the matter. When the *Enterprise* encounters the "Intruder" it turns out to be an enormous mechanical organism whose power source is a NASA spacecraft, Voyager 6, launched three centuries earlier to collect data and return its findings to Earth, and that is precisely what the evolved Voyager is trying to do. With the sacrifice of the lives of lovers Commander Willard Decker and beautiful advisor Ilia, Voyager is able to release its findings and terminate itself.

Paramount Pictures, 1979 (original). Director: Robert Wise; screenwriter: Harold Livingston, based on a story by Alan Dean Foster. Cast: William Shatner (Adm. James T. Kirk), Leonard Nimoy (Mr. Spock), De Forest Kelley (Dr. Leonard "Bones" McCoy), Stephen Collins (Cmd. Willard Decker), Persis Khambatta (Ilia), James Doohan (Montgomery "Scotty" Scott), George Takei (Sulu), Nichelle Nichols (Uhura), Walter Koenig (Chekov), Majel Barrett, Grace Lee Whitney, Mark Leonard, Billy Van Zandt.

• ***Star Trek: The Wrath of Khan*** (sequel). Paramount Pictures, 1982. Director: Nicholas Meyer; screenwriter: Jack B. Sowards. Cast: William Shatner (Kirk), Leonard Nimoy (Spock), Ricardo Montalban (Khan), De Forest Kelley, Ike Eisenmann, James Doohan, George Takei, Nichelle Nichols, Walter Koenig.

• ***Star Trek 3: The Search for Spock*** (sequel). Paramount Pictures, 1984. Director: Leonard Nimoy; screenwriter: Harve Bennett. Cast: William Shatner (Kirk), De Forest Kelley (McCoy), James Doohan, Nichelle Nichols, Walter Koenig, Robert Hooks, Leonard Nimoy, George Takei.

Even though the cost of special effects for the first Star Trek movie exceeded that spent for the entire television series, many trekkies were disappointed in the big screen version of their favorite fantasy. It is possible that plenty of money and a lot of time to develop a story took something away from the simple space adventure that captured so much interest in its far-out episodes. In the first sequel, the crew of the *Enterprise* has a run-in with the evil genius Ricardo Montalban. In the next installment, it's discovered that Spock isn't really dead, but has been reborn as a Vulcan child. Well, I'll be a green, pointed-ears alien! In 1986, *Star Trek 4: The Voyage Home,* was released and it has captured some of the charm and wit of the TV shows, as Kirk and Spock find themselves in contemporary San Francisco.

Star Trek 2: The Wrath of Khan *see* **Star Trek: The Motion Picture**

Star Trek 3: The Search for Spock *see* **Star Trek: The Motion Picture**

Star Trek 4: The Voyage Home *see* **Star Trek: The Motion Picture**

849 Star Wars

Based on an original screenplay by George Lucas. Story: In this spectacular space adventure, young Luke Skywalker, "in a galaxy far, far away," sets out to rescue Princess Leia, who has been kidnapped by the Empire's villainous rulers, Grand Moff Tarkin and Darth Vader. Helping and sharing his dangerous adventures are Obi-Wan Kenobi, last of the Jedi Knights, Hans Solo, a cocky mercenary spaceship pilot, his anthropoid sidekick, Chewbacca, and two robots, R2-D2 and C3PO. Although this team succeeds in rescuing Leia and destroying the Empire's enormous battlestation, the *Death Star,* the story isn't over.

Twentieth Century–Fox, 1977 (original). Director and screenwriter: George Lucas. Cast: Mark Hamill (Luke Skywalker), Harrison Ford (Hans Solo), Carrie Fisher (Princess Leia), Peter Cushing (Grand Moff Tarkin), Alec Guinness (Ben Obi-Wan Kenobi), Anthony Daniels (C3PO), Kenny Baker (R2-D2), Peter Mayhew (Chewbacca), David Prowse (Lord Darth Vader), James Earl Jones (voice of Darth Vader), Phil Brown, Shelagh Fraser, Jack Purvis, Alex McCrindle, Eddie Byrne, Drewe Henley.

• ***The Empire Strikes Back*** (sequel). Twentieth Century–Fox, 1980. Director: Irvin Kershner; screenwriter: George Lucas. Cast: Mark Hamill, Harrison Ford, Carrie Fisher, Billy Dee Williams, Alec Guinness, Anthony Daniels, Kenny Baker, Peter Mayhew, David Prowse, James Earl Jones.

• ***Return of the Jedi*** (sequel). Twentieth Century–Fox, 1983. Director: Richard Marquand; screenwriters: Lawrence Kasdan and George Lucas. Cast: Mark Hamill, Harrison Ford, Carrie Fisher, Billy Dee Williams, Anthony Daniels, Peter Mayhew, Kenny Baker, David Prowse, James Earl Jones.

The real stars of these three films are the special effects. Combined, the movies are salutes to the serials of the youth of George Lucas and others like your authors, pleased to find all missed episodes brought together to be seen in single showings. For many the best scene in the three movie series is the intergalactic bar early in the first film, which allowed audiences to know that they were no longer in Kansas. In the first sequel, audiences got more of the same mindless and exhilarating entertainment. In the second sequel, Hamill as Luke Skywalker finally masters the force and then must take on his father, Darth Vader. One movie dedicated to Lucas' fantasy would be enough for most people.

850 Star Witness

Based on a story by Lucien Hubbard. Story: The Leeds family is witness to a battle of rival gangs. They are terrorized into perjuring themselves when followers of a captured gang leader realize that their testimony can send their boss to the electric chair. This includes a brutal beating of the father and the kidnapping of a young son. In the end, Grandfather Summerville is

instrumental in rescuing the boy and forces his way to the stand to testify against the gunman, resulting in the conviction of the headman.

Warner Bros., 1928 (original). Director: William Wellman; screenwriter: Lucien Hubbard. Cast: Walter Huston (D.A. Whitlock), Chic Sale (Grandad Summerville), Frances Starr (Ma Leeds), Grant Mitchell (Pa Leeds), Sally Blane (Sue Leeds), Edward Nugent (Jackie Leeds), Ralph Ince, Dickie Moore, George Ernest.

• ***The Man Who Dared*** (remake). Warner Bros., 1939. Director: Crane Wilbur; screenwriter: Lee Katz. Cast: Charley Grapewin (Grandfather Carter), Henry O'Neill (Mr. Carter), Dickie Jones (Billy Carter), Jane Bryon, Elisabeth Risdon, James McCalion.

Charles (Chic) Sale, as the aging war veteran who refuses to be intimidated by a gang of crooks, is in fine form. However, in the remake, Charley Grapewin plays the old man as something of a senile jerk, so his actions seem less courageous and more lacking in awareness of the real dangers of his actions in rescuing his grandson and telling what he knows in the courtroom.

851 State Fair

Based on the novel by Philip Strong. Story: Iowa farmer and hog raiser Abel Frake, his wife Melissa, daughter Margy and son Wayne eagerly await their annual trip to the State Fair, where Abel hopes his prize hog, Blue Boy, will win a blue ribbon. Melissa has her heart set on winning ribbons for her pickles and mincemeat pie. The younger Frakes hope to find adventure and romance. Before Ma and Pa fulfill their dreams, Margy falls in love with newspaperman Pat Gilbert and Wayne is attracted to trapeze artist Emily Joyce. Wayne proposes marriage to Emily, but the experienced girl suggests that he return home to his childhood sweetheart. Pat, who generally loves 'em and leaves 'em, also proposes marriage to Margy, but she puts him off, but not for long.

Fox Film Corporation, 1933 (original). Director: Henry King; screenwriters: Paul Green and Sonya Levien. Cast: Will Rogers (Abel Frake), Janet Gaynor (Margy Frake), Lew Ayres (Pat Gilbert), Sally Eilers (Emily Joyce), Norman Foster (Wayne Frake), Louise Dresser (Melissa Frake), Frank Craven, Victor Jory, Frank Melton.

• ***State Fair*** (remake). Twentieth Century–Fox, 1945. Director: Walter Lang; screenwriters: Oscar Hammerstein II, Paul Green and Sonya Levien. Cast: Jeanne Crain (Margy Frake), Dana Andrews (Pat Gilbert), Dick Haymes (Wayne Frake), Vivian Blaine (Emily Joyce), Charles Winninger (Abel Frake), Fay Bainter (Melissa Frake), Donald Meek, Frank McHugh, Percy Kilbride, Harry Morgan.

• ***State Fair*** (remake). Twentieth Century–Fox, 1962. Director: Jose Ferrer;

Opposite, top: *Just before the youngsters take off for a night on the midway of the* State Fair *(20th Century–Fox, 1945), they get some advice from Ma and Pa. From left to right: Fay Bainter, Dick Haymes, Jeanne Crain and Charles Winninger.* Bottom: *Here's an All-American farm family in the 1962 20th Century–Fox remake of* State Fair. *From left to right: Tom Ewell, Alice Faye, Pamela Tiffin and Pat Boone.*

screenwriters: Richard Breen, Oscar Hammerstein II, Paul Green and Sonya Levien. Cast: Pat Boone (Wayne Frake), Bobby Darin (Jerry Dundee), Pamela Tiffin (Margie Frake), Ann-Margret (Emily Porter), Tom Ewell (Abel Frake), Alice Faye (Melissa Frake), Wally Cox, David Brandon, Clem Harvey, Robert Foulk.

Each of the three films celebrated Americana as found in small-town life, with each starring a different member of the Frake family. In the original, Will Rogers nicely represents country people, being his usual witty self. Rogers is ably assisted by Janet Gaynor, Louise Dresser and Norman Foster, all of whom are simply delightful, guileless folk, who can be tempted by the sharpies but not completely taken in. Even the hog Blue Boy was adored by the movie-going public, to the extent that his passing was noted by *Time* magazine in 1934.

In the 1945 musical remake, lovely 20-year-old Jeanne Crain as daughter Margy moves front and center, looking very fetching sitting in her window as she sang Richard Rodgers and Oscar Hammerstein II's "It Might As Well Be Spring" (actually, Louanne Hogan supplied the singing for the Academy Award–winning song). Dick Haymes falls for band singer Vivian Blaine, who's married to a man she doesn't love, but this wrinkle is ironed out and the couple are united. Crain completely bowls over ladies' man Andrews, to such a point he's begging to settle down in the country. As in the original, Pa's hog wins Best of Show and Ma's mincemeat, spiked with brandy, is given the blue ribbon by the tipsy judges. This remake, which is even better than the original, also features the songs "It's a Grand Night for Singing," "Isn't It Kinda Fun?" "Our State Fair" and "All I Owe Iowa."

In the third and least successful version of the rustic story, Pat Boone of the white bucks fame is clearly the center of attraction as the Frake's son who meets worldly-wise Ann-Margret at the State Fair, now moved to Texas. In her first film since 1945, Alice Faye is by far and away the class act in the picture, with Boone and Pamela Tiffin none too impressive as the youngsters, and Tom Ewell's hammy performance less enjoyable than that of his hog. Bobby Darin, as Tiffin's romantic interest at the fair, is an untrustworthy wise guy whom Pamela's parents should disapprove of. Besides the hold-over songs "It Might As Well Be Spring," "It's a Grand Night for Singing," etc., Richard Rodgers added "More Than Just a Friend" sung by Ewell, "Willing and Eager" featuring Boone and Ann-Margret, "This Is Heaven" by Darin and "It's the Little Things in Texas" sung by Ewell and Faye.

852 State's Attorney

Based on a screenplay by Gene Fowler and Rowland Brown. Story: Tom Cardigan is a brilliant criminal lawyer who works for mobster Vanny Powers. Circumstances have Cardigan switching from a defense lawyer to first assistant D.A., who sends Vanny to the hangman in a dramatic courtroom scene in which he confesses his own shady past and announces that he is retiring from his position as a final gesture of atonement for his misuse of the law.

RKO, 1932 (original). Director: .George Archainbaud; screenwriters: Gene Fowler and Rowland Brown. Cast: John Barrymore (Tom Cardigan), Helen

Twelvetrees (June Perry), William Boyd (Vanny Powers), Jill Esmond, Mary Duncan, Oscar Apfel.

• ***Criminal Lawyer*** (remake). RKO, 1937. Director: Christy Cabanne; screenwriters: Louis Stevenson, G.V. Atwater and Thomas Lennon. Cast: Lee Tracy (Brandon), Margot Grahame (Madge Carter), Eduardo Ciannelli (Larkin), Erik Rhodes, Betty Lawford, Frank M. Thomas, Wilfrid Lucas, William Stack.

In the '30s, there was considerable movie interest in the activities of lawyers with questionable ethics. All right-thinking people know that even the most despicable criminal and crazed, animallike felon deserve the best defense possible. However, one could wish that the world was not so litigious over matters of questionable appropriateness for settlement in a court. These two films didn't deal with cases for Judge Wopner but had lawyers who were in the back pocket of mobsters, only later to develop consciences and jump to the other side of the court to "burn" their former mentors, and salve their own sense of guilt. Lee Tracy almost makes things credible and Ciannelli is as ever, a magnificent heavy.

853 Stella Dallas

Based on the novel by Olive Higgins Prouty. Story: When his father commits suicide, socialite Stephen Dallas moves to a small town where he marries Stella, a crude-mannered woman far below his social station. The marriage doesn't work out and the couple separate, Stephen returning to New York while Stella stays behind with their daughter, Laurel. Years pass and Stella realizes that she cannot provide the opportunities for sensitive Laurel that her father could. Stella finally agrees to give Stephen a divorce so he can marry Helen Morrison on the condition that a good home be provided for Laurel. At first Laurel refuses to leave her mother, but to force the issue, Stella marries a drunkard, and Laurel consents to live with her father and step-mother. Sometime later, at the marriage of Laurel to charming society lad Richard Grovesnor, Stella stands outside the Morrison home in the rain and watches the ceremony through a window.

Samuel Goldwyn/United Artists, 1925 (original). Silent. Director: Henry King; screenwriter: Frances Marion. Cast: Ronald Colman (Stephen Dallas), Belle Bennett (Stella Dallas), Alice Joyce (Helen Morrison), Jean Hersholt (Ed Munn), Beatrix Pryor (Mrs. Grovesnor), Lois Moran (Laurel Dallas), Douglas Fairbanks, Jr. (Richard Grovesnor), Vera Lewis, Maurice Murphy, Jack Murphy, Newton Hall, Charles Hatten, Robert Gillette, Winston Miller.

• ***Stella Dallas*** (remake). United Artists, 1937. Director: King Vidor; screenwriter: Harry Wagstaff Gribble. Cast: Barbara Stanwyck (Stella Martin Dallas), John Boles (Stephen Dallas), Anne Shirley (Laurel Dallas), Barbara O'Neil (Helen Morrison), Alan Hale (Ed Munn), Marjorie Main (Mrs. Martin), Edmund Elton (Mr. Martin), George Walcott, Gertrude Short, Tim Holt, Nella Walker, Bruce Satterlee, Jimmy Butler.

The Olive Higgins Prouty novel is a real weeper and most critics felt one experience with the story as a movie was enough, but they had not counted on what could be done if talent was gathered together under the supervision of a sensitive director and using good production values. The result is an emotionally satisfying picture which is sentimental without it becoming overly so. Goldwyn's original choices for Stella and Laurel Dallas were Ruth Chatterton and Gladys George, but the producer must have been more than satisfied with Barbara Stanwyck and Anne Shirley, both of whom were nominated for but did not win Academy awards. In both films there is little to like or admire about Stella Dallas, save her constant struggle to see that Laurel comes out alright despite having such an uncouth mother. The role of Stephen Dallas is a difficult one, being so restrictive, and while Ronald Colman rose to the occasion, John Boles finds the part a struggle. It's an A-number-one tearjerker and for those who enjoy a good cry watching a "woman's movie," here's an excuse for really turning on the waterworks.

Step Down to Terror *see* **Shadow of a Doubt**

Step Lively *see* **Room Service**

Step Lively Jeeves *see* **Thank You, Jeeves**

854 The Sting

Based on the screenplay by David S. Ward. Story: It's a delightful period piece about two con men, Henry Gondorff and Johnny Hooker, who to revenge the death of a friend ordered killed by racketeer Doyle Lonnegan, plan an elaborate racehorse sting to hit the latter for a quarter of a million dollars. The scam is complicated but well-pieced together with beautiful bits by assorted con men in on the play, and enough switches and surprises to keep everyone's interest as audiences look forward to seeing if Lonnegan will be taken, before Hooker is either arrested by the feds or assassinated by one of Lonnegan's hired killers.

Universal Pictures, 1973 (original). Director: George Roy Hill; screenwriter: David S. Ward. Cast: Paul Newman (Henry Gondorff), Robert Redford (Johnny Hooker), Robert Shaw (Doyle Lonnegan), Charles Durning (Lt. Snyder), Ray Walston (Singleton), Eileen Brennan (Billie), Harold Gould (Kid Twist), John Hefferman, Dana Elcar, Jack Kehoe, Dimitra Arliss.

• ***The Sting 2*** (sequel). Universal Pictures, 1983. Director: Jeremy Paul Kagan; screenwriter: David S. Ward. Cast: Jackie Gleason (Henry Gondorff), Mac Davis (Johnny Hooker), Oliver Reed (Doyle Lonnegan), Karl Malden, Bert Remsen, Teri Garr.

The Sting won the Academy Award for Best Picture, David S. Ward was a winner for Best Screenplay, George Roy Hill for directing and Marvin Hamlisch for Best Musical Arrangement, featuring the music of Scott Joplin. In addition Robert Surtees and Robert Redford received nominations, the former for best Cinematography and the latter for Best Actor.

The sequel is a boring reprise of the leading characters and the villain of the first piece. Lonnegan learns that he has been taken by Gondorff and Hooker, that they are not dead, and he wants revenge. With the help of Teri Garr who is the con-woman daughter of Jackie Gleason, Mac Davis is able to work another scam with Karl Malden an additional victim—but don't feel sorry for him, he deserves it, being a mean and rotten crook, just as bad as Oliver Reed as Lonnegan. When they put in the second team in making the sequel, they doomed the film to a bit of effectively made ho-hum.

The Sting 2 *see* **The Sting**

Stolen Hours *see* **Dark Victory**

855 A Stolen Life

Based on the novel by Karel J. Benes. Story: Twin sisters Sylvina and Martina are staying at an Alpine resort with their father and aunt. Sylvina is lighthearted and gay; Martina is more serious. While climbing a mountain, Martina meets and is smitten with Alan McKenzie. Later he encounters Sylvina and thinking she is Martina, proposes marriage to the wrong girl. Martina sacrifices herself, keeps her silence and the marriage takes place. While McKenzie is away on a mountain-climbing expedition, the two sisters go for a sail, the boat capsizes and Sylvina is drowned, and Martina is taken for her. After some hesitancy, Martina decides to assume her sister's identity, only to discover that Sylvina had been unfaithful to McKenzie while he was away and he knew of it. Alan tells Martina, whom he believes to be his wife, that he feels a divorce is the best thing. But finally the truth comes out.

Orion Productions/Paramount Pictures, Great Britain, 1939 (original). Director: Paul Czinner; screenwriter: Margaret Kennedy. Cast: Wilfred Lawson (Thomas Lawrence), Elisabeth Bergner (Sylvina/Martina), Mabel Terry Lewis (Aunt Helen), Michael Redgrave (Alan McKenzie), Richard Ainley, Kenneth Buckley, Pierre Jouvenet, Stella Arbenina.

• ***A Stolen Life*** (remake). Warner Bros., 1946. Director: Curtis Bernhardt; screenwriter: Margaret Buell Wilder. Cast: Bette Davis (Kate and Patricia Bosworth), Glenn Ford (Bill Emerson), Dane Clark (Karnok), Walter Brennan (Eben Folger), Charlie Ruggles (Freddie Linley), Bruce Bennett, Peggy Knudsen, Esther Dale, Joan Winfield, Clara Blandick.

The remake placed the setting for this actress showcase in New England, with Bette Davis appearing as a sweet, sincere, artistic girl and her man-crazy, bad-tempered sister. When the latter, who by trickery has married the man the former loves, drowns in a boating accident, the sweet girl assumes her sister's identity. Her deception doesn't turn out satisfactorily and only when her identity is straightened out does she find happiness. Both pictures move slowly, developing the character differences of the two sisters which will prove so important to the plot in the more dramatic second half. Both Bergner and Davis acquit themselves nicely, but one must admit the story is just short of ridiculous—maybe not even short.

Stop, Look and Listen *see* **The Family Upstairs**

Stop, You're Killing Me *see* **A Slight Case of Murder**

856 The Storm

Based on the play *Men Without Skirts* by Langdon McCormack. Story: Three people are snowbound in a log cabin in the Canadian wild. They are a woodsman, his friend from the city and a stranded French girl. Besides the inevitable romantic triangle, the three must survive avalanches, snow drifts, pounding rapids, blinding storms, howling gales and a spectacular forest fire. The woodsman gets the girl.

Universal Pictures, 1922 (original). Director: Reginald Barker; screenwriter: J.C. Hawks. Cast: House Peters (Burr Winston), Matt Moore (Dave Stewart), Virginia Valli (Manette Fachard).

• ***The Storm*** (remake). Universal Pictures, 1930. Director: William Wyler; screenwriters: Wells Root and Charles A. Loue. Cast: Lupe Velez (Manette Fachard), William "Stage" Boyd (Burr Winston), Paul Cavanaugh (Dave Stewart), Alphonse Ethier, Ernie Adams, Tom London, Nick Thompson, Erin La Bissoniere.

The appeal of these movies was not the romantic triangle but the way the studio was able to demonstrate nature's wrath. The performances were adequate, the screenplays workmanlike and the direction enthusiastic. The 1938 Universal picture *The Storm* has no relation to the earlier two. It deals with a storm at sea.

Storm Over the Nile *see* **The Four Feathers**

The Story of Mankind *see* **Cleopatra**

The Story of Robin Hood *see* **Robin Hood**

857 The Story of Temple Drake

Based on the novel *Sanctuary* by William Faulkner. Story: Temple Drake, neurotic granddaughter of a Southern judge, rejects the marriage proposal of a young attorney, becomes involved with a bootleg gang, is raped by sadistic hood Trigger, finds she likes the rough stuff, and allows him to set her up in a brothel in the big city. Eventually, she kills her gangster-lover with his own gun, stands trial and finally comes to repent the degradation to which she had fallen.

Paramount Pictures, 1933 (original). Director: Stephen Roberts; screenwriter: Oliver H.P. Garrett. Cast: Miriam Hopkins (Temple Drake), Jack LaRue (Trigger), William Gargan (Stephen Benbow), William Collier, Jr. (Toddy Gowan), Irving Pichel (Lee Goodwin), Sir Guy Standing (Judge Drake), Elizabeth Patterson, Florence Eldridge, James Eagles, Harlan E. Knight, James Mason, Jobyna Howland.

• ***Sanctuary*** (remake). Twentieth Century–Fox, 1961. Director: Tony Richardson; screenwriter: James Poe. Cast: Lee Remick (Temple Drake), Yves Montand (Candy Man), Bradford Dillman (Gowan Stevens), Harry Townes (Ira

Bobbitt), Odetta (Nancy Mannigoc), Howard St. John (Governor Drake), Jean Carson, Reta Shaw, Strother Martin, William Mims, Marge Redmond, Jean Bartel.

When Paramount purchased the movie rights to Faulkner's notorious 1931 novel of Southern decadence, sexual bondage, rape and murder, the Hays Office advised the studio that no reference to "Sanctuary" would be permitted in bringing the story to the screen. Miriam Hopkins, who admitted she enjoyed portraying women like Temple Drake, gave a first rate performance in a role of a woman for whom it was not possible to have any sympathy, because she reveled in her degradation. Jack LaRue was brought in when George Raft refused the part, and gave perhaps the best performance of his career as the sadistic gangster who gives Hopkins the kind of treatment she craves.

The remake incorporated not only Faulkner's *Sanctuary* but also its sequel, *Requiem for a Nun*, and stuck closer to the Mississippi author's intent and story. Temple, a flirtatious college girl, is taken to a backwoods still by young Gowan Stevens. There she is brutally raped by Cajun bootlegger Candy Man. The next morning she willingly submits to some more of this cruel man's lovemaking and agrees to live with him in a New Orleans brothel. She loves her life until Candy Man is reported killed in an automobile accident and she is forced to go home, taking a brothel maid, Nancy, with her. She marries Gowan and has a child, but is bored with her life and longs for the old days in New Orleans. Suddenly Candy Man reappears and Temple is ready to abandon everything to be with him. At this point, in an effort to bring Temple to her senses, Nancy smothers to death Temple's child. Nancy is condemned to death despite Temple's explanation of everything to her father, the governor. This version, despite sticking closer to Faulkner's novels, didn't work as well as the earlier picture and the acting was definitely inferior.

The Story of the Compte of Monte Cristo *see* **The Count of Monte Cristo**

Straight Is the Way *see* **Four Walls**

Strange Confession *see* **The Man Who Reclaimed His Head**

Strange Conquest *see* **The Crime of Dr. Hallet**

858 The Stranger

Based on the novel *The First and the Last* by John Galsworthy. Story: A poor nameless scrubman assumes the blame when Larry Darrant kills ex-convict Jim Wallenn, who had attacked Larry's fiancée, Peggy Bowlin, on the eve of their wedding. This stranger whom Peggy had befriended refuses to defend himself at his trial and is sentenced to death by hanging. Durrant marries Peggy, who had witnessed the killing, and intends to live life to the fullest with her until the time of the man's execution and then give himself up. While standing on the scaffold, awaiting the execution, the stranger has a heart attack and dies a natural death, just as Larry is making his way forward to confess. The timeliness and nature of the poor unfortunate's death saves Larry's family from a scandal and clears his conscience enough to allow him to look forward to a happy future with Peggy.

Famous Players–Lasky/Paramount Pictures, 1924 (original). Silent. Director: Joseph Henabery; screenwriter: Edfrid Bingham. Cast: Betty Compson (Peggy Bowlin), Richard Dix (Larry Darrant), Lewis Stone (Keith Darrant), Tully Marshall (the Stranger), Robert Schable, Mary Jane Irving, Frank Nelson, Marian Skinner.

• ***Twenty-One Days*** (remake). Columbia Pictures, Great Britain, 1939. Director: Basil Dean; screenwriter: Graham Greene. Cast: Vivien Leigh (Wanda), Leslie Banks (Keith Darrant), Laurence Olivier (Larry Darrant), Francis L. Sullivan (Mander), Hay Petrie (John Evan), Esme Percy (Henry Wallenn), Robert Newton (Tolly), Victor Rietti, Morris Harvey, Meinhart Maur.

These melodramas have a happy ending for everyone except the innocent man who must have suffered the agony of the condemned and then had a convenient heart attack that made it unnecessary for the real slayer to confess his crime. Somehow the films seem to be saying that the fact the deceased was a bounder, his killing was in self-defense, and the stranger was no one of importance; the guilty party had a right to act as he did. The appeal of the performances in the two films does not outweigh this unacceptable position.

859 Strangers of the Night

Based on the play *Captain Applejack: An Arabian Night's Adventure* by Walter Hackett. Story: Ambrose Applejohn, an English gentleman seeking adventure, finds it when burglars arrive at his estate to steal a treasure hidden by his pirate ancestor, Captain Applejack. Temporarily getting the better of the robbers, he falls asleep and dreams of his ancestor's adventures and on awakening, filled with new courage, he completely thwarts the crooks. He then finds himself greatly admired by his aunt's ward, Poppy Faire.

MGM, 1923 (original). Silent. Director: Fred Niblo; screenwriter: Bess Meredyth. Cast: Matt Moore (Ambrose Applejohn), Enid Bennett (Poppy Faire), Barbara La Marr (Anna Valeska), Robert McKim, Mathilde Brundage, Emily Fitzroy, Otto Hoffman.

• ***Captain Applejack*** (remake). Warner Bros., 1931. Director: Hobart Henley; screenwriter: Maude Fulton. Cast: John Halliday (Ambrose), Mary Brian (Poppy), Kay Strozzi (Anna), Louise Closser Hale, Alec B. Francis, Arthur Edmund Carewe.

The Walter Hackett play was popular and these two adaptations did alright at the box office, but it's unlikely that they will show up anywhere for viewing today. The acting of the two casts of performers was not inspiring. Both John Halliday and Mary Brian would find better vehicles for their talents in the years to come.

860 Strangers on a Train

Based on the novel by Patricia Highsmith. Story: Tennis star Guy Haines encounters Bruno Antony while riding a train. Bruno seems to know a bit too much about Guy's life, such as his unhappy marriage to Miriam and his love for Anne, daughter of Senator Morton. In what Guy believes is just talk from his strange traveling companion, Bruno suggests that they trade murders. Bruno will kill Guy's wife and Guy will kill Bruno's hated father. The theory being since neither has a motive, they will never be suspected. Bruno leaves the train, believing that the two men have a deal and promptly goes about strangling Miriam at an amusement park. When Guy learns of his wife's death, the thought of what Bruno proposed comes back to him as he is questioned by the police. Seems he can't prove where he was at the time of the murder. Bruno shows up a little later, put out that Guy hasn't kept his part of the bargain. When Bruno finally decides that Guy will not kill his father, he plans to shift the blame for Miriam's death onto Guy by planting the latter's cigarette lighter at the scene of the crime. Things don't go according to Bruno's plan, and he and Guy fight on an out of control merry-go-round, resulting in Bruno's death and the clearing of Guy from further suspicion.

Warner Bros., 1951 (original). Director: Alfred Hitchcock; screenwriters: Raymond Chandler and Czenzi Ormonde. Cast: Farley Granger (Guy Haines), Ruth Roman (Anne Morton), Robert Walker (Bruno Antony), Leo G. Carroll (Senator Morton), Patricia Hitchcock (Barbara Morton), Laura Elliott (Miriam Haines), Marion Lorne, Jonathan Hale, Howard St. John, John Brown, Norma Varden, Robert Gist.

• ***Once You Kiss a Stranger*** (remake). Warner Bros., 1969. Director: Robert Sparr; screenwriters: Frank Tarloff and Norman Katlov. Cast: Paul Burke (Jerry), Carol Lynley (Diana), Martha Hyer (Lee), Peter Lind Hayes (Peter), Philip Carey (Mike), Stephen McNally (Lt. Gavin), Whit Bissel (Dr. Haggis), Elaine Devry, Kathryn Givney, Jim Raymond, George Fenneman, Orville Sherman.

The performances in the Hitchcock movie were of mixed quality with Farley Granger, Robert Walker and Laura Elliott being top notch, while Ruth Roman and some of the supporting players might have tried a bit harder. Nevertheless, the suspense is marvelous. The remake, with the sex of Bruno being changed, is only so-so, partially because the master is not directing and partially because Carol Lynley can't portray a mad person like Robert Walker could. She proposes to a drunken pro golfer, Paul Burke, she has seduced that they exchange murders. She'll take care of his rival Philip Carey and Burke will rid her of psychiatrist Whit Bissel. She carries through on her part and is outraged when Burke reneges. After an attempt by Lynley to implicate Burke in the death of Carey fails, Carol is arrested and put away as a mental case.

The Strawberry Blonde *see* **One Sunday Afternoon**

861 Street Girl

Based on the story *The Viennese Charmer* by William Carey Wonderly. Story: On the way home from a shabby New York restaurant where they play jazz, the Four Seasons (Mike Fall, Joe Spring, Pete Summer and Happy Winters) come across a masher annoying a pretty blonde. Mike saves her and she introduces herself as a destitute Hungarian violinist, named Freddie Joyzelle. Mike persuades his partners to let her stay with them and join their group. When they are fired from their job, she finds them a better one with a Hungarian restaurant. One night Prince Nicholas of Aragon pays the club a visit and makes Mike jealous by kissing Freddie after she plays a song for him. Due to the prince's patronage, the club and the group becomes famous and the owner plans to build a new one to accommodate the crowds. Mike, still unhappy, quits, but the prince reunites Mike and Freddie and everyone is happy.

RKO, 1929 (original). Director: Wesley Ruggles; screenwriter: Jane Murfin. Cast: Betty Compson (Freddie Joyzelle), John Harron (Mike Fall), Ned Sparks (Happy Winter), Jack Oakie (Joe Spring), Guy Buccola (Pete Summer), Ivan Lebedeff (Prince Nicholas), Joseph Cawthorn, Eddie Kane.

• ***That Girl from Paris*** (remake). RKO, 1937. Director: Leigh Jason; screenwriters: P.J. Wolfson and Dorothy Yost. Cast: Lily Pons (Nikki Monet), Gene Raymond (Windy MacLean), Jack Oakie (Whammo), Herman Bing (Hammacher), Lucille Ball (Claire), Mischa Auer (Butch), Frank Jenks, Patricia Wilder, Vinton Hayworth, Willard Robertson.

• ***Four Jacks and a Jill*** (remake). RKO, 1941. Director: Jack Hively; screenwriters: John Twist and Monte Brice. Cast: Ray Bolger (Nifty), Anne Shirley (Nine), June Havoc (Opal), Desi Arnaz (Steve), Jack Durant (the Noodle), Eddie Foy, Jr. (Happy), Fritz Feld, Henry Daniell, Jack Briggs, William Blees.

Street Girl was the first "official" RKO production. Its songs included "My Dream Melody" and "Huggable and Sweet" by Oscar Levant and Sidney Claire. The first remake was meant to be a showcase for the talents of Lily Pons and she was mostly delightful singing "Una Voce Poco Fa" from Rossini's "The Barber of Seville" and "Seal It with a Kiss" by Arthur Schwartz and Edward Heyman. Jack Oakie supplies most of the comedy including a dandy closing sequence. Another nice bit has Pons picking out "The Blue Danube" which the boys can't play so they vamp til ready creating a pleasant syncopated version of the classic Strauss piece. The final entry has Anne Shirley being picked by Ray Bolger to replace his group's singer when the incumbent, June Havoc, retires at the insistence of her gangster boyfriend. Complications arise in the form of taxi driver Desi Arnaz who masquerades as a fugitive king. Musical numbers include "I'm in Good Shape for the Shape I'm In" and "Boogie Woogie Conga" by Mort Greene and Harry Revel.

862 Street of Chance

Based on the story by Oliver H.P. Garrett. Story: New York gambler John Marsden is devoted to his wife, Alma, and his younger brother "Babe." He gives the latter a $10,000 wedding gift on the condition that Babe not gamble. Alma insists that John take his winnings, leave New York and give up his life as a gambler. He agrees but when he discovers that his brother insists on gambling and is winning, John sits in the game to teach his brother a lesson. It's not easy to do as Babe continues to win. Desperate, John cheats, is caught at it by another gambler and is mortally wounded.

Paramount Pictures, 1930 (original). Director: John Cromwell; screenwriter: Howard Estabrook. Cast: William Powell (John B. Marsden/"Natural" Davis), Jean Arthur (Judith Marsden), Kay Francis (Alma Marsden), Regis Toomey ("Babe" Marsden), Stanley Fields, Brooks Benedict, Betty Francisco, John Risso.

• ***Now I'll Tell*** (remake). Fox Film Corporation, 1934. Director: Edwin Burke; screenwriters: Edwin Burke and Ernest Palmer, based on a story by Mrs. Arnold Rothstein. Cast: Spencer Tracy (Murray Golden), Helen Twelvetrees (Virginia), Alice Faye (Peggy), Robert Gleckler (Mositer), Henry O'Neill, Hobart Cavanaugh, G.P. Huntley, Jr., Shirley Temple.

• ***Her Husband Lies*** (remake). Paramount Pictures, 1937. Director: Edward Ludwig; screenwriters: Wallace Smith and Eve Greene. Cast: Gail Patrick (Natalie Martin), Ricardo Cortez (Spade Martin), Akim Tamiroff (Bullock), Tom Brown (Chick), Louis Calhern (Sordoni), June Martel, Dorothy Peterson, Ralf Harolde, Adrian Morris, Ray Walker, Jack LaRue.

The three films are supposedly based on the exploits of infamous gambler Arnold Rothstein, a nice guy devoted to his wife and family but not above improving his odds of winning by fixing things (including perhaps baseball's 1919 World Series—although this is not alluded to in these movies). The first film in which king of the gamblers William Powell's supremacy is challenged by his younger brother, Regis Toomey, made Powell a top star. In the second and totally different feature, Tracy's fling as the gambler also enhanced his rapidly growing star, but by 1937 the magic must have worn off, because the role in the straight remake of the 1930 picture did little for the career of Ricardo Cortez. Shirley Temple's role in *Now I'll Tell* didn't change her then unknown status, but it did bring Alice Faye front and center as one who would surely be heard from again.

863 The Street with No Name

Based on an original screenplay by Harry Kleiner. Story: This documentary-like movie pegs itself as part of the crusade against teenage punks who grow up to be full-fledged mobsters. Menacing Alec Stiles leads the gang of youngsters with Cordell, an all–American boy, joining the gang. He's really an FBI agent sent to infiltrate and get evidence against Stiles and the other modern-day Fagins. In the finale, the cops and the hoods shoot it out in a factory, with the good guys naturally winning.

Twentieth Century–Fox, 1948. Director: William Keighley; screenwriter: Harry Kleiner. Cast: Mark Stevens (Cordell), Richard Widmark (Alec Stiles), Lloyd Nolan (Inspector Briggs), Barbara Lawrence (Judy), Ed Begley, Donald Buka, Joseph Pevney, John McIntire, Walter Grenza, Howard Smith.

• ***House of Bamboo*** (remake). Twentieth Century–Fox, 1955. Director: Samuel Fuller; screenwriters: Fuller and Harry Kleiner. Cast: Robert Ryan (Sandy Dawson), Robert Stack (Eddie Spanier), Shirley Yamaguchi (Mariko), Cameron Mitchell (Griff), Brad Dexter (Capt. Hanson), Sessue Hayakawa (Inspector Kita), Biff Elliot, Sandra Giglio, Elko Hanabusa, Harry Carey, Peter Gray, DeForest Kelley.

Richard Widmark was reprising his Johnny Udo character from *Kiss of Death* of the previous year and Lloyd Nolan his role as Inspector Briggs of *The House on 92nd Street* (1945). The remake is set in Tokyo with Robert Stack as an undercover military policeman out to find the murderer of a GI and help American and Japanese authorities break up a gang of American gangsters headed by personable, suave and psychotic Robert Ryan. This routine crime melodrama is not worth a permanent place in one's library of films recorded from the TV with a VCR but certainly worth a look before the tape is put to better use.

864 Strictly Dishonorable

Based on the play by Preston Sturges. Story: Count Di Ruva, Gus to his friends, a philandering and suave Italian singer, falls in love with petite southern belle Isabelle Parry one night at a speakeasy. Even though Isabelle has a fiancé, inebriated Henry Greene, she returns the singer's affection, even when he announces that his intentions are "strictly dishonorable."

Universal Pictures, 1931 (original). Director: John M. Stahl; screenwriter: Gladys Lehman. Cast: Paul Lukas (Count Di Ruva—Gus), Sidney Fox (Isabelle Parry), Lewis Stone (Judge Dempsey), George Meeker (Henry Greene), William Ricciardi, Sidney Toler, Samuel Bonello, Carlo Schipa, Natalie Moorhead.

• ***Strictly Dishonorable*** (remake). MGM, 1951. Director and screenwriter: Melvin Frank and Norman Panama. Cast: Ezio Pinza (Augustino Caraffa), Janet Leigh (Isabelle Parry), Millard Mitchell (Bill Dempsey), Gale Robbins (Marie Donnelly), Maria Palmer, Esther Minciotti, Silvo Minciotti, Arthur Franz.

Paul Lukas gave an engaging performance as the singer in this racy and humorous story, but Lewis Stone ran off with the acting honors as a former judge who likes his liquor, giving an impressive and amusing performance. In the remake of the Preston Sturges play, Ezio Pinza is an opera star, also famous for his amours, during the days of Prohibition. Into his life pops lovely Janet Leigh, a wide-eyed innocent miss from Mississippi who has long admired the great star. The two enter into a marriage of convenience, both quite willing to make it more than that, but first Pinza must deal with a breach-of-promise suit brought by a countess, played by Maria Palmer. Besides some operatic arias which Pinza plays for laughs, he sings "Everything I Have Is Yours." For those who look for such things, there is a movie within this movie, as a scene is shown from the 1929 film *A Woman of Affairs* starring Greta Garbo and John Gilbert. Despite a generally good performance by Pinza in this and in *Mr. Imperium,* the public showed little interest in the opera star's talents.

Strictly Modern *see* **Cousin Kate**

Strictly Unconventional *see* **The Circle**

Stronger Than Desire *see* **Evelyn Prentice**

The Student Prince *see* **The Student Prince of Heidleberg**

865 The Student Prince of Heidelberg

Based on the novel *Alt Heidèlberg* by Wilhelm Meyer-Forster and the operetta by Dorothy Donnelly and Sigmund Romberg. Story: Crown Prince Karl Heinrich, nephew of the king of a small European country, attends the University of Heidelberg, and falls in love with Kathi, the neice of the owner of the inn where he and his tutor, Dr. Juttner, have taken rooms. His happiness is shattered when his uncle dies and he must return home to assume the throne and marry an ugly princess. Lonely and still in love, he returns to Heidelberg for a visit and finds that everything has changed. His former fellow students and friends now treat him with deference, with only Kathi still the same. After a brief reunion with his beloved he returns to his fiancée, realizing that his duties take preference over his personal happiness.

• ***The Student Prince of Heidelberg*** (remake). MGM, 1927. Silent. Director: Ernst Lubitsch; screenwriter: Hans Kraly. Cast: Ramon Novarro (Prince Karl Heinrich), Norma Shearer (Kathi), Jean Hersholt (Dr. Juttner), Gustav von Seyffertitz (King Karl VII), Philippe De Lacy, Edgar Norton, Bobby Mack, Edward Connelly, Otis Harlan, John S. Peters.

• ***The Student Prince*** (remake). MGM, 1954. Director: Richard Thorpe; screenwriters: William Ludwig and Sonia Levien. Cast: Edmund Purdom (Prince Karl), Ann Blyth (Kathi), Edmund Gwenn (Dr. Juttner), Louis Calhern (King Karl), John Williams, S.Z. Sakall, John Ericson, Betta St. John, Evelyn Varden.

Without music, it's a rather heavy story and less fascinating than many others which have had similiar themes of a member of royalty choosing duty over love. Not everyone can be King Edward of England. The story has also been filmed in 1915 and 1916 in the United States as *Old Heidelberg,* in Germany in 1923 and 1926 as *The Student Prince* and in 1959 as *Old Heidelberg.* A story very much like it was filmed in Great Britain in 1935 under the title *The Student's Romance* with Patric Knowles, Mackenzie Ward and Carol Goodner.

In the 1954 picture, Mario Lanza had been cast to portray Prince Karl, but his weight had ballooned too much to make him convincing as a romantic lead. Dull Edmund Purdom was chosen to give his fine physique to the cause with Lanza supplying the voice. Among the Romberg songs that enlivened the uneven production were "Deep in My Heart," "The Drinking Song," "Golden Days" and "Serenade." The music was lovely, the movie was so-so. With all due respect to the charm of Ann Blyth, it must be pointed out that Betta St. John, to whom Purdom is bethrothed, could never be described as ugly.

The Student's Romance *see* **The Student Prince of Heidelberg**

866 A Study in Scarlet

Based on the story by Arthur Conan Doyle. Story: It appears that one member of a secret crime ring is eliminating the others one-by-one to cut down the final split of their loot. There are enough murders to satisfy even the most bloodthirsty and all the characters, save Holmes and Watson, look and act guilty.

Samuelson Film Manufacturing Company, Ltd., England, 1914 (original). Silent. Cast: James Bragington (Sherlock Holmes).

• ***A Study in Scarlet*** (remake). Universal Pictures, 1914. Silent. Cast: Francis Ford (Sherlock Holmes).

• ***A Study in Scarlet*** (remake). World-Wide Pictures, 1933. Director: Edwin L. Marin; screenwriter: Robert Florey. Cast: Reginald Owen (Sherlock Holmes), Warburton Gamble (Dr. Watson), J.M. Kerrigan (Jabez Wilson), Allan Dinehart (Thaddeus Merrydew), John Warburton (John Stanford), June Clyde (Eileen Forrester), Anna May Wong (Mrs. Pyke), Alan Mowbray (Inspector LeStrade), Doris Lloyd, Billy Bevan, Leila Bennett, Cecil Reynolds, Tetsu Komai, Halliwell Hobbes, Tempe Pigott, Wyndham Standing.

We can't say much about the two silent films, except to note that Frances Ford is the brother of director John Ford and as a young man was quite a mantinee idol. The 1933 movie has a definite English look to it, although it is an American production. In this film, Owen as Holmes dropped some of the once familiar trappings of the master detective, such as the deerslayer hat and his magnifying glass. Rathbone later would pick these up again, at least in the period pieces.

A Study in Scarlet *see* **The Lodger** *and* **Sherlock Holmes**

867 Submarine D-1

Based on a story by Frank Wead. Story: It's the documentary-like presentation of life aboard a submarine, with a lot of time spent detailing the technical phases of the operation of the underwater vessels. The story is of little importance, with sailors Butch Rogers and Sock McGillis vying for the affection of Ann Sawyer when ashore, but waving the flag rather effectively when aboard the sub.

Warner Bros., 1937 (original). Director: Lloyd Bacon; screenwriters: Frank Wead, Warren Duff and Lawrence Kimble. Cast: Pat O'Brien (Butch Rogers), George Brent (Lt. Cmdr. Matthews), Wayne Morris (Sock McGillis), Frank McHugh (Lucky), Doris Weston (Ann Sawyer), Ronald Reagan (Paul), Henry O'Neill, Dennie Moore, Veda Ann Borg, Regis Toomey, Broderick Crawford.

• ***Dive Bomber*** (remake). Warner Bros., 1941. Director: Michael Curtiz; screenwriters: Frank Wead and Robert Buckner. Cast: Errol Flynn (Doug Lee), Fred MacMurray (Joe Blake), Ralph Bellamy (Dr. Lance Rogers), Regis Toomey (Tim Griffin), Herbert Anderson (Chubby), Louis Jean Heydt, Craig Stevens, Robert Armstrong, Allen Jenkins, Addison Richards.

These films served to satisfy the public's curiosity about the country's military preparedness as the rest of the world went to war. In the first, although the sub was silent running, it had the best lines. If anything the horseplay of sailors like O'Brien, Morris and McHugh got in the way of the real story, the operation of the submarine. The second film stressed the importance of flight surgeons in devising medical research to keep pilots in the best of shape for their strenuous duties. Flynn is a naval doctor who loses Louis Jean Heydt on the operating table and incurs the enmity of the lad's friends, Fred MacMurray and Regis Toomey. To get first-hand information of the power-dive blackout that doomed Heydt, Flynn enrolls for a flying course at the U.S. Naval Station at San Diego where MacMurray is the flight commander and Toomey, his aide. The animosity is played up for awhile until it is dropped for the good of the service as Flynn and his superior, Ralph Bellamy, make important progress in stratosphere reactions of pilots and devices for their protection. As in the first film, the story of the particular branch of the service and how it functions is of far greater interest than the modest story.

Sudden Impact *see* **Dirty Harry**

Summer Holiday *see* **Ah, Wilderness**

Summer Love *see* **Rock, Pretty Baby**

Summer Magic *see* **Mother Carey's Chickens**

868 Summer of '42

Based on an original screenplay by Herman Rauscher. Story: It is the simple and touching story of the sexual awakenings of three adolescent boys on Nantucket during the summer of 1942. One, Hermie, becomes infatuated with Dorothy, a beautiful young woman, whose husband is away at war. When she learns that he has been killed, her anguish leads her to take him to her bed for comfort.

Warner Bros., 1971 (original). Director: Robert Mulligan; screenwriter: Herman Rauscher. Cast: Gary Grimes (Hermie), Jennifer O'Neill (Dorothy), Jerry Houser (Oscy), Oliver Conant (Benjie), Katherine Allentuck (Aggie), Christopher Norris, Lou Frizzell, Walter Scott.

• ***Class of '44*** (sequel). Warner Bros., 1973. Director: Paul Bogart; screenwriter: Herman Rauscher. Cast: Gary Grimes (Hermie), Jerry Houser (Oscy), Oliver Conant (Benjie), William Atherton (Fraternity President), Sam Bottoms (Marty), Deborah Winters (Julie), Joe Ponazecki, Murray Westgate.

The first film beautifully caught the feeling for the period and the way that boys of the era behaved. The attempt to recapture the magic in the sequel was not completely successful. Although the film was good, the sexual innocence of Hermie could no longer be a topic and his further exploitations seemed more selfish than giving as was the case in the original.

The Sun Shines Bright *see* **Judge Priest**

869 Superfly

Based on a screenplay by Phillip Fenty. Story: A drug-pusher named Priest plans one last big killing before going straight but discovers quitting is easier said than done in this well-made film.

Warner Bros., 1972. Director: Gordon Parks, Jr.; screenwriter: Phillip Fenty. Cast: Ron O'Neal (Priest), Carl Lee (Eddie), Shelia Frazier (Georgia), Julius W. Harris (Scatter), Charles McGregor (Fat Freddie), Nate Adams, Polly Niles, Yvonne Delaine, Henry Shapiro, Jim Richardson.

• ***Superfly T.N.T.*** (sequel). Paramount Pictures, 1973. Director: Ron O'Neal; screenwriter: Alex Haley, Ron O'Neal and Sig Shore. Cast: Ron O'Neal (Priest), Roscoe Lee Browne (Dr. Lamine Sonko), Sheila Frazier (Georgia), Robert Guillaume (Jordon Gaines), Jacques Sernas (Matty Smith), William Berger (Lefevre), Roy Bolserm, Silvio Nardo, Olga Bisera, Rik Boyd.

The first movie does seem to be glorifying drug pushers and despite the fact that it has its comical and exciting moments, this makes it rather hard to find much good in the tedious story line. In the inferior sequel, Ron O'Neal becomes mixed up in foreign politics and has successfully quit the drug racket. Now he's running guns.

Superfly T.N.T. *see* **Superfly**

870 Superman

Based on the comic strip characters created by Jerry Siegel and Joe Schuster. Story: According to the opening of each *Superman* radio show, the super hero who first appeared in 1938 in Action Comics is "a strange visitor from another planet who came to Earth with powers and abilities far beyond those of mortal men. Superman, who can change the course of mighty rivers, bend steel in his bare hands; and who, disguised as Clark Kent, mild-mannered reporter for a great metropolitan newspaper, fights a never ending battle for truth, justice and the American way." As a baby, Superman had been sent from his home planet Krypton, on a collision course with its own sun, by his father Jor-El. He lands on Earth, millions of miles away, near Smallville, and is raised as their own son by Martha and John Kent. When he grows up, he moves to Metropolis, and posing as Clark Kent, gets a job as a reporter with *The Daily Planet*. This then is his base for fighting crime and any other threat to "truth, justice and the American way."

• ***Superman*** (remake). Warner Bros., 1978. Director: Richard Donner; screenwriters: Mario Puzo, David Newman, Leslie Newman and Robert Benton. Cast: Christopher Reeve (Superman/Clark Kent), Marlon Brando (Jor-El), Gene Hackman (Lex Luthor), Ned Beatty (Otis), Jackie Cooper (Perry White), Glenn Ford (John Kent), Phyllis Baxter (Martha Kent), Margot Kidder (Lois Lane), Valerie Perrine (Eve Terchmacher), Trevor Howard, Jack O'Halloran, Maria Schell, Terence Stamp, Susannah York, Jeff East, Harry Andrews, Sarah Douglas, Lee Quigley, Marc McClure, Aaron Smolinski.

• ***Superman 2*** (sequel). Warner Bros., 1980. Director: Richard Lester; screenwriters: Mario Puzo, David Newman and Leslie Newman. Cast: Christopher Reeve (Superman/Clark Kent), Gene Hackman (Lex Luthor), Ned Beatty (Otis), Jackie Cooper (Perry White), Sarah Douglas (Ursa), Margot Kidder (Lois Lane), Valerie Perrine (Eve), Terence Stamp (General Zod), Jack O'Halloran (Non), E.G. Marshall, Susannah York, Mark McClure.

Columbia Pictures produced two Superman serials, the first consisting of 15 episodes in 1948 with Kirk Alyn as Superman, Noel Neill as Lois Lane and Tommy Bond as Jimmy Olsen. The second serial, released in 1950 under the name *Atom Man vs. Superman,* consisted of 15 episodes and once again starred Kirk Alyn as the super hero. The Warner Bros. Superman series starred a pleasant enough Christopher Reeve and allowed the Man of Steel to have a bit of sex with Lois Lane in the 1980 remake. In 1983, the studio brought out *Superman 3* in which computer expert Richard Pryor manufactures some synthetic Kryptonite that warps Superman's personality, but he recovers in time to fight it out with his resourceful enemies, Robert Vaughn and Annie Ross, matching his strength against their supposedly indestructible and unbeatable computer. In *Superman 4* (1987), the Man of Steel wishes to put an end to the threat of a nuclear arms race. There's nothing worse that a comic book character who takes himself too seriously.

Superman 2 ***see*** **Superman**

Superman 3 ***see*** **Superman**

Superman 4 ***see*** **Superman**

Svengali ***see*** **Trilby**

871 Swamp Water

Based on a story by Vernon Bell. Story: Tom Keefer hides out in a swamp after escaping hanging for a murder. There he meets Ben, whom he convinces of his innocence. They begin a fur-trapping partnership, with Tom's share to go to his daughter, Julie. But Ben's girlfriend Mabel catches on to what's up and in a jealous rage, because of Ben's developing interest in Julie, gives the secret away. Ben refuses to tell the whereabouts of Tom. Instead he forces the man whose testimony convicted Tom to confess that he had perjured himself to allow the real murderer go free. The film ends with Ben triumphantly leading Tom from the swamp.

Twentieth Century–Fox, 1941 (original). Director: Jean Renoir; screenwriter: Dudley Nichols. Cast: Walter Brennan (Tom Keefer), Walter Huston (Thursday Ragan), Anne Baxter (Julie), Dana Andrews (Ben), Virginia Gilmore (Mabel McKenzie), John Carradine (Jesse Wick), Mary Howard, Eugene Pallette, Ward Bond, Guinn Williams.

• ***Lure of the Wilderness*** (remake). Twentieth Century–Fox, 1952. Director: Jean Negulesco; screenwriter: Louis Lantz. Cast: Jean Peters (Laurie Harper), Jeffrey Hunter (Ben Tyler), Constance Smith (Noreen), Walter Brennan (Jim Harper), Tom Tully (Zack Tyler), Harry Shannon, Will Wright, Jack Elam, Harry Carter.

In the remake of the story of a man wanted for murder who hides out in the swamps of the Okefenokee Swamp in southeast Georgia, Walter Brennan reprises his role, only this time he takes his daughter Jean Peters with him.

Jeffrey Hunter is the young man who helps Brennan find justice and falls for the sulky-looking jungle girl Peters. Neither film is as good as one might hope for from their casts. The story just isn't that interesting and the screenplays don't provide any exciting twists or unexpected developments.

872 The Swan

Based on the play by Ferenc Molnar, translated into English by Melville C. Baker. Story: Princess Beatrice would like to arrange a marriage between her daughter Princess Alexandra and the heir-apparent, Prince Albert. To distract Albert from other possible brides, Beatrice instructs Alexandra to openly flirt with the handsome court tutor, which she does willingly because she has come to love him. Nevertheless she follows her aristocratic heritage to marry Albert, realizing that she is like the swan, graceful and regal in her own setting, but awkward and unhappy away from it.

Paramount Pictures, 1925 (original). Silent. Director and screenwriter: Dimitri Buchowetzki. Cast: Frances Howard (Alexandra), Adolphe Menjou (H.R.H. Albert of Kersten-Rodenfels), Ricardo Cortez (Dr. Walter), Claire Eames (Princess Dominica), Ida Waterman (Princess Beatrice), Helen Lindroth, Joseph Depew, George Walcott, Michael Visaroff, Mikhael Vavitch.

• ***One Romantic Night*** (remake). United Artists, 1930. Director: Paul L. Stein; screenwriter: Melville Baker. Cast: Lillian Gish (Alexandra), Rod La Rocque (Prince Albert), Conrad Nagel (Dr. Nichols Haller), Marie Dressler (Princess Beatrice), O.P. Heggie (Father Benedict), Albert Conti (Count Lutzen), Edgar Norton, Billie Bennett, Phillipe DeLacy, Bryon Sage, Barbara Leonard.

• ***The Swan*** (remake). MGM, 1956. Director: Charles Vidor; screenwriter: John Dighton. Cast: Grace Kelly (Princess Alexandra), Alec Guinness (Prince Albert), Louis Jourdan (Dr. Nicholas Agi), Agnes Moorehead (Queen Maria Dominika), Jessie Royce Landis (Princess Beatrix), Brian Aherne (Father Hyacinth), Leo G. Carroll (Caesar), Estelle Winwood (Symphorosa), Robert Coote, Van Dyke Parks, Christopher Cook, Edith Barrett.

The star of the silent version of the Molnar story, Frances Howard, soon after retired to marry her own prince of Hollywood, Samuel Goldwyn. Five years later, Lillian Gish made the picture expecting the services of German director Max Reinhardt, but before shooting began, he had his fill of Hollywood and went back to Europe. The result in the hands of journeyman director Paul Stein is dull and lifeless, hardly noticeable as a comedy. The only thing of note about the film is that it was Gish's talking picture debut. The timing for the MGM picture couldn't be better. Within a week of its release, its star, Grace Kelly, married Prince Ranier of Monaco and truly became a princess. The making of the picture and the engagement of its star to minor European royalty was mere coincidence. All in all, it wasn't a bad piece, with some unexpected funny scenes involving Brian Aherne.

The Sweater Girl ***see*** **College Scandal**

873 Sweeney

Based on the TV series created by Ian Kennedy Martin. Story: While investigating a suicide, Flying Squad Inspector Regan exposes a plot to blackmail the energy minister at an oil conference.

Euston Films, Great Britain, 1977 (original). Director: David Wickes; screenwriter: Ronald Graham. Cast: John Thaw (Insp. Regan), Dennis Waterman (Sgt. Carter), Barry Foster (McQueen), Ian Bannen (Charles Baker), Colin Welland (Chadwick), Diane Keen (Bianca), Michael Coles (Johnson), Joe Melia, Brian Glover, Lynda Bellingham, Morris Perry, Nick Brimble.

• ***Sweeney 2*** (sequel). Euston Films, Great Britain, 1978. Director: Tom Clegg; screenwriter: Troy Kennedy Martin. Cast: John Thaw (Insp. Regan), Dennis Waterman (Sgt. Carter), Denholm Elliott (Jupp), Barry Stanton (Big John), John Flanagan (Willard), David Casey (Godyear), Derrick O'Connor (Llewellyn), John Atkin, James Warrior, Guy Standeven, Ken Hutchison.

In the sequel to the big screen adventures of Scotland Yard's Flying Squad, the detectives track down an armed robbery gang of expatriates who return from a luxurious Malta development for each job. As is often the case when a successful TV series is the basis for a movie, the producers, used to an hour's time frame, don't have enough action to sustain or justify a longer program.

874 Sweeney Todd

Based on the play by George Dibden-Pitt and C. Hazelton. Story: Sweeney Todd dreams that he is a "demon barber" who slits sailors' throats to get their valuables and deposes of their corpses in pies which he sells to unsuspecting customers who enjoy the "meat" pies' special flavor.

QTS Productions/Ideal, Great Britain, 1928 (original). Silent. Director: Walter West; screenwriters: George Dibden-Pitt and C. Hazelton. Cast: Moore Marriott (Sweeney Todd), Zoe Palmer (Johanna), Charles Ashton (Mark Ingestre), Iris Darbyshire (Amelia Lovett), Judd Green (Simon Podge), Philip Hewland, Brian Glenny, Harry Lorraine.

• ***Sweeney Todd: The Demon Barber of Fleet Street*** (remake). King/MGM, Great Britain, 1936. Director: George King; screenwriter: Frederick Hayward and H.F. Maltby. Cast: Tod Slaughter (Sweeney Todd), Bruce Seton (Mark Ingestre), Eve Lister (Johanna Oakley), Stella Rho (Mrs. Lovatt), Ben Soutten (Beadle), D.J. Williams, Jerry Verno, John Singer, Aubrey Mallalieu, Billy Holland, Ben Williams.

The remake, set in 1760 London, actually has the barber who shaves and murders his customers in his waterfront barber shop and then, working with Mrs. Lovatt, turns their corpses to more good use as ingredients for meat pies. One young sailor, Mark Ingestre, is robbed but survives due to a quarrel between the two accomplices. The sailor later returns and the demon barber is caught in his own trap. Tod Slaughter gives a swaggeringly good performance in his most famous role.

Sweeney Todd, The Demon Barber of Fleet Street *see* **Sweeney Todd**

Sweeney 2 *see* **Sweeney**

875 Sweepings

Based on the novel by Lester Cohen. Story: After the Chicago fire, Daniel Pardway works with great dedication to become a mercantile prince, the founder and owner of one of the city's great department stores. Throughout the years of struggle what keeps him going is the dream that his three sons will carry on the commercial empire that he is building. Disappointingly, one by one his sons either go bad, or spoiled by easy living turn to other, easier pursuits than running a department store. Pardway's one daughter is no better, being a social butterfly who buys herself a penniless nobleman. In the end, Pardway entrusts the running of his empire to a trusted associate, Abe Ullman, who has been with the old man all along.

RKO, 1933 (original). Director: John Cromwell; screenwriters: Lester Cohen, Howard Estabrook and H.W. Hannemann. Cast: Lionel Barrymore (Daniel Pardway), Alan Dinehart (Thane), Eric Linden (Freddie), William Gargan (Gene), Gloria Stuart (Phoebe), Gregory Ratoff (Ullman), Lucien Littlefield, Nan Sunderland, Helen Mack.

• ***Three Sons*** (remake). RKO, 1939. Director: Jack Hively; screenwriter: John Twist. Cast: Edward Ellis (Daniel Pardway), William Gargan (Thane Pardway), Kent Taylor (Gene Pardway), J. Edward Bromberg (Abe Ullman), Katharine Alexander (Abigail Pardway), Virginia Vale (Phoebe Pardway), Robert Stanton (Bert Pardway), Dick Hogan, Grady Sutton, Adele Pearce, Alexander D'Arcy.

Both films effectively show a father's disappointment in his sons who do not share his dream, his drive, or his horse sense. On the other hand the author, screenwriters and director fail to suggest why they should. Expecting children who have been manipulated and spoiled during all their formative years to suddenly develop dear old dad's values and get-up-and-go is unrealistic. There's also the point of why should a child follow in a parent's footsteps. That's not how father became successful.

Sweet Kitty Bellairs *see* **The Incomparable Bellairs**

Sweet Rosie O'Grady *see* **Love Is News**

876 The Sweetheart of Sigma Chi

Based on the story by George Waggoner. Story: It's a light and highly unlikely story of fraternity and sorority life on campus. Boys and girls enjoy each other's company. The only discouraging word in the whole plot is that some gamblers attempt to fix a rowing race. Of course they aren't successful.

Monogram Pictures, 1933 (original). Director: Edwin L. Marin; screenwriters: Luther Reed and Albert E. Demond. Cast: Mary Carlisle (Vivian), Buster Crabbe (Bob North), Charles Starrett (Morley), Florence Lake (Dizzy),

Eddie Tamblyn, Sally Starr, Mary Blackford, Tom Dugan, Burr McIntosh, Major Goodsell.

• ***The Sweetheart of Sigma Chi*** (remake). Monogram Pictures, 1946. Director: Jack Bernhard; screenwriter: Frank L. Moss. Cast: Phil Regan (Lucky Ryan), Elyse Knox (Betty Allan), Phil Brito (Phil Howard), Ross Hunter (Ted Sloan), Tom Harmon (Coach), Paul Guilfoyle, Anne Gillis, Edward Brophy, Fred Colby, Alan Hale, Jr., David Holt.

It must have been wonderful in college during the '20s and '30s. "Students" seldom had to worry about how they would pay the tuition. Athletes were admired. Girls had interest in only one degree, "Mrs." Things are a bit more complicated nowadays. In the musical remake, songs include "Penthouse Serenade" sung by Irish tenor Phil Regan, and Phil Brito delivering "Five Minutes More," "It's Not That I'm Such a Wolf, It's Just You're Such a Lamb" and the title song. Among the other songs, "Cement Mixer (Putty Putty)" by the Slim Galliard Trio became a novelty hit.

Sweetie ***see*** **The Charm School**

Swell Guy ***see*** **The Hero**

Swing High, Swing Low ***see*** **Burlesque**

877 Swiss Family Robinson

Based on the novel by Johann David Wyss. Story: It's the familiar story of a shipwrecked family that builds a new home on a desert island. It delivers a message about the evils of civilization at the same time it shows the pluck needed to survive when one leaves a familiar world with all its trappings.

RKO, 1940. Director: Edward Ludwig; screenwriters: Walter Ferris, Gene Towne and Graham Baker. Cast: Thomas Mitchell (William Robinson), Edna Best (Elizabeth Robinson), Freddie Bartholomew (Jack Robinson), Terry Kilburn (Ernest Robinson), Tom Holt (Fritz Robinson), Baby Bobby Quillan (Francis Robinson), Christian Rub, John Wray, Herbert Rawlinson.

Disney/Buena Vista, 1960. Director: Ken Annakin; screenwriter: Lowell S. Hawley. Cast: John Mills (Father), Dorothy McGuire (Mother), James MacArthur (Fritz), Janet Munro (Roberta), Sessue Hayakawa (Pirate Chief), Tommy Kirk (Ernst), Kevin Corcoran (Frances), Cecil Parker, Andy Ho, Milton Reid, Larry Taylor.

Swiss Family Robinson was also filmed in England in 1972 and in 1973. The 1940 film was one of "The Play's the Thing Productions." The production partners, Gene Towne and Graham Baker, chose stories that were in the public domain, saving money by not having to pay an author. Despite this policy and the fact that it was a fairly good picture, the film lost nearly $200,000. The Disney remake did much better at the box office but the screenwriters took certain liberties with the story, including introducing Janet Munro as a girl the family rescues from pirates, thus providing a little unmarried romantic interest for James MacArthur and Tommy Kirk.

The Sword and the Rose *see* **When Knighthood Was in Flower**

The Sword and the Stone *see* **Knights of the Roundtable**

The Sword of Ali Baba *see* **Chu Chin Chow**

Sword of Monte Cristo *see* **The Count of Monte Cristo**

Sword of Sherwood Forest *see* **Robin Hood**

T

878 T-Men

Based on a story by Virginia Kellog. Story: In one of the best of the "B" movies, Treasury agents O'Brien and Genaro go undercover in an attempt to break a counterfeit ring. Assuming the roles of two small-time hoods, they get taken into the Vantucci mob in Detroit. They produce a phony bill for which they claim to have the plates. Genaro is innocently betrayed by his wife, whom he runs into accidently when with members of the gang; her momentary recognition of him signs his death warrant. Genaro has found the key to coded information which will break the case. While O'Brien stands by helplessly, the gang members kill Genaro, but not before he is able to impart the information about the key to O'Brien. Ultimately, O'Brien takes revenge for the killing of his partner by shooting down his murderer as other T-Men break up the gang.

El Productions, 1948 (original). Director: Anthony Mann; screenwriter: John C. Higgins. Cast: Dennis O'Keefe (Dennis O'Brien), Alfred Ryder (Tony Genaro), Mary Meade (Evangeline), Wallace Ford (Schemer), June Lockhart (Mrs. Genaro), Charles McGraw (Moxie), Jane Randolph (Diana), Art Smith (Gregg), Herbert Heyes, Jack Overman, John Wengraf, Jim Bannon.

• ***The File of the Golden Goose*** (remake). United Artists, 1969. Director: Sam Wanamaker; screenwriter: John C. Higgins. Cast: Yul Brynner (Pete Novak), Charles Gray (Nick "The Owl" Harrison), Edward Woodward (Peter Thompson), John Barrie (Sloane), Bernard Archard (Collins), Ivor Dean (Reynolds), Anthony Jacobs, Adrienne Corri, Karel Stepanek, Walter Gotell.

In the remake, Yul Brynner is an American treasury agent who narrowly escapes an assassination attempt in which his girl friend is killed just before he leaves for London to investigate an international counterfeit ring known as the Golden Goose. He is dismayed when Scotland Yard assigns family man Edward Woodward to work with him. Brynner is correct, of course, as later Woodward is tricked into revealing his identity when the two go undercover and Woodward is killed for his trouble, almost ensuring the same fate for Yul. The film is a cliche-filled crime thriller with few surprises and every character a one-dimensional stereotype.

879 A Tailor Made Man

Based on the play by Harry James Smith. Story: John Paul Burt, who presses clothes for a living, borrows an expensive suit to wear to an exclusive function. Apparently "clothes do make the man" as Burt is offered a position of handling labor problems in the shipping firm of Abraham Nathan. Despite no experience and no great brains, Burt is successful, but returns to the tailor's shop when he is exposed as an imposter by adversary Gustavus Sonntag. Nathan goes after Burt, giving him a permanent position. Burt is now in a position to marry Tanya Huber.

United Artists, 1922 (original). Silent. Director: Joseph De Grasse; screenwriter: Albert Ray. Cast: Charles Ray (John Paul Burt), Thomas Ricketts (Anton Huber), Ethel Grandin (Tanya Huber), Stanton Heck (Abraham Nathan), Douglas Gerrerd (Gustavus Sonntag), Victor Potel, Edythe Chapman, Irene Lentz, Frederick Stanton.

• ***A Tailor Made Man*** (remake). MGM, 1931. Director: Sam Wood; screenwriter: H.J. Smith. Cast: William Haines (John Paul Burt), Dorothy Jordan (Tanya), Joseph Cawthorn (Huber), Marjorie Rambeau (Kitty DePuy), William Austin (Jellicott), Ian Keith, Hedda Hopper, Hale Hamilton, Joan Marsh, Martha Sleeper.

Charles Ray was a popular performer in the early silent days and hoped that this story would revive his career. It didn't and he soon found himself as an extra. People just didn't seem to buy the absurd story of a hard-working poor boy who moved into corrupt and superficial society when he passes himself off as a dandy by wearing some fancy clothes that he borrowed from the tailor shop where he worked. Things didn't improve nine years later with the same preposterous story of a man becoming a success merely because he's wearing a stolen dress suit. The performances of William Haines, Dorothy Jordan and Joseph Cawthorn didn't help, either.

Tale of 1001 Nights *see* **Arabian Nights**

880 A Tale of Two Cities

Based on the novel by Charles Dickens. Story: "It was the best of times, it was the worst of times. . . ." In late eighteenth-century France, cynical, unhappy lawyer Sydney Carton is in love with Lucie Manette, but she loves Charles Darnay, who looks somewhat like Carton. Darnay is the nephew of the cruel French aristocrat Marquis St. Evremonde. Shortly after Darnay and his new wife, Lucie, have moved to England, Evremonde's coach runs over a child and the former's only concern is for his prize horses. This is the last straw. The father of the dead boy rushes into Evremonde's mansion and kills the aristocrat in his bed. The blood lust quickens among the oppressed peasants, and soon aristocrats are being brought by tumbrel to the guillotine where the cheers of each decapitation are led by Madame de Farge. With Evremonde the most hated name in France, Madame de Farge plots to lure Darnay back to France where he is condemned to death. Carton visits Darnay, drugs him and takes his place, going the next morning to the guillotine in Darnay's place, thinking "It

Ronald Colman looks with pained admiration at Elizabeth Allan, the woman for whom he will sacrifice his life to save her husband from the guillotine in A Tale of Two Cities *(MGM, 1935).*

is a far, far better thing that I do than I have ever done, it is a far, far better rest that I go to than I have ever known."

• ***A Tale of Two Cities*** (remake). Fox Film Corp., 1917. Silent. Director: Frank Lloyd; screenwriter: uncredited. Cast: William Farnum (Charles Darnay/Sydney Carton), Jewell Carmen (Lucie Manette), Charles Clary (Marquis St. Evremonde), Herschel Mayall (Jacques de Farge), Rosita Marstini (Madame de Farge), Josef Swickard (Dr. Alexandre Manette), Ralph Lewis, Marc Robbins, Willard Louis.

• ***A Tale of Two Cities*** (remake). MGM, 1935. Director: Jack Conway; screenwriters: W.P. Lipscomb and S.N. Behrman. Cast: Ronald Colman (Sydney Carton), Elizabeth Allan (Lucie Manette), Edna May Oliver (Miss Pross), Blanche Yurka (Madame de Farge), Reginald Owen (Stryver), Basil Rathbone (Marquis St. Evremonde), Donald Woods (Charles Darnay), Henry B. Walthall (Dr. Manette), Walter Catlett, Fritz Leiber, H.B. Warner, Mitchell Lewis, Claude Gillingwater, Isabel Jewell.

• ***A Tale of Two Cities*** (remake). Rank, Great Britain, 1972. Director: Ralph Thomas; screenwriter: T.E.B. Clarke. Cast: Dirk Bogarde (Sydney Carton), Dorothy Tutin (Lucie Manette), Christopher Lee (Marquis St. Evremonde), Athene Seyler (Miss Pross), Rosalie Crutchley (Madame de Farge), Ernest

Dorothy Tutin and Dirk Bogarde appear in a quiet moment from A Tale of Two Cities *(Rank, 1958).*

Clark (Stryver), Stephen Murray (Dr. Manette), Paul Guers (Charles Darney), Donald Pleasence, Ian Bannen, Cecil Parker, Alfie Bass.

The great Dickens novel of the world coming apart during the time of the French Revolution was also filmed in 1911, 1913 and 1925. Each time, audiences were enthralled with the passions that were explored in the productions. In the three pictures detailed above, Farnum, Colman and Bogarde came in for the greatest amount of deserved praise for their portrayal of the cynical and despondent Carton, but plenty of others did their fair share to make the films good drama. The role of Madame de Farge, important and pivotal, was safely in the hands of talented actresses Rosita Marstini, Blanche Yurka and Rosalie Crutchley. Sad to say none of the actresses who portrayed Lucie Manette were convincing as women who could inspire a man to sacrifice his life so she could be happy with another. The villainous St. Evremonde was sneeringly played by Charles Clary, Basil Rathbone and Christopher Lee. All in all, each production successfully captured the mood of a world gone mad.

Tales of Robin Hood *see* **Robin Hood**

881 Tall, Dark and Handsome

Based on an original screenplay by Karl Tunberg. Story: Shep Morrison is a

Chicago gang leader in the '20s, noted for his murderous nature and the number of guys he has had taken for "rides." The truth is he's a pussycat. The basement of his mansion is a pleasantly arranged prison for those he supposedly has had knocked off. To evade a one-way ride for himself from his North Side adversary, he plays dead long enough to pin a murder rap on his rival, then heads out for South America and a new life with innocent and sweet Judy, a girl with whom he has fallen in love.

Twentieth Century–Fox, 1941 (original). Director: H. Bruce Humberstone; screenwriter: Karl Tunberg. Cast: Cesar Romero (Shep Morrison), Virginia Gilmore (Judy), Charlotte Greenwood (Winnie), Milton Berle (Frosty), Sheldon Leonard (Pretty Willie), Stanley Clements, Frank Jenks, Barnett Parker, Marc Lawrence.

• ***Love That Brute*** (remake). Twentieth Century–Fox, 1950. Director: Alexander Hall; screenwriters: Karl Tunberg, Darrell Ware and John Lee Mahin. Cast: Paul Douglas (Big Ed Hanley), Jean Peters (Ruth Manning), Cesar Romero (Pretty Willie), Keenan Wynn (Bugs), Joan Davis (Mamie), Arthur Treacher (Quentin), Peter Price, Jay C. Flippen, Harry Kelley, Leon Belasco.

These two gangster comedies with their Damon Runyan–like characters remind one of *A Slight Case of Murder,* but neither is quite as good as that film. Cesar Romero appears in both, in the first as the soft-hearted mobster and in the second as the rival who gets framed for killing Paul Douglas, when the latter substitutes another body for his own. Jean Peters plays the country girl with whom Douglas falls in love. He goes so far to hide his occupation from her that he hires some kids to play his children so he can employ her as their governess. She finds out about his rackets and murderous reputation and storms out of his life, but he's able to win her back when he demonstrates that his crimes are not of the capital nature. Both casts do a fine job in this gangster yarn with a twist.

882 The Taming of the Shrew

Based on the play by William Shakespeare. Story: Rich Paduan merchant Baptista has two beautiful daughters, the wild-tempered shrew Katharina and the sweet and loveable Bianca. He has decreed that Bianca cannot wed one of her many suitors until Katharina first takes a husband. This seems unlikely because of her vile temper, but as fate would have it, a fortune-hunting scoundrel named Petruchio arrives in Padua seeking a wealthy wife. Although he immediately feels Katharina's scorn and abuse, after warding off her blows, Petruchio announces that he will wed her the following Sunday. The ceremony goes off despite Petruchio arriving late, drunk and improperly dressed for the occasion. He then takes his wildly protesting wife to his dilapidated home where under a pretext of great love for her, he rejects all manner of comfort and luxury, maintaining he is unworthy of her. Eventually they are invited to Bianca's wedding to young poet Lucentio. Here Petruchio wagers that Katharina is the most devoted and obedient of wives. To the amazement of all, she gives the other women a lecture on the virtues of wifely obedience.

• ***The Taming of the Shrew*** (remake). British & Colonial, Great Britain, 1923.

Silent. Director: Edwin J. Collins; screenwriter: Eliot Stannard. Cast: Dacia Deane (Katharina), Lauderdale Maitland (Petruchio), Cynthia Murtagh (Bianca), M. Grey Murray (Baptista), Roy Beard (Lucentio), Somers Bellamy (Gremio).

• ***The Taming of the Shrew*** (remake). United Artists, 1929. Director and screenwriter: Sam Taylor. Cast: Mary Pickford (Katherine), Douglas Fairbanks (Petruchio), Edwin Maxwell (Baptista), Joseph Cawthorn (Gremio), Clyde Cook (Grumio), Geoffrey Warwell (Hortensio), Dorothy Jordan (Bianca).

• ***Kiss Me Kate*** (remake). MGM, 1953. Director: George Sidney; screenwriter: Dorothy Kingsley, based on the Samuel and Bella Spewack play. Cast: Kathryn Grayson (Lilli Vanessi—"Katherine"), Howard Keel (Fred Graham—"Petruchio"), Ann Miller (Lois Lane—"Bianca"), Keenan Wynn (Lippy), Bobby Van ("Gremio"), Tommy Rall (Bill Calhoun—"Lucentio"), James Whitmore (Slug), Kurt Kasznar ("Baptista"), Bob Fosse ("Hortensio"), Ron Randall, Willard Parker.

• ***The Taming of the Shrew*** (remake). Columbia Pictures, 1967. Director: Franco Zeffirelli; screenwriters: Paul Dehn, Suso Cecchi and Zeffirelli. Cast: Elizabeth Taylor (Katharina), Richard Burton (Petruchio), Cyril Cusack (Grumio), Michael Horden (Baptista), Alfred Lynch (Tranio), Alan Webb (Gremio), Natasha Pyne (Bianca), Michael York (Lucentio), Giancarlo Cobelli, Vernon Dobtcheff, Ken Parry.

Other movie versions of the shrew were produced in 1908, 1911, 1913, 1914, 1915, 1941 and 1944. The 1953 version was a musical with songs by Cole Porter including "So in Love," "From This Moment On," "Always True to You in My Fashion," "Brush Up Your Shakespeare" and "Where Is the Life That Late I Led." Elizabeth Taylor and Richard Burton took advantage of audiences' enjoyment of seeing them together by producing a passable version of the play. The other versions were fair-to-middling, but nothing to get very excited about.

883 Tammy and the Bachelor

Based on the novel *Tammy Out of Time* by Cid Ricketts Sumner. Story: Backwoods gal Tammy Tyree nurses Peter Brent back to health when his plane crashes near her grandpapy's still. He invites her to visit him at his home, Brentwood Hall. Here, Tammy's naturalness influences not only Peter, but his dreadfully insecure mother, his father who has retreated into the world of his books, and his maiden aunt, frustrated at never having become the artist she hoped to be. After a good dose of Tammy's optimism and happy outlook on life, all are better for the experience, and of course, Tammy and Peter fall madly in love.

Universal Pictures, 1957 (original). Director: Joseph Pevney; screenwriter: Oscar Brodney. Cast: Debbie Reynolds (Tammy Tyree), Leslie Nielsen (Peter Brent), Walter Brennan (Grandpa Tyree), Mala Powers (Barbara), Sidney Blackmer (Professor Brent), Mildred Natwick (Aunt Renie), Fay Wray (Mrs. Brent), Philip Ober, Craig Hill, Louise Beavers, April Kent.

• ***Tammy Tell Me True*** (sequel). Universal Pictures, 1961. Director: Harry Keller; screenwriter: Oscar Brodney. Cast: Sandra Dee (Tammy Tyree), John

Gavin (Tom Freeman), Beulah Bondi (Mrs. Call), Virginia Grey (Miss Jenks), Charles Drake (Buford Woodley), Julia Meade, Cecil Kellaway, Edgar Buchanan, Gigi Perreau, Catherine McLeod, Ross Elliot.

• ***Tammy and the Doctor*** (sequel). Universal Pictures, 1963. Director: Harry Keller; screenwriter: Oscar Brodney. Cast: Sandra Dee (Tammy Tyree), Peter Fonda (Dr. Mark Chadwick), Macdonald Carey (Dr. Wayne Bentley), Beulah Bondi (Mrs. Call), Margaret Lindsay (Rachel Coleman), Reginald Owen (Jason Tripp), Alice Pearce, Adam West, Joan Marshall, Stanley Clements.

• ***Tammy and the Millionaire*** (sequel). Universal Pictures, 1967. Directors: Leslie Goodwins, Sidney Miller and Ezra Stone; screenwriter: George Tibbles. Cast: Debbie Watson (Tammy Tarleton), Donald Woods (John Brent), Dorothy Green (Lavinia Tate), Jay Sheffield (Steven Brent), George Furth (Dwayne Witt), Frank McGrath, Denver Pyle, David Macklin.

About the only thing one can conclude about these four pictures is that Tammy can't seem to keep a man—she gets a new love in each one. She also seems to grow younger. As is usually the case, the first is the best of this series. Debbie Reynolds, just as cute as a bug, radiated innocence and confidence, even when way out of her element. She also had a million-selling hit with the title song. In the first sequel, Sandra Dee, just as cute as Debbie, decides to get herself a college education and falls in love with one of her teachers, played by John Gavin. In the 1963 movie, Sandra Dee as Tammy gets a job as a nurse's aide at a hospital and falls for handsome intern Peter Fonda. In 1967 we have a new Tammy, cute little Debbie Watson, and she even has a new last name. This time our fresh young thing gets a job as a secretary for a millionaire and is rushed by his son.

Tammy and the Doctor *see* **Tammy and the Bachelor**

Tammy and the Millionaire *see* **Tammy and the Bachelor**

Tammy Tell Me True *see* **Tammy and the Bachelor**

884 Tarzan of the Apes

Based on the novel by Edgar Rice Burroughs and the play by Herbert Woodgate and Arthur Carlton. Story: After his parents are killed, the infant son of Lord and Lady Greystoke is adopted by a female ape in West Africa. Given the name of Tarzan, he is taught to communicate with animals and live in the jungle. Years later, when he has grown to manhood, he is discovered by a search party led by Dr. Charles Porter. The latter identifies the Ape Man as the missing Greystoke, teaches him English and takes him back to England where Tarzan accepts civilization and his title, and marries Dr. Porter's daughter, Jane.

National Film Corporation, 1918 (original). Silent. Director: Scott Sidney; screenwriters: Fred Miller and Lois Weber. Cast: Elmo Lincoln (Tarzan/Lord Greystoke), Enid Markey (Jane Porter), Gordon Griffith (Tarzan as a boy), Kathleen Kirkham (Tarzan's mother), True Boardman (Tarzan's father),

Thomas Jefferson (Dr. Porter), Colin Kenny, Jack Wilson, George French, Bessie Toner.

• ***Tarzan, the Ape Man*** (remake). MGM, 1932. Director: William S. Van Dyke; screenwriter: Cyril Hume. Cast: Johnny Weissmuller (Tarzan), Maureen O'Sullivan (Jane Porter), Neil Hamilton (Harry Holt), C. Aubrey Smith (James Porter), Doris Lloyd (Mrs. Cutten), Forrester Harvey, Ivory Williams.

• ***Tarzan, the Ape Man*** (remake). MGM, 1959. Director: Joseph Newman; screenwriter: Robert Hill. Cast: Dennis Miller (Tarzan), Joanna Barnes (Jane Parker), Cesare Danova (Harry Holt), Robert Douglas (Colonel Parker), Thomas Yangha (Riano).

• ***Greystoke, the Legend of Tarzan of the Apes*** (remake). WEA/Warner Bros., Great Britain, 1984. Director: Hugh Hudson; screenwriters: Robert Towne and Michael Austin. Cast: Ralph Richardson (Earl of Greystoke), Ian Holm (Capt. Phillippe D'Arnot), James Fox (Lord Esker), Christopher Lambert (John Clayton/Tarzan), Andie MacDowell (Jane Porter), Cheryl Campbell (Lady Alice Clayton), Paul Geoffrey (Lord Jack Clayton), John Wells, Nigel Davenport, Ian Charleson, Nicholas Farrell, Richard Griffiths.

There have been more than fifty movies featuring Tarzan. In some, he is little more than an ape, in others he is a noble savage, and in still others he speaks perfect English. Johnny Weissmuller is the best known of the movie Tarzans, having appeared in 12 features, some with Maureen O'Sullivan as Jane and Johnny Sheffield as Boy. There even has been an X-rated version in 1981 starring Bo Derek, who rides and writhes nakedly, thus arousing the beast—no, make that man, in her Tarzan. Explicit as the film is, Bo's appearance is not as sexy as Maureen O'Sullivan's in her skimpy loin-cloth outfit. Among other "actors" who have appeared as Tarzan in the movies are Gene Pollar, P. Dempsey Tabler, James H. Pierce, Frank Merrill, Buster Crabbe, Herman Brix (Bruce Bennett), Glenn Morris, Lex Barker, Gordon Scott, Jock Mahoney, and Mike Henry.

Tarzan, the Ape Man *see* **Tarzan of the Apes**

Tea for Two *see* **My Lady Friends**

The Teeth of the Tiger *see* **Arsene Lupin**

885 The Telephone Girl

Based on the play *The Woman* by William Churchill De Mille. Story: Political boss Jim Blake, backing his son-in-law, Mark Robinson, for governor, discovers that Robinson's opponent, Matthew Standish, had three years earlier registered in a hotel with someone who was not wife. Blake traps Standish into trying to warn the girl in question to keep quiet, but Kitty O'Brien, a telephone operator important in Blake's plan, refuses to cooperate. It takes awhile but everything gets sorted out and Kitty ends up marrying Blake's son, Tom.

Famous Players–Lasky/Paramount Pictures, 1927 (original). Silent. Director: Herbert Brenon; screenwriter: Elizabeth Meehan. Cast: Madge Bellamy (Kitty

O'Brien), Holbrook Blinn (Jim Blake), Warner Baxter (Matthew Standish), Mary Allison (Grace Robinson), Lawrence Gray (Tom Blake), Hale Hamilton, Hamilton Revelle, W.E. Shay.

• ***The Secret Call*** (remake). Paramount Pictures, 1931. Director: Stuart Walker; screenwriter: Eve Unsell. Cast: Richard Arlen (Tom Blake), Peggy Shannon (Wanda Kelly), William B. Davidson (Jim Blake), Charles Trowbridge (Phil Roberts), Jane Keith, Selmer Jackson, Ned Sparks, Jed Prouty.

In the remake, Peggy Shannon plays the daughter of a once-wealthy politician who committed suicide. She's now a switchboard operator with a hotel. She won't help other politicians destroy a career by telling what she knows of a man registering at the hotel with some woman not his wife. Neither film will win any elections; in fact a recall may be in order.

886 Temple Tower

Based on the novel by Herman Cyril McNeile. Story: When Bulldog Drummond discovers that a gang of thieves are hiding out in a house located in his part of town, he is determined to capture them. The gang is headed by one Blackton, who has doublecrossed his partners, and known only as the Strangler. Though Blackton tries many fiendish tricks to prevent his arrest, he's no match for Drummond and his Scotland Yard associates.

Fox Film Corp., 1930 (original). Director: Donald Gallagher; screenwriter: Llewellyn Hughes. Cast: Kenneth McKenna (Capt. Hugh Drummond), Marceline Day (Patricia Verney), Henry B. Walthall (Blackton), Cyril Chadwick (Peter Darrell), Peter Gawthorne, Ivan Linow, Frank Lanning, Yorke Sherwood.

• ***Bulldog Drummond's Secret Police*** (remake). Paramount Pictures, 1939. Director: James Hogan; screenwriter: Garnett Weston. Cast: John Howard (Capt. Hugh Drummond), Heather Angel (Phyllis Clavering), H.B. Warner (Colonel Neilson), Elizabeth Patterson (Aunt Blanche), Reginald Denny (Algy Longworth), E.E. Clive, Leo G. Carroll, Forrester Harvey.

Bulldog Drummond certainly had his followers among readers, but many film adaptations of the cases of McNeile's hero were at best routine, as is the case with the two now under consideration. The remake barely counts as a feature-length picture, running only 55 minutes and meant to fill out the lower portion of a double bill. In it, Drummond has to contend with a foe, Leo G. Carroll, whose castle is equipped with a series of torture devices. John Howard, Reginald Denny, H.B. Warner and Heather Angel appeared together in several pictures in the series.

Temptation *see* **Bella Donna**

887 The Ten Commandments

Based on the Book of Exodus from the Bible. Story: It's the well-known story of the mistreatment of the Jewish captives by the Egyptians, God's plagues on the Egyptians until the Pharaoh agrees to "Let My People Go," their escape across the parted Red Sea, Moses being given the Ten Commandments by God, and his coming down from the mountain to find the Israelites worshipping a golden idol.

Famous Players/Paramount Pictures, 1923 (original). Director: Cecil B. De Mille; screenwriter: Jeanie Macpherson. Cast (Prolog): Theodore Roberts (Moses), Charles De Roche (Rameses, the Pharaoh), Estelle Taylor (Miriam), Julia Faye (Pharaoh's wife), Terrence Moore (Pharaoh's son), James Neill (Aaron), Lawson Butt (Dathan), Clarence Burton, Noble Johnson. Part 2: Edythe Chapman (Mrs. McTavish), Richard Dix (John McTavish), Rod La Rocque (Dan McTavish), Leatrice Joy (Mary Leigh), Nita Naldi (Sally Lung), Robert Edeson, Charles Ogle, Agnes Ayres, Viscount Glerawly.

• ***The Ten Commandments*** (remake). Paramount Pictures, 1956. Director: Cecil B. De Mille; screenwriters: Aeneas MacKenzie, Jesse Lasky, Jr., Jack Gariss and Fredric M. Frank. Cast: Charlton Heston (Moses), Yul Brynner (Rameses), Anne Baxter (Nefertiti), Edward G. Robinson (Dathan), Yvonne De Carlo (Sephora), Debra Paget (Lilia), John Derek (Joshua), Sir Cedric Hardwicke (Sethi), Nina Foch (Bithiah), Martha Scott (Yochabel), Judith Anderson (Memnet), Vincent Price (Baka), John Carradine (Aaron), Eduard Franz, Olive Deering, Donald Curtis, Douglas Dumbrille, H.B. Warner, Henry Wilcoxon.

De Mille's spectaculars were always good entertainment if not great cinema. The original version actually had two disconnected stories, the familiar Exodus and a modern tale of two brothers in San Francisco, John and Dan McTavish, both of whom love Mary Leigh. She chooses Dan, who becomes a wealthy building contractor by using shoddy materials. When this is discovered, his downfall is under way. He kills his oriental mistress, Sally Lung, while trying to obtain bribe money from her and discovers that he may have contracted leprosy from her. Drunk and frightened, he runs his motorboat onto the rocks and is killed. Mary then marries John.

In 1932, in the film *Forgotten Commandments,* a melodrama of the loose morals at a Russian university starring Sari Maritza, Gene Raymond and Marguerite Churchill, religious motifs are illustrated by clips from De Mille's 1923 movie.

The 1956 movie ran 219 minutes, 69 more than De Mille's earlier version. It was nominated for Best Picture of the Year, losing out to another all-star spectacular, *Around the World in 80 Days.* This version concentrated on the biblical story with no modern accompanying feature. The acting is generally second-rate but the scenes and the special effects sustain one over the long haul. It's almost better to see it on television, so one has the commercial breaks to stretch and refresh one's self.

888 The Ten Dollar Raise

Based on the short story by Peter Bernard Kyne. Story: Wilkins, a bookkeeper for 20 years with Bates & Stryker, has long expected a raise promised annually so that he can marry his sweetheart Emily, a stenographer with the same company. Bates' son Don, desperately in debt, cons the timid Wilkins into buying some land that turns out to be underwater, but the good news is that it also contains oil. Now rich, Wilkins buys up stock in the company, makes himself president, keeps Bates on as general manager and marries the ever-faithful and patient Emily.

Frothingham/Associated Producers, 1921 (original). Silent. Director: Edward Sloman; screenwriter: Albert S. Le Vino. Cast: William V. Mong (Wilkins), Marguerite De La Motte (Dorothy), Pat O'Malley (Jimmy), Helen Jerome (Emily), Hal Cooley (Don), Lincoln Plummer (Bates), Charles Hill Mailes (Stryker).

• ***The Ten Dollar Raise*** (remake). Fox Film Corp., 1935. Director: George Marshall; screenwriters: Henry Johnson and Louis Breslow. Cast: Edward Everett Horton (Hubert T. Wilkins), Karen Morley (Emily Converse), Alan Dinehart (Fuller), Glen Boles (Don Bates), Berton Churchill (Mr. Bates), Rosina Lawrence, Ray Walker, Frank Melton, William Benedict.

• ***He Hired the Boss*** (remake). Twentieth Century–Fox, 1943. Director: Thomas Z. Loring; screenwriters: Ben Markson and Irving Cummings, Jr. Cast: Stuart Erwin (Hubert Wilkins), Evelyn Venable (Emily Conway), Thurston Hall (Mr. Bates), Vivian Blaine (Sally Conway), William T. Orr (Don Bates), Bennie Bartlett, Chick Chandler, Hugh Beaumont, Ken Christy.

This comedy about a timid milquetoast who finally gets the gumption to assert himself drags and one wonders why producers thought it should be twice remade. In the first rehash, Edward Everett Horton, always good for a laugh or two, provides the only bright spot in the otherwise dreary comedy. In the 1943 version, Stu Erwin is okay but that wasn't a good enough reason for viewers to plunk down a quarter of their hard-earned money to see it.

Ten Little Indians *see* **And Then There Were None**

889 Ten Nights in a Bar Room

Based on the story by Timothy Shay Arthur and the play by William W. Pratt. Story: Joe Morgan, a lumberman, becomes an alcoholic when a new a saloon is opened in town. Things get so bad that he can no longer work and he neglects his wife and child. When his daughter comes to the tavern to get him to come home, a thrown beer glass hits her in the head and she later dies from the injury. Realizing at last where alcohol has led him, Joe at first seeks revenge for his daughter's death, but following a spectacular fire and a logjam, he reunites with his wife, all thoughts of revenge gone.

Arrow Film Corp., 1921 (original). Silent. Director: Oscar Apfel; screenwriter: L. Case Russell. Cast: Baby Ivy Ward (Little Mary Morgan), John Lowell (Joe Morgan), Nell Clarke Keller (Fanny Morgan), Charles McKay (Simon Slade), James Phillips, Ethel Dwyer, Charles Beyer, John Woodford, Kempton Greene.

• ***Ten Nights in a Bar Room*** (remake). Roadshow Productions, 1931. Director: William O'Connor; screenwriter: Norton S. Parker. Cast: William Farnum (Joe Morgan), Thomas Santschi (Simon Slade), Patty Lou Lynd (Mary Morgan), Robert Frazer (Dr. Romaine), Phyllis Barrington (Ann Slade), Rosemary Thebe (Sarah Morgan), John Darrow, Lionel Belmore.

Variety wondered if exhibitors would be willing to show the remake and split the communities into those who were "wet" and the "drys." Whatever the outcome, town by town, on that question, the movie is tiresome and never rings true. Among the evils of alcohol are bad films about the evils of alcohol.

Ten Weeks with a Circus *see* **Circus Days**

The Tenderfoot *see* **The Butter and Egg Man**

The Terrible Lovers *see* **Private Lives**

890 The Terror

Based on the play by Edgar Wallace. Story: The Terror, an unknown killer, makes his headquarters in an old English home which has been converted to an inn. The Terror frightens his guests with strange noises and mysterious organ recitals. Among those visiting the inn are a Scotland Yard detective, Ferdinand Fane, who makes people think he's not too bright to throw them off the track; a spirtualist, Mrs. Elvery, and a couple of crooks, Joe Connors and Soapy Marks, who wish to take vengeance against their former gang leader, the Terror. After a night of murder, the identity of the mysterious and deadly host is revealed.

Warner Bros., 1928 (original). Part-talkie. Director: Roy Del Ruth; screenwriter: Harvey Gates. Cast: May McAvoy (Olga Redmayne), Louise Fazenda (Mrs. Elvery), Edward Everett Horton (Ferdinand Fane), Alec B. Francis (Dr. Redmayne), Matthew Betz (Joe Connors), Holmes Herbert (Goodman), Otto Hoffman (Soapy Marks), Joseph W. Girard, John Miljan, Frank Austin.

• ***Return of the Terror*** (remake). First National Pictures, 1934. Director: Howard Bretherton; screenwriters: Eugene Solow and Peter Milne. Cast: Mary Astor (Olga), Lyle Talbot (Dr. Goodman), John Halliday (Dr. Redmayne), Frank McHugh (Joe), Irving Pichel (Burke), Frank Reicher, J. Carroll Naish, Renee Whitney, Robert Barrat, George E. Stone, Robert E. O'Connor.

• ***The Terror*** (remake). Alliance Pictures, Great Britain, 1941. Director: Richard Bird; screenwriter: William Freshman. Cast: Wilfrid Lawson (Mr. Goodman), Bernard Lee (Ferdie Fane), Arthur Wonter (Colonel Redmayne), Linden Travers (Mary Redmayne), Henry Oscar (Connor), Alastair Sim (Soapy Marks), Iris Hoey (Mrs. Elvery), Leslie Wareing, Stanley Lathbury, John Turnbull.

Roger Corman and Francis Ford Coppola produced a film called *The Terror* for American International in 1963, but it isn't based on the Edgar Wallace play. Instead it has Boris Karloff as a baron living in a creepy castle, mourning the death of his wife of 20 years. Jack Nicholson had a leading role in the picture.

An interesting thing about the 1928 film was that it was the first movie without a listing of the production and acting credits; all the credits were spoken. The 1934 film, although based on the Wallace story and with some of the same characters, really had little to do with the original. It deals with a physician on trial for murder by poisoning. The English production in 1941 had a nice character case but is defective because the audience is not given enough clues, false or otherwise, to allow them to figure out the identity of the Terror. As any fan of detective mystery stories knows, that's the appeal of the genre.

Tess ***see*** **Tess of the D'Urbervilles**

891 Tess of the D'Urbervilles

Based on the novel by Thomas Hardy. Story: When John Durbeyfield learns that he is a relative of the wealthy D'Urbervilles, he sends his daughter Tess to the current lord, Alec, who employs her as a maid. He seduces her and she finds herself pregnant. She stalks out of his life but loses her baby. She finds happiness with Angel Clare, although when he learns of her past, he deserts her. To free herself from the influence of Alec, she is forced to kill him, for which she is executed.

MGM, 1924. Silent. Director: Marshall Neilan; screenwriter: Dorothy Farnum. Cast: Blanche Sweet (Tess), Conrad Nagel (Angel Clare), Stuart Holmes (Alec D'Urberville), George Fawcett (John Dubeyfield), Victory Bateman, Courtenay Foote, Joseph J. Dowlin.

• **Tess** (remake). Renn/Burrill, France-Great Britain, 1979. Director and screenwriter: Roman Polanski. Cast: Nastassia Kinski (Tess), Peter Firth (Angel Clare), Leigh Lawson (Alec D'Urberville), Rosemary Martin, Sylvia Coleridge, John Collin, Tony Church, Brigid Erin Bates.

The Polanski remake was a critical success but it didn't catch on at the box office, seemingly from a word-of-mouth description of the movie as being unexciting and rather strange, despite having the lovely Nastassia Kinski in the title role. The film won Academy awards for photography, art direction and costume design. Polanski and the picture were nominated for Oscars as was Philippe Sarde for the score, but all came away empty-handed.

892 Tess of the Storm Country

Based on the novel by Grace Miller White. Story: Elias Graves wishes to move squatters off of his land. Leading the squatters' fight for survival is Tess Skinner, who wins the sympathy and love of Graves' son, Frederick. She loses both when she is discovered with a child whom Frederick assumes to be hers. Tess and Frederick are reunited when his sister, Teola, reveals at the baptism that the child is hers. Graves and the squatters' differences are finally resolved when it is shown that Tess' father is innocent of murdering Graves' right-hand man, Dan Jordan.

• ***Tess of the Storm Country*** (remake). Pickford Co./United Artists, 1922. Silent. Director: John S. Robertson; screenwriter: Elmer Harris. Cast: Mary Pickford (Tess Skinner), Lloyd Hughes (Frederick Graves), Gloria Hope (Teola Graves), David Torrence (Elias Graves), Forrest Robinson (Daddy Skinner), Jean Hersholt (Ben Letts), Robert Russell (Dan Jordan), Danny Hoy, Gus Saville, Mme. De Bodamere.

• ***Tess of the Storm Country*** (remake). Fox Film Corp., 1932. Director:

Alfred Santell; screenwriter: Rupert Hughes. Cast: Janet Gaynor (Tess Howland), Charles Farrell (Frederick Garfield, Jr.), Dudley Digges (Captain Howland), June Clyde (Teola Garfield), George Meeker (Dan Taylor), Edward Pawley (Ben Letts), Claude Gillingwater (Frederick Garfield, Sr.), Matty Kemp, De Witt Jennings, Louise Carter.

This aged melodrama was also filmed in 1914 and in 1960 it starred Diana Baker as a Scottish girl who arrives in the Pennsylvania Dutch country and must endure the prejudice of the local farmers against the Mennonites. The tear-jerker had its cinematic heyday when filmed as a vehicle for Mary Pickford. At least then, audiences didn't have to hear the trite dialog. The 1932 film teamed Gaynor and Farrell, really just Gaynor, as Farrell had little to do and didn't appear on screen very often.

La Testament du Docteur Cordelier *see* **Dr. Jekyll and Mr. Hyde**

893 Thank You Jeeves

Based on the stories by P.J. Wodehouse. Story: Filming Wodehouse can't be an easy task and it has rarely been attempted. The plot's not the thing, in fact it's hardly anything, the movie being the story of a competent and very correct butler who with the questionable assistance of his sappy employer rescues a maiden from some villains involved in gun-running or something equally vile. It's a madcap farce with good use of Wodehouse's dialog and Arthur Treacher is at his pompous best as the reserved butler, with David Niven showing good comedy style in his first leading role.

Twentieth Century–Fox, 1936 (original). Director: Arthur Grenville Collins; screenwriters: Joseph Hoffman and Stephen Gross. Cast: Arthur Treacher (Jeeves), David Niven (Bertie Wooster), Virginia Field (Marjorie Lowman), Lester Matthews (Elliott Manville), Colin Tapley, John Graham Spacey, Willie Best.

• ***Step Lively, Jeeves*** (sequel). Twentieth Century–Fox, 1937. Director: Eugene Forde; screenwriters: Frances Hyland, Frank Fenton and Lynn Root. Cast: Arthur Treacher (Jeeves), Patricia Ellis (Patricia Westley), Robert Kent (Gerry Townsend), Alan Dinehart (Hon. Cedric B. Cromwell), George Givot (Prince Boris Caminov), Helen Flint, John Harrington, George Cooper.

By the sequel, David Niven had moved onto more important roles and so Bertie Wooster was absent. To make matters worse, the story wasn't written by Wodehouse, being an original effort by Frances Hyland, who didn't have P.G.'s style or way with dialog. Treacher was still excellent but that was about it in this muddled film. Treacher is chosen by two con men to be transported to America as a phony earl and the heir to Sir Francis Drake's buried treasure and land grants. Their mark is a wealthy gangster with a social-climbing wife. The scheme is exposed by reporter Patricia Ellis and her fiancé, Robert Kent.

Thanks for the Memory *see* **Up Pops the Devil**

That Certain Woman *see* **The Trespasser**

That Girl from Paris *see* **Street Girl**

That Kind of Woman *see* **The Shopworn Angel**

That Lady in Ermine *see* **The Lady in Ermine**

That Way with Women *see* **The Ruling Passion**

That Wonderful Urge *see* **Love Is News**

There Goes Kelly *see* **Up in the Air**

894 There's Always a Woman

Based on a story by Wilson Collinson. Story: It's a briskly paced comedy about a detective and his somewhat dotty wife who beats him to the solution of a murder. This is another imitation of the "Thin Man"–type story, with the flattery not too bad, having plenty of laughs and some nice surprise twists.

Columbia Pictures, 1938. Director: Alexander Hall; screenwriter: Gladys Lehman. Cast: Joan Blondell (Sally Reardon), Melvyn Douglas (William Reardon), Mary Astor (Lola Fraser), Frances Drake (Anne Calhoun), Jerome Cowan (Nick Shane), Robert Paige, Thurston Hall, Pierre Watkin, Walter Kingsford, Lester Matthews.

• ***There's That Woman Again*** (sequel). Columbia Pictures, 1939. Director: Alexander Hall; screenwriters: Philip G. Epstein, James Edward Grant and Ken Englund. Cast: Melvyn Douglas (Bill Reardon), Virginia Bruce (Sally Reardon), Margaret Lindsay (Mrs. Nacelle), Stanley Ridges (Tony Croy), Gordon Oliver (Charles Crenshaw), Tom Dugan, Don Beddoe, Jonathan Hale, Pierre Watkin, Paul Harvey.

While the title of the sequel is in error, Joan Blondell was replaced as detective Melvyn Douglas' dumbbell wife by Virginia Bruce, and the level of the comedy didn't suffer much. However, the combination wasn't enough to make the producers extend the teaming after this story of jewel robberies and two murders. Margaret Lindsay made a very attractive villain but things quickly boil down to hokum.

895 There's Always Tomorrow

Based on the novel by Ursula Parrott. Story: Joseph White, a likeable, mild-mannered husband and father, is neglected by his wife and five children. He strikes up an innocent friendship with Alice who has always secretly loved him. She makes him feel wanted again, but his children, keeping the relationship from their mother, put an end to what they consider a scandalous affair.

Universal Pictures, 1934 (original). Director: Edward Sloman; screenwriter: William Hurlburt. Cast: Frank Morgan (Joseph White), Binnie Barnes (Alice), Lois Wilson (Sophie White), Louise Latimer (Janet), Elizabeth Young (Helen),

Alan Hale (Harry), Robert Taylor (Arthur), Maurice Murphy, Dick Winslow, Helen Parrish, Margaret Hamilton.

• ***There's Always Tomorrow*** (remake). Universal Pictures, 1956. Director: Douglas Sirk; screenwriter: Bernard C. Schoenfeld. Cast: Barbara Stanwyck (Norma Miller), Fred MacMurray (Clifford Groves), Joan Bennett (Marion Groves), Pat Crowley (Ann), William Reynolds (Vincent Groves), Gigi Perreau (Ellen Groves), Judy Nugent (Frances Groves), Jane Darwell, Hal Smith, Paul Smith, Race Gentry.

Frank Morgan was superb as the neglected husband and father, and Binnie Barnes made an impressive American film debut as the understanding "other woman." In the remake, it's Fred MacMurray who is taken for granted by his wife, Joan Bennett, and his three kids. Things get better for him when he renews his acquaintance with an old flame, Barbara Stanwyck, but when the kids object to what appears to be the breaking-up of their family life, Barbara gracefully backs out of the picture. All this happens without Bennett ever being the wiser, so her relationship with her husband undergoes no changes.

There's That Woman Again *see* **There's Always a Woman**

These Three *see* **The Children's Hour**

They Call Me Mr. Tibbs *see* **In the Heat of the Night**

They Knew What They Wanted *see* **The Secret Hour**

They Live by Night *see* **The Twisted Road**

They Made Me a Criminal *see* **The Life of Jimmy Dolan**

896 The Thief of Bagdad

Based on a fairy tale. Story: Until he meets the Princess, the Thief of Bagdad has no use for the teachings of Allah. Pretending to be a prince, the scoundrel wins her love. After suffering humility when she discovers his deception and confessing the truth to a holy man, he is sent on a quest to recover a magic chest to prove his worthiness. Overcoming many obstacles, he finds what he was sent for, and rescues the Thief of Bagdad and the Princess from an invasion of Mongols.

Fairbanks Productions/United Artists, 1924 (original). Silent. Director: Raoul Walsh; screenwriters: Lotta Woods and Elton Thomas (Douglas Fairbanks). Cast: Douglas Fairbanks (the Thief of Bagdad), Snitz Edwards (His Evil Associate), Charles Belcher (the Holy Man), Julanne Johnston (the Princess), Anna May Wong (the Mongol Slave), Winter-Blossom (the Slave of the Lute), Etta Lee (the Slave of the Sand Board), Brandon Hurst (the Caliph), Tote Du Crow (the Soothsayer), Sojin, K. Nambu, Sadakichi Hartmann, Noble Johnson, Mathilde Comont.

• ***The Thief of Bagdad*** (remake). London Films, 1940. Directors: Ludwig Berger, Michael Powell, Tim Whalen, Zoltan Korda, William Cameron

Menzies and Alexander Korda; screenwriters: Lajos Biro and Miles Malleson. Cast: Conrad Veidt (Jaffar), Sabu (Abu), June Duprez (the Princess), John Justin (Ahmad), Rex Ingram (Djinni), Miles Malleson (the Sultan), Morton Selten (Old King), Mary Morris (Halima/Mechanical Doll), Bruce Winston, Hay Petrie, Adelaide Hall, Roy Emerton, Allan Jeayes.

Costing the unheard of $2,000,000, the Fairbanks film was the most opulent of the smiling, swashbuckling silent star's career. The special effects of the movie, for the time, were viewed as simply amazing. Fairbanks had to brave the Caverns of Fire, the Valley of Monsters, the Flight of a Thousand Stairs and the Flying Horse as part of the tests he had to endure to earn the love of the Princess. The final shot has Fairbanks and Julanne Johnston sailing over Baghdad on a Magic Carpet while the stars spell out the message, "Happiness Must be Earned."

The 1940 Alexander Korda production is one of those magical movie events that comes along all too infrequently. Seeing it on its initial release as a child or years later in re-release or on television, one recalls that some of the most memorable and vivid movie images of a lifetime come from this perfect example of an Arabian Nights–like story. Beyond the marvelous special effects of flying carpets, killer mechanical dolls, flying mechanical horses, giant genies, etc., the casting is splendid. Who could be more evil than Conrad Veidt as the magician who usurps a throne by blinding the caliph and changing his loyal friend, the thief of Baghdad, Sabu, into a mongrel dog? Sabu is the childlike thief who fears nothing, least of all a giant genie who gives him three wishes. Speaking of the Djinni, Rex Ingram is delightful in the role of this laughing menace who has spent thousands of years in a bottle, and is just as likely to kill the one who released him as to reward him. John Justin and June Duprez are horrible actors, but they seem just right for the young lovers. That this film is such a spectacular entertaining fairy tale is amazing considering the number of cooks involved in its direction, some whom received credit and others, including the brothers Korda, who did not.

The fairy tale has also been brought to the screen in various countries in 1928, 1934, 1957, 1960, 1961, 1965 and 1968.

Thief of Damascus *see* **Chu Chin Chow**

Thieves Like Us *see* **The Twisted Road**

Thin Ice *see* **My Lips Betray**

897 The Thin Man

Based on the novel by Dashiell Hammett. Story: This classic detective story, combining some of the best elements of a screwball comedy, has tipsy retired detective Nick Charles and his lovely but eccentric wife Nora called upon to solve the murder of an inventor, Clyde Wynant, the thin man of the title.

MGM, 1934 (original). Director: W.S. Van Dyke; screenwriters: Albert Hackett and Frances Goodrich. Cast: William Powell (Nick Charles), Myrna

Loy (Nora Charles), Maureen O'Sullivan (Dorothy Wynant), Nat Pendleton (John Guild), Minna Gombell (Mira Wynant Jorgensen), Porter Hall (MacCauley), Cesar Romero (Chris Jorgensen), Edward Ellis (Clyde Wynant), Edward Brophy (Morelli), Gertrude Short (Julia), Henry Wadsworth, William Henry, Harold Huber.

• ***After the Thin Man*** (sequel). MGM, 1936. Director: W.S. Van Dyke; screenwriters: Albert Hackett and Frances Goodrich. Cast: William Powell (Nick Charles), Myrna Loy (Nora Charles), James Stewart, Elissa Landi, Joseph Calleia, Jessie Ralph, Alan Marshal, Sam Levene.

William Powell and Myrna Loy also starred as Nick and Nora Charles in *Another Thin Man, Shadow of the Thin Man, The Thin Man Goes Home* and *Song of the Thin Man.* These lighthearted murder mysteries featuring a husband and wife who thoroughly enjoy each other and their marriage (demonstrated through their charming playfulness and high spirits) delighted Depression audiences and they still have appeal for those who pick them up on TV. The fact that it was Edward Ellis and not William Powell who was the "thin man" of the title, did not faze the producers. If the public wanted Nick Charles to be also known as the "Thin Man," then so be it. The first sequel contains an interesting bit of trivia. The murderer is none other than Jimmy Stewart—can you buy that? And he's pretty emotional about the whole thing.

The Thin Man Goes Home ***see*** **The Thin Man**

The Third Round ***see*** **Bulldog Drummond**

898 The Third String

Based on a story by W.W. Jacobs. Story: Ginger Dick is a sailor on leave who falls for barmaid Julia. He poses as an Australian boxing champion to impress her and finds himself in the ring with a real champion, Bill Lumm. Ginger arranges with Lumm for the former to win, but it's to no avail, Julia goes off with her boss at the pub.

London Films, Great Britain, 1914 (original). Silent. Director: George Loane Tucker; screenwriter: W.W. Jacobs. Cast: Jane Gail (Julia), Frank Stanmore (Ginger Dick), George Bellamy (Peter Russett), Charles Vernon (Bill Lumm), Judd Green, Charles Rock.

• ***The Third String*** (remake). Welsh/Pearson, Great Britain, 1932. Director: George Pearson; screenwriters: Pearson, James Reardon and A.R. Rawlinson. Cast: Sandy Powell (Ginger Dick), Kay Hammond (Julia), Mark Daly (Pete Russett), Alf Goddard (Bill Lumm), Charles Paton, Sydney Fairbrother, Pollie Emery, James Knight.

The plot of these films has been used time and time again and these versions are neither the best nor the worst examples of the comedy sub-sub-genre.

899 The Thirteenth Chair

Based on the play by Bayard Veiller. Story: When the police are stumped by the mysterious killing of writer Spencer Lee in Calcutta, they call on Madame

La Grange to hold a seance to see if the dead man can be called upon to give his version of his murder. Lee is about to reveal his murderer's identity when his best friend, Edward Wales, is killed. In a reconstruction of the events of the seance the killer is frightened into giving a confession.

• ***The Thirteenth Chair*** (remake). MGM, 1929. Part talkie. Director: Tod Browning; screenwriter: Elliott Clawson. Cast: Conrad Nagel (Richard Crosby), Leila Hyams (Helen O'Neill), Margaret Wycherly (Madame Rosalie La Grange), Helene Millard (Mary Eastwood), Holmes Herbert (Sir Roscoe Crosby), Mary Forbes (Lady Crosby), Bela Lugosi (Inspector Delzante), John Davidon (Edward Wales), Charles Quartermaine, Moon Carroll, Cyril Chadwick, Bertram Johns.

• ***The Thirteenth Chair*** (remake). MGM, 1937. Director: George Seitz; screenwriter: Marion Parsonnet. Cast: Dame May Whitty (Mme. La Grange), Madge Evans (Nell O'Neill), Lewis Stone (Marney), Elissa Landi (Helen Trent), Thomas Beck (Crosby), Henry Daniell (Wales), Janet Beecher (Lady Crosby), Ralph Forbes (Trent), Holmes Herbert (Crosby), Heather Thatcher, Charles Trowbridge.

First filmed by Pathe in 1919, *The Thirteenth Chair* is a good if very-dated whodunit. The two actresses who play the medium, Margaret Wycherly in the first (best remembered as Ma Jarrett in *White Heat*) and Dame May Whitty in the remake, keep the focus of attention on themselves and carry much of the plot. In the first, Bela Lugosi, not yet established as the evil villain, played a Scotland Yard inspector, a role handled very well by Lewis Stone in the remake. The filming in the darkness has it's intended eerie audience effect.

900 The Thirteenth Guest

Based on a story by Armitage Trail. Story: The complex story of this mystery melodrama deals with relatives and a strange will in a cobwebby old house, with several persons being electrocuted by trick telephones. Detective Winston unravels the mystery with some help from a rather stupid assistant called Grump. The flashes of a masked figure at work at an electric switch are just enough to give the audience a chance to discover the killer before the detectives do.

Monogram Pictures, 1932 (original). Director: Albert Ray; screenwriters: Francis Hyland and Arthur Hoerl. Cast: Ginger Rogers (Marie Morgan), Lyle Talbot (Winston), J. Farrell MacDonald (Capt. Ryan), James Eagles (Harold Morgan), Eddie Phillips (Thor Jensen), Erville Alderson (Adams), Paul Hurst (Grump), Robert Klein, Crauford Kent, Frances Rich, Ethel Wales, Bill Davidson.

• ***Mystery of the 13th Guest*** (remake). Monogram Pictures, 1943. Director: William Beaudine; screenwriters: Charles Marion and Tim Ryan. Cast: Dick Purcell (Johnny), Helen Parrish (Marie), Tim Ryan (Burke), Frank Faylen (Speed), John Duncan (Harold), Jon Dawson (Jackson), Paul McVey, Jacqueline Dalya, Cyril King.

The hackneyed story is that of an uncle trying to eliminate all the beneficiaries of a will. In the remake, Dick Purcell is the detective who exposes the murderer and prevents his new love interest, Helen Parrish, from getting knocked off. Like Ginger Rogers before her, Parrish is proven to be the occupant of the title chair. The acting and direction are less than ordinary.

901 The 39 Steps

Based on the novel by John Buchan. Story: Richard Hannay meets a spy named Margaret who is murdered in his flat and the police believe he is the culprit. To exonerate himself he is forced to flee all over Scotland, sometimes chased by the police, sometimes by the real murderers, sometimes by both. In the process he becomes very attached to beautiful Pamela, in fact they are handcuffed together, much against her will, she thinking him a murderer. She is finally convinced of his innocence and the danger to both of them. Ultimately, Hannay discovers the meaning of the 39 steps while watching a performance by Mr. Memory. He's cleared and the spies and murderers are caught and their plot thwarted.

Gaumont, Great Britain, 1935 (original). Director: Alfred Hitchcock; screenwriters: Charles Bennett, Ian Hay and Alma Reville. Cast: Robert Donat (Richard Hannay), Madeleine Carroll (Pamela), Godfrey Tearle (Prof. Jordan), Lucie Mannheim (Anabella Smith), Peggy Ashcroft (Margaret), John Laurie (John), Helen Haye (Mrs. Jordan), Frank Cellier (Sheriff Watson), Wylie Watson (Mr. Memory), Gus McNaughton, Jerry Verno.

• ***The 39 Steps*** (remake). Rank, Great Britain, 1959. Director: Ralph Thomas; screenwriters: Frank Harvey, Charles Bennett, Ian Hay and Alma Reville. Cast: Kenneth More (Richard Hannay), Taina Elg (Miss Fisher), Brenda de Banzie (Nellie Lumsden), Barry Jones (Prof. Logan), Reginald Beckwith (Lumsden), Sidney James (Perce), Faith Brook (Nannie), Jameson Clark (McDougal), Michael Goodliffe (Brown), James Hayter (Mr. Memory), Andrew Cruickshank, Leslie Dwyer.

• ***The 39 Steps*** (remake). Rank, Great Britain, 1978. Director: Don Sharp; screenwriter: Michael Robson. Cast: Robert Powell (Richard Hannay), David Warner (Edmund Appleton), Eric Porter (Insp. Lomas), Karen Dotrice (Alexandra Mackenzie), John Mills (Col. Scudder), George Baker (Sir Walter Bullivant), Ronald Pickup (Bayliss), Donald Pickering (Marshall), Timothy West, Miles Anderson, Andrew Keir, Robert Fleming, William Squire, Paul McDowell.

The 1935 film is among the best directed by Alfred Hitchcock and depicts his special talents and approaches to thrillers admirably. The cast, headed by Robert Donat, is superb. The film is not only exciting and suspenseful, but it is humorous and touching as well. The remakes are adequate if judged by themselves but if compared to the first production, they must be declared wanting. While the first of these is pretty much the same tale as the Hitchcock picture, the 1978 film has Hannay as a mining engineer, pursued by spies for a notebook he has that contains the secret of a bomb in Big Ben. Understanding what it is that everyone is after doesn't make for a better thriller, as Hitchcock well knew.

Robert Donat and Madeleine Carroll pose as their characters in a beautiful profile in The 39 Steps *(Gaumont British, 1935).*

902 This Gun for Hire

Based on the novel by Graham Greene. Story: Gunman Raven is hired by foreign agents to kill a scientist and obtain secret documents which contain the formula for a new kind of explosive. When he completes the assignment, he is paid off by Willard Gates with marked stolen money to get rid of him. But Raven resolves to have his revenge for being turned into a fugitive. Nightclub singer Ellen Graham is recruited by the FBI to help trap Gates. She agrees but insists that her police detective boyfriend, Michael Crane, be kept in the dark about her activities. Raven and Ellen's paths cross and a romance is budding between them when both Gates and Raven are killed in a hail of bullets.

Paramount Pictures, 1942 (original). Director: Frank Tuttle; screenwriters: Albert Maltz and W.R. Burnett. Cast: Veronica Lake (Ellen Graham), Robert

Something to the left has caught the attention of Kenneth More and Brenda de Banzie in The 39 Steps *(Rank, 1959).*

Preston (Michael Crane), Laird Cregar (Willard Gates), Alan Ladd (Raven), Tully Marshall (Alvin Brewster), Mikhail Rasumny (Sluky), Marc Lawrence, Pamela Blake, Harry Shannon, Frank Ferguson, Bernadene Hayes.

• ***Short Cut to Hell*** (remake). Paramount Pictures, 1957. Director: James Cagney; screenwriters: Ted Berkman and Raphael Blatt. Cast: Robert Ivers (Kyle), Georgann Johnson (Glory Hamilton), William Bishop (Stan), Jacques Aubuchon (Bahrwell), Peter Baldwin, Yvette Vickers, Murvyn Vye, Milton Frome.

The role of the quiet but determined gunman was Alan Ladd's big movie break. Prior to this role, his appearances in films were brief and unimportant. Critics were not fast to rave about his performance, but audiences took to him right away and particularly liked his time spent in the movie with Veronica Lake. These two short people might as well have been ten feet tall for the sparks that they set off. Laird Cregar, the large and talented actor who tragically died much too soon, gave another fine performance as the enemy agent. In Cagney's first attempt at directing a movie he chose to bring out an updated version of the 1942 hit. In the story, ruthless killer Robert Ivers is searching for Jacques Aubuchon, who has paid him off in marked stolen money for two murders for hire. Ivers picks up Georgann Johnson, girlfriend of William Bishop, the detective in charge of the murder cases, and keeps her with him until he is gunned down by the police in a good climax. It's not that the movie is bad, but Cagney was dealing with a cast of never-had-beens and never-would-be's, and none of them had Jimmy's ability to be hardboiled. It was better for Cagney to be on the other side of the camera.

This Is the Night *see* **Good and Naughty**

903 This Love of Ours

Based on the play *As Before, Better Than Before* by Luigi Pirandello. Story: In this romantic melodrama, Michel Tuzac gives his wife, Karin, the heave-ho after listening to gossip that she was unfaithful. He allows their daughter to believe that her mother is dead. Michel bumps into Karin many years later in Chicago, where she is working as an assistant to artist Targel in a nightclub act. Michel convinces Karin that he knows he was wrong about her, and that he wants to start their life together again. Taking Karin home, Michel does not reveal her true identity to daughter Susette, and the latter is not happy about this strange woman taking her mother's place. It all works out before the finish, with everyone as happy as can be.

• ***This Love of Ours*** (remake). Universal Pictures, 1945. Director: William Dieterle; screenwriters: Bruce Manning, John Klorer and Leonard Lee. Cast: Merle Oberon (Karin Tuzac), Charles Korvin (Michel Tuzac), Claude Rains (Targel), Carl Esmond (Uncle Robert), Sue England (Susette Tuzac), Jess Barker, Harry Davenport, Ralph Morgan, Fritz Leiber, Helen Thimig, Ferike Boros.

• ***Never Say Goodbye*** (remake). Universal Pictures, 1956. Director: Jerry Hopper; screenwriter: Charles Hoffman. Cast: Rock Hudson (Dr. Michael Carrington), Cornell Borchers (Lisa), George Sanders (Victor), Ray Collins (Dr. Bailey), David Janssen (Dave), Shelley Fabares (Suzy Carrington), Raymond Greenleaf, Frank Wilcox, Casey Adams, Else Neft.

Luigi Pirandello's play was the basis of the 1931 MGM film *As You Desire Me* starring Greta Garbo as the amnesiac mistress of an artist, Erich von Stroheim, who rediscovers her real husband, Melvyn Douglas, and falls in love with him again. The presentation of the story in these two Universal entries is pure soap opera but audiences seemed to enjoy them. In the 1956 remake, Rock Hudson had angrily walked out on wife Cornell Borchers (in her American film debut), taking their child with them. His attempts at reconciliation were frustrated by Borchers being arrested in the Russian section of Berlin and being sent behind the Iron Curtain. When he does run into her again, she is an assistant to a cabaret caricaturist, George Sanders. Seeing Hudson, she bolts from the theater and is hit by a truck. Hudson, who is a surgeon, successfully operates on her and convinces her to return to him. However, daughter Shelley Fabares refuses to accept Borchers as her mother, but with love Borchers wins the child over.

This Man in Paris *see* **This Man Is News**

904 This Man Is News

Based on a screenplay by Roger MacDougall, Allan MacKinnon and Basil Dearden. Story: Another comedy-thriller of the "Thin Man" school, this British film tells the tale of Simon Drake, a reporter who is fired because of failure to follow up on a lead for a front-page crime story. To get even, the intoxicated Simon phones in an anonymous tip to his former editor. When his tip turns out to be right on the nose, the criminals figure he knows too much and he's soon engulfed in a series of beatings and killings. Through it all, his droll wife chips in with some rather amazing pieces of deductions which save him from ending up in the morgue.

Pinebrook Ltd./Paramount Pictures, 1938 (original). Director: Donald MacDonald; screenwriters: Roger MacDougall, Allan MacKinnon and Basil Dearden. Cast: Barry K. Barnes (Simon Drake), Valerie Hobson (Pat Drake), Alastair Sim (MacGregor), John Warwick (Johnnie Clayton), Philip Leaver ("Harelip" Murphy), James Birrie, David Keir, Tom Gill, Edward Lexy, Garry Marsh.

• ***This Man in Paris*** (sequel). Pinebrook Ltd./Paramount Pictures, 1939. Director: David MacDonald; screenwriters: Allan MacKinnon and Roger MacDougall. Cast: Barry K. Barnes (Simon Drake), Valerie Hobson (Pat Drake), Alastair Sim (MacGregor), Jacques Max Michel (Beranger), Mona Goya (Torch Bernal), Edward Lexy, Garry Marsh, Anthony Shaw, Cyril Chamberlain.

Barry K. Barnes and Valerie Hobson made lively British Nick and Nora Charles clones working together to outwit the criminals, Scotland Yard and Barnes' editor. In the sequel, the Drakes take on a counterfeiting gang in Paris. This one wasn't quite as spry as the first and no more films in the proposed series were made.

905 This Thing Called Love

Based on the play by Edwin Burke. Story: Seeing the constant fights between her sister Clara and the latter's husband, Harry Bertrand, and their ultimate break-up, Ann Marvin holds out little hope for marriage. She receives a proposal from millionaire gold miner Robert Collings, but counters with the suggestion that although they will marry, she will work as his housekeeper at a salary of $25,000 a year, to see how they like each other's company, before consummating the marriage. He accepts with the agreement that each is free to consort with one's own friends. When she remains indifferent to him, he arouses her jealousy by flirting with Alvarez Guerra; she responds by romancing De Witt. Having gone to the trouble to make each other jealous and learning that the Bertrands have reconciled, they realize that their love is strong enough to try a conventional arrangement.

Pathe Exchange, 1929 (original). Director: Paul L. Stein; screenwriter: Horace Jackson. Cast: Edmund Lowe (Robert Collings), Constance Bennett (Ann Marvin), Roscoe Karns (Harry Bertrand), Zasu Pitts (Clara Bertrand), Carmelita Geraghty (Alvarez Guerra), John Roche (De Witt), Stuart Erwin, Ruth Taylor, Wilson Benge, Adele Watson.

• ***This Thing Called Love*** (remake). Columbia Pictures, 1940. Director: Alexander Hall; screenwriters: George Seaton, Ken Englund and P.J. Wolfson.

Cast: Rosalind Russell (Ann Winters), Melvyn Douglas (Tice Collins), Binnie Barnes (Charlotte Campbell), Allyn Joslyn (Harry Bertrand), Gloria Dickson (Florence Bertrand), Lee J. Cobb, Gloria Holden, Paul McGrath, Leona Marcie, Don Beddoe.

These comedies deal with some very suggestive sexual situations and can get away with doing so because the couple is married, but just haven't got around to doing anything about it as of yet. This must have been particularly satisfying to the producers and a pain to the Hays Office, because surely a man and his wife can spar about going to bed together. In the remake, it is Rosalind Russell's notion, which Melvyn Douglas reluctantly accepts, that they should test their love during a three-month abstainment period. Although agreeing to her terms, Douglas fully intends to break her down and get her to abandon the trial period. By the time he's won her over to his way of thinking, he's contacted a bad case of poison oak and—well, you get the point. It's adult fun, something that one sees now on television's *Moonlighting* with Bruce Willis and Cybill Shepherd, although because of the prevailing attitudes of their time, the films were much more daring than the TV show.

This Time for Keeps *see* **Keeping Company**

906 Those Who Dance

Based on a story by George Kibbe Turner. Story: It's a tale of the lives that are wrecked by involvement with bootleg liquor during Prohibition. It caused the death of Bob Kane's sister in an automobile accident and his blindness. He declares war on the trafficking and all moonshiners. He helps Rose Carney save her brother Matt from the electric chair, when the latter, who works for bootleggers, is framed for murdering a government agent.

Thomas H. Ince/First National Pictures, 1924 (original). Silent. Director: Lambert Hillyer; screenwriters: Hillyer and Arthur Statter. Cast: two versions: Blanche Sweet (Rose Carney/Ruth Jordan), Bessie Love (Vida-Veda Carney), Warner Baxter (Bob Kane), Robert Agnew (Matt Carney/Matt Jordan), John Sainpolis (Monahan), Lucille Rickson (Ruth Kane/Mary Kane), Mathew Betz (Joe the Greek/Red Carney), Lydia Knott, Charles Delaney, Frank Campeau, W.S. McDonough, Jack Perrin.

• ***Those Who Dance*** (remake). Warner Bros., 1930. Director: William Beaudine; screenwriter: Joseph Jackson. Cast: Monte Blue (Dan Hogan), Lila Lee (Nora Brady), William Boyd (Diamond Joe Jennings), Betty Compson (Kitty), William Janney (Tim Brady), Wilfred Lucas (Big Ben Benson), Cornelius Keefe (Pat Hogan), De Witt Jennings, Gino Corrado, Bob Perry.

In the remake of this underworld melodrama, detective Benson, secretly in league with a gang of thieves, arrests Tim Brady for murder. He is tried, convicted and sentenced to die. Diamond Joe Jennings promises Tim's sister Nora to use his influence with the governor to free Tim. Nora learns that Diamond Joe is really the one behind her brother's frame-up. She seeks help from the police, who assign Dan Hogan to the case. Dan is the brother of the man Tim Brady is supposed to have murdered. Dan goes undercover, is unmasked but is able to make some arrests and solve the case, with Diamond Joe being shot by Benson, trying to appear on the right side. He doesn't get away with it and is also arrested. The execution is stayed and Tim is freed. Dan and Nora appear to be ready to take up a more permanent relationship.

A Thousand and One Nights *see* **Aladdin and His Wonderful Lamp** *and* **Arabian Nights**

907 Three Blind Mice

Based on the play *Blind Mice* by Stephen Powys, also the play *Loco* by Dale Eunson and Katherine Albert. Story: It's the pleasant comedy about three sisters from Kansas, Pamela, Moira and Elizabeth Charters, who move to California hoping to land a rich husband for the eldest girl, Pamela. Posing as a wealthy woman in order to meet the right kind of men, she finds herself pursued by two presumably rich suitors, Van Smith and Steve Harrington. Pamela falls for Smith who has a fine lineage but no money. It's okay because her sister Elizabeth marries the one with money.

Twentieth Century–Fox, 1938 (original). Director: William A. Seiter; screenwriters: Brown Holmes and Lynn Starling. Cast: Loretta Young (Pamela Charters), Joel McCrea (Van Smith), David Niven (Steve Harrington), Stuart Erwin (Mike Brophy), Marjorie Weaver (Moira Charters), Pauline Moore (Elizabeth Charters), Binnie Barnes (Miriam), Jane Darwell, Leonard Kinskey, Spencer Charters.

• ***Moon Over Miami*** (remake). Twentieth Century–Fox, 1941. Director: Walter Lang; screenwriters: Vincent Lawrence and Brown Holmes, adapted by George Seaton and Lynn Starling. Cast: Don Ameche (Phil O'Neil), Betty Grable (Kay Latimer), Robert Cummings (Jeffrey Bolton), Charlotte Greenwood (Susan Latimer), Jack Haley (Jack O'Hara), Carole Landis (Barbara Latimer), Cobina Wright, Jr., Lynne Roberts, Robert Conway.

• ***Three Little Girls in Blue*** (remake). Twentieth Century–Fox, 1946. Director: Bruce Humberstone; screenwriter: Valentine Davies. Cast: June Haver (Pam), George Montgomery (Van Damm Smith), Vivian Blaine (Liz), Celeste Holm (Miriam), Vera-Ellen (Myra), Frank Latimore (Steve), Charles Smith (Mike), Charles Halton, Ruby Dandridge, Thurston Hall.

• ***How to Marry a Millionaire*** (remake). Twentieth Century–Fox, 1953. Director: Jean Negulesco; screenwriter: Nunnally Johnson. Cast: Betty Grable (Loco), Marilyn Monroe (Pola), Lauren Bacall (Schatze Page), David Wayne (Freddie Denmark), Rory Calhoun (Eben), Cameron Mitchell (Tom Bookman), William Powell (J.D. Hanley), Alex D'Arcy, Fred Clark, George Dunn, Percy Helton.

These movies differ very little from the "Golddiggers" series of Warner Bros., although supposedly based on different material. The notion of a beautiful woman believing it's just as easy to love a rich man as a poor one and more rewarding, has long been exploited on the stage and in movies. Fox jumped on the bandwagon with a 1931 piece called *Working Girls.* The 1941 film was merely a musical remake of the 1938 picture, featuring Leon Robin and Ralph

Rainger songs including the title number, "Loveliness and Love" and "You Started Something." The 1946 musical version added Technicolor, serving up the Mack Gordon, Josef Myrow and Harry Warren songs "On the Boardwalk," "Somewhere in the Night," "You Make Me Feel So Young" and the title song. In the 1953 film, Betty Grable gets first billing, but the star of the film is clearly Marilyn Monroe with Lauren Bacall carrying most of the important action, as the three girls plot to get themselves a rich husband, but only Bacall is totally successful and she doesn't even know it when she picks her guy, Cameron Mitchell.

Three Cockeyed Sailors *see* **Sailor's Three**

908 Three Coins in the Fountain

Based on the novel *Coins in the Fountain* by John H. Secondari. Story: Three American girls, Miss Francis, Anita and Maria, find romance in Rome with Mr. Shadwell, Georgio and Prince Dino Di Cessi, respectively. The title refers to the girls throwing coins in the Treve Fountain which is supposed to do things for their love life.

Twentieth Century–Fox, 1954 (original). Director: Jean Negulesco; screenwriter: John Patrick. Cast: Clifton Webb (Shadwell), Dorothy McGuire (Miss Francis), Jean Peters (Anita), Louis Jourdan (Prince Dino Di Cessi), Maggie McNamara (Maria), Rossano Brazzi (Georgio), Howard St. John, Kathryn Givney, Cathleen Nesbitt, Vincent Padula, Mario Siletti.

• ***The Pleasure Seekers*** (remake). Twentieth Century–Fox, 1964. Director: Jean Negulesco; screenwriter: Edith Sommer. Cast: Ann-Margret (Fran Hobson), Tony Franciosca (Emilio Lacaye), Carol Lynley (Maggie Williams), Gardner McKay (Pete Stenello), Pamela Tiffin (Suzie Higgins), Andre Lawrence (Dr. Andreas Briones), Gene Tierney (Jane Barton), Vito Scotti, Isobel Elsom, Maurice Marsac, Shelby Grant.

The first film was a pleasant little nothing which enjoyed tremendous popularity, probably because of the Academy Award–nominated title song which became a big hit for the Four Aces. The remake is much the same, only now the location is Madrid. In both films the three young American women don't have it easy from the beginning in their romantic pursuits but by the end of the films things have worked out fairly well for almost all concerned. The remake surely could have used a hit song.

Three Daring Daughters *see* **Three Smart Girls**

909 Three Faces East

Based on the play by Anthony Paul Kelly. Story: During World War I, Frank Bennett, a prisoner of war in Germany, is cared for by a nurse named Fraulein Marks. When she is captured in a British raid, it is revealed that she is actually a British Secret Service agent by the name of Miss Hawtree. Her new instructions are to discover the identity of a German spy named Boelke. While at the home of the head of the British War Office, Arthur Bennett (Frank's father),

Miss Hawtree seems to be falling for a wounded servant named Valdar, but no, he's really Boelke in disguise and due to Miss Hawtree his mission is a failure and he is killed. As the war ends, Miss Hawtree and Frank look forward to a happy and peaceful future.

Cinema Corp. of America/PDC, 1926 (original). Silent. Director: Rupert Julian; screenwriters: C. Gardner Sullivan and Monte Katterjohn. Cast: Jetta Goudal (Miss Hawtree/Fraulein Marks), Robert Ames (Frank Bennett), Henry Walthall (George Bennett), Clive Brook (Valdar), Edythe Chapman, Clarence Burton, Ed Brady.

• ***Three Faces East*** (remake). Warner Bros., 1930. Director: Roy Del Ruth; screenwriter: Oliver H.P. Garrett. Cast: Constance Bennett (Frances Hawtree), Erich von Stroheim (Valdar), Anthony Bushell (Arthur Chamberlain), William Courtenay (Mr. Yates), Crauford Kent, Charlotte Walker, William Holden.

• ***British Intelligence*** (remake). Warner Bros., 1940. Director: Terry Morse; screenwriter: Lee Katz. Cast: Boris Karloff (Valdar), Margaret Lindsay (Helene von Lorbeer), Maris Wrixon (Dorothy), Bruce Lester (Frank Bennett), Leonard Mudie (James Yeats), Holmes Herbert (Arthur Bennett), Winifred Harris, Lester Matthews, John Graham Spacy, Austin Fairman.

As these things go, *Three Faces East* and it's 1940 remake *British Intelligence* are pretty good spy stories. In the last version, the producers wisely withhold the information that the female spy is actually a British agent until near the end, although there are enough clues for the astute to discover her true allegiance. Boris Karloff gets the most of his role as the German spy chief, cleverly disguised as a servant in the home of a high British war official. Erich von Stroheim, "the man you love to hate," also had a field day with the role in 1930.

Three for the Show *see* **My Favorite Wife** *and* **Too Many Husbands**

910 Three Hours

Based on the story *Purple and Fine Linen* by May Eddington. Story: Madeline Durkin, once married to one of San Francisco's richest businessmen, has been reduced to begging in the streets. James Finlay is about to give her some money, when a moment's distraction allows her to run off with his wallet. Findlay traces Madeline to a shop where she is busily buying herself the finest of clothes. Finlay drags her off with the intention of turning her over to the police. She begs for a three-hour reprieve and he finally agrees. She goes with him to his apartment where in a flashback she tells her tragic story. She had been falsely accused by her husband of having had an affair and in the divorce action she lost custody of her child. She is permitted to see the child but once, this very evening. This was why she was trying to look her very best and led her to steal from Finlay. He goes with Madeline to the home of her ex-husband and they find the child is dead. Madeline turns to Finlay for consolation, and their love can be seen to bloom.

Corinne Griffith Productions/First National Pictures, 1927 (original). Silent. Director: James Flood; screenwriter: Paul Bern. Cast: Corinne Griffith

(Madeline Durkin), John Bowers (James Finlay), Hobart Bosworth (Jonathan Durkin), Paul Ellis (Gilbert Wainwright), Anne Schaefer, Mary Louise Miller.

• ***Adventures in Manhattan*** (remake). Columbia Pictures, 1936. Director: Edward Ludwig; screenwriters: Joseph Krumgold, Sidney Buchman, Harry Sauber and Jack Kirkland. Cast: Jean Arthur (Claire Peyton), Joel McCrea (George Melville), Reginald Owen (Blackton Gregory), Thomas Mitchell (Phil Bane), Herman Bing, Victor Kilian, John Galludet, Emmet Vogan, George Cooper, Robert Warwick.

Although based on the same source, the remake bears little resemblance to the original tearjerking melodrama. It's supposed to be a comedy about a criminologist, Joel McCrea, hired by a newspaper to write about a mysterious criminal who is stealing every thing of value that's not nailed down. McCrea does so well at his job that he is able to make predictions as to which job the thief will pull next. If that sounds like a lead-up to McCrea being the crook, it isn't. Actually McCrea's foresight enables him to capture the criminal. The last caper is a dandy. The master criminal is putting on a war play in a theater next to a bank, whose vault contains a valuable necklace he fancies. While cannons are blazing on stage, henchmen are below, blasting into the vault.

911 Three Kids and a Queen

Based on the story by Harry Poppe, Chester Beecroft and Mary Marlind. Story: Three boys, Blackie, Flash and Doc, the latter only six years old and a real charmer, decide to kidnap elderly bad-tempered and wealthy Mary Jane Baxter. She enjoys the experience and goes along with the kidnapping, suggesting her ransom be $50,000 to be used to help Tony Orsatti's impoverished family.

Universal Pictures, 1935 (original). Director: Edward Ludwig; screenwriters: Barry Trivers and Samuel Ornitz. Cast: May Robson (Mary Jane Baxter), Frankie Darro (Blackie), Charlotte Henry (Julia), William Benedict (Flash), Billy Burrud (Doc), Henry Armetta (Tony Orsatti), Herman Bing, Lillian Harmer, John Miljan, Lawrence Grant, Hale Hamilton, Noel Madison.

• ***Little Miss Big*** (remake). Universal Pictures, 1946. Director: Erle C. Kenton; screenwriter: Erna Lazarus. Cast: Beverly Simmons (Nancy Bryan), Fay Holden (Mary Jane Baxter), Frank McHugh (Charlie Bryan), Fred Brady (Eddie Martin), Dorothy Morris (Kathy Bryan), Milburn Stone (Father Lennergan), John Eldredge (Sanford Baxter), Samuel S. Hinds, Houseley Stevenson.

May Robson was nicely nasty as the eccentric spinster, the queen of the title, in the first version of this work. The children, Frankie Darro, William Benedict and especially Billy Burrud, did themselves proud as the three kids. In the remake, Fay Holden is an irritable old crone, committed to an asylum by her nephew. She escapes and takes refuge with the family of poor barber Frank McHugh. His young daughter, Beverly Simmons, improves Holden's disposition and after the old lady passes her sanity hearing, she makes certain that McHugh's family is rewarded.

Three Little Girls in Blue *see* **The Gold Diggers** *and* **Three Blind Mice**

912 Three Live Ghosts

Based on the play by Frederic Stewart Isham and Max Marcin. Story: Three men who have escaped from a German prison camp and are reported missing in action, arrive in England on the night of the Armistice. The arrival of the three, Jimmy Grubbins, Billy Foster and Spoofy, is not exactly opportune. Billy is wanted by the police for some crimes committed by another and is turned in by Grubbins' mother when she learns there is a reward. Spoofy, who suffers from shellshock, burglarizes a home that turns out to be his own. Before the final curtain of this comic melodrama, everything is straightened out, and the lads get a proper welcome home.

Famous Players–Lasky/Paramount Pictures, 1922 (original). Silent. Director: George Fitzmaurice; screenwriter: Ouida Bergere. Cast: Anna Q. Nilsson (Ivis Ayers), Norman Kelly (Billy Foster), Curil Chadwick (Spoofy), Edmund Goulding (Jimmy Grubbins), Claire Greet (Mrs. Grubbins), John Miltern, Annette Benson.

• ***Three Live Ghosts*** (remake). United Artists, 1929. Director: Thorton Freeland; screenwriters: Helen Hallett, Max Marcin and Sally Winters. Cast: Beryl Mercer (Mrs. Grubbins), Hilda Vaughn (Peggy Woofers), Harry Stubbs (Bolton), Joan Bennett (Rose Gordon), Nancy Price (Alice), Charles McNaughton (Jimmie Grubbins), Robert Montgomery (William Foster), Claud Allister (Spoofy), Arthur Clayton, Tenen Holtz.

• ***Three Live Ghosts*** (remake). MGM, 1935. Director: H. Bruce Humberstone; screenwriter: C. Gardner Sullivan. Cast: Beryl Mercer (Mrs. Grubbins), Richard Arlen (Billy Foster), Claude Allister (Spoofy), Charles McNaughton (Jimmie Grubbins), Cecila Parker, Dudley Digges, Robert Greig.

The 1922 stage comedy really isn't funny enough to have been filmed three times, but it did give a number of performers some steady work. Beryl Mercer is quite enjoyable as the mother who wished her son had stayed dead until the last insurance payment had been collected. Claude Allister turns in a credible job as the soldier with amnesia who later discovers the jewels he stole and the baby he kidnapped are actually his and he is Lord Leicester. All ends well for the other two live ghosts as well, as one finds all charges against him being dropped and that he is the heir to his father's fortune, while the remaining lad, Mrs. Grubbins' pride and joy, marries his sweetheart.

913 Three Men in a Boat

Based on the novel by Jerome K. Jerome. Story: It's the tale of the comical misadventures in 1890 of three friends on a Thames boating holiday.

Artistic, Great Britain, 1920 (original). Silent. Director: Challis Sanderson; screenwriters: Manning Haynes and Lydia Hayward. Cast: Lionelle Howard (J.), Manning Haynes (Harris), Johnny Butt (George), Eva Westlake, Edward C. Bright.

• ***Three Men in a Boat*** (remake). Associated Talking Pictures, Great Britain, 1933. Director: Graham Cutts; screenwriters: D.B. Wyndham-Lewis and Reginald Purdell. Cast: William Austin (Harris), Edmund Breon (George), Billy Milton (Jimmy), Davy Burnaby (Sir Henry Harland), Iris March (Peggy),

Griffith Humphreys, Stephen Ewart, Victor Stanley, Frank Bertram, Sam Wilkinson, Winifred Evans.

• ***Three Men in a Boat*** (remake). Remus, Great Britain, 1957. Director: Ken Annakin; screenwriters: Hubert Gregg and Vernon Harris. Cast: Laurence Harvey (George), Jimmy Edwards (Harris), David Tomlinson (J.), Shirley Eaton (Sophie Clutterbuck), Jill Ireland (Bluebell Porterhouse), Lisa Gastoni (Primrose Porterhouse), Martita Hunt, Adrienne Corri, Noelle Middleton, Robertson Hare, Campbell Cotts.

A bit of romance was added to the second and third versions of the celebrated comic novel. This didn't noticeably improve the pictures, which were not he funniest of burlesques to begin with.

914 The Three Musketeers

Based on the novel by Alexandre Dumas, *père.* Story: Cardinal Richelieu, Prime Minister of France in the court of King Louis XIII, holds power through intrigue, often using as his agents the mysterious and beautiful Milady de Winter and the devotedly deadly De Rochefort. As part of his plot to control France, he plans to subtly expose the queen's love affair with England's Duke of Buckingham. Into the fray arrives D'Artagnan of Gascony, coming to Paris to join the Musketeers and find some adventure. He earns his membership by proving his prowess as a swordsman and quickly forms an alliance with musketeers Athos, Porthos and Aramis. When the Queen presents Buckingham, as a token of her affection, a gift of some diamond studs which she had received from Louis, Richelieu, learning of this, dispatches Milady de Winter to England to get the jewels from Buckingham. D'Artagnan is sent on a like mission on behalf of the Queen. He recovers them in time to save the queen from the wrath of the king, frustrate Richelieu, run De Rochefort through, put an end to Milady de Winter's treachery and win the hand of Constance, a lady-in-waiting to the Queen.

• ***The Three Musketeers*** (remake). Fairbanks/United Artists, 1921. Silent. Director: Fred Niblo; screenwriters: Lotta Woods and Edward Knoblock. Cast: Douglas Fairbanks (D'Artagnan), Leon Barry (Athos), George Siegmann (Porthos), Eugene Pallette (Aramis), Boyd Irwin (De Rochefort), Thomas Holding (Duke of Buckingham), Nigel De Brulier (Cardinal Richelieu), Mary MacLaren (Queen Anne), Marguerite De La Motte (Constance Bonacieux), Barbara La Marr (Milady de Winter), Adolphe Menjou (Louis XIII), Sidney Franklin, Charles Stevens, Willis Robards, Lon Poff, Walt Whitman, Charles Belcher.

• ***The Three Musketeers*** (remake). RKO, 1935. Director: Rowland V. Lee; screenwriters: Dudley Nichols and Rowland V. Lee. Cast: Walter Abel (D'Artagnan), Paul Lukas (Athos), Margot Grahame (Milady de Winter), Heather Angel (Constance), Ian Keith (De Rochefort), Moroni Olsen (Porthos), Onslow Stevens (Aramis), Rosamond Pinchot (Queen Anne), Ralph Forbes (Duke of Buckingham), Lumsden Hare (de Treville), Miles Mander (King Louis XIII), Nigel De Brulier (Cardinal Richelieu).

• ***The Three Musketeers*** (remake). Twentieth Century–Fox, 1939. Director: Allan Dwan; screenwriters: M.M. Musselman, William A. Drake and Sam

Hellman. Cast: Don Ameche (D'Artagnan), The Ritz Brothers (The Three Lackeys), Binnie Barnes (Milady de Winter), Lionel Atwill (De Rochefort), Gloria Stuart (Queen Anne), Pauline Moore (Constance), Joseph Schildkraut (King Louis XIII), Miles Mander (Cardinal Richelieu), Douglass Dumbrille (Athos), John King (Aramis), Russell Hicks (Porthos), John Carradine (Naveau), Lester Matthews (Duke of Buckingham), Gregory Gaye, Egon Brecher, Moroni Olsen.

• ***The Three Musketeers*** (remake). MGM, 1948. Director: George Sidney; screenwriter: Robert Ardrey. Cast: Lana Turner (Milady de Winter), Gene Kelly (D'Artagnan), June Allyson (Constance), Van Heflin (Athos), Angela Lansbury (Queen Anne), Frank Morgan (King Louis XIII), Vincent Price (Cardinal Richelieu), Keenan Wynn (Planchet), John Sutton (Duke of Buckingham), Gig Young (Porthos), Robert Coote (Aramis), Reginald Owen (de Treville), Ian Keith (De Rochefort), Patricia Medina, Richard Stapley.

• ***The Three Musketeers*** (remake). Film Trust, 1973. Director: Richard Lester; screenwriter: George MacDonald Fraser. Cast: Michael York (D'Artagnan), Oliver Reed (Athos), Richard Chamberlain (Porthos), Frank Findlay (Aramis), Raquel Welch (Constance), Geraldine Chaplin (Queen Anne), Faye Dunaway (Milady de Winter), Charlton Heston (Cardinal Richelieu), Christopher Lee (De Rochefort), Jean-Pierre Cassel (King Louis XIII), Simon Ward (Duke of Buckingham).

• ***The Four Musketeers*** (remake). Film Trust/20th Century–Fox/Este, 1974. Director: Richard Lester; screenwriter: George MacDonald Fraser. Cast: Michael York, Oliver Reed, Frank Findlay, Faye Dunaway, Raquel Welch, Charlton Heston, Simon Ward, Christopher Lee, Geraldine Chaplin, Jean-Pierre Cassel, Roy Kinnear.

It would almost be easier to list the years that the Dumas adventure story was not filmed. However, screen productions throughout the world occurred at least once in each of the following years in addition to those mentioned above: 1903, 1980–09, 1911–14, 1916, 1919, 1921–23, 1929, 1932, 1942, 1946, 1950–55, 1960–64, 1970 and 1973. While the acting of the numerous important characters to the story of *The Three Musketeers* has been a mixed bag in the various productions, the excitement of the adventure yarn has made almost all film versions popular. Douglas Fairbanks, Sr., made a dashing D'Artagnan; Walter Abel, an earnest one; Don Ameche, a singing duelist; Gene Kelly, an acrobatic swordsman; and Michael York, an eager-to-please young musketeer. The heroes and villains in the piece did not have to wear white and black hats to distinguish themselves. Evil was evil, purity was purity, and good was good. Richelieu, De Rochefort and Milady de Winter were bad ones, alright, but the beauty and allure of the latter made it seem a shame that she had to lose her head to the executioner's axe. Constance was loyal, steadfast and pure; while Queen Anne was a foolish woman in an unhappy arranged marriage, looking for love with the enemy of her adopted country. Each of the films is enough to stir the emotions and warm the blood of anyone looking for some good, exciting, vicarious adventure.

915 Three on a Match

Based on a story by Kubee Glasman and John Bright. Story: Three girls raised in the slums meet for the first time after a 12-year separation. Ruth Wescott is a secretary, Vivian Deverse is a wealthy socialite and Mary Keaton is a showgirl. Defying the superstition that the last person to light a cigarette from the same match will die, they do just that with Vivian being the last to light up. There must be something to the curse as Vivian gets involved with a lover and dope, and when the latter gets to be too much for her, she throws herself to her death.

First National Pictures, 1932 (original). Director: Mervyn LeRoy; screenwriter: Lucien Hubbard. Cast: Joan Blondell (Mary Keaton), Warren William (Henry Kirkwood), Ann Dvorak (Vivian Deverse), Bette Davis (Ruth Westcott), Buster Phelps (Junior), Lyle Talbot (Mike), Humphrey Bogart (the Mug).

• ***Broadway Musketeers*** (remake). Warner Bros., 1938. Director: John Farrow; screenwriters: Don Ryan and Kenneth Gamet. Cast: Margaret Lindsay (Isabel Dowling), Ann Sheridan (Fay Reynolds), Marie Wilson (Connie Todd), John Litel (Stanley Dowling), Janet Chapman (Judy Dowling), Dick Purcell (Vincent Morrell), Richard Bond, Anthony Averill, Horace MacMahon, Dewey Robinson, Dorothy Adams.

In the remake, the three girls, who meet years later after leaving the orphanage where they were raised, are Margaret Lindsay, Ann Sheridan and Marie Wilson. Lindsay leaves her husband, John Litel, to run off with Richard Bond who gets involved with mobsters over a gambling debt. This results in the kidnapping of Lindsay and her baby, plus Margaret's suicide as the gangmen plan to kill her. Ann Sheridan as a nightclub entertainer sings "Has It Ever Occurred to You" and "Who Said That This Isn't Love" by M.K. Jerome and Jack Scholl.

Three Russian Girls *see* **The Girl from Leningrad**

Three Sailors and a Girl *see* **The Butter and Egg Man**

916 Three Sinners

Based on the play *The Second Life* by Rudolf Bernauer and Rudolf Osterreicher. Story: When she sees that her husband, Count Dietrich Wallentin, no longer loves her, Gerda agrees to go to Vienna to visit relatives, leaving the Count to his dalliances with Baroness Brings. On the train, she is seduced by famous musician Raoul Stanislav. She briefly leaves the train, and it pulls out of the station without her. Later she learns that the train crashed, killing everyone aboard. Because of her shame about her affair, she does not tell her husband that she is alive. Later her husband encounters her in a Viennese gambling casino, where she is a hostess. He is attracted to her as he says because of her remarkable resemblance to his late wife. Gerda discloses her identity and returns to her husband. Later, perceiving that he doesn't really love her, Gerda takes her child and sails to America with a wealthy patron of the gambling house.

Paramount/Famous Lasky Corp., 1928 (original). Silent. Director: Rowland V. Lee; screenwriters: Doris Anderson and Jean De Limur. Cast: Pola Negri (Baroness Gerda Wallentin), Warner Baxter (James Harris), Paul Lukas (Count Dietrich Wallentin), Tullio Carminati (Raoul Stanislav), Olga Baclanova (Baroness Hilda Brings), Anders Randolph, Anton Vaverka, Ivy Harris.

• ***Once a Lady*** (remake). Paramount Pictures, 1931. Director: Guthrie McClintic; screenwriters: Zoe Akins and Samuel Hoffenstein. Cast: Ruth Chatterton (Anna Keremazoff), Ivor Novello (Bennett Cloud), Jill Esmond (Faith Fenwick, the girl), Suzanne Ransom (Faith Fenwick, the child), Geoffrey Kerr (Jimmy Fenwick), Doris Lloyd (Lady Ellen), Herbert Bunston, Gwendolyn Logan, Stella Moore.

Pola Negri's career in the United States was coming to an end after only six years. She would make one final film for Paramount, *The Woman from Moscow*, but tests had demonstrated that her heavy accent would make her inappropriate for U.S. talkies. In the remake of this dreary drama, screenwriters Zoe Akins and Samuel Hoffenstein added a bit of a mother-love twist to the story of a loose woman who abandons her husband and daughter, letting them believe she is dead, but coming into their lives once again some twenty years later. She is made to be of Russian origin and has come up with a rather inventive Russian dialect in this *Madame X*–like melodrama.

917 Three Smart Girls

Based on a story by Adele Commandini. Story: The Craig sisters, Penny, Joan and Kay, conspire to break up the relationship between their divorced father, Judson, and a golddigger, Donna Lyons, who are planning to marry. They are so successful that dear old dad is reunited with his wife, Dorothy.

Universal Pictures, 1936 (original). Director: Henry Koster; screenwriters: Adele Commandini and Austin Parker. Cast: Deanna Durbin (Penny Craig), Nan Grey (Joan Craig), Barbara Read (Kay Craig), Binnie Barnes (Donna Lyons), Alice Brady (Mrs. Lyons), Ray Milland (Lord Michael Stuart), Charles Winninger (Judson Craig), Nella Walker (Dorothy Craig), Mischa Auer, Ernest Cossart, Hobart Cavanaugh, John King, Lucile Watson.

• ***Three Smart Girls Grow Up*** (sequel). Universal Pictures, 1939. Director: Henry Koster; screenwriters: Bruce Manning and Felix Jackson. Cast: Deanna Durbin (Penny "Mouse" Craig), Nan Grey (Joan Craig), Helen Parrish (Kay Craig), Charles Winninger (Judson Craig), Robert Cummings (Harry Loren), William Lundigan (Richard Watkins), Nella Walker (Dorothy Craig), Ernest Cossart, Felix Bressart.

• ***Hers to Hold*** (sequel). Universal Pictures, 1943. Director: Frank Ryan; screenwriter: Lewis R. Foster. Cast: Deanna Durbin (Penny Craig), Joseph Cotten (Bill Morley), Charles Winninger (Judson Craig), Nella Walker (Dorothy Craig), Gus Schilling (Rosey Blake), Evelyn Ankers (Flo Simpson), Ludwig Stossel, Irving Bacon, Nydia Westman, Murray Alper.

A disguised remake of *Three Smart Girls* was released by MGM in 1948, called *Three Daring Daughters*, starring Jeanette MacDonald, Jose Iturbu, Jane

Powell, Anne Todd and Mary Elinor Donahue. In this version, it was the mother that the three daughters didn't want to remarry.

Deanna Durbin was Universal's biggest money maker in the latter part of the '30s and early '40s. Audiences loved her pretty face, winning personality and especially her spectacular coloratura singing voice. In the first film, she favored audiences with renditions of "My Heart Is Singing" and "Someone to Care for Me" by Gus Kahn, Walter Jurmann and Bronislau Kaper, as well as "Il Bacio" by Luigi Arditi. In the first sequel, Deanna put her energies to work to find husbands for her two elder sisters, and find them she did, in the persons of Robert Cummings and William Lundigan. For herself, she kept on singing; her numbers including the blockbuster hit "Because" by Edward Beschemacher and Guy D'Hardelot, and "The Last Rose of Summer" by Thomas Moore and Richard Alfred Milliken. In the weeper *Hers to Hold*, Deanna is finally grown up and looking for her own romantic interest, finding a pretty good one in pilot Joseph Cotten. She still had time to sing "Say a Little Prayer for the Boys Over There" by Jimmy McHugh, "Begin the Beguine" by Cole Porter and "The Seguidilla" from Bizet's *Carmen*.

Three Smart Girls Grow Up *see* **Three Smart Girls**

Three Sons *see* **Sweepings**

918 Three Wise Fools

Based on the play by Austin Strong and Winchell Smith. Story: Sydney Fairchild, the daughter of Rena Fairchild (once loved by three bachelors, Theodore Findley, Judge James Trumbull and Dr. Richard Gaunt), surprises her mother's former suitors with a visit. They honor the memory of their former love by agreeing to her dying request that they take responsibility for Sydney. All goes well until Sydney is suspected of helping a crook who breaks into their houses. She is arrested, but Findley's nephew proves she is innocent of any wrongdoing.

Goldwyn Pictures, 1923 (original). Silent. Director: King Vidor; screenwriters: June Mathis, John McDermott and James O'Hanlan. Cast: Claude Gillingwater (Theodore Findley), Eleanor Boardman (Rena and Sydney Fairchild), William H. Crane (Hon. James Trumbull), Alec B. Francis (Dr. Richard Gaunt), John Sainpolis, Brinsley Shaw, Fred Esmelton, William Haines, Zasu Pitts.

• ***Three Wise Fools*** (remake). MGM, 1946. Director: Edward Buzzell; screenwriters: John McDermott and James O'Hanlan. Cast: Margaret O'Brien (Sheila O'Monohan), Lionel Barrymore (Dr. Richard Gaunt), Lewis Stone (Judge Thomas Trumbull), Edward Arnold (Theodore Findley), Thomas Mitchell (Terence Aloysius O'Tavern), Ray Collins, Jane Darwell, Charles Dingle, Harry Davenport, Henry O'Neill, Cyd Charisse, Warner Anderson, Billy Curtis.

In the remake, an ancient leprechaun is trying to convince younger ones of the existence of humans. He tells the story of three young men on whose life was put the Irish curse that they would realize all of their ambitions but never have any friends. As old men, the granddaughter of the curse-maker shows up in their lives, firmly believing in the "little people" and intent on teaching the men how to be human. This is not an easy job as the three are ornery old cusses. With pixie-like aplomb young colleen Margaret O'Brien charms the three and in doing so they see the "little people" and the little people see them, both henceforth believing in the existence of the other. The cast of the film is loaded with some great character actors, but the picture is all Margaret O'Brien. It's reported that Lionel Barrymore denied that she was a child, believing had it been the Middle Ages, she would have been burned as a witch.

Thunder in the Valley *see* **Owd Bob**

Thunderhead, Son of Flicka *see* **My Friend Flicka**

919 The Ticket of Leave Man

Based on the story by Tom Taylor. Story: Tiger Dalton offers hand outs and a place to stay to ex-convicts with the idea of drawing them further into crime. One such man, Bob Brierly, gets a job in a bank and Tiger blackmails him into rifling the safe. However, Tiger's girlfriend, May, tips off the police, for which Tiger repays the "squealer" by shooting her. The police pursue him into a cemetery, where Tiger falls into an open grave, breaking his neck.

Barker/Moss, Great Britain, 1918 (original). Silent. Director: Bert Haldane; screenwriter: Tom Taylor. Cast: Daphne Glenne (May Edwards), George Foley (Bob Brierly), Wilfrid Benson (James Tiger Dalton), Aubrey Fitzmaurice (Hawkshaw), Rolf Leslie, Rachel de Solla, George Harrington.

• ***The Ticket of Leave Man*** (remake). King/MGM, Great Britain, 1937. Director: George King; screenwriters: H.F. Maltby and A.R. Rawlinson. Cast: Tod Slaughter (the Tiger), Marjorie Taylor (May Edwards), John Warwick (Bob Brierly), Robert Adair (Hawkshaw), Frank Cochran, Peter Gawthorne, Jenny Lynn, Arthur Payne.

The story has some of the aspects of *Oliver Twist* without being that well-written or half as interesting. In the remake, Slaughter is everything one would want or expect in such a minor-league criminal mastermind, all brute strength, few brains.

920 Tiger Shark

Based on the story *Tuna* by Houston Branch and material by Bryan Foy. Story: Portuguese tuna fisherman Mike wouldn't have any luck at all if it wasn't for bad luck. He has lost one hand to a shark, his wife, Quita, to his best friend, Pipes, and ends up in the jaws of a man-eating shark who this time finishes the job.

First National Pictures, 1932 (original). Director: Howard Hawks; screenwriter: Wells Root. Cast: Edward G. Robinson (Mike), Zita Johann (Quita), Richard Arlen (Pipes), Leila Bennett (Lady Barber), Vince Barnett, J. Carroll Naish.

• ***Bengal Tiger*** (remake). Warner Bros., 1936. Director: Louis King;

screenwriters: Roy Chanslor and Earl Felton. Cast: Barton MacLane (Cliff Ballenger), June Travis (Laura), Warren Hull (Joe Larsen), Paul Graetz (Carl Homan), Joseph Grehan, Richard Purcell, Carlyle Moore, Jr.

• ***Slim*** (remake). Warner Bros., 1937. Director: Ray Enright; screenwriter: W.W. Haines. Cast: Pat O'Brien (Red Blayd), Henry Fonda (Slim), Margaret Lindsay (Cally), Stuart Erwin (Stumpy), J. Farrell MacDonald, Dick Purcell, Joe Sawyer, John Litel.

• ***King of the Lumberjacks*** (remake). Warner Bros., 1940. Director: William Clemens; screenwriter: Crane Wilbur from a story by Sid Hickox. Cast: John Payne (Slim), Gloria Dickson (Tina), Stanley Fields (Dominic), Joe Sawyer (Jigger), Victor Kilian, Earl Dwire, Herbert Haywood, G. Pat Collins, John Sheehan.

• ***Manpower*** (remake). Warner Bros., 1941. Director: Raoul Walsh; screenwriters: Richard Macaulay and Jerry Wald. Cast: Edward G. Robinson (Hank McHenry), Marlene Dietrich (Fay Duvall), George Raft (Johnny Marshall), Alan Hale (Jumbo Wells), Frank McHugh, Eve Arden, Barton MacLane, Walter Catlett, Joyce Compton.

This entry illustrates how a studio can recycle a script, even when other sources are credited for the story. Each of these movies tells the tale of men in dangerous occupations, with two good friends loving the same woman; the one losing out in the romantic triangle being killed on the job.

In *Bengal Tiger,* Barton MacLane, a drunken lion tamer, marries an orphan, June Travis, but discovers that she loves a daring young trapeze artist, Warren Hull. These two are the closest of friends, but one night MacLane knocks out Hull and puts him into a cage with a tiger. As the cat moves in for the kill, Travis calls out her love for Hull. MacLane enters the cage, pulls Hull out, locks himself inside, and turns just as the cat springs, effectively eliminating the triangle.

In *Slim,* Pat O'Brien and Henry Fonda repair high tension wires on the top of electrical towers. Margaret Lindsay is the girl who switches allegiances from O'Brien to farm boy Fonda. O'Brien is killed when the two linemen repair a downed "hot" wire during a blizzard.

In *King of the Lumberjacks,* Stanley Fields is the title character who marries former nitery singer Gloria Dickson, but along comes her old sweetheart, John Payne. Fields sacrifices his life to allow the two young people to be together when he uncouples a car on a runaway train, with them on the safe side.

Finally, in *Manpower,* George Raft and Edward G. Robinson are buddies on a construction and maintenance crew for power lines. Marlene Dietrich is a cheap tart who works in a clip joint. Raft sees through her right away but Robinson falls in love with her and they get married. Now of course, love develops between Raft and Dietrich, leading to a fight between the two men on a power tower, with Robinson falling to his death. All these movies prove that one surefire way to resolve a love triangle is to have one of the three die—preferably the extra man.

921 Till Death Do Us Part

Based on the British TV series created by Johnny Speight. Story: It's life in war and peace with a cockney family from the thirties to the sixties featuring loudmouthed, bigoted Londoner Alf Garnett.

Associated London/British Lion, Great Britain, 1968 (original). Director: Norman Cohen; screenwriter: Johnny Speight. Cast: Warren Mitchell (Alf Garnett), Dandy Nichols (Else Garnett), Anthony Booth (Mike), Una Stubbs (Rita Garnett), Liam Redmond (Father), Bill Maynard (Bert), Brian Blessed, Sam Kydd.

• ***The Alf Garnett Saga*** (remake). Associated London/Columbia-Warners, 1972. Director: Bob Kellett; screenwriter: Johnny Speight. Cast: Warren Mitchell (Alf Garnett), Dandy Nichols (Else Garnett), Adrienne Posta (Rita), Paul Angelis (Mike Garnett), John Le Mesurier (Frewin), John Bird, Roy Kinnear, Roy Hudd, Joan Sims, Tom Chadbon, Patsy Byrne.

The TV series on which these two comedies are based inspired Norman Lear to produce *All in the Family* in the United States with Carroll O'Connor as the loveable bigot Archie Bunker. In the sequel, Alf's main exasperation is with his son-in-law and the possibility that his daughter is pregnant with a black man's baby. It was even more crude than the original and not nearly as funny.

'Til We Meet Again *see* **One Way Passage**

922 Tillie the Toiler

Based on the newspaper comic strip by Russ Westover. Story: Beautiful but dumb stenographer Tillie Jones is encouraged by her mother to accept the marriage proposal of wealthy Pennington Fish, despite the fact that Tillie loves Mac, a simple office worker. To satisfy her mother's ambitions, she agrees to marry Pennington, but at the last moment bolts back to Mac, who has at last rebelled against his inferior career position and has been made office manager, replacing underhanded Mr. Whipple.

Cosmopolitan/MGM, 1927 (original). Silent. Director: Hobart Henley; screenwriter: A.P. Younger. Cast: Marion Davies (Tillie Jones), Matt Moore (Mac), Harry Crocker (Pennington Fish), George Fawcett (Mr. Simpkins), George K. Arthur (Mr. Whipple), Estelle Clark (Sadie), Bert Roach, Gertrude Short, Claire McDowell, Arthur Hoyt.

• ***Tillie the Toiler*** (remake). Columbia Pictures, 1941. Director: Sidney Salkow; screenwriters: Karen DeWolf and Francis Martin. Cast: Kay Harris (Tillie Jones), William Tracy (Mac), George Watts (Simpkins), Daphne Pollard (Mumsy), Jack Arnold (Whipple), Marjorie Reynolds (Bubbles), Bennie Bartlett, Stanley Brown, Ernest Truex, Franklin Pangborn, Sylvia Field.

The two films, meant to be B programmers to fill out double bills, were just about what one would expect from stories based on four-panel comic strips. Most of the running time of the two films is used to establish the comic strip characters, with too little time to make much of the possibilities of the beautiful but bungling Tillie as she tries to make a go of it in the business world as a stenographer, and find a husband.

923 Tilly of Bloomsbury

Based on the play by Ian Hay. Story: A boardinghouse keeper's daughter, Tilly, falls in love with a wealthy aristocrat who takes the girl down to his country house for the weekend, where his mother makes things very unpleasant for Tilly. She tries to break off the relationship with her young man, but he chooses her over his mother and wins her back.

• ***Tilly of Bloomsbury*** (remake). Sterling Productions, Great Britain, 1931. Director: Jack Raymond; screenwriter: W.P. Lipscomb. Cast: Phyllis Konstam (Tilly), Sydney Howard (Broker's man), Richard Bird (Dick), Ellis Jeffreys, Edward Chapman, Mabel Russell, Marie Wright, W.R. Hignett.

• ***Tilly of Bloomsbury*** (remake). Hammersmith Productions/RKO, 1940. Director: Leslie Hiscott; screenwriters: Nils Holstius and Jack Marks. Cast: Jean Gillie (Tilly), Michael Denison (Dick), Sydney Howard (Broker's man), Henry Oscar, Athene Seyler, Michael Wilding, Kathleen Harrison, Athole Stewart, Martita Hunt, Joy Frankau.

The Ian Hay play was filmed as a silent in Great Britain in 1921. In the two talkies, the only thing interesting about the threadbare farces is the work of Sydney Howard, who in an almost cameo role, appears as the broker's man who agrees to pose as the butler for Tilly's family when the aristocrats come to visit. The results are disastrous—but the boy defies his snobbish mother and marries Tilly anyway.

924 Time to Kill

Based on the novel *The High Window* by Raymond Chandler and a character created by Brett Halliday. Story: Detective Michael Shayne is called upon to recover a valuable coin for rich Mrs. Murdock. While on the trail of the missing currency, Shayne encounters three murders committed to cover up the counterfeiting of the collector's item.

Twentieth Century–Fox, 1942 (original). Director: Herbert I. Leeds; screenwriter: Clarence Upson Young. Cast: Lloyd Nolan (Michael Shayne), Heather Angel (Merle), Doris Merrick (Linda Conquest), Ralph Byrd (Louis Venter), Ethel Griffies (Mrs. Murdock), Richard Lane, Sheila Bromley, Morris Ankrum.

• ***The Brasher Doubloon*** (remake). Twentieth Century–Fox, 1947. Director: John Brahm; screenwriters: Dorothy Hannah and Leonard Praskins. Cast: George Montgomery (Philip Marlowe), Nancy Guild (Merle Davis), Conrad Janis (Leslie Murdock), Roy Roberts (Lt. Breeze), Fritz Kortner, Florence Bates, Marvin Miller, Houseley Stevenson, Bob Adler.

The title of the remake refers to a rare coin that tough detective Philip Marlowe, poorly played by George Montgomery, is hired to find after it had been stolen from a rich old lady's collection. After the mandatory number of killings, Marlowe recovers the coin and puts the wrongdoers away, some permanently. This is the least effective filming of the adventures of Raymond Chandler's detective, and the fault clearly lies with the casting. Marlow was gritty, clever and quick-witted; Montgomery, sad to say, acts like the juvenile lead in a minor drawing-room farce.

Times Square Playboy *see* **The Home Towners**

925 Timothy's Quest

Based on the novel by Kate Douglas Wiggins. Story: Rather than be sent to an orphanage, Timothy, a slum child, and "Lady Gay," a little girl he protects, head for the country. They arrive at the home of Miss Avilda Cummins and ask to be adopted. Miss Cummins, who lives with a spinster servant, Samantha Ann Ripley, lets them spend the night, but has no plans of allowing them to become permanent members of the household. After a while she softens her position and when Timothy overhears her plan of adopting "Lady Gay" and sending Timothy to an orphange, he decides it's time to move on. Before leaving, he tells Miss Ripley of hearing the voice of a man living in a nearby lonely house, calling out "Samanthy." She recognizes the man as her former suitor and goes to be with him. Avilda now wishes that she had been more understanding and helpful to her sister, who had "died in sin." She retrieves Timothy and officially adopts both children.

Dirigo Films/American Releasing Corporation, 1922 (original). Silent. Director: Sidney Olcott; screenwriter: Katherine Stuart. Cast: Joseph Depew (Timothy), Baby Helen Rowland (Lady Gay), Marie Day (Miss Avilda Cummins), Margaret Seddon (Samantha Ann Ripley), Bertram Marburgh, Vivia Ogden, Gladys Leslie, William F. Haddock.

• ***Timothy's Quest*** (remake). Paramount Pictures, 1936. Director: Charles Barton; screenwriters: Virginia Van Upp, Dore Schary and Gilbert Pratt. Cast: Dickie Moore (Timothy), Virginia Weidler (Samantha Tarbox), Eleanore Whitney (Martha), Tom Keene (David Masters), Elizabeth Patterson (Vilda Cummins), Samuel S. Hinds (Rev. Fellows), Esther Dale, Bennie Bartlett, J.M. Kerrigan, Irene Franklin.

The Kate Douglas Wiggin novel was a wholesome homey tale, just about right to be read under a tree somewhere in the country on a summer afternoon, with a pitcher of lemonade handy. Such a setting would make the experience enjoyable if not exciting or riveting. Watching these two film versions makes one call out for the tree, the summer afternoon and the lemonade; as it's difficult to enjoy the movie exploits of a bit-too-precocious child and a set of stereotyped country folk short on humor, lacking in sparkling dialog and cumbersome in plot.

926 Titanic!

Based on a historical event. Story: The sinking of H.M.S. *Titanic* in 1912 provides the factual basis for this screen drama reenacting the tragedy which took over 1500 lives. The story chooses a group of passengers and crew to follow, first as they are enjoying the maiden voyage of the grand ship and its luxurious appointments, and then as they must deal with the reality that the ship will sink and some of them are about to die while others must live with the knowledge that loved ones are still aboard the doomed ship.

Twentieth Century–Fox, 1953 (original). Director: Jean Negulesco; screenwriters: Charles Brackett, Walter Reisch and Richard Breen. Cast: Clifton

Webb (Richard Sturges), Barbara Stanwyck (Mrs. Sturges), Robert Wagner (Giff Rogers), Audrey Dalton (Annette), Thelma Ritter (Mrs. Young), Brian Aherne (Capt. Smith), Richard Basehart (Healey), Allyn Joslyn (Earl Meeker), James Todd (Sandy Comstock), William Johnstone, Charles Fitzsimmons, Barry Bernard, Harper Carter, Edmund Purdom.

• ***A Night to Remember*** (remake). Rank, Great Britain, 1958. Director: Roy Baker; screenwriter: Eric Ambler from Walter Lord's book. Cast: Kenneth More (Lightoller), Honor Blackman (Mrs. Lucas), Anthony Bushell (Capt. Rostron), Jill Dixon (Mrs. Clarke), Jane Downs (Mrs. Lightoller), James Dyrenforth (Col. Gracie), Michael Goodliffe (Andrews), Kenneth Griffith (Phillips), Harriette Johns, Frank Lawton, Richard Leech, David McCallum, Alec McCowen, Tucker McGuire, John Merivale, Laurence Naismith, George Rose.

Both of the films are suspenseful, even though it's a foregone conclusion that the ship will go down. In both instances the showing of the bravery, cowardice, foolishness, sacrifice, selfishness, love, despair, fear and all the other emotions associated with a great tragedy is handled with great care and in excellent taste. The surprising thing is that there did not seem to be any panic among the passengers until the end, and apparently this reflects what really happened. That is a tribute to the training and dedication of the crew who worked valiantly to save their passengers, knowing full well there would be little room in the inadequate number of lifeboats for them.

927 To Be or Not to Be

Based on a story by Ernst Lubitsch and Melchoit Lengyel. Story: Maria and Joseph Tura lead a Polish theatre troupe, with his speciality being a hammy Hamlet. When the Germans invade Poland, he and his wife get involved in impersonations of Nazi agents; even Tom Dugan takes on the role of Adolf Hitler, as the troupe and a Polish flyer escape in the Fuehrer's plane to England.

United Artists, 1942 (original). Director: Ernst Lubitsch; screenwriter: Edwin Justus Mayer. Cast: Carole Lombard (Maria Tura), Jack Benny (Joseph Tura), Robert Stack (Lt. Stanislas Sobinski), Felix Bressart (Greenberg), Lionel Atwill (Rawitch), Stanley Ridges (Prof. Siletsky), Sig Ruman (Col. Ehrhardt), Tom Dugan, Charles Halton, George Lynn, Henry Victor, Maude Eburne, Armand Wright, Erno Verehes, Halliwell Hobbes, Miles Mander.

• ***To Be or Not to Be*** (remake). Twentieth Century–Fox, 1983. Director: Alan Johnson; screenwriters: Thomas Meehan and Ronny Graham. Cast: Mel Brooks (Frederick Bronski), Anne Bancroft (Anna Bronski), Tim Matheson (Lt. Andre Sobinski), Charles Durning (Col. Erhardt), Jose Ferrer (Prof. Siletski), Christopher Lloyd, James Hoake.

The title refers to the bit repeated several times in both films of a handsome young officer getting up from his seat in the audience each time the Polish actor begins Hamlet's soliloquy to have a rendezvous with the actor's wife. Carole Lombard was killed in an airplane crash before the movie was completed, although most of her scenes had been shot. Her performance was as effortless as was Benny's perfectly timed. The remake with Mr. and Mrs. Brooks was a nice reprise of the story, but it would be too much to expect that Mel Brooks would be on a par with Benny at portraying an egotistical ham or Anne Bancroft with Carole Lombard as a comedienne.

928 To Have and Have Not

Based on the novel by Ernest Hemingway. Story: Harry Morgan is an American fishing skipper out of the Caribbean island of Martinique during World War II. The Free French want to hire his boat to smuggle some resistance leaders to safety. He resists their pleas for help and concentrates his attention on Marie, a tall beautiful girl stranded on the island. Ultimately, Harry discovers that he can't sit out the war and must get involved. From then on, the story is almost a typical cops and robbers story, only this time the robbers are the good guys, as Morgan picks up the wounded resistance leader and his wife, has to outrun a police gun boat and act nonchalant when the local constabulatory, all Nazi puppets, question him about his involvement.

Warner Bros., 1944 (original). Director: Howard Hawks; screenwriters: James Furthman and William Faulkner. Cast: Humphrey Bogart (Harry Morgan), Lauren Bacall (Marie), Walter Brennan (Eddie), Dolores Moran (Helene De Bursac), Hoagy Carmichael (Crickett), Walter Molnar (Paul De Bursac), Sheldon Leonard, Marcel Dalio, Walter Sande, Dan Seymour, Aldo Nadi, Paul Marion, Patricia Shay.

• ***The Breaking Point*** (remake). Warner Bros., 1950. Director: Michael Curtiz; screenwriter: Ranald MacDougall. Cast: John Garfield (Harry Morgan), Patricia Neal (Leona Charles), Phyllis Thaxter (Lucy Morgan), Juano Hernandez (Wesley Park), Wally Ford (Duncan), Edmon Ryan (Rogers), Ralph Dumke, Guy Thomajan, William Campbell, Sherry Jackson, Victor Sen Yung.

• ***The Gun Runners*** (remake). United Artists, 1958. Director: Don Siegel; screenwriters: Dan Mainwaring and Paul Monash. Cast: Audie Murphy (Sam Martin), Eddie Albert (Hanagan), Patricia Owens (Lucy Martin), Everett Sloane (Harvey), Gita Hall (Eva), Richard Jaeckel, Paul Birch, Jack Elam.

The producers of the two remakes may have believed that the success of the 1944 film was due to the Ernest Hemingway story and thus a new version would also score. The truth to tell, the Hemingway story, at least as it was made into a screenplay by Jules Furthman and William Faulkner, was a mishmash of action and talk, with a confused plot and not much real suspense. However, the interplay between the aging Bogie and the 19-year-old Lauren Bacall was something to see. It's in this movie that the catlike "Baby" lets Bogie know she was his for the having, and all he had to do was whistle. Bacall was never better and Bogie, never more openly pursued, both on and off the screen, by this enchanting beauty. Adding to the fun was Walter Brennan as a likeable drunk and Hoagy Carmichael as a stereotyped cigarette-smoking piano player. The latter collaborated with Johnny Mercer on the great tune "How Little We Know."

In the first remake, John Garfield didn't have Lauren Bacall to liven up the proceedings and so he was just stuck with the story of a relatively minor Hemingway novel. Garfield is a former PT-boat skipper who owns a power cruiser which he rents to private fishing parties out of a Southern California port. When a client skips out without paying the bill, impoverished Garfield is reduced to smuggling coolie labor into the country. Besides being left holding the bag, Garfield inherits his client's mistress, Patricia Neal, as well. He's already married to loyal Phyllis Thaxter, so this just adds a bit of spice to his exciting life. The film with Audie Murphy is more of the same with the ex-army hero portraying the captain of a cabin cruiser who's sucked into an illegal cruise. It's really a ho-hum yarn by this time, with the second crew trying valiantly but with little success to make the story work.

Toby Tyler *see* **Circus Days**

929 Tol'able David

Based on the story by Joseph Hergesheimer. Story: Young David Kinemon hero worships his older brother Allen, driver of the stagecoach that carries the U.S. mail in the Virginia mountains. Moving into the quiet community are the three Hatburns, fugitives from justice, who bully everyone they encounter. When Allen catches the Hatburns attacking David's dog, he moves in to protect the animal. Iscah Hatburn strikes Allen with a large rock, crippling him for life. The attack on his son causes David's father to have a fatal heart attack. Now forced to become the man of the house and bowing to his mother's fear, David puts off avenging his brother, thus convincing the villagers that he is a coward. David takes over his brother's job of driving the stagecoach and encounters the Hatburns and engages them in an uneven fight, but proves to be a worthy successor to his brother.

Inspiration Pictures/First National Pictures, 1921 (original). Silent. Director: Henry King; screenwriters: King and Edmund Goulding. Cast: Richard Barthelmess (David Kinemon), Gladys Hulette (Esther Hatburn), Walter P. Lewis (Iscah Hatburn), Ernest Torrence (Luke Hatburn), Warner Richmond (Allen Kinemon), Ralph Yearsley, Forrest Robinson, Laurence Eddinger, Edmund Gurney, Marion Abbott.

• ***Tol'able David*** (remake). Columbia Pictures, 1930. Director: John G. Blystone; screenwriter: Benjamin Glazer. Cast: Richard Cromwell (David Kinemon), Noah Beery (Luke), Joan Peers (Esther Hatburn), Henry B. Walthall (Amos Hatburn), George Duryea (Alan Kinemon), Edmund Breese, Barbara Bedford, Helen Ware, Harlan Knight, Peter Richmond, James Bradbury, Sr.

The David and Goliath–like story of a peace-loving boy who has to deal with three marauding fugitives was filmed almost identically in the remake as in the original, except that the second time around David dispatches the baddies in a gunfight. The 1921 film was very popular at the time of its release, but by 1930, audiences weren't in the mood for rural melodrama.

The Toll of the Sea *see* **Madame Butterfly**

930 Tom Brown of Culver

Based on a story by George Green and Dale Van Every. Story: A moody, rebellious boy, Tom Brown, is supported through school at Culver Military Academy by the American Legion. He becomes a model cadet and patriotic citizen, despite learning that the father he thought had died heroically in battle during World War I was actually a shell-shocked deserter who survived.

Universal Pictures, 1932 (original). Director: William Wyler; screenwriters: George Green, Dale Van Every, Clarence Marks and Tom Buckingham. Cast: Tom Brown (Tom Brown), H.B. Warner (Dr. Brown), Slim Summerville (Slim), Richard Cromwell (Bob Randolph), Ben Alexander (Ralph), Sidney Toler (Major Wharton), Russell Hopton, Andy Devine, Willard Robertson, Norman Phillips, Jr., Tyrone Power, Jr., Alan Ladd.

• ***Spirit of Culver*** (remake). Universal Pictures, 1939. Director: Joseph Stanley; screenwriters: Whitney Bolton and Nathaniel West. Cast: Jackie Cooper (Tom Allen), Freddie Bartholomew (Bob Randolph), Andy Devine (Tubby), Henry Hull (Doc Allen), Jackie Moran (Perkins), Tim Holt (Captain Wilson), Gene Reynolds, Kathryn Kane.

The predominately male cast of these two pictures gave fine if not outstanding performances. Tom Brown gave his name to his character, and a couple of youngsters, Tyrone Power, Jr. (his dad was a movie actor as well), and Alan Ladd, who would later make their marks on the motion picture industry, appeared in small roles. The remake is just a repetition of the story, but with Jackie Cooper as the boy who learns his supposedly heroic father was a coward.

931 Tom Brown's School Days

Based on the novel by Thomas Hughes. Story: Unlike the novel which concentrated on the adventures of frightened schoolboy Tom Brown, bullied by upperclassmen at Rugby School, the movie versions concentrated on the institution's headmaster and founder, Dr. Arnold, who is made out as a combination Mr. Chips, Sigmund Freud and miracle worker as he successfully converts unruly little monsters into dignified and courteous gentlemen.

• ***Tom Brown's School Days*** (remake). RKO, 1940. Director: Robert Stevenson; screenwriters: Walter Ferris, Frank Cavett, Gene Thomas and Graham Baker. Cast: Cedric Hardwicke (Dr. Arnold), Freddie Bartholomew (East), Jimmy Lydon (Tom Brown), Josephine Hutchinson (Mrs. Arnold), Billy Halop (Flashman), Polly Moran, Hughie Green, Ernest Cossart, Alec Craig, Gale Storm, Barlowe Borland, Forrester Harvey.

• ***Tom Brown's School Days*** (remake). Minter/Renown, Great Britain, 1951. Director: Gordon Perry; screenwriter: Noel Langley. Cast: John Howard Davies (Tom Brown), Robert Newton (Doctor Arnold), Diana Wynyard (Mrs. Arnold), Francis De Wolff (Squire Brown), Kathleen Byron (Mrs. Brown), Hermione Baddeley (Sally Harrowell), James Hayter, Rachel Gurney, Amy Veness, John Charlesworth.

The story of Rugby School was filmed as a silent in 1910 and 1916. Neither talkie production of the classic novel was a success. Audiences didn't seem very interested in the story and then the first suffered in comparison with *Goodbye, Mr. Chips.* Seen today one can find much to admire in the performances and the settings. Jimmy Lydon, like John Howard Davies, is a bit wimpy in the title role but then we suppose that's the way the character was meant to be. Billy Halop, in the first film, made a nice bully and Cedric Hardwicke came across as a genuine, dedicated pedagogue. In the remake, Robert Newton was excellent as the good Doctor Arnold. But the superiority of his performance showed how thin was the work of the rest of the cast.

932 Tom, Dick and Harry

Based on a story by Paul Jarrico. Story: Janie, a naive and fickle switchboard operator, aims for romance with a millionaire, on the proposition that's it's just as easy to love a rich man as a poor one. She accepts a marriage proposal from breezy automobile salesman Tom, but when she mistakes Harry for a rich man, she becomes engaged to him as well. To complete matters she finally meets millionaire Dick and wrangles a third proposal. The rest of the film concentrates on her making a decision as to whom to marry. She ends up with auto mechanic Harry, because bells ring when he kisses her. So much for her maxim about rich men and poor men.

RKO, 1941 (original). Director: Garson Kanin; screenwriter: Paul Jarrico. Cast: Ginger Rogers (Janie), George Murphy (Tom), Alan Marshal (Dick), Burgess Meredith (Harry), Joe Cunningham, Jane Seymour, Leonore Lonergan, Vicki Lester, Phil Silvers, Betty Breckenridge.

• ***The Girl Most Likely*** (remake). RKO, 1957. Director: Mitchell Leisen; screenwriter: Devery Freeman. Cast: Jane Powell (Dodie), Cliff Robertson (Pete), Keith Andres (Neil), Kay Ballard (Marge), Tommy Noonan (Buzz), Una Merkel, Kelly Brown, Judy Nugent, Frank Cady.

The musical remake found Jane Powell with two too many suitors, and like Ginger Rogers before her she chooses the one that rings her chimes, Cliff Robertson, over those with money and ambition. In the last picture started and finished at RKO's studios, Jane's musical numbers included the title song by Nelson Riddle and Bob Russell and "All the Colors of the Rainbow" by Hugh Martin and Ralph Blane. RKO's refusal to give Paul Jarrico any credit for the remake got the studio into hot water with the Writer's Guild.

933 Tom Jones

Based on the novel by Henry Fielding. Story: In eighteenth-century England, Squire Allworthy returns to his manor to find a baby in his bed. A serving maid named Jenny Jones is believed to be the mother and is banished from the manor. The squire raises the child, named Tom Jones, along with his legitimate heir, Blifil. Tom grows up to be a lusty lad, and although he loves Sophie, daughter of neighboring Squire Western, he disgraces himself with Molly, a local trollop. When Sophie refuses to marry Blifil because she loves Tom, the latter is sent away to make his fortune. On the way and in London, he has several affairs, until Sophie shows up, having run away from home. Blifil frames Tom for robbery and he is sentenced to be hanged, but he is rescued at the last moment, when it is revealed that although indeed illegitimate, his mother was actually Squire Allworthy's deceased sister. Reinstated in the house of Squire Allworthy, Tom is at last free to marry Sophie.

Lopert Pictures, Great Britain, 1963 (original). Director: Tony Richardson; screenwriter: John Osborne. Cast: Albert Finney (Tom Jones), Susannah York

(Sophie Western), Hugh Griffith (Squire Western), Edith Evans (Miss Western), Joan Greenwood (Lady Bellaston), Diane Cilento (Molly Seagrim), George Devine (Squire Allworthy), David Warner (Blifil), Joyce Redman (Mrs. Waters-Jenny Jones), George A. Cooper, David Tomlinson, Rosalind Atkinson, Angela Baddeley, Peter Bull, James Cairncross.

• ***The Bawdy Adventures of Tom Jones*** (remake). Universal Pictures, Great Britain, 1976. Director: Cliff Owen; screenwriter: Jeremy Lloyd, based on the musical play *Tom Jones* by Dan MacPherson. Cast: Nicky Henson (Tom Jones), Trevor Howard (Squire Western), Terry-Thomas (Mr. Square), Arthur Lowe (Dr. Thwackum), Georgia Brown (Jenny Jones/Mrs. Waters), Joan Collins (Black Bess), William Mervyn, Murray Melvin, Madeleine Smith, Geraldine McEwan, Jeremy Lloyd, Janie Greenspun.

The 1963 movie won the Best Picture Academy Award, with other Oscars going to screenwriter John Osborne, director Tony Richardson and composer John Addison. In addition, Albert Finney, Hugh Griffith, Edith Evans, Diane Cilento and Joyce Redman all received nominations. It was an astonishing box-office success because of its zany pace, not despite it. The musical remake is a trashy piece with but three actual musical numbers. It's more tiresome than titillating.

934 Tom Sawyer

Based on the novel by Mark Twain. Story: When Tom Sawyer has an argument with his sweetheart Becky Thatcher, he seeks comfort from town ragamuffin Huckleberry Finn. They agree to visit the town graveyard at midnight where they see Injun Joe, a halfbreed, kill one of his companions. Muff Potter, who is also present, but badly drunk, is convinced that it was he who killed the man. Tom and Huck swear a blood oath that they will never divulge what they have seen this night. Later, unfairly rebuked by his guardian, Aunt Polly, Tom runs away from home, joining Huck and Joe Harper on an expedition to an island on the Mississippi River, where they spend three carefree days. They return home and learn that they are believed to have drowned and so attend their own obsequies at the church. Discovered, Tom confesses to what he has seen at the graveyard, but Injun Joe escapes. At a school picnic near a cavern, Tom and Becky get lost and run across Injun Joe with a chest of gold. They are pursued by Injun Joe, but the latter falls to his death. Huck finds Tom and Becky, leading them to safety and retrieving the chest of gold.

• ***Tom Sawyer*** (remake). Paramount Pictures, 1930. Director: John Cromwell; screenwriter: Sam Mintz. Cast: Jackie Coogan (Tom Sawyer), Junior Durkin (Huckleberry Finn), Mitzi Green (Becky Thatcher), Tully Marshall (Muff Potter), Clara Blandick (Aunt Polly), Dick Winslow (Joe Harper), Charles Stevens (Injun Joe), Lucien Littlefield, Mary Jane Irving, Ethel Wales, Jane Darwell, Jackie Searle.

• ***The Adventures of Tom Sawyer*** (remake). United Artists, 1938. Director: Norman Taurog; screenwriter: John V.A. Weaver. Cast: Tommy Kelly (Tom Sawyer), May Robson (Aunt Polly), Jackie Moran (Huck Finn), Walter Brennan (Muff Potter), Victor Jory (Injun Joe), Marcia Mae Jones (Mary Sawyer), Ann

Gilles (Becky Thatcher), Victor Kilian, Nana Bryant, Mickey Rentschler, Cora Sue Collins, Charles Richman, Spring Byington, Margaret Hamilton.

• ***Tom Sawyer*** (remake). United Artists, 1973. Director: Don Taylor; screenwriters: Richard M. and Robert B. Sherman. Cast: Johnny Whitaker (Tom Sawyer), Celeste Holm (Aunt Polly), Warren Oates (Muff Potter), Jeff East (Huck Finn), Jodie Foster (Becky Thatcher), Lucille Benson (Widow Douglas), Kunu Hank (Injun Joe), Henry Jones, Noah Keen, Dub Taylor, Richard Eastham, Sandy Kenyon.

Tom Sawyer, Huck Finn, Aunt Polly, Becky Thatcher and Injun Joe also appeared together on the screen in 1917, 1918, 1967 and 1972. It's a toss-up as to whether the 1930 or 1938 version is the best of the several productions, with the edge probably going to the 1938 Technicolor picture. Tommy Kelly and Jackie Moran were excellent, while Jackie Coogan may have been a bit too old for the title role. The 1973 musical is just too tame, taking much of the bite out of the story, giving a genteel rendition, instead, which just doesn't make it.

Tonight Is Ours ***see*** **The Queen Was in the Parlour**

935 Tons of Money

Based on the play by Will Evans and Arthur Valentine. Story: Bankrupt inventor Aubrey Allington stages his own "death" and returns as his long lost cousin George to evade his creditors. But then "George" himself shows up, but he also turns out to be a phony, but then another George appears on the scene, and so forth.

Stoll, Great Britain, 1924 (original). Silent. Director: Frank Crane; screenwriters: Lucita Squier and Tom Webster. Cast: Leslie Henson (Aubrey Allington), Clifford Seyler (George Maitland), Flora le Breton (Louise Allington), Mary Brough (Mrs. Mullet), Jack Denton (Henry), Elsie Fuller, Douglas Munro, Roy Byford, Willie Warde, Ena Mason.

• ***Tons of Money*** (remake). British & Dominions, Great Britain, 1931. Director: Tom Walls; screenwriters: Herbert Wilcox and Ralph Lynn. Cast: Ralph Lynn (Aubrey Allington), Yvonne Arnaud (Louise Allington), Mary Brough (Benita Mullet), Robertson Hare (Chesterman), Gordon James (George Maitland), Madge Saunders (Jane Everard), Philip Hewland, Willie Warde, John Turnbull, Peggy Douglas.

It's a complicated and energetic comedy, but not anything that will rank among Britain's best examples of a fine sense of humor. It's a rather silly story, played even sillier by the leading performers.

936 Tony Rome

Based on the novel *Miami Mayhem* by Marvin H. Albert. Story: Seedy Miami private eye Tony Rome runs into murder and blackmail when he agrees to guard millionaire Rudy Klosterman's daughter Diana. He's aided in his investigation of the complex case by predatory divorcee Ann Archer.

Twentieth Century–Fox, 1967 (original). Director: Gordon Douglas; screenwriter: Richard Breen. Cast: Frank Sinatra (Tony Rome), Jill St. John (Ann

Tommy Kelly as Tom Sawyer (left), Jackie Moran as Huckleberry Finn and Victor Jory as Injun Joe pose for this scene from The Adventures of Tom Sawyer *(United Artists, 1938), one of several filmings of the Mark Twain story.*

Archer), Richard Conte (Lt. Santini), Sue Lyon (Diana Pines), Gena Rowlands (Rita Kosterman), Simon Oakland (Rudolph Kosterman), Jeffrey Lynn, Lloyd Bochner, Robert J. Wilke, Virginia Vincent, Joan Shawlee, Richard Krisher, Lloyd Gough, Babe Hart, Jeanne Cooper, Stan Ross, Buzz Henry.

• ***Lady in Cement*** (sequel). Twentieth Century–Fox, 1968. Director: Gordon Douglas; screenwriter: Marvin H. Albert and Jack Guss. Cast: Frank Sinatra (Tony Rome), Raquel Welch (Kit Forrest), Richard Conte (Lt. Santini), Martin Gabel (Al Mungar), Lainie Kazan (Maria Baretto), Pat Henry (Rubin), Dan Blocker (Gronsky), Steve Peck, Virginia Wood, Richard Deacon, Frank Raiter.

Sinatra is surprisingly good in these surprisingly bad detective stories. The original and its sequel have too many characters, too much violence and too many kinky sexual references to allow audiences to concentrate on the story line—if there really is one. In the sequel, Frank discovers the nude corpse of a blonde with her feet encased in cement while taking his morning swim. It's pretty much downhill from there as he's hired by Dan Blocker to determine if the unrecognizable victim is his missing girlfriend, and if so who killed her and why.

Too Busy to Work *see* **Doubting Thomas**

937 Too Many Husbands

Based on the play by W. Somerset Maugham. Story: After Bill Cardew is reported dead on a boat cruise, his wife Vicky marries his publishing partner Henry Lowndes. The couple is stunned when Bill is discovered on a desert island and on his return, moves in with Vicky and Henry. Their attention makes her in no great hurry to choose which one she wants as her husband. When both walk out on her she sends the police after them. The judge rules what should have been clear all along: Bill is Vicky's only legal husband and the two go home together with Henry still hanging around, waiting his opportunity to supplant Bill.

Columbia, 1940 (original). Director: Wesley Ruggles; screenwriter: Claude Binyon. Cast: Jean Arthur (Vicky), Fred MacMurray (Bill Cardew), Melvyn Douglas (Henry Lowndes), Harry Davenport (George), Dorothy Peterson (Gertrude Houlihan), Melville Cooper, Edgar Buchanan, Tom Dugan.

• ***Three for the Show*** (remake). Columbia, 1955. Director: H.C. Potter; screenwriters: Edward Hope and Leonard Stern. Cast: Betty Grable (Julie), Marge Champion (Gwen Howard), Gower Champion (Vernon Lowndes), Jack Lemmon (Marty Stewart), Myron McCormick (Mike Hudson), Paul Harvey, Robert Bice, Hal K. Dawson.

These movies are similiar in plot to *My Favorite Wife* and its remake, *Move Over Darling,* but are not as sparkling as the former, nor as dull as the latter. The 1955 musical found Betty Grable with one too many husbands when number one, reported dead in the war, comes back after she has married his best friend. It takes her the rest of the film to decide which one to stick with, while cute Marge Champion stands around waiting to scoop up the loser. Among the songs heard are George and Ira Gershwin's "Someone to Watch Over Me" and "I've Got a Crush on You," "How Come You Do Me Like You Do" by Gene Austin and Roy Bergere, and "I've Been Kissed Before" by Bob Russell and Lester Lee.

Too Young to Marry *see* **Broken Dishes**

938 Topaze

Based on the play by Marcel Pagnol, translated to English by Benn W. Levy. Story: When impeccably honest and dedicated Professor Topaze refuses to alter the grade of the incorrigible son of his school's wealthy patrons, he is fired. The naive man is befriended by Coco who induces her lover, corrupt city councilor Henri, to give the ex-professor a position. Although he realizes that he is being used by his benefactor for illegal schemes, Topaze becomes an apt student of corruption, mastering the art of it. So much so, that he is honored for his efforts with the ribbon and palm from the French Academy. Topaze replaces the grafting Henri, takes Coco as his mistress and lives his life according to the maxim "dishonesty does pay."

RKO Pictures, 1933 (original). Director: Henri d'Abbadia d'Arrast; screenwriter: Benn W. Levy. Cast: John Barrymore (Topaze), Myrna Loy (Coco), Albert Conti (Henri), Luis Alberni (Dr. Bomb), Jobyna Howland (Baroness de Latour-Latour), Reginald Mason (Baron de Latour-Latour), Jackie Searle, Frank Reicher.

• ***Topaze*** (remake). Paramount Pictures, France, 1935. Director and screenwriter: Louis Gasnier. Cast: Louis Jouvet (Topaze), Edwige Feuillere (Suzy), Pierre Larguary (Tamise), Marcel Vallee (Muche), M. Pawley (Castel-Blanc), Jeanne Loury, Maurice Remy, Simone Heliard.

• ***Topaze*** (remake). Discina International Films, France, 1951. Director and screenwriter: Marcel Pagnol. Cast: Fernandel (Topaze), Helene Perdriere (Suzy Courtois), Pierre Larquary (Tamise), Jacques Morel (Castel-Vernac), Marcel Vallee (Muche), Milly Mathis, Jacqueline Pagnol, Jacques Castelot.

• ***Mr. Topaze*** (remake). Twentieth Century–Fox, Great Britain, 1962. Director: Peter Sellers; screenwriter: Pierre Rouve. Cast: Peter Sellers (Topaze), Nadia Gray (Suzy), Herbert Lom (Castel-Benac), Leo McKern (Muche), Martita Hunt, John Neville, Billie Whitelaw, Michael Gough, Joan Sims, John Le Mesurier.

John Barrymore plays against type in his performance as the initially meek pedagogue who allows himself to be exploited and then takes happily to corruption. Howard Hughes had announced plans to remake the film with Vincent Price, but nothing came of the project. Both of the French versions received critical praise and the performances of both Louis Jouvet and Fernandel in the title role were considered excellent—but less so than that of Barrymore. The Peter Sellers version demonstrated that he was unable as director to pull a top-rate performance from himself as an actor.

939 Topper

Based on a story by Thorne Smith. Story: Marion and George Kirby are a wealthy, fun-loving couple killed in an automobile accident after a night of drinking and carousing. Their astral bodies rise from the wreckage and their witty conversation continues as if nothing had happened. They decide that until they have done someone a good deed, they will be forced to spend their afterlife in their present unsatisfactory between-state. They choose to help out their banker, Cosmo Topper, who has lived a dull, routine life. Their playfulness and the fact that he alone is allowed to see them makes for many amusing situations.

MGM, 1937 (original). Director: Norman Z. McLeod; screenwriters: Jack Jevne, Eric Hatch and Eddie Moran. Cast: Constance Bennett (Marion Kirby), Cary Grant (George Kirby), Roland Young (Cosmo Topper), Billie Burke (Mrs. Topper), Alan Mowbray (Wilkins), Eugene Pallette (Casey), Arthur Lake, Hedda Hopper, Virginia Sale, Theodore Von Eltz, J. Farrell McDonald.

• ***Topper Takes a Trip*** (sequel). United Artists, 1939. Director: Norman Z. McLeod; screenwriters: Eddie Moran, Jack Jevne and Corey Ford, based on the novel of the same name by Thorne Smith. Cast: Constance Bennett (Marion Kirby), Roland Young (Cosmo Topper), Billie Burke (Mrs. Topper), Alan Mowbray (Wilkins), Verree Teasdale (Mrs. Parkhurst), Franklin Pangborn

(Louis), Alexander D'Arcy, Paul Hurst, Eddy Conrad, Spencer Charters, Irving Pichel.

• ***Topper Returns*** (sequel). United Artists, 1941. Director: Roy Del Ruth; screenwriters: Jonathan Latimer and Gordon Douglas. Cast: Joan Blondell (Gail Richards), Roland Young (Cosmo Topper), Carole Landis (Ann Carrington), Billie Burke (Mrs. Topper), Dennis O'Keefe (Bob), Patsy Kelly, H.B. Warner, Eddie "Rochester" Anderson, George Zucco, Donald MacBride, Rafaela Ottiano, Trevor Bardette.

The Topper films came at the end of the screwball comedy era and were well received by audiences and are still fun to view today, although the sequels are seldom seen on TV. In the first sequel, Constance Bennett, sans husband Cary Grant, shows up in her astral form to help Roland Young who is being sued for divorce on the basis that he had a woman (Miss Bennett's spirit) in his hotel room. Bennett, still intent on doing Young a good deed, finally reunites him with his wife, Billie Burke. In what may be the funniest entry of the nonsensical trio, Young's strange affinity for spirits is put to test once again in the second sequel, only this time it's Joan Blondell, recently murdered, who enlists Young's aid in solving the crime.

Topper Returns ***see*** **Topper**

Topper Takes a Trip ***see*** **Topper**

Tovarich ***see*** **Tovaritch**

940 Tovaritch

Based on the play by Jacques Deval. Story: Russian Imperial Princess Tatiana and her husband, General Mikail, are refugees in Paris after the Russian Revolution, forced by circumstances to take positions as servants in a French home where their identity is unknown to their employers. The couple does have a credit in the Bank of France of two billion francs, a sum entrusted to them by the czar himself. Their loyalty is such that it does not occur to them to use any portion of the money for themselves. Their identities are revealed at a dinner party by a guest, Gorotchenko, a Soviet representative, and former cruel persecutor of Tatiana and Mikail. Finally, the royal couple signs over the funds to the new Russian government to be used for the common good of the people.

Jacques Deval Production/Romain Pines, France, 1935 (original). Director and screenwriter: Jacques Deval. Cast: Irene de Zlahy (Tatiana), Andre Lefaur (Mikail), Pierre Renoir (Gorotchenko), Georges Mauloy (Chauffourier-Dubieff), Marguerite Deval (Madame Arbeziah), Wina Winifred, Olga Muriel, Jean Forest.

• ***Tovarich*** (remake). Warner Bros., 1937. Director: Anatole Litvak; screenwriter: Casey Robinson. Cast: Claudette Colbert (Tatiana), Charles Boyer (Mikail), Basil Rathbone (Gorotchenko), Anita Louise (Helene Dupont), Melville Cooper (Charles Dupont), Isabel Jeans (Fernande Dupont), Morris

Carnovsky (Chauffourier-Dubieff), Maurice Murphy, Gregory Gaye, Montagu Love.

The comedy of the two films seems dated and somewhat obvious now, but the performances hold up, particularly those of Colbert, Boyer and Rathbone in the remake. It's a charming story with heart and pleasantly developed characters. It's not an award winner but it still amuses and pleases.

Tower of London *see* **Richard III**

The Toy Tiger *see* **Mad About Music**

941 Trader Horn

Based on the novel by Alfred Aloysius Horn and Etheldreda Lewis. Story: Experienced African hunter Trader Horn enters the jungle with a safari. They encounter a tribe whose queen, Nina, countermands an order of torture death for the explorers. This gets her in dutch with her own people and she must escape with the white men. Although she can only make the guttural sound of her tribesmen, her scantily attired figure and expressive eyes let Peru know that she is interested in him. Several of the party die, but the principals make it to safety and Horn returns to his beloved jungle.

Metro, 1930 (original). Director: W.S. Van Dyke; screenwriter: Richard Schayer. Cast: Harry Carey (Trader Horn), Edwina Booth (Nina), Duncan Renaldo (Peru), Mutia Omoolu (Renchario), Olive Golden (Edith Trend), C. Aubrey Smith (Trader).

• ***Trader Horn*** (remake). MGM, 1972. Director: Reza Badiyi; screenwriters: William Norton and Edward Harper. Cast: Rod Taylor (Trader Horn), Anne Heywood (Nicole), Jean Sorel (Emil), Don Knight (Col. Sinclair), Ed Bernard (Apaque), Stack Pierce (Malugi).

Between the primitive 1930 talkie and the 1972 picture, Hollywood had made many treks to Africa. The latter film included every conceivable cliche that had been learned over the years. And even with all of this, cowboy star Harry Carey looked more like he belonged in the jungle than did Rod Taylor. The original, shot on location, resulted in an illness to Miss Booth from which she never did fully recover and she successfully sued the company for damages. Despite its disjointedness, the film was a big box-office success.

Tragodie im Hause Habsburg *see* **Mayerling**

The Trail of the Pink Panther *see* **The Pink Panther**

Transatlantic Tunnel *see* **The Tunnel**

La Traviata *see* **Camille**

942 Treasure Island

Based on the novel by Robert Louis Stevenson. Story: It's the familiar adventure yarn of young Jim Hawkins who comes into possession of a pirate treasure map and sails with Doctor Livesey, Captain Smollett and Squire Trelawney aboard the *Hispañola* to seek the fortune. Unfortunately, their crew, led by one-legged Long John Silver, are pirates out to get the riches for themselves. The friendship that develops between Jim and Silver is put to the test once they reach the island and the crew's true colors are known.

• ***Treasure Island*** (remake). MGM, 1934. Director: Victor Fleming; screenwriter: John Lee Mahin. Cast: Wallace Beery (Long John Silver), Jackie Cooper (Jim Hawkins), Lionel Barrymore (Billy Bones), Otto Kruger (Doctor Livesey), Lewis Stone (Captain Smollett), Nigel Bruce (Squire Trelawney), Charles "Chic" Sale (Ben Gunn), William V. Mong (Pew), Charles McNaughton (Black Dog), Dorothy Peterson (Mrs. Hawkins).

• ***Treasure Island*** (remake). RKO, 1950. Director: Bryon Haskin; screenwriter: Lawrence E. Watkin. Cast: Bobby Driscoll (Jim Hawkins), Robert Newton (Long John Silver), Basil Sydney (Captain Smollett), Walter Fitzgerald (Squire Trelawney), Dennis O'Dea (Doctor Livesey), Ralph Truman (George Merry), Finlay Currie (Captain Bones), John Laurie (Pew), Francis de Wolff (Black Dog), Geoffrey Wilkinson (Ben Gunn), Geoffrey Keen, William Devlin, Diarmuid Kelly.

Robert Louis Stevenson's great adventure classic for children (aged seven to seventy), has been filmed many times including in 1908, 1911, 1915; a 1920 silent with Lon Chaney in two roles and a female star, Shirley Mason, as Jim Hawkins; another in 1938; and in 1954, Robert Newton once again played the title role in *Long John Silver*, planning a new trip to Treasure Island with additional clues as to the location of the booty. Other versions appeared in 1968, 1970, and 1971. There was a poorly produced 1972 version, notable only for having Orson Welles as Silver; and in 1973, viewers were presented with *Scalawag*, a overdone reworking of the story with Kirk Douglas as a one-legged pirate and Mark Lester as the boy who joins with him to trace a hidden treasure in Mexico in 1840. Rounding things out there was one more entry in 1975.

For most movie buffs, the definitive screen rendition occurred in 1934 with Wallace Beery the only possible choice for Long John Silver. Some will argue that in the 1950 movie, Robert Newton seemed very comfortable in the part. While this is true, he was about the only member of the cast of that picture that did seem suitably cast. Back in 1935, the whole roster of players couldn't have been much better had Stevenson picked them out himself. Particularly impressive and in character were Lionel Barrymore as Billy Bones and Chic Sale as poor old Ben Gunn. Jackie Cooper scores high marks as Jim Hawkins, who proves to be a match for the treacherous Silver and his pirate colleagues.

Treasure of the Golden Condor *see* **Son of Fury**

943 Trent's Last Case

Based on the novel by E.C. Bentley. Story: When Sisbee Manderson is apparently murdered, Inspector Trent interrogates the various suspects: Manderson's wife, Mabel; his secretary, John Marlow, who is in love with Mabel; Manderson's uncle; the butler; and the maid. Inspector Murch suspects that

Marlow is the murderer, but Trent proves that Manderson committed suicide in such a way as to throw suspicion onto his secretary.

Broadwest, Great Britain, 1920 (original). Silent. Director: Richard Garrick; screenwriter: P.L. Mannock. Cast: Gregory Scott (Philip Trent), Pauline Peters (Mabel Manderson), Clive Brook (John Marlow), George Foley (Sisbee Manderson), Cameron Carr (Insp. Murch), P.E. Hubbard, Richard Norton.

• ***Trent's Last Case*** (remake). Fox Film Corp., 1929. Silent with sound effects and musical score. Director: Howard Hawks; screenwriter: Scott Darling. Cast: Donald Crisp (Sisbee Manderson), Raymond Griffith (Philip Trent), Raymond Hatton (Joshua Cupples), Marceline Day (Evelyn Manderson), Lawrence Gray (Jack Marlowe), Nicholas Soussanin, Anita Garvin, Ed Kennedy.

• ***Trent's Last Case*** (remake). Republic/British Lion, Great Britain, 1952. Director: Herbert Wilcox; screenwriter: Pamela Wilcox Bower. Cast: Margaret Lockwood (Margaret Manderson), Michael Wilding (Philip Trent), Orson Welles (Sisbee Manderson), John McCallum (John Marlowe), Miles Malleson (Burton Cupples), Hugh McDermott, Sam Kydd, Jack McNaughton, Henry Edwards, Kenneth Williams, Eileen Joyce.

In the second remake, Michael Wilding as the reporter turned detective sets out to prove that financier Orson Welles did not commit suicide, but rather was killed by his wife, Margaret Lockwood, and secretary, John McCallum, but Trent is wrong. Welles did kill himself, trying to make it look like murder by McCallum, but his wife foiled his plan. It's a talky piece which could have been done without.

944 The Trespasser

Based on an original screenplay by Edmund Goulding. Story: Marion Donnell elopes with wealthy Jack Merrick but while in the midst of their honeymoon, Jack's father induces him to annul the marriage so a proper society wedding can be arranged. Marion is furious and walks out on Jack, but she is with child. A year later, she and her son are living in a Chicago tenement where she suffers a breakdown because of their poverty. Her former employer, Hector Ferguson, who always loved her, comes to her assistance, providing her with a luxurious apartment and leaving her half a million dollars when he dies. Meanwhile, Jack has married Flip who has become an invalid after an automobile accident. John Merrick, Sr., starts proceedings to take custody of his grandson. Marion gives the child up willingly, believing he will have a better future with his father's family. The sad tears of this sad parting turn to tears of happiness when Marion and Jack are reunited after Flip's death.

Gloria Productions/United Artists, 1929 (original). Director and screenwriter: Edmund Goulding. Cast: Gloria Swanson (Marion Donnell), Robert Ames (Jack Merrick), Purnell Pratt (Hector Ferguson), Henry B. Walthall (Fuller), Wally Albright (Jackie), William Holden (John Merrick, Sr.), Blanche Frederici, Kay Hammond, Mary Forbes, Marcelle Corday.

• ***That Certain Woman*** (remake). Warner Bros., 1937. Director and screenwriter: Edmund Goulding. Cast: Bette Davis (Marion Donnell), Henry Fonda

(Jack Merrick), Ian Hunter (Lloyd Rogers), Anita Louise (Flip), Donald Crisp (Merrick, Sr.), Hugh O'Donnell, Katherine Alexander, Mary Phillips, Minor Watson, Ben Welden, Sidney Toler.

In another variation of the self-sacrificing mother theme, we have two fine actresses, Gloria Swanson and Bette Davis, providing their special interpretations of a self-reliant young woman who at the age of 16 married a gangster, since deceased, and then decided to make something of herself. She becomes the secretary of a prominent lawyer who falls in love with her, but he doesn't press his case. She finally marries a rich young wastrel, only to suffer the embarrassment of having the marriage annulled by her husband's father who has learned of her past. While the story cannot withstand close scrutiny, the performance of Bette Davis in the remake is letter-perfect, while Henry Fonda scores as the weakling wealthy son and Ian Hunter as the loving employer.

The Trial of Billy Jack *see* **Billy Jack**

The Trial of Joan of Arc *see* **Joan of Arc**

945 The Trial of Mary Dugan

Based on the play by Bayard Veiller. Story: Pretty Mary Dugan is on trial for the murder of her lover, multimillionaire Edgar Rice. Her brother, Jimmy, a fledgling lawyer, disgusted with the casual examination of witnesses by Mary's attorney, Edward West, insists in taking over her defense. When Jimmy puts Mary on the stand, vitriolic prosecuting attorney Galway forces Mary to admit that Rice was just one of a number of lovers that she had taken. However, she points out that the money she got from the men was used to put her brother through law school. Jimmy produces a witness, Dr. Welcome, who proves that the murderer had to be a powerful left-handed individual, and therefore could not be Mary. Jimmy goes further and proves that attorney West, who was also one of Mary's ex-lovers, was the one who killed Rice.

MGM, 1929 (original). Director: Bayard Veiller; screenwriters: Veiller and Becky Gardiner. Cast: Norma Shearer (Mary Dugan), Lewis Stone (Edward West), H.B. Warner (D.A. Galway), Raymond Hackett (Jimmy Dugan), Lilyan Tashman (Dagmar Lorne), Olive Tell (Mrs. Edgar Rice), Adrienne D'Ambricourt, De Witt Jennings, Wilfred North, Landers Stevens, Mary Doran, Westcott B. Clarke, Charles Moore, Claud Allister, Myra Hampton.

• ***The Trial of Mary Dugan*** (remake). MGM, 1941. Director and screenwriter: Norman Z. McLeod. Cast: Laraine Day (Mary Dugan), Robert Young (Jimmy Blake), Henry O'Neill (D.A. Galway), John Litel (Edward West), Marsha Hunt (Agatha Hall), Tom Conway (Edgar Wayne), Freida Inescourt (Mrs. Wayne), Marjorie Main (Mrs. Collins), Alma Kruger, Pierre Watkin, Addison Richards, George Watts, Sara Haden, Francis Pieriot, Ian Wolfe, Cliff Danielson, Milton Kibbee.

There was a Spanish- and a French-language version of the 1929 production, with a young Charles Boyer appearing in the Jimmy Dugan role in the latter film. Norma Shearer made her talking film debut in the 1929 movie, and both she and the film were acclaimed as being superb. While this film was almost a literal translation of the Broadway play, the 1941 version had new evidence and many characters giving different testimony. There is also a change of venue from New York for the first film to Los Angeles for the second. One additional difference: Robert Young, who serves as Laraine Day's legal protector, is no longer her brother, but her sweetheart. The changes in the film were not made to make the story more dramatic, but to satisfy the more stringent production codes dealing with morality. Whereas Norma Shearer could tearfully tell on the witness stand of her shame for having been so promiscuous, Laraine Day had to be a victim of corrupt men and really as pure as the driven snow. In transforming the leading character from sinner to saint, the film loses much of its punch and becomes a rather ordinary courtroom drama, seen on the screen hundreds of times.

946 Trilby

Based on the novel *Trilby and Little Billee* by George du Maurier. Story: In Paris in the 1890s, hypnotist Svengali turns Trilby O'Ferrall into a great opera star, but he cannot compel her to reciprocate his love.

London Films, Great Britain, 1914 (original). Silent. Director: Harold Shaw; screenwriter: Bannister Merwin. Cast: Sir Herbert Tree (Svengali), Viva Birkett (Trilby O'Ferrall), Ion Swinley (Little Billee), Charles Rock (Sandy McAllister), Phillip Merivale (Taffy Wynne), Wyndham Guise, Cicely Richards, Douglas Munro.

• ***Svengali*** (remake). Warner Bros., 1931. Director: Archie Mayo; screenwriter: J. Grubb Alexander. Cast: John Barrymore (Svengali), Marian Marsh (Trilby), Bramwell Fletcher (Little Billee), Donald Crisp (the Laird), Lumsden Hare (Taffy), Carmel Myers, Luis Alberni, Ferike Boros.

• ***Svengali*** (remake). Alderdale/Renown, Great Britain, 1954. Director and screenwriter: Noel Langley. Cast: Hildegarde Neff (Trilby), Donald Wolfit (Svengali), Terence Morgan (Billy Bagot), Derek Bond (the Laird), Paul Rogers (Taffy), David Grossoff, Hubert Gregg, Noel Purcell, Alfie Bass, Harry Secombe, Peter Iling, Hugh Cross, Toots Pound, Michael Craig.

Having once seen the imaginative and forceful performance of John Barrymore as Svengali it is difficult to imagine anyone else in the role, although Donald Wolfit is a fine actor and gave a creditable performance in his appearance as the hypnotist who is able to transform a model of little talent into a great opera singer, being able to turn her on and off at will. But where apparently hypnotism can alter talent, it is not strong enough to force love.

A Trip to Paradise *see* Liliom

The Triumph of the Rat *see* The Rat

947 The Trouble with Angels

Based on the novel *Life with Mother Superior* by Jane Trahey. Story: When Mary Clancy and Rachel Devery reluctantly arrive at St. Francis Convent

School, Mother Superior correctly spots them as troublemakers. The girls pull all kinds of harmless to dangerous pranks, but Mother Superior is convinced that she can tame them. Her determination and friendly understanding win the day, to such a point that Mary decides to enter the order.

Columbia Pictures, 1966 (original). Director: Ida Lupino; screenwriter: Blanche Hanalis. Cast: Rosalind Russell (Mother Superior), Hayley Mills (Mary Clancy), June Harding (Rachel Devery), Binnie Barnes (Sister Celistine), Camilla Sparv (Sister Constance), Mary Wickes (Sister Clarissa), Gypsy Rose Lee, Marge Redmond, Barbara Hunter, Bernadine Withers, Jim Boles.

• ***Where Angels Go—Trouble Follows!*** (sequel). Columbia Pictures, 1968. Director: James Neilson; screenwriter: Blanche Hanalis. Cast: Rosalind Russell (Mother Simplicia), Stella Stevens (Sister George), Binnie Barnes (Sister Celistine), Mary Wickes (Sister Clarissa), Susan Saint James (Rosabelle), Barbara Hunter (Marvel Ann Clancy), Dolores Sutton, Milton Berle, Arthur Godfrey, Van Johnson, Robert Taylor, Alice Rawlings.

These comical films can best be appreciated by those who attended schools with nuns as teachers. For them, it may be amusing to see the "good sisters" being given a hard time for a change. In truth, none of these nuns reminds one of the formidable ladies who were almost as infallible as the Pope and seemed just about as approachable—at least in the eyes of youngsters in awe of their authority and ability to wither the most incorrigible child with a look, and occasionally a whack with a ruler, hand or rosary.

In the sequel, despite severe misgivings Mother Superior agrees to accompany progressive young Sister George and a busload of girls from St. Francis in Pennsylvania to an ecumenical rally in California. On the way they have to fend off a gang of motorcyclists intent on rape, attend a rock concert, spend an exciting (for the kids, that is) night at a Catholic boy's school, stay as guests on a ranch in New Mexico run by Robert Taylor and his six strapping sons, try to keep the old bus running, and withstand an attack by Indian extras on a film location in Arizona. As has been said, traveling with children (okay, teenagers) is like traveling third-class in Albania.

948 True Confession

Based on the novel *Mon Crime* by Louis Verneuil and the play by Verneuil and Georges Berr. Story: In this crazy comedy, Helen Bartlett, not surprisingly, buys herself a lot of trouble when she confesses to murdering her boss, a crime which she did not commit. She chose to do this so her struggling lawyer husband, Ken, would have a major case to win, and she hoped as a result he would attract a lot of clients. Everything goes according to plan when Ken wins fame by getting an acquittal, on a plea of self-defense. Helen is hounded by a zany criminologist, Charley, who knows what she has done and why. After a lot of wild comedy, everyone ends up happy—or perhaps slap-happy would be a better way to put it.

Paramount Pictures, 1937 (original). Director: Wesley Ruggles; screenwriter: Claude Binyon. Cast: Carole Lombard (Helen Bartlett), Fred MacMurray (Kenneth Bartlett), John Barrymore (Charley), Una Merkel (Daisy

McClure), Porter Hall (Prosecutor), Edgar Kennedy, Richard Carle, John T. Murray, Lynne Overman, Fritz Feld, Hattie McDaniel.

• ***Cross My Heart*** (remake). Paramount Pictures, 1946. Director: John Berry; screenwriter: Harry Tugend and Claude Binyon. Cast: Betty Hutton (Peggy Harper), Sonny Tufts (Oliver Clarke), Rhys Williams (Prosecutor), Ruth Donnelly (Eve Harper), Alan Bridge (Detective Flynn), Iris Adrian, Howard Freeman, Lewis L. Russell, Michael Chekhov.

Let it be said with all charity that Betty Hutton is no Carole Lombard, Sonny Tufts is no Fred MacMurray and director John Berry is no Wesley Ruggles. Getting that out of the way, the 1946 remake of *True Confession* is better than it should have been. Where Lombard was the fantasy-prone beauty who demonstrated her great confidence in her lawyer-husband's ability by confessing to a murder she didn't commit, Hutton in her usual St.-Vitus'-dance bouncy approach to her roles played a similarly trusting dame to boyfriend Sonny Tufts, one of the most charming, talentless actors ever to appear on the screen. The musical numbers in the remake included Johnny Burke and Jimmy Van Heusen's "That Little Dream Got Nowhere," "How Do You Do It?" and "Love is the Darndest Thing." Both films are good fun and some people claim *True Confession* is the best work of Carole Lombard's career.

True to the Army *see* **She Loves Me Not**

The Truth About Spring *see* **Satan's Sister**

The Truth About Youth *see* **When We Were Twenty-One**

949 Tugboat Annie

Based on the *Saturday Evening Post* series by Norman Reilly Raine. Story: Annie is the female skipper of a harbor tugboat. Her husband, Terry, is a shiftless, soused but likeable failure. Their son, Alec, captains an ocean liner. After getting the family into all kinds of scrapes because of his boozing, Terry redeems himself by crawling into the tug's steaming boiler to plug a leak, thus saving his son's ship and passengers.

MGM, 1933 (original). Director: Mervyn LeRoy; screenwriters: Zelda Sears and Eva Greene. Cast: Marie Dressler (Annie), Wallace Beery (Terry), Robert Young (Alec), Maureen O'Sullivan (Pat), Willard Robertson, Tammany Young, Frankie Darro.

• ***Tugboat Annie Sails Again*** (remake). Warner Bros., 1940. Director: Lewis Seller; screenwriter: Walter DeLeon. Cast: Marjorie Rambeau (Tugboat Annie), Alan Hale (Capt. Bullwinkle), Jane Wyman (Peggy Armstrong), Ronald Reagan (Eddie Kent), Clarence Kolb, Charles Halton, Paul Hurst, Victor Kilian.

Is *Tugboat Annie* hokey? Unbelievably so! Is the story filled with inconsistencies? Enough to drive a truck through! Do the leads give hammy performances? They're high on the hog! Are Dressler and Beery marvelous? You better believe it! Is the sequel in the same league as the original? No way! Tugboat Annie is one of the most enjoyable cinematic characters from the early years of talkies, and Marie Dressler just couldn't have been more delightful, ably abetted in the sentimental comedy by Wallace Beery doing what he did best, portraying a simple, boozy sweetheart. We give Marjorie Rambeau an A for effort in the sequel but neither the story nor the performances of her supporting cast could match that filmed in 1933.

Tugboat Annie Sails Again *see* **Tugboat Annie**

950 The Tunnel

Based on the novel by Bernhard Kellermann. Story: Engineer Mac Allen is in charge of the construction of a tunnel under the Atlantic Ocean from New York to Europe. Over a period of 15 years he fights every possible obstacle, natural and man-made, including the accidental death of his neglected wife, but ever goes forward to his eventual triumph.

Bavaria-Film Production, Germany, 1933 (original). Director: Kurt Bernhardt; screenwriters: Bernhardt and Reinhart Steinbickler. Cast: Paul Hartmann (Max), Olly von Flint (Mary), Gustaf Gruendgens (Woolf), Attila Hoerbiger, Max Weydner, Elga Brink, Otto Wernicke.

• ***The Tunnel*** (remake). Vandor Film, France, 1933. Director: Kurt Bernhardt; screenwriters: Bernhardt, Reinhardt Steinbickler and Alexandre Arnoux. Cast: Jean Gabin (Mac Allan), Madeleine Renaud (Mary), Van Daele (Baillere), Gustaf Gruendgens (Wood), Andre Nox, Raymonde Allain, Le Vigran.

• ***Transatlantic Tunnel*** (remake). Gaumont British Production, 1935. Director: Maurice Elvey; screenwriters: Kurt Siodmak, L. duGarde Peach and Clemence Dane. Cast: Richard Arlen (McAllen), Leslie Banks (Robbie), Madge Evans (Ruth McAllen), Helen Vinson (Varlia), C. Aubrey Smith (Lloyd), Basil Sydney, Henry Oscar, Jimmy Hanley, Walter Huston, George Arliss.

The first two films were produced by Kurt Bernhardt for Vandor Productions, a French concern with a studio in Munich, where the two pictures were made simultaneously. The English remake had an excellent cast, good direction and quality production features, but it didn't turn out to be the hit producers had hoped for in the United States. The combination of a science-fiction plot with human dedication and determination wasn't enough to pull the customers into the theaters.

The Twelve Chairs *see* **Keep Your Seats, Please**

20th Century Oz *see* **The Wizard of Oz**

Twenty-One Days *see* **The Stranger**

951 20,000 Years in Sing Sing

Based on the novel by Lewis E. Lawes. Story: Sing Sing's warden's advanced theories on prison reforms are detailed in this unbelievable but highly enjoyable drama about tough con Tom Connors, who becomes putty in the hands of Warden Long. When he is given a furlough to visit his critically injured girlfriend, he is on his honor to return. The girl, Fay, kills a man and Connors takes the blame for the crime, returns to prison as he promised the warden, is tried for the killing and is sent to the chair.

First National Pictures, 1933 (original). Director: Michael Curtiz; screenwriters: Wilson Mizner and Brown Holmes. Cast: Spencer Tracy (Tom Connors), Bette Davis (Fay), Lyle Talbot (Bud), Shelia Terry (Billie), Edward McNamara (Chief of Guards), Arthur Bryon (Warden Long), Warren Hymer, Louis Calhern, Spencer Charters, Sam Godfrey, Grant Mitchell, Nella Walker.

• ***Castle on the Hudson*** (remake). Warner Bros., 1940. Director: Anatole Litvak; screenwriter: Seton I. Miller. Cast: John Garfield (Tommy Gordon), Ann Sheridan (Kay), Pat O'Brien (Warden Long), Burgess Meredith (Steven Rockford), Henry O'Neill (D.A.), Jerome Cowan (Ed Crowley), Guinn Williams, John Litel, Margot Stevenson, Willard Robertson.

The remake tells basically the same story. Garfield is a tough kid who gets a 25 to 30-year stretch at Sing Sing for knocking over a jewelry store. While he's being reclaimed as a human being by Warden Pat O'Brien, his loyal girlfriend, Ann Sheridan, is working to get him released. When she's seriously injured in an automobile accident, O'Brien puts Garfield on his honor and lets him loose to visit her. When Sheridan kills Jerome Cowan, Garfield returns to the prison and the chair to save the warden from his political enemies.

952 23½ Hours' Leave

Based on the story by Mary Roberts Rinehart. Story: Sgt. William Gray is a lively sort, always up to some kind of devilment in an encampment of troops just about to be shipped overseas during World War I. Peggy Dodge is the general's daughter who falls in love with him, without either knowing much about each other. Her father and his mischief-making are the main ingredients for providing the laughs in this small-potatoes military comedy.

Paramount Pictures (original). Director and screenwriter: Henry King. Cast: Douglas MacLean (Sgt. William Gray), Doris May (Peggy Dodge), Thomas Guise (General Dodge), Maxfield Stanley, Wade Boteler, Alfred Hollingsworth, N. Leinsky.

• ***23½ Hours' Leave*** (remake). Grand National Pictures, 1937. Director: John Blystone; screenwriters: Harry Ruskin and Henry McCarty. Cast: James Ellison (Sgt. Gray), Terry Walker (Peggy), Morgan Hill (Tommy), Arthur Lake (Turner), Paul Harvey (General), Wally Mather, Andy Andrews, Murray Alper, Pat Gleason, John Kelly.

James Ellison was one of the "B" picture stars who never got promoted to first run features and this training camp yarn wasn't designed to do much for his prospects. The comedy—what there is of it—is almost slapstick with Paul Harvey as the General getting most of the abuse and laughs. Give Ellison credit, however, even though he can't sing, he manly attempts three numbers—all very forgettable.

Twice Around the Daffodils *see* **Carry on Nurse**

953 Twin Beds

Based on the play by Margaret Mayo and Salisbury Field. Story: Elsie Dolan, a telephone operator, meets and marries Danny Brown, a show doctor and composer. Their first night together in their new apartment is interrupted when Danny is called to a theater to rehearse the understudy to the show's intoxicated star, Monty Solari. In his haste, Danny leaves the front door of the apartment open, and Solari, who lives in the same apartment building, drunkenly wanders in and climbs into Danny's twin bed. This sets the stage for a series of wild and slapstick episodes as Elsie attempts to conceal Solari's presence from her husband. After an extended round of horseplay and hijinks, everything is explained satisfactorily and the Browns go to Europe to complete their honeymoon.

• ***Twin Beds*** (remake). First National Pictures, 1929 (original). Part-talkie. Director: Alfred Santell; screenwriter: F. McGrew Willis. Cast: Jack Mulhall (Danny Brown), Patsy Ruth Miller (Elsie Dolan), Edythe Chapman (Ma Dolan), Knute Erickson (Pa Dolan), Jocelyn Lee (Maizie Dolan), Armand Kaliz (Monty Solari), Nita Martan, Zasu Pitts, Gertrude Astor, Carl Levinus, Alice Lake.

• ***Twin Beds*** (remake). United Artists, 1942. Director: Tim Whelan; screenwriter: Curtis Kenyon, Kenneth Earl and E. Edwin Moran. Cast: George Brent (Mike Abbott), Joan Bennett (Julie Abbott), Mischa Auer (Nicolai Cherupin), Una Merkel (Lydia), Glenda Farrell (Sonya), Ernest Truex, Margaret Hamilton, Charles Coleman, Charles Arnt.

The story of a married couple's problems with the wanderings of a drunken neighbor was also filmed as a silent in 1920 by First National Pictures. The pretext for the story is mighty thin, but it results in an enjoyable and slightly naughty farce nevertheless. In the 1942 version, newlyweds George Brent and Joan Bennett live in a swank apartment where concert singer and neighbor Mischa Auer makes romantic overtures to Joan. To prevent complications the couple moves to another apartment building and at about the same time so does Auer. Brent is sure this is no mere coincidence and angrily leaves. Later an inebriated Auer wanders into Bennett's apartment by mistake. Joan tries hiding Auer in a clothes hamper when Brent returns and soon to complicate things further, Auer's wife, played by Glenda Farrell, shows up as well. The star of this film is clearly the zany Auer. Brent and Bennett don't appear too comfortable in their comical roles and as a result aren't as funny as the situations call for.

954 The Twisted Road (They Live by Night)

Based on the novel *Thieves Like Us* by Edward Anderson. Story: It's the moving, somber story of a young escaped convict, Bowie, who falls in love and marries Keechie, a girl whose circumstances are not much better than his.

RKO, 1948 (original). Director: Nicholas Ray; screenwriter: Charles Schance. Cast: Cathy O'Donnell (Keechie), Farley Granger (Bowie), Howard Da Silva (Chickamaw), Jay C. Flippen (T-Dub), Helen Craig (Mattie), Will Wright, Marie Bryant, Ian Wolfe, William Phillips, Harry Harvey.

• ***Thieves Like Us*** (remake). United Artists, 1974. Director: Robert Altman; screenwriters: Altman, Calder Willingham and Joan Tewksbury. Cast: Keith

Carradine (Bowie), Shelly Duvall (Keechie), John Schuck (Chicamaw), Bert Remsen (T-Dub), Louise Fletcher (Mattie), Ann Latham, Tom Skerritt, Al Scott.

The appeal to these unusual period crime thrillers is limited. There's not much action as the directors concentrate on character development and the relationship of this Bonnie and Clyde–like couple with other lowlifes and psychotic criminals. It's moody storytelling, with the supporting players better than the leads in both cases, but not by much.

Two Against the World *see* **5-Star Final**

Two-Faced Woman *see* **Her Sister from Paris**

The Two Faces of Dr. Jekyll *see* **Dr. Jekyll and Mr. Hyde**

Two-Fisted *see* **Is Zat So?**

U

The Ugly Duckling *see* **Dr. Jekyll and Mr. Hyde**

Under Flaschen Flaggen *see* **Man, Woman and Sin**

955 Under the Red Robe

Based on the novel by Stanley J. Weyman. Story: In this movie, supposedly based on events in the life of Cardinal Richelieu, prime minister of France under King Louis XIII, the cardinal demands that Gil de Berault, who is under a death sentence for dueling, capture Henri de Cocheforet, a suspected leader of a plot to overthrow the king. Berault succeeds but also becomes captivated by de Cocheforet's beautiful sister, Renee. He abandons his assignment and returns to Richelieu empty-handed, prepared to meet his fate. Meanwhile, the king's brother, the Duc d'Orleans, a conspirator against Richelieu, persuades the king to dismiss his prime minister. Berault reveals Orleans' treachery and the cardinal is returned to favor with Berault praised as a patriot.

• ***Under the Red Robe*** (remake). Cosmopolitan Corporation/Goldwyn, 1923. Silent. Director: Alan Crosland; screenwriter: Bayard Veiller. Cast: Robert B. Mantell (Cardinal Richelieu), John Charles Thomas (Gil de Berault), Alma Rubens (Renee de Cocheforet), Otto Kruger (Henri de Cocheforet), William H. Powell (Duc d'Orleans), Ian MacLaren (King Louis XIII), Genevieve Hamper, Mary MacLaren, Rose Coghlan, Gustav von Seyffertitz, Sidney Herbert, Arthur Houseman.

• ***Under the Red Robe*** (remake). Twentieth Century–Fox/Denham Studios, Great Britain, 1937. Director: Victor Seastrom; screenwriters: Edward Rose, Lajos Biro, Philip Lindsay and J.L. Hodson. Cast: Conrad Veidt (Gil de Berault), Annabella (Lady Marguerite), Raymond Massey (Cardinal Richelieu),

Romney Brent (Marius), Sophie Stewart (Duchess of Foix), F. Wyndham Goldie (Duke of Foix), Lawrence Grant, Baliol Holloway, Shale Gardner, Frank Damer, James Regan.

Under the Red Robe, first filmed in 1915, is an interesting historical costume drama with the accent on the costumes and only fleeting attention given to history. In the remake Conrad Veidt impresses as Cardinal Richelieu's chief undercover agent, sent to corral an elusive duke but lets the latter go and risks the cardinal's displeasure, rather than lose the love of the duke's lovely sister. Also making fine contributions to the success of the film is Raymond Massey as the cardinal and Romney Brent as the prime minister's stooge. Annabella as the love interest is good to look at but her performance is rather ordinary.

956 Under Two Flags

Based on the novel by Ouida. Story: In a plot which in parts is reminiscent of *Destry Rides Again,* an English nobleman, Victor, arrives in Algiers and joins the French Foreign Legion, without revealing his true identity. A French-Arab camp follower named "Cigarette" falls in love with him, but he does not reciprocate her feelings. She is furious when she learns of Victor's background and goes to his true love, Princess Corona, with intentions of killing her. Instead she reveals Victor's real identity to the princess, learns of plots against Victor and Algiers by Sheik Ben Ali Hammed, clears Victor of treason and takes a bullet meant for Victor, dying in his arms.

• ***Under Two Flags*** (remake). Universal Films, 1922. Silent. Director: Tod Browning; screenwriter: Edward T. Lowe. Cast: Priscilla Dean (Cigarette), James Kirkwood (Corporal Victor), John Davidson (Sheik Ben Ali Hammed), Stuart Holmes (Marquis de Chateauroy), Ethel Grey Terry (Princess Corona), Robert Mack, Burton Law, Albert Pollet, W.H. Bainbridge.

• ***Under Two Flags*** (remake). Twentieth Century–Fox, 1936. Director: Frank Lloyd; screenwriters: W.P. Lipscomb and Walter Ferris. Cast: Ronald Colman (Sgt. Victor), Claudette Colbert (Cigarette), Victor McLaglen (Major Doyle), Rosalind Russell (Lady Venetia), Gregory Ratoff (Ivan), Nigel Bruce (Captain Menzies), C. Henry Gordon, Herbert Mundin, John Carradine, Lumsden Hare, J. Edward Bromberg, Onslow Stevens, Fritz Leiber.

First filmed in 1916 with tempestuous Theda Bara as Cigarette, *Under Two Flags* is sturdy fare for those fascinated with the romance of the French Foreign Legion, a place where men go to forget, and the women they forget with. In the sound version, Claudette Colbert enthusiastically portrays the bawdy cafe hostess with whom Ronald Colman dallies and Rosalind Russell appears as the English lady, quite willing to overlook any indiscretions in his past. The highlight of the film is the battle between the marauding Arabs and a handful of Legionnaires manning a fort until rescued by troops led to the spot by Colbert, whose character here gives up the ghost to save the man she loves.

The Unfaithful ***see*** **The Letter**

957 Unfaithfully Yours

Based on a story by Preston Sturges. Story: Symphony orchestra leader Sir

Alfred de Carter believes that his wife Daphne has been unfaithful. This drives him to such a fury that while conducting a concert, he fantasizes three long plans of revenge. During a number by Rossini, he imagines himself slashing Daphne with a razor and then pinning the murder on her lover, while Wagner causes him to daydream of nobly giving up his wife in favor of the other man. Finally with Tchaikovsky, he imagines playing Russian roulette with his rival. The payoff is of course that Daphne is innocent.

Twentieth Century–Fox, 1948 (original). Director and screenwriter: Preston Sturges. Cast: Rex Harrison (Sir Alfred de Carter), Linda Darnell (Daphne de Carter), Barbara Lawrence (Barbara), Rudy Vallee (August Henschler), Kurt Krueger (Anthony), Lionel Stander (Hugo), Edgar Kennedy, Alan Bridge, Julius Tannen, Torben Meyer, Robert Greig, Evelyn Beresford, Georgia Caine, Harry Seymour.

• ***Unfaithfully Yours*** (remake). Twentieth Century–Fox, 1983. Director: Howard Zieff; screenwriters: Valerie Curtin, Barry Levinson and Robert Klane. Cast: Dudley Moore (Claude Eastman), Natassia Kinski (Daniella Eastman), Armand Assante (Maxmillian Sten), Albert Brooks (Norman Robbens), Cassie Yates (Carla Robbens), Richard Libertini, Richard B. Shull, Jan Triska.

In the remake, Moore only thinks of one plot to take revenge on the believed infidelity involving his wife, Natassia Kinski, and guest artist Armand Assante, but in his imagination it is the perfect crime with Assante getting the blame for the murder of Kinski. When he tries to carry through with his plan, everything goes wrong, hilariously, or at least that's what the producer, director and star hoped. Actually, it's not all that amusing.

Unholy Love *see* **Madame Bovary**

958 The Unholy Three

Based on the novel by Clarence Aaron Robbins. Story: Professor Echo, a ventriloquist, Hercules, a strongman, and Tweedledee, a dwarf, work in a sideshow. As they perform, their partner, Rosie O'Grady, moves through the audience picking pockets. Seeking bigger profits, the gang opens a pet shop, stocked with parrots that do not talk; but when customers are present, Echo, disguised as an old lady and using ventriloquism, makes them appear to talk. When the customers get the bird home and they find it has nothing to say, their complaints bring a visit by Echo, still dressed as an old lady, pushing Tweedledee, disguised as a baby, in a carriage. While Echo is throwing his voice, demonstrating to the customers that the bird indeed does talk, Tweedledee is casing the place for a robbery to be later performed by Hercules. The gang hires a gentle clerk, Hector McDonald, with whom Rosie falls in love. When Hercules and Tweedledee kill one of their victims on a job, they see that Hector takes the blame. Rosie and "the Unholy Three" skip town. She promises to stay with Echo if he will save Hector. Echo is successful in getting Hector acquitted and later allows Rosie to be reunited with him. Meantime, Hercules and Tweedledee are killed by a gorilla.

MGM, 1925 (original). Silent. Director: Tod Browning; screenwriter:

Waldemar Young. Cast: Lon Chaney (Echo), Mae Busch (Rosie O'Grady), Matt Moore (Hector MacDonald), Victor McLaglen (Hercules), Harry Earles (Tweedledee), Harry Betz, Edward Connelly, William Humphreys, A.E. Warren.

• ***The Unholy Three*** (remake). MGM, 1930. Director: Jack Conway; screenwriters: J.C. and Elliott Nugent. Cast: Lon Chaney (Echo), Lila Lee (Rosie), Elliott Nugent (Hector), Harry Earles (Midget), Ivan Linow (Hercules), John Miljan, Clarence Burton, Crauford Kent.

The Unholy Three is an unusual production, clearly intended to demonstrate the talented eccentricities of "The Man with a Thousand Faces," Lon Chaney. The remake, released after Chaney's death, was the only sound film he ever made. Most critics feel the silent version is the better of the two, but this one sound example makes one wonder what the very talented character actor might have accomplished had he had additional chances to integrate his vocal impersonations with his physical ones.

The Unholy Wife *see* **The Secret Hour**

Unmarried *see* **Lady and Gent**

Untamed *see* **Mantrap**

959 Up for the Cup

Based on the story by Con West. Story: Yorkshire loom inventor John Willie Entwhistle comes to London for the Cup Final and has his wallet containing his money and tickets stolen. There's more. His sweetheart, Mary Murgatroyd, disappears and Entwhistle arrives just in time to save her from a fate worse than death at the hands of his employer's son. He learns he's to be richly rewarded for his invention, leaving him and Mary happy, at last.

British & Dominions, Great Britain, 1931 (original). Director: Jack Raymond; screenwriters: Con West, R.P. Weston and Bert Lee. Cast: Sydney Howard (John Willie Entwhistle), Joan Wyndham (Mary Murgatroyd), Stanley Kirk (Cyril Hardcastle), Sam Livesey (John Cartwright), Marie Wright (Mrs. Entwhistle), Moore Marriott (James Hardcastle), Hal Gordon, Herbert Woodward, Jack Raymond.

• ***Up for the Cup*** (remake). Citadel/Byron, Great Britain, 1950. Director: Jack Raymond; screenwriters: Con West and Jack Marks. Cast: Albert Modley (Albert Entwhistle), Mai Bacon (Maggie Entwhistle), Helen Christie (Jane), Harold Berens (Auctioneer), Wallas Eaton (Barrowboy), Jack Melford (Barrowboy), Charmian Innes, Fred Groves, John Warren.

One of the best of the regional farces, the remake has Yorkshire mill worker Albert Entwhistle and his wife in London to see the Cup Final. First he loses her, then his wallet with the ticket for the match in it. Which he misses most is questionable in this wild comedy.

Up from the Beach *see* **The Longest Day**

960 Up Front

Based on the novel by Bill Mauldin. Story: Based on Bill Mauldin's popular World War II cartoon characters of "Joe" and "Willie," the film lacks the poignancy and irony of Mauldin's strips, settling for just another spoof of army life. Willie and Joe get involved in a black-market scheme, resulting in a final chase scene with the boys driving a truck of army contraband.

Universal Pictures, 1951 (original). Director: Alexander Hall; screenwriter: Stanley Roberts. Cast: David Wayne (Joe), Tom Ewell (Willie), Marina Berti (Emi), Jeffrey Lynn (Captain Ralph Johnson), Richard Egan (Capa), Maurice Cavell (Vuaglio), Vaughn Taylor, Silvio Minciotti, Paul Harvey.

• ***Back at the Front*** (sequel). Universal Pictures, 1952. Director: George Sherman; screenwriters: Lou Breslow, Don McGuire and Oscar Brodney. Cast: Tom Ewell (Willie), Harvey Lembeck (Joe), Mari Blanchard (Nida), Richard Long (Sgt. Rose), Palmer Lee (Capt. White), Barry Kelley (Gen. Dixon), Russell Johnson, Vaughn Taylor, Aram Katcher.

Both films were presented as broad farces with war being treated more as slapstick than a horrible tragedy. In the sequel, Willie and Joe are now in Japan as guinea pigs in an Army experiment. This time they get involved with a gang of smugglers and they feign numerous rare illnesses, hoping to be discharged from the service. It's ho-hum material.

Up in Arms *see* **The Nervous Wreck**

961 Up in Mabel's Room

Based on the play by Wilson Collinson and Otto Harbach. Story: Mabel Ainsworth obtains a quickie divorce from her husband, Garry, when she discovers him buying lingerie that he will not explain. Later she finds out that the purchase of the frilly thing was meant to be an anniversary present, embroidered with her name. Mabel follows Garry from Paris back to the States, determined to get him back. At a party, Mabel pretends not to recognize Garry and plants the chemise, which had caused all the misunderstanding, in Garry's pocket to cause him some difficulties with his current flame, Sylvia Wells. The latter discovers the intimate item, faints and is taken to Mabel's room, where Garry is hiding under the bed. After some further mishaps and misunderstandings, Mabel claims her chemise and, discovering that her divorce is not valid, the couple decides to give the marriage another try.

Christie Film Co., 1926 (original). Silent. Director: E. Mason Hopper; screenwriter: F. McGrew Willis. Cast: Marie Prevost (Mabel Ainsworth), Harrison Ford (Garry Ainsworth), Phyllis Haver (Sylvia Wells), Harry Myers (Jimmy Larchmont), Sylvia Breamer, Paul Nicholson, Carl Gerard, Maude Truax.

• ***Up in Mabel's Room*** (remake). United Artists, 1944. Director: Allan Dwan; screenwriter: Tom Reed. Cast: Marjorie Reynolds (Geraldine Ainsworth), Dennis O'Keefe (Gary Ainsworth), Gail Patrick (Mabel Essington), Mischa Auer (Boris), Charlotte Greenwood (Martha), Lee Bowman, John Hubbard, Binnie Barnes, Janet Lambert.

The material in these bedroom farces is extremely dated, but one can see the laughs they must have once caused. In the remake, timid Dennis O'Keefe, recently married, has made only one indiscretion in his life. Before he got married to Geraldine, he had made a present of a slip with her name embroidered on it to Mabel Essington, played by Gail Patrick. Geraldine, played by Marjorie Reynolds, suspects O'Keefe of more serious dalliance with Mabel, now engaged to O'Keefe's best friend, Lee Bowman, and this leads to more mix-ups and misunderstandings before everything is resolved and the proper pairings are once more in place. For today's audiences the naughty double entendre dealing with what O'Keefe slipped to Patrick in Mexico surely will seem rather tame.

962 Up in the Air

Based on an original screenplay by Edward Kelso. Story: Rita Wilson, a female singer for a radio station, is shot dead as she faces a microphone. A bit later a cowboy star, Tex, also is killed. Pageboy Frankie, with the reluctant help of Jeff, shows the cops exactly how the murders were committed and by whom. As a reward, his girlfriend, Anne, is given the job of the girl singer, while he and Jeff are given their own radio show.

Monogram Pictures, 1940 (original). Director: Howard Bretherton; screenwriter: Edward Kelso. Cast: Frankie Darro (Frankie), Marjorie Reynolds (Anne), Mantan Moreland (Jeff), Gordon Jones (Tex), Lorna Grey (Rita Wilson), Tristam Coffin, Clyde Dilson, Dick Elliott, John Holland, Carleton Young.

• ***There Goes Kelly*** (sequel). Monogram Pictures, 1945. Director: Phil Karlstein; screenwriter: Edward Kelso. Cast: Jackie Moran (Jimmy), Wanda McKay (Anne), Sidney Miller (Sammy), Ralph Sanford (Marty), Dewey Robinson (Delaney), Jan Wiley, Anthony Warde, Harry Depp, George Eldredge.

These stories about wide-eyed page boys who solve murder mysteries are suitable to their purpose, to fill out the lower half of a double bill, and drive the people out of the theater to make room for more to see the primary feature. There's little to choose between Frankie Darro and Jackie Moran, or for that matter between the respective comic reliefs, Mantan Moreland and Sidney Miller.

963 Up Pops the Devil

Based on the play by Albert Hackett and Frances Goodrich. Story: The simple plot of this romantic comedy about bohemian inhabitants of Manhattan's Greenwich Village concentrates on a young dancer, Anne Merrick, who works in order that her author husband can spend all of his time writing. Eventually he comes to resent being "kept" and breaks up with his wife, only to reconcile with her when he makes good.

Paramount Pictures, 1931 (original). Director: A. Edward Sutherland; screenwriters: Arthur Kober and Eve Unsell. Cast: Skeets Gallagher (Binny Hatfield), Stuart Erwin (Stranger), Carole Lombard (Anne Merrick), Lilyan Tashman (Polly Griscom), Norman Foster (Steve Merrick), Edward J. Nugent, Theodore von Eltz, Joyce Compton, Eulalie Jensen.

• ***Thanks for the Memory*** (remake). Paramount Pictures, 1938. Director:

George Archainbaud. Cast: Bob Hope (Steve Merrick), Shirley Ross (Anne Merrick), Charles Butterworth (Biney), Otto Kruger (Gil Morrell), Hedda Hopper (Polly Griscom), Laura Hope Crews, Emma Dunn, Roscoe Karns, Eddie Anderson.

The authors of the play which was the basis for these two comedies would go on to greater success with *The Thin Man.* The 1931 film gave Paramount an opportunity to put to work some of their young talent. Of these only Carole Lombard would become a big star, although Stu Erwin had some comedy success later in the '30s. The remake was put together quickly to take advantage of the popularity of the teaming of Bob Hope and Shirley Ross in *The Big Broadcast of 1938.* All in all, those who enjoyed their duet of what was to become Hope's theme song, "Thanks for the Memories," from *The Big Broadcast,* were sure to enjoy their harmonizing on the million-record selling "Two Sleepy People" by Hoagy Carmichael and Frank Loesser. Other than that the story of the bumpy marriage of a young bohemian couple hasn't got a lot going for it.

964 Up the Creek

Based on a screenplay by Val Guest, John Warren and Len Heath. Story: Missile-mad Lt. Humphrey Fairweather, having conducted numerous disastrous experiments at various postings, is assigned to a mothballed cruiser anchored at the end of a creek. Here he finds the crew, led by bo'sun CPO Docherty, has founded a thriving black market in the ship's stores with the locals. Everyone escapes a potential court-martial when visiting Admiral Foley fires off one of Fairweather's home-made rockets and sinks the ship.

Byron/Warner Bros., Great Britain, 1958 (original). Director: Val Guest; screenwriters: Guest, Len Heath and John Warren. Cast: David Tomlinson (Lt. Humphrey Fairweather), Peter Sellers (CPO Docherty), Wilfrid Hyde-White (Admiral Foley), Liliane Sottane (Susanne), Lionel Jeffries (Steady Barker), Lionel Murton, Sam Kydd, John Warren, David Lodge, Reginald Beckwith, Vera Day, Michael Goodliffe, Frank Pettingell.

• ***Further Up the Creek*** (sequel). Byron-Hammer/Columbia, Great Britain, 1958. Director: Val Guest; screenwriters: Guest, John Warren and Len Heath. Cast: David Tomlinson (Lt. Fairweather), Frankie Howard (Bosun), Shirley Eaton (Jane), Thora Hird (Mrs. Galloway), Lionel Jeffries (Steday Barker), Lionel Murton, David Lodge, John Warren, Sam Kydd, Edwin Richfield, Stanley Unwin, Michael Goodliffe, Patrick Holt, Walter Hudd.

In the sequel, the crew of the antiquated frigate *Aristotle,* led by their wily bo'sun, abandon their bookmaking business when the ship is sold to the president of Algerocco. They advertise a Mediterranean cruise and book a number of passengers. They escape court-martial this time, because led by their new commander, Lt. Fairweather, they foil a revolution in Algerocco.

965 Up the River

Based on a screenplay by Maurine Watkins. Story: A pair of con artists, St. Louis and Dannemora Dan, are sent to prison where they become stars of the baseball team. Fellow prisoner Steve learns that his mother is being fleeced by crooks. Using the annual prison show as an excuse, St. Louis and Dan escape and arrive in New England to appropriate the bonds that Steve's mother had turned over to the crooks and return to prison in time to win the annual baseball game.

Fox Film Corporation, 1930 (original). Director: John Ford; screenwriter: Maurine Watkins. Cast: Spencer Tracy (St. Louis), Warren Hymer (Dannemora Dan), Humphrey Bogart (Steve), Claire Luce (Judy), Joan Lawes (Jean), Sharon Lynn (Edith La Verne), George MacFarlane, Gaylord Pendleton, William Collier, Sr., Robert E. O'Connor, Louise MacIntosh.

• ***Up the River*** (remake). Twentieth Century–Fox, 1938. Director: Alfred Werker; screenwriters: Lou Breslow and John Patrick. Cast: Preston Foster (Chipper Morgan), Tony Martin (Tommy Grant), Phyllis Brooks (Helen), Slim Summerville (Slim Nelson), Arthur Treacher (Darby Randall), Alan Dinehart, Eddie Collins, Jane Darwell, Sidney Toler, Bill Robinson, Edward Gargan.

The most notable thing about the 1930 prison comedy is that it was Spencer Tracy's first film and Humphrey Bogart's second. Both versions are decent parodies of the usual prison yarns with some funny business for the times. The remake has no top names to carry it and so it didn't do much at the box office. The songs written by Sidney Clara and Harry Akst included "It's the Strangest Thing," sung by Tony Martin (who is a much better singer than he is an actor). Oh yes, the game won by the cons this time around is football.

Uptight *see* **The Informer**

V

The Vagabond King *see* **If I Were King**

966 The Valiant

Based on the play by Holworthy Hall and Robert M. Middlemass. Story: When James Dyke kills a man in a tenement, he gives himself up to the police. Refusing to give his name or offer any defense, he is quickly tried and sentenced to die. His aged mother, Mrs. Douglas, spots a badly reproduced picture of him in a newspaper and sends his sister, Mary, to determine if this is their long-lost son and brother. James convinces Mary that he is not her brother, telling her that James Douglas had died a hero in World War I. After she is gone, James goes calmly and resignedly to his death.

Fox Film Corp., 1929 (original). Director: William K. Howard; screenwriters: John Hunter Booth and Tom Barry. Cast: Paul Muni (James Dyke), John Mack Brown (Robert Ward), Edith Yorke (Mrs. Douglas), Marguerite Churchill (Mary Douglas), Richard Carlyle, De Witt Jennings, Clifford Dempsey, Henry Kolker.

• ***The Man Who Wouldn't Talk*** (remake). Twentieth Century–Fox. Director: David Burton; screenwriter: Robert Ellis, Helen Logan, Selter Ziffren and Edward Ettinger. Cast: Lloyd Nolan (Joe Monday), Jean Rogers (Alice Stetson),

Richard Clarke (Steve Phillips), Onslow Stevens (Frederick Keller), Eric Blore (Horace Parker), Joan Valerie, Mae Marsh, Paul Stanton, Douglas Wood.

Paul Muni made his screen debut in the somber 1929 melodrama. The remake has a happier ending. Bitterly resigned to his death, Lloyd Nolan refuses all appeals to reveal his true identity, during his trial for an inadvertent killing. He had changed his name to protect his family and he does not wish to cause them further shame. But the law is not satisfied to convict a man without all the facts and when the events leading up to the killing are disclosed, his life is spared.

The Vampire of Dusseldorf *see* **M**

967 Vanity Fair

Based on the novel by William Makepeace Thackery. Story: Using her wits and charms, Becky Sharp climbs from humble beginnings to a place in society. Although she is unable to lure Joseph Smedley, brother of her friend Amelia, to the altar, she has better luck with Rawdon Crawley, son of her employer. His family feels she is common, and cuts off Rawdon from his share of the family wealth. While Rawdon is away at the Napoleonic wars, she has a number of affairs including one with George Osborne; soon after he marries Amelia. Everything goes wrong for the adventuress when none of the men in her life will have anything further to do with her. After touring Europe under an assumed name she returns to London to live a quiet life.

• ***Vanity Fair*** (remake). Ballin Productions/Goldwyn, 1923. Silent. Director and screenwriter: Hugo Ballin. Cast Mabel Ballin (Becky Sharp), Hobart Bosworth (Marquis of Steyne), George Walsh (Rawdon Crawley), Harrison Ford (George Osborne), Earle Foxe (Capt. Dobbin), Eleanor Boardman (Amelia Smedley), Willard Louis (Joseph Smedley), Robert Mack, William Humphreys, Dorcas Matthews, Laura La Varnie, James A. Marcusi, Eugene Acker, Leo White.

• ***Vanity Fair*** (remake). Hoffman Productions/Allied Pictures, 1932. Director: Chester M. Franklin; screenwriter: F. Hugh Herbert. Cast: Myrna Loy (Becky Sharp), Conway Tearle (Rawdon Crawley), Barbara Kent (Amelia Smedley), Walter Bryon (George Osborne), Anthony Bushell (Dobbin), Billy Bevan (Joseph Smedley), Montagu Love (Marquis of Steyne), Herbert Bunston, Mary Forbes, Lionel Belmore, Lilyan Irene.

• ***Becky Sharp*** (remake). RKO, 1935. Director: Rouben Mamoulian; screenwriter: Francis Edward Faragough. Cast: Miriam Hopkins (Becky Sharp), Frances Dee (Amelia Sedley), Cedric Hardwicke (Marquis of Steyne), Billie Burke (Lady Bareacres), Alison Skipworth (Miss Crawley), Nigel Bruce (Joseph Sedley), Alan Mowbray (Rawdon Crawley), Colin Tapley (William Dobbin), G.P. Huntley, Jr., William Stack, George Hassell, William Faversham.

Thackeray's novel was also filmed in 1911 and 1915. The first talkie remake, starring Myrna Loy, pulled Becky Sharp from Regency England and sat her down in the present dáy (that is, the early 1930s). Without updating the story and minus the costumes, the ancient story looked creaky and dated. The 1935 piece is most remembered for being the first film to employ the three-color Technicolor technique. Cinematographically interesting, the story still is nothing to get excited about. Miriam Hopkins' performance wins few raves, as she routinely goes through a series of men until they all have abandoned her and she faces a life of growing old alone with her beauty gone. The best of the lot in this unexciting picture is Cedric Hardwicke as the one man who uses Becky as much as she uses him.

Die Vetsera *see* **Mayerling**

A Very Young Lady *see* **Girl's Dormitory**

La Veuve Joyeuse *see* **The Merry Widow**

Vicki *see* **I Wake Up Screaming**

Victor and Victoria *see* **Viktor und Viktoria**

Victory *see* **Dangerous Paradise**

968 Viktor und Viktoria

Based on a story by Hans Hoemburg. Story: A starving singer, Viktoria, who can't find a job in post–World War I Germany, is a smash hit when she impersonates a man, Viktor, who is a female-impersonator. Her life is complicated when she falls for a manly man. He discovers her secret and they become lovers, but to the rest of the world it is thought to be a homosexual liaison. Before the fade-out, the sexes get straightened out to everyone's satisfaction.

UFA Productions, Germany, 1933 (original). Director and screenwriter: Reinhold Schuenzel. Cast: Renate Mueller (Viktor/Viktoria), Adolf Wohlbrueck, Hermann Thimig, Hilde Hildebrand, Fritz Odemar, Friedel Pisetta, Arlbert Waescher.

• ***First a Girl (Once a Woman)*** (remake). Gaumont British, 1935. Director: Victor Saville; screenwriter: Marjorie Gaffney. Cast: Jessie Matthews (Elizabeth), Sonnie Hale (Victor), Anna Lee (Princess), Griffith Jones (Robert), Alfred Drayton (McLintock), Constance Godridge, Eddie Gray, Martita Hunt, Donald Stewart.

• ***Some Like It Hot*** (remake). Mirisch Company, 1959. Director: Billy Wilder; screenwriters: Billy Wilder and I.A.L. Diamond. Cast: Marilyn Monroe (Sugar Kane Kovalchick), Tony Curtis (Joe/Josephine), Jack Lemmon (Jerry/Daphne), George Raft (Spats Columbo), Pat O'Brien (Mulligan), Joe E. Brown (Osgood Fielding III), Nehemiah Persoff, Joan Shawlee, Billy Gray, George E. Stone.

• **Victor/Victoria** (remake). MGM, 1982. Director and screenwriter: Blake Edwards. Cast: Julie Andrews (Victor/Victoria), James Garner (King), Robert Preston (Toddy), Lesley Ann Warren (Norma), Alex Karras (Squash), John Rhys-Davies (Cassell), Graham Stark, Peter Arne, Sherloque Tanney.

Viktor und Viktoria was a very successful German comedy and a splendid vehicle for singer Renate Mueller who impersonates the original "Victoria," played amusingly and foolishly by Hermann Thimig. *First a Girl* has a similar story with seamstress Jessie Matthews achieving theatrical success when she impersonates a man impersonating a woman. Her secret is discovered by admirer Griffith Jones when he catches her swimming.

The classic comedy *Some Like It Hot* is not a direct descendant of *Viktor und Viktoria* but the main device of female impersonation and resulting problems of romance are enough alike to include it here. The story is of two '20s era musicians, Curtis and Lemmon, who are innocently present at the St. Valentine's Day Massacre. To escape pursuing mobsters, they disguise themselves as women and get jobs with an all-girls band on its way to Florida. Curtis falls for the band's singer, Monroe, who is hoping to catch a millionaire husband. Curtis tries to play the part, while Lemmon is pursued by a real millionaire, Joe E. Brown. Things get hectic when the gangsters arrive and recognize Tony and Jack. All ends well with Curtis getting Monroe and Lemmon engaged to Brown. The latter is unperturbed when Lemmon confesses he's a man, saying "Well, nobody's perfect."

Julie Andrews is excellent as the starving singer who is talked into pretending she is a homosexual female impersonator. She falls in love with Chicago nightclub operator James Garner who discovers her secret while she is bathing. For her career he goes along with the world thinking that he also is gay, but can only take so much of a threat to his masculinity. Alex Karras portrays the ex–pro football player bodyguard of Garner, who is delighted to admit he's gay when he believes his boss is. The real star of the film is Robert Preston as a delightful old queen who arranges Andrews' deception.

969 The Virgin Soldiers

Based on the novel by Leslie Thomas. Story: It's the semi-serious, semi-comic adventures of British Army recruits in Singapore in 1950. Most of the action is of a sexual nature and most of the comical jabs land below the belt, as these young men have exploits both with guerillas and the sergeant's daughter.

Columbia British, Great Britain, 1969 (original). Director: John Dexter; screenwriters: John Hopkins, John McGrath and Ian La Fresnais. Cast: Lynn Redgrave (Phillipa Raskin), Hywel Bennett (Pete Brigg), Nigel Davenport (Sgt. Driscoll), Nigel Patrick (RSM Raskin), Rachel Kempson (Mrs. Raskin), Jack Shepherd, Michael Gwynn, Christopher Timothy, Don Hawkins, Geoffrey Hughes, Roy Holder, Jolyon Jackley.

• ***Stand Up Virgin Soldiers*** (remake). Maidenhead/Smith/Warner Bros., Great Britain, 1977. Director: Norman Cohen; screenwriter: Leslie Thomas. Cast: Robin Askwith (Pte. Brigg), Nigel Davenport (Sgt. Driscoll), George Layton (Pte. Jacobs), John Le Mesurier (Col. Bromley Pickering), Warren Mitchell (Morris Morris), Robin Nedwell, Edward Woodward, Irene Handl, Fiesta Mei Lung, Pamela Stephenson, Lynda Bellingham, David Auker.

The remake was just more of the sexual adventures of national servicemen in Singapore in 1950, but something seemed to have happened during the eight-year lay-off. While the second picture is certainly bawdy, it's not particularly enjoyable, even for those looking for titillation.

The Virgin Queen *see* **The Private Life of Henry VIII**

970 Virginia's Husband

Based on the play by Florence Kilpatrick. Story: Virginia Trevor, something of a man-hater and early women's libber, is forced to hire an ex-officer, Bill Hemingway, to pose as her husband, in order to satisfy wealthy Aunt Janet, who has been sending Virginia a nice allowance from abroad, but who is now arriving in London to visit her niece and her husband.

Nettlefolf/Butcher, Great Britain, 1928 (original). Silent. Director: Harry Hughes; screenwriter: H. Fowler Mear. Cast: Lillian Oldland (Virginia Trevor), Mabel Poulton (Joyce), Pat Aherne (Bill Hemingway), Marie Ault (Aunt Janet), Fewlass Llewellyn, Ena Grossmith, Charles Dormer.

• ***Virginia's Husband*** (remake). Smith/Fox Film Corp., Great Britain, 1934. Director: Maclean Rogers; screenwriter: H. Fowler Mear. Cast: Dorothy Boyd (Virginia Trevor), Reginald Gardiner (John Craddock), Enid Stamp-Taylor (June Haslett), Ena Grossmith (Elizabeth), Annie Esmond (Mrs. Elkins), Sebastian Smith, Wally Patch, Tom Helmore, Andrea Malsndrinos, Hal Walters.

Both the silent film and its sound remake are so-so comedies, whose story line has been exploited often elsewhere with more amusing results.

W

Wasbash Avenue *see* **Coney Island**

Wagons Roll at Night *see* **Kid Galahad**

Wake Island *see* **The Lost Patrol**

Walk, Don't Run *see* **The More the Merrier**

971 The Wandering Jew

Based on the play by E. Temple Thurston. Story: Matathias is a Jew who demands the release of Barabbas and the crucifixion of Christ. For this he is cursed with eternal life, forced to wander through the centuries until Christ comes to him and grants him death, which comes during the Spanish Inquisition.

• ***The Wandering Jew*** (remake). Stoll, Great Britain, 1923. Silent. Director: Maurice Elvey; screenwriter: Alicia Ramsey. Cast: Matheson Long (Matathias), Hutin Britton (Judith), Malvina Longfellow (Gianella), Isobel Elsom (Olalla Quintana), Florence Sanders (Joanne), Shayle Gardner, Hubert Carter, Jerrold Robertshaw, Winifred Izard, Fred Raynham, Lewis Gilbert, Hector Abbas, Lionel D'Aragon, Gordon Hopkirk.

• ***The Wandering Jew*** (remake). Twickenham/Gaumont, Great Britain, 1933. Director: Maurice Elvey; screenwriter: H. Fowler Mear. Cast: Conrad Veidt (Matathias), Marie Ney (Judith), Cicely Oates (Rachel), Basil Gil (Pontius Pilate), Anne Grey (Joanne de Beaudricourt), Dennis Hoey (de Beaudricourt), Joan Maude (Gianella), Peggy Ashcroft (Olla Quintana), Jack Livesey, Bertram Wallis, John Stuart, Arnold Lucy, Francis L. Sullivan, Felix Aylmer, Ivor Barnard, Abraham Sofaer.

This questionable story of a perhaps symbolic Jew, a "Christ-killer," has been also filmed in 1904, 1913, 1915, 1918, 1926 and 1949. Putting aside for the moment the clearly betrayed prejudice inherent in the story, the best known version of the film, the 1933 version, was praised for its production values, but generally described as boring. Audiences didn't seem much interested in the four pictured periods in Matathias' life, the time of Christ, the Crusades, Medieval Italy and the Spanish Inquisition. One can find much to commend in Conrad Veidt's portrayal of the wandering Jew.

972 The Ware Case

Based on the play by George Pleydell Bancroft. Story: Sir Hubert Ware, who admits to being in dire financial straits, is brought to trial for the drowning murder of his wife's odious but wealthy brother Eustace Ede. His solicitor, Michael Ayde, is able to get Ware acquitted due to the testimony of a surprise witness. Returning home, Ware realizes that Michael and his wife are in love. He declares that he is really guilty of the crime and kills himself with poison.

Broadwest, Great Britain, 1917 (original). Silent. Director: Walter West; screenwriter: J. Bertram Brown. Cast: Matheson Lang (Sir Hubert Ware), Violet Hopson (Lady Magdalen Ware), Ivy Close (Marian Scales), Gregory Scott (Michael Ayde), George Foley (Sir Henry Egerton).

• ***The Ware Case*** (remake). Film Manufacturing Co., Great Britain, 1928. Silent. Director: Manning Haynes; screenwriter: Lydia Hayward. Cast: Stewart Rome (Sir Hubert Ware), Betty Carter (Lady Magda Ware), Ian Fleming (Michael Adye), Cameron Carr (Inspector Watkins), Wellington Briggs (Sir Henry Egerton), Patrick Ludlow (Eustace Ede), Patrick Stewart, Syd Ellery, John Valentine.

• ***The Ware Case*** (remake). Ealing, Great Britain, 1938. Director: Robert Stevenson; screenwriters: Robert Stevenson, Roland Pertwee and E.V.H. Emmett. Cast: Clive Brook (Sir Hubert Ware), Jane Baxter (Lady Margaret Ware), Barry K. Barnes (Michael Adye), C.V. France (Judge), Francis L. Sullivan (Attorney-General), Frank Cellier (Skinner), Peter Bull (Eustace Ede), Edward Rigby, Dorothy Seacombe, Athene Seyler, Elliot Mason.

These films made for absorbing viewing. One change in the two remakes, aside from the use of more characters, has Ware jumping to his death rather than taking poison when he discovers that his wife and his attorney are in love.

Watch the Birdie *see* **The Cameraman**

973 Waterloo Bridge

Based on the play by Robert E. Sherwood. Story: Myra, a ballerina, meets an army officer, Roy Wetherby, with whom she falls in love. They plan to marry despite the opposition of his wealthy family. He is forced to join his troops in World War I, and is reported as having been killed in action. His family will have nothing to do with Myra and she sinks into prostitution. He's not dead, of course, and their paths cross once again.

Universal Pictures, 1931 (original). Director: James Whale; screenwriters: Tom Reed and Benn W. Levy. Cast: Mae Clarke (Myra), Kent Douglas (Roy Wetherby), Doris Lloyd (Kitty), Ethel Griffies (Mrs. Holby), Enid Bennett (Mrs. Wetherby), Frederick Kerr, Bette Davis, Rita Carlisle.

• ***Waterloo Bridge*** (remake). MGM, 1940. Director: Mervyn LeRoy; screenwriters: S.N. Behrman, Hans Rameau and George Froeschel. Cast: Vivien Leigh (Myra), Robert Taylor (Roy Cronin), Lucile Watson (Lady Margaret Cronin), Virginia Field (Kitty), Maria Ouspenskaya (Madame Olga Kirowa), C. Aubrey Smith (the Duke), Janet Shaw, Janet Waldo, Steffi Duna, Virginia Carroll, Leda Nicova.

• ***Gaby*** (remake). MGM, 1956. Director: Curtis Bernhardt; screenwriters: Albert Hackett, Frances Goodrich, and Charles Lederer. Cast: Leslie Caron (Gaby), John Kerr, Cedric Hardwicke, Taina Elg, Margalo Gillmore.

In the remake, sweet ballet dancer Vivien Leigh meets British officer Robert Taylor on Waterloo Bridge, the night before he is to depart for the front. It's love at first sight for both of them, but marriage must be delayed until his first furlough. Fate steps in as Taylor is erroneously reported as having been killed in battle. With no help from his family, the unsophisticated girl turns to prostitution. Taylor returns and finds her at the railroad station where she is plying her trade and the romance is on again. But she chooses suicide rather than besmirch his family's name because of her means of making a living.

This was Vivien Leigh's first film released after *Gone with the Wind* and audiences were anxious to see Scarlett O'Hara again. However, Myra is quite another girl, weak where Scarlett was strong, sacrificing where Scarlett was willful. Still, Leigh proved once again that she was quite a force on the screen. Robert Taylor, on the other hand, was just a good-looking hunk who, loving, would cause Vivien such pain and misery. It was a fine woman's picture and scored high at the box office. The 1956 remake, updating the story to World War II with Leslie Caron as the girl who became round-heeled when her soldier was reported killed, was a flabby picture, totally unappealing even with a happy ending.

Watusi *see* **King Solomon's Mines**

974 Way Down East

Based on the play by Lottie Blatt Parker. Story: Young orphan Anna Moore is seduced and abandoned by a rake, Lennox Sanderson. She is sent out into the frozen wastes of New England by the farming family for whom she works when her past is discovered. She is rescued from drowning in the icy river just in time by the farmer's son, David Bartlett, who then marries her.

United Artists, 1920 (original). Silent. Director: D.W. Griffith; screenwriters: Griffith, Anthony Paul Kelly and Joseph R. Grismer. Cast: Lillian Gish (Anna Moore), Mrs. David Landau (her Mother), Josephine Bernardi (Mrs. Tremont), Mrs. Morgan Belmont (Diana Tremont), Lowell Sherman (Lennox Sanderson), Burr McIntosh (Squire Bartlett), Kate Bruce (Mrs. Bartlett), Richard Barthelmess (David Bartlett), Vivia Ogden, Patricia Fruen, Florence Short, Porter Strong.

• ***Way Down East*** (remake). Twentieth Century–Fox, 1935. Director: Henry King; screenwriter: Howard Estabrook and William Hurlbut. Cast: Rochelle Hudson (Anna Moore), Henry Fonda (David Bartlett), Slim Summerville (Constable Seth Holcomb), Edward Trevor (Lennox Sanderson), Margaret Hamilton (Martha Perkins), Andy Devine (Hi Holler), Russell Simpson (Squire Bartlett), Spring Byington (Mrs. Bartlett), Astrid Allwyn, Sara Haden, Al Lydell, Harry C. Bradley, Clem Bevans.

The D.W. Griffith production of the creaky Victorian melodrama became a silent classic. The climax in which Gish is floating down the river on a cake of ice while Richard Barthelmess quickly makes his way from one flow to another to reach her is exciting, touching and beautiful. Gish gave one of her most memorable and moving performances and the camera work of Billy Blitzer and Hendrick is superb for any era. The remake, while a beautiful production—the tearjerker of stern righteousness, bigotry and a wronged girl—was no longer attuned to the times. The crack-up of the ice flow at the end is still spectacular and the work of Fonda and Hudson is commendable, but it's not a classic like the earlier version.

975 The Way of All Flesh

Based on a story *The Whispering Chorus* by Perley Poore Sheehan. Story: Bank cashier August Schiller prides himself on being a good man, a good husband and a good father. On a trip for his bank to deliver some bonds, a momentary indiscretion changes the course of his life. He becomes involved with Mayme, who seduces him and steals the bonds. When her lover, the Tough, beats August and tries to steal his watch, the banker resists, resulting in the Tough being killed by a passing train. August changes clothes with the Tough and it is reported that the banker died a hero's death protecting his employer's property. August wanders through the years as a broken derelict. Years later he learns that his oldest son has become a famous violinist, and he hoards enough money to buy a gallery seat for a Christmas Day concert. He follows his son home and peers through the window of his home to find his wife and grown children, happy and still revering their father's memory. August then walks away.

• ***The Way of All Flesh*** (remake). Paramount–Famous Lasky, 1927. Silent. Director: Victor Fleming; screenwriters: Jules Furthman and Lajos Biro. Cast: Emil Jannings (August Schiller), Belle Bennett (Mrs. Schiller), Phyllis Haver (Mayme), Donald Keith (August Junior), Fred Kohler (the Tough), Philippe De

Lacey, Mickey McBan, Ann Lisle, Carmencita Johnson, Gordon Thorpe, Jackie Coombs.

• ***The Way of All Flesh*** (remake). Paramount Pictures, 1940. Director: Louis King; screenwriter: Leonore Coffee. Cast: Akim Tamiroff (Paul), Gladys George (Anna), William Henry (Paul, Jr.), John Hartley (Victor), Muriel Angelus (Mary Brown), Berton Churchill (Reginald L. Morten), Fritz Leiber (Max), Marilyn Knowlden, Betty McLaughlin, James West, Darryl Hickman, June Hedin, Norma Nelson.

Cecil B. De Mille made a silent film in 1918 based on Perley Poore Sheehan's story using the author's original title, *The Whispering Chorus.* Emil Jannings, who was very good at portraying decent men who are ruined by lust, was very good in this film, appearing as a proud, happy family man who is seduced and robbed by luscious Phyllis Haver—and as far as his happy life and prominent career, that's all she wrote. Akim Tamiroff, a greatly underappreciated actor, gave a very tidy performance as the unfortunate banker in the remake. The morality of the notion that one mistake should ruin one for life is a bit hard to take and wouldn't be at all accepted in our now more permissive society of almost everything goes. Neither would the saccharine sentimentality of the story and films.

We Were Dancing *see* **Tonight at 8:30**

Wedding Rings *see* **The Dark Swan**

976 Wednesday's Child

Based on the play by Leopold L. Atlas. Story: Young Bobby is forced to testify during the divorce proceedings of his parents, and then finds himself in a military boarding school because neither his mother nor father have any time for him. However, by the end of the film, the father has a change of heart and takes the lad home with him.

RKO, 1934 (original). Director: John S. Robertson; screenwriter: Willis Goldbeck. Cast: Frankie Thomas (Bobby), Edward Arnold (his Father), Karen Morley (his Mother), Shirley Grey, Robert Shayne, David Durand.

• ***Child of Divorce*** (sequel). RKO, 1946. Director: Richard O. Fleischer; screenwriter: Lillie Hayward. Cast: Sharyn Moffet (Bobby), Regis Toomey (Ray), Madge Meredith (Joan), Walter Reed, Una O'Connor, Doris Merrick, Harry Chesire, Selmer Jackson.

These are message pictures about the effect of divorce on children. In the sequel, the sex if not the name of the child is changed with the principals, Sharyn Moffet as the child and Regis Toomey and Madge Meredith as her parents, giving performances of sad conviction. The story is presented in an almost documentary style, and the agony of all involved in the break up of a family is painfully demonstrated.

Weekend at the Waldorf *see* **Grand Hotel**

Weib im Dschungel *see* **The Letter**

977 Welcome Home

Based on the play *Minick* by George S. Kaufman and Edna Ferber. Story: When old man Prouty arrives unexpectedly at the small apartment of his son Fred and daughter-in-law Nettie, announcing that he's come to stay, the young couple try to make the best of things, but it soon becomes apparent that his presence is seriously affecting their life style. Old man Prouty and his cronies ruin one of Nettie's luncheons for friends, an act she considers the last straw. She tells Fred either his father leaves or she does. The old man visits some friends at an old folks' home and likes it well enough to decide to move in, especially when he discovers that Nettie is pregnant. He finally recognizes that the old must move aside for the young.

Famous Players–Lasky/Paramount Pictures, 1925 (original). Silent. Director: James Cruze; screenwriters: Walter Woods and F. McGrew Willis. Cast: Luke Cosgrove (Old Man Prouty), Warren Baxter (Fred Prouty), Lois Wilson (Nettie Prouty), Ben Hendricks, Margaret Morris, Josephine Crowell, Adele Watson.

• ***No Place to Go*** (remake). Warner Bros., 1939. Director: Terry Morse; screenwriters: Lee Katz, Lawrence Kimble and Fred Niblo, Jr. Cast: Dennis Morgan (Joe Plummer), Gloria Dickson (Gertrude Plummer), Fred Stone (Andrew Plummer), Sonny Bupp, Aldrich Bowker, Charles Halton, Georgia Caine, Frank Faylen, Donnie Moore.

The Kaufman and Ferber play from the story *Old Man Minick* was also brought to the screen in 1932 by Warner Bros. under the title of *The Expert.* The humor found in what to do with an unwanted oldster depends upon where you stand in terms of age. If young, one can empathize with the young couple. A bit older and the problems of the old man seem worthy of concern. In the remake, the son and daughter-in-law take his father from the old soldier's home where he is content when they become wealthy. This version demonstrates that the amount of money one has makes little difference when two generations with extremely different life styles try to live together.

We're Not Dressing *see* **The Admirable Crichton**

We're on the Jury *see* **Ladies of the Jury**

978 West of Zanzibar

Based on the play by Chester De Vonde and Kilborne Gordon. Story: Flint loses the use of his legs because of a fight with ivory trader Crane who has taken an interest in Flint's wife. When Flint's wife dies in childbirth, he is convinced that her daughter is Crane's child, not his. He takes the child, named Maizie, with him to Africa, where years later he arranges for her to become a prostitute in one of the native fleshpots. Crane arrives and convinces Flint that Maizie is really his child, not Crane's. Crane is killed by the natives, and Flint sacrifices his own life so Maizie can escape with a hop-headed doctor.

MGM, 1928 (original). Silent. Director: Tod Browning; screenwriters: Elliott

Clawson and Waldemar Young. Cast: Lon Chaney (Flint), Lionel Barrymore (Crane), Mary Nolan (Maizie), Warner Baxter (Doc), Jacquelin Gadson (Anna), Roscoe Ward, Kalla Pasha, Curtis Nero.

• ***Kongo*** (remake). MGM, 1932. Director: William Cowen; screenwriter: Leon Gordon. Cast: Walter Huston (Flint), Lupe Velez (Tula), Conrad Nagel (Kingsland), Virginia Bruce (Ann), C. Henry Gordon (Gregg), Mitchell Lewis, Forrester Harvey, Curtis Nero.

The remake follows the same story as the Chaney-Barrymore silent, with Walter Huston as a crippled tyrant in an African settlement who degrades Virginia Bruce by setting her up as a prostitute in a Congo "house" after she arrives from a convent school. He learns that she's really his daughter, not that of his arch-enemy, C. Henry Gordon. Lupe Velez is Huston's "woman" and Conrad Nagel is a drug-maddened doctor who is totally at the mercy of Huston's will. The films are so filled with bitterness and hate by all concerned that it's rather difficult to work up any sympathy for anyone other than the unfortunate Miss Bruce.

West of Zanzibar (1954) ***see*** **Where No Vultures Fly**

West Side Story ***see*** **Romeo and Juliet**

979 What a Man

Based on the novel *The Dark Chapter* by E.J. Rath and the play *They All Want Something* by Courtenay Savage. Story: Overhearing a train conductor describe wealthy Mrs. Kilbourne's weakness for helping worthless humanity, Wade Rawlins takes advantage of the information and wrangles the job of chauffeur to the woman's family. The other members of the family do not share Mrs. Kilbourne's joy in works of kindness for hobos and tramps, but one by one Wade wins them over, particularly the elder daughter, Eileen, who falls in love with him. Finally, the butler, William, who was the most suspicious of the motives of Mrs. Kilbourne's latest reclamation case, recognizes Wade as a former British army officer, at which point Wade reveals his past as a well-bred English gentleman and Canadian bootlegger.

Sono-Art Production, 1930 (original). Director: George J. Crone; screenwriters: A.A. Kline and Harvey Gates. Cast: Reginald Denny (Wade Rawlins), Miriam Seegar (Eileen Kilbourne), Harvey Clark (Mr. Kilbourne), Lucille Ward (Mrs. Kilbourne), Carlyle Moore (Kane Kilbourne), Anita Louise (Marion Kilbourne), Charles Coleman (William), Norma Drew, Christiane Yves, Greta Granstedt.

• ***Merrily We Live*** (remake). MGM, 1938. Director: Norman Z. McLeod; screenwriters: Eddie Moran and Jack Jevne. Cast: Constance Bennett (Jerry Kilbourne), Brian Aherne (Wade Rawlins), Billie Burke (Mrs. Kilbourne), Alan Mowbray (Grosvenor), Patsy Kelly (Cook), Ann Dvorak (Minerva), Bonita Granville (Marion), Tom Brown (Kane), Clarence Kolb, Marjorie Rambeau, Philip Reed, Willie Best, Sidney Bracey.

A Spanish version of the 1930 film was released under the name of *Asi Es la*

Vida. These entertaining screwball comedies still can produce some laughs. The remake combines some of the charm and business of films such as *My Man Godfrey* (1936), *You Can't Take It With You* (1938) and *The Passing of the Third Floor Back* (1935). In it Brian Aherne is a successful author who hadn't bothered to shave or clean up much the day he stopped by the Kilbourne house to ask to use the phone because his car had broken down. When Billie Burke takes him for a poor unfortunate, Aherne decides to go along with it in case there's some material for a book in the experience. In his calm and self-possessed way he starts to bring a semblance of order to the muddled Kilbourne clan and in the process wins the love of beautiful Constance Bennett.

980 What Every Woman Knows

Based on the play by James Matthew Barrie. Story: Alick Wylie offers to pay for John Strand's education on the condition that he marry the former's daughter, Maggie. Within five years, Strand is a Member of Parliament mainly on the strength of his brilliant speeches which Maggie types, edits and into which she incorporates her own wit and judgement. Strand strays from his marriage vows with Lady Sybil and unaware of this infatuation, Maggie arranges for her husband and rival to visit a country estate of a cabinet minister. There Strand is honored when his host asks him to prepare a speech for him, but without Maggie's touches, it is unimpressive. When Maggie at John's request makes revisions, the result is brilliant. Strand finally realizes the source of his success and breaks off his relationship with Lady Sybil.

• ***What Every Woman Knows*** (remake). Famous Players–Lasky/Paramount Pictures, 1921. Director: William C. DeMille; screenwriter: Olga Printzlau. Cast: Lois Wilson (Maggie Wylie), Conrad Nagel (John Strand), Charles Ogle (Alick Wylie), Fred Hunter (David Wylie), Lilian Tucker (Sybil Tenterden), Guy Oliver, Winter Hall, Claire McDowell.

• ***What Every Woman Knows*** (remake). MGM, 1934. Director: Gregory La Cava; screenwriters: Monckton Hoffe, John Meehan and James K. McGuinness. Cast: Helen Hayes (Maggie), Brian Aherne (John), Madge Evans (Sybil), Lucille Watson (Comtesse), Dudley Digges (James), Donald Crisp (David), David Torrence, Henry Stephenson, Boyd Irwin.

These were enjoyable features based on the period, not so long ago, when women had to bask in the glory of their men, even if they were superior in ability and intelligence. The Barrie play was first filmed in 1917. In the remake, Helen Hayes felt right at home in the part of the brains of the family, having performed the role for a season on Broadway in 1926. Brian Aherne is quite good as the vigorous zealot who doesn't recognize his wife's role in the success of his career until he almost dumps her for Madge Evans.

981 What Price Glory

Based on the play by Lawrence Stallings and Maxwell Anderson. Story: Two hardboiled marines, Captain Flagg and Sergeant Quirt, are fierce but friendly rivals, particularly when it comes to women. In a small French village they meet Charmaine who seems quite willing to share her favors and love with both men. This is not satisfactory to the two marines and they gamble for her, with Flagg winning. The latter bows out when he discovers that she actually prefers Quirt. On two occasions the friends come back from action in the trenches but on their third trip to the front, Quirt is wounded in no-man's land and calls out for help from his friend. Flagg goes to his aid, but as Charmaine sadly reflects, her men will not come back a third time.

Fox Film Corp., 1926 (original). Silent. Director: Raoul Walsh; screenwriter: James T. O'Donohoe. Cast: Victor McLaglen (Captain Flagg), Edmund Lowe (Sgt. Quirt), Dolores Del Rio (Charmaine), William V. Mong, Phyllis Haver, Elena Jurado, Leslie Fenton, August Tollaire, Barry Norton, Sammy Cohen.

• ***What Price Glory*** (remake). Twentieth Century–Fox, 1952. Director: John Ford; screenwriters: Phoebe and Henry Ephron. Cast: James Cagney (Capt. Flagg), Dan Dailey (Sgt. Quirt), Corinne Calvet (Charmaine), William Demarest (Corporal Kiper), Craig Hill (Lt. Aldrich), Robert Wagner, Marisa Pavan, Casey Adams, James Gleason.

John Ford converted the celebrated silent war melodrama into a comedy involving James Cagney and Dan Dailey with Corinne Calvet being the main squeeze who is passed back and forth between the two men without any complaint on her part, seemingly happy to share the company of whomever happens to be handy. The film, while it won't drive one out of a theater, is not particularly interesting, nor funny, nor are the three leads probably the best performers for the roles. Give it a C-rating.

982 When Knighthood Was in Flower

Based on the novel by Charles Major. Story: For political reasons, King Henry VIII of England wishes his sister, Mary Tudor, to marry King Louis XII of France. She prefers commoner Charles Brandon, so the two lovers run away, but Henry has them brought back. Mary agrees to the arranged marriage if she is free to choose her own second husband. Shortly after the wedding, Louis dies and although King Francis I wants Mary for his wife, Henry lives up to his promise and allows Mary to wed Brandon with his blessing.

Cosmopolitan Productions/Paramount Pictures, 1922 (original). Silent. Director: Robert G. Vignola; screenwriter: Luther Reed. Cast: Marion Davies (Princess Mary Tudor), Forrest Stanley (Charles Brandon), Lyn Harding (King Henry VIII), Theresa Maxwell Conover, Pedro De Cordoba, Ruth Shepley, Ernest Glendenning, Arthur Forrest, Johnny Dooley, William Kent.

• ***The Sword and the Rose*** (remake). Walt Disney Productions, 1952. Director: Ken Annakin; screenwriter: Laurence E. Watkin. Cast: Richard Todd (Brandon), Glynnis Johns (Mary Tudor), James Robertson Justice (Henry VIII), Michael Gough, Jane Barrett, Peter Copley, Rosalie Crutchley, Jean Mercure.

The 1922 piece was a spectacular romantic drama. The 1952 picture was a spectacular disappointment. Disney Studios had done better and would again in live-action movies. This version of the ancient novel about the loves of Henry VIII's willful sister was boring. None of the performers seemed comfortable in their roles and the direction showed a definite lack of direction. The silent movie wasn't all that wonderful either.

983 When Knights Were Bold

Based on the play by Charles Marlowe. Story: Sir Guy de Vere is a commoner who inherits a title, and finds the ancestral home filled with stuffy relatives and other strangers. A suit of armor falls on him and he dreams he is back in medieval days. When he recovers he routs his unwanted guests but impresses Rowena enough that she stays to be his wife.

London Films/Jury, Great Britain, 1916 (original). Silent. Director: Maurice Elvey; screenwriter: Frank Miller. Cast: James Welch (Sir Guy de Vere), Janet Ross (Lady Rowena), Gerald Ames (Sir Brian Ballymote), Hayford Hobbs (Widdicombe), Gwynne Herbert (Isaacson), Philip Hewland, Bert Wynne.

• ***When Knights Were Bold*** (remake). Britain & Dominions, Great Britain, 1929. Silent. Director: Tim Whelan; screenwriters: Whelan and Herbert Wilcox. Cast: Nelson Keys (Sir Guy de Vere), Miriam Seegar (Lady Rowena), Eric Bransby Williams (Sir Brian Ballymote), Wellington Briggs (Widdicombe), Lena Haliday, Martin Adeson, Hal Gordon, Edith Kingdon, E.L. Frewen.

• ***When Knights Were Bold*** (remake). Capital/General Film, Great Britain, 1936. Director: Jack Raymond; screenwriters: Austin Parker and Douglas Furber. Cast: Jack Buchanan (Sir Guy de Vere), Fay Wray (Lady Rowena), Garry Marsh (Brian Ballymote), Kate Cutler (Aunt Agatha), Martita Hunt (Aunt Esther), Robert Horton, Aubrey Mather, Aubrey Fitzgerald, Robert Nainby, Moore Marriott.

The best of the three versions of this *A Connecticut Yankee in King Arthur's Court*-like story is surely the last. Jack Buchanan is the whole show, with scream queen Fay Wray having little to do but look like what one would expect of someone named Lady Rowena.

984 When Ladies Meet

Based on the play by Rachel Crothers. Story: It's the smart comical tale of an ambitious young writer, Mary Howard, loved by Jimmie Lee, who launches a romance with her publisher, Rogers Woodruff, and then is confronted with a love triangle both in her book and in her life. It follows Rachel Crothers' play very closely and is fairly predictable, but is generally amusing and a fun piece of entertainment.

MGM, 1933 (original). Director: Harry Beaumont; screenwriters: John Meehan and Leon Gordon. Cast: Ann Harding (Clare Woodruff), Robert Montgomery (Jimmie Lee), Myrna Loy (Mary Howard), Alice Brady (Bridget Drake), Frank Morgan (Rogers Woodruff), Martin Burton, Luis Alberni.

• ***When Ladies Meet*** (remake). MGM, 1941. Director: Robert Z. Leonard; screenwriters: K. Lauren and Anita Loos. Cast: Joan Crawford (Mary Howard), Robert Taylor (Jimmie Lee), Greer Garson (Clare Woodruff), Herbert Marshall (Rogers Woodruff), Spring Byington (Bridget Drake), Rafael Storm, Mona Barrie.

While theoretically the main character in these two films is the writer, in the first case (Myrna Loy) and in the second (Joan Crawford), it is the wifely member of the triangle (or is it quadrangle?) who is given the best lines, and in the cases of both Ann Harding and Greer Garson, the best acting. The male contingent in both features is merely necessary so the women will have something to fight over. These are talky pieces but the talk is good.

When My Baby Smiles At Me *see* **Burlesque**

985 When Tomorrow Comes

Based on the novel by James M. Cain. Story: Waitress Helen falls in love with pianist Philip Durand. They have a passionate meeting in an organ loft on Long Island when she loses her job because of a strike by waitresses and a hurricane assures their privacy. Then, sob, she discovers he's already married.

Universal Pictures, 1939 (original). Director: John M. Stahl; screenwriter: Dwight Taylor. Cast: Irene Dunne (Helen), Charles Boyer (Philip Durand), Barbara O'Neil (Madeline Durand), Onslow Stevens (Holden), Nydia Westman (Lulu), Fritz Field, Nella Walker, Harry Bradley, Milton Parsons, Greta Meyer.

• ***Interlude*** (remake). Universal Pictures, 1957. Director: Douglas Sirk; screenwriters: Daniel Fuchs and Franklin Coen. Cast: June Allyson (Helen Banning), Rossano Brazzi (Toni Fischer), Marianne Cook (Reni Fischer), Francoise Rosay (Countess Reinhart), Keith Andes (Dr. Morley Dwyer), Frances Bergen, Lisa Helwig, Herman Schwedt, Anthony Tripoli, John Stein.

The producers hoped to cash in on the box-office appeal of the team of Irene Dunne and Charles Boyer that was demonstrated by *Love Affair*, released earlier in the year. They should have waited until they had a better vehicle for this talented pair. The story of the waitresses' strike is more interesting than the love story. In the remake, June Allyson is an American librarian who falls in love with a pianist, Rossano Brazzi, who is married to a mentally ill woman, Marianne Cook. It doesn't get better the second time around.

986 When We Were Twenty-One

Based on the play by Henry V. Esmond. Story: Affectionately known as the Imp, Dick Audaine becomes engaged to Phyllis Ericson, who secretly loves Dick's guardian, Richard Carewe. Dick becomes infatuated with Kara Glynesk, a gold digger. Phyllis comes into possession of a letter from Kara to the Imp, but anxious to protect the Imp, Carewe allows her to believe it was intended for him. Still, Carewe and others can do nothing to prevent the Imp from marrying Kara, who, after she discovers he has no money, deserts him. Phyllis is now free to marry Carewe, which she does.

Pathe Exchange, 1921 (original). Silent. Director and screenwriter: Henry King. Cast: H.B. Warner (Richard Carewe), Claire Anderson (Phyllis), James Morrison (Richard Audaine), Christine Mayo (Kara Glynesk), Claude Payton, Minna Grey.

• ***The Truth About Youth*** (remake). First National Pictures, 1930. Director: William Seiter; screenwriter: Harrison Orkow. Cast: Loretta Young (Phyllis Ericson), David Manners (Richard Dane—the Imp), Conway Tearle (Richard Carewe), J. Farrell MacDonald (Col. Graham), Myrna Loy (Kara, the Firefly), Harry Stubbs, Myrtle Stedman, Ray Hallor, Dorothy Mathews, Yola D'Avril.

In the remake, Conway Tearle plans for his ward, David Manners, to marry the daughter, Loretta Young, of his housekeeper. However, Manners falls in love with nightclub entertainer Myrna Loy. When Tearle's housekeeper finds a note from Kara, he lets on that it was meant for him rather than Manners. He goes so far as to offer Loy $5,000 to pretend she loves him, not knowing that she had just the day before eloped with Manners. When her real love shows up again with plenty of money, Loy dumps Manners and gives Tearle back his money. Manners decides to take Horace Greeley's advice and heads west, leaving Young to declare her long-felt love for Tearle.

Where Angels Go—Trouble Follows *see* **The Trouble with Angels**

987 Where Are Your Children?

Based on a story by Hilary Lynn. Story: Judy, a somewhat wild teenager, lives with her brother and sister-in-law, develops a romance with Danny, a rich boy without parental guidance, and eventually becomes involved in a murder of which she is ultimately cleared.

Monogram Pictures, 1943 (original). Director: William Nigh; screenwriters: Hilary Lynn and George W. Sayre. Cast: Gale Storm (Judy), Jackie Cooper (Danny), Patricia Morison (Linda), John Litel (Judge Evans), Gertrude Michael (Nell), Addison Richards, Herbert Rawlinson, Betty Blythe, Anthony Ward.

• ***Are These Our Parents?*** (remake). Monogram Pictures, 1944. Director: William Nigh; screenwriters: Michel Jacoby and Harry Newmann. Cast: Helen Vinson (Myrna Salisbury), Lyle Talbot (George Kent), Ivan Lebedeff (Alexis), Noel Neill (Terry Salisbury), Richard Bryon (Hal Bailey), Addison Richards, Emma Dunn, Anthony Warde.

If the youngsters in these two pictures were the worst juvenile deliquents that society had to worry about, the nation could feel justifiably proud. In the second film, Noel Neill is fed up with her fashionable boarding school and her mother's lack of interest in her. She sneaks away to a cheap roadhouse where she meets Richard Byron, a boy disgusted with the knowledge that his father is neglecting his defense job for another woman. The pair become suspects in a murder case, but a juvenile delinquency officer places the blame for their problems squarely on the shoulders of their parents. The rebukes are just the ticket; the parents amend their ways and promise to be better, more concerned parents in the future. This might have been palatable once upon a time, but today it seems ridiculous.

988 Where No Vultures Fly

Based on a story by Harry Watt. Story: Game warden Bob Payton, appalled at the slaughter of animals in East Africa, pushes for the formation of a national park to protect the wildlife. He and his wife have trouble with poachers, whose leader is eventually killed fleeing the law. Ultimately, Payton's dream comes true and a national safari park "where no vultures fly" becomes a reality.

Ealing, Great Britain, 1952 (original). Director: Harry Watt; screenwriters: Ralph Smart, W.P. Lipscomb and Leslie Norman. Cast: Anthony Steel (Bob

Payton), Dinah Sheridan (Mrs. Payton), Harold Warrender (Mannering), Meredith Edwards (Gwyl), William Simons, Orlando Martins, Philip Birkinshaw.

• ***West of Zanzibar*** (sequel). Ealing, 1954. Director: Harry Watt; screenwriters: Jack Whittingham and Max Catto. Cast: Anthony Steel (Bob Payton), Sheila Sim (Mary Payton), Edric Connor (Ushingo), Orlando Martins (M'Kwongwi), William Simons, Martin Benson, Peter Illing, Juma, Howard Marion-Crawford, R. Stuart Lindsell.

The 1952 film was panned by critics but applauded by viewers, becoming the top British moneymaker of the year. In the sequel, Steel is determined to put an end to the work of ivory smugglers and does. His wife, Sheila Sim, has a wardrobe that's hard to believe for the African bush.

Where Sinners Meet *see* **The Little Adventuress**

989 Where the Boys Are

Based on the novel by Glendon Swarthout. Story: The movie is set in Fort Lauderdale, site of an annual spring invasion by vacationing college students looking for some casual mating. Well, in this version at least, the guys are, whereas the girls mostly are holding out for wedding rings. The tale follows the romantic adventures of Merritt, Melanie, Tuggle and Angie, and the fellows in their lives, Ryder, T.V., Franklin and Dill.

MGM, 1960 (original). Director: Henry Levin; screenwriter: George Wells. Cast: Dolores Hart (Merritt Andrews), George Hamilton (Ryder Smith), Yvette Mimieux (Melanie), Jim Hutton (T.V. Thompson), Barbara Nichols (Lola), Paula Prentiss (Tuggle Carpenter), Connie Francis (Angie), Chill Wills, Frank Gorshin, Rory Harrity, Ted Berger, John Brennan, Vito Scotti.

• ***Where the Boys Are '84*** (sequel). ITC, 1984. Director: Hy Averback; screenwriters: Stu Kreiger and Jeff Burkhart. Cast: Lisa Hartman, Lorna Luft, Wendy Schaal, Lynn-Holly Johnson, Russel Todd, Howard McGillin, Alana Stewart.

The most memorable thing about the 1960 movie was Connie Francis' warbling of the title song. The difference between it and its 1984 reincarnation is that whereas their mothers worried about losing their hearts and virginity far from home, the girls of 1984 had mostly divested themselves of that excessive baggage long before arriving in Florida. The only questions in this cheap sexual exploitation movie are with whom, when and where.

Where the Boys Are '84 *see* **Where the Boys Are**

Where the Bullets Fly *see* **Licensed to Kill**

Where's Charley *see* **Charley's Aunt**

990 Whistling in the Dark

Based on the play by Laurence Gross and Edward Chiles Carpenter. Story:

After eloping, Wallace Porter and his new bride, Toby Van Buren, happen upon the hideout of a bootlegging mob. Porter is required to use his ingenuity to plot the murder of the bootlegger's legitimate brewer rival, and then be just as clever in getting out of carrying out the plan.

MGM, 1933 (original). Director and screenwriter: Eliott Nugent. Cast: Ernest Truex (Wallace Porter), Una Merkel (Toby Van Buren), Edward Arnold (Dillon), John Miljan (Charlie), C. Henry Gordon (Lombarde), Johnny Hines, Joseph Cawthorn, Nat Pendleton, Tenen Holtz, Marcelle Corday.

• ***Whistling in the Dark*** (remake). MGM, 1941. Director: S. Sylvan Simon; screenwriter: Robert MacGunigle. Cast: Red Skelton (Wally Benton), Conrad Veidt (Joseph Jones), Ann Rutherford (Carol Lambert), Virginia Grey (Fran Post), Rags Ragland (Sylvester), Henry O'Neill (Philip Post), Eve Arden (Buzz Parker), Paul Stanton, Don Costello, William Tannen, Reed Hadley, Lloyd Corrigan.

Una Merkel is a unique treat, and has not been given sufficient credit for her fine comedy talent. Similarly, Ernest Truex, known mainly for his silent films, is a very amusing man. Putting the two together in this fast-paced comedy was good casting, and resulted in a fun little piece. In the remake Red Skelton is a radio personality who solves ingenious crimes, on the air. He, his fiancée, Ann Rutherford, and the sponsor's daughter, Virginia Grey, are kidnapped by a gang of racketeers headed by Conrad Veidt, who want him to plot the perfect murder of a man whose existence stands in the way of Veidt collecting a million dollars. Skelton comes up with a good poisoning plan and from then on it's up to the three kidnap victims to prevent his plan from being implemented. If you enjoy the antics of Skelton, this one's for you.

991 White Cargo

Based on the novel by Ida Vera Simonton and the play by Leon Gordon. Story: The tough manager of a West African rubber plantation, Weston, must wet-nurse a series of novices from the home country. One of these, Langsford, despite the warnings of Weston, marries a half-caste girl, Tondeleyo, and becomes a derelict. Weston catches the girl trying to poison her husband and forces her to take the poison herself. Broken, Langsford is shipped home as "white cargo."

W.P. Film Co., 1929 (original). Silent and sound versions. Directors: J.B. Williams and Arthur Barnes; screenwriter: J.B. Williams. Cast: Leslie Faber (Weston), Gypsy Rhouma (Tondeleyo), John Hamilton (Ashley), Maurice Evans (Langsford), Sebastian Smith, Humberstone Wright, Henri de Vries, George Turner.

White Cargo (remake). MGM, 1942. Director: Richard Thorpe; screenwriter: Leon Gordon. Cast: Hedy Lamarr (Tondelayo), Walter Pidgeon (Harry Witzel), Frank Morgan (the Doctor), Richard Carlson (Langsford), Reginald Owen (Skipper), Henry O'Neill, Bramwell Fletcher, Clyde Cook, Leigh Whipper, Oscar Polk.

When *White Cargo* first appeared on the stage it was considered off-color and very hot, dealing with an interracial marriage and a steamy half-caste who radiates sex. The British version was actually more torpid than torrid, but still encountered opposition from American censors. It was barred from production in the United States by the Hays Office. The 1942 film with Hedy Lamarr managed to live up to its reputation due to the sultry sarong-slithering sexuality of its star. Although she doesn't appear in the first 30 minutes of the film, when she delivers the classic line "I am Tondelayo" in her slow suggestive drawl, the temperature in moviehouses rose several degrees. Besides her sizzling performance as the two-timing trollop, Walter Pidgeon is excellent as the man who can handle her and Richard Carlson is convincing as Tondelayo's weak victim.

992 White Lightning

Based on a screenplay by William Norton. Story: Gator McKlusky, a moonshiner and convict, escapes and helps the feds put away a crooked sheriff who had his brother killed.

United Artists, 1973 (original). Director: Joseph Sargent; screenwriter: William Norton. Cast: Burt Reynolds (Gator McKlusky), Jennifer Billingsly (Lou), Ned Beatty (Sheriff Connors), Bo Hopkins (Roy Boone), Matt Clark (Dude Watson), Louise Latham (Martha Culpepper), Diane Ladd, R.G. Armstrong, Conlan Carter, Dabbs Greer, Lincoln Demyan.

• ***Gator*** (sequel). United Artists, 1976. Director: Burt Reynolds; screenwriter: William Norton. Cast: Burt Reynolds (Gator), Jack Weston (Irving Greenfield), Lauren Hutton (Aggie Maybank), Jerry Reed (Bama McCall), Alice Ghostly, Dub Taylor, Burton Gilliam, Mike Douglas, William Engesser.

In the first movie, Burt Reynolds is in one of his familiar roles as a "good old boy" but at the time of its filming he was taking the role seriously. It would only be later that he would be making a parody of this type of character. He began "funnin'" with the role in the sequel in which as a convicted moonshiner, he is blackmailed into becoming an undercover agent in a hoodlum's gang.

993 The White Sister

Based on the novel by Marion Crawford. Story: When her father dies, Angela Chiaromonte, heir to a vast Italian estate, is left penniless, because her half-sister, the Marchesa di Mola, destroyed the will dividing the property evenly between the two women. Angela's fiancé, Giovanni Severini, leaves for war in Africa, with plans to marry her on his return. When reports of his death reach Angela, she enters a convent. Severini, who had been a captive and had finally escaped back to Italy, goes to her and tries to convince her to renounce her vows and marry him. She refuses and Severini is killed helping townspeople escape an erupting Vesuvius.

• ***The White Sister*** (remake). Inspiration Pictures/Metro, 1923. Silent. Director: Henry King; screenwriters: George V. Hobart and Charles E. Whittaker. Cast: Lilian Gish (Angela Chiaromonte), Ronald Colman (Capt. Giovanni Severini), Gail Kane (Marchesa di Mola), J. Barney Sherry (Monsignor Saracinesca), Charles Lane (Prince Chiaromonte), Juliette La Violette, Signor Serena, Alfredo Bertrone, Ramon Ibanez, Alfredo Martinelli.

• ***The White Sister*** (remake). MGM, 1933. Director: Victor Fleming; screenwriter: Donald Ogden Stewart. Cast: Helen Hayes (Angela Chiaromonte), Clark Gable (Giovanni Severini), Lewis Stone (Prince Chiaromonte), Louise Closser Hale (Mina), May Robson (Mother Superior), Edward Arnold, Alan Edwards.

The play about the Italian noblewoman who takes the veil when she believes her fiancé has been killed was also filmed in 1915 and 1960. Both versions mentioned here are expensive women's pictures, considered very prestigious at the time of their release, but today they would not hold much interest. At the time of the films, and particularly at the time the story was set, a nun who "jumped over the wall" for whatever reason would have been considered dishonorable and in disgrace. Such is no longer the case. The acting, acceptable in the times of their release, also will not set well with modern audiences. Lilian Gish, Ronald Colman, Helen Hayes and Clark Gable were names that brought in the customers in great numbers, but their performances here were anything but outstanding.

994 White Woman

Based on the play by Norman Reilly Raine and Frank Butler. Story: Beautiful blonde "entertainer" Judith Denning faces deportation from Malaya until she receives a wedding proposal from Horace Prin, overseer of a rubber plantation. She has no love for the unattractive man and he is straightaway cuckolded by handsome David von Eltz. Horace takes out his displeasure on the native workers, leading them to revolt and kill him.

Paramount Pictures, 1933 (original). Director: Stuart Walker; screenwriters: Samuel Hoffenstein and Gladys Lehman. Cast: Charles Laughton (Horace Prin), Carole Lombard (Judith Denning), Charles Bickford (Ballister), Kent Taylor (David von Eltz), Percy Kilbride, Charles B. Middleton, James Bell, Claude King, Ethel Griffies, Jimmie Dime, Noble Johnson.

• ***Island of Lost Men*** (remake). Paramount Pictures, 1939. Director: Kurt Neumann; screenwriters: William R. Lipman and Horace McCoy. Cast: Anna May Wong (Kim Ling), J. Carroll Naish (Gregory Prin), Eric Blore (Herbert), Ernest Truex (Frobenius), Anthony Quinn (Chang Tai), William Haines (Hambly), Broderick Crawford (Tex Ballister), Rudolf Forster, Richard Loo.

In the first film, the heat and humidity of the Malayan jungle seemed to have little effect on the beautiful Miss Lombard. She always looked as if she just came from Rodeo Drive in Beverly Hills, complete with a pretty new frock and her hair freshly done. The film was compared unfavorably to *The Island of Lost Souls* which also starred Charles Laughton as a hard taskmaster for some native types. In the remake, J. Carroll Naish is the menace into whose hands falls a variety of lawbreakers, including Anna May Wong, daughter of a Chinese general who had been accused of fleeing the country with a large sum of money which didn't belong to him. It's Anna's intention to clear her father's name. She succeeds with the help of Anthony Quinn and a few others who take the chance on defying the cruel Naish. Natives eventually finish off the latter with spears.

995 The Whole Town's Talking

Based on the play by John Emerson and Anita Loos. Story: Wounded World War I veteran Chester Binney mistakenly believes that he has had a silver plate embedded in his head and must avoid all excitement. When he returns to his hometown to claim a fortune that he has inherited, his former employer, George Simmons, tries to arrange a match between Chester and his daughter Ethel. She finds Chester unexciting and says so. To counter this her father comes up with a photograph of famous movie star Rita Renault, with a dedication to Chester. Naturally, Rita and her jealous husband, Jack Shields, arrive in town, with the latter discovering not only the photograph but Chester kissing Rita. This provokes a running fight and when Chester discovers that his health requires no particular restrictions, he punches out Jack and another suitor for Ethel, winning the girl and pleasing her father.

Universal Pictures, 1926 (original). Silent. Director: Edward Laemmle; screenwriter: Raymond Cannon. Cast: Edward Everett Horton (Chester Binney), Virginia Lee Corbin (Ethel Simmons), Trixie Friganza (Mrs. Simmons), Otis Harlan (Mr. Simmons), Dolores Del Rio (Rita Renault), Malcolm Waite (Jack Shields), Robert Ober, Aileen Manning, Hayden Stevenson, Margaret Quimby.

• ***Ex-Bad Boy*** (remake). Universal Pictures, 1931. Director: Vin Moore; screenwriter: Dale Van Every. Cast: Robert Armstrong (Chester Binney), Jean Arthur (Ethel Simmons), Lola Lane (Letta Lardo), George Brent (Donald Swift), Jason Robards, Sr. (Roger Shields), Grace Hampton, Mary Doran, Spencer Charters, Tony Stakenau.

These movies should not be confused with the 1935 film called *The Whole Town's Talking*, based on a story by W.R. Burnett, in which Edward G. Robinson plays the dual roles of a mild-mannered bookkeeper and the gangster for whom he is a dead ringer. The 1931 remake is a fairly straightforward retelling of the story of a small-town boy who gets in trouble when a beautiful movie star comes to town and everyone believes she's in love with him.

Whoopee! ***see*** **The Nervous Wreck**

996 Who's That Knocking at My Door?

Based on an original screenplay by Martin Scorsese. Story: J.R. has grown up in New York's "Little Italy" with the two biggest influences on his life being the Roman Catholic church and the law-of-the-jungle rule of the streets. He rarely strays from his neighborhood where he spends most of his time drinking with his buddies, playing cards and "horsin' around with the broads." While riding on the Staten Island Ferry, he meets a girl unlike anyone he has ever known before. She reads, speaks French, lives alone and has thoughts about things beyond her little world. As their feelings for each other deepen, she offers herself to J.R., but believing she is a virgin, he refuses. When he discovers that she had been raped by a former boyfriend, he holds her responsible and leaves her. Unable to get her out of his mind or fall back into his old patterns he tries for a reconciliation by telling the girl he forgives her for not being chaste. She sees this as a sign that he could never accept her for herself and she rejects him. Flying in a rage, he goes to his church but can find no solace there.

Timrod Films, 1968 (original). Director and screenwriter: Martin Scorsese. Cast: Zina Bethune (the Girl), Harvey Keitel (J.R.), Lennard Kuras, Ann Colette, Michael Scala, Wendy Russell, Catherine Scorsese, Philip Carlson, Vic Magnotta, Paul Di Biondi, Robert Uricola, Bill Minkin, Marissa Joffrey, Harry Northrup, Saskia Holleman, Tsuai Yu-Lan, Marieka, Susan Wood.

• ***Mean Streets*** (sequel). Warner Bros., 1973. Director: Martin Scorsese; screenwriters: Mardik Martin and Scorsese. Cast: Harvey Keitel (Charlie), Robert De Niro (Johnny Boy), David Proval (Tony), Amy Robinson (Teresa), Richard Romanus (Michael), Cesar Danova (Giovanni), Vic Argo, Robert Carradine, David Carradine, Jeannie Bell, D'Mitch Davis, George Memmoli, Murray Mosten.

The second film is not a sequel in the usual sense. However, since "Little Italy" is almost a character being studied in both films as is the sordid and meaningless existence of the punks whose existence director Scorsese is examining, it seems an appropriate pairing. In the second film, the director follows the lives of four low-level Italian-American hoods who use Tony's Bar as their base for drinking, brawling and hustling. The film has an overpowering sense of grim reality and although the entire cast is excellent, De Niro walks away with acting honors as the slightly psychotic Johnny Boy.

Why Leave Home *see* **Cradle Snatchers**

997 The Wicked Lady

Based on the novel *The Life and Death of the Wicked Lady Skelton* by Magdalen King-Hall. Story: In the days of Charles II, self-centered, ambitious Barbara Worth steals Sir Ralph Skelton away from her friend Caroline but soon grows bored with life on his manor in the country. She amuses herself by becoming a highway (wo-)man, which brings her into contact with Captain Jerry Jackson, a serious scoundrel. They have a passionate love affair but because of her treachery he is hanged, a ceremony which he survives, escaping only to be shot by Barbara. Badly wounded herself, she makes it back to her room before dying under the care of Kit Locksby, another of Caroline's lovers, who is the only man that Barbara ever really loved.

Gainsborough, Great Britain, 1945 (original). Director: Leslie Arliss; screenwriters: Arliss, Aimee Stuart and Gordon Glennon. Cast: Margaret Lockwood (Barbara Worth), James Mason (Capt. Jerry Jackson), Patricia Roc (Caroline), Griffith Jones (Sir Ralph Skelton), Michael Rennie (Kit Locksby), Felix Aylmer (Hogarth), Enid Stamp Taylor (Henrietta Kingsclere), Jean Kent (Doxy), Martita Hunt, Francis Lister, Emrys Jones, David Horne, Muriel Aked, Aubrey Mallalieu.

• ***The Wicked Lady*** (remake). Columbia/EMI/Warners, Great Britain, 1983. Director: Michael Winner; screenwriters: Leslie Arliss, Michael Winner, Gordon Glennon and Aimee Stuart. Cast: Faye Dunaway (Lady Barbara Skelton), Alan Bates (Capt. Jerry Jackson), John Gielgud (Hogarth), Denholm Elliott (Sir

Ralph Skelton), Prunella Scales (Lady Henrietta Kingsclere), Oliver Tobias (Kit Locksby), Glynis Barber (Lady Caroline), Joan Hickson, Helena McCarthy, Mollie Maureen, Derek Francis, Nicholas Gecks, Hugh Millais.

Both versions of the story relied as much on the low-cut gowns of Margaret Lockwood and Faye Dunaway as they did on the innate evilness of Lady Barbara Skelton. Lockwood was a delicious villainess, ideally cast as the selfish, murderous, unfaithful wife and lover. Dunaway was equally as beautiful but her evilness seemed to have a mental deficiency as its basis, which showed clearly in her face whenever she was being particularly bad. Lockwood's evil was a bit more subtle. Critics panned both versions, but the first became the year's biggest moneymaker in Great Britain. The second shared the critics' scorn but not the box-office success.

Wide Open *see* **The Narrow Street**

998 Wife, Husband and Friend

Based on the novel by James M. Cain. Story: Doris Borland is a socialite who wants to become a singer and is encouraged in her ambition by her husband, Leonard. While Doris is discouraged by constant rejections, Leonard secretly has been taking singing lessons and it seems he has a bit of talent. Doris' friend Cecil Carver, an opera star, persuades Leonard to appear with her in a grand opera, where he flops. Doris and Leonard are then happy to put aside their musical ambitions and concentrate on each other.

Twentieth Century–Fox, 1939 (original). Director: Gregory Ratoff; screenwriter: Nunnally Johnson. Cast: Loretta Young (Doris Borland), Warner Baxter (Leonard Borland), Binnie Barnes (Cecil Carver), Cesar Romero (Hugo), George Barbier (Major Blair), J. Edward Bromberg, Eugene Pallette, Helen Westley.

• ***Everybody Does It*** (remake). Twentieth Century–Fox. Director: Edmund Goulding; screenwriter: Nunnally Johnson. Cast: Paul Douglas (Leonard Borland), Linda Darnell (Cecil Carver), Celeste Holm (Doris Borland), Charles Coburn (Major Blair), Millard Mitchell (Mike Craig), Lucille Watson (Mrs. Blair), John Hoyt, George Tobias, Leon Belasco, Tito Vuolo.

In the first version of the James M. Cain story, it's not quite clear whether Binnie Barnes wants to get her hooks into Warner Baxter or just is being helpful in his coping with his wife's overriding ambition to be a singer. In the remake, there's no doubt that opera singer Linda Darnell would be happy to snatch Paul Douglas away from Celeste Holm, whose yearning to be a concert star is driving hubby crazy. In both movies, the potential gags are all milked completely dry, but one must admit some of the humor is cream.

The Wife of Monte Cristo *see* **The Count of Monte Cristo**

999 The Wild Geese

Based on the novel by Daniel Carney. Story: Rich British industrialist Sir Edward Matherson hires mercenaries Col. Allen Faulkner, Shawn Fynn and Rafer

Janders to go to Rhodesia and rescue a captured humanist leader so Matherson's firm can again have the copper rights in the country. It becomes a bloody war.

Richmond/Rank, Great Britain, 1978 (original). Director: Andrew V. McLaglen; screenwriter: Reginald Rose. Cast: Richard Burton (Col. Allen Faulkner), Roger Moore (Shawn Fynn), Richard Harris (Rafer Janders), Hardy Kruger (Peter Coetzee), Stewart Granger (Sir Edward Matherson), Jack Watson, Winston Ntshona, John Kani, Frank Finlay, Kenneth Griffith, Barry Foster, Jeff Corey, Ronald Fraser, Ian Yule, Brook Williams, Percy Herbert, Patrick Allen.

• ***Wild Geese II*** (sequel). Frontier Films/Thorn–EMI, Great Britain, 1985. Director: Peter Hunt; screenwriter: Reginald Rose, based on Daniel Carney's novel *The Square Circle.* Cast: Scott Glenn (John Haddad), Barbara Carrera (Kathy Lucas), Edward Fox (Alex Faulkner), Laurence Olivier (Rudolf Hess), Robert Webber (Robert McCann), Robert Freitag, Kenneth Haigh, Stratford Johns, Derek Thompson, Paul Antrim, John Terry, Ingrid Pitt, Patrick Stewart.

The first film had some interesting moments and decent performances from a cast mostly beyond their prime, but the sequel about an American TV company hiring the Wild Geese mercenaries to break Nazi war criminal Rudolf Hess from his Berlin prison is just absurd nonsense made sad by the fact that Laurence Olivier's quest for money made him agree to appear as Hess in this atrocious piece.

Wild Geese II *see* **Wild Geese**

1000 Willard

Based on the novel *Ratman's Notebooks* by Stephen Gilbert. Story: Lonely Willard Stiles' only friends are his pet rats. He decides to take revenge on those who had been unkind to him, and he trains an army of rats to be killers.

Cinerama, 1971 (original). Director: Daniel Mann; screenwriter: Gilbert A. Ralston. Cast: Bruce Davison (Willard Stiles), Ernest Borgnine (Al Martin), Elsa Lanchester (Herietta Stiles), Sondra Locke (Joan), Michael Dante (Brandt), Jody Gilbert (Charlotte Stassen), Joan Shawlee, William Hansen, J. Pat O'Malley, John Mhyers.

• ***Ben*** (sequel). Cinerama, 1972. Director: Phil Karlson; screenwriter: Gilbert A. Ralston. Cast: Lee H. Montgomery (Danny Garrison), Joseph Campanella (Cliff Kirtland), Arthur O'Connell (Billy Hatfield), Rosemary Murphy (Beth Garrison), Meredith Baxter, Kas Garas, Paul Carr, Richard Van Vleet, Kenneth Tobey.

For some any film with rats is a horror movie. The authors do not subscribe to this classification. This is an unusual melodrama and suspenseful thriller that attracted good numbers at the box office, being so successful, that the sequel was produced with the lead rat of the first being the title character of the second. Michael Jackson had a hit song called "Ben" and for those not knowing of the movie, it sounded like a tender little love song—and it was.

Wine, Women and Horses *see* **Dark Hazard**

1001 The Witching Hour

Based on the play by Augustus Thomas. Story: While Jack Brookfield is entertaining guests at his Louisville gambling house, Tom Denning taunts Clay Whipple, who has a deadly fear of cat's-eye jewelry, with a scarfpin possessing the fearful stone. In desperation, Clay kills Denning, is arrested, tried and sentenced to death. Brookfield, whose neice Viola loves Clay, intercedes with the judge in the case, convincing him that Clay should have another trial as he was acting under a hypnotic suggestion that went astray. This is all tied in with an attorney, Frank Hardmuth, with gubernatorial ambitions whom Brookfield ties to the murder of the governor-elect. When Hardmuth attempts to shoot Brookfield, the latter thwarts the plan by hypnotizing his assailant. In the second trial, Clay is acquitted.

• ***The Witching Hour*** (remake). Famous Players–Lasky/Paramount Pictures, 1921. Silent. Director: William D. Taylor; screenwriter: Julia Crawford Ivers. Cast: Elliott Dexter (Jack Brookfield), Winter Hall (Judge Prentice), Ruth Renick (Viola Campbell), Robert Cain (Frank Hardmuth), Edward Sutherland (Clay Whipple), Fred Turner, Genevieve Blinn, Charles West, L.M. Wells.

• ***The Witching Hour*** (remake). Paramount Pictures, 1934. Director: Henry Hathaway; screenwriters: Salisbury Field and Anthony Veiller. Cast: Sir Guy Standing (Martin Prentice), John Halliday (Jack Brookfield), Judith Allen (Nancy Brookfield), Tom Brown (Clay Thorne), Olive Tell, William Frawley, Richard Carle, Ralf Harolde, Purnell Pratt, Frank Sheridan.

The Witching Hour was first filmed as a silent in 1916, but by 1934 the story was rather old-fashioned and the 64-minute film suffered from a lack of box-office players. The movie still packs a punch if one doesn't require plausibility and enjoys the effects of hypnotism.

1002 Within the Law

Based on the play by Bayard Veiller. Story: When Mary Turner is unjustly convicted by theft, she vows vengeance on Edward Gilder, her employer and prosecutor. On release from prison, she joins Aggie Lynch and Joe Garson in a scheme to blackmail rich men with threats of breach-of-promise suits. To Mary's glee, Dick Gilder, son of the man she hates, falls into her hands. To complicate matters, Mary falls in love with Dick, but she is determined to go through with her plan for revenge. Dick is nearly framed for a murder committed by Joe Garson, but when another girl confesses to the crime for which Mary was sent to prison, she admits her love for Dick.

• ***Within the Law*** (remake). First National Pictures, 1923. Silent. Director: Frank Lloyd; screenwriter: Francis Marion. Cast: Norma Talmadge (Mary Turner), Lew Cody (Joe Garson), Jack Mulhall (Dick Gilder), Eileen Percy (Aggie Lynch), Joseph Kilgour (Edward Gilder), Arthur S. Hull, Helen Ferguson, Lincoln Plummer.

• ***Paid*** (remake). MGM, 1930. Director: Sam Wood; screenwriters: Charles

MacArthur and Lucien Hubbard. Cast: Joan Crawford (Mary Turner), Robert Armstrong (Joe Garson), Marie Prevost (Agnes Lynch), Kent Douglass (Bob Gilder), John Miljan (Inspector Blake), Purnell B. Pratt (Edward Gilder), Hale Hamilton, Polly Moran, Robert Emmett, Tyrell Davis.

• ***Within the Law*** (remake). MGM, 1939. Director: Gustav Machaty; screenwriters: Charles Lederer and Edith Fitzgerald. Cast: Ruth Hussey (Mary Turner), Tom Neal (Richard Gilder), Paul Kelly (Joe Garson), William Gargan (Cassidy), Paul Cavanaugh ("English Eddie"), Rita Johnson (Agnes), Samuel S. Hinds (Mr. Gilder), Lynne Carver, Sidney Blackmer, Jo Ann Sayers.

In the third film version of the Bayard Veiller work (there was a silent production in 1917), bitter Joan Crawford, on leaving prison for a crime she did not commit, becomes associated with three criminals with whom she instigates numerous barely legal activities. To gain revenge on her former employer who had her sent to prison, she marries his son, played by Kent Douglass. When the father is unsuccessful in getting the marriage annulled, he arranges for two of Crawford's associates to rob his son's home. His plan is to make the police believe that Joan is involved in the crime. Things go better than he planned when one of the robbers kills the other and the police arrest her for the killing. However, the other robber is ultimately captured and confesses after exposure to the third degree, allowing Joan to be reunited with her husband. The 1939 version shows the age of the story, although Ruth Hussey is excellent as the innocent clerk railroaded to a three-year jail term.

Without Regret *see* **Interference**

Wives Under Suspicion *see* **The Kiss Before the Mirror**

The Wiz *see* **The Wizard of Oz**

1003 The Wizard of Oz

Based on Lyman Frank Baum's *The Wonderful World of the Wizard of Oz.* Story: As she nears her eighteenth birthday, Dorothy learns from her "aunt" that she was a foundling, left on the doorstep as an infant. The only thing left with the baby is a letter with instructions to not open it until Dorothy is 18. Before she can read the letter, a cyclone sweeps Dorothy, her uncle, and two hired men into the Land of Oz. The letter establishes that Dorothy is the Queen of the realm and she is accepted as such by Prince Kynde, but Prime Minister Kruel is not pleased. He asks the wizard to put a spell on Dorothy and her followers, but having no real magical powers, the wizard is unable to do so. The two hired men disguise themselves as a scarecrow and a tin woodsman, are put into jail, but escape and run into a lion in his den. The two try to escape by climbing a high tower. The scarecrow reaches for a ladder hanging from an airplane. The ladder breaks, and the scarecrow tumbles . . . and at that point Dorothy wakes up—it was all a dream.

• ***The Wizard of Oz*** (remake). Cadwick Pictures, 1925. Silent. Director and screenwriter: Larry Semon. Cast: Larry Semon (Scarecrow), Bryant Washburn

(Prince Kynde), Dorothy Dwan (Dorothy), Virginia Pearson (Countess Vishuss), Charles Murray (the Wizard), Oliver Hardy (the Tin Woodsman), Josef Swickard (Prime Minister), Mary Carr, G. Howe Black.

• ***The Wizard of Oz*** (remake). MGM, 1939. Directors: Victor Fleming (uncredited), Richard Thorpe and King Vidor; screenwriters: Noel Langley, Florence Ryerson and Edgar Allan Woolf. Cast: Judy Garland (Dorothy), Frank Morgan (Professor Marvel/the Wizard of Oz), Ray Bolger (Hunk/the Scarecrow), Bert Lahr (Zeke/the Cowardly Lion), Jack Haley (Hickory/the Tin Woodsman), Billie Burke (Glinda), Margaret Hamilton (Miss Gulch/Wicked Witch), Charley Grapewin (Uncle Henry), Clara Blandick (Auntie Em), the Munchkin Midgets.

• ***The Wiz*** (remake). Universal/Motown, 1978. Director: Sidnet Lumet; screenwriter: John Schumacher, from play by Charlie Smith and William Brown. Cast: Diana Ross (Dorothy), Michael Jackson (Scarecrow), Nipsy Russell (Tin Man), Ted Ross (Cowardly Lion), Richard Pryor (The Wiz), Mabel King (Evil Witch Evilene), Lena Horne (Glinda), Theresa Merritt (Aunt Em), Thelma Carpenter, Stanley Greene, Clyde J. Barrett.

Frank Baum's charming stories were also brought to the screen by Selznick in 1910 as *Dorothy and the Scarecrow of Oz* and a sequel the same year, *Land of Oz.* Paramount brought audiences *The Patchwork Girl of Oz* in 1914. Baum himself produced *His Majesty, the Scarecrow of Oz* in 1914, *The Magic Cloak of Oz* in 1914, and *The Ragged Girl of Oz* in 1919. There was a Spanish version, *Fantasy . . . 3,* in 1967; a Childhood production, *The Wonderful Land of Oz,* in 1969; an animated production, *Journey Back to Oz,* in 1977 with Liza Minnelli following in her mother's footsteps in a manner of speaking by supplying Dorothy's voice; Australia's *Oz* in 1976; and independent productions, *The Wizard of Oz* in 1977 and *20th Century Oz* in 1978.

Little can be added to the millions of words that have been written about the 1939 production of *The Wizard of Oz,* which was nominated for but did not win the Academy Award for Best Picture. Anyone above the age of the five has probably seen the film several times on its yearly television appearance. Some who first saw it in the theater as children have had an opportunity to share its magic with their children and grandchildren.

The cast seems about as perfect as could possibly be assembled. Judy Garland, in the role that launched her to stardom, is the girl Dorothy, wistfully dreaming of adventure beyond her own backyard in Kansas. Her appealing rendition of the marvelous Academy Award–winning song "Over the Rainbow" is unforgettable. On her trip to Oz, she meets Ray Bolger as the very wise and engagingly floppy scarecrow, whose lifelong desire is to replace his head full of stuffing with a brain; Bert Lahr as the delightful cowardly lion, afraid of his own tail, who wails that he would be king of the forest if he only had "the noive"; and Jack Haley as the sentimental tin woodsman, told by Frank Morgan, who played several fine roles including the Wizard, "As for you, my galvanized friend, you want a heart. You don't know how lucky you are not to have one. Hearts will never be practical until they can be made unbreakable."

In addition, Margaret Hamilton has the role of her career as the mean Miss

Gulch and the scary Wicked Witch of the West who threatens Dorothy, thusly, "Well, my little pretty, I can cause accidents, too." Billie Burke is a lovely Glinda, the good witch and of course the Munchkins are merely enchanting. Even Dorothy's dog Toto deserves praise. Other Harold Arlen and E.Y. Harburg songs which have delighted audiences for 50 years include "Follow the Yellow Brick Road," "We're Off to See the Wizard," and "Ding, Dong, the Witch Is Dead."

The glossy black version of *The Wizard of Oz* has Diana Ross as a 24-year-old Harlem school teacher who while chasing her dog Toto in a snowstorm disappears into a vortex of snow crystals only to reappear in another part of Manhattan where her experiences more or less parallel those of the earlier Dorothy. The musical numbers by Quincy Jones and Charlie Smalls include the showstopping "Don't Bring Me No Bad News," sung by Mabel King and her Flying Monkeys, "Believe in Yourself," a black-pride number sung by Lena Horne, Ted Ross' "I'm a Mean Old Lion," and "Is This What Feeling Gets (Dorothy's Theme)" sung by Diana Ross and "Ease on Down the Road" with Ted Ross, Michael Jackson, Nipsy Russell and Diana Ross. For all of the films, Baum's message keeps coming through—"There's no place like home."

Wolf Larsen *see* **The Sea Wolf**

1004 The Woman Disputed

Based on the story *Boule de Suif* by Guy de Maupassant and the play by Denison Clift. Story: Friends Paul Hartman, an Austrian officer, and Nika Turgenov, a Russian lieutenant, together bring about the regeneration of Mary Ann Wagner, a prostitute of Lemberg, Austria. When war is declared between the two nations, the men are ordered to join their regiments. Mary promises to marry Paul, and Nika promises to avenge what he considers a slight. Later, when a Russian army unit led by Nika occupies Lemberg, Mary submits to Nika to obtain the release of a captured spy. The next day, the Austrian army recaptures Lemberg, guided by the spy's report. Paul learns of Mary's capitulation to Nika's lust and at first cannot bring himself to forgive her for being unfaithful to him, but relents when 10,000 of his men kneel at her feet in thanks for her courage and sacrifice that saved many of their lives.

United Artists, 1928 (original). Musical score and sound effects. Director: Henry King; screenwriter: Sam Taylor. Cast: Norma Talmadge (Mary Ann Wagner), Gilbert Roland (Paul Hartman), Arnold Kent (Nika Turgenov), Boris De Fas, Michael Vavitch, Gustav von Seyffertitz, Gladys Brockwell, Nicolas Soussanin.

• ***Mademoiselle Fifi*** (remake). RKO, 1944. Director: Robert Wise; screenwriters: Josef Mischel and Peter Ruric. Cast: Simone Simon (Elizabeth Rousset), John Emery (Jean Cornudet), Kurt Krueger (Lt. von Eyrick), Alan Napier (Count de Breville), Helen Freeman, Jason Robards, Norma Varden, Romaine Callendar, Fay Helm, Edmund Glover.

• ***Angel and Sinner*** (remake). WIPS Production, France, 1947. Director and screenwriter: Christian Jacque. Cast: Micheline Presle (Boule de Suif), Louis

Salou (Lt. Eyrik), Palau (Carre-Lamadon), Roger Karl (Lt. Major Falsborg), Marcel Simon, Alfred Adam, Jean Broucahard, Michel Saline, Denise D'Ines.

The story of the noble prostitute who's damned if she does and damned if she doesn't was also filmed in 1934 and 1935 based on the de Maupassant story and in numerous other movies with similar plots. The 1944 movie has Simone Simon as a French prostitute aboard a stagecoach of refugees, which is held up because she refuses to sleep with a Prussian officer. Her fellow passengers urge her to submit and when she does they shun her. She takes a measure of revenge by killing the officer. It's a low budget film with some high quality production values, an interesting story and interestingly acted, particularly by Simon. The 1947 French version of the story updates it to World War II and the conflict between the French and the Germans. It has the same plotline as the 1944 film with Micheline Presle as a round-heeled Joan of Arc who is urged by her fellow passengers to submit to a German so they can all escape, and when she does they treat her as a moral leper. The next German officer with a similiar proposition she kills and then takes off for the countryside.

The Woman from Monte Carlo *see* **The Night Watch**

1005 The Woman God Changed

Based on the short story "Changeling" by Brian Oswald Donn-Byrne. Story: Dancer Anna Janssen kills her common-law husband, Alastair De Vries, for fooling around with a chorus girl. She escapes to Tahiti but is pursued by detective Tom McCarthy, who arrests her. On the trip back, their ship sinks, with only Anna and Tom surviving, cast ashore on a deserted island. After two years, they realize that they are in love and, no longer expecting to be rescued, exchange marriage vows. When a ship is sighted, Anna insists on returning with Tom to face the charges against her. Tom tells her story at her trial and she is sentenced to spend the rest of her natural life in the custody of husband Tom.

Cosmopolitan Productions/Paramount Pictures, 1921 (original). Silent. Director: Robert G. Vignola; screenwriter: Doty Hobart. Cast: Seena Owen (Anna Janssen), E.K. Lincoln (Thomas McCarthy), Henry Sedley (Alastair De Vries), Lillian Walker (Lilly), H. Cooper Cliffe, Paul Nicholson, Joseph Smiley.

• ***His Captive Woman*** (remake). First National Pictures, 1929. Director: George Fitzmaurice; screenwriter: Carey Wilson. Cast: Milton Sills (Thomas McCarthy), Dorothy MacKaill (Anna Janssen), Gladden James (Alastair de Vries), Jed Prouty, Sidney Bracey, Gertrude Howard, Marion Bryon, George Fawcett.

The plot of these movies is ridiculous but somehow the redemption of a cabaret dancer who kills her sugar daddy when stranded on a deserted island with the officer charged with bringing her to justice is enjoyable. However, we wonder if their love can really survive the life sentence as man and wife on their island.

Woman Hungry *see* **The Great Divide**

The Woman I Love *see* **L'Equipage**

1006 Woman in Room 13

Based on the play by Samuel Shipman, Max Marcin and Percival Eilde. Story: A daring detective schemes to have the wrong man convicted of a murder by using a dictaphone. His motive is to take revenge on the man's wife who had earlier divorced him and ruined his career. His plan is foolproof until he accepts his ex-wife's invitation to talk the case over and she gets him to confess without knowing that she has concealed a dictaphone herself.

Goldwyn, 1920 (original). Silent. Director: Frank Lloyd; screenwriters: E. Richard Schayer and D. Nash. Cast: Pauline Frederick (Laura Bruce), John Bowers (Paul Ramsey), Charles Clary (John Bruce), Robert McKim (Dick Turner), Sidney Ainsworth (Andy Lewis), Charles Arling, Marguerite Snow, Emily Chichester.

• ***Woman in Room 13*** (remake). Fox Film Corp., 1932. Director: Henry King; screenwriter: Guy Bolton. Cast: Elissa Landi (Laura), Ralph Bellamy (John Bruce), Neil Hamilton (Paul Ramsey), Myrna Loy (Sari Lodar), Gilbert Roland (Victor Legrand), Walter Walker, Luis Alberni, Charley Grapewin.

Pauline Frederick was praised for her performance in the silent. In fact the whole picture was merely a vehicle for her peculiar talents as a woman who will suffer for her man. The same was not said about Elissa Landi, an actress whose star never shone very brightly. Critics also didn't feel the mystery of who was the real killer held much suspense.

1007 The Woman in White

Based on the novel by Wilkie Collins. Story: Sir Percival Glyde marries Laura Fairlie for her money but is thwarted by her sister, Marian. Percival seizes the opportunity provided by Laura's exact double, "the woman in white," the vengeful, deranged and dying daughter of the real Glyde, who had been one of the imposter's several murder victims, to put Laura in an asylum. She is rescued by an admirer, Walter Hartwright, and the imposter perishes in a church fire set ablaze by himself.

• ***The Woman in White*** (remake). Britain & Dominions, Great Britain, 1929. Silent. Director: Herbert Wilcox; screenwriters: Wilcox and Robert J. Cullen. Cast: Blanche Sweet (Laura Fairlie/Anne Catherick, the woman in white), Haddon Mason (Walter Hartwright), Cecil Humphreys (Sir Percival Glyde), Louise Prussing (Marian Fairlie), Frank Perfett (Count Fosco), Minna Grey (Countess Fosco).

• ***Crimes at the Dark House*** (remake). Ealing, Great Britain, 1940. Director: George King; screenwriters: Edward Dryhurst, Frederick Hayward and H.F. Maltby. Cast: Tod Slaughter (Sir Percival Glyde), Hilary Evans (Marian Fairlie), Sylvia Marriott (Laura Fairlie), Hay Petrie (Dr. Fosco), Geoffrey Wardwell (Paul Hartwright), David Horne (Mr. Fairlie), Margaret Yarde (Mrs. Bullen), Rita Grant (Anne Catherick).

• ***The Woman in White*** (remake). Warner Bros., 1948. Director: Peter Godfrey; screenwriter: Stephen Morehouse Avery. Cast: Eleanor Parker (Laura Fairlie/Anne Catherick), Alexis Smith (Marian Halcombe), Sydney Greenstreet (Count Fosco), Gig Young (Walter Hartright), Agnes Moorehead (Countess Fosco), John Abbott (Frederick Fairlie), John Emery (Sir Percival Glyde), Curt Bois, Emma Dunn, Matthew Boulton, Anita Sharp-Bolster.

The Wilkie Collins novel was also filmed in 1912, 1914, 1917 and 1920 as *Twin Pawns.* The 1940 film was done somewhat tongue-in-cheek, but the 1948 production takes everything very seriously in the ancient crime mystery, where a mysterious lady in white arrives on the scene from time to time to warn of the evil scheme. Eleanor Parker looks splendid in the costumes she wears in her dual roles and does nothing to shame herself, but it's not possible to say too much in positive praise of her performance. The character performances of Sydney Greenstreet, John Abbott and John Emery are the most praiseworthy in the film.

1008 A Woman of Affairs

Based on the novel *The Green Hat* by Michael Arlen. Story: Diana Merrick's love for aristocratic Neville Holderness is not to result in marriage because his father does not approve of her family's way of life. Later Diana marries David Furness, a friend of her brother's, without knowing that he is a thief. On their honeymoon in France, David kills himself when he learns the police are on his trail. Diana takes it to be her responsibility to repay all those from whom her husband has stolen. Returning home to England some years later, she rejects Neville when he tries to return to her, noting his father's attitude and the fact that he is married. Her brother dies of a fatal bout with alcoholism and Diana deliberately drives her car into a tree where she and Neville first declared their love, and dies.

MGM, 1929 (original). Silent. Director: Clarence Brown; screenwriter: Bess Meredyth. Cast: Greta Garbo (Diana), John Gilbert (Neville), Lewis Stone (Hugh), John Mack Brown (David), Douglas Fairbanks, Jr. (Jeffrey), Hobart Bosworth, Dorothy Sebastian.

• ***Outcast Lady*** (remake). MGM, 1934. Director: Robert Z. Leonard; screenwriter: Zoe Atkins. Cast: Constance Bennett (Iris), Herbert Marshall (Napier), Mrs. Patrick Campbell (Lady Eve), Hugh Williams (Gerald), Elizabeth Allan (Venice), Henry Stephenson (Sir Maurice), Robert Loraine, Lumsden Hare, Leo Carroll, Ralph Forbes, Alec B. Francis.

The 1929 version of the Michael Arlen story didn't sizzle the screen as had earlier collaborations of Greta Garbo and John Gilbert. The piece was a throwaway story popular at the time that allowed the beautiful actress a few fine moments before the camera. The remake with Constance Bennett and Herbert Marshall is less, partially because the censors had their say but also because the story development is too sketchy and little things like suicides occur without audiences being right sure why or what the event has to do with the plot. Constance Bennett handles the acting adequately. Too bad someone did not provide a better, filmable screenplay.

Woman of Glamour *see* **Ladies of Leisure**

1009 Woman of the Year

Based on the screenplay by Ring Lardner, Jr., and Michael Kanin. Story: Tess Hardin and Sam Craig each write newspaper columns. Her beat is world affairs; his is sports. She disparages baseball on an "Information Please" broadcast and he takes her to task in his column. They meet and despite their differences send off sparks which lead to love and marriage. However, Tess is so busy with diplomats, speeches and receiving awards as "Outstanding Woman of the Year" that she has little time for Sam. He finally grows tired of the arrangement and moves out. By a strange coincidence, the very next night Tess attends the marriage of her widower father and an old friend, listens closely to the vows that are exchanged and gives up her career to become the housewife type that Sam seems to want.

MGM, 1942 (original). Director: George Stevens; screenwriters: Ring Lardner, Jr., and Michael Kanin. Cast: Spencer Tracy (Sam Craig), Katharine Hepburn (Tess Harding), Fay Bainter (Ellen Whitcomb), Reginald Owen (Clayton), Minor Watson (William J. Harding), William Bendix ("Pinkle" Peters), Gladys Blake, Dan Tobin, Roscoe Karns, William Tannen.

• ***Designing Woman*** (remake). MGM, 1957. Director: Vincente Minnelli; screenwriters: George Wells and Helen Rose. Cast: Gregory Peck (Mike Hagen), Lauren Bacall (Marilla Hagen), Dolores Gray (Lori Shannon), Sam Levene (Ned Hammerstein), Tom Helmore (Zachary Wilde), Mickey Shaughnessy (Maxie Stulz), Jesse White, Chuck Connors, Edward Platt, Alvy Moore, Carol Veazle, Jack Cole.

The ending of the 1942 movie must have been galling to the very independent Ms. Hepburn, but times being what they were, it's probably too much to expect that both husband and wife could compromise and accommodate. The film, despite it's anti-feminist message (at least by today's standards), was quite pleasant as the initial teaming of the wonderful pair of Hepburn and Tracy. Besides the ending another thing that may offend some of today's audiences is a scene where Tracy takes a seat on the stage where Hepburn is making a speech in an auditorium filled with people and lights up a cigarette.

The 1957 film is not strictly a remake but the story is similiar enough to believe that George Wells and Helen Rose had the original story in mind when they came up with theirs. Peck, a crusading sports reporter, marries Bacall, a prominent fashion designer, and abandons his comfortable but cluttered Greenwich Village apartment for her elegant East Side penthouse. Her friends and his friends don't mix, and before long the marriage is on the rocks because the two combatants don't seem to have anything in common. Of course, everything gets straightened out before the final clinch as Bacall and her friends help Peck deal with a crooked fight promoter who wishes to get Greg for exposing his racket. One leaves the picture with the sense that they still have very little in common, and they can't count on life-threatening situations all the time to draw them together. Still, it's an amusing if incongruous picture.

1010 Woman to Woman

Based on the play by Michael Morton. Story: English officer David Compton has an affair with French ballerina Louise. He becomes an amnesiac and after World War I marries barren socialite Mrs. Anson-Pond. He comes across former lover Louise and their son, whom he adopts as his own when Louise dies of a heart condition.

Balcon, Freedman & Saville, Great Britain, 1923 (original). Silent. Director: Graham Cutts; screenwriter: Alfred J. Hitchcock. Cast: Betty Compson (Louise), Clive Brook (David Compton), Josephine Earle (Mrs. Anson-Pond), Marie Ault (Henriette), Myrtle Peter (Davy), A. Harding Steerman, Madge Tree.

• ***Woman to Woman*** (remake). Gainsborough, Great Britain, 1929. Director and screenwriter: Victor Saville. Cast: Betty Compson (Lola), Juliette Compton (Vesta), George Barraud (David), Winter Hall (Dr. Garvin), Marguerite Chambers (Florence), George Billings (Little David).

• ***Woman to Woman*** (remake). British National, Great Britain, 1946. Director: Maclean Rogers; screenwriters: James Seymour and Marjorie Deans. Cast: Douglass Montgomery (David Anson), Joyce Howard (Nicole Bonnet), Adele Dixon (Sylvia Anson), Yvonne Arnaud (Henriette), Paul Collins (David, Jr.), John Warwick, Eugene Deckers, Lily Khan, Martin Miller.

The tear-drenched silent was a very successful "woman's picture," but the remakes didn't seem to capture audiences' esteem. It had all the ingredients: a brief love affair at the time of war, an unwed mother with the father seemingly gone forever, his amnesia, her heart condition, his wife who can't have children and who won't give him a divorce when he remembers that he has a son by a French ballerina, the latter conveniently dying, and the adoption of the child by his father.

1011 Womanpower

Based on the short story "You Can't Always Tell" by Harold MacGrath. Story: Johnny Bromley, a rich young man, is considered a worthless idler by his father and a coward by a young vamp he fancies, named Dot. He takes himself to a remote prizefighter's training camp to learn the manly art of self-defense. There he meets and falls in love with the camp owner's daughter, Jenny Killian. With her encouragement he overcomes the memories of Dot's sneering accusations of cowardice. He makes something of himself, wins back the approbation of his father and Jenny's hand in marriage. On running into Dot and a former rival, the broker who had previously humiliated him in front of the callous girl, he surprises both by flooring the larger man with a single punch.

Fox Film Corp., 1926 (original). Silent. Director: Harry Beaumont;

Opposite, top: *Columnist Katharine Hepburn wins the title* Woman of the Year *in the 1942 MGM film of that name, but when she marries sportswriter Spencer Tracy, he expects her to act like a more traditional wife.* Bottom: *In* Designing Woman *(MGM, 1957), sportswriter Gregory Peck falls in love and marries clothes designer Lauren Bacall and then they settle down to see if they have anything in common.*

14
14A
AA

screenwriter: Kenneth B. Clarke. Cast: Ralph Graves (Johnny White Bromley), Kathryn Perry (Jenny Killian), Margaret Livingston (Dot), Ralph Snipperly (Gimp Conway), William Walling (Jake Killian), Lou Tellegen (the Broker), Anders Randolf (Bromley Sr.), David Butler, Robert Ryan.

• ***Right to the Heart*** (remake). Twentieth Century–Fox, 1942. Director: Eugene Forde; screenwriter: Walter Bullock. Cast: Brenda Joyce (Jenny Killian), Joseph Allen, Jr. (John T. Bromley, III), Cobina Wright, Jr. (Barbara Paxton), Stanley Clements (Stash), Don De Fore (Tommy Sands), Ethel Griffies (Minerva Bromley), Hugh Beaumont, Charles D. Brown.

These are two more examples of entertaining and mostly comical B programmers, both very short on name performers who would pull in the customers. In the remake, Joseph Allen gets disowned by his rich aunt for his irresponsible behavior, which action leads to his immediate dumping by fortune-hunting Cobina Wright when he is flattened in a brawl by a boxer. He enrolls in a backwoods training camp to condition himself for a planned rematch. Here he falls in love with Brenda Joyce and learns enough humility to get back in the good graces of his aunt.

1012 The Women

Based on the play by Clare Boothe. Story: In this bitchy comedy drama, Sylvia Fowler takes delight in arranging for her friend Mary Haines to learn from a gossipy manicurist that her husband, Stephen Haines, is having an affair with showgirl Crystal Allen. Mary heads for Reno, staying at the Double Bar T Ranch with other women establishing residency before being granted divorces. Among them are frequently married Countess De Lage and worldly-wise dancer Miriam Aarons. They are soon joined by the shocked Sylvia who gets into a brawl with Miriam when it is learned that the latter will be the next Mrs. Fowler. Stephen Haines marries Crystal Allen but when Mary learns that Crystal is having an affair with Countess de Lage's newest husband, cowboy actor Buck Winston, Mary exposes Crystal and takes her husband back.

MGM, 1939 (original). Director: George Cukor; screenwriters: Anita Loos and Jane Murfin. Cast: Norma Shearer (Mary Haines), Rosalind Russell (Sylvia Fowler), Joan Crawford (Crystal Allen), Phyllis Povah (Edith Potter), Florence Nash (Nancy Blake), Joan Fontaine (Peggy Day), Lucille Watson (Mrs. Moorehead), Mary Boland (Countess de Lage), Paulette Goddard (Miriam Aarons), Marjorie Main, Muriel Hutchinson, Margaret Dumont, Dennie Moore, Mary Cyril, Esther Dale, Hedda Hopper, Virginia Weidler, Ruth Hussey, Mary Beth Hughes, Cora Witherspoon.

• ***The Opposite Sex*** (remake). MGM, 1956. Director: David Miller; screenwriters: Fay and Michael Kanin. Cast: June Allyson (Kay), Dolores Gray

Opposite, top: *Hedda Hopper, Norma Shearer and Joan Fontaine are having a laugh at the expense of Rosalind Russell in* The Women *(MGM, 1939).* Bottom: *Whatever bitchy thing Agnes Moorehead, right, has to say, she's getting a variety of reactions from Ann Sheridan, Ann Miller, Joan Collins, Dolores Gray, Alice Pearce and June Allyson in* The Opposite Sex, *the 1956 MGM remake of* The Women.

(Sylvia), Joan Collins (Crystal), Ann Sheridan (Amanda), Ann Miller (Gloria), Leslie Nielsen (Steve Hilliard), Jeff Richards (Buck Winston), Agnes Moorehead (Countess de Lage), Charlotte Greenwood (Lucy), Joan Blondell (Edith), Sam Levene (Mike Pearl), Bill Goodwin (Howard Fowler), Alice Pearce, Barbara Jo Allen, Sandy Descher, Carolyn Jones, Jim Backus.

The first version had an all-female cast, advertised as "135 Women with Men on Their Mind." The bitchy production was one of the highlights of a very good movie year. It's still funny and filled with memorable scenes of cats literally and figuratively scratching at each other. The color remake allowed the men before the camera, and this didn't make things better. In fact it may have distracted from the nasty behavior of the "ladies."

Women Love Once *see* **Daddy's Gone A-Hunting**

Women Without Names *see* **Ladies of the Big House**

The Wonderful Land of Oz *see* **The Wizard of Oz**

1013 The Wonderful Story

Based on the story by I.A.R. Wylie. Story: Both Robert and Jimmy Martin are in love with Kate Richards. She marries Robert but he becomes paralytic, so she marries Jimmy. Robert still dominates their lives but eventually accepts the situation when their child reforms him.

Astra-National, Great Britain, 1922 (original). Silent. Director: Graham Cutts; screenwriter: Patrick L. Mannock. Cast: Lillian Hall Davis (Kate Richards), Herbert Langley (Robert Martin), Olaf Hytten (Jimmy Martin).

• ***The Wonderful Story*** (remake). Fogwell/Sterling, Great Britain, 1932. Director and screenwriter: Reginald Fogwell. Cast: Wyn Clare (Mary Richards), John Batten (John Martin), Eric Bransby Williams (Bob Martin), Moore Marriott, J. Fisher White, Sam Livesey, Ernest Lester.

One is tempted to say it's not a wonderful story and leave it at that. However, fairness requires the observation that at least in the remake, the acting just about makes the picture bearable.

Wonders of Aladdin *see* **Aladdin and His Wonderful Lamp**

1014 The Working Man

Based on a story by Edgar Franklin. Story: While on a fishing trip, shoe manufacturer Reeves runs into Jenny and Tommy, the orphaned heirs of a competing shoe manufacturer. Because he once loved their mother but was turned down when he proposed, he joins their troubled firm and runs things so well that he almost puts his own company, being run by nephew Benjamin, whom he wishes to teach a lesson, out of business. In the end the two companies merge as do Jenny and Benjamin.

Warner Bros., 1933 (original). Director: John Adolfi; screenwriters: Charles Kenyon and Maud Powell. Cast: George Arliss (Reeves), Bette Davis

(Jenny), Hardie Albright (Benjamin), Theodore Newton (Tommy), Gordon Westcott.

• ***Everybody's Old Man*** (remake). Twentieth Century–Fox, 1936. Director: James Flood; screenwriters: Patterson McNutt and A.E. Thomas. Cast: Irvin S. Cobb (William Franklin), Rochelle Hudson (Cynthia Sampson), Johnny Downs (Tommy Sampson), Norman Foster (Ronald Franklin), Alan Dinehart.

The first film was made to change George Arliss' image as a distant character actor of costume pieces to some kind of regular Joe. In this it wasn't particularly successful, but the film had its moments. In the remake, humorist Irvin C. Cobb, groomed to replace the late Will Rogers, was given his first starring role as a tough industry leader in a fight with a rival canner, with Cobb in a "no quarter asked, no quarter given" mode. Just as Cobb is about to deliver the fatal blow to the competitor's business, that worthy dies. Now Cobb is very sad. It turns out that the deceased was once Cobb's partner but had married the only woman Cobb ever loved. Cobb ends up helping the children of his competitor and his deceased wife to run their business properly.

The World of Wonderful Reality ***see*** **The City of Beautiful Nonsense**

1015 The World, the Flesh and the Devil

Based on the play by Laurence Cowan. Story: With such an imposing title one might expect something very powerful, but it's only the name of a London pub, where a crooked lawyer plots—but fails to achieve—the disposal of the heir to a baronetcy.

Kinema, Great Britain, 1914 (original). Director: F. Martin Thornton; screenwriter: Laurence Cowan. Cast: Frank Esmond (Nicholas Brophy), Stella St. Audrie (Caroline Stanger), Warwick Welington (Sir James Hall), Charles Carter (Rupert Stanger/Dyke), Rupert Harvey, Jack Denton, Gladys Cunningham, Frances Midgeley, Mercy Hatton, H. Agar Lyons.

• ***The World, the Flesh and the Devil*** (remake). Real Art/Radio, Great Britain, 1932. Director: George A. Cooper; screenwriter: H. Fowler Mear. Cast: Harold Huth (Nicholas Brophy), Isla Bevan (Beatrice Elton), S. Victor Stanley (Jim Stanger), Sara Allgood (Emma Stanger), James Raglan, Fred Groves, Frederick Leister, Felix Aylmer, Barbara Everett.

The original of this ordinary drama about a baronet's bastard's schemes to dispose of the true heir was filmed in natural color, something of an achievement for 1914. Other than that the two films make a dull combination.

1016 The Wrecker

Based on the play by Arnold Ridley and Bernard Merivale. Story: Railroad employees Roger Doyle and Mary Dalton unmask the saboteur who is wrecking a railway's trains to be none other than the company's manager, who secretly heads a motorcoach (bus) company in competition with the railway.

Gainsborough, Great Britain, 1928 (original). Director: Geza M. Bolvary; screenwriter: Angus Macphail. Cast: Carlyle Blackwell (Ambrose Barney), Benita Hume (Mary Shelton), Joseph Striker (Roger Doyle), Winter

Hall (Sir Gerald Bartlett), Gordon Harker, Pauline Johnson, Leonard Thompson.

• ***Seven Sinners*** (remake). Gaumont, Great Britain, 1936. Director: Albert de Courville; screenwriters: Frank Launder, Sidney Gilliat, L. DuGarde Peach and Austin Melford. Cast: Edmund Lowe (John Harwood), Constance Cummings (Caryl Fenton), Thomy Bourdelle (Paul Turbe), Henry Oscar (Axel Hoyt), Felix Aylmer (Sir Charles Webber), Joyce Kennedy, Allan Jeayes, O.B. Clarence.

In the remake, American detective Edmund Lowe is hunting those responsible for a series of train crashes. The London insurance agent assigned to work with him is the attractive Constance Cummings. Between them they expose those responsible who had been using the train wrecks to cover up a murder.

1017 The Wrong Road

Based on an original story by Gordon Rigby. Story: The prospects for bank clerk Jimmy Caldwell and his girl, Ruth Holden, don't look very good, so they decide to steal $100,000 from the bank where he works, hide it away, serve their sentences for the crime, gather up the loot on their release and live happily ever after. All goes according to plan until they try to live happily ever after. It's not as easy as they think to reclaim the music box in which they hid the loot. And they hadn't counted on a former cellmate of Jimmy's showing up demanding a cut, or a parole officer appealing to their consciences.

Republic Pictures, 1937 (original). Director: James Cruze; screenwriters: Gordon Rigby and Eric Taylor. Cast: Richard Cromwell (Jimmy Caldwell), Helen Mack (Ruth Holden), Lionel Atwill (Mike Roberts), Horace MacMahon (Blackie), Russ Powell, Billy Bevan, Marjorie Main, Rex Evans.

• ***Out of the Storm*** (remake). Republic Pictures, 1948. Director: R.G. Springsteen; screenwriter: John K. Butler. Cast: James Lydon (Donald Lewis), Lois Collier (Ginny Powell), Marc Lawrence (Red Stubbins), Richard Travis (R.J. Ramsey), Robert Emmett Keane, Helen Wallace, Roy Barcroft, Iris Adrian.

In the remake of this implausible story, Jimmy Lydon is a clerk in a shipbuilding plant whose payroll has been robbed by a gang of crooks. The latter in their hurry to get away leave behind $100,000, which Lydon decides to smuggle out of the plant, figuring the hold-up gang will be blamed. After this is accomplished the rest of the movie deals with how his conscience bothers him, leading eventually to his decision to return the money and face the consequences.

1018 Wuthering Heights

Based on the novel by Emily Bronte. Story: Cathy Earnshaw, the daughter of an unhappy Yorkshire family, falls passionately in love with a gypsy stableboy, Heathcliff, who has been brought up with her and her brother, Hindley. The latter hates Heathcliff and constantly reminds him of his origins and lack of rank or fortune. This treatment and Cathy's developing interest in a nearby wealthy neighbor, Edgar Linton, lead to Heathcliff running away and Cathy marrying Linton. Later Heathcliff returns, now wealthy and successful. He buys up Hindley's notes and takes ownership of the latter's land, allowing the drunken former master to stay on so that his ever-deepening descent into degradation can be enjoyed up close by Heathcliff. To spite Cathy, Heathcliff courts and marries Linton's sister Isabella but makes her miserable because of his all-consuming love for Cathy. Cathy becomes ill and Heathcliff goes to her. After declaring her love for him, she expires in his arms. Heathcliff runs off into the night and freezes to death so they can be together once more.

Ideal, Great Britain, 1920 (original). Silent. Director: A.V. Bramble; screenwriter: Eliot Stannard. Cast: Milton Rosmer (Heathcliff), Anne Trevor (Cathy), Warwick Ward (Hindley Earnshaw), John L. Anderson (Edgar Linton), Colette Bretel (Catherine Hareton), Cecil Morton York (Earnshaw), Cyril Raymond, Dora de Winton, Aileen Bagot, George Trail.

• ***Wuthering Heights*** (remake). United Artists, 1939. Director: William Wyler; screenwriters: Ben Hecht and Charles MacArthur. Cast: Laurence Olivier (Heathcliff), Merle Oberon (Cathy), David Niven (Edgar Linton), Hugh Williams (Hindley Earnshaw), Geraldine Fitzgerald (Isabella Linton), Flora Robson, Donald Crisp, Leo G. Carroll, Cecil Kellaway, Miles Mander.

• ***Wuthering Heights*** (remake). American International, Great Britain, 1970. Director: Robert Fuest; screenwriter: Patrick Tilley. Cast: Anna Calder-Marshall (Catherine Earnshaw), Timothy Dalton (Heathcliff), Julina Glover (Hindley Earnshaw), Ian Ogilvy (Edgar Linton), Hilary Dwyer (Isabella Linton), Judy Cornwell, Hugh Griffith, Harry Andrews, Pamela Brown, James Cossins, Rosalie Crutchley, Peter Sallis.

The Emily Bronte story has also been filmed in 1953 and 1960. In the 1920 silent, Heathcliff wins Squire Earnshaw's estate, brutalizes his adopted son, and makes him wed his dead step-sister's daughter. The 1939 film, one of the most romantic and memorable movies ever made, received Academy Award nominations for Best Picture, Best Script, Best Director, Best Musical Score, Best Photography, Best Leading Actor, Best Leading Actress and Best Supporting Actress. Only Gregg Toland for his haunting photography won.

Screenwriters Hecht and MacArthur followed Bronte's novel up to a point and then moved swiftly ahead to the tragic ending twenty years later, when Heathcliff joins Cathy in death. Merle Oberon's death scene is one of the most unforgettable in screen history. With her last breath, she asks Olivier to take her to the window: "Let me look at the moors once more with you." Then, "I'll wait for you, until you come," and her body goes limp in his arms. Heathcliff's reaction is, "What do they know of heaven or hell, Cathy, who know nothing of life? Oh, they're praying for you, Cathy. I'll pray one prayer with them. I'll respect till my tongue stiffens: Catherine Earnshaw, may you not rest while I live on. I killed you. Haunt me, then! Haunt your murderer! I know that ghosts have wandered on the earth. Be with me always—take any form—drive me mad! Only do not leave me in this dark alone where I cannot find you. I cannot live without my life! I cannot die without my soul. . . ." And then he goes out for one final search for his Cathy and dies, the film ending with the appearance of the ghostly lovers gathering heather on Penniston Crag.

The 1970 film, despite a competent cast, hardly had a chance since it would be compared to one of the all-time favorite romantic movies. There was just no way most people, including critics, could objectively view or re-view it without thinking of the 1939 masterpiece and seeing how the 1970 version fell short in every respect. Some movies just shouldn't be remade.

Y

1019 The Yellow Ticket

Based on the play by Michael Morton. Story: The title refers to the badge of prostitution in Russia the secret police gives exclusively to Jewish girls, which provides the only legal manner in which they can travel in Czarist Russia. This is the passport that Anna Mirrel is given when she applies for the right to travel to visit her dying father in St. Petersburg. Believing that she can accept the ticket and still be virtuous, Anna finds herself the subject of every coarse joke and jive from officials all along the route of her journey. She meets a young newspaperman writing about Russia and he naturally takes her for what her passport says she is. The story deals with Russian persecution of the Jews and only in a limited way suggests the horrible treatment these people would endure at the hands of the Germans in only a few years.

Pathe Pictures, 1918 (original). Silent. Director: William Parks; screenwriter: Michael Morton. Cast: Milton Sills (Julian Rolfe), Fannie Ward (Anna Mirrel), Warner Oland (Baron Andrey), Armand Kaliaz (Count Rostov), J.H. Gilmour, Leon Bary, Anna Lehr, Dan Mason.

• ***The Yellow Ticket*** (remake). Fox Film Corp., 1931. Director: Raoul Walsh; screenwriter: Michael Morton. Cast: Elissa Landi (Mary Kalish), Lionel Barrymore (Baron Andrey), Laurence Olivier (Julian Rolfe), Walter Bryon (Count Nikolai), Sarah Padden, Arnold Korff, Mischa Auer, Boris Karloff, Rita La Roy.

Perhaps not too strangely, but sadly, some critics questioned the appropriateness of telling the story of a "Jewish problem" as if that were the case. The producers were not on any crusade. They merely felt they had a story with some dramatic impact. They did not display much outrage in portraying the treatment of the Jews.

1020 Yes Madam

Based on the novel by K.R.G. Browne. Story: According to his uncle's will, Bill Quinton must act as a chauffeur for two months. If he's fired within that period, the £80,000 his uncle left him will go to his cousin Hugh Tolliver. The latter does his best to see that Bill gets the sack in his job with nouveau riche Mr. Peabody, but Bill's girlfriend, Pansy, makes certain he gets the money.

British Lion/Fox Film Corp., Great Britain, 1933 (original). Director: Leslie Hiscott; screenwriter: Michael Barringer. Cast: Frank Pettingell (Albert

Peabody), Kay Hammond (Pansy Beresford), Harold French (Bill Quinton), Muriel Aked (Mrs. Peabody), Peter Haddon (Hugh Tolliver), Wyn Weaver, Hal Walters.

• ***Yes Madam?*** (remake). Associated British Pictures, Great Britain, 1938. Director: Norman Lee; screenwriters: Clifford Grey, Bert Lee and William Freshman. Cast: Bobby Howes (Bill Quinton), Diana Churchill (Sally Gault), Wylie Watson (Albert Peabody), Bertha Belmore (Emily Peabody), Vera Pearce (Pansy Beresford), Billy Milton (Tony Tolliver), Fred Emney, Cameron Hall.

In the musical remake two cousins, Bobby Howes and Sally Churchill, stand to inherit £80,000 apiece if they take jobs as servants and don't get sacked within a month's time. A third cousin, Tony Tolliver, who will benefit from their misfortune should either lose their job, tells their employer, Mr. Peabody, that Bill is a burglar. Seems that's just what Peabody has been looking for. He asks Bill to get back some incriminating letters that Peabody wrote. Bill's burglary attempt is a disaster and no one gets the inheritance, but Bill and Sally get each other.

Yes, Madam? *see* **Yes Madam**

1021 You Belong to Me

Based on a story by Dalton Trumbo. Story: Many humorous stories have been told about a busy doctor whose wife becomes jealous of his practice and the attention he pays to his female patients. This film merely reverses the roles. Helen Hunt is the physician and Peter Kirk is the rich playboy who becomes her husband. To discover the rest of the plot of this comedy, imagine all the usual situations such a story suggests. The clever reader will think of them all, and perhaps a few more which if incorporated into this movie would have made it better.

Columbia Pictures, 1941 (original). Director: Wesley Ruggles; screenwriter: Claude Binyon. Cast: Barbara Stanwyck (Helen Hunt), Henry Fonda (Peter Kirk), Edgar Buchanan (Billings), Roger Clark (Vandemer), Ruth Donnelly (Emma), Melville Cooper (Moody), Ralph Peters, Maude Eburne, Renie Riano.

• ***Emergency Wedding*** (remake). Columbia Pictures, 1950. Director: Edward Buzzell; screenwriters: Nat Perrin and Claude Binyon. Cast: Larry Parks (Peter Kirk), Barbara Hale (Helen Hunt), Willard Parker (Vandemer), Una Merkel (Emma), Alan Reed (Tony), Eduard Franz (Dr. Heimer), Irving Bacon, Don Beddoe, Jim Backus, Teru Shimada, Myron Welton, Ian Wolfe.

Henry Fonda and Barbara Stanwyck worked well together in comedies, notably in *The Lady Eve.* This farce is not on a par with that marvelous collaboration, but the two are able to make the most of an ordinary story. The remake, with far less talented leads, doesn't work as well. Larry Parks merely pouts angrily every time he thinks of his wife with a male patient. Barbara Hale, who most people remember in the undemanding role of Della Street on television's *Perry Mason,* walks through her part with no apparent enthusiasm. The notion that a woman shouldn't be a doctor to men or shouldn't work at all because she has a husband rich enough to take care of her is a view that deservedly would be most unpopular today.

You Can't Escape Forever *see* **Hi, Nellie**

You Can't Run Away from It *see* **It Happened One Night**

1022 Young America

Based on the play by Frederick Ballard and the *Mrs. Doray* stories by Pearl Franklin. Story: Poor boy Art Simpson and his mongrel dog, Jasper, are all each other has in the world and their association constantly leads to the threat of one or the other losing his liberty. Art's efforts to find the money to pay the dog tax for Jasper brings him into conflict with the law, but the two eventually find a loving home with the Dorays.

Essanay Film Co., 1922 (original). Silent. Director and screenwriter: Arthur Berthelet. Cast: Charles Frohaman Everett (Art Simpson), Jasper (Himself), Wilson Reynolds, Marlow Bowles, William Wadsworth, Leona Ball, Florence Barr, Evelyn Ward, Frances Raymond.

• ***Young America*** (remake). Fox Film Corp., 1932. Director: Frank Borzage; screenwriter: William Counselman. Cast: Spencer Tracy, Doris Kenyon, Tommy Conlon, Ralph Bellamy, Beryl Mercer, Sarah Padden.

• ***Young America*** (remake). Twentieth Century–Fox, 1942. Director: Louis King; screenwriter: Samuel S. Engel. Cast: Jane Withers, Jane Darwell, Lynne Roberts, William Tracy, Robert Cornell, Roman Bohnen, Irving Bacon, Ben Carter, Louise Beavers.

They don't make films like these anymore—fortunately. The first remake, even with Spencer Tracy and Ralph Bellamy, had no chance because the story of two boys in trouble with the law was old, dull and hokey in 1932, even in 1922. By 1942, the story had been reworked as a vehicle for Jane Withers as a spoiled city brat, sent to a farm to work under the auspices of the Four-H clubs, where she turns into a decent sort through her association with other youngsters, animals, a county fair and a boy.

Young As You Feel *see* **Handy Andy**

Young at Heart *see* **Four Daughters**

Young Bess *see* **The Private Life of Henry VIII**

Young Doctor Kildare *see* **Internes Can't Take Money**

Young Doctors in Love *see* **The Interns**

Young Donovan's Kid *see* **Big Brother**

Young Lady Chatterly *see* **Lady Chatterly's Lover**

Your Obedient Servant *see* **Black Beauty**

1023 You're a Sweetheart

Based on a story by Warren Wilson, Maxwell Shane and William Thomas. Story: Hal Adam goes to great lengths to produce a successful new Broadway musical starring Betty Bradley. Someone should have done the same for this nonsensical movie.

Universal Pictures, 1937 (original). Director: David Butler; screenwriters: Monte Brice and Charles Grayson. Cast: Alice Faye (Betty Bradley), George Murphy (Hal Adam), Ken Murray (Don King), William Gargan (Fred Edwards), Frances Hunt, Frank Jenks, Andy Devine, Caspar Reardon, Charles Winninger, Donald Meek, David Oliver, Andrew A. Trimble.

• ***Cowboy in Manhattan*** (remake). Universal Pictures, 1943. Director: Frank Woodroff; screenwriter: Warren Wilson. Cast: Frances Langford (Babs Lee), Robert Paige (Bob Allen), Leon Errol (Hank), Walter Catlett (Ace Robbins), Joe Sawyer (Louie), Jennifer Holt, George Cleveland, Will Wright.

Alice Faye made only this one movie for Universal and it might have been better had she made none. It's a dull story with dull performances and dull song and dance routines, including the title number by Harold Adamson and Jimmy McHugh, performed by Faye and Murphy. The second film, *Cowboy in Manhattan,* has songwriter Robert Paige pretending he's a millionaire cowboy to impress Frances Langford, the star of a musical show. There's even less here of value than in the 1937 movie, but it only runs a very long 54 minutes.

You're Never Too Young *see* **The Major and the Minor**

You're Only Young Once *see* **A Family Affair**

You're Telling Me *see* **So's Your Old Man**

Z

1024 Zaza

Based on the play by Pierre Berton and Charles Simon. Story: Zaza, a Paris music hall soubrette, falls in love with Bernard Dufresne, a French diplomat, without knowing that he is married. When she finds out, he offers to divorce his wife, but she will not allow him to ruin his career and they part until the wife dies years later.

• ***Zaza*** (remake). Famous Players–Lasky/Paramount Pictures, 1923. Silent. Director: Allan Dwan; screenwriter: Albert Shelby Le Vino. Cast: Gloria Swanson (Zaza), H.B. Warner (Bernard Dufresne), Ferdinand Gottschalk (Duke de Brissac), Lucille La Verne (Aunt Rosa), Mary Thurman (Florianne), Yvonne Hughes, Riley Hatch, Roger Lytton, Ivan Linow.

• ***Zaza*** (remake). Paramount Pictures, 1938. Director: George Cukor; screenwriter: Zoe Atkins. Cast: Claudette Colbert (Zaza), Herbert Marshall (Dufresne), Bert Lahr (Cascart), Helen Westley (Annis), Constance Collier (Nathalie), Genevieve Tobin (Florianne), Walter Catlett, Ann Todd, Rex O'Malley.

Zaza was filmed in Italy in 1909 and 1943, and in France in 1955. In 1915, there was a Famous Players production starring Pauline Frederick in the title role. In the 1938 movie, Claudette Colbert was brought in for a replacement for the injured Isa Miranda who would four years later star in the Italian production of *Zaza*. Fanny Brice coached Miss Colbert for her songs "Hello, My Darling" and "Zaza" written by Frederick Hollander and Frank Loesser. Bert Lahr is impressive in his first dramatic role as the partner and counselor of the mischievous, flirtatious and tempestuous music hall singer. Herbert Marshall is capable as the married diplomat, doing what he did best in so many movies—not stealing any scenes from the female lead.

1025 Zulu

Based on historical fact and a story by John Prebble. Story: While attending a Zulu ceremony in Natal, South Africa, in 1879, the Reverend Otto Witt and his daughter Margaretta learn that the Zulus have slaughtered 1,200 British soldiers and that they plan to attack the small garrison stationed at Rorke's Drift. Alcoholic Witt rushes to warn the commanding officers, Lieutenants Chard and Bromhead, but doesn't convince them to withdraw. With 4000 to 100 advantage, the Zulus attack in waves with nerve-shattering intervals of waiting between assaults. The undermanned force hangs on until surprisingly the Zulus withdraw, saluting the valor of their enemy as they move off. Later Chard, Bromhead and nine others are awarded the Victoria Cross for bravery.

Embassy Pictures, Great Britain, 1964 (original). Director: Cy Endfield; screenwriters: John Prebble and Cy Endfield. Cast: Stanley Baker (Lt. John Chard), Jack Hawkins (Otto Witt), Ulla Jacobsson (Margaretta Witt), James Booth (Pvt. Henry Hook), Michael Caine (Lt. Gonville Bromhead), Nigel Green (Colour-Sgt. Bourne), Ivor Emmanuel (Pvt. Owen), Paul Daneman, Glynn Edwards, Neil McCarthy, David Kernan, Gary Bond, Peter Gill, Tom Gerard, Patrick Magee, Richard Davies, Denys Graham.

• ***Zulu Dawn*** (prequel). Samarkand, U.S./Netherlands, 1979. Director: Douglas Hickox; screenwriters: Cy Endfield and Anthony Storey. Cast: Burt Lancaster, Peter O'Toole, Simon Ward, John Mills, Nigel Davenport, Michael Jayston, Denholm Elliott, Ronald Lacey, Freddie Jones, Bob Hoskins, Christopher Cazenove, Ronald Pickup, Anna Calder-Marshall.

Baker co-produced the 1964 film in which cockney Michael Caine made his film debut as an upper-class aristocrat with perfect diction. The boss, Baker, as everyone knows, was the workingman's British actor. The second film is in fact a prequel to the first, depicting the British command's ineffectual handling of the Zulu nation—first in diplomacy and then on the battlefield at Ulandi where 1,200 troops were massacred, as Jack Hawkins was to learn.

Zulu Dawn ***see*** **Zulu**

Index

Numbers in this index refer to entry, not page numbers. Entries in quotation marks are titles of songs in their respective films, and italicized entries are titles of books, plays and stories upon which films are based. Titles of original movies and their sequels or remakes do not appear here since they are listed in alphabetical order in the book, unless they are mentioned in the discussion of another movie. In that case, the entry number refers to the movie under discussion.

A

B

C

D

E

F

G

H

J

K

L

M

N

O

S

T

U

V

W

Y

Z